THE OXFORD HANDBOOK OF
SCIENCE FICTION

THE OXFORD HANDBOOK OF

SCIENCE FICTION

Edited by
ROB LATHAM

OXFORD
UNIVERSITY PRESS

Oxford University Press is a department of the University of Oxford.
It furthers the University's objective of excellence in research, scholarship,
and education by publishing worldwide.

Oxford   New York
Auckland   Cape Town   Dar es Salaam   Hong Kong   Karachi
Kuala Lumpur   Madrid   Melbourne   Mexico City   Nairobi
New Delhi   Shanghai   Taipei   Toronto

With offices in
Argentina   Austria   Brazil   Chile   Czech Republic   France   Greece
Guatemala   Hungary   Italy   Japan   Poland   Portugal   Singapore
South Korea   Switzerland   Thailand   Turkey   Ukraine   Vietnam

Oxford is a registered trademark of Oxford University Press
in the UK and certain other countries.

Published in the United States of America by
Oxford University Press
198 Madison Avenue, New York, NY 10016

© Oxford University Press 2014

All rights reserved. No part of this publication may be reproduced, stored in a
retrieval system, or transmitted, in any form or by any means, without the prior
permission in writing of Oxford University Press, or as expressly permitted by law,
by license, or under terms agreed with the appropriate reproduction rights organization.
Inquiries concerning reproduction outside the scope of the above should be sent to the
Rights Department, Oxford University Press, at the address above.

You must not circulate this work in any other form
and you must impose this same condition on any acquirer.

Library of Congress Cataloging-in-Publication Data
The Oxford Handbook of Science Fiction / edited by Rob Latham.
pages cm
Includes bibliographical references and index.
ISBN 978-0-19-983884-4 (hardcover : acid-free paper)—ISBN 978-0-19-983885-1 (ebook)   1. Science
fiction—History and criticism.   I. Latham, Rob, 1959- editor of compilation.
PN3433.5.O94 2014
809.3'8762—dc23
2014004219

1 3 5 7 9 8 6 4 2
Printed in the United States of America
on acid-free paper

Contents

Contributors   ix

Introduction   1

PART I. SCIENCE FICTION AS GENRE

1. Extrapolation and Speculation   23
   BROOKS LANDON

2. Aesthetics   35
   PETER STOCKWELL

3. Histories   47
   ARTHUR B. EVANS

4. Literary Movements   59
   GARY K. WOLFE

5. Fandom   71
   FARAH MENDLESOHN

6. The Marketplace   81
   GARY WESTFAHL

7. Pulp Science Fiction   93
   JESS NEVINS

8. Literary Science Fiction   104
   JOAN GORDON

9. Slipstream   115
   VICTORIA DE ZWAAN

10. The Fantastic   127
    BRIAN ATTEBERY

11. Genre vs. Mode 139
VERONICA HOLLINGER

PART II. SCIENCE FICTION AS MEDIUM

12. Film 155
MARK BOULD

13. Radio and Television 169
J. P. TELOTTE

14. Animation 184
PAUL WELLS

15. Art and Illustration 196
JEROME WINTER

16. Comics 212
COREY K. CREEKMUR

17. Video Games 226
PAWEŁ FRELIK

18. Digital Arts and Hypertext 239
JAMES TOBIAS

19. Music 252
JOHN CLINE

20. Performance Art 263
STEVE DIXON

21. Architecture 277
NIC CLEAR

22. Theme Parks 291
LEONIE COOPER

PART III. SCIENCE FICTION AS CULTURE

23. The Culture of Science 305
SHERRYL VINT

24. Automation 317
    ROGER LUCKHURST

25. Military Culture 329
    STEFFEN HANTKE

26. Atomic Culture and the Space Race 340
    DAVID SEED

27. UFOs, Scientology, and Other SF Religions 352
    GREGORY L. REECE

28. Advertising and Design 364
    JONATHAN M. WOODHAM

29. Countercultures 383
    ROB LATHAM

30. Sexuality 395
    PATRICIA MELZER

31. Body Modification 408
    ROSS FARNELL

32. Cyberculture 421
    THOMAS FOSTER

33. Retrofuturism and Steampunk 434
    ELIZABETH GUFFEY AND KATE C. LEMAY

PART IV. SCIENCE FICTION AS WORLDVIEW

34. The Enlightenment 451
    ADAM ROBERTS

35. The Gothic 463
    WILLIAM HUGHES

36. Darwinism 475
    PATRICK B. SHARP

37. Colonialism and Postcolonialism 486
    JOHN RIEDER

38. Pseudoscience 498
    ANTHONY ENNS

39. Futurology 513
    ANDREW M. BUTLER

40. Posthumanism 524
    COLIN MILBURN

41. Feminism 537
    LISA YASZEK

42. Libertarianism and Anarchism 549
    NEIL EASTERBROOK

43. Afrofuturism 561
    DE WITT DOUGLAS KILGORE

44. Utopianism 573
    PHILLIP E. WEGNER

Index 585

Contributors

Brian Attebery alternates between scholarly projects in fantasy and science fiction, with occasional forays into children's literature and other areas of cultural study. His latest books are *Parabolas of Science Fiction*, edited with Veronica Hollinger (Wesleyan, 2013), and *Stories about Stories: Fantasy and the Remaking of Myth* (Oxford, 2014).

Mark Bould is reader in film and literature at the University of the West of England, and co-editor of the journal *Science Fiction Film and Television*. His books include *Science Fiction: The Routledge Film Guidebook* (2012), *The Routledge Concise History of Science Fiction* (2011), *The Routledge Companion to Science Fiction* (2009), *Fifty Key Figures in Science Fiction* (Routledge, 2009), and *Red Planets: Marxism and Science Fiction* (Pluto/Wesleyan, 2009).

Andrew M. Butler is the author of *Solar Flares: Science Fiction in the 1970s* (Liverpool, 2012) and Pocket Essentials volumes on Philip K. Dick, cyberpunk, Terry Pratchett, film studies, and postmodernism. He is a winner of the SFRA Pioneer Award and an editor of *Extrapolation*.

Nic Clear is head of the Department of Architecture and Landscape Architecture at the University of Greenwich, where he also teaches a postgraduate design unit that specializes in the use of film and animation in the generation, development, and representation of speculative architectural spaces.

John Cline received his Ph.D. in American studies from the University of Texas. He is the co-editor of two collections of essays on film, *From the Arthouse to the Grindhouse: Highbrow and Lowbrow Transgression in Cinema's First Century* (Scarecrow, 2010) and *Cinema Inferno: Celluloid Explosions from the Cultural Margins* (Scarecrow, 2010), as well as numerous scholarly articles, including entries in the revised *Grove Dictionary of American Music*. He contributes regularly to *The Los Angeles Review of Books* and *The Oxford American*.

Leonie Cooper is a lecturer in the Faculty of Art, Design and Architecture, Monash University. Her research field is screen cultures and the construction of new heuristic tools to think through its epistemological and perceptual transitions. She has had essays published in *Stars in Our Eyes: The Star Phenomenon in the Contemporary Era* (Praeger, 2002) and *Star Voyager: Exploring Space on Screen* (Hardie Grant, 2011). While having addressed digital media and SF at international conferences, she is also concerned with their relationship to the material practices and methods of creative research.

Corey K. Creekmur is an associate professor of English and film studies at the University of Iowa, where he also directs the Institute for Cinema and Culture. In addition to his own publications on topics ranging from popular Hindi cinema to representations of race, gender, and sexuality in American mass culture, he is the general editor of the Comics Culture book series for Rutgers University Press and recently provided a critical afterword for Gilbert Hernandez's graphic novel *Marble Season*.

Steve Dixon is president of LASALLE College of the Arts in Singapore. He has published on digital arts, robots, artificial intelligence, critical theory, theater studies, and pedagogy. His book *Digital Performance: A History of New Media in Theater, Dance, Performance Art and Installation* (MIT, 2007) has won two international awards.

Neil Easterbrook teaches comparative literature, theory, and science fiction at TCU in Fort Worth, Texas. He has published widely on SF, including essays on authors such as Heinlein, Le Guin, Delany, Gibson, McDonald, Miéville, Dick, Egan, Vonnegut, Calvino, and Lem and on topics such as Singularity, metafantasy, slipstream, and bad SF films. He won the 2009 Pioneer Award from the Science Fiction Research Association.

Anthony Enns is an associate professor in the Department of English at Dalhousie University in Halifax, Nova Scotia. His co-edited collections include *Screening Disability* (University Press of America, 2001), *Sonic Mediations: Body, Sound, Technology* (Cambridge Scholars, 2008), and *Vibratory Modernism* (Palgrave Macmillan, 2013), and his essays on science fiction and popular culture have appeared in such journals as *Science Fiction Studies, Screen, Journal of Popular Film and Television, Quarterly Review of Film and Video, Popular Culture Review*, and *Studies in Popular Culture*.

Arthur B. Evans is professor of French at DePauw University and managing editor of the journal *Science Fiction Studies*. He has published numerous books and articles on Jules Verne and early French science fiction, including the award-winning *Jules Verne Rediscovered* (1988). He is also general editor of the Wesleyan University Press "Early Classics of Science Fiction" book series and co-editor of the *Wesleyan Anthology of Science Fiction* (2010).

Ross Farnell completed a doctorate with a thesis on the posthuman condition in contemporary SF and cultural theory in 1998, and has published related writings and interviews. Since that time, his primary focus has been on arts and cultural management, community development, and contemporary arts practice. He is currently director of the Burrinja Cultural Centre in Melbourne, Australia. He continues to pursue his ongoing passion for music, recording, and performing with various bands and projects.

Thomas Foster is a professor of English at the University of Washington and the author of *The Souls of Cyberfolk: Posthumanism as Vernacular Theory* (Duke, 2005). He has published numerous articles on modernism, postmodernism, and science fiction and is currently working on a book tentatively entitled *Ethnicity and Technicity: Race, Nature, and Culture in the Cyberpunk Archive*.

Paweł Frelik teaches at Maria Curie-Skłodowska University in Lublin, Poland. His research and writing interests include visual science fictions, cross-media storytelling, (un)popular culture, and contemporary experimental fiction. He serves on the boards of the journals *Science Fiction Studies*, *Extrapolation*, and *Journal of Gaming and Virtual Worlds*.

Joan Gordon is a professor of English at Nassau Community College and an editor of the journals *Science Fiction Studies* and *Humanimalia: A Journal of Human/Animal Interface Studies*. She has served as president of the Science Fiction Research Association and was a Fulbright Distinguished Chair at Maria Curie Skłodowska University. She has also written a number of articles and co-edited several books.

Elizabeth Guffey is professor of art and design history at SUNY-Purchase. She is also founding editor of the peer-review journal *Design and Culture*. She is the author of numerous articles on design history and of the books *Retro: The Culture of Revival* (Reaktion, 2006) and *Poster: A Material History* (Reaktion, 2014).

Steffen Hantke is the author of *Conspiracy and Paranoia in Contemporary Literature* (Peter Lang, 1994), as well as the editor of *Horror: Creating and Marketing Fear* (Mississippi, 2004), *Caligari's Heirs: The German Cinema of Fear after 1945* (Scarecrow, 2007), and *American Horror Film: The Genre at the Turn of the Millennium* (Mississippi, 2010). He teaches at Sogang University in Seoul, South Korea.

Veronica Hollinger is a professor of cultural studies at Trent University in Ontario, Canada. She is the co-editor of five scholarly collections, the most recent of which is *Parabolas of Science Fiction* (Wesleyan, 2013). She is a long-time co-editor of *Science Fiction Studies* and the author of many essays on feminist and cyberpunk SF, on postmodernism and posthumanism, and on the increasingly science-fictional character of contemporary technoculture.

William Hughes is professor of Gothic studies at Bath Spa University and an immediate past president of the International Gothic Association. He is the author, editor, or co-editor of 15 books on the Gothic including, most recently, *Bram Stoker's "Dracula": A Reader's Guide* (Continuum, 2009), *The Historical Dictionary of Gothic Literature* (Scarecrow, 2012), and *Ecogothic* (Manchester, 2013), co-edited with Andrew Smith. He is the founder and editor of the refereed journal *Gothic Studies*, and his media appearances in the United Kingdom have included interviews on *Most Haunted Live* and BBC Radio 4's *Questions, Questions*.

De Witt Douglas Kilgore is an associate professor of English and American studies at Indiana University. He is the author of *Astrofuturism: Science, Race and Visions of Utopia in Space* (Pennsylvania, 2003) and the co-editor of a special issue of *Science Fiction Studies* on the work of Octavia E. Butler. His recent publications include essays on racial reformation in Kim Stanley Robinson's novels and Marvel Comic's *Black Panther*.

Brooks Landon teaches courses in contemporary literature and culture, science fiction, and prose style in the English Department of the University Iowa, where he is Herman J. and Eileen S. Schmidt Professor. He is the author of *The Aesthetics of Ambivalence: Rethinking Science Fiction Film in the Age of Electronic (Re)Production* (Greenwood, 1992) and *Science Fiction After 1900: From the Steam Man to the Stars* (Routledge, 2002).

Rob Latham is professor of English at the University of California, Riverside, where he co-directs the Science Fiction and Technoculture Studies Program. He is the author of *Consuming Youth: Vampires, Cyborgs, and the Culture of Consumption* (Chicago, 2002) and co-editor of *The Wesleyan Anthology of Science Fiction* (Wesleyan, 2010). A senior editor of the journal *Science Fiction Studies*, he also serves as an editorial consultant for *The Journal of the Fantastic in the Arts* and *Science Fiction Film and Television*.

Kate C. Lemay is assistant professor of art history at Auburn University-Montgomery, where she teaches courses on American art. Her research interests include the American memorials, art, and architecture in France dedicated to World War II. Her projects have been supported by fellowships from IIE Fulbright, the Terra Foundation in American Art, the Smithsonian American Art Museum, le Centre Nationale pour les Recherches Scientifiques and the Mémorial de Caen, and the Emily Landau Research Center at the Georgia O'Keeffe Museum.

Roger Luckhurst teaches literature at Birkbeck College, University of London. He is the author of *Science Fiction* (Polity, 2005), a technocultural history of the genre, as well as of *The Invention of Telepathy, 1870–1901* (Oxford, 2002), *The Trauma Question* (Routledge, 2008), and *The Mummy's Curse: The True History of a Dark Fantasy* (Oxford, 2012).

Patricia Melzer is assistant professor in German and women's studies at Temple University and the author of *Alien Constructions: Science Fiction and Feminist Thought* (Texas, 2006). Her second book, *Death in the Shape of a Young Girl: Gender and Political Violence in West German Terrorism*, which is forthcoming in 2015 from NYU Press, examines the implications of gendered political violence for feminist theories of violence as they emerge in the case of the left-wing terrorist group Red Army Faction.

Farah Mendlesohn is professor of English at Anglia Ruskin University in Cambridge. Among her publications are the Hugo Award–winning *Cambridge Companion to Science Fiction* (2003) and *Rhetorics of Fantasy* (Wesleyan, 2008). She edited the semi-prozine/academic journal *Foundation: The International Review of Science Fiction* from 2001 to 2007. She has run British Science Fiction Association author evenings, served as president of the International Association of the Fantastic in the Arts, chaired an Eastercon in 2006, run the program for the Montréal Worldcon in 2009, and will be director of exhibits for the 2014 Worldcon in London.

Colin Milburn holds the Gary Snyder Chair in Science and the Humanities at the University of California, Davis. His research focuses on the relations of literature, science, and media technologies. He is the author of *Nanovision: Engineering the Future* (Duke, 2008) and *Mondo Nano: Fun and Games in the World of Digital Matter* (Duke, 2014).

Jess Nevins is a librarian at Lone Star College in Tomball, Texas. He is the author of the *Encyclopedia of Fantastic Victoriana* (Monkeybrain, 2004) and *The Encyclopedia of Pulp Heroes* (forthcoming, 2014) and has written widely on the pulps for the website io9.com.

Gregory L. Reece writes about religion and popular culture, new religious movements, and the philosophy of religion. His books include *Irony and Religious Belief* (Mohr Siebeck, 2002), *Elvis Religion: The Cult of the King* (Tauris, 2006), *UFO Religion: Inside Flying Saucer Cults and Culture* (Tauris, 2007), *Weird Science and Bizarre Beliefs: Mysterious Creatures, Lost Worlds and Amazing Inventions* (Tauris, 2008), and *Creatures of the Night: In Search of Ghosts, Vampires, Werewolves and Demons* (Tauris, 2012). He has a Ph.D. in religious studies from the Claremont Graduate University and lives in Montevallo, Alabama.

John Rieder, author of *Colonialism and the Emergence of Science Fiction* (Wesleyan, 2008), is a professor of English at the University of Hawai'i at Mānoa, a senior editor of *Extrapolation*, and winner of the Science Fiction Research Association's 2011 Pioneer Award.

Adam Roberts is professor of nineteenth-century literature at Royal Holloway, University of London. He is the author of *The Palgrave History of Science Fiction* (2006) and many other works of criticism in SF and other fields. He has also written a dozen science fiction novels, the most recent of which, *Jack Glass* (2012), won the British Science Fiction Association and John W. Campbell Memorial Awards.

David Seed holds a chair in American literature at Liverpool University. He has edited the *Companion to Science Fiction* (Blackwell, 2005) and edits the Science Fiction Texts and Studies series for Liverpool University Press. His writings on the culture of the Cold War include *American Science Fiction and the Cold War: Literature and Film* (Edinburgh, 1999), *Brainwashing: The Fictions of Mind Control* (Kent State, 2004), and *Under the Shadow: The Atomic Bomb and Cold War Narratives* (Kent State, 2013).

Patrick B. Sharp is professor and chair of liberal studies at California State University, Los Angeles. His book publications include *Savage Perils: Racial Frontiers and Nuclear Apocalypse in American Culture* (Oklahoma, 2007) and the edited anthology *Darwin in Atlantic Cultures: Evolutionary Visions of Race, Gender, and Sexuality* (Routledge 2009). He has also published articles on nuclear narratives, race, gender, and science fiction in journals such as *Twentieth Century Literature* and *Science Fiction Film and Television*.

Peter Stockwell is chair in literary linguistics at the University of Nottingham, United Kingdom. He has worked on the language and cognition of science fiction starting with his book *The Poetics of Science Fiction* (Longman, 2000), and has since published over 20 books and 70 research papers. His most recent work draws together literary analysis and cognitive science as a cognitive poetics.

J. P. Telotte is a professor and former chair of the School of Literature, Media, and Communication at Georgia Institute of Technology. He co-edits the journal *Post Script*; teaches courses in film history, film genres, and animation; and has published extensively on science fiction film and television. Among his books are the following volumes on science fiction: *Replications: A Robotic History of Science Fiction Film* (Illinois, 1995), *A Distant Technology: Science Fiction Film and the Machine Age* (Wesleyan, 1999), *Science Fiction Film* (Cambridge, 2001), *The Essential Science Fiction Television Reader* (Kentucky, 2008), and (with Gerald Duchovnay) *Science Fiction Film, Television, and Adaptation: Across the Screens* (Routledge, 2012). He is currently completing a study of science fiction television.

James Tobias is associate professor in the Department of English at the University of California, Riverside. Holder of a doctorate in critical studies from the University of Southern California's School of Cinematic Arts, he is the author of *Sync: Stylistics of Hieroglyphic Time* (Temple, 2010), a study of musicality across time-based media of the twentieth and twenty-first centuries, among many other publications.

Sherryl Vint is professor of science fiction media studies at the University of California, Riverside, and co-director of the program in science fiction and technoculture studies. She has published widely on science fiction, including the books *Bodies of Tomorrow: Technology, Subjectvity, Science Fiction* (Toronto, 2007) and *Animal Alterity: Science Fiction and the Question of the Animal* (Liverpool, 2010), and she co-edits the journals *Science Fiction Studies* and *Science Fiction Film and Television*.

Phillip E. Wegner is the Marston-Milbauer Eminent Scholar in English at the University of Florida. He is the author of *Imaginary Communities: Utopia, the Nation, and the Spatial Histories of Modernity* (California, 2002), *Life Between Two Deaths, 1989–2001: U.S. Culture in the Long Nineties* (Duke, 2009), and *Shockwaves of Possibility: Essays on Science Fiction, Globalization, and Utopia* (Peter Lang, 2014).

Paul Wells is director of the Animation Academy at Loughborough University in the United Kingdom and chair of the Association of British Animation Collections (ABAC). He has published widely in animation studies, including *Understanding Animation* (Routledge, 1998), *Re-imagining Animation: The Changing Face of the Moving Image* (Ava, 2008), and *The Animated Bestiary: Animals, Cartoons, and Culture* (Rutgers, 2009). He is also an established writer and director for radio, television, and theater, recently completing documentaries on Geoff Dunbar and John Halas, and conducting workshops and consultancies worldwide based on his book *Basics Animation 101: Scriptwriting* (Basics Animation, 2007).

Gary Westfahl, an adjunct professor at the University of La Verne, is the author, editor, or co-editor of 24 books about science fiction and fantasy, including the Hugo Award–nominated *Science Fiction Quotations: From the Inner Mind to the Outer Limits* (Yale, 2005), the three-volume *Greenwood Encyclopedia of Science Fiction and Fantasy* (2005), and the author study *William Gibson* (Illinois, 2013). He has also written hundreds of essays and reviews for various books, journals, magazines, and websites, including a long series of film reviews for the website *Locus Online*. In 2003 he received the Science Fiction Research Association's Pilgrim Award for his lifetime contributions to science fiction and fantasy scholarship.

Jerome Winter is a Ph.D. candidate studying science fiction and contemporary American literature at the University of California, Riverside. His essay "Epistemic Polyverses and the Subaltern: The Postcolonial World-System in Ian McDonald's *Evolution's Shore* and *River of Gods*" appeared in a special "Globalization" issue of *Science Fiction Studies* in 2012. He works as the associate editor of *Los Angeles Review Book*'s SF page.

Jonathan M. Woodham is professor of design history and director of research and development (arts and humanities) at the University of Brighton in the United Kingdom. He has been active in design history research and publication for almost four decades and has been invited to deliver keynotes in 20 countries on four continents. His best-known work is *Twentieth Century Design* (Oxford, 1997), which has sold more than 50,000 copies worldwide and been translated into Korean and Chinese.

Gary K. Wolfe is professor of humanities at Roosevelt University in Chicago, where he also served as dean of University College and as dean of graduate studies. His *Evaporating Genres: Essays on Fantastic Literature* (Wesleyan, 2011) received the Locus Award for nonfiction. Earlier studies include *The Known and the Unknown: The Iconography of Science Fiction* (Kent State, 1979), which received the Eaton Award; *David Lindsay* (Borgo, 2007); *Critical Terms for Science Fiction and Fantasy* (Greenwood, 1986); and *Harlan Ellison: The Edge of Forever* (Ohio State, 2001), with Ellen R. Weil. He received the Science Fiction Research Association's Pilgrim Award, the International Association for the Fantastic in the Arts' Distinguished Scholarship Award, and a World Fantasy Award for criticism and reviews. He edited *American Science Fiction: Nine Classic Novels of the 1950s* for the Library of America in 2012. He has been a contributing editor and reviewer for *Locus* magazine since 1991.

Lisa Yaszek is professor in the School of Literature, Media, and Communication at Georgia Tech. Her research interests include science fiction, cultural history, critical race and gender studies, and science and technology studies. Her essays on science fiction as a global language have appeared in *Extrapolation*, *NWSA Journal*, and *Rethinking History*. She is the author of *Galactic Suburbia: Recovering Women's Science Fiction* (Ohio State, 2008) and coeditor of the *Configurations* special issue on Kim Stanley Robinson (Winter–Spring 2012).

Victoria de Zwaan is associate professor of cultural studies at Trent University in Peterborough, Canada. She works in the field of literary cultural studies, teaches courses in experimental fiction and literary theory, and has published articles and given conference papers on a diverse, international range of experimental writers such as Pynchon, Acker, Pavic, Kundera, Rushdie, Danielewski, and Coover. Her book *Interpreting Radical Metaphor in the Experimental Fictions of Donald Barthelme, Thomas Pynchon, and Kathy Acker* was published by Mellen Press in 2002.

THE OXFORD HANDBOOK OF
SCIENCE FICTION

INTRODUCTION

The problem for science fiction studies for much of its early history as an academic discipline essentially involved determining the nature and boundaries of its putative object, deciding *what counts* as science fiction (SF). Broadly speaking, for the first two decades of its existence most scholarly work on SF tended to take three forms: theoretical efforts at definition that established the historical compass of the genre and elicited a canon of major works (see, for example, Alkon and also Malmgren); formalist studies that traced important iconic or ideational features of the field (see, for example, Wolfe); and critical investigations that purported to show the alignment of science fiction with specific trends in literary-cultural theory, such as feminism (see, for example, Wolmark). For all their many differences in orientation and emphasis, these approaches tended to treat SF as a more or less fixed genre, whether defined discursively (in terms of narratological features), theoretically (in terms of epistemological structures), or institutionally (in terms of publishing categories). The overall thrust of this body of work was to argue for SF as a significant form of modern literature that raised consequential issues and intersected with major modes of criticism.

The evolution of such a problematic is entirely understandable in context, given the recentness of SF's entry into the academy. The first serious effort at a comprehensive bibliography of the English-language genre was Everett F. Bleiler's *Checklist of Fantastic Literature*, published in 1948, a year after the first book-length survey of the field, J. O. Bailey's *Pilgrims in Space and Time: Trends and Patterns in Scientific and Utopian Fiction*, appeared. The first dedicated journal, *Extrapolation*, was founded in 1959, colleges and universities started offering regular courses in SF in the early 1960s (see Hillegas), and academic presses began featuring studies specifically of science fiction—as opposed to utopian literature, the imaginary voyage, fiction anthologies with critical commentary, or works on major authors such as H. G. Wells—in the 1970s (see Ketterer; Rose; and Philmus, *Unknown*). In the early decades of its existence, SF studies was under significant critical and institutional pressure to both delimit and legitimate its subject matter. As Robert Philmus remarked in 1973, in the very first issue of the journal *Science Fiction Studies*: "Generic names must mean something. The problem SF poses in this regard is that its name . . . does not in itself and by convention evoke the 'shape' and identity of what it designates; and because it does not, what *science fiction* designates must be identified—that is, stipulated" ("Shape" 37; emphasis in original). Moreover, as Edward

James points out in his survey of early SF criticism, the process of devising definitions and constructing a historical canon tended to function to "giv[e] modern SF writers a respectable ancestry" and thus "greater respectability in the halls of academe" (32–33).

The signal accomplishment of these initial decades, in terms of scope and influence, was unquestionably Darko Suvin's *Metamorphoses of Science Fiction* (1979). Suvin's definition of SF as "*a literary genre whose necessary and sufficient conditions are the presence and interaction of estrangement and cognition*" (7–8; emphasis in original); his claim that this estrangement was achieved primarily through "*the narrative dominance or hegemony of a fictional 'novum' (novelty, innovation) validated by cognitive logic*" (63; emphasis in original); and his historical conspectus tracing the genre's origins to Thomas More's *Utopia* (1516) and Jonathan Swift's *Gulliver Travels* (1726) enshrined a very specific and compelling vision of SF: it was a literary form that functioned to defamiliarize, critique, and/or satirize present-day reality through the projection of alternative worlds, an effect accomplished through the mobilization of both technoscientific methods ("cognitive logic") and objects ("fictional 'novum[s]'"). Suvin's conception had the virtue of rigor and clarity, its epochal intervention registered by the rampant italics he used throughout the book to underline his key ideas. Yet it was also, as several critics have pointed out, narrowly prescriptive and sociopolitically tendentious. In the words of Istvan Csicsery-Ronay Jr., "[m]any of SF's most typical novums [such as time machines] are only ostensibly scientifically rational" (73), and Patrick Parrinder has observed that Suvin's central assumption that true SF must necessarily be socially critical "turns the text's function of 'commenting on the author's collective context' into the measure of aesthetic achievement" (47). Surely, there is something curious about a definition of SF that, by Suvin's own admission, rules out the vast majority of texts published and consumed as such—especially the American magazine tradition—as insufficiently cognitive, or insufficiently estranging, or both.

Despite its shortcomings, Suvin's definition of the genre has exerted an enormous influence on subsequent critics, and there can be little doubt that the Suvinian model has produced trenchant and compelling studies of the work of authors such as Wells, Stanisław Lem, Karel Čapek, and Ursula K. Le Guin, among others. But as this list suggests, the canon it has generated has been a fairly narrow one, often unapologetically so. In his book *Critical Theory and Science Fiction* (2000), Carl Freedman, Suvin's most significant contemporary follower, asserted that the pulp tradition was an unfortunate distraction from the main line of true SF, which descended from the classical utopia through Wells to major "literary" writers such as Le Guin and Samuel R. Delany, and that the ongoing legacy of pulp SF "continues to obscure the critical vitality of the genre" (90). This vitality lay in science fiction's ability to "foreground and demystify the actual, and thereby to point to some authentic plenitude with which the deprivations of mundane reality are contrasted" (72); works that failed to accomplish this heady mission were necessarily inferior, if they even deserved the name of "science fiction" at all. For his part, Suvin had called pulp SF a "misshapen subgenre," more or less indistinguishable from "supernatural or occult fantasy," whose perpetuation and popularity were merely "the result of an ideological or commercial habit" (68).

Yet another consequence of the dominance of Suvin's approach in the early decades of academic SF studies was a general neglect of science fiction in other media. In his award-winning essay "Kubrick's *2001* and the Possibility of a Science-Fiction Cinema," Freedman argued that SF film was essentially impossible given the dominance of special effects over "literary quality" within the medium, especially its Hollywood incarnation. Indeed, only those rare films that managed to sustain "a close alliance . . . to literary science fiction" achieved anything like the "critical and oppositional potential" of which the genre was capable (312). In short, SF films substituted technological spectacle for genuine cognitive estrangement. The journal Suvin co-edited, *Science Fiction Studies*, generally scanted coverage of film, television, and other forms of mass-media SF in its early years, the title of its November 1980 special issue, "Science Fiction and the Non-Print Media" (published the year that Suvin stepped down from the editorial board), only serving to underscore this omission with a belated effort at inclusion. Even the articles in this special issue, as the lead editorial proclaimed, functioned "to 'demythologize' . . . the images the visual media present us with" ("Editorial" 246), rather than seeing those images as themselves authentic vehicles of demythologization, as the novums of literary SF would be. A significant result of this marginalization of nonprint science fiction was that a separate discourse about SF film, more or less segregated from SF studies proper, developed within the discipline of cinema studies, beginning in 1980 with Vivian Sobchack's pioneering study *The Limits of Infinity: The American Science Fiction Film, 1950–1975* and continuing with Constance Penley's 1986 special issue of *Camera Obscura* on "Science Fiction and Sexual Difference" (eventually published as *Close Encounters: Film, Feminism, and Science Fiction* in 1991). A few critics attempted to bridge this divide—for example, Brooks Landon, who asserted in 1992 that "to expect SF films . . . to pursue only the same goals as does SF literature is . . . critically narrow-minded" (*Aesthetics* 8)—but they were decidedly in the minority. It was not until 2008 that a journal devoted specifically to *Science Fiction Film and Television* would appear (though *Science Fiction Studies* did, especially after 1990, become more catholic in its coverage of mass-media SF).

The critical hegemony of the Suvinian paradigm began to be effectively challenged by the rise of cultural-studies perspectives in the 1980s and 1990s. Less concerned with normative definitions and literary canons than with the varying and contradictory ways that the genre had been configured at particular historical moments, cultural-studies scholarship tended to see SF as in constant dialogue with other forms of cultural production, as well as with unfolding events in social and political history. More specifically, cultural-studies work focused on connections between the genre and the many formal and informal discourses that made up nineteenth- and twentieth-century "technoculture"—that complex of institutions and attitudes, predictions and inventions linking high-tech research with popular culture. Technoculture studies brought together issues and contexts related to the industrial production, textual refraction, and sociopolitical deployment of technological advances; and SF had a central place within this corpus, given its longstanding history of tracking the futuristic fallout of technoscientific "progress." As a form of literature devoted, in large part, to evoking the potential futures and possible worlds engendered by mechanical innovation, SF emerged, so these critics claimed, as the preeminent site within Euro-American popular culture, where the vast social impact of modern technology could be creatively explored and critically interrogated.

Important works in the cultural study of SF powerfully displayed the genre's unparalleled capacity to illuminate the technological culture that had radically transformed modern life. H. Bruce Franklin's *War Stars: The Superweapon and the American Imagination* (1988), for example, showed how the technophilic perspectives of classic pulp SF converged with the imperatives of the militarist state to sanction the high-tech warfare of the postwar atomic age. Similarly, Andrew Ross's *Strange Weather: Culture, Science and Technology in the Age of Limits* (1991) analyzed the implication of SF in two key events in the history of modern technoculture—the "enlightened technocracy" movement of the 1920s, with which early SF was affiliated through the career of science popularizer Hugo Gernsback (editor of the first SF pulp, *Amazing Stories*), and the computer counterculture of the 1980s, which cyberpunk SF both championed and critiqued. Indeed, cyberpunk and its affiliated cybercultures were at the center of much of this early cultural-studies work. Scott Bukatman's *Terminal Identity: The Virtual Subject in Postmodern Science Fiction* (1993), for example, argued for cyberpunk as a quintessential postmodern genre, defining it broadly enough to include not only print SF by the likes of William Gibson but also films, graphic novels, and even theme parks. And N. Katherine Hayles's *How We Became Posthuman: Virtual Bodies in Cybernetics, Literature, and Informatics* (1999) showed how major SF texts since the 1950s—including the work of cyberpunk authors such as William Gibson—had participated, along with postwar cybernetics theory and recent innovations in artificial intelligence and artificial life research, in formulating a "posthumanist" cultural paradigm.

This spate of fresh critical-historical work, emanating largely from scholars of American studies, visual culture studies, and science and technology studies, may seem to have developed in relative isolation from the tradition of classical SF studies pioneered by Suvin (only Bukatman and Hayles mention his work, in passing). Yet both schools are deeply rooted in Western Marxist thought, though their specific debts and therefore critical emphases vary. Where Suvin adapted Brechtian ideals of estrangement and Ernst Bloch's notion of the utopian novum, cultural-studies theorists returned to the Gramscian concept of hegemony and the critiques of popular culture pioneered by Raymond Williams and the Birmingham School. What made the late 1980s and early 1990s a turning point in SF criticism was what appeared at the time to be the signal accomplishment of cyberpunk, which emerged as a trenchant form of postmodern discourse that offered compelling futuristic visions of the intersection of corporate power and global technoculture. Fredric Jameson, for example, called the subgenre "the supreme *literary* expression, if not of postmodernism, then of late capitalism itself" (418 n1; emphasis in original). In 1988 the *Mississippi Review* released a special issue on cyberpunk edited by Larry McCaffery, which was eventually published in book form as *Storming the Reality Studio: A Casebook of Cyberpunk and Postmodern Fiction* (1992) and featured the work of a new generation of SF scholars such as Csicsery-Ronay, Landon, David Porush, and Veronica Hollinger.

When Csicsery-Ronay and Hollinger joined the new editorial board of *Science Fiction Studies* in 1991 (along with Arthur B. Evans and Richard D. Mullen, who had originally founded the journal), the transition away from the Suvinian paradigm seemed complete. Yet there was still significant shared ground thanks to their mutual roots in Marxist critical theory, and the cultural study of SF came to adopt, in modified form, some of Suvin's key ideas—in particular, his emphasis on the centrality of an estranging novum linked to technoscientific development (see Csicsery-Ronay 47–75)—while shedding the more problematic baggage of formalist genre studies, especially its inclination to construct narrow and exclusionary canons. Moreover, contra Suvin, for whom works of science fiction were either cognitively estranging and therefore socially critical or else reactionary deformations, technoculturally oriented SF studies operated with an understanding that SF can be at once critical of *and* complicit with the technological culture with which it is inextricably entwined.

The development of SF criticism since the 1990s is thus marked by both rupture *and* continuity, yet technoculture studies has clearly made possible significant new ways of understanding the history of SF. Roger Luckhurst's 2005 "cultural history," for example, melds an internal survey of the genre's characteristic institutions and textual strategies with an external focus on the cultural politics of technological development; indeed, the chief accomplishment of his book is to render such facile inside–outside distinctions moot, since a genuine *cultural* history requires meticulous attention to both genre adaptation and technosocial transformation. Luckhurst's book shares with the aforementioned works of Franklin, Bukatman, Ross, and Hayles a perspective that persistently moves past the borders of genre to trace larger systems of meaning-making in which technology has a central—if not preeminent—place. While Luckhurst's focus remains largely on SF literature, technocultural studies of SF have often had a multimedia orientation, breaking the stranglehold on literary studies that had marked the discipline for its first two decades. As noted above, Bukatman's book found examples of cyberpunk in texts ranging from the film *TRON* (1982) and the TV movie *Max Headroom: Twenty Minutes into the Future* (1985) to Howard Chaykin's comic book *American Flagg!* (1983–88) and Disney's Tomorrowland. And recent works of reference in the field have taken note of this shift, with *The Routledge Companion to Science Fiction* (2009), edited by Mark Bould et al., featuring chapters not just on SF literature, but on film, television, and comics—even a chapter "SF Tourism" by Landon.

Indeed, if the problem for SF studies in the 1970s was to establish what counts as science fiction, the problem today is to determine *what does not count* as science fiction. *The Oxford Handbook of Science Fiction* takes up this critical challenge, attempting to descry the historical and cultural contours of SF in the wake of technoculture studies. Rather than treating the genre as an isolated aesthetic formation, it examines SF's many lines of cross-pollination with technocultural realities since its inception in the nineteenth century, showing how SF's unique history and subcultural identity have been constructed in ongoing dialogue with popular discourses of science and technology. Moreover, the scope of what qualifies as science fiction is also expansive, encompassing not only literary texts but also speculative technocultural work in a wide range of media. The scope of SF's sociocultural influence has never been greater, almost keeping pace with the magnitude of technological change itself. As cyberpunk author Bruce Sterling pointed out in 1986, his generation was the first "to grow up in . . . a truly science-fictional world"; as a result, "the techniques of classical 'hard SF'—extrapolation, technological literacy—are not just literary tools, but an aid to daily life" (xi). This *Handbook* acknowledges this extraordinary explosion and proliferation of science-fictional texts and modalities, which have made SF today less a genre than a way of being in the world. As Landon puts it, SF is now "the new realism of technological society," a "meta-genre so broad and so pervasive as to be a concept and force quite outside the boundaries of fiction, and of art itself" (*Science Fiction* xiii). In Csicsery-Ronay's words, "science-fictionality" has becomes nothing less than "a way of thinking about the world" (ix).

This volume consists of four broadly themed parts, each divided into eleven chapters. Part I, "Science Fiction as Genre," considers the internal history of SF literature, examining its characteristic aesthetic and ideological modalities, its animating social and commercial institutions, and its relationship to other fantastic genres. Part II, "Science Fiction as Medium," presents a more diverse and ramified understanding of what constitutes the field as a mode of artistic and pop-cultural expression, canvassing extra-literary manifestations of SF ranging from film and television to video games and hypertext to music and theme parks. Part III, "Science Fiction as Culture," examines the genre in relation to cultural issues and contexts that have influenced it and been influenced by it in turn, the goal being to see how SF has helped to constitute and define important (sub)cultural groupings, social movements, and historical developments during the nineteenth, twentieth, and twenty-first centuries. Finally, Part IV, "Science Fiction as Worldview," explores SF as a mode of thought and its intersection with other philosophies and large-scale perspectives on the world, from the Enlightenment to the present day. The topics covered in these four parts are designed to be exemplary rather than exhaustive, treating a selective but significant array of issues that, taken altogether, communicate a rich sense of SF as a literary, artistic, pop-cultural, social, and ideological formation.

In other words, this is not a comprehensive work of reference designed to survey the field systematically or to summarize consensus views. The chapters do have some overview function, and their range is designed to present a representative sample of relevant topics in the four areas covered; but their purpose is generally more argumentative than expository, seeking to intervene in current debates and to broaden the scope of what usually counts as science fiction. While each chapter is designed to stand on its own, there is inevitable overlap among them in terms of contextual information presented and specific texts cited. The overall effect, I hope, is to convey a strong sense of the heterogenous discourses and debates, histories and cultures, that have gone to make science fiction, broadly conceived, what it is today.

Part I opens with Brooks Landon's careful anatomy of two key terms in SF critical discourse: extrapolation and speculation. The former is generally seen as indexing the genre's predictive capacity, while the latter is taken to refer to its more visionary tendencies; in other words, they are two contrasting ways of understanding the essential narrative logic of the genre. Yet, as Landon shows, the actual evolution of these ideas within SF discourse has been considerably more confused and contradictory, with critics sometimes conflating the terms while at other times seeing one as a derivation or subset of the other. These critical peregrinations, Landon argues, have been linked to shifts in the relative status of scientific "plausibility" and thus to debates over the centrality of science itself to an understanding of the genre. The second chapter, by Peter Stockwell, moves from debates over the ideological function of SF narratives to a focus on their aesthetic modalities. SF, Stockwell asserts, has been traditionally associated with the sublime due to its vaunted appeal to the reader's "sense of wonder"—an association that has damaged the genre's critical standing given the influence of Kant's disparagement of the category of the sublime in favor of the beautiful. Stockwell turns to recent work in the area of cognitive aesthetics in order to recast the way SF's artistic value is understood, ultimately seeing SF as an "immersive" literature whose linguistic and narratological allure lies in placing the reader in "a position of assumed familiarity with the imagined world."

Just as Landon and Stockwell take issue with prevailing critical models for understanding SF's narrative operations, so Arthur B. Evans contests some of the ways its history has traditionally been constructed. Evans presents a three-stage history of SF historiography that, in its final two stages, roughly correlates with the distinction drawn in this Introduction between a genre-studies model and a cultural-studies model: before 1970 (during the prehistory of academic SF criticism per se), histories tended to focus on authors or themes, at which point there was a shift to more "semiotic" approaches devoted to analyzing the characteristic "protocols" of the genre, followed by a move toward "sociological" histories that viewed SF as an expression of prevailing sociocultural trends. Cutting across these divisions were the "origin stories" that SF historians told about the roots and evolution of the genre; again tallying with claims made in this Introduction, Evans shows how earlier SF histories—produced during the period of the genre's academic legitimation—devoted a significant portion of their attention to prestigious British ancestors such as Shelley and Wells, whereas more recent histories have focused on the legacy of the American pulp genre during the twentieth century and after. Gary K. Wolfe's chapter builds on Evans by analyzing the consolidation of a conventional view of SF history as a series of literary movements—the hard SF of the 1940s, the 1960s New Wave, cyberpunk in the 1980s, and so on. Yet these movements were not all of a piece: some were genuine alliances of editors and authors with a common purpose, whereas others were more amorphous groupings or even retrospective projections.

The next two chapters, by Farah Mendlesohn and Gary Westfahl, focus on two important institutions supporting SF as a commercial genre: fandom and the literary marketplace. Mendlesohn gives a sense of the global scope of SF fandom, as well as the complex bureaucracy that has evolved to sustain its plethora of conventions, publications, and awards, ultimately arguing for fandom as a "knowledge economy" that privileges seniority of experience as a way of nurturing institutional memory. For his part, Westfahl shows how US science fiction, despite developing within a strong market milieu, has always spawned authors and editors who chafed at prevailing commercial norms for SF storytelling, pushing for innovation and diversity in a context where market pressures tended toward the crystallization of repeatable formulas. In Westfahl's view, this struggle has been settled definitively in favor of the marketplace, and "authors still striving to produce provocative, original science fiction . . . are becoming a disregarded minority, with little impact on the genre."

Following this pair of chapters are three that discuss dominant modalities of generic expression. Jess Nevins argues that "pulp SF" is actually a more capacious category than has traditionally been assumed, encompassing not merely work in magazines specifically designated as "science fiction" but also a vast amount of material published in the general pulps; if the latter were taken into account to a greater degree by critics and historians, pulp SF would be viewed in a considerably different light, seen as more pessimistic in its treatment of technoscientific topics and more complex in its depiction of women and nonwhite characters. Joan Gordon analyzes the development of "literary" science fiction into three main groupings: SF that foregrounds the specific aesthetic qualities characteristic of the genre, SF that mimics some of the styles of writing of the literary mainstream, and SF that prominently alludes to works of canonical literature. All three approaches, she suggests, are converging in an era of rampant technological change and saturation. Victoria de Zwaan's chapter addresses the "postmodernization" of SF during the cyberpunk era, showing how Bruce Sterling's category of "slipstream," while theoretically incoherent, continues to appeal to critics as a way of registering the ongoing hybridization between SF and experimental writing.

The final two chapters in Part I serve to unsettle the category of science fiction itself, opening our understanding of the genre to a range of literary techniques and cultural manifestations. Brian Attebery demonstrates how SF has always had a strong—if uneasy—relationship with fantasy, with many of its most characteristic narrative devices, from time machines to faster-than-light travel, having little warrant in actually existing science. As Attebery observes, this intermingling with fantasy renders problematic some of the core assumptions of Suvinian genre theory, which draws a sharp line between these forms; the "incursion of the fantastic" into an SF text complicates the status of science fiction as "a vector for disseminating scientific ideas or as a mode of social critique." Attebery proposes replacing conventional genre theory, concerned as it is with the clear demarcation of borders, with a more fluid sense of SF as a spectrum of possibilities characterized by the varying intensity of the copresence of fantastic elements. Veronica Hollinger goes further, arguing that SF perhaps no longer deserves to be seen as a genre at all; instead, it may now be a *mode*, a method of "thinking and speaking about contemporary reality so that SF becomes integrated with other discourses about late-capitalist global technoculture." Echoing the general perspectives of this *Handbook*, Hollinger claims that the traditional view of SF as a settled genre formation has become increasingly untenable as "contemporary reality and science fiction have become inextricably bound up with each other."

Hollinger's argument, positioned at the end of the first part, opens the critical conversation to include the media modalities in which SF finds expression, which is the subject of the chapters in Part II. The chapters proceed from more familiar media forms of SF, such as film and television, which already have fairly well-developed critical discourses surrounding them, to forms that have long been recognized as having a significant relationship with the genre—such as comics and video games—but have not been extensively treated in the extant scholarship, to forms that have seldom been considered in relation to SF at all, such as music, performance art, and architecture. Mark Bould's chapter on film addresses the continuing marginalization of mass-media forms in SF studies, seeing this as a legacy of the academic legitimation crisis of the discipline's early decades. Yet he also shows the limitations of a genre-based model in general, even in SF film studies: the "purifying, categorizing impulse" it expresses is inadequate to grapple with the "fluid and tenuous discursive constructions" most films are, especially today. In particular, the distinction between cognition and affect—so central to Suvin's model and to understandings of the distinctions between SF and horror film—needs to be rethought in an era when special effects may have complex ways of addressing viewers, encoding significant critical information. J. P. Telotte's chapter on radio and television sets a pattern for a number of the chapters to come, showing how these media were not peripheral but central to twentieth-century SF history. Citing pulp pioneer Hugo Gernsback's career as a popularizer of radio technology, Telotte argues that these "new, science-fictional media would not only provide powerful platforms for staging tales of scientific imagination, but also forms that would, self-consciously, draw the media into their exploring and contesting of the genre's nature."

Paul Wells pursues a similar argument, seeing animation as a "thick text" whose technocultural elements have an inherently science-fictional quality. Historically, animation functioned as "a new way of seeing, a modern engagement with the simultaneity of the emergence of new science and technology with fresh codes and conditions of visual interpretation." Its affective tone of "enchanted rapture" made it uniquely suited to serve as a kind of self-reflexive embodiment of SF's mission to chronicle the experiential effects of change, from Segundo de Chomón's use of stop-motion techniques to depict "the magical technologies of electrically imbued objects" to Pixar Studios' deployment of CGI to register the wonder of "scientific and technological interfaces with human creativity." Jerome Winter's chapter points to the paucity of serious scholarship on SF art and illustration, "not simply as a supplement to the history of SF literature, but as a significant shaper of the image culture of twentieth-century technological modernity." Winter analyzes the impact of SF visual art—in a number of formats, including pulp magazine covers, film promotional art, album sleeve design, and digital illustration—in helping to shape modern technocultural consciousness in ways that have been arguably more pervasive and influential than the impact of SF literature itself. Similarly, Corey Creekmur's chapter essays an "alternative history" of science fiction in which comic strips and comic books are accorded a more central place, in terms of both the sheer quantity of their output and their enormous and ongoing popularity (not to mention their outsized influence, in recent years, on other forms of SF media). For example, the figure of Buck

Rogers, incubated in the SF pulp *Amazing Stories*, went on to have a long career in newspaper (and subsequently film) serialization, doing more to disseminate science-fictional imagery among a mass audience than the specialized SF magazine culture that spawned him. Creekmur considers more contemporary examples as well, from Osamu Tezuka's wildly popular manga *Astro Boy* (1952–68) to more sophisticated graphic novels such as Warren Ellis and Darick Robertson's *Transmetropolitan* (1997–2002).

Three pairs of chapters follow, examining SF in digital media (video games, digital arts and hypertext), performance-based media (music, performance art), and media of the built environment (architecture, theme parks). Paweł Frelik's chapter on video games continues the argument for moving forms of visuality to the center of SF critical discourse; indeed, it makes an ambitious argument seeking to displace the presumed superiority of print SF in mediating the genre's key strengths (such as the depiction of alternative worlds or the critique of present-day reality), which, Frelik claims, visual-culture modes of expression can display just as—if not more—powerfully. Moreover, the close historical connection between the medium and SF themes and ideas—one of the earliest video games was *Spacewar!* (1962), which was adapted into the first arcade game *Computer Space* (1971)—has ensured that SF video games would not suffer the relative marginalization that SF has in other media, including visual media such as film and television, thus allowing it to become one of the prime vehicles for popular experiences (and understandings) of technological interactivity and simulation. James Tobias finds a similar connection between medium and SF in the representational and haptic strategies of digital textuality: both are "allegorical index[es] of technocultural change" that operate across a spectrum from the utopian to the dystopian. Tobias analyzes the "discursive performativities of utopian program-as-narrative" in a range of digital forms, from hypertexts to museum installations to web-based narratives, identifying potent critiques of instrumentalized technoscientific agency in the ludic power of their interfaces.

John Cline's chapter expands the scope of what counts as "science fiction music" from SF film soundtracks, which are already the subject of some scholarship, to critically neglected forms such as popular songs whose lyrics express SF themes, as well as musical instruments—in particular, the Theremin and other electronic modalities—whose technological substrate makes them inherently science-fictional. Like prevailing treatments of SF music, scholarship on performance art within technocultural SF studies is rather skewed, with certain key figures—such as Stelarc or Orlan—tending to be highlighted due to the science-fictional nature of their cyborg personae, at the expense of a more wide-ranging consideration of the links between the medium and SF. While providing insightful commentary on the careers of these two artists, Steve Dixon's chapter goes further, arguing for an intimate aesthetic and ideological connection: performance art "inhabits an interesting, tension-filled liminal space that is *precisely science fiction*. This space, like popular SF notions of outer space, mixes a reality of the known here-and-now with a 'will' to the unknown, the alien, and the future" (emphasis in original). The ritualized and affecting technocultural spectacles in SF performance art, Dixon asserts, especially those of cyborgized bodies and machinic transformations, powerfully activate the cognitive estrangement Suvin locates at the heart of the genre. Nic Clear's chapter on architecture is similar to Cline's on music and Dixon's on performance art in that all three seek to shift the focus from a finding of SF themes *in* the medium to a consideration of the medium's inherent science-fictionality. Like Dixon, Clear borrows a key concept from Suvin—"the novum"—to explain the aesthetic and ideological power of architectural novelties, ranging from the ambitious utopian technoscapes of Futurism and Constructivism to the more playful Pop visions of the Archigram Group. Clear provocatively claims that contemporary science-fictional architecture—including the "liquid architectures" of cyberspace—operates as a compelling critique of the profession's entrenched technocratic corporatism. By contrast, Leonie Cooper finds, even in the most corporate of architectural forms, the Disney theme parks, a series of "transitional spaces" and "ambiguous zones" whose liminality allows a "science-fictional mode of engagement" with the popular imaginary of the future. In short, the theme park "can become a kind of prophetic tool for forecasting a future that is already predestined by its simulations, or it can become evidence that the future must be imagined in ways other than how it has already been imagineered by theme-park designers."

Cooper's chapter, with its consideration of the theme park as a cultural as well as a medium-specific form, could readily have been included in Part III of this *Handbook*, "Science Fiction as Culture," which canvasses cultural phenomena or formations that have a clear relationship with SF and/or a strong science-fictional component. Taken overall, the chapters convey a sense of the range of ways that cultural values and practices have been informed or inflected by modern technoscience. As Sherryl Vint points out in her chapter on the culture of science, the "staying power of the term '*science* fiction,' which stubbornly resisted displacement by the more evocative and perhaps more accurate '*speculative* fiction,' suggests that something about the culture of science remains at the genre's core" (emphasis in original). She examines not only the presence of SF in scientific culture but also the genre's role in mediating "science" as an institution or a set of ideas to the public at large, as well as the influence of scientistic assumptions on the theorization of SF's narrative dynamics by, for example, Darko Suvin. Deploying perspectives from the sociology of science, Vint argues for SF as "a supplement to the official discourses of science," registering the ways in which technoscience, rather than being the disinterested intellectual pursuit one might imagine it to be, is always encountered precisely in and as a cultural form, saturated with cultural assumptions and values. Roger Luckhurst's chapter on the culture of automation provides a case study of Vint's basic claims, exploring the ways that forms of industrial and cybernetic automation encoded a technocratic worldview with effects not only on the kinds of SF stories that could be told but also on popular modes of self-understanding and ways of life. Luckhurst excavates a prehistory of modern automation in the eighteenth-century culture of clockwork automata and in the nineteenth-century Industrial Revolution, attending at once to their cultural fallout and their crystallization in early SF texts. Just as Wells's *The Time Machine* (1895), with its degeneration of the human race into two starkly opposed classes, is an allegory of the long-term effects of automated routines of industrial production and consumption, so in the twentieth century the *Terminator* films (1984, 1991, 2003) explore the dire prospects of cybernetic automation systems that reduce human agency to a mere feedback process.

The next two chapters examine a particular post–World War II technocultural complex that has had a profound impact on the SF genre but whose dissemination to the public at large has also been deeply science-fictional. Steffen Hantke's chapter studies the reciprocal militarization of SF and science-fictionalization of military culture, particularly in the postwar period, which produced both a popular sci-fi movie called *Star Wars* (1977) and a system of nuclear deterrence—the Strategic Defense Initiative—that was popularly dubbed with the same moniker. As Hantke demonstrates, the sheer volume of the US defense budget during these decades inevitably impacted public culture in significant ways, making it more or less "explicitly *militaristic*" (emphasis in original). As a result, military imagery and values became "an indispensable part of the national imaginary," manifesting in a range of media, from films and television programs to first-person shooter video games. David Seed likewise shows the cultural ramifications of atomic technology and the "space race" during the immediate postwar decades, in familiar SF novels and films but also in comics, animation, and popular music that is relatively obscure today. Since postwar technoscientific achievements in these areas had been prefigured in the SF pulps decades earlier, a major consequence of their realization was to usher the genre "[f]rom a place of cultural marginality" to "a central position ... as a source of fictional and cinematic representations." Gregory L. Reece's chapter explores some of the subcultural effects of this postwar technocratic regime in the rise of cult belief systems with a strong science-fictional flavor, from the writings of UFO contactees to fringe religions such as the Heaven's Gate and Raëlian movements. The phenomenon with the deepest genre roots was clearly Dianetics (later the Church of Scientology), which was founded by erstwhile pulp SF writer L. Ron Hubbard.

A focus on the cross-over traffic between mainstream culture and marginal subcultures marks a number of the remaining chapters in this part. Jonathan M. Woodham's chapter on midcentury advertising and design positions itself at the interface between pulp and mass imagery, showing how science-fictional iconography and themes were absorbed into mainstream marketing culture through the mediation of popular spectacles like GM's Motoroma, Futurama, and Kitchens of Tomorrow exhibitions, "powerful three-dimensional futuristic advertisements that consumers likened to a science-fictional world depicting new concepts of domestic lifestyles, interior spaces, and technology." While a few rare SF novels—most famously, Frederik Pohl and C. M. Kornbluth's *The Space Merchants* (1953)—commented satirically on the metastasizing of this marketing culture, the vast amount of traffic went in the opposite direction, with the genre pouring its image repertoire into the popular consciousness in the form of "science-fictional stylings" and language (for example, Dynaflow, Thermopane) that evoked a future of easeful leisure and mechanized abundance. It is precisely this vision of the future against which postwar countercultures such as the Beats and hippies, which I treat in my chapter, rebelled. These countercultures, as I show, drew upon a different set of genre resources for their inspiration, specifically the social utopianism of

SF texts and SF fans' sense of possessing a privileged form of subcultural insight. Just as avid fans divide the social world between a small corps of foresightful SF readers and a stolid mass of "mundanes" trapped in consensus "reality," so the Beats and hippies perceived a "split between enlightened hipsters and blinkered 'squares.'" My chapter reads how this division is figured in two bodies of work—the SF-inflected stories and poems of the 1950s Beat writers and the early-1960s craze for "beatnik SF" stories—as well as the legacy it has left for later forms of countercultural expression, whether within the genre (for example, Samuel R. Delany's 1966 novel *Babel-17* futuristically allegorizing the hip-square dichotomy) or outside it (for example, hippie religions drawing inspiration from SF works like Robert A. Heinlein's *Stranger in a Strange Land* [1961]).

The next two chapters delve into (sub)cultural identities and practices that feature complex dialectics of embodiment and science-fictionality. Patricia Melzer's chapter on sexuality examines the way traditional SF stories, rife with heteronormative assumptions and attitudes, were transformed by the advent of gay liberation, leading both to the growing inclusion on nonstraight characters in SF texts and to the establishment of institutions, such as the fan-based Gaylactic Network, that work within the genre to promote awareness about LGBT issues. Yet Melzer also shows the many ways in which traditional SF, though on the surface seemingly chaste, was actually permeated with sexual themes and topics, from Gernsback's postpulp career as a popularizer of sexology to Heinlein's occasional depictions of futuristic polyamory. Melzer traces in detail the ways that science fiction has borrowed ideas from "scientific" theories of gender and sexuality, while at the same time, in its projections of radical alterity, "destabiliz[ing] the naturalization of knowledge about bodies and desires produced by the natural sciences as well as by sexology and psychoanalysis." Ross Farnell's chapter explores the recent mainstreaming of body-modification practices, once the province of subcultures such as modern primitivism and S/M fetishism, via reconceptualizations of the body that have deep roots in SF—especially "the transgressive aesthetics and ideologies of cyberpunk and the cyborg, which have moved from the page to the catwalk and piercing parlor." The availability of the body for radical self-fashioning, a malleable surface for futuristic inscription and even surgical alteration, has been a theme of SF since at least Wells's *The Island of Dr. Moreau* (1897), but it reached a peak of intensity in the work of cyberpunk authors during the 1980s. For example, Bruce Sterling's popular "Shaper-Mechanist" series extrapolates divergent posthuman futures, one involving the genetic reconfiguration of the body and the other its prosthetic augmentation, the latter in particular having significant overlap with contemporary practices of neotribalist self-surgery. What cyberpunk SF and body-modification subcultures also share, in Farnell's view, is an uneasy yet complicit relationship with a commodified mainstream technoculture that has been progressively pushed into the most intimate reaches of the embodied self.

Thomas Foster scrutinizes the other half of cyberpunk's mind–body dualism in his chapter on cyberculture. On the one hand, he shows how cyberpunk's fantasies of disembodiment and prosthetic agency are rooted in the perspectives of the postwar cybernetics movement, especially its vision of living organisms as informational machines with indefinite borders; on the other hand, he shows how cyberpunk's extrapolations of cybernetic ideas have been folded back into contemporary cyberculture, leading to innovations in computer interface design. The final chapter in Part III looks at an offshoot of cyberpunk, steampunk, and its relationship to the larger cultural phenomenon of retrofuturism, both of which reflect "current dissatisfaction with the present while creating a nostalgia for what we once considered the future." As Elizabeth Guffey and Kate C. Lemay demonstrate, the optimism of midcentury technoculture, as expressed not only in the SF produced during the period but also in mainstream cultural phenomena such as the space age design canvassed in Woodham's chapter, has become an object of both fascination and skeptical reconsideration within retrofuturist subcultures. The most emblematic of these is steampunk, which began as an SF subgenre and has morphed into a lifestyle movement that bypasses twentieth-century technoculture in favor of earlier forms of technology more amenable to a culture of "tinkering." Yet for all their quirky earnestness, "most retrofuturism and steampunk forms contain an ironic note, lending the entire genre a kind of subversive power."

Guffey and Lemay's chapter straddles the divide between Parts III and IV, focusing on both an SF subculture (steampunk) and its animating perspective on the world (retrofuturism). Of course, the division between culture and worldview (like that between medium and culture, which separates the chapters in Parts II and III) is essentially artificial, since cultures are shot through with ideologies and ideologies manifest themselves as cultural forms. Part IV, entitled "Science Fiction as Worldview," offers critical assessments of the science-fictional qualities of 11 ideological systems, as well as analyses of the impact of these systems on the development of SF itself. Just as Part III endeavors to provide a sense of just how thoroughly twentieth-century cultural formations have been science-fictionalized, so the overall goal of Part IV is to convey an appreciation for the deep penetration of SF ideas and values into some of the major forms of thought characteristic of the modern period, broadly construed. The first two chapters, by Adam Roberts and William Hughes, address the Enlightenment and the Gothic, respectively—two seemingly opposed worldviews that nonetheless drew upon proto-SF discourses and had a significant influence upon the subsequent evolution of the genre. Obviously, the Enlightenment's notion of the emancipatory power of reason and scientific knowledge has deeply informed modern SF, but, as Roberts shows, Enlightenment thinkers often had recourse to SF themes of cosmic voyaging and vertiginous shiftings of scale, as in Voltaire's "Micromégas" (1752), a satirical story of first contact between benighted Earthmen and the eponymous alien philosopher, a gigantic being of unfathomably enlightened understanding. For his part, Hughes shows how the worldview of Gothic fiction, though considerably darker in tone than that produced by Enlightenment *philosophes*, was still complexly entangled with the emergent SF genre. Indeed, according to Hughes, the Gothic and SF share a close textual and ideological kinship: each genre functions as "a literary laboratory, a projected experimental space that, if it does not satisfactorily claim a didactic imperative, almost invariably interrogates the limits of the human as much as those of the imaginary technological." Starting with Mary Shelley's *Frankenstein* (1818), the Gothic becomes as obsessed as does SF with scientific figures and practices, a concern evident in works of Victorian Gothic such as Bram Stoker's *Dracula* (1897), thus paving the way for modern SF-Gothic hybrids such as Richard Matheson's *I Am Legend* (1954).

The next three chapters also consider the subsequent careers of nineteenth-century worldviews, perspectives ready-made for SF appropriation due to the inherently science-fictional aspect of some of their core ideas. Patrick B. Sharp's discussion of Darwinism not only traces its clear influence on the development of science fiction, especially in the genre's treatment of race, gender, and technology, but also discusses the science-fictionality of Darwinism itself, from the voyage of scientific discovery aboard the *Beagle* that helped lead to its birth to the various pseudoscientific mutations, such as eugenics, that it spawned. What Darwinism bequeathed to SF, above all, was a set of "colonial assumptions," deeply embedded in the fabric of Victorian science, that have since become "an inseparable part of the plots, characterizations, and framing logics of the SF genre as a whole." John Rieder's chapter develops this connection further, building on his 2008 study *Colonialism and the Emergence of Science Fiction*, which demonstrated the imbrication of early SF with colonialist ideologies. Here, Rieder turns his attention to postcolonial theory, showing how its themes of cultural hybridization and zones of contact at once manifest an implicitly science-fictional dynamic and readily lend themselves to extrapolation in SF narratives. His chapter draws a distinction between the forms of postcolonial thought and expression—including works of SF—that engage with the histories of settler colonialism, where one culture displaces and virtually exterminates another, and dependent colonialism, where two cultures coexist in a hierarchy of domination and subordination. Anthony Enns, in his chapter on pseudoscience, analyzes three Victorian fringe theories—of the hollow earth, Martian canals, and extrasensory perception—that were themselves deeply science-fictional and that, perhaps not surprisingly, "migrated to science fiction after they were rejected by orthodox science." Moreover, the modern genre itself has been a prolific incubator of pseudoscientific belief systems; indeed, as Enns shows, John W. Campbell, during the last two decades of his career as editor of *Astounding Science-Fiction* (later *Analog*), ostensibly the most hard-scientific of the SF magazines, became an avid promoter of ideas that "official science . . . dismisses with annoyance."

While not exactly a pseudoscience, Futurism or futurology, which is the subject of Andrew M. Butler's chapter, is not precisely a social science either. Butler surveys the explosion of professional Futurism during the 1960s, with new think tanks such as the World Future Society and the Institute for the Future generating quasi-science-fictional forecasts of coming trends. A highly technocratic discourse, Futurism nonetheless, according to Butler, has links back to Christian eschatology, as well as obvious affinities with science fiction. The genre is indeed sometimes seen as a variant of Futurism, seeking to predict the effects of social and technological change (for example, the "Future History" plotted out by Heinlein in the 1940s). Eminent popular Futurists such as Alvin Toffler recommended SF as "a kind of sociology of the future" that "has immense value as a mind stretching force for the creation of the habit of anticipation" (qtd. Butler), and historical cross-over between the two discourses has been significant (for example,

Arthur C. Clarke was both a major SF writer *and* a Futurist). Yet to conflate the two is to ignore the specifically *aesthetic* character of SF's extrapolations, Butler argues, and the necessary estrangement attendant on any science-fictional depiction of futurity. Colin Milburn's chapter on posthumanism focuses on a particular manifestation of Futurist thinking: the anticipation of an imminent transcendence of the fetters of embodied existence thanks to massive biotechnological or cybercultural advances. This vision links fringe sciences like cryonics with science fiction; indeed, as Milburn shows, the idea of immortality via cryogenic suspension was actually pioneered by a minor SF writer of the 1940s, Robert Ettinger. Milburn analyzes the rhetorical and discursive conflation of posthumanism and SF, with each plundering ideas and vocabulary from the other; echoing Hollinger, he suggests that "science fiction" today designates less a cohesive genre than a distributed "mode of discourse" that can be found equally "in literary texts, pop-science books, or futurological documentaries."

The following two chapters cover sociopolitical philosophies with strong currents of connection with SF. Lisa Yaszek's chapter argues that "SF is naturally compatible with the project of feminism": both are at their cores utopian discourses that outline speculative scenarios for the radical reconfiguration of social roles and relationships. Yaszek tracks the historical exchanges between these discourses over the "three waves" of feminist thought and activism since the nineteenth century, showing how feminist writers consistently turned to the resources of SF and the utopian novel to drive home their ideas, from Charlotte Perkins Gilman's depiction of a female-only community in *Herland* (1915) to Shulamith Firestone's imagination of a postbiological destiny for women in *The Dialectics of Sex* (1970) to Donna Haraway's embrace of the cyborg as a progressive gender mythology in her "Cyborg Manifesto" (1985). At the same time, SF authors as diverse as Melissa Scott, Octavia E. Butler, and Geoff Ryman have been inspired by feminist insights, while Joanna Russ wrote major works of both SF and feminist criticism. Neil Easterbrook, in his chapter on libertarianism and anarchism, explores a similar collusion between modes of sociopolitical thought and science fiction. Just as libertarian thinkers such as Ayn Rand have penned quasi-SF novels to espouse their ideas, so SF writers such as Heinlein and L. Neil Smith have crafted futures extrapolating ideals of unconstrained commerce and individual liberty. Since 1979 the Libertarian Futurist Society has given a Prometheus Award for SF novels that best reflect a libertarian worldview; as might be expected, the winners have been largely right-wing works, yet a handful of left-wing anarchist novels—especially those of Ken MacLeod—have also won. Easterbrook carefully distinguishes between these social philosophies, while showing their mutual imbrication in a worldview suspicious of centralized authority, an attitude that has long informed SF itself; indeed, to the extent that SF depicts "alternate future[s] or ask[s] readers to reflect on alternate presents, it is," says Easterbrook, "oppositional by definition."

While Yaszek and Easterbrook trace dialectics linking sociopolitical worldviews and SF, De Witt Douglas Kilgore analyzes Afrofuturism as an overarching mode of thought and creative expression that *includes* science fiction alongside other technocultural forms, such as hip-hop and experimental jazz, that make "self-conscious use of a speculative-fictional style" in order to muse on the collective fate of the descendants of the African diaspora. Citing anthologies on black and postcolonial SF edited by Sheree R. Thomas and Nalo Hopkinson, as well as a range of SF novels, Kilgore shows the long history of Afro-diasporic engagement with the genre. In Kilgore's view, Afrofuturism deploys utopian perspectives to critique dystopian realities, locating alternative trajectories that frame the future as "complex and contradictory rather than destructive." With the recent advent of Chicano/a and indigenous Futurisms, it is clear, says Kilgore, that Afrofurism has become "a model for how other peoples of color might view the futuristic art they create, allowing them to become conscious of their own imbrication in a technoscientific culture and to resist erasure from the narratives it sponsors." The utopian outlook characteristic of Afrofuturism and many of the other worldviews canvassed in this part makes it only appropriate that the volume should end with a chapter on utopianism itself. Phillip E. Wegner sees utopianism not as a mode of thought that intermingles with SF but rather as essential to the genre's very existence; indeed, "It is precisely its utopianism that distinguishes modern science fiction both from precursor forms ... and from the contemporary practices of futurology and prognostication." Given that I have taken issue in this Introduction with the Suvinian model of literary genre studies, it is also appropriate that this book should conclude with a stout defense of Suvin's critical legacy. According to Wegner, Suvin's key ideas of cognitive estrangement and the novum, his quintessential features of SF as a narrative form, both necessarily depend upon a utopian worldview; the basic task of an SF text "is to give figurative form to such a dramatic break from the status quo" that a reader's mindset is scrambled and reordered, opened to the "anticipatory illumination" of an alternative mode of being or form of social organization. Wegner shows this latent utopianism at work in both SF criticism and neo-Marxist theory, as well as in SF novels by Alfred Bester, Arkady and Boris Strugatsky, and Ken MacLeod.

Despite the wide range of topics covered in this *Handbook*, no one is more aware than I of all that has been omitted. As noted above, the essential problem for SF studies today is to determine *what does not count* as science fiction, and I could easily have included chapters on SF toys, SF theater, the science-fictional qualities of portable electronic devices, the "social science fiction" movement in anthropology and sociology, the discourse of human–animal studies, and much more. But as I have indicated, my goal in assembling this volume was to be representative rather than exhaustive, to convey a powerful sense of how deeply science-fictional ideas and attitudes have permeated the social fabric during the past two centuries, making SF today less a fixed and coherent genre than a diverse and distributed ensemble of phenomena that resists totalization or even ready summary. In many ways, science fiction has become the master discourse of our technocultural experience, the privileged chronicler of what Csicsery-Ronay has called "the *technologiade*, the epic of the struggle surrounding the transformation of the cosmos into a technological regime" (217). While the cosmos this *Handbook* maps is a relatively modest one, I hope that it will serve to inspire future projects of critical cartography, within science fiction studies and beyond.

I would like to close with some brief acknowledgments and a dedication. Most obviously, I want to thank the 44 contributors, both for their prompt and gracious responses to my queries and for their tremendous patience as this book has wended its way toward completion. I am grateful to my colleagues in the English Department at the University of California, Riverside (UCR) for their unstinting support of my research on science fiction, and to Stephen Cullenberg, dean of the College of Humanities, Arts, and Social Sciences, whose visionary leadership has made UCR's Science Fiction and Technoculture Studies (SFTS) program a reality, thus giving me a home base from which to mount projects such as this. I would also like to thank my co-editors at *Science Fiction Studies*, several of whom contributed chapters to this book, and especially to the managing editor, Arthur B. Evans, for all his wise mentorship over the years. And I am more grateful than words can express to my indefatigable Research Assistant, Lorenzo Servitje, for the painstaking efforts he took to secure the permissions for the numerous illustrations included in this volume, and to my editor at Oxford, Brendan O'Neill, for his great patience and understanding.

Finally, I would like to dedicate *The Oxford Handbook of Science Fiction* to two cherished colleagues and friends: Brooks Landon, with whom I worked for over a decade at the University of Iowa and without whose groundbreaking criticism, consistently aimed at expanding the perceived borders of our field, this book would never have been possible, and Sherryl Vint, my SFTS collaborator and comrade in arms, whose brilliance and diligence as a scholar have been a continuous inspiration. *Per aspera ad astra.*

Rob Latham

Works Cited

Alkon, Paul K. *Origins of Futuristic Fiction*. Athens: Georgia UP, 1987. Print.
Bailey, J. O. *Pilgrims in Space and Time: Trends and Patterns in Scientific and Utopian Fiction*. New York: Argus, 1947. Print.
Bleiler, Everett F. *The Checklist of Fantastic Literature: A Bibliography of Fantasy, Weird, and Science Fiction Books Published in the English Language*. Chicago: Shasta, 1948. Print.
Bould, Mark, Andrew M. Butler, Adam Roberts, and Sherryl Vint, eds. *The Routledge Companion to Science Fiction*. New York: Routledge, 2009. Print.
Bukatman, Scott. *Terminal Identity: The Virtual Subject in Postmodern Science Fiction*. Durham, NC: Duke UP, 1993. Print.
Csicsery-Ronay Jr., Istvan. *The Seven Beauties of Science Fiction*. Middletown, CT: Wesleyan UP, 2008. Print.
"Editorial." Special Issue: Science Fiction and the Non-Print Media. *Science Fiction Studies* 7.3 (Nov. 1980): 245–46. Print.
Franklin, H. Bruce. *War Stars: The Superweapon and the American Imagination*. New York: Oxford UP, 1988. Print.
Freedman, Carl. *Critical Theory and Science Fiction*. Hanover, NH: Wesleyan UP, 2000. Print.
———. "Kubrick's *2001* and the Impossibility of a Science-Fiction Cinema." *Science Fiction Studies* 25.2 (July 1998): 300–18. Print.

Hayles, N. Katherine. *How We Became Posthuman: Virtual Bodies in Cybernetics, Literature, and Informatics*. Chicago: U Chicago P, 1999. Print.

Hillegas, Mark. "The Course in Science Fiction: A Hope Deferred." *Extrapolation* 9 (Dec. 1967): 19–21. Print.

James, Edward. "Before the *Novum*: The Prehistory of Science Fiction Criticism." *Learning from Other Worlds: Estrangement, Cognition and the Politics of Science Fiction and Utopia*. Ed. Patrick Parrinder. Liverpool: Liverpool UP, 2000. 19–35. Print.

Jameson, Fredric. *Postmodernism, or, The Cultural Logic of Late Capitalism*. 1991. Durham, NC: Duke UP, 1992. Print.

Ketterer, David. *New Worlds for Old: The Apocalyptic Imagination, Science Fiction, and American Literature*. Bloomington: Indiana UP, 1974. Print.

Landon, Brooks. *The Aesthetics of Ambivalence: Rethinking Science Fiction Film in the Age of Electronic (Re)Production*. Westport, CT: Greenwood, 1992. Print.

———. *Science Fiction After 1900: From the Steam Man to the Stars*. New York: Twayne, 1997. Print.

Luckhurst, Roger. *Science Fiction: A Cultural History*. London: Polity, 2005. Print.

Malmgren, Carl. *Worlds Apart: Narratology of Science Fiction*. Bloomington: Indiana UP, 1991. Print.

McCaffery, Larry, ed. *Storming the Reality Studio: A Casebook of Cyberpunk and Postmodern Fiction*. 1991. Durham, NC: Duke UP, 1992. Print.

Parrinder, Patrick. "Revisiting Suvin's Poetics of Science Fiction." *Learning from Other Worlds: Estrangement, Cognition and the Politics of Science Fiction and Utopia*. Ed. Patrick Parrinder. Liverpool: Liverpool UP, 2000. 36–50. Print.

Penley, Constance, Elisabeth Lyon, Lynn Spigel, and Janet Bergstrom, eds. *Close Encounters: Film, Feminism, and Science Fiction*. Minnesota: U of Minnesota P, 1991. Print.

Philmus, Robert. *Into the Unknown: The Evolution of Science Fiction from Francis Godwin to H.G. Wells*. Berkeley: U of California P, 1970. Print.

———. "The Shape of Science Fiction: Through the Historical Looking Glass." *Science Fiction Studies* 1.1 (Spring 1973): 37–41. Print.

Rieder, John. *Colonialism and the Emergence of Science Fiction*. Middletown, CT: Wesleyan UP, 2008. Print.

Rose, Mark. *Alien Encounters: Anatomy of Science Fiction*. Cambridge, MA: Harvard UP, 1981. Print.

Ross, Andrew. *Strange Weather: Culture, Science and Technology in the Age of Limits*. New York: Verso, 1991. Print.

Sobchack, Vivian. *The Limits of Infinity: The American Science Fiction Film, 1950–1975*. South Brunswick, NJ: Barnes, 1980. Print.

Sterling, Bruce. "Preface." *Mirrorshades: The Cyberpunk Anthology*. New York: Ace, 1986. ix–xvi. Print.

Suvin, Darko. *Metamorphoses of Science Fiction: On the Poetics and History of a Literary Genre*. New Haven, CT: Yale UP, 1979. Print.

Wolfe, Gary K. *The Known and the Unknown: The Iconography of Science Fiction*. Kent, OH: Kent State UP, 1979. Print.

Wolmark, Jenny. *Aliens and Others: Science Fiction, Feminism, and Postmodernism*. Iowa City: U of Iowa P, 1994. Print.

PART I

SCIENCE FICTION AS GENRE

CHAPTER 1

EXTRAPOLATION AND SPECULATION

BROOKS LANDON

In one of the early sustained critical attempts to introduce readers to the protocols of science fiction, *Inquiry into Science Fiction* (1955), Basil Davenport opened his chapter "Speculative Science Fiction" by referring to a couple of humorous quotations that introduce a number of recurrent issues in the ongoing attempt to explain the nature of SF. The first he attributes to a Frank Stockton character who muses, "If some things were different, other things would be otherwise" (45). The second he attributes to a character in a *Punch* cartoon who sadly observes, "Things might be so different if they wasn't as they is" (45). These comments point toward two of science fiction's most important rhetorical approaches: trying to imagine the future in terms of extrapolating from the present, in effect asking what might be "if this goes on...," and trying to imagine conditions significantly different from those of the writer's reality by posing the question "what if...?"

Davenport's chapter title implicitly suggests that science fiction has to do with "speculation," one of a cluster of terms largely understood as limiting the science-fictional imagination to a necessary concern with science and associating its narrative with forms of extrapolation and questions of plausibility. Accordingly, in many—if not most—of the discourses of science fiction, "extrapolation" and "speculation" are both understood as means to a crucial end: science fiction, in whatever fashion, must somehow go beyond what is currently known and must represent the unknown through some rhetoric of "plausibility." Plausibility, in turn, has largely been discussed in the discourse of SF in terms of the centrality of science, whether understood narrowly and monolithically or broadly and metaphorically.

As is true of so many ostensible binary oppositions in the discourse of science fiction, this one has been complicated by years of polemical and prescriptive constructions and definitions that have so blurred distinctions between the two terms as to make them impossible of definitional clarity or even of historical recovery. Speculation has been variously discussed in contrast with extrapolation, as an extension or further stage of extrapolation, as a category of which extrapolation is a subset, and so on.

And these two terms are particularly problematic, since as frequently as they are cast in opposition to each other, they are used as if they are interchangeable. For example, an overview of the genre by Lisa Yaszek suggests in its first sentence that science fiction is seen by literary and cultural historians "as the premiere narrative form of modernity because authors working in this genre extrapolate from Enlightenment ideals and industrial practices to imagine how educated people using machines and other technologies might change the material world," and then adds in her second sentence: "This kind of future-oriented technoscientific speculation lends itself to social and political speculation as well" (385). As we can see, Yaszek uses the terms interchangeably, and her comment suggests how comparison of these two nouns can be further complicated by the wide use of verb and modifier forms of each in which "speculate" or "speculative," "extrapolate" or "extrapolative" may be deployed without any necessary reference to the more bounded concepts of "speculation" and "extrapolation."

A contemporary interrogation of extrapolation and speculation as tools of scientific thinking must be understood more diachronically, as emerging from specific historical conditions and taking shape and changing over time, than as synchronic or capable of fixed, unchanging definition. It may be best to think of three different constructed relationships between the two terms. Historically, there is a line of SF thinking that opposes extrapolation to speculation, with the former term suggesting the fidelity to known and possibly even existing science and technology associated with the narratives of Jules Verne and the latter suggesting the more sociologically focused and less obviously plausible narratives of H. G. Wells. Another relationship can be seen in such works as Hal Clement's *Mission of Gravity* (1954), where speculation forms an initial set of "rules" as the starting point for a narrative not extrapolated from known facts, but that is then developed as rigorously as possible by extrapolating consequences from these starting "rules." And still another, particularly found in the contemporary discourses based on the idea of the Singularity, starts from extrapolation, but then claims that developments reach a point beyond which not only extrapolation but also speculation is no longer possible. So, one relationship posits extrapolation and speculation as near binary opposites, roughly alignable with other binaries such as that between "hard" and "soft" SF, while the other two position them as sequential stages, one starting from speculation and then becoming the baseline for extrapolation, the other starting from extrapolation and leading to speculation.

Both extrapolation and speculation have been understood at various times and by various writers as beginning not from a baseline scientific or sociological "reality," but from the textual base of a preceding SF story. In this way, James Patrick Kelley's "Think Like a Dinosaur" (1995) can be seen as a critical extrapolation from Tom Godwin's "The Cold Equations" (1954), Karen Joy Fowlers "What I Didn't See" (2003) can be thought of as an extrapolation from James Tiptree's "The Women Men Don't See" (1973), and countless artificial life stories can all be seen as extrapolations from Mary Shelley's *Frankenstein* (1818).

To complicate matters further still, extrapolation and speculation are popularly associated with quite different semantic registers, with extrapolation being a widely used mathematical term that denotes precision and extension from the known to the unknown, while speculation is a widely used financial term, with connotations of risk, lack of firm evidence, and uncertainty. Despite widespread invocation of both terms in discussions of SF, systematic treatments are very hard to find. *The Encyclopedia of Science Fiction* (1993) not only does not have an entry on "speculation," but declines a direct definition of "extrapolation," referring readers instead to "prediction" (397), whose corresponding entry immediately rules out prediction as an essential goal of SF. Similarly, neither extrapolation nor speculation is indexed in Roger Luckhurst's *Science Fiction* (2005), Istvan Csicsery-Ronay's *The Seven Beauties of Science Fiction* (2008), or Mark Bould and Sherryl Vint's *The Routledge Concise History of Science Fiction* (2011). Indeed, almost all discussions of extrapolation and/or speculation fail to specify the characteristics of either term, much less establish any rigorous sense of their relationship to each other.

One noteworthy exception, however, was Robert A. Heinlein's "Pandora's Box," first published under the title "Where To?" in 1952, that set the terms for most subsequent discussions of extrapolation and speculation. Heinlein tends to use these terms normatively and somewhat interchangeably: speculation is clearly the more expansive idea, but it is grounded in adherence to the "scientific method," and *both* terms function only in terms of plausibility. For Heinlein, scientific possibility is necessary for both extrapolation and speculation, and most SF writers make use of both methods. His explanation, which has been highly influential, if not originary, has a certain axiomatic ring to it:

> "Extrapolation" means much the same in fiction writing as it does in mathematics: exploring a trend. It means continuing a curve, a path, a trend into the future, by extending its present direction and continuing the *shape* it has displayed in its past performance—i.e., if it is a sine curve in the past, you extrapolate it as a sine curve in the future, not as an hyperbola, nor a Witch of Agnesi, and *most certainly not* as a tangent straight line.
>
> "Speculation" has far more elbowroom than extrapolation; it starts with a "What if?"—and the new factor thrown in by the what-if may be both wildly improbable and so revolutionary in effect as to throw a sine-curve trend (or a yeast-growth trend, or any trend) into something unrecognizably different. What if little green men land on the White House lawn and invite us to join a Galactic union?—or big green men land and enslave us and eat us? What if we solve the problem of immortality? (238–39; emphasis in original)

In another of his well-known ruminations on SF, "Science Fiction: Its Nature, Faults and Virtues" (1959), Heinlein expands the notion of "awareness" of scientific method, charging the SF writer with speculating from "such facts as there are" concerning seemingly impossible phenomena such as time travel and ghosts and doing so "as grandly and sweepingly as his imagination permits" (8). "Every new speculation necessarily starts by kicking aside some older theory," he notes, adding that phenomena that may seem "impossible, contrary to scientific fact," are actually only "contrary to present orthodox theory," and therefore fair game for science-fictional exploration (7).

Heinlein offers the most sustained rationale for the kind of science fiction strongly associated with John W. Campbell's influential editorship of SF's flagship magazine, *Astounding Science-Fiction* (renamed *Analog* in 1960) from 1937 to 1971. Possibly the most extended revelation of what "science" meant to Campbell may be found in his "The Place of Science Fiction" (1953), where he personifies it as a cold, inhuman, unemotional, rigid monolith. If Heinlein serves as Campbell's chief spokesperson for the importance of SF's fidelity to science through extrapolation, another celebrated writer closely associated with Campbell was Isaac Asimov, who also hewed to the Campbell view of science and scientific method, but who famously expanded the purview of science in his essay "Social Science Fiction" (1953). Asimov's discussion provides several new valuable perspectives for the comparison of extrapolation and speculation. Asimov divides SF into three forms of narrative: adventure stories, gadget stories, and social science fiction, illustrating each category with brief glosses on how a writer in 1880 might construct a story about "an imaginary vehicle that can move without horses by some internal source of power" (40). Asimov suggests that adventure SF and gadget SF both depend on the extrapolation of a "horseless carriage" from what is known of other mechanized transport combined with rudimentary knowledge of the workings of an internal combustion engine. The social science fiction narrative, however, might start from the assumption that something called a horseless carriage or an automobile had somehow been perfected and this technology had led to unforeseen problems connected with the oil industry, roadway infrastructure, and accidents. As Asimov drily notes: "It is easy to predict an automobile in 1880; it is very hard to predict a traffic problem. The former is really only an extrapolation of the railroad. The latter is something completely novel and unexpected" (41). Asimov shifts focus from extrapolation to speculation, but also specifies a necessary limit to the science-fictional presentation of "the completely novel and unexpected" by noting that there "is a great difference between taking liberties with the unlikely and taking liberties with the impossible" (42).

In a 1977 essay, "The Science in Science Fiction," another former Campbell writer, and later an editor of *Analog* himself, Stanley Schmidt, offered a sustained consideration of the relationship between extrapolation and speculation and the roles both play in establishing the plausibility of science as imagined in SF. Schmidt replaces "speculation" as a category with what he calls "innovation." Extrapolation, according to Schmidt, means "speculation based on extensions, developments, and applications of well-established knowledge." He adds: "No new principles are postulated, so it can be said with a fair degree of assurance that these speculations are things that we know are possible" (30). He distinguishes "innovation" from "extrapolation," stipulating that the former "does depend on the assumption of new—i.e., now unknown—principles" (31), offering faster-than-light travel, anti-gravity, and time travel as examples. For this kind of innovation to count as science-fictional, it "cannot be proved possible," but it is also important that "nobody should be able to prove it's *impossible* at the time of its writing" (31; emphasis in original). Edging back somewhat from insistence on strict standards of possibility or impossibility, Schmidt cites the need in an SF story for "internal consistency" and calls for the SF writer to "make at least a passing attempt at explaining any new principles" (33). Even such "a passing attempt" to establish plausibility may be successful because SF readers have read a lot of stories in which plausible explanations for implausible phenomena have been offered. As a result of reader familiarity with the larger SF megatext, "There are some things which once were innovative, have not even remotely become part of accepted scientific knowledge, and yet are now readily accepted by readers without explanation" (33).

A more expansive view of this phenomenon has been advanced by Stanislaw Lem, who explains that science fiction's ties to the real world are quite elastic as "the real world—the world which realism describes in its contemporary shape" is something SF "tries to describe at other points on the space-time continuum" (35). In effect, this shifts the issue from asking whether a fictional semblance *is* plausible to the question of whether it *could be* plausible, a question the answer to which, as Schmidt suggests, may be found in the reader's knowledge of the SF megatext. If the reader is familiar with other SF works that offer at least a gesture toward a plausible explanation for their departures from everyday reality, that might suffice. As a result, it may be the case that the evaluation of the plausibility of both extrapolation and speculation depends as much on the reader's familiarity with the SF megatext as on any cognitive connection to science or technology. Accordingly, SF's claim to plausibility frequently rests on a consensual hoax. It is the specific premise of SF, Lem specifies, "that anything shown shall in principle be interpretable empirically and rationally" (35). And that "in principle" is key, since, as Lem reminds us, much narrative machinery in "realistic" fiction is already patently fantastic, as when the thoughts of dying man are enlisted in telling a story.

Joining Heinlein and Schmidt as one of the very few writers or critics who offer their views of both extrapolation and speculation, and joining Lem in his acceptance of the essential rhetorical hoax of SF, Basil Davenport freely acknowledges that SF writers frequently resort to rhetorical "jiggery pokery" (1) or "scientific double-talk" (2) or "scientific hocus pocus" (14) to ground their narratives in the plausible. This is not difficult, he notes, because "readers will apparently accept anything if they are told it is scientific" (14). Having identified the idea of a "space-warp" as the kind of jiggery pokery necessary to make some SF narratives possible, Davenport explains extrapolation in a way that makes it sound more like what Heinlein calls speculation, associating it both with the jiggery pokery of space-warps and parallel universes and locating its starting point in the social rather than the exact sciences: "We take some tendency in our present society, toward sexual license, say, or the prolonging of the life span, or the dominance of women, imagine it enormously increased, and show the probable consequences" (12).

If Davenport shifts our understanding of extrapolation and speculation further from the science-fetishizing pole represented by Campbell, Heinlein, and Asimov, Judith Merril is the SF writer and editor who most clearly wants to leave that pole far behind. The "speculative fiction" Merril is known for championing has some features in common with the "speculative fiction" promoted by Heinlein, but it resists the assumption that "science" is the prime arbiter of plausibility and argues that speculation has more in common with "mainstream" literature than with Campbell-style genre SF. Merrill developed her views of the nature and role of speculative fiction in the yearly summations featured in her series of twelve "Year's Best S-F" anthologies (edited from 1956 through 1969), as well as in the long 1966 essay, "What Do You Mean: Science? Fiction?" As those two provocative question marks in her title suggest, Merril's essay sets out to challenge "certain axiomatic assumptions" about both terms (53). According to Merril, speculative fiction consists of "stories whose objective is to explore, to discover, to *learn*, by means of projection, extrapolation, analogue, hypothesis-and-paper-experimentation, something about the nature of the universe, of man, of "reality" (60; emphasis in original). As she elaborates:

> I use the term "speculative fiction" here specifically to describe the mode which makes use of the traditional "scientific method" (observation, hypothesis, experimentation) to examine some postulated approximation of reality, by introducing a given set of changes—imaginary or inventive—into the common background of "known facts," creating an environment in which the responses and perceptions of the characters will reveal something about the inventions, the characters, or both. (60)

Merril's overview of the evolution of science fiction into speculative fiction centers on the roles of influential editors in promoting an ever-more-capacious aesthetic, starting with Hugo Gernsback in the 1920s and moving to Campbell in the 1940s, Anthony Boucher and Horace L. Gold in the 1950s, and Michael Moorcock in the 1960s. She sees Gernsback's limited view of science leading to stories containing "endless expositions of technical, technological, technophiliac and Technocratic ideas" (63) and Campbell's "engineering" view offering a still limited but "broader concept of the scope of 'science'" (68). Campbell, she suggests, actually "created an audience for new speculative idea fiction, which his own magazine was no longer supplying" (77). Enter Boucher and Gold, editors of *The Magazine of Fantasy and Science Fiction* and *Galaxy*, respectively, both encouraging fresh ideas not so closely tied to a limited construction of science.

Proclaiming Reginald Bretnor's "The Future of Science Fiction" (1953) "the outstanding critical insight into the nature and direction" of SF, Merril credits Bretnor with matching Boucher's call for a new literature "whose special province is science," but that would represent a true synthesis between science and literature (83). Indeed, Bretnor seems to offer the blueprint for Merril's "speculative fiction," including an implicit distinction between extrapolation and speculation that starts from the assumption that areas of inquiry exist for which we not only "have no scientific maps" but "as yet no mapping instruments" (Bretnor 286). These uncharted areas, Bretnor insists, "are a proper study for the scientist and for the science fiction writer, both of whom have as their function, not outright affirmation, not flat denial, but the exploring of every possibility—and of a great many apparent impossibilities as well" (287).

In the synthesis of two kinds of extrapolation, that which extrapolates from known "maps" of science and that which extrapolates from areas for which no "new maps" have been drawn, Bretnor sees the "seed of an entire new literature" (288), an "integrated literature" equally driven by scientifically informed mainstream writers and artistically informed SF writers. Clear signs of Bretnor's messianic aesthetic can be found everywhere in Merril's writings about SF, especially her advocacy for the 1960s British "New Wave" as just such a newly relevant speculative literature, with Moorcock, editor of the New Wave flagship *New Worlds*, the driving force. Commensurate with this succession of editors, Merril proposes a succession of writers offering ever-broader instances of speculation, with Cordwainer Smith's "Scanners Live in Vain" (1950) the first example of the kind of "integrative" SF called for by Bretnor and envisioned in her normative use of "speculative fiction." And J. G. Ballard becomes for Merril the writer who best exemplifies the "new literature" she sees emerging (94).

Merril is well known for her own editing of *Year's Best S-F*. The very titles of these anthologies reflect her impatience with "science fiction" as a term, as she cycles through various permutations of *s* and *f*, the hyphen between coming and going. As she eventually explains in her sixth volume, her insistence on initials was intended to signal that her concern was not just with genre science fiction, but with "the whole field of science-fantasy, of speculative literature" ("Summation" 375). In 1967 Merril edited *SF: The Best of the Best*, collecting her favorite stories from the first five annuals, reminding her readers that science fiction "is not fiction about science, but fiction which endeavors to find the meaning in science and the scientific-technological society we are constructing" ("Introduction" 3). What she wants speculative fiction to be is "a special sort of contemporary writing which makes use of fantastic or inventive elements to comment on, or speculate about, society, humanity, life, the cosmos, reality. And any other topic under the general heading of philosophy" (3). In her comments for the last volume in the series, *SF 12*, published in 1969, Merril announces that she has finally settled on what she wants SF to stand for, embracing Robert Scholes's concept of "fabulation," which she sees as an answer to Bretnor's call for an "integrated literature." "Speculative Fabulation" is what she opts for, hopefully announcing: "SF: Speculative Fabulation. A satisfactory solution at last for my abbreviation-in-search-of an-extension?" ("Fish" 11). Whatever Merrill means by SF, it is clearly *not* tied to the rigorous "plotting the curve" understanding of extrapolation so dear to Campbell, Heinlein, Asimov, et al. Serious fiction that reflects a disciplined mind and that emphasizes "humanics" over mechanics seems to meet Merril's standards for extrapolation from known science. Indeed, her view of speculative literature is similar in many respects to more recent discussions of slipstream.

As this brief overview of some of the most prominent originary discussions of extrapolation and speculation suggests, no two writers seem to use the terms in the same way, and thus rigorous consideration of these terms is quite difficult. Either explicitly or implicitly, all questions about extrapolation and speculation have somewhere in their background concerns with plausibility—its nature, its standards, and its degree of importance. Plausibility in science fiction may be created by a number of different strategies and may refer to a wide range of realities, but is characteristically linked, however loosely, to some aspect of science or technology. Plausibility in SF nods toward the real and the known, while the "sense of wonder" frequently invoked to explain the affective appeal of SF nods toward the fabulous, if not the fantastic; extrapolation and speculation are the imaginative processes that negotiate the difference between those two ends. Accordingly, important to any understanding of extrapolation and/or speculation are assumptions having to do with the role of "science" in science fiction.

Science is unmistakably and irrevocably associated with SF, whether through its presence or absence. "Imaginary Science" is only one of the seven cognitive "beauties" of science fiction studied by Csicsery-Ronay, but it is arguably the most widely referenced of the beauties. Csicsery-Ronay's chapter starts from the proposition that "science is sf's pretext," leading to "the illusion that SF stories are dramatizations of scientific knowledge," never more than "an image of science, a poetic illusion disguising its illusionary status" (111). His noteworthy point is that extrapolation is essentially *a ludic process*. As particularly opposed to Campbell's view that science is deadly serious stuff, Csicsery-Ronay holds that "exaggeratedly rationalistic theories ignore SF's fundamentally playful performance of scientific thinking":

> Even when it is written by professional scientists with established reputations, SF requires its science to violate scientific correctness, even plausibility. Writers take known, plausible, or just widely entertained scientific ideas and extend them speculatively into the unknown, exceeding their contexts, revealing their fantastic dimensions, and undermining obliquely their claims to universal applicability. Most SF writers, far from pushing an agenda of scrupulous respect for scientific truth, toy with it, making it a source of metaphors, rationalized by realistic representation, and embedded in quasi-mythic narrative traditions that express social concerns. (112)

Just as surely as the understanding of extrapolation and speculation has shifted over time, so the understanding of the science in science fiction, whether imaginary or "real," has also shifted and must be approached diachronically. It is ironic that so much discussion acknowledging that SF is first and foremost "the literature of change" has insisted on fixed, synchronic approaches to define or characterize the genre. If science fiction is, as most writers, critics, and readers seem to agree, the literature of change, it follows that, whatever meaning we ascribe to terms such as extrapolation and speculation, their meaning must have inexorably changed over the hundred or so years they have been used in the discourse of SF, and it is equally certain that the relationship between the two terms has changed over that period, with "speculation" gradually supplanting "extrapolation" as the favored term. Moreover, the understanding of known science as the baseline for both terms has also changed. In this sense, the pertinent question may not so much concern the plausibility of the endpoint of extrapolation or speculation as the starting point: what is meant by science. In his excellent "Science Fiction and the Scientific World-View" (1979), Patrick Parrinder has explored this problem, explaining that "science" in SF is frequently used as a sliding signifier variously understood as "the scientific world-view," "the scientific outlook," "scientific thought," or "an ideology justifying scientific research as intrinsic to the nature and purpose of human existence" (67). Locating all these constructions somewhere between the two conceptual poles of the Darwinian theory of evolution and the certainty of entropy posited by the Second Law of Thermodynamics, Parrinder charts developments in the scientific worldview, periodizing its ascendencies and declines, and contextualizing its concerns in terms of individual actants and cultural and ideological forces. Parrinder reminds us that disillusion and distrust of science have been as prevalent in SF as has its championing and persuasively demonstrate why generalizations about the nature of SF's relations to the scientific worldview can only be understood in terms of change.

Parrinder's approach anticipates both Roger Luckhurst's effort to understand SF texts "as part of a constantly shifting network that ties together science, technology, social history and cultural expression with different emphases at different times" (6) and John Rieder's argument for a historical genre theory, in which our understanding of SF would take into account "the motives, the contexts, and the effects" of those characterizing the genre, "and the many ways of intervening in the genre's production, distribution, and reception" (204). Against the well-entrenched tradition of SF critical discourse that constructs extrapolation and speculation as static terms closely tied to scientific plausibility is the contemporary view that these terms and indeed SF itself should not be thought of as fixed categories or classifications, but as subject to negotiations at particular times and framed by particular circumstances and purposes. Such an elastic approach to the genre is outlined by Mark Bould and Sherryl Vint in their *Routledge Concise History of Science Fiction* and illustrated more fully in their 2009 polemical essay "There Is No Such Thing as Science Fiction." Bould and Vint argue directly in that essay (and only slightly more obliquely in their Routledge book) that "genres are never, as frequently perceived, objects which already exist in the world and which are subsequently studied by genre critics, but fluid and tenuous constructions made by the interaction of various claims and practices by writers, producers, distributors, marketers, readers, fans, critics and other discursive agents" (48). Their approach to genre also accounts for many discussions of extrapolation and speculation, since particular SF texts are routinely "enrolled," however breezily, as shining examples of extrapolation or of speculation.

Today, even critics who would disagree with Bould and Vint are finding it ever more difficult to sustain static classificatory efforts—due in great part to the changing nature of science. James Gunn, whose SF writing and criticism have been prominent and influential for over sixty years, resignedly acknowledged this in 2006:

> Increasingly, from the quanta to the cosmos, uncertainty has become the one constant. At the subatomic level, the only reality is illusory, at the cosmic level, the latest theory imagines the natural world as the three-dimensional aspect of cosmic strings that exist in a ten-dimensional reality. Fantasists seem authorized to let their imaginations soar, and more scientifically minded authors can resort to the magic of nanotechnology. (231)

Gunn is not alone in noting the obvious blurring of the line between fantasy and reality in science as well as in SF. Old-school linear extrapolation, usually confined to the near future, has become problematic even in hard SF, as Kathryn Cramer details, noting that "facts" age badly in science, making contemporary science "a moving target" (189). Moving away from the mathematical model of extrapolation, Cramer suggests the need for hard SF to construct science *as a mythology*: "What science gives to hard SF is a body of metaphor that provides the illusion of both realism and rationalism" (188). And yet the ideal of extrapolation based on confidence in the reality of baseline science remains strong in some SF writers, as can be seen in a comment Cramer offers from Greg Egan, one of the preeminent current writers of hard SF. Responding to the situation lamented by Gunn, Egan addresses this phenomenon as a gain rather than as a loss, claiming

> what happens in my novels is that the border between science and metaphysics shifts: issues that originally seemed completely metaphysical, completely beyond the realms of scientific enquiry, actually become part of physics. I'm writing about extending science into territory that was once believed to be metaphysical, not about abandoning or "transcending" science at all. (qtd. Cramer 195)

Paolo Bacigalupi, author of the award-winning *The Windup Girl* (2009), joins Egan in insisting on the importance of "extending" science but from a greatly expanded understanding of what can be extended. Bacigalupi believes that science fiction is supposed to display an "extrapolative quality," but his notion of extrapolation is expansive, and seems to value *affective* extrapolation along with technoscientific (including the extrapolation of current fears), while suggesting that just because a writer can "work out the physics" of a fantastic idea doesn't mean the idea isn't "silly stuff." For him, contemporary relevance seems to trump rigor, as he dismisses "lines of speculation which are pretty interesting but not necessarily connected to today's questions" (54).

Like so many before him, Bacigalupi seems to use extrapolation and speculation nearly interchangably, allowing for a broad understanding of extrapolation, but distinguishing it from speculation of the "thought experiment" or merely interesting kind. Comments such as Egan's and Bacigalupi's suggest that while there may never be agreement on the nature of the relationship between extrapolation and speculation, the history of SF suggests an inexorable merging of the two terms, with speculation becoming the more widely used, even by adherents to the hard-science end of the SF continuum. "Genre-morphing" is what John Clute terms this phenomenon (77), while Gary Wolfe writes about *Evaporating Genres* (2011), both eminent critics noting the passing of an era in which standards of plausibility could be relied upon to demarcate genre boundaries, with obvious implications for older understandings of extrapolation/speculation in terms of plausibility. While SF nominally based on extrapolation and/or speculation with plausible ties to the technoscientific worldview has flourished as a literature of interrogation and contemplation rather than as a literature of prediction, its strained allegiance to plausibility has been in place long enough for SF's claim on extrapolative rigor to have worn thin. Clute suggests that extrapolation, even when not evaluated in terms of predictions, now has a record of failure, as "there is a decreasing resemblance between the world we inhabit today and the future worlds advocated with some consistency of voice and vision, in the American SF of the previous half-century" (66). His point is that "the old story of sf" turns out *not* to have been a story of scientific extrapolation or speculation, but of something else entirely—of "the American Dream of progress" (66).

Finally, Singularity discourse may take these two terms to a self-cancelling extreme as fairly conventional mathematical-style extrapolation is being invoked by Vernor Vinge, Ray Kurzweil, Eric Drexler, Damien Broderick, and other Singularitarians to predict a moment beyond which not even the wildest speculation will be possible. The concept of Singularity thus becomes another argument in the growing recognition that historically freighted and fraught terms such as extrapolation and speculation may have reached the end of their usefulness in the discourse of SF.

Works Cited

Asimov, Isaac. "Social Science Fiction." 1953. *Turning Points: Essays on the Art of Science Fiction*. Ed. Damon Knight. New York: Harper & Row, 1977. 29–61. Print.

Bacigalupi, Paolo. "*Locus* Interview: The Windup Boy." *Locus* 67.2 (Aug. 2011): 6–7, 54–55. Print.

Bould, Mark, and Sherryl Vint. *The Routledge Concise History of Science Fiction*. New York: Routledge, 2011. Print.

———. "There Is No Such Thing As Science Fiction." *Reading Science Fiction*. Ed. James Gunn, Marleen Barr, and Matthew Candelaria. New York: Palgrave, 2009. 43–51. Print.

Bretnor, Reginald. "The Future of Science Fiction." *Modern Science Fiction: Its Meaning and Its Future*. Ed. Reginald Bretnor. New York: Coward-McCann, 1953. 265–94. Print.

Campbell Jr., John W. "The Place of Science Fiction." *Modern Science Fiction: Its Meaning and Its Future*. Ed. Reginald Bretnor. New York: Coward-McCann, 1953. 3–22. Print.

Clute, John. "Science Fiction from 1980 to the Present." *The Cambridge Companion to Science Fiction*. Ed. Edward James and Farah Mendlesohn. Cambridge, UK: Cambridge UP, 2003. 64–78. Print.

Clute, John, and Peter Nicholls, eds. *The Encyclopedia of Science Fiction*. 2nd ed. New York: St. Martin's, 1993. Print.

Cramer, Kathryn. "Hard Science Fiction." *The Cambridge Companion to Science Fiction*. Ed. Edward James and Farah Mendlesohn. Cambridge, UK: Cambridge UP, 2003. 186–96. Print.

Csicsery-Ronay Jr., Istvan. *The Seven Beauties of Science Fiction*. Middletown, CT: Wesleyan UP, 2008. Print.

Davenport, Basil. *Inquiry into Science Fiction*. New York: Longmans, Green and Co., 1955. Print.

Gunn, James. *Inside Science Fiction*. 1992. 2nd ed. Lanham, MD: Scarecrow, 2006. Print.

Heinlein, Robert A. "Pandora's Box." 1952. *Turning Points: Essays on the Art of Science Fiction*. Ed. Damon Knight. New York: Harper & Row, 1977. 238–58. Print.

———. "Science Fiction: Its Nature, Faults and Virtues." 1959. *Turning Points: Essays on the Art of Science Fiction*. Ed. Damon Knight. New York: Harper & Row, 1977. 3–28. Print.

Lem, Stanislaw. "On the Structural Analysis of Science Fiction." 1973. Trans. Franz Rottensteiner et al. *Microworlds: Writings on Science Fiction and Fantasy*. Ed. Franz Rottensteiner. New York: Harvest/HBJ, 1984. 31–44. Print.

Luckhurst, Roger. *Science Fiction*. Malden, MA: Polity, 2005. Print.

Merril, Judith. "Introduction." *SF: The Best of the Best*. New York: Dell, 1967. 1–7. Print.

———. "Introduction: Fish Out of Water, Man Beside Himself." *SF:12*. New York: Dell, 1968. 9–11. Print.

———. "Summation: The Year in S-F." *6th Annual Edition: The Year's Best S-F*. New York: Dell, 1963. 374–78. Print.

———. "What Do You Mean: Science? Fiction?" 1966. *SF: The Other Side of Realism: Essays on Modern Fantasy and Science Fiction*. Ed. Thomas D. Clareson. Bowling Green, OH: Bowling Green U Popular P, 1971. 53–95. Print.

Parrinder, Patrick. "Science Fiction and the Scientific World-View." *Science Fiction: A Critical Guide*. Ed. Patrick Parrinder. London: Longman, 1979. 67–88. Print.

Rieder, John. "On Defining SF, or Not: Genre Theory, SF, and History." *Science Fiction Studies* 37.2 (July 2010): 191–209. Print.

Schmidt, Stanley. "The Science in Science Fiction." *Many Futures, Many Worlds: Theme and Form in Science Fiction*. Ed. Thomas D. Clareson. Kent, OH: Kent State UP, 1977. 27–49. Print.

Wolfe, Gary K. *Evaporating Genres: Essays on Fantastic Literature*. Middletown, CT: Wesleyan UP, 2011. Print.

Yaszek, Lisa. "Science Fiction." *The Routledge Companion to Literature and Science*. Ed. Bruce Clark with Manuela Rossini. New York: Routledge, 2011. 385–95. Print.

CHAPTER 2

AESTHETICS

PETER STOCKWELL

SCIENCE fiction is extremely diverse as a genre, encompassing a wide range of narrative types and expressive patterns: you will find stories cast in the form of crime and detective puzzles, theological and philosophical explorations, ripping yarns, shoot-outs and battles, and meditative extrapolations; both pacy narrative drive and lyrical contemplation; characters that resonate as rich fictional people and characters that are everyman tokens and plot devices. You will find magical realism, modern gothic, postmodernism and the absurd, omniscient narration, and psychological stream of consciousness; the registers of action-adventure, experimental narrative, science, humor, and psychobabble; stories both heavy with demotic dialogue and elsewhere brimming with specialized terminology; and a rich and still expanding set of subgenres across the many media forms of print and screen. All of this diversity makes it very difficult to delineate a single unifying aesthetic that can be said to identify science fiction as a cultural phenomenon. However, it seems to me that this is a fault of our traditional understanding of aesthetics, rather than a problem unique to science fiction.

The term "aesthetics" gained widespread usage only in the late eighteenth century. At its most scholarly, aesthetics has been the term that encompasses discussions of artistic value, based on setting out the principles and beliefs that underscore a particular art object or movement: this is aesthetics as philosophy (see Janaway). At the same time, aesthetic discussions have often centered upon considerations of the nature of beauty and the measurement of a particular work of art: this is aesthetics as (literary) criticism (see Armstrong). The beauty or otherwise of an artwork can be considered not only in terms of its own properties or creative intentions but also for the effect it has on a viewer or culture: this approach treats the aesthetic value of a work in terms of its social impact. Finally, there is a sense in which the aesthetic of an object relates in journalistic and popular usage to the "look and feel" of the work: this is aesthetics as fashion.

Across these different senses and applications, there is a general set of uses that pertains to the internal properties and features of the literary text, and another related set that inclines toward the generic and social positioning of the work. To give a simple example, here are the openings to five short stories from the same collection by science fiction writer Roger Zelazny:

1. Roger Zelazny "The Doors of His Face, the Lamps of His Mouth" (1965):

    I'm a baitman. No one is born a baitman, except in a French novel where everyone is. (In fact, I think that's the title, *We are All Bait*. Pfft!) How I got that way is barely worth the telling and has nothing to do with neo-exes, but the days of the beast deserve a few words, so here they are. (1)

2. "The Keys to December" (1966):

    Born of man and woman, in accordance with Catform Y7 requirements, Coldworld Class (modified per Alyonal), 3.2-E, G.M.I. option, Jarry Dark was not suited for existence anywhere in the universe which had guaranteed him a niche. This was either a blessing or a curse, depending on how you looked at it.
    So look at it however you would, here is the story.... (33)

3. "Divine Madness" (1966):

    "... I is this? hearers wounded-wonder like stand them makes and stars wandering the conjures sorrow of phrase Whose..."
    He blew smoke through the cigarette and it grew longer. (199)

4. "The Great Slow Kings" (1963):

    Drax and Dran sat in the great Throne Hall of Glan, discussing life. Monarchs by virtue of superior intellect and physique—and the fact that they were the last two survivors of the race of Glan—theirs was a divided rule over the planet and their one subject, Zindrome, the palace robot. (181)

5. "A Rose for Ecclesiastes" (1963):

    I was busy translating one of my *Madrigals Macabre* into Martian on the morning I was found acceptable. The intercom had buzzed briefly, and I dropped my pencil and flipped on the toggle in a single motion. (71)

On the social and cultural dimension, Zelazny is widely regarded as a "literary" science fiction author, with an MA in Renaissance literature and with a style of writing that often blended classical mythologies, literary allusion, and quotations from French, Latin, and Greek (see Lindskold). The first example above illustrates the blend of what appears to be scholarly and literate allusion with a demotic dialogic style, and even a science-fictional neologism ("neo-exes"). Excerpt 2 exemplifies the immersive and idiomatic style that can often be found in science-fictional openings. Like the first extract ("a few words, so here they are"), the introduction refers to itself as text ("here is the story"), which is both informal and self-consciously artsy, blending conversational idioms with technical terms that the experienced SF reader might decode: a genetically modified person in the form of a Cat suited for Alyonal, a cold planet that has 3.2 times the Earth's gravity.

Excerpt 3 is the most literate and self-conscious of all, with graphological marking drawing attention to the opening sentence in italics and reversed word-order: corrected, it is a quotation from Shakespeare's *Hamlet*. It retains internally the science-fictional suggestion in "stars," and then introduces an oddity in the sentence that describes the smoked cigarette growing longer. The reversal is iconic in the rest of the story, which deals with a character who—between seizures—lives backward through the immediate future, in what turns out to be a redemptive love story. Excerpt 4 displays the grandiose register of overblown mythological science fiction, quickly undermined in bathos. The final extract immerses the reader into the futuristic world, presented as if it were familiar—a common technique in SF that is here lyrically enriched with the alliterative "m" and the anachronistic blend of pencil and toggle.

These examples have been selected because they neatly illustrate—within one book—several different features of science-fictional writing. Any comprehensive aesthetics of science fiction would have to allow a principled account of all of these features (and more) and also recognize that Zelazny is at one (literate and allusive) end of a spectrum that stretches to more action-driven and one-dimensional examples of formulaic genre fiction.

One possible way of dealing with genre diversity would be to work out different aesthetic principles for the different forms of SF. So we could explain separately the characteristically appealing features and effects of the writing of the interwar US pulp magazines, or the 1960s British New Wave, or cyberpunk in the 1980s, and so on. However, this approach neglects to recognize the intuitive sense shared by many readers that SF is generically and wholly a particular thing. Subgenres have family resemblance with each other, even if those at extended ends of the spectrum appear superficially dissimilar.

An alternative approach is to claim that SF is not easily amenable to the customary perspectives of literary scholarship, because the latter arose alongside a literature of character, a lyrical sensibility, and an artistic self-referentiality that has diverged from the history of SF writing. Science fiction therefore requires its own unique aesthetic account. The most famous proponents of this position are SF authors and critics Samuel R. Delany and Joanna Russ. Delany argues that science fiction is necessarily and by definition richer (an aesthetic judgment) than what he terms "mundane" fiction because of its greater potential for world-building, freed from the restrictions of the parochial and everyday. However, this position is an evaluation of *poetics* rather than aesthetics proper: the enhanced richness is a matter of larger scope for propositional content and meaning; Delany does not claim that SF allows a wider or qualitatively different intensity of emotional attachment than other literary art. Russ contrasts the emphasis and value placed in literary criticism on lyrical intensity with SF's "drastically different form of literary art" (112). She describes science fiction as essentially didactic rather than contemplative, with characters that are collective or representational rather than individual psychologies and with an emphasis on phenomena possessing a quality of almost religious awe. Criticism of science fiction cannot possibly look like the criticism we are accustomed to. It will—perforce—employ an aesthetic in which the elegance, rigorousness, and systematic coherence of explicit ideas is of great importance (Russ 118).

This position might appeal to anyone with a contrarian streak who enjoys being an SF fan as an act of alterity, but it smacks of special pleading. Rather than engaging with the common processes of aesthetic reception all art shares, treating SF as aesthetically sui generis only serves to marginalize it further. It is not psychologically plausible to imagine a separate type of reading and appreciative process evolved solely for SF, and it is not socially plausible to separate SF out from the continuity of human experience. For her part, Russ points out the similarities between medieval literature and science fiction (indeed, it is notable that many SF scholars, such as Edward James and Tom Shippey, are also medievalists). Medieval and science-fictional literature share, she claims, many features of didacticism and exposition, everyman character tokens, materialism, and a "sense of wonder"—the last named capturing their common aesthetic effect. However, this continuity undermines the argument that SF needs to be treated differently from other forms of literary art. Later in this chapter, I suggest three ways that science fiction is aesthetically engaging, ways that are common to all other forms of literature; but it is worth arguing at this point that there are good theoretical reasons for asserting this continuity.

From classical times up until the early modern era, beauty has largely been understood in terms of proportion, balance, harmony, planned design, and symmetry. Ugliness in this understanding is not a thing in itself but a turning away from beauty, a failure of proportion, balance, and so on. Nonbeauty is therefore formless. In our contemporary terms, we might say that beauty has been understood as figure (a good, well-formed gestalt shape) possessing psychological prominence and attraction, while nonbeauty has been conceived as ground (the indistinct, property-less background that simply defines the space behind the figure). Much of what we would now call aesthetics scholarship, from Plato and Aristotle to St. Thomas Aquinas and St. Bonaventure, was concerned with setting out the rules and principles for achieving artistic beauty in literature, painting, sculpture, architecture, landscape, and so on. Up until the seventeenth century in Western philosophy, beauty was a matter of identifying and articulating prescriptive rules, even if those prescriptions were based on an educated consensus of what constituted beautiful objects.

During the late Renaissance and into the Enlightenment, observations on aesthetics take a turn toward a more subjective understanding that we might recognize as modern: beauty is not (just) a property of objects but a perceived property. Differences in feeling become important in delineating and categorizing different aesthetic effects. So Edmund Burke, for example, differentiates between the beautiful and the sublime as mutually exclusive effects: the sublime allows for intensity of feeling caused by pleasurable terror at immensity or transcendence. He also emphasizes the personal and subjective in understanding such feelings and the power of language to convey them:

> Certain it is, that the influence of most things on our passions is not so much from the things themselves, as from our opinions concerning them; and these again depend very much on the opinions of other men, conveyable for the most part by words only. (335)

In his *Critique of Judgment* (1790), Kant also develops the distinction between beauty and the sublime by further subdividing the latter into the noble sublime, splendid sublime, and terrifying sublime. In maintaining this distinction, he proposes what we might now see as a very modern, cognitive psychological understanding of the perceptual basis of figure and ground: beauty is a judgment of an object in the world, while the sublime transcends objects and is a more formless and intense feeling.

This is a distinction in which the SF tradition from *Frankenstein* (1818) onward tends to come off badly, since SF is firmly placed in the sublime category. This is evident in the genre's key feature of awe-some-ness, sense of wonder, or what in mid-twentieth-century American SF was called the "gosh-wow!" effect (see Stockwell, *Poetics* 76–106). The reason this is a bad outcome for SF is that, by contrastive implication, it denies the genre access to the category of beauty. Even if beauty and sublimity are scaled prototypically along an axis, with one blending into the other as proposed by Schopenhauer, SF still remains located in both senses at the "other-worldly" pole with awe, terror, and wonder, rather than alongside lyric, passion, emotion, and other effects of pure observed beauty. Schopenhauer's sublime is self-effacing, as the observer forgets his or her own situation and is transported elsewhere in transcendence.

Now it must be said at this point that not all science fiction achieves this sort of sublimity! Part of the problem of the history of aesthetics is that commentary tends to be reserved for examples of high art, with the prescriptions expressed often functioning in a circular way to define what counts as value and what does not. Either way, SF loses out, being seen either as low art unworthy of scholarly study or else as a type of art that appeals to simple reason and childish wonder, rather than anything more resonant, tasteful, or emotionally sophisticated.

In a valiant attempt to reappropriate some of these values for SF, Istvan Csicsery-Ronay Jr. has set out what he calls the "seven beauties" of science fiction. His approach aims at description rather than prescription, though there is certainly a sense that he intends a persuasive element to his scheme:

> Rather than a program-like set of exclusive rules and required devices, this mode is a constellation of diverse intellectual and emotional interests and responses that are particularly active in an age of restless technological transformation. I consider seven such categories to be the most attractive and formative of science-fictionality. (5)

His seven beauties are: the SF sublime, the SF grotesque, imaginary science, future history, fictive neology, the fictive novum, and the technologiade. It should be immediately clear that most of these features primarily concern poetics (content and technique) rather than aesthetics (effect), though one of the attractive aspects of Csicsery-Ronay's scheme is the implicit assertion that technique and effects cannot be neatly separated. His set of features is also presented as a "constellation" rather than necessary criteria, so different SF works will possess different combinations of these aspects. Csicsery-Ronay's features represent the elements that differentiate SF from other forms of literature. In this respect, and in spite of its advance on earlier delineations of the genre, it functions still as an argument for SF as special, odd, or deviant, separated from other literary art, even as it promotes this otherness as valuable.

Instead, we might turn to our current best understanding of the psychological processes of literary appreciation to construct an aesthetics of science fiction. Though there has been a shift in aesthetic theory from prescription to description, the prescriptive tradition remains alive in journalistic and popular discourses that defend differences between high and low culture, whereas most modern scholarly work in aesthetics is concerned with the anthropology and social psychology of artistic value, or with the comparative study of art across cultures and histories, and is mainly descriptive. However, even the most anthropologically descriptive discussion of aesthetics has a persuasive element, indicating that aesthetics as a field is neither purely objective nor subjective but necessarily *intersubjective*. As a result, we need to draw on those aspects of human experience that are common to us, while trying to describe them in as transparent and systematic a way as possible. The best current framework for achieving this resides in the insights for art and literature emerging from cognitive science (see Hogan; Stockwell, *Cognitive*).

The cognitive turn in the humanities rejects Cartesian dualities of mind and body, reason and emotion, poetics and aesthetics. These are replaced by continuities such as the embodied mind, the interanimation of meaning and feeling, and the assertion that our processes and experiences of life and art are not separate. In essence, real emotion and literary emotion, real people and literary characters, remembered experiences and recounted experiences are processed very similarly, with the only difference being their ontological status. One consequence is that science-fictional aesthetics cannot be treated separately from literary aesthetics, because literary feeling is still fundamentally the same as feeling in general (see Stockwell, *Texture*). We can identify—drawing on cognitive science—the common aesthetic patterns that SF shares with other art and experience in general; and we can also identify the particular patterns of science-fictional singularity.

For example, it is clear from different sources such as gestalt psychology and the cognitive psychology of visual perception that certain shapes and concepts are universally regarded as more attractive than others, in the sense both of attracting attention and being aesthetically appealing (see Stafford; *Styles*). And it is possible to apply the same principles to the effects of literary reading to produce a usable toolkit of the linguistic features of good attractors in a literary text. Literary works exploit these linguistic resources to generate aesthetic effects in readers, and these patterns are as effective in science fiction as in other forms of literature. This is not to say that SF is identical to other forms of literary art, of course: the task of the literary critic ought to be in identifying where SF draws on culturally shared aesthetic patterns as well as identifying where SF adapts those patterns in a singular way. The literary critic needs to be adept at a close cognitive poetic analysis of style as well as aware of aspects of literary historiography and both scholarly and popular reception. This ideal critic should blend—in a way that can itself be seen as science-fictional—scientific awareness and cultural sensibility.

The distinction between beauty and wonder only works for a narrow understanding of experience and in relation to a (self-defined) narrow section of artistic enterprise. Instead, I would like to propose the encompassing notion of *compulsion* as the power that literary reading generates. This is the feeling that the book is compelling and gripping, important beyond its mere materiality or the world it designates, and the feeling that readers are transported or self-effaced or transformed in the process (see Gerrig). Science fiction—at least, those works that people think of as good science fiction—is compelling in this sense, just as much as any sort of literature can be. At its best, it is utterly compelling to the point of enthusiastic immersion.

Understanding SF aesthetics as a compulsive effect requires a holistic grasp of its textual and narratological features together with the creative enrichment and enthusiasm brought by its readers. Science-fictional sublimity and beauty are thus essentially different emphases for the same phenomenon. In the rest of this chapter, I outline very briefly and mainly by example three forms of beauty in which science fiction excels: beauty of expression, beauty of structure, and beauty of world.

Science fiction is not generally regarded as poetic in the common sense, though in fact I would argue that the creative neologism and fictive novum identified by Csicsery-Ronay are poetic forms of expression at different levels that are more richly exploited in SF than in other genres. Nevertheless, there are examples of great poetic and lyrical writing in the SF canon. The obvious example is the prose style of Ray Bradbury, an appreciation of which grows the more closely it is examined. Consider this example from "The Golden Apples of the Sun" (1953):

> The captain stared from the huge dark-lensed port and there indeed was the sun, and to go to that sun and touch it and steal part of it forever away was his quiet and single idea. In this ship were combined the coolly delicate and the coldly practical. Through corridors of ice and milk-frost, ammoniated winter and storming snowflakes blew. Any spark from that vast hearth burning out there beyond the callous hull of this ship, any small firebreath that might seep through would find winter, slumbering here like all the coldest hours of February. (*Golden Apples* 165)

The success of this passage lies in its aptness at the semantic level and its balance at the syntactic level. The poetically striking nature of its meaning is carried by the metaphors: some compressed as noun-phrase modifiers ("milk-frost"), others displaying empathetic personification ("callous hull"), or both of these qualities together as a personifying lexical blend ("firebreath"); there is metaphor as explicit analogy ("like all the coldest hours") and other examples in which the referential target of the metaphor remains stylistically invisible but still present ("that vast hearth"). This metaphoric exuberance is not simply a modernist technique for its own sake: the short story itself (like much SF) literalizes a metaphor—about going to the sun—and does it by overlaying a science-fictional spaceflight scenario onto W.B. Yeats's poetic lines "And pluck till time and times are done, the silver apples of the moon, the golden apples of the sun." The sense of space-travel motion, delicacy, and the contrast of the safe interior and sublimely dangerous exterior are captured in the continuous feeling of the additive syntax and the locative expressions ("that sun" in contrast to "slumbering here") and the spatial prepositions ("from," "Through," "beyond"). In one paragraph, Bradbury conveys not simply the denotation of the story but the sensation of it simultaneously. He even deploys /k/ and /l/ sounds systematically throughout to associate these sounds iconically with coldness.

The following passage from Bradbury's 1950 novel *The Martian Chronicles* is even more striking:

> They had a house of crystal pillars on the planet Mars by the edge of an empty sea, and every morning you could see Mrs. K eating the golden fruits that grew from the crystal walls, or cleaning the house with handfuls of magnetic dust which, taking all dirt with it, blew away on the hot wind. Afternoons, when the fossil sea was warm and motionless, and the wine trees stood stiff in the yard, and the little distant Martian bone town was all enclosed, and no one drifted out their doors, you could see Mr. K himself in his room, reading from a metal book with raised hieroglyphs over which he brushed his hand, as one might play a harp. And from the book, as his fingers stroked, a voice sang, a soft ancient voice, which told tales of when the sea was red steam on the shore and ancient men had carried clouds of metal insects and electric spiders into battle. (14)

The long syntactic addition, coordination, and compounding in each of these three sentences literally take your breath away when the passage is read aloud. Each added phrase is framed definitely and by precise specification, so the effect is of assuming a familiarity with golden fruits and crystal walls that only increases the thrilling alienness of the metal insects and electric spiders from ancient Martian history. Again, Bradbury sets up particular consonant clusters (/kl/, /dz/, and /tl/) that echo through the passage and bind it together subliminally, so that when these phonetic patterns reach a crescendo in the final lines, the reference to ancient history appears to be prefaced by the future in a peculiarly iconic science-fictional manner.

Examples such as these are not restricted to Bradbury: any list would only make a start with the stylistic richness of Brian W. Aldiss, Kurt Vonnegut, Charles Stross, Ursula K. Le Guin, Russell Hoban, Octavia Butler, Jeff Noon, Margaret Atwood, and scores of others—prose styles of intricacy, poetic resonance, and thematic relevance that are the equal of any literature. SF poetic style is often motivated and immediately thematically relevant to the world being evoked, rather than being an experiment in artistic self-referentiality; this is what distinguishes the wildly creative stylistic experimentation of Aldiss's *Barefoot in the Head* (1969) from James Joyce's superficially similar *Finnegans Wake* (1939).

SF poetic style often serves an immersive function, placing the reader's interior narrative voice (as narratee or implied reader) into a position of assumed familiarity with the imagined world. William Gibson's style is often cited as the paradigmatic example of this, though, in fact, it is pervasive in SF. The effect is often conversational, intimate, and slick—rendering an impression of SF style as cool. This Gibsonesque extract is from John Brunner:

> At present I am being Arthur Edward Lazarus, profession minister, age forty-six, celibate: founder and proprietor of the Church of Infinite Insight, a converted (and what better way for a church to start than with a successful conversion?) drive-in movie theatre near Toledo, Ohio, which stood derelict for years not so much because people gave up going to the movies—they still make them, there's always an audience for wide-screen porn of the type that gets pirate three-vee satellites sanded out of orbit in next to no time—as because it's on land disputed between the Billykings, a Protestant tribe, and the Grailers, Catholic. No one cares to have his property tribaled. However, they normally respect churches, and the territory of the nearest Moslem tribe, the Jihad Babies, lies ten miles to the west.
> My code, of course, begins with 4GH, and has done so for the past six years.
> *Memo to selves:* find out whether there's been any change in the status of a 4GH, and particularly whether something better has been introduced . . . a complication devoutly to be fished. (5)

This is a style on the boundary of recognition, not so far from contemporary idiom as to be obscurely alien, but sufficiently unfamiliar to feel as if you are inhabiting another mind. The efforts of decoding required here ("three-vee," "tribaled," "4GH") maintain the self-awareness that there is a tension between the reader's world and the narrator's, and this dialogic pattern is a significant part of the characteristic SF aesthetic.

The second aesthetic characteristic of science fiction I will examine is beauty of structure. The narrative drive of most SF is part of its compelling nature: SF texts are often page-turners, with a resolution, dilemma, or catastrophe to be fulfilled or averted. Most science fiction is end-directed, and rarely if ever ends in the sort of aporia that is characteristic of many modernist short stories and postmodern novels. Even where the end of an SF story is not resolved, such works tend to close with apocalypse or a gesture toward transcendence. Arthur C. Clarke's work provides good examples of this, especially his 1953 novel *Childhood's End* and both the screenplay and novelization of *2001: A Space Odyssey* (1968). The former ends with a witness escaping the apocalypse on Earth and the latter ends with a witness attempting to articulate transcendence.

SF literary narrative has been deeply influenced by cinematic editing techniques: flashbacks, parallel storylines, a strong third-person narrative voice, and other features are part of the shared poetic techniques of both art-forms, and the aesthetic experience of both can also be regarded as somewhat comparable. Such structural fragmentation in the context of SF narrative resolution tends to be felt not as disjunction, as it might in another genre, but as a sense of paciness and excitement. The work of China Miéville provides good examples of this. *The City and the City* (2009) begins as a detective novel, but the peculiarity of the setting soon distracts the reader: one city is overlaid on another, occupying the same space, with each population prohibited (apparently by threat of alien punishment) from seeing the other city. The murder inquiry ensures the novel is a page-turner, but the achievement of the work lies in the way it lines up crime story, political satire, ontological contemplation, and uncertainty over whether the framework is science-fictional or psychological—and then fires each of these structures at the reader at once. *Kraken* (2010) similarly has a heist mystery at its heart, but quickly expands into a wild pursuit narrative that encompasses religion, politics, and magic.

Miéville's (2011) *Embassytown* displays all the features of beauty of structure, with an alien race whose language and thought are so intertwined that they cannot conceive of a lie or utter it. Human contact almost destroys their civilization, and the novel again combines politics, philosophy, and narrative excitement, with a brilliant resolution. As Ursula Le Guin said in her review of the novel:

> *Embassytown* is a fully achieved work of art [that] . . . works on every level, providing compulsive narrative, splendid intellectual rigour and risk, moral sophistication, fine verbal fireworks and sideshows, and even the old-fashioned satisfaction of watching a protagonist become more of a person than she gave promise of being.

In science fiction, often, the narrative structure itself is sublime.

Finally, it is in the richness of its evocation of nonactual worlds that science fiction distinguishes itself from most other forms of literature. Most SF worlds are overengineered for the fictional purpose at hand, with a wealth of detail and texture that is not necessary for the mechanics of the plot or the enactment of meaning. Technologies are invented, named, and described even where they do not advance the story, civilizations appear that are incidental to the main account, languages are created that are sophisticated far beyond the requirements of the narrative at hand (see Adams). This richness of world-building is compelling and is one of the features that clearly makes authors return to their own invented universes to write sequels and sequences. There are numerous examples that are particularly rich and wide-ranging in historical and spatial sweep, such as the novels and novellas in Alastair Reynolds's "Revelation Space" series (2000–), or Iain M. Banks' "Culture" universe (1987–), or Isaac Asimov's "Foundation" and "Robot" series (1939–93). Although each book is self-contained, there is an additional pleasure for the reader who recognizes cross-textual references and the elaboration of motifs from elsewhere within the same universe. The literary theorist Gerard Genette proposed the term "architext" to account for the web of possibilities that any single literary work with all its intertextual and paratextual features could point toward, but science fiction materializes Genette's abstract notion. Not only do many SF sequences provide an overprofusion of elaborated detail for its own sake (Neal Stephenson's "Baroque Cycle" [2003–2004], for example), but they often also gesture toward an even richer, unstated universe than is actually described directly. Where in a realist and naturalist literary novel a reader focuses only on the imaginary setting within a backgrounded but indistinct familiar world, in a science-fictional universe the spaces between the worlds and each narrated setting are also available for readerly engagement. The aesthetic effect is often vertiginous, immersive, and overwhelming.

It is possible, then, to talk about the beauty of SF in terms that are not exclusive to the genre, that draw on our best current knowledge of the psychology of reading, and that are neither straightforwardly prescriptive nor merely descriptive. An analysis of the aesthetics of SF (or anything) needs to be based on human commonalities as well as on particular textual variations. Science fiction sometimes displays a beauty of style that can be poetic, iconic, and immersive. It can have a beauty of structure that engages a narrative drive, aims at a satisfying resolution, and feels pacy and urgent. And it characteristically evokes the beauty of the world in a rich immersion, architectural consistency, resonance, and persistence of effect. All of this makes science fiction a compulsive genre of literary art.

Works Cited

Adams, Michael, ed. *From Elvish to Klingon: Exploring Invented Languages*. New York: Oxford UP, 2011. Print.
Armstrong, Isobel. *The Radical Aesthetic*. Oxford: Blackwell, 2000. Print.
Bradbury, Ray. "The Golden Apples of the Sun." *The Golden Apples of the Sun*. London: Hart-Davis, 1953. Print.
_____. *The Martian Chronicles*. 1950. London: Hart Davis, 1951. Print.
Brunner, John. *The Shockwave Rider*. London: Dent, 1975. Print.
Burke, Edmund. *A Philosophical Enquiry into the Origin of our Ideas of the Sublime and Beautiful*. London: J. Dodsley, 1767. Print.
Csicsery-Ronay Jr., Istvan. *The Seven Beauties of Science Fiction*. Middletown, CT: Wesleyan UP, 2008. Print.
Delany, Samuel R. *The Jewel-Hinged Jaw: Notes on the Language of Science Fiction*. Elizabethtown, NY: Dragon, 1977. Print.
Genette, Gérard. *The Architext: An Introduction*. 1979. Trans. Jane E. Lewin. Berkeley: U of California P, 1992. Print.
Gerrig, Richard. *Experiencing Narrative Worlds: On the Psychological Activities of Reading*. New Haven, CT: Yale UP, 1993. Print.
Hogan, Patrick Colm. *Cognitive Science, Literature, and the Arts*. New York: Routledge, 2003. Print.
Janaway, Christopher. *Reading Aesthetics and Philosophy of Art*. Oxford: Blackwell, 2006. Print.
Le Guin, Ursula K. Review of China Miéville's *Embassytown*. *The Guardian* (May 6, 2011). Web. July 20, 2013. http://www.guardian.co.uk/books/2011/may/08/embassytown-china-mieville-review.
Lindskold, Jane M. *Roger Zelazny*. New York: Twayne, 1993. Print.
Russ, Joanna. "Toward an Aesthetic of Science Fiction." *Science Fiction Studies* 2.2 (July 1975): 112–19. Print.
Stafford, Barbara Maria. *Echo Objects: The Cognitive Work of Images*. Chicago: U of Chicago P, 2007. Print.
Stockwell, Peter. *Cognitive Poetics*. London: Routledge, 2002. Print.
_____. *The Poetics of Science Fiction*. London: Longman, 2000. Print.
_____. *Texture: A Cognitive Aesthetics of Reading*. Edinburgh: Edinburgh UP, 2009. Print.

Styles, Elizabeth. *The Psychology of Attention*. 2nd ed. Hove: Psychology Press, 2006. Print.

Zelazny, Roger. "Divine Madness." *The Doors of His Face, the Lamps of His Mouth, and Other Stories*. London: Faber and Faber, 1971. 199–206. Print.

———. "The Doors of His Face, The Lamps of His Mouth." 1965. *The Doors of His Face, the Lamps of His Mouth, and Other Stories*. London: Faber and Faber, 1971. 1–32. Print.

———. "The Great Slow Kings." 1963. *The Doors of His Face, the Lamps of His Mouth, and Other Stories*. London: Faber and Faber, 1971. 181–88. Print.

———. "The Keys to December." 1966. *The Doors of His Face, the Lamps of His Mouth, and Other Stories*. London: Faber and Faber, 1971. 33–56. Print.

———. "A Rose for Ecclesiastes." 1963. *The Doors of His Face, the Lamps of His Mouth, and Other Stories*. London: Faber and Faber, 1971. 71–106. Print.

CHAPTER 3

HISTORIES

ARTHUR B. EVANS

HISTORY is fiction. Not the events, but the telling of them. From Herodotus to Jules Michelet to Howard Zinn, historians not only chronicle the past, they also invent its meaning. Writing history is not a scientific enterprise. As Brian Stableford once remarked, unlike natural scientists who "frame explanations by setting particular events in the context of general laws," historians engage in a narrative process that is "more closely akin to fiction than most other kinds of nonfiction" (*Science Fact* 231). History, as the word itself implies, always tells a story.

There are many histories of science fiction. But all of them are partial and partisan—that is, each has its own interpretive purpose, its own limitations of scope, and its own ideological biases. It is possible to classify these different SF histories into three distinct (but overlapping) groups according to their methodological approach: thematic/authorial, semiotic, and sociological.

Not taking into account the many amateur fanzines and reader commentaries in the SF pulp magazines, or early academic treatises on "imaginary voyage" literature (Atkinson, Gove), or a handful of seminal studies on utopias, the gothic, and fictional trips to the Moon (Mumford, Scarborough, Nicholson) produced before 1940, one could claim that the first monographic history of the SF genre was J. O. Bailey's *Pilgrims Through Space and Time: Trends and Patterns in Scientific and Utopian Fiction* (1947). In this pioneering academic study, Bailey examines a wide range of SF authors and works, organizing them according to a host of recognizably SF themes (what is today often referred to as the SF "megatext"): for example, space travel, robots, time travel, aliens, world catastrophes, utopias, dystopias, hollow earths, and wonderful machines. Other SF histories of this general type soon followed, first from the nonacademic SF authorial and fan community (Damon Knight, Sam Moskowitz, Sam Lundwall) and then from the ranks of literary scholars in colleges and universities (Thomas D. Clareson, Everett Bleiler, Kingsley Amis, James Gunn). These early theme/author-based SF histories have a number of strengths, including the broad, inclusive scope of their vision and the historical genealogy they seek to establish for the genre. Bailey's book, for example, has been called "a remarkable catalogue of centuries of novels and stories" (Delany xvi) that "helped give the genre its own archeology and at least something of a pedigree" (Wolfe, "History and Criticism" 525). But many of these theme/author-based SF histories also have some inherent weaknesses: they rely too heavily on plot description and rarely discuss the formal structure of the SF stories they treat, and they give little attention to the work's reading public(s) or sociohistorical context. Further, at least in the case of the "populist" SF historian Sam Moskowitz, the documentational apparatus often seems maddeningly sketchy (prompting the founder of *Science Fiction Studies*, R. D. Mullen, to decry his "cavalier, disdainful dismissal" of the basic evidentiary procedures necessary for good scholarship). Although the thematic/authorial approach remains the most common way that people tend to identify the SF genre, it does not take into account the full range of SF subgenres (prehistoric, alternate history, steampunk, singularity fiction, and so on). And it would no doubt stumble badly when confronting contemporary "metafictional" or "slipstream" SF by authors such as Thomas Pynchon or China Miéville—that is, narratives whose referentiality goes well beyond the themes of the traditional SF megatext.

The second category of SF histories might be termed semiotic because they focus on the genre's narrative structure and how readers interact with it—a variant of what is sometimes referred to as "reader response" criticism. Although a few SF writers and critics first began talking about the protocols of reading SF during the 1950s and 1960s (Judith Merril, Samuel R. Delany), the most prominent practitioner of this approach is probably Darko Suvin in his watershed study *Metamorphoses of Science Fiction: On the Poetics and History of a Literary Genre* (1979). In this book, Suvin analyzes SF as a popular (and subversive) literature of "cognitive estrangement," and he traces its evolution from Thomas More's *Utopia* (1516) to the work of Karel Čapek in the 1920s and 1930s. Suvin's now-famous opus followed in the footsteps of an earlier trailblazing study by Robert M. Philmus (the first SF history to be published by an American university press) and was soon joined by those examining SF as rhetorical technique: Gary K. Wolfe, Robert Scholes, Samuel R. Delany, Christine Brooke-Rose, Carl Malmgren, and others.

One reason why Suvin's *Metamorphoses* became so renowned was because his semiotic approach to defining SF offered an especially useful way to distinguish between SF and other fictional genres. Contrary to what occurs in realist narratives, the estrangement-causing novum portrayed in SF must be radically different from the reader's actual empirical environment. And, contrary to most fantasy and horror, it must eschew the supernatural and present a certain level of scientific (or pseudoscientific) verisimilitude. Finally, as a result of the "what if. . .?" alternate reality it implies, the SF novum must trigger cognition and stimulate reader reflection on the nature of the real. In doing so, it not only elicits a certain sense of wonder (which attracts many to the genre) but also duplicates the scientific method as the reader engages in a thought experiment and follows that through to its logical conclusion.

The most obvious weakness in SF histories using a semiotic approach is that their preferred analytical vantage point tends to be synchronic rather than diachronic and their chronological coverage is often woefully incomplete—for example, Suvin's "history" ignores most of the twentieth century. But this approach does have another useful advantage: it serves as a handy tool for distinguishing between good science fiction ("SF" or "sf") and bad science fiction ("sci-fi"). For example, it shows how science-fictional novels and films that generate significant amounts of cognition—such as Stanislaw Lem's *Solaris* (1961) or Ridley Scott's *Blade Runner* (1982)—are more challenging and ultimately more rewarding than those requiring much less—such as Edgar Rice Burroughs's *A Princess of Mars* (1912) or Danny Cannon's *Judge Dredd* (1995).

The third category of SF histories leans heavily on the sociological. It defines the genre not in terms of its thematic content or how it activates a specific set of reading protocols but, rather, according to how SF grew out of and/or manifests certain sociohistorical trends. It may, for example, chronicle the emergence and development of a national SF tradition: for example, France (Lofficier), Canada (Ketterer), Great Britain (Ruddick), Japan (Bolton et al.). It may explore the evolution of a particular type of SF: for example, "futuristic fiction" (Alkon), "future-war fiction" (Clarke), "scientific romance" (Stableford), or "feminist SF" (Lefanu, Larbalestier, Merrick). Or it may discuss the place of SF in society, either through its publishing venues (Ashley), its fandom (Del Rey), its ideology (Huntington, Rieder), or even its "science fiction thinking" (Landon, Csicsery-Ronay). One excellent example of this kind of cultural SF history is Roger Luckhurst's *Science Fiction* (2005), in which SF is treated as a by-product of "technologically saturated societies" (3).

The advantages of this particular approach include its interpretive breadth (according to Luckhurst, it seeks "to situate SF texts in a broad network of contexts and disciplinary knowledges" [2]) as well as its objectivity in exploring the political and anthropological historicity of the genre—for example, how SF expressed the impact of evolving technologies on human subjectivity, what social mechanisms caused it to be judged a "low" literary genre, or how it interacted with and was influenced by the dominant institutions and ideologies of its time. But, at least in Luckhurst's book, its field of vision remains limited both geographically (to only two national traditions) and chronologically (to only the post-Victorian)—that is, it concentrates exclusively on the two paradigms of British SF and American SF from the late 1880s onward. As a result, it ignores the contributions of important non-Anglophone SF authors (such as J.-H. Rosny aîné, Kurd Lasswitz, Karel Čapek, Stanislaw Lem, Arkady and Boris Strugatsky, or Kobo Abé, among many others) as well as SF authors and works from before the 1880s. In all fairness, Luckhurst openly acknowledges his narrow Anglo-American prejudice, saying, "This bias reflects only the question of space and the limits of my own competencies, rather than any hierarchical value given to Anglo-American SF" (10). But there is no such acknowledgment of limitation—or even the slightest hint of flexibility—in what he sees as the definitive chronological starting point for the genre: "In my view, it makes little sense to talk about 'science fiction' before 1880" (16).

It is true that every SF history must tell its own origin story. And this story influences both how the SF historian goes about defining the genre (as themed speculation, as hermeneutic practice, or as cultural artifact) and how he or she conceives the genre's historical identity. As one critic summed it up: the "starting point inevitably affects what we see as the history (and the prehistory) of the genre, which in turn changes our perception of what science fiction is. It is a mobius loop: the definition affects the perception of the historical starting point, which in turn affects the definition" (Kincaid 45). But the logical possibilities are finite in number, and most SF historians trace the genesis of the genre from one of three historical time periods: from before the nineteenth century (starting, for example, with Lucian of Samosata, More, Kepler, or Godwin), from the nineteenth century (with Shelley, Poe, Verne, or Wells), or from the early twentieth century (with Hugo Gernsback, John W. Campbell, and the American pulp magazines).

Before the explosion of academic SF criticism that began during the 1970s, most SF writers and critics took it for granted that the genre originated in Jules Verne's "extraordinary voyages" and H. G. Wells's "scientific romances." Kingsley Amis, for example, in his popular SF history *New Maps of Hell* (1960), expressed what was common knowledge at the time when he said: "Whatever else he may or may not have been, Jules Verne is certainly to be regarded as one of the two creators of modern science fiction; the other, inevitably enough, is H. G. Wells" (31). In terms of the thematic and ideological content of their tales, both Verne and Wells were universally seen as exemplars of what SF should be—a composite grafting of the scientific onto the fictional ("hard" in Verne, "soft" in Wells) and a socially conscious brand of literature glorifying the quest for new knowledge (Verne) while cautioning against the dangers that such knowledge might bring to an imperfect and ever-changing world (Wells).

This traditional view of Verne and Wells as complementary "fathers" of science fiction was challenged in 1973 by a new and highly influential SF history called *Billion Year Spree* by noted British writer and critic Brian Aldiss. In it, Aldiss proposed Mary Shelley's 1818 novel *Frankenstein* as the original ur-text for all SF. And he put forward an entirely new definition of the genre, claiming that it is "characteristically cast in the Gothic or post-Gothic mode" (25). Aldiss's book and its Hugo-winning expansion *Trillion Year Spree* (1986)—probably due, at least in part, to the immense upsurge of the "feminist '70s" and the many feminist critical studies of the 1980s (see Attebery)—had great success. And his strong valorization of Mary Shelley opened the door to a complete reevaluation of the traditional Verne–Wells origins story for the SF genre.

By the 1980s and 1990s, the study of SF was already well established in college classrooms and a growing number of academic scholars were publishing in the field. Some of these scholars—such as Paul K. Alkon in his *Science Fiction Before 1900* (1994)—followed Aldiss's lead, stating unequivocally that "science fiction starts with Mary Shelley's *Frankenstein*" (1). Some—such as Edward James in his *Science Fiction in the 20th Century* (1994)—championed H. G. Wells as an important turning point in the development of modern SF. Some—such as Tom Moylan in his *Scraps of the Untainted Sky* (2000)—treated the genre as inextricably linked to the development of early utopias and dystopias. And, in their own search for SF's origins, some critics—such as Everett F. Bleiler in his *Science-Fiction: The Early Years* (1990) and Adam Roberts in his *The History of Science Fiction* (2006)—ventured back to Johannes Kepler and the birth of science during the Renaissance or even further back to the speculative literature and myths of Ancient Greece.

Finally, the newest wrinkle in this ongoing debate about SF's earliest prototypes began to emerge in the 1990s. It argued that true science fiction (the genre as well as the name) was born in the American pulp magazines of the 1920s and 1930s, midwifed by Hugo Gernsback. It was Gernsback who, in the 1926 inaugural issue of *Amazing Stories*, famously defined SF as "the Jules Verne, H. G. Wells, and Edgar Allan Poe type of story—a charming romance intermingled with scientific fact and prophetic vision" (3). The primary promoter of this new SF origin story was Gary Westfahl who, in his *The Mechanics of Wonder* (1998) and in many other writings, energetically proselytized Gernsback's importance as the unsung father of SF. Westfahl states categorically, for example, that Gernsback "made science fiction a recognized literary form" (1) and "stands as the first person to create and announce a history of science fiction" (67). Mostly as a result of Westfahl's advocacy, the idea that Gernsback and the American pulp magazines were the ontological source for the SF genre has resonated among some contemporary SF critics and historians. Mark Bould and Sherryl Vint, for instance, in their excellent *The Routledge Concise History of Science Fiction* (2011) openly acknowledge that certain SF-like literary "traditions" and "rubrics" did indeed exist before the twentieth century and were "in circulation long before anyone thought to call them 'SF.'" But they still find it "problematic to label any of these texts—or the traditions they exemplify—as 'SF' since it is only as the *name* and the *idea* of the genre were introduced that actants began, retrospectively and inconsistently, to understand them as belonging, as least potentially, to SF" (35; emphasis added). Such an argument—demanding that a literary genre have a fixed name and that its practitioners self-consciously identify themselves by that name before the genre can be deemed to exist—seems unduly reductive. And it also seems to give too much credence to the (mistaken) belief that *all* of today's SF is necessarily derived from what we now call "genre SF"—the variety of SF popularized in the pulp magazines of the 1920s and 1930s.

This unresolved question of SF's "true origins" has been the source of another ongoing debate: whether to use the epithet "proto" or "early" when discussing works of pre-1920s SF. At stake is more than just semantics. The term "proto" implies that *real* science fiction came into being at a later date, whereas "early" implies that it came into being at some time prior. For example, SF historians who believe that Mary Shelley's novel *Frankenstein* was SF's original source text would no doubt classify the works of Verne and Wells as "early SF." Others who believe that SF did not truly emerge as a genre until the term "science fiction" came into widespread use in the 1930s would probably classify Verne and Wells as "proto-SF." I would suggest, however, that the term "proto-sf" is intrinsically biased and dismissive toward SF produced before the pulp era. The term "early sf," though admittedly more vague, offers the distinct advantage of not defining its subject exclusively and retroactively in terms of a later narrative form. It allows premodern science-fictional texts to stand on their own and to be considered in their own historical specificity, rather than viewed simply as a kind of quaint and unfinished "pre"-version of the "real" SF yet to come.

SF histories can also be found in a variety of published formats. Most of the titles cited above are monographs and books, some written by fans or SF authors and some by academics, some produced by popular presses and some by university presses. But other shorter essay-length histories of the genre have also regularly appeared in SF encyclopedias such as those authored or edited by Brian Ash (1977), George Mann (2001), or, more notably, by John Clute and Peter Nicholls (1993). They can also be found in a growing number of SF handbooks, critical guides, and reference volumes such as Edward James and Farah Mendlesohn's *The Cambridge Companion to Science Fiction* (2003), Neil Barron's *Anatomy of Wonder* (5 editions, 1976–2004), David Seed's *A Companion to Science Fiction* (2005), and *The Routledge Companion to Science Fiction* (2009) edited by Mark Bould, Andrew M. Butler, Adam Roberts, and Sherryl Vint. Histories of the genre are also implicit in most SF historical anthologies, not only in their introductions and headnotes but also in the stories that are chosen for inclusion. Consider the differing range of SF authors featured, for example, in the anthologies by August Derleth (1950, from Plato to Ray Bradbury); James Gunn (1977–98, from Lucian to Herbert W. Franke); Eric S. Rabkin (1983, from Cyrano to Ursula K. Le Guin); Tom Shippey (1992, from Wells to David Brin); Garyn G. Roberts (2003, from Shelley to Jack Williamson); and in the recent *Wesleyan Anthology of Science Fiction* by Arthur B. Evans, Istvan Csicsery-Ronay Jr., Joan Gordon, Veronica Hollinger, Rob Latham, and Carol McGuirk (2010, from Hawthorne to Ted Chiang).

Of special interest in this category of SF anthologies is *The Secret History of Science Fiction* (2009), edited by James Patrick Kelly and John Kessel. In their introduction, the editors bemoan the lack of literary quality in most contemporary SF and explain: "What we hope to present in this anthology is an alternative vision of sf from the early 1970s to the present, one in which it becomes evident that the literary potential of sf was not squandered" (8). A similar editorial strategy was attempted over a decade earlier in *The Norton Book of Science Fiction* (1993), edited by Ursula K. Le Guin and Brian Attebery. Marketed as a teaching anthology, it featured over sixty short stories from 1960 to 1990 that were described as presenting a "glimpse of the story of science fiction itself during the first thirty years of its maturity" when the genre experienced an "increase in the number of writers and readers, the breadth of subject, the depth of treatment, the sophistication of languages and technique, and the political and literary consciousness of the writing" (18). Although the editors were careful to deny any "historical intent" (17) or genre representativeness in their selection of stories, the anthology was nevertheless criticized by many SF critics as presenting a skewed and inaccurate picture of the genre. One went so far as to characterize the book as "a Big Lie of Orwellian dimensions, useful only to people who wish to falsify and distort science fiction, not those who wish to teach it" (Westfahl, "Review").

Gary K. Wolfe, in his essay "History and Criticism" (1995), contends that all critical discourse about SF came out of three traditions: fan discussions in the pulp magazines of the 1920s and 1930s, commentaries on each other's work by SF authors in the 1940s and 1950s, and academic studies from the 1960s onward (483–85). But, as I have pointed out in "The Origins of Science Fiction Criticism" (1999), how one defines the first texts of SF criticism is closely tied to how one defines the genre itself and its starting point. For example, Kepler's *Somnium* (1634) and his appended *Notes* might well qualify as

Western literature's first work of SF, of SF criticism, and perhaps even of SF history (since he speaks of the influence of Plutarch and Lucian on his story). In the late eighteenth century, the anthologist Charles Garnier was certainly acknowledging the existence of a separate and identifiable literary tradition of speculative fiction when he gathered together and annotated a 39-volume collection called *Voyages imaginaires, songes, visions, et romans cabalistiques* (Imaginary Voyages, Dreams, Visions, and Cabalistic Novels, 1785–89). Included in the collection was an impressive array of 71 early SF works by authors such as Lucian, Holberg, Cyrano de Bergerac, Defoe, Swift, Paltock, Grivel, and many others. Another candidate for the honor of first SF critic might be Camille Flammarion, whose *Les Mondes imaginaires et les mondes réels* (Imaginary and Real Worlds, 1864) is described by Brian Stableford as "an early historical analysis of speculative fiction in its scientific context" (*Science Fact* 180). Critical writing about SF is not and has never been exclusive to the editorial pages of the American pulp magazines, to the "tips of the trade" columns written by established SF authors such as James Blish or Damon Knight, or to the scholarly exegeses produced in the halls of academe.

In terms of their point of view, methodology, and scope, today's SF histories have evolved a great deal from Bailey's *Pilgrims in Space and Time*. Some reflect new trends in social awareness and gender identity: witness, for example, the huge surge of (often historical) feminist SF criticism by scholars such as Sarah Lefanu, Jenny Wolmark, Marleen S. Barr, Jane Donawerth, Justine Larbalestier, Lisa Yaszek, and Helen Merrick. Some offer new sociopolitical and epistemological insights on "SF theory," such as the studies by Fredric Jameson, Carl Freedman, and Istvan Csicsery-Ronay Jr. And some explore SF's long and complex relationship with ideologies of race and imperialism in critical works by DeWitt Douglas Kilgore and John Rieder. But beyond their more specialized focus, the most visible difference between today's SF histories and earlier ones from the 1960s and 1970s has to do with their respective chronological coverage. There has been a discernible shift during the past few decades in how SF historians are configuring the genre's past. In a nutshell, the earlier histories gave a disproportionately large amount of attention to pre-1900 SF, whereas today's SF histories seem to be progressively de-emphasizing it.

As evidence of this shift, let us first consider two traditional SF histories from the earlier period: Moskowitz's *Explorers of the Infinite* (1963) and Aldiss's *Billion Year Spree* (1973). In each, *more than half* of the chapters are devoted to SF authors and works dating from before the pulp era. Or note the studies by H. Bruce Franklin (1966), Robert M. Philmus (1970), and David Ketterer (1974), all of which concentrate entirely on the nineteenth century or before. Or look at the historical overviews appearing in the first edition of Barron's *Anatomy of Wonder* (1976), which features three essays on pre-Golden Age SF, covering 1870 to 1937, and only one essay on the modern period from 1938 to 1975. Even the history of SF showcased in Darko Suvin's *Metamorphoses of Science Fiction* (1979), as mentioned, extends no further than H.G. Wells, Russian SF, and Karel Čapek—all listed in the table of contents under the rubric "Introduction to Newer SF History." One reason why these (mostly academic) literary historians from the 1960s and 1970s spent so much time and expended so much exegetical energy on SF authors and works from the pre-twentieth century was because they were consciously trying to establish an honorable—that is, mainstream—lineage for SF in order to make it more acceptable as a literary genre. As Franklin has explained, "Those of us who escorted science fiction into the formal parties of the academy in the mid-1960s labored hard to make it look respectable. That was one reason we documented its long pedigree and heritage from the literary canon" ("Transforming" 197).

Let us now time-travel four decades or so to the present and examine some recent SF histories. The historical overviews contained in James and Mendlesohn's *Cambridge Companion* (2003) are evenly divided into four distinct periods: "origins to 1926," "1926–1960," "1960–1980," and "1980 to the present." The fifth edition of Barron's *Anatomy of Wonder* (2005) now features two essays on pre-Golden Age SF (1516–1939) and three on more modern SF (since 1940). Even more telling is the chronological focus of Bould and Vint's *Concise History* (2011), which offers a single chapter on "science fictions before Gernsback" followed by seven chapters on SF after 1930. The pattern is clear: today's SF historians have sharply reduced the amount of coverage they are giving to pre-twentieth-century SF. Is the genre now sufficiently "mapped" so that it no longer needs to identify its roots? Has it become so academically respectable that its inclusion in university curricula no longer demands canonical justification? Has the consensus about the genre's origins among SF scholars begun to shift away from the nineteenth century (or before) and gravitate toward the early twentieth? There are no definitive answers to these questions. But the perceived importance of authors such as Jules Verne in the history of the genre has changed dramatically in recent years. In 1963 Moskowitz described Verne as SF's patriarch, saying: "[H]e was the first author to develop consciously and consistently an approach to the genre which turned it into a specialized form of literature, quite distinct from fantasy, the Gothic horror tale, the fictional political utopia, or the imaginatively embroidered travel tale" (73). In 2005, in his well-regarded cultural history, Luckhurst ignores Verne entirely.

Finally, historians of the genre have, since the 1980s, frequently ventured beyond the literary, beyond Anglo-American SF, and beyond the standard subgenres of the field. This development is especially appropriate since today's SF, as Brooks Landon has aptly observed, "is no longer 'just' fiction, but has become a universally recognized category of film, television, music, music videos, electronic games, theme parks, military thinking, and advertising, and its concepts and icons are now routinely appropriated for the development and marketing of products ranging from breakfast cereals to pickup trucks" (xv). The medium of SF film and television has been expertly explored by scholars such as Vivian Sobchack and J. P. Telotte. Several non-Anglophone SF histories are now available by Jean-Marc and Randy Lofficier for France; by Christopher Bolton, Istvan Csicsery-Ronay Jr., and Takayuki Tatsumi for Japan; by Rachel Haywood Ferreira for Latin America; and by Russell Blackford, Van Ikin, and Sean McMullen for Australia; among others. And, finally, a growing number of works produced during the early years of the twenty-first century have demonstrated the remarkable breadth of today's SF scholarship. Some—such as Robert Crossley's *Imagining Mars* (2011)—remain steadfastly traditional in their historical approach. Others—such as Peter Fitting's

Subterranean Worlds (2004) and Nicholas Ruddick's *The Fire in the Stone* (2009)—focus our attention on important and yet neglected SF subgenres. And still others—such as Rob Latham's *Consuming Youth* (2002) and several essays in the collection *Queer Universes* (2008), edited by Wendy Pearson, Veronica Hollinger, and Joan Gordon—are helping to push the envelope of SF critical inquiry toward exciting new frontiers.

Works Cited

Aldiss, Brian W. *Billion Year Spree: The True History of Science Fiction.* Garden City, NY: Doubleday, 1973. Rev. and expanded, with David Wingrove, as *Trillion Year Spree: The History of Science Fiction.* London: Gollancz, 1986. Print.

Alkon, Paul K. *Origins of Futuristic Fiction.* Athens: U of Georgia P, 1987. Print.

———. *Science Fiction Before 1900: Imagination Discovers Technology.* New York: Twayne, 1994. Print.

Amis, Kingsley. *New Maps of Hell.* New York: Ballantine, 1960. Print.

Ash, Brian. *The Visual Encyclopedia of Science Fiction.* New York: Harmony, 1977. Print.

Ashley, Mike. *The Story of Science-Fiction Magazines.* 3 vols. Liverpool: Liverpool UP, 2000–2007. Print.

Atkinson, Geoffrey. *The Extraordinary Voyage in French Literature before 1700.* New York: Columbia UP, 1920. Print.

———. *The Extraordinary Voyage in French Literature from 1700 to 1720.* Paris: Champion, 1922. Print.

Attebery, Brian. *Decoding Gender in Science Fiction.* New York: Routledge, 2002. Print.

Bailey, J. O. *Pilgrims Through Space and Time: Trends and Patterns in Scientific and Utopian Fiction.* New York: Argus, 1947. Print.

Barr, Marleen. *Lost in Space: Probing Feminist Science Fiction and Beyond.* Chapel Hill: U of North Carolina P, 1993. Print.

Barron, Neil, ed. *Anatomy of Wonder: A Critical Guide to Science Fiction.* 4 editions. New York: Bowker, 1976, 1981, 1986, 1995, 2004. Print.

———, ed. *Anatomy of Wonder: A Critical Guide to Science Fiction.* 5th ed. Westport, CT: Libraries Unlimited, 2004. Print.

Blackford, Russell, Van Ikin, and Sean McMullen, eds. *Strange Constellations: A History of Australian Science Fiction.* Westport, CT: Greenwood, 1999. Print.

Bleiler, Everett F. *The Checklist of Fantastic Literature.* Chicago: Shasta, 1948. Print.

———. *Science-Fiction: The Early Years.* Kent, OH: Kent State University Press, 1990. Print.

Bolton, Christopher, Istvan Csicsery-Ronay Jr., and Takayuki Tatsumi, eds. *Robot Ghosts and Wired Dreams: Japanese Science Fiction from Origins to Anime.* Minneapolis: U of Minnesota P, 2007. Print.

Bould, Mark, Andrew M. Butler, Adam Roberts, and Sherryl Vint, eds. *The Routledge Companion to Science Fiction.* London: Routledge, 2009. Print.

Bould, Mark, and Sherryl Vint. *The Routledge Concise History of Science Fiction.* London: Routledge, 2011. Print.

Brooke-Rose, Christine. *A Rhetoric of the Unreal: Studies in Narrative and Structure, Especially of the Fantastic.* Cambridge, UK: Cambridge UP, 1981. Print.

Clareson, Thomas D. *Some Kind of Paradise: The Emergence of American Science Fiction.* Westport, CT: Greenwood, 1985. Print.

Clarke, I. F. *Voices Prophesying War: 1763–1984*. 2nd ed. Oxford: Oxford UP, 1992. Print.
Clute, John, and Peter Nicholls, eds. *The Encyclopedia of Science Fiction*. New York: St. Martin's, 1993. Print.
Crossley, Robert. *Imagining Mars: A Literary History*. Middletown, CT: Wesleyan UP, 2011.
Csicsery-Ronay Jr., Istvan. *The Seven Beauties of Science Fiction*. Middletown, CT: Wesleyan UP, 2008. Print.
Delany, Samuel R. *The Jewel-Hinged Jaw*. 1978. Middletown, CT: Wesleyan UP, 2009. Print.
Del Rey, Lester. *The World of Science Fiction: 1926–1976, The History of a Subculture*. New York: Ballantine, 1979. Print.
Derleth, August. *Beyond Space and Time*. New York: Pellegrini and Cudahy, 1950. Print.
Donawerth, Jane. *Frankenstein's Daughters: Women Writing Science Fiction*. Syracuse, NY: Syracuse UP, 1997. Print.
Evans, Arthur B. "The Origins of Science Fiction Criticism: from Kepler to Wells." *Science Fiction Studies* 26.2 (July 1999): 163–86. Print.
Evans, Arthur B., Istvan Csicsery-Ronay Jr., Joan Gordon, Veronica Hollinger, Rob Latham, and Carol McGuirk, eds. *The Wesleyan Anthology of Science Fiction*. Middletown, CT: Wesleyan UP, 2010. Print.
Fitting, Peter. *Subterranean Worlds: A Critical Anthology*. Middletown, CT: Wesleyan UP, 2004. Print.
Flammarion, Camille. *Les Mondes imaginaires et les mondes réels*. Paris: Didier, 1864. Print.
Franklin, H. Bruce, ed. *Future Perfect: American Science Fiction of the Nineteenth Century*. Oxford: Oxford UP, 1966. Print.
———. "Transforming Futures." *Science Fiction Studies* 36.2 (July 2009): 197–98. Print.
Freedman, Carl. *Critical Theory and Science Fiction*. Hanover, NH: Wesleyan UP, 2000. Print.
Garnier, Charles George Thomas, ed. *Voyages imaginaires, songes, visions et romans cabalistiques*. 39 vols. Amsterdam and Paris, 1787–89. Print.
Gernsback, Hugo. "A New Sort of Magazine." *Amazing Stories* 1.1 (Apr. 1926): 3. Print.
Gove, Philip Babcock. *The Imaginary Voyage in Prose Fiction, 1700 to 1800*. New York: Columbia UP, 1941. Print.
Gunn, James. *Alternate Worlds: The Illustrated History of Science Fiction*. Englewood Cliffs, NJ: Prentice-Hall, 1975. Print.
———. *The Road to Science Fiction*. 6 vols. 1977–1998. Lanham, MD: Scarecrow, 2002. Print.
Haywood Ferreira, Rachel. *The Emergence of Latin American Science Fiction*. Middletown, CT: Wesleyan UP, 2011. Print.
Huntington, John. *Rationalizing Genius: Ideological Strategies in the Classic American Science Fiction Short Story*. New Brunswick, NJ: Rutgers UP, 1989. Print.
James, Edward. *Science Fiction in the 20th Century*. Oxford: Oxford UP, 1994. Print.
James, Edward, and Farah Mendlesohn, eds. *The Cambridge Companion to Science Fiction*. Cambridge, UK: Cambridge UP, 2003. Print.
Jameson, Fredric. *Archaeologies of the Future: The Desire Called Utopia and Other Science Fictions*. New York: Verso, 2005. Print.
Kelly, James Patrick, and John Kessel, eds. *The Secret History of Science Fiction*. San Francisco: Tachyon, 2009. Print.
Ketterer, David. *Canadian Science Fiction and Fantasy*. Bloomington: Indiana UP, 1992. Print.
———. *New Worlds for Old: The Apocalyptic Imagination, Science Fiction, and American Literature*. Bloomington: Indiana UP, 1974. Print.

Kilgore, DeWitt Douglas. *Astrofuturism: Science, Race, and Visions of Utopia in Space.* Philadelphia: U of Pennsylvania P, 2003. Print.
Kincaid, Paul. "On the Origins of Genre." 2003. *Speculations on Speculation.* Ed. James Gunn and Matthew Candelaria. Lanham, MD: Scarecrow, 2005. 41–53. Print.
Knight, Damon. *In Search of Wonder: Essays on Modern Science Fiction.* Chicago: Advent, 1967. Print.
Landon, Brooks. *Science Fiction After 1900: From the Steam Man to the Stars.* New York: Twayne, 1997. Print.
Larbalestier, Justine. *The Battle of the Sexes in Science Fiction.* Middletown, CT: Wesleyan UP, 2002. Print.
Latham, Rob. *Consuming Youth: Vampires, Cyborgs, and the Culture of Consumption.* Chicago: U of Chicago P, 2002. Print.
Lefanu, Sarah. *In the Chinks of the World Machine: Feminism and Science Fiction.* London: Women's Press, 1988. Print.
Le Guin, Ursula K., and Brian Attebery, eds. *The Norton Book of Science Fiction.* New York: Norton, 1993. Print.
Lofficier, Jean-Marc, and Randy Lofficier. *French Science Fiction, Fantasy, Horror and Pulp Fiction.* Jefferson, NC: McFarland, 2000. Print.
Luckhurst, Roger. *Science Fiction.* Cambridge, UK: Polity, 2005. Print.
Lundwall, Sam. *Science Fiction: What It's All About.* New York, Ace, 1971. Print.
Malmgren, Carl. *Worlds Apart: Narratology of Science Fiction.* Bloomington: Indiana UP, 1991. Print.
Mann, George, ed. *The Mammoth Encyclopedia of Science Fiction.* New York: Carroll and Graf, 2001. Print.
Merrick, Helen. *The Secret Feminist Cabal: A Cultural History of Science Fiction Feminisms.* Seattle, WA: Aqueduct, 2009. Print.
Merril, Judith. "What Do You Mean? Science? Fiction?" 1966. *SF: The Other Side of Realism.* Ed. Thomas D. Clareson. Bowling Green, OH: Bowling Green UP, 1971. 53–95. Print.
Moskowitz, Sam. *Explorers of the Infinite.* Cleveland, OH: World, 1963. Print.
Moylan, Tom. *Scraps of the Untainted Sky: Science Fiction, Utopia, Dystopia.* Boulder, CO: Westview, 2000. Print.
Mullen, R. D. "In Response." *Science Fiction Studies* 24.3 (Nov. 1997): 529–34. Print.
Mumford, Lewis. *The Story of Utopias.* New York: Boni and Liveright, 1922. Print.
Nicholson, Marjorie. *A World in the Moon.* Northampton, MA: Smith College, 1936. Print.
Pearson, Wendy, Veronica Hollinger, and Joan Gordon, eds. *Queer Universes: Sexualities in Science Fiction.* Liverpool: Liverpool UP, 2008. Print.
Philmus, Robert M. *Into the Unknown: The Evolution of Science Fiction from Francis Godwin to H.G. Wells.* Berkeley: U of California P, 1970. Print.
Rabkin, Eric S. *Science Fiction: A Historical Anthology.* Oxford: Oxford UP, 1983.
Rieder, John. *Colonialism and the Emergence of Science Fiction.* Middletown, CT: Wesleyan UP, 2008. Print.
Roberts, Adam. *The History of Science Fiction.* New York: Palgrave Macmillan, 2006. Print.
Roberts, Garyn G. *The Prentice Hall Anthology of Science Fiction and Fantasy.* Upper Saddle River, NJ: Prentice-Hall, 2003. Print.
Ruddick, Nicholas. *The Fire in the Stone: Prehistoric Fiction from Charles Darwin to Jean M. Auel.* Middletown, CT: Wesleyan UP, 2009. Print.

———. *Ultimate Island: On the Nature of British Science Fiction.* Westport, CT: Greenwood, 1993. Print.

Scarborough, Dorothy. *The Supernatural in Modern English Fiction.* New York: Putnam, 1917. Print.

Scholes, Robert. *Structural Fabulation: An Essay on Fiction of the Future.* Notre Dame, IN: U of Notre Dame P, 1975. Print.

Seed, David, ed. *A Companion to Science Fiction.* Oxford: Blackwell, 2005. Print.

Shippey, Tom, ed. *The Oxford Book of Science Fiction Stories.* Oxford: Oxford UP, 1992. Print.

Sobchack, Vivian. *Screening Space: The American Science Fiction Film.* 1980. New Brunswick, NJ: Rutgers UP, 2001. Print.

Stableford, Brian. *Science Fact and Science Fiction: An Encyclopedia.* London: Routledge, 2006. Print.

———. *Scientific Romance in Britain, 1830–1950.* London: Fourth Estate, 1985. Print.

Suvin, Darko. *Metamorphoses of Science Fiction: On the Poetics and History of a Literary Genre.* New Haven, CT: Yale UP, 1979. Print.

Telotte, J. P. *A Distant Technology: Science Fiction Film and the Machine Age.* Middletown, CT: Wesleyan UP, 1999. Print.

———. *Science Fiction Film.* Cambridge, UK: Cambridge UP, 2001. Print.

Westfahl, Gary. *The Mechanics of Wonder: The Creation of the Idea of Science Fiction.* Liverpool: Liverpool UP, 1998. Print.

———. Review of *The Norton Book of Science Fiction.* Ed. Ursula K. Le Guin and Brian Attebery. "World of Westfahl." *SFSite.* N.d. Web. Jan. 30, 2012. http://www.sfsite.com/gary/ww-review06.htm.

Wolfe, Gary K. "History and Criticism." *Anatomy of Wonder: A Critical Guide to Science Fiction.* 4th ed. New Providence, NJ: Bowker, 1995. 483–546. Print.

———. *The Known and the Unknown: The Iconography of Science Fiction.* Kent, OH: Kent State UP, 1979. Print.

Wolmark, Jenny. *Aliens and Others: Science Fiction, Feminism, and Postmodernism.* Iowa City: U of Iowa P, 1994. Print.

Yaszek, Lisa. *Galactic Suburbia: Recovering Women's Science Fiction.* Columbus: Ohio State UP, 2007. Print.

CHAPTER 4

LITERARY MOVEMENTS

GARY K. WOLFE

TRADITIONALLY, literary and artistic movements are characterized by some form of special pleading, whether it be for a return to origins (as with the Pre-Raphaelites), a social or political agenda (as with German Expressionism), a liberation from bourgeois artistic restrictions (as with Dada and Surrealism), or even the imposition of formal constraints (as with the French Oulipo movement or the Danish Dogme in film). For much of its history, however, science fiction developed in a popular commercial environment that scarcely permitted its writers to advocate anything beyond persuading editors to read their work and pay them within a reasonable time frame. While its sister genre of fantasy may have occasionally benefitted from association with such movements as the Pre-Raphaelites or the Arts and Crafts Movement (William Morris) or fin-de-siècle aestheticism (Oscar Wilde), or from more informal alliances such as Oxford's Inklings (J. R. R. Tolkien, C. S. Lewis, Charles Williams), American science fiction—at least as a self-aware phenomenon—was arguably a market before it settled in as a genre, and it would take several decades before the notion of a literary movement—complete with manifestos, principles, and adherents—could gain any real traction. Science fiction first had to develop a substantial enough body of work for any hypothetical movement to respond to or react against. Even today, it is relatively easy for readers to confuse movements with subgenres (such as sword and sorcery or space opera), themes (such as nuclear war), modes (such as slipstream), marketing trends, or social groups of fans and writers such as the Futurians (founded in 1938) or the Hydra Club (founded in 1947).

In fact, one can argue—as Gary Westfahl has in *The Mechanics of Wonder: The Creation of the Idea of Science Fiction* (1998)—that science fiction was initially promoted as a movement itself. Hugo Gernsback's editorial in the very first issue of *Amazing Stories* (April 1926) was titled "A New Sort of Magazine," which featured fiction that he rather vaguely described as "a charming romance intermingled with scientific fact and prophetic vision" (qtd. Westfahl, *Mechanics* 38). A few years later, in *Writer's Digest*, Gernsback was a bit more direct in stating the rules for this sort of fiction: "LET it be understood, in the first place, that a science fiction story must be an exposition of a scientific theme and it must be also a story. As an exposition of a scientific theme, it must be reasonable and logical and must be based upon known scientific principles" (Gernsback 269). This more prescriptive article was directed at writers wanting to sell to the magazine Gernsback was then editing, *Scientific Detective Monthly*, but it retains something of the tone of a manifesto, and Westfahl has argued that, through such editorials and essays, Gernsback "personally launched the movement" that became modern genre science fiction ("Hugo Gernsback" 274).

By 1930, this "movement" had taken hold in the letter columns of *Amazing Stories* (and later of other science fiction pulps), and it seemed clear that these enthusiastic readers believed themselves to be part of something radically innovative in popular literature. If the contributors to the pulp magazines viewed them mainly as one fiction market among many, the readers seemed to feel that a "movement" of some sort was indeed afoot, and Gernsback shrewdly took advantage of this by announcing the formation of the Science Fiction League, complete with lapel buttons, in the May 1934 *Wonder Stories*. Fan historian Dave Kyle has argued that in "the history of science fiction fandom, nothing has had greater significance, importance, and universal effect than the formation in 1934 of the Science Fiction League." While it probably did not represent the beginning of science fiction fandom, it provided a focal point leading to similar organizations such as the International Science Fiction Guild, the Science Fiction Advancement Association, and the Legion of Science Fiction Improvement (Kyle). Many of these early organizations amounted to little more than correspondence science clubs, but attention gradually shifted to the quality and purpose of the fiction itself, and by the time of the first World Science Fiction Convention in 1939, distinct factions had evolved.

The faction most clearly identified as a self-conscious movement initially revolved around a fan named John Michel, whose speech "Mutation or Death" at a 1937 Philadelphia convention argued for greater political commitment among SF fans and writers. The following year a group including Donald A. Wollheim and Frederik Pohl formed the Committee for the Political Advancement of Science Fiction, promoting what they now called "Michelism" (Knight 12). After failing to reach alliances with more politically conservative fan groups, Wollheim, Pohl, and others formed the Futurian Science Literary Society in September 1938—and were promptly excluded from the following year's World Science Fiction Convention in what, with characteristic fannish hyperbole, came to be known as "the Great Exclusion Act of 1939."

Whether these internecine squabbles among very young fans had any measurable effect on the fiction of the time is questionable, but the Futurians came to include several writers and editors whose own later fiction indeed seemed to reflect its liberal proclivities—not only Pohl and Wollheim, but also C. M. Kornbluth, James Blish, Isaac Asimov, Damon Knight, and Judith Merril. By the early 1940s, Futurian members Pohl, Wollheim, and Lowndes were editing nearly half the SF pulps, while authors such and Blish and Asimov had become regular contributors to these and other magazines. By then, science fiction had long since evolved beyond Gernsback's simple idea of a "new kind of magazine," and it might well be argued that the Futurians, with their lingering echoes of Michelism and the "political advancement of science fiction," were among the first of the fan movements to have a lasting effect on the direction and shape of the genre.

But for the most part, movements that deliberately sought to refocus and influence the direction of SF writing remained the work of individual editors with individual agendas. By far the most prominent of these after Gernsback was John W. Campbell Jr., who in 1937 became editor of *Astounding Stories*, soon changing the title (in March 1938) to *Astounding Science-Fiction*—thus becoming the first magazine to employ "science fiction" as part of its title. In a January 1938 editorial titled "Mutation," Campbell asked, "Does evolution apply to *Astounding Stories*? Certainly" (qtd. Panshin and Panshin 259). He introduced a series of "Mutant issues," each of which would "help to determine the *direction* that the evolution of *Astounding Stories* and science fiction must take" (qtd. Panshin and Panshin 260; emphasis in original). But more than his editorials or the introduction of new features, Campbell's most significant influence came in the writers he recruited—including Isaac Asimov, Robert A. Heinlein, A. E. Van Vogt, Theodore Sturgeon, and Jack Williamson—and in his famously long and hectoring letters to authors about what science fiction should be: rigorously extrapolated narratives based on engineering and scientific concepts, with narrative frameworks drawn more from the realistic fiction of the day rather than the "charming romances" or pulp "space operas" of the preceding decade. Campbell's influence over the next two decades became so pervasive—what Asimov dubbed the "Golden Age" of science fiction—that it hardly now seems like a "movement," but that is exactly how it appeared to readers (and writers) by the end of the 1930s: a deliberate effort, with the cooperation of a number of talented writers, to "reboot" science fiction from its pulp adventure-story roots (though these roots remained alive and healthy in other pulp magazines).

The war years took their toll on such activity, but by the early 1950s, with science fiction seemingly divided between Campbell's technological realism on the one hand and pulp adventure on the other, new magazine editors began to promote their own alternative visions of the field, in each case developing stables of authors who, while probably not identifying themselves with specific movements, nevertheless enthusiastically embraced these shifting visions of what the field could accommodate. In 1949 Anthony Boucher and J. Francis McComas founded *The Magazine of Fantasy*, changing its title to *The Magazine of Fantasy and Science Fiction* with the second issue. By combining science fiction, fantasy, and horror stories with reprints of classic or little-known stories by literary figures, the editors sought to bridge the gap between genre and literary fiction, even down to a page layout that resembled that of a literary journal. Only a year later, *Galaxy Science Fiction* debuted under H. L. Gold, whose editorial choices emphasized social and satirical science fiction over simple technological extrapolation, leading to the publication of some of the most influential SF satires of the era, such as Pohl and C. M. Kornbluth's "Gravy Planet" (1952), later revised as the novel *The Space Merchants* (1953)—ironically bringing to fruition some of the goals of the old Michelist movement of the 1930s. As *Astounding*'s influence waned, partly because of John W. Campbell's growing infatuation with pseudoscientific or cultish ideas, what began as deliberate editorial movements to promote literary or satirical science fiction increasingly became the mainstream of the field during the following decade.

While Boucher, McComas, and Gold did not issue manifestos or concoct labels for the movements they promoted, the first clearly self-proclaimed literary movement in postwar science fiction was also the work of a single editor, Michael Moorcock, who assumed editorship of the British magazine *New Worlds* in 1964. Britain, like the United States, had had its share of fan organizations dating back to the 1930s, such as the Science Fiction Association with its fanzine *Novae Terrae* (Greenland 15). Editor E. J. Carnell changed the title to *New Worlds* in 1939, eventually transforming it into a professional magazine in 1946, with one of its chief aims being to develop a home-grown alternative to the American magazines, which had been imported since the war years. Folding after only three issues, the magazine was revived by Carnell in 1949, this time surviving until 1964, already beginning to publish authors who would later be associated with the New Wave, such as J. G. Ballard and Brian W. Aldiss. Faced with declining sales, it was again announced that the magazine would fold, leading to a passionate letter from the young Moorcock, arguing that the magazine should "be far out—it needs editors who are willing to take a risk on a story and run it even though this may bring criticism on their heads" (qtd. Ashley and Tymn 427). When the magazine was rescued by yet another publisher, Carnell (by then committed to editing a series of science fiction anthologies) recommended Moorcock for the editorship.

From his first editorial, Moorcock proclaimed "a kind of SF which is unconventional in every sense." "A *popular* literary renaissance is around the corner," he continued. "Together we can accelerate that renaissance" (qtd. Greenland 17). The model of that renaissance, celebrated in an essay by Ballard in that same issue, was the pointedly transgressive work of William S. Burroughs. But Moorcock also proved to be a cautious and canny editor; along with the more radical fiction of Ballard, Aldiss, and others, he continued to feature traditional, familiar forms of science fiction. The term "New Wave" itself, likely adapted from the *nouvelle vague* of 1950s French cinema, had been used by American reviewer P. Schuyler Miller as early as 1961 to refer to British authors such as Aldiss and John Brunner (Prucher 130), but its enthusiastic promotion in connection to *New Worlds* was largely the work of anthologist Judith Merril, first in a 1966 book review column in *The Magazine of Fantasy and Science Fiction* and later in her controversial (and appallingly titled) 1968 anthology *England Swings SF*. No fewer than 16 of the 28 stories in that anthology had appeared in *New Worlds*, including stories that became emblems of the movement, such as Pamela Zoline's "The Heat Death of the Universe" and Ballard's "The Assassination of John Fitzgerald Kennedy Considered as a Downhill Motor Race" (both 1967). Merril seemed determined to draw a line in the sand for the older American SF community, and that community responded with vehemence: Lester del Rey argued that "much of the New Wave seemed to be an effort to peddle the work of one group of writers by propaganda, rather than by merit" (257), and Donald Wollheim claimed it represented "a departure from the science-fiction directives for mankind," concerned primarily with "shock words and shock scenes, hallucinatory fantasies, and sex" (105).

The Moorcock *New Worlds*, though, included a number of younger American writers clearly sympathetic with its aims, including Thomas M. Disch, Pamela Zoline, Kit Reed, Carol Emshwiller, and Norman Spinrad. The fact that many Americans felt a similar need for literary innovation in science fiction was evidenced by the enormous success of Harlan Ellison's huge original anthologies *Dangerous Visions* (1967) and *Again, Dangerous Visions* (1972), which featured the work of not only British writers, but also established Americans such as Pohl, Fritz Leiber, and Philip José Farmer, along with newer writers like Roger Zelazny, David R. Bunch, and R. A. Lafferty. Though Ellison shied away from identifying his anthology with the New Wave, the terms he uses in its introduction—"'the new thing'—the *nouvelle vague*, if you will, of speculative writing" (*Dangerous* xx)—make the association fairly clear. The anthology "was intended to shake things up. It was conceived out of a need for new horizons, new forms, new styles, new challenges in the literature of our times" (xix). But already, innovative editors such as Cele Goldsmith at *Amazing* and Damon Knight with his series of *Orbit* anthologies (and later Terry Carr with his series of "specials" for Ace books and his anthology series *Universe*) had begun to reflect the "revolution" in their editorial choices. The New Wave had become part of the ongoing dialogue of science fiction.

But not entirely. There remained a cultural divide between most of the science fiction world and what was coming to be known as the counterculture, dramatized at the 1968 World Science Fiction Convention in Berkeley, California, which some fans described as the first large-scale encounter between science fiction and the hippie movement. The passion for cultural and political relevance, which had been a subtext among liberal SF fans and readers since the early Michelist movement, was clearly expressed in Philip José Farmer's effort, in his guest of honor address, to recruit science fiction writers and readers to subscribe to the Triple Revolution Statement, an open letter sent to President Lyndon Johnson in 1964 signed by prominent academics and social activists including Linus Pauling, Tom Hayden, and Irving Howe—and which Farmer himself had promoted in his story in Ellison's *Dangerous Visions*, "Riders of the Purple Wage." By emphasizing the "three revolutions" of cybernetic automation, thermonuclear weaponry, and human rights, the document seemed almost designed to bring some of the major recurring concerns of science fiction into the arena of public discourse, but Farmer's speech would be remembered more for its length than its content, and the Triple Revolution must be counted among several abortive attempts at creating an activist movement within science fiction.

Another, less overtly political movement to emerge from the 1960s was the drug subculture, which had influenced the New Wave through Moorcock and Ballard's championing of William S. Burroughs and which later appeared in the fiction of Ellison, Spinrad, and others. During the 1970s, the author who most prominently explored this intersection was Philip K. Dick—but the incipient movement that he inadvertently spawned had less to do with drug culture than with his habit of combining autobiographical, hallucinatory, and science fiction elements within the same work. Reading his 1977 novel *A Scanner Darkly*, writer Rudy Rucker conceived what he called "transrealism," a kind of self-consciously postmodern technique of introducing fantastical or

SF elements into naturalistic or autobiographical material, sometimes even using the author's name as a character, as Rucker would later do in his 1999 novel *Saucer Wisdom*. Rucker wrote a "Transrealist Manifesto" in 1983, but while the movement never developed a coherent group of followers, it did lead to a full-length study by Australian author and critic Damien Broderick, *Transrealist Fiction: Writing in the Slipstream of Science* (2000), which identified transrealism less as a movement than as a narrative strategy, citing authors from John Barth and J. G. Ballard to Joanna Russ and James Tiptree Jr.

Another effect of the uneasy 1960s encounters between the SF community and the rock counterculture was the emergence of Philip K. Dick as a kind of countercultural guru, which may in part be traced to a long profile by Paul Williams in the November 6, 1975, issue of the rock magazine *Rolling Stone*, later expanded into Williams's book *Only Apparently Real* (1986). Dick's combination of his own personal struggles with a persistent questioning of the stability of reality,—and a kind of urban street sensibility already evident in science fiction through the work of Ellison, Spinrad, and others—would prove over the next few decades to be broadly appealing, and while it cannot be claimed that Dick's work spawned a particular movement, it nevertheless had a profound effect on what proved to be the most significant movement in science fiction since the New Wave. Viewing Ridley Scott's 1982 adaptation of Dick's novel *Do Androids Dream of Electric Sheep?*, the novelist William Gibson wrote, "BLADERUNNER [sic] came out while I was still writing Neuromancer. I was about a third of the way into the manuscript. When I saw [the first twenty minutes of] BLADERUNNER [sic], I figured my unfinished first novel was sunk, done for. Everyone would assume I'd copped my visual texture from this astonishingly fine-looking film." The relatively modest response to the film's initial release, however, allayed Gibson's fears, and when *Neuromancer* (commissioned by editor Terry Carr) was published in July 1984, it won the Hugo, Nebula, and Philip K. Dick awards, quickly becoming the defining text in a movement, largely articulated by Gibson's friend Bruce Sterling, called cyberpunk.

"Cyberpunk" was originally the coinage of writer Bruce Bethke, who used it for the title of a 1980 story about teenage hackers, published in the November 1983 *Amazing Stories*, but the term gained wide currency after Gardner Dozois used it in an essay for the *Washington Post Book World* the following year. This sort of streetwise, cyberspace-drenched *noir* fiction had of course been around well before *Neuromancer*—Michael Levy cites earlier works by Sterling, John Shirley, Rudy Rucker, Lewis Shiner, Pat Cadigan, Vernor Vinge, Greg Bear, and Gibson himself—and more than half the stories in Sterling's *Mirrorshades: The Cyberpunk Anthology* (1986) pre-date Gibson's novel. While Sterling's preface to that anthology most fully articulates what he believed cyberpunk to be (he mentions alternative labels such as Radical Hard SF, neuromantics [a somewhat derisive coinage by Norman Spinrad], the Mirrorshades Group, and the Outlaw technologists), he had been promoting it between 1983 and 1986 in his *samizdat*-like fan newsletter *Cheap Truth*, whose first issue complained that "American SF lies in a reptilian torpor" ("Quest for Decay"). Even before *Neuromancer*, Sterling (writing as Vincent Omniaveritas) proclaimed Gibson as its possible savior; in reviewing the story "Burning Chrome" in *Cheap Truth* #2, he wrote, "THIS is the shape for science fiction in the 1980's: fast-moving, sharply extrapolated, technologically literate, and as brilliant and coherent as a laser. Gibson's focused and powerful attack is our best chance yet to awaken a genre that has been half-asleep since the early 1970's" ("Public Shudders").

Like the New Wave, cyberpunk inevitably generated a response within the SF community. Michael Swanwick, in a 1986 essay titled "A User's Guide to the Postmoderns," identified what he characterized as a contrasting 1980s movement to the cyberpunks, the "humanists," among whom he named Connie Willis, Kim Stanley Robinson, John Kessel, James Patrick Kelly, Lucius Shepard, and Nancy Kress. As Michael Levy notes, these humanists "did not issue manifestos or shout from the rooftops about the differences between their work and earlier sf" (157). In fact, much of their work shared qualities with the best of cyberpunk, and it eventually led to a theme anthology edited by Fiona Kelleghan, *The Savage Humanists* (2008), prefaced by Kelleghan's lengthy essay that argued for viewing it as a movement.

One of the most lasting legacies of cyberpunk, however, may lie simply in the construction of its name. "Punk" quickly became the default suffix for any perceived, proposed, or hypothetical aggregation of writers who shared specific themes and concerns, and the SF and fantasy field was soon awash in "-punk" movements, some more ironic than others: biopunk (biotechnology); nanopunk (nanotechnology); nowpunk (featuring present-day settings but SF themes); witpunk (humorous science fiction, after an anthology edited by Claude Lalumiere and Marty Halpern); steampunk (usually set in the Victorian era); and various steampunk derivatives such as dieselpunk (generally set between the world wars) and even Teslapunk (involving electrical devices, usually during the period of Tesla's own experiments). Even related fantastic genres embraced the promise of franchise labeling: particularly graphic horror became splatterpunk, while fantasy developed mannerpunk (fantasy influenced by Jane Austen, P. G. Wodehouse, and others), mythpunk (coined by author Catherynne Valente to describe fantasy that combines myth and folklore with postmodern literary technique), even elfpunk (in which folkloristic creatures are portrayed in contemporary settings). Few of these came with specific manifestos, although a variation of biopunk called ribofunk by author Paul di Filippo (from "ribosome" and "funk") was defined in his own "manifesto" as speculative fiction that recognizes that "the next revolution—the only one that really matters—will be in the field of biology."

Of all these constructions, steampunk is the only one since cyberpunk to have escaped the world of genre fiction to become a popular cultural meme. Cyberpunk had become a *TIME* magazine cover story in February 1993, and steampunk reached the cover of the *New York Times* Style section in May 2008—though the article focused more on fashion, film, design, and lifestyle than on the fiction that provided its name. "Steampunk" was apparently coined by the writer K. W. Jeter in a letter to *Locus* magazine in April 1987; referring to fiction by himself and his friends James P. Blaylock and Tim Powers, he predicted, "I think Victorian fantasies are going to be the next big thing, as long as we can come up with a fitting collective term for Powers, Blaylock, and myself. Something based on the appropriate technology of that era; like 'steampunks,' perhaps...." Ironically, although Powers, Blaylock, and Jeter *did* see themselves as a group, it would be several years before the term came into widespread usage following the publication of Bruce Sterling and William Gibson's novel *The Difference Engine* (1990), which clearly allied the movement to cyberpunk, and Paul di Filippo's *The Steampunk Trilogy* (1990), which represented its first use in a title. Although it has become popular in both science fiction and fantasy (in film as well as literature), steampunk is now more properly described as a subgenre (or, on a wider scale, as a microculture) rather than an organized and self-conscious movement.

As we have seen, both cyberpunk and steampunk were *post facto* formulations derived from fiction that had appeared over several prior years, and this would prove true as well of two of the prominent movements to emerge in the 1990s and 2000s: slipstream and the New Weird. "Slipstream" is used as a term of convenience here, not in the sense that John Clute defined, in his 1993 *Encyclopedia of Science Fiction*, as referring primarily to nongenre works "piggybacking" on SF tropes, but more in the sense that Bruce Sterling suggested in 1989 as an alternative term to "novels of Postmodern sensibility" (see Prucher 189). In fact, the tendency toward mixing genres within a single work, or combining genre tropes with postmodern literary techniques, has seen many labels: New Humanism, transrealism, nonrealist fiction, postgenre fiction, New Wave Fabulism, postmodern fantasy, cross-genre fiction, liminal fantasy, "span" fiction, Artists without Borders, and interstitial arts. In a 2003 column in *Asimov's Science Fiction*, James Patrick Kelly identified Kelly Link, Karen Joy Fowler, and Carol Emshwiller as the "muses" of this movement, arguing that their fiction deliberately seeks to undermine conventional categories, and in 2006 he and John Kessel defined it further in *Feeling Very Strange: The Slipstream Anthology*, where they described it as a literary effect rather than a movement or subgenre.

A self-conscious movement did emerge from such fiction in 2002, when writers Ellen Kushner, Terri Windling, and Delia Sherman, along with SUNY professor Heinz Fenkl, organized what they called the Intersitial Arts Foundation, holding its first symposium the following year and later sponsoring a series of anthologies beginning with *Interfictions: An Anthology of Interstitial Writing*, edited by Sherman and Theodora Goss in 2007. While the organization's avowed purpose is to support "interstitial" art, music, and performance as well as literature—"art found *in between* categories and genres" (Kushner; emphasis in original)—its principal activities (conferences, essays, blogs, anthologies) have focused largely on literature and on supporting and recognizing particular kinds of genre-bending work rather than promoting a specific activist agenda.

Another cross-genre movement, the New Weird, emerged primarily from a question posed by English novelist M. John Harrison on his online message board in April 2003: "The New Weird. Who does it? What is it? Is it even anything? Is it even New?" (qtd. VanderMeer and VanderMeer 317). Soon the discussion was joined by a variety of writers and editors, including Jeff VanderMeer, Michael Cisco, Steph Swainston, Jonathan Strahan, Kathryn Cramer, Jeffrey Ford, Justina Robson, Cheryl Morgan, and most prominently China Miéville, whose own novels, beginning with *King Rat* (1998) and *Perdido Street Station* (2000), were most often cited as exemplars of the movement. With roots as diverse as the earlier weird fiction of Lovecraft and Clark Ashton Smith, the experimentalism of the New Wave, and works such as M. John Harrison's *Viriconium* series (1971–85), the movement came to be identified with a variety of authors, including Cisco, Swainston, VanderMeer, di Filippo, K. J. Bishop, Jay Lake, Sarah Monette, and Hal Duncan, and eventually gave rise to its own anthology, Ann and Jeff VanderMeer's *The New Weird*, in 2008.

Although both the Interstitial and New Weird movements sought to celebrate works and authors who challenged the boundaries between science fiction, fantasy, and weird fiction, neither movement seemed particularly interested in prescribing particular modes or approaches to writing fiction. That was not quite the case with other movements that emerged in the first decade of the twenty-first century. The "New Space Opera" has been traced by Paul J. McAuley as far back as a 1984 editorial by David Pringle and Colin Greenland in *Interzone*, calling for a "radical, hard SF," "critical and investigative." While this same editorial has been cited as promoting the cyberpunk movement in England, McAuley, Stephen Baxter, and others saw it as a call that "*all* science fiction . . . was overdue for renovation" (McAuley; emphasis in original). This included refurbishing and updating the sort of large-scale adventures that had drawn them as young readers into science fiction, but without the crudeness of characterization and militaristic (and mostly American) chauvinism. In the view of McAuley's colleague Ken MacLeod, the New Space Opera had been invented even earlier, with M. John Harrison's 1974 novel *The Centauri Device*, which "took a British New Wave sensibility to the stars." But Harrison's seminal work only seemed to bear fruit decades later, as a younger generation of novelists, including McAuley, MacLeod, Baxter, Alastair Reynolds, Peter Hamilton, and others (along with such American writers as Greg Bear, Vernor Vinge, and Robert Reed), began to reexamine the political and social possibilities of the space opera form. The New Space Opera may never have developed a manifesto, but it, too, soon received its own anthologies, with Jonathan Strahan and Gardner Dozois's *The New Space Opera* (2007) and *The New Space Opera 2* (2009), and David Hartwell and Kathryn Cramer's *The Space Opera Renaissance* (2006).

Almost as a rebuke to the New Space Opera, however, came a movement arguing that much that was wrong with science fiction had to do with those very galaxy-spanning epics. Reacting to a complaint by British writer Julian Todd that science fiction had nearly abandoned the real technological and environmental challenges facing society, Geoff Ryman and a group of students at the 2002 Clarion Writers' Workshop concocted the idea of "Mundane SF," which argued that such common narrative devices as interstellar travel, contact with aliens, the engineering of wormholes, or quantum indeterminacy not only were radically unlikely, but also tended to shift attention away from more immediate near-future problems closer to home. While the movement has produced a blog and generated a fair amount of debate among other SF writers, its most prominent proponent remains Ryman himself, although its advocates might point to popular younger writers such as Paolo Bacigalupi as echoing its basic tenets. Ryman edited an anthology in 2010, *When It Changed: 'Real Science' Science Fiction*, in which he and others wrote stories related to the work of scientists at Manchester University, where Ryman teaches. The movement shares some goals with the Hieroglyph project developed by writer Neal Stephenson and a varied group of other writers, scientists, and academics to promote science fiction that might inspire younger researchers toward achievable technologies—the "big stuff" that Stephenson feels has been lacking in recent technological innovation. "Time for the SF writers to start pulling their weight and supplying big visions that make sense," Stephenson wrote in an essay in *World Policy Journal*. "Hence the Hieroglyph project, an effort to produce an anthology of new SF that will be in some ways a conscious throwback to the practical techno-optimism of the Golden Age." Though the anthology was still in the planning stages at the end of 2012, Stephenson had recruited an impressive array of participants in the project's closed discussion board.

The "techno-optimism" that Stephenson refers to also resonates with various efforts to promote a less pessimistic tone in science fiction. The British magazine *Interzone* has periodically faced such complaints from readers, and in 2008 co-editor Jetse de Vries resigned his position partly over such differences. This eventually led to an ongoing web discussion involving de Vries, Damien Walter, Jason Stoddard, Kathryn Cramer, Lou Anders, and others on the need for a more optimistic science fiction, eventually articulated by Stoddard in a blog post titled "Stranger and Happier: A Positive Science Fiction Platform" and in a 2010 anthology edited by de Vries, *Shine: An Anthology of Optimistic SF*. As with Stephenson's Hieroglyph project, it is too early to tell as of this writing whether the movement is likely to have any lasting effects beyond web discussions and an anthology—which has been the fate of many proposed advocacy movements in science fiction.

It is fair to say that science fiction, in general, has not been a movement-driven literature (although some of its most profound shifts have been related to broader cultural movements such as feminism and libertarianism, discussed elsewhere in this volume). The most significant efforts to define or redefine the field were initially the work of editors such as Gernsback and Campbell, who could promote their agendas through simple economics—buying the stories they felt reflected their views—and only later by editors who characterized their choices in terms of revolutionary or revisionist movements (such as Moorcock or Ellison). Other, even later movements, such as cyberpunk, slipstream, or the New Weird, were essentially retroactive descriptions of fiction that had already been appearing for some years prior to the initial manifestos—less a genuine call for a new kind of fiction than the expression of a desire to see more fiction "like this," whether "this" referred to William Burroughs, William Gibson, or China Miéville. In almost all cases, the key works of a given movement have preceded the critical and editorial formulations of the movement, and science fiction has continued to evolve, as it always has, through individual visionary writers assimilating diverse aspects of the field's history and, on occasion, creating a magnetic node around which other writers, critics, readers, and (almost always) anthologists could find a point of coalescence.

Works Cited

Ashley, Michael, and Marshall B. Tymn, eds. *Science Fiction, Fantasy, and Weird Fiction Magazines.* Westport, CT: Greenwood, 1985. Print.

Broderick, Damien. *Transrealist Fiction: Writing in the Slipstream of Science.* Westport, CT: Greenwood, 2000. Print.

Del Rey, Lester. *The World of Science Fiction: The History of a Subculture.* New York: Del Rey, 1979. Print.

Di Filippo, Paul. "Ribofunk: The Manifesto." *streettech.com.* 1998. Web. Jan. 4, 2013. http://www.streettech.com/bcp/BCPtext/Manifestos/Ribofunk.html.

Ellison, Harlan. "Introduction: Thirty-Two Soothsayers." *Dangerous Visions.* Ed. Harlan Ellison. Garden City: Doubleday, 1967. xix–xxix. Print.

Farmer, Philip José. "Guest of Honor Speech, Baycon: The Twenty-Sixth Annual World Science Fiction Convention, San Francisco, CA, 1968." *Worldcon Guest of Honor Speeches.* Ed. Mike Resnick and Joe Siclari. Deerfield, IL: ISFIC, 2006. 114–32. Print.

Gernsback, Hugo. "How to Write Science Stories." Ed. Gary Westfahl. *Science Fiction Studies* 21.2 (July 1994): 268–72. Print.

Gibson, William. "Oh Well, While I'm Here: BLADERUNNER [sic]." www.williamgibsonbooks.com. Jan. 17, 2003. Web. Jan. 4, 2013. http://www.williamgibsonbooks.com/archive/2003_01_17_archive.asp.

Greenland, Colin. *The Entropy Exhibition: Michael Moorcock and the British "New Wave" in Science Fiction.* London: Routledge & Kegan Paul, 1983. Print.

Jeter, K. W. Letter to the Editor. *Locus: The Newspaper of the Science Fiction Field* 20.4 (Apr. 1987): 57. Print.

Kelly, James Patrick. "Slipstream." 2003. *Speculations on Speculation: Theories of Science Fiction.* Ed. James Gunn and Matthew Candelaria. Lanham, MD: Scarecrow, 2005. 343–51. Print.

Kelly, James Patrick, and John Kessel, eds. *Feeling Very Strange: The Slipstream Anthology.* San Francisco: Tachyon, 2006. Print.

Knight, Damon. *The Futurians: The Story of the Science Fiction "Family" of the 1930s That Produced Today's Top SF Writers and Editors.* New York: John Day, 1977. Print.

Kushner, Ellen. "IAF Origins." *The Interstitial Arts Foundation Website.* June 2004. Web. Jan. 4, 2013. http://www.interstitialarts.org/wordpress/?page_id=8.

Kyle, Dave. "The Science Fiction League." *Mimosa* 14. 1993. Web. Jan. 4, 2013. http://www.jophan.org/mimosa/m14/kyle.htm.

Levy, Michael. "Fiction, 1980–1992." *The Routledge Companion to Science Fiction.* Ed. Mark Bould, Andrew M. Butler, Adam Roberts, and Sherryl Vint. New York: Routledge, 2009. 153–62. Print.

MacLeod, Ken. "Singularity Skies." *Locus: The Magazine of the Science Fiction and Fantasy Field* 51.2 (Aug. 2003): 41. Print.

McAuley, Paul. "Junk Yard Universes." *Locus: The Magazine of the Science Fiction and Fantasy Field* 51.2 (Aug. 2003): 42. Print.

Panshin, Alexei, and Cory Panshin. *The World Beyond the Hill: Science Fiction and the Quest for Transcendence.* Los Angeles: Tarcher, 1989. Print.

Prucher, Jeff. *Brave New Words: The Oxford Dictionary of Science Fiction.* New York: Oxford UP, 2007. Print.

Ryman, Geoff, et al. "The Mundane Manifesto." *The New York Review of Science Fiction* 19.10 (June 2007): 4–5. Print.

Stephenson, Neal. "Innovation Starvation." *World Policy Journal* (Fall 2011). Web. Jan. 4, 2013. http://www.worldpolicy.org/journal/fall2011/innovation-starvation.

Sterling, Bruce (as Vincent Omniaveritas). "Public Shudders at 'Best of the Year.'" *Cheap Truth* 2. N.d. Web. Jan. 4, 2013. http://www.csdl.tamu.edu/~erich/cheaptruth/cheaptru.2.

———. "Quest for Decay." *Cheap Truth* 1. N.d. Web. Jan. 4, 2013. http://www.csdl.tamu.edu/~erich/cheaptruth/cheaptru.1.

Sterling, Bruce, ed. *Mirrorshades: The Cyberpunk Anthology*. New York: Arbor House, 1986. Print.

Stoddard, Jason. "Stranger and Happier: A Positive Science Fiction Platform." www.strangeandhappy.com. Sept. 27, 2008. Web. Dec. 28, 2011. http://strangeandhappy.com/2008/09/27/stranger-and-happier-a-positive-science-fiction-manifesto/.

Swanwick, Michael. "A User's Guide to the Postmoderns." 1986. *Speculations on Speculation: Theories of Science Fiction*. Ed. James Gunn and Matthew Candelaria. Lanham, MD: Scarecrow, 2005. 313–30. Print.

Vandermeer, Ann, and Jeff VanderMeer, eds. *The New Weird*. San Francisco: Tachyon, 2008. Print.

Westfahl, Gary. "Hugo Gernsback and His Impact on Modern Science Fiction." *Science Fiction Studies* 21.2 (July 1994): 273–79. Print.

———. *The Mechanics of Wonder: The Creation of the Idea of Science Fiction*. Liverpool: Liverpool UP, 1998. Print.

Wollheim, Donald A. *The Universe Makers: Science Fiction Today*. New York: Harper & Row, 1971. Print.

CHAPTER 5

FANDOM

FARAH MENDLESOHN

ONE of the perennial debates in science fiction centers upon the question "What is a fan?" In this chapter, I will define fans as those who engage with others over their shared interest in science fiction and fantasy. At one end of the spectrum, this may mean a small cluster of people who meet for gaming; at the other, it may mean individuals so far absorbed into and obsessed by the mechanisms and rituals of fan culture that they spend more time organizing events than they do actually reading/watching/playing the products of the genre. Fans go to SF conventions, and fans run conventions; fans play games, and fans organize games; fans read books, and fans argue about books. Some of them, as we will discover, go on to write books (and video games, TV shows, films, and other media).

The second debate focuses on the question "When does fandom emerge?" Official SF fandom is connected to the rise of the American pulp magazines during the 1920s and 1930s, but a dialogue was already present during the late nineteenth century: in reviews of such authors as H. Rider Haggard, H. G. Wells, and Jules Verne; in letters in literary journals; in the discussions among utopian socialists led by William Morris; and in the phenomenon of people writing books in reply to other books (Morris's *News From Nowhere* [1890], for example, is a response to Edward Bellamy's *Looking Backward: 2000–1887* [1888]). By the 1920s and 1930s, we can see small groups of people writing and reading together, of whom the Inklings in Oxford and the H. P. Lovecraft circle in New England are perhaps the most famous.

The technology necessary for fandom arose before official fandom did: thanks to the availability of cheap, efficient, international postal rates, and the absence of the telephone from most houses, the late nineteenth and early twentieth centuries were the golden age of letter writing. The rise of the toy printing press also fueled the habit of childhood magazines among the affluent, while handwritten magazines were a feature of many of the school stories of the 1920s and 1930s. The relative isolation of many middle-class people (especially women) in villages and small towns encouraged the emergence of what was from at least 1876 called an amateur press association (or APA), in which acquaintances would submit writing that was collated by one person and then circulated among the group (see Bailey). Writing to be read by friends was enough of a tradition that when SF fanzines (mimeographed amateur publications) emerged, people recognized them and knew how to respond, with LoCs (or letters of comment).

Hugo Gernsback, the founder and editor of the first dedicated sf magazine, *Amazing Stories,* actively encouraged readers to think of themselves as a collective entity, attempting to create a fan club around his publication, with its own logo and means of identification. Gernsback tapped into a particular social class, the (mostly) male upper-working, lower-middle class in search of advancement through technical education. SF fandom emerged in the first real period of mass mobility—at least for men—that America experienced, and it contributed in its own way to the nation-building of the interwar years, as state identities gradually became absorbed into a more homogenous notion of Americanness. At the same time, early SF fandom showed clear hallmarks of American localism: it tended to be organized into official local chapters that resembled the chapters of many American movements from labor unions to rotary clubs. Some were simply gatherings of friends to discuss science fiction, but others acquired particular tones, such as the New York–based Futurians, co-founded by Frederik Pohl in 1938, who had a distinct leftwing orientation and a belief that politics was crucial to the SF project—or, later, the Madison, Wisconsin, group whose annual convention (WisCon) was to become for a long time the only specifically feminist fan meeting in the United States. Many of these clubs still exist: the oldest continually operating is the Los Angeles Science Fantasy Society (LASFS), named in 1940 but already extant for some years before that. Other major groups include the San Francisco Science Fiction Conventions Inc. (SFSFC) and the New England Science Fiction Association (NESFA) in Boston, which mounts an annual convention, Boskone, and runs its own well-regarded small press. These organizations also compete to host the World Science Fiction Convention (or Worldcon), decided by bids submitted two years in advance through a campaign and vote organized by the World Science Fiction Society (WSFS), on which we will later have more to say. These groups also produce many of the Big Name Fans (established through a combination of reputation and longevity), who also emerge from the fanzines.

Of the other countries that have an active fandom (rather than simply fans), only Australia, with its huge distances, still has clearly defined local groups connected to well-known conventions: Swancon (held in Perth since 1975) is Australia's longest-running regional convention, and there is also a National Convention (NatCon) that has been meeting since the 1950s and that bestows (since 1969) the Ditmar Awards. In Europe, Germany is perhaps the closest to the US model, though its fandom is mostly centered around the popularity of the "Perry Rhodan" series; German fandom is city-based, with clusters around Hamburg, Berlin, and Frankfurt, reflecting perhaps the traditionally federal nature of that country. Sweden was arguably one of the earliest European countries to establish a fandom; largely based around Stockholm, it coalesced in the 1950s out of groups of fans who had been conversing about the genre for decades. Swedish and Norwegian fandoms have traditionally been closely connected to UK fandom, as has Irish fandom, and there are active fandoms in Finland, Croatia, Denmark, and Russia.

Before the 1980s, British fandom, which emerged before the Second World War and thrived on the magazines shipped as "ballast" from the United States, displayed a widescale regional fragmentation centered on major cities: Leeds, Glasgow, Birmingham, and London had strong but informal centers, and this was reflected in the frequently contested bids to hold the national convention, Eastercon. By the 1990s, however, local affiliations were becoming somewhat less important: Birmingham has one of the few strong groups, centered for over 40 years on Rog Peyton's bookshop Andromeda, and another cluster runs Bristolcon. Although the British Science Fiction Association is a nominally national body, it has been unable to change its London-centric orientation. Similarly in Canada, the Toronto group that formed around SF editor Judith Merrill's donation of her personal collection to the Public Library of Toronto is a quite loose affiliation, with strong ties to other groups of Canadian fans. Although there are regional conventions, they lack the sense of loyal local identities. When Canada, the United Kingdom, or Australia bid for a Worldcon, the bidders tend to be drawn from across the country, and groups collaborate over the bid rather than compete. Some of this is due to their relatively smaller fandoms, but it is also clear that the phenomenon reflects a muted local identity compared to the often fierce regionalism that still marks US fandom.

In continental Europe, the European Science Fiction Society began running conventions in 1972: the first was in Trieste, Italy, and subsequent events moved around the continent, including behind the Iron Curtain (Poland in 1976 and Yugoslavia in 1986). In Poland, East Germany, and the Soviet Union, samizdat copies of Western SF circulated alongside the very healthy native traditions. Many of these groups received external support from an organization called Fans Across the World, which sent shipments of books and fanzines. One split in Europe, however, occurred between the alliance of Anglo and Nordic nations on the one hand and the Latinate speakers on the other: most Finnish, Scandinavian, and German fans speak English and have been historically eager to engage UK fandom. In contrast, there are large fandoms in Italy and Spain that have instead pursued extensive links with growing Latin American fandoms in Argentina and Brazil. The biggest genre events in Europe every year are the French Utopiales in Nantes and the French comic conventions in Angoulême, which dwarfs the annual Comic-Con in San Diego. However, there is relatively little exchange between French fandom and the Anglo-Nordic fan world.

Many UK Worldcons are also Eurocons (a separate institution), drawing on the expertise of fans across the continent and with a particularly strong link with Dutch and Scandinavian fans. The European Science Fiction Association has functioned to establish contacts across Europe, and the Worldcons in the Hague in 1990 and in Glasgow in 1995 and 2005 helped to bring European fans closer. There were over 500 Nordic fans at the 2005 Worldcon, and Nordic fans retain very close links to North America and the United Kingdom.

Although science fiction and fantasy are beginning to thrive in India, and Indian writers are being published in the US and UK markets, fandom there is very new. However, a conference on science fiction in Indian literature is in its second decade. For large non-Western fandoms we must look to China and Japan. The Chinese magazine *Science Fiction World* has been going strong for more than 20 years, with a circulation of 200,000. In China, most of the mass organizations of SF fans exist at universities and colleges. The most famous of these—Beijing University, Qinghua University, Fudan University, Zhejiang University—all have students' SF societies that organize many activities for their members (film screenings, writing contests, and the like). A few societies publish their own fanzines. There is no annual convention, but *Science Fiction World* has organized several fan meetings, at which it has presented its Galaxy Awards. The most influential fan events historically were the 1997 Beijing International SF Conference and the 2007 China (Chengdu) SF/Fantasy Conference, which brought together fans from all over China to celebrate the genre and hear lectures by SF and fantasy writers. Virtually all of this activity is sponsored by the government: *Science Fiction World* is under the control of the Sichuan branch of the Science and Technology Association, while the annual Xingyun (Nebula) Awards are organized by the World Chinese Science Fiction Association.

Japan has its own distinct fandom focused on anime and manga, as well as "cosplay" (costuming combined with performance). Although a bilingual convention, HALcon, has been held since 2010, language barriers have kept Japanese and Anglophone fans separated. At the same time, there is much translation of US and UK work, and the prestigious Seiun Award, like many in non-English-speaking countries, has categories for foreign language fiction. One effect of this is that there is always a small but prominent Japanese presence at Worldcons, a fact that enabled Japan's bid for the 2007 Worldcon in Kyoto, a convention that was revealing of the very different interests of Japanese and Anglophone fans. Arguably, the most famous Japanese fan was Takumi Shibano, a translator, who began in 1957 as a fanzine editor and chaired the country's first SF convention in 1962. He was guest of honor at the 1996 Los Angeles Worldcon and again in 2007 in Kyoto.

The first international convention was held in Leeds in 1937, and the first Worldcon (a service mark owned by WSFS) took place in New York in 1939. These events consisted of a few hundred people and a single track of programming focused almost exclusively on literature and science. By the twenty-first century, Worldcons had come to attract—depending on the footprint of the host city—between 4,000 and 6,000 people and offer programs consisting of up to 20 tracks covering SF in all media, science, history, politics, and crafts. Individual Worldcons are usually named for their host cities—for example, Chicon (in Chicago), Detention (in Detroit), or the Millenium Philcon (in Philadelphia).

Invisible to many fans are the political and bureaucratic aspects of fandom: most conventions require collaboration, and where the Worldcon is concerned, this includes elaborate committee structures. The early Worldcons were riven by fan politics (some still are), which led to infighting about their location and content. This divisiveness was resolved through the development of a process that coalesced into a business meeting, with a set of rules and a process to update them. The role of WSFS (World Science Fiction Society), an unincorporated literary society, is to determine three things: the selection of Worldcon sites, the process for bestowing the Hugo Awards, and the conduct of the business meeting. Although everyone who is a member can go to the business meeting, in practice a group of around 100 forms the active core; it is nonetheless a participatory democracy that is not incorporated and does not elect officers.

Fan organizations can be roughly divided into those that run conventions and those that give awards; where voted awards exist, the two often overlap, as in the case of the Hugos (Worldcon), Ditmars (Australian NatCon), Seiun (Japan), and BSFA awards (Eastercon). Then there are the Nebula Awards, which are chosen by the membership of the Science Fiction and Fantasy Writers of America membership (a professional union), and the Locus Award, which are tied to the trade magazine (and erstwhile fanzine), *Locus*. Some awards—the Arthur C. Clarke Award (UK), the Philip K. Dick Award for best paperback original, the Tiptree Award for best writing about gender and sexuality, and the World Fantasy Awards—are juried and require layers of administration. Particularly active Big Name Fans who regularly run conventions and sit on juries are sometimes playfully referred to as "smof" (for Secret Master(s) of Fandom). The first official Smofcon was held in 1984, which was also the year of the largest Worldcon (over 8,000 members) and the largest Eastercon (over 1,700). Smofcon is both a training session and management retreat for con-runners.

It has been argued that fandom is graying, yet there are enormously diverse offerings within fandom that constantly renew, refresh, and change the field. The sense of what science fiction *is* has expanded enormously, while the sense of what science fiction fans are interested in appears to have no boundaries. As the Worldcons increased in size, however, fandom fractured into a range of different interest groups. Worldcon remains the largest general and book-oriented convention in the English-speaking world, but the US anime conventions are far larger, and Dragon Con in Atlanta, best known for its cosplay and interest in TV and film, attracts 40,000 attendees. Comic-Con in San Diego draws over 100,000 people. GenCon (a 40-year-old gaming convention) attracts over 120,000. All three of these are professionally run events with full-time staff, while Worldcon remains an amateur, participatory event. Alongside these are many small special-interest conventions focused on gaming, costume, anime, or a particular TV show such as *Blake's 7* or *Star Trek*. These conventions each have their own distinctive fandoms, but there is almost always an overlap with the Worldcon demographic, which has ensured that the Worldcon, while invisible to many fans, remains an amorphous core. That fandom can be said to exist as a whole amidst this national, regional, and thematic fragmentation is due to a range of mechanisms, such as the preservation of historical memory within the community through fanzines and exhibits and fans' longstanding willingness to travel widely from site to site.

Fannish culture is a "knowledge economy": activities and people are valued for what they know and can pass on. This aspect of the culture can be seen in the kind of program items often offered at conventions that might appear to the outsider to be irrelevant: items on geocaching, on linguistics, on medieval history, or on Japanese embroidery. The attitude that all knowledge is valuable and that *someone else will want to know what you know* underpins much of the extracurricular culture of SF fandom. The earliest manifestation of this knowledge economy can be found in the letters columns of *Amazing Stories*, where readers reviewed and corrected the fiction in the confidence that others would want to know what they thought; often the result was a lively exchange among correspondents over subsequent issues. One of the earliest Big Name Fans, Forrest J. Ackerman, was an active letter writer in these early magazines during his youth. Arguments that began in letter columns quickly spilled over into the amateur presses: the form seems to have been peculiarly suited for a new genre that was concentrated in a small number of publications, for it was possible for everyone to read everything.

SF fanzines began to be published in the 1930s, though there is difference of opinion as to which was the first. The early fanzines were a product of the early fan communities, largely teenaged American boys talking to one another about the stories they read and about amateur science. During the 1940s, a shift took place as fanzines began to talk about the community itself rather than the fiction and about what interested members of that community. What could appear in a fanzine was remarkably broad. During the war years, a Leeds fan, J. Michael Rosenblum, used his fanzine—*The Futurian War Digest* or FIDO, which was produced on old off-cuts of paper—to promote his pacifism and his life as a conscientious objector and farmworker. For the SF historian, fanzines offer a fascinating insight into a uniquely interactive cultural space and the personalities that shaped the field.

The technology that supported the fanzines was varied. It is not clear how common mimeograph machines were before the 1960s, and in this early period many fanzines were simply letters typed with multiple carbons, so that "editions" might run to eight or ten copies. Ackerman would write many notes on one piece of paper and send the paper to a "hub" person, such as Ken Slater in the United Kingdom, who would cut up the slips and send them out. In contrast, Harry Turner's 1940s fanzine *Zenith* was beautifully duplicated. Most people producing fanzines in this early period were tied to local communities, and travel was expensive and limited. In the early 1960s, for example, around 200 people went to a UK Eastercon; most were engaged in fanzine culture. Pete Weston's popular fanzine, also called *Zenith*, featured contributions from the Birmingham fan group, while the Manchester group produced *Alien* (see Weston). Jeanne Gomoll, one of the leading Wiscon fans, became engaged in fandom first through the local fanzine *Janus* (1975). Fanzines continue to reflect the continuing diversification in the field. The first media-oriented fanzine may have been the one produced by SF writer Lois McMaster Bujold and Lillian Stewart Carl in 1968.

Since 1955 the Hugo Awards have featured a regular category for fanzines. Until the 1970s, the distinction between fanzines and professional magazines was clear, but with the rise of *Locus*, now a trade magazine but once a mimeographed fanzine, the lines became blurred and the current category of "semiprozine" recognizes the sense of a continuum. The category of fan writer is defined not by the amateur status of the author but by the venue of the material; hence, professional author Frederik Pohl won the best fan writer Hugo for his blog memoir in 2010.

Paper fanzines have retained their popularity despite challenges from other media, in part, because new technologies have continually brought in new fans.

Pieces written as blog posts eventually appear in fanzines, while fanzines provide conversation fodder for podcasts. Ease of publication means that an individual letter of comment may go on to become the basis of a new fanzine. Online publishing and archiving have given this ephemeral form a new lease on life. Earl Kemp, an old-time Chicago fan who rediscovered fandom through the Internet in the late 1990s as a result of googling his name, began to produce an online fanzine (or ezine) called *eI*, which was partially his own memoirs. *eI* has published articles on the early presses and fan culture, including the occasional article by an academic scholar. PDF versions of ezines are circulated by e-mail, and many appear in the repository efanzines.com. While mimicking paper fanzines in their layout, most are only ever read onscreen. In 2004 Cheryl Morgan's *Emerald City* was the first electronically distributed fanzine to win a Hugo; in 2010 Tony Smith's *Star Ship Sofa* became the first podcast to be selected best fanzine.

Fans are knowledge-hungry, interested in new technologies. They like to exchange ideas, and they are often isolated, the only SF fan in the classroom or the workplace. Fanzines were a way of surmounting these barriers. The Internet could have been invented for the SF community. Although other groups have made extensive use of the new modes of electronic communication, SF fans are a dominant online presence. Fanzines not only embody the history of the field and its fans, but they also create that history: across the years, feuds and schisms were played out in the fanzines, often—because of the speed of surface mail—at glacial rates. Delphi discussion groups and later usenet and sff.net allowed people to have conversations in real time, as if they were at conventions, but due to the lack of moderators and the typical inhibiting factors of face-to-face conversation, "flame wars" often erupted. People discovered quite quickly that a common interest in *Star Trek* or the works of Robert A. Heinlein or a desire to write science fiction did not guarantee any other kind of commonality.

The emergence of blogging had somewhat of a calming effect since, like the fanzine, it involved a more passive mode of reading in which it was difficult to comment directly. People were more likely to use their own blog to comment at length than to append a short comment on someone else's. LiveJournal changed this because it allowed commentators to respond to other comments and allowed people to link journals. It also offered a particularly potent set of connections: whereas mailing lists tended to attract the like-minded, and usenet lists to attract people with a shared topic in common, the LiveJournal circles that have developed are overlapping configurations of interests, politics, and friendship groups. People "friend" a livejournal because they like a post someone else has referred them to in a series of "blind dates." The result—now mirrored on the competing but also collaborating site Dreamwidth—can be very creative as people encounter new ideas, but the response rate at which a debate can move has also speeded up. In 2009 an argument broke out over the treatment of writers and fans of color in the SF and fantasy communities, a debate that became known as RaceFail. SF fans, editors, and authors interacted publicly and contentiously, while many "lurkers" were able to track a discussion that ranged from the economics of publishing through the definition and workings of racial privilege. The format also allowed fans of color to be heard in ways that were difficult to achieve in the structured programming of conventions; frequently, they received signal boosts from the ability of LiveJournal writers to link to their sites. New stars emerged, often pseudonymously, but pseudonyms have always been common in fan writing.

Fanzines have generated not just fan writing but also fan art, and a Hugo Award exists to honor it. Fancartography—the production of maps of imaginary landscapes—is less often recognized by the community but has developed alongside the SF publishing industry (see Ekman). Some of the first maps produced came in the wake of the paperback publication of Tolkien's *Lord of the Rings* trilogy in the 1960s, in reprints of Robert E. Howard's "Conan the Barbarian" stories. Since then, the project of mapping fantasy worlds has produced J. B. Post's *An Atlas of Fantasy* (1973); Karen Wynn Fostad's *Atlas of Pern* (1985) devoted to the work of Anne McCaffrey, which has been expanded by the online Pern Museum hosting a range of maps; Alberto Manguel's *Dictionary of Imaginary Places* (1980); and others. One of the most popular fictional cartographers is Stephen Briggs who has published several maps of Ankh-Morpork, a fantasy world created by Terry Pratchett. These have been commercially released with Pratchett's permission.

Fan fiction is the most controversial production emanating from fandom. In one sense, fan fiction—that is, freestanding SF stories written by fans—has always existed; it is creator-copyright fiction that is the new invention since authors, of course, own their characters and their worlds. The dissemination of fan fiction using characters and settings from professionally published works began in the 1960s and was for the most part ignored by the authors affected—although Marion Zimmer Bradley decided to publish a collection of fan fiction set in her "Darkover" universe. The Internet provided a new forum for "fan-fic" writers not only to write but also to read and critique each others' work (see Jenkins; Pugh; Hellekson and Busse). Although some authors have refused permission for fan fiction, others have decided to accept it as an homage and, like Eric Flint, to actively encourage it on the condition that certain protocols are observed, the main being a standard disclaimer appearing at the beginning of each story. Online communities have grown up around fan-fic, such as An Archive of Our Own, and some who began as fan-fic writers—for example, Naomi Novik, Deborah Doyle, Paul Cornell, and Mark Gatiss—have gone on to develop careers as SF professionals.

There has always been a strong overlap and engagement between the fan community and the world of SF authors and editors. Most authors were, of course, once readers of the genre. Many major professional authors and artists appeared first as fan writers, fanzine editors, fan artists, and convention runners. Ray Bradbury and Ray Harryhausen were founding members of the Los Angeles Science Fantasy Society, and E. C. Tubb helped to found the British Science Fiction Association. Frederik Pohl and Judith Merril were founding members of the Futurian Society (see Knight), and the young Isaac Asimov crops up first as a letter writer, then as an author, and then as one of only six Futurians allowed into the first Worldcon in New York in what became known as the Great Exclusion Act of 1939 (see Moskowitz). Pohl has continued to be active in fandom as a writer and reviewer. Among younger authors, Gregory Benford and his brother Jim were fanzine editors, and Lois McMaster Bujold was drawn into the field at least initially through *Star Trek* fandom. Jeanne Gomoll's life as a professional artist began in the fanzines. Julian May was the first woman to chair a Worldcon, in 1952. In the United Kingdom, Jainne Fenn, Jo Walton, and Charles Stross are well-known fans who have succeeded as SF writers. Terry Pratchett, who published his first story at the age of 15, was an active fan and, in turn, has created an entire fandom of his own.

Emerging from fandom to join the ranks of SF professionals can be a mixed blessing. Stross observed that, within 1980s British fandom, aspiring to be a "filthy pro" could cause some fans to look down their noses. On the other hand, fandom provided a tremendous infrastructure for the young writer: fanzines needed material, local workshops such as the Northampton group ran a mailing workshop providing peer criticism for isolated aspiring writers, and there were yearly workshops where one could be critiqued by a Big Name. Having roots in fandom could also lead to professional accomplishments, such as winning a Hugo or another award bestowed by one's former peers, which was especially gratifying. The connection between writers and fandom has been memorialized in literary texts, such as *Bimbos of the Death Sun* (1988), a crime novel by Sharon McCrumb, and Diana Wynne Jones's *Deep Secret* (1997), in which an SF convention proves the perfect place to cast works of power, transit to other worlds, and hide an injured centaur. In 2011 Jo Walton published *Among Others*, a fantasy novel set in the 1970s that recaptures the moment when the works of such authors as Robert Silverberg and Joanna Russ and Samuel R. Delany were new, freshly discovered by fans through reading clubs and conventions. Over the years, some connections between writers and fandom have become formalized, for example, through writing workshops such as Clarion (established in 1968), a six-week intensive training ground for aspiring SF writers based for a long time at Michigan State University and now at San Diego State University.

Many SF editors are also fans, particularly the team at TOR Books. Patrick Nielsen Hayden and Teresa Nielsen Hayden are both celebrated fan writers, and senior editor David Hartwell is a board member for the World Fantasy Convention and the editor-publisher of *The New York Review of Science Fiction*, a semiprozine. In the United Kingdom, Malcolm Edwards was the driving force behind Gollancz's science fiction line, and John Jarrold is a senior editor at Orbit and Simon and Schuster; both are well-known fans. Although also a published author, David Langford is best known for his award-winning fanzine *Ansible*. Begun in August 1979 as a double-sided sheet of paper, passed by hand and mail, it has migrated to the Internet as a news-sheet filled with announcements and satirical pieces. The other magazine editor to come out of fandom was Charles N. Brown, whose *Locus* began as a mimeographed fanzine in 1968 as part of the promotion for a bid to host the 1971 Worldcon in Boston; it eventually developed into the field's premier trade journal. Throughout this time, Brown built a reputation as a book collector and an expert with a thorough knowledge of the field. He remained a convention-goer to the last, dying on a flight home from the 2009 Readercon.

Acknowledgments

For their assistance and advice as I prepared this chapter, I would like to thank Claire Brialey, Vince Docherty, Jeanne Gomoll, Zhao Haihong, Cheryl Morgan, Mark Plummer, Charles Stross, and Gary K. Wolfe.

Works Cited

Bailey, Jenna. *Can Any Mother Help Me?* London: Faber and Faber, 2007. Print.
Ekman, Stefan. *Writing Worlds, Reading Landscapes: An Exploration of Settings in Fantasy.* Middletown, CT: Wesleyan UP, 2012. Print.
Hellekson, Karen, and Kristina Busse, eds. *Fan Fiction and Fan Communities in the Age of the Internet.* Jefferson, NC: McFarland, 2006. Print.
Jenkins, Henry. *Fans, Bloggers and Gamers: Exploring Participatory Culture.* New York: NYU, 2006. Print.
Knight, Damon. *The Futurians: The Story of the Science Fiction "Family" of the 30's That Produced Today's Top SF Writers and Editors.* New York: John Day, 1977. Print.
Moskowitz, Sam. *The Immortal Storm: A History of Science Fiction Fandom.* Westport, CT: Hyperion, 1954. Print.
Pugh, Sheenagh. *The Democratic Genre: Fan Fiction in a Literary Context.* Bridgend, UK: Seren, 2006. Print.
Weston, Pete. *With Stars in My Eyes: An Amazing Story of the Brummie Spaceways.* Boston: NESFA, 2004. Print.

CHAPTER 6

THE MARKETPLACE

GARY WESTFAHL

Although science fiction was created in the marketplace and always seemed comfortable in that milieu, its leading figures, paradoxically, constantly struggled against the natural pressures that the market exerts upon its products; and after several decades of successful resistance, they finally lost that battle. Many lament this outcome, but there are also reasons to celebrate this triumph of the marketplace.

The story of science fiction and the marketplace begins with Hugo Gernsback, who introduced science fiction in his science magazines with his serialized novel *Ralph 124C 41+: A Romance of the Year 2660* (1911–12), found that readers enjoyed similar stories by other authors, and finally launched the first magazine entirely devoted to science fiction, *Amazing Stories*, in 1926. Though not officially a pulp magazine, *Amazing* soon adopted that format, and was later joined by other science fiction pulps that employed garish covers to attract readers who were mostly young males.

Gernsback recognized that the stories he was presenting, which he christened "scientifiction," represented a new form of popular fiction, as announced in his first editorial: "There is the usual fiction magazine, the love story and the sex-appeal type of magazine, the adventure type, and so on, but a magazine of 'scientifiction' is a pioneer in its field in America" ("New Sort" 3). He promoted his new genre by distinguishing it from other varieties of popular fiction: unlike the less scientific stories published elsewhere, which Gernsback dismissed as "fairy tale[s]" that "have no place in Amazing Stories" ("Fictions Versus Facts" 291), scientifiction was, he claimed, solidly based upon scientific facts, so stories could educate young readers and provide scientists with useful ideas; and unlike the "'sex-appeal' type of story," scientifiction offered wholesome entertainment "that appeals to the imagination, rather than carrying a sensational appeal to the emotions" ("Thank You!" 99). In 1929, providently forced by bankruptcy to devise a new term, Gernsback renamed his genre "science fiction," but his arguments on its behalf remained the same.

In defining science fiction, Gernsback stipulated no particular patterns for stories to follow; as long as their science was correct and predictions were scientifically defensible, any sort of narrative was suitable. In this respect, the genre he delineated defied standard expectations that popular fiction should feature stock characters in formulaic plots, such as detectives tracking down murderers, beautiful heroines romanced by mysterious strangers, or explorers trekking through jungles in search of treasure. As Walter Nash notes, "In popular fiction the conventions are simplified and more or less fixed. . . . [P]opfiction is nothing if not predictable" (3–4). When writers realized that science-based content was Gernsback's only requirement, with no other conditions imposed, they relied upon patterns from other pulp genres, so issues of *Amazing Stories* included comic tales of inept inventors, globe-spanning adventure stories, detective fiction involving cutting-edge science, and horror stories with a scientific patina. Sensing two of these hybrid forms might be especially appealing, Gernsback launched new magazines to feature them: *Air Wonder Stories* (1929–30) for futuristic aviation stories, and *Scientific Detective Monthly*, later *Amazing Detective Tales* (1930), for scientific crime stories.

Yet his efforts to promote these forms of science fiction based on other generic models were unsuccessful, as they were overshadowed by another sort of story modeled upon a novel Gernsback published in 1928: E. E. "Doc" Smith's *The Skylark of Space*. Its bold story of interstellar space travel, with heroic scientists in conflict with both alien and human villains, proved enormously popular, inspiring many other writers to produce similar tales, ranging from the renowned John W. Campbell Jr., Edmond Hamilton, and Jack Williamson to the forgotten Frank K. Kelly, Leslie F. Stone, and Harl Vincent. By the 1930s, such adventures, which Wilson Tucker derisively labeled "space opera" in 1941, were so common,—and so formulaic—that Gernsback's *Wonder Stories* held contests encouraging readers to offer new "Interplanetary Plots" that professional authors could turn into stories; instructions warned contestants that a "plot submitted that simply relates a war between two planets, with a lot of rays and bloodshed, will receive little consideration." Instead, the magazine sought "some original 'slant' on interplanetary travel" (Gernsback, "Wanted" 437).

Yet Gernsback was fighting a losing battle against a generic pattern that remained ubiquitous in science fiction magazines and was gaining a toehold in other media aimed at the same young men who read the science fiction pulps. Although Philip Francis Nowlan's 1928 stories about Anthony Rogers, a present-day man who awakens in the future, involved no space travel, they became the basis for a comic strip, *Buck Rogers in the 25th Century* (1929–67), that evolved into a standard space opera; it was followed by a similar comic strip, *Flash Gordon* (1934–92), which also inspired a short-lived pulp magazine, *Flash Gordon Strange Adventure Magazine* (1936). Both characters soon appeared in film serials destined to become models for countless films and television programs.

By the decade's end, science fiction was apparently settling into the sorts of narrative conventions that characterized other forms of popular fiction: its central trope was space travel; its typical protagonists were heroic space pilots; and its standard plots were battles in space or adventures on other planets, involving adversaries ranging from space pirates to loathsome aliens. It is not surprising that a new magazine specializing in these stories, *Planet Stories*, debuted in 1939, and that another magazine launched the following year, *Captain Future*, took formulaic plotting to its next logical step, with space adventures starring a set of recurring characters: a brilliant scientist accompanied by a robot, an android, and a "living brain." There was every reason to believe, then, that science fiction in the 1940s and beyond would predominantly consist of such "predictable" products.

Yet this did not occur, and while Great Men theories of history are inherently suspect, the best explanation is that one man single-handedly prevented science fiction from gelling into a conventional generic pattern. After saying that "[t]he true history of the field can be written as the story of that dialectic between creative impulses and market forces," Norman Spinrad argues that "[t]he battle began when John W. Campbell, Jr. became editor of *Astounding Science-Fiction*" (26), for Campbell struck the first effective blow against the growing standardization of science fiction.

Although Campbell first became known in the 1930s for writing expansive space operas, he garnered more praise for the innovative stories he wrote as "Don A. Stuart" (since his true identity was widely known), including "Twilight" (1934), a moody look at humanity's future decline, and "Who Goes There?" (1938), an intriguing mystery involving a shapeshifting alien that inspired three films entitled *The Thing* (1951, 1982, 2011). Thus, when Campbell was named the new editor of *Astounding Stories* in 1937, he not only inherited the practical advantage of editing the science fiction magazine with the highest rates, but also his reputation could attract writers whose interests ranged beyond routine space adventures. Consider Clifford D. Simak, who authored several unmemorable stories in the early 1930s before he grew discouraged and gave up writing science fiction. However, when Campbell took over *Astounding*, he resolved to try again, telling his wife, "I can write for Campbell. . . . He won't be satisfied with the kind of stuff that is being written. He'll want something new" (qtd. Moskowitz 273).

Indeed, Campbell immediately signaled his desire for "something new": he retitled the magazine *Astounding Science-Fiction* to suggest a shift in new directions; his early editorials aggressively solicited new writers with scientific backgrounds; borrowing a device from previous editor F. Orlin Tremaine, who labeled inventive works as "Thought-Variant" stories, he promoted unusual narratives as "Nova" stories for other writers to emulate; and he published a special "Mutant" issue to suggest that his form of science fiction was evolving in novel ways. Soon, he recruited contributors with new and distinctive approaches to science fiction, including Simak, who developed a unique style of gentle, pastoral science fiction; A. E. van Vogt, who enthralled readers with fast-paced, hallucinogenic adventures; Theodore Sturgeon, who specialized in emotional, character-driven narratives; and Isaac Asimov, who became noted for stories involving the solution of scientific mysteries.

But one writer more than any other enabled Campbell to achieve his goal of publishing new and different forms of science fiction: Robert A. Heinlein. Using his own name and three pseudonyms, Heinlein appeared almost continuously in *Astounding* and its sister magazine *Unknown* (later *Unknown Worlds*) from 1939 to 1942, impressing readers with his streetwise characters, well-developed backgrounds, skill at imparting information through casual references, and insights garnered from diverse experiences in engineering, the military, and politics. Most significantly, Heinlein recognized that Campbell did not want formulaic work and provided him with a dizzying variety of stories. These twenty-three tales included a few space adventures—one occurring in the asteroids ("Misfit" [1939]), three others on generation starships traveling to other stars ("Universe" [1941], "Common Sense" [1941], *Methuselah's Children* [1942]); other space stories more idiosyncratically focused on oppressive labor conditions on Venus ("Logic of Empire" [1941]), a dying entrepreneur's poignant trip to the Moon ("Requiem" [1940]), and a company devoted to solving odd problems ("'We Also Walk Dogs'" [1941]). His Earthbound stories for Campbell were a cloistered tale of an inventor and his amazing discovery ("Life-Line" [1939]); adventures on a future Earth involving a bureaucrat thwarting a strike ("The Roads Must Roll" [1940]), a nuclear power plant about to explode ("Blowups Happen" [1940]), rebels opposing totalitarian governments ("'If This Goes On—'" [1940], *Sixth Column* [1941]), and unique utopias ("Coventry" [1940], *Beyond This Horizon* [1942]); innovative treatments of time travel ("By His Bootstraps" [1941]), travel into other dimensions ("Elsewhen" [1941]), and psychic powers ("Waldo" [1942]); a comic excursion into the fourth dimension ("'And He Built a Crooked House—'" [1941]); what we would now term a near-future technothriller ("Solution Unsatisfactory" [1941]); a strange encounter with enigmatic aliens ("Goldfish Bowl" [1942]); a paranoid, solipsistic vision anticipating Philip K. Dick ("They" [1941]); and fantasies developed with a rigorous logic that recalled science fiction ("Magic, Inc." [1940], "The Unpleasant Profession of Jonathan Hoag" [1942]).

Inspired by Heinlein's example, Campbell was soon arguing that "science-fiction is the freest, least formalized of any literary medium" ("Introduction" 5), and he described "*Astounding*'s policy" as "free and easy—anything in science fiction that is a good yarn is fine" ("Science" 100). He maintained that science fiction writers, driven solely by scientific ideas, could take stories into unpredictable territory: "The plotting is as nearly 100% uninhibited as anything imaginable ... because the author feels that freedom, he can let the story have its head, let it develop in any direction that the logic of the developing situation may dictate" ("Introduction" 5). Such stories, by following premises to their logical conclusions, could then offer guidance to scientists and policymakers who needed to anticipate and deal with future advances. And while these thoughtful works might not appeal to young readers, who gravitated in the 1940s toward magazines like *Planet Stories* that offered more juvenile fare, Campbell maintained his high circulation by attracting scientifically trained adult readers. (As early as 1938, Campbell boasted that "over thirty percent of *Astounding*'s readers are *practicing technicians*—chemists, physicists, astronomers, mechanical engineers, radio men—technicians of every sort" ["In Times to Come" 11; emphasis in original].)

Ironically, just as he was promulgating the ideas that would long shape science fiction, Campbell was about to lose his status as the field's dominant editor, for coming revolutions in science fiction publishing would first marginalize Campbell and later marginalize all editors like Campbell.

Initially, these changes were not harmful to Campbell's goals since his commitment to a variegated genre was shared by the people involved in these new developments.

First, during the 1950s, all of science fiction's pulp magazines either vanished or, like *Astounding*, converted to the smaller digest format, which looked more dignified and, unlike the science fiction pulps, implicitly sought adult readers who were presumably not interested in routine space operas. Reflecting such an intent, H. L. Gold, editor of the new digest magazine *Galaxy*, entitled his first editorial "For Adults Only" and went on to publish a wide variety of sophisticated stories. Another new digest, Anthony Boucher and J. Francis McComas's *The Magazine of Fantasy and Science Fiction*, similarly attracted adults with diverse stories of a high literary quality. Since these magazines paid just as well as *Astounding*, they could draw major writers away from Campbell, who also began alienating readers and writers as he became obsessed with psychic powers and pseudoscience.

Another development—the rise of paperback books—would undermine the status of all magazine editors by providing an alternative—and more profitable—market for science fiction writers. Yet Campbell's influence remained pervasive since paperback companies were often controlled by strong-willed editors who were in their own ways equally committed to avoiding generic formulas. Thus, while Donald A. Wollheim's Ace Books did reprint many space operas from the 1930s and 1940s and published new novels along similar lines, he also nurtured diverse new talents such as Dick, John Brunner, Samuel R. Delany, and Ursula K. Le Guin; and Ian and Betty Ballantine's Ballantine Books became renowned for publishing highly regarded original works such as Arthur C. Clarke's *Childhood's End* (1953) and Frederik Pohl's *Star Science Fiction* anthologies (1953–59).

As an additional force influencing science fiction, reviewers and commentators, publishing in professional magazines, fanzines, and books, became more numerous and prominent in the 1950s, and they supported Campbell's view that science fiction should be variegated and far-ranging in its speculations. In a compilation of his reviews, *In Search of Wonder* (1956), Damon Knight called science fiction "the last stronghold of independent thought" (6) and a genre that was "more fruitful and various than we generally (in our biased impatience) imagine" (8). Fanzine writer Norman Siringer, after approvingly noting "the decline of the space opera in the late thirties," acknowledged that "[u]nder the able guidance of John W. Campbell, *Astounding Science-Fiction* has rescued science fiction from the formula type action story" (22). Siringer also pioneered in calling for science fiction to be freed from "confinement to the pulp magazines" since "[e]ven the better American pulps are subject today to the same codes and taboos that restricted the writer for [other pulps such as] the *Golden Argosy, Hoffman's Adventure, All Story*, and *Blue Book*" (21). This desire to break taboos became central to science fiction's "New Wave" in the 1960s: Michael Moorcock dedicated his magazine *New Worlds*, in Spinrad's words, to "stylistic and formal experimentation" (28), and Harlan Ellison did the same in his anthology *Dangerous Visions* (1967), whose introduction promised to address "a need for new horizons, new forms, new styles, new challenges in the literature of our times" (3).

Still, despite these ongoing efforts to nurture diversity in science fiction throughout the 1950s and 1960s, there also emerged new efforts to produce a more standardized genre, though mostly for juvenile audiences. The Stratemeyer Syndicate revived inventor-hero Tom Swift in a series of "Tom Swift, Jr." books, beginning in 1954, that were mostly space adventures; around the same time, its publisher Grosset & Dunlap also published eight books featuring television's Tom Corbett, Space Cadet; in 1952 Doubleday recruited Asimov to write six juveniles, under the pseudonym "Paul French," starring space pilot Lucky Starr; and in 1961 the same company hired Wollheim to write eight novels about astronaut Mike Mars. Another new market for science fiction writers—film and television—offered lucrative, if not stimulating, opportunities for writers who were willing to produce formulaic work for younger viewers; among others, Clarke briefly wrote for the television series *Captain Video* (1949–55), and Jerome Bixby, previously noted for the story "It's a *Good* Life" (1953), authored screenplays for the films *It! The Terror from Beyond Space* (1958) and *The Lost Missile* (1958). As for adult science fiction, pulp writers had regularly produced numerous sequels to popular magazine stories, and the practice continued in the 1950s and 1960s, though writers could now repackage and republish related stories as books or produce new novels continuing their series. Examples include Zenna Henderson's "People" stories (1952–95), involving telepathic aliens who migrate to Earth, and James White's "Sector General" stories (1957–99), chronicling medical mysteries in a futuristic space hospital. However, such series never developed the generic rigidity of the juvenile series, allowed characters to mature and change over time, and generally remained the exception, not the norm, in science fiction publishing.

In the 1970s, though, a notoriously disastrous experiment in selling formulaic science fiction to adult readers lasted only two years. As Mike Resnick relates,

> the short-lived ill-fated Laser Books was published by wealthy and wildly-successful (to this point) Harlequin, its first attempt to infiltrate the science fiction field. But because all Harlequin books at that time were essentially interchangeable, written to a rigid formula, they assumed that *all* category fiction must work that way. So they hired [Frank] Kelly Freas, who was probably the best science fiction artist going at that time, to do the cover of every Laser book, and then tied his hands by giving him a formula which had the books look as interchangeable as the romances. . . . [N]o one could sell 50 near-identical-in-appearance science fiction novels in those pre-Trekbook days, and the line went down the tubes. (175; emphasis in original)

Yet Resnick acknowledges that Harlequin's project was not really dumb, only premature, as he then says, "You had to wait for television audiences, reared on the same plots and characters week in and week out, to *want* to read the same books over and over before that concept would work" (175; emphasis in original). Indeed, soon after Laser Books collapsed, a very successful series of formulaic science fiction books, inspired by a television series, would be launched.

Arguably, after Gernsback's and Campbell's editorial careers, the third most important event in the history of science fiction literature came in 1979, when Pocket Books began publishing novels based on the television series *Star Trek* (1966–69). True, *Star Trek* novels dated back to 1968, when Mack Reynolds's juvenile *Mission to Horatius* appeared; Bantam Books published a second *Star Trek* novel in 1971, followed by several others between 1976 and 1981. But it was Pocket Books that turned the production of *Star Trek* novels into a steady and profitable business by packaging them in standardized covers, numbering each book, and imposing increasingly inflexible guidelines upon authors. Soon, Pocket stopped publishing other science fiction books to focus exclusively on the franchise, and it has now offered readers over 500 *Star Trek* novels, including long series featuring the casts from all five television franchises and other series starring original characters inhabiting the *Star Trek* universe.

The popularity of *Star Trek* novels inspired publishers to launch similar series based on other science fiction franchises. There were earlier precedents—short-lived lines in the 1960s based on the television series *The Man from U.N.C.L.E.* (1964–68) and *The Prisoner* (1967–68)—but such books proliferated in the 1980s and thereafter. *Star Wars* novels enjoyed the greatest success, but there were also innumerable books based on the TV series *Doctor Who* (1963–89, 2005–), as well as books based on the *Terminator*, *Alien*, and *Godzilla* films and the series *The X-Files* (1993–2002), *Babylon 5* (1994–98), and *Stargate SG-1* (1997–2007), among many others.

To explain why such books became so common in the 1980s, there is merit in Resnick's suggestion that they reflected the growing popularity of science fiction television, but other factors were in play. By this time, Campbell had long been dead, the writers he published in the 1940s were dying or fading from view, and his readers represented an aging minority within an audience of mostly new readers who did not know or care about Campbell's crusade for constant originality in science fiction. Instead, they had learned to enjoy science fiction by watching *Star Trek* and *Star Wars* and were perfectly content to embrace their written equivalents: packaged, predictable books, guaranteed to provide the sorts of adventures they craved. Unaffected by Campbell or his concerns, they were simply typical readers of popular fiction, and publishers regularly attract such readers with repetitive books that minimize the risks of publishing. Setting up rigid guidelines eliminates any need for talented authors—any professional who can follow instructions will suffice—and new books can be printed with precise expectations as to how many copies will be sold. These are standard practices in popular fiction; in the case of science fiction, the surprise is not that such policies came to dominate the industry but that they took so long to emerge.

To further explain these developments, ongoing changes in the publishing industry increasingly marginalized what David G. Hartwell has termed the "heroic" editors who had long fought to prevent science fiction from descending into formulaic patterns ("The Distortion of the Product" 38). As their sales plummeted, all but a handful of science fiction magazines ceased publishing, and the few major magazines that survived had to adjust to shrinking circulation figures and their diminishing influence on writers who were understandably more attentive to the greater financial rewards from publishing books. One can praise creative editors of the 1980s and 1990s, such as Gardner Dozois of *Asimov's Science Fiction* and Gordon Van Gelder of *The Magazine of Fantasy and Science Fiction*, whose magazines published many award-winning stories, but such editors were no longer the most important figures in the field.

As for book publishers, the increasing consolidation of companies into large corporate conglomerates meant that individual editors had less control over what they published, as decisions were dictated by sales figures, the calculations of marketing experts, and the demands of chain bookstores. Today, only a few editors retain a degree of power to publish what they please: Betsy Wollheim, daughter of Donald A. Wollheim, inherited his company, DAW Books, and has remained an independent force though her company was acquired by Penguin; Hartwell earned three Hugo Awards as an adventurous editor for Tor Books; and Lou Anders oversees Prometheus's Pyr Books, dedicated to publishing meritorious original works. One is hard-pressed, though, to think of other examples among the trade publishers.

Furthermore, no survey of science fiction's history can ignore the growing prominence—and eventual dominance—of fantasy. After the 1960s, when the works of J. R. R. Tolkien became enormously popular, fantasy novels were regularly found in the science fiction sections of bookstores, soon renamed the science fiction and fantasy sections; and fantasies, unencumbered by traditions requiring novelty or originality—indeed, governed by principles that almost demanded fidelity to time-honored patterns—faced no barriers to quickly adopting the format of interminable series, some by single authors (such as Terry Brooks or David and Leigh Eddings, who annually produced new novels set in their fantasy worlds), others as multiple-author franchises (such as the "Forgotten Realms" novels based on the *Dungeons & Dragons* role-playing game). And when such products were crowding science fiction out of bookstore shelves, the genre inevitably began to borrow moves from its competitor's playbook by offering similar series.

To be sure, there were still writers and readers in the 1980s who remained committed to Campbell's philosophy, believing that science fiction should be variegated and daringly imaginative, and they resented the growing number and prominence of these sequels and series. Several jeremiads condemning these works and predicting the death of science fiction inevitably emerged; prominent examples include Cristina Sedgewick's "The Fork in the Road: Can Science Fiction Survive in Postmodern, Megacorporate America?" (1991) and three essays in a 1996 anthology: Spinrad's "Science Fiction in the Real World—Revisited," Hartwell's "The Distortion of the Product: Stresses on Science Fiction Literature," and Kathryn Cramer's "Our Pious Hope: Science Fiction Marketing, Counter-Marketing, and Transcendence." Still, while gloomy about the present situation, these pieces expressed the hope that the combined efforts of concerned writers, readers, and critics might somehow spark a counterrevolution that would restore the freedom and diversity that had once characterized science fiction. Surveying what has happened since they wrote, one can safely say that these hopes were naïve. Indeed, the only discernible result of their outcries was that bookstores resolved to mollify readers who disliked formulaic products with a policy of segregation: *Star Trek* novels and other series, instead of being incorporated into the regular section for science fiction and fantasy, were isolated in a separate area, which was convenient for readers looking for the latest installments of favorite series but also meant that the eyes of traditional connoisseurs would not be sullied by rows of books they despised.

Nevertheless, the mentality of series fiction gradually and inexorably invaded the sections of bookstores that theoretically excluded such works, as editors and agents encouraged writers to create recurring characters and worlds that could attract regular followings, instead of writing singletons incapable of ensuring steady audiences. The examples of Lois McMaster Bujold and David Weber, whose novels featuring Miles Vorkosigan and Honor Harrington are highly profitable, inspired many writers to launch similar series about space travelers in the tradition of *Star Trek*–inspired space opera, with an emphasis on military matters, but other repetitive approaches also proved successful. As a result, science fiction today has finally become what Gernsback, Campbell, and others had vigorously resisted, a genuine form of popular fiction, with an overwhelming majority of its works rigidly following some standard conventions.

To document this claim, I visited a Barnes & Noble bookstore in Montclair, California, on January 3, 2012, for a snapshot of the science fiction being offered to customers. Ignoring 19 shelves devoted to "Teen Fantasy/Adventure," 19 shelves for "Teen Paranormal Romance," 9 shelves for comic books and graphic novels, and 24 shelves for manga, I only examined the section devoted to science fiction and fantasy books for adults, which had 48 shelves for general science fiction and fantasy, 23 shelves for series, and 24 shelves for new books of all varieties. Though not obsessive enough to examine every single book to first distinguish science fiction from fantasy, and then distinguish original books from series books, I surveyed the 75 "New" books in this fashion. Some might quarrel with certain classifications (novels about vampires, werewolves, and zombies were considered fantasy, though stories may include scientific rationales, while a Terry Pratchett "Discworld" novel was counted as science fiction despite its kinship with fantasy), but different decisions in borderline cases would not have significantly changed the results. Books were classified into three groups: "classic" works first published decades ago; original works that to my knowledge had no related predecessors or successors; and works in series, ranging from a single sequel to the proudly proclaimed 100th novel in the series.

Overall, the "New" section featured 6 "classic" books (8 percent), 12 original books (16 percent), and 57 series books (76 percent). If this configuration is representative, it suggests that three out of every four science fiction books now being published are parts of series and undoubtedly formulaic, at least to some extent. Further, while a few series books came from authors who have garnered critical attention, such as Bujold, Larry Niven, Pratchett, Vernor Vinge, and Connie Willis, the vast majority have authors who are unknown to scholars. To use myself as an example, I have never read anything by Taylor Anderson, Jack Campbell, William C. Dietz, Karen Traviss, and the team of Sharon Lee and Steve Miller, the only authors who had two books in the "New" section. And while series books featured a few detectives with special powers and post-apocalyptic warriors, most were examples of military science fiction set in outer space, precisely the sorts of stories that Gernsback dismissed as "a lot of rays and bloodshed" and Siringer condemned as "the formula type action story."

To be sure, determined optimists would note that the section not reserved for new books did feature many examples of the variegated science fiction championed by Campbell, represented by at least one or two books from respected authors of the past and present: Poul Anderson, Asimov, Paolo Bacigalupi, Iain M. Banks, Greg Bear, Octavia E. Butler, Orson Scott Card, Clarke, Dick, Neil Gaiman, William Gibson, Joe Haldeman, Heinlein, Frank Herbert, Le Guin, Ian MacDonald, Jack McDevitt, China Miéville, Robert J. Sawyer, Dan Simmons, Neal Stephenson, Charles Stross, H. G. Wells, and Gene Wolfe. There were even classics no one would expect to find in a 2012 bookstore, such as John Brunner's *Stand on Zanzibar* (1968), Pat Frank's *Alas, Babylon* (1959), Walter M. Miller Jr.'s *A Canticle for Leibowitz* (1960), and Yevgeny Zamyatin's *We* (1921). Still, these books only filled the gaps between lengthy arrays of contemporary works in series.

However, optimists might continue, one cannot dismiss all series fiction as derivative junk until one has read it, for talented writers may find ways to stimulatingly stretch generic boundaries even within such confines. For example, in the section devoted to series, I noticed a Doctor Who novel by Moorcock and two novels based on video games by Bear and John Shirley. Surely, if anyone could produce memorable texts in franchised universes, it would be writers like these, and some of the other series authors, though unheralded, might be equally skilled. It seems more probable, though, that these novels are no better or worse than others of their kind, despite the best efforts of their writers.

Optimists might finally argue that science fiction has always been a literature with a few worthwhile works surrounded by mediocrities, as stipulated by "Sturgeon's Law," with nostalgia editing from memory the many second-rate stories that appeared in *Astounding* and cluttered paperback racks in the 1950s; discerning readers, they would say, have always had to seek scattered gems amid the dross. But today's situation is significantly different. Writers in earlier generations shared certain ideas about science fiction, largely derived from Campbell, that they endeavored to apply when writing; some did this well, others did this poorly, accounting for the gap between memorable stories and forgettable ones. But most contemporary writers grew up without any exposure to the genre's traditions, having learned their trade from watching *Star Trek* and *Star Wars*, and they never even attempt to write anything exceeding those expectations; if asked why they were not drawing upon cutting-edge science to produce innovative, groundbreaking stories, they would be baffled to discover that anyone might expect them to do so. Moreover, in the past, authors who best matched Campbell's ideals were the genre's stars, featured on magazine covers and bookstore shelves, while lesser writers lurked in the background; today, successful writers of popular series garner more attention and shelf space in bookstores, while writers admired by discerning readers are overlooked. The authors still striving to produce provocative, original science fiction, then, are becoming a disregarded minority, with little impact on the genre.

It is only natural for those who remain committed to Campbell's ideals to be displeased by this development; however, one might respond, devotees of a literature founded upon the principle that the world is changing should not be so resistant to change. For it is easy to argue that what has happened to science fiction is both natural and beneficial: the marketplace discovered what sorts of stories people want to read, and it devised mechanisms to provide them with products they desire. The notion that publishers, to fulfill a dead man's agenda, should instead endeavor to provide readers with stories they do not want to read runs counter to bedrock principles of democracy and free choice. To reverse Hartwell's argument, it is not the marketplace that "distorts the product" of science fiction; rather, it is people like Hartwell who have struggled to distort science fiction into the forms they prefer, instead of the forms most readers feel it should have assumed long ago. One might also question whether there is any reason for traditional science fiction to remain in existence. Yes, decades ago, when few people understood how technology would radically transform the world and the literary establishment seemed resistant to change, there might have been a need for fiction that would foreground the coming impact of science and break time-honored rules. But now, when examining the future is a cottage industry and calls for innovative literature are clichés, Campbell's variety of science fiction no longer seems essential. If science fiction is instead focusing on the standard purpose of popular fiction—to entertain undemanding readers—that hardly seems a catastrophe.

And for readers and scholars who still esteem the sort of science fiction that Campbell espoused, they can keep it alive by means of small presses, webzines, and other forums for creative people on society's margins. Their works may garner increasingly little attention and income, but dedicated writers will find ways to carry on, and the resulting literature might become something like poetry, ignored by most readers but still a vibrant tradition to the minority that values it. We should, however, stop describing such texts as "science fiction," for my survey indicates that science fiction, as it is now defined by a vast majority of readers, has become something entirely different from the literature that Campbell championed and many still cherish. Instead, one might revive a term long promoted as a more dignified alternative to "science fiction," "speculative fiction," to identify the innovative stories preferred by discerning readers and critics.

Indeed, however one feels about science fiction and the marketplace, the literary tradition inspired by the foes of the marketplace definitely seems worth maintaining, even though its champions do not always acknowledge its originator, John W. Campbell Jr. Thus, the editors of the sometimes-valuable, sometimes-infuriating reference *Fifty Key Figures in Science Fiction* found space for several figures of questionable significance (such as critics Jean Baudrillard and Donna J. Haraway) but excluded Campbell, despite the fact that the sort of superior science fiction written by most writers in that volume came into existence solely because Campbell insisted that it must (see Bould et al.). No figure in that book, even Gernsback, had such a pervasive and significant impact on the genre; and even if his herculean efforts to resist the inexorable forces of the marketplace ultimately proved unsuccessful, he deserves the attention and respect of everyone today who is still committed to innovative science fiction.

WORKS CITED

Bould, Mark, Andrew M. Butler, Adam Roberts, and Sherryl Vint, eds. *Fifty Key Figures in Science Fiction*. London: Routledge, 2009. Print.

Campbell Jr., John W. "In Times to Come." *Astounding Science-Fiction* 22.2 (Oct. 1938): 11. Print.

―――. "Introduction." *Who Goes There?* Chicago: Shasta, 1948. 3–6. Print.

―――. "The Science of Science Fiction Writing." *Of Worlds Beyond: The Science of Science Fiction Writing*. Ed. Lloyd Arthur Eshbach. 1947. Chicago: Advent, 1964. 91–101. Print.

Cramer, Kathryn. "Our Pious Hope: Science Fiction Marketing, Counter-Marketing, and Transcendence." *Science Fiction and Market Realities*. Ed. Gary Westfahl, George Slusser, and Eric S. Rabkin. Athens: U of Georgia P, 1996. 56–70. Print.

Ellison, Harlan. "Introduction: Thirty-Two Soothsayers." *Dangerous Visions #1*. Ed. Harlan Ellison. 1967. New York: Berkley, 1969. 19–31. Print.

Gernsback, Hugo. "Fiction Versus Facts." *Amazing Stories* 1.4 (July 1926): 291. Print.

―――. "A New Sort of Magazine." *Amazing Stories* 1.1 (Apr. 1926): 3. Print.

―――. "Thank You!" *Amazing Stories* 1.2 (May 1926): 99. Print.

―――. "Wanted: Still More Plots." *Wonder Stories Quarterly* 3.4 (Summer 1932): 437. Print.

Gold, H. L. "For Adults Only." *Galaxy* 1.1 (Oct. 1950): 2–3. Print.

Hartwell, David G. "The Distortion of the Product: Stresses on Science Fiction Literature." *Science Fiction and Market Realities*. Ed. Gary Westfahl, George Slusser, and Eric S. Rabkin. Athens: U of Georgia P, 1996. 36–55. Print.

Knight, Damon. *In Search of Wonder: Essays on Modern Science Fiction*. 1956. 2nd ed. Chicago: Advent, 1967. Print.

Moskowitz, Sam. *Seekers of Tomorrow: Masters of Modern Science Fiction*. Cleveland: World, 1966. Print.

Nash, Walter. *Language in Popular Fiction*. London: Routledge, 1990. Print.

Resnick, Mike, and Barry N. Malzberg. "Really Dumb Ideas." 2006. *The Business of Science Fiction: Two Insiders Discuss Writing and Publishing*. Jefferson, NC: McFarland, 2010. 168–78. Print.

Sedgewick, Cristina. "The Fork in the Road: Can Science Fiction Survive in Postmodern, Megacorporate America?" *Science Fiction Studies* 18.1 (Mar. 1991): 11–52. Print.

Siringer, Norman. "Literature and Science Fiction." *The Rhodomagnetic Digest* 2.1 (Aug. 1950): 19–22. Print.

Spinrad, Norman. "Science Fiction in the Real World—Revisited." *Science Fiction and Market Realities*. Ed. Gary Westfahl, George Slusser, and Eric S. Rabkin. Athens: U of Georgia P, 1996. 20–35. Print.

CHAPTER 7

PULP SCIENCE FICTION

JESS NEVINS

PULP magazines, named for the wood pulp paper they were printed on, grew out of the cheap fiction magazines of the nineteenth century. The pulps began when *Argosy* went to an all-fiction format in 1896; they came of age in the 1920s, peaked in the 1930s, and endured a long senescence that ended in 1971 when the last pulp, *Ranch Romances*, stopped publishing. The genres of pulps ranged from mystery to sports to westerns, and many writers who began in the pulps went on to establish long and successful careers as novelists. But the pulps hold a special place in the history of science fiction because, more than any other genre, science fiction cohered and matured in the pulps.

Traditionally, the focus of science fiction criticism has been on the stories that appeared in the SF pulps, but a substantial amount of science fiction—in fact, the majority of science fiction in the pulps—appeared outside of the SF pulps, in what will be referred to in this essay as the "general pulps." The story of pulp science fiction is of two competing communities: that of the SF pulps and that of the general pulps.

The science fiction that appeared in both kinds of pulps had more similarities than differences. Pulp fiction, regardless of genre, has some easily identifiable characteristics: an emphasis on adventure and drama and an avoidance of the mimetic mundane; a privileging of plot over characterization; use of dialogue and narration as means for delivering information rather than displaying authorial style; regular use and exploitation of the exotic, whether racial, sexual, socioeconomic, or geographic; simple emotions strongly expressed; repeated use of common tropes, motifs, and plot devices, to the point of rendering them clichés; adherence to the real or perceived limits of specific genres, with a concurrent lack of literary experimentation; and a clear-cut moral stance, with good usually triumphing over evil.

Fiction in the SF pulps, especially during the 1926–1945 period, displays all of these characteristics as well as others that are more common in the SF pulps than in the general fiction pulps. Most notably, pulp science fiction labored under the requirements and rules of specific editors and magazines. Hugo Gernsback and John W. Campbell Jr. published in *Amazing Stories* and *Astounding Stories* only a certain type of science fiction; as discussed below, the outlines of Campbellian SF imposed limitations of style and content on stories and authors. This was not the case with analogous major editors at non-SF pulps, including Arthur S. Hoffman at *Adventure*, Joseph T. Shaw at *Black Mask*, and Dorothy Hubbard at *Western Story Magazine*. Similarly, the influence of dime novels was more heavily felt, and for a longer period, in the SF pulps than in the general fiction pulps. The heavy use of amateur writers, the adherence to a journalistic narrative mode, the excessive use of what Brian Attebery has described as "expository lumps" (33), the emphasis on adventure and mystery formulas and the de-emphasis on romance (Attebery 33)—all can be traced to the dime novels. The pulps of other genres defined themselves in ways different from their dime novel predecessors long before the SF pulps did.

The origin of "science fiction" as a genre is usually located in the pulps. The traditional narrative in SF criticism is that Gernsback, editor of *Amazing Stories*, did more than just coin a phrase in 1929 when he described what he published as "science fiction"; he is supposed to have created the literary genre. Proponents of this point of view object to calling the stories and novels that came before Gernsback "science fiction" on the grounds that there was not a widespread consciousness of SF as something distinct. As John Rieder puts it, before Gernsback "what we now call early sf was perhaps nothing more than the loose aggregation" of Victorian science-fictional tropes and motifs (25). But this "loose aggregation" was seen by both writers and readers as something distinct from other genres. Throughout the nineteenth century, a limited group of phrases were used to describe, advertise, and criticize SF stories and novels: "a romance of science" in the 1840s and 1850s, "scientific romance" from the 1850s until the end of the century, and "scientific fiction" in the 1870s and 1880s. The wording changed, but the meaning remained the same: scientifically fantastic fiction. When science fiction began appearing in the pulps, it was neither new nor surprising.

Nor was it long in appearing. *Argosy* changed to the pulp format with its October 1896 issue. *Argosy*'s January 1897 issue featured H. Wellington Vrooman's "The Avenging Tiger," a story about the transmigration of souls and revenge. Over the next 60 years, until the end of the pulp era in the mid-1950s, thousands of SF stories would appear in nearly every kind of pulp, from general to single-subject, including railway and sports. In fact, more science fiction appeared in the general pulps than in the SF pulps: roughly 60 percent of all science fiction published from 1926 to 1936 was published in the general pulps, and roughly 55 percent of all science fiction published from 1937 to 1942 was published in the general pulps.

Only a minority of the stories in the general pulps utilize the framework of the science fiction of the era, including aliens, futuristic settings, and fantastic scientific principles. But these stories have a preponderance of science-fictional tropes, motifs, and plots. That these stories *also* incorporate the framework, tropes, motifs, and plots of other genres does not make them any less science-fictional. If, as Farah Mendlesohn has argued, the SF pulps actively incorporated aspects of other genres, such as locked room mysteries (52), the reverse was also true: other genre pulps actively incorporated the material of science fiction. Some genres were friendlier to science fiction than others. General fiction pulps, detective pulps, and air fiction pulps often ran SF stories, while romance and western pulps rarely did. But most genre pulps, even sports pulps, featured science fiction at least occasionally, and some, like the hero pulps, published mostly science fiction. Gary Westfahl writes that Gernsback was the first to give science fiction "characteristic content, a characteristic form, and characteristic purposes" (qtd. Landon 54), but a more accurate statement would be that Gernsback was the first to give Gernsbackian science fiction characteristic content, form, and purposes. The majority of the science fiction published from 1926 to 1942 was not Gernsbackian.

In 1896 science fiction was regularly appearing in the dime novels. The *Frank Reade Library*, describing the world adventures of a boy inventor, was still being published, and in 1901 twice as many SF stories appeared in dime novels as in the pulps. But in a relatively short amount of time this situation reversed itself, and in 1910, 31 science fiction stories appeared in the 13 pulp magazines published that year, compared to no stories in the 40 dime novels published that year. The number of SF stories appearing in the pulps from 1896 to 1918 almost equals that of all other sources combined, including dime novels, slicks, novels, and movies.

Most of the people writing these stories were not professionals. Brian Stableford has described the "assiduous new recruits" who made up a "new generation" of SF writers in England in the beginning of the twentieth century (27). In the United States there was not a new generation of professional writers but instead a prolific group of amateurs, now-obscure men and women such as Ion Arnold, James Barr, and J. A. Tiffany. The pulp SF these men and women wrote was primarily influenced by contemporary sources, including novels and movies, rather than influencing these other sources. In this, pulp SF is not unique; during this period, the content driver of other genres, including mysteries, romance, and westerns, was novels and movies. Nonetheless, while individual authors and stories in the pulps, such as Edgar Rice Burroughs with his "Tarzan" (1912–65) and "Mars" (1912–41) series, became famous and/or influential (and have become synonymous with SF during the 1896–1918 period), the flow of common tropes, motifs, and plots was from novels and movies to the pulps and not the other way around.

Genre SF's split from the general pulps, and the transformation of pulp science fiction from echo box to broadcaster, did not begin with the 1926 debut of *Amazing Stories* but rather in 1919. For the pulp industry as a whole, 1919 was notable as the year in which both the supply and the demand for stories increased dramatically. Many veterans returning from the war became new readers and new writers, and the pulp industry responded by branching out into previously unexplored genres. 1919 was also the first year in which the number of pulp titles published exceeded the number of dime novels published. 1919 was more significant for science fiction. The total number of SF stories published more than tripled from its 1918 total. As part of a strategy to test the pulp market and to begin the transition from dime novels to pulps, Street and Smith published *Thrill Book*. *Thrill Book* begun as a pulp devoted to the weird, occult, and fantastic, but in its final eight issues it regularly published science fiction, making *Thrill Book* the first pulp to be dedicated, as part of its editorial policy, to publishing SF.

Thrill Book only lasted for 16 issues, through October 1919, but its existence is representative of the changes that science fiction would undergo over the next seven years.

SF went from being split roughly between pulp and nonpulp sources to clearly being the province of pulps. From 1901 to 1918, 49 percent of science fiction appeared in the pulps, while from 1919 to 1925, 57 percent of science fiction did so. Only three and a half years after the end of *Thrill Book* did *Weird Tales* appear, adding another pulp that would regularly print science fiction.

Behind the appearance of *Thrill Book* and *Weird Tales* was the larger publishing reality that genre fiction was suddenly popular enough and profitable enough to support single-subject pulps. Pulps devoted to mystery, romance, sports, and westerns all appeared during this time period. Science fiction lagged behind these genres in adding titles but was otherwise popular. Fan favorite writers such as Burroughs, Johnston McCulley, Will McMorrow, and Victor Rousseau wrote science fiction. More SF novels were published between 1919 and 1925 than in any other preceding seven-year period. Seventeen non-English-language SF novels, plays, and short story collections were translated and published in English during this period, 50 percent more than in the 1901–1918 period. If, as Stableford says, one of the aftereffects of the First World War was a lingering distaste for science fiction among British novel readers (27), the reverse was true among American readers.

By the end of 1925, science fiction seemed to be in a healthy state in the pulps. Its rate of appearance in *Weird Tales* was increasing (15 stories in 1924, 30 stories in 1925), and its rate of appearance in other pulps continued to slowly increase. If science fiction was a minority interest in publishing compared to heavyweight genres like romance, adventure, and detective, it was nonetheless a genre that authors and publishers regularly made use of. Then came Hugo Gernsback. The debate over how much credit Gernsback deserves in fostering the genre continues, with both partisans and critics often using overheated rhetoric to support or condemn him. There is little debate that he was *the* dominant figure among SF pulp editors of the 1926–1936 period. However, his position in pulp SF needs to be reexamined.

Indisputably, Gernsback did more than anyone else to make science fiction a permanent category for magazine publishers. As an editor of various science magazines in the 1910s and 1920s, he published more science fiction, by himself and other writers, than any single editor in the pulps or slicks. As the publisher and editor of *Amazing Stories* (from 1926 to 1929) and six other pulps during this period, Gernsback created the SF pulp. He was the first editor to emphasize the need for scientific accuracy in SF stories, and in so doing laid the groundwork for all hard science fiction (Westfahl 167). But the claims for Gernsback need qualifying. The single-subject fiction pulp devoted to SF was hardly an inspiration, given the appearance of many similar single-subject pulps before 1926. Gernsback, after moving to the United States, would have seen two ongoing SF dime novels: *Frank Reade Weekly* (96 issues, 1902–1906) and *Motor Stories* (32 issues, 1909). Similarly, Gernsback's fostering of a fan community via the letters page of his pulps was not original to him. Brooks Landon describes this act as "instrumental in the development of SF 'fandom,' surely one of the phenomena that most distinguish SF from other literatures" (54). But Gernsback's cultivation of SF fandom was only a duplication of the way in which the editors of dime novels had previously developed various fandoms.

More broadly, what might be called Gernsback's sphere of influence has to be called into question. Roughly 60 percent of all science fiction during this period was published in the general pulps rather than the SF pulps, by editors and publishers who paid little attention to what Gernsback was doing, and authors such as Paul Ernst, Perley Poore Sheehan, and Robert M. Wilson were highly successful without wanting or needing Gernsback's help. During the 1926–1936 period, SF pulps never had more than 7 percent of the overall market and were never higher than the sixth most popular genre, trailing far behind the detective/mystery, romance, spicy, and western genres. As far as most pulp writers and editors were concerned, Gernsback might as well not have existed.

Critics also continue to overestimate Gernsback's effect on pulp science fiction. A recurring charge laid against him is that he relegated SF to the pulp "ghetto" (Clareson 17). But numerous SF stories were published in the pulps before Gernsback, and as mentioned, most science fiction during this period was published in the general pulps, not the SF pulps. Contra Peter Nicholls's claim that "magazine sf was at ... a low ebb" in the 1930s (570), the amount of science fiction published in the general pulps continued to rise throughout this period, as it had since 1919. The story of pulp SF during the 1926–1936 period is not one of Gernsbackian science fiction, but of two communities: the SF pulps and the general pulps. The distance between the two was great.

The SF pulps paid less than the pulps of other genres, appeared less frequently, and were for the most part Gernsback productions, meaning that they were what E. F. Bleiler has called a "closed shop" (xxii). Moreover, Gernsback's dictates for science fiction in his pulps—that it must be both instructive and promote research and experimentation (Clareson 15)—were restrictive to writers; the editors of the pulps of other genres did not impose their vision on their writers so overtly. What Attebery says was the first "attempt to define the genre" (33) was a prescriptive definition, designed to exclude material of which Gernsback disapproved. Gernsback's definition of science fiction not only assembled "various narrow orthodoxies inimical to any thriving literature," as Brian W. Aldiss says (202), it ignored the thriving science fiction that happened to appear in the general pulps.

Unsurprisingly, SF pulps during these years were largely the province of what Thomas Clareson calls "enthusiasts" (14), while the general pulps were the province of professional writers, such as Frank Triem, Robert J. Hogan, and Donald Keyhoe. If the difference between these two groups was not quite that of C. P. Snow's "Two Cultures," there is nonetheless a distinct feeling of fiction-as-written-by-scientists in the SF pulps and fiction-as-written-by-humanists in the general pulps. Whatever similarities exist between the two groups must be understood as a parallel development rather than a process of adaptation or mutual influence. The general pulps were wholly unconcerned with what Gernsback and the other SF pulp editors were doing in their magazines, and Gernsback followed his vision rather than imitated the stories in the general pulps.

The nine-year period beginning when Campbell took over as editor of *Astounding Stories* is generally regarded as the "Golden Age" of the SF pulps. Campbell transformed *Astounding* into the dominant pulp in the field: *Astounding* was able to recruit or otherwise attract the best writers, and as a result, he dictated the direction and philosophy of mainstream science fiction. More generally, the 1937–1945 period saw the number of SF pulps grow, from a low of 7 in 1937—the genre's lowest point since 1929—to a high of 23 in 1941. But throughout this period, science fiction remained less important to the industry than all other genres; at the high point there were fewer SF pulps than those of any other major genre. The general pulps remained dominant from 1937 to 1942, with more science fiction appearing outside the SF pulps than in them, even during the apex of 1941. In 1943 the situation changed, with stories in SF pulps becoming more numerous than stories in the general pulps, but even as late as 1945 the numeric difference between the two was not large. During this period, the SF pulps finally began to edge out the general pulps as the source of the majority of pulp science fiction, but the gap between the two never became significant during this period. It was only beginning in 1946 that the SF pulps truly became the dominant market.

The 1936–1945 period was when the most diverse and numerous single-subject pulps were published. Reflecting this fact, the genres in which SF stories appeared were less concentrated than in the previous period. Detective pulps remained the primary location for SF stories, but the number of adventure/SF stories dropped. It is notable that both groups of pulps, general and science fiction, featured professional writers, but there was little interaction between the two. Some of the professional writers of science fiction wrote for the general pulps, but none of the professional writers of other genres wrote for the SF pulps. This was an extension of the Gernsbackian community into the professional sphere. SF pulp writers, like the fans who read those pulps, were a community. To writers and fans wanting to join that community, they were welcoming. But to writers outside that community, individuals such as Lester Dent, Gunnar Hjerstedt, and John Reynolds, who routinely published in non-SF pulps, they were less so.

These writers had a number of reasons for not submitting to the SF pulps, especially *Astounding*, but pay was not one of them—*Astounding* was known for paying as well as any pulp. Many of the professional pulp writers had been writing stories for various pulps for years or even decades, and they would likely have seen Campbell's editorial style as heavy-handed and unpleasant. Campbell's philosophy of science fiction—that it should show the "consequences of scientific development in terms of the changes occurring in society" (Clareson 24)—was quite different from the ways in which the non-SF-pulp writers approached science fiction, as a genre with broad contours rather than one with specific philosophical underpinnings.

Science fiction in the general pulps began to lessen from 1943 on. The overall appetite for science fiction did not diminish—the number of SF novels published in 1945 was virtually the same as in 1939—but there was a gradual dwindling of science fiction accompanying the cancellation of general pulps. The professional pulp writers gradually stopped writing science fiction and moved on to other genres, so that by 1945 less science fiction was being published in the general pulps than at any time since 1929. Aldiss writes that "a wartime mood of 'realism' spread over stories that were often far from realistic in essence" (216); this was even truer among the general pulps than the SF pulps.

The pulps rebounded quickly from the war, reaching a ten-year high in terms of numbers in 1950. The general genres held steady or grew slightly from 1946 to 1950, but science fiction recovered more slowly than the other genres. The new pulps that appeared through 1950 were for the most part amateurish in appearance and content, though the mainstay SF pulps generally published a high level of science fiction. But 1950 was the last efflorescence of the pulps. After 1950 the number of pulps published began a slow, permanent decline. New pulps appeared in every genre until 1953, especially romance and western, but with the emergence of digest magazines and paperback books during this period, the death of the pulp medium was clearly imminent.

As with the dime novels, the death of the pulp format took place over the course of several years rather than abruptly. The rise of the digests played a large part, especially the 1949 appearance of *The Magazine of Fantasy* (soon renamed *The Magazine of Fantasy and Science Fiction*) with its near-immediate success in capturing most of *Astounding's* market share. The rise of original paperback novels, beginning in 1950 when Fawcett Publications introduced Gold Medal Books, was similarly devastating to the pulps. Nonetheless, the death of the pulps was a gradual rather than sudden thing: in 1955 there were 48 pulps published, and as late as 1960 there were still 11 pulps being published, 2 of which were science fiction.

The divide between science fiction in the general pulps and science fiction in the SF pulps disappeared during this time period, as science fiction essentially vanished from the general pulps. By 1950 none of the authors who had regularly written SF stories in the general pulps were doing so, and save for the very occasional one-shot story, the genre was moribund if not dead in the general pulps. The writers who had written science fiction in the general pulps embraced other genres, while the SF writers had a relatively large number of outlets in which to publish science fiction: from 1950 to 1953, the SF pulps lost the least number of titles to cancellation, in terms of percentage, of all genres except romance.

As critics have often noted, science fiction matured during this period. Numerous stories with both "grace and genuine invention" (Mendlesohn 54) appeared, and the first true classics were written. The change was one of quality and approach rather than a variation of tropes and motifs. Mike Ashley describes the transformation as being "from technocentric to psychocentric" (174), with character development emphasized more than it had previously been. This was accompanied by a general disenchantment with technology; the devastation of the war was reflected in the numerous stories in which war, technology, and especially nuclear power were portrayed in at least ambiguous if not overtly negative terms. Expanding on a trend begun in the early 1940s, an increasing number of light-hearted stories were published during this period, mitigating the influence of Campbellian seriousness. Science fiction had at last reached the stage where the mystery and western pulps had begun: any sort of science fiction, from grimly serious to amusing comedy, could now appear in the pulps.

The primary theme of much early science fiction was technology, and on this subject the divide between the general pulps and the SF pulps grew as time passed. A suspicion of technology, science, and scientists in the pre-World War I years flowered into open distrust of the war, and in the pre-*Amazing* years, scientists and technology were portrayed as evil more often than as good. In the 1926–1936 period, the SF pulps were if anything more suspicious of scientists and technology than the general pulps, which showed an increase in heroic scientists from the earlier period. But with the advent of Campbell at *Astounding*, this situation reversed itself: the SF pulps portrayed scientists as heroic and technology in a positive light, while the general pulps largely portrayed them in negative terms. The mad scientists and evil technology of Lester Dent's "Doc Savage" series (1933–49) stand in stark contrast to the typical Campbellian hero-scientist and his inventions.

Similarly, the portrayal of "others"—whether aliens and robots (common in the SF pulps) or women and people of color (not so common)—differed in the general and SF pulps. In the pre-1919 years, aliens and robots were portrayed in largely positive ways, and while there were few female or nonwhite protagonists, their numbers did increase during the war. But beginning in 1919, the portrayal of aliens and robots changed, becoming negative twice as often as positive, although the rate of female and nonwhite protagonists remained the same. Xenophobia toward nonhuman life forms remained a constant in both the general and the SF pulps, but the treatment of women and people of color differed. After 1926 female protagonists were more common in the general pulps than in the SF pulps; the portrayal of people of color was similarly more positive in the general pulps. *Astounding* experienced high sales in black neighborhoods, including Harlem and Chicago's South Side (Cioffi 27), but it was in the general pulps rather than the SF pulps that blacks would have seen recognizable faces. With their black-skinned robots used as slaves and tools of a would-be world conqueror, Philip Scruggs's two "Kosmacs" stories, published in *Excitement* in 1930, had layers of racial commentary that would have been unthinkable in *Astounding*.

In the scope and scale of their stories, the general pulps were less ambitious than the SF pulps. Before the First World War, the preferred setting for SF stories was the present or the near future on Earth, with far fewer stories set in the far future or in outer space. But in the 1919–1925 era, stories set in the present decreased and the number of stories set in the far future increased. After 1926 the SF pulps generally emphasized far future settings, with outer space being relatively common, and the general pulps emphasized the near-future Earth.

The most obvious difference between the general pulps and the SF pulps was their approach to the genre itself. During the pre-*Amazing* years, there was a consciousness on the part of writers that science fiction was something different, but they viewed it primarily as a toolbox of motifs, tropes, and plots to be used in other genre contexts rather than as a flourishing genre of its own. Only 40 percent of the stories from this era are solely science-fictional in orientation, the rest being mixtures of various genres with SF material. One typical story, Gertrude Bennett's "The Citadel of Fear" (*Argosy*, Sept.–Oct. 1918), features a mad scientist with bioengineered monsters but is nonetheless recognizably a part of the "Lost Race" subgenre of adventure fiction. From 1926 to 1936, science fiction became recognizably *generic* in both the general and the SF pulps, but only in the SF pulps was science fiction the dominant form.

Forty-five percent of the SF stories in the general pulps were mixed with other genres. From 1937 to 1945, this trend continued: SF pulps published pure science fiction, while the general pulps strongly trended toward genre hybridity. For every overtly science-fictional story, such as H. Bedford-Jones "Strato-Shooters" series (*Blue Book*, 1943–44), with its near-future high-tech aviation police, there are three like Gunnar Hjerstedt's "Silent Smith and the Hounds of Death" (*Detective Tales*, Jan. 1945), in which the titular amateur detective pursues a group of Nazi mad-scientist spies loose in New York City.

Stylistically, pulp SF stories varied in quality, much like the stories of other genres. In the pre-*Amazing* years, some authors stood out, but the quality of the majority of stories was low; as one critic put it, they suffered from "the same fluent slovenly expression, impersonal, standardized, never halted by any concern for the right word" (Burgum 38). It is notable that those authors seen as being stylistically distinct—H. P. Lovecraft and C. L. Moore among them—stand out in stark contrast to their peers in the SF pulps. Meanwhile, in the general pulps, authors as different as H. Bedford-Jones, Arthur O. Friel, and Walker Tompkins were publishing science fiction of markedly higher quality than the material regularly appearing in the SF pulps. It was not until the 1940s that the quality of some of what was published in the SF pulps outweighed the quality of what was published in the general pulps. During this period, the SF pulps began to feature mature, professional writers who had spent years honing their craft, as the writers in the general pulps always had, with the result that the best science fiction in the SF pulps was markedly superior to the best science fiction in the general pulps. This was not true of the *average* story in both, however.

Likewise, the standardization that Burgum decried was far more of a problem in the SF pulps than in the general pulps. With some rare exceptions, the stories in the SF pulps post-1926 followed the rules of the genre and the dictates of the editors, so that one can speak with relative accuracy of a standard pulp SF story. By contrast, the SF stories in the general pulps were not produced under similar constraints, so that there is greater variation in plot and style than may be found in the SF pulps. Similarly, hybrid genre stories—adventure/science fiction, detective/science fiction, horror/science fiction—in the general pulps venture farther from their generic ideals than their counterparts in the SF pulps. In this sense, the science fiction in the general pulps represents a lost opportunity for science fiction. Had Gernsback and Campbell never appeared on the scene, science fiction might well have matured a decade earlier. Minus the Gernsbackian and Campbellian requirements and limitations, science fiction as a genre might have followed the path of the general pulps and been less concerned with big ideas or popularizing science and more concerned with literary ideals of characterization and narrative style. SF writers did concern themselves with such things, but only in the 1940s. Absent Gernsback and Campbell, SF writers might have imitated their general pulp counterparts and made such things a part of their stories during the 1930s.

In the broadest sense, the general pulps and the SF pulps differed in their approaches to the future. During the Gernsback years, science fiction in both the SF pulps and the general pulps is "marked by an enormous cultural malaise" (Bleiler xv) resulting from the effects of the First World War and the Depression. But during the Campbell years, the SF pulps generally reversed course from the previous decade in alignment with the editor's ideology, depicting hopeful worlds in which scientists were more heroic than wicked, in which technology was more used to help rather than harm, and in which humanity was an active participant rather than a helpless bystander in the emergence of the future. Conversely, the general pulps continued to portray science, scientists, and technology in negative ways, largely unchanged from the 1926–1936 period. For every positive portrayal of scientific breakthroughs and technological achievements, there were nearly two negatives, and portrayals of a hopeful SF future were far less common than those of evil and/or mad scientists.

The death of the pulp medium did not mean the death of pulp science fiction. The term itself, "pulp," acquired a broader meaning as early as the 1930s, with H. L. Mencken (among others) using it to describe a style of fiction and approach to storytelling, rather than just a type of magazine, and this is now the term's primary meaning. How the pulp *style* survived is relatively easily told. The popularity of the pulps during their heyday meant that the medium became a content driver of other media: comics, radio, and genre films took their cues from the pulps. While these other media eventually matured and admitted influences beyond the pulps, the pulp style continued to be common in visual media, and with the ascendancy of visual media in the modern era, pulp style has become widespread in popular entertainment. The film *Star Wars* (1977), for example, is a virtual compendium of pulp motifs from the 1930s.

Analyzing why the pulp style survived is slightly more complicated. On a surface level, it is easy to understand: the energy, narrative drive, pacing, and inventiveness of concept characteristic of pulp fiction are as appealing to mass audiences today as they were during pulp's heyday. Pulp style's avoidance of literary flourishes, difficult vocabulary, and subtle characterization, and its general embrace of formulaic storytelling, remove blocks to an audience's understanding. Pulp style can also be produced more quickly and in higher quantities compared to more "literary" material. More broadly, the pulp style ultimately appeals to base sensations: excitement, fear, desire. Just as the horror (or "male") Gothic, with its appeal to physical sensation, ultimately proved more popular with audiences than the terror (or "female") Gothic, with its emphasis on characterization and motivation, the pulp style has triumphed over its competitors because of its more basic and therefore more widespread appeal.

Uniquely among literary genres, the SF short story came of age in the pulps. Its transition from dime novel juvenilia to the equal of canonical mimetic fiction is perhaps the most radical change any genre underwent in the pulps. The difference in quality between the short science fiction of the turn of the century and that of the late 1940s and early 1950s is so stark, in fact, that it is fair to say that science fiction in previous periods had been a genre, but in its final period it became a *literary* genre. That change is unique in the pulps; other genres were essentially literary before they appeared in the pulps or became literary outside of the pulps. Only science fiction used the pulps as its vehicle to maturity.

WORKS CITED

Aldiss, Brian W., with David Wingrove. *Trillion Year Spree: The History of Science Fiction*. New York: Atheneum, 1986. Print.

Ashley, Mike. *The Time Machines: The Story of the Science-Fiction Pulp Magazines from the Beginning to 1950*. Liverpool: Liverpool UP, 2000. Print.

Attebery, Brian. "The Magazine Era: 1926–1960." *The Cambridge Companion to Science Fiction*. Ed. Edward James and Farah Mendlesohn. Cambridge, UK: Cambridge UP, 2003. 32–48. Print.

Bleiler, Everett F. *Science Fiction: The Gernsback Years*. Kent, OH: Kent State UP, 1998. Print.

Burgum, Edwin Berry. "Six Authors in Search of Their Future." *Partisan Review* 1.5 (1934): 38. Print.

Cioffi, Frank. *Formula Fiction? An Anatomy of American Science Fiction, 1930–1940*. Westport, CT: Greenwood, 1982. Print.

Clareson, Thomas D. *Understanding Contemporary American Science Fiction: The Formative Period (1926–1970)*. Columbia: U of South Carolina P, 1990. Print.

Landon, Brooks. *Science Fiction After 1900: From the Steam Man to the Stars*. New York: Twayne, 1997. Print.

Mendlesohn, Farah. "Fiction, 1926–1949." *The Routledge Companion to Science Fiction*. Ed. Mark Bould, Andrew M. Butler, Adam Roberts, and Sherryl Vint. New York: Routledge, 2009. 52–60. Print.

Nicholls, Peter. "History of SF." *The Encyclopedia of Science Fiction*. Ed. John Clute and Peter Nicholls. New York: St. Martin's, 1993. 566–72. Print.

Rieder, John. "Fiction, 1895–1926." *The Routledge Companion to Science Fiction*. Ed. Mark Bould, Andrew M. Butler, Adam Roberts, and Sherryl Vint. New York: Routledge, 2009. 23–31. Print.

Stableford, Brian. "Science Fiction Before Genre." *The Cambridge Companion to Science Fiction*. Ed. Edward James and Farah Mendlesohn. Cambridge, UK: Cambridge UP, 2003. 15–31. Print.

Westfahl, Gary. "'The Closely Reasoned Technological Story': The Critical History of Hard Science Fiction." *Science Fiction Studies* 20.2 (1993) 157–75. Print.

CHAPTER 8

LITERARY SCIENCE FICTION

JOAN GORDON

JONATHAN Lethem's 1998 *Village Voice* essay "Close Encounters: The Squandered Promise of Science Fiction" generated quite a bit of discussion within the SF community, resulting in re-publication in *The New York Review of Science Fiction* and a subsequent exchange there with Ray Davis. The gist of Lethem's argument is that the SF community missed a chance to merge with the literary mainstream in 1973 when Arthur C. Clarke's *Rendezvous with Rama* (1973) won the Nebula Award over Thomas Pynchon's *Gravity's Rainbow* (1973). The article's scathing, and apparently unintended, implication was, as Davis put it, that the "the mainstream 'A Lists' are where the best writing is to be found and that 'genre' publishing is restricted to immature types who don't really know what's going on" (1)—or, for the purposes of this chapter, that science fiction is not literature.

Of course, science fiction *is* literature if we accept that word's broadest definition, "a body of writings in prose or verse," or even its second broadest definition, "imaginative or creative writing, esp. of recognized artistic value" ("Literature"), although some still may quibble about "*recognized* artistic value." Davis, in his response to Lethem, points out that Pynchon, with or without a Nebula, would be recognized as a writer of literature, while many great SF writers (he cites Samuel R. Delany and Joanna Russ) would not (1). It is not my purpose here to justify whether SF has literary value, which to me seems self-evident. Like any body of writing, however, not all SF is of *artistic* value; or, as Theodore Sturgeon legendarily summarized the situation, "Ninety-nine percent of everything is crud" (qtd. Landon 3). Instead, this chapter will consider how the category of literary science fiction reflects the genre's history, its culture, and its reception. As a historical term, it points to the genre's precursors; as a cultural label, it embraces practitioners from within the genre who emphasize the "literary" in several ways; as a reflection of the genre's reception, it points to writers who move beyond or defy genre classification. The remainder of this chapter will only briefly discuss the before and beyond, since other chapters—for instance, those on SF histories and slipstream—will explore that material. My three primary topics will be SF within the genre's traditional boundaries that employs specifically literary qualities characteristic of the genre, SF that employs many of the literary techniques associated more commonly with non-genre writing, and SF that uses the "megatext" of non-SF literature.

SF critics have claimed many precursors for the genre, from *The Epic of Gilgamesh* to *Frankenstein* (1818). Enlightenment-era utopias, gothic novels, scientific romances, and travel adventures are other sources. H. Bruce Franklin cites American origins in the stories of Poe, Melville, Hawthorne, Irving, Bierce, Bellamy, and Twain, among others, asserting, with strong evidence, that "[t]here was no major nineteenth-century American writer of fiction . . . who did not write some science fiction or at least one utopian romance" (ix) and that, with its grand social experimentation and its embrace of progress and change, "America . . . was from the start especially congenial to science fiction" (viii). Not that it was called "science fiction": that term—and the separation anxiety it caused—appeared in the twentieth century when Hugo Gernsback coined the term in 1929 in his magazine *Science Wonder Stories*. And even though Gernsback may have been responsible for creating the ghetto separating science fiction from something else called "literature," he was also reprinting works by Poe, Verne, Wells, Twain, and others so as to create distinguished literary precursors for his new genre.

Now the boundaries were drawn. With the rise of the paperback novel in the 1950s, as Gary K. Wolfe explains, "Science fiction had become a widely recognized and readily identifiable genre" (22) and a marketing category that would forever separate SF from other forms of literature. Also during this time, from the 1920s to the 1950s, SF developed its own distinct culture in the form of fans, fanzines, and conventions, devoted to defending SF's unique merits while shunning any taint of social respectability (one infamous rallying cry was "out of the classroom and back to the gutter"). And all during this genre-fication of SF, other writers continued to use its conventions outside the growing culture/ghetto: George Orwell, Aldous Huxley, Olaf Stapledon, and so on.

This background explains how the word "literary" could come to designate none, or some, but not all of science fiction. We might also consider, briefly, how the word could differentiate written SF from other manifestations—film, television, games, comics, music, art, and other media covered elsewhere in this volume.

Within SF culture, certain qualities are particularly admired, and these may be considered the literary qualities of science fiction. A number of writers and critics (among them Russ, Delany, and Damon Knight) have delineated these qualities, including scientific verisimilitude and plausibility, stimulating and innovative ideas, and that nebulous attribute, a sense of wonder. These are all perceived as positive qualities, but negative elements have also been associated with SF: a lack of psychological depth or convincing characterization, clumsy or merely serviceable prose, wooden dialogue, awkward intrusions of information sometimes referred to as expository lumps or info-dumps, and unlikely or wildly extravagant plots.

In the periodic attacks on SF from outside the field, there is an assumption that these negative traits are both characteristic of the genre and absent in other literature, and therefore proof of SF's nonliterary status. Perhaps typical of such complaints is a review by Sven Birkerts of Margaret Atwood's novel *Oryx and Crake* (2003) that begins:

> I am going to stick my neck out and just say it: science fiction will never be Literature with a capital "L," because it inevitably proceeds from premise rather than character. It sacrifices moral and psychological nuance in favor of more conceptual matters, and elevates scenario over sensibility.

Here, Birkerts describes SF's negative attributes as the inevitable result of its positive ones while using Atwood's novel to prove that, since it does have "moral and psychological nuance" and so on, it cannot be science fiction.

Birkerts advances without question Henry James's view that psychological and aesthetic considerations far outweigh ideational or didactic ones. This division was central to the epistolary and essayistic battle between James—a sometime writer of ghost stories, we might remember—and H. G. Wells, one of the precursors of SF. As Leon Edel and Gordon N. Ray put it:

> The essential difference between the two lay . . . in the fact that Wells's scientific training, combined with his need for self-assertion, made him an exponent of a materialistic kind of artistry to which James was utterly opposed. Wells could not for long accept beauty and art as ends in themselves. (18)

One argument against Birkerts admits that his Jamesian accusations may be true to some extent but also asserts that they can be excused *because of* the importance of other qualities. Such an argument has been advanced by Joanna Russ in her essay "Towards an Aesthetic of Science Fiction" (1975), where she claims that SF is definitely literature but that it cannot be "judged by the usual literary criteria" (112). She goes on to enumerate the qualities intrinsic to a fiction of ideas, qualities that we recognize and enjoy in many writers, even those who may proceed, as Birkerts puts it, "from premise rather than character" and whose prose may not sing.

Many writers of SF illustrate the premise that its "literariness" has different demands—and offers different rewards—than the Jamesian tradition: Hugo Gernsback himself, Isaac Asimov, E. E. "Doc" Smith, John W. Campbell Jr., and Larry Niven, for instance, all would align themselves with Wells. There are certainly moments in Clarke's *Childhood's End* (1953), to name a canonical SF text, that disappoint in terms of character development and style. The novel's characters are primarily representatives of certain types: Stormgren the diplomat, Karellen the alien Overlord, Jean the appallingly clichéd wife and mother. Speculations are presented in large, sometimes clumsy expository lumps ("As you know, for the past five years we have tried to awaken. . .," and the like [8]). Prose is often flat and uninspired ("After all, it was not every day that one had a chance of talking to one of the masters of Earth" [74]). Yet while it is easy to find these flaws, if we judge the novel instead by the standards adhering to SF, we can see why it has become a classic within the field. Clarke is a trained scientist, and he takes great care to be scientifically accurate. His descriptions of space travel fit the current understandings of physics: one example occurs in a long letter full of calculations that might bore a nonfan, but whose verisimilitude pleases SF readers

(115–16). At times Clarke's speculations even seem predictive, as when he imagines "an . . . infallible method—as certain as fingerprinting, and based on a very detailed analysis of the blood—of identifying the father of any child" (66), well before DNA testing had been developed. Clarke's speculations about a utopian future with ample leisure, wide education, racial and social equality, increasing secularity, and so on provide much to think about and argue with. And the novel's imagining of alien environments and the next stage of human evolution provides a striking sense of wonder. Given these rewards, SF readers are able to forgive the novel's inability to imagine the future evolution of gender roles, or other limitations of the author's time and place, along with any lapses in style.

Clarke excels in another characteristically science-fictional literary trait, what Delany calls its "subjunctivity," or the way in which his novel literalizes metaphor. When Clarke writes, "the island rose to meet the dawn" (182), this is not only a metaphorical description (of a sunrise), but also a literal one: a massive nuclear explosion causes the island to disintegrate and fly up into the sky. Further, it represents the way in which humanity itself has been utterly destroyed by the rising dawn of a new phase of cosmic evolution.

Istvan Csicsery-Ronay Jr. has provided a particularly rich exploration of the literary qualities characteristic of SF, positing and exploring "a constellation of diverse intellectual and emotional interests and responses" that he judges to be "the most attractive and formative of science-fictionality" (5). These qualities neither excuse nor substitute for perceived lacks but demonstrate what he calls the "seven beauties" of science fiction: fictive neology, fictive novums, future history, imaginary science, the science-fictional sublime, the science-fictional grotesque, and the Technologiade (or the myth of technological transformation). *Childhood's End* illustrates a number of these beauties. While the novel does not provide much in the way of neologisms, the benign alien invaders are given an otherwise sinister name—Overlords—that here becomes a "neoseme," a term produced by "semantic shifts of words . . . that remain familiar in structure and appearance, but have been appropriated by imaginary new social conditions to mean something new" (Csicsery-Ronay 19). *Childhood's End* is full of fictive novums, from the Overlords, to a successful world government, to the utopian community that attempts to restart innovation in a world become stagnant and complacent. Most obviously this is a future history: one that both mirrors and critiques the narrow views of the 1950s. The novel's imaginary science includes not only trips to alien worlds but also metaphors of what Csicsery-Ronay calls "materialized transcendence" (169). Clarke's real power lies in his evocation of the science-fictional sublime, "a shock of imaginative expansion, a complex recoil and recuperation of self-consciousness coping with phenomena suddenly perceived to be too great to be comprehended" (Csicsery-Ronay 146). When we finally see the Overlords and realize that they are the source of our "race memory" of Satan, when the utopian community commits mass nuclear suicide and "the island rose to meet the dawn" (Clarke 182), and when the entire generation of children ascend to the Overmind, we feel this shock in a way impossible to evoke except through science fiction.

The rigor and detail of Csicsery-Ronay's development of SF's characteristic literary traits neatly refute the claim that SF is not "literary" while avoiding the pitfall of apologizing for the genre. Indeed, he assigns to science fiction an important literary stature: "SF narrative ... has become the leading mediating institution for the utopian construction of technoscientific Empire. And for resistance to it" (8). "It is," he goes on to say, "one of the cultural tasks of sf to draw [the beauties] into an aesthetic constellation. This is also its primary pleasure" (9). Looking for these beauties in science fiction both within the genre walls and beyond opens up a new perspective on the field that refutes the demand that all literature adhere to standards only relevant in particular times and places.

There has always been a vein of SF writing that employs, along with the field's own particular beauties, those of the wider literary world: subtle metaphor, stylistic grace, allusion, "moral and psychological nuance." This too is literary science fiction, of a more Jamesian kind. Even in the pulp era, which had the reputation of sacrificing "literariness" to sense of wonder, grace to innovative speculation, and art to science, these extra-SF qualities were present. An early example is C. L. Moore's "Shambleau" (1933), first published in the pulp magazine *Weird Tales*. Its plot is, of course, thinly disguised horse opera, and it features the typical square-jawed hero, but all of this is in service to a tale of psychic vampirism and a revision of Keats's "La Belle Dame Sans Merci" and the legend of Medusa, scrutinizing the vulnerability of men who attempt to live up to stereotypical gender roles. And it does so in prose that is often sensuous and lyrical. Describing the eponymous creature's eyes, Moore writes, "They were frankly green as young grass, with slit-like, feline pupils that pulsed unceasingly, and there was a look of dark, animal wisdom in their depths—that look of the beast which sees more than man" (115). The passage exemplifies a number of Csicsery-Ronay's beauties, particularly the science-fictional grotesque, which collapses the divisions between states of being (here, between human and nonhuman), while also employing powerful appeals to the senses and taking great care with cadence and rhythm. The story's extra-SF literary qualities neither diminish nor are diminished by its science-fictional literary qualities, and the author has paid equal attention to both kinds of literariness.

By the late 1940s, with the genre well-established and with the threat of nuclear apocalypse ascendant, Theodore Sturgeon was writing his evocative and compassionate short stories and novels well within the SF fold. "Thunder and Roses" (1947) is representative. Taking place after nuclear war, as the population of the United States is slowly dying, a famous singer comes to an army post to persuade the men there not to release the bomb that would destroy the rest of the world. The story focuses on individual reactions to intense physical and emotional trauma rather than on political, broad-stroke issues. In addition to lyrical passages representing the singer's inspirational anthem, the story uses the devices of SF (near-future setting, dystopian apocalypse) to examine individual psychology and moral responsibility. We find these qualities in Sturgeon's novels as well, notably in *The Dreaming Jewels* (1950), *More Than Human* (1953), and *Venus Plus X* (1960). While SF is often chastised for sacrificing character development to ideational engagement, here the focus is squarely on individual psychology.

While the collection of related stories that made Ray Bradbury's career, *The Martian Chronicles* (collected in 1950), is clearly SF (and was marketed as such), his later work was often marketed outside the genre and has been accepted by a wider audience. "There Will Come Soft Rains" (1950) also deals with nuclear fears. This story, however, has no characters at all, proceeding "from premise [nuclear war] rather than character," as Birkerts would say, but doing so in order not only to comment on those particular fears but also to reflect the mechanization of modern life by describing the automated house that continues its routine after its inhabitants have died. The house becomes the story's character, and it and its mechanical contents are personified in many ways, in an elegy for the human inhabitants who are now only shadows and ash. The result is a story that does not elevate "scenario over sensibility" but uses scenario to reflect sensibility sharply. Sturgeon and Bradbury both make clear how SF's particular literary concerns can enhance extra-SF qualities, and vice versa.

By the 1960s some SF writers, associated with the so-called New Wave, had developed more aggressively literary aspirations. In 1962 J. G. Ballard wrote an editorial for the British SF magazine *New Worlds*, "Which Way to Inner Space," calling for more introspective, psychological, and experimental writing, work that reflected not the conservative style and attitudes present in much SF but the absurdism and surreality of the avant-garde. The New Wave set itself in opposition to SF's old guard, seeing the rest of the field as antiliterary in the "capital L" sense. The Golden Age of SF, usually associated with John W. Campbell Jr.'s *Astounding* in the early 1940s, was condemned for sacrificing extra-SF literary qualities. As Roger Luckhurst puts it, the New Wave "regarded Golden Age SF as an exhausted mode of low culture, trapped in a ghetto of its own construction" (142). He quotes Judith Merril's view: "The genre is returning from its forty years of self-imposed wandering away from the well-springs of literature" (147). Among the British writers associated with *New Worlds* and with the New Wave were Ballard, Brian W. Aldiss, Michael Moorcock, and John Brunner. In the United States, Harlan Ellison, Thomas M. Disch, and Robert Silverberg were among the young Turks, with Ellison using his series of *Dangerous Visions* anthologies (beginning in 1967) as a vehicle for the movement. New Wave style generally favors achronology, stream of consciousness, and metaphor, and its visions of the future are usually dark: the belief that progress and technology are inevitably positive is gone.

Ballard's "The Cage of Sand" (1962) is exemplary of the New Wave. It begins with a moody evocation of a surreally lit wasteland of abandoned beach hotels, examining the obscure motives of three people who live in this wasteland as they pay homage to the capsules containing dead astronauts that pass overhead each night. The reader puzzles for more than half the story to account for the presence of Martian sands on this Florida beach, and the story ends in entrapment and delusion. Instead of portraying a progressive vision of triumphant space travel, the story reveals the hardship that transit to the stars has wrought, and the story's wasteland is a literalization of its characters' wasted interior lives, what T. S. Eliot might have called an objective correlative. Certainly, the New Wave had much in common with the earlier rise of modernism, seeing even the most literary of previous SF as stylistically conservative, if not politically reactionary.

By the time the New Wave had crested and covered the field, science fiction had certainly matured in terms of its concern for extra-SF literary qualities. In the early 1970s, Ursula K. Le Guin and Gene Wolfe, for example, were developing their important bodies of work. In her 1975 essay "Science Fiction and Mrs. Brown," Le Guin refers to Virginia Woolf's personification of the central importance of character to the novel and asks whether such concern has a place in SF. Her answer is, predictably, yes, an answer she strives to live up to in her own writing. Her 1969 story "Nine Lives" uses clones and planetary exploration to imagine the strain that isolation puts on individuals and the importance of social interaction in building individual identity. When all but one of the clones are killed in a mining disaster, the remaining "singleton" struggles to survive as an individual, deprived of the collectivity of his multiple selves: he must learn how, in E. M. Forster's words, to "only connect." While Le Guin is careful to speculate plausibly on cloning, she is more interested in what its social implications would be for both the clones and others who interact with them. These more sociological and psychological considerations, focused through a diligent character study, provide a rich metaphorical engagement with themes of selfhood and alienation, traditionally seen as the province of "capital L" literature.

Gene Wolfe, on the other hand, looks farther back than Woolf's psychological realism for much of his inspiration. While he, like Le Guin, uses traditional SF icons (spaceships, clones, the far future, and the like), his work is characterized by allusions to ancient history, mythology, and medieval allegory, often ambiguous or otherwise subtle symbolism, and complex religious and ethical concerns. His work rewards the careful examination customary in literary scholarship. Take, for example, his 1992 story "Useful Phrases," which seems on the surface to be a tale of alien contact, but if one considers each element as a literalization of metaphor (another beauty of science fiction), it becomes much more, suggesting everything from the power of literature, to the longing for human connection, to the search for higher meaning and eternal life. Near the end of the story, the narrator says, "Again and again I find myself drawn to the window; clouds gravid with snow hang low over the city, hiding every star but one" (682). The reader—and this is a story not only for but also about readers—is struck both by the beauty and poignancy of the description, its echo of the end of Joyce's "The Dead" (1914), and by the multiple metaphorical and symbolic possibilities it presents. Surely, this is literary science fiction in a sense that cannot meaningfully be separated from the wider understanding of literature.

Wolfe's nod to Joyce, like Ballard's to Eliot, points to another meaning of "literary science fiction." Science fiction is characterized by what Damien Broderick has called the "megatext," the vast confluence of all past SF texts, novums, plots, settings, characters, and so on; detecting these allusions thus becomes a significant part of the experience of reading SF. But, as Ballard and Wolfe remind us, those allusions can also refer to works outside SF, to canonical works of mainstream literature. As one might expect, there are many references to SF's precursors in the field, especially to Shelley's *Frankenstein*

(Aldiss's *Frankenstein Unbound* [1973] and Michael Bishop's *Brittle Innings* [1994], for instance), as well as to Wells and Verne. But SF mines many other sources: Conrad's "Heart of Darkness" in Ballard's *The Day of Creation* (1987) and Silverberg's *Downward to the Earth* (1970); Melville's *Moby Dick* (1851) in John Kessel's "Another Orphan" (1982) and Philip José Farmer's *The Wind Whales of Ishmael* (1971). Mark Twain's influence is evident in Kathleen Ann Goonan's *Queen City Jazz* (1994), while Sheri S. Tepper uses Euripides's *The Trojan Women* in *The Gate to Women's Country* (1988). Dan Simmons mines a vast number of sources in *Hyperion* (1989), as does Farmer in his *Riverworld* series (1971–83). Such allusion serves to root the work in the larger conversation that literature provides, linking SF to a wider tradition, enriching its repertoire of imagery and metaphor, and providing the pleasures of homage, pastiche, and parody.

To demonstrate this way of understanding literary science fiction, I want to turn to Joe W. Haldeman's *The Hemingway Hoax* (1990), focusing on its quite obvious use of the literary megatext, specifically the work of Ernest Hemingway. Readers of Haldeman's other SF, from *The Forever War* (1974) to *Camouflage* (2004), may be aware of Hemingway's influence, from the carefully controlled and constructed sentences that reveal the narrators' inner states to the often strikingly similar autobiographical elements. The plot of *The Hemingway Hoax* is a mobius time loop (similar to that of Heinlein's "'All You Zombies—'" [1959]) that offers a science-fictional explanation for the historical theft of Hemingway's suitcase full of manuscripts in 1922. The protagonist, John Baird, is a Vietnam vet and literature professor who shares a number of traits with both Hemingway and Haldeman. A crook persuades Baird to forge the lost manuscripts, but if he were to succeed, it would alter future history over many dimensions, prompting mysterious entities to intervene to prevent him. This complex SF plot permits Haldeman to build up parallels among Hemingway, Baird, and himself, culminating in an extensive list of points (134–35). The chapter headings are all names of works by Hemingway, from the famous ("The Sun Also Rises") to the obscure and unpublished ("The Time Exchanged"), evidence of the author's extensive research. The very first paragraph includes a clear allusion ("It is neither clean nor well-lighted" [9]) to one of Hemingway's most famous short stories.

The novel also contains several pastiches of Hemingway's style in Baird's attempts to forge the manuscripts. Early on, Haldeman states the problem: "Hemingway is easy enough to parody . . . but parody was exactly what one would not want to do" (16). Instead, Haldeman shows the pastiches gradually improving in quality. Midway through the story, Baird writes, "Nick had fired through the gauze six times, perhaps killing three enemy, and the gause [sic] now had a ragged hole in the center" (56). Not particularly inspired, just descriptive, and Baird is having trouble figuring out how to make it clearer. Near the end, he produces a more effective passage: "Fever stood up. In the moonlight he could see blood starting on his hands. His pants were torn at the knee and he knew it would be bleeding there too" (139). More sequence of motion and fact, as Hemingway himself advised, than in the first example. In these and other examples, Haldeman carefully modulates the faithfulness of the imitation, providing pleasure for seasoned readers of the Nobel Prize–winning author.

Baird's forged passages are never as good as those in which Haldeman himself writes in a style clearly inspired by Hemingway's work. A particularly powerful example occurs toward the end of the novel in a tour-de-force description of time running backward:

> And the unending lightless desert of pain becomes suddenly one small bright spark and then everything is dark red and a taste, a bitter taste, Hoppe's No. 9 gun oil and the twin barrels of the fine Boss pigeon gun cold and oily on his tongue and biting hard against the roof of his mouth. (29)

The sentence marries lyricism to violence and vivid specificity, as Hemingway does, but far more successfully than Baird ever can.

The lesson here is not that we must hope Haldeman never decides to forge Hemingway's style, but that his use of the literary megatext is complex and skilled, employed in the service of the story's unfolding. The allusions to Hemingway's life and work enrich character development, with the Hemingway style giving clues to the narrator's state of mind. The allusions work in reverse as well, since their employment of that distinctive style, and the information provided about Hemingway's work, expand the reader's appreciation of the source. The parallels among Hemingway, Baird, and Haldeman provide a triangulation that suggests further parallels between the world in the aftermath of World War I and that prevailing after the Vietnam War. The mobius time loops of the story not only deploy string theory physics but also explore the effects of memory, circumstance, and accident on individual fate, demonstrating that SF can be both Wellsian and Jamesian at the same time.

Science fiction provides such powerful metaphors, and has so much to say about fears and hopes for the future, that it is not surprising when it transcends the boundaries of the perceived ghetto. Just as people wrote science fiction before the term existed, they continue to write it, sometimes aware of the SF megatext, sometimes denying its existence, sometimes seemingly unaware of it. The chapter on slipstream will explore this phenomenon more thoroughly, but here, I will sketch some of the ways in which mainstream literature uses the devices of SF. Some writers work both within the field and outside it as their interests change: Jack Womack, William Gibson, Neal Stephenson, China Miéville, and Geoff Ryman have all done this. They continue to acknowledge their roots and the atmosphere of SF continues to surround their fiction. Other writers have never written genre SF but have often used its tropes with varying degrees of acknowledgment: Thomas Pynchon, Margaret Atwood, Jonathan Lethem, Michael Chabon, and Haruki Murakami, for instance. These writers may be most associated with slipstream. Still others have written one or two examples of science fiction without publishing them within the field: P. D. James, Philip Roth, Michael Cunningham, Kazuo Ishiguro. This last category often produces the most problematic examples. Without much knowledge of the field, these writers often reinvent its ideas but not always with success. Certainly, they bring their literary gifts to their SF writing, but often they struggle with the basic difficulties of constructing SF stories: using plausible science, avoiding expository lumps, developing innovative ideas and original forms of speculation. Compelling characterization, vivid details of everyday life, and graceful prose are generally among their strengths.

The whole of a science fiction story is a conceit, a vehicle for the tenor of the world we know, to use I. A. Richards's terms defining metaphor. Who can resist such a grand ride? As with any good car (or spaceship, for that matter), the vehicle is as important as the destination, and much of the energy of SF, much of its literariness, both intra- and extra-generic, is devoted to constructing fresh horizons. In a world where modern technoscience has come more and more to construct people's lives, it is increasingly difficult to make a meaningful separation between SF and capital-L literature, between intra- and extra-SF literariness. Science and technology have become irresistible vehicles for all writers, not only those who self-identify as SF authors and readers.

This chapter began with Jonathan Lethem's dream that Thomas Pynchon's *Gravity's Rainbow* had won the Nebula Award bestowed by SF writers. In 2008, some 35 years later, Michael Chabon's *The Yiddish Policemen's Union* (2007), marketed as a mainstream novel and reviewed as such but indistinguishable from SF in its content, did indeed win the Nebula; it also won the 2008 Hugo Award voted on by SF fans. A similarly marketed novel won a Hugo in 2010: China Miéville's *The City and the City* (2009). With the major exception of SF writer Octavia E. Butler's 1995 MacArthur Award, the literary mainstream has not yet been so generous. *The Road* (2006) by Cormac McCarthy won the 2007 Pulitzer Prize, and Chabon's *The Amazing Adventures of Kavalier & Clay* (2000) won the 2001 Pulitzer, but even though they were works of SF, they were not identified as such. Ray Davis, in his response to Lethem, pointed out that while "Pynchon's lack of a Nebula did not damage his career . . . the National Book Award (or any attention at all) to *Dhalgren* or *The Female Man* . . . would have helped Delany's or Russ's careers." The ghetto walls may have been dismantled, but that is only a preliminary step toward full acceptance of SF as a serious and powerful form of contemporary literature.

Works Cited

Ballard, J. G. "The Cage of Sand." 1962. *The Wesleyan Anthology of Science Fiction*. Ed. Arthur B. Evans et al. Middletown, CT: Wesleyan UP, 2010. 337–58. Print.

———. "Which Way to Inner Space?" *New Worlds* 118 (May 1962): 2–3, 116–18. Print.

Birkerts, Sven. "Present at the Re-Creation." Rev. of *Oryx and Crake* by Margaret Atwood. *The New York Times*. May 18, 2003. Web. Jan. 9, 2012. http://www.nytimes.com/2003/05/18/books/present-at-the-re-creation.html?pagewanted=all&src=pm.

Bradbury, Ray. "There Will Come Soft Rains." 1950. *The Wesleyan Anthology of Science Fiction*. Ed. Arthur B. Evans et al. Middletown, CT: Wesleyan UP, 2010. 234–40. Print.

Broderick, Damien. *Reading by Starlight: Postmodern Science Fiction*. New York: Routledge, 1995. Print.

Clarke, Arthur C. *Childhood's End*. 1953. New York: Del Rey, 1990. Print.

Csicsery-Ronay Jr., Istvan. *The Seven Beauties of Science Fiction*. Middletown, CT: Wesleyan UP, 2008. Print.

Davis, Ray, and Jonathan Lethem. "Mistakes Were Made: An Exchange." *New York Review of Science Fiction* 1.4 (Dec. 1998). *Pseudopodium.org*. Web. Nov. 22, 2011. http://www.pseudopodium.org/repress/shorts/Davis_and_Lethem-Mistakes_Were_Made.html.

Edel, Leon, and Gordon N. Ray. *Henry James and H.G. Wells: A Record of Their Friendship, Their Debate on the Art of Fiction, and Their Quarrel*. Urbana: U of Illinois P, 1958. Print.

Franklin, H. Bruce, ed. *Future Perfect: American Science Fiction of the Nineteenth Century*. New York: Oxford UP, 1978. Print.

Haldeman, Joe W. *The Hemingway Hoax*. New York: Morrow, 1990. Print.

Landon, Brooks. *Science Fiction After 1900: From the Steam Man to the Stars*. New York: Twayne, 1997. Print.

Le Guin, Ursula K. "Nine Lives." 1969. *The Wesleyan Anthology of Science Fiction*. Ed. Arthur B. Evans et al. Middletown, CT: Wesleyan UP, 2010. 452–76. Print.

———. "Science Fiction and Mrs. Brown." 1975. *The Language of the Night: Essays on Fantasy and Science Fiction*. Rev. ed. New York: HarperCollins, 1989. 97–117. Print.

Lethem, Jonathan. "Close Encounters: The Squandered Promise of Science Fiction." *The Village Voice*. June 1998. *hipsterbookclub.livejournal.com*. Dec. 22, 2008. Web. 20 July 2013. http://hipsterbookclub.livejournal.com/1147850.html.

"Literature." *Webster's II: New College Dictionary*. New York: Houghton Mifflin, 2001. Print.

Luckhurst, Roger. *Science Fiction*. Malden, MA: Polity, 2005. Print.

Moore, C. L. "Shambleau." 1933. *The Wesleyan Anthology of Science Fiction*. Ed. Arthur B. Evans et al. Middletown, CT: Wesleyan UP, 2010. 110–35. Print.

Russ, Joanna. "Towards an Aesthetic of Science Fiction." *Science Fiction Studies* 2.2 (July 1975): 112–19. Print.

Sturgeon, Theodore. "Thunder and Roses." 1947. *The Wesleyan Anthology of Science Fiction*. Ed. Arthur B. Evans et al. Middletown, CT: Wesleyan UP, 2010. 189–210. Print.

Wolfe, Gary K. *Evaporating Genres: Essays on Fantastic Literature*. Middletown, CT: Wesleyan UP, 2011. Print.

Wolfe, Gene. "Useful Phrases." 1992. *The Wesleyan Anthology of Science Fiction*. Ed. Arthur B. Evans et al. Middletown, CT: Wesleyan UP, 2010. 675–82. Print.

CHAPTER 9

SLIPSTREAM

VICTORIA DE ZWAAN

"Slipstream," a term used in such activities as bicycling, boating, and bird flight to indicate a type of movement that benefits from or is caught up in an energy stream that comes from elsewhere, was introduced into the world of SF writing and criticism by Bruce Sterling in 1989. Despite wide skepticism among SF critics about the term's value, and its general absence from literary-critical worlds outside SF, it has developed and continues to have a sustained if somewhat perplexing function in SF criticism and writing. In what follows, I will examine the emergence of the term and its history inside SF discourse and writing, but I will also try to account for its continuing presence in the critical and creative worlds of SF, by examining some of the cultural, theoretical, and institutional contexts that help explain why it was of interest in the first place and also why it has had staying power for more than 20 years.

In 1989, in the first and by far more important and influential of his two essays on the subject, Bruce Sterling responds directly to an argument made by Carter Scholz that, because nongenre SF writers, by adapting "SF's best techniques to their own ends," had begun to write better speculative fictions than SF itself could produce, SF would therefore never be able to "become a worthy literature" (qtd. Sterling, "Slipstream" 77). In his "Catscan" column in the July 1989 issue of *Science Fiction Eye*, Sterling agreed that modern SF was irrelevant to current social realities, having about it "the reek of decay" ("Slipstream" 77). In order to escape "the Iron Curtain of category marketing," the most interesting speculative writing—"a contemporary kind of writing which has set its face against consensus reality"—could be gathered into a genre called "slipstream" (78). Sterling famously defines this genre as follows:

> This is a kind of writing which simply makes you feel very strange; the way that living in the late twentieth century makes you feel, if you are a person of a certain sensibility. We could call this kind of fiction Novels of Postmodern Sensibility, but that looks pretty bad on a category rack, and requires an acronym besides; so for the sake of convenience and argument, we will call these books "slipstream." (78)

He acknowledges that the term "slipstream," simply "a parody of mainstream," is perhaps "an artificial construct, a mere grab-bag of mainstream books that happen to hold some interest for SF readers" (78); but he goes on to say that he believes nevertheless that there is, in fact, some family resemblance between the long list of texts he then gives us of the books that would be included in this new marketing category, which include a wide range of novels—some of which fall under the rubric, generally speaking, of SF, but most of which do not.

Notwithstanding the way in which this relatively coherent line of argument can be summarized, it needs to be noted here that Sterling's polemical piece, though certainly engaging and provocative, does not present itself as a coherent and sustained argument. Rather, in the course of this brief piece, Sterling shifts his ground, sometimes quite wildly and in contradictory directions. For example, the whole argument is initially based on an all-out attack on SF as "the sprawling possessor of a dream that failed" (77), but there are also references to SF's unnamed "intrinsic virtues" (80); he describes slipstream fiction as expressing a "zeitgeist" whose main feature is an "aggression against reality" (78), embodied in stylistic experimentation, but elsewhere he suggests that slipstream writing, in fact, reflects "the perverse, convoluted, and skeptical tenor of the postmodern era" (80), implying thereby a mimetic relationship with the real. Toward the end of his article, Sterling acknowledges that the term "slipstream" has no particular value except for marketing books; but elsewhere he suggests that this is, in fact, a new genre, to be defined by a "Postmodern Sensibility" that makes the reader "feel very strange." Put differently, Sterling gestures in many different directions in his attempt to define slipstream, including reception/affect, style, worldview, period, ideology, to name just a few options, and subsequently denies that he has any real grasp on the genre, though he voices a hope that others, whether it be booksellers or literary critics, might develop and clarify it.

One of the claims that Sterling makes is that "once the notion of slipstream is vaguely explained, almost all SF readers can recite a quick list of books that belong there by right" (78), and he includes a long list of his own selections. He argues that the existence of this list, and of others that critics and fans might develop, constitutes the best argument that the term "slipstream" refers to something real. The list of names that Sterling gives us contains at least three different "families" of writers, and the slippage among them is instructive, especially in relation to both the critical and creative discourses of contemporary SF. It is not possible to cover the whole list, so I restrict myself to three sets of names that strike me as most pertinent to this chapter.

First, a significant number (but far from a majority) of the authors have overt associations with SF, but may also be known for non-SF, "literary" (in SF parlance, "mainstream") novels. These "crossover" figures include: Brian W. Aldiss, J. G. Ballard, William S. Burroughs, Thomas M. Disch, Russell Hoban, Doris Lessing, Michael Moorcock, Marge Piercy, Kurt Vonnegut, and Jack Womack. Sterling's choice of book titles in these cases is not always one of their SF works, but when it is, it is generally more "literary" and avant-garde than what he refers to as "hard-SF." For example, Piercy's *Woman on the Edge of Time* (1976) uses what is now a familiar SF frame of time travel as a basis for a thought experiment about a possibly utopian future. The novel has all the elements of social critique and political activism familiar to us in the speculative tradition, but it has neither the clarity nor the realism of more conventional works of utopian literature or SF. On the contrary, there is a vertiginous and hallucinatory counterrealist quality to the narrative, narrated by the sociopathic and "insane" Consuelo, that undermines the reader's confidence in the solidity or reality of the possible world he or she is entering. This is also the kind of "world" we find in many of the other texts in this category, especially in Burrough's *Naked Lunch* (1959), which is, of course, not SF per se: there is no solid frame that allows us, in more realist works in any genre, to determine the nature of the "reality" of the text that, though fictional, nevertheless provides a stable foundation for action and meaning.

This particular selection of authors and books, taken on its own, can bring us some way toward understanding Sterling's argument. If, as he argues, "hard-SF"—which we might also understand as "mainstream SF"—once had a realist and objectivist "coherent social vision" about the world that is now outmoded (77), it has lost its raison d'être and ought to be replaced by the new genre of slipstream, which does a better job of capturing contemporary realities. This is a complicated and problematic argument, which, for reasons I will discuss in more detail below, has been quite persuasive to SF critics and writers, not only in relation to the idea of slipstream but also to the idea of the status and function of SF in contemporary culture. For the moment, however, it is enough to say that this part of the list speaks directly to the idea of a crossover between genre SF and the literary mainstream, with the latter being the "senior partner," so to speak.

Second, there are a number of writers on Sterling's list whose work is not SF at all but rather works of mainstream literature or of other genres. Their presence here may be understood in terms of their creation of a sense of existential instability or "weirdness" by way of some or all of the following: surrealist or magic realist elements; a sometimes confounding mixture of genres; unstable or defective narration; or any other disruptive or disorienting elements that undermine realist habits of reading. Some of the authors in this "category" are: Peter Ackroyd, Isabel Allende, Kingsley Amis, Paul Auster, Julian Barnes, J. M. Coetzee, Lawrence Durrell, W. P. Kinsella, Elmore Leonard, Norman Mailer, Toni Morrison, Philip Roth, Muriel Spark, and Nancy Willard. While these highly idiosyncratic inclusions make for a lovely reading list for those of us who enjoy books of the nonrealist variety, the random nature of this part of the list serves to muddy rather than clarify the ideas Sterling wants to promote about both marketing categories and genre. That is, even though many fictions defy tidy genre boundaries and can and should therefore be grouped into different sets of literary constellations, it is nevertheless vital that any given genre, if it is to be heuristically useful, should have specificity beyond the level of "sensibility." An aesthetic preference for counterrealism may bring together readers in an appreciation for the books Sterling lists, but that does not by itself "prove" the existence of or need for the supposed genre-category of slipstream.

Even at the most prosaic level of Sterling's concerns, shelving in bookstores, this part of his own list indicates that his slipstream category is so wide, and that it invites us to add so many titles, that the generic specificity and categorical precision he is arguing for would disappear into a broad distinction between realism and nonrealism, which would then require new distinctions in the form of subcategories and/or subgenres in order to make it possible to navigate the bookshelves. More importantly, however, Sterling's essay, addressed to and influential within the SF world, has as its original inspiration the idea voiced by Scholz that writers outside SF are now "doing our job," by which I understand him to mean that the avant-garde literary mainstream engages with contemporary technoculture in more interesting ways than genre SF does. It is curious, then, that so few of the titles on Sterling's list could be said to perform this specific kind of speculative task.

Third, Sterling's list includes a large number of writers who can be grouped into the category of "experimental fiction," itself a problematic term but one that is generally understood to refer to fictions that play with and reflect upon the conventions and codes of realism. This list includes American metafictionists Donald Barthelme, Robert Coover, Raymond Federman, and Ronald Sukenick, and writers of (in)famous maximalist experimental fictions such as Günter Grass, Russell Hoban, Gabriel García Márquez, Thomas Pynchon, Salman Rushdie, and David Foster Wallace. Kathy Acker and Harry Matthews are also notable examples of this third category. As with the first two categories above, it is easy for anyone looking at this list to be reminded of other experimental titles and authors that could and should be added, in an endless chain of association. In this respect, the list is generative and has its own interest for that reason. However, the criteria for inclusion on the master list are so elastic that, in the end, the exercise seems self-defeating as anything beyond the creation of a personal "top 100 weird books I like," as is demonstrated by the inclusion of a number of somewhat obscure choices (for example, H. F. Saint, Rupert Thomson), as well as by the creation of "slipstream lists" by other people, which would include Sterling's own "revised" list in 1999 (with Lawrence Person).

Of these authors, Thomas Pynchon can be singled out as a writer interested in what might be called SF themes, especially in his 1973 novel *Gravity's Rainbow*, a complex experimental work organized loosely around themes of technology and science. Pynchon is often named by SF writers as a strong influence on their writing, and *Gravity's Rainbow* was, in fact, nominated for a Best Novel Nebula Award by the Science Fiction Writers of America. One or two others, perhaps most notably Kathy Acker, engages from time to time with SF themes or plots: Acker reworks the plot of William Gibson's *Neuromancer* (1984) for her own ends in *Empire of the Senseless* (1988). I have examined the claims of the slipstream on Pynchon and Acker in some detail elsewhere (see my "Slipstream" and "Rethinking the Slipstream"). Here, my point is simply that the inclusion of these texts, like the second category of texts mentioned above, confuses rather than clarifies the argument, primarily because there are already other terms available for them, such as magic realist, experimental, postmodern, counterrealist, critifictional, metafictional, avant-garde, surfictionist, or Surrealist. It is not clear what value the term "slipstream" adds to these established categories. In fact, as it turns out, except for Ronald Sukenick and Curtis White's *In the Slipstream*, a 1999 anthology of exciting and innovative American experimental writing across different genre boundaries including SF (by such figures as John Shirley, Mark Leyner, and Samuel R. Delany), the term "slipstream" has not so far had a discernible impact on the so-called (non-SF) mainstream literary-critical culture.

In his second and less-well-known essay on the subject, "Slipstream 2" (originally published in the fanzine *Nova Express* in 1999 and reprinted in the special slipstream issue of *Science Fiction Studies* in 2011), Sterling acknowledges that, although "slipstream was a literary term that needed to be coined, ... the phenomenon doesn't actually exist" (6). The article then goes on to define what does and does not constitute—or rather would or would not belong to—this nonexistent but necessary and possibly emergent genre. It is *not* any of the following, according to Sterling: "science fiction that is written to high literary standards," "futuristic," "written with an engineer's temperament," magic realism; New Age, or ideological (7–8). It *is* "fantastic, antirealistic novels of a postmodern sensibility" (6), "polyvalent and decentered," "at home in the mess that we have" (8), "the literary reflection of a new way to be alive" (10), and perhaps best understood as "Cultural Studies Fiction," driven in part by an interest in cultural theory (9).

It is worth noting that, although Sterling includes a half-hearted attack on SF as "increasingly stale and self-involved" (9), his main and—given his statement that slipstream doesn't exist—somewhat quixotic argument is not so much against SF as in favor of the development of slipstream as a recognizable and distinct genre:

> A genre arises out of some deeper social need; a genre is not some independent floating construct. Genres gratify people, they gratify a particular mindset. They gratify a cultural sensibility, and there is a cultural sensibility that is present today that would like to have a literature of its own and just can't quite get it together to create one. This would be a nonrealistic genre of a postmodern sensibility. ("Slipstream 2" 7)

Sterling deems Mark Leyner and Kathy Acker, authors of complicated experimental postmodernist fictions that engage—or perhaps "sample"—multiple (literary and nonliterary) genres and cultural objects (including SF), but neither of whom are primarily associated with SF, the examples par excellence of slipstream writing. Their invocation here is somewhat paradoxical: these authors create texts that defy, undermine, and complicate genres, but this does not mean that they thereby create a new genre, though they may share some formal characteristics under the umbrella term "experimental fiction" as well as an aesthetic sensibility. Sterling's insistence on "sensibility" as the basis for genre formation in both slipstream essays is not without some merit, of course; but Sterling himself acknowledges that "perhaps [slipstream] will never come to fruition" (6), primarily because it is simply too broadly defined on the one hand and too subjective on the other.

In both these essays, Sterling argues that SF, unlike other fictions available to us in the avant-garde of mainstream literature, is not "doing the job" of imaginatively engaging with contemporary technoculture in a way that expresses a "postmodern sensibility." While he talks of these "other fictions" as having some interest to SF readers, his focus is not primarily on SF in either article, and indeed he states in the later one that slipstream writing will not emerge out of SF. It is somewhat puzzling, then, that the idea of slipstream has taken hold and retains currency in SF discourse. The reasons for this are complex, even contradictory, and worth exploration. In what follows, then, I will examine some of the relevant contexts that help to account for the positive reception of Sterling's ideas about slipstream fiction in the world of SF, in the face of his overt attack on SF itself, before returning to the history of slipstream discourse as it pertains to creative and critical work in SF between 1989 and the present day.

In my view, the idea of slipstream emerged out of a confluence of literary, critical, and theoretical developments in the 1980s, which included at least the following: cyberpunk science fiction, which made an extraordinary splash both inside and outside SF literary-critical circles, but which, inside SF circles, was heralded as one avatar of "postmodernized SF"; "the age of theory" brought about by the arrival of poststructuralism into the center of North American academic life over the previous two decades; debates and discussions about the meaning, range, and applicability of the term "postmodernism" in general; and, more particularly, assessments of texts generally understood under the rubric "postmodernist experimental fiction" and thought to have some connection to SF, either as precursors to cyberpunk and other postmodern SF texts or as fellow travelers. The leading characters associated with this particular confluence or moment as it impacts SF discourse—apart from Bruce Sterling, self-appointed spokesman for the cyberpunk movement as well as inventor of slipstream—are Larry McCaffery, whose edited volume *Storming the Reality Studio* (1991) specifically pulled together the different threads mentioned above, and Fredric Jameson, whose work on "the cultural logic of late capitalism" provides the foundational premises for understanding cyberpunk's relationships not only with postmodernist experimental fiction, but more crucially with postmodern culture, an association that essentially governs the McCaffery volume.

Storming the Reality Studio is organized around what McCaffery refers to as the convergence of postmodernized SF and quasi-SF in the mainstream, as exemplified in the "case" of cyberpunk SF, which overtly draws on literary influences on cyberpunk outside SF proper (including Burroughs, Pynchon, and Don De Lillo), as well as some "insider" precursors (including J. G. Ballard and Delany), cyberpunk "practitioners" (including Rudy Rucker, Sterling, and John Shirley), and some contemporary "others" (including Acker and William T. Vollmann). Excerpts from these authors' texts are complemented by a series of critical articles, including seminal poststructuralist texts by Baudrillard and Jacques Derrida; literary-theoretical chapters on the relations between cyberpunk and postmodernism by Brian McHale and two editors of *Science Fiction Studies* (Veronica Hollinger and Istvan Csicsery-Ronay Jr.); excerpts from Jean-François Lyotard and Jameson on the subject of postmodern culture; and a range of other articles on the topic of cyberpunk.

Notwithstanding the apparently pluralist nature of the volume as concerns theories of postmodernism, its guiding premise may be found, not in Lyotard's argument that postmodernism is defined by a skepticism for metanarratives, but rather in Jameson's reading of postmodern culture in general and cyberpunk in particular as an exemplar of late capitalism, which renders "postmodernized SF" such as cyberpunk a "paradoxical form of realism" (Csicsery-Ronay 182). As McCaffery puts it in his introduction:

> I hope to establish that Jameson's eloquent and timely call for new art forms capable of assisting us in clarifying the nature and meaning of our lives has in fact already begun to be answered by some of the artists and critics who are represented here. Their work represents the most concerted effort yet by artists to find a suitable means for displaying the powerful and troubling technological logic that underlies the postmodern condition. (16)

This particular idea, that cyberpunk and postmodernism somehow follow the same "cultural logic of late capitalism"—an idea that Sterling prefigured in his suggestion that slipstream fiction is "the literary reflection of a new way to be alive"—is echoed in several different ways in the volume, in addition to the inclusion of an excerpt from Jameson's famous essay on postmodernism. Csicsery-Ronay suggests that "[b]y the time we get to cyberpunk, reality has become a case of nerves—that is, the inter-fusion of nervous system and computer matrix, sensation and information" (190); Stephen P. Brown states that "the cyberpunks . . . did not originate their vision, but picked up bits and pieces of what was actually coming true, and fed it back to readers who were already living in Gibson's Sprawl, whether they knew it or not" (177); and the term "late capitalism" is sprinkled throughout the volume (see McCaffery's introduction and Hollinger's article, for example).

There are also a couple of casual references to Sterling's notion of slipstream, coined at the same time as the book was in development (it was expanded from a special "cybperunk" issue of *Mississippi Review* published in 1988). Hollinger mentions the term as referring to "postmodernist writing that has been influenced by SF" (203), and McCaffery also invokes it early on when he discusses that same phenomenon of quasi-SF mainstream fiction, about which he makes this comment: "One gets less a sense of these authors consciously borrowing from genre SF norms than of their introducing these elements simply because the world around them demands that they be present" (11).

I would note here that, while Sterling does not invoke Jameson or any other theorist in his "Slipstream" essay, he invokes the same "logic" as does the McCaffery volume when he suggests that "this is a kind of writing which simply makes you feel very strange; the way that living in the late twentieth century makes you feel." Put differently, although the term "slipstream" does not seem to have a direct connection to cyberpunk, it is clear that Sterling's conceptualization of the term, with its contradictory commitments both to antirealism and to slipstream fiction reflecting contemporary realities, initially either emerges out of or coincides serendipitously with discussions about cyberpunk's precursors and fellow travelers in the literary mainstream (the issue of *Science Fiction Eye* in which it was originally published is entitled "Beyond Cyberpunk"). In any case, I would argue that slipstream only came to be taken seriously inside SF literary circles in the first place because of theoretical and critical developments in SF that were made concrete in the McCaffery volume and that specifically sought on the one hand to undermine the separation of SF from mainstream fiction and on the other to elevate "postmodernized SF" as the "apotheosis" of late capitalism (Csicsery-Ronay 182).

The idea of slipstream came along at a crucial moment for SF theorists and critics, who found it attractive on (at least) two counts. First, the erasure of the generic walls between non-SF and SF, defined up to that point by way of style, subject matter, publishing markets, and a still persistent academic differentiation of SF from the more "legitimate" literary mainstream, opened up the field of inquiry belonging to SF, in what Niall Harrison would later describe as "a land-grab by the ghetto." Second, the emergence of this term, more or less coincident with the McCaffery volume, gave a name to a set of texts that seemed to exist in the liminal space between (in McCaffery's terms) "postmodern SF" and "quasi-SF works in the mainstream" but extended the possibilities for inclusion beyond the cyberpunk family that was the nominal focus of McCaffery's *Casebook*.

A number of SF critics have examined the "legitimation of SF writing" aspect of the slipstream phenomenon and its potentially entropic and destructive consequences for the specificities—or what Sterling refers to as the "intrinsic virtues"—of genre SF itself (see, for three quite different examples of this line of inquiry, Luckhurst, Westfahl, or my own "Re-thinking the Slipstream"). It has to be said, however, that the idea of slipstream has not done any discernible damage to SF, mainly because the term has never come to refer to some new genre distinct from or replacing genre SF in the way that Sterling advocated. Instead, and in spite of an ongoing skepticism in SF circles as to its genuine value, it has become common currency inside SF discourse since 1989, both for writers and for critics, used primarily to refer to a set of texts that match in some respects McCaffery's comparatively domestic formula of "postmodern SF" and/or "quasi-SF" mainstream fictions. It should be noted that the term "quasi-SF" does not refer simply to mainstream fiction that examines traditional SF themes—which is what Carter Scholz talked about in the article that inspired Sterling's original argument for slipstream—but also to "speculative" fictions beyond the materials that have been the traditional hallmarks of SF. This usage has, in fact, been consistent since Sterling's article appeared in 1989 and is best exemplified in two anthologies: the 2006 volume of "slipstream" writing, *Feeling Very Strange*, edited by James Patrick Kelly and John Kessel, and the 2011 *Science Fiction Studies* special issue on slipstream, edited by Rob Latham.

In their introduction to *Feeling Very Strange*, Kelly and Kessel foreground the difficulties of the term "slipstream," which they refer to on the first page as both a "brave new genre" and "the genre that might not be" (vii), and which they acknowledge only has meaning "to those coming from the genre side of the divide" (ix)—that is, from the world of science fiction. They conclude that "slipstream is a literary effect rather than a fully-developed genre" (xii), that it is characterized by postmodernist and genre-defying antirealism, that it is committed to "cognitive dissonance"—or what Freud would refer to as the "uncanny" effect that makes "the familiar strange or the strange familiar" (xiii), and that has as its precursors primarily prominent figures from the "experimental" tradition, such as Kafka, Borges, Calvino, and Coover. Further, they concede that most of the writers included in the anthology do not think of their own writing as slipstream. Kelly and Kessel's emphasis in their introduction, like Sterling's in his two essays, is primarily on an aesthetic sensibility, as defined by readers and critics, rather than any definition having to do with formal or stylistic characteristics deliberately adopted by writers operating within a specific genre.

The critical consensus regarding *Feeling Very Strange* is that this anthology does not bring clarity to the concept/genre of slipstream in a convincing way (see the reviews by Harrison, Johnson, and Soyka). Quite apart from the ongoing definitional ambiguities apparent in the introduction—and also in the discussions reprinted from David Moles's blog, which are interspersed throughout the text—the combination of stories also fails to demonstrate a discernible set of characteristics aside from having some counterrealist features, such as Surrealist or hallucinatory surfaces, disruptive plot structures, or other subversive narrative devices, most of which do not have particularly science-fictional or speculative aspects, but many of which do contain elements of fantasy.

More specifically, of all the stories, only Jonathan Lethem's "Light and the Sufferer" (1995) demonstrates one of the more formal definitions of slipstream: the intrusion of SF themes or motifs into other genres, thereby creating bizarre effects. More specifically, the story foregrounds a rather familiar, though compellingly written, plot about the narrator's futile attempt to rescue his brother, Light, from a life of addiction and drug-dealing in, again, a familiar setting, New York City. This story gives us believable characters, a cause–effect development of action, and a predictable and probable closure (the murder of Light by the dealer whose drugs he stole); in this respect, it is a kind of gritty realism. What presumably makes this story slipstream is the incongruous introduction of science-fictional elements in the form of two aliens known as "Sufferers," who participate in the action but whose origins and intentions remain shrouded in mystery. I would note, though, that the mysterious alien element does not substantially undermine the main plot; further, it does not make one "feel very strange."

Other stories in the volume, such as Amy Bender's "The Healer" (1998), a series of vignettes organized around two mutant girls, one with a hand of ice and the other with a hand of fire, are far more strange in conception and affect. Ted Chiang's "Hell is the Absence of God" (2001), an insightful story about grief and faith, which introduces the fantastic in the form of angelic visitations, also falls short, in my view, either of disrupting genre on the formal side or of making one feel very strange on the affective side. I would echo here Greg Johnson's view that the volume does not demonstrate a new emerging genre but rather "succeeds totally as a showcase of mostly young, talented writers." Like the other showcases of slipstream writers listed by Kelly and Kessel in their introduction (xiv), and like Sterling's original list, the anthology has a generative function of providing excellent reading lists for readers, critics, and writers covering the literary realms of experimentalism, fantasy, and SF. More specific to SF, these lists and anthologies open up questions about the relationships between SF and fantasy and between SF and the "mainstream," as well as the manner in which figures and themes are leaking out of fantasy and SF into both popular culture and the literary mainstream, though to serve purposes other than speculation.

In 2011 the scholarly journal *Science Fiction Studies* published a special issue on slipstream, which is instructive in its balancing of the ongoing theoretical and critical skepticism about the term, as exemplified in the range of views gathered in the symposium on slipstream included in the issue, in the persistence of the term as a heuristic tool in the articles about specific texts, and in the lists of slipstream works generated by members of the journal's editorial board. In his introduction to the volume, Latham suggests that ours is a "post-genre" period, which has generated a number of different terms to respond to "a consensus that seems to be building" that there is a breakdown of traditional demarcations between genres: New Wave fabulism, New Weird, interstitial fiction, and, of course, slipstream (1). I would note here the irony of this fertile generation of potentially overlapping genre categories in the face of the purported breakdown of genre distinctions. This is not to say that the phenomenon is not real; but it does indicate the problems in creating terminology that can adequately describe it.

Most interestingly, the symposium, a series of short statements about slipstream by a range of critics and writers, reveals a near consensus that the term remains quite problematic and obscure: for Andrew Butler, the "definition disappears in a puff of logic" ("Symposium" 11); John Kessel questions whether the term is needed at all (14); Gary Wolfe suggests that slipstream may be an "enhancement" rather than a genre (19); and Jonathan Lethem claims that, despite trying, he has been unable to "invest in the need for the slipstream label" (15). The annotated list of texts offered by the editorial board provides a marvelous, extensive reading list (see "Suggested Further Readings"), but, as with Sterling's original list, its sheer range serves to obscure rather than clarify the term. And, though eloquent and interesting, the article-length analyses of challenging contemporary fictions do not really seem to require the term "slipstream": see, for example, N. Katherine Hayles's focus on the phenomenon of invisible databases as a source in the real world for slipstream's affect of strangeness or Justin St. Clair's emphasis on narrative dimensionality as one hallmark of slipstream writing. Criticism and doubt about the term "slipstream" notwithstanding, the special *Science Fiction Studies* issue on the topic, like the inclusion of this chapter on the subject in the present volume, demonstrates a strangely persistent attachment to the term "slipstream" that remains hard to explain. Perhaps the best explanation is that it continues to be the most efficient way to talk about the expansion of SF writing and of critical discourse beyond the strict genre boundaries of hard, largely realist SF into a more hybrid kind of postmodernist writing that straddles, while revealing itself to be most comfortable within, the liminal spaces between SF, fantasy, speculative fiction, and experimental fiction.

Works Cited

Brown, Stephen P. "Before the Lights Came On." *Storming the Reality Studio: A Casebook of Cyberpunk and Postmodern Science Fiction*. Ed. Larry McCaffery. Durham, NC: Duke UP, 1991. 173–77. Print.

Csicsery-Ronay Jr., Istvan. "Cyberpunk and Neuromanticism." 1988. *Storming the Reality Studio: A Casebook of Cyberpunk and Postmodern Science Fiction*. Ed. Larry McCaffery. Durham, NC: Duke UP, 1991. 182–93. Print.

de Zwaan, Victoria. "Rethinking the Slipstream: Kathy Acker Reads *Neuromancer*." *Science Fiction Studies* 24.3 (Nov. 1997): 459–70. Print.

———. "Slipstream." *The Routledge Companion to Science Fiction*. Ed. Mark Bould, Andrew M. Butler, Adam Roberts, and Sherryl Vint. New York: Routledge, 2009. 500–504. Print.

Harrison, Niall. "Review of *Feeling Very Strange*, edited by James Patrick Kelly and John Kessel." *Strange Horizons*. Sept. 5, 2006. Web. July 7, 2013. http://www.strangehorizons.com/reviews/2006/09/feeling_v-comments.shtml.

Hayles, N. Katherine. "Material Entanglements: Steven Hall's *The Raw Shark Texts* as Slipstream Novel." *Science Fiction Studies* 38.1 (Mar. 2011): 115–33. Print.

Hollinger, Veronica. "Cybernetic Deconstructions: Cyberpunk and Postmodernism." 1990. *Storming the Reality Studio: A Casebook of Cyberpunk and Postmodern Science Fiction*. Ed. Larry McCaffery. Durham, NC: Duke UP, 1991. 203–18. Print.

Jameson, Fredric. *Postmodernism, or, The Cultural Logic of Late Capitalism*. Durham, NC: Duke UP, 1991. Print.

Johnson, Greg. "Review of *Feeling Very Strange*, edited by James Patrick Kelly and John Kessel." *SF Site*. 2006. Web. July 7, 2013. http://www.sfsite.com/10a/fs233.htm.

Kelly, James Patrick, and John Kessel. "Introduction." *Feeling Very Strange: The Slipstream Anthology*. Ed. James Patrick Kelly and John Kessel. San Francisco: Tachyon, 2006. vii–xv. Print.

Latham, Rob. "Introduction and Critical Bibliography." Special Issue: Slipstream. Ed. Rob Latham. *Science Fiction Studies* 38.1 (Mar. 2011): 1–5. Print.

Lethem, Jonathan. "Light and the Sufferer." 1995. *Feeling Very Strange: The Slipstream Anthology*. Ed. James Patrick Kelly and John Kessel. San Francisco: Tachyon, 2006. 53–86. Print.

Luckhurst, Roger. "The Many Deaths of Science Fiction: A Polemic." *Science Fiction Studies* 21.1 (Mar. 1994): 35–50. Print.

Lyotard, Jean-Francois. *The Postmodern Condition: A Report on Knowledge*. 1979. Trans. Geoff Bennington and Brian Massumi. Minneapolis: U Minnesota P, 1984. Print.

McCaffery, Larry. "Introduction: The Desert of the Real." *Storming the Reality Studio: A Casebook of Cyberpunk and Postmodern Science Fiction*. Ed. Larry McCaffery. Durham, NC: Duke UP, 1991. 1–16. Print.

Moles, David. "I Want My 20th Century Schizoid Art." May 3–June 2, 2005. *Feeling Very Strange: The Slipstream Anthology*. Ed. James Patrick Kelly and John Kessel. San Francisco: Tachyon, 2006. 36–8, 112–15, 181–84, 246–49. Print.

Person, Lawrence, and Bruce Sterling. "The Master List of Slipstream Books." 1999. Web. July 6, 2013. http://home.roadrunner.com/~lperson1/slip.html.

Piercy, Marge. *Woman on the Edge of Time*. New York: Knopf, 1976. Print.

Soyka, David. "Review of *Feeling Very Strange*, edited by James Patrick Kelly and John Kessel." *SF Site*. 2006. Web. July 7, 2013. http://www.sfsite.com/08b/fv230.htm.

St. Clair, Justin. "Borrowed Time: Thomas Pynchon's *Against the Day* and the Victorian Fourth Dimension." *Science Fiction Studies* 38.1 (Mar. 2011): 46–66. Print.

Sterling, Bruce. "Slipstream." *Science Fiction Eye* 1.5 (July 1989): 77–80. Print.

———. "Slipstream 2." 1999. *Science Fiction Studies* 38.1 (Mar. 2011): 6–10. Print.

"Suggested Further Readings in the Slipstream." *Science Fiction Studies* 38.1 (Mar. 2011): 208–19. Print.

Sukenick, Ronald, and Curtis White, eds. *In the Slipstream: An FC2 Reader*. Salt Lake City: Fiction Collective 2, 1999. Print.

"Symposium on Slipstream." *Science Fiction Studies* 38.1 (Mar. 2011): 11–19. Print.

Westfahl, Gary. "Who Governs Science Fiction?" *Extrapolation* 41.1 (Spring 2000): 63–72. Print.

CHAPTER 10

THE FANTASTIC

BRIAN ATTEBERY

"And taking a handful of sun I platted the twishers and set the boulder back on the hillside where it belonged," says a character in a well-known story by Zenna Henderson ("Ararat" 23). Such a statement hardly seems to belong in a science fiction narrative. There is no technology. The hillside is not on some alien world but in a canyon community in the American Southwest. The invented terminology is not derived from Latinized Greek, like most scientific language, but adapted from vernacular English: "twishers" suggests something that twists or swishes—rays of sunlight seen as motion—and "platting" is just plaiting or braiding. The activity being described is pure magic: someone has miraculously "lifted" a boulder off the ground and someone else manipulates sunlight to bring it back down.

Henderson's story was published in 1952 in *The Magazine of Fantasy and Science Fiction*. A reader dipping into its middle, where this scene occurs, might logically conclude that it would fall under the first of the magazine's two named purviews, fantasy rather than science fiction. Yet the full story, and the larger arc of stories of which it became a part (generally known as "The People" series), deal with space travel and a colony of stranded aliens on earth. Plots of individual stories revolve around genetics, cultural contact, and forgotten technology. The emphasis is often on knowledge: recovering old knowledge or combining it with new discoveries to solve problems. Logic and memory and conceptual breakthroughs are validated. The seemingly magical operations, which also include prophecy, clairvoyance, and telepathy, are part of the aliens' genetic inheritance and inform their scientific worldview. The story does not term them magic but rather "Persuasions and Designs" (32)—words at least marginally more rational in their connotations than "Incantations and Spells." The SF readership embraced the story, and the reading practices to which it responds best are those described by Samuel R. Delany as SF's protocols: inferring physical and cultural information from verbal clues to form a coherent, scientifically valid model of a hypothetical world.

Henderson represents one of the major strands within the SF tradition: the use of the fantastic in otherwise extrapolative narratives. The kind of SF she wrote is sometimes called "science fantasy," a term that reflects the hybrid nature of the subgenre (see Attebery, *Strategies* 105–06). Henderson was not the first writer to incorporate the fantastic within SF: she was working in a tradition that goes back at least to Edgar Rice Burroughs and his "John Carter of Mars" books (1917–1964), in which barbarian warriors pal around with scientific wizards and the fictional rules include both spirit travel and alien biology. Science fantasy was the dominant mode in the early-twentieth-century publication *Weird Tales*, represented by writers such as H. P. Lovecraft and C. L. Moore, and it continued to play a major role in the paperback era beginning in the 1950s. Henderson's contemporary Andre Norton moved freely back and forth between the two parent genres and not infrequently blended them. Norton's first two "Witch World" books (1963 and 1964), for instance, juxtapose witchcraft with dimensional portals and robots.

A number of fictional frameworks have evolved within SF to allow for the inclusion of blatant fantasy. The fantastic in the form of rationalized myth was employed to great effect by Delany in his *The Einstein Intersection* (1967) and by Roger Zelazny in *Lord of Light* (1967), both award-winning novels. Zelazny's rationalizations have to do with far-future technological advances, Delany's with paradigm shifts in the nature of rationality. The common fictional device of the lost colony world can be used to justify the presence of the fantastic within SF. For example, Anne McCaffrey's *Dragonflight* (1968) fits the plot and emotional affect of a fairy tale into an at least nominally SF setting; many of Marion Zimmer Bradley's "Darkover" books are high romance with a space-opera backdrop. It is impossible to imagine McCaffrey's lost colony world of Pern without its gravity-defying dragons or Bradley's similar Darkover without its magical blue matrix jewels. Both are pure fantasy except that they are not: the stories insist that they fit into a scientific worldview, and the stories are frequently compelling enough to make readers grant the claim, at least as a sort of legal fiction. There is an entire subgenre of far-future dying-world stories, in which barbaric remnants of humanity encounter wizards wielding forgotten high-tech devices. Clark Ashton Smith and Jack Vance pioneered this form; Gene Wolfe (in "The Book of the New Sun" [1980–83]), Elizabeth Hand (in her "Winterlong" trilogy [1988–93]), Terry Dowling (in the Tom Rynosseros stories of a future Australia [1990–2007]), and many others have found this kind of fantastically shaded SF artistically congenial. Most of these varieties of science fantasy operate under a single mantra: Arthur C. Clarke's famous comment that "[a]ny sufficiently advanced technology is indistinguishable from magic" (36).

Yet is it not always clear what constitutes the fantastic within SF, and many theories of the genre would rule out the possibility—or desirability—of combining fantastic elements with SF. "The fantastic" has been defined in many ways, some of which do not involve the kind of supernatural elements I have been talking about. Most definitions cluster around the idea of a departure from reported reality—a violation of natural law—but there are a few interesting outliers among them. One is the often cited structuralist approach of Tzvetan Todorov, which defines the fantastic as the moment of hesitation between natural and supernatural explanations of an event (with James's "The Turn of the Screw" [1898] as the best-known English-language instance). Another is Eric Rabkin's definition of the fantastic as a deliberate reversal of a narrative's own internal logic (using Carroll's *Alice's Adventures in Wonderland* [1865] as the type case). However, Kathryn Hume's identification of two fundamental and usually complementary modes—fantasy and mimesis—is more representative of practice within the English-language critical community and ultimately more useful. Hume distinguishes between the two on the basis of their relationship to reality, which she defines not in absolute terms but as a consensus about what exists or is possible (a consensus that can shift over time or from culture to culture). Mimetic writing sticks to that consensus, while fantastic writing goes beyond or outside it. Many narrative texts, especially those close to oral tradition, are a combination of the two rather than being all in one mode or the other. Hume's binary is a useful one, although it does not clearly distinguish between content and treatment. When C. S. Lewis makes the point that even a dragon can be described with more or less "Realism of Presentation" (57), is he talking about fantasy or mimesis? How can one fictional dragon be realer than another? When we find ourselves talking about the mimesis—or imitation—of something that does not exist, we have wandered into the realm of the postmodern—yet another version of Jean Baudrillard's simulacra. However, that is true of all fantasy rather than just science-fictional uses of the fantastic and so falls outside the boundaries of this chapter.

Despite such definitional complications, so long as there are only two possibilities to consider, the distinction between the fantastic and the not-fantastic (for which no standard term exists) is fairly clear. As soon as other related words come into play, however, things get considerably muddier. It is not at all clear, for instance, how fantasy is related to the fantastic—what happens, that is, when the adjective "fantastic" is turned into a noun denoting an abstract quality? How does this substantive adjective differ from the noun, which is associated with both genres and psychological states? What about other adjectival absolutes: the marvelous, the uncanny, the impossible, the absurd? Such constructions evade the necessity of naming the thing that is marvelous, uncanny, or absurd, and so we are free to fill in the blank however we like. One critic might be talking about impossible events, another about particularly imaginative settings—that is, scenes that are fantastic in the sense of being extravagantly imaginative or ornate. Gary K. Wolfe groups most genre definitions under the heading "fantasy," even those that, like Rabkin's, actually use the adjectival form "fantastic." The latter term he reserves for Todorov's moment of irresolution, though he also mentions Roger Caillois's use of "fantastic" to designate a moment not of hesitation but of aberration: a "break in reality"—or, in other words, a temporary intrusion of the supernatural into a mimetically conceived fictional environment (37).

Discussions of the fantastic within SF often deplore its use. Darko Suvin set the tone with his *Metamorphoses of Science Fiction*, in which he magisterially declared fantasy to be no more than "a subliterature of mystification" (9). Science-fictional uses of the fantastic, he said, constitute the "misshapen subgenre" of science fantasy (68). Mingling the two genres, SF and fantasy, is thus not only aesthetically incongruous but also a betrayal of SF's epistemological validity and historical relevance. Though Suvin softens his stance considerably in a later essay on fantasy, allowing that "the divide between cognitive (pleasantly useful) and non-cognitive (useless) does not run between SF and fantastic fiction but inside each" ("Considering" 211), his earlier position represents a common viewpoint. Even a writer as even-handedly committed to both genres as Ursula K. Le Guin has written with regret of her earlier tendency to mix the two. "At first," she says, "I knew too little science to use it as the framework, as part of the essential theme, of a story, and so wrote fairy tales decked out in space suits"; later on, though, "I finally got my pure fantasy vein separated off from my science fiction vein, by writing *A Wizard of Earthsea* and then *Left Hand of Darkness*, and the separation marked a very large advance in both skill and content" ("Citizen" 28, 29–30).

If SF is defined only in terms of rational cognition, then the fantastic may appear to be incompatible with its aims and techniques—or, more importantly, its aspirations to literary respectability. As Mark Bould observes, such "[s]harply-drawn distinctions between SF, fantasy and horror have long been characteristic of SF criticism. This has often seemed to be more a consequence of the desire to make SF seem more important than other, 'lesser' genre fictions than of any particularly necessary distinction between the genres" (52, n. 4). Many apologists for SF refer to its social function either as a vector for disseminating scientific ideas or as a mode of social critique. The incursion of the fantastic makes either claim problematic. The presence of the inexplicable makes the relationship between the text-created universe and the world of experience more obscure or at least more complicated. In a work such as Frederik Pohl and C.M. Kornbluth's *The Space Merchants* (1953), both the science and the social commentary are relatively clear-cut. We can see how the book's imagined society caricatures certain tendencies in capitalist culture, and we can imagine how one might get to that future by following certain already evident lines of technological development and social evolution. It works as both extrapolation and analogy, the two commonly identified modes of science-fictional thinking. More recently, Geoff Ryman's concept of "Mundane SF"—which rehabilitates a term employed by some lovers of SF and fantasy to dismiss the rest of literature—eschews the fantastic in favor of the probable, encouraging writers to avoid even such generically accepted but unlikely premises as faster-than-light travel and telepathy:

> Well the word Mundane means of the world. So by and large Mundane SF sticks to Earth or the nearby solar system. For example if we can't get to the stars, aliens can't get to us. Quantum uncertainty works only at the micro level. Parallel universes are unlikely. So two years ago, out of Clarion [Writers' Workshop] a bunch of young writers decided they wanted to limit themselves to the most likely future. This meant facing up to what we know is coming, dealing with it and imaging good futures that are likely. (Reed)

Rather like the Danish cinematic manifesto called Dogme 95, Mundane SF is more of an ideal than a widespread movement. Both advocate eschewing showy tricks—space empires and psychic powers on the one hand, special lighting and mood-setting music on the other—in favor of stripped-down emotional truth. However, even in Ryman's own largely Mundane and deeply moving novel *Air* (2005), he incorporates bits of the fantastic, such as an impossible pregnancy and a sort of time slippage. These fantastic elements pique the reader's curiosity and advance the novel's themes, so it ultimately matters little whether they meet the Mundane test, but they do suggest that the fantastic is more deeply interwoven into SF than discussions such as Suvin's would allow. It is always there; the pleasures of even the most technological hard-SF depend on fantastic effects. Hence, scholar R. D. Mullen suggested that both SF and fantasy belong to a "supergenre" of Fantastic Romance (Wolfe 38)—a reasonable solution, albeit one that introduces an equally loaded term. If "fantastic" is an adjective in search of a noun, "romance" is a noun in need of a modifier. It means very little by itself, but a great deal when it becomes, for instance, "scientific romance" or "women's romance" or "Arthurian romance" (see Attebery, "Romance"). The nature and limits of Fantastic Romance have yet to be defined.

The multitude of common uses of the adjective "fantastic," compounded by the lack of any specific noun, leads to considerable ambiguity about the sorts of details that might fall under the heading. These do, however, fall into a number of relatively distinct categories within SF: not "the fantastic" but what we might call "the fantastics." First, there is what we might call the Natural Fantastic: the depiction of any natural process or product of technology in such a way as to strike us as extraordinary or astonishing. Second, there is the Rationalized Fantastic, in which an apparently impossible operation turns out to be explicable through some extrapolation of contemporary science (or, often, the application of scientific terminology in a way that *looks* like an explanation). Third, there is the Situated Fantastic: the imposition of alternative viewpoints upon a situation such that one character's magic is another's high tech. Fourth, there is fiction that places scientific materialism within a larger conceptual framework that includes the supernatural: the Dissensus Fantastic. In it, either the text or its writer dissents from the kind of common-sense, rationalist beliefs implied in Hume's idea of consensus reality. Such framing can be justified by religious conceptions of the universe shared by many, such as C. S. Lewis's Medieval-style Christianity in *Out of the Silent Planet* (1938), or philosophies shared by a few, like H. P. Lovecraft's cosmic paranoia in the various stories of the Cthulhu mythos. (This is not to say that Lovecraft believed literally in Cthulhu and his gang of Elder Gods, but that the portrait of an animate and malevolent universe matched up with his stance toward the world.) Altogether, these four versions of the fantastic are so commonly part of even the hardest of SF that they reveal something of the nature and purposes of the genre—ruling them out would leave SF without faster-than-light ships, telepaths, tractor beams, or time machines. Few writers so scrupulously avoid anything fantastic, although, interestingly, most utopian fiction—to which I will return in a moment—makes an effort to do so. If we borrow Ryman's "mundane" and pair it with "fantastic," we have a binary comparable to Hume's fantasy and mimesis, and this binary, I would suggest, offers another way to think about Todorov's moment of fantastic hesitation.

The first of these versions of the fantastic, the Natural Fantastic, falls well within Suvin's definition of SF as the literature of cognitive estrangement. It sometimes involves changes of scale—imagining microscopic or subatomic phenomena as working at a macro level, projecting human institutions and activities across a whole galaxy, moving a narrative through broad sweeps of time. George Gamow's *Mr. Tompkins in Wonderland* (1940) represents the purest form of this sort of fantastic narrative: the title character hears a series of lectures about quantum physics and then dreams that phenomena such as the time distortion of near-light speed might be perceptible at a human scale. Other ways to achieve the scientifically grounded fantastic include transferring characteristics from one category to another: from plants to animals (imagining humans with a haploid generation, for instance) or animals to people (e.g., hive societies) or people to machines. Such fictional devices are only fantastic so long as they violate common sense; once something like artificial intelligence begins to seem achievable, and especially once smart (if not yet truly intelligent) machines become part of daily life, the fantastic drains away and can only be replenished by upping the ante. Instead of manlike machines, writers begin to imagine godlike machines, as in Harlan Ellison's "I Have No Mouth, and I Must Scream" (1967) or William Gibson's *Neuromancer* (1984).

Even though this form of the fantastic does not fit most definitions of fantasy because it stays within the realm of the possible and avoids the outright supernatural, the term "fantastic" is appropriate in that it describes the stories' intended affect. All those words bandied about in pulp magazine titles—"thrilling," "wonder," "startling," "amazing"—suggest something well beyond intellectual curiosity. One of SF's functions is to throw the reader into another state of consciousness, what Istvan Csicsery-Ronay Jr. calls the "science fictional sublime": "a powerful expansion of quotidian awareness to the insight that the physical universe involves far more than anyone can imagine" (146). We respond to natural sublimity the same way we do to the supernatural: the same gooseflesh, the same vertigo, the same sense of our own insignificance combined with immersion in something greater than ourselves. In actual practice, the natural and technological versions of the fantastic frequently cross over into the inexplicable, as in the examples of computer-generated deities mentioned above. The same writers who excel at producing awe through scientifically derived images also move into more mystical versions of the sublime: Arthur C. Clarke's *Childhood's End* (1953) and Clarke and Kubrick's *2001: A Space Odyssey* (1968) both begin in the former and end in the latter.

The endings of those two texts might fit into the second category, the Rationalized Fantastic, in which seemingly supernatural events are given materialist explanations, although neither *2001*'s Starchild nor *Childhood's End*'s Overmind can be fully explained by the sorts of extrapolative logic that governs earlier parts of their stories—both require a sort of imaginative leap of faith. Other examples mentioned earlier better illustrate the technique. McCaffrey makes a considerable effort, for instance, to justify the existence of her dragons in scientific terms. In the later volumes of the series, McCaffrey explains the dragons' fire-breathing as a chemical process, their ability to stay aloft as the unconscious use of telekinesis to boost otherwise inadequate wings, and their existence as a species as the result of deliberate genetic modification. Their psychic powers of telekinesis and telepathy are treated as scientific possibilities rather than magical operations—a rhetorical move made possible by the genre's history rather than any convincing scientific evidence. Andre Norton's SF often involves characters with extraordinary powers such as psychometry, or the "reading" of objects to determine their history and emotional associations, but Norton herself was a believer in such practices. This belief might put her outside the "consensus reality" of most scientists and place her work in the category of the Dissensus Fantastic, but her fictional depictions in novels such as *Forerunner Foray* (1973) are essentially science-fictional: she makes an effort to justify and limit the paranormal through scientific language and direct observation. As she says, "When I use such a definite occult matter as psychometry, the tarot, etc., in a book, I have a definite demonstration by an expert in order to get a material correct" ("Andre Norton" 1019).

The Situated Fantastic depends upon establishing within a given narrative two distinct, culturally based views of the universe. My term is derived from Donna Haraway's concept of "situated knowledges," which represents a midpoint between the empiricist "facts are facts" approach to science and the "that's just your opinion" permissiveness of social constructivism. For Haraway, facts are facts, but depending on one's social identity and cultural perspective, those facts are known differently. They grow out of different bodily experiences; they fit into different patterns of belief and practice, they arise out of different priorities, and they assign power differently. These variations are especially evident in Haraway's field of primate studies, in which what we think we know about apes is inevitably colored by what we believe about humans. Hence, Haraway propounds a localized theory of knowledge that, without denying the empirical world, takes personal responsibility for what one finds: her theory presents "an argument for situated and embodied knowledges and against various forms of unlocatable, and so irresponsible, knowledge claims" (191).

The Situated Fantastic takes this insight and dramatizes it in the form of mutually contradictory models of reality. William Blake invokes the Situated Fantastic when he describes two ways of thinking about the sun:

> "What," it will be Question'd, "When the Sun rises, do you not see a round disk of fire somewhat like a Guinea?" O no, no, I see an Innumerable company of the Heavenly host crying, 'Holy, Holy, Holy is the Lord God Almighty.'" (565–66)

This passage nicely conveys the dialogic quality of the Situated Fantastic. One speaker, the questioner, represents the scientific viewpoint. The other, the poet, argues for a mythic, supernatural universe. Neither is allowed to silence the other. In the next lines, Blake implicitly acknowledges that the sensory information brought to him by his "Corporeal or Vegetative eye" gives him the "guinea" version of the sun, but that he chooses to "look thro' it & not with it" to see spiritual truth as well as material fact (566).

The Situated Fantastic is a way of validating non-Western, nonmodern conceptions of the universe. Not surprisingly, it shows up in the work of anthropologically informed SF writers such as Le Guin and writers with a complex cultural heritage such as Nalo Hopkinson. Le Guin's early story "Semley's Necklace" (1964), which became the opening segment of her novel *Rocannon's World* (1966), is far from the haphazard mixture of magic and fantasy that she later makes it out to be. Instead, the story offers two sympathetic viewpoint characters, one an anthropologist from a technological culture and the other a member of a Bronze-Age alien society. Rocannon, the anthropologist, sums up the divergence in their systems of belief: "What I feel sometimes is that I . . . meeting these people from worlds we know so little of, you know, sometimes . . . that I have as it were blundered through the corner of a legend, or a tragic myth, maybe, which I do not understand" (21). It is his confession of his own lack of understanding that makes this Situated rather than Rationalized Fantastic: he is seeking a more complex relationship to truth than that offered by either magic or science alone. A similar kind of binary vision is central to the work of Hopkinson, whose science fiction transcribes non-European beliefs—often drawn from Caribbean folklore—into high-tech futures; examples include both *Brown Girl in the Ring* (1998) and *Midnight Robber* (2000).

Sometimes the two perspectives are represented not by contrasting characters but by locations: one realm in which magic works and one in which it does not but scientific technology is operative. This is the set-up in works as diverse as Andre Norton's *Judgment on Janus* (1963), Roger Zelazny's *Jack of Shadows* (1971), Garth Nix's "Abhorsen" trilogy (1995–2003), and Jim Grimsley's *The Ordinary* (2004). In each, there is a clear boundary between the two realms but the story involves border crossings and category violations that force characters ultimately to acknowledge multiple realities. The success of such versions of the Situated Fantastic depends on the degree to which both the science-fictional and the fantastic perspectives are fully worked out, logically consistent, and metaphorically sophisticated. In other words, the Situated Fantastic requires that a story be both exemplary fantasy and exemplary SF in order to function at the level of epistemological commentary. By pointing out a common linguistic evasion, Le Guin reveals the similar demands made by both genres if they are to function at that high level:

> "Somehow" is a weasel word; it means the author didn't want to bother thinking out the story—"Somehow she just knew. . . ." "Somehow they made it to the asteroid. . . ." When I teach science fiction and fantasy writing I ban the word. Nothing can happen "somehow." (*Steering* 61–62)

Yet even when "somehows" are allowed to creep into a work of science fantasy and the level of intellectual rigor is turned down to low, the hybrid genre can still offer entertainment, often through comic juxtapositions and unexpected turns of plot that arise from the Situated Fantastic. Popular examples include Christopher Stasheff's "Warlock" series (beginning with *The Warlock in Spite of Himself* [1969]) and Piers Anthony's "Apprentice Adept" series (starting with *Split Infinity* [1980]), but an earlier and better instance is Fletcher Pratt and L. Sprague de Camp's series of Harold Shea adventures, the first of which occurred in "The Roaring Trumpet" (1940). The science-fictional aspect in them is rather perfunctory, involving alternative dimensions to which one can travel by manipulating symbolic logic, but throughout the series, Shea uses something like scientific reasoning to counter magic, and the result is more or less a draw. Suzette Haden Elgin's "Ozark Trilogy" (1981) uses linguistics for similar ends. Though the science-fictional underpinnings of the trilogy are understated, in a related book, *Yonder Comes the Other End of Time* (1986), Elgin introduced her space opera hero Coyote Jones to the world of Planet Ozark and let the two worldviews collide openly.

The Dissensus Fantastic differs from the Situated in favoring one viewpoint over the other. It might be called the De-Rationalized Fantastic in that the text seems to consider offering scientific explanations for extraordinary things but then ultimately opts for the supernatural instead. Usually, the characters who speak for the scientific viewpoint are revealed to be at best misguided and at worst demonic, as in *That Hideous Strength* (1945), the final volume of C. S. Lewis's "Space Trilogy." As mentioned above, Lewis used the Dissensus Fantastic to articulate a Christian vision of the universe and thereby to critique the materialist ethos of SF. Lewis's hero Ransom starts out as an accidental traveler to Mars in a more or less conventional rocket ship but ends up as an incarnation of the Arthurian Fisher King in a battle between good and evil, in which the scientific institute and its figurehead (a caricature of H. G. Wells) are revealed to be in the service of the devil and the forces of good are aided by the angelic tutelary spirits of the planets. There is no question of which worldview is both right and good; faith and the supernatural roundly defeat science.

The Dissensus Fantastic need not be based in Christian belief, however. Amitav Ghosh's *The Calcutta Chromosome* (1995) is doubly science-fictional. One thread of the novel looks back at scientific history—the search for causes and cures for malaria—and another posits a near-future, postcolonial world. Yet midway through, explanations of events subtly shift from microbiology and genetics to mysticism, and a minor female character turns out to be a Hindu goddess controlling much of the action. As in Hindu epics, the world of appearances is revealed to be *maya*, "illusion," and thus science, the study of observable phenomena, is equally illusory. A similar skepticism about natural phenomena can be found in Gnosticism, which is not so much a religion as a tendency within many religious traditions, including Christianity and Buddhism. From a Gnostic perspective, the material universe is a trap, often the creation of a malevolent demiurge masquerading as a god, and the only escape is through suffering, which leads to discovery of secret knowledge, or "gnosis." H. P. Lovecraft's fiction, like Lewis's or Ghosh's, also pulls the scientific rug out from under the reader, but in this case on the basis of a worldview that is essentially Gnostic—except without the Gnostic idea of salvation through knowledge. For characters in Lovecraft's universe, penetrating to the secret heart of things results in damnation. The stable world of reason and order is false, but the truth is worse. A more conventional sort of Gnosticism shows up in David Lindsay's *A Voyage to Arcturus* (1920), in which a spiritual voyage to and around the planet of Tormance leads the protagonist Maskull through a series of disillusionments until the only reality he accepts is pain. Despite their philosophical differences, Lindsay's work strongly influenced Lewis's approach to the SF fantastic.

A more recent example of the Dissensus Fantastic, again with Gnostic implications, is John Crowley's novel *The Deep* (1975). Crowley begins the work entirely within the point of view of characters who believe in magic. Gradually, it is revealed that the magic is really technology: the strange flat earth is an artificial world, one of the main characters is an android, and humanity has been placed in this situation by a powerful alien. Yet the unveiling does not end there. The alien—or rather two complementary alien powers—might as well be divine. When one of the characters reaches the Deep beneath and outside the habitable earth and speaks with its denizen, Leviathan, the latter's utterances are both scientific and biblical. Leviathan talks of solar sails, "like woven air, that fine; large as the world" but also of a sort of second Genesis: "It was I who dropped the pillar into the placeless deeps . . . I who set this roof, to protect me from the heaven-stones" (162). The reader is taken through science and beyond into mystery. A similar philosophical-theological journey structures Gene Wolfe's grand, multivolume science fantasies: "The Book of the New Sun," "The Book of the Long Sun" (1994–96), and "The Book of the Short Sun" (2000–01). Many see Wolfe's version of the Dissensus Fantastic as being grounded in his Catholicism. Much Dissensus Fantastic has a quasi-religious quality, though it may reflect a writer's investigation of, rather than a testimonial to, faith. The Dissensus Fantastic nearly always involves the gradual penetration of ever-deepening mysteries. These mysteries may be dark, as in the case of Lovecraft and Lindsay, or consoling, as in Lewis's space fiction or Madeleine L'Engle's science fantasies, best represented by *A Wrinkle in Time* (1962).

Most evident in the Dissensus Fantastic, but common to all varieties of the science-fictional fantastic, is a pull toward the "numinous." This term, popularized in the early twentieth century by Rudolf Otto, conveys an aspiration shared by religious writers like L'Engle and nontheological ones like Carl Sagan: to move the reader into a state of rapt contemplation of the sublime and the transcendent, which may be seen in terms of nature or the supernatural. Encounters with the numinous can inspire fear and trembling or ecstatic joy. What they do not do is motivate rational, collective action. Hence the avoidance of all forms of the fantastic within most utopian fiction. The devoutly Catholic Thomas More left miracles and mysteries out of his *Utopia* (1516). Nineteenth-century utopias such as Edward Bellamy's *Looking Backward* (1887) are strong on gadgetry and social engineering but decidedly short on sublimity. Le Guin's most utopian novel, *The Dispossessed* (1974), is also her least fantastic: in it she eschews even the modest touches of the fantastic that mark most hard-SF novels, such as telepathy and faster-than-light travel. Kim Stanley Robinson's utopian *Pacific Edge* (1988) focuses on personal interactions and pragmatic solutions; it avoids the fantastic touches that mark Robinson's more visionary work, such as *The Years of Rice and Salt* (2002). It seems that the pull toward utopia is a force equal but opposite to the yearning for the numinous. The utopian imagination requires a Mundane approach in order to convince the reader that ordinary human beings, working together rationally, can make the world better.

Within any given SF text, a strange image or extraordinary action can be explained away or validated. At the moment when the fantastic is evoked, the reader does not necessarily know which version it is: Natural, Rationalized, Situated, or Dissensus. Only after the moment of strangeness is integrated into a complete conceptual and narrative structure does it become clear whether we are in the realm of the numinous or the mundane—or, if the former, whether we are being invited to admire the infinite variety of the cosmos or look beyond the universe to something transcendent. Thus, the presence of the fantastic within SF creates a moment of hesitation comparable to that described by Todorov. In a narrative like the Zenna Henderson story with which I began, that hesitation becomes a permanent suspension: the reader is left to decide how her alien People acquired their mysterious Persuasions and Designs, whether they represent an as-yet-undiscovered law of nature or the intercession of the divine, and whether we might all one day learn to plat the twishers and toss boulders around the landscape.

The answers to these questions determine which kind of SF the story might be, but they do not particularly affect its ability to intrigue and charm the reader. Science fiction has always been more of a hybrid than its apologists and theoreticians acknowledge. As Roger Luckhurst points out, "The genre has always been a mixed, hybrid, bastard form, in the process of constant change" (243). If there is a significance to the hesitation among forms of SF fantastic, that significance is not necessarily structural or psychological, as Todorov would have it, but rather an indicator of the slipperiness of the categories of fantasy, science fantasy, and science fiction. Because readers often do not know until after the fact—if then—which sort of fantastic they have encountered, the different constituencies that make up the SF community can come together in appreciating a range of textual experiences, from the mundane to the mystical.

Works Cited

"Andre Norton." *Science Fiction and Fantasy Literature: A Checklist 1700–1974*. Vol. 2: *Contemporary Science Fiction Authors II*. Ed. Robert Reginald. Farmington Hills, MI: Gale, 1979. 1018–19. Print.

Attebery, Brian. "Romance." *The Encyclopedia of Fantasy*. Ed. John Clute and John Grant. New York: St. Martins, 1997. 820–21. Print.

———. *Strategies of Fantasy*. Bloomington: Indiana UP, 1992. Print.

Blake, William. "A Vision of the Last Judgment." 1810. *The Complete Poetry and Prose of William Blake*. Ed. David V. Erdman. Charlottesville, VA: Institute for Advanced Technology in the Humanities, 2001. 554–56. Print.

Bould, Mark. "The Dreadful Credibility of Absurd Things: A Tendency in Fantasy Theory." *Historical Materialism* 10.4 (2002): 51–88. Print.

Clarke, Arthur C. "Hazards of Prophecy: The Failure of Imagination." *Profiles of the Future: An Enquiry into the Limits of the Possible*. 1962. Rev. ed. 1973. New York: Popular Library, 1977. 30–39. Print.

Crowley, John. *The Deep*. New York: Berkley, 1975. Print.

Csicsery-Ronay Jr., Istvan. *The Seven Beauties of Science Fiction*. Middletown, CT: Wesleyan UP, 2008. Print.

Delany, Samuel. "About Five Thousand Seven Hundred and Fifty Words." *The Jewel-Hinged Jaw: Notes on the Language of Science Fiction*. New York: Berkley, 1978. 21–37. Print.

Haraway, Donna. "Situated Knowledges: The Science Question in Feminism and the Privilege of Partial Perspective." 1988. *Simians, Cyborgs, and Women: The Reinvention of Nature.* New York: Routledge, 1991. 183–201. Print.

Henderson, Zenna. "Ararat." 1952. *Ingathering: The Complete People Stories of Zenna Henderson.* Framingham, MA: NESFA, 1995. 13–32. Print.

Hume, Kathryn. *Fantasy and Mimesis: Responses to Reality in Western Literature.* London: Methuen, 1984. Print.

Le Guin, Ursula K. "A Citizen of Mondath." 1973. *The Language of the Night: Essays on Fantasy and Science Fiction.* Ed. Susan Wood. New York: Perigee, 1979. 25–30. Print.

———. "Semley's Necklace." 1964. *The Wind's Twelve Quarters.* New York: Harper, 1975. 1–24. Print.

———. *Steering the Craft: Exercises and Discussions on Story Writing for the Lone Navigator or the Mutinous Crew.* Portland, OR: Eighth Mountain, 1998. Print.

Lewis, C. S. *An Experiment in Criticism.* Cambridge, UK: Cambridge UP, 1961. Print.

Luckhurst, Roger. *Science Fiction.* Cambridge, UK: Polity, 2005. Print.

Rabkin, Eric. *The Fantastic in Literature.* Princeton, NJ: Princeton UP, 1976. Print.

Reed, Kit. "Geoff Ryman Interviewed by Kit Reed." *Infinity Plus: SF, Fantasy, Horror.* Aug. 7, 2004. Web. Jan. 14, 2012. http://www.infinityplus.co.uk/nonfiction/intgr.htm.

Suvin, Darko. "Considering the Sense of 'Fantasy' or 'Fantastic Fiction': An Effusion." *Extrapolation* 41.3 (Fall 2000): 209–47. Print.

———. *Metamorphoses of Science Fiction: On the Poetics and History of a Literary Genre.* New Haven, CT: Yale UP, 1979. Print.

Todorov, Tzvetan. *The Fantastic: A Structural Approach to a Literary Genre.* 1970. Trans. Richard Howard. 1973. Ithaca, NY: Cornell UP, 1975. Print.

Wolfe, Gary K. *Critical Terms for Science Fiction and Fantasy: A Glossary and Guide to Scholarship.* Westport, CT: Greenwood, 1986. Print.

CHAPTER 11

GENRE VS. MODE

VERONICA HOLLINGER

In his admiring review of *Pattern Recognition* (2003), William Gibson's first novel to be set in the present, John Clute cites a very familiar passage spoken by the immensely up-to-date and very sinister marketing genius Hubertus Bigend:

> Fully imagined cultural futures were the luxury of another day, one in which "now" was of some greater duration. For us, of course, things can change so abruptly, so violently, so profoundly, that futures like our grandparents' have insufficient "now" to stand on. We have no future because our present is too volatile. . . . (Gibson 57; qtd. Clute 403)

For Clute, "a novel like *Pattern Recognition*, where passages like the above are both embedded into the text and intrinsic to the understanding of that text, can be understood as a kind of sf. Sf for the new century." According to Clute, it is no longer possible to write "First SF"—that is, the SF typified by such Golden Age classics as *I, Robot* (1950), *Childhood's End* (1953), and *Starship Troopers* (1959). These are, in Clute's words, "novelizations of the prior," productions of a historical period whose extrapolative imagination was as expansive as the open-ended future promised to be. In contrast, science fiction "for the new century" is a discourse about "the case of the world," a way of producing meanings about the contemporary world of global capital, information overload, technoscientific imperialism, and geopolitical upheaval. As he summarizes, "Sf is no longer about the future as such, because 'we have no future' that we can do thought experiments about, only futures, which bleed all over the page, soaking the present" (403).

Clute, in other words, is not reading *Pattern Recognition* for narrative—its patterns, not its plot, are of paramount interest—but as a kind of rhetorically precise thick description of the Westernized technoscientific future-present whose outlines have been coming into focus since the mid-twentieth century. Building on an increasing number of commentaries since the 1980s, Clute reads science fiction not (only) as genre, but (also) as mode. In this view, SF now signifies something more than a particular kind of narrative complex—generally understood to be an archive of stories with particular themes, motifs, and figures, a kind of storytelling oriented toward the future, closely related to the realist novel in its rhetorical verisimilitude, at once an estranged mirror of the present and an imaginative extrapolation of worlds to come.

In contrast, mode implies not a kind but a method, a way of getting something done. In this instance, it is a way of thinking and speaking about contemporary reality so that SF becomes integrated with other discourses about late-capitalist global technoculture, including science and technology studies, cyberculture studies, and studies of posthumanism (see Vint). One of the most influential examples of this integration is N. Katherine Hayles's reading of cybernetics theory and science fiction as complementary discourses in *How We Became Posthuman* (1999). Mary Flanagan and Austin Booth's co-edited *Reload: Rethinking Women and Cyberculture* (2002) contains both critical-theoretical chapters—on, for instance, cyberfeminism, medical technologies, and virtual subjectivities—and SF stories by writers such as C. L. Moore, James Tiptree Jr., and Octavia E. Butler, with neither form given precedence over the other. Darren Tofts et al.'s mammoth *Prefiguring Cyberculture* (2002) opens with a section titled "I, Robot: AI, Alife and Cyborgs" and closes with a section titled "Futuropolis: Postmillennial Speculations." And Colin Milburn's *Nanovision* (2008) traces the symbiotic relationship between SF discourse and the discourses of nanotechnological development to argue that "nanotechnology should be viewed as simultaneously a science and a science fiction" (25).

It is perhaps no coincidence that, from the perspective of genre criticism, science fiction is currently suffering a crisis of "enrollment," having become transformed over time into "a fuzzily-edged, multidimensional and constantly shifting discursive object" (Bould and Vint, *Routledge Concise History* 4–5). Given its affinities with both fantasy and horror, is China Miéville's *Perdido Street Station* (2000), which won the Arthur C. Clarke Award, science fiction? In spite of Clute's admiration, is *Pattern Recognition*—a novel in which any distance between the "real" and the science-fictional has definitively collapsed—science fiction?

Recent genre studies have tended to focus on science fiction's increasingly permeable boundaries, as well as its ongoing fragmentation into various hybrid forms (not to mention its transformations in nonprint media). This is suggested, for example, in the title of Gary K. Wolfe's recent collection, *Evaporating Genres* (2011). In "Twenty-First-Century Stories," Wolfe and his co-writer Amelia Beamer list some of the new "postgenre" designations that have begun to circulate among fans and critics: "Slipstream. Interstitial. Transrealism. New Weird. Nonrealist fiction. New Wave Fabulist. Postmodern fantasy. Postgenre fiction. Cross-genre. Span fiction. Artists without Borders. New Humanist. Fantastika. Liminal fantasy. . ." (164). So much for Derrida's iron(ic) "law of genre": "Genres are not to be mixed" (55).

It is entirely appropriate that one of the earliest critical considerations of science fiction was speculation about a kind—a genre—of novel that did not yet exist but that might come to be in the future. In 1834 Félix Bodin, in the preface to his *Roman de l'avenir* [The Novel of the Future], speculated on what he called "the epic of the future":

> New paths are needed for literature, new fields for the imagination.... Those who complain that the past has been exploited enough will not say the same, I hope, about the future.... [T]he marvellous of the future ... is entirely believable, entirely possible ... an environment utterly fantastic and yet not lacking in verisimilitude. (qtd. Evans 172)

In Bodin's speculations, one can already see in outline some of the features conventionally associated with SF as genre: its strategy of imaginative extrapolation, its significant intersections with and differences from the historical novel, its commitment to a certain kind of logical plausibility, and its evocation of the "sense of wonder."

Since Bodin's prescient speculations about "the novel of the future," science fiction has come into focus as a more or less recognizable cultural product, its features constituted by and historicized in the very many critical-theoretical commentaries of the past century by fans, scholars, writers, and academics. It is this coherent sense of genre that allowed American SF writer and editor Frederik Pohl to claim, only somewhat flippantly, that science fiction "is that thing that people who understand science fiction point to, when they point to something and say 'That's science fiction!'" (qtd. Jakubowski and Edwards 257). In academic SF studies, science fiction has become identified with, for example, terms such as "cognition," "estrangement," and "novum" (see Suvin), and with rhetorical strategies such as the dialectical play of extrapolation and metaphor. From another perspective, Samuel R. Delany has argued that SF is, like every genre, "a reading protocol complex" (235) with which readers become familiar through the accumulation of experience with its stories.

The very breadth and variety of critical and theoretical studies published to date, however, demonstrate that science fiction as a particular *kind* has never been as coherent as Pohl's statement about experienced SF readers might suggest. Is SF "a literature of cognitive estrangement" or is it a complex of reading protocols? Is it "a literature of ideas" or is its most attractive feature its capacity to evoke "the sense of wonder"? Is it first and foremost a literary genre or must theorists also take account of the different representational strategies of nonprint media? Is it a fixed and ahistorical category or a system of generic effects that changes over time? In their challenge to conventional genre studies, "There Is No Such Thing as Science Fiction," Mark Bould and Sherryl Vint make the case that, while there "never was such a *thing* as SF[,] . . . ways of producing, marketing, distributing, consuming and understanding texts as SF . . . are in a constant, unending process of coming into being" (43; emphasis in original). This essay appeared in a collection co-edited by James Gunn, whose own contribution, "Reading Science Fiction as Science Fiction," takes strong exception to its argument. As its title suggests, Gunn's arguments rely heavily on Delany's ideas about the "reading protocols" that guide experienced readers to respond to a text's generic demands.

For another aphorism about genre, we might turn to Tom Shippey's ironic observation that "science fiction is hard to define because it is the literature of change and it changes while you are trying to define it" (qtd. Jakubowski and Edwards 258). In spite of the desire of many fans, critics, and scholars for some kind of unified field theory of science fiction, what has accumulated are very many—often contradictory—theories, perspectives, positions, and descriptions, from scholars, editors, readers, and writers, about SF in any number of cultural and historical moments and in any number of different media. As Istvan Csicsery-Ronay Jr. has observed, "Critical provocation is part of SF's generic identity" ("Science Fiction/Criticism" 43).

Recent studies have tended to reflect this sense of the diffuse nature of the genre. Roger Luckhurst's cultural history of SF concludes that it "has always been a mixed, hybrid, bastard form, in a process of constant change" (*Science Fiction* 243). Rob Latham usefully reminds us that "[t]here is nothing new about this intermixing of genre tropes.... Indeed, it is virtually impossible fully to disentangle elements of SF, fantasy, horror, and detection in the work of major US and UK popular writers whose careers were launched prior to the advent of the specialty pulps during the 1920s and 1930s." Bould and Vint's *Concise History of Science Fiction* (2011) introduces its object as radically heterogeneous, constantly "translated and transformed as it moves across different media and into different contexts of circulation" (5). In "Science Fiction and the Literary Field" (2011), Andrew Milner examines SF's conditions of possibility in the context of Pierre Bourdieu's theoretical work, taking account of publishing practices, fan activities, class distinctions, and media developments, as well as the history of SF's various "movements" such as New Wave and cyberpunk.

As if to confirm at least a temporary cessation of critical attempts to fix SF as a coherent generic project, the Science Fiction Research Association presented its 2011 Pioneer Award for best critical essay of the year to John Rieder's "On Defining SF, or Not: Genre Theory, SF, and History" (2010), which argues for a revisionary reading of science fiction in the context of a paradigm shift in genre theory "from identifying and classifying fixed, ahistorical entities to studying genres as historical processes" (191). He offers five propositions consequential on this historical turn:

1. sf is historical and mutable;
2. sf has no essence, no single unifying characteristic, and no point of origin;
3. sf is not a set of texts, but rather a way of using texts and of drawing relationships among them;
4. sf's identity is a differentially articulated position in a historical and mutable field of genres;
5. attribution of the identity of sf to a text constitutes an active intervention in its distribution and reception. (193)

For Rieder, "The notorious diversity of the genre is not a sign of confusion, nor the result of a multiplicity of genres being mistaken for a single one, but rather, on the contrary, the identity of sf is constituted by this very web of sometimes inconsistent and competing assertions" (192). Rieder also sets his historical sights on SF criticism, reminding us that "the labeling itself is crucial to constructing the genre," so that critical-theoretical commentaries are themselves "part of the history of sf" (193).

Here is a different set of questions. What happens to science fiction when, as Zoë Sofia and Istvan Csicsery-Ronay Jr. (see his "Futuristic Flu") argue, the future collapses onto the present? when the future, as Fredric Jameson contends ("Progress Versus Utopia"), is no longer available as the site of meaningful (utopian) difference? when the present, as I have argued elsewhere, is itself the site of unremitting and radically estranging transformations? These are some of the questions that have exerted pressure on the idea of sf as simply "a generic effects engine of literature and simulation arts" (Csicsery-Ronay, "SF of Theory" 387). As early as 1980, SF began to be theorized differently in an increasingly technologized and globalized context. Perhaps we might view such commentaries as a kind of "slipstream" criticism relative to more "centered" genre studies.

One of the earliest discussions to shift the emphasis from genre to mode appears in Mark Rose's *Alien Encounters* (1981). Rose's opening chapter on "Genre" introduces Pamela Zoline's classic New Wave story "The Heat Death of the Universe" (1967) as "an extreme example of the transformation of the generic field into metaphor" (17), where conventionally SF's worlds have been "presented as logical extensions of reality," as metonymical extrapolations. For Rose, the shift from metonymy to metaphor in a story such as "Heat Death" signals "[t]he movement from the specificity of 'genre' to the vague and more generalized status of 'mode'" (23). For Rose, this is perceptible in the "texts themselves" and it heralds the eventual end of science fiction as a distinctive genre. In an earlier study (cited by Rose) aptly titled "The Life and Death of Literary Forms," genre theorist Alastair Fowler argues that "genre tends to mode":

> The genre . . . eventually exhausts its evolutionary possibilities. But the equivalent mode, flexible, versatile, and susceptible to novel commixtures, may generate a compensating multitude of new generic forms. For the mode was abstracted from an existing concrete historical genre. The latter, closely linked to specific social forms, is apt to perish with them. But the mode corresponds to a somewhat more permanent poetic attitude or stance, independent of particular contingent embodiments of it. (214)

Fowler gives as example the "gothic mode," which has long outlasted the gothic novel or romance "and was applied to forms as diverse as . . . the psychological novel . . . not to mention various science fiction genres. . ." (214). His analysis is certainly confirmed by the recent collection compiled by Sara Wasson and Emily Alder, *Gothic Science Fiction* (2011), as well as by the chapter on "Gothic" in this *Handbook*.

There is certainly a case to be made that SF is increasingly being read as an "attitude or stance" toward contemporary technoscientific reality, less concerned with extrapolating "fully imagined cultural futures" (to recall Hubertus Bigend's statement) and more concerned with examining, in estranged terms, the technoscientific features of the everyday—in Rose's terms, this is reading SF as a figural discourse about the constantly shrinking distance between the present and the future.

Rose's aim is relatively straightforward, to trace the transformation from genre to mode of a literary form. Some other (perhaps more familiar) theoretical studies have been more concerned to attempt a sociocultural analysis of the thorough imbrication of technology and culture in Westernized societies—these are efforts at what

Jameson has termed "cognitive mapping" (*Postmodernism* 54) of the increasingly estranged zones of the contemporary real. Jameson himself famously situated cyberpunk SF as "the supreme literary expression if not of postmodernism then of late capitalism itself" (*Postmodernism* 419 n.1). In a similar vein, Jonathan Benison's "Science Fiction and Postmodernity" emphasizes a particular way of reading SF, arguing that it is "as a *mode* rather than as a genre that SF speaks to postmodernity" (139; emphasis in original). For Benison, the penetration of technology into almost every facet of human life and the penetration of SF imagery into the social imaginary mean that "SF emerges through social theory as one way of talking about certain recent developments in advanced industrial society" (139). While for Benison this by no means spells the end of genre, it does mean (re)reading SF specifically for "its contemporary social and historical significance" (141) as a privileged discourse of technoscientific postmodernity.

Going even further, Benison asserts that "SF in some sense does not exist any more as such," and, in a statement that echoes the provocative formulations of Jean Baudrillard, he concludes that "as mode it is everywhere and nowhere" (150). Baudrillard's theorization of hyperreality and the "precession of simulacra" provides one of the most influential, if hyberbolic, treatments of the postmodern world as technological simulation. In "Simulacra and Science Fiction," Baudrillard calls for a new SF imaginary appropriate to the world of universal hyperreal simulation, because "the 'good old' SF imagination is dead"; his privileged text is *Crash*, J. G. Ballard's 1973 novel about sex, death, and car crashes, and he concludes that "SF of this sort is no longer an elsewhere, it is an everywhere: in the circulation of models here and now, in the very axiomatic nature of our simulated environment" (312).

Debra Benita Shaw has explained the importance of science fiction to critiques such as Baudrillard's. In her words,

> Hyperreality is an intensified reification in which the excessive worlds of science fiction are our daily reality and the mode in which this excess exists is cybernetic: a function of the control, manipulation and dissemination of electronic communication which is the postmodern mode of production. We live in the matrix and it lives through us. (24)

Shaw notes that, for Baudrillard as for many other social theorists, "in contemporary hi-tech postmodern culture, the space between that cultural moment and the extrapolated 'other' world has collapsed" (23). This is not dissimilar to Jameson's influential disclaimer that it has become impossible to imagine futures of genuine difference, so that SF's role in postindustrial technoculture is to "to dramatize our incapacity to imagine the future" ("Progress Versus Utopia" 153): the "temporal structure" of SF is "not to give us 'images' of the future . . . but rather to defamiliarize and restructure our experience of our own *present*, and to do so in specific ways distinct from all other forms of defamiliarization" (151; emphasis in original). Or, in Clute's words, "Cognitive estrangement is us" (403).

From within the field of science fiction studies, Csicsery-Ronay has also suggested SF's usefulness as a mode of imaginative response to the present. In "The SF of Theory," he argues that sf "is not a genre of literary entertainment only, but a mode of awareness, a complex hesitation about the relationship between imaginary conceptions and historical reality unfolding into the future" (388). It is from this perspective that he examines the function of science fiction in both Baudrillard's disquisitions on the hyperreal and Donna Haraway's socialist/feminist "Manifesto for Cyborgs," her ironic rehabilitation of this science-fictional figure to represent allegorically potential (networked) resistances to the dominant regimes of technoscience. Haraway describes SF writers such as Joanna Russ and Octavia Butler as "storytellers exploring what it means to be embodied in high-tech worlds. They are theorists for cyborgs" (197).

"The SF of Theory" usefully reminds us that, especially since the 1980s and the many excited critical discussions about cyberpunk as postmodern SF, science fiction's "use value" has been increasingly deployed outside the immediate field—not only by such disparate social theorists as Baudrillard and Haraway but also in such diverse theoretical fields as STS (science and technology studies) and HAS (human–animal studies). As an aspect of the social imaginary, furthermore, in many instances it no longer retains any necessary links to narrative, as demonstrated in studies of SF tourism (Landon) and World's Fairs (Telotte), as well as of science fiction's intersections with architecture, performance art, and advertising (see the chapters by Clear, Dixon, and Woodham in this *Handbook*).

Although his later study *The Seven Beauties of Science Fiction* (2008) offers an in-depth genre analysis of SF's aesthetic and rhetorical conventions, Csicsery-Ronay opens it with a discussion of "science-fictionality," which he describes as "a mode of response that frames and tests experiences as if they were aspects of a work of science fiction" (2). Consider the awful logic of this apparently random list of "science-fictional moments":

> the postmodern hecatomb of the World Trade Center; Chernobyl's lost villages and mutant flora; CGI pop stars; genocide under surveillance satellites; . . . Internet pornography raining down in microwaves; . . . Artificial Life; global social movements (and even nations) without territories; the ability to alter one's gender; the evaporation of the North Pole. (2)

It is as a response to such "moments" that we might read Margaret Atwood's recent forays into science fiction in novels such as *Oryx and Crake* (2003) and its sequel *The Year of the Flood* (2009). It is as if for Atwood—in spite of her often uneasy relationship with SF as a popular genre—it remains the only language through which to examine critically the out-of-control world of global technoscience. In the dizzying pile-up of genetic hybrids, animal extinctions, radical corporate greed, and environmental collapse, it is often difficult to distinguish between what Atwood has taken from current technoreality ("spoat/giders") and what she has imagined for her near-future dystopia ("wolvogs"). Or, in William Gibson's words, "I found the material of the actual twenty-first century richer, stranger, more multiplex, than any imaginary twenty-first century could ever have been. And it could be unpacked with the toolkit of science fiction" (*Distrust* 46).

In 1999 the authors of "A History of Science Fiction Criticism" published in *Science Fiction Studies* noted that

> [t]here is no consensus as to when and where sf criticism originated, who its major figures were, or what they were talking about. Contemporary sf critics, after paying brief homage to a few iconic predecessors, may proceed as if unaware that the issues they are discussing were first raised in the introduction to a nineteenth-century novel, debated at length in the letter columns of certain 1930s' sf magazines, or intensely analyzed in a 1970s' critical essay. (Evans et al. 161)

In the intervening years, this meta-critical gap has been addressed in a number of very good overviews of SF's rich critical and theoretical conversations. These include, in addition to the expansive four-part chronological history by Evans and colleagues, overviews by Csicsery-Ronay ("Science Fiction/Criticism") and Wolfe ("Pilgrims of the Fall"), Peter Nicholls's substantial entry on "Critical and Historical Works About SF" in the *Encyclopedia of Science Fiction*, and Wolfe's chapter on "History and Criticism" in the fifth edition of Neil Barron's *Anatomy of Wonder*. An extensive "Chronological Bibliography of Science Fiction History, Theory, and Criticism," dating back to 1634, is maintained on the *Science Fiction Studies* website. Also of interest is Delany's early challenge to some already established critical conventions, "Some Reflections on SF Criticism" (1981).

My own focus here has been on what I see as a significant shift in some critical perspectives to "science-fictionality" as a theoretical framework and to science fiction as one of the significant discourses of technoculture—a key element of the technosocial imaginary, to recall Benison's position. A "first generation" of theoretical inquiries exploring SF's deep imbrication with the environments of technoscience—by Baudrillard, Jameson, and Haraway—has been followed by studies such as Hayles's *How We Became Posthuman* (1999), Chris Hables Gray's *Cyborg Citizen* (2002), Neil Badmington's *Alien Chic* (2004), Takayuki Tatsumi's *Full Metal Apache* (2006), and Milburn's *Nanovision* (2008), all of which rely heavily on science-fictional figures to ground their analyses. We might consider that each of them is the performance of a kind of *critical* "science-fictionality," examples of what Csicsery-Ronay has called "the SF of theory."

Rose's *Alien Encounters* traces a perceived wearing out of genre materials and the waning of SF's conventional powers of imaginative extrapolation. For Rose, the horizon of SF's disappearance is already in sight. It is SF's capacity metaphorically to distance us from the present that is now its most significant feature, its capacity as discourse to estrange the present in order to map the "now" that, in Bigend's words, "can change so abruptly, so violently, so profoundly" (Gibson, *Pattern Recognition* 57). As this suggests, in many cases the impetus for this valorization of SF as a privileged technocultural discourse is the perceived breakdown in conventional ways of experiencing historical time. Thus, Jameson and Baudrillard, in different ways, signal the end of the authentic utopian imagination, and, much like Baudrillard, Benison aligns science fiction with the era of simulation, as a discourse participating in the disappearance of the "real" even as it is particularly attuned to addressing that same disappearance. Echoing Haraway, however, for some later scholars such as Hayles and Milburn, who write about the posthuman rather than the postmodern, the present is the site of a necessary critical resistance to the pressures of hegemonic technoculture, and science fiction is a potentially powerful discourse of resistance.

But is Rose correct in assuming that science fiction is showing signs of genre wear and tear? Or is this Rose's version of what Luckhurst refers to as "science fiction's death wish"? In his essay "The Many Deaths of Science Fiction," Luckhurst makes the case that "SF moves from crisis to crisis, but it is not clear that such crises come from outside to threaten a once stable and coherent entity. SF is *produced* from crisis, from its intense self-reflexive anxiety over its status as literature" (47; emphasis in original). What seems clear is that science fiction as a narrative genre continues—at least for now—to offer itself as a rich and complex site for examination, and genre criticism continues to thrive in full-length studies, in journals such as *Science Fiction Studies, Extrapolation,* and *Science Fiction Film and Television*, and in collections such as this *Handbook*— even as it must also now take account of the diffusion of science fiction into every facet of the social world.

As genre, science fiction is succinctly described by Luckhurst as "speculation on the diverse results of the conjuncture of technology and subjectivity" (222), which is very much in keeping with conventional ideas about science fiction as "thought experiment." As mode, science fiction offers itself as a kind of image-bank for a present that is itself deeply science-fictional, but to read SF in this way does not imply its disappearance as narrative. Indeed, Hayles makes a convincing case for the importance of narrative to her own theoretical studies of cybernetics and information systems:

> The literary texts do more than explore the cultural implications of scientific theories and technological artifacts. Embedding ideas and artifacts in the situated specificities of narrative, the literary texts give these ideas and artifacts a local habitation and a name through discursive formulations whose effects are specific to that textual body. (22)

And, just as Hayles emphasizes the links between story and theory, so too is it appropriate to emphasize the affinities between reading for genre and reading for mode in science fiction's estranged representations of the technoscientific present.

Who are some of our SF "theorists for technoculture," to borrow from Haraway? Jameson has often privileged cyberpunk texts, specifically Gibson's work, which almost single-handedly propelled science fiction into the purview of postmodernist theory. In his earlier work, both he and Baudrillard—and there are many others— have taken special account of Philip K. Dick's fiction, as a kind of world-building that renders transparent the workings of technocapitalism and its regimes of simulation. Haraway's "Manifesto" is a scattershot homage to some of the great feminist writers of the 1970s and 1980s, including Russ, Butler, and Delany. In her critical analysis of theories of posthumanism, Hayles also turns to Dick's writing, while also paying close attention to texts such as Greg Bear's novel of viral apocalypse, *Blood Music* (1985), and Richard Powers's slipstream fiction about artificial intelligence, *Galatea 2.2* (1995). Milburn references a multiplicity of SF materials, ranging from stories by James Blish and Theodore Sturgeon to episodes of *Star Trek*, to aid in his astute critique of the science-fictional rhetoric in which visions of the nanotechnological future are so often couched. Shaw reads Milburn's *Nanovision* as, in part, a demonstration that "the scientific imaginary and the science-fictional imaginary are inseparable in that they both emerge from within a culture that cannot imagine a future *other than* in terms of technology and its application" (169; emphasis in original). Or, as Csicsery-Ronay puts it, "It is impossible to map the extent to which the perception of contemporary reality requires and encourages science-fictional orientations" (*Seven Beauties* 3).

There are, of course, very many science fictions that strike readers as particularly attuned to the technocultural zeitgeist. Jack Womack's *Random Acts of Senseless Violence* (1992), as near-future a novel as it is possible to be without actually being set in the present, focuses on the economic decline of the American middle class, the increase in urban violence, and the rising power of global corporations. Maureen McHugh's *Nekropolis* (2004) explores the lives of the very poor in an Islamic future of intelligent androids and artificial slavery. Geoff Ryman's "mundane" SF novel, *Air (or, Have Not Have)* (2004), also moves outside the West to recount the experiences of an impoverished "third-world" village as a global communications network is about to come online. Cory Doctorow's *Eastern Standard Tribe* (2004) is concerned with time zones in the context of global culture, end-user design, and the legalities of music file-sharing. Ian McDonald's collection *Cyberabad Days* (2009) focuses on a near-future India where out-of-control technological development is on a collision course with traditional ways of being human. Paolo Bacigalupi's *The Windup Girl* (2009), another novel that examines global technoculture from the "margins" of the developed world, is concerned with international conflicts over food security and the fate of "lesser" nations in such conflicts. These are fictional works, set for the most part in near futures, that immerse their readers in the experiences of the contemporary, each performing its own tactics of pattern recognition.

From this perspective, Gibson's *Pattern Recognition*, in which contemporary reality and science fiction have become inextricably bound up with each other, is simply the logical end-point of science fiction's obsession with the present. It is, finally, impossible to maintain any significant distinction between SF as genre and SF as mode, or between SF as symptomatic of the regimes of simulation and SF as privileged perspective on technoscientific reality. SF serves not only as a narrative project finely attuned to the environment of technoculture but also as "the thesaurus of images" (Csicsery-Ronay, *Seven Beauties* 2) through which we "map" our lives in this environment. It is not only a body of stories about these lives, but also the discursive imaginary that constructs these stories.

And if, indeed, "we have no future," this is not necessarily a cause for lament, because it can imply something other than a failure of imagination or paralysis in the hyperreal. As Gibson puts it,

> This newfound state of No Future is . . . a very good thing. It indicates a kind of maturity, an understanding that every future is someone else's past, every present, someone else's future. Upon arriving in the capital-F Future, we discover it, invariably, to be the lower-case now.
> The best science fiction has always known that. . . . (*Distrust* 45)

Works Cited

Atwood, Margaret. *Oryx and Crake.* New York: Doubleday, 2003. Print.

Badmington, Neil. *Alien Chic: Posthumanism and the Other Within.* New York: Routledge, 2004. Print.

Baudrillard, Jean. "Two Essays: Simulacra and Science Fiction/Ballard's *Crash.*" 1981. Trans. Arthur B. Evans. *Science Fiction Studies* 18.3 (Nov. 1991): 309–20. Print.

Benison, Jonathan. "Science Fiction and Postmodernity." *Postmodernism and the Re-reading of Modernity.* Ed. Francis Barker, Peter Hulme, and Margaret Iversen. Manchester, UK: Manchester UP, 1992. 138–58. Print.

Bould, Mark, and Sherryl Vint. *The Routledge Concise History of Science Fiction.* London: Routledge, 2011. Print.

———. "There Is No Such Thing as Science Fiction." *Reading Science Fiction.* Ed. James Gunn, Marleen S. Barr, and Matthew Candelaria. New York: Palgrave, 2009. 43–51. Print.

Clute, John. "The Case of the World, Two" (review of *Pattern Recognition* by William Gibson). *Scores: Reviews 1993–2003.* Harold Wood, UK: Beccon, 2003. 403–06. Print.

Csicsery-Ronay Jr., Istvan. "Futuristic Flu, or, The Revenge of the Future." *Fiction 2000: Cyberpunk and the Future of Narrative.* Ed. George Slusser and Tom Shippey. Athens: Georgia UP, 1992. 26–45. Print.

———. "Science Fiction/Criticism." *A Companion to Science Fiction.* Ed. David Seed. Oxford: Blackwell, 2005. 43–59. Print.

———. *The Seven Beauties of Science Fiction.* Middletown, CT: Wesleyan UP, 2008. Print.

———. "The SF of Theory: Baudrillard and Haraway." *Science Fiction Studies* 18.3 (Nov. 1991): 387–404. Print.

Delany, Samuel R. "Some Reflections on SF Criticism." *Science Fiction Studies* 8.3 (Nov. 1981): 233–39. Print.

Derrida, Jacques. "The Law of Genre." Trans. Avital Ronell. *Critical Inquiry* 7.1 (Autumn 1980): 55–81. Print.

Evans, Arthur B. "The Origins of Science Fiction Criticism." *Science Fiction Studies* 26.2 (July 1999): 163–86. Print.

Evans, Arthur B., Donald M. Hassler, Veronica Hollinger, and Gary Westfahl. "A History of Science Fiction Criticism." *Science Fiction Studies* 26.2 (July 1999): 161–283. Print.

Flanagan, Mary, and Austin Booth, eds. *Reload: Rethinking Women and Cyberculture.* Cambridge, MA: MIT, 2002. Print.
Fowler, Alastair. "The Life and Death of Literary Forms." *New Literary History* 2 (1971): 199–216. Print.
Gibson, William. *Distrust That Particular Flavor.* New York: Putnam's, 2012. Print.
_____. *Pattern Recognition.* New York: Putnam's, 2003. Print.
Gray, Chris Hables. *Cyborg Citizen: Politics in the Posthuman Age.* New York: Routledge, 2002. Print.
Gunn, James. "Reading Science Fiction as Science Fiction." *Reading Science Fiction.* Ed. James Gunn, Marleen S. Barr, and Matthew Candelaria. New York: Palgrave, 2009. 159–67. Print.
Haraway, Donna. "A Manifesto for Cyborgs: Science, Technology, and Socialist Feminism in the 1980s." 1985. *Coming to Terms: Feminism, Theory, Politics.* Ed. Elizabeth Weed. 1989. New York: Routledge, 2013. 173–204. Print.
Hayles, N. Katherine. *How We Became Posthuman: Virtual Bodies in Cybernetics, Literature, and Informatics.* Chicago: U of Chicago P, 1999. Print.
Hollinger, Veronica. "Stories about the Future: From Patterns of Expectation to Pattern Recognition." *Science Fiction Studies* 33.3 (Nov. 2006): 452–72. Print.
Jakubowski, Maxim, and Malcolm Edwards. "Twenty Definitions of Science Fiction." *The SF Book of Lists.* New York: Berkley, 1983. 256–58. Print.
Jameson, Fredric. *Postmodernism, or, The Cultural Logic of Late Capitalism.* Durham, NC: Duke UP, 1991. Print.
_____. "Progress Versus Utopia; or, Can We Imagine the Future?" *Science Fiction Studies* 9.2 (July 1982): 147–58. Print.
Landon, Brooks. "SF Tourism." *The Routledge Companion to Science Fiction.* Ed. Mark Bould, Andrew M. Butler, Adam Roberts, and Sherryl Vint. London: Routledge, 2009. 32–41. Print.
Latham, Rob. Review of *The City and the City* by China Miéville. *eI* 9.6 (Nov. 2010). Web. May 14, 2012. http://efanzines.com/EK/eI53/index.htm#city.
Luckhurst, Roger. "The Many Deaths of Science Fiction: A Polemic." *Science Fiction Studies* 21.1 (Mar. 1994): 35–50. Print.
_____. *Science Fiction.* Cambridge, UK: Polity, 2005. Print.
Milburn, Colin. *Nanovision: Engineering the Future.* Durham, NC: Duke UP, 2008. Print.
Milner, Andrew. "Science Fiction and the Literary Field." *Science Fiction Studies* 38.3 (Nov. 2011): 393–411. Print.
Nicholls, Peter. "Critical and Historical Works About SF." *The Encyclopedia of Science Fiction.* Ed. John Clute and Peter Nicholls. New York: St. Martin's, 1993. 277–81. Print.
Rieder, John. "On Defining SF, or Not: Genre Theory, SF, and History." *Science Fiction Studies* 37.2 (July 2010): 191–209. Print.
Rose, Mark. *Alien Encounters: Anatomy of Science Fiction.* Cambridge, MA: Harvard UP, 1981. Print.
Shaw, Debra Benita. *Technoculture: The Key Concepts.* Oxford: Berg, 2008. Print.
Sofia, Zoë. "Exterminating Fetuses: Abortion, Disarmament, and the Sexo-Semiotics of Extraterrestrialism." *Diacritics* 14 (Summer 1984): 47–59. Print.
Suvin, Darko. *Metamorphoses of Science Fiction: On the Poetics and History of a Literary Genre.* New Haven, CT: Yale UP, 1979. Print.
Tatsumi, Takayuki. *Full Metal Apache: Transactions between Cyberpunk Japan and Avant-Pop America.* Durham, NC: Duke UP, 2006. Print.

Telotte, J. P. "'I Have Seen the Future': The New York World's Fair as Science Fiction." *A Distant Technology: Science Fiction Film and the Machine Age.* Hanover, NH: Wesleyan UP, 1999. 162–82. Print.

Tofts, Darren, Annemarie Jonson, and Allesio Cavallero, eds. *Prefiguring Cyberculture: An Intellectual History.* Cambridge, MA: MIT, 2002. Print.

Vint, Sherryl. "Science Studies." *The Routledge Companion to Science Fiction.* Ed. Mark Bould, Andrew M. Butler, Adam Roberts, and Sherryl Vint. London: Routledge, 2009. 413–22. Print.

Wasson, Sara, and Emily Alder, eds. *Gothic Science Fiction, 1980–2010.* Liverpool: Liverpool UP, 2011. Print.

Wolfe, Gary K. "History and Criticism." *Anatomy of Wonder: A Critical Guide to Science Fiction.* 5th ed. Ed. Neil Barron. Westport, CT: Libraries Unlimited, 2004. 523–612. Print.

———. "Pilgrims of the Fall." *Evaporating Genres: Essays on Fantastic Literature.* Middletown, CT: Wesleyan UP, 2011. 189–213. Print.

Wolfe, Gary K., with Amelia Beamer. "Twenty-First Century Stories." 2009. *Evaporating Genres: Essays on Fantastic Literature.* Middletown, CT: Wesleyan UP, 2011. 164–85. Print.

PART II
SCIENCE FICTION AS MEDIUM

CHAPTER 12

FILM

MARK BOULD

WESTERNS and crime movies played a key role in the early development of film studies, but serious critical discussion of SF film—like them, also typically gendered as a masculine genre—was surprisingly belated, presumably because of SF's cultural associations with the fantastic rather than the realistic, and with juvenility. The first major monograph did not appear until Vivian Sobchack's *The Limits of Infinity: The American Science Fiction Film, 1950–75* (1980; expanded as *Screening Space: The American Science Fiction Film* in 1987), the first major edited collection until Annette Kuhn's *Alien Zone: Cultural Theory and Contemporary Science Fiction Cinema* (1990), the first substantial retrospective collection until Sean Redmond's *Liquid Metal: The Science Fiction Film Reader* (2005), and the first dedicated journal until the 2008 launch of *Science Fiction Film and Television*. There are now a number of useful introductory volumes and critical treatments of specific periods, national cinemas, individual films, franchises, filmmakers, and technical/aesthetic issues, and SF films frequently provide extended examples for more overtly critical-theoretical matters. Substantial monographs remain relatively rare, however, and there is still no sustained critical treatment of non-Anglophone SF.

SF studies also marginalizes film, with less than 10 percent of the articles published in such journals as *Science Fiction Studies*, *Extrapolation*, and *Foundation* being concerned with nonprint media. Arguably, this neglect arises from the discipline's struggle for legitimacy: allying itself closely with literary studies and critical theory enabled it to disavow popular conceptions of SF as pulp fiction for socially awkward adolescents. Similarly, SF fandom—with which many early figures in SF studies were affiliated—has often sought to legitimate prose SF by differentiating it sharply from fantasy and horror, as well as from SF in other media. For example, John Baxter's *Science Fiction in the Cinema* (1970) claims that "[t]hroughout the history of science fiction it has been an article of faith among its readers that filmed SF was an abomination, that it degraded the field and provided nothing of interest to the serious mind" (7). Having claimed the spurious authority of dubious tradition (positive fan commentary on SF films appears as early as the 1930s [see Bould and Vint 44–45]), Baxter contends that SF films are so debased—their plots "tawdry," their "visual conventions . . . crude and unformed"—that "in a sense" they "are neither science fiction nor films" (7). A decade later, James Gunn's essay on teaching SF film begins with the claim that "there are virtually no good films that are also good science fiction" (205). A decade after that, in his history of SF film, John Brosnan stated that, "[b]y reading the real stuff over the years, I became increasingly annoyed with SF movies because they seemed to ignore most of the potential offered by science fiction" (xii) and concluded that "intellectually satisfying and visually evocative" SF films "remain the occasional happy accident" (388). Confirming Pierre Bourdieu's observation that when tastes "have to be justified, they are asserted . . . by the refusal of other tastes" (49), Baxter, Gunn, and Brosnan each suppress their own cultural situatedness so as to purvey their own preferences as either more or less objective truths or as representative of a general consensus.

Their statements contain other problematic obfuscations. In a synecdochic spiral, they equate a favored part of the US-British magazine-and-paperback SF tradition with the whole of that tradition, which in turn they treat as the whole—and, contradictorily, the *telos*—of not only prose SF but also the entire genre. Simultaneously, they homogenize a diverse body of films into an undifferentiated category from which they can extract an occasional exception. While they do effectively register a felt dissonance between SF cinema in general and the kinds of prose SF that they prefer, they do nothing with such insights beyond using them to perpetuate a quasi-Leavisite project of judgment, hierarchy, and canonization.

In contrast, Sobchack, having identified the unexamined premises of several similar statements and unpicked their faulty logic, attempts to distinguish SF from horror without constructing a hierarchical opposition:

> The horror film is primarily concerned with the individual in conflict with society or with some extension of himself, the SF film with society and its institutions in conflict with each other or with some alien other. . . . Both genres deal with chaos, the disruption of order, but the horror film deals with moral chaos, the disruption of natural order (assumed to be God's order), and the threat to the harmony of hearth and home; the SF film . . . is concerned with social chaos, the disruption of social order (man-made), and the threat to the harmony of civilized society going about its business. (29–30)

Although this distinction might appear value-neutral, its recursivity—like all genre definitions, it "infer[s] the defining characteristics of" each genre "from films that are already deemed to belong to" them (Moine 60)—suggests a similar, underlying cultural politics. Not only is Sobchack's conclusion—"the horror film evokes fear, the SF film interest" (43)—also her premise, but it perpetuates a hierarchy of taste articulated through the mind/body split, with SF connoting the (sophisticated, white, bourgeois, masculine, rational) mind and horror the (primitive, nonwhite, proletarian, feminine, irrational) body.

Having made this distinction, however, Sobchack notes the frequency with which it is muddied by individual films. For example, "the Monster or Creature film," which some consider to "most typify... the 'miscegenation' of the two genres," "causes purist critics the most trouble when they try to make abrupt distinctions between" them (30). Sobchack's oscillation between her categorizing impulse and her awareness of genres' heterogeneity serves as a reminder that Jacques Derrida's proclamation that "Genres are not to be mixed" (55) is not an iron law but an ironic observation. Phenomena tend to exceed the classificatory structures imposed upon them; and any boundary that can be drawn can also be erased, relocated, reinscribed, ignored, penetrated, permeated, abandoned. As Bruno Latour observes, it is only the urge to separate phenomena into purified categories that enables the creation of hybrids; and it is only because the world is heterogeneous—that is, full of phenomena that will subsequently be rediscovered as hybrids—that the purifying, categorizing impulse exists. Taxonomies designed to order and manage phenomena simultaneously—inevitably—generate exceptions, excesses, and omissions for which they cannot account. The abject critical language of generic miscegenation and impurity—and more celebratory discourses of creolization, syncretism, transgression, abjection, liminality, interstitiality, teratology, and the grotesque—register the shortcomings of such conceptual contrivances, while also leaving them intact.

Furthermore, the very notion of generic hybridity is challenged by poststructuralist conceptualizations of the text as, in Robert Stam's words, an "open... structuration... reworked by a boundless context," "feed[ing] on and... fed into an infinitely permutating intertext, which is seen through ever-shifting grids of interpretation" (Stam 57; see also Staiger, Bould). Genres are similarly heterogeneous and unstable. As Rick Altman demonstrates, they are not objects that already exist in the world but fluid and tenuous discursive constructions formed by the interactions of various claims made and practices undertaken by writers, producers, distributors, marketers, readers, fans, critics, and other discursive and material agents.

An example of this kind of discursive struggle can be seen in the critical reception of *Jigureul jikyeora!* (*Save the Green Planet!* [2003]), in which an amphetamine-gulping UFOlogist abducts a chemical company's celebrity CEO to torture him into confessing that he is an alien from Andromeda. Drawing on a range of national and transnational sources, it delights in foregrounding its open structuration and heterogeneous textuality. For example, when the CEO, strapped into a chair like Alex in *A Clockwork Orange* (1971), eventually admits to his extraterrestrial origins, the history of Andromedan interventions in terrestrial life he recounts is accompanied by a montage of biblical, pop-science, and pseudoscience illustrations, actual footage of wars and atrocities, and pastiches of *2001: A Space Odyssey* (1968). However, in an overt allusion to *The Usual Suspects* (1995), he has concocted this improbable narrative from words and images he found among the items littering his abductor's basement.

Unusually, *Sight and Sound* reviewed *Jigureul jikyeora!* twice. Kim Newman compared it unfavorably to the baroque revenge thriller *Oldeuboi* (*Oldboy* [2003]). He complains that it is incoherent, "scattershot," "ramshackle," and "keeps changing its mind" as to what kind of film it is, and finds its conclusion, which "takes a definitive leap into science fiction" as the fleeing Andromedans destroy the Earth, "simply wayward for its own sake" and "wildly out of place" (66). Significantly, although Newman alludes to other East Asian films, the cinematic references he evokes in describing, and identifying the flaws of, *Jigureul jikyeora!* are prompted by generic connections: wish-fulfillment superhero comedies, such as *Hero at Large* (1980) and *Blankman* (1994), and crime movies involving abduction and/or torture and/or a surprise apocalypse, such as *Ôdishon* (Audition [1999]), *Misery* (1990), *Calvaire* (The Ordeal [2004]), and *Dead or Alive* (1999). In contrast, Tony Rayns's review decries *Oldeuboi* as having "little or no interest in social realities" and argues that *Jigureul jikyeora!*, "far from being uncertain where it is going," is "a complex but entirely coherent lament for the fate" of the director's generation, who were "born and raised in" South Korea's "military dictatorship," which institutionalized violence, crushed political opposition, and massacred civilians (84). Rayns identifies the influence of Hollywood and Hong Kong action movies on the film's "tone, colour and . . . narrative drive," but argues that it "is not itself a conventional genre movie," even evoking Hitchcock as an auteur *sui generis* to praise the director's skill at "maintaining [audience] empathy" with such a damaged, brutal protagonist (84). Broadly, then, Newman judges *Jigureul jikyeora!* and other East Asian films through the lens provided by his understanding of American-derived genres, while Rayns does so through the lens of Korean culture and cinema, treating "genre" as if it were synonymous with "formulaic" and thus incompatible with the authentically cinematic. Newman looks for genre but finds chaos and generic failure, whereas Rayns finds significance in the film's supposed "transcendence" of genre. In both cases, these conclusions are largely determined not so much by the film as by the cultural situatedness of the critic and his attitude toward genre filmmaking.

Complaints that SF film fails to live up to the potential of prose SF are often accompanied by the suggestion that filmmakers should turn to SF writers for assistance; but when such collaboration takes the form of adapting an SF novel, the resulting film is often immediately dismissed as inferior to its source (see Landon 45–58). Such instances of the fidelity fallacy—the notion that an adaptation should somehow perfectly reproduce its source text in another medium—typically cast any divergence from the source as a failure to adapt it "properly." But, drawing on broader cultural prejudices about the superiority of older and linguistic arts over newer and visual ones (Stam 58), and deployed to articulate a specific taste-hierarchy as neutral and consensual, the cumulative dismissals of SF adaptations function to maintain such hierarchies by rendering adaptations axiomatically inferior to their sources (and thus SF film to prose SF).

Rather than arguing that many SF adaptations are at least as "good" or "interesting" as their sources (albeit perhaps in different ways), it is more productive to engage with the points of divergence between source and adaptation—these are likely to be the moments of greatest cinematic interest and, counterintuitively, of the greatest fidelity because, in negotiating between the capacities of the different media, the adaptation's choices often address the source's conscious and unconscious premises. For example, since contemporary blockbuster SF typically privileges spectacle and affect, adaptations commonly identify and extensively elaborate upon the source's more melodramatic, action-oriented, or spectacular elements. Therefore, while the stories collected in Isaac Asimov's *I, Robot* (1950) are little more than narrativized logic problems, a peculiarly limited form of story often popular in SF and detective fiction, the adaptation, *I, Robot* (2004), is little more than narrativized kinesis. However, while the film might minimize or ignore logic, it draws upon the full array of big-budget cinematic resources to depict futuristic places and spaces—something that consistently eludes Asimov's limited powers of description. These contrasts obscure certain of the adaptation's fidelities to its source, such as the cursory characterization (especially of women) and the uncanny replication of Asimov's slightly befuddled, liberal, and well-meaning antiracism, dependent on stereotypes and incapable of complexity (but not of creating contradictions). Some might dismiss such fidelities as merely coincidental or symptomatic rather than as representing a critical understanding of the source text, especially since doing so would enable the continued veneration of the author and prose SF over a director and a blockbuster movie that had the audacity to refuse more obvious similarities of plot and tone. So let us instead consider *Fahrenheit 451* (1966), which has frequently been decried in terms that pit its "auteur" director, François Truffaut, against beloved author Ray Bradbury.

Bradbury's relationship to the mid-century American magazine SF tradition was more vexed in the period in which he came to prominence than his subsequent canonization suggests. Unable to sell fiction to *Astounding*, generally considered the leading SF magazine of the 1940s, he was the first writer in the American pulp tradition to publish regularly in such middlebrow venues as *Collier's*, *The Saturday Evening Post*, *The New Yorker*, *The Best American Short Stories of 1946*, and *O. Henry Prize Stories of 1947*. Consequently, the SF community simultaneously used Bradbury to demonstrate the genre's growing maturity and considered him an SF author "for those who do not like SF" (Aldiss 296). James Blish praised his "artistry" but considered him "a scientific blindworm": while Bradbury's privileging of style and character over the dully written but "scientifically accurate story" associated with the decline of *Astounding* "did us good," he was nonetheless "in some respects . . . bad for the field" (100). Popular criticism of Truffaut's adaptation of Bradbury's *Fahrenheit 451* (1953) generally prefers the novel to the film, but nonetheless betrays a similar ambivalence. John Brosnan and Peter Nicholls suggest that "[t]he film is more ambiguous than the book and, so to speak, lacks its fire; Truffaut seems not altogether to accept Bradbury's moral simplicity" (401). Phil Hardy argues that "Truffaut's worst film . . . suffers from the director's commitment to character . . . at the expense of the novel's vision of life" but also praises the transformation of the Fire Captain into "a rounded, sympathetic character" (251–52). Frederik Pohl and Frederik Pohl IV contradictorily bemoan the absence of both Kubrick's "attention to detail" and Bradbury's "disdain for plausibility" (193). David Wingrove argues, even more contradictorily, that, because film is a more "passive medium" than literature, the film could not retain the novel's "black-and-white argument" (90). Taken together, these criticisms indict the adaptation for being more nuanced and sophisticated than its source.

This peculiar inversion of critical norms stems from the default privileging of source over adaptation, of prose SF over SF film, and of American narrative cinema over European art-house cinema, and also from the tradition of pulp storytelling, with its preference for unadorned prose and linear plotting over character, mood, style, and ambiguity. Curiously, though, critiquing the film from within this framework requires a transvaluation of the qualities of Bradbury's fiction for which it had previously been criticized. For example, Damon Knight sarcastically attributed Bradbury's broad popular success to his tendency to depict "radar and rocket ships and atomic power [as] big, frightening, meaningless things" and "to shrink all the[se] big frightening things to the compass of the familiar" (109–10). But in dismissing Truffaut's film, Bradbury's simplistic jeremiad against nonliterary media is reconstituted—and valorized—as "polemical sharpness" (Hardy 251), the fiery expression of moral clarity. Moreover, by distancing the novelist from the filmmaker, Bradbury is further recuperated by the US magazine SF tradition for which he had previously posed such a problem.

These ambivalences and transvaluations trouble the notion of adaptation if it is understood as "the process of adapting one original, culturally defined 'standard whole' in another medium" (Cardwell 19) by indicating the extent to which Bradbury's novel is not some fixed and pristine object but a heterogeneous, open, and fluid text whose meaning is the product of the discursive struggles around it. Treating the novel as precisely this kind of "standard whole," however, leads John Baxter to locate the source of the film's supposed failure in its contamination by another source: apparently, Truffaut was "unfortunately ... truer to his spiritual father Hitchcock than to Bradbury, and his *hommages* to the master—a fascination with the colour red, scenes directed more for tension than point, a black and cynical humour—leave little room for any but a vague retelling of the original story" (202). Baxter's suggestion that it is utterly inappropriate for the film to draw upon more than one source implies—yearns for— the possibility of an unmediated, ahistorical relationship between source and adaptation. Furthermore, Baxter's revulsion at this impurity causes him to overlook the role the Hitchcock allusions play in Truffaut's fidelity to, and critique of, Bradbury's novel.

In Bradbury's dystopian future, in which firemen are charged with burning books rather than putting out fires, Montag, a renegade fireman enamored of books, is forced to flee the city. He joins the book people, a band of hobos dedicated to memorizing texts. The novel ends on a euphoric note as, after a long-foreshadowed nuclear war, the book people advance on the devastated city. In contrast, the film ends with a static shot of a wintry lake, with the book people passing back and forth, muttering to themselves, memorizing. While Bradbury celebrates "the book people's transformation of themselves into a living library and arsenal for future revolutionaries," Truffaut "sees them as zombies," circling "in the snow endlessly intoning the world's literature," as "brainwashed in their commitment to that which they don't understand as [are] their book-burning persecutors" (Hardy 251). Such complaints about the film's divergence from the novel are premised on a failure to interrogate—as Truffaut does—the novel's peculiar fetishization of literature. Bradbury's book people have no engagement with the texts they memorize: they merely memorize them, destroy the hard copies, and seek to

FIGURE 12.1 Montag and the book people. *Fahrenheit 451* (1966).

stay alive until someone else has fought the revolution, after which they will speak the texts aloud to be transcribed and published. While Bradbury imagines the book people as a friction-free conduit between original texts, discrete and pristine, and their later, magically unmediated reproduction, Truffaut engages with the textuality and texturality of texts and with the processes of mediation (indeed, while Bradbury's book people have photographic memories, Truffaut's must labor at their task of preservation).

In a key passage, Faber, one of Bradbury's mouthpiece characters, defines the literary text in terms of its informational density and depth, its accumulation of observed and recorded detail that expresses a genuine experience of life. While this might hint at a conceptualization of the novel as, to use Roland Barthes's terms, a "scriptable" text that invites the reader's active participation in a critical and creative dialogue, *Fahrenheit 451* generally treats texts as "lisible," locating agency with the author, or perhaps the text, but not the reader—as can be seen, in exaggerated form, in the complete subordination of his book people to the books they memorize.

Despite the apparent wishes of his critics, Truffaut refuses to merely memorize and extrude Bradbury's novel on cue. For example, Truffaut's numerous allusions to Hitchcock's films, most explicitly to *Rope* (1948), *The Wrong Man* (1956), *Vertigo* (1958), and *The Birds* (1963), not only function—like Truffaut's very fast cuts, long takes, reversed footage, superimpositions, slow motion, repetition, negative footage, jump cuts, irises, wipes, extreme close-ups, whip pans, and dissolves to colored frames between sequences—to bring a sense of artifice and texture to the film, but also, by foregrounding the friction involved in the process of reworking a text in another medium, to disrupt the calm flow of faithful, unmediated transcription. By opening outward to admit intertexts, the film questions the putative purity of its major source (Bradbury's novel itself is a tissue of borrowings from the dystopian tradition of Yevgeny Zamyatin, Aldous Huxley, and George Orwell, and from contemporary media discourses about tranquilizers, sleeping pills, psychiatry, juvenile delinquency, drag-racing, rock and roll, credit, consumer durables, comic books, lurid paperbacks, pornography, censorship, abstract art, divorce, abortion, homosexuality, civil rights, and so on). Furthermore, the Hitchcock allusions function as an active remembering, rather than a passive memorization, of their sources, and their presence enlivens the film's relationship to the novel in the same way. The ability to perceive and appreciate this depends upon cultural situatedness, however (not least upon generational differences), and upon the transition from the new criticism of the 1920s through 1950s, which treated texts as self-contained and self-referential, to a poststructuralist paradigm starting in the 1960s, which is concerned with contingency, relationality, textual instability, and the death of the author.

Truffaut's careful, critical adaptation of Bradbury's novel indicates some of SF film's potential to be every bit as thoughtful and intellectually demanding as prose SF is purported, by many of its champions, to be. However, since the nature of the global media economy arguably confines such film-making to lower-budget, independent, and non-Anglophone cinemas, both popular criticism and theoretical work on SF film tend to focus on contemporary Hollywood and its imitators. The apparent dominance of cinematic SF since *Star Wars* (1977) and *Close Encounters of the Third Kind* (1977) by the spectacular blockbuster has led to the common refrain that contemporary SF "relies too heavily on . . . expensive and essentially 'empty' special effects" (King and Krzywinska 63), rather than on narrative, characterization, mood, tone, ideas, and so on. For example, Sean Cubitt describes films such as *Star Wars: Episode II—Attack of the Clones* (2002) in terms of a "clothes-line model" of "perfunctory narrative" along which "effects sequences" are hung:

> Each set piece sequence acts to trigger a rush of emotions: putting a clock on the action, staging the spin-off computer game. . . . The scream, the laugh, the tear, the white knuckles, the racing pulse: the stimuli are clichés because the emotions they elicit and that audiences seek are clichés. Market research ensures, as far as anything can, that expectations will be met. Of course, such expectations derive from the past, never from the future, and so the hectic overproduction of affects is only ever repetitive of old emotions. . . . [E]ach set-piece sequence miniaturizes the older classical plot into a few minutes of film, condensing as it simplifies the emotional content, delivering the intensified segment as an event in itself, and building, from the succession of events, a montage of affects. (238)

Steven Shaviro, discussing the frenetic *Gamer* (2009), argues that "contemporary film editing is oriented, not towards the production of meanings (or ideologies), but directly towards a moment-by-moment manipulation of the spectator's affective state (118); moreover, "The frequent cuts and jolting shifts of angle have less to do with orienting us towards action in space, than with setting off autonomic responses in the viewer" (124). Such criticisms can be understood as manifestations of an older, Frankfurt School-inspired suspicion of the audience's susceptibility to spectacular media, which also underpins Carl Freedman's argument—logically flawless but built on questionable premises—about the impossibility of SF cinema. Following Darko Suvin, Freedman conceptualizes prose SF as the literature of "cognitive estrangement," which, by depicting materially rationalized counterfactual worlds, prompts a Brechtian recognition of the constructedness—and thus radical reconstructability—of our own world. He conceptualizes SF cinema in terms of the dominance of special effects; for him, special effects are "filmic moments of a *radically* filmic character," drawing on the full resources of cinema *and* "self-consciously *foreground*[ing] their own radicality" (305, 307; emphasis in original). In SF, "special effects are deliberate triumphs of cinematic *technology*" that "*enact*, on one level, the technological marvels that the typical science-fiction film thematizes" on another (307; emphasis in original). However, if the cinematic experience reduces the viewer "to a passive, atomized spectator in a darkened room," then special effects' tendency "to overwhelm the viewer" intensifies "the authoritarian aspect of film" (306) by minimizing the "breathing room in which anything like a cognitive response might be formulated" (311). Therefore, the contradiction between critical cognition and authoritarian spectacle is irresolvable, and the only options are films that are "less radically cinematic (as with Ridley Scott) or less authentically science-fictional (as with Spielberg or Lucas)" (315).

Following work by Tom Gunning, André Gaudreault, and others on "the cinema of attractions" (see Strauven; Bukatman), it has become increasingly common to recognize the extent to which film has, since its origins, been as concerned with spectacle as with narrative. Consequently, there are a number of recent efforts to engage with SF spectacle in more nuanced ways. For example, Geoff King observes that denunciations of spectacular blockbusters are usually predicated upon an idealized classical narrative cinema that never actually existed, while also betraying a specific "politics of taste":

> An appreciation of "restraint," delayed gratification or the development of more complex, modulated narrative structures is the product of particular circumstances [and thus] built into the pleasures taken by those whose social, class or educational backgrounds provide a cultural capital that can be expended enjoyably in the celebration of such qualities. (166–67)

Despite their theoretical sophistication, Cubitt, Shaviro, and Freedman reiterate this hierarchy of taste and several associated oppositions—powerful apparatus/powerless subject, spectacle/narrative, affect/reason—and thus neglect the utopian sensations of abundance, energy, intensity, transparency, and community that entertainment spectacle can produce (see Dyer). Indeed, one of the key challenges facing the study of SF cinema is how to overcome these hierarchical oppositions, and "the affective turn" in cultural studies can provide some useful tools. If, as Laura U. Marks contends, "[f]ilm is grasped not solely by an intellectual act but by the complex perception of the body as a whole" (145), the appeal of cinematic spectacle is not necessarily just an affective one. Furthermore, Eve Kosofsky Sedgwick argues that affect should be understood not just as a response to "distinct transitory physical or verbal events" but also as a "complex interleaving of . . . causes, effects, feedbacks, motives, long-term states such as moods and theories" (104). Consequently, any serious discussion of SF film must allow for a greater complexity that reflects the synaesthesia of experience—we encounter the world through all our senses at once—rather than falling back unreflexively into thinking based on arbitrary analytical distinctions (for example, cognition vs. affect, narrative vs. spectacle).

Some preliminary engagements with SF in related terms have emerged in recent work on special effects. Michele Pierson describes the spectator as constantly "combining, overlapping, and alternating between consciousness of the illusion of reality produced by the film and surrender to the aleatory play of fantasy and remembering that the film's illusionistic effects invite" (20–21). The sense of wonder that special effects can produce partially depends upon this spectatorial double-consciousness that entertains belief in the images they produce while simultaneously "speculating about how they were achieved or ... identify[ing] their improvement on older methods" (Pierson 10). Dan North argues that "every film in which special effects play a significant part" is about "illusionism"—"*about* special effects," "techniques of visualisation," and "the real and its technological mediation" (2; emphasis in original). Furthermore, the visibility of the special effect as a special effect—and they all become visible eventually—provides a point "of access for the spectator's critical engagement with the film" (North 5).

To explore the inseparability of cognition and affect in response to special effects, let us turn to *Resident Evil: Extinction* (2007), the third entry in a popular but critically maligned, ad hoc film series derived from a video game franchise. It was written and produced—like all of the series—by Paul W. S. Anderson, who is best known and frequently derided for his financially successful video game adaptations, and directed by Russell Mulcahy, who was responsible for the cult hits *Razorback* (1984) and *Highlander* (1986), but who has mostly worked in television or direct-to-video since such high-profile underperformers as *Highlander II: The Quickening* (1991) and *The Shadow* (1994). The film opens with the series protagonist Alice waking, naked, in a shower. In scenes familiar from *Resident Evil* (2002), an earlier installment in the franchise, she puts on a red dress and boots, wanders through a mansion's hallway and into a glass-lined corridor, avoids its laser defenses, and finds herself in a Raccoon City hospital corridor. Making for the exit, she avoids one lethal booby-trap but is killed by another. Dr. Isaacs, an Umbrella Corporation scientist, orders two environment-suited technicians to dispose of Alice's body.

Cut to an isolated weather station shack in the Nevada desert. The floor slides open, the technicians emerge from the city-sized Umbrella Corporation facility hidden far underground, and they throw Alice's corpse into a concrete-lined ditch. The (virtual) camera tracks back, revealing dozens and dozens of identical corpses digitally composited into a single shot, and climbs up past the compound's fence to reveal the zombie hordes massing beyond. This Alice is not the protagonist after all, but Isaacs's 86th unsuccessful attempt to clone her so as to synthesize the cure to the zombie virus carried in her blood. The moment is simultaneously shocking and banal, thought-provoking and a reminder of the film's medium-sized ($45 million)

FIGURE 12.2 Alice's discarded clones. *Resident Evil: Extinction* (2007).

budget, and it raises questions on multiple levels: Is Alice really dead? Has the lead actress, Milla Jovovich, quit the franchise? Who are all these other Alices? Who is going to be the protagonist of this movie? Why does Anderson take such delight in displaying multiple, mutilated corpses of his actress wife? How was that shot filmed? Are all the corpses played by Jovovich? Are some of them body doubles? Are some of them purely digital creations? How much more convincing would the film have been if the producers spent more money making it? And would such efforts have rendered the film more convincing or would the number of dead Alices have simply increased?

Many consider the *Resident Evil* films to be disposable commodities: the animated corpse-form of an utterly reified product, splicing together fragments from a subcultural episteme—characters, incidents, and images from elsewhere in the multimedia franchise, and also, in this particular installment, from such diverse sources as *The Birds*, *The Andromeda Strain* (1971), *Mad Max 2* (1981), *Day of the Dead* (1985), and, via Richard Stanley's *Hardware* (1990) and *Dust Devil* (1992), spaghetti westerns—to produce a soulless revenant, reproducing endlessly for no purpose beyond simple profit-taking. But the revelation of dozens of dead Alices is the first of several complexly self-reflexive moments in the film that speak about the commodity form (including actresses and images of women) and its structuration of late-capitalist subjectivity. From the outset, this clone-Alice questions her identity, pondering her scars and her reflection in mirrored surfaces. Later, the "real" Alice meets Claire Redfield—a character from the second game introduced into the films as a potential replacement protagonist, as was Jill Valentine, a character from the first game, in *Resident Evil: Apocalypse* (2004)—who dresses like the Sarah Connor of *Terminator 2: Judgment Day* (1991) and is accompanied by K-Mart, a teenager who looks and dresses like her. Close-ups of Alice's face are sometimes digitally airbrushed, as if willing her to become a game avatar or animated character so as to be able to dispose of the actress playing her entirely—as happened to Claire in the feature-length motion-captured CG *Resident Evil: Degeneration* (2008).

Amid the simulacral architecture protruding from the sands that have engulfed Las Vegas (now doubly a desert of the real), Alice, who has spent five years "off the grid," avoiding detection by sidestepping the Umbrella Corporation's surveillance satellites, is reacquired, and Isaacs takes over her motor coordination, freezing her in place. This intervention is signaled by CG images of the Corporation's global communications infrastructure—part of the series' self-conscious pattern of utilizing certain kinds of CGI, including wire-frame three-dimensional maps of Umbrella's facilities, to signal a crude auctorial intervention to redirect the narrative so as to meet the expectations of contemporary commercial cinema (while also transforming a budgetary constraint into a house style). Alice uses psychic powers to burn out the control chip and regain control of her body; but no matter how much affective freedom and agency Alice's actions (or the gameplayer's gameplay) might s(t)imulate, the film, like the games, is relentlessly goal-oriented. She eventually, inevitably, infiltrates the Corporation's facility and kills Isaacs, broadcasting a threat to Umbrella's remaining board members that she and "a few of [her] friends" are coming for them. In the final shot of the film, Alice and the newly "born" 88th clone stand side by side in front of a window, and the (virtual) camera tracks back from them, revealing dozens of additional clones stirring into consciousness. Revising the earlier image of numerous Alice corpses, it offers the illusion of Alice(s) escaping the control of—and wreaking further revenge upon—the Corporation, and thus an upbeat ending to the film (and potentially the series), while also implying further installments if this one proves financially successful. (It did, leading so far to *Resident Evil: Afterlife* [2010] and *Resident Evil: Retribution* [2012], as well as an as-yet-untitled sixth film scheduled for 2015 release, and two CG films, *Resident Evil: Degeneration* and *Resident Evil: Damnation* [2012].)

As even such a brief account of *Resident Evil: Extinction* demonstrates, by engaging simultaneously with SF and medium specificity (even in an age—and product—of media convergence), one can move beyond the construction of taste-hierarchies to a richer, critical understanding of individual texts. Furthermore, the serious treatment of SF in film and other media has the potential to expose the extent to which the critical truisms and theoretical shibboleths of SF studies are as much about the prose medium as the genre, and to provide tools with which to better recognize and understand prose SF's own extensive fascination with spectacle and affect.

Works Cited

Aldiss, Brian W. *Billion Year Spree: The History of Science Fiction*. 1973. London: Corgi, 1975. Print.

Altman, Rick. *Film/Genre*. London: BFI, 1999. Print.

Barthes, Roland. *The Pleasure of the Text*. 1973. Trans. Richard Miller. New York: Hill and Wang, 1975. Print.

Baxter, John. *Science Fiction in the Cinema*. 1970. London: Tantivy, 1979. Print.

Blish, James (as William Atheling, Jr.). *The Issue at Hand: Studies in Contemporary Magazine Science Fiction*. 1964. 2nd ed. Chicago: Advent, 1973. Print.

Bould, Mark. "Genre, Hybridity, Heterogeneity; Or, The Noir-SF-Vampire-Zombie-Splatter-Romance-Comedy-Action-Thriller Problem." *A Companion to Film Noir*. Ed. Andrew Spicer and Helen Hanson. Oxford: Blackwell, 2013. 33–49. Print.

Bould, Mark, and Sherryl Vint. *The Routledge Concise History of Science Fiction*. London: Routledge, 2011. Print.

Bourdieu, Pierre. *Distinction: A Social Critique of the Judgement of Taste*. 1979. Trans. Richard Nice. 1984. London: Routledge, 2010. Print.

Bradbury, Ray. *Fahrenheit 451*. New York: Ballantine, 1953. Print.

Brosnan, John. *The Primal Screen: A History of Science Fiction Film*. London: Orbit, 1991. Print.

Brosnan, John, and Peter Nicholls. "*Fahrenheit 451*." *The Encyclopedia of Science Fiction*. 1979. 2nd ed. Ed. John Clute and Peter Nicholls. London: Orbit, 1993. 401. Print.

Bukatman, Scott. *Matters of Gravity: Special Effects and Supermen in the 20th Century*. Durham, NC: Duke UP, 2003. Print.

Cardwell, Sarah. *Adaptation Revisited: Television and the Classic Novel*. Manchester, UK: Manchester UP, 2002. Print.

Cubitt, Sean. *The Cinema Effect*. Cambridge, MA: MIT, 2004. Print.

Derrida, Jacques. "The Law of Genre." Trans. Avital Ronell. *Critical Inquiry* 7.1 (1980): 55–81. Print.

Dyer, Richard. "Entertainment and Utopia." *Only Entertainment*. London: Routledge, 1992. 17–34. Print.

Fahrenheit 451. Dir. François Truffaut. 1966. Universal Pictures UK, 2003. DVD.

Freedman, Carl. "Kubrick's *2001* and the Possibility of a Science-Fiction Cinema." *Science Fiction Studies* 25.2 (July 1998): 300–18. Print.

Gunn, James. "The Tinsel Screen: Science Fiction and the Movies." *Teaching Science Fiction: Education for Tomorrow*. Ed. Jack Williamson. Philadelphia: Owlswick, 1980. 205–18. Print.

Hardy, Phil. "*Fahrenheit 451*." *The Aurum Film Encyclopedia: Science Fiction*. Ed. Phil Hardy. London: Aurum, 1995. 251–52. Print.

I, Robot. Dir. Alex Proyas. 2004. Twentieth Century Fox, 2004. DVD.

King, Geoff. *Spectacular Narratives: Hollywood in the Age of the Blockbuster*. London: I.B. Tauris, 2000. Print.

King, Geoff, and Tanya Krzywinska. *Science Fiction Cinema: From Outerspace to Cyberspace*. London: Wallflower, 2000. Print.

Knight, Damon. *In Search of Wonder: Essays on Modern Science Fiction*. 1956. 2nd ed. Chicago: Advent, 1967. Print.

Kuhn, Annette, ed. *Alien Zone: Cultural Theory and Contemporary Science Fiction Cinema*. London: Verso, 1990. Print.

Landon, Brooks. *The Aesthetics of Ambivalence: Rethinking Science Fiction Film in the Age of Electronic (Re)Production*. Westport, CT: Greenwood, 1992. Print.

Latour, Bruno. *We Have Never Been Modern*. 1991. Trans. Catherine Porter. Brighton, UK: Harvester, 1993. Print.

Marks, Laura U. *The Skin of the Film: Intercultural Cinema, Embodiment, and the Senses*. Durham, NC: Duke UP, 2000. Print.

Moine, Raphaëlle. *Cinema Genre*. Trans. Alistair Fox and Hilary Radner. Oxford: Blackwell, 2008. Print.

Newman, Kim. "Save the Green Planet!" *Sight & Sound* 14.11 (Nov. 2004): 66. Print.

North, Dan. *Performing Illusions: Cinema, Special Effects and the Virtual Actor*. London: Wallflower, 2008. Print.

Pierson, Michelle. *Special Effects: Still in Search of Wonder*. New York: Columbia UP, 2002. Print.

Pohl, Frederik, and Frederik Pohl IV. *Science Fiction Studies in Film*. New York: Ace, 1981. Print.

Rayns, Tony. "Shock Tactics." *Sight & Sound* 15.5 (May 2005): 84. Print.

Redmond, Sean, ed. *Liquid Metal: The Science Fiction Film Reader*. London: Wallflower, 2005. Print.

Resident Evil: Extinction. Dir. Russell Mulcahy. Prod. and written by Paul W. S. Anderson. 2007. Sony Pictures, 2008. DVD.

Save the Green Planet! [*Jigureul jikyeora!*]. Dir. Joon-Hwan Jang. 2003. Tartan, 2003. DVD.

Sedgwick, Eve Kosofsky. *Touching Feeling: Affect, Pedagogy, Performativity*. Durham, NC: Duke UP, 2003. Print.

Shaviro, Steven. *Post-Cinematic Affect*. Hampshire, UK: Zero, 2010. Print.

Sobchack, Vivian. *Screening Space: The American Science Fiction Film*. New York: Ungar, 1991. Print.

Staiger, Janet. "Hybrid or Inbred: The Purity Hypothesis and Hollywood Genre History." *Perverse Spectators: The Practices of Film Reception*. New York: New York UP, 2003. 61–76. Print.

Stam, Robert. "Beyond Fidelity: The Dialogics of Adaptation." *Film Adaptation*. Ed. James Naremore. London: Athlone, 2000. 54–76. Print.

Strauven, Wanda, ed. *The Cinema of Attractions Reloaded*. Amsterdam: Amsterdam UP, 2006. Print.

Wingrove, David. *Science Fiction Film Source Book*. Harlow, UK: Longman, 1985. Print.

CHAPTER 13

RADIO AND TELEVISION

J. P. TELOTTE

JEFFREY Sconce's comment about the emergence of uncanny electronic texts—"[w]herever streams of consciousness and electrons converge in the cultural imagination, there lies a potential conduit to an electronic elsewhere" (92)—offers an appropriate lead for considering the development of radio and television science fiction, because it recalls an important convergence that has helped to define the "elsewhere" that is today's media SF. Early in the twentieth century, even as radio was beginning to find a mainstream audience and as television was largely a subject of conjecture and experimentation, a parallel was emerging in the popular consciousness between SF's development and that of these two electronic media. In fact, both radio and television were often framed in the same context of science and speculation that pushed the growth of SF literature, thereby linking these media to the new genre in which they often served as key icons. We might recall how Hugo Gernsback, the "father" of contemporary SF, in his various electronics and popular science magazines (for example, *Radio News, Radio and Television, Science and Invention*), anticipated this intersection of speculative discourses by freely interspersing articles on radio and television technology with SF stories. In the process he forecast a relationship wherein our electronic media and SF not only shared in each other's evolving identities but also suggested the key role that would be played by these delivery technologies. For those new, science-fictional media would not only provide powerful platforms for staging tales of scientific imagination but also forms that would, self-consciously, draw the media into their exploring and contesting of the genre's nature.

The substance of much early SF radio shows another element of convergence, for it traces from the same background that would later inspire SF film serials and fledgling television efforts—the pulp magazines and comics prominent in the 1920s and 1930s. These first radio efforts told a very appropriate *radio story*, for they were essentially about new technologies, like radio, that could take audiences "elsewhere": space operas that emphasized rocket-powered adventuring, action usually played out on a grand scale, packaged within a formulaic, violence-spiced narrative, aimed at young male listeners. This is the model of such early radio series as *Buck Rogers* (1932–36, 1939–40,

1946–47) and *Flash Gordon* (1935–36), both of which would generate film adaptations and later short-lived television versions. But more than space adventures, they foregrounded the new-found ability to communicate over vast distances—as Sconce notes, this era even associated "wireless with distant, interplanetary communication" (97)— and the use of technology, given emphasis through various promotional giveaways and toy products, to expand the reach of human culture, to suggest the reality of that "electronic elsewhere" and a possible future for radio.

However, as radio became a feature of every home and a center of domestic activities—as it became less science-fictional and less pointedly "elsewhere"—the medium itself began to generate other possibilities, ones that pointedly exploited its character. In fact, by the late 1930s radio SF had become almost as diverse as that appearing in the popular pulp magazines. Recognizing the genre's potential appeal to an adult audience, as well as its narrative flexibility, programmers began including SF or fantasy narratives in the anthology-type shows that were a broadcast staple from the mid-1930s into the 1950s. Hardly the first example of such programming, but easily the most famous, was Orson Welles's 1938 adaptation of *The War of the Worlds* for his *Mercury Theater on the Air*. Broadcast on Halloween and in the wake of the recent war posturings in Europe, this single episode incited a public panic and media uproar that demonstrated the potential of an SF that was rooted in reality, that tapped into contemporary cultural anxieties, and that exploited radio's implicit promise of communication from anywhere. Indeed, the power of such programming was further illustrated when Howard Koch's radio script was translated into Spanish, the events given a local setting, and the show broadcast in Chile in 1944 and, five years later, in Ecuador. In both instances, panic again ensued, despite "a systematic press campaign . . . warning the public that the play was going to be presented and that it should not be taken literally" (Lucanio and Coville 63).

To less spectacular impact, but also reaching for a growing SF audience, other anthology shows began mixing in an archive of canonical SF literature with original SF scripts or story adaptations. *Radio Guild*, for example, adapted Karel Čapek's landmark 1920 play about robots, *R.U.R.* (1933), while also broadcasting the futuristic story "The Man Who Was Tomorrow" (1939). *Columbia Workshop*, devoted to more experimental programming, also adapted *R.U.R.* (1937); aired a story by journalist Paul Y. Anderson, "An Incident of the Cosmos" (1937), in which aliens witness and comment upon a minor cosmic "incident," the destruction of Earth; and later aired William N. Robson's time-travel tale "Do Not Open for 5,000 Years" (1939). And the popular *Favorite Story* program adapted numerous classic SF works, including *Frankenstein* (in 1946), *Twenty Thousand Leagues Under the Sea* (in 1947), and *The Time Machine* (in 1949). This anthologizing of SF, interspersed with other narrative types, was especially attractive programming because it capitalized on radio's implicit appeal to the imagination, while also allowing for various sorts of spectacular aural effects.

Further exploiting those appeals were specialized shows of the 1940s and 1950s devoted to the fantastic in its various forms. Long-running series like *Suspense* (1940–62), *Escape* (1947–54), and *Inner Sanctum* (1941–52) usually began with the implicitly reflexive call for listeners to let their imaginations go, to let the fantasy take over. What typically followed was a formulaic, highly dramatic program emphasizing sound effects and sudden twist endings, with material recalling the best of the pulp magazines, again mixed with adaptations of classic SF. The most successful series, *Suspense*, originally emphasized murder and mystery stories, but it also provided an early forum for such figures as Curt Siodmak and H. P. Lovecraft, offering adaptations of *Donovan's Brain* (a two-episode show of 1944) and "The Dunwich Horror" (1945), as well as pulp magazine authors like Robert Arthur Jr., who contributed the time-travel story "The Man Who Went Back to Save Lincoln" (1962). *Escape*, which began with an announcer's promise to "free you from the four walls of today for a half-hour of high adventure," twice broadcast versions of *The Time Machine* (1948, 1950), as well as space and time-travel stories like "Mars is Heaven" (1950) and "The Man from Tomorrow" (1953). And while *Inner Sanctum* was most noted for its eerie atmosphere—iconically established with its signature opening sound of a creaking door—it regularly interspersed stories that straddled genres, with titles that readily betrayed the SF pulps' influence, including "The Man of Steel" (1941), "The Mad Doctor" (1941), "The Man Who Couldn't Die" (1945), and "The Conquest of Death" (1947), all tales in which disembodied sounds melded with fantastic narrative to form a highly effective "electronic elsewhere."

As SF found new prominence in film and the fledgling television medium in the 1950s, radio entered into a difficult time, one Erik Barnouw terms a "period of desperation" (288); as the medium's place in the entertainment industry was threatened, its *elsewhere* looked to become a *nowhere*. Yet this "desperation" also produced "spurts of boldness and creativity" (Barnouw 288), including the first appearance of dedicated SF radio series. Recalling the best of the pulps, these shows include *Beyond Tomorrow* (1950, scripted by Robert A. Heinlein), *2000 Plus* (1950–52), *Dimension X* (1950–51), *Tales of Tomorrow* (1953), and the *Dimension X* revival, *X Minus One* (1955–58). All were anthology shows that anticipated some of the groundbreaking television programs that would follow, such as *Science Fiction Theatre* (1955–57) and *The Twilight Zone* (1959–64). Especially noteworthy is *Dimension X*, described by one commentator as "the first science fiction show for adults" (Nachman 189). It featured adaptations of some of the era's leading SF writers, including Heinlein, Isaac Asimov, Ray Bradbury, Frederik Pohl, and Clifford D. Simak, and its audio drama gained an otherworldly assist from musical director Albert Berman's introduction of the theremin, the electronic instrument whose eerie effects would, after its use in films like *The Thing from Another World* (1951) and *The Day the Earth Stood Still* (1951), become an aural signature for many later media efforts in SF and fantasy. *Dimension X*'s successor, *X Minus One*, aimed for a similar adult audience of genre fans, allying itself with one of the period's top SF publications. Thus, its opening narration each week promised listeners "stories of the future, adventures in which you'll live in a million could-be years on a thousand maybe worlds . . . in cooperation with *Galaxy Magazine*." While none of these series were long-lived, their primary clustering in the early to mid-1950s is significant, attesting to a growing fascination with media SF, even as radio itself was beginning to seem old-fashioned and its original technological link to the genre—its own science-fictional character—was disappearing.

In fact, another wave of SF radio in this era would look not so much to the world of SF literature, but rather to another technology, to television itself. Thus, the early 1950s saw a group of juvenile-oriented programs that, while recalling the space operas of the 1920s and 1930s, was obviously tracking the genre's sudden impact on television. Shows like *Planet Man* (1950), *Space Patrol* (1950–55), *Tom Corbett, Space Cadet* (1952), and *Captain Starr of Space* (1953–54) provided young audiences with a connection to television's wildly popular and quickly proliferating space operas, such as *Captain Video, Space Patrol*, and *Tom Corbett, Space Cadet*. In fact, the casts for *Space Patrol* and *Tom Corbett* were the same in both media, with plot points often overlapping so that audiences might see these space adventures as electronic extensions of the televisual ones, as part of an expanding *media elsewhere*. But with this modeling of the new television series, these programs were already pointing up the new medium's seeming takeover of the genre and its own role in establishing a new elsewhere for SF.

Yet even as television was altering radio's role in popular entertainment, radio programming continued—and continues to this day—to contribute on a regular basis to the SF imaginary. In the United Kingdom especially, the BBC has sustained a strong record of quality SF series and specials on radio, including such notable programs as *Satellite Seven* (1958), *The Day of the Triffids* (1960), *Orbit One Zero* (1961), *Host Planet Earth* (1965), *The Slide* (1968), *The Foundation Trilogy* (1973), *Out of the Silent Planet* (1977), *The Hitchhiker's Guide to the Galaxy* (1978, 1980, 2004, 2005), *Earth Search* (1981–82), *Space Force* (1984–85), *The Quatermass Memoirs* (1996), *Blake's Seven* (1996–98), and *Planet B* (2009, 2011). And in keeping with that tradition, various other countries of the former British Empire have also regularly experimented with such programming, aimed at both children and adults, among them South Africa's *SF68* (1968) and *Challenge of Space* (1972), Australia's *Dr. Jekyll and Mr. Hyde* (1943–44) and *Rocky Starr* (1950–63), and Canada's *The Kraken Wakes* (1965), *The Secret of Dominion* (1984), *Johnny Chase, Secret Agent of Space* (1978–81), and *Canadia: 2056* (2007).

And in the United States as well, while SF television has reached new heights of popularity and largely replaced radio as a key venue for new series, radio SF retains a measure of popularity, both as nostalgic performance and as a delivery vehicle for new sorts of marvelous and uncanny stories. National Public Radio's productions of *Tales from the Other Side* (1992) and *Radio Tales* (1996–2002), the latter subsequently airing from 2002 to the present on satellite radio, have tried to recapture the spirit of the anthology shows of the 1940s and 1950s, while also reviving the classics of the genre, among them *Frankenstein* (1999), *Journey to the Center of the Earth* (2000), *20,000 Leagues Under the Sea* (2001), and *War of the Worlds* (2001). And a modern classic, George Lucas's *Star Wars* saga (1977–), has also been adapted for NPR (1981, 1983, 1996), with many of the film actors reprising their roles for the radio dramatizations. Interspersed with contemporary SF stories, these various adaptations demonstrate not only that radio retains the power to move the imagination, but also that some element of the early link between SF and radio technology may linger and can still be tapped for powerful effect.

While radio SF continues to demonstrate its own appeal, television SF has probably had a far more significant impact on the genre's development, in part because of its own implicitly science-fictional nature. In fact, Gerald Nachman argues that "radio really wasn't as good a medium for science fiction" because "futuristic high-tech wizardry has to be seen to be thrilled to" (191). And indeed television, like early radio, was initially framed in a science-fictional mode—as a regular feature of SF discourse and as a recurrent icon of the genre. It was featured in the various popular science magazines (including Gernsback's *Radio and Television* and *The Electrical Experimenter*); it was a common element in the literature; and in SF films and serials of the 1920s and 1930s, from *Metropolis* (1927) to *S.O.S.—Tidal Wave* (1939), television appeared as a ubiquitous, intrusive, and sometimes dangerous technology. Indeed, as Joseph Corn and Brian Horrigan suggest—and in a way that practically describes SF itself—in that period "the idea of television in our future heated the popular imagination as few technologies ever have" (24). It was, as the movies presented it, a sign of technological modernity, of a promising temporal "elsewhere" that, especially given the horrors of the two world wars, was much to be desired.

Yet capitalizing on its technological promise proved difficult, due to the limited budgets of early television and the constraints of the technology—as John Ellis offers, it was marked by a "characteristically pared down" image (112). Thus, while the United Kingdom's first efforts at public television broadcasting included several ambitious adaptations of classic SF, versions of Çapek's *R.U.R.* in both 1938 and 1948, and of Wells's *The Time Machine* in 1948, these were stagey, dialogue-heavy efforts. And the first real explosion of televised SF in postwar America essentially replayed the pattern of radio SF's emergence, with the space opera taking center stage, albeit in a rather earth-bound mode, again due to budget limitations. But these series—*Captain Video* (1949–55), *Tom Corbett, Space Cadet* (1950–55), *Space Patrol* (1950–55), *Rod Brown of the Rocket Rangers* (1953–54), *Rocky Jones, Space Ranger* (1954–55)—despite their minimalist special effects, pointed to what a contemporary commentator termed "video's magic world of tomorrow" (Robinson 31). For they were clearly marked, as Lincoln Geraghty notes, by an "aesthetics of technological innovation and visualizations of the future" (27)—that is, suggestions of the sort of visual excitement viewers normally associated with cinematic SF. And their repeated depictions of video screens and video monitoring devices, their stylistic reliance on reaction shots and looks of outward regard, and, especially in the case of *Captain Video*, their embedding of other narratives—old serial episodes—that viewers, along with the onscreen characters, were enjoined to watch, demonstrated a remarkable self-consciousness about television storytelling, as if they were all engaged in another sort of SF adventuring: exploring how SF might best function in this newest electronic elsewhere.

And indeed, this impulse would be further developed in another wave of SF programming: the anthology shows that, while recalling the radio anthologies of earlier years, introduced a new level of narrative sophistication, adult focus, and visual development. Programs like the Ivan Tors and Maurice Ziv-produced *Science Fiction Theatre*, which began each episode with the pledge to "show you something interesting"; Rod Serling's justly famous and expensively produced *The Twilight Zone*, which promised to "unlock…another dimension"; and the more special effects–oriented

The Outer Limits (1963–65), which told viewers, "We will control the horizontal. We will control the vertical. We can roll the image, make it flutter. . . . [S]it quietly and we will control all that you see and hear"—all directly addressed their implicitly adult audiences, promising them something that would capitalize on television's possibilities. And with their generally first-rate scripts, written by such figures as Jack Finney (*Science Fiction Theatre*), Richard Matheson and Rod Serling (*The Twilight Zone*), Joseph Stefano and Harlan Ellison (*The Outer Limits*), they consistently provided SF drama that competed well with the conventional theaterlike drama so popular on American television in the 1950s and 1960s, shows like *General Electric Theater, Kraft Television Theater,* and *Playhouse 90.*

Indeed, *The Twilight Zone*—arguably the most important of television SF shows and one that would twice be revived (in 1985–89 and 2002–03)—helped counter a growing sense that the genre, as embodied in those early space operas, represented "a subliterary form of culture designed to appeal to children or to . . . lowbrow plebeian tastes" (Booker 8). It did so not only with higher budgets, talented writers, and obvious parallels to the highbrow live-action dramatic anthologies, but also with its cinematic style. For *Twilight Zone* was shot on film by veteran cinematographers like George T. Clemens, it used the prop and set resources from the MGM movie studio, and it was helmed by talented Hollywood directors, including Richard Donner, Don Siegel, and Jacques Tourneur. Moreover, it demonstrated a sophisticated self-consciousness through episodes that focused on the power and nature of the media. It formed, as a result, more than what Sconce terms a "perverse 'unconscious' of television" (134); it was also a link to the cultural unconscious, suggesting the media-haunted—as well as science and technology-haunted—nature of contemporary America.

Besides lending sophistication to television SF, *The Twilight Zone* also set in motion the exploration of a broad spectrum of narrative possibilities, as it ranged across the genre: space adventures, utopias/dystopias, alien encounters and alien invasions, time and dimensional travel, tales of extraordinary technology, alternate worlds, and comic takes on conventional SF forms, all with an adult appeal. Consequently, *Twilight Zone* helped make possible the revisioning of earlier forms, a revisioning that would show in two of the most influential of subsequent SF series, *Doctor Who* (1963–89, 1996, 2005–) and *Star Trek* (1966–69). Both have roots in that earlier flood of space operas, with *Doctor Who*, the longest-lived of all SF series, recalling early television's *Captain Z-Ro* (1951–56) and its educational tales of travels to real historical events, and *Star Trek*, which has generated more spinoffs than any other series, linking those other, often Earth-centric adventure shows to the infinite wonders of "space, the final frontier," as its pre-credits voiceover weekly announced.

Both of these series also underscored the very promise of their medium, their televisuality. For *Doctor Who*, with the Doctor's TARDIS as his iconic travel vehicle, literally opened up a new dimension for audiences—surprised companions repeatedly observed, "It is larger inside than out," only to exit the TARDIS and encounter some new time and place, a different reality. And *Star Trek*'s starship *Enterprise*, with its panoramic viewing screen—pointedly having a wider aspect ratio than a conventional

FIGURE 13.1 "Nightmare at 20,000 Feet," an episode of *The Twilight Zone*.

FIGURE 13.2 Tom Baker, the fourth Doctor, menaced by Daleks in *Doctor Who*.

television screen—always seemed not only to propel viewers "where no man has gone before," as its introduction promised, but also, like the anthology shows, to permit them to *see* what no one had seen before, at least on network television. While justly praised for exploring topics that were seldom the stuff of broadcast television—racism, women's rights, social prejudice—both shows also provided viewers, in a way that previous SF television had seldom managed, an immediate visual correlative to that "aesthetic experience of wonder" that Michele Pierson (168) and others have identified as one of media SF's essential appeals.

While its own visual appeal was significant—indeed, the starship *Enterprise* quickly became an SF icon—*Star Trek* is most noteworthy for the work of another of the most influential figures in the form's development, Gene Roddenberry. Already a well-established media writer, Roddenberry created the concept for *Star Trek* by pitching it as "*Wagon Train* in space"—an allusion to one of the period's top western programs, as well as to its own effort at offering audiences a new elsewhere. Although the resulting adventures of the *Enterprise* in the twenty-third century would in its initial run prove only moderately successful (in its peak season, it ranked 52nd among all series [Brooks and Marsh 1119])—it attracted a new and highly loyal audience in syndication, inspired a series of feature films, spawned an animated series (1973–75), and provided the seed for a host of more ambitious and successful spinoffs. Behind this longevity and continued success, Roddenberry would claim, was a consistent narrative emphasis on social commentary, on addressing our "cultural consciousness." He believed that, by focusing on "a new world with new rules, I could make statements about sex, religion, Vietnam, unions, politics and intercontinental missiles" (qtd. Fulton 429). Yet just as crucial to its reception was its optimistic visualization of the future, or as Booker terms it, a "compelling (and heartening) future image" (51) that showed our problems being worked out, technology serving us usefully, and humanity successfully encountering other life forms. In such effects, *Star Trek*—and no less later versions of *Doctor Who*—reflexively engage and illuminate the very nature of media SF, as a form that continually struggles to bring its technologically based vision to the screen, while also suggesting a place for this vision beyond the limits of that same screen, as if its narratives were always trying to reach beyond, to escape the screen of fiction, to argue for their possible reality and pertinence to life itself.

With their ability to take viewers anywhere and to immerse them in almost any sort of narrative, these series also point up the larger trajectory of SF television during this period. For the 1960s ushered in a wide array of SF programming: shows about extraordinary explorations (*Lost in Space* [1965–68], *Time Tunnel* [1966–67]), extraordinary technology (*Voyage to the Bottom of the Sea* [1964–68]), extraordinary encounters (*The Invaders* [1967–68], *Land of the Giants* [1968–70]), comic encounters (*My Favorite Martian* [1963–66]), and even animated SF (*The Jetsons* [1962–63], *Astroboy* [Japan, 1963–66], *The Adventures of Jonny Quest* [1964–65]). Inflected by the space race of the era and by the appearance of such big-budget SF films as *Fantastic Voyage* (1966), *Planet of the Apes* (1968), and especially *2001: A Space Odyssey* (1968), these series demonstrate not only how SF was becoming highly popular programming, but also visually and

FIGURE 13.3 Captain James T. Kirk and Science Officer Mr. Spock, from the original *Star Trek* TV series.

narratively ambitious, challenging film's own version of that "aesthetic experience of wonder."

Contributing to that development was another key figure in SF television, Irwin Allen. An Academy Award–winning director, writer, and producer, he created four series and, like Serling, brought a highly cinematic sensibility to each. His most successful program, *Voyage to the Bottom of the Sea*, was adapted from his 1961 film of the same title, and it established a popular formula for scientific adventure, usually centered around a piece of extraordinary technology—a stand-in for television itself—such as a submarine, flying saucer, or time machine. Although Allen seldom explored the sorts of cultural issues that marked Serling's or Roddenberry's work, he gave his visually spectacular narratives a basic human focus, as they explored how people respond when faced with unusual or extraordinary circumstances, and that focus arguably helped broaden their appeal beyond that of the usual SF audience. At the same time, Allen's series, with their larger budgets, large casts, and use of filmlike special effects, brought a big-screen look to television SF, and with that, greater audience expectations for the genre. While they have received scant critical praise, Allen's effects-heavy adventure series led viewers to expect to *see* more from television SF, to see images and effects that until then had been the province of film.

Moreover, Allen's work paved the way for another moment of media convergence, and indeed what suggests a kind of identity struggle for SF television in the 1970s. Following *Voyage to the Bottom of the Sea* came other efforts at copying big-screen hits, notably *Planet of the Apes* (1974) and *Logan's Run* (1977–78). Both drew heavily on popular cinematic originals, the former using some original cast members and striking make-up developed for the film, and the latter borrowing the original's model work and costuming. However, both would prove short-lived. The main, if moderate successes of this period were two linked series that explored a new area for SF, biotechnology, while also examining how individuals might respond to such developments. *The Six Million Dollar Man* (1975–78) and its spinoff *The Bionic Woman* (1976–78) told the stories of government employees who, following serious injuries, were reconstructed by government scientists and turned into realistic superheroes. But as Geraghty observes, each was "as much a crime or detective series as a science fiction drama" (63). They did effectively foreground various media effects—slow motion, special sound effects, and point-of-view shots—to suggest the activated superpowers of their protagonists, in the process inserting a reflexive commentary on technological manipulation. However, their real-world context, evoking the current headlines scientists were making with the creation of various human prostheses, along with their more commonplace crime-fighting plots, represented a marked shift from the fantastic worlds of shows like *Planet of the Apes* and *Logan's Run*, and suggested a genre in search of a new, more realistic identity within the cultural imagination.

For a time, that identity struggle was resolved not in favor of real-world concerns and contemporary science, but by more efforts at copying film, as the sudden and phenomenal success of *Star Wars* (1977) and its sequels reenergized fantasy and space-adventure formulas. *Battlestar Galactica* (1978–80), *Buck Rogers in the 25th Century* (1979–81), and the British *Blake's 7* (1978–81) were all highly ambitious series, having fairly large budgets—*Battlestar Galactica*'s was the highest to date for a prime-time series (Brooks and Marsh 93)—big casts, elaborate special effects, and epic plots that recalled the *Star Wars* universe George Lucas had quickly but firmly implanted in the popular imagination. The first of these detailed the epic wanderings of a space fleet, bearing humanity's ancestors after their home planets were destroyed by rebellious robots. While nominally updating the earlier comic strip, radio series, and film serial, *Buck Rogers* clearly patterned its protagonist on *Star Wars'* Han Solo, even giving him a robot assistant that recalled the film's droids, R2D2 and C3PO. And *Blake's 7*, in chronicling the efforts of a small group of rebels to subvert the dominant Federation, similarly echoed *Star Wars'* story of rebel resistance to a repressive galactic empire. Moreover, the scope of these series was matched by their advances in television effects and model work—a point underscored by *Battlestar Galactica*'s employment of John Dykstra, responsible for many of *Star Wars'* innovative effects. In these series—and others that followed—we also see the continuing shift from an SF radio aesthetic to a television one, or as Jan Johnson-Smith characterizes it, "from a predominantly verbal medium into a predominantly visual medium" (61).

The convergence of cinematic and televisual models of SF would be furthered throughout the 1980s, as a spate of successful films emphasizing themes of alien encounters and alien invasion—works like *E.T.: The Extra-Terrestrial* (1982), *Aliens* (1986), *Predator* (1987), and *Alien Nation* (1988)—found their reflection in such series as *The Powers of Matthew Star* (1982–83), *V* (1984–85), *Starman* (1986–87), *War of the Worlds* (1988–90), *Alien Nation* (1989–91), the situation comedy *ALF* (1986–90), and a reinvigorated *Doctor Who*. As in the films, the aliens depicted in these series were both threatening and benevolent, even comic. They would lend new possibilities to various familiar narrative types, as in *Alien Nation*'s revamping of the police drama and *The Powers of Matthew Star*'s vision of the high school student as not only an alienated character but also a true alien—a concept further explored in *Roswell* (1999–2002). And they would offer repeated testimony to a growing cultural paranoia and sense of insecurity, attitudes brought into sharp focus in the long-running *The X-Files* (1993–2002).

Yet arguably more influential in this period was another sort of encounter with aliens and another sort of self-referentiality—that found in Gene Roddenberry's return with *Star Trek: The Next Generation* (1987–94). As Johnson-Smith observes, Roddenberry did not want to risk upsetting "the established audience dynamic" (108) of the original series, which had produced a dedicated cult following of "Trekkers," immersed in the *Star Trek* mythos. So the new series, while set 80 years beyond the first program's events, largely followed its predecessor's model. Although the cast and crew were new, it had the same sort of multiracial—and multispecies—composition as the original. They carried out their interstellar explorations in an updated starship *Enterprise-D*. And thanks to a larger budget, the new series sported first-rate special effects. But most important, like the original series, it too deployed its more convincingly realized futuristic settings and situations to explore contemporary cultural concerns.

If not quite as obviously conscious of its status as media product as some other series, *The Next Generation* would soon develop another sort of self-referentiality—one suggesting its mindfulness of what Paul Virilio terms the "media nebula" of contemporary culture (69). Exploiting the new dynamic of television consumption provided by cable—and later satellite—broadcasting, which produced the possibility for reaching niche audiences and a demand for more product, it would spin off other series, creating narrative lines that allowed for cross-series character appearances and cross-referencing of key events and issues. Thus, before *The Next Generation* finished its original run, and despite Roddenberry's death in 1991, another syndicated effort was launched in 1993, *Star Trek: Deep Space Nine* (1993–99), which was eventually followed by *Star Trek: Voyager* (1995–2001) and the prequel narrative *Enterprise* (aka *Star Trek: Enterprise*, 2001–05). These series would elaborately expand on the *Star Trek* mythos, not only by narrative cross-referencing, but also by tracing out a history of the United Federation of Planets and the work of its Starfleet, and by elaborating on several popular motifs or plot threads, such as the menace of the Borgs or the interspecies conflict between the Cardassians and the Bajorans, woven throughout the series. If at times these sequels and prequels, because of their mutual referentiality, tended to become "backward—not forward-looking" like the original series (Johnson-Smith 109), they also helped ring in what Booker terms "an unprecedented period of richness and innovation" (108) in SF television, as their narratives branched out, intersected, and produced a compelling future history that increasingly resonated with our own. Moreover, these and other series of the 1990s demonstrated the medium's new-found ability to generate, largely independent of the film industry, a powerful narrative world that could flourish in the new television viewing environment.

FIGURE 13.4 Captain Jean-Luc Picard kidnapped by the Borg in *Star Trek: The Next Generation*.

Taking a new approach to the SF mission of exploring and expanding that "electronic elsewhere," and launched by one of those new outlets, was another highly resonant and trajectory-shifting series, Fox Network's *The X-Files*. Rather than taking viewers on exploratory interstellar voyages, this program argued, as protagonist Fox Mulder repeatedly asserts, that "the truth is out there"—that is, in our world, waiting to be seen and explored. It little resembled anything then available on the film screen, as it ranged across a variety of fantasy concerns, including horror, supernatural phenomena, and urban legends, while binding them within the series' larger and gradually clarified focus on a government cover-up of alien activity. The show's two central characters, FBI agents Mulder and Dana Scully, effectively represented two sides in the public debate about UFOs and other unexplained phenomena, with the former, because of earlier experiences, a firm believer in such things and the latter, a trained forensic scientist, always skeptical about the incidents they investigate. When Scully is abducted by aliens, becoming an X-file case herself, the series' prime emphasis becomes the investigation of an elaborate alien plot for Earth's conquest. Yet that investigation is never simple or complete; it repeatedly takes audiences towards that "truth…out there," only to swerve off, become involved with other mysteries, or pull back from a final revelation. If *The X-Files*' contemporary setting and police-procedural scenarios often made it seem more like a detective mystery than SF, its foregrounding of what Booker describes as a "postmodernist mode of epistemological skepticism" (142) and its emphasis on an unfolding approach to narrative—coupled with an increasing media self-consciousness—would prove appealing and influential. Its success would lead to two feature film versions (1998, 2008); generate a short-lived spinoff about conspiracy investigators, *The Lone Gunmen* (2001); and build a cult following of "x-philes," as they called themselves, that nearly rivaled that of *Star Trek*.

Given its narrative convolutions and its skeptical/paranoiac vision, it is hardly surprising that *The X-Files* initially had few imitators, apart from NBC's *Dark Skies* (1996–97), which lasted just 19 episodes. Yet eventually *The X-Files*' postmodern patterns, its emphasis on narrative—and media—convergences, translated into a string of SF-inflected investigation and conspiracy series, among them: *Taken* (2002), *Lost* (2004–10), *Invasion* (2005–06), *Eureka* (2006–12), *Fringe* (2008–13), *Dollhouse* (2009–10), and *Warehouse 13* (2009–14), as well as a somewhat un-SF-like but successful and ultimately genre-stretching series by Joss Whedon, *Buffy the Vampire Slayer* (1997–2003). In these series, a realistic, mostly present-day setting provides the unexpected context for narratives involving time travel, dimensional travel, teleportation, or simple unexplained occurrences, often associated with either real or suspected alien activity. And that amazing amalgam of the everyday and the fantastic, and of constantly intersecting narratives, is commonly marked by a mixture of tone as well, as episodes slide into a comic or absurd register that, as with *The X-Files*, corresponds to the suspicion of reality itself that is one of the driving forces of most postmodern narrative.

Yet while these paranoid investigations of reality, with their implicit commentary on the medium itself, have become a dominant mode of SF television in the early twenty-first century, an earlier narrative model still proves a powerful vehicle for the cultural imagination. For the contemporary viewing environment, with its ability to target specific audiences and offer inexpensive digital special effects, has also given new life to the narrative model of the various *Star Trek* series. Of particular note are shows like the syndicated *Babylon 5* (1992–98) and *Stargate SG-1* (1997–2007), the longest-running SF series on US television; the SyFy Channel's *Farscape* (1999–2003) and the Fox network's *Firefly* (2002), both of which developed dedicated cult followings; the computer-animated *Star Wars: The Clone Wars* (2008–13), a continuation of George Lucas's SF film epic; and the ambitious remake of *Battlestar Galactica* (2003–09), whose tale of apocalyptic conflict between humans and their robot creations foregrounds contemporary issues of gender, race, class, and genocide. All of these series offer variations on the space opera, all depend heavily on digital effects, and, apart from *Stargate SG-1* and *Star Wars: The Clone Wars*, all draw more on television traditions than the cinema. In fact, the ability of these postmodern space operas to find great popularity at the same time as the skeptical/paranoiac series attests not just to a struggle for generic identity, but to the health and broad popularity of SF on television.

One might well argue that today television is the most important venue for media SF. Having a cable outlet, SyFy Channel, dedicated to the genre is one sign of that importance, especially since that channel is constantly developing new content, while also making available to a new generation of viewers such classic series as *Twilight Zone* and *Star Trek*. In Britain, the BBC has dedicated nights to SF and fantasy programming and is funding a variety of such series: the revival of *Doctor Who* by Russell T. Davies; the spinoffs from that series, *Torchwood* (2006–11) and *The Sarah Jane Adventures* (2007–10), and the animated *The Infinite Quest* (2007); the time-travel police shows *Life on Mars* (2004–07) and *Ashes to Ashes* (2008–10); the dimensional travel adventure *Primeval* (2007–11), resulting in a Canadian spinoff, *Primeval: New World* (2012–13); and the comic space adventure *Red Dwarf* (1988–99, 2009, 2012–). Significantly, the contemporary spate of television SF has generated a new relationship with the cinema, affording a number of opportunities for direct-to-video movie adaptations and inspiring big-screen offshoots, such as the two *X-Files* films, a host of *Star Trek* movies, and the highly successful translation of the *Firefly* series, *Serenity* (2005). SF television has, in effect, hit the big time.

Of course, television was from its early days itself seen as science-fictional and presented as an icon of the form. So its ability today—like radio earlier—to serve as a home for all manner of SF narratives should seem quite fitting. But as Johnson-Smith reminds us, "As broadcast technology has advanced and increased, so have our expectations, and we demand so much more" (252). In the media, though, the genre incorporates that very demand, not only in the way it speaks of our hopes for progress and the future but also in its own consistent efforts at visualizing an "experience of wonder," at modeling its own responses to such "expectations." We might only expect that television, in its current or some evolved 3D, holographic, new-media form, and delivered on a variety of personal electronic devices, will continue to provide us with a "conduit to an electronic elsewhere"—in fact, continue to envision various elsewheres. In effect, in SF television's very success we can find one more sure reflection of the form, of its constant struggle for identity, and of its future potential.

Works Cited

Barnouw, Erik. *The Golden Web: A History of Broadcasting in the United States.* New York: Oxford UP, 1968. Print.

Booker, M. Keith. *Science Fiction Television: A History.* Westport, CT: Praeger, 2004. Print.

Brooks, Tim, and Earle Marsh. *The Complete Directory to Prime Time Network and Cable TV Shows, 1946–Present.* 1979. 8th ed. New York: Ballantine, 2003. Print.

Corn, Joseph J., and Brian Horrigan. *Yesterday's Tomorrows: Past Visions of the American Future.* Baltimore, MD: Johns Hopkins UP, 1996. Print.

Ellis, John. *Visible Fictions: Cinema, Television, Video.* 1982. Rev. ed. London: Routledge, 1992. Print.

Fulton, Roger. *The Encyclopedia of TV Science Fiction.* 1990. 3rd ed. London: Boxtree, 1997. Print.

Geraghty, Lincoln. *American Science Fiction Film and Television.* New York: Berg, 2009. Print.

Johnson-Smith, Jan. *American Science Fiction TV: Star Trek, Stargate and Beyond.* Middletown, CT: Wesleyan UP, 2005. Print.

Lucanio, Patrick, and Gary Coville. *Smokin' Rockets: The Romance of Technology in American Film, Radio and Television, 1945–1962*. Jefferson, NC: McFarland, 2002. Print.

Nachman, Gerald. *Raised on Radio*. New York: Pantheon, 1998. Print.

Pierson, Michele. *Special Effects: Still in Search of Wonder*. New York: Columbia UP, 2002. Print.

Robinson, Murray. "Planet Parenthood." *Collier's* 129 (Jan. 5, 1952): 31, 63–4. Print.

Sconce, Jeffrey. *Haunted Media: Electronic Presence from Telegraphy to Television*. Durham, NC: Duke UP, 2000. Print.

Virilio, Paul. *A Landscape of Events*. Trans. Julie Rose. Cambridge, MA: MIT, 2000. Print.

CHAPTER 14

ANIMATION

PAUL WELLS

ANIMATION has a long and prominent place in the history of the science fiction film, from the early trick-film works of Segundo de Chomón to the 3D stop-motion classics of Ray Harryhausen to dystopic anime and the visual-effects-laden blockbusters of the contemporary era. As Susan Napier has noted, "The free space of the animated medium . . . is ideal for depicting the free spaces of science fiction and fantasy. . . . The overt technology of the animation medium highlights in a self-reflexive way the technological basis of the science fiction genre and the artificiality of fantasy" (106). These self-reflexive qualities of animation enable the form to absorb the common signifiers of the SF genre—future worlds, spaceships, aliens, megalomaniac scientists, and so on—and offer a commentary on technology, representation, social mores, and cultural practices. Kaveney draws upon the concept of the "thick text" to explain such an approach, noting "the precondition of reading or recognizing a thick text is that we accept that all texts are not only a product of the creative process but contain all the stages of the process within them like scars or vestigial organs" (5). SF animation should also be understood as a thick text on the basis that it is essentially defined by its process, its embrace of generic elements, and, crucially, its self-conscious interrogation of the interface between its reference points and sources. King and Krzywinska have commented that there is sometimes a disparity in the perception of SF cinema as dumbed-down spectacle and SF literature as inherently "intellectual" (56). I wish to suggest that animation reconciles this apparent anomaly by occupying a self-consciously constructed space between a concentration upon the image as a heightened aesthetic expression and the image as an expression of a core concept or metaphor.

Animation predominantly engages with mainstream SF cinema by echoing or parodying its core iconography. Thereafter, its thick text is composed of two key aspects: first, the ways in which science-fictional concepts emerge in coincidence with the presence of animation as an experimental aspect of film form (this has occurred in the development of early cinema and throughout the history of special effects), and second, in relation to the rich tradition of SF illustration present in pulp magazines, graphic narratives, comics, concept art, and the covers of major novels. The latter aspect also locates animation within the broader literary context epitomized in the imagery of Jules Verne, Edgar Allan Poe, and H. G. Wells.

Illustrator and artist J. J. Grandville, though best known for his anthropomorphized caricatures of creatures, provides a starting place by which the tracking of animated science fiction begins. "Another World" (1844), his pretechnological engagement with mid-nineteenth-century culture, has a lengthy but highly pertinent subtitle: "Transformations, visions, incarnations, ascensions, locomotions, explorations, peregrinations, excursions, stations, cosmologies, fantasmagories, reveries, folâteries, facéties, lubies, metamorphoses, zoomorphoses, lithomorphoses, metempsychoses, apotheoses et autres choses" (Holland and Summersby 18). Such a list effectively defines both animation as a form and science fiction as a burgeoning genre, but, crucially, it does so as a model of processes and transitions in the representation, perception, and experience of change and development. It is this that fundamentally allies animation and science fiction as visual forms, and was first properly evidenced through the global reach of the illustrated stories of Jules Verne.

Verne's *Journey to the Center of the Earth* (1864) and *From the Earth to the Moon* (1865) remain seminal and influential texts, and even though the narratives may have suffered in translation, the illustrations of Edouard Riou and Henri de Montaut remained unchanged in numerous editions worldwide. The impact and effect of this imagery, given the commercial popularity of Verne's work, are beyond question, and it operates not merely as illustration but as an interpretation of the narratives, often with pedagogic value. Verne's alternative worlds prompted visual representation, which in turn suggested alternative ideas, and the possibility that the modern world could be viewed as a platform for experimentation and progressive agendas—an idea taken up by the early pioneers of proto-SF cinema.

It is customary to suggest that the Lumière brothers, Auguste and Louis, defined early cinema's preoccupation with the everyday world in what might be regarded as the primitive documentary shooting of short reels like *Workers Leaving the Lumière Factory* (1895). It was not long, though, before Georges Méliès's work came to emblematize the counterthrust of early film as a vehicle for fantasy, in over 500 films made between 1895 and 1914, most characterized by in-camera visual effects. His *A Trip to the Moon* (1902) and *The Impossible Voyage* (1904) have been retrospectively seen as some of the first SF films, embracing Verne-style imagery alongside the more outward-facing imperatives of twentieth-century modernity. Right from the beginning of cinema itself, then, visual effects were a staple of science fiction, effectively and efficiently depicting alternative worlds. Some of these effects are essentially the frame manipulations and stop-motion animation later properly identified as a technique, or a specific trick, rather than simply experimental "play" in the service of amusing or seemingly magical outcomes.

As the work of Grandville and particularly the illustrations in Verne's stories passed into the popular imagination, so, too, did the illustration of Frenchman Albert Robida, who initially pastiched the work of Verne but later brought his prolific skills to works like *The Twentieth Century: The Electric Life* (1890). Anticipating the rise of contemporary media, fast global travel, consumer culture, and modern industrial warfare, Robida amusingly drew the world as manufactured and man-made, often implying that embedded in such activity was humankind's inevitable downfall. Such themes were echoed in Segundo de Chomón's films, in which, like those of Méliès's (whose films he hand-tinted at Pathé Frères), there is a conscious engagement with the modernity of the cinematic apparatus. Chomón helped to move early cinema from the initial attractions in short vignettes of comic or exaggerated action to a more narrative-focused preoccupation with the meaning of stop-motion animated effects. *The Electric Hotel* (1907) simultaneously exhibits the joys and anxieties imbued in a futuristic hotel, where luggage unpacks itself and brushes autonomously clean shoes, straighten hair, and shave beards. Too much electric current, however, renders all the furniture subject to chaotic motion and the breakdown of the previously elegant order of the hotel. Here, then, Chomón anticipates the utopian/dystopian tension in many progressive visions but distilled into comparable metaphorically charged vignettes. In one moment, the magical technologies of electrically imbued objects serve men and women, bestowing passivity and calm upon humanity, yet later the same technology renders their world in disarray. More than 100 years later, Pixar's *Wall-E* (2008) takes up the same theme. Overindulgent passivity makes humankind literally unable to move, their world already lost to the chaos of misused technologies.

Chomón also echoed Méliès's Vernian journeys in *Excursion to the Moon* (1908) and *Voyage to Jupiter* (1909), using a whole range of visual effects, effectively illustrating human aspiration to explore space and the desire to experience the other worlds revealed by the increasing quality of astronomical images and their mediation through popular publications. As Lynda Nead has pointed out (201–46), this kind of film-making emerged from the views of figures like astrologer Camille Flammarion, who believed that astronomical photographs should be seen as creative acts of transportation in which the viewer might imagine other worlds and embrace the universe as an infinite space, of both sacred and secular possibility. The shift from the still image to the moving one required a new way of seeing, a modern engagement with the simultaneity of the emergence of new science and technology with fresh codes and conditions of visual interpretation. Animation mediated this new way of seeing: as Nead again suggests, "Animation is a consequence of the long, lingering and penetrating gaze into the image. Looking becomes an aesthetic and erotic reverie, a kind of enchanted rapture that creates life..." (58). This enchanted rapture was to inform animation's engagement with science-fictional themes thereafter.

Such was the dynamic nature of change in the early twentieth century; it was clear that the impact of science and technology on everyday life needed mediating to ordinary people. Flammarion published his best-selling book *Popular Astronomy* (1880; English translation 1894), and periodicals emerged in the United States such as *Popular Science Monthly*, edited in 1915 by one Max Fleischer, who noted, "I realised that I was not only artistically inclined but had a keen and instinctive sense of mechanics" (Cabarga 18). Once the Fleischer brothers established their animation studio, they, like Disney (and early pioneers such as J. Stuart Blackton, Emile Cohl, and Winsor McCay, who preceded them), were essentially developing a modern medium in animation to engage with the modern world. As such, cartoons in this period can be read as a quasi-science-fictional tool for the projection of, and reflection upon, a world in transition—a modernity taking shape by negotiating its relationship with antiquity and by establishing new rhythms and speeds of social and cultural existence (see Leslie; Klein, *Seven Minutes*; and Wells, *Animation*).

This tension with the old world is perhaps best expressed through the seminal stop-motion features *The Lost World* (1925) and *King Kong* (1933) (see Wells, *Animated Bestiary* 1–18, 88–90). Essentially, these are tales in which the primordial order is arrayed against the commercial and intellectual ethos of the new America, engaging with issues of exploitation and alienation as well as visions of progress grounded in scientific inquiry. Crucially, though, what was at stake in these films was the deployment of animated effects that had to sustain the narrative. *King Kong* could only work if its 12-foot-tall animated puppet became persuasive as a giant gorilla, inflamed by a plausible but only implied anthropomorphic tendency. The audience had to accept Kong's "animality" as the embodiment of a passion, frustration, and anger caused by the denial of his freedom and by love thwarted. Beauty ultimately killed the beast, but clearly the underlying issues relate powerfully to the deep anxieties of modernity in relation to identities revealed and changed by industrial and commercial progress. Consequently, the very empathy prompted by Kong in the light of his alienation and death makes him one of science fiction's most engaging characters.

Brian W. Aldiss has noted that many skeptics view science fiction as lacking such characters but insists anyway that its key character is actually the environment—changing landscapes that effectively act as narratives with complex messages and projections of human ideas and values (see Holland and Summersby 8). It is this theme that animation explicitly defines and explores throughout its history, but especially during the early to mid-twentieth century. "Space" is both a conceptual idea and a creative context, and in essence, despite the familiarity of much of their content in rural tales and broad slapstick, all cartoons seemed to function as alternative worlds. Crucially, though, some undertook an explicit engagement with the emergent scientific ideas of the period. In 1923 the Fleischers made *Einstein's Theory of Relativity*, featuring the earth spinning compared to a speeding bullet, demonstrating that, compared to the earth's rotation, the bullet seemed as if it was traveling backward. Animation could clearly reveal the broad conceptual premise of scientific ideas but present them with an almost science-fictional visual veneer.

The biggest impact in relation to the animated SF cartoon, though, was clearly the artwork for illustrated fiction in publications like *Amazing Stories* and *Astounding Stories*, where the sometimes lurid color palettes and space-opera vistas of Frank R. Paul, Leo Morey, and Howard Brown influenced the war-time Superman cartoons by the Fleischers and Chuck Jones's designer, Maurice Noble, in masterpieces such as *Duck Dodgers in the 24½th Century* (1953). Both the Fleischer and Warner Brothers studios realized at one and the same time that they needed to reflect the cultural zeitgeist yet project such topicality into more timeless contexts of adventure and comic surreality.

The notion of "space" as concept and context very much informs the thematic agendas of these works. J. P. Telotte has noted that the Superman cartoons "cue us to see their stereoptical effects *not* as coded signs of the real, as demonstrations of this world's three-dimensionality, but rather as atmospheric and even thematic tropes, even as another voice through which the narrative might speak of the dark and subversive forces at work in this world" (*Animating Space* 105; emphasis in original). In *The Mechanical Monsters* (1941), for example, Superman is not merely challenged by thieving flying robots, but by entrapment in telephone wires and abandonment on an alien natural world, the latter a consistent challenge to the ultimately ultra-urbane Superman. The Fleischers embraced the art deco designs and scale of William Dold and Hubert Rogers's imagery, prioritizing the ways in which Superman essentially mediated the space between the everyday modernism of New York City and the interventions of mad scientists and alien technologies. In *The Magnetic Telescope* (1942), a scientist defies a ban to magnetize a comet into the earth's atmosphere for study and research, only to see the reckless approach of the police prompt his machine to go wrong and genuinely endanger the city. The comet defeats Superman's initial attempts to merely break it apart, destroying trains, vehicles and buildings, and the situation is only brought under control when Superman harnesses the power of the scientist's original magnet and his own strength and stamina. This is surely a veiled message about aligning brain and brawn—and rethinking scientific policy in periods of conflict—rather than relying merely on brute force.

In *The Electric Earthquake* (1942), a Native American claims that New York actually belongs to his people and insists the *Daily Planet* publish the truth. When his request is refused, he threatens, "Maybe modern science will make you think differently." His machine induces an earthquake in the city, but he is thwarted by Superman, who prevents further damage, wrecks the scientist's lab, and, of course, saves Lois Lane—all of this, for the most part, taking place underwater. Superman must necessarily prevent disaster, but there remains an ambivalence in the cartoon about the Native American's original claims and the role and function of the press—the destruction of the city coordinated from beneath the sea, here, almost operating as a literal illustration of the return of the repressed.

While the Superman cartoons played their part in axis-crushing propaganda in shorts such as *Japoteurs* (1942) and *Jungle Drums* (1943), it is the more localized stories like *The Arctic Giant* (1942) that display science fiction's customary tension between utopian ambition and dystopian outcomes, often reconciled in a reactionary status quo. Advanced technology has excavated and preserved a huge Godzilla-like creature from the prehistoric world, but a small accident when an oil can falls into its refrigerated container at the Museum of Natural Science causes the creature to thaw, come to life, and rampage across the city. Superman saves civilians from broken bridges and ravaged buildings, and eventually entraps the giant for display in the zoo. Echoing the Kong narrative, and anticipating the creature-feature B movies of the 1950s, it demonstrates animation's ability to reconcile time and space and to determine plausible speculations as a consequence of the ontological equivalence of its imagery. Superman is a quintessential SF figure, in that his co-presence as Clark Kent and as a superhero helps mediate the relationship between past securities and reasonable projection.

This same relationship is played out in a highly literal way in Chuck Jones's space-related cartoons. Jones casts Daffy Duck as hero in his parody of Buck Rogers, *Duck Dodgers in the 24½th Century*, and uses the premise of the science fiction quest for something needed, lost, or life-saving to determine the theme of the cartoon: "The earth's supply of Illudium Phosdex, the shaving cream atom, is alarmingly low" (Jones, *Chuck Amuck* 150). Most important, though, it is the cartoon environment that simultaneously contextualizes and provokes the gags while foregrounding SF imagery. As Jones points out,

> Far from imitating Buck Rogers, we go way beyond the clutching bonds of the earth-bound live action camera and what were then the miniature cities of the future. We do it because we *can*, because we have that great and imaginative designer, Maurice Noble, to create the city of the future, a city that, even with today's advances in technology, still stands as the city to stimulate live action directors such as George Lucas and Steven Spielberg. (*Chuck Amuck* 149; emphasis in original)

Noble's designs anticipated the largesse of Cape Canaveral's rockets in the 1960s and reimagined gantries and infrastructures after the style of the 1930s pulps. Planet X was characterized by huge crosses of rocks, cloud, and fauna, and ACME's finest weaponry, and was populated by Marvin Martian, a Jones mainstay, mainly as an adversary for Bugs Bunny in *Haredevil Hare* (1948), *The Hasty Hare* (1951), *Hareway to the Stars* (1958), and *Mad as a Mars Hare* (1963). Throughout the 1950s and early 1960s, Jones maintained a simultaneous commentary on science fiction B movies and the popular preoccupation with aliens and UFOs. Jones recognized that the presence of an "alien" effectively offered the possibility of positing different ways of seeing. By the time of *Martian Through Georgia* (1962), Jones had consolidated this perspective by showing an alien utopia in which the alien had become bored with his own ability to levitate or to psychically project and sought solace on Earth, which ultimately rejects him as an unwelcome monster. Typically, Jones's erudition manifests itself by using the SF tension between utopian aspiration and dystopian inevitability as a vehicle for the comedy of disappointment. Jones's outlook was in some sense bound up with his view of fanaticism or obsession, which he defined as the redoubling of effort without proper reflection upon or thought about the same inevitable consequence (*Chuck Amuck* 1). Jones's interpretation of science-fictional narratives and tropes was, therefore, always couched within an absurdist frame and a quasi-philosophic stance about human folly.

In 2009 Dreamworks released *Monsters vs. Aliens*, an affectionate homage to 1950s science fiction creature features. There is some irony in the fact that this is the first computer animation film developed in stereo 3D, celebrating the less-than-state-of-the-art effects of the 1950s B movie. The key characters are based on those from *The Blob* (1958), *The Fly* (1958), *Creature from the Black Lagoon* (1954), *Mothra* (1961), and *Attack of the Fifty Foot Woman* (1958), and the film references numerous other scenes and images, most notably the destruction of the Golden Gate Bridge in San Francisco alluded to in *It Came From Beneath the Sea* (1955).

The San Francisco "City Fathers" initially forbade the filmmakers to destroy the Golden Gate Bridge in the mid-1950s film on the basis that it would undermine public confidence, but master 3D stop-motion animator Ray Harryhausen had already animated an atomically aroused and enlarged octopus tearing down the bridge, so the sequence remained. Harryhausen had previously animated the destruction of a city by a prehistoric monster in *The Beast from 20,000 Fathoms* (1953) and was later to do the same, but this time with flying saucers, in *Earth vs The Flying Saucers* (1956). Harryhausen's animation essentially facilitated the action sequences in which the alien Other threatened the urban political, economic, and cultural status quo—a common Cold War theme in 1950s SF—but once more, his work also spoke to the complex resolution of past and present, tradition and modernity, evolution and resolution. In *20 Million Miles to Earth* (1957), a Venusian reptile, an Ymir, hatches when brought back from a US interplanetary expedition and becomes subject to the traditional dichotomy of either being of interest for preservation and research or an inherent threat, liable to be harmed or killed. The rampaging Ymir finds itself in Rome, and the set-piece finale sees him fall from the Colosseum—again representing the tension between values and culture of antiquity and the deep anxiety about change. As Dr. Judson Uhl asks after the Kong-like demise: "Why is it always, always so costly for man to move from the present to the future?"

At the philosophic level, this has been a question at the heart of science fiction since its inception; at the practical level, the question is concerned with technology, practice, and cost. Harryhausen's "Dynamation," the combination of live action with integrated animation, was expensive enough, but it successfully enabled the plausible interaction of different worlds and historic periods, partly anticipating the "steampunk" aesthetic in later science fiction but, crucially, always casting the present as a precarious balance between the expectations of the past and the shock of the new, from whatever its source. This was also the key theme of Czech feature animator and visual effects master Karel Zeman, who used and extended the pioneering craft practices of Georges Méliès and anticipated the digital interventions of George Lucas at Industrial Light and Magic in the contemporary era. Consequently, Zeman's work speaks to Manovich's discussion of "new media" in the light of pre/proto cinematic forms, casting digital cinema as a mode of animation (293–333). This marks out Zeman's practice as a highly self-conscious engagement with the ways an image could be constructed, drawing upon a number of arts-and-crafts idioms as pertinent methods to achieve his effects, while also thinking about animating within a layered, physically composited, quasi-photographic environment, long anticipating approaches to CGI.

Zeman worked as a commercial illustrator in Paris in the 1930s and was influenced by the playful surreal juxtapositions in the work of Achille Mauzan and Leonetto Cappiello. Once back in the former Czechoslovakia, he worked in the spirit of more politically driven artists like Karel Teige, Toyen, and Vaclav Pikal, finding his niche in creating metaphorically charged narratives, inspired by and adapting the work of Jules

Verne. His most notable films, *Journey to the Centre of the Earth* (1956), *The Invention of Destruction* (1958), and *Baron Münchausen* (1961), all drew upon Verne's original illustrators, Riou and de Montant, and their construction, as with much animation/live action combining different historical and metaphysical contexts, is informed by Klein's concept of the "scripted space":

> Scripted Spaces are a walk through or click through an environment.... They are designed to *emphasize* the viewer's journey—the space between—rather than the gimmicks on the wall. The audience walks into the story.... By scripted spaces, I mean primarily a *mode of perception*, a way of seeing.... They are a Scripted phenomenology, where the shock that is a "special" effect can be very, very brief—brief yet scrupulously designed again, three acts in a few seconds. (*Vatican to Vegas* 11–12; emphasis in original)

Zeman's imagery—dirigibles, flying bikes, giant machines—is concerned with recalling the narratives embedded in illustration, objects, and environments, and prompting the phenomenological recollection of stories and pictures when realized in a new context. When *Baron Münchausen* was released, Soviet cosmonaut Yuri Gagarin had become the first man to orbit Earth. Consequently, the film references both the work of Chesley Bonestell, whose visualization of the planets in *The Conquest of Space* (1949) and in films like *Destination Moon* (1950) was the new hyperrealist benchmark for space illustration, and the science fiction writing of Cyrano de Bergerac—who appears here, spinning his hat into space as if it were a flying saucer, saying, "We are journeying towards the mighty embrace called the Universe." It was an embrace that had already been undertaken and was to endure in the animated science fiction from Japan.

First published as a manga in 1952, Osamu Tezuka's *Tetsuwan Atomu* (literally, "Iron-Arm Atom") became *Astro Boy*, an animated series, in 1963, initially lasting for 193 episodes. It was the first anime broadcast outside Japan and proved its enduring appeal in remakes in the 1980s and early 2000s, before receiving a treatment as a full-length CGI feature in 2009. Astro Boy's status as a "boy-robot," both in the original manga and in the animation, enabled his character to strongly reflect the key themes of Japan's postwar recovery and its move toward economic stability and growth by the end of the 1960s. *Astro Boy* embodied progressive technology, increasing industrialization and urbanization, and also emergent tensions with the natural environment and ancient orders saturated with spiritual and philosophic meaning. *Astro Boy* also toys with generic icons from Frankenstein's monster to Pinocchio to Superman, successfully combining the pathos of the boy robot's social and cultural alienation with his inherent moral fortitude in saving the world from seemingly imminent disaster. Indeed, Astro Boy's desire to love and be loved distinguishes him from the tradition of Japanese *mecha* that follows, most robots being merely veiled metaphors for the legacy of the atomic bomb, militarist agendas, and apocalyptic anxiety in works such as *Robot Carnival* (1987), *Patlabor* (1990), and *Roujin Z* (1999).

Astro Boy became very popular in the United States, constantly balancing the sentiment and slapstick that resulted from his status as a "boy" untutored in everyday life with the spectacle resulting from his special powers as a superhero: searchlight eyes; jet propulsion and flight; amplified hearing; a computer brain that enabled him to speak 60 languages; an atomic reactor in his chest; and guns available in his bottom. Astro Boy was created as a response to a scientist's grief about his own son's death in a traffic accident—echoing the core theme of much contemporary anime: the seemingly contradictory ambition of seeking emotional comfort and progress in technology as a substitute for the inherent spiritual loss Japan experienced at Hiroshima and Nagasaki.

The more apocalyptic agenda prompted by this tension is expressed in major breakthrough anime like Katsuhiro Otomo's *Akira* (1988), in which the disaffected youth and terrorists of post-apocalyptic Tokyo seek to re-create the eponymous bioweapon of the title. In essence, though, this film, like much anime, becomes a vehicle by which the animation itself can be used to illustrate the new mutabilities in personal identities and social environments as humankind and technology become increasingly allied, elided, and effaced. This is the theme of Mamuro Oshii's *Ghost in the Shell* (1990) and its sequel, *Innocence* (2004), in which the "ghost" of human essence inhabits a state-of-the-art "machine," at times rendering the soul, as well as the flesh and blood understanding of human life, as mere data—a freely transferable artificial intelligence desperately seeking to maintain its own singularity and identity.

At one level, this demonstrates a deep ambivalence about the advances in postwar technology, and Japan's place at the forefront of such innovation. Satoshi Kon's *Paprika* (2006) features Dr. Atsuko Chiba, who is equipped with a device—the DC mini—by which she can enter others' dream-states as her alter-ego Paprika. As in all scenarios dealing with advanced technologies, their impact—positive or negative—is determined by those who use them. When some DC minis are stolen, this sets in train a thriller plot by which Chiba seeks their return, but such is secondary to the free play of visual invention in the representation of dreams and interior states. The carnival of objects, figures, machines, memorabilia, and phenomena—the material evidence of Japan's buoyant postwar economy—that marches through the film is a symbol for the freedom of consciousness and the language of animation that apprehends and records it. In consequence, Kon plays with dates and times to shift dimensions and space in acts of creative daring that reinvent SF anime as a vehicle for psychological inquiry rather than apocalyptic meltdown. Crucially, though, Kon's approach freely interrogates the contradictory yet progressive sensibility of modern Japan, a "thick text" foregrounding a protean form as it impacts upon an already protean genre.

The protean dynamics of SF animation may be demonstrated in a wide range of unsung and important works. John Halas and Joy Batchelor's *Automania 2000* (1963) imagines a future in which cars overtake the world, while *Dilemma* (1981) anticipates humankind's inevitable abuse of technology in the service of global destruction. Nazim Tulyakhodzhayev's 1984 adaptation of Ray Bradbury's 1950 short story "There Will Come Soft Rains" chillingly renders a future automated world in which humankind is already absent, the victims of atomic dissolution, and shows the further impact of nuclear fallout when the mechanized systems seek to kill a living dove and destroy a hanging crucifix. Lighter, less symbol-laden versions of the future occur in TV series like *The Jetsons* (1962–63), *Dexter's Laboratory* (1996–2003), *The Powerpuff Girls* (1998–2004), and *Futurama* (1999–), but a summation of the impact and effect of SF animation may be best achieved by addressing the work of René Laloux and the Pixar animation, *WALL-E*.

Laloux's work is consistently characterized by a playful mix of inventive science-fantasy aesthetics and the interrogation of ideological struggle. While clearly the signature author of his work, Laloux's collaboration with distinctive designers and illustrators—Roland Topor, Moebius, and Philippe Caza—has enabled the depiction of complex organic worlds, mutable forms, and cultures in flux. There are implicit tensions about control and conformity that attend such shape-shifting, and Laloux's films work as allegories about animation itself as much as they address significant political concerns. Like most science fiction, though, Laloux is always talking about the "here and now" of human folly, even though his preoccupations are consistently grounded in bigger anxieties about the conditions that create and permit quasi-Fascist regimes, or the oppressions of authoritarian government. In Laloux's masterpiece, *Fantastic Planet* (1973), humanlike "Oms" are brutalized by blue giant "Draags," and though never a precise metaphor, the intimations of Stalinism or allusions to the genocidal horrors of the Nazi concentration camps are clear. In *Gandahar* (1988), Laloux's solar system is made up of alternative worlds, requiring metaphysical as well as narrative exploration, each planet initially a version of Paradise until the veneer of its idyllic orthodoxies is stripped away to lay bare the conditions of its inevitable "fall." Laloux's intention is not to labor this inevitability, or to stress any kind of Christian infrastructure, however, but to offer up metaphors of resistance, which insist upon warning humanity about its folly, an idea taken up in more recent work like Pixar's *WALL-E*.

An eco-parable, the film uses the SF trope of the "last person in the world" and the idea of autonomous antihuman technologies, telling the story of an empathetic, human-serving robot and a romance between two sentient machines. Corporate irresponsibility and commercial exploitation are viewed as the cause of an eco-apocalypse, yet human values are somehow sustained through the innocence and endeavor of Wall-E. Though a machine, Wall-E's feelings are completely transparent, though his only companion is a small cockroach, and with each action he insists upon and ensures that there is hope in the world.

When Eve arrives on the planet to check for any living flora or fauna, she initially has the profound and dangerous inscrutability of a Gort, shooting at anything that moves, yet provoking in Wall-E awe and wonder as she flies freely through the air and peruses the planet with beautiful, laserlike, blue-ray precision. His attempts to impress her lead to a series of slapstick mishaps, and in this, and the film's sustained visual storytelling and limited dialogue, *Wall-E* signals its daring in making a latter-day "silent film," drawing on the pathos of the Chaplin and Keaton era. Such an approach merely reinforces the sense of loss and seeming hopelessness of the situation Wall-E finds himself in, but his love for Eve gives him new purpose. Though Eve is initially "shut down" once she finds a living organism—a small shoot cultivated in a boot, proffered by Wall-E as a

FIGURE 14.1 Robotic romance on a ruined Earth. *Wall-E* (2008).

romantic gift—this merely becomes another imperative for Wall-E to find the spirit to endure and achieve connection with Eve by attempting to hold her hand, a visual motif drawn from his viewings of the film *Hello Dolly* (1969). If his role has been only to serve humanity, Wall-E's sense of service develops a more chivalric code as he pursues Eve back to her home spaceship—coincidentally, the *Axiom*, the ship upon which humanity sailed away from Earth some 700 years before and that now floats aimlessly about the Universe.

Wall-E and Eve represent a return to a hard-bodied agenda imbued with the spirit of traditional notions of romantic love, and an intrinsic "humanity" that both redefines the robot/cyborg and, crucially, reminds the disorientated, powerless, fragmented, disintegrated, boundary-less, hybridized humankind afloat on the *Axiom*, and alienated from its "home" or source, that it must fundamentally change. Instead of retreating into the virtual and the insularity of cyberworlds, humankind needs to reinvent itself and know again what it is to be human, what it is to experience genuine connection, and what it might require to use its technologies for the preservation rather than destruction of the world. While this might seem like a counterculture message from the 1960s, it is a contemporary message that gains greater purchase from the insistence that "machines" can achieve "modernity," but only if they are not taken for granted, misused, or trusted wholly as the inevitable facilitator of successful progress. In essence, Wall-E takes responsibility, finds beauty in the world around him despite all of its bleakness and abuse, embraces service in the face of the profound needs of humanity, and is characterized only by love and generosity of spirit. The fact that he is a machine is irrelevant; he is a role model by which humankind can see what it has lost.

Indeed, this theme may be viewed as a key aspect of animated science fiction in general. Pixar's John Lasseter insists "the art challenges technology and the technology inspires the art" (Lasseter, personal interview, November 3, 2001), and this view has constantly ensured that animation, in general, has remained experimental even as it has entered the mainstream. Wall-E becomes but one animated metaphor for the ways in which technology and creativity can combine to engage with the most serious problems and complexities facing humankind. Animated science fiction has self-consciously used its overt illusionism to ask questions about identity, relationships, and political action. The art and technology of animation have, therefore, consistently facilitated visions that self-reflexively foreground the how and why of the scientific and technological interfaces with human creativity, and consistently offered an astute and increasingly pertinent insight into the late-capitalist, postindustrial human condition.

Works Cited

Cabarga, Leslie. *The Fleischer Story: A History of the Fleischer Cartoon Studio in the Golden Age of Film Animation 1920–1942*. New York: Da Capo, 1988. Print.

Holland, Stephen, and Alex Summersby. *Sci-fi Art: A Graphic History*. New York: Collins Design, 2009. Print.

Jones, Chuck. *Chuck Amuck: The Life and Times of an Animated Cartoonist*. London: Simon & Schuster, 1990. Print.

Kaveney, Roz. *From* Alien *to* The Matrix: *Reading Science Fiction Film*. London: I.B. Tauris, 2005. Print.

King, Geoff, and Tanya Krzywinska. *Science Fiction Cinema: From Outerspace to Cyberspace*. London: Wallflower, 2000. Print.

Klein, Norman M. *Seven Minutes: The Life and Death of the American Animated Cartoon*. London: Verso, 1993. Print.

——. *The Vatican to Vegas: A History of Special Effects*. New York: New Press, 2004. Print.

Leslie, Esther. *Hollywood Flatlands: Animation, Critical Theory and the Avant-Garde*. London: Verso, 2002. Print.

Manovich, Lev. *The Language of New Media*. Cambridge, MA: MIT, 2002. Print.

Napier, Susan J. "When the Machines Stop: Fantasy, Reality, and Terminal Identity in *Neon Genesis Evangelion* and *Serial Experiments: Lain*." *Robot Ghosts and Wired Dreams: Japanese Science Fiction from Origins to Anime*. Ed. Christopher Bolton, Istvan Csicsery-Ronay Jr., and Takayuki Tatsumi. Minneapolis: U of Minnesota P, 2007. 101–22. Print.

Nead, Lynda. *The Haunted Gallery: Painting, Photography, Film c.1900*. New Haven, CT: Yale UP, 2007. Print.

Telotte, J. P. *Animating Space: From Mickey to WALL-E*. Lexington: U of Kentucky P, 2010. Print.

Wells, Paul. *The Animated Bestiary: Animals, Cartoons, and Culture*. New Brunswick, NJ: Rutgers UP, 2009. Print.

——. *Animation and America*. New Brunswick, NJ: Rutgers UP, 2002. Print.

CHAPTER 15

ART AND ILLUSTRATION

JEROME WINTER

SINCE the 1970s, numerous coffee-table books have chronicled the growing body of science fiction art, amply meeting the demands of collectors, SF aficionados, and casual readers. In addition to titles showcasing the portfolios of individual artists, notable works attempting a sweeping historical scope on the subject are James E. Gunn's *Alternate Worlds* (1975), Brian W. Aldiss's *Science Fiction Art* (1975), Vincent Di Fate's *Infinite Worlds* (1997), Frank M. Robinson's *Science Fiction of the Twentieth Century: An Illustrated History* (1999), and Steve Holland's *Sci-Fi: A Graphic History* (2009). Oversized, with high-grade, glossy paper and galleries of retouched reproductions, these handsome hardcovers generally eschew scholarly argument, captioning the arrays of stunning images with sidebars filled with biographical snippets, historical background, and homages to individual artists. There has been to date, however, very little sustained critical attention to SF visual art not simply as a supplement to the history of SF literature, but as a significant shaper of the image culture of twentieth-century technological modernity. In fact, the visual culture of SF, considered broadly, has perhaps been more influential than SF texts themselves in terms of its impact on the general culture.

In *Picture Theory*, W. J. T. Mitchell argues for a "critical iconology" that examines the means by which the human sensorium, trained by visual and literary cultures, has become inextricably linked in an "imagetext" situated within historically contingent institutions and discourses. Contrary to received notions, Mitchell contends that the distinction between the verbal and the visual modalities is not a rigid dichotomy but a complex sensory ratio; immanent within literary texts are visual descriptions, implied representations, and cultural regimes of seeing, just as immanent within images are narratives, literary intertexts, and an underlying tissue of reading practices. With Mitchell's imagetext in mind, it is important to note that, whether visually or verbally represented, depictions of the future in SF have often had a common iconological reference point. This context might perhaps best be grasped in terms of what David E. Nye has described as the "American technological sublime"—those modern engineering marvels (skyscrapers, the Hoover Dam, the Apollo moon landing) that dwarf and overwhelm the individual. In SF art and illustration, however, the technological sublime can be traced back at least to nineteenth-century Europe and onward into a twentieth-first-century global future.

To give a sense of the sheer profusion of material in this niche of cultural production, this chapter analyzes images and discourses of the future in a wide spectrum of SF visual media—from the trail-blazing photorealist interior illustrations and frontispieces of Jules Verne's *Voyages Extraordinaire* to the serial technocratic iconography of Frank R. Paul's painterly magazine covers and interior drawings in the 1920s pulps; from the "imagination of disaster" in 1950s SF movie posters to the technosurreal iconoclasm captured in Richard M. Power's paperback cover art; from the seductions of hyperreal simulacra of Chris Foss's illustrations to the postcyberpunk digital imaging of global diversity realized by Stephan Martinière. My overarching contention is that the history of SF art and illustration reveals a recurring tendency to transform and reconfigure icons of imminent futures in ways that have proven both timely and influential.

As I. F. Clarke, in his seminal futurological study *The Pattern of Expectation*, observes, the meteoric rise of Jules Verne's popularity exploited the growing technocultural need for future-oriented literature that became "the most effective means of examining, describing and prescribing whatever writers thought would happen, or feared would happen, or considered should happen in the years ahead" (91). The woodcut illustrations by various skilled artists that accompanied the Hetzel editions of Verne's texts were instrumental and decidedly not incidental in catalyzing the experience of the transfigured future these tales evoke (Evans 241). Verne's extraordinary voyages initiated a defamiliarizing future shock that invited responses celebrating both the progressive adventure of heroic technological innovation and a blissful obliviousness to the woeful costs of rapid industrialization. In an illustration from Verne's *Robur, The Conquerer* (1886), for instance, artist Léon Benett depicts a skyway brimming with hot-air balloons in a motley assortment of shapes, sizes, design, and rigging. This striking image and its photography-simulating illusion of realism project the contemporary technocultural enthusiasm for balloon racing into a romanticized, fantastic near future.

Likewise, the remarkably gifted artist Albert Robida anticipated the boisterous trend-watching that would characterize science fiction in the twentieth century with his drawings of a vibrantly progressive future on the foreseeable horizon. In an image from his illustrated novel *The Twentieth Century* (1883), for example, the Verne-influenced Frenchman anticipates the red-light district of a future Paris in which brazen prostitutes in short skirts designed for rocket-powered aerocabs hail potential customers in a city congested with billboards and a tangle of telephone lines. In more terrifying fashion, the weaponized airships depicted in Robida's *The Infernal War* (1908) forecast the importance of aerial dogfights in a then-hypothetical Second World War. Some of Robida's predictions seem especially prescient in retrospect, but regardless of their status as plausible premonitions, these illustrations display a fertile imagination of the future that consistently registered the impact of technological change on a wide spectrum of social life.

FIGURE 15.1 Léon Benett, interior illustration from Jules Verne's *Robur, The Conqueror* (1904).

Discovered by Hugo Gernsback in 1914, Frank R. Paul followed quickly in the footsteps of Robida and Verne's illustrators, proving to be an immensely prolific and facile artist. Over his career, Paul produced hundreds of water-color cover paintings and pen-and-ink interior drawings and calligraphy for *Modern Electrics* (later renamed *Science and Invention*), *Amazing Stories, Wonder Quarterly,* and *Air Wonder Stories.* To increase sales of these magazines, Gernsback promoted Paul not as an incidental incentive but as a primary marketing tool: the interior advertisement for *Amazing Stories* in the April 1926 issue of *Science and Invention,* for instance, entices its readers with the prospect that "every story [is] illustrated" (qtd. Frank 19). Moreover, Gernsback was quick to use Paul's talents for profit-making publicity through inventive stunts such as

FIGURE 15.2 Albert Robida, interior illustration from his novel *The Twentieth Century* (1883).

selling reproductions of Paul's covers for a dollar or—as outlined in the editorial for the December 1926 issue of *Amazing Stories*—devising a contest for readers to craft a story around the Paul cover for that issue (Gernsback).

Paul's cover art used arresting, bright-toned colors—chrome yellow, crimson red, cerulean blue. Puritanical crusaders campaigned against pulp covers much more explicit but no less garish than Paul's work: Margaret Brundage's covers for the pulp *Weird Tales* typify the raw eroticism that moral guardians castigated as lurid and obscene. But it was partly this controversy swirling around the magazine stands that all but determined that the pulps would become big business in the United States beginning in the 1920s (see Boyer 155). Paul was by no means immune from the censure of this so-called vice movement—as exemplified by Mrs. L. Silberberg's letter to the editor, "A Lady Reader's Criticism," in the October 1928 issue of *Amazing Stories*. Mrs. Silberberg pleads with the magazine to "tone down Paul," begging for "more subdued illustration" that would spare her the "barrage of eyes" from genteel onlookers and the furtive need to "sneak unnoticed that blatant pictorial atrocity under [her] arm" (1145).

In this sensational climate, Paul set the template for science-fictional iconography that would soon consolidate and dominate the evolving genre of SF art, directly influencing signal pulp-artist colleagues such as Leo Morey, Howard Brown, H. W. Wesso, and Hubert Rogers. Paul's work quickly became the visual gold standard for depicting hulking machines, renegade robots, alien creatures and landscapes, careening rockets, future cities, flying saucers, fringe-science experiments, and astronauts. It cannot be overstated how representative, wide-ranging, and foundational Paul's work was in constituting science fiction as a genre. On the one hand, Ray Bradbury could credit Paul and the speculative-fantastic power of his glittering future cityscapes and giant mutated ants, while at the same time, Arthur C. Clarke could hail the meticulousness of his accurate rendering of the planet Jupiter, complete with the Great Red Spot and turbulent equatorial belt, which graced the cover of the November 1928 issue of *Amazing Stories*.

Paul sowed the seeds of a burgeoning genre with his gaudy iconography, and his career can be seen as illustrative of not only pulp-era science fiction but also interwar visions of the modernizing future as a whole. His sketchwork rendering of outlandish but believable aliens, such as the ostrichlike Tweel from Stanley G. Weinbaum's "The Martian Odyssey" in the July 1934 issue of *Wonder Stories*, represents a complex alterity that the author's influential stories also perform. Similarly complex, his spectacular depiction of the almost gleeful destruction wrought by the Martian tripods of H. G. Wells's *War of the Worlds* (1898), on the cover of the August 1927 issue of *Amazing Stories*, evokes both the allure and the menace of the futuristic weapons of the pulp era—dirigibles, submarines, airplanes, tanks, machine guns, and so on.

On this iconic cover, Paul lavishes attention on the gleaming chromium surfaces of the streamlined, saucer-shaped tripods. The nightmarish scene of technologized massacre and destruction, as well as the incursion of the alien futuristic machine into the rural English countryside, shows the chaos and panic of the hysterical crowd. Dynamic action is implied as long, thin tentacles pluck men off fleeing horses. And a masterly illusion of depth is achieved through lighting and shading techniques. In a striking touch, the flames of the background inferno are reflected off the shining surfaces of the tripods. All in all, Paul deftly captures the terror of the heat rays, which are figured in the novel as inscrutably advanced weapons wreaking "flaming death, this invisible, inevitable sword of heat" (Wells 261). These war machines, of course, were embedded in an extra-generic, emergent technocultural framework.

The interwar Technocracy Movement contested this framework, targeting the capitalist system for its egregious inefficiency, hostile division of labor, and hijacking of industry-derived abundance by greedy, myopic business interests. As Andrew Ross has argued, the Technocracy Movement, like the left-wing avant-garde in SF, shared "the dominant values of modernity and progress," but they "promised to be more creative, more productive, more efficient, more growth-oriented, and more humane than the fettered capitalist management of society was proving to be" (120). Paul was clearly influenced by this pervasive technocratic zeitgeist: in a keynote address given to the First World Science Fiction Convention in 1939, he claimed that SF readers were youthful "rebels" capable of resisting the deadening conformity of the "well-ordered society" for the sake of the "advance guard of progress" (qtd. Pohl 223). As a testament to the anxiety such potentially radical rhetoric invoked in the genre at the time, the socialist-identified Futurian group of SF writers was barred from this inaugural convention and never heard Paul's speech in person.

Paul's interior art for Gernsback's *Ralph 124C 41+* suggests a bright technocratic utopia of urban splendor, featuring a retro-Renaissance courtly couple, Alice and Ralph, rollerskating on a balcony against the background of a sprawling metropolis. First serialized in *Modern Electrics* in 1911 and published in book form in 1925, the story depicts vast solar-powered "Metero-Towers" dominating the future city of New York in 2660. An architect by training, Paul designed the Johnson & Johnson building in New Brunswick, New Jersey, in 1938, and his future cities are not so much wild speculation as direct extrapolations of popular 1920s and 1930s trends in building design. Paul's future cities invoke the sleek, utilitarian Manhattan of tomorrow that Hugh Ferris and Harvey Wiley Corbett promoted, and that exist to this day in Rockefeller Center, the Chrysler Building, and the Empire State Building. Paul's euphoric vision of a buoyant architectural future can be glimpsed in the back-cover art for the April 1942 issue of *Amazing Stories*, which includes all the staples of his optimistic, marvelous cities of tomorrow: private helipads, downtown pedestrian malls, towering megastructures, freeways, orchestrated traffic of teardrop starships, efficient municipal planning, and curvilinear design flourishes that anticipate the Space Age. By contrast, the back cover of the November 1941 issue features a "Golden City on Titan" that is an ominous, forbidding anticipation of the future city. Reminiscent of the menacing towers of Babel in Fritz Lang's *Metropolis* (1927), the regimented array of zigguratlike skyscrapers inspires ritual worship from the dwarfed alien denizens gesticulating and gazing upward at the totemic towers, colored in lurid yellows, oranges, and greens, ornamented by gargoyles with Aztec headdresses. The image elicits a nightmarish, perhaps xenophobic terror as much as a sublime sense of wonder, suggesting that Paul's futurism was not single-mindedly optimistic.

The flying saucer is one of the Paul-derived SF icons that thoroughly saturated mass entertainment by the 1950s. Appearing in its most recognizable, perfectly disklike shape on the November 1929 cover of *Science Wonder Stories*, this circular spaceship design would achieve kitsch status by way of such 1950s films as *The Day the Earth Stood Still* (1951), *War of the Worlds* (1953), *Earth vs. the Flying Saucers* (1956), and *Forbidden Planet* (1956) before becoming the paranoid object of UFOlogical cults as sentimentalized in *Close Encounters of the Third Kind* (1977). Although the newspaper comic strips featuring Buck Rogers and Flash Gordon were instrumental, alongside Paul's pulp covers, in disseminating the look and feel of SF art during the 1930s and 1940s, the role of 1950s film poster art in transmitting the icons of the SF pulps to a popular audience has often been overlooked. These commercial posters were frequently quite accomplished works of art as well as advertisements for the films they promoted. Reynold Brown's

FIGURE 15.3 Frank R. Paul, back cover for April 1942 issue of *Amazing Stories*. Image courtesy of the Frank R. Paul Estate.

panoramic poster for *This Island Earth* (1955), for instance, is a dynamic, fiery collage of literally explosive scenes from the movie, capturing the plot-driven character of 1950s SF film as well as its hypnotically seductive apocalypticism. As Alan Nadel argues, the terrors invoked by 1950s SF films often became conflated with broader cultural concerns—anti-Communist rhetoric, nuclear anxiety, a suffocating suburban ethos—that seemed to foreclose the future possibilities of the post–World War II boom (41–53).

In her famous essay "The Imagination of Disaster," Susan Sontag contends that 1950s SF films, with their evocation of the seductive terrors of worldwide devastation, threaten to debase not only discriminating taste but also our capacity to contend with an "aesthetics of destruction, with the peculiar beauties to be found in wreaking havoc, making a mess" (213). Sontag views SF films of this period as producing a spectacular, depoliticizing inoculation against the looming menace of a near future dominated by apocalyptic violence. For Sontag, such popular, commercial cinema glamorizes and aestheticizes technological violence and disorder to an audience rendered helpless and complicit.

However, Brown's poster for *This Island Earth*, contra Sontag, displays a mutant energy that defies such a pat analysis, injecting its iconography with a dissident edge that suggests a vibrant technoculture moving rapidly forward, yet perpetually on the brink of destruction. SF films—and the promotional art that attended them—channeled and repackaged this future-oriented anxiety to captivate a mainstream audience.

In a curious feedback loop, the cover art for the burgeoning ranks of SF paperbacks reinterpreted and reabsorbed such apocalyptic visions but, especially as the 1950s gave way to the 1960s, with a newly countercultural emphasis that further broadened the appeal of SF iconography. In a bid to wrest market share away from flourishing competitors like Ace and Dell, Ballantine Books ran an experimental, nonrepresentational painting by a young Richard Powers on the cover of Arthur C. Clarke's *Childhood End* (1953). By the late 1960s, Ballantine Books had tapped such a rich vein of demand for surreal covers that the editor of Ace Books, Donald A. Wollheim, requested that artists like Jack Gaughan and Paul Lehr emulate Powers's successful model while at the same time holding steadfast to their time-honored representational techniques (Ortiz 142). Influenced by abstract Surrealists such as Joan Miró, Roberto Matta, and Yves Tanguy, Richard Powers set the tone for this countercultural trend in cover art with his breathtakingly psychedelic style that catered to an increasingly receptive audience.

Powers saw what he called his constantly evolving "absurrealismus" style (qtd. Frank 28) as evoking an antiestablishment and countercultural subversiveness that sought to smash the hallowed icons of not only commercial SF art and illustration but fine-arts museum and gallery circuits as well. In the early 1970s, for instance, Powers issued acerbic hoaxes like the pamphlet *Menschifesto* at the May 1970 Rhen Show exhibit in New York City, signing his work with reference to the fictitious Lazarus Organization, which was meant to lambaste Andy Warhol's Factory system since, as Powers explained in a 1964 interview, "Pop Art is getting so much publicity [that w]e are living in a sensation-saturated age" (qtd. Frank 24). As a result of his distaste for both art-world trends and commercially driven conventions, Powers continually toggled back and forth between the commercial and artistic realms but always with an unchanging antipathy for the overly commodified: "I experimented with styles.... I could do a commercial assignment and get paid for it and at the same time work it out of my system" (qtd. Frank 109).

To social theorists like Guy Debord in the 1960s, a media-saturated "society of the spectacle" had supplanted the politics of everyday life with a self-referential system only interruptible by the guerilla tactics of consumer-culture jamming. Caught up in these broader antitechnocratic technocultural discourses, the SF fiction and art of what came to be known as the "New Wave" were directly influenced by Situationist International aesthetics as articulated by Debord, in strategic combination with the Surrealist aesthetics practiced by Salvador Dalí, Paul Éluard, Max Ernst, and many others. In a review-essay entitled "The Coming of the Unconscious" in the August 1966 issue of *New Worlds*, a principal organ of the New Wave movement, J. G. Ballard argued that "the techniques of surrealism have a particular relevance at this moment when the fictional elements in the world around us are multiplying to the point that it is almost impossible to distinguish between the 'real' and the 'false'—the terms no longer have any meaning" (145–46). Richard Powers did the cover art for Ballard's 1962 collection *The Voices of Time* and, in a rare effusion of praise for the craft of literary science fiction, exclaimed that Ballard's work was "one of the best pieces of Surrealist writing I've ever read" (qtd. Frank 61). Like Ballard, Powers honed an elaborate arsenal of abstract Surrealist techniques with a keen eye to disrupting a ubiquitous media-dominated reality.

In his first Surrealist manifesto, issued in 1924, André Breton claimed Surrealism manifested the "marvelous in the everyday" in part out of a spirit of social protest and revolt against technocultural stagnation. "Surrealism, such as I conceive it," Breton avers, "asserts our complete non-conformism.... [It] does not allow those who devote themselves to it to forsake it whenever they like. There is every reason to maintain that it acts on the mind very much as drugs do; like drugs, it creates a certain state of need and can push men to frightful revolts" (438–39). Rebelling against the deadening machinery of modern life, Powers constructed nightmarish visions of the future that placed a high premium on deploying the surreally macabre and grotesque to contest a realist aesthetic dependent on traditional representational techniques that prized harmony, symmetry, and perspective. Often using acrylics, Powers painted fantastic tableaus and collages, dreamlike assemblages of hallucinatory and disjointed images suggesting what Lautréamont famously aphorized as the "chance encounter of a sewing machine and an umbrella on an operating table." Powers recontextualized amorphous objects and barren landscapes in a bizarre, defamiliarizing process similar to what Belgian Surrealist Marcel Mariën labeled *détournement*—or the guerilla misdirection and repurposing of a cultural artifact that subverts and resists its intended use or meaning (see Plant 86–88). A typical Powers cover puts a mysterious combination of nonmimetic, symbolic images in odd juxtaposition. Some recurring images Powers frequently deploys are mannikins, biomorphs, skeletons, barbs and thorns, gelatinous shapes, distorted landscapes and skyscapes. These images constitute iconoclastic reinterpretations of such conventional SF genre material as biotechnology, alien worlds, genetic mutations, and future cities.

Participating in the evolving imagetext of SF visual culture, Powers's playful, disturbing distortions and heightening of the perceptual reality of everyday life resonate equally with the SF literature of the period as with its art. Powers's dissident style expresses an impulse to recover a pragmatic, future-oriented politics from the enervating, phantasmagoric grip of media spectacle. Moreover, Powers's complex oeuvre is generally illustrative of the paradoxical moment when Surrealist and Situationist images advocating a critique of consumer culture became not only acceptable but also normative for commercial SF cover art. The semi-hallucinatory images mirrored the fiction they adorned—as exemplified by Powers's cover art for Berkley's 1981 paperback reprint of Philip K. Dick's *The Man in the High Castle* (1962). In a cover particularly suggestive of Yves Tanguy, Powers illustrates the novel through what appears to be a sinking and melting version of the titular, semi-fictionalized castle of Hawthorne Abendson; the deep-saturated color scheme is striking for its hellish reds and yellows and the vague detournement of metallic objects reminiscent of what the novel describes

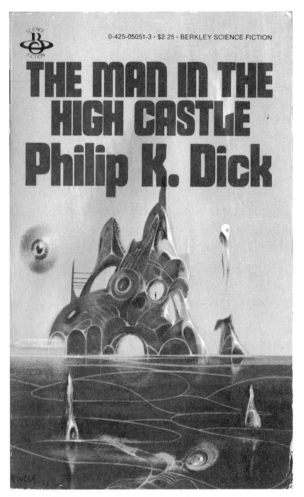

FIGURE 15.4 Cover art for paperback edition of Philip K. Dick's *The Man in the High Castle* (1962). Image courtesy of the Estate of Richard Powers.

as "guns all over the place" and "charged barb wire" (Dick 88). In the novel, the castle is the imagined mountaintop fortress of Abendson, the alternate-history author of a subversive, banned book-within-the-book in which, counterfactually to the novel's universe but parallel to our own, the Axis Powers lost World War II. Powers's cover succeeds in capturing how the castle symbolizes Abendson's mystic paranoia and vainly defends against the authoritarian depredations of a moribund, delusive technoculture.

Recoiling against perceived New Wave excesses, subsequent SF art and illustration grew more technically and representationally conservative, offering, at its most sleek and savvy, de-realized simulacra as indexes of a brave new world dominated by the accelerating vertigo of technocapitalist speed and power. This artwork eschewed stylistic experimentation in favor of the pleasures of gleamingly rendered technological hardware and future weaponry. In his believable depictions of the shock and awe of future technology seemingly devoid of a place for the human, Chris Foss's cover art aptly demonstrates what Rian Hughes has described as "techno-porn" (10). Hughes contends that Foss deftly weds the commercial and the avant-garde, but Foss's own estimation of himself is less generous. As opposed to the delicate compromise of New Wave artists like Powers, Foss blusters that "the real talent is in commercial art. Fine art is hot air" (qtd. Hughes 10). His concept art for Alejandro Jodorowski's abortive film adaptation of Frank Herbert's 1965 novel *Dune* suggests both the emerging backlash against the antitechnocratic positions of countercultural artists like Powers as well as a less extreme, more seductive continuation of their tactical uses of media. His micro-precise images of vast Spacing Guild starships look as if they can travel intergalactic distances faster than light while carrying whole cities as cargo. Foss's sleek high-tech visions show the clear influence of the meticulous verisimilitude in the representation of futuristic hardware found in Stanley Kubrick and Arthur C. Clarke's *2001: A Space Odyssey* (1968). Yet Foss can also reveal a more abrasive, sensationalist, and photorealistic aesthetic in his work, as evidenced by his cover for Ballard's *Crash*, which showcases a hallucinatory hyperrealism, its lurid pulp-influenced style vividly demonstrating Ballard's traumatized cathexis of death-driven technology, consumer capitalism, and aggressive sexuality. Exposing the gadget fetishism of all his work, Foss's *Crash* cover is a rare moment where the cruelly dehumanizing reality of technological progress is shown with an unflinching, hard-edged artistry.

A consummate professional working in a variety of media, including the pornographic illustrations for the sex manual *The Joy of Sex* (1972), Foss also painted one of his lurid, bulky starships for the album cover of *Clear Air Turbulence* (1977) by the Ian Gillian Band. The prevalence of SF iconography in rock-music cover art shows the deep seepage of science fiction into the gestalt of popular culture by the second half of the twentieth century. The rampant cross-pollination and interbreeding of SF-related music, fiction, and art are readily apparent, for example, in the Foss-like album cover of *Hall of the Mountain Grill* (1974) by Hawkwind (with whom the SF author Michael Moorcock was an occasional collaborator). From the countercultural turn in the 1960s on, SF rock-star personas became integral to the myriad album covers of David Bowie, Jimi Hendrix, Pink Floyd, and Jefferson Airplane, all of whom relied explicitly on a well-established template of SF visuals to convey their cosmic vibes and timbers. This nexus of SF and popular music also merged with the civil rights movements and morphed into the utopian Afrofuturism of Herbie Hancock, Sun-Ra, and Parliament-Funkadelic. For the album cover of *News from This World* (1977), the stadium rock band Queen even grandfathered in pulp-era iconography by asking Frank Kelly Freas to modify one of his 1950s *Astounding* covers to show a renegade robot cupping in his giant hand the maimed band members. The widespread popularity of such SF iconography persists to this day, as exemplified by the album covers of Janelle Monáe's *Metropolis* suite (2007–10) that visually performs extended riffs on Fritz Lang's film of that title and Philip K. Dick's 1968 novel *Do Androids Dream of Electric Sheep?*, or the haute fashion flaunted in the transmedial blitz of Lady Gaga's *Born This Way* (2011), which variously attempts a campy pastiche of 1970s-era science-fictionality.

The rise of the Internet and the World Wide Web in the 1980s and 1990s not only instantaneously distributed and circulated accumulating archives of digital images in dispersed worldwide networks but also exacerbated the hegemony of transnational corporations based in the global North and the neoimperial divide between a few rich, developed nations and a majority of poor, underdeveloped ones. Recent SF artists have updated New Wave and postmodern aesthetics to respond in part to what theorists of globalization such as Manuel Castells and David Harvey contend is a signal feature of our times—namely, the recent unprecedented acceleration of the information technology industry that has bound the world into ever-smaller, ever-faster circuits. In many of these analyses, informational globalization betrays a key ideological split: the jet-setting cosmopolitan technoelite, corporate networkers, and transnational nomads are privy to a globally integrated system of instantaneous electronic transactions and communications, while at the same time, new "narrow-casting" or "long tail" models of multimedia communication, identity politics, and cultural interactions have positioned themselves against this reigning information technocracy.

No pithier encapsulation (or Surrealist detournment for that matter) of this longtail phenomenon has been crafted than William Gibson's description of the black-marketing of memory-enhancing drugs in his story "Burning Chrome," where the narrator claims "the street finds its own use for things" (199). In *Count Zero*, Gibson links his techno-Surrealist aesthetics with the onset of globalization as the informational network of cyberspace breeds a proliferating series of semi-sentient artificial intelligences that identify as Afro-Caribbean deities—crucially including the voodoo loa Legba, "master of roads and pathways, the loa of communication" (58). In this novel, Gibson also pays self-conscious homage to Joseph Cornell, the Surrealist diorama artist, by making the biochip that unleashes the evolution of megacorporate artificial intelligence a "Cornell box." This technosurreal artifact evokes nostalgia for a globe unaffected by the radical space-time compression of globalization: "In its evocation of impossible distances, of loss and yearning[, it] was somber, gentle, and somehow child-like" (18). Since cyberpunk's controversial inception, cover artists have tried to capture the visual equivalent of Gibson's literary techniques; the various covers of Gibson's iconic first novel, *Neuromancer* (1984), have over the years emphasized the author's ambivalent attitude toward the machinations of technological modernity and its prospects for the near future. A recent Brazilian edition from Aleph Press of Gibson's globally influential novel can get away with reducing the art to a minimalist icon that merely features a close-up of the black-and-white face of "razorgirl" Molly Millions, a weaponized female cyborg who has proven a pivotal touchstone for SF art and letters around the world.

The technologies of digital and electronic image manipulation have also reconfigured the photomontage techniques pioneered by New Wave artists into a new media of virtual futuristic iconography. Hugo-winning French artist Stephan Martinière's cover art for Ian McDonald's 2007 novel *Brasyl* reveals the debt it owes to cyberpunk in its *Blade Runner*-esque rendering of a future Rio de Janeiro teeming with cyborgized people and flying cars, soaked in the glow of all-pervasive neon. Recalling Paul's utopian future cities, the covers for McDonald's *River of Gods* (2004) and *The Dervish House* (2010) similarly depict glittering future cities but make a point to hybridize elements of the local culture with a global futurity: a hyperdeveloped urban concentration filled with pedestrians in rickshaws and *sherwani* jackets for the former's Mumbai; a 20-minutes-into-the-future, LA-inspired downtown cheek-by-jowl with star-and-crescent bunting, trollies, and women in *burqa*s for the latter's Istanbul. In an interview for *SF Revu*, Martinière freely acknowledges the instrumental utility of computer-graphics software like Photoshop, Painter, and other three-dimensional imaging tools, avowing that "in the expression 'digital art' I would say the 'art' part is the brain, the knowledge, the skills and imagination of the artist and the 'digital' part is like an electronic canvas" (Surrette).

FIGURE 15.5 Cover art for Ian McDonald's *Brasyl* (2007). Image courtesy of Prometheus Books.

Drawing attention to the digital divide explored in McDonald's novels, Martinière's stunning skill at digital-image manipulation both resists and reiterates the fetishizing cultural imperialism of transnational corporations and the homogenizing imperatives of hegemonic nation-states in the global North. In *The Practices of Everyday Life*, Michel de Certeau contends that whereas strategic actors wield a seemingly impregnable position within a consumer-oriented cyberculture, the excluded working classes and the neocolonized can only perform an aleatory array of "innumerable tactics" and subtle subterfuges that disrupt and challenge the hegemonic priorities of technological modernity (de Certeau 40). Certainly, the political valence of Zapatista warfare against the Mexican state or the hacker-aided protests against the November 1999 World Trade Organization meeting in Seattle are a decidedly different form of cultural expression than the Photoshop wizardry of contemporary commercial SF art and illustration. But, as Rita Raley contends, tactical media recognizes the postrevolutionary intractability of global capitalism and offers critique and dissent from within a consumer culture that aims to be "dynamic, decentralized, and bottom-up" (11).

A diorama artist before personal computers allowed him to perfect his craft, Dave McKean used digital techniques to paint the cover art for Cory Doctorow's *Someone Comes to Town, Someone Leaves Town* (2005), evoking the noirish, horrific urgency and evolving potential for SF art in a rapidly accelerating cyberculture. The piece depicts a photomontage of the abused angel Mimi from the novel, with jagged angular wings jutting out of a scarred back, discrepant blots and streaks silk-screening the image, expressionistic textures and layers, and a sepia-toned chiaroscuro coloring. On its most mimetic level, Doctorow's novel involves the securing of free Wi-Fi Internet access for Toronto by two dumpster-diving anarcho-punks, and the subplot involving Mimi seems to refract anxiety that casts bottom-up, longtail computer activity as shadowy and criminal. The debunking of this myth resonates with the novel's publication history: attempting to pioneer a new business model for fiction writers, Doctorow released the book for free online with a Creative Commons license while at the same time publishing it in print under the aegis of the Sci-Fi Channel. Extending his "copyleft" activism to a global reach, Doctorow explains, on the download page for the novel, that the noncommercial use clause does not extend to third world countries: "What's more, if you live in the developing world—a country not on the World Bank's list of high-income countries—you can do much more. You can make your own editions, charge money for them, make movies, translations, plays and anything else you care to, and charge whatever you want, without sending me one cent—you don't even need my permission." A far cry from the bold appeals of pulp-era iconography or the avant-garde visions of New Wave artists, contemporary digital art frequently participates in a global cyberculture that deploys modest, semi-oppositional tactics alongside canny commercial ploys.

In their book *Yesterday's Tomorrows*, Joseph Corn and Brian Horrigan claim that the emergence, evolution, and sudden disappearance of buoyant optimism and heedless confidence in the visionary futures purveyed by pulp-era American SF art can be understood according to a trajectory of political-cultural bad faith, compromise, and disillusion. What began as "radical political visions defying the capitalist leviathan" devolved into the idle delusions and daydreams of a "singular brand of zealots" (xii). Corn and Horrigan trace this paradigm shift in the gradually darkening tastes and expectations for SF aesthetic renderings of the future back to a naïve technological determinism. In their view, pulp-era exuberance betrays a telltale cognitive dissonance: "Such technological utopianism presumes that material means can ameliorate social problems and even perfect society" (xiii); this conflation of the social and technological produces a "smokescreen" that serves as an "obstacle to action" (xiii). While conceding Corn and Horrigan's inarguable premise that grandiose technocratic utopias dramatically lost their luster and cultural capital after the pulp era of SF art (until perhaps very recently), this chapter qualifies and counters this notion, showing the consistent recognition of the potential radical transformation of technoculture that constitutes SF art and illustration conceived as a crucial preview of coming attractions for our collective futures.

Works Cited

Aldiss, Brian W. *Science Fiction Art: The Fantasies of SF*. New York: Bounty/Crown, 1975. Print.
Ballard, J. G. "The Coming of the Unconscious." *New Worlds* 164 (Aug. 1966): 141–46. Print.
Boyer, Paul S. *Purity in Print: Book Censorship in America from the Gilded Age to the Computer Age*. Madison: U of Wisconsin P, 2002. Print.
Breton, André. "The Surrealist Manifesto." 1924. *Art in Theory 1900–1990: An Anthology of Changing Ideas*. Ed. Charles Harrison and Paul Woods. Oxford: Blackwell, 1992. 447–53. Print.
Castells, Manuel. *The Information Age: Economy, Society, and Culture*. 3 vols. 1996–1998. Oxford: Blackwell, 2010. Print.
Clarke, I. F. *The Pattern of Expectation, 1644–2001*. London: Cape, 1979. Print.
Corn, Joseph J., and Brian Horrigan. *Yesterday's Tomorrows: Past Visions of the American Future*. New York: Summit, 1984. Print.
de Certeau, Michel. *The Practice of Everyday Life*. 1980. Trans. Steven Rendall. Berkeley: U of California P, 1984. Print.
Debord, Guy. *The Society of the Spectacle*. 1967. Trans. Donald Nicholson-Smith. Cambridge, MA: Zone, 1994. Print.
Di Fate, Vincent. *Infinite Worlds: The Fantastic Visions of Science Fiction Art*. London: Virgin/Wonderland, 1997. Print.
Dick, Philip K. *The Man in the High Castle*. 1962. New York: Putnam, 1966. Print.
Doctorow, Cory. *Someone Comes to Town, Someone Leaves Town* [free download page]. *Cory Doctorow's Craphound.com*. 2007. Web. June 6, 2013. http://craphound.com/someone/?page_id=1589.
Evans, Arthur B. "The Illustrators of Jules Verne's *Voyages Extraordinaires*." *Science Fiction Studies* 25.2 (July 1998): 241–70. Print.
Frank, Jane. *The Art of Richard Powers*. London: Paper Tiger, 2001. Print.
Gernsback, Hugo. "$500 Prize Story Contest." *Amazing Stories* 1.9 (Dec. 1926): 773. Print.
Gibson, William. "Burning Chrome." 1982. *Burning Chrome and Other Stories*. New York: Harper Voyager, 2003. 179–205. Print.

———. *Count Zero*. New York: Arbor House, 1986. Print.
Gunn, James E. *Alternate Worlds: The Illustrated History of Science Fiction*. New York: Prentice-Hall, 1975. Print.
Harvey, David. *Spaces of Global Capital: A Theory of Uneven Geographical Development*. New York: Verso, 2006. Print.
Holland, Steve. *Sci-Fi: A Graphic History*. New York: Collins Design, 2009. Print.
Hughes, Rian. *Hardware: The Definitive SF Works of Chris Foss*. London: Titan, 2011.
Mitchell, W. J. T. *Picture Theory: Essays on Verbal and Visual Representation*. Chicago: U of Chicago P, 1994. Print.
Nadel, Alan. *Containment Culture: American Narratives, Postmodernism, and the Atomic Age*. Durham, NC: Duke UP, 1995. Print.
Nye, David E. *American Technological Sublime*. Cambridge, MA: MIT, 1994. Print.
Ortiz, Luis. *Outermost: The Art + Life of Jack Gaughan*. New York: Nonstop, 2010. Print.
Plant, Sadie. *The Most Radical Gesture: The Situationist International in a Postmodern Age*. New York: Routledge, 1992. Print.
Pohl, Frederik, ed. *Science-Fiction Roll of Honor*. Random House: New York, 1975. Print.
Raley, Rita. *Tactical Media*. Minneapolis: U of Minnesota P, 2009. Print.
Robinson, Frank M. *Science Fiction of the Twentieth Century: An Illustrated History*. Portland, OR: Collector's P, 1999. Print.
Ross, Andrew. *Strange Weather: Culture, Science, and Technology in the Age of Limits*. New York: Verso, 1991. Print.
Silberberg, L. "A Lady's Criticism." *Amazing Stories* 3.7 (Oct. 1928): 1145–46. Print.
Sontag, Susan. "The Imagination of Disaster." *Against Interpretation: And Other Essays*. New York: Dell, 1966. 212–28. Print.
Surrette, Gayle. "Artist: Stephan Martinière." *SFRevu*. Apr. 12, 2007. Web. June 15, 2013. http://sfrevu.com/php/Review-id.php?id=5487.
Wells, H. G. *The War of the Worlds*. 1898. *The Time Machine, The Invisible Man, The War of the Worlds*. New York: Everyman's Library, 2010. 237–412. Print.

CHAPTER 16

COMICS

COREY K. CREEKMUR

SCIENCE fiction comics have accompanied the production of SF literature and cinema for over a century yet remain marginalized despite increased recognition that the cultural manifestations of SF, or what Istvan Csicsery-Ronay Jr. more broadly calls "science-fictional habits of mind" (2), extend well beyond fiction, film, and television. Historical studies of SF consistently emphasize the genre's development through pulp magazines and paperbacks but have generally ignored the simultaneous publication formats (newspaper strips, comic books, and graphic novels) supporting SF comics. However, the historical origins of the American comic book, and the superhero stories most often associated with the format, are embedded in the simultaneous history of early SF fandom, with key figures moving between both cultural realms. If comics *are* considered within SF criticism, there's a tendency to select isolated examples—such as Alan Moore and Dave Gibbons's Hugo Award–winning (in the "Other Forms" category) revisionist superhero series *Watchmen* (1985)—from a very large corpus, allowing the rare, privileged exception to deflect attention from typical generic production.

Increased attention to SF within an international frame also often fails to acknowledge the steady flow of SF comics across national borders, perhaps most visibly through the worldwide popularity of Japanese manga. It's especially unclear why SF comics don't share the status now typically accorded to SF film and television since all of these media have been intertwined for decades through adaptations and marketing tie-ins, as well as creative personnel. SF comics are, in fact, produced more often and in more international locations than SF films, and the best examples of both are equally ambitious and sophisticated. Yet despite the rapid development and legitimation of comics studies, comics remain undervalued as contributions to the overall genre and culture of SF, much in the way that SF literature was once itself categorically dismissed from serious critical consideration. Nonetheless, comics have played a significant historical role in the popularity and public visibility of SF, and should play a greater role in future critical and historical accounts of the genre, especially when approached as a cultural category defining a wide range of increasingly globalized, transnational multimedia. Moreover, many of the best examples of SF comics take full advantage of their status *as comics*, presenting SF content through inventive use of the distinctive (even "science-fictional") formal elements that distinguish comics from other media, as this essay seeks to demonstrate.

While a number of histories of SF as a literary and cinematic genre mention SF comics, these references are often perfunctory and dismissive, relegating comics to the margins of significant SF. In some cases, SF comics are linked to other media through shared content (as in the case of comics to film adaptations), but the specific medium through which this content is conveyed remains ignored. While it might be unconvincing to attempt to challenge these accounts with a history of SF that privileges comics, it seems reasonable to suggest an "alternative history" of SF that locates SF comics on equal footing with other media, given their sheer quantity and simultaneous production and consumption alongside most of the history of SF literature and film.

Indeed, very soon after the consolidation of SF as a popular genre (and well before its secure naming), comics began to employ what would become familiar SF tropes and icons. Each historical period of modern SF offers easily identifiable parallels in comics: the first SF comic, appearing a few years after H. G. Wells's *The First Men in the Moon* (1901) and Georges Méliès' film *A Trip to the Moon* (1902), may be editor and cartoonist Harry Grant Dart's color Sunday strip *The Explorigator* (1908), which ran in the *New York World* for 14 weeks and depicted an expedition to the moon via airship by a group of boys. Drawn in large, detailed color panels evidently inspired by Winsor McCay's contemporary masterpiece *Little Nemo in Slumberland* (1905–14), *The Explorigator* followed the influential model of fantastic voyages pioneered by Jules Verne by substituting a potential future reality for the fantastic travel McCay confined to a child's dreams.

Following such early correspondences between comics and the development of SF as a popular genre, one can continue to trace similar parallels: the extremely successful newspaper strips *Buck Rogers* (1929–67) and *Flash Gordon* (1934–2003) unfolded alongside the "space operas" in early SF pulp magazines like *Amazing Stories* and *Planet Stories*, founded in 1926 and 1939, respectively. The rapid rise of the superhero comic book in the late 1930s mirrored SF's ongoing fascination with supermen (and women) in the form of advanced aliens, telepaths, or mutants. As Gerard Jones discovered, many of the key creators of the American comic book came directly out of early, loosely organized SF fandom, which built its collective identity, in part, through the interactive letters columns of SF pulp magazines. Jerry Siegel, who would create Superman with his childhood friend Joe Shuster a decade later, promoted his self-published fanzine *Cosmic Stories* in Hugo Gernsback's *Science Wonder Stories* in 1929, and the imaginations of other future comics authors and editors like Mort Weisinger and Julius Schwartz were informed by the consolidation of SF fandom as a group with unusual access to creators (an inheritance comics fandom has largely maintained).

In some cases, creators regularly moved back and forth between pulp SF and the early comic book industry: although Gernsback himself abandoned comics after publishing only three issues of *Superworld Comics* (1940) drawn by his regular pulp cover artist Frank R. Paul, emerging SF authors like Alfred Bester, Theodore Sturgeon,

Henry Kuttner, Manly Wade Wellman, and Edmond Hamilton regularly cranked out prose for the pulps as well as (often unsigned) scripts for comics. A full account of this intertwined history might emphasize that Fiction House, the publisher of the SF pulp magazine *Planet Stories* (1939–55), also published *Planet Comics* (1940–53), the first long-running comic book devoted exclusively to SF stories, or that Avon Publications, the important early publisher of SF paperbacks, also published SF comics like *Strange Worlds* (1950–55) featuring the early work of artist Wally Wood, eventually among the greatest SF artists in the history of American comics. Predictably, this cross-fertilization also resulted in shared content: Brian Attebery has traced the origins of early "supermen" and "wonder women" comics to their SF predecessors—Philip Wylie's 1930 SF novel *Gladiator* directly inspired the creation of Superman, for instance—exploring various forms of human evolution, "arguably the preeminent story form for 1940s and

FIGURE 16.1 Joe Doolin cover for *Planet Comics* No. 65 (1951).

'50s SF" (63), which editor John W. Campbell Jr. encouraged from authors writing for his influential *Astounding Science-Fiction*.

Additional highlights in a comics-centered history of SF might emphasize the direct link in the early 1950s between EC comics—which published the SF titles *Weird Science* (1950–53), *Weird Fantasy* (1950–53), *Weird Science-Fantasy* (1954–55), and *Incredible Science Fiction* (1955–56)—and the widely influential work of Ray Bradbury, a dozen of whose short stories EC adapted after Bradbury noticed that others had been "borrowed" as story sources without his permission. EC's exceptional artists on their SF titles, especially Wally Wood and Al Williamson, also brought an unprecedented degree of realism to the pages of comic books in their incredibly detailed representations of aliens as well as the interior hardware of spaceships, for stories that (like Bradbury's) employed SF tropes to comment indirectly on current social ills, as in writer Al Feldstein and artist Joe Orlando's famous allegory of racial tolerance, "Judgment Day," in *Weird Fantasy* 18 (1953).

Following the near-collapse of the comic-book industry brought about by the self-censoring Comics Code in 1954 (which directly targeted EC's notorious crime and horror titles), SF comics returned to prominence in the early 1960s in response to the "space race" and "atomic age," most successfully through the preeminence of Marvel's anguished superheroes (discussed below). In the 1960s and 1970s, the international impact of New Wave SF was best represented via the poetic and psychedelic comics of European artists like Moebius (Jean Giraud) and Phillipe Druillet, both associated with the groundbreaking magazine *Metal Hurlant* (which inspired the American *Heavy Metal*). New Wave SF also inspired early independent comics in the United States, including Mike Friedrich's anthology *Star*Reach* (1974–79) and Jack Katz's sprawling SF fantasy *The First Kingdom* (1974–86), both of which took advantage of their independent status to add more explicit sexuality and philosophical themes to SF comics designed for adult readers.

The appearance of explicitly feminist SF in the 1970s and 1980s was also matched in independent comics by the work of previously marginalized female creators including Colleen Doran, Carla Speed McNeil, and Teri Sue Wood, the individual creators of, respectively, *A Distant Soil* (1983–), *Finder* (1996–), and *Wandering Star* (1993–97), which all build rich, coherent worlds featuring unconventional gender and sexual identities.

More recently, comics have included numerous cyberpunk titles, including Warren Ellis and Darick Robertson's paradigmatic *Transmetropolitan* (1997–2002) as well as steampunk variants, most notably Alan Moore and Kevin O'Neill's pastiche of popular Victorian genres and characters (including Verne's Captain Nemo and Wells' Invisible Man), *The League of Extraordinary Gentlemen* (1999–). Finally, equivalents of boundary-transgressing "slipstream" fiction are evident in boldly experimental comics grounded in popular SF elements such as Gary Panter's widescreen *Dal Tokyo* strips (collected 2012) or Jeffrey Brown's willfully naïve volumes of *Incredible Change-Bots* (2007, 2011) which rely upon self-consciously "ugly," "childlike," or "primitive" art to suggest an outsider artist's ambivalent relationship to a mainstream genre increasingly defined by expensive state-of-the-art special effects. Brown's riff on the Transformers toys thus returns them, following their own transformation into blockbuster movies, to their junky origins as cheap objects of childish (and perhaps destructive) play. My goal in this limited sketch of a comics-centered history of SF is, again, to simply argue for the persistent interaction of SF comics with SF as a genre for at least the past century. Arguably, no account of the broadly "science-fictional" turn of contemporary popular culture or art should ignore such regular and often significant contributions to the genre, yet most accounts of SF media continue to do so.

While the international status of SF film and literature is increasingly acknowledged, SF comics have been equally prominent within specific national traditions or have functioned as a conduit bridging cultural traditions, as another brief sketch may demonstrate. Curiously, British SF comics (unlike literature and film) have enjoyed only limited crossover success in the United States and elsewhere. Despite the enormous impact of early British SF writers on the genre, the first major British SF comic was Frank Hampson's *Dan Dare, Pilot of the Future*, launched in the boys' weekly *Eagle* in 1950 (discussed more fully below). Although *Dan Dare* was revived in the first issue of *2000 AD* in 1977, establishing a loose continuity between earlier and later SF traditions, *2000 AD* was a punk-era game-changer, replacing the wholesome and patriotic stories of the past with a new blend of parody and dystopian gloom. The paper's iconic figure, introduced in its second issue, was future Mega-City One lawman *Judge Dredd*, created by editor Pat Mills, writer John Wagner, and artist Carlos Ezquerra, and eventually taken up by dozens of others. *2000 AD*, in vivid contrast to the visions of *Eagle* and other boys' weeklies, offered SF strips with a balance of wicked social satire and unapologetic adolescent mayhem, in effect summarizing the large-scale shift in SF in the post–World War II period.

Unsurprisingly, the legacy of Verne has had a continual impact on French-language comics (*bandes desinées*) since at least the 1930s, in the European album format and *ligne claire* ("clear line") style that would define Franco-Belgian comics for decades to come. Even the most famous comic in this tradition, Hergé's massively popular Tintin series (1929–76), while commonly appreciated as boy-detective/adventure stories, took a notable detour into SF with the two-album narrative *Destination Moon* (1953) and *Explorers on the Moon* (1954), anticipating the actual moon landing by over a decade, in perhaps the most widely read SF comics ever published.

Although the New Wave of SF writing emerging in the 1960s is commonly associated with the United Kingdom, as noted earlier, no other comics so fully embraced the new erotic and expansive visual potential of SF as French comics. For sheer visual impact, little could match Philippe Druillet's or Moebius's albums employing panoramic, intricately composed pages merging SF and mystical traditions. The main successors to this tradition can be found in later publications from *Les Humanoïdes Associés*, including the work of brothers François and Luc Schuiten and artist Enki Bilal, among others.

Certainly, the most famous SF comic from Latin America is *El Eternauta* (1957) from Argentina, written by H. G. Oesterheld and drawn by Francisco Solano Lopez; the story, centered on a small human group's resistance to an invasion of aliens known as "Them," was remade in 1969 and redrawn by Alberto Breccia, and a sequel (drawn again by Solano Lopez) appeared in 1976, by which time the leftist Oesterheld was in hiding before his arrest in 1977 and presumed murder in 1978 by the ruling military junta. Originally serialized, the story is now often viewed as a political allegory: in the revised version, Western powers sell South America to the aliens. References to the now decades-old SF comic still resonate in Latin American political and cultural discourse.

Perhaps the most extensive body of SF comics—closely linked to Japanese animated films (or anime)—exists within Japanese manga. Examples can be found as early as Noburu Oshiro's *Voyage to Mars* in 1940, but the massive post–World War II development of manga is largely associated with the prolific career of Osamu Tezuka, whose works are credited with bringing cinematic energy to a more static earlier form. Tezuka's most popular contribution to SF is his long-running *Astro Boy* (1952–68), centered around a cute but heroic boy robot; Astro Boy's status as a key icon of Japanese SF would much later allow for revisionist texts like Naoki Urasawa's *Pluto* (2003–09), an elaborate update and expansion of one of the most popular stories featuring Tezuka's legendary character.

Mitsuteru Yokoyama's *Tetsujin 28-go* (1956), in Tezuka's wake, was an equally popular series centered on a robot and a boy that would influence a steady production of "mecha" manga focused on robots. Notably, the large market for *shojo manga* (girl's comics) also makes Japan perhaps the largest producer of SF for young female readers: the *shojo manga* pioneer Moto Hagio's *They Were 11* (1975–76), dramatizing the testing of a group of young space cadets, is a key example of intelligent SF manga for girls. More recently, the prolific female comics collective Clamp created the wildly popular *Chobits* (2001–02), featuring "persocoms"—personal computers in human form; like many other examples, the multivolume manga has spawned an anime series, video games, and a vast range of merchandise. One of the first translated manga to reach a large Western audience, Katsuhiro Otomo's massive, action-packed *Akira* (1982–90), set in a postapocalyptic neo-Tokyo, had a wide-ranging impact on the visual representation of what would become known as cyberpunk, as did the cyborg thriller *Ghost in the Shell* (1989–90) by Masumune Shirow.

As these few examples seek to demonstrate, SF and manga have been deeply and consistently intertwined throughout the period that extends from the destruction of Hiroshima and Nagasaki to Japan's current high-tech status (a history often represented as science-fictional). Moreover, the international popularity of manga, especially among younger female readers, represents a unique dissemination of non-Western SF—albeit influenced by Western models—to audiences that otherwise do not avidly consume the genre (or comics, for that matter).

Roger Luckhurst, one of the few scholars to fully acknowledge the role early SF comic strips played in the "growth of SF outside the relatively narrow cultural base of the pulps," emphasizes that, by the late 1920s, SF comics "began to insert themselves into everyday life (and popular memory)" and thus started "that perennial difficulty of constraining analysis of SF to a single aesthetic mode" (66). More persistently and elaborately—and, for decades, more colorfully—than early cinema, SF comics helped realize the futuristic, the alien, and the cosmic as visual spectacles as well as visionary concepts. Transforming the evocative descriptions in prose SF into powerful images, comics more fully rendered the look—and at times evoked the scale—of the objects, events, and locations of SF, pushing the "wonder" generated by its narratives closer to plausible material reality. Moreover, whereas the illustrators of SF pulp magazine and later paperback covers were often limited to creating a single striking image condensing a story—if not the entire genre—contained within, SF comics do not merely feature supplemental illustrations but provide fully narrativized images arranged in sequential panels animated with a propulsive energy that seems to transcend the stasis of their actual pages.

In addition to their creative juxtapositions of language and image in the service of SF stories, the impact of newspaper comic strips and comic books might also be understood in terms of Luckhurst's important suggestion that "new literatures produced in mass quantities by publishing syndicates," such as SF pulp magazines, "were a product of the transformative power of Mechanism itself" (52). The regularity of daily, weekly, or monthly serial publication and consumption guiding most comics in itself sustains a tacit belief in the functional, efficient science embodied in the very technologies ensuring that modern life (and the future) is systematic, punctual, and rational, even when engineered to divert and entertain. Thus, the black-and-white daily and color Sunday strips featuring futuristic spacemen and their advanced machines not only visualized the scientific miracles of the future but also attested to an increasingly efficient mass culture that produced otherwise fantastic stories like clockwork.

As noted earlier, superhero comic books, initiated by the immediate success of Siegel and Shuster's character Superman in *Action Comics* in 1938, derive directly from creators steeped in early SF fandom. However, the rapid proliferation in the late 1930s and revitalization of superhero comics in the early 1960s, leading eventually to the common misperception that they define the American comic book, have often led to their isolation from rather than affiliation with mainstream SF, and thus to their treatment as a somewhat distinct genre (as the current designation of "superhero" films quite apart from SF movies affirms). Certainly, not all superhero narratives bear clear links to SF: some superheroes are based in mythology (Thor, Wonder Woman) or magic (Dr. Strange), and thus ignore the fundamental scientific basis of SF; others are derived from different popular genre traditions, such as detective fiction (Batman, The Spirit), even if they include SF elements, such as Batman's high-tech gadgets. Nonetheless, many superheroes from the periods that comics fans designate as the Golden Age (the late 1930s to the early 1950s) and the Silver Age (1956 to around 1970) are explicit SF figures: DC characters like Adam Strange (a space-age update of Edgar Rice Burroughs's John Carter of Mars, first appearing in 1958), the Green Lantern (in his 1959 revision as test pilot and intergalactic policeman Hal Jordan), and the Atom (physicist Ray Palmer, first appearing in 1961) all attempt to explain their bizarre adventures through scientific principles.

Marvel's wildly successful revitalization as a comics publisher in the early 1960s followed suit, locating the origins of its often anguished heroes in the troubling possibilities of scientific experimentation gone wrong, with Stan Lee and Jack Kirby's *The*

Fantastic Four (1961–), Lee and Steve Ditko's *Spider-Man* (1962–), Lee and Kirby's *The Hulk* (1962–), and Lee and Kirby's *X-Men* (1963–) all explicitly the products (or victims) of scientific error or uncontrolled mutation. Since their first appearances, continual revisions and reinventions of these (and many other) superhero characters have refined such initially naïve, vaguely "scientific" explanations, drawing upon advances in—as well as popular fears surrounding—genetics, cybernetics, and nanotechnology, among other areas that might be exploited for fictional purposes.

Despite their success among SF fans, however, the reluctant embrace of superhero comics by SF critics may stem from their persistent reliance on "space opera" adventures rather than "hard science" speculations, even if the latter are more frequent than in the past. For decades, the critical legitimation of SF seemed to demand the trivialization of space opera as a remnant of the genre's embarrassing past, even if contemporary variations on the space opera have been some of SF's most commercially popular products. The common perception after World War II that comics were largely for children, a condition virtually imposed upon them by the tight restrictions of the Comics Code after 1954, also obviously limited the ambitions of SF comics creators who might have otherwise wished to produce more sophisticated narratives. And, of course, many superhero comics with SF trappings do rely upon ludicrous or at best implausible explanations within a genre that still values logic and plausibility as a basis for even its most fantastic narratives.

Aside from their ostensible SF content and trappings, whether silly or reasonably scientific, however, perhaps the most "science-fictional" component of the experience of superhero comics emerged through the growth of a dedicated comics fandom and its somewhat unanticipated activity of carefully collecting what were originally designed as disposable publications. Letters columns in superhero comic books allowed for the seemingly direct interaction between creators and fans established by earlier SF pulp magazines, and these revealed that regular readers increasingly demanded a coherence to the narratives they were reading with which editors had been largely unconcerned. In their desire for what came to be identified as "continuity," readers were less interested in scientifically convincing explanations for superhero narratives than in an overarching narrative logic that might explain how the many adventures of a single character over many years (despite being the product of many different authors and artists) were linked.

Moreover, following the frequent crossovers and team-ups that drew together a publisher's roster of characters, readers insisted that the logic linking different titles narratively (rather than industrially or economically) should be articulated. Eventually, it became necessary for DC to explain the relationship between its character the Flash from the Golden Age (introduced in 1940 as Jay Garrick) and the Flash from the Silver Age (introduced in 1956 as Barry Allen), or its superhero teams the Justice Society of America (first seen in 1940) and the Justice League of America (first seen in 1960), which curiously shared some members. This was done through the editorial staff's increasingly elaborate establishment of an ever-growing number of parallel worlds, or a vast multiverse, implying that virtually all of DC's properties could be linked (unless the stories were explicitly presented, curiously, as "imaginary stories"). Again, fans led creators to maintain this narrative logic, tying together hundreds of stories from decades of comics, with each new story adding another piece to the massive puzzle.

In addition to encouraging fans of any single superhero to now buy all of DC's titles because they were implicitly linked, this increasingly complex interaction provided readers with an active fantasy of their participation in the construction of DC's "universe," a practice that would take place with equally fervent dedication by Marvel's new fans from the early 1960s onward and eventually fuel the active creation of fan fiction derived from copyrighted properties that would define a major segment of SF fandom in later decades. In their dedication to the DC or Marvel universes, fans understood their consumption of superhero comics to be anything but passive: reading comics demanded distinctive skills of narrative comprehension and a store of knowledge that separated true fans from casual readers and thus reinforced the cultish ties that bind fandom as a community. But such "world building" by fans still derived from the worlds provided in vivid detail by comics creators.

Arguably, the most prominent function of SF comics has been to actually depict the "visionary" aspects that are seen as fundamental to the genre. If this is an obvious point, its importance remains undervalued. In an illuminating essay "The Icons of Science Fiction," Gwyneth Jones asserts that "[m]ore than in any other fiction[,] in SF the imaginary setting is a major character in the story—and this fictional surface is held together by the highly foregrounded description of unreal objects, customs, kinships, fashions, that can be identified and decoded by the reader" (163). SF comics, however, provide readers with actual images, often in place of what in prose would be "highly foregrounded description"; even if literary SF engages the "mind's eye," the ability of comics to literally envision the future or other or alternative worlds (far more inexpensively than cinema) has contributed significantly to our shared sense of what robots, spaceships, ray guns, or aliens might look like, and in many cases one suspects that images from comics have directed actual design and engineering choices. "World building," the often highly valued skill of SF creators to fully flesh out the details of coherent, imaginary futures or alternative worlds or universes, thus shifts from (often extended) description in prose to (often compact) drawing in SF comics, although the historical privileging of verbal over visual information has perhaps blinded us to an appreciation of this function of comics.

Despite their status as mass-produced and consumed artifacts, the fact that comics are first drawn ensures that they exhibit stylistic differences and even individual artistic "signatures" in spite of their frequent, generic conventionality or reliance on a company-defined "house style." (Historically, of course, many early comics creators worked in anonymity or under pseudonyms, much like the prolific creators of pulp SF.) The question of authorship in mainstream comics remains somewhat vexed since most comic books—especially before the self-expressive function of underground comix of the 1960s and subsequent independent comics could be imagined—were produced in a factory mode by teams of workers, typically isolated as writers, pencillers, inkers, colorists, and letterers. Comics fans have thus tended to inconsistently privilege some writers and some artists as the primary authors of their works, maintaining an artisanal appreciation of what is, in fact, an industrial product.

Significantly, most comics fans do not view them as simply illustrated stories but engage with the intricate coordination of word and image, and sequential narration as significant style, viewing images and layout as fundamental rather than merely supplemental to meaning. Throughout the history of comics, many artists have made distinctive, often self-reflexive, use of these formal elements, while less adventurous artists have employed these reliable devices as a basic template. Put more abstractly, comics offer distinctive devices for the manipulation of narrative time and space, and in the creation of SF comics, some writers and artists have recognized that the ambitious subject matter of much SF—time and space themselves as concepts or scientific categories—might be approached through the exploration of the temporal and spatial possibilities offered by comics.

For instance, although the *Flash Gordon* newspaper strip (which only appeared in color on Sundays) was clearly modeled upon the earlier and wildly successful *Buck Rogers* strip (which appeared in daily as well as Sunday newspapers), its artist, Alex Raymond, quickly moved away from the standard 12-panel grid employed with only minor variations by Sunday *Buck Rogers* artists Dick Calkins, Russell Keaton, and Rick Yager. (After a short while, however, the Sunday strip regularly used its final panel to provide diagrams for the many gadgets or rocket ships introduced within the strip, suggesting that Buck's advanced technology was currently in the planning stages and perhaps could be built by "popular mechanics" in their own garages.) Within a year, Raymond's *Flash Gordon* pages, drawn in a realist style akin to the era's book and magazine illustrations rather than newspaper "funnies," expanded from cramped, small panels to fewer but larger panels to depict both greater detail and sweeping action, culminating in a legendary 1935 page that depicts a hawkman army diving the full length of the entire newspaper page, an action presented as too grand to be contained within a typical panel. Through Raymond's exquisite brushwork, the rather bulbous rocketships of *Buck Rogers* were also transformed into sleek missiles, with Raymond's incredibly thin lines of ink effectively rendering speed on the static page.

The appearance in 1950 of Frank Hampson's *Dan Dare, Pilot of the Future* had a similar impact: each weekly segment appeared in two full-color, originally painted rotogravure pages featuring meticulously rendered depictions of the futuristic 1990s, often based upon actual models and research (SF author Arthur C. Clarke was a consultant). As artist Dave Gibbons has recalled, the bright *Dan Dare* pages appeared in a Britain that was otherwise gray: "Every Friday a new issue would glow, like a radioactive gem buried amongst seams of anthracite newsprint," providing "[a] future that was sharply defined, solidly real, and intensely colourful, in every sense of the word" (n.p.). On the very first page of the very first *Dan Dare* strip, a panel depicting at some distance a rocket blasting off from the ground is followed by a panel that shifts our perspective to the sky above the airborne rocket as it approaches us, a transition that not only implies movement in space and time but also offers us an unrestricted, literally inhuman view. In other words, part of the appeal of an SF comic strip like *Dan Dare* was not just in its vivid rendering of the fantastic near future but in its offer of new perspectives, through its formal construction, of that future.

FIGURE 16.2 Full-page Sunday panel from Alex Raymond's *Flash Gordon* comic strip.

Two additional examples might serve to make the general point that the form or style as well as the content of SF comics constitutes a significant element of their "science-fictionality." EC illustrator Wally Wood typically drew scripts written by others; however, Wood's meticulous detail—again, the visual equivalent to the descriptive detail common in SF prose—might be viewed as a hindrance to the "quick read" comics are often assumed to provide. Wood's SF panels, especially the larger "splash pages" that typically begin his stories set within spaceships, are packed with visual detail (which poor printing and color often blurred) that generally serves no narrative purpose but that renders the future fantasy material plausible: it's worth recalling that Wood drew such interiors at a time when the control panels on view in SF films were laughably simplistic.

In contrast to Wood's detailed realism, the prolific artist Jack Kirby—often illustrating Stan Lee's scripts, although the nature of their collaboration remains disputed—was increasingly led by his inexhaustible imagination toward wildly cosmic themes supported by appropriately awe-inspiring images of vast stretches of space or enormous, crazy machines, often surrounded by what came to be known as "Kirby krackle," patterns of semi-abstract imagery that effectively visualized concepts like negative space and pure energy. Charles Hatfield has emphasized that Kirby's early devotion to pulp SF as well as his later interest in pseudoscientific phenomena informed his regular exploration of what Hatfield (following historian David E. Nye) calls "the technological sublime." Kirby's predilection for intricate, sometimes nightmarish machines, as well as narratives taking place at the edge of human comprehension and perception, were often rendered, by the mid-1960s, in semi-experimental full-page or double-page collages, with images maintaining an SF perspective of awe amidst plots steeped in muscular, action-driven heroics.

As many have noted, comics (with notable exceptions) have seemed an overwhelmingly urban phenomenon, despite their widespread circulation. Early newspaper comics often represented the modern city's advanced technologies and soaring skyscrapers, and, as Scott Bukatman has forcefully argued, by the late 1930s "American superheroes encapsulated and embodied the same utopian aspirations of modernity as the cities themselves" (185). Superman's shiny Metropolis, Batman's gritty Gotham City, and even the relatively realistic New York City inhabited by Spider-Man or the Fantastic Four (in their high-tech Baxter Building) all tended to be depicted as both contemporaneous and futuristic, locations supporting both everyday activities and extraordinary adventures or catastrophic destruction. Earlier comic strips like *Buck Rogers* and *Flash Gordon* also offered compelling views of futuristic or otherworldly cities, typically gleaming and streamlined, before images of densely overpopulated and polluted cities began to dominate European SF comics, ranging from the crammed and trash-strewn city in Alejandro Jodorowsky and Moebius's *The Incal* (1981–89) to the hundreds of Judge Dredd stories in Britain's *2000 AD* set in the vast, postapocalyptic sprawl of Mega-City One. The large European comic album format has ironically allowed for beautifully detailed drawings of notably ugly urban spaces.

In addition to the use of the modern or futuristic city as a common SF setting, as Bukatman emphasizes, the distinctive location of urban superheroes, especially those with the power of flight, is above the city, a position readers are also allowed to inhabit. The crush of the urban crowd and congested transportation on the ground are literally transcended via flight above skyscrapers and the mastery of aerial perspectives. The bird's (or god's) eye view also allows the city to be comprehended from a distance as a grid, a mapped view that lends itself to analogy with the common panel organization of most comics. The urban narratives of most superhero and many SF comics are thereby modeled by the organization of the panels on their pages. Thierry Groensteen has emphasized the doubling or mirroring devices employed throughout the page and panel compositions of *Watchmen*, for example, most extensively in the double-page spread at the heart of the chapter appropriately entitled "Fearful Symmetry" (99). Howard Chaykin's satirical SF series *American Flagg!* (1983–89), set in Chicago in the early 2030s, perhaps most fully took advantage of the impact of pages often organized through repetitive images (and famously visualized sound effects) to portray a world dominated by the reproductive technologies of unrelenting media and advertising. The work clearly influenced similar and equally effective design strategies in the subsequent and better-known *Watchmen* and Frank Miller's dystopian Batman comic *The Dark Knight Rises* (1986), in which pervasive television screens function as comic panels.

More contemporary comics have represented the modern city through the postmodern lens of "retrofuturism," employing simultaneously nostalgic and ironic images of the future from the past in such works as Kurt Busiek's series (with many artists) *Astro City* (1995–98, 2003–) and especially a number of titles written by Dean Motter, including *Mister X* (1983–90), *Terminal City* (1997–98), and *Electropolis* (2001–02). The setting of Motter's comics can't be considered mere background but occupies a primary place in our reception. According to Henry Jenkins, Motter's carefully designed Art Deco comics present "science fiction as a mode of historical critique," demonstrating "that past imaginings of the future need to be understood as historical artifacts of older ideologies about human progress and that their remobilization in the present can be used as a means of reflecting on the failures of those dreams to become realities" (64).

While the ongoing production of mainstream superhero comics now functions more or less as "research and development" for the creation of far more profitable blockbuster films and video games featuring copyrighted characters owned by media conglomerates, the publication format of the "graphic novel" (whether reprinting series comics or containing original material) and the relative freedom of independent comics publishers demonstrate the ongoing appeal of SF for contemporary comics creators. Titles launched in 2012 alone, including Brian K. Vaughan and Fiona Staples's *Saga*, Jonathan Hickman and Nick Patarra's *The Manhattan Projects*, Brian Wood and Kristian Donaldson's *The Massive*, or Brandon Graham and Simon Roy's major revamp of *Prophet*, all constitute sophisticated and ambitious SF comics, suggesting that a solid future remains for this long-lasting alignment between the format of comics and the genre of SF.

Works Cited

Attebery, Brian. *Decoding Gender in Science Fiction*. New York: Routledge, 2002. Print.
Bukatman, Scott. "The Boys in the Hoods: A Song of the Urban Superhero." 2000. *Matters of Gravity: Special Effects and Supermen in the Twentieth Century*. Durham, NC: Duke UP, 2003. 184–223. Print.
Csicsery-Ronay Jr., Istvan. *The Seven Beauties of Science Fiction*. Middletown, CT: Wesleyan UP, 2008. Print.
Gibbons, Dave. "Introduction." *Frank Hampson, Dan Dare, Pilot of the Future: Voyage to Venus Part I*. London: Titan, 2004. Print.
Groensteen, Thierry. *The System of Comics*. 1999. Trans. Bart Beaty and Nick Nguyen. Jackson: UP of Mississippi, 2007. Print.
Hatfield, Charles. *Hand of Fire: The Comics Art of Jack Kirby*. Jackson: UP of Mississippi, 2012. Print.

Jenkins, Henry. "'The Future That Never Was': Retrofuturism in the Comics of Dean Motter." *Comics and the City: Urban Space in Print, Picture, and Sequence.* Ed. Jorn Ahrens and Arno Meterling. New York: Continuum, 2010. 63–83. Print.

Jones, Gerard. *Men of Tomorrow: Geeks, Gangsters, and the Birth of the Comic Book.* New York: Basic Books, 2004. Print.

Jones, Gwyneth. "The Icons of Science Fiction." *The Cambridge Companion to Science Fiction.* Ed. Edward James and Farah Mendlesohn. Cambridge, UK: Cambridge UP, 2003. 163–73. Print.

Luckhurst, Roger. *Science Fiction.* Cambridge, UK: Polity, 2005. Print.

CHAPTER 17

VIDEO GAMES

PAWEŁ FRELIK

AS most histories of video games aptly demonstrate, the origins of the medium seem to be inextricably tied to science fiction—one of the earliest known computer games was *Spacewar!* (1962) designed as a demonstration program for the PDP-1 machine at MIT. It featured battling spaceships, each armed with a supply of missiles and a hyperspace switch for evasion tactics, and was controlled by a player using a keyboard/joystick console. Although conceived as purely utilitarian, *Spacewar!* became the prototype for the first mass-marketed, coin-operated arcade game, *Computer Space* (1971), and morphed into a range of titles involving staple SF scenarios: from alien invasion (*Space Invaders* [1978] and *Galaxian* [1979]) to space navigation (*Asteroids* [1979]) to nuclear warfare (*Missile Command* [1980]). The kinetic visual spectacle of these early arcade games strongly influenced SF cinema during the period, especially *Star Wars* (1977), *Tron* (1982), and *The Last Starfighter* (1984).

Doom (1993), widely regarded as one of the most important titles in gaming history, was also essentially a science fiction game. It spawned numerous clones and marked the trajectory of development for the first-person shooter genre, 3D graphics, and networked play. *Doom*'s burgeoning community of players, developers, and fans also became a model for the entire gaming subculture based on participation not only in gameplay itself but also in extended commentary, level development, and online resources building. Compared to later titles, *Doom* is technically and conceptually relatively simple, but it still exemplifies a range of critical issues at the intersection of the gaming medium and science fiction as a genre, major among which has been the question of narrative. Much of the critical dissent around the issue of narrative is grounded in the vastly different definitions of this term—unless stated otherwise, I use it to denote a fixed and predetermined sequence of events (see Prince; Bordwell).

While early video games presented very little background information, forcing players to imagine stories behind the clusters of pixels on the screen, newer titles have capitalized on the development of gaming technologies by inserting increasingly large chunks of textual and visual data and significantly expanding story-worlds presented in the games. Such information can be coded in the form of in-game diaries, TV broadcasts, recorded phone messages, or abandoned notes that the player encounters but also as cinematic "cutscenes" (game sequences over which the player has relatively little control) and diegetic and nondiegetic archive logs and databases. In science fiction video games, this tendency to infuse game-space with narrative elements coincides with the genre's privileging of the plot-driven narrative. While early SF pulp fictions were often little more than excuses to proselytize about the virtues of technology and rationality, with time fans—and particularly the scholarly community—have come to regard SF as a literature of ideas whose primary vehicle is a coherent and well-constructed plot with well-rounded characters. Such a focus has carried over to other science fiction media, most notably film and television.

In video-game criticism, the narrative-centric approach constitutes a significant strand that tends to group video games with other forms of new media and seeks to identify in them both the continuation of traditional narrative strategies and their permutations, affected by the constraints and affordances of these new forms. The compulsion to see video games as a new frontier of storytelling, however, remains at odds with the character of digital visual culture, which "endorses form over content, the ephemeral and superficial over permanence and depth, and the image itself over the image as referent" (Darley 81). The problems facing those attempting to combine spectacular gameplay with strong narrative are perfectly exemplified by Richard Morgan, a British novelist known for complexly plotted and politically involved SF novels. A self-confessed gamer, Morgan has repeatedly criticized video-game scripts, including those of the *Halo* franchise renowned for its extensive narrative universe, but has himself failed to achieve narrative sophistication in *Crysis 2* (2009) and *Syndicate* (2012), for which he was a lead writer and that have been criticized for their exaggerated dialogue and flat characters. Critically, high narrative expectations have resulted in scathing denunciations—like SF cinema, many SF video games suffered at the hands of narrative-based approaches, which tend to cast visual spectacle as hollow because it serves no "higher" narrative function (Ndalianis 258) and which completely fail to account for the participatory dimension of gaming. The fact that many video-game scholars have imported their theoretical apparatus from literary or cinematic theory has only aggravated the situation. On the other hand, it is impossible to deny that, when measured against the standards of literary or filmic storytelling, even the most narratively acclaimed video games are driven by clichéd storylines "that would make a B-movie writer blush, and characters so wooden that they make *The Flintstones* look like Strindberg" (Aarseth 51). Although they did constitute significant improvements over earlier gaming titles, in traditional narrative terms *Half-Life* (1998), with its linear plotting, or *DeusEx* (1999), with rich cultural allusions and three alternate conclusions, still fail to measure up to the complexity of many 1950s SF novels.

At the core of the conflicted claims concerning the narrative potential of SF video games is an erroneous conviction that the set of generic protocols formulated from an analysis of literary SF can be applied to any medium without consequences for the protocols themselves. In reality, SF video games are merely pseudo-morphs of both literary and cinematic science fictions, a media form whose "surface deceit . . . conceals a number of internal differences" and "a basic discontinuity in genus and species" (Gunning 355). Naturally, games share a number of characteristics with novels or films, but they are also distinctly different from them because of the very nature of the medium. Consequently, they require a new set of approaches that recalibrates critical attention to those aspects that are inherent in the medium's unique deployment of the SF repertoire. The following discussion is thus grounded in the assumption that the exclusive narrative approach imported from SF literary and film studies is biased, unproductive, and—most important—insufficient to address some of the most relevant aspects of the medium: its species of visuality as well as its interactivity and performativity.

Differences between video games and other narrative media are already apparent in the very classification of texts and the lack of agreement among critics regarding a system of gaming genres. Many researchers suggest taxonomies largely reflective of cognitive or haptic interactions required from the player. Wolf enumerates as many as 42 different types (117), including adventure, flying, platform, role-playing, and strategy, many of which can accommodate different thematics. For instance, the genre of first-person shooter (FPS) can be equally successfully packaged in narrative conventions as diverse as mafia stories, technothrillers, military tales, or science fiction with little influence on the core experience of gameplay. In addition, game genres are inherently impure. It is not uncommon for a title to integrate FPS, role-playing, action, and puzzle-solving—all three installments of *Mass Effect* (2007, 2010, 2012) are a case in point. Simultaneously, more traditional thematic distinctions have also been used, including those belonging to the broad field of what John Clute has dubbed "fantastika"—the related genres of science fiction, fantasy, and horror.

Compared to other cultural forms, video games are unique in that, unlike literature or cinema, they do not suffer from the schizophrenic split into mainstream and genre productions. This is important for SF video games, which, at least within their own cultural sphere, have not confronted the generic prejudice so prevalent in other media. It seems unlikely that ghetto lines will be drawn between SF video games and, for instance, "newsgames" or educational games such as *Food Force* (2005). While evaluations of individual titles may naturally vary, game studies scholarship has manifested no signs of discrimination against, for instance, science fiction first-person shooters as a form. One of the main reasons for this absence of discrimination between mainstream and genre is the fact that in fiction or film such a bias has been largely predicated on issues of thematics and narrative form (or occasionally on the material circumstances of production): mainstream texts are by definition more complex in structure and ideation. In games, which obviously use narrative and thematics but are inherently concerned with simulation and participation, the cognitive and haptic demands do not differ across genres, thus producing much less risk of conceptual apartheid among differently inflected renderings of the interactive component.

Games may be "themable," as Jesper Juul has argued (189, 199), but on the level of rules so are novels—at the core of William Gibson's celebrated *Neuromancer* (1984) is simple hard-boiled plotting. This does not, however, preclude the theme from imprinting its character on a game's title as well as using the game's structure to its own ends. Consequently, while certain science fiction games may be animated by the same mechanics and gameplay principles as some James Bond games, as texts the former are likely to figure and signify differently from the latter and can be analyzed from a specifically science-fictional perspective. To date, there has been little critical work on how video games in general and specific gaming genres in particular engage and transform traditional genre codes as derived from fiction and film. Nevertheless, while aware that medium-specific rules, the component of video games that distinguishes them from fiction or film, are genre-blind, I would like to postulate a genre-specific analysis of SF video games. Such an analysis will both illuminate how SF video games in general are different from SF literature or SF film and suggest the areas of intersection between the genre and the medium.

It is immaterial whether the relative paucity of (traditionally understood) narrative complexity, and the attendant deficit of entryways for traditional interpretation, are a result of the medium's recency or its inherent inability to tell stories in the same ways as other media do—waiting for a *Casablanca* of video games is as fallacious as expecting a *Ulysses* of hypertext. Narrative is not the only interesting element of science fiction video games; it is also not the most productive avenue to be pursued when approaching them, either. This does not mean that SF video games are a minor form of the genre, critically or (especially) commercially. Quite the opposite, in fact: I would like to suggest that video games, as well as such related forms as Alternate Reality Games (ARGs), are a crucial form through which science fiction can seek to convey a more active sense of futurity. Also, by capturing wide audiences, they can contribute to a more universal understanding of the ideas that SF has promoted in its many forms. If science fiction is, indeed, the only arena of contemporary culture that actively constructs and interrogates utopian/dystopian futures beyond the consumption-driven world of the present, then SF video games are suited for the task as well as—and in some ways even better than—SF films or novels. Marie-Laure Ryan goes so far as to claim that science fiction and other fantastic genres are much better suited for "the interactive and fundamentally visual nature of games than 'high' literature focused on existential concerns, psychological issues, and moral dilemmas" (195).

Despite the problematic relationship between video games and earlier narrative traditions in science fiction, as well as the disparate ways in which these forms operate culturally, there are at least four compelling and productive intersections between SF as a cultural mode and video games as a medium. These are: video games as narratives of space, a focus central to both science fiction and postmodernity; video games as integral elements of distributed narratives spanning multiple media and forms; video games as instances of visual science fictions invested in the pictorial portrayal of futurity; and video games as performative simulations, conveying a sense of the malleability of the future. SF video games share the first three of these intersections with earlier cultural forms such as film, while the last one is specifically inherent in the gaming medium. Underlying the discussion of these four nexuses is the assumption that science-fictionality does not need to reside in the strength of a plot-driven narrative.

The emergence of science fiction as a literary form has often been tied to the changed perceptions of time as a new dimension of modernity that has replaced space. While this transition has also imprinted itself on SF film and television, genre video games reverse this focus—like all new media objects, they privilege spatial imagination (Manovich 244–84). For Lev Manovich, navigable space has become "an accepted way for interacting with any type of data" (252), while McKenzie Wark notes that "[g]amespace turns descriptions into a database, and storyline into navigation" (69). Furthermore, Ryan states that games do not need to tell stories "that would provide suitable literary material to immerse the player in the fate of its fictional world, because the thrill of being in a world, of acting in it and of controlling its history, makes up for the intellectual challenge, the subtlety of plot, and the complexity of characterization that the best of literature has to offer" (195). All these assertions aptly describe science fiction games, whose spatial turn not only extends the genre's ontological underpinning but also, unwittingly, reconnects it with its early roots in utopia and fantastic voyage. Two specific aspects of video-game spatiality are pertinent here.

Most obviously, the spatial turn resonates with the strong world-building focus of the genre generally. Even in traditional SF media, the spaces circumscribed in texts such as *Blade Runner* (1982) or *Neuromancer* (1984) are as important as their narrative trajectories or philosophical import. As spectacular examples of science-fictional topography, the panoramas of alien planets and architecture in the *Halo* franchise, the underwater city in *Bioshock* (2007), the postapocalyptic landscapes of the *Fallout* series (1997–2010), or the spatially disorienting alien spacecraft in *Prey* (2006) extend the preoccupation with what Brian McHale has called "worldliness." At the same time, SF video games not only provide the visual shapes of narrated visions but also, unlike SF cinema, provide spaces that the player may enter. The degree of immersion largely depends on the gaming genre—it is significantly lower in real-time strategy games such as *Emperor: Battle for Dune* (2001) or *Rage of War* (2008) than in shooters such as *Halo*, the *Half-Life* series (1998–), or *Crysis 2* (2011)—but the experience of moving through space is crucial to the affective experience of the genre's sense of alterity.

The traversal of futuristic space is particularly central to the FPS genre—those using the first-person perspective (FPP) such as the *F.E.A.R.* series (2005–11) and those utilizing third-person perspective (TPP) such as the *Dead Space* games (2008–13). The differences between the two types include the graphical perspective of the character-controlling player and the design (TPP titles often tend to feature more spacious environments), but in both cases the player's movement through space is a pretext to showcase an array of virtual locations. As in other non-SF games, it is not uncommon to structure levels as diverse environments. Depending on the storyline, levels in some titles will be unified: *F.E.A.R.* (2005) predominantly deploys the player in abandoned office buildings and urban locales, while *Dead Space* (2008) is mostly set on a starship and right outside it. Other games, including a number of titles in the *Alien vs. Predator* franchise (1982–2011), alternate between indoor (ground facilities, spacecraft) and outdoor (jungle) environments. Regardless of their character, such spaces foreground the science-fictionality of individual titles.

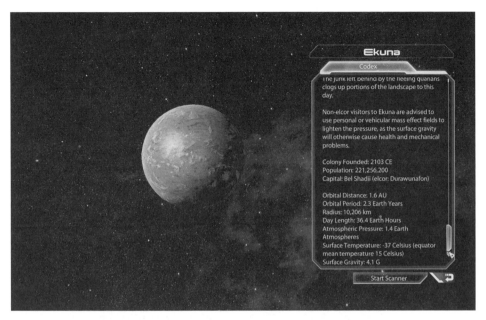

FIGURE 17.1 Video games as texts of imperial possession. *Mass Effect 2*.

The second sphere of SF video-game spatiality is the genre's frequent deployment of territorial expansion, which makes the genre video games almost handbook examples of "the fantastic model of achieved technoscientific Empire" (Csicsery-Ronay Jr., "Science Fiction and Empire" 231). This aspect is most clearly articulated through the player's activity. Regardless of their genre allocation, there are few SF games that do not involve the rhetoric of spatial control and possession: exploration, colonization, conquest, or territorial mapping. These are particularly important in various types of strategy games. While both the fairly rudimentary 2D graphics of such older titles as *StarCraft* (1998) or *Emperor: Battle for Dune* and the visual lushness of newer 3D games like *Earth 2150* (2000) or *StarCraft 2: Wings of Liberty* (2011) may lack the spectacular immediacy of the shooter genre, all these games are ultimately narratives of imperial control and possession. Unlike non-SF strategy games derived from *SimCity* (1989–) and *Civilization* (1991–), which represent gamespace by a blank or black-out map that is uncovered as the player acquires and develops land, most SF strategy games foreground the discourse of military conflict. Gaming environments, both planetary and interplanetary, thus become theaters of competition and war, in which resource management and army deployment are privileged forms of gaming activity.

In terms of distributed narratives, the second science-fictional modality of video games, over the last few decades games have entered the circulation of adaptations, within which they can be situated as both a source and a target medium. In the latter category, many video-game adaptations are little more than cursory borrowings of story elements from fiction or cinema. *Neuromancer* (1988), *Dune* (1992), and *S.T.A.L.K.E.R.: Shadow of Chernobyl* (2007) very loosely follow the plots of Gibson's,

Frank Herbert's, and Arkady and Boris Strugatsky's originals, respectively. The same is true of the two gaming versions of *Blade Runner* (1992): due to licensing problems, the 1985 game is reportedly based on Vangelis's film soundtrack, while the 1997 game is set in the same universe but features a story running parallel to the film's plot. Occasionally, games can extend the original, as was the case with *I Have No Mouth and I Must Scream* (1995), based on Harlan Ellison's 1967 short story: Ellison co-wrote the script of the game and even lent his voice to the AM computer. While the gameplay largely reflects the story's plot, the game contextualizes the events in the text, most prominently by developing the background stories of the five principals in such graphic detail that it led to the partial censoring of the game in France and Germany and the removal of the module devoted to one of the characters.

The rise of what Henry Jenkins has called "convergence culture" and the development of narrative franchises (see Lauer and Rodrigo 241–62) have opened new opportunities for game developers. Most importantly, video games function as integral nodes in networks of transmedia narratives incorporating books, films, comics, websites, and TV shows. Because of its preoccupation with open-ended world-building, science fiction has been a genre particularly inviting such interactions. Apart from providing a more tactile and participatory experience of story arcs present in other nodes, video games can also serve as containers of plot-related information. On their own, the narrative components found in the games may be proportionally minor in relation to those in novels or films, but their potential importance in such transmedial "Works as Assemblage" (Hayles 279) should not be underestimated.

The position of video games in such narrative universes may vary—from a marginal position (*Star Wars* games), to a function as bridging "interquels" between other nodes (*Terminator Salvation* [2009]), to centrality (*Mass Effect* trilogy [2007–12], *Halo* games [2001–])—as may the degree of their relevance for the distributed narrative in question. The franchises enumerated above are characterized by a degree of relaxed continuity in which the events invoked in the games do not have decisive importance to the plots of nodes central to their narrative universes (most typically, a novel, a comic book, or a film), but this does not always need be the case. Some of the information contained in the *Matrix* video games (2003–09) is critical to understanding the overarching story; Jenkins discusses in detail the interlocked complexity of a franchise in which, despite appearances, all media components are equally important (93–130).

A special position in such transmedia narratives is occupied by alternate-reality games, which blur the boundary between a storytelling component and a promotional tool. Examples include *The Beast* (2001), which preceded the release of Steven Spielberg's *A.I.: Artificial Intelligence* (2001); *I Love Bees* (2004), which promoted *Halo 2* (2004); or *Year Zero* (2007), which was tied to Nine Inch Nails' eponymous SF concept album. Although technically not video games, ARGs heavily rely on digital technologies and mobilize online communities in pursuit of an unfolding narrative; the notorious difficulty of their puzzles and the time constraints require coordinated collaboration between players. At the same time, their storytelling import becomes appreciable only when considered a part of larger narrative ecologies.

The third science-fictional modality of video games is their powerful ability to visualize future worlds. In 2001 James Newman pointed out that the pleasures of video games "are not primarily visual, but kinaesthetic, functional and cognitive" (see Aarseth 52)—an assertion arguably true at the time but hardly valid any more. Their procedurality and narrativity notwithstanding, contemporary video games are most immediately visual artifacts in which the primacy of kinetic imagery has emerged as a result of software and hardware advances. In many instances, the relationship between narrative and visuality in SF video games mirrors that found in "spectacular narratives" (see King) and "post-continuity cinema" (see Shaviro), in which the storytelling component is played down—although never eliminated—in favor of pure spectacle. Despite this, graphics have received relatively little attention (see Keane 105). Many game critics insist that it is the procedures governing gameplay that are the defining element of the medium and that if the rules are interesting, then the fictional world can be changed (Juul 189). This seems to underplay the potency of the game's theme. Given the relative simplicity of most storylines and the fact that various titles within the same gaming genre—for example, first-person shooter—may share the software engine responsible for the prominent majority of core functionalities (graphics rendering, sound, animation, and so on), which results in broadly comparable gameplay, it seems that at least a portion of a given title's popularity relies precisely on its "skinning"—the individual graphic design of the game. Integral to the awe, wonder, and estrangement of many SF video games are their majestic vistas of alien worlds, futuristic cities, gigantic spaceships, and outer space. Their early depictions might have been marred by pixelated screens, generic textures, and jolting movement, but more recent games have vastly benefited from the converging trajectories of digital graphics in games and cinema.

The aesthetic pleasure of SF games is inextricably connected with the genre's world-building and its construction of spaces, which are evocative of SF iconicity in general and adaptive texts in particular. Naturally, this aesthetic focus does not preclude the importance of gameplay and storytelling, but the study of SF video games can benefit from a more systematic concentration on their ocular aspects. In that regard, SF video games are related to other SF visualities, including art, illustration, or visual paratexts. Several more specific approaches are possible here. Given the economies of production in which digitally generated video-game imagery allows creators to sidestep the economic demands of large-scale cinema and enhance the material limitations of illustration, SF video games can be treated as a privileged visual expression of the genre. Collectively, they can be read as an iconographic archive of science fiction in which signature images (future cities, spacecrafts, time machines, or cyborgs) are not only deployed in various permutations but also literally mobilized and made available to the players. Individually, in their variety of types of visual representations (static images, cinematic cutscenes, interactive environments) that remediate virtually every other visual medium (see Bolter and Grusin 88–103), SF video games are also like moving paintings, still lifes, landscapes, and *Wunderkammern*. All these forms can be enjoyed aesthetically and affectively but also, to use Gérard Genette's term, hypertextually—in

FIGURE 17.2 Video games as visual science fiction. *Eve Online*.

dialogue with preceding texts, both visual and nonvisual. Consequently, *Bioshock* and *Singularity* (2010) can be analyzed as retrofuturistic deployments of art deco aesthetics and Soviet-era iconography, respectively, but also in terms of how their retro-visuality contributes to the former's critique of Ayn Rand's philosophy of Objectivism and the latter's recreation of the West's Cold War perception of the Soviet Union.

Video-game visuals can also be discussed in terms of the dialectic of style and "stylisticality" (Davis 75–119), including the ways in which they reflect the historical transformation of icons and signatures in various SF media and also the ways in which these icons express the changing modes of thinking about technology or progress. One can, for instance, trace the evolution of the iconography of spacecraft in video games and how it coincided and departed from similar depictions in magazine illustration, film, and television. Given the importance of spaces, in-game architectures are another visual aspect open to interpretation, as is the racial and gender construction of alien beings, an aspect performed in games predominantly through appearance, which may or may not be additionally developed in the game's narrative. Finally, with a view toward the importance of video-game concept art (see Taylor 226–37), it is possible to discuss the relationship between the original graphics and its particular in-game iterations, also across several games in a series.

The final science-fictional modality, video games as performative simulations that convey a sense of the malleability of the future, is dependent on the fact that playing a video game is an experience of immersion, "of being transported to an elaborately simulated place" (Murray 98). Such immersion remains in a dialectical relationship with "the incongruent perspective of *remote control*" (Venus 434; emphasis in original) that renders engagement with a game in an alienated, stylized way. Beyond the distinction of rules vs. narrative, video games are simulations, rehearsals of "what could happen" and ways "to explore the mechanics of dynamic systems" (Frasca 86). Even more specifically, they are emblematic of "a new stage in SF thinking where media offers the realization rather than just the representation of SF narratives" (Landon xxv). As a medium, SF video games stand at the very intersection of simulation "as a major new hermeneutic discourse mode" (Aarseth 53), while at the same time underscoring SF's traditional role as "a complex hesitation about the relationship between imaginary conceptions and historical reality unfolding into the future" (Csicsery-Ronay Jr., *Seven Beauties* 4).

Some of the most basic video-game options remain thematically science-fictional. Unlimited "lives" available to players, the creation and customization of in-game identities and their avatars, or the ability to save and reload a character's in-game "subjectivity" can be thought of as expressions of a desire to transcend technologically the innate constraints of the body. Even these extremely simple in-game tasks, however, bespeak underlying cultural assumptions: Galloway suggests that "acts of configuration in video games express processes in culture that are large, unknown, dangerous, and painful, but they do not express them directly" (16). Since it is masses of players, and not the few select writers or directors, that engage in configuring gameplay, the choices they make and later share online in the form of screenshots, blog posts, or gameplay videos (and the demands they make from producers in subsequent versions of the title) become indicative of larger social realities.

If science fiction is, among other things, a discourse concerned with unhumanizing and posthumanizing our points of view, then SF video games also offer a tentative sense of what we think it would be like to look at the world through eyes not our own. Many FPS titles feature so-called cyborg vision, clearly modeled after films such as *The Terminator* (1984) and *Robocop* (1987), which simulates the posthuman gaze by overlaying the visual field with various electronic displays and data feeds. In *Aliens vs. Predator* (2001), playing a predator allows access to several vision modes, including infrared, while directing an alien grants a radical extension of mobility, as a result of which any surface becomes available for traction. Approximate and mediated as they are, these options attempt to transport the player into other sensoria and offer a perspective rarely represented in fiction and only occasionally imitated in cinema.

More universally, SF video games can offer simulations of global or even galactic politics and economy. *Eve Online* (2003), an MMORPG (massively multiplayer online role-playing game) set 21,000 years in the future when humanity has dispersed across the stars, is a highly complex modeling of the processes of empire—its steep learning demands are matched by the high realism of its simulation. For Darren Jorgensen, *Eve Online* is "a metatext for both space opera and . . . the numerical verisimilitude of sf" ("Numerical" 144), but it can equally easily serve as a tool for those interested in learning to navigate the mazes of political survival and economic success in a world in which mining, piracy, manufacturing, trading, exploration, and combat exist side by side. The *Eve* database of star systems, ships, weapons, and other resources is more inclusive of SF novums than any number of novels, but the goal of the game is not to construct a narrative but to challenge the players to use a set of profoundly realistic skills. *Eve Online* engages the very processes of neoliberal late capitalism, and its success seems to owe much precisely to its futuristic setting.

This potential for simulation extending beyond mere play was most clearly demonstrated in *Superstruct*, a massively multiplayer forecasting game, created by the Institute for the Future, and involving over 8,000 players, between September and November 2008. Although not featuring the customary graphical interface and relying instead on forums, blogs, videos, wikis, and other online spaces, the game very effectively harnessed the crowdsourced wisdom of the Internet and combined it with the thrill of a gamelike challenge. Set in 2019, *Superstruct* opened with the premise that the supercomputer Global Extinction Awareness System (GEAS) had reset the "survival horizon" for *Homo sapiens* to 23 years. Five "Superthreats" were identified: viral infection ("Quarantine"), hunger ("Ravenous"), political instability ("Power Struggle"), criminality ("Outlaw Planet"), and population displacement ("Generation Exile"). After choosing one of them, the players could investigate a full Superthreat report, including stories, micro-scenarios, discussions, and videos. The goal of the game was to develop solutions to the posited problems, the more systemic and far-reaching the better. Since no clear win conditions were set, the game channeled the players' creativity into a thoroughly realistic thinking about the world. Blurring the boundaries between social simulation and fiction, *Superstruct* demonstrated the potential of SF video games as simulations of real-life potentialities. Although most SF video games are, of course, far more invested in providing entertainment than in raising players' consciousness regarding global problems, it is the genre's future-oriented mode of perceiving the world that elevated the game's problem-solving, an integral element of so many video games, to an actual engagement with the world outside the game.

Tempting as it may be to say that simulation games are a more serious realization of the medium's potential than first-person shooters, this claim would amount to a critical flattening of a rich landscape of possibilities. Just as video games perform their cultural work in ways different from film or literature, various gaming genres appeal to different aesthetic or cognitive faculties. At the same time, the medium's partial shift of agency from author to player retains what most critics consider the most valuable quality of science fiction—its capacity to mobilize critical thinking about the world. The futures of SF video games can become tools of ideology-critique and anamorphic devices of thought. If playing "a military/shooter type game might be understood as one part of a broader cultural investment in [a] kind of mind-set or cultural attitude" (King and Krzywinska 201), then playing SF video games in general and SF simulation games in particular may contribute to a better awareness of the nature of our current cultural position. If, as Jorgensen suggests, it is possible to think about science fiction as an experimental science ("Towards" 205), genre video games seem to be better equipped to convey this possibility to their audiences than fiction or film by directly involving them in the performance or, in some cases, the creation of their sense of futurity.

It needs to be stressed that these four approaches to understanding the nexus linking video games and science fiction do not exclude other vantage points from which to analyze SF video games. Despite their paucity of storytelling sophistication, narrative analysis can still be undertaken. Other approaches—for example, feminist, postcolonial—are also possible, although in most cases they will not result in analyses much different from those obtained in other SF media. On the other hand, the four aspects of SF video games addressed here consider those elements of the medium that, to a lesser or greater extent, make it qualitatively and functionally different from SF literature, film, or television.

Works Cited

Aarseth, Espen. "Genre Trouble: Narrativism and the Art of Simulation." *First Person: New Media as Story, Performance, and Game*. Ed. Noah Wardrip-Fruin and Pat Harrigan. Cambridge, MA: MIT, 2004. 45–55. Print.

Bolter, J. David, and Richard A Grusin. *Remediation: Understanding New Media*. Cambridge, MA: MIT, 1999. Print.

Bordwell, David. *Narration in the Fiction Film*. New York: Routledge, 1985. Print.

Clute, John. *Pardon This Intrusion: Fantastika in the World Storm*. Essex, UK: Beccon, 2011. Print.

Csicsery-Ronay Jr., Istvan. "Science Fiction and Empire." *Science Fiction Studies* 30.2 (July 2003): 231–45. Print.

———. *The Seven Beauties of Science Fiction*. Middletown CT: Wesleyan UP, 2008. Print.

Darley, Andrew. *Visual Digital Culture: Surface Play and Spectacle in New Media Genres*. London: Routledge, 2004. Print.

Davis, Whitney. *A General Theory of Visual Culture*. Princeton, NJ: Princeton UP, 2011. Print.

Frasca, Gonzalo. "Videogames of the Oppressed: Critical Thinking, Education, Tolerance, and Other Trivial Issues." *First Person: New Media as Story, Performance, and Game*. Ed. Noah Wardrip-Fruin and Pat Harrigan. Cambridge, MA: MIT, 2004. 85–94. Print.

Galloway, Alexander R. *Gaming: Essays on Algorithmic Culture*. Minneapolis: U of Minnesota P, 2006. Print.

Genette, Gérard. *Palimpsests: Literature in the Second Degree*. 1982. Trans. Channa Newman and Claude Doubinsky. Lincoln: U of Nebraska P, 1997. Print.

Gunning, Tom. "An Unseen Energy Swallows Space: The Space in Early Film and Its Relation to American Avant-Garde Film." *Film Before Griffith*. Ed. John L. Fell. Berkeley: U of California P, 1983. 355–66. Print.

Hayles, N. Katherine. *My Mother Was a Computer: Digital Subjects and Literary Texts*. Chicago: U of Chicago P, 2005. Print.

Jenkins, Henry. *Convergence Culture: Where Old and New Media Collide*. New York: NYU P, 2006. Print.

Jorgensen, Darren. "The Numerical Verisimilitude of Science Fiction and *Eve Online*." *Extrapolation* 51.1 (2010): 134–47. Print.

———. "Towards a Revolutionary Science Fiction: Althusser's Critique of Historicity." *Red Planets. Marxism and Science Fiction*. Ed. Mark Bould and China Miéville. Middletown, CT: Wesleyan UP, 2009. 196–212. Print.

Juul, Jesper. *Half-Real: Video Games Between Real Rules and Fictional Worlds.* Cambridge, MA: MIT, 2005. Print.

Keane, Stephen. *Cinetech: Film, Convergence and New Media.* Basingstoke, UK: Palgrave Macmillan, 2007. Print.

King, Geoff. *Spectacular Narratives: Hollywood in the Age of the Blockbuster.* London: I.B. Tauris, 2000. Print.

King, Geoff, and Tanya Krzywinska. *Tomb Raiders and Space Invaders: Videogame Forms and Contexts.* London: I.B. Tauris, 2006. Print.

Landon, Brooks. *The Aesthetics of Ambivalence: Rethinking Science Fiction Film in the Age of Electronic (Re)production.* Westport, CT: Greenwood, 1992. Print.

Lauer, Jean Anne, and Shelley Rodrigo. "Resident Franchise: Theorizing the SF Genre, Conglomerations, and the Future of Synergy." *Playing the Universe: Games and Gaming in Science Fiction.* Ed. David Mead and Paweł Frelik. Lublin, Poland: Maria Curie-Sklodowska UP, 2007. 241–62. Print.

Manovich, Lev. *The Language of New Media.* Cambridge, MA: MIT, 2002. Print.

McHale, Brian. *Postmodernist Fiction.* New York: Routledge, 1987. Print.

Murray, Janet Horowitz. *Hamlet on the Holodeck: The Future of Narrative in Cyberspace.* New York: Free P, 1997. Print.

Ndalianis, Angela. "Special Effects, Morphing Magic, and the 1990s Cinema of Attractions." *Meta-Morphing: Visual Transformation and the Culture of Quick-change.* Ed. Vivian Sobchack. Minneapolis: U of Minnesota P, 2000. 251–71. Print.

Prince, Gerald. *Dictionary of Narratology.* 1987. Rev. ed. Lincoln: U of Nebraska P, 2003. Print.

Ryan, Marie-Laure. *Avatars of Story.* Minneapolis: U of Minnesota P, 2006.

Shaviro, Steven. "Post-Continuity." *The Pinocchio Theory.* Mar. 26, 2012. Web. Mar. 30, 2012. http://www.shaviro.com/Blog/?p=1003.

Taylor, Laurie. "Networking Power: Videogame Structure from Concept Art." *Videogames and Art.* Ed. Andy Clarke and Grethe Mitchell. Bristol, UK: Intellect, 2007. 226–37. Print.

Venus, Jochen. "Beyond Play and Narration: Videogames as Simulations of Self-Action." *Beyond the Screen: Transformations of Literary Structures, Interfaces and Genres.* Ed. Jörgen Schäfer and Peter Gendolla. Bielefeld, Germany: Transcript, 2010. Print.

Wark, McKenzie. *Gamer Theory.* Cambridge, MA: Harvard UP, 2007. Print.

Wolf, Mark J. P. "Genre and the Video Game." *The Medium of the Video Game.* Ed. Mark J. P. Wolf. Austin: U of Texas P, 2001. 113–34. Print.

CHAPTER 18

DIGITAL ARTS AND HYPERTEXT

JAMES TOBIAS

ALAN Turing's 1950 essay "Computing Machinery and Intelligence" marks an important milestone in the long and tangled trajectory of computing machines deployed in the arts, letters, and modern media at large. More than just an argument about the computability of intelligence, the essay proposes the pursuit of both the computation of cognition and the composition of machine perception—the latter in the suggestion of a "child-machine" to be trained through "sense organs" (459). In effect, if Turing's emphasis is on intelligence, like other key figures in computing during this period, he understood computing methods to apply potentially to automating learning as well as to synthesizing living processes. (Turing's formulation of the potentials and limits of a "universal computer" in his 1936 essay "On Computable Numbers" is widely acknowledged to have been crucial both to the development of modern computing as well as to the field later known as "artificial intelligence"; Turing's 1952 essay "The Chemical Basis of Morphogenesis" helped to lay the groundwork for the field later known as "artificial life.") The conclusion makes the point clear; whether a more top-down mapping of abstract cognition or a more bottom-up processing of sense data, "both approaches should be tried" ("Computing" 460). The emphasis is on the demonstration of intelligent effects understood in terms of learning, not given values, and regardless of the material substrate conducting the symbolic process. For Turing, there is no final boundary between abstraction and materiality; distinctions of theory or practice give way to a demonstration of the effects of processes that can be "blackboxed."

Turing's seminal essay on machine learning and sense-aware child-machines, then, sees abstraction as not bounded off from expressive materiality yet, at the same time, demonstrably alienable from it. Turing's description of practical intelligence takes on, in historical retrospect, sociotechnical and biopolitical characteristics. In this chapter, I show the ways in which digital arts and letters enact Turing's demonstrative and expressive practical intelligence in ways that echo the issue of utopia and dystopia in SF literature, but what is allegorized in SF as the problem of utopian programs becomes, instead, a question of *how* to demonstrate the potentials and limits of programming contemporary life. I conclude that the most meaningful effects of contemporary, hyperindustrial works of digital media art is that their fictive, ludic contingency in terms of human–computer interaction tends to work reflexively as a demonstration confirming or disconfirming their factic, programmatic power, and thus prompting allegorical readings of everyday experience with program media in terms of our use of everyday computing machinery. In short, digital arts and letters constitute a key site at which we engage contemporary hyperindustrialism's power to enframe everyday temporal experience: they compose the equivalent of utopian or dystopian allegories of global technoscience into our use of the machines we equip ourselves with for life in globalizing capitalism.

In his 1950 essay, Turing first describes a game of imitation conducted via the separation of a respondent, whose gender identity is to be determined, from an interlocutor. Turing posits that such a parlor game revolving around the difficulty of discerning gender through a conversation in which the participants' physical identities are screened from one another would be little different than one in which the intelligence of a machine process is to be determined as human by a human interlocutor similarly screened from the machine. Turing's positing of intelligence as a game of imitation, of course, has been frequently understood in terms of representation or simulation and, as "the Turing Test," derived in computing contests, philosophical thought experiments, and narratives—the latter especially indicating a strengthened need for—and the increasingly complex difficulty of—determining self-identity in contemporary technocultures. A familiar instance is the "Voight-Kampff Machine," used to determine humanness and detect lies, featured in Philip K. Dick's novel *Do Androids Dream of Electric Sleep?* (1968), famously adapted in Ridley Scott's 1982 film *Blade Runner*.

Yet Turing's claim was not that machines can be programmed to be intelligent in the ways that humans are intelligent. His claim was rather that intelligence, like gender, is a complex game of self-identity achieved through engagements with the world and the Other, a game in which self-identity is what Donna Haraway would later describe as "material-semiotic"—that is, constructed of complex entanglements of material substance as well as of educational or social influence. Turing claimed that self-identity in this complex construction of physical nature, educational entrainment, and sociotechnical encoding is something at which we may routinely fail to understand or to perceive accurately (here, too, between understanding and perception the boundary is a matter of orientation).

Turing's arguments for machine intelligence invoke human disability or failure not only in terms of identifications like those encoded in terms of gender but also in terms of racial or ethnic difference or of developmental difference (see Turing, "Computing Machinery" 448, 460). Computers also routinely demonstrate failures of logical self-identity; on the basis of demonstrably shared failure, human or machine communication and learning become analogous and, in ways yet to be determined fully, substitutable for one another. Whether the apparatus functions or malfunctions, the fail-prone actors' utterances are nonetheless registered and enframed, so even if no intelligent value is performatively enacted, intelligence may nonetheless be potentially demonstrated in terms of a larger, ongoing, and open process.

Turing's "Computing Machinery" essay, then, is not only a key instance in which programmed computation and lived identity become factically and fictively entangled in technoscientific life. It is significant in its own right for placing intelligence and self-identity within what is in effect a "posthumanist" framework where play and contingency are as important as determination and necessity, and, moreover, where demonstrability is more important than performativity. In Turing's developmental entangling of computing equipment with lived social identity, play, contingency, and demonstrability make intelligence an emergent aspect of computer-mediated conduct whereby the machine may "win" by default to the degree that both computers or humans each routinely commit fundamental errors of identity. Embodied cognition as a given human faculty gives way to embodied cognition as a sociotechnical disability indexing the potential to revise perceptual and analytical failure (hence, Turing's invocation of Helen Keller [456]).

The important role failure plays in Turing's account of machine intelligence is frequently lost even in sympathetic accounts of Turing's ludic pragmatics of disability. Judith Halberstam argues that Turing makes essentialist pairings of gender with biology and of cognition with culture and inadvertently "fails to realize the full import of his negotiations between machine and human" (443). But Halberstam neglects Turing's work on metabolic development processes, failing to note that, for Turing, even biological materiality is subject to the contingencies of material-semiotic composition. After Turing, the status of what constitutes "discourse" brooks no easy distinction between nature or culture, male or female body, human or animal, computer program or social project. Cybernetics, of course, as a science of regulating machine, human, or animal behavior comprises the default site of such distinctions as its own technoscientific project. Further, the behavior Turing construed as conversation between interlocutors, whether male and female or human and machine, is a contingent, never finally determinable conduct—a semi-conducted conduct, as it were—distributed between human and nonhuman actors in networks of sociotechnical power relations, in the sense that Bruno Latour has described.

Mimesis as an only partially technically determined poesis that constructs conduct in the way Turing described has less to do with gender essentialism or a reserving of intelligence for culture, and more to do with a semi-conducted material-semiotics subsequently radically extended in biopolitical terms. Biopolitics after Turing produces surplus "biovalue" familiar in postcybernetic, postgenomic technoculture (see Waldby 31). In this context, as SF narratives allegorize sociotechnical risks or interventions, digital arts and letters dramatize and enact the ways in which living bodies, the body politic, the "body" of cultural forms (distributing, exhibiting, and interpreting media), and historical temporality itself all become subject to both technical programming and aesthetic intervention. These hypermedia works produce not simply, say, ideological values, but as Nikolas Rose argues, new ways of configuring biotechnical truths (142). Thus, famously, Alba, the bioluminescent bunny that transgenic artist Eduardo Kac claimed to have created, became embroiled in struggles over contested ownership and image manipulation scandals before expiring in 2002; even her age was disputed on her death (see Wolfe).

That SF can productively allegorize biotechnological culture and its truth-power relations seems clear; Haraway's seminal essay on the cyborg famously argues that science fiction offers allegorical resources for waging feminist resistance as cyborg writing. Jameson more recently argues that SF literature offers four allegorical registers allowing us to read SF less for a literal utopian program (always problematic and anachronistic since the literary imagination of utopia is inevitably undone by history) than for a "utopian impulse." SF as allegorical index of technocultural change, as postmodern, has often been read in much the ways Jameson suggests: Kellner has argued that William Gibson's *Neuromancer* (1984) offered a more useful "social theory" both of postmodernism generally and of web-based cultural production and social interaction specifically than did Jean Baudrillard's dystopian criticism (319). Electronic literature or literary hypertexts routinely have allegorized the kinds of values Jameson finds in SF's utopian impulse, with critics assigning them utopian or dystopian valuations by turns and degrees. Shelley Jackson's *Patchwork Girl* is the canonical example, having served as exemplar text for a host of critical interpretations of both electronic literature and technocultural conditions since its digital publication in 1995. Yet what electronic literature or hypermedia can specify *in addition to* discursive performativities of utopian program-as-narrative is the ludic and contingent value of technical *demonstrativity* operating reflexively on the equipmental substrate of the digital work of art.

As a result, our "interactive" interpretation of narrative "lexia" and "map" on navigating Jackson's *Patchwork Girl* bridges the kinds of allegorical reading strategies theorized by Haraway or Jameson, but, given the needs assigned to hypertext or hypermedia production then and since, it also affords the kinds of allegorical readings Samuel R. Delany has posited as available through SF fiction. For Delany, any literary production can be read as a problem of aesthetic values in terms of its own coherence or achievements (the "new critical" allegory), but also, and more interesting for him, as an allegory of its own interpretive problems and aporias—the kind of reading that Jameson attempts to resolve for SF literature by emphasizing utopian impulse over any utopian program depicted diegetically.

Delany offers other possibilities, though: SF might depict power relations in the text as allegorical of the power relations structuring SF as a minor "paraliterary" genre in relation to other genres. Delany also suggests that SF futurist narratives be read against the "lacunaic" structure of history in order to discern the ways in which "the relation between the SF writer's life and the SF writer's text allegorizes the historical critique dramatized by the text itself." Finally, rather than reading SF as a prediction or critique of technological progress (or a deferral from social to technological progress), we might read for the ways in which an SF text "extrapolates on science" and thus "always poses a critique of one or another aspects of the current philosophy of science," so that we can "read in detail the way in which the relation between a specific SF text and the larger SF genre allegorizes the critique of the philosophy of science dramatized" in that text (44). If we transpose "SF narrative" in Delany's comments to "hypertext narrative," "futurist narrative" to "navigable or interactive narrative," and the lacunaic structure of history to a lacunaic structure of technocultural history, we get the kinds of critical accounts given for *Patchwork Girl* in terms of the actions this hypertext prompts as "reading" becomes equivalent to "usage": the interactive hypertext becomes a critical allegory of hypertext's ability to reconfigure the form's relationship to modern literatures (Landow 239–45), of hypertextual women's writing in relation to historically gendered literary authorship (Hayles, *My Mother* 143–68), and of technoscientific history (Clayton 92–94). In hypermedia demonstration, allegorization functionalizes—or alternatively, functionally disables, as *Patchwork Girl* tends to do, I think—biopolitical, sociotechnical action as semi-conducted conduct subject to new ways of configuring biotechnical truth. In this way, it also makes possible the manifestation of new, as yet to be programmed, potentials for other demonstrations of interpretation and use in digital computing.

Disabling as a dystopian configuring of hypermedia programs need not be literally destructive in the sense of erasing digital data; it can also be ludic, comedic, both in the registers of allegorical content and of enacted "navigation." Christine Tamblyn's 1993 CD-ROM essay on women and technology, *She Loves It, She Loves It Not*, provided an earlier instance of hypermedia deploying the kinds of allegorical demonstratives that *Patchwork Girl* raised to the level of an interpretable analytic of authorship's historical gendering. In *She Loves It*, though, the demonstration of gendered authoring and reading is extended to gendered inventing or hacking (a strategy seen in work by other cyberfeminist artworks of the day), as an alternative usage of computing machinery is laid out not simply as allegory encoded into hypertext threads that the user-reader reconstitutes for herself in the form of sentences never quite written by the author (as *Patchwork Girl* does), but rather as navigational functions mirroring potential paths of reading that the user-reader accepts as the manifest content of the disc-computer-apparatus. Tamblyn's ironic presentation of these navigational paths as accessed through absurd collages of audiovisual icons (appearing comedically, for instance, as a kind of cyber-Amelia Earhart) offsets the overt and programmatic mapping of feminist manifesto to hypertextual navigation, intimating unintended consequences and asserting comedic value (see Tamblyn).

Delany's sense of what the SF text can do—the affordances that allow it to "produce more interesting critical fictions, more informative and interesting stories" (45), is very much, I think, the sense that motivated hypermedia and hypertext authors like Tamblyn or Jackson to prompt their readers to demonstrate certain modalities of use of computing machines over others. And just as Delany pointed out for reading SF, reading hypertext allegorically for its ability to reveal cultural value is likely to fail in important ways. The problem for Delany was the threat of closure: reading the text as an allegory of the life of its author becomes, in effect, a biopolitical containment of the author that can only confirm "the very monologic subject," "stalled among the sundered and essentialist concepts of Individual, Culture, and Society, each alienated from the other" (45), that Delany's theory and practice of SF literature have sought to complicate. In Tamblyn's case, humor upsets and resists the tendency toward a monologic mapping of user reading, material text, and authorial program. Jackson's celebrated text is, of course, celebrated precisely because it defers any such monologism, urging the reader herself to resist it or configure it differently while giving her access to the generative material-semiotics of what Hayles has called, in *How We Became Posthuman*, the "flickering signifier" (25–49).

I'm arguing, then, that digital arts and media are the site where the threat of monologic closure that Delany diagnosed—and against which he devised multiform and complex allegorical writing and reading strategies—becomes a matter of the play of computational demonstration and technocultural contingency operative in biotechnical cultures after Turing. On the one hand, the capacity of the reader to actively recompose a digital text is definitively sustained by the software and hardware formats that determine its delivery (rather than by, say, language, literature, or historical change as such); on the other hand, just as history overtakes any utopian program in an SF text, technological history quickly overtakes any determination of "open writing" offered in a hardware-software platform, as platforms obsolesce or are updated in ways that don't support earlier functions, making digital narrative or art impossible to display let alone actively use and explore without the availability of now antiquated equipment. Little wonder, then, that Kellner offered Gibson's *Neuromancer* as a "social theory" of postmodern media culture; in all likelihood, whether or not Kellner was aware of or interested in the history of the digital arts, by 1995 access to important instances of many of them would have been hard to achieve in the first place as they were dedicated to highly specific configurations of platform and content difficult to maintain in the long term. Far worse than the monologics of the Other for digital arts and media is the risk of technical closure, that radical contingency that determines the limits of their demonstrability in obsolescing configurations of conduct, interpretation, and hardware-software programming.

Nowhere was this double risk of monologic and technical closure thematized as clearly, perhaps, as in Perry Hoberman's installation *Bar Code Hotel* (exhibited at the Los Angeles Interactive Media Festival in 1994). Designed for simultaneous use by multiple participants wearing 3D glasses, *Bar Code Hotel* "recycles the ubiquitous symbols found on every consumer product" in order to upset their prescriptive function as indicators of consumer value. Visitors to *Bar Code Hotel* "check in" by donning a pair of stereoscopic glasses and picking up a bar code wand. The "hotel" is the complex of exhibition room, interaction design, active objects, computer processing, and stereoscopic display; the user interface is the wall and surfaces of the room itself. On one wall, a stereoscopic projection displayed the rapid changes each user can make to the system's memory of bar-coded indices; the user makes such changes using the bar-code wand to read bar codes displayed on tables in graphic white and black. Each user is able to introduce rapid changes into the overall memory of the system; objects corresponding to each coded table area move, bounce, scale, or otherwise respond to a specific user's actions and to other objects.

The result, as Hoberman describes (and as I remember the effect), is a kind of slapstick comedy produced in a computational environment that is at once entirely alienated yet paradoxically, given the physical installation space shared by the be-goggled participants, also highly social. This demonstration of a pleasurably distracted sociality through computational alienation is achieved in part by the installation's emphasis on the graphic nature of the black-and-white bar codes covering the surfaces of the room. The user feels as if she has entered an alien, totally programmed system. At the same time, though, screenic actions are "intuitive" to achieve by scanning bar codes, and the screen objects responding to user actions are semi-autonomous, so you can't completely control what they do; you're as curious to see others demonstrate the system as you are to try it yourself and show off what you learn. Here, the monologics of use, function, and display by which consumer bar codes warrant normative usability and exchange value at the digital interface of production and consumption is diverted to produce, as Hoberman puts it, "a game without rules" generating the effect of a chaotic "musical ensemble," where what we might call *affective* use value rules. *Bar Code Hotel* turned the partially automated biopolitical consumer biography afforded by bar code systems, RFD tags, or more contemporary web-based mining of metadata into a playful moratorium, providing a brief but spectacular exception to the double-faced marketing description of the computer user as both biopolitical actor and data profile to be marketed and consumed.

Other digital products of that period similarly resisted the tendency for the computer subject to be defined as the biographical object of data functions by mounting innovative combinations of fictive and factual historical biography. DNA Media's *Glenn Gould: The New Listener* (1999), for instance, combined the navigation of both hypertextual and hypermedia materials in an attempt to use the specificities of CD-ROM media to redefine biographical criticism and narrative. The disc deploys rich, navigable audiovisual media through which the user explores beautifully rendered scenes modeling Gould's radio essays in audiovisual form, or providing demonstrations of his experiments with spatial quadrophony or other aspects of sound recording. In some instances, the presentation of Gould's life and work draws intertextually from the opening and closing sections of the 1988 film *32 Short Films About Glenn Gould,* in which an actor playing Gould is seen ambling across a frozen expanse in a cinematic evocation of Gould's 1967 radio essay "The Idea of North." Then again, while referencing a biopic that also deployed historical fact against audiovisual fiction, *The New Listener* further provides a database affording the CD-ROM user a text-based search of documents relevant to Gould's life. *The New Listener's* combination of an elaborately fictive demonstration of Gould's biography with access to otherwise hard-to-access archival materials mobilizes multiple, differential oppositions: fictive vs. factic, rich audiovisual navigation vs. textual database search. In the turn from one to another, the project mitigates against either a monologic or technical closure of action, use, or operation; such closure would only do violence to Gould's own aims of turning the audio program itself into an "open work."

While *Bar Code Hotel* or *Glenn Gould: The New Listener,* as different as they were in format and configuration, both allegorized the investments Jameson associates with the utopian impulse while also displaying the kinds of allegorical capacities Delany argues the SF text can hold for a critique of the genre's relation to dominant discourses of history and technoscience, they did so while complicating the tendency for "data-subjectivity" demonstrated by the contingent user of the digital artwork to stand in for biographical narrative—and thus for digital media's operational power to close down the data-subject's relationship to different technical histories (including those whose affordances digital media inherit and then subject intensively to a reductive logic of computational functionality). Whether or not digital artworks begin with noticeably familiar science fiction elements or thematics, these projects nevertheless routinely complicate the rhetoric of "the technoscientific new" and its routinized accompaniment of nostalgia for technologies of the past by mobilizing affective use value and thus by mapping navigability—along with the programmed memory constituting the hypermedia work—in ways that reflexively trouble any presumed monologic mapping between user and system. Such works also trouble the monologic mapping of data subjectivity and marketable biovalue that underlies, say, web-based behavioral marketing or web-celebrity promising "media democratization." Very often, hypertext or hypermedia art seems to spring from Turing's interests in, say, machine learning or the dynamics of chess, to dramatize digital life on the screen as a dystopian game and thereby suggest the limits rather than the potentials of these forms of technocultural expression.

Dan Shiovitz's *Bad Machine* (1999) deploys the text-based adventure-game format familiar from early 1980s games to present, as a summary description puts it, the point of view of "a member of a collective of mechanical entities completely controlled by a central Queen." The text-based feedback presented to the machine reader of the piece dramatizes the "protagonist's non-standard viewpoint." Language and code interfere with one another in a dystopian interruption of the dream of a transparent digital interface. Here, as in much of the work designated as "electronic literature," a primary concern is to effect in hypermedia the kind of allegorical critique of paragenre's relationship to genre (here, the hypertext program's relationship to hyperindustrial programming) or of philosophies of technoscience or technological history that Delany suggests SF can perform for the philosophy of science or for modern history generally.

At the same time, much of what has been collected as "electronic literature," in fact, reflexively emphasizes the features of the digital medium while highlighting the role of user interaction as a kind of authorship—in effect, itself a utopian impulse that suggests that replacing "writing" by "digital programming" might emancipate the data consumer. In many works, though, this impulse turns literally into a program. For example, in the sound-and-image composition and playback of *Nio* (2001), inspired by the classic cinema animation style known as Visual Music, Jim Andrews includes a module that he hopes will enable the production of further such works (although none, to my knowledge, have been produced and distributed to any significant degree). Such works, whether playfully simulating user interaction as failed authorship or alienated human positionality (*Bad Machine*) or providing a new instrument for musical, audiovisual poetry (*Nio*), tend to fall on one of two sides of a utopian tendency to frame user interaction—as either frustrated by the opacity of a technically conditioned mode of aesthetic experience or as enhancing the user's ability to compose "new" forms of aesthetic material (postmodern metanarrative, neo-Visual Music).

In this regard, Hayles's sense that effective "electronic literature" affords an entangled, emergent generation of meaningful technical-aesthetic experience, where "the body and the machine interact in fluid ways that are co-determining" (*Electronic* 128), is useful to keep in mind. If this entanglement is as extensive as Hayles suggests, no single program module, no single programming language, will have the kind of effect that the utopian impulses of Andrews's programming envisage. Programming writing as emancipatory media composition risks, without the larger context and consideration Hayles outlines, rendering hypermedia composition as utopian, technoscientistic fiction—since, in these instances, neither the body nor the text necessarily change their material-semiotic capacities in any particular "reading" of the electronic literary text. The body may tire in reading these hypertexts, but the software machine does not—and, in fact, registers no effect by the readerly body at the level of the underlying programming that allows it to be displayed and distributed, especially when presented as a production tool in its own right. Such works of hypermedia function as technoscientistic fiction revealing, even as they instrumentalize it, that commonplace that Jameson identified as a shared feature of SF literature and literary modernism: "its *public introuvable* and the breakdown of traditional cultural institutions, in particular, the social 'contract' between writer and reader," which has as a structural consequence "the transformation of the text into an *auto-referential* discourse, whose content is a perpetual interrogation of its own conditions of possibility" (292; emphasis in original).

That is to say, to the degree that the hypermedia artwork prompts discernment of its meanings in reception in terms of either a failed allegory of human–machine interpretation, or in terms of successful engineering of a new capacity for authoring as the literary, visual, or audiovisual display becomes an expressive tool in its own right, it is to that degree that hypermedia art as technoscientistic fiction is beset by—and falters upon—its own utopian imagination and impulses. In the projection of a coherent technological imaginary that might be instantiated in a particular computing machine, and in the delivery of a single hypermedia work, it closes itself off from the public of reader-authors it imagines (positively or negatively) and enframes the homeostatic, interactive engagement with cybernetic technologies of authoring and interpretation as an essentially auto-reflexive activity that might be redeemed by the future production of hypermedia work *within* the conditions of the software: monologism of the encoded, machine Other.

"Participatory expression" engendered within a given configuration of software, networked or not, is of course precisely what will never happen, not only because software reception is not conditioned according to the political contexts in which citizenship might be, but also because software reception is never conditioned according to the conditions of software production. Software innovation proceeds precisely by producing the obsolescence of contemporary software functionalities and the attendant expressive capacities software affords, not by empowering software interpreters as producers whose actions transcend the operations of the hardware machines they operate.

Thus, in Erik Loyer's web-based SF narrative *Chroma* (2001), Duck-at-the-Door decides not to engage a technically possible immersion and projection of the self in a networked communication environment recreating an ancient, archetypal memory substance that "transmits information just as air transmits sound"—rather, she resists doing just that. "Mnemonos," the realm of memory transmitted as data, she finds, is a bad bet on a dangerously nostalgic investment in pure cognition devoid of sense that can never be commensurate with temporal duration given to experience as impersonal memory data. In *Chroma*, user interaction is most meaningful when our gestural actions produce the least programmatically functional, most decoratively effective algorithmic variations, or when they produce disorienting effects. In Chapter 2, the user frantically gestures to assemble a collage of diversely raced and gendered subjects, but finds herself displacing the very images she seeks to assemble into a vital whole; any gestural revelation of a new photographic detail prevents the identities of others from appearing more completely. Or again, in Chapter 3, user gesture contributes to a graphical, musical animation—recalling both classic jazz-album-cover designs as well as those of more recent electronic music—set into dynamic motion, with a jazz-inflected, down-tempo ambient electronic soundtrack, but there is no functionally instrumental manipulation of sound via visual music animation. Here, visual music animation appears to be an inspiration, as it is for *Nio*, but it is presented in a way that asks the user to conceive of electronic music as technical memory, commodity memory, or cultural memory. The need and the capacity to differentiate modalities of memory rest upon the user. And if the user takes Duck-at-the-Door as her avatar, she will finally demonstrate a conscious refusal of the desire to immerse her subjectivity in a display of memory mounted and made accessible in terms of technicized possibility rather than in, say, historically enduring community, culture, or communication.

Duck explains why in Chapter 6, after we learn of the science experiment's intent to create avatar bodies with cognitive functions parceled out in advance in Chapter 5. "I've had experience with invented bodies before," says Duck: "I live in one." Duck goes on to explain that her parents had had to play an older version of this very old game, a version that was all about race, where each body is assigned only one race, and which her parents subverted by checking more than one race for her, making her both black and white, breaking the encoded rules by assigning her the combined codes of both. But now people don't see her at all since, according to the rules of the game, "I shouldn't even exist." Now, the rules are being invented again, the game renewed: Duck "can already tell: I'm going to have to cheat to win."

Loyer's critique of online identity here recalls Loretta Todd's description of cyberspace as a functionalized neo-Platonism (180); here, though, rather than an alternative understanding to be found in other notions of nature, technology, and poetic experience, there is no easy out: those who don't or can't be configured within the functional rules already understand that they will have to cheat to win—and, thus, fail. For "winning" here correlates not simply to finishing the game narrative, which ends with Duck's soliloquy, but synecdochically, as Duck explains, by obtaining social legibility and a recognition of the complexly raced body's historical agency whose meanings have already been undercut by participation in "the game" in the first place.

We learn that the game mechanics dramatizing Loyer's hypermedia demonstration of disagreement between action and code, use and software, have transformed: from more utopian, connoted by the user's actions as enacting fluid, visual music, to more dystopian, in Duck's final soliloquy, where we learn her actual name, Alisha Reynolds, as we struggle to navigate through the "new game" Alisha/Duck describes. Here, Loyer has programmed the game's navigation as cognitive disorientation: our visual orientation on the graphical labyrinth is at odds with the control mechanism we are given to navigate it. Nonetheless, we still learn and discordantly find our way to the end of the text—but only because Alisha/Duck has already critiqued its ideological potentials and limits before we arrived in the game at which we were destined to fail. An allegory of future potential and risk turns out—in thematics, narrative, and usability of game mechanics—to demonstrate a contemporary and resistant use of digital technologies, a use grounded in the historical past and in analogous uses of other historical media.

In *Chroma*, the sensorium attributed to digitized embodiment also, as in Jameson's description of the colonial politics of Kim Stanley Robinson's "Mars" trilogy (1993–96), enacts "the coexistence of multiplicities" (411). Yet here, rather than a coexistence of Mars and Terra effected in the reader's cognitive response, a structural parallelism is enacted between the everyday use of networked communications and the reading-playing of the hypermedia work of fiction that *Chroma* is, even while that parallelism connotes a technological dysfunction historically rooted in histories of unequal application of laws and, thereby, of imperial, colonial, and technological violence (rather than being demonstrated as a utopian program worked out according to a computational program). The flattened, two-color register of the screen in this episode, along with the diagrammatic architectural rendering of an online world of play, such as the one Duck is faced with, deliberately avoid a more fully "fleshed out" CGI body inhabiting a cyberrealistic three-dimensional space that demonstrates full capacities for spatial navigation, as in massively multiplayer online role-playing games (MMORPGs) such as *Everquest* (1999) or *World of Warcraft* (2004–11).

Chroma's graphically flattened yet aesthetically multilayered demonstration of the historical legacies immanent to online "memory theaters" parallels the high-fidelity texture of Alisha/Duck's incisive, demythifying vocal (or textual) commentary. Presaging Loyer's more recent design work in his own "Opertoons" series of multimedia narrative apps including *Ruben and Lullabye* (2009) and *Upgrade Soul* (2012–) and in his documentary hypermedia design for Sharon Daniel's *Public Secrets* (2007) or Radical Imaginations' *The Knotted Line* (2012), *Chroma*'s demonstrates a counterposition of everyday life rendered as the visual elaboration of programmed rules requiring some bodies to falsify themselves (or their reflexive truths) *against* a highly musical soundtrack, where offscreen voice may clarify tensions animating the visual progression of the narrative. Gestural manipulation establishes the relation or lack of relation between the two in a dynamic, carefully designed modulating movement that is in itself musical.

The resulting dissonance of narrative form and gestural articulation ultimately suggests media program and historical program as proceeding in complex entanglements that can never become fully commensurate to one another within a purely functionalist mapping of encoded gestural action to digital screen (or to the meaning of some programmed effect that would be the "output" of some such mapping). The result is that a narrative of dystopian or utopian programming of user action and self-presence results in a ludic intervention into our ability to think and feel life as programmed but contingent—and the digital interface becomes, to this degree, "aneconomical" rather than functional. The ludic, contingent gesture that does appear at this interface, though, while demonstrating the possibility for a critical understanding of history and of technoscience, does not arise from "within the program." In *Chroma*, the gesture of navigating through the digital labyrinth as a recapitulation of the everyday social labyrinth demands a new response arising in Duck/Alisha's recovery of her memory of—and in her ability to speak about—historical difference in both critical and experiential registers. Duck/Alisha's turn to the complex material-semiotic composition of race and gender, as well as her suggestion of technical logics as both augmenting and disabling, recall Turing's argument for computational intelligence as demonstrative, ludic, and contingent.

In the hands of artist-authors such as Tamblyn, Jackson, Hoberman, Loyer, and many more, the merits of the hypermedia work of art become clear: these complex projects, whether fictive or documentary in orientation, whether demonstrating essayistic, poetic, or rhetorical strategies, encapsulate the drama of configurable corporealities and subjectivities supposedly enabled by the powerful affordances of computationally programmed biotechnics. More broadly, their mobilization of the reflexive dimensions of hypermedia calls our attention to the ways in which digital arts and letters may demonstrate our desire to reflexively engage and work through allegorical critiques of technoculture familiar to SF readers and critics. Digital arts and letters' effects, then, range from revealing sociotechnical composition and biopolitical forces to acting on bodies so composed. To the extent that contemporary production of data underlies the grounding of political power in programmatic, functionalist frames, the digital arts' embrace of ludic, contingent composition over sheer programmatic, algorithmic power is also the degree to which the digital arts and letters demonstrate their own allegorical force.

Works Cited

Andrews, Jim. *Nio*. 2001. Web. July 20, 2013. http://www.vispo.com/nio/.
Clayton, Jay. "Frankenstein's Futurity: Replicants and Robots." *The Cambridge Companion to Mary Shelley*. Ed. Esther Schor. Cambridge, UK: Cambridge UP, 2003. 84–99. Print.
Delany, Samuel R. "Interview: Samuel R. Delany." *Diacritics* 16.3 (Autumn 1986): 26–45. Print.
Glenn Gould: The New Listener. DNA Media, 1999. CD-ROM.
Halberstam, Judith. "Automating Gender: Postmodern Feminism in the Age of the Intelligent Machine." *Feminist Studies* 17.3 (Autumn 1991): 439–60. Print.

Haraway, Donna. "A Manifesto for Cyborgs: Science, Technology, and Socialist Feminism in the 1980s." 1985. *Coming to Terms: Feminism, Theory, Politics.* Ed. Elizabeth Weed. New York: Routledge, 173–204. Print.

Hayles, N. Katherine. *Electronic Literature: New Horizons for the Literary.* Notre Dame, IN: U of Notre Dame P, 2008. Print.

———. *How We Became Posthuman: Virtual Bodies in Cybernetics, Literature, and Informatics.* Chicago: Chicago UP, 1999. Print.

———. *My Mother Was a Computer: Digital Subjects and Literary Texts.* Cambridge, MA: MIT, 2006. Print.

Hoberman, Perry. "Bar Code Hotel." *perryhoberman.com.* Web. July 20, 2013. http://www.perryhoberman.com/page24/.

Jackson, Shelley. *Patchwork Girl.* Eastgate Systems, 1995. CD-ROM.

Jameson, Fredric. *Archaeologies of the Future: The Desire Called Utopia and Other Science Fictions.* New York: Verso, 2005. Print.

Kellner, Douglas. *Media Culture: Cultural Studies, Identity, and Politics Between the Modern and the Postmodern.* New York: Routledge, 1995. Print.

Landow, George. *Hypertext 3.0.* Baltimore, MD: Johns Hopkins UP, 2006. Print.

Latour, Bruno. *Science in Action: How to Follow Scientists and Engineers Through Society.* Cambridge, MA: Harvard UP, 1987. Print.

Loyer, Eric. *Chroma.* 2001. *Electronic Literature Collection,* vol. 2. Web. July 20, 2013. http://collection.eliterature.org/2/works/loyer_chroma.html.

Rose, Nikolas. *The Politics of Life Itself: Biomedicine, Power, and Subjectivity in the Twenty-First Century.* Princeton, NJ: Princeton UP, 2009. Print.

Shiovitz, Dan. "Author Description." *Bad Machine.* 1999. Electronic Literature Collection, vol. 1, 2008. CD-ROM.

Tamblyn, Christine, Marjorie Franklin, and Paul Thompson. "*She Loves It, She Loves It Not: Women and Technology,* an Interactive CD-ROM." 1993. *Leonardo* 28.2 (1995): 99–104. Print.

Todd, Loretta. "Aboriginal Narratives in Cyberspace." *Immersed in Technology: Art and Virtual Environments.* Ed. Mary Anne Moser and Douglas Macleod. Cambridge, MA: MIT, 1996. Print.

Turing, Alan. 1952. "The Chemical Basis of Morphogenesis." *The Essential Turing: Seminal Writings in Computing, Logic, Philosophy, Artificial Intelligence, and Artificial Life: Plus The Secrets of Enigma.* Ed. Jack Copeland. New York: Oxford UP, 2004. 519–61. Print.

———. "Computing Machinery and Intelligence." 1950. *Mind: A Quarterly Review of Philosophy and Psychology* 59.236 (Oct. 1950): 433–60. Print.

———. "On Computable Numbers, with an Application to the Entscheidungsproblem." 1936–37. *The Essential Turing: Seminal Writings in Computing, Logic, Philosophy, Artificial Intelligence, and Artificial Life: Plus The Secrets of Enigma.* Ed. Jack Copeland. New York: Oxford UP, 2004. 58–90. Print.

Waldby, Catherine. *The Visible Human Project: Informatic Bodies and Post-Human Culture.* New York: Routledge, 2000. Print.

Wolfe, Cary. "From Dead Meat to Glow-in-the-Dark Bunnies: Seeing 'the Animal Question' in Contemporary Art." *Parallax* 12.1 (2006): 95–109. Print.

CHAPTER 19

MUSIC

JOHN CLINE

In practical terms, "SF music" does not exist: there are no SF sections in record stores, nor any comprehensive studies of SF music in either book or essay form. There is a substantial bibliography of works treating the scores of SF films, but this inevitably excludes both experimental/art music and popular songs with SF themes. Furthermore, as Vivian Sobchack notes, "Not only does most music from one SF film sound like the music from another SF film . . . but most of the music sounds like all of the music from most other narrative film" (208). The definitional problem regarding what actually constitutes "science fiction music" presents a unique challenge for discussing the intersection of sound and SF.

To begin with, the same issues involved in identifying the distinguishing general characteristics of SF also apply here. Although lyrical content can be an important indicator of SF themes (for example, David Bowie's 1969 hit "Space Oddity"), it cannot account for instrumental music. One preliminary solution to the problem, to borrow a concept from SF literary studies, is to switch over to the realm of the "speculative." A "speculative music" would additionally negate the old division between representational (or "program") music and absolute (or "abstract") music, since functionally, if not intentionally, a speculative music would invoke a phenomenological world distinct from the quotidian environment of the listener. The concept of speculative fiction encompasses a whole host of genres—gothic horror, for instance. But whereas the auditory realm of gothic horror can be invoked by relatively traditional instrumentation (for example, tritones on a pipe organ), SF music is historically dependent on the development of sound devices that have no prior precedent in acoustics—namely, electronic modalities.

Before the advent of electronic instruments, changes in instrumentation worldwide were merely of type rather than kind; from the standpoint of organology, the relatively modern saxophone is just an extremely sophisticated extension of a bullroarer, since both are reed instruments. Tones generated through purely electronic means were thus the first totally unique form of music to emerge in human culture in several thousand years. Although, according to Thom Holmes, a few unique electronic musical devices existed in the first two decades of the twentieth century (including the massive

Telharmonium), the first to be widely disseminated was the theremin, invented by the Russian scientist Leon Theremin in 1920. With the theremin and, eventually, other developments like the Ondes Martenot, magnetic tape, and modular synthesizers, technology allowed for historically unique sounds to be heard, at frequencies unattainable by traditional acoustic instruments and in patterns impossible for human musicians. The emergence of many of the future-oriented elements of SF in literature and film speaks to a burst of imagination that occurred parallel to the widespread technological developments of which electronic instruments were one small part.

Technology is not the only factor to consider with regard to SF and music, however. Paradigmatic shifts in technology do not necessarily entail an equivalent shift in aesthetics, and it is in this light that Leon Theremin is emblematic. Theremin was a scientist first, and specifically a scientist in early Soviet Russia; he was also a trained cellist. Consequently, his first great protégé on the instrument, Clara Rockmore, utilized the device to reproduce the string parts from nineteenth-century classical music, particularly Tchaikovsky. In context, Theremin's paradoxical approach to how his namesake instrument would be used seems like a result of the conflicted world of the 1920s Soviet Union: between the Leningrad Polytechnical Institute and the peasants of the countryside, or between futurists like Malevich and Mayakovsky and socialist realism with its valorization of certain aspects of the Russian cultural past. At the same time, Theremin's conjunction of the most cutting-edge technology with relatively conservative ideology and aesthetics suggests an analogy with space opera, a subgenre of SF literature whose heyday was in the 1920s and 1930s, wherein a future or outer space world accessible via new and imaginary technologies (often treated in a cursory way) allows the author to stage a return of "traditional" values.

However, while SF literary history has been characterized by a more or less coherent chronological succession of ideologically and aesthetically dominant styles (space opera, hard-SF, New Wave, among others), SF musical history, rather than tracing an arc from the conservative to the radical, has instead displayed a concurrent set of spectral options for composers at any given point in time. Even in Theremin's own era and within his circle of associates, there existed numerous figures that more fully embraced the approach to music-making made possible by new technologies. A very short list of key figures would include Arthur Honegger, George Antheil, Luigi Russolo, and Henry Cowell, though the real foil to Theremin was the French-American composer Edgard Varèse. Despite their personal and professional association (Theremin actually built instruments for Varèse), the composer's enthusiastic attitude toward the musical possibilities opened up by the new technologies stands in stark contrast to the scientist's more conservative aesthetics. Varèse pioneered the idea that music was nothing more or less than "organized sound," and his body of work is a demonstration that organization was not dependent on any of the forms inherited from the nineteenth century. In fact, one explanation for Varèse's rather slim oeuvre is that he wasn't able to make the music of his imagination until technology actually caught up in the 1950s, when he composed *Poème électronique* for the Philips Pavilion at the 1958 Brussels World's Fair—this despite his excitement decades earlier at the theremin. Positing Theremin and Varèse as opposite ends of an ideological and aesthetic spectrum is essential to understanding the dynamics of SF and music across the twentieth and into the twenty-first centuries.

As noted earlier, Vivian Sobchack has made some astute observations regarding the SF soundtrack. Sobchack's book was one of the first attempts at a sustained critique of SF film (it was published in an earlier edition as *The Limits of Infinity* in 1980); as such, it also contained the earliest analysis of sound in SF film, a chapter entitled "The Leaden Echo and the Golden Echo." Most of the SF film scholars who have followed in Sobchack's wake have taken up some of her underlying assumptions, specifically the authors included in Philip Hayward's anthology *Off the Planet: Music, Sound, and Science Fiction Cinema* and in Mathew J. Bartkowiak's *Sounds of the Future: Essays on Music in Science Fiction Film*. Although the topics and approaches in these collections are varied, they repeat what I believe is a false distinction that Sobchack established in *Screening Space*.

Sobchack's position regarding the mediocrity of the majority of SF soundtracks is clear enough. However, after providing ample justification for this position (as well as highlighting the exceptions), Sobchack writes, "Interestingly, in contrast to the lack of musical adventurousness in the SF film, the use of innovative and dramatically expressive sound effects has been widespread from science fiction's beginnings in the fifties as a film genre" (216). From a film-studies perspective, the distinction that Sobchack creates here between the diegetic sounds created by Foley artists and the nondiegetic scores is understandable, since it coincides with the division of labor that exists within the film industry. At the same time, this distinction is not very helpful if we are trying to consider SF music as a whole, beyond its use in film, and it is extremely problematic given developments in musical aesthetics that arose around the same time as the 1950s SF films that Sobchack discusses.

In particular, I would cite John Cage's *Imaginary Landscape No. 1* (1939), Pierre Schaeffer's *Cinq études de bruits* (1948), and Cage's *4'33"* (1952)—the famed "silent" piece—as crucial for understanding how Varèse's suggestion of music as "organized sound" was applied during this period. This conceptual shift is significant because it allows a dismantling of the music/sound division Sobchack deploys. The pieces I refer to above were not chosen at random. Cage's *Imaginary Landscape* is an excellent example of "speculative music," and the point of *4'33"* was to force an epiphany on the audience that the environmental sounds were actually the "music." Schaeffer's earliest piece of *musique concrète* used prerecorded sounds—the same types of things a Foley artist would work with—as the raw material for composition. It is indubitable that Louis and Bebe Barron, normally avant-gardists, were aware of these developments, and it is probable that even a veteran film scorer like Bernard Herrmann was as well; respectively, they were the composers for *Forbidden Planet* (1956) and *The Day The Earth Stood Still* (1951)—the most widely noted SF soundtracks of the decade. Furthermore, I believe it is far more productive to consider the Foley artists that Sobchack praises as peers of the trio I refer to above, given their approach to sound and despite whatever their private intentions were as employees of the Hollywood studios.

If many of the SF writers of the 1940s and 1950s were concerned with the ways that technocracy could remake society, for better or worse, their peers in music were often actual employees of the kinds of technocratic institutions that appear in the era's fiction. For instance, according to Dave Tompkins, a very young Ray Bradbury, who was in New York for the 1939 World's Fair, won a free long-distance call to his parents in Los Angeles—as a demonstration of the superiority of the Bell telephone system—and was on hand to witness the "Voder," a manually operated speech synthesis machine that, as the "vocoder" during World War II, was used to send encoded military messages, and that 30 years later would become a staple in "futuristic" music. The vocoder was the brainchild of the researchers at Bell Laboratories, a place where the future was quite literally invented for most of the twentieth century. Twenty-two years after the World's Fair demonstration, Bell Lab scientists programmed an IBM 7094 to sing "Daisy Bell" (a.k.a., "Bicycle Built for Two"), an event referenced in Arthur C. Clarke and Stanley Kubrick's *2001: A Space Odyssey* (1968) when the HAL 9000 computer is shut down. Furthermore, HAL's birthplace, the University of Illinois at Urbana-Champaign, was the home of the first supercomputer, the ILLIAC, although an identical machine was built for the US military called the ORDVAC during the same period (they were completed in 1952 and 1951, respectively).

While these references in Clarke and Kubrick's work are easy enough to substantiate, it is less clear whether they were aware that the University of Illinois also housed one of the premier electronic music studios of the postwar period. It is one of the curious facts of postwar music in the Western world that the vast majority of cutting-edge electronic music was produced in laboratories created and funded as a kind of by-product of the military-industrial-university complex: on top of the Experimental Music Studios at Illinois, there was also the Westdeutscher Rundfunk in Cologne (Karlheinz Stockhausen's home base), the Radiodiffusion-francaise (where Schaeffer produced his *musique concrète* pieces), the BBC Radiophonic Workshop, the Columbia-Princeton Electronic Music Center, and the Sonic Arts Union at the University of Michigan. The San Francisco Tape Music Center, while originally an independent entity, eventually attached itself to Mills College. The only truly "independent" electronic music studio of the period, Raymond Scott's appropriately bureaucratic-sounding Manhattan Research, Inc., was able to remain solvent mostly because Scott provided jingles for use by General Motors, IBM, Baltimore Gas and Electric, and numerous consumer product manufacturers (see Scott et al.).

While it is unfair to say that the music produced by composers given access to these facilities was aligned ideologically with the technocratic tendencies of the Cold War, it is worth noting that the cost of the machinery necessary to produce this radical music was simply out of reach for anyone who did not associate themselves with such institutions. Not that all institutions were created equal, however; according to Louis Niebur, unlike their peers in Germany, France, and the United States, Britain's BBC Radiophonic Workshop operated on limited budgets and was explicitly tasked with providing the kinds of sound effects that their Foley-artist peers in Hollywood were also making—including the famous original *Doctor Who* theme. Although this theme is a fairly clear instance of SF music, not all the music produced within these various institutions can be described as such, electronic though it may be. Nevertheless, the technologies and compositional techniques that emerged from these laboratories have had a profound influence on the development of most SF music ever since.

Following *The Day the Earth Stood Still* and *Forbidden Planet*, the real turning point in SF soundtracks are two films directed by Kubrick, the aforementioned *2001* and *A Clockwork Orange* (1971). Neither film uses the kind of generic Hollywood narrative score Sobchack critiques, but at the same time, neither fits neatly into the "experimental" type of score composed by Bernard Herrmann or Louis and Bebe Barron. Both films use music innovatively—though they do not necessarily use innovative music. *2001*'s soundtrack consists of a mix of classical nineteenth-century Germanic music (one piece by Johan Strauss II, another by the unrelated Richard Strauss) and two by the Soviet-Armenian neoclassical composer Aram Khachaturian. The elegance and grandeur of these pieces are contrasted by four comparatively harsh and dissonant compositions by the modernist György Ligeti. If Kubrick had only used the classical music, his film would have perhaps been subject to the criticisms Sobchack offers of typical Hollywood scores in SF films. The effectiveness of the music in the film comes from the juxtaposition of these pieces with the Ligeti: the resulting effect for a listener-viewer is one of ambivalence, an uneasy stance that meshes well with the interplay of Clarke's screenplay and Kubrick's direction.

By contrast, the score for *A Clockwork Orange* is made up almost entirely of nineteenth-century classical music. The juxtaposition of sound in the film actually occurs entirely through the instrumentation used for the classical pieces: traditional orchestration in some instances, and Walter (now Wendy) Carlos's synthesizer versions of others, occasionally the exact same pieces of music (for example, excerpts from Beethoven's *Ninth Symphony*). Kubrick's decisions regarding what the film's soundtrack should contain thus reflexively stage the aesthetic/ideological contrast of perspectives between Theremin and Varèse discussed above. *A Clockwork Orange* also works another set of juxtapositions, however: between image and sound. The "ultraviolence" taking place onscreen is not exactly contrasted by the Beethoven (orchestral or synthesized); instead, it effectively reveals the violence and will to dominate that lurks at the heart of the "heroic" swoop of the nineteenth-century German classical canon (see McClary). Very few directors have Kubrick's astute sense of music: later SF films that have attempted to create the kind of dissonances and revelations *2001* achieves, such as *Liquid Sky* (1982) with its entirely synthesized score that veers between electro-punk and baroque, fail to sustain the same aesthetic and ideological complexities.

Kubrick's use of music in film is ultimately inimitable. (The same cannot be said for the continuum that runs from Kenneth Anger to Martin Scorsese to Quentin Tarantino, with their skillful use of pop-song juxtapositions, but this technique is much simpler to execute.) The scores to other SF films of the 1970s and 1980s are far easier to categorize—a fact that is particularly evident in the career of composer Jerry Goldsmith. Defying the pigeonholing that marks the careers of most authors of Hollywood scores (Herrmann once quipped that he got all the thrillers, while Henry Mancini got the comedies), Goldsmith reveals in his SF scores from the end of the 1960s and into the 1980s a remarkable adaptability, which may just be a nice way of saying that he followed the fashions of the day. In sequential order, the soundtracks he created went from the conventionally orchestrated *Planet of the Apes* (1968) to a mixture of orchestra and electronics in *Logan's Run* (1976) to the heavily treated acoustic instruments and electronics of *Alien* (1979) and finally to the entirely electronic score of *Outland* (1981). This trajectory, while it doesn't correlate to his approach to other types of films, is an effective demonstration of the spectrum of ideology and aesthetics in SF film music, especially in its increasing use of electronics as compositional tools. By 1990's *Total Recall*, however, when electronic soundtracks had mostly fallen out of vogue, Goldsmith was back to composing conventionally orchestrated SF scores.

Most of the other composers who worked on SF films during this period did not exhibit the same range, in some cases for explicitly held aesthetic positions. At the conservative end are the soundtracks for *The Omega Man* (1971), *Silent Running* (1972), *The Day of the Dolphin* (1973), *Westworld* (1973), and *Soylent Green* (1973). The most extraordinarily obstinate in their devotion to the conventions of nineteenth-century classical music, however, are the soundtracks for *Star Wars* (1977) and *Close Encounters of the Third Kind* (1977), both by John Williams—whose scores are almost devoid of any indication that significant developments in compositional technique or instrumental technology have taken place in a century (I say "almost" because the five-note mothership motif from *Close Encounters* and the alien cantina music in *Star Wars* are exceptions, but both are diegetically motivated). Williams undoubtedly possessed an enormous talent, but it seems hardly accidental that the directors with whom he is most closely associated, Steven Spielberg and George Lucas, have turned out to be the most conservative to emerge from the "New Hollywood" of the late 1960s and 1970s.

At the more radical and experimental end of movie soundtracks during the period are the scores for *The Andromeda Strain* (1969) and *Zardoz* (1974), but even more interesting is the music for John Carpenter's SF films and Vangelis's work on *Blade Runner* (1982). Carpenter is unusual among film directors in that he often composes his own music, occasionally in conjunction with collaborators; his minimalist, synthesizer-based soundtracks for films like *Assault on Precinct 13* (1976), *Halloween* (1978), and *Escape from New York* (1981) are legendary. Even though only *Escape* could be classified as an SF film, the soundtracks for *Dark Star* (1974) and—with Ennio Morricone, himself a highly unconventional composer—*The Thing* (1982) are similarly devoted to a stripped-down, anxiety-producing repetition of electronic tones. Despite his later films' use of more traditional types of scores (for example, *Starman* [1984]), during the 1970s and early 1980s Carpenter's approach to music was almost militantly opposed to the one used by John Williams. During the same period, the Greek composer Vangelis produced perhaps the most heralded electronic soundtrack in history, his Academy Award–winning work on *Chariots of Fire* (1981). Appropriate to that film's narrative, Vangelis's score has an epic sweep—somewhat unusual for purely electronic music. Similar compositional elements also exist in his score for *Blade Runner* alongside more atmospheric electronic work, and that film's soundtrack, while perhaps not as radical as Carpenter's, remains a milestone in SF music.

The SF scores of the 1990s appear, on reflection, to have been widely conscious of the ideological/aesthetic oppositions that were an integral part of SF soundtrack music of the preceding decades. Individual composers and music supervisors addressed these issues in different ways. Despite the vogue for purely electronic soundtracks from the late 1970s to the early 1980s, the next decade's films largely returned to conventional orchestration. Brad Fiedel, however, continued to produce electronic soundtracks, primarily with the *Terminator* franchise, though also notably for Robert Longo's *Johnny Mnemonic* (1995). Three scores, in particular, seem to have been particularly invested in reconciling the old aesthetic divisions: Danny Elfman's for *Mars Attacks!* (1996), Eric Serra's for *The Fifth Element* (1997), and the interplay between Don Davis's score and the pop songs used in *The Matrix* (1999).

Elfman's score for *Mars Attacks!*, like the film it accompanies, is part homage, part satire of 1950s SF films. Elfman occasionally uses rather generic orchestral music, but within those elements are spliced the kinds of electronic sounds that in the 1950s were typically relegated to the arena of "sound effects"—a conjunction that effectively eliminates the division Sobchack assumes in *Screening Space*. In *The Matrix*, the juxtaposition of score and pop songs operates as an update to Kubrick's use of music in *2001*, with Davis's orchestral score functioning in counterpoint to the electronic dance music and metal songs. Serra's score for *The Fifth Element* is quite varied, since he created pieces heard from the radios of flying taxis in the film, in addition to the incidental music. In the most revealing scene, the characters witness a performance by the "Blue Diva," an alien opera singer, whose vocal begins as what could easily be a Mozart aria but then shifts into a kind of futuristic Donna Summer-meets-Giorgio Moroder mode. In this scene, electronic music is reconciled with the classical grandeur beloved by John Williams (who, following his 1970s SF scores, became conductor of the Boston Pops in 1980).

The first popular songs to take up SF themes were novelty hits such as Billy Lee Riley's rockabilly "Flying Saucer Rock'n'Roll" in 1957 and Sheb Wooley's "Purple People Eater" in 1958 (see Ortfinoski). These songs are best understood as cash-ins on the popularity of SF films with teenagers and, possibly, the mass-folk cultural interest in UFOs that grew out of the events in Roswell, New Mexico, in 1947. Although in some respects still "novelty," specific songs within the oeuvre of British producer Joe Meek stand out as the earliest attempts to blend SF-themed pop with futuristic music. "Telstar" by the Tornados (a studio group Meek produced) was the first British single to reach number one on the Billboard charts in 1962—predating the Beatles by two years. Its title a reference to communications satellites that entered the popular consciousness with the launch of the Soviet *Sputnik I* in 1957, this instrumental is reminiscent of then-popular "surf" music, though it takes the echo and reverb effects common to that genre to new heights. Even more "out there" was Meek's 1960 concept album *I Hear a New World*; not as popular as "Telstar" by many miles, the title track featured vocals using the same tape-speed manipulation that had scored a hit for Alvin and the Chipmunks two years earlier (the rest of the album consists of instrumentals). Unlike his high-art peers housed in the cutting-edge electronic sound labs, Meek's electronics are kitchen sink: *musique concrète* on the cheap. Still, Meek was innovative in his use of the studio—almost a British Phil Spector—and it is interesting to consider what kind of work he would have produced had he not committed suicide in 1967, the point at which the relatively affordable synthesizers produced by Robert Moog became available for purchase (see Unterberger 144–48).

Although not as intimately connected with the Cold War's technocratic empire as the avant-garde, rock musicians like the Beatles began to have access to electronic instruments in high-end commercial studios like Abbey Road during the late 1960s. None of the Beatles music can legitimately be considered SF (though perhaps Jimi Hendrix's contemporaneous "3rd Stone From the Sun" and "Are You Experienced?" could), even if they did use, in simplified form, techniques developed by composers like Stockhausen. This technological access, combined with an aesthetic associated with psychedelic drugs, did inspire SF-themed rock compositions, most notably "Interstellar Overdrive" from Pink Floyd's 1967 album *The Piper at the Gates of Dawn*.

Concurrently, several musicians whose training lay within the technocratic institutions were freed by the introduction of the Moog, including Gershon Kingsley and Walter/Wendy Carlos. Kingsley, both with Jean-Jacques Perrey and separately, released a series of novelty Moog records in the late 1970s, as did Carlos, whose 1968 album *Switched-On Bach* was probably many people's introduction to purely synthetic music. (Earlier electronic instruments, including the theremin, were common enough from SF soundtrack music and the Beach Boys' "Good Vibrations," and the Ondes Martenot, Ondioline, and Mellotron popped up occasionally in rock music from the era.) Carlos's music, like Theremin and Rockmore's collaborations decades earlier, was often devoted to rendering classical standards in electronic form. By contrast, Perrey and Kingsley, while generally light-hearted and pop-oriented, frequently took up SF themes in their compositions. Christopher Tyng would eventually rework another piece from the era, *Psyché Rock* by Pierre Schaeffer protégé Pierre Henry, as the theme to the SF animated series *Futurama* (1999–2003, 2008–13).

It is also worth noting that this era saw the development of a critical apparatus devoted to rock music, and many of the early fan-critics were also fans of SF. The founder of *Crawdaddy!*, the late Paul Williams, promoted SF in his magazine, and later became the literary executor of Philip K. Dick, helping to shepherd his unpublished novels into print. Writing on Williams's website, Johan Kugelberg observes that "rock fandom Big-Name-Fans had been SF-fans: Paul Williams, Lenny Kaye, Greg Shaw, even Lester Bangs had dabbled in the world of science-fiction fanzines and SF-conventions." Moreover, during the 1960s and 1970s, SF literature either frequently referenced rock music directly—for example, Norman Spinrad's 1971 story "No Direction Home," which borrows its title from Dylan's lyric for "Like a Rolling Stone" (1965)—or featured rock stars as protagonists (for example, Michael Moorcock's "Jerry Cornelius" series [1968–]).

SF fandom and rock music really hit a rich vein with the surprise success of David Bowie's 1969 single "Space Oddity." Although in many ways a conventional folk-rock tune, the song did feature the Stylophone, a small electronic instrument. Bowie's relationship to SF is complex. The genre's themes have been fairly consistent lyrical reference points in his work, but early on his music was rarely as out-there as his costumes; his 1972 concept album *The Rise and Fall of Ziggy Stardust and the Spiders from Mars* owes a greater debt to 1950s rock and roll than it does to Stockhausen. This is in contrast to less popular but more innovative music made during the same period by groups like 50 Foot Hose, White Noise, The United States of America, the Silver Apples, Lothar and the Hand People, and Tonto's Expanding Headband.

The real battleground in the early 1970s for popular SF music, however, lay between two interpretations of what constituted "progressive" (or "prog") rock. Simplified a great deal, one side consisted of the likes of Emerson, Lake and Palmer, Yes, King Crimson, Genesis, and the post-Syd Barrett Pink Floyd (along with Rush's 1976 album *2112* and Styx's 1983 song "Mr. Roboto"), all of whom displayed pretentions toward the virtuosity and grandiosity of nineteenth-century classical music and a simultaneous attraction to medieval romance themes alongside their SF-oriented material—perhaps functioning together as a peculiar iteration of the "space opera" end of the aesthetic spectrum. At the other lay the more modernist wing containing Hawkwind (who sometimes featured Moorcock as a collaborator), Van der Graaf Generator, and what the English music press dubbed "Krautrock"—Kraftwerk, Faust, Neu!, and Cluster, among others. By the late 1970s, this group would also count David Bowie among its adherents after he began working with Brian Eno, a great admirer and occasional collaborator with the Krautrock bands. The music produced by this group of artists tended to be more abstract rather than narrative-oriented, Hawkwind being the exception. It also leaned a bit more toward the bleakly dystopian—although, as with SF literature and film of the period, such attitudes were the order of the day.

Johnny Rotten may never have taken up SF themes in his music, either with the Sex Pistols or with Public Image, Ltd., but his 1977 radio broadcast "A Punk and His Music" made it clear where his allegiances fell in the prog-rock divide: with the Germans and Van der Graaf Generator. With the exception of the Misfits, who sang basic rock-and-roll songs based on the plots of old SF and horror movies, the music within the punk orbit that could be described as SF was all fairly radical musically, at least in a pop context. Probably the earliest group to blend SF with punk attitude was Devo, whose futuristic stage-wear and devotion to the belief that humanity was in the process of "de-evolution" were evident as early as 1972. Emerging from the industrial wasteland of northern Ohio, and formed in part in response to the shootings at Kent State (a disillusionment with the 1960s that finds parallel in much contemporaneous SF literature), the band was at its more grimly humorous prior to the massive success of their first major release, 1978's *Q: Are We Not Men? A: We Are Devo!* Subsequently, while they retained elements of the bleak outlook evident on their self-released singles, they became more conventionally, if perhaps ironically, pop with their song structures (see Heylin 298–304). Somewhat similarly, Gary Numan, both with Tubeway Army and as a solo artist, made a virtue out of coldness and ironic distance—characteristics that he, unlike Devo, inherited from Kraftwerk and that are apparent in songs like "Are 'Friends' Electric?" and "Cars" (both 1979). Numan and his fellow Brit Thomas Dolby (for example, "She Blinded Me With Science" [1982]) were also innovative in their use of electronics, as was the early incarnation of the Human League with their 1979 concept album *The Dignity of Labour*, a tribute of sorts to Soviet cosmonaut Yuri Gagarin.

Many English bands during this period took to naming themselves or individual songs after SF novels and short stories, often those written by J. G. Ballard, including the band Comsat Angels, Joy Division's song "The Atrocity Exhibition" (1980), and The Normal's "Warm Leatherette" (1978, based on Ballard's 1973 novel *Crash*). With producer Martin Hannett at the boards, Joy Division's music creatively utilized electronic effects, and The Normal's Daniel Miller used his single to launch Mute Records, home of much innovative electronic music since. The Comsat Angels, however, were indicative of the trend, which began in England in the early 1980s, of recreating the structure of 1960s pop via mass-produced electronics, a tendency that both quashed the SF element from rock music for most of the next 20 years and represented, relatively speaking, an aesthetic retreat to the conservative ground established by once-new pop forms.

Rock music's interest in SF waned after the early 1980s, and much of the music of the 1990s focused instead on working-class or pseudo-working-class masculine themes. (The ubiquitous flannel shirt of the grunge era is a fairly good indicator of how far away from SF music had come at that point.) One exception was the band Stereolab, who built an entire career out of a kind of retrofuturism rooted in spacey bachelor pad/lounge music and novelty Moog records of the 1960s. Mainstream dance music normalized synthesizers after the early 1980s but reiterated the themes of love and partying that had been ubiquitous in the disco era; for SF, one has to look to underground rave culture, where the combination of the elements of 1960s and 1970s spacey psychedelia and new electronic innovations was much more typical.

During the early 2000s, "electroclash" emerged in New York City, continuing in Stereolab's retrofuturist vein but shifting forward to nostalgia for the early 1980s. Although relatively short-lived, it did initiate a revival of interest in minimalist electronic music, most of it dance-oriented and some of it concerned with SF themes. Radiohead, an enormously popular group compared to the others mentioned in this section, released a series of dystopian SF concept albums in the late 1990s and early 2000s (especially *OK Computer* in 1997 and *Kid A* in 2000) that, while not retrofuturist, certainly took stylistic cues from 1970s Krautrock and the more experimental end of British prog-rock from the same period.

Although "SF music" does not exist in the conventional sense of other musical genres, the intersection of sound and science fiction has, in fact, resulted in many instances of music that can be considered SF, and in this regard SF music does exist across a fairly wide spectrum of political aesthetics, using a variety of technologies. This topic is desperately in need of further research: virtually the only area that has shown sustained critical investigation is Afrofuturist music (see Eshun; Zuberi; and the chapter on the topic in this handbook). Yet there is a wide range of SF music out there, for those who care to listen.

Works Cited

Bartkowiak, Mathew J., ed. *Sounds of the Future: Essays on Music in Science Fiction Film.* Jefferson, NC: McFarland, 2010. Print.

Eshun, Kodwo. *More Brilliant Than the Sun: Adventures in Sonic Fiction.* London: Quartet, 1998. Print.

Hayward, Philip, ed. *Off the Planet: Music, Sound and Science Fiction Cinema.* Eastleigh, UK: John Libbey, 2004. Print.

Heylin, Clinton. *From the Velvets to the Voidoids: The Birth of American Punk Rock.* Chicago: Chicago Review, 2005. Print.

Holmes, Thom. *Electronic and Experimental Music: A History of New Sound.* 2nd ed. New York: Routledge, 2002. Print.

Kugelberg, Johan. Blurb for *Crawdaddy!* Magazine. *Paulwilliams.com.* Web. Jan. 12, 2012. http://www.paulwilliams.com/writings.html.

McClary, Susan. *Feminine Endings: Music, Gender, and Sexuality.* Minneapolis: U of Minnesota P, 2002. Print.

Niebur, Louis. *Special Sound: The Creation and Legacy of the BBC Radiophonic Workshop.* New York: Oxford UP, 2010. Print.

Ortfinoski, Steve. *The Golden Age of Novelty Songs.* New York: Watson-Guptill, 2000. Print.

Scott, Raymond, Jim Henson, and Dorothy Collins. *Manhattan Research, Inc.* Basta Records, 2000. CD.

Sobchack, Vivian. *Screening Space: The American Science Fiction Film.* 2nd ed. New Brunswick, NJ: Rutgers UP, 1997. Print.

Tompkins, Dave. *How to Wreck a Nice Beach: The Vocoder from World War II to Hip-Hop. The Machine Speaks.* New York: Melville House, 2011. Print.

Unterberger, Richie. *Unknown Legends of Rock 'n' Roll.* Milwaukee, WI: Backbeat, 1998. Print.

Zuberi, Nabeel. "Is This the Future?: Black Music and Technology Discourse." *Science Fiction Studies* 34.2 (July 2007): 283–300. Print.

CHAPTER 20

....

PERFORMANCE ART

....

STEVE DIXON

We must note from the start that what we here call performance art (as it is known in the United States, or Live Art as it is known in the United Kingdom) is entirely different from theater and eschews theater's artifice and pretense. As one of performance art's preeminent figures, Marina Abramović, puts it: "To be a performance artist, you have to hate theatre" (qtd. Hickling). Emerging from—and allied closely with—the fine arts, for the most part it does not aim to tell a story, nor are its artists actors playing characters: they are themselves and they perform actions and events, often within site-specific or gallery installation settings. Crucially, performance art is *not fiction*. This is precisely why the exploration of science fiction in performance art is so potent and revolutionary: its artists are not acting out some narrative of scientific futurity, they are inventing and inhabiting it. While their works are narratives of sorts and "texts" in the broad literary sense, they are not engaged with fictionalizing but rather *actualizing*.

"Actuals" lie at the center of the history, theory, and creative impulse of performance art. Most famously theorized by Richard Schechner, performance art events are actuals that follow similar patterns to tribal rituals, whereby actions are performed in order to effect an *actual* result: shamanistic trance rituals actually cure patients, a rain dance makes rain actually happen. Performance art is efficacious and effects a real change in the real world, in contrast to theater (and fictional forms in general) that normally only effect change in the minds of the audience. Schechner elucidates five qualities and characteristics of actuals including: "1) *process*, something happening in the *here and now*; 2) *consequential, irredeemable*, and *irrevocable* acts . . . 3) *contest*, something is at stake . . . 4) *initiation*, a *change in status* for participants; 5) space is used *concretely* and *organically*" (18; emphasis in original).

At first, these ideas seem to fly in the face of understandings of science fiction: making concrete change in a concrete space would appear by definition to require authentic, real-life acts that negate fictionality, scientific or otherwise. Yet when performance art turns its imagination into the realms of science fiction, by dint of its historical roots in tribal rituals, its allegiances with shamanism, and its egalitarian philosophies granting it interdisciplinary permission to embrace fiction as metaphor and to employ any media (even the much-hated theater), it inhabits an interesting, tension-filled liminal space that is *precisely science fiction*. This space, like popular SF notions of outer space, mixes a reality of the known here-and-now with a "will" to the unknown, the alien, and the future; and in the extreme territories and rituals of performance art, this will is as Nietzschean and hardcore as that of any SF protagonist or monster.

The actual changes in the real world made by performance artists include cyborgic bodily modifications, literalizing Richard Feynman's maxim that "the best way to predict the future is to invent it" (qtd. Thacker, "Science Fiction of Technoscience" 155). The Brazilian-born American artist Eduardo Kac was the first to have a microchip surgically implanted in his body "for art's sake" in a performance entitled *Time Capsule* (1997), and Australian artist Stelarc, starting in 2003, underwent multiple surgical procedures—and experienced seriously real-world septic complications—to have an Internet-enabled third ear developed on his left arm. In *3rd I* (2010–11), Iraqi-American performance artist Wafaa Bilal had a 10-megapixel digital camera surgically implanted into the back of his head, which web-streamed an image of its point of view once a minute for an entire year. As is often the case in performance art, its concept proved stronger than its content, as his "allegorical statement about the things we don't see and leave behind" (Bilal) inevitably comprised endless shots of daytime walls and nighttime blackness.

Many such futuristically conceived pieces give birth to spectacularly mundane results since performance art elevates concepts, actions, behaviors, and statements above aesthetics, and process is considered equally as or more important than product. But since these performance actions are actuals effecting concrete, real-world change in the bodies of the artists and their interactions with the world, even the mundane results become genuinely "estranged," to borrow a term from Darko Suvin's classic definition of science fiction: "*the presence and interaction of estrangement and cognition . . . [in] an imaginative framework alternative to the author's empirical environment*" (7–8; emphasis in original).

The work of French performance artist Orlan provides a perfect demonstration of these ideas in action, adopting a cruel politics of estrangement aligned with a vivid cognitive exercise regime for her audience as she performs visceral hyridizations and bastardizations of classical art, culture, and myth. Her *Self-Hybridization* project (1998–2000) draws on mythological themes and ancient Mayan iconography to create grotesque and frightening digital reconfigurations of her visage, while *The Reincarnation of St. Orlan* (1993) takes her theater of cruelty to the physical operating theater. Like a living *Photoshop* model, Orlan's face, through a long series of plastic-surgery operations, is transformed into a composite montage of elements of some of the most beautiful women from art history: the chin of Botticelli's Venus, the mouth of Gustave Moreau's Europa, and the forehead of the Mona Lisa. But it is the process of performance through each surgery, rather than their facial results, that provides the impact and power, and that has assured a revered place in performance-art history. Under local anesthetic, Orlan reads philosophical texts out loud (ensuring that Suvin's "cognition" is stimulatingly in play) and talks cheerily via satellite to a global audience as her face is literally ripped open and sawn apart by masked surgeons. It is an ultimate act of estrangement; it is also a scene from the most gorily outlandish science fiction horror movie (Georges Franju's *Eyes Without a Face* [1960], say)—and it happens live, *actually*.

The contemporary SF-inspired performance artist has a notable historical lineage spanning the entire twentieth and twenty-first centuries. In the 1910s and 1920s, the futuristic was very literally proclaimed by performance makers among the Italian Futurists: "Today it is the MACHINE that distinguishes our era. . . . We feel mechanically, and we sense that we ourselves are made out of steel, we too are machines, we too have been mechanized. . . . [T]his is the principle of a new aesthetic" (Pannaggi and Paladini 272–73). The very first exhibition of the German Bauhaus was entitled "Art and Technology: A New Unity" (1923), and throughout the 1930s artists like Oscar Schlemmer conceived artificial performers (wired and wireless remote-controlled), while Russian Constructivist theater director Vsevolod Meyerhold and choreographer Nikolai Foreger trained their performers to act as man–machine cyborgs. By the 1960s, performance artists such as Bruce Lacey and Nam June Paik were inventing robots to do their bidding, and Andy Warhol continued the Futurists' calls, quipping: "I want to be a machine, I think everyone should be a machine" (qtd. Dixon 271). The 1970s saw Stelarc's naked body suspended high in the sky like an astronaut (held up entirely by hooks piercing his skin), and Christopher Burden opened his own *Doorway to Heaven* (1973) by stabbing two live electrical wires directly into his chest, with explosive, near-fatal results.

By the twilight years of the twentieth century, the industrial machine age had shifted to a digital one, where the prevailing SF prophecy of a convergence of humans and machines would become a distinctive and dazzling, if sometimes disquieting, image in performance art. In the 1990s, the digital revolution prompted a renaissance in performance art. Traditionalists stubbornly resisted the technological onslaught by probing their visceral, analogue bodies with increasing intensity, while others adopted new technologies to either critique and deconstruct, or to herald and pioneer, their implications for the body. Every aspect of the SF genre was seemingly explored: from Chicano cyborgs (Guillermo Gómez-Peña's *The Ethno-Cyberpunk Trading Post & Curio Shop on the Electronic Frontier* [1994]) to cyberpunk robot wars (Survival Research Laboratories' *The Unexpected Destruction of Elaborately Engineered Artifacts* [1997]) and from VR sex (Stahl Stensie and Kirk Woolford's *CyberSM* [1994]) to the ethics and disaster scenarios of biotechnology (Critical Art Ensemble's *BioCom* [1997]).

Fakeshop's take on the biotech theme, *Multiple_Dwelling* (1999), presented at the Ars Electronica festival, combined a reworking of the SF movie *Coma* (1978) with multiple networked spaces and real and virtual bodies. Through various performance events, including real bodies suspended in space (à la *Coma*), surgical images of real and avatar organ transplants, and VRML worlds, it attempted to construct what the ensemble call "fake biologies" ("Lifescience"). While critiquing ideas of fragmented, objectified and surgically altered bodies and societies, it also operated as an interdisciplinary actual, as collaborator Eugene Thacker suggests:

> a hybrid mix of biomedical science, computer science, and science fiction ... uneasy with the notion of simply being an art project ... complex, ambiguous, and affective zone where the bodies that we are and the bodies that we own are consistently inscribed by science, culture, and embodied networks and linkages. ("SF, Technoscience, Net.art" 69)

Performance artists, then, have taken the core element and medium of their art—their physical selves—and have sought, through the paradigm of actuals, to inscribe the vocabulary and language of science fiction onto their bodies and to imbricate the technologies of science fact into their bodies in the act of performance.

Nobody does this better than Stelarc; and if, in Orlan's work, "no longer does art imitate life ... [,] life imitates art" (Giannachi 49), then with Stelarc, both his life and his art imitate—and realize—science fiction. Stelarc is the quintessential cyborg performance artist who has been testing the limits of his body since piercing his skin with multiple hooks and suspending himself in mid-air in various configurations in performances ranging from 1976 to 1988. Since then, he has used numerous technologies, including high-tech robotic prostheses, to explore what he calls "alternate, intimate and involuntary interfaces with the body" (Stelarc, "Biography"). These include swallowing an expanding, endoscope-style probe to create a Cronenbergian *Stomach Sculpture* (1993), involuntarily "dancing" in response to electrical shocks sent by remote gallery visitors in different cities simultaneously touching his computer-screen avatar (*Fractal Flesh* [1995]), and writing the word EVOLUTION on a sheet of glass using three hands, one of them a sophisticated robotic third hand, a Perspex-and-metal forearm and hand appendage, custom-designed for him in Japan and controlled by muscle activity in different parts of his body (*Handswriting* [1982]).

Stelarc's philosophical mantra and website slogan for many years—"The Body Is Obsolete"—was distinctly cyberpunk, and he genuinely considers his body (always referred to in the third person: "the" body, "this" body—never "my" body) as an evolutionary entity. Suvin's estrangement is stretched to its logical conclusion with Stelarc's consideration of his body "not as a subject but as an object—NOT AS AN OBJECT OF DESIRE BUT AS AN OBJECT FOR DESIGNING" ("Prosthetics" 391). It is an experimental site and laboratory specimen for enhancements, but unlike Orlan, Stelarc is a self-surgeon who takes no interest in or influence from classical art: he is a Futurist conceiving his own modifications. Stelarc's performance actuals are not Orlan's postmodern critiques that hold up a mirror to society's notions of beauty, art, and the body as canvas. Rather, and in true SF style, they attempt to smash the mirror and have us fly off into an entirely new world. He is, in his own words: "an evolutionary guide, extrapolating new trajectories ... [,] a genetic sculptor, restructuring and hypersensitizing the human body; an architect of internal body spaces; a primal surgeon, implanting dreams, transplanting desires; an evolutionary alchemist, triggering mutations, transforming the human landscape" ("Strategies" 154).

These ideas of transforming both internal bodily spaces and external landscapes close the circle of accord with Suvin's definition of science fiction as operating not only

FIGURE 20.1 Stelarc with muscle-controlled robotic third hand. Photo by K. Oki. Courtesy of the artist.

through the interaction of estrangement and cognition but also within "an imaginative framework alternative to the author's empirical environment" (7), and this would include Stelarc's performances in the online world of *Second Life* (since 2005), where multiple avatars of the artist ascend, descend, float, and rotate in gravitationless space around a huge 3D heart and alongside other disembodied organs. In his accompanying voice-over, Stelarc refers to "Organs without Bodies," deliberately reversing Deleuze and Guattari's formulation (first coined by Antonin Artaud) of "bodies without organs," while other performances such as *Exoskeleton* (1998) ignite correspondences with the philosophers' notions of Becoming. Stelarc stands on a rotating turntable atop a giant six-legged pneumatically powered robot, controlling its spiderlike walking movements via computer-translated arm gestures. Other examples of Stelarc "becoming animal" include his *Walking Head* (2006), another perambulatory robotic creation, this time without the artist on board; in his corporeal stead is an LED screen with his animated 3D avatar head, and its positioning almost directly on top of the legs bears an eerie resemblance to the horrific spider-with-human-head mutation in John Carpenter's 1982 film *The Thing*. Such images are metaphors for the conjunction and co-evolution of humans and machines that are the very stuff of science fiction—but also, of course, of science fact.

As Ursula K. LeGuin has put it: "All fiction is metaphor. Science fiction is metaphor. What sets it apart from older forms of fiction seems to be its use of new metaphors" (vi). Among her examples is a future "alternative society," a theme that has consistently fascinated performance artists, particularly in relation to depictions of utopia. In 1964 Ernst Bloch and Theodor W. Adorno famously argued over the political interpretations and contemporary meanings of this term, with Bloch arguably winning the hermeneutic joust, acknowledging that while the importance of utopia as a concept had declined or been discredited, utopian thinking was still very much alive and well; it just comes in new names and guises, he said, most notably "Science Fiction" ("Something's Missing" 2). In his 1982 essay "Progress versus Utopia, or, Can We Imagine the Future?," Fredric Jameson added to the debate, suggesting that science fiction not only shows how visions of the future position and illuminate understandings of the historical present and reflect our own limits and closures but also demonstrate the increasing difficulty of relating to historicity or imagining future utopias (see Jameson 281–95). Carol McGuirk reminds us that utopian science fiction provides us with important parables because "utopia is inherently didactic" (138), while Matthias Bottger and Ludwig Engel discuss the genre as "our favorite form of reflection on society . . . a poetic and an indirect form of social critique" (159).

The idea that utopian science fiction simultaneously invents the future while poetically critiquing the present comes vibrantly to life in Hayden Fowler's art-gallery–based performance installation *Anthropocene* (2011). Featuring a utopian "floating island" dominated by three large white spheres fronted by a curved platform and surrounded by lush, tall grasses, the performance shows Fowler emerging from a circular hole in the center sphere (as if through the iris of a huge eyeball) dressed only in loincloth-style shorts and a small piece of white animal skin draped around his shoulders. He surveys the surroundings, sits, and eats. Living in a white futuristic utopia, he has become caveman and animal zoo exhibit—the mise-en-scène is the idealized zoo enclosure of polar bears and penguins in captivity. But while apparently returning to a Garden of Eden and a state of nature, closer inspection reveals that Fowler's food is junk from tins, and rats surround him.

The future casting of SF and utopian thinking in general (be it from artists, philosophers, politicians, or urban planners) have always contributed to human development and social evolution. They—or we—envision a future and try to shape it accordingly, whether toward the construction of a dreamed utopia or the avoidance of a dystopian nightmare. In the 1920s, architect and technosociologist Lewis Mumford made clear that the real function and value of utopia are social progress and change, and his contemporary Anatole France echoed the sentiment with words that resonate vividly in relation to Fowler's "caveman-utopia" performance: "Without the utopians of other times, men would still live in caves, miserable and naked. It was Utopians who traced the lines of the first city. . . . Out of generous dreams come beneficial realities. Utopia is the principle of all progress, and the essay into a better future" (qtd. Mumford 22). By definition, utopia is where you are not, and *Anthropocene* functions like any utopian discourse or SF vision to provide a commentary on where we might go—or what we might become—but in strict and absolute relation to where we are *now*. As composer John Cage noted in the 1950s, a fundamental purpose of art is "not to bring order out of chaos nor to suggest improvements in creation, but simply to wake [us] up to the very life we're living" (qtd. King 264). Fowler's performance installation takes that great staple theme of SF—a speculation on where and how people might live one day—and simultaneously offers a pastiche and critique of contemporary utopian thinking around "designer living." In Jameson's terms, it can be viewed as a parodic "anti-Utopia" (176). This is an idyll with a dark side, encapsulating the increasing desire for—and seductive allure of—antiseptic aesthetics and inauthentic lifestyles.

Fowler himself muses on "whether this is a post-apocalyptic scene, a vision of the last surviving biological inter-relationship [man and rats], or the dawn of a whole new nature" (Fowler). The themes of his hyperreal diorama fit neatly across all three of Jean Baudrillard's celebrated "orders of simulacra" (natural, productive, simulation):

> To the first category belongs the imaginary of the *utopia*. To the second corresponds science fiction, strictly speaking. To the third corresponds—is there an imaginary that might correspond to this order? The most likely answer is that the good old imaginary of science fiction is dead and that something else is in the process of emerging (not only in fiction but in theory as well). (121; emphasis in original)

Baudrillard conceives that the "real" has vanished since the three different orders of simulacra increasingly absorb/reabsorb one another, and the distance between the real and the imaginary abolishes itself. His ideas are pertinent to—and even literalized in—*Anthropocene* since, as Baudrillard puts it: "This projection is maximized in the utopian, in which a transcendent sphere, a radically different universe takes form (the romantic dream is still the individualized form of utopia . . . the island of utopia stands opposed to the continent of the real)" (122). For Baudrillard, science fiction "is no longer anywhere, and it is everywhere" (126), and thus he pronounces, in typically dramatic and nihilistic style, "the end of science fiction" (124). With trademark panache, he miraculously reconfigures this end as a new beginning. This entails a cessation of excess and "romantic expansion . . . [,] freedom and naïveté," and a reversed trajectory and implosive evolution that looks to the past rather than the future in order to "requotidianize" ourselves and recapture fragments of the "so-called real world" (124).

These notions are important in relation to expressions of science fiction within live performance art, since it is an art-form that exists quintessentially in the real world—a corporeal body in a palpable space—and all its theories and histories are steeped in discourses of flesh-and-blood materiality, of here-and-now liveness and ephemerality. Performance artists are congenital manipulators (and lovers) of the concrete, the visceral, the actual. Perhaps more than in any other medium, the performance artist (as in Fowler's work) is able to activate and actualize both Baudrillard's theory of the three orders of simulacra *and* his own hopes for science fiction. While staging SF images and narratives of futurity, performance artists can simultaneously exist in the quotidian and recapture/reinterpret the real, as well as operate within and across the potent, sliding territories that comprise the three orders of simulacra: "[b]etween the *operatic* (the theatrical status of theatrical and fantastical machinery) . . . the *operative* (the industrial) . . . and the *operational* (the cybernetic)" (Baudrillard 127; emphasis in original).

Baudrillard's own narratives of apocalypse—from the collapse of the real and the inexorable march of simulacra to the end of science fiction—find embodiment in the singularity machine that is the ultraintelligent, sentient robot. A simultaneously alluring and fearful figure at the heart of many of the greatest science fictions, robots have a long lineage as artificial "performance artists" stretching back through antiquity. Both Aristotle and Pindar record anthropomorphic automata performing, and a Turkish sorcerer automaton smoking a hookah famously defeated Napoleon in a game of chess in 1807 (see Kang 16–17, 178), a portentous event echoing another science fiction: the supercomputer HAL in Stanley Kubrick's film of Arthur C. Clarke's *2001: A Space Odyssey* (1968) taking murderous control of the spaceship after defeating Frank Poole at chess.

Kubrick's scientific consultant on supercomputers for the film was an originator of the theory of the technological singularity, I. J. Good. His musings on an "intelligence explosion" (33) resulting from an ultraintelligent machine designing ever-better machines would inspire Vernor Vinge to talk of machines "awaken[ing]," Damien Broderick to conceive a "futurological abyss" called *The Spike* (2002), and Ray Kurzweil to pronounce that *The Singularity is Near* (2005). Good's original 1965 article describes how "[m]an will construct the *deus ex machina* in his own image," and many artists have attempted such robot god-machines, often in a lighthearted vein. In 1988 Canadian artist Laura Kikauka assembled a female robot from junkyard items, including a squirting oil pump, bedsprings, a sewing machine treadle, and a boiling kettle. Separately and independently, her collaborator Norman White built an anthropomorphic male mechanical robot that sported assorted flickering gauges and rotating appendages. They brought the two machines together for a "blind date" that turned distinctly sexual, in a performance called *Them Fuckin' Robots* (1988). Kikauka and White connected different pipes and pistons from one robot to the other (connection points were the only technical specifications they had revealed to each other), and the robots proceeded to copulate while a robotic voice redolent of early sci-fi B-movies repeated the mantra "Abnormal Sex Behavior." The two machines responded to one another's motions and magnetic fields, charging capacitors and increasing the speed of pumps and pistons until the performance reached an electrically sparked and beautifully comic "climax" as gooey fluid spurted intermittently from one of the male robot's tubes.

What is interesting here is that the traditions of performance art—as a bodily practice—guide the SF narrative and subvert its implications. All genres are "drenched in ideologies" (Schenck 282), and "the body" remains the abiding and absolute one within performance art, even in its convergences with science fiction. Therefore, where "singularity" in most SF concerns an "immanent transcendence" of machine consciousness (Broderick 113) or a self-cognition (as in the Skynet computer system becoming self-aware in *Terminator 2: Judgment Day* [1991]), the singularity moment in this robot performance does not lead to machine messianism, apocalypse, or transcendence, but to a much simpler and biological impulse: "*fuckin'*." The event horizon of this singularity is not an "intelligence explosion" but an ejaculation of a quite different order, heralding the onset of lustful and procreating monstrous machines. Although an ironic and comic performance, this "becoming animal" (or becoming human) of the machines has depth and significance. It is an actual dramatization of contemporary culture's increasing fascination with the conjunction of technology and sexuality (see Springer), as well as a warning about the humanization of the machine, robot sexual desire, and the promise of their ultimate procreation: "Put a Dog Machine and a Bitch Machine side by side, and eventually a third little machine will be the result" (Bernard de Fontenelle, qtd. Laqueur 155).

Performance art's excursions into science fiction emphasize that nature and robots are not oppositional forces, but rather are the closest and most intimate allies. Indeed, in the realms of robot performance art, they have become one and the same. Performance artists sometimes celebrate this notion in their work, but just as often they present cautionary tales: warnings about a reciprocal process whereby there is an increasing humanization of machines and a gradual dehumanization and "machinization" of humans (see Dixon 276). Eduardo Kac and Ed Bennett's performance *A-Positive* (1997) depicts this theme graphically, with a robot machine being "humanized" with the actual blood of the performer Kac. Like the technological "jacking in" of William Gibson's *Neuromancer* (1984) or the battery-cell human slaves of the film *The Matrix* (1999), Kac is corporeally connected to the robot via an intravenous needle, and his blood actually "feeds" it, visibly pumping through a clear tube. But the blood-sucking "biobot" is more than a vampiric parasite: it extracts oxygen from the plasma to keep a tiny flame burning and is catalyzed into a reciprocal feeding gesture, sending intravenous shots of dextrose into Kac's body. The cybernetic man–machine symbiosis is mutually beneficial.

Like many of the most significant performance artworks, it is a quiet but efficacious ritual that is conceptually simple and intensely distilled and focused. And like many of the most significant science fictions, it tells a hypnotic, multifaceted story with deep psychological, sociopolitical, and existential resonances. This blood kinship ritual between man and machine is performed with dignity and grace—like an idealized wedding photo, formal and elegant, a dignified and apparently spiritualized union. It is, in the utopian reading, reassuring and serene, an image of man and machine in perfect harmony, but from the dystopian perspective, it is a Gothic wet dream of the "undead" feeding on the living—a *Frankenstein* meets *Dracula* meets *Alien* SF-horror par excellence. But what is most resonant—and most deeply unsettling—about the piece is not this conceptual sense of ambiguity but rather the lack of it when seen in performance: the blissful and casual state of compliance that Kac conjures about where we (and the robots) are, where we are heading, and what we will become.

Kac's varied Deleuzian becomings throughout his oeuvre provide a fascinating case study of performance art as actual and performance artists as embodiments of science fiction. In *Time Capsule* (1997), Kac became the first artist to actually implant a microchip into himself, injecting it into his left leg using a special hypodermic syringe during a live performance broadcast on Brazilian television. He put his leg into a scanner and a remote telerobotic finger (thousands of miles away in Chicago), then activated the scanner, which displayed the chip's embedded ID number. He completed the

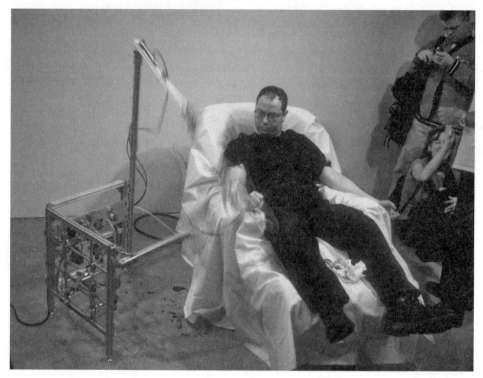

FIGURE 20.2 Eduardo Kac attached to "biobot" in *A-Positive* (1997). Photo courtesy of the artist and the Julia Freedman Gallery.

performance by going online to a database that utilizes the same technology to identify pets, whereupon he registered himself as an owner *and* as an animal. Kac's particular take on Deleuze and Guattari's notion of "becoming animal" took a different line of flight when, using a process of zygore microinjection, he genetically modified an albino rabbit, integrating an enhanced green fluorescent protein into its genome. On May 14, 2000, the rabbit gave birth to Alba, *GPF Bunny* [Green Florescent Protein Bunny], an independent and autonomous, genetically engineered and highly controversial live-performance artwork actual that glows in the dark under the right lighting conditions and was raised as a member of Kac's family. As he put it, aesthetics "in the context of transgenic art must be understood to mean that creation, socialization, and domestic integration are a single process" (qtd. Elwell 8).

As Rosi Braidotti notes, "Contemporary culture has shifted the issue of genetic mutations from the high-tech laboratories into popular culture," raising "metamorphosis to the status of a cultural icon" (178–79); and Kac is the self-styled "first transgenic artist" investigating what he calls "a new art form based on the use of genetic engineering techniques to create unique living beings" (Kac, qtd. Elwell 7). His first was a petri-dish-dwelling, live, and evolving bacteria called *Genesis* (1999), which had been implanted with a "God code" formed by converting a piece of text from the Bible (beginning "And God said, Let us make man in our image, after our likeness . . .") into Morse code and translating the dots and dashes into a base pair of genes that were then created in a laboratory and implanted into a nonspecific bacterium. Kac's casting of "God" at the living (if not breathing) center of this performance piece is conceptually blatant and as hermeneutically clear as a divine thunderbolt of retribution. It provides an interesting take on creationism, opens important debates around ethics in both genetic science and art, and turns a microscopic organism into a cross-genre SF blockbuster: Frankensteinian Gothic meets messianic cloning meets genetic mutation.

As Deleuze and Guattari point out: "Science fiction has gone through a whole evolution taking it from animal, vegetable and mineral to becomings of bacteria, viruses, molecules and things imperceptible" (248). Kac continued his own SF molecular narrative into full parthenogenesis territory when he integrated his own genetic material into a petunia to create (if not quite give birth to) a new living being called *A Natural History of the Enigma* (2009). It won the Golden Nica for Hybrid Art at the Ars Electronica Festival, a notable arts honor that was awarded to another performance artist, Stelarc, for his *Extra Ear* project in 2011.

In philosophical theory, "becoming" (at least in Deleuze and Guattari's formulation) is a continual process of progressive iterations and potentials, seemingly a new poetics and a metaphysics of transformation. But it actually opposes metaphysics by making an ontological distinction between being and becoming, denying the metaphysical notion of "pure being" and elevating pure becoming in its place. Moreover, as Slavoj Žižek puts it: "This pure becoming is not a particular becoming *of* some corporeal entity, a passage of this entity from one to another state, but a becoming-it-itself, thoroughly extracted from its corporeal base" (9; emphasis in original). Where being's temporality is the present, becoming never "actually occurs"; rather, like the starting point of all science fiction, which Deleuze and Guattari praise for its nomadic force, it is "always forthcoming" but equally, for Deleuze, "already past" (qtd. Žižek 9).

Becoming is the philosophical paradigm with arguably the closest empirical fit with science fiction, and science fiction in its turn propounds its own distinctive theories of becoming. In dystopian SF texts, the plots are almost by definition about (disastrous) becomings and have a frequent habit of suddenly reaching apocalyptic endpoints—anti-Deleuzian "becoming-finalities"—as certain metamorphoses are recognized as irreversible, with terminal results. Yet in more optimistic SF texts, a category in which I would include the majority of performance artworks dealing with similar themes of futurity, becoming is explored and depicted as adventurous and liberating, desirable, playful, joyful, and—perhaps most important—inevitable and necessary.

Science fiction in performance art is simultaneously a political gesture, a technical feat, and an embodied art process that both looks forward to "becoming the future" and actualizes a version of it in the present, live in front of us. This actualization in real time and space operates dialectically as an estrangement of the actual, eschewing the quotidian. As Carl Freedman has noted: "SF, like dialectics, refuses any simple acceptance of the mundane; and in evoking a world which is not ours but which could, at least in principle, become ours, it estranges the actual through an insistence on the primacy of historical specificity" (200). As potently as any SF writers or filmmakers, performance artists have taken on what Braidotti calls "the visionary and didactic role" of science fiction: to enact, with corporeal bodies in real time and space, a powerful "post-humanist, bio-centred egalitarianism" that estranges and displaces our worldview and establishes "a continuum with the animal, mineral, vegetable, extraterrestrial and technological worlds" (183). Eugene Thacker describes the construction of "narratives of progress . . . on the contingencies of the future, and the necessity of re-imagining the present" ("SF, Technoscience, Net.art" 73), and as Deleuze makes clear: "Men's only hope lies in a revolutionary becoming" (171).

Crucially, in the quotidian world, the evolutionary becomings of humans and machines have for some time now operated in parallel, both metamorphoses moving on their own revolutionary trajectories. Their symbioses and dazzling lines of flight toward, across, into, and through one another are captured compellingly in live performance art through a disquieting and breathtaking dance of ideas, bodies, technologies, and actuals.

Acknowledgments

I am grateful to Malar Villi Nadeson, Library Director, the Ngee Ann Kongsi Library at LASALLE College of the Arts, Singapore, for her excellent assistance in researching for this chapter.

Works Cited

Baudrillard, Jean. "Simulacra and Science Fiction." *Simulacra and Simulation*. 1981. Trans. Sheila Faria Glaser. Ann Arbor: U of Michigan P, 1994. 121–27. Print.

Bilal, Wafaa. "Artist Implants Camera in the Back of His Head." *The Telegraph* (Nov. 23, 2010). Web. July 20, 2013. http://www.telegraph.co.uk/culture/art/art-news/8154643/Artist-has-camera-implanted-in-his-head.html.

Bottger, Matthias, and Ludwig Engel. "They Promised Us Jetpacks! Of Futures and Utopias." *Utopia Forever: Visions of Architecture and Urbanism*. Ed. Robert Klanten and Lukas Feireiss. Berlin: Gestalten, 2011. 158–61. Print.

Braidotti, Rosi. *Metamorphoses: Towards a Materialist Theory of Becoming*. Cambridge, UK: Polity, 2002. Print.

Broderick, Damien. *The Spike: How Our Lives Are Being Transformed by Rapidly Advancing Technologies*. London: Tor, 2002. Print.

Deleuze, Gilles. "Control and Becoming." 1990. Trans. Martin Joughin. *Negotiations: 1972–1990*. New York: Columbia UP, 1995. 169–76. Print.

Deleuze, Gilles, and Felix Guattari. *A Thousand Plateaus: Capitalism and Schizophrenia*. 1980. Trans. Brian Massumi. London: Athlone, 1988. Print.

Dixon, Steve. *Digital Performance: A History of New Media in Theater, Dance, Performance Art and Installation*. Cambridge, MA: MIT, 2007. Print.

Elwell, J. Sage. *Crisis of Transcendence: A Theology of Digital Art and Culture.* Lanham, MD: Lexington, 2011. Print.

Fowler, Hayden. "Artist's Statement." *Performance Space.* Web. February 26, 2012. www.performancespace.com.au/2011/hayden-fowler/.

Freedman, Carl. "Science Fiction and Critical Theory." *Science Fiction Studies* 14.2 (July 1987): 180–200. Print.

Giannachi, Gabriella. *Virtual Theatres: An Introduction.* London: Routledge, 2004. Print.

Good, I. J. "Speculations Concerning the First Ultraintelligent Machine." 1965. *Accelerating Future.* Web. July 20, 2013. http://www.acceleratingfuture.com/pages/ultraintelligentmachine.html.

Hickling, Alfred. "Interview: Marina Abramović." *The Guardian* (Oct. 2, 2010). Web. July 20, 2013. http://www.guardian.co.uk/artanddesign/2010/oct/03/interview-marina-abramovic-performance-artist?intcmp=239.

Jameson, Fredric. *Archaeologies of the Future: The Desire Called Utopia and Other Science Fictions.* London: Verso, 2005. Print.

Kang, Minsoo. *Sublime Dreams of Living Machines: The Automaton in the European Imagination.* Cambridge, MA: Harvard UP, 2011. Print.

King, Bruce. *Contemporary American Theatre.* London: Macmillan, 1991. Print.

Kurzweil, Ray. *The Singularity Is Near: When Humans Transcend Biology.* New York: Viking, 2005. Print.

Laqueur, Thomas. *Making Sex: Body and Gender from the Greeks to Freud.* Cambridge, MA: Harvard UP, 1990. Print.

LeGuin, Ursula K. "Introduction." *The Left Hand of Darkness.* New York: Ace, 1987. i–vi. Print.

"Lifescience: Fakeshop's *Multiple_Dwelling*." *Ars Electronic Archive.* 1999. Web. July 20, 2013. http://90.146.8.18/en/archives/festival_archive/festival_catalogs/festival_artikel.asp?iProjectID=8345.

McGuirk, Carol. "On Darko Suvin's Good-Natured Critique." *Science Fiction Studies* 22.1 (Mar. 1995): 138–40. Print.

Mumford, Lewis. *The Story of Utopias.* 1922. Whitefish, MT: Kessinger, 2003. Print.

Pannaggi, Ivo, and Vinici Paladini. "Manifesto of Futurist Mechanical Art." 1922. Trans. Lawrence Rainey. *Futurism: An Anthology.* Ed. Lawrence Rainey, Christine Poggi, and Laura Whitman. New Haven, CT: Yale UP, 2009. 272–73. Print.

Schechner, Richard. *Essays on Performance Theory, 1970–1976.* Michigan: Drama Book Specialists, 1977. Print.

Schenck, Celeste. "All of a Piece: Women's Poetry and Autobiography." *Life/Lines: Theorizing Women's Autobiography.* Ed. Bella Brodzki and Celeste Schenck. Ithaca, NY: Cornell UP, 1993. 281–305. Print.

"Something's Missing: A Discussion Between Ernst Bloch and Theodor W. Adorno on the Contradictions of Utopian Longing." 1964. Ernst Bloch, *The Utopian Function of Art and Literature: Selected Essays.* Trans. Jack Zipes and Frank Mecklenberg. Cambridge, MA: MIT, 1988. 1–17. Print.

Springer, Claudia. *Electronic Eros: Bodies and Desire in the Postindustrial Age.* Austin: U of Texas P, 1996. Print.

Stelarc. "Biography." *Stelarc.org.* Web. July 20, 2013. http://stelarc.org/?catID=20239.

———. "Prosthetics, Robotics and Remote Existence: Postevolutionary Strategies." *Leonardo* 24.5 (1991): 389–400. Print.

———. "Strategies and Trajectories." *Obsolete Body/Suspensions/Stelarc*. Ed. James D. Paffrath with Stelarc. Davis, CA: JP Publications, 1984. 76. Print.
Suvin, Darko. *Metamorphoses of Science Fiction: On the Poetics and History of a Literary Genre*. New Haven, CT: Yale UP, 1979. Print.
Thacker, Eugene. "The Science Fiction of Technoscience: The Politics of Simulation and a Challenge for New Media Art." *Leonardo* 34.2 (Apr. 2001): 155–58. Print.
———. "SF, Technoscience, Net.art: The Politics of Extrapolation." *Art Journal* 59.3 (2000): 64–73. Print.
Vinge, Vernor. "Technological Singularity." 1993. Web. July 20, 2013. http://www-rohan.sdsu.edu/faculty/vinge/misc/WER2.html.
Žižek, Slavoj. *Organs without Bodies: On Deleuze and Consequences*. New York: Routledge, 2004. Print.

CHAPTER 21

ARCHITECTURE

NIC CLEAR

When discussing science fiction's relationship with architecture, the usual practice is to look at the architecture "in" science fiction—in particular, the architecture in SF films (see Kuhn 75–143) since the spaces of literary SF present obvious difficulties as they have to be imagined. In this essay, that relationship will be reversed: I will instead discuss science fiction "in" architecture, mapping out a number of architectural movements and projects that can be viewed explicitly *as* science fiction. It is not my contention that the concept of science fiction should be applied to every aspect of architectural production; however, the domination of the architectural profession by conservative, even reactionary views of the built environment as simply an extension of late capitalism needs to be critiqued, and the possibilities afforded by an engagement with the discourse of science fiction are therefore much needed.

But *which* science fiction? The definition used here to discuss science-fictional architecture takes as a central idea Darko Suvin's conception of the "novum." Suvin contends that science fiction is a "literature of cognitive estrangement" (372) expressing an "exclusive interest in a strange newness, a novum" (373) that distinguishes the represented world of a text as "an alternative to the author's empirical environment" (375). The concept of the "novum" will be a cornerstone of my assessment of those architectural projects best described as science fiction. Following China Miéville, however, I reject Suvin's sharp distinction between science fiction and fantasy, as well as any rigid conceptions of "hard" vs. "soft" SF. An insistence that the science has to hold up, which as Miéville points out it rarely does, is for this chapter of little importance. What is of more importance is whether it can be used in a creative and useful way.

Of equal relevance is Adam Roberts's conception that science fiction should more correctly be called "technology fiction" in that technological instrumentalities "enframe" the world in a way that abstract science does not (see Roberts 11). Roberts's argument suggests that it is technology rather than "science" that is the motive force of science fiction, something that is also true for much of the architecture developed from the late nineteenth century onward. Or, to put it more accurately, it is *representations* of technology that both SF and architecture tend to deal with, and this too will be one of the main themes developed throughout my chapter. My focus will be on the ways in which those representations are used to critically define an imagined future. My main intention is to make an explicit connection between the genre of science fiction, as a system that uses conceptions of novelty and alterity, and examples of technologically "speculative" architectures that are largely un-built, even unbuildable. Technical considerations alone do not define and constrain the novum: it can also include the social and political dimensions of a project an architect is attempting to imagine.

In *Archaeologies of the Future*, Fredric Jameson, following Suvin, argues that utopian writing is a subset of SF (xiv). Given that architectural theory has had such a close affinity with utopian ideas, it seems strange that the claim of utopian architecture *as* science fiction has not been made more explicitly before. One of the issues that may have contributed to this confusion is the terminology that surrounds many of these projects. Within architectural discourse, the terms "speculative," "utopian," and "visionary" are often seen as interchangeable, and they are frequently used within the same context and applied to the same projects (see Spiller, *Visionary Architecture*). Throughout this chapter, the term "speculative" is preferred for a number of reasons. First, it emphasizes projects that have not been realized, whereas many utopian blueprints have been attempted, if not actually "realized." (As architectural historian Manfredo Tafuri argues, utopian transformations cannot be achieved through architectural means alone, requiring wider social and political changes.) Second, not all speculative projects are utopian, in the same way that not all science fiction is utopian, even if the utopian is always a part of science fiction. Third, the term "speculative" has interesting connotations within SF itself, since "speculative fiction" is often used as an alternative point of reference by ambitious "literary" SF writers who wish to distance themselves from the genre mainstream—an ironic fact given that the term was coined by Golden Age legend Robert A. Heinlein.

Unlike literary science fiction, there are few nineteenth-century figures, such as Mary Shelley, H. G. Wells, or Jules Verne, who might be seen as founding figures for a technologically speculative architecture. Throughout the nineteenth century, architectural technology made some dramatic shifts: these advances enabled buildings to be taller, with longer spans and more open facades, and enabled people and materials to travel longer distances more quickly. The introduction of these new technologies, combined with the development of other advances in sciences as diverse as physiology and psychology, even transformed, as Jonathan Crary has argued, the way the world was perceived and represented. Given the advance of industrialization and the social and political possibilities it offered, and combined with the onset of more technologically advanced construction techniques, it still took some time before a truly futuristic vision of architecture became possible, and even then the deployment of those ideas lay within the practical realm rather than the speculative. Buildings such as Joseph Paxton's Crystal Palace, designed for the Great London Exhibition of 1851, employed advanced techniques in prefabrication and was a visual tour de force, representing a new form of global consumption and communication. All Paxton essentially did, however, was to scale up existing construction technologies (see Piggott 6–8).

It was not until the emergence of the architectural avant-gardes at the beginning of the twentieth century that the conditions to create technologically inspired speculative architectures arose, and it is significant that two of the most advanced uses of speculative architecture came from countries whose economies were still essentially agrarian: Italy and Russia. Perhaps it was the absence of those new technologies that created the most potent conditions for the architectural experimentation that took place. Of all the early-twentieth-century avant-gardes, the Italian Futurists were perhaps the most extreme expression of a rejection of older forms and values and an almost ecstatic embrace of the new. Founded by the poet Filippo Tommaso Marinetti with the publication of "The Futurist Manifesto" in 1909, the movement became infamous for its proselytizing of speed, dynamism, and new technologies, including the technologies of war.

The main expression of Futurist architecture was La Città Nuova (The New City) designed by Antonio Sant'Elia and largely developed as a series of small, exquisite perspective drawings that were exhibited as part of the Futurist Architectural Exhibition, Nuove Tendenze, in Milan in 1914. The technological ambition, combined with the scale and social vision, of La Città Nuova clearly marks it as a science fiction project: the New City envisioned by Sant'Elia completely erases existing structures and replaces them with a series of massive buildings that house both industrial works and the population. This population was expected to be mobile and dynamic, and the buildings deployed a scale and aesthetic that might have been more appropriate for civil engineering projects. In "Futurist Architecture," originally written by Sant'Elia alone and then transformed by Marinetti (largely by inserting the word "Futurism" wherever he could), the authors pronounce:

> We must invent and rebuild the Futurist city: it must be like an immense, tumultuous, lively, noble work site, dynamic in all its parts; and the Futurist house must be like an enormous machine. The lifts must not hide away like lonely worms in the stairwells; the stairs become useless, must be done away with, and the lifts must climb like serpents of iron and glass up the housefronts. (36)

Sant'Elia was, like many other pioneers of Futurism, killed in World War I, and while his influence can be seen directly in a few architectural projects, his significance lies in how broadly his ideas were subsumed into the mainstream of European modernism.

A Soviet offshoot of Futurism, Kazimir Malevich's Suprematism, developed an architectural language that combined abstract expressive forms, the tectonics of industrial construction, and an agitprop sensibility of social transformation. Working under the collective title of Constructivism, this group of designers attempted to create an architecture that would fuse radical politics with radical aesthetics via the use of advanced technology. One of the major projects from this period was Vladimir Tatlin's plan for a monument for the Third International (1919–20), often referred to as "Tatlin's Tower." This tower, designed as the headquarters of the Comintern, was to be a 400-meter-high, double-helical steel structure; inside were four rotating substructures: a cube, a pyramid, a cylinder, and a hemisphere, each of which would house a

FIGURE 21.1 Drawing for Antonio Sant'Elia's exhibit La Città Nuova (1914).

particular department and rotate at a different speed. The plans also contained a radio station and a projection facility that could project messages onto passing clouds. Given the available technology in Russia at the time (or indeed anywhere), the tower was a work of pure science fiction: if built, it would have been a third higher than the Eiffel Tower. Moreover, given the scale of the design proposed by Tatlin, it is unlikely that the substructures could have been supported, let alone rotated. However, the project was always more a symbol than an actual proposal, a clear articulation of a future in which Soviet Socialism would make the creation of such structures possible (see Lynton). So confident in Russia's technological destiny was Tatlin that he was depicted in Dadaist Raoul Haussman's collage "Tatlin at Home" (1920) as half man, half machine.

If Tatlin's Tower was science fiction because it required resources and technologies that did not yet exist, the works of artist and architect Lazar Markovich Lissitzky (a.k.a. El Lissitzky) can be seen as SF because he was attempting to describe a type of *space* that didn't yet exist—through the construction of a series of drawings and paintings that he called "Proun." Proun developed ideas from Malevich's Suprematism as well as from Futurism and Cubism; they are not simply drawings for architectural designs but combine different techniques and projections to map out a new spatial and tectonic language appropriate for the new social order. Proun, principally through the use of axonometric

FIGURE 21.2 "Proun" painting by El Lissitzky (early 1920s).

projection (a kind of 3D planar rotation), created spaces that were "atopical and polymorphous" (Bois 57)—literally, "out of place" and "multiple." Lissitzky's ambitious plans were never realized, though he did design displays for the U.S.S.R.'s pavilions at international exhibitions, including the 1939 World's Fair in New York City.

Perhaps the most explicit synthesis of Constructivist programs to operate within the realms of science fiction were the speculative proposals designed by Iakov Chernikhov. In his 1933 book *101 Architectural Fantasies*, Chernikhov explicitly called for an architecture that aspires to think the unthinkable: "Architectural fantasies show us new compositional processes, new modes of depicting; they nurture a feeling for form and colour; they are a training ground for the imagination; they excite creative impulses; they draw out further new creativity and ideas; they help find solutions for new architectural intentions" (62). The fantasies themselves constitute an imaginative taxonomy of form and representation, ranging from highly abstract plays on light, color, and even musical composition to proposals for new towns and factories (see Chibireva). Chernikhov later produced industrial miniatures that developed the fantasies as hard black-and-white illustrations looking almost like woodcuts, along with a series of industrial tales that were never published in his lifetime. A highly respected teacher, Chernikhov's graphic works remain deeply influential on architectural avant-gardes.

Many other theoretical works produced by other Constructivist architects can be seen as science fiction: the Vesnin Brothers' Palace of Labor (1922), Ivan Leonidov's Lenin Institute (1927), Mosei Ginsburg's Palace of the Soviets (1934), all show an approach to technology that was well beyond the capabilities of Russia at the time. By 1934 the dreams of the Revolution and the progressive ideals of Constructivism were being suppressed by the reactionary nightmares of Stalinism, and Russian architecture took a major step backward into monumental neoclassicism. Yet the legacy of the Russian avant-garde has been picked up by numerous architects both formally and politically and is still of major importance today.

At the same time that the Futurists and Constructivists were developing the idea that the city needed to be designed and (re)organized along industrial and technological principles, French architect Tony Garnier articulated a similar proposal with his Une Cité Industrielle (An Industrial City) in 1917. Une Cité Industrielle was a call for an industrialized form of socialist town planning where there were no churches or police force. The Cité itself was rigorously engineered, structured according to programmatic zoning, and with the construction of all the components meticulously mapped out; Garnier's drawings show blast furnaces represented with the same exquisite detail as the civic center. The systematic application of an advanced use of materials and technology integrated into a proposal for a new social and political organization—what Anthony Vidler calls Garnier's "social utopianism" (271)—is what makes Une Cité Industrielle a work of science fiction.

While the Cité was never built, Garnier's ideas were extremely influential in developing theories of urbanism during the early twentieth century, especially those of Swiss architect Charles-Édouard Jeanneret, better known as Le Corbusier. While often derided as emblematic of the airy hubris of modern town planning, Le Corbusier's architecture, especially in its earliest stages, is much more radical than its detractors are usually willing to credit. Completely rejecting the historic form of the city, Le Corbusier fervently believed that new technologies would be key to creating a modern urbanism, free from the ills of traditional cramped and overcrowded urban centers. With his radical town planning proposals, the Ville Contemporaine (The Contemporary City, 1922), the Plan Voisin (1925), and the Ville Radieuse (The Radiant City, 1931), Le Corbusier set out an agenda for wholesale transformation, formally through the development of innovative building techniques, spatially through the application of a new urban syntax, and politically—in the Ville Radieuse at least—through the imposition of an egalitarian technocracy. His new, abstract, highly mechanized conception of the city constitutes a science fiction, which he unsuccessfully attempted to apply to various real situations throughout the 1930s. Le Corbusier's urban visions have often been seen as prototypes for many twentieth-century dystopias, literary and filmic (see Hayward), with critics particularly focusing on his supposed hyperrationalism—for example, citing his dictum that the house should merely be seen as a "House Machine" (Le Corbusier 227). But a close inspection of what he designed, rather than what he said about his designs, reveals a much more sensuous and playful architecture. His large-scale housing blocks, the "Unites," are far from the sterile, repetitive, Brutalist nightmares that the term "Corbusianism" stereotypically conjures up.

In 1951 the nationwide Festival of Britain promoted the desire for a futuristic United Kingdom based around science and technology and breaking away from the urgent need for reconstruction and the mundanities of rationing and postwar austerity. It also marked the 100th anniversary of the 1851 Great Exhibition at which the Crystal Palace had debuted. The main exhibition venue, on London's South Bank, presented postwar Britain as forward-thinking and technologically sophisticated. Its centerpiece was the Dome of Discovery, a structure that resembled a flying saucer, which at the time of its construction was the largest dome in the world. Adding to the skyline was the Skylon Tower, a cigar-shaped, steel "tensegrity" structure—a floating design of cables and structural masses. The Festival was hugely successful, with the main site attracting nearly 8.5 million visitors, though it could be argued that its futuristic stylings were a glossy attempt to conceal a Britain very much in decline (see Forty).

Another major influence on the "futuristic" sensibilities of postwar Britain was the 1956 exhibition held at the Institute of Contemporary Arts in London called "This Is Tomorrow." A multidisciplinary show featuring the work of 12 artistic teams, it was to prove a seminal influence on the burgeoning culture of Pop Art. Its most iconic image is a delirious collage from Richard Hamilton entitled "Just what is it that makes today's homes so different, so appealing?"—an image that, with its excerpts from houseware ads and its address to modish urbanites, does as much as any to set the tone for postwar consumerism. The event—and Hamilton's collage in particular—mightily impressed an ambitious young British author named J. G. Ballard, who claimed that it was "a vote of confidence, in effect, in my choice of science fiction" (*Miracles* 188). And indeed, Ballard's mature work would grapple with many of the same themes: the consumerist appeal of stark, iconic, sexual imagery; the ambivalent repulsion with and fascination for hyperurban venues; the lurking fear that "the future is just going to be a vast, conforming suburb of the soul" (Ballard, "Interview" 8).

Riding the wave of queasy optimism unleashed by the "This Is Tomorrow" exhibit were a group of young architects who took the possibilities of technological innovation to new extremes and blurred the lines between science fiction and architecture in ways that had not been seen before (or since). Known collectively as the Archigram Group, they came to public attention with the publication of the first issue of their eponymous magazine in 1961 and their exhibition at the Institute of Contemporary Arts in 1963. Archigram were celebrants of new technology and the possibility that a new architecture would do away with the old, "boring" ways; their use of garish collages and Pop graphics created the promise of an architecture of pleasure and liberation, facilitated by consumerism. Archigram's ideas were developed through a series of playful projects such as Peter Cook's Plug-In City (1964) and Instant City (1968), Ron Herron's Walking Cities (1964), and David Greene's Rokplug and LogPlug (1969)—all of which (as their titles suggest) celebrated the mobility and transience of modern life, where we have all become technonomads. Herron's Walking Cities, for example, imagined intelligent, mobile structures, while Cook's Plug-In City, by contrast, imagined modular dwellings that could be removed from and inserted into any number of architecture frameworks. The inspiration of the American space missions was clearly evident in Greene's Living Pod (1966) and Mike Webb's Cushicle and Suitaloon (also 1966), the latter envisioning portable environments of membraneous shells, almost like waldoes. Within these

FIGURE 21.3 Drawing for Ron Herron's Walking Cities project (1964). Image courtesy of the Estate of Ron Herron.

projects, however, there was also the possibility of a darker, more hermetic aspect to modern technology, a technocratic claustrophobia.

One of the great influences on the development of Archigram's generation was the engineer Richard Buckminster Fuller, best known for his Dymaxion projects and his adaptations of the geodesic dome. (Fuller's own great SF project, "Dome over Manhattan," was a floating structure projected to cover midtown from 64th to 22nd Streets.) The majority of Archigram's projects are quite clearly within the science fiction genre; there is often little attempt to disguise their fantastical aspirations. They use science fiction as an attack on the banality of mainstream architecture, even modernist architecture, which they felt had become hidebound and normative, unable to respond to changing social conditions. The main critique of Archigram is that their work is narcissistic, lacks rigor, and is politically naïve, if there is even a politics present at all (see Hejduk); however, their influence, particularly as teachers in fine arts schools, cannot be underestimated, and their experimental exuberance should not be dismissed.

If Archigram saw the movement to a society of consumerism as benign, then the Italian design group Superstudio took the opposite view completely, resisting and opposing consumer culture. Led by Adolfo Natalini and Cristiano Toraldo di Francia, both committed Marxists, Superstudio spawned conceptual projects such as a "Continuous Urban Monument: An Architectural Model for Total Urbanization" (1969), which envisioned a single building that spanned the entire surface of the earth.

Composed of interlocking grids, this hypertrophied global megalopolis—echoed in many contemporaneous New Wave SF texts—was an ironic comment on the banality of modern architecture. Displayed as a series of beautifully composed collages, the Continuous Urban Monument is a work of SF architecture at its purest, pitched in a dystopian vein. By contrast, Paolo Soleri's vision of "arcologies"—immense, self-sustaining architectural ecologies designed as an alternative to wasteful suburban sprawl—is more utopian and futuristic, subtly critiqued in Robert Silverberg's 1971 novel *The World Inside*, with its vision of vast, teeming "urbmons" ("urban monads").

The Situationist International emerged in 1957 from a number of Marxist avant-garde groups. Led by Guy Debord, who had been a key member of the Letterist International, the Situationists were concerned with the transformation of everyday life and a total reimagining of the city. Situationist ideas regarding the city were first developed through the Letterist International's theory of "Unitary Urbanism," consisting principally of the concepts of "psychogeography" (the ludic, personally motivated mapping of urban landscapes) and the "derive" (a mode of subconscious wandering). The spirit of this attitude toward urbanism can be gleaned from a text written by Gilles Ivain (a.k.a. Ivan Chtchetglov), "Formulary For a New Urbanism" (1958), which calls for a completely new spirit in architecture, with cities predicated on emotion and desire rather than function and utility. "Everyone will live in their own personal 'cathedral,'" he writes. "There will be rooms more conducive to dreams than drugs, and houses where one cannot help but love. Others will be irresistibly alluring to travelers" (38).

The Dutch architect Constant Nieuwenhuys, who had also been a member of the Letterists, developed the most comprehensive proposal for a Situationist architecture with his "New Babylon" project. New Babylon went through various iterations, but there were a number of consistent themes and ideas. It was to be constructed on the principles of "homo ludens" rather than "homo faber"; the overall layout and construction would be determined by the inhabitants and in a constant state of flux; and the use of robotic systems would ensure freedom to roam the extended city structure, which expanded from a series of nodal points. Constant maintained that New Babylon was an unrealizable utopian dream impossible in capitalist consumer society, yet like any good work of science fiction, he saw it as way of critiquing existing social and political conditions. In Simon Sadler's words, New Babylon's "dynamic labyrinth" could only be conceived as "an ongoing project founded upon degrees of social freedom and creativity unimaginable in utilitarian society" (146–47).

Ironically, the generation of architects that followed Archigram and the Situationists, while adopting many of the visual elements of those movements' playful architectures, replaced their flights of fancy with a more utilitarian approach. For this generation, speculation was of secondary importance to construction, the use of industrialized imagery to highlight the functional aspects of architecture within a "high-tech" aesthetic that expressed this functionalism stylistically. High-tech architecture is one of the first clear examples of a late-capitalist style, and its techniques echo Jameson's famous anatomy of postmodern art. Its methods are historical pastiche, borrowing from nineteenth-century neoclassicism, paying lip service to the Futurists and Constructivists, mimicking 1950's sci-fi and Meccano. It is totally consumerist and highly corporate. High-tech has had nothing truly interesting to say about the city; its sleek mechanical surfaces sit seamlessly within an urban landscape of banks and insurance buildings.

As British high-tech became the favored architecture of big business, its stylistic flourishes giving way to a slick corporatism, another generation of architects—many of them American—was preparing to take up the science-fictional mantle. Neil Denari's early projects, such as the West Coast Gateway (1988) and the Tokyo Forum (1989), develop a mechanical language through a series of ultra-cool black-and-white images: the drawings look as if they were produced by a machine but are, in fact, hand-drawn, their smooth forms suggesting the surfaces of spacecraft and rocketships (at the very least new forms of hybrid car). His early perspectives eschew the traditional Cartesian point of view, rendered as if from a helicopter, complete with head-up display. Denari's contemporaries in the Los Angeles–based partnership collectively known as Holt Hinshaw Pfau Jones used similar aesthetic devices and shared an equally mechanistic approach to architecture (see McCarter), as did the work of Bryan Cantley, whose company Formula wears its SF credentials like a badge of honor. The debt owed by these architects, whether consciously or not, to the work of SF illustrators such as Chris Foss and to the stylings of Ridley Scott's *Blade Runner* (1982), especially the work of designer Syd Mead, cannot be overstated.

The pages of contemporary architectural magazines, websites, and blogs are filled with images of buildings created using complex double-curved geometries and composed of apparently seamless materials; they are always sustainable, "smart" buildings with programmable systems and interactive facades, seeming to promise that the future we had always dreamed of is already here. The skies are always blue, the streets are always clean, and the spaces are populated by photo-shopped models drinking cappuccinos. Much of this architecture has been developed using computational software that allows the generation of complex shapes, the justification for this methodology being that it allows for optimum structural solutions and a more efficient use of space. Moreover, when linked into computer-aided manufacturing techniques, these forms can be produced cost-effectively. Such "parametric" tools are held by digital evangelists such as Patrick Schumacher of Zaha Hadid Architects to be a completely new style of architecture and the "only" way forward.

We should not allow ourselves to be seduced by the SF look and techniques of these projects, however. The real technologies that drive this architecture are the technologies of global finance, management, and procurement. Jameson's words have never seemed more apposite: "Architecture is . . . of all the arts the closest constitutively to the economic, with which, in the form of commissions and land values, it has a virtually unmediated relationship" (56). Yet despite founding one of the most megacorporate entities in the field, the Office for Metropolitan Architecture, Rem Koolhaas is one of the most articulate critics of the "new" architecture. In his essay "Junkspace," which itself reads like a frenzied stream-of-consciousness SF story, Koolhaas creates a vivid indictment of a culture trapped by its own hubris, technological addiction, and vapidity. It might seem contradictory that one of the main practitioners of contemporary architecture should be so vociferous in his condemnation of the practices of the architectural mainstream, but Koolhaas knows three important things: clients don't read architectural theory, the essay in its original form is almost unreadable anyway, and its aggressive pugnacity makes him seem to be even more of a genius. In contemporary architecture, there really is no such thing as bad publicity.

With the growth of the Internet since the mid-1990s and the development of virtual and augmented realities, the assumption that architecture and architectural spaces have to be physical has been questioned by a few architects on the periphery of the profession and in the academies. Mainstream architectural practice has not embraced these new technologies in any way other than the commissioning of business websites, and so the possibilities of virtual and augmented reality as spaces of architectural inquiry are still largely unexplored. Indeed, given the rise of practices that require spatial skills in creating new digital environments and designing games and films, web-design architecture should be well placed to grow, but to date its main achievements have been theoretical (see Carpo).

Neil Spiller's two issues of *Architectural Design Profile* devoted to "Architects in Cyberspace" were among the first attempts to deal with the concept of the virtual in a mainstream architectural publication. They both featured a wide variety of contributions from architects, artists, cyberneticians, environmental psychologists, product designers, and philosophers, but unfortunately Spiller's lead has not been taken much further. Spiller's own projects show a restless eclecticism borrowing from heavy metal music, Surrealism, alchemy, nanotechnology, synthetic biology, Pataphysics—and also science fiction, with the work of William Gibson, Jeff Noon, and Neal Stephenson being particular influences. One of the architects featured in both issues was Marcos Novak, a self-styled (trans)architect, theorist, composer, and artist whose "liquid architectures" tackle many themes of the Situationists while placing them within virtual worlds. His utopian ideas on virtual environments and his seductive data-driven forms represent one of the few attempts to synthesize the virtual and real-world aspects of architecture.

Of all the architects using the new spaces offered by speculative architecture, Lebbeus Woods is perhaps the most radical and inspiring. Through a series of projects that are formally innovative, programmatically challenging, and beautifully illustrated, Woods has produced some of the most exquisite drawings since Piranesi. Woods cares little for traditional architectural protocols, not to mention physics and gravity. His interventions are nearly always bricolaged from various elements directly inserted, sometimes improbably, into the existing city, and it is difficult to tell whether Woods's insertions are acting as sutures to hold the scarred city together or working as irritants to force them further apart. Often situating his projects in contested areas such as Berlin (before the wall came down), Sarajevo, and Havana, or in disaster areas such as earthquake zones, Woods rejects the notion that architecture can remain neutral: his "Anarchitecture" manifesto calls for architecture to be "a political act."

As this chapter has I hope shown, it is possible to trace a history of modern architecture as a form of science fiction. Yet few SF critics or historians have included architecture in the forms of media encompassed by the genre. John Clute and Peter Nicholls's magisterial *Encyclopedia of Science Fiction* contains very few references to architecture, and Adam Roberts, in his otherwise excellent history of SF, never mentions architecture despite having a final chapter that covers painting, sculpture, performance, and digital art. One of the principal aims of this essay has thus been to alert SF scholarship to the centrality of architecture in the genre's history—not just in the form of inspiration for specific SF texts (for example, the Crystal Palace as the model for the dystopian glass towers in Yevgeny Zamyatin's *We* [1921]) but also as a crucial mode of science fiction in its own right. At the same time, I hope to provoke architecture into recognizing its own place within the history of SF and to embrace the field's speculative possibilities in order to generate a critical alternative to the banalities of the corporate-architectural complex. Despite its often superficially futuristic appearance, architecture has lost its utopian desire to create a better society; it has at best contented itself with the goal of creating a slightly less worse society, for some.

We are clearly at a moment of great technological change. One hundred years ago, architects were imagining how the technologies of the Industrial Revolution might impact and transform our cities. Currently, the most interesting speculations involve a whole range of new technologies, from nanotech and synthetic biology to artificial intelligence and virtual reality. While SF literature is industriously exploring these domains, architecture has been content to sit timidly on the sidelines. Architecture needs to regain its curiosity and begin to ask "what if . . . ?" questions again. The importance of science fiction, as numerous SF critics have pointed out, is that it provides an opportunity to develop a socially critical perspective on society. Science fiction creates the kind of "cognitive maps" that Jameson calls for at the end of his postmodernism essay, offering us the possibility of navigating the "unmappable" technological spaces of late capitalism (89). Given the tools at architecture's disposal, it, too, should be embracing these possibilities more fully.

Works Cited

Ballard, J. G. "Interview with Andrea Juno and V. Vale." *J. G. Ballard*. San Francisco: RE/Search, 1984. 6–35. Print.

——. *Miracles of Life, Shanghai to Shepperton: An Autobiography*. London: Fourth Estate, 2008. Print.

Bois, Yve-Alain. "Metamorphosis of Axonometry." *Daidalos* 1 (1981): 41–58. Print.

Carpo, Marco, ed. *The Digital Turn in Architecture, 1992–2010: A Reader*. London: Wiley, 2012. Print.

Chernikhov, Iakov. "Architectural Fantasies 1929–1933." Special Issue: Russian Constructivism & Iakov Chernikhov. Ed. Catherine Cooke. *Architectural Design* 59.7–8 (1989): 61–67. Print.

Chibireva, Natasha. "Yakov Chernikhov: An Architect of His Time." *Building.co.uk*. July 26, 2012. Web. July 20, 2013. http://www.building.co.uk/comment/blogs/yakov-chernikhov-an-architect-of-his-time/5040301.article.

Crary, Jonathan. *Suspension of Perception: Attention, Spectacle, and Modern Culture*. Cambridge MA: MIT, 1999. Print.

Forty, Adrian. "Festival Politics." *A Tonic to the Nation: The Festival of Britain, 1951*. Ed. Mary Banham and Bevis Hillier. London: Thames and Hudson, 1976. 26–38. Print.

Hayward, Susan. "Luc Besson's *Cinquième element* (1997) and the Spectacular: The City-Body and the Sci-Fi Movie." *The Seeing Century: Film, Vision, and Identity*. Ed. Wendy Everett. Amsterdam: Rodopi, 1994. 136–46. Print.

Heinlein, Robert A. "On the Writing of Speculative Fiction." 1947. *Turning Points: Essays on the Art of Science Fiction*. Ed. Damon Knight. New York: Harper & Row, 1977. 199–204. Print.

Hejduk, Renata. "A Generation on the Move: The Emancipatory Function of Architecture in the Radical Avant-garde." *Transportable Environments: Theory, Context, Design and Technology*. Ed. Robert Kronenberg and Fritz Klassem. New York: Taylor & Francis, 2006. 40–52. Print.

Ivain, Gilles (a.k.a. Ivan Chtchetglov). "Formulary for a New Urbanism." 1958. *The Situationists and the City: A Reader*. Ed. Tim McDonough. London: Verso, 2009. 32–40. Print.

Jameson, Frederic. *Archaeologies of the Future: The Desire Called Utopia and Other Science Fictions*. London: Verso, 2005. Print.

———. "Postmodernism, or The Cultural Logic of Late Capitalism." *New Left Review* 146 (July-Aug. 1984): 53–92. Print.

Koolhaas, Rem. "Junkspace." *The Harvard Design School Guide to Shopping*. Ed. Chuihua Judy Chung, Jeffrey Inaba, Rem Koolhaas, and Leong Sze Tsung. Cambridge, MA: Taschen, 2001. 408–21. Print.

Kuhn, Annette, ed. *Alien Zone II: The Spaces of Science Fiction Cinema*. London: Verso, 1999. Print.

Le Corbusier. *Towards a New Architecture*. 1923. Trans. Frederick Etchells. New York: Dover, 1986. Print.

Lynton, Robert. *Tatlin's Tower: Monument to Revolution*. New Haven, CT: Yale UP, 2008. Print.

McCarter, Robert. "Building Machines." Pamphet Architecture No. 12. New York: Princeton Architectural P, 1987. Print.

Miéville, China. "Cognition as Ideology: A Dialectic of SF Theory." *Red Planets: Marxism and Science Fiction*. Ed. Mark Bould and China Miéville. London: Pluto, 2009. 231–48. Print.

Novak, Marcos. "Liquid Architectures in Cyberspace." *Cyberspace: First Steps*. Ed. Michael Benedikt. Cambridge, MA: MIT, 1991. 225–54. Print.

Piggott, Jan. *Palace of the People: The Crystal Palace at Sydenham, 1854–1936*. London: C. Hurst, 2004. Print.

Roberts, Adam. *The History of Science Fiction*. Basingstoke, UK: Palgrave Macmillan, 2005. Print.

Sadler, Simon. *The Situationist City*. Cambridge, MA: MIT, 1998. Print.

Sant'Elia, Antonio, and Filippo Tommaso Marinetti. "Futurist Architecture." 1914. Trans. Michael Bullock. *Programs and Manifestoes on 20th-Century Architecture*. Ed. Ulrich Conrads. 1964. Cambridge, MA: MIT, 1971. 34–38. Print.

Spiller, Neil. "Architects in Cyberspace II." *Architectural Design Profile* 136. Ed. Neil Spiller. London: Academy Editions, 1998. Print.

———. *Visionary Architecture: Blueprints of the Modern Imagination*. London: Thames and Hudson, 2006. Print.

Spiller, Neil, and Martin Pearce. "Architects in Cyberspace." *Architectural Design Profile* 118. Ed. Neil Spiller. London: Academy Editions, 1995. Print.

Suvin, Darko. "On the Poetics of the Science Fiction Genre." *College English* 34.3 (Dec. 1972): 372–82. Print.

Tafuri, Manfredo. *Architecture and Utopia: Design and Capitalist Development*. Cambridge, MA: MIT, 1987. Print.

Vidler, Anthony. "The Modern Acropolis: Tony Garnier from *La cité antique* to *Une cité industrielle*." 1989. *The Scenes of the Street and Other Essays*. New York: Monicelli, 2011. 258–73. Print.

Woods, Lebbeus. *Anarchitecture: Architecture Is a Political Act*. London: Academy Editions/ St Martin's, 1992. Print.

CHAPTER 22

THEME PARKS

LEONIE COOPER

Pleasure gardens at Vauxhall in the mid-1800s; Worlds Fairs and Expositions in Chicago (1893 and 1933–34) and New York (1939), with their engineered visions of a soon-to-arrive future already actualized within these specially built arenas; and the amusement parks at Coney Island that appeared in the late 1800s and offered such culinary inventions as hot dogs as well as the illicit possibility of an accidental embrace as strangers passed through attractions like the Barrel of Love at Steeplechase Park—all are antecedents to the theme park. A unique merging of architecture and entertainment, designed to elicit feelings of wonder, surprise, shock, and delight far greater than those apparently available in quotidian life, the theme park has emerged from what Scott A. Lukas calls a "rhizomatic" history (23). Yet its geographical and cultural borders are equally porous. If limited to American terrain, iterations of the theme park extend far beyond the artificial berm that encircles the worlds built by Disney's Imagineers in Anaheim and Florida to include diversely themed destinations such as Kennywood, Holiday World, Cedar Point, Knoebels, and Dollywood (see Lukas 14–18). Scholars have also moved beyond borders to explore other cultural precincts such as the Japanese science city of Odaiba, which Angela Ndalianis views as a further iteration of Disney's desire to build worlds founded upon both science fact and science fiction (112–13). Moreover, another complication is that, while Walt Disney, like the showmen at Coney Island, announced that his theme parks would transport guests to other worlds, the boundaries between the theme park and everyday life have increasingly blurred. The principles upon which theme parks have been built now underpin the construction of shopping malls, museums, and art galleries, as well as emerging urban destinations such as a *Star Trek*–inspired attraction at an entertainment resort called the Red Sea Astrarium in Aqabla Jordan (see Flanagan).

The Star Trek Experience, situated at the Las Vegas Hilton until it was decommissioned on September 1, 2008, is exemplary of the complexities of the theme park. Visiting this attraction in its heyday, visitors could banter with Ferengi and Klingons in Quark's Bar (a reproduction of a tavern from the series *Star Trek: Deep Space Nine* [1993–99]) and encounter other characters from the franchise, all kin to the costumed "walkarounds" that are key to Disney's operations. Offering a kinetic thrill designed to be superior to those generated by attractions such as the *Rocket to the Moon* ride built for the original Tomorrowland at Disneyland, which owed, in turn, a debt to the cyclorama of the same title created for the 1901 Pan-American Exposition in New York and moved to Luna Park at Coney Island in 1902, the *Star Trek Experience* simulated a voyage to the stars. It was a journey, however, that was as much about Las Vegas itself as a theme park as it was about the futuristic imagining of space travel. When the footage that simulated this journey to the stars concluded with the starship *Enterprise* gliding above the Vegas strip, the occupants of this starship were almost forced to acknowledge that the delights offered by Vegas were no different from those made possible by the simulation technologies they had just experienced.

While cognizant of the ever-evolving form that is the theme park, the focus of this chapter will be on Disney. This term—Disney—does designate the parks designed by Walt Disney and his Imagineers; and two particular parks that are most typically associated with science fiction (SF), Tomorrowland at the original Anaheim Disneyland and Epcot (formerly the EPCOT Center) at Orlando's Disney World, are the focus of this chapter. However, Disney is also a term strategically deployed to position this study of the theme park within established scholarship. In his extensive study of the theme park as a global phenomenon, Salvador Clave acknowledges that the Disney parks have generated the most scholarship but goes on to argue that focusing on the "Disney experience gives rise to considerable bias" (xx). Disney has been chosen here, however, because of this bias, not in spite of it. If "like a virus, the theme park spreads [to] infect the world around it" (Lukas 13), then Disney has to be considered the most contagious variant of all. The name itself is capable of invoking a generic brand while also indicating its various and specific iterations—Disneyland in Anaheim and Disney World in Orlando, as well as Euro-Disney in Paris and the Disneylands in Tokyo and Hong Kong. Disney can mean the Disney Studios, the figure of Walt Disney himself, as well as the various creations and enterprises of the company (see Jackson and West). This semiotic slippage between the man himself, the enterprise, and the environments that they designed is embedded in Disney's own historiography: an article on the newly opened Disneyland, which appeared in *Look* magazine on July 26, 1955, described the newest of Disney's enterprises—with its heart-shaped plan carved out of 160 acres of orange groves—as a "surprisingly accurate map of the complicated mass of little grey cells that make up the mind of Walt Disney" (qtd. Jackson xiii).

Importantly, "Disney" has become symbolic of the complex and shifting relations between the theme park and the everyday world. Alan Bryman, for instance, in his seminal book on the Disney parks argues that Disney has acted as a synecdoche for America itself and the symbolic economies through which it has (re)defined itself on the global stage since the 1950s. Bryman speaks of "the sense of Utopia attained (or nearly so) in the form of the contemporary USA," with Disney serving as "both signifier (of Utopia) and signified (by the parks)" (*Disney and His Worlds* 140). These recursive relations between America and Disney were hyperbolized by Jean Baudrillard in his now (in)famous claim that Disneyland "is presented as imaginary in order to make us believe that the rest is real, whereas all of Los Angeles and the America that surrounds it are no longer real, but belong to the hyperreal order and to the order of simulation" (2). Subsequently, Disney not only gestures toward the viral nature of the theme park but also, at least for some scholars, its almost hallucinogenic effects, exemplified by Ada Louise Huxtable's claim that the design principles deployed in the parks are symptomatic of a broader cultural confusion between the symbolic work of the artificial and the real.

The invocation of Disney by Baudrillard haunts accounts of the theme park: it informs Bryman's notation of the "sometimes confusing" relations between utopia and the Disney parks that have arisen within a variety of critical contexts (*Disney and His Worlds* 140), and Lukas begins his chapter-length study of the theme park as a "text" by invoking Baudrillard (212–45). When Baudrillard invoked Disney, it was a provocative gesture designed to destabilize the construction of analogical relations between the real and its simulations that underpin arguments such as Huxtable's. In Baudrillard's "implosive era" of third-order simulacra, models (and here Disney is operating as one such model) "no longer constitute the imaginary in relation to the real" (122). Utopia, for instance, cannot be counterpoised as an "ideal alternative world" to the real, and neither can Disney act as its doubled and doubling Other. "[T]here is no more double; one is always already in the other world, which is no longer an other, without a mirror, a projection, or a utopia that can reflect it" (125). Moreover, Baudrillard's parallel engagement with the work of SF remains unrecognized. Even if Disney operates as a kind of ultimate cybernetic model that absorbs any possible distance between the real and the imaginary, then it does so, at least for Baudrillard, because the work of "science fiction" itself has been destabilized. As Istvan Csicsery-Ronay Jr. explains, SF and "its tissue of mediating connections [has become] compressed, until all that is left is its monogram, SF"—and SF, in turn, operates as an "insignia that clings to its traces but has no fixed referent" (390).

Significantly then, both SF and Disney are complex tropes, insignia of domains that extend beyond cultural and conceptual borders. The theme park "expands as a text and interpretative object" to achieve the "status [of] a life form" (Lukas 222, 216), and SF undergoes a series of displacements from a "generic effects engine of literature and simulation arts (the usual sense of the phrase 'science fiction') [to] a mode of awareness" (Csicsery-Ronay 387). According to Clave, Disney's theme parks "represent and give shape and sense to the societies in which they exist [by] selectively interpreting the reality, transferring emotions and feelings from the personal to the commercial sphere and generating specific spaces of control and transgression" (xx). To understand how Disney grants "shape and sense" to lived experience, however, these extended models of SF must be recognized. With such shifts in mind, Brooks Landon and Scott Bukatman have extended the understanding of SF from a fixed genre to a set of experiential phenomena determined by a global technological apparatus that includes theme parks: Landon's essay "SF Tourism," for example, argues that we should conceive science fiction today as a series of "material embodiments of [the] 'sense of wonder'" (33), including World's Fairs and Disneyland, while Bukatman's study of virtual environments in SF examines not only cyberpunk fiction but also the retrofuturistic nostalgia of Tomorrowland (*Terminal Identity* 227–40). Ndalianis has also invoked Disney to characterize this expanded sense of what constitutes SF, arguing for new "science fictional modes of engagement . . . that escape the science fiction genre to become their own unique experiences" (6).

Such shifts in understanding science fiction mean that critical analysis of the theme park must move beyond identifying the SF motifs, concepts, and scenarios that may be found *within* the text—or in this case, Disney's parks—to explore how these environments invite a science-fictional mode of engagement. Recognizing how Disney grants "shape and sense" to lived experience, moreover, means addressing the "complex hesitation about the relationship between imaginary conceptions and historical reality unfolding into the future" that Csicsery-Ronay attributes to SF (388). This science-fictionality emerges from the imaginary and symbolic operations of the Disney theme park as well as Disney's function as a kind of insignia for a world that has itself become science-fictional. In turn, the fact that Disney "gives shape" to this SF experience as it is lived in the historical present is equally important, and the science-fictionality of Disney should be embedded within material and historical conditions of our lived experiences. Thus, the following discussion focuses on one particular attraction at Epcot called Mission: Space to explore how this SF experience is instantiated within one of Disney's most recent attractions, while framing its specific work through the complex symbolic terrain of the future that operates in Tomorrowland, designed by Disney for the original park in Anaheim. With its iconic rocketship guiding guests forward, Tomorrowland seems the most likely site for Disney and SF to align, a "place where Walt could try to articulate a future so compelling that his guests and their children would want to go home and make it all come true, down to the moving sidewalks and the dancing fountains" (Marling 143). With its emphasis on kinetic motion and its billing as a "World on the Move," Tomorrowland was designed to catapult guests into a promising future that was never more than a step or two away. With a propensity for architecture that looked like "NASA's moonshot hardware" (Marling 146), this park was planned to be Disney's instrument for predicting the future, but it would be one already predetermined by his own Imagineers—reinforced by the fact, as Marling points out, that imagineering "is the ultimate Tomorrowland word, redolent of rocket fuel and derring-do" (146). Guests who entered Disney's Land of Tomorrow were asked to have faith that the rocketship's symbolic thrust upward was evidence of a future soon to be realized—as it was when the Soviet Union launched *Sputnik 1* into the skies, less than two years after Disneyland first opened.

Yet "Tomorrow" has been tricky terrain for Disney to imagineer, refusing to "stand still quite long enough to solidify into meaningful architecture" (Marling 143). In fact, the Tomorrow imagineered by Disney's designers was not new; it was deliberately based upon the futures envisaged at the Chicago Century of Progress Exposition in 1933–34 and the 1939 New York World's Fair. These "proto-theme parks" (Lukas 30) have been considered as a melding of SF with science fact because they "combined the speculation familiar to science fiction with the realities of the scientific and technological innovations of the time" (Ndalianis 116). The Futurama exhibit sponsored by General Motors at the 1939 World's Fair, for example, transported visitors in time machines so that, like characters in SF novels, they could experience a future where the social problems haunting the Great Depression could be safely dismissed, solved by innovations in science and technology (see Kihlstedt 105–07). While the imagined future to which Futurama transported its visitors was a temporary zone, Disney's Tomorrowland was meant to last—to be "timeless," as Disney merchandise for Epcot's Millennium Celebration reassured its guests (*Walt Disney*). Ironically then, for a land in perpetual motion, Tomorrow's symbolic architecture was based upon signs and symbols of an already imagined future and designed, ultimately, to remain static.

While the future is bubble-wrapped as Tomorrowland, Disney's Tomorrow is also a troubling matter because this symbolic architecture was meant to invoke an ambiguous nowhere, one that is (and was) neither past, present, nor future—designed, in the words of imagineer John Hench, so that "things are as they might once have been, or yet could be" (65). In fact, even the Tomorrow articulated at the World's Fair had nothing to do with the "future": planners were wary of any prophetic notions, and while the marketing catchphrase "The World of Tomorrow" spoke of the future, it was also meant to convey that great change was imminent and already evident in the design of a Fair that "embodied" the way of life that was fast approaching (Kihlstedt 99). Yet conjuring up an ambiguous future was actually necessary for Disney's particular "version of science fiction," as Ndalianis claims (77). Tomorrow needed to be flexible enough to change in response to the urban environment that surrounded it and that was itself in constant transition—as the skyscrapers and motorways envisaged as science fiction in General Motors' Futurama at the Fair became the actual landscape of Los Angeles. Indeed, Tomorrowland itself has over the years undergone a series of revisions, resulting in a form of reprogrammable architecture that, when combined with Disney's strategy of constantly updating or "plus-ing" attractions, articulates Tomorrow as inevitably in need of revisions.

Disney's designs on a Tomorrow that could remain in a state of transition are no surprise, given that creating transitional spaces has been integral to Disney's imagineering. Hench describes how transitional spaces function within the parks themselves to guide guests from one themed site to another and thus maintain spatio-temporal continuity between different attractions and their worlds. One such transitional space is the Planetary Plaza just outside the entrance to the Mission: Space attraction. While not located in Tomorrowland but rather in Future World, one of the two sections of Epcot, this attraction is situated in an environment that evolved from the same ethos that drove Disney's construction of Tomorrowland. Initially named Project X by Disney, the EPCOT (Experimental Community for Tomorrow) Center was conceived not just as an embodiment of advances in science and technology in the form of symbolic architecture, it would *be* a City of Tomorrow inhabited today. After Walt Disney's death, his dream was not realized, and the buildings that would have housed the inhabitants of his planned community became instead a series of pavilions, each containing exhibits of state-of-the-art technology and scientific innovations sponsored by such corporations as Compaq, Bell, Exxon, General Electric, and General Motors. In the first instance, the Plaza of Mission: Space is a transitional space typical of Disney: the sculptural landmarks and cast members dressed as Goofy in astronaut gear act as subtle cues that distinguish the attraction's grounds and space theme from neighboring pavilions but also maintain continuity with the overall science-factual theme of Epcot. Yet the transition that it signifies is far more complex for it promises to transport guests into Disney's particular Tomorrow—and in this ambiguous zone that is not the present, the past, or the future, they are transfigured into astronauts.

Mission: Space promises to outdo previous space-themed rides and attractions with the Disney parks and its historical predecessors by providing the first truly "astronaut-like" experience. Located between Test Track (a slot-car attraction mounted by General Motors) and the Wonders of Life pavilion, the building was designed to showcase a corporate alliance among Disney, NASA, Compaq, and Hewlett-Packard. The architecture of the attraction itself—with its luminescent "Tech White" shell encasing both the Red Planet (mocked-up from 100 shades of red and deliberately alluding to NASA's current logo) and the X-2 shuttle that will allow guests to experience a few seconds of weightlessness—evokes Epcot's corporate version of Tomorrow. With Mars and Earth nestled within the façade's sweeping curves, the attraction performs symbolic maneuvers and these, in turn, are easily co-opted by its corporate sponsors. Compaq CEO Michael Capellas thus praised the attractions as a "rare glimpse" into a future where the "possibilities for computers and spaceflight are apparently endless" (qtd. Verrier).

This transitional space acts as a kind of stage for the reenactment of what Marling identifies as "Scene One," which asks guests to symbolically "shake off" the outside world before they enter Disneyland (83). What they also shake off, however, are any residual traces of the lived present so that they might be retrofitted as suitable inhabitants of Disney's Tomorrow. Thus, the Plaza draws guest's attention to artifacts from Disney/NASA's "science-factual" imagineering of (American) space travel, including a scale model of the moon embedded with metallic nodes that indicate the 30 landing sites of NASA missions between 1959 and 1976, a plaque that was flown into space and returned to Earth aboard the shuttle *Atlantis* attached to the façade with steel rods, and the marks left by a Mars rover that was driven over wet concrete not long after the attraction officially opened on October 9, 2003. The Plaza does not just exhibit relics through its symbolic architecture, however; it also acts as a material façade upon which these science-factual data are imprinted through the use of various media (sculpture, text, and other materials).

It is the transfiguration of guests into occupants of Disney's and NASA's particular version of Tomorrow, however, that is the real purpose of the Plaza. Ironically and suitably so, both the attraction and the artifacts within it are hollow—media releases remind guests that it would require 22,702,080 jelly beans to fill up the moon sphere (see Mongello). Marling has attributed a certain "commodiousness" to Disney's architecture (83), arguing that the outside of a building is always designed to reflect the activities and experiences offered inside it. Purposed to perform the same function, the Plaza is a kind of hollow vessel within which guests congregate, reading the historical quotes and touching the objects. Bryman, in his 2004 book *The Disneyization of Society*, has identified "performative labour" as a key strategy devised by Disney, and tributes to the extensive "backstage work" are often littered throughout the attractions, exemplifying Disney's ethos that "before there can be magic there must be work" (Tuan 197). The costumed characters that greet guests in the Plaza (like Goofy in his spacesuit) may be cast members put to work in the Disney parks, but in this space, guests must also undertake their own form of labor, *excavating* (that is, hollowing out) a historiography of a Tomorrow that has already been written.

A further transitional stage occurs as guests are funnelled through more "preshows" to undergo "preflight training." Rope barricades guide them past a series of staged tableaux such as the Space Simulation Lab displaying a 35-foot gravity wheel, which demonstrates how astronauts will live and work in space in 2036, into a corridor where a futuristic chronology of space travel, inscribed upon the wall, gives the years for the first family in space (2030) and the first deep-space mission aboard the X-2 (2035). With the motion simulator (the X2 trainer) functioning like the rocketship of Tomorrowland as a "beckoning hand," guests are induced "to follow the script" (Marling 86). Their journey is inherently teleological, not only because Disney's storytelling depends on these kinds of coherent, orderly, and sequenced layouts but also because they must move onward if they are to fulfill a rite of passage and "really" become the astronauts who will, like those articulated in the science-factual and science-fictional stories on exhibit, journey to the stars. While the Plaza asks guests to excavate the future as it has already been written in the hands of NASA and Disney, their passage past these exhibits depends upon signs of a future that still awaits them.

The promise of experiencing weightlessness, just like an astronaut, might be the hand that beckons guests to move onward, but it is also the means to ensure that they perform as is required for Disney's Tomorrow. The technology of motion exhibited to guests as they journey through the attractions is an ironic measure of the fact that they are ultimately harnessed to an invisible assembly line, their movement from entrance to exit as perfectly synchronized as the circular motions of the gravity wheel. "It's a primal ordering," Michael Sorkin declares, a "Newtonian vision of the universe, bodies intricately meshing and revolving like ticking clock-work, on . . . [t]he driverless people-mover—its motions seemingly dictated by the invisible hand . . . symbol of this economic fantasy of perfect self-government" (221). In this light, the guest's work in excavating a future that has already been written in the Plaza prepares them to enact the "science of people-moving" (Sorkin 221) upon which Disney's Tomorrow actually depends. As they labor, guests are conscripted into a custodial system that has used advances in engineering not only to manage the crowds but also to enforce the ethos of cleanliness and order that was so important for Walt Disney as it would distinguish his park from its predecessors in carnivals and amusement parks (Bryman 64; Adams 99). A piece of rubbish appears for no longer than 4 minutes before it is gathered up by the Disney AVAC (Automatic Vacuum Collection system), the largest waste management system in the world, able to process 3 tons of refuse per hour and whisk garbage down vacuum tubes at a velocity of up to 60 mph (Adams 132). Though stomachs may churn, heart rates quicken, and palms sweat as guests anticipate their "astronautlike" experience, this custodial system ensures that glitches and interruptions such as vertigo and vomiting will be efficiently contained (though Disney has not always been successful in containing accidents as, during 2005–06, two people died after riding on Mission: Space [Ortega]). These transitional spaces not only guide guests through a process of symbolic transition but also assure them that the flesh of those who will accompany them aboard the X2 has been suitably retrofitted to meet the parameters of Disney's custodial system.

Mission: Space is emblematic of what Marling has called Disney's "architecture of reassurance" as it promises that those who seek the stars will undergo safe passage into a future hermetically sealed from the messy contingencies of the present. If guests willingly perform what is required in the Mission: Space attraction, then they might magically become occupants of Disney's Tomorrow. Bukatman has written of Tomorrowland and argued that the "narrative strategies of Disney's worlds . . . move guests through a technologically informed yet ultimately conservative and historically bound vision of 'the future'" ("There's Always" 26). Disney, it appears, offers a science-fictional experience of the future that typifies the "sense and sensibility" of the lived conditions of postmodernism that Vivian Sobchack identifies as the rationale of SF in its "postfuturist" phase. As with the SF film during the 1980s with which she is particularly concerned, at Disney "time has decelerated . . . but is not represented as static. It is filled with curious things and dynamized as a series of concatenated events rather than linearly pressured to stream forward by the teleology of plot" (228). As a kind of microcosm of the parks, those who choose to enter Mission: Space are also asked to "linger on 'random' details," to take "a certain pleasure . . . in holding the moment to sensually engage its surfaces, to embrace its material collections as 'happenings' and collage" (228). Extending on Sobchack, then, when guests encounter NASA spacesuits carefully arranged as if they are to be worn when visitors enter the X2 trainer, it can only mean their "*incorporation* of" the values of late multinational capitalism as well as their "*absorption* by" them (252; emphasis in original).

However, as Marling also points out, the development of Disney's architecture of reassurance was driven by an ambivalent recognition on the part of the Imagineers that the "issues raised by the iconography of the park were, at some level, profoundly disturbing" (169). Designing a future that promised but never threatened was a difficult, potentially impossible, mission. Equally, the subjugation to the technological apparatus that is Disney's own form of spaceship is not necessary preordained by the machinations of these Imagineers. Random irruptions into the seamless and hermetic world of Disney are not uncommon and even actively sought by scholars such as Karen Klugman, a founding member of the Project on Disney, who discovered a Mickey Mouse paper cup sandwiched between the boards of a park bench. Not yet (and perhaps never) erased by Disney's vast custodial system, this piece of forgotten trash enabled Klugman to partake in an "alternative ride" where Mickey is no longer a Disney operative but a disenfranchised subversive who, like herself, has managed to escape detection (179). J. P. Telotte has suggested that the Disney parks require a form of "double vision," one that acknowledges the utopian possibilities for technologies while recognizing that they are used as instruments of social control (111–12). Like Klugman, guests of Mission: Space might adopt this double vision, recognizing that their transfiguration into astronauts requires a necessary submission to Disney's technological operations and its symbolic architectures of Tomorrow.

For Csicsery-Ronay, SF is an experience characterized by a doubled and doubling form of "hesitation" activated by a gap existing "between, on the one hand, belief that certain ideas and images of scientific-technological transformations of the world can be entertained and, on the other hand, the rational recognition that they may be realized" (387). As guests labor to excavate a Tomorrow that is already realized by Disney and NASA, but which is nonetheless a future that is not yet manifest, they must negotiate the gap between the conceivable and its actualization. If SF is a mode of awareness that involves such hesitations toward the technological (in its social, lived, and ethical dimensions), then the ambivalence that is activated when Disney tries to transfigure its guests into astronauts is significant. The designers of Mission: Space may have used science-fictional (and factual) motifs, symbols, and themes such as the long-term habitation of space stations in the attraction, but it is the ambivalence that is activated by the figurative transfiguration of guests into occupants of Disney's own Spaceship Earth that is science-fictional. Scholars such as Bukatman, Landon, and Ndalianis have provided important contributions to understanding how theme parks and urban destinations invite a science-fictional form of experience. By turning to Disney's Tomorrow and situating a particular attraction within it, this chapter argues that the ambivalence activated by Disney's designs on its guests as both future and present occupants of its own Spaceship Earth is as significant to an SF analysis as traditional SF icons like the rocketships at Tomorrowland or even the technological and engineering developments that enable Disney and NASA to offer "astronautlike" experiences.

Even studies on the theme park that are not explicitly concerned with SF are haunted by its concerns. The theme park can become a kind of prophetic tool for forecasting a future that is already predestined by its simulations, or it can become evidence that the future must be imagined in ways other than how it has already been imagineered by theme-park designers. Baudrillard's form of SF theory would find this kind of thinking faulty for it depends upon the "pantographic excesses" of an SF that once existed and allowed for imaginary and alternative futures but is no longer operational. As he warns, there is no alternative: "Simulation is unsurpassable . . . without exteriority" (125). An approach is required, instead, that is the "opposite" of a science fiction invested in a possible distance between the imaginary and the real (Baudrillard 121). Csicsery-Ronay has suggested that the "substantialization of SF's objects has created a new form of haunted consciousness, haunted by the uncanny spectral actuality of its properly imaginary objects" (392). The theme park is itself such an object and, as such, its study might meet Baudrillard's criteria for SF theory that will "revitalize, reactualize, requotidianize fragments of simulation, fragments of this universal simulation that have become for us the so-called real world" (124). The "things" that we encounter within it, like the paper cup forgotten by the trash collectors and discovered by

Klugman or the empty spacesuits on display at Mission: Space, can also activate the kind of "decentred situations" that Baurdillard seeks in SF (124). Given that Baudrillard has historically been invoked in scholarship to suggest that the theme park is the simulation within which the real has disappeared, this is an important revisioning. If we grant the theme park "the feeling of the real, of the banal, of lived experience," then the science-fictional experiences it offers could enable the reinvention of "the real as fiction, precisely because it has disappeared from our life" (124) and, in turn, a further understanding of the science-fictional worlds we now inhabit.

Works Cited

Adams, Judith. A. *The American Amusement Park Industry: A History of Technology and Thrills*. Boston: Twayne, 1991. Print.

Baudrillard, Jean. *Simulacra and Simulation*. 1981. Trans. Sheila Faria Glaser. Ann Arbor: U of Michigan P, 1994. Print.

Bryman, Alan. *Disney and His Worlds*. New York: Routledge, 1995. Print.

_____. *The Disneyization of Society*. London: SAGE, 2004. Print.

Bukatman, Scott. *Terminal Identity: The Virtual Subject in Postmodern Science Fiction*. Durham, NC: Duke UP, 1993. Print.

_____. "There's Always... Tomorrowland: Disneyland and the Hypercinematic Experience." 1991. *Matters of Gravity: Special Effects and Supermen in the 20th Century*. Durham, NC: Duke UP, 2003. 13–31. Print.

Clave, Salvador Anton. *The Global Theme Park Industry*. Cambridge, UK: CABI, 2007. Print.

Csicsery-Ronay Jr., Istvan. "The SF of Theory: Baudrillard and Haraway." *Science Fiction Studies* 18.3 (Nov. 1991): 387–404. Print.

Flanagan, Ben. "Jordan Theme Park Treks Ahead." *The National* (Aug. 1, 2011). Web. Jan. 8, 2012. http://www.thenational.ae/business/travel-tourism/jordan-theme-park-treks-ahead.

Hench, John (with Peggy Van Pelt). *Designing Disney: Imagineering and the Art of the Show*. New York: Disney Editions, 2003. Print.

Huxtable, Ada Louise. *The Unreal America: Architecture and Illusion*. New York: New Press, 1997. Print.

Jackson, Kathy Merlock. "Introduction." *Walt Disney: Conversations*. Ed. Kathy Merlock Jackson. Jackson: U of Mississippi P, 2006. ix–xix. Print.

Jackson, Kathy Merlock, and Mark I. West, eds. *Disneyland and Culture: Essays on Theme Parks and Their Influence*. Jefferson, NC: McFarland, 2010. Print.

Kihlstedt, Folke T. "Utopia Realized: The World's Fairs of the 1930s." *Imagining Tomorrow: History, Technology and the American Future*. Ed. Joseph J. Corn. Cambridge, MA: MIT, 1986. 97–117. Print.

Klugman, Karen. "Reality Revisited." *Inside the Mouse: Work and Play at Disney World*. Ed. The Project on Disney. Durham, NC: Duke UP, 1995. 163–79. Print.

Landon, Brooks. "SF Tourism." *The Routledge Companion to Science Fiction*. Ed. Mark Bould, Andrew M. Butler, Adam Roberts, and Sherryl Vint. New York: Routledge, 2009. Print.

Lukas, Scott A. *Theme Park*. London: Reaktion, 2008. Print.

Marling, Karal. "Imagineering the Disney Theme Parks." *Designing Disney's Theme Parks: The Architecture of Reassurance*. Ed. Karal Marling. New York: Flammarion, 1998. 29–178. Print.

Mongello, Lou. "Mission: Space." *WDWRadio.com*. Sept. 17, 2007. Web. July 21, 2013. http://www.wdwradio.com/2007/09/mission-space/.

Ndalianis, Angela. *Science Fiction Experiences*. Washington, DC: New Academia, 2011. Print.

Ortega, Juan. "Woman Dies After Riding Disney's 'Mission: SPACE." *Space.com*. Apr. 13, 2006. Web. July 21, 2013. http://www.space.com/2292-woman-dies-riding-disney-mission-space.html.

Sobchack, Vivian. *Screening Space: The American Science Fiction Film*. 2nd ed. New Brunswick, NJ: Rutgers UP, 1999. Print.

Sorkin, Michael. "See You in Disneyland." *Variations on a Theme Park: The New American City and the End of Public Space*. Ed. Michael Sorkin. New York: Hill and Wang, 1992. 205–32. Print.

Telotte, J. P. "Negotiating Disney and Technology." *Studies in the Humanities* 29.2 (Dec. 2002): 109–24. Print.

Tuan, Yi-Fu (with Steven D. Hoelshcher). "Disneyland: Its Place in World Culture." *Designing Disney's Theme Parks: The Architecture of Reassurance*. Ed. Karal Marling. New York: Flammarion, 1998. 191–200. Print.

Verrier, Richard. "Disney's Mission: Space Ride at Epcot." *Los Angeles Times*, Sept. 18, 2002. Web. July 24, 2013. http://www.latimes.com/topic/g02-1795,0,4744192.story?track=rss-topicgallery.

Walt Disney World Resort: A Pictorial Souvenir: Millennium Edition. Orlando, FL: Roundtable, 1999. Print.

PART III

SCIENCE FICTION AS CULTURE

CHAPTER 23

THE CULTURE OF SCIENCE

SHERRYL VINT

The relationship between science and science fiction (SF) is both self-evident and extremely complex. Although William Wilson first used the term "science fiction" in 1851, it came into common usage only during the 1930s, when Hugo Gernsback adopted it for pulp magazines publishing stories that engaged with emergent science and technology. The label "science fiction" signals dialogue with the culture of science, but this self-evident aspect is not the whole story. When one scratches the surface of this relationship, a whole series of difficulties arises in defining the terms "science," "culture," and "science fiction." Gernsback claimed he was inaugurating a new literature for the modern age, but at the same time he drew on existing traditions exemplified, in his analysis, by the combined genius of H. G. Wells, Jules Verne, and Edgar Allan Poe. He thereby unwittingly initiated an ongoing series of critical scrimmages regarding the origins of SF and its precise demarcation from similar genres such as fantasy and horror. Such critical battles are far from resolved: indeed, they seem to be gaining new life in recent discussions about what Gary K. Wolfe has called the potential "evaporation" of the genre as it becomes indistinguishable from a culture in which many of SF's motifs and techniques—and, most pertinent here, plots and themes entwined with science and technology—have become pervasive.

The very staying power of the term "*science* fiction," which stubbornly resisted displacement by the more evocative and perhaps more accurate "*speculative* fiction," suggests that something about the culture of science remains at the genre's core. At the same time, however, this *something* remains elusive, and contradictory claims abound. Gernsback tirelessly promoted the role of SF not only in popularizing scientific knowledge and cultivating a scientifically literate population, but also in contributing to a future in which such stories will "hav[e] blazed a new trail, not only in literature and fiction, but in progress as well" (3). Most of the pulp stories published by Gernsback and his successors were stronger on adventure narrative than on patentable ideas, however, and much of the "science" included in them was simply a vision of magnificent and powerful technology without any attempt to explain how its wonders were achieved. Science was important in these early years and its possibilities were actively debated by readers, but it was always subordinate to story, paving the way for the commonplace acceptance of things deemed impossible, at least by current scientific understanding, such as faster-than-light (FTL) travel.

Works now considered SF were published before this magazine tradition disseminated the name. The existence of a subgenre called hard-SF admits that much of the genre fails to embrace the standards of scientific rigor demanded by some critics and fans. Roger Luckhurst dates the emergence of SF to the late nineteenth century, defining it as "the literature of technologically saturated societies" (*Science Fiction* 3) and stressing its role in reflecting upon and interrogating the impact of changes in science and technology on culture and daily life. He links its emergence to a number of concomitant shifts in the cultures of modernity, for which the Enlightenment and the practice of science are crucial precursors. This definition is instructive for it also sheds light on critical claims that SF is perhaps now disappearing as a distinct genre: SF springs from the growing presence of scientific ways of knowing the world and of technology in quotidian life, factors that stand out in the late Victorian period; it begins to fade from view, camouflaged as it were, when the influence of science and technology becomes commonplace rather than transformative.

Public understandings of science are often filtered through SF, with journalists treating the genre as a repository of shorthand concepts for the implications of new discoveries or inventions. Often framed as reality having "caught up with" SF, such accounts demonstrate ongoing exchanges between the cultures of science and SF since the emergence of widespread technological development. Inventions such as flying machines, automata, and television broadcasts were presented as marvels of a modern age once imaginable only in fiction. Showcases of technology such as World's Fairs seamlessly combine cutting-edge scientific achievement with the promotion of commercial products and with the "sense of wonder" fan discourse describes as the core of SF. Together, commercial science and the SF imagination worked to promote a vision of the future, an impulse particularly evident in the title of the 1939 World's Fair, "The World of Tomorrow," and embodied in its most famous exhibit, General Motors's Futurama. This ride promised more than cars with improved features: it remade the social world in its vision of increased mobility via the infrastructure of highways, one example of the ways in which Western culture since at least the late nineteenth century is inevitably a culture of science.

Such conflations of science and the SF imagination define moments of intense technological change, such as the Space Race of the 1960s, propelled by a combination of Cold War rhetoric and Golden Age SF, or the Human Genome Mapping Project of the 1990s. Labels such as "Frankenstein foods" to describe GM produce demonstrate how vocabulary from SF has become part of the public understanding of science. Such connections create vivid images that connect discoveries to familiar experiences, such as when a planet with two suns, discovered in 2011, was popularly referred to as Tatooine—Luke Skywalker's birthplace—rather than by its official designation, Kepler 16b (see Fazekas). The visionary rhetoric characteristic of the 1939 World's Fair remains evident in popular reporting about otherwise abstruse research, such as graphene, a carbon allotrope for which Russian scientists Andre Geim and Konstatantin Novoselov won a Nobel Prize in 2010. Graphene's properties have been popularly explained as promising such SF technologies as human–computer interfaces, folding smartphones, and cloaking devices (see Waugh). Similarly, reporting on the discovery of the Higgs boson particle, which might unlock the secrets of everything from the Big Bang to gravity to dark matter, led to journalistic speculations about finally achieving *Star Trek* technologies such as transporters, holodecks, and replicators (see Klotz). Connections between SF and popular science are at times dystopic, such as fears that the black holes created by particle accelerators will destroy the universe or that eating GM foods will alter one's DNA. Yet SF should not be understood as simply exaggerating or misrepresenting risks; indeed, scenarios that may seem "like science fiction" can outline legitimate but hard-to-imagine consequences, such as the evidence that artificial plastics leach chemicals into the water supply that our bodies perceive as organic hormones.

To understand SF's interactions with science, we must first define more precisely the phrase "culture of science." A dogmatic definition of science would exclude most of what circulates under the name SF, at least retroactively, as new evidence—such as the lack of conditions that might sustain life on Mars—rules out scenarios perhaps once plausible when it appeared the planet had canals. Further, SF is still *fiction*, invested in imagining a science beyond what is already known. One critical tradition has responded to this difficulty by suggesting that SF embraces the *values* rather than the facts of science: it is rational, its narratives are thought experiments that explore the logical consequences of ideas, its extrapolative techniques mirror the practices of scientific method, its themes address universal and objective truths just as scientific knowledge does. For example, James Gunn sees Tom Godwin's 1954 story "The Cold Equations"—in which a stowaway on an emergency supply ship has to be jettisoned into space to save the mission—as the epitome of the genre, praising its portrait of the immutable and impersonal laws of physics and arguing that anyone who fails to see the inevitability of its downbeat conclusion "isn't reading the story correctly" (199).

Godwin's tale exemplifies one pole of the relationship between science and SF, not only adopting the exactitude of scientific method but also relying on established laws of physics. Such a strategy allows a certain degree of latitude in the science included in the story, but once the premises of the created world have been set, the author cannot violate them any more than we can adjust gravity. From this point of view, Stanley Kubrick's *2001: A Space Odyssey* (1968) is SF, while the *Star Wars* franchise (1977–) is not: in this reading, the former is distinguished by meticulous attention to details of scientific verisimilitude (the difficulty of eating in a zero-gravity environment, the absence of sound in the vacuum of space), while the latter is simply an adventure story with the props of space travel, lacking any real engagement with the putative science behind its technologies. Yet what are we to make of the scientific "realism" of a film such as *Alien* (1979), which focuses on science's embedded relationships with capitalism and the military rather than on the physics of space travel? These economic and political conditions, too, are the culture of science.

Darko Suvin's hugely influential definition of SF as the "*literature of cognitive estrangement*" (4; emphasis in original) adds nuance to understanding SF as scientific method. Suvin equates "cognitive" with science but expands his use of the term to include the social as well as physical sciences, thus creating a space for political and social critique. Carl Freedman goes further, arguing that "the crucial issue for generic discrimination is not an epistemological judgment external to the text itself on the rationality or irrationality of the latter's imaginings, but rather ... the *attitude of the text itself* to the kind of estrangements being performed" (18; emphasis in original). Thus, texts that are skeptical or critical about the consequences of science and technology, and that take a scientific "attitude" toward not strictly scientific phenomena, are included in the genre. Under this rubric, highly experimental New Wave works such as J. G. Ballard's *The Atrocity Exhibition* (1970) or Michael Moorcock's *A Cure for Cancer* (1971), which question whether the Enlightenment project is inevitably tainted by its implication in the depredations of modernity, from urban sprawl to Vietnam, can be understood as SF. These events, too, were products of the culture of science, as much as were enhanced communication and transportation networks, improved medical treatment, and other technologies celebrated in the more technophilic SF of the 1940s Golden Age. This range within SF points to the problems with rigidly insisting that the genre must be objective and impersonal, like "The Cold Equations" and supposedly like science itself: this view is premised on a limited understanding of the culture of science. Science, too, is multiple and has a history, but it has popularized an image of itself as the neutral and objective pursuit of universal truth, purified by methods that isolate its observations and conclusions from the flux of contemporary political and social struggles.

In *The Sociology of Science* (1973), Robert Merton argues that science is defined by the cultural values of communalism, skepticism, disinterestedness, and universality; these values are central to the discourse of the culture of science, its investment in the Enlightenment ideal of reason, and its experimental method of objective witnessing in controlled laboratory conditions. Yet, as historian of science Steven Shapin points out, "Knowledge free of prejudice has not been obtained in historical practice, and ... it is probably impossible to obtain in principle. The Republic of Science seems rather to reflect the most widely distributed prejudices of its time and of its citizens" (54). In striving to comprehend the culture of science, then, we are faced with the challenge of tracing both its discursive claims and its material practices, much as defining SF requires examining both proffered critical rubrics and the fiction published under this designation. The dialectical relationships among the discourses and practices of science and those of SF are thus multifaceted since science and SF are multiple and changing.

It is not a coincidence that the celebrated Golden Age of SF is coeval with the increased funding for science in the postwar period. Although experimental science begins in the eighteenth century, it remains in the hands of gentlemen scholars able to fund their own research until the late nineteenth century, when the second Industrial Revolution made scientific education a priority. Science becomes a *system* in this period, as it gains cultural authority and begins to displace both theology in public culture and the humanities in education. Reflecting these economic shifts, early pulp SF often shows a nostalgic investment in the individual entrepreneur or amateur experimenter. Thomas Edison, who used his skill to market himself and his technologies and to amass a sizable fortune, is an exemplar figure of this ideal, although the commercial side of his legacy is often downplayed in SF. During the Golden Age, Robert A. Heinlein continued this tradition in works such as "The Roads Must Roll" (1946) and "The Man Who Sold the Moon" (1949), which are suspicious of both education—frequently contrasted with pragmatic experience—and organized labor. From the opposing ideological perspective, writers such as C. M. Kornbluth, Fredrick Pohl, Robert Silverberg, and Norman Spinrad, during the 1950s and 1960s, look at the same conjunction of science and industry to critique commercial and militarized science that has lost even the pretense of service to the greater good.

Advocates of the tradition of hard-SF are quick to point to genre ideas and inventions that have become part of our material world. The communication satellites first imagined by Arthur C. Clarke and the remotely operated arms that take their name from Robert Heinlein's "Waldo" (1942) are famous examples. If one is willing to be generous in the credit given to SF, it becomes clear that there is a considerable degree of overlap between the gadgets it imagines and the technologies eventually materialized in practice. Many of our quotidian tools have their antecedents in the SF imagination, from the smartphones that also serve as cameras, miniature computers, and navigation systems, to the immense telecommunications industry of on-demand programming, to remotely piloted military drones. The term "cyberspace," like the term "waldo," was coined in SF—in William Gibson's 1982 story "Burning Chrome"—but it is also pertinent that Gibson *typed* his famed cyberpunk novel *Neuromancer* (1984) and that the Internet as we know it today is as much a product of ARPANET and military research as it is of the SF imagination. Contra Gernback's proclamations, SF has generally not played a role in imagining the scientific *how* of new technologies, but nonetheless its visions of a world made otherwise by the development of technoscience have been an important source of inspiration and energy for scientific researchers, as is demonstrated in Allucquère Roseanne Stone's work on cyberculture and Colin Milburn's on nanotech. Constance Penley pithily encapsulates this relationship: "*Star Trek* is the theory, NASA the practice" (19).

The question of how SF is related to the culture of science extends to thinking about what we mean by "science." Currently, nanotech and biotech personalized medicine are "real" fields of research, for example, but neither has yet delivered much in the way of technological applications. Thus, while both have the status of "real" science, it may be that further research will change this classification, just as genomics research shifted from viewing the gene as a master code for making an organism to a focus on the multiple variations of SNPs (single nucleotide polymorphisms) or as research in physics abandoned the concept of ether. Thomas Kuhn's influential *The Structure of Scientific Revolutions* (1962) irrevocably changed the way Western societies think about the culture of science. Kuhn rejects the idea that science is a single, homogenous practice of uncovering objective truths about nature, arguing instead that science is always culturally constrained by a normative paradigm. Science periodically goes through moments of crises, Kuhn explains, when the number of anomalies that challenge the dominant paradigm make visible the uncertainty that always haunts science's image of itself as objective, universal, and immutable. In these periods of "extraordinary science," multiple explanations compete. Once a new paradigm becomes dominant, science erases these traces of struggle, and any theories left behind become pseudoscience or nonscience, thus maintaining the image of "real" science as singular and true.

Science is thus a culture defined by the erasure of its own history, an attempt to appear as nature rather than culture. Until relatively recently, histories of science used "nature" to account for the emergence of "real" science (that is, facts are found by observation), while "culture" was enlisted to account for any wrong turns or foolish suppositions (that is, religious dogma promoting a heliocentric model of the universe). Science studies challenges this practice of bifurcation, following David Bloor whose *Knowledge and Social Imagery* (1976) argues for the principle of symmetry—that one must use the same criteria to explain both "real" and failed science, since both nature and culture inform both medieval alchemy and modern chemistry. SF often finds itself in a similar quandary during border scrimmages seeking to define the genre: for example, are works based on telepathy, such as A. E. Van Vogt's *Slan* (1946) or John Wyndham's *The Midwich Cukoos* (1957), SF? In the period contemporary to their publication, research on ESP and similar phenomena was conducted scientifically, as in J. B. Rhine's program at Duke University. Now that telepathy is no longer regarded as science, should such works be considered fantasy? Generally, such retroactive policing of the genre's boundaries has not been advocated. Luckhurst argues for the term "marginal" rather than "pseudoscience," claiming that SF might be regarded as "the cultural record of these multiple, speculative possibilities—sometimes right, accurately predicting the trajectory of normal science in advance, but often gleefully, delightfully, gorgeously wrong" ("Pseudoscience" 405). These stories of "wrong" science enable a clearer understanding of how interwoven the cultures of official and marginal science are, and of the reciprocal exchanges between these cultures of science and other social, political, and aesthetic contexts. Works such as Craig Baldwin's found-footage SF films, which blend original narrative, research documentaries, popularized science, commercials, SF film, and more, provide a fuller picture of the culture of science than do the sanitized reports of its official culture, which diligently work to strip away all these social factors that are ingredients in its production as much as are chemical reactions, molecules, the laws of physics, and cellular structures.

I have argued elsewhere that we might see SF as a parallel project to science studies because SF often returns to science the full material world of people and passions and politics that is carefully excluded by its official culture. By embedding projected scientific breakthroughs or novel technologies within a full world, the best SF makes visible the considerable influence of the broad set of discourses, practices, and beliefs called "culture" on science. Some writers have made the practice and cultures of science a specific focus of their work, such as Kim Stanley Robinson. His *Years of Rice and Salt*

(2002), set in an alternative world in which Islamic rather than Christian colonization is dominant, demonstrates how experimental practice is different, yet still scientific, in a culture premised on reincarnation and thus the continuity of human and animal souls. His "Science in the Capital" trilogy (2005–07) shows issues of funding applications, internal department hierarchies, and external political exigencies as central to the question of whether science can mitigate the climate crisis. *Galileo's Dream* (2009) considers the struggle between science and religion as paradigms for explaining the world, ultimately suggesting that a science that works cooperatively rather than competitively with a religious sensibility gives us the benefits of progress without the excesses of the Enlightenment project turned into totalitarianism. Such work on the cultures of science is as important to the genre as is true hard-SF, such as Hal Clement's *Mission of Gravity* (1954), an adventure tale on the difficulties of recovering a probe on a planet whose gravity is as high as 700g, or Greg Egan's *Schild's Ladder* (2002), whose title comes from a construction in differential geometry (included in an explanatory appendix).

One of the best examples of the complex interchange between SF and the culture of science is Gwyneth Jones's *Life* (2004). Biologist Anna Senoz, whose brilliant career is derailed by encounters with institutional and structural sexism, discovers an exchange she calls Transferred Y that she predicts will result in the elimination of the Y chromosome. Focusing on gender difference as a product of human culture rather than biology, *Life* suggests that even if the Y chromosome were to disappear and transform the biology of sex, changing the genetic program will not remove the social position of inferiority called femininity. Reflecting on the relationship between science and SF, Jones describes the SF writer as an "inhabitant of the boundary area between our knowledge of the world out there, our science and its technologies, and the reports we have from the inner world of subjective experience: ideology, interpretation, metaphor, myth" ("Fools" 77). She claims that, although science and society present themselves as separate systems, they always permeate one another, and SF is an interface between them. The novel's themes mirror the insights of feminist science studies scholars such as Evelyn Fox Keller and Sandra Harding. In her essay "True Life Science Fiction," Jones comments on the parallels between *Life* and the biography of Barbara McClintock, a story she learned only after the novel was conceptualized. Like Anna, McClintock was a female scientist whose work on gene transposition in the 1950s did not fit into the genetic model of the time. McClintock's work was finally recognized with a Nobel Prize in 1983, but only after science had continued to pursue an inadequate paradigm for the intervening 25 years and only once male researchers reproduced McClintock's results. Jones concludes her essay by stating, "The story I told in *Life* is true. I wonder when it will be out of date. *Eppur si muove*" (163).

Harding's work incorporates feminist standpoint theory—which is concerned "with the assumptions generated by 'ways of life' and apparent in discursive frameworks, conceptual schemes, and epistemes, within which entire dominant groups tend to think about nature and social relations" (150)—to argue that scientific knowledge is inevitably shaped by the gender, race, class, and historical contexts of those who produce it. Harding's work challenges the distinction often made between knowledge produced by

Western institutions of legitimated science and that produced in the so-called private space of women (such as medical aptitude gained from horticulture or the lore of midwives) or that produced in the so-called unscientific cultures of non-Western people. Similarly, histories of SF long refused to recognize the contributions of female authors and fans, a view corrected in recent scholarship such as Justine Larbelestier's *The Battle of the Sexes in Science Fiction* (2002) and Lisa Yaszek's *Galactic Suburbia* (2008). Yaszek argues that despite the cultural association of science with masculinity, the technological changes experienced by most Americans in the early twentieth century overwhelmingly had to do with experiences in the home and with the impact of domestic technologies such as electricity, indoor plumbing, and refrigeration.

Harding draws on postcolonial science studies, not only to argue that non-Western epistemological frameworks can produce valid "scientific" knowledge equal to that produced by Western experimental science, but also to critique science's implication in projects of colonialism. As John Rieder makes clear in *Colonialism and the Emergence of Science Fiction* (2008), SF was shaped as much by the social and intellectual changes brought about by imperialism as by the concomitant rise of modern technoculture. Similarly, as Harding notes, colonialism depended on advancements in cartography and geology and on improved technologies for shipbuilding, and often succeeded because of better understandings of biology, particularly immunology. A critical perspective on this history has been absent until recently in both science and SF. Recent work by Vandana Shiva and Kavita Philip has demonstrated the degree to which Western science has participated in the imperialist project, not only by supplying these technologies but also by appropriating knowledge from non-Western cultures and then discounting their contributions. Shiva argues, for example, that pharmaceutical companies patenting the genetic information in plants that are the product of hundreds of years of indigenous agriculture is an ongoing colonialism she calls "biopiracy." Similarly, Elizabeth Ginway's *Brazilian Science Fiction* (2004) and Rachel Haywood Ferreira's *The Emergence of Latin American Science Fiction* (2011) reveal the ways that SF thinks differently about the nexus of science, technology, and the ideal of progress when the genre emerges in colonized nations. Such work challenges definitions of science and SF that make them the exclusive property of the West.

Paolo Bacigalupi's 2009 novel *The Windup Girl* is a postcolonial critique of ongoing scientific colonization, focusing on the biotech industry's extraction of genetic resources from countries it treats as economic colonies and on the privatization of food through genetically modified, nongerminating, patented seeds. Set in twenty-second-century Thailand, the novel recounts the political struggles between the Ministry of Environment, committed to maintaining a strict biological quarantine to protect Thailand from an infection that destroyed most of the world's food supply, and the Ministry of Trade, which is contemplating commerce with multinational agribusiness corporations. Bacigalupi's novel is an incisive critique not only of the culture of colonialism that produced dystopian climatic conditions but also the culture of science, whose location within corporate structures defined by profit-making ensures that it will inevitably be shaped by short-term perspectives.

The Windup Girl, with its combined focus on science and society, exemplifies one of the assertions of science-studies scholar Bruno Latour. What Latour calls the "modern Constitution"—that is, the discourses of science and politics as they were formulated during the scientific and political revolutions of the seventeenth century—have created a false regime of ontological purification comprising "two entirely distinct ontological zones: that of human beings on the one hand; that of nonhumans on the other" (10–11). We associate science with nature, a realm whose actions we deem separate from the cultural-political order. Yet, Latour points out, the stories in the local newspaper link "the most esoteric sciences and the most sordid politics, the most distant sky and some factory in the Lyon suburbs, dangers on a global scale and the impending local elections for the next board meeting" (1): we never encounter technology or nature (e.g., the chemical contaminants of pollution) in a context that is not simultaneously a cultural and human one (e.g., laws regarding emissions, the decisions of CEOs). In order to understand and respond to a reality in which science and technology influence and shape human lives, we need to understand that "half of our politics is constructed in science and technology. The other half of Nature is constructed in societies" (144). Latour eschews science's traditional subject/object binary, focusing instead on what he calls quasi-objects, entities that are always and simultaneously constructed by their surrounding culture *and* objects in a material world that preexists and exceeds human knowledge. "We can keep the Enlightenment without modernity" (135), he contends, by recognizing the inevitable hybridization of nature and culture and focusing on the network that connects seemingly social things such as dietary habits or transportation systems with seemingly natural things such as viruses or the behavior of electrons. Our error has been in denying these links and thereby recognizing only "essences of Nature or Society" (135).

Neal Stephenson's ambitious, complex, and sweeping "Baroque Cycle" (2003–04) reads like a primer for comprehending Latour's worldview. Set in the seventeenth century, it explores the rise of the experimental method through the practices of the Royal Society, the blurry distinction between alchemy and "real" science, changes in social practices as new products such as coffee and chocolate become available in England through imperialism, and much more. Stephenson's achievement lies in his clarity of vision, his ability to show how the social, economic, political, and scientific forces of the seventeenth century were not simply temporally coincident but rather mutually constitutive. His vast cast of characters, ranging from the vagabond Jack Shaftoe to a fictionalized Sir Isaac Newton, carefully traces the networks that link the vivisection experiments of the Royal Society with the Puritans' challenge to contemporary religious authority, the ongoing alchemical project to find the philosopher's stone with anxieties about the deflation of the English currency. The "Baroque Cycle" delineates how the insights we now consider modern scientific knowledge come increasingly into focus through the experiments of the Royal Society and others, but the books insist on a science that remains connected to the individual particularities of those who practice it and to the specificities of the larger episteme. Commenting on slavery, for example, a character reminds herself how easily its link to newly available commodities could be forgotten, "*I am as guilty as the next person of putting sugar in my coffee without considering the faraway Negroes who made it for me*" (*Quicksilver* 737; emphasis in original).

The rise of experimental science that claims to represent universal nature, and the rise of a system of currency that represents physical stores of precious metals, both emerge from a common episteme in which credibility is a key term: just as Newton's calculus relies on the power of his reputation to convince people that his equations stand for physical relationships of force that cannot be seen, so too does the credibility of a sovereignty issuing currency determine whether such notes will be taken as legitimate signs of material wealth. This affinity parallels arguments made by Steven Shapin and Simon Schaffer that the conflict over experimental method between chemist Robert Boyle and political philosopher Thomas Hobbes shows how the emergence of scientific protocols for the establishment of fact, for appropriate kinds of disagreements over interpretation, and ultimately for the status of "truth" was deeply influenced by concurrent struggles over how to establish political authority and adjudicate disagreements about governance.

The main theme of Stephenson's "Baroque Cycle" is summed up by the title shared by the final volume, the final book within that volume, and the final book of Newton's *Principia Mathematica* (1687): *The System of the World*. Newton sought to outline the mathematical principles of gravitation, to explain the system by which all of physical reality and motion, from apples to planetary systems, is organized. The system of the world in Stephenson's seventeenth century is equally expansive in scope, but consistent with Latour's caveat, it is a hybrid of nature and culture, not simply a purified and abstract mathematics. As a character comments, "We are at a fork in the road just now. One way takes us to a wholly new way of managing human affairs . . . the Royal Society, the Bank of England, Recoinage, the Whigs, and the Hanoverian Succession are all elements of it. The other way leads us to Versailles" (*System* 575). The new, modern system of the world is the Enlightenment project, moving away from superstition and toward rational knowledge, one that will lead to maps "with more of geography and fewer of monsters and mermaids" (*System* 674). Stephenson's vision demonstrates the power of SF as a kind of science studies, celebrating science's ability to make a better world but simultaneously acknowledging the limits of science and the need to recognize that just because "phenomenae that we think of as diverse, and unrelated: free will, God's presence in the Universe, miracles, and the transmutation of chymical elements" (*System* 685) does not mean they are unconnected.

The best SF can function as a supplement to the official discourses of science. Jacques Derrida defined a supplement as something that serves as an aid to something "original" or "natural." Drawing attention to how a supplement can be either "a plenitude enriching another plenitude" (144) or a replacement for the thing it is intended to supplement—that is, an adding-in or a substitution—Derrida concludes that it is both at once. We can understand the relationship between SF and the culture of science in a similar way. Because SF requires a good story as well as a scientific premise, it includes the messy, contingent details that are part of how science happens in the real world but that are removed from sight in experimental design and the publication of results. Although some might argue that SF is a "bad" substitution for an understanding of the "real" (rather than "imagined") consequences of technological innovation, it serves two cultural functions that outweigh this potentially negative effect. First, it is a barometer of contemporary cultural anxieties and preoccupations, relevant data for understanding our episteme, even if such fears—such as late-twentieth-century visions of AIs run amuck—do not come to pass. Second, its narrative features require the technologies it presents to be embedded in a full social world, and thus it helps us to remember that science does not exist in a vacuum but is produced by, and in turn shapes, a contingent, malleable, complex social world.

WORKS CITED

Bacigalupi, Paolo. *The Windup Girl*. San Francisco: Night Shade, 2009. Print.

Bloor, David. *Knowledge and Social Imagery*. 1976. 2nd ed. Chicago: U of Chicago P, 1991. Print.

Derrida, Jacques. *Of Grammatology*. 1967. Trans. Gayatri Spivak. Baltimore: Johns Hopkins UP, 1976. Print.

Fazekas, Andrew. "New Saturn-Like Planet Has Two Suns, NASA Says." *National Geographic* (Sept. 15, 2011). Web. July 20, 2013. http://news.nationalgeographic.com/news/2011/09/110915-nasa-new-planet-two-suns-star-wars-tatooine-space-science/.

Freedman, Carl. *Critical Theory and Science Fiction*. Hanover, NH: Wesleyan UP, 2000. Print.

Gernsback, Hugo. "A New Sort of Magazine." *Amazing Stories* 1.1 (Apr. 1926): 3. Print.

Ginway, Elizabeth. *Brazilian Science Fiction: Cultural Myths and Nationhood in the Land of the Future*. Lewisburg, PA: Bucknell UP, 2004.

Gunn, James "A Touch of Stone." *The Road to Science Fiction*. Vol. 3: *From Heinlein to Here*. Clarkston, GA: White Wolf, 1996. 198–99. Print.

Harding, Sandra. *Is Science Multicultural?: Postcolonialisms, Feminisms, Epistemologies*. Bloomington: Indiana UP, 1998. Print.

Haywood Ferreira, Rachel. *The Emergence of Latin American Science Fiction*. Middletown, CT: Wesleyan UP, 2011. Print.

Jones, Gwyneth. "Fools: The Neuroscience of Cyberspace." 1995. *Deconstructing the Starships: Science, Fiction, and Reality*. Liverpool: Liverpool UP, 1999. 77–90. Print.

———. *Life*. Seattle, WA: Aqueduct, 2004. Print.

———. "True Life Science Fiction: Sexual Politics and the Lab Procedural." 2008. *Imagination/Space: Essays and Talks on Fiction, Feminism, Technology, and Politics*. Seattle, WA: Aqueduct, 2009. 141–65. Print.

Klotz, Irene. "Is the Higgs Boson the First Step to a 'Star Trek' Transporter?" *NBCNews.com*. July 5, 2012. Web. July 20, 2013. http://www.nbcnews.com/id/48087875/ns/technology_and_science-science/t/higgs-boson-first-step-star-trek-transporter/#.UeyivBaHroc.

Kuhn, Thomas. *The Structure of Scientific Revolutions*. 1962. 3rd ed. Chicago: U of Chicago P, 1996. Print.

Latour, Bruno. *We Have Never Been Modern*. 1991. Trans. Catherine Porter. Cambridge, MA: Harvard UP, 1993. Print.

Luckhurst, Roger. "Pseudoscience." *The Routledge Companion to Science Fiction*. Ed. Mark Bould, Andrew M. Butler, Adam Roberts, and Sherryl Vint. London: Routledge, 2009. 403–13. Print.

———. *Science Fiction*. Cambridge, UK: Polity, 2005. Print.

Merton, Robert. *The Sociology of Science: Theoretical and Empirical Investigations*. Chicago: U of Chicago P, 1973. Print.

Milburn, Colin. *Nanovision: Engineering the Future*. Durham, NC: Duke UP, 2008. Print.

Penley, Constance. *NASA/Trek: Popular Science and Sex in America*. New York: Verso, 1997. Print.

Philip, Kavita. *Civilizing Natures: Race, Resources, and Modernity in Colonial South India*. New Brunswick, NJ: Rutgers UP, 2003. Print.

Rieder, John. *Colonialism and the Emergence of Science Fiction*. Middletown, CT: Wesleyan UP, 2008. Print.

Shapin, Steven. *Never Pure: Historical Studies of Science as If It Was Produced by People with Bodies, Situated in Time, Space, Culture and Society, and Struggling for Credibility and Authority*. Baltimore: Johns Hopkins UP, 2010. Print.

Shapin, Steven, and Simon Schaffer. *Leviathan and the Air Pump: Hobbes, Boyle, and the Experimental Life*. Princeton, NJ: Princeton UP, 1985. Print.

Shiva, Vandana. *Stolen Harvest: The Hijacking of the Global Food Supply*. Cambridge, MA: South End, 2000. Print.

Stephenson, Neal. *Quicksilver*. New York: HarperCollins, 2003. Print.

———. *The System of the World*. New York: HarperCollins, 2004. Print.

Stone, Allucquère Rosanne. "Will the Real Body Please Stand Up? Boundary Stories About Virtual Cultures." *Cyberspace: First Steps*. Ed. Michael Benedikt. Cambridge, MA: MIT, 1991. 81–118. Print.

Suvin, Darko. *Metamorphoses of Science Fiction. Metamorphoses of Science Fiction: On the Poetics and History of a Literary Genre*. New Haven, CT: Yale UP, 1979. Print.

Vint, Sherryl. "Science Studies." *The Routledge Companion to Science Fiction*. Ed. Mark Bould, Andrew M. Butler, Adam Roberts, and Sherryl Vint. London: Routledge, 2009. 413–22. Print.

Waugh, Rob. "'Invisibility Cloak' Created by Scientists, But There's One Hitch—So Far, It Works Underwater." *Daily Telegraph* (Oct. 4. 2011). Web. July 20, 2013. http://www.dailymail.co.uk/sciencetech/article-2045118/Invisibility-cloak-created-scientists-theres-hitch-works-UNDERWATER.html.

Wolfe, Gary K. *Evaporating Genres: Essays on Fantastic Literature*. Middletown, CT: Wesleyan UP, 2011. Print.

Yaszek, Lisa. *Galactic Suburbia: Recovering Women's Science Fiction*. Columbus: Ohio State UP, 2008. Print.

CHAPTER 24

AUTOMATION

ROGER LUCKHURST

The word "automation" was consolidated in the English language in a flurry of debates during the early 1950s. The journals *Automation* and *Instruments and Automation* began in 1954, a major conference "The Automatic Factory" was held in England in the summer of 1955, and a US Congressional inquiry on the matter began in October 1955. The same year, the *Saturday Review* published a special issue "Atoms and Automation," and even the high-culture bastion of England's BBC Third Programme asked an engineer to deliver a set of radio talks on the question of automatic production (see Macmillan). The *Oxford English Dictionary* claims that the term was originally coined by Delmar Harder, Vice-President of the Ford Motor Company, in 1948, but it was conceptually sharpened in John Diebold's 1959 pamphlet for the National Planning Association, which described the process as a significant threshold moment in the history of technology: "Now, through systematic application of the principle called feedback, machines can be built which control their own operations, so that production processes do not have to be designed to take account of the limitations of a human worker" (3). By 1955 there was a fully automated factory prototype working in Rockford, Illinois—although a spokesman had announced the first completely automated factory in the Soviet Union at an Eastern bloc congress in 1954.

Automation was allied to terms like "automatic control," "control engineering," or "cybernetics." The last of these, coined by Norbert Weiner in 1947, radically conflated human, animal, and machine informational systems, seeing them all as reducible to programmable processes and codes. With the rise of servo-mechanisms using feedback loops, humans were increasingly inserted into technical systems less as operators than as units in a complex assembly. For many, automation thus heralded something beyond a mere extension of the possibilities of mechanization in the workplace. In the first major sociological study of automation, Frederick Pollock claimed that "economic and social consequences of a revolutionary character may well follow from the increasing use of new machines which operate with amazing efficiency and have an almost fantastic output" (6). To grasp the full implications of automation, it was necessary to avoid what Diebold called "excessive enchantment with the hardware of the machine"

(4), for such technological fetishism concealed the transformation of nearly every aspect of civil society the process portended.

Automation announced the second Industrial Revolution. Many accounts were utopian, suggesting a postscarcity world of three-day workweeks and equally distributed wealth within 10 years. The rhetoric of the boosters was always proleptic, using glossy science-fictional tones to evoke the sort of world led by an elite of engineers familiar from the work of H. G. Wells. Technocracy, a movement that rose and fell in the 1930s, was now about to be realized. "We shall expect to find an *economic general staff*—the real masters of both machines and men—at the apex of the social pyramid," Pollock predicted (83; emphasis in original). For others, automation was a dystopian possibility that lurked amidst the new, shiny machines. In one trade union pamphlet from 1956, the latest danger was that electronic technology, "under the control and ownership of some few men, could become a weapon for the destruction of other men, depriving them of work, their families of food, and the life of the great masses of the people of all joy" (*Automation* 6). The frontispiece of R. H. Macmillan's 1956 account of automation was a menacing woodcut of a monstrous robotic creature arriving at the gates of a small factory.

In November 1955, the SF magazine *Galaxy*, known for its emphasis on social-satirical SF, published Philip K. Dick's story "Autofac," in which the remnants of a postholocaust America are serviced by automated delivery trucks from entirely sealed underground factories. The autonomous, cybernetic network of production continues on a war footing, and the survivors "can't transmit our information to the factories—the news that the [nuclear] war is over and we're ready to resume control of industrial operations" (5). They can only resort to machine breaking and eventually contrive an automated war *within* the network over diminishing raw materials, which eventually destroys their local factory. Humans regain a freedom that is primitive subsistence in a denatured, toxic landscape, improvising feeble tools from the postindustrial rubble. With profound ambivalence, they discover that the factories are self-repairing, at the start of a cycle that will build to full-scale automation again. As a result, humans will lose agency but paradoxically regain something of their retooled humanity, now that they have realized they are irreversibly dependent on the network. In other stories, Dick imagines automated factories that actively deceive humans to perpetuate a war-production economy (*The Penultimate Truth* [1964]), turn against humans with ingenious weapons ("Second Variety" [1953], filmed as *Screamers* [1995]), or continue in manic cycles of production long after humanity has gone ("Some Kinds of Life" [1953]).

Dick's work, which gave instant narrative shapes to the possible futures implicit in contemporary discussions of automation, foregrounded crucial questions about agency, labor, and subjectivity in moments of rapid technological transformation. Dick recognized that the boundaries of the human were under substantial pressure with the advent of automation and the equivalence of communicational codes in cybernetics. The default subjective condition in this technologized environment was, for Dick, one of paranoia. Yet although automation was understood as a postwar condition, the product of the military-industrial complex of what Andy Pickering has called the

"World War II Regime," these ideas had a long history. Indeed, they are intrinsic to any definition of industrial modernity in the West. In what follows, therefore, I want to sketch out an historical span through which we can track the insistence of these questions of agency, labor, and subjectivity, and the ways in which SF as a distinctive literature of technologically saturated societies didn't just become a register of ambiguous reactions to these developments but substantively helped to shape the future-oriented, promissory discourse of automation itself.

In March 1811, in the English town of Nottingham, which contained one of the largest concentrations of industrial mills and factories, a mass gathering to complain about the reduction of wages in the depressed textile industry, rising food prices, and increasing taxes developed into a riot and then into an attack on machine looms. There had been machine breaking of the framework loom and the spinning jenny during the eighteenth century, but this time the violence against property was not an empty expression of rage but a targeted and discriminating attack on factories with particularly draconian policies and on specific wide-loom machines. It was these machines that were creating structural unemployment in industrial environments that had only recently been created by the demand for high labor concentrations. That frame-breakers were organized soon became clear: manifestos were issued under the name Ned Ludd or General Ludd. The Luddites remained an anonymous collective throughout their activities during the 1810s. The town clerk of Nottingham wrote urgently to the Home Office that the movement, which soon spread throughout industrial Nottinghamshire, needed to be put down by military force, asserting that "the endeavours of the labouring Classes by terror to compel their Employers to increase the price of their labour" threatened not only the capitalist foundations of the Industrial Revolution but also British society as a whole, since it was widely assumed to be agitation fermented by provocateurs sent from Revolutionary France (qtd. Bailey 22). In response, agents of the state infiltrated working populations, targeting those who agitated for the illegal cooperative action on wages and conditions. Luddism was but one symptom of a conspiratorial age.

If the Luddites targeted identifiable machines, it was because this was a transitional moment in industry. Mechanical devices might still be considered wonders or uncanny intrusions into an order organized by natural and human forces. The celebrated automata—the mechanical "self-movers"—of the eighteenth century were diversions because they temporarily confounded the natural and artificial orders, producing an uncanny moment of hesitation about their ontological status. It is this moment of category crisis that places E. T. A. Hoffmann's "The Sandman" (1816), a fevered tale about a mechanical device mistaken for a woman, at the heart of Sigmund Freud's study of the uncanny. The automaton was a constant in early Gothic writing, even if the actual automata of that age might initially seem more diverting than horrifying. Jacques de Vaucanson's quacking and shitting duck, an elegant device with 400 moving parts, was displayed at many courts in Europe in the 1740s. Wolfgang von Kempelen's The Turk, a chess-playing automaton with apparently self-motored mechanical intelligence, had a longer life; it was first displayed in Europe in 1770 and recreated periodically in America into the 1850s (where it was seen by Edgar Allen Poe), although it proved to be a trick of puppetry rather than self-authored mechanical action. Perhaps the implications of Pierre Jaquet-Droz's trio of dolls—the musician, the draughtsman, and the writer—from the 1770s were more ominous, since a machine could now appear to write that Cartesian assertion of human certainty, "I think therefore I am." Indeed, these diversions proved to be intimately connected with the nascent technological revolution in industry. In 1741 De Vaucanson was appointed to advise on improvements to the silk industry and invented the first fully automated silk loom. His workshop was destroyed by rioting weavers, and the inventor was forced to flee Lyon (see Kang; Wood).

The automaton was merely an early signal of major social transformations. The monstrous creature created by Victor Frankenstein is a biological automaton self-motored by electrical spark and self-educated by reading C. F. Volney's revolutionary text *Ruins of Empire* (1791). No wonder Mary Shelley's overdetermined monster has been read as an emanation of vengeful workers or slaves, or as a text that shares the radical subcultures of London's electrical engineers, meeting in pubs to discuss the consequences of materialist and mechanistic conceptions of life (see Morus). The anxiety induced by the automaton could also be measured, in 1796, by the bizarre psychosis of James Tilly Matthews, who was confined to Bethlehem asylum in London because he believed that government policy was being orchestrated by an elaborate machine hidden in a London basement that pumped out mesmeric fluid coercing cabinet ministers from a distance (see Jay). Matthews has been regarded as modernity's first "schizophrenic"—a mental illness that, according to psychoanalyst Victor Tausk, commonly produced fantasies of elaborate "influencing machines" that persecuted individuals "by means of waves or rays or mysterious forces which the patient's knowledge is inadequate to explain" (521). These symptoms are the early tremors of new forms of technosocial assembly.

Thomas Carlyle announced the arrival of "The Mechanical Age" in 1829 (34), expecting it to refashion not just the economic but also the social and spiritual spheres, too. A strain of organicism in Victorian intellectual life regarded the machine as a horrific intrusion into a rapidly vanishing pastoral ideal, which accounts for John Ruskin's raillery against a mechanistic industrial order or Matthew Arnold's complaints about the anarchy embodied in "that mechanical character which civilization tends to take everywhere" (33). "Faith in machinery," Arnold claimed, was "our besetting danger" (34). Leo Marx has analyzed the pervasive trope of "the machine in the garden" in American discourse as well, pointing to an emblematic scene in Nathaniel Hawthorne's writing where the "startling shriek" of a locomotive slices through the quietude (13). Of course, the railway was how many Victorians first experienced what it meant to be inserted into what one commentator in 1851 called "a vast machine": the traveler no longer had active agency but was subject to the complex infrastructure and timetabling of the network, and the entire experience was "filtered through the machine ensemble" (Schivelbusch 24). This early cultural experience of technological enframement was directly related to the emergence of notions of psychological trauma, which emerged from medical and legal discussions of the physical and mental consequences of train crashes; what is now called posttraumatic stress disorder was first termed "railway spine" (see Luckhurst).

Nineteenth-century industrial transformation is best grasped in the writings of Karl Marx. Marx understood the immensely liberating and transformative potential of technological innovation in industrial modernity, yet under capitalism, he claimed, the machine was primarily "a means for producing surplus-value" (492): it did not liberate men from labor but immiserated them either by increasing their workload or entirely replacing their labor-power. Marx saw human labor being progressively displaced as the agent of production in the shift from handicraft to manufacture and finally to "large-scale industry," which he defined as the development of a cooperation of machines placed in complex assembly, an "automatic system of machinery" (503) that inserted workers into an "entirely objective organisation of production" (508). "A system of machinery," Marx concluded, "constitutes a vast automaton" (502)—a phrase he borrowed from Andrew Ure, who had dreamed of a factory "composed of various mechanical and intellectual organs, acting in uninterrupted concert" (544). The industrial rhythms of this automaton dictated not just the working hours but also every aspect of social existence through various forms of "time-discipline," including—as E. P. Thompson has shown—a moral discourse against the dangers of idleness in the hours beyond the factory gates.

The most concrete way of encountering Victorian modernity, with its continuous disturbances and transformations, was through the space-time compressions of not factory assemblages but the more intimate technologies that reinvented everyday life: accelerating transportation, revolutions in print technology, the telegraph, the new machine inscription devices of the 1870s (microphones, phonographs, telephones, typewriters), and the odd transience of city spaces as they were subject to the permanent revolution of unceasing urban expansion. These ongoing changes opened up the possibility of future projections, visions of the future that foregrounded technology as the principal marker of social change. Some of the resulting treatments, such as Edward Bellamy's *Looking Backward: 2000–1887* (1888), were utopian, but as Brian Stableford has observed, it is the modern genre of dystopia that makes the "dangers of automation" one of its fundamental themes (76). Jane Loudon's *The Mummy!: A Tale of the Twenty-Second Century* (1828) is a conservative account of feudal order restored after the chaos of the Regency, yet the story is staged in a future London as cluttered with new-fangled steam and pneumatic technologies as the influential etchings of Albert Robida's *Le Vingtième Siècle* (1883), which helped fix a certain vision of the utopian "electric" future.

One of the earliest fictions to use machinery less as furniture than as an agency tending toward automation was Samuel Butler's *Erewhon* (1872), a response to Darwinian theory that fused biological with technological change. This tonally tricky and subversive portrait signals the central importance of machines by depicting a society that elected to banish them nearly 300 years before because "the machines were ultimately destined to supplant the race of man, and to become instinct with a vitality as different from, and superior to, that of animals, as animal to vegetable life" (97). In extracts from "The Book of Machines" interpolated in the narrative, machine consciousness—a great leap in evolution that, for humans already dependent on them, rapidly inverts the master–servant relationship—renders humanity "a sort of parasite upon the machines" (206). These projections include a striking portrait of a fusion of human and machine, a creature with "many extra-corporeal members" (224) that advances from the Enlightenment automaton to the modern cyborg in impressively short order. Butler was a maverick biological theorist who grasped, in his work on hereditary memory, that physiologists were constantly extending the terrain of the autonomic functions of the central nervous system, eroding the powers of conscious will by finding evidence of what William Carpenter called "unconscious cerebration" (Wilson 10). Psychological "automatism," a coinage of the 1880s, would soon be intrinsically related to fears of automation: late Victorians were constantly at risk of having their wills supplanted by automated habit. One of the spookiest spectacles of the age was to witness a medium fall into a trance and take dictation from the spirits of the dead, or perhaps only from their "subliminal" consciousness: this was called *automatic writing*.

The key figure in this utopian/dystopian projection of future automation was H. G. Wells. His early, quixotic essays and scientific romances of the 1890s had a satirical edge informed by his education in biology at T. H. Huxley's Normal School of Science, which gave him a wry evolutionary perspective on any future social projections. The dethronement of man was his sardonic theme—this at a time when "Greater" Britain was stretching to its full imperial extent. Wells was also socialist enough to write, in reaction to the phenomenal success of Bellamy's utopia, a complacent vision of a cooperative world of nationalized capitalism where technology benignly underpins the resolution of labor conflict, his 1905 novel *A Modern Utopia*. Wells was similarly unimpressed by William Morris's anti-Bellamy socialist utopia, *News from Nowhere* (1890), which depicts a pastoral future in which ugly industrial mechanism is once more expelled to the edges of Eden, ushering in a faux-medieval revival of craft guilds as models of unalienated labor. Instead, Wells embraced the fact that technology would be central and transformative to both social and biological futures.

In *The Time Machine* (1895), the dullard Time Traveller repeatedly fails to understand what it is that he sees: he reads the society of the Eloi as a Morrisian pastoral idyll, underpinned perhaps by invisible modes of automation, when in fact they have biologically degenerated in the absence of the need to labor. Mechanism, however, has not been banished: underground workshops, "full of the throb and hum of machinery" (48), are tended by simian Morlocks, descendants of the laboring classes now imprinted with the automated habits, efficiency ratios, and absence of empathy of the machines they tend. The Traveller proves extraordinarily ambivalent about this social vision, his identification torn between the benign but decadent Eloi and the malignant but energetic Morlocks. The Traveller shares "a certain weakness for mechanism" (59) yet is revolted by the slightest touch of the blanched bodies of the workers; he cannot escape the social conflicts of Victorian capitalism that he brings into the future, even though the sight of his own ruined civilization—abandoned machinery rotting in a museum—speaks of the deathly consequences of that social organization. The framing narrator too, his narcissism unraveled by the Time Traveller's tale, orders the reader not to countenance the future vision.

Wells's vision of a technocratic future is perhaps most famously realized in the mise-en-scène—automated pavements, skyscrapers, busy aerial transports, and clean art deco lines—of William Cameron Menzies's film *Things to Come* (1936), which Wells scripted. Yet many of these developments were worked out decades earlier in Wells's *Anticipations of the Mechanical and Scientific Progress upon Human Life and Thought* (1902), a set of essays that virtually founded the discourse of extrapolative futurology. His earlier novella "A Story of the Days to Come" (1899) has been decidedly ambivalent about technological "progress," regarding class conflict as an inevitable driver of the process, even in technologically advanced futures; yet after *Anticipations*, Wells generally held to a more rigid sense of human improvement through technological modernity and one-state world government, dictated by "a large fairly homogenous body … of more or less expert mechanics and engineers" (93). The apocalyptic potential of increasingly technologized war shadowed this proposal ever more urgently until Wells's death in 1946, as his predictions about the industrialization of war were grimly realized.

Insistent repetition of this Wellsian utopia prompted some remarkable, influential rebuttals, which have fixed the conception of dystopia as a genre predominantly concerned with attacking the dangers of automation. E. M. Forster's "The Machine Stops" (1909), a direct riposte to Wells's *A Modern Utopia*, offers a vision of a postscarcity future where humanity is entirely controlled and contained by a centralized automated machine, to the extent that unmediated human contact has become taboo and human reproduction has been consigned to a eugenic calculus, so "that the Machine may progress eternally" (148). The plot follows a rebel who tries unsuccessfully to wake his fellow citizens to the danger of the Machine's imminent collapse, their parasitical dependence on it rendering this inevitable catastrophe fatal for humankind. Aldous Huxley's *Brave New World* (1932) was begun as a response to Wells's *Men Like Gods* (1923) but showed considerably less hope that there might be an unalienated space outside the machinic orchestration of social and natural worlds. Indeed, Huxley suggests that mechanization has reached a point where it is virtually impossible to sustain a notion of nature "outside" the machine. Philosopher Martin Heidegger referred to this problem as "Enframing," a condition in which the very essence of being human risked oblivion under the "planetary imperialism of technologically organized man" (152). The immediate target of Huxley's bleak satire was not Wells, however, but the industrialist Henry Ford, who had inaugurated a new stage in the history of automation with his perfection of assembly-line mass production in the early decades of the twentieth century.

These decades were dominated, in Great Britain, by a rhetoric of "national efficiency" geared to fight off the perceived threats of Western economic, social, and moral decline (see Searle). The working classes were the renewed target of this discourse, seen as degenerate, work-shy, and—more important—newly unionized. In 1910 Frederick Winslow Taylor gave a lecture to the American Society of Engineers that was published a year later as *The Principles of Scientific Management*. Taylor's premise was that laborers worked as slowly and sullenly as they dared and that industrial efficiency could be increased only by "replac[ing] the judgment of the individual workman" with mechanized processes (22). To achieve this, Taylor worked with the photographers

Frank and Lillian Gilbreth to analyze the repetitive movements of basic manual labor, using a stopwatch to determine the most efficient patterns of muscular action (in, for instance, bricklaying). Close surveillance of workers using these time-and-motion studies sought to eliminate "deliberate loafing" (48). Moreover, in Taylor's view, heavy manual labor required only the "mental make-up of an ox" (35) and would shortly be entirely replaced by machines anyway. Ford took the consequences of this atomization of the laboring body in a new direction, using it to disassemble factory work into a sequence of simple repeated actions along a moving assembly line. Ford thus revolutionized automobile production, driving down unit labor costs and product prices. He openly approved of the de-skilling of workers, since it standardized outputs while placing power in the hands of efficiency managers rather than shop-floor trade unionists. In *My Philosophy of Industry*, Ford waxed lyrical about "Machinery, the New Messiah" (the title of his first chapter) and gave individual sections titles suggesting surreal predictions of the future wonders of automation, such as "Repairing Men Like Boilers" (10).

The industrial system formed by "Taylorism" and "Fordism" had enormous cultural and political effects across the globe during the 1920s. It is associated with the triumph of American mass production and consumption, and was famously satirized in Charlie Chaplin's 1936 film *Modern Times*. Chaplin's comedy embodied Peter Wollen's observation that "Fordism turned the factory into a kind of super-machine in its own right, with both human and mechanical parts" (36), once again deepening the imbrication of human beings with the technosocial assembly. This new stage of automated labor produced visions of oppressed masses in Fritz Lang's *Metropolis* (1927) and Karel Capek's 1920 play *R.U.R. (Rossom's Universal Robots): A Fantastic Melodrama*, which coined the word "robot." But Taylorism was not intrinsically capitalist: the dominant faction of the Communist Party in the Soviet Union also embraced it, setting up the Central Labor Institute to roll out Taylorist principles. The strongest advocate, head of the CLI, was the proletarian poet Alexei Gastev, who advocated "mechanized collectivism" (Bailes 538). His fellow poet, Andrei Platonov, proclaimed that "[e]very machine is a genuine proletarian poem. . . . Electrification is the first proletarian novel, our big book in an iron jacket. Machines are our poems and the artistry of machines, the beginning of proletarian poetry, which is the revolt of humanity against the Universe" (qtd. Cardew 18). It was Gastev, however, who regarded the standardization of the psychology of the proletariat as the key virtue of Taylorism: his talk of "proletarian units" rather than individuals functioned to reduce people to codes of numbers and letters, prompting Yevgeny Zamyatin to write his dystopian masterpiece, *We* (1921), a scathing satire of an entirely Taylorized, postindividual future. Suppressed in Zamyatin's native Russia, the novel was published in English translation in the United States in 1924, its American readers misconstruing it as a critique of Communism rather than of the principles that underpinned American industrialism. Zamyatin, like so many others, was in direct dialogue with Wells, preferring the "strange, paradoxical combinations" of Wells's earlier fictions (268) to the "machines, machines, machines" that drove his undialectical utopias (259).

The concrete results of Taylorism in industry energized calls for national efficiency in America. In 1921 Thorstein Veblen argued that a "Soviet of Technicians" of "trained technological experts" should take over the economy in order to lead a "progressive advance of this industrial system towards an all-inclusive mechanical balance of interlocking processes" (58). In the wake of the economic collapse inaugurated by the stock market crash of 1929, arguments for undemocratic economic management became more extreme. The Committee on Technocracy, for example, suggested that the accelerating advance of mechanism had produced a structural crisis that could only be managed by "engineers and technologists" in permanent control of a "productive and distributive system which will harness the energy resources of the country" (Akin 137).

This viewpoint fed directly into the emergent ideology of several foundational American SF magazines. Hugo Gernsback briefly edited the *The Technocracy Review* alongside *Amazing Stories* during the 1920s, and John W. Campbell's editorship of *Astounding Science-Fiction* during the late 1930s and 1940s embedded the paradigm of heroic scientists and engineers crafting technical solutions to social problems into the genre's DNA. Campbell also wrote a fine pair of stories of far-future automation, "Twilight" (1934) and "Night" (1935), in which mechanized factories and machine intelligences have outlasted humanity. More important, Campbell fostered the early career of key SF writer Robert A. Heinlein, whose 1940 story "The Roads Must Roll" is an explicit engagement with technocracy whose ultimate conclusion is that "the real hazard . . . is not the machinery but the men who run the machinery" (63)—thus making the hegemony of trained experts crucial to social harmony. In an echo of Rudyard Kipling, whose 1912 story "As Easy as A.B.C." was a futuristic fiction about the abandonment of democracy in favor of global rule by engineers, Heinlein advocates an ostensibly purely "technical" solution that is nevertheless authoritarian and contemptuous of the weak institutions of the democratic state.

Heinlein was more of a libertarian than a Fascist, although Fascism was another vector of response to the same historical conditions of economic and social catastrophe during the 1930s. The work of Ernst Jünger, an important influence on Hitler's formulation of national socialism, gives a taste of the delirious Fascist discourse on technology. Jünger saw Taylorism not in factories but in the vast machinic armies that ground through the mud of the Great War. A survivor of the front, which he considered a "gripping spectacle" (123), he wrote ecstatic visions of gigantic factories "producing armies on the assembly line . . . the precise labour of a turbine fuelled with blood" (129). In Jünger's frenetic vision, the future revealed a prospect of "total mobilization" in a society entirely geared for war and saturated with technologies of death. Total mobilization, Jünger said, "expresses the secret and inexorable claim to which our life in the age of masses and machines subjects us" (128).

This deathly prophecy was surely fulfilled by the Second World War, where the erasure of any distinction between combatants and civilians was taken to new levels of atrocity that required a wholly new language: the term "genocide" was coined in 1944 to name this new dispensation. The massive and secret assemblage known as the Manhattan Project, which built the atomic bombs dropped on Japan, not only escalated the formation of an economic infrastructure later to be dubbed the "military-industrial complex" but also produced a weapon that, in the instant of its explosion over Hiroshima on August 6, 1945, fully realized the concept of total mobilization. Nothing and no one on the planetary level could ever consider themselves outside this new and deadly technological framework. The postwar nuclear arms race inflected the question of automation with a particular concern over whether military technocrats might unleash a "push-button war" (see Plotnick). The most sardonic fictional account of the alienated, abstracted bureaucrats who administer computerized global annihilation is Mordecai Roshwald's *Level 7* (1959), which offers a chilling finale to two centuries of proleptic imaginings of obedient, automated human labor.

In subsequent decades, SF would project visions of entirely automated weapons systems controlled by Artificial Intelligences whose goal is nothing less than the extermination of humanity. The scenario of the *Terminator* franchise (the first film appeared in 1984, its sequels in 1991 and 2003), in which the orbiting Skynet A.I. launches a lovingly depicted nuclear annihilation, has its origins in the "secret confluence of war sciences" that lay at the heart of Norbert Wiener's cybernetics (Galison 248), which emerged from experiments to ensure greater efficiency in antiaircraft batteries by creating a symbiotic feedback loop between human operators and servo-mechanisms for targeting and release. Katherine Hayles has shown how the interdisciplinary Macy conferences, held between 1943 and 1954, consolidated cybernetics as a discourse that conflated machines, animals, and humans as informational systems. Many different lines of science-fictional modeling of the automated future derive from this source, from the conservative humanism of Kurt Vonnegut's *Player Piano* (1952), set in the ruins of an automated factory built on the site of Thomas Edison's first workshop, to the ecstatic embrace of uploaded selves typical of defiant posthumanist SF like Charles Stross's 2005 novel *Accelerando*, which happily disarticulates the informational bundle of the human in a potentially infinite number of iterations far into the future.

The word "automation" has a vaguely antique feel to it now, summoning images of data punch cards or vast rooms humming with magnetic-tape memory-storage systems, a dystopian Alphaville that carries an odd tinge, still, of heady utopian possibilities. Automation is a discourse about hardware, whereas the scientific revolution of the twenty-first century is in the "wetware" of genome mapping and the reshaping of the human from within. Perhaps this is why the cardboard-creaky futures of Philip K. Dick convey so precisely a specific postwar sensibility of free-floating anxiety regarding the fate of human labor and agency produced by the triumphalist discourse of the automated future. Dick's work compulsively suggests that humans and machines are switching places: the androids may be "among us, although morphologically they do not differ from us" ("Man, Android and Machine" 211), and this confusion provokes his classic tales of paranoia. Yet Dick also mournfully recognized that humans had been hollowed out, had become "the true machines" while "those objective constructs . . . the electronic hardware we build . . . may be the cloaks for authentic living" (227–28). From first to last, the history of automation, especially as refracted through SF, cannot be thought without the alienated schizoid states it creates.

WORKS CITED

Akin, William E. *Technocracy and the American Dream: The Technocrat Movement, 1900–41.* Berkeley: U of California P, 1977. Print.

Arnold, Matthew. *Culture and Anarchy.* 1869. Ed. S. Lipman. New Haven, CT: Yale UP, 1994. Print.

Automation: A Challenge to Trade Unions and Industry. London: Association of Supervisory Staffs, Executives and Technicians, 1956. Print.

Bailes, Kendall E. "Alexei Gastev and the Soviet Controversy over Taylorism, 1918–24." *Soviet Studies* 29.3 (1977): 373–94. Print.

Bailey, Brian. *The Luddite Rebellion.* New York: NYU P, 1998. Print.

Butler, Samuel. *Erewhon.* 1872. Ed. Peter Mudford. London: Penguin, 1985. Print.

Cardew, Patricia. "Utopia and Anti-Utopia: Alexei Gastev and Evgeny Zamyatin." *The Russian Review* 46 (1987): 1–18. Print.

Carlyle, Thomas. "Signs of the Times." 1829. *A Carlyle Reader.* Ed. G. B. Tennyson. 1969. Cambridge, UK: Cambridge UP, 1984. 31–54. Print.

Dick, Philip K. "Autofac." 1955. *Minority Report: Collected Stories IV.* London: Gollancz, 1987. 1–20. Print.

———. "Man, Android and Machine." 1976. *The Shifting Realities of Philip K. Dick: Selected Literary and Philosophical Writings.* Ed. Lawrence Sutin. New York: Vinage, 1995. 211–32. Print.

Diebold, John. *Automation: Its Impact on Business and Labor.* Washington, DC: National Planning Association, 1959. Print.

Ford, Henry. *My Philosophy of Industry.* Ed. Ray Leone Faurote. 1929. Whitefish, MT: Kessinger, 2003. Print.

Forster, E. M. "The Machine Stops." 1909. *The Science Fiction Century.* Ed. David G. Hartwell. New York: Tor, 1997. 139–60. Print.

Galison, Peter. "The Ontology of the Enemy: Norbert Wiener and the Cybernetic Vision." *Critical Inquiry* 21.1 (Aug. 1994): 228–66. Print.

Hayles, N. Katherine. *How We Became Posthuman: Virtual Bodies in Cybernetics, Literature, and Informatics.* Chicago: U of Chicago P, 1999. Print.

Heinlein, Robert A. "The Roads Must Roll." 1940. *The Science Fiction Hall of Fame. Vol. 1: 1929–1964.* Ed. Robert Silverberg. 1970. New York: Orb, 1998. 53–87. Print.

Heidegger, Martin. "The Age of the World Picture." 1938. *The Question Concerning Technology and Other Essays.* Trans. William Lovitt. New York: Harper, 1977. 115–54. Print.

Jay, Mike. *The Air Loom Gang: The Strange and True Story of James Tilly Matthews, His Visionary Madness and His Confinement in Bedlam.* London: Bantam, 2003. Print.

Jünger, Ernst. "Total Mobilization." 1930. Trans. Joel Golb and Richard Wolin. *The Heidegger Controversy: A Critical Reader.* Ed. Richard Wolin. 1991. Cambridge, MA: MIT, 1993. 119–39. Print.

Kang, Minsoo. *Sublime Dreams of Living Machines: The Automaton in the European Imagination.* Cambridge, MA: Harvard UP, 2011. Print.

Luckhurst, Roger. *The Trauma Question.* London: Routledge, 2008. Print.

Macmillan, R. H. *Automation: Friend or Foe?* Cambridge, UK: Cambridge UP, 1956. Print.

Marx, Karl. *Capital. Vol. 1.* 1867. Trans. Ben Fowkes. London: Penguin, 1976. Print.

Marx, Leo. *The Machine in the Garden: Technology and the Pastoral Ideal in America.* New York: Oxford UP, 1964. Print.

Morus, Iwan Rhys. *Frankenstein's Children: Electricity, Exhibition, and Experiment in Early-Nineteenth-Century London*. Princeton, NJ: Princeton UP, 1998. Print.

Pickering, Andy. "Cyborg History and the World War II Regime." *Perspectives in Science* 3.1 (1995): 1–48. Print.

Plotnick, Rachel. "Predicting Push-Button Warfare: US Print Media and Conflict from a Distance, 1945–2010." *Media, Culture & Society* 34.6 (2012): 655–72. Print.

Pollock, Frederick. *The Economic and Social Consequences of Automation*. Oxford: Blackwell, 1957. Print.

Schivelbusch, Wolfgang. *The Railway Journey: The Industrialization of Time and Space in the Nineteenth Century*. 1977. New York: Berg, 1986. Print.

Searle, G. R. *The Quest for National Efficiency: A Study in British Politics and Political Thought, 1899–1914*. Berkeley: U of California P, 1971. Print.

Stableford, Brian. "Automation." *Encyclopedia of Science Fiction*. 1979. Ed. John Clute and Peter Nicholls. 2nd ed. 1993. London: Orion, 1999. 74–76. Print.

Tausk, Victor. "On the Origin of the 'Influencing Machine' in Schizophrenia." *Psychoanalytic Quarterly* 2 (1933): 519–56. Print.

Taylor, Frederick Winslow. *The Principles of Scientific Management*. New York: Harpers, 1911. Print.

Thompson, E. P. "Time, Work-Discipline, and Industrial Capitalism." *Past and Present* 38 (1967): 56–97. Print.

Veblen, Thorstein. *The Engineers and the Price System*. New York: B.W. Huebsch, 1921. Print.

Wells, H. G. *Anticipations of the Mechanical and Scientific Progress upon Human Life and Thought*. London: Chapman & Hall, 1902. Print.

———. *The Time Machine*. 1895. London: Dent, 1995. Print.

Wilson, Timothy D. *Strangers to Ourselves: Discovering the Adaptive Unconscious*. Cambridge, MA: Harvard UP, 2002. Print.

Wollen, Peter. "Modern Times: Cinema/Americanism/The Robot." 1991. *Raiding the Icebox: Reflections on Twentieth-Century Culture*. London: Verso, 1993. 35–71. Print.

Wood, Gaby. *Living Dolls: A Magical History of the Quest for Mechanical Life*. London: Faber, 2003. Print.

Zamyatin, Yevgeny. "Wells's Revolutionary Fairy-Tales." 1922. Trans. Lesley Milne. *H.G. Wells: The Critical Heritage*. Ed. Patrick Parrinder. London: Routledge & Kegan Paul, 1972. 258–74. Print.

CHAPTER 25

MILITARY CULTURE

STEFFEN HANTKE

SCIENCE fiction is at its most American when it addresses military themes. Other national traditions have, of course, also dealt with war and the military, as late-nineteenth and early-twentieth-century British works, from George Tomkyns Chesney's *The Battle of Dorking* (1871) to H. G. Wells's *The War in the Air* (1907), testify (see Clarke; Gannon). Though these traditions deserve scrutiny in their own right, they constitute a prehistory of science fiction. From the moment when World War II ended and the Cold War began, which also marked the transition of SF as a fully self-aware genre from the cultural margins to the cultural mainstream, the convergence of science fiction and the military has nowhere been as central to matters of national identity as in the United States. This is not to suggest that the military theme in American SF is *inevitably* a product of the nation's history and culture, but that American history and culture provide conditions under which science fiction aligns itself creatively, productively, and critically with the realm of politics, drawing legitimacy from this alignment. This convergence is present in crass, propagandistic military SF in fiction and film, in first-person shooter games, and in numerous television series. But it lurks as a subtext of much mainstream SF as well. If, for example, the "continuing mission" of the starship *Enterprise* is "to explore strange new worlds, to seek out new life, new civilizations," then why does the "uniformed, militarily-hierarchical crew" often go to battle stations and engage in armed conflict, "despite its nominally peaceful aims"? (Rabkin).

Historical evidence shows that the United States has existed on a persistent war footing throughout what Henry Luce in 1941 famously called the American Century. Since the Cold War, America has pursued an agenda requiring it to "maintain a *global military presence*, to configure its forces for *global power projection*, and to counter existing or anticipated threats by relying on a policy of *global interventionism*" (Bacevich, *Washington Rules* 14; emphasis in original). Within this framework, US troops provided most of the Allied occupational force in Europe and Asia following World War II. After the Korean War (1950–53), the United States engaged in the Vietnam War (1961–73), the Iran hostage rescue attempt (1980), deployment in Beirut (1982–84), the invasion of Grenada (1983), the raid on Tripoli (1986), the invasion of Panama (1989), the Persian Gulf War (1991–92), the invasion of Somalia (1992–93), the invasion of Haiti (1994), the air raids on Bosnia (1995), and Operation "Allied Force" in Kosovo (1999). Most recently, the United States has waged war in Afghanistan (2001–) and Iraq (2003–11), and has engaged in military action in Libya (2011). Moreover, formal declarations of war, as issued at the onset of the First and Second World Wars, have largely been replaced in the discourse of US foreign relations by a more euphemistically obscurantist vocabulary declaring specific conflicts to be, for example, a "police action," a necessary element in the process of "nation building," or a "kinetic military operation."

Necessary for the creation and maintenance of this permanent state of war is a national economy that, in 2001, channeled over 300 billion dollars into defense spending, a number that increased to over 700 billion a decade later; as a result, the United States accounts for over 40 percent of global military spending (Walker). A military machinery of this size and scope, spread throughout national society, is certain to have far-reaching economic, social, political, and ideological manifestations. Yet the number of citizens directly involved in the US military makes up only a small percentage of the overall population, especially since the abolition of the draft in 1973 and the increasing use of private contractors. A culture of war may be spread throughout US society, but in terms of its direct effects, it has also been contained within a narrow segment of the population, which tends to render it less visible. Battlefields, invariably, are elsewhere, as are civilian casualties; images of military deaths have been scrubbed from mainstream media since the 1970s. The fact that most of the wars the United States has engaged in since World War II are conflicts in which it has enjoyed a vastly asymmetrical advantage over its enemies has contributed to a broad acceptance of military action.

Whether this condition of constant war and war-preparedness, which permeates the political and economic life of the United States, also renders its culture explicitly *militaristic* is more difficult to assess. Attempts to grasp the complex interrelation between military and civilian life tend to take as their point of departure the "military-industrial complex," a term famously deployed by President Dwight Eisenhower in his 1961 farewell address and amended periodically to fit newly weighted configurations of power—for example, the "military-industrial-academic complex" (Lieven 156), indicating the prominent role of university research, or the "military-industrial-entertainment complex" (Turse, "Bringing the War Home"), pointing to the nexus of military and media influence. Examples of the cultural ubiquity of the military abound. Unlike "the situation that had existed prior to World War II, when the American military profession was a marginal institution and senior military officers figures of marginal importance" (Bacevich, *New American* 52), military service during the postwar era has been a virtually indispensable asset in US politics, catapulting Allied General Dwight D. Eisenhower into the presidency, aiding the political ascent of John F. Kennedy, serving as an advantage for George H. W. Bush and John McCain, and, when called into question, damaging the public images of Bill Clinton, George W. Bush, or John Kerry. (The presidential election of 2012 was the first since 1944 that did not feature a military veteran on either major party ticket.) "To state the matter bluntly," Bacevich argues, "Americans in our own time have fallen prey to militarism, manifesting itself in a romanticized view of soldiers, a tendency to see military power as the truest measure of national greatness, and outsized expectations regarding the efficacy of force" (*New American* 2). Writing in 1959, C. Wright Mills complained that "the American elite does not have any real image of peace—other than as an uneasy interlude existing precariously by virtue of the balance of mutual fright. The only seriously accepted plan for 'peace' is the fully loaded pistol" (qtd. Lieven 156).

Accepting the military as an indispensable part of the national imaginary is considered a cultural and social value across the political spectrum. Doctrinal debates about the true essence of the nation according to its Founding Fathers (for example, as a republic or an empire), or about the strategic framework of American foreign policy (for example, whether the Bush doctrine of "preemption" is to be preferred over Cold War "containment") never advance beyond the baseline assumption that war is the continuation of diplomacy by other means. To insist that war is not the extension but the *failure* of diplomacy, that voluntary enlistment constitutes a lack of moral imagination, that deserters and conscientious objectors should be recognized as figures of courage and personal integrity, or that dissent and even insubordination can constitute moral and civic virtues—such attitudes are unthinkable within the American political imagination. Even when a war is unpopular with a broad swath of the public, as with the recent conflicts in Iraq or Afghanistan, citizens still proudly proclaim that they "support the troops."

If one were to name a single text that represents SF to those who are neither fans of the genre nor have any particular interest in it—a mainstream audience, in other words—it would most likely be George Lucas's *Star Wars*, an intertextual behemoth comprising feature films (starting in 1977), novels, animated television series, toys, games, and many other spinoff products. More than other popular SF franchise—*Star Trek* (1967–) in its many incarnations comes to mind as a close second—it is *Star Wars* that has come to define, for better or worse, the genre as it appears to average consumers. Whatever the reason might have been that elevated Lucas's franchise to this exalted position—the putative mythic universality of its narrative, or the fortuitous moment in the history of American cinema when the first film was released, or its paradigm-altering special-effects technologies—even those who loathe the films will admit that, for most people, the first thing that comes to mind when asked for a "typical" example of SF is *Star Wars*.

Obviously, Lucas's creation is central to the discussion of military SF because of the word "wars" in its title. Although *Star Wars* represents a very specific type of science fiction, which means that Lucas self-consciously ignored much of the 1960s and 1970s New Wave and began instead "plunder[ing] Flash Gordon serials and other pulp sci-fi of the '30s" (Biskind 324), the enduring popularity of the franchise has moved it to a central position within the genre's canon—from which perch its long shadow obscures other types, modes, or subgenres that may be critically more highly valued (that is, more relevant to an audience deeply invested in, and more widely familiar with, the genre). To the extent that *Star Wars* deals with intergalactic war and futuristic weaponry, heroic action on a personal scale and technological conflict on a massive scale, imperial domination and occupation and insurgence, armies and fleets, battles, victory, defeat, surrender, courage, and cowardice—in other words, to the extent that *Star Wars* mobilizes the well-established generic inventory of the war story—its sheer popularity suggests to a mainstream audience that all science fiction, like *Star Wars*, is military science fiction.

Yet *Star Wars* merely culminated a tradition of militaristic SF cinema, the roots of which extend back to the Cold War, passing this heritage along to subsequent generations of SF filmmakers. A casual survey of the most popular specimens of SF film released since the late 1970s reveals a ubiquity of military themes. Starting in 1984, the *Terminator* franchise was built on the narrative and thematic premise of a future atomic war, deriving its urgency from Cold War anxieties visible in films about nuclear accidents such as *Fail-Safe* (1964) and *Dr. Strangelove* (1964), and turning contemporary urban America into a battlefield where futuristic soldiers struggle for control over an essential military asset. Starting in 1979, the *Alien* franchise has featured military themes, especially its second installment, James Cameron's *Aliens* (1986), which was not only the most commercially successful of the franchise but also transformed Ridley Scott's original SF/horror hybrid into a military action film. Add to this cinematic canon the immense popularity of first-person shooter games such as *Doom* (1993–2012), *Quake* (1996–2010), and *Halo* (2001–13); multiplayer online games like *World of Warcraft* (2004–11) and its analog predecessor, *Warhammer* (1983); not to mention cross-promotional properties such as Hasbro's G.I. Joe and Transformers, which have recently spawned popular film series, and what emerges is a profile of the genre in which the military theme stands out as a crucial marker of commercial viability.

These franchises make a compelling case that the key medium of military SF is no longer the printed word but visual-culture texts, especially films and, to a lesser yet steadily increasing extent, television and computer gaming. This is not to diminish the critical or commercial significance of SF literature. Robert A. Heinlein's *Starship Troopers* (1959), jingoistic though it might be, remains a novel crucial to the canon of science fiction, just as Joe Haldeman's *The Forever War* (1975) is likely to remain an antiwar staple on college syllabi for some time to come; and Jerry Pournelle, a writer wedded to military themes, has maintained an impressive readership over many decades. More recent military SF is also doing well commercially: Baen Books, home to an extensive cadre of authors specializing in the subgenre of military science fiction, caters to a small if avid audience with a varied list of creative talents, including writers like David Weber, David Drake, Harry Turtledove, and Timothy Zahn. Despite their appeal, however, these more recent authors of military SF have little chance of being as readily adopted into the canon as were Heinlein or Haldeman, catering more clearly as they do to a niche market. Writers with slightly more sterling critical credentials, such as Lucius Shepard, Orson Scott Card, or John Scalzi, may also have solid sales figures, but even at their most popular, they reach smaller audiences than Paul Verhoeven's 1997 adaptation of *Starship Troopers* or Steven Spielberg's 2005 adaptation of H. G. Wells's *War of the Worlds* (1898). In short, literary science fiction has ceded its central position in the cultural mainstream to film, television, and games: the novelizations of *Star*

Wars, often written by significant SF authors such as Terry Bisson, Elizabeth Hand, and Steven Barnes, emerged as a commercial afterthought to the blockbuster movies.

Generically speaking, *Star Wars* suggests that the cinematic representation of war in science fiction tends to neglect aspects of the topic incompatible with the broader genre of adventure narratives and their affective aesthetics. The war film tends to be more flexible and inclusive in its depiction of military preparation and battle than its SF variant; Jeanine Basinger's description of the combat film—with its primary focus on battle by land, sea, or air, featuring a large cast of characters and recurrent narrative and thematic tropes in subtle variations—stresses the genre's pliability, its capacity for melding with other forms, including SF (198). Yet by contrast, one would be hard-pressed to find a science fiction film that devotes itself to the theme of physical trauma or personal loss and their psychological consequences as doggedly as Dalton Trumbo's *Johnny Got His Gun* (1971) or Hal Ashby's *Coming Home* (1978) does; the protagonist of *Avatar* (2009) may be a paraplegic veteran, but the spectacular scenes of warfare provide the film's true thrills, not its engagement with the trauma of its protagonist's mutilated body. In some cases, specific war films have clearly influenced major SF texts—as, for example, Akira Kurosawa's samurai epic *The Hidden Fortress* (1958) provided an inspiration for the Jedi knights and light-sabers of *Star Wars* (Jamilla 22).

Representations of military occupation and its consequences, on the other hand, are frequently treated in SF literature, including such novels as Ursula K. Le Guin's *The Word for World Is Forest* (1976) and M. J. Engh's *Arslan* (1976), and they tend to de-emphasize physical action by contrast with thematically equivalent films and television series, such as John Milius's *Red Dawn* (1984), ABC's miniseries *Amerika* (1987), or the AMC series *Falling Skies* (2011–). Rather than psychological introspection, domestic settings, and an exploration of the repercussions of military action in the civilian sphere, military SF films favor the battlefield, physical action, the kinetic display of bodies interacting with each other and their material and technological environments, dynamic spectacles of acceleration and velocity, collision and impact, risk and danger. Ideologically, these elements are packaged in the format of the adventure narrative, which means that, aesthetically, the danger and violence of warfare are coded in the affective register of thrills and spills. In *Star Wars*, the violent deaths of multitudes of people in the vaporization of the planet Alderaan or the explosion of the Death Star attain little emotional gravity compared to the delirious rush of superbly choreographed individual dogfights in space.

What distinguishes military SF films from their pulp-fiction precursors is that they achieve this representation of war as thrilling adventure by mobilizing sophisticated special-effects technologies, which allow viewer immersion in imagined natural and technological environments, as well as proximity to the visually and aurally accelerated and intensified sites of violent conflict. Lucas revolutionized special effects in SF film, introducing "motion control," which "liberate[d] the camera, allowing the dizzying rushes of speed for which *Star Wars* became famous" (Shone 47), and creating the firm Industrial Light and Magic as an autonomous entity within his production facility. Not by coincidence, it was ILM that would be responsible for pioneering the use of CGI (computer-generated imagery) in film, and the later films in the *Star Wars* franchise have deployed "computers whose amassed power was a little less than that used by NASA but more than that used by the Pentagon" (Shone 281). SF cinema, in particular, has profited from increasingly affordable access to this technology as its superficially mimetic qualities and its decidedly nonmimetic visual flexibility nudge the genre further toward military themes and, more specifically, the combat film. The recent cycle of 3D movies, given great impetus by the box-office success of *Avatar*, has further underwritten this trend.

The centrality of technologically driven special effects in *Star Wars* points to an unlikely convergence of George Lucas's cinematic imagination with the political fantasies of Ronald Reagan. Reagan's Strategic Defense Initiative—a space-based system purportedly capable of intercepting ballistic missiles directed at the United States—was popularly branded as "Star Wars," which points to the fact that, increasingly, military technologies of surveillance, simulation, and control spring from the same scientific sources as the cinematic apparatus that puts them to civilian use. Dave Grossman has reported how the US military uses visual media for the conditioning of reflexes and attitudes to overcome soldiers' innate aversion to kill. "In real life," Scott Connors adds, "the military is not only receptive to military SF (indeed, both *Starship Troopers* and Orson Scott Card's *Ender's Game* are required reading in many service schools) but actively looks to SF for new ideas." A clear synergy links these two domains: writers of military SF such as Heinlein, Pournelle, and Larry Niven are reported to be favorites among employees of the Lawrence Livermore National Laboratory working on weapons research (Seed 189–90), while right-wing SF writers like Ben Bova have written works of nonfiction supporting such high-tech military programs as Reagan's SDI (see Franklin 202). Moreover, production designer Ron Cobb, who worked not only on *Star Wars* but also *Aliens* and *Total Recall* (1990), has, as Nick Turse reminds us, lent "his creative skills to a program to design the Army's super soldier of the future, the Objective Force Warrior," a "future soldier system" integrating the individual combatant, cyborg-style, with an array of portable and lethal technological apparatuses. Peter Warren Singer argues that SF fiction and film have been central in innovating and promoting processes of automated conventional warfare, such as military robotics, since the end of World War II (150–69).

Star Wars marks the convergence between the respective technocratic imaginations of entertainment and military politics, a convergence that retrospectively reconfigures the history of American warfare. Though Lucas draws from different periods of history in his conceptualization of futuristic war—using fantasy versions of weapons as diverse as swords, handguns, airplanes, and aircraft carriers—the underlying historical analogy for the war between rebels and imperial troops is the American Revolution. This use of a foundational historical trope of the American imagination points to a strategy that makes military science fiction politically powerful. This is not to say that *Star Wars* deserves to be read merely as political propaganda, despite its endorsement of war through its heavy dependence on thrilling spectacles of combat, but rather that military SF, in general, should be examined for the specific historical imagery it mobilizes in its efforts to conceptualize, visualize, and narrativize future war. Whether it be *The Last Starfighter* (1984) imagining space battles as World War II–style dogfights or *Falling Skies* depicting an armed insurrection by a tattered militia against a technologically superior occupying army à la the Revolutionary War, the metaphorical invocation of hallowed battles functions to frame war as justified, reasonable, inevitable, winnable, enjoyable, and/or heroic.

Though *Star Wars* may serve remarkably well as *the* emblematic text of American military SF, it is also a product of its specific historical moment. As conditions change during the course of the American Century, so too does the political alignment of forces converging within a text. Though its overall shape and function remain essentially unaltered, military science fiction, from one period to the next, continues to shift its thematic emphasis among its various constituent elements. To capture a sense of periodic dominants, of themes that emerge more prominently with each shift, I would like to look at the trajectory that extends from the early years of the Cold War to the so-called global war on terror to show how military SF aligns itself with specific agendas at specific times.

Military science fiction from the 1950s and 1960s appears during a period that is transitional in three respects, marking shifts from pre–World War II isolationism to aggressive global engagement, from demobilization to massive remobilization on the occasion of the Korean War, and from a reliance on conventional military assets to the development of an arsenal dominated by nuclear weaponry. Given these massive realignments of US foreign policy and military strategy, military SF aided in the broader effort to enlist Americans in the project of the American Century by familiarizing them with the nation's new military technologies and strategies, the new global mapping of the American sphere of influence, and the attitudes that would legitimize and further this agenda within civil society. Rezoning the global terrain for American interests, from the polar regions to outer space, military SF launched futuristic technologies that would lay claim to far regions around the globe. The US Navy secures safe passage under the Arctic ice in Spencer Gordon Bennet's *The Atomic Submarine* (1959), the climax of which features alien invaders being shot down by a nuclear missile launched from the film's eponymous vessel; television extended the concept into series format with Irwin Allen's *Voyage to the Bottom of the Sea* (1964–68). In Robert Day's film *First Man into Space* (1959), test pilots break free of Earth's gravitational field, undeterred by technical obstacles and the human costs of such expansion. Even time posed no barriers to American expansionism, as the secret military project in ABC's television series *Time Tunnel* (1966–67) propelled two scientists to remote temporal locations.

Such global remappings were matched by domestic rezonings in response to the emerging security state, which was turning vast stretches of the nation into military no-go areas, thus inadvertently helping to produce the Area 51 mythology. Especially when it came to the American Southwest, where the development and testing of the nuclear arsenal had been concentrated, SF films acknowledged the military as the prime agent of this rezoning: radiation produced by nuclear testing is the cause of mutation in giant-creature films like Gordon Douglas's *Them!* (1954) and Jack Arnold's

Tarantula (1955). Despite their alarmist tone, however, these movies also see the military as the only force capable of containing these threats; both films end with scenes in which giant insects are beaten back and incinerated by a highly mobile, vigilant, and competent military force—the same force ensuring the nation's safety during alien incursions into the American heartland in films such as William Cameron Menzies's *Invaders from Mars* (1953) and Fred F. Sears's *Earth vs. the Flying Saucers* (1956).

Cold War-era SF films occasionally depicted the military as threat rather than savior (in Robert Wise's *The Day the Earth Stood Still* [1951], the priorities of national security stand in the way of global peace), and military science fiction generally remained ambivalent as the United States negotiated the transition from a conventional to a nuclear arsenal. The threat of nuclear war is ever-present in these movies, but ironically, it is often the display of America's conventional weaponry that wins the day. Since the use of nuclear weapons by the United States was predicated on their defensive, second-strike capabilities only, displaying them in action would have necessitated showing a first strike by the Soviet Union. The depiction of nuclear warfare is not something the combat film—including the subgenre of SF combat films—has tended to favor, largely because it diminishes the occasion and efficacy of heroic agency, eliminates proper battlefields, causes mostly civilian casualties, and results in no clear winners or losers. Depicting the level of American casualties and countrywide devastation that would legitimize a retaliatory use of nuclear weapons was an unsavory proposition. As a result, film and television during this period largely refrained from showing the US nuclear arsenal in action, except for scenarios in which SF permitted displacement of its use into outer space or against alien invaders. By contrast, celebration of the conventional arsenal not only served to compensate for the problematic framing of nuclear weapons, it also had the added advantage of aiding in the remobilization of conventional forces during the Korean War.

One feature of military SF during this period is particularly striking. The way in which *Star Wars* modeled its central military struggle on the American Revolutionary War illustrates a recurring ideological theme with particular relevance to the types of conflicts typical of post-9/11 military engagement. According to this pattern, which recurs also in war films like Stephen Spielberg's *Saving Private Ryan* (1998) and Ridley Scott's *Black Hawk Down* (2001), Americans consistently appear as an outgunned and outnumbered underdog confronted with a seemingly insurmountable enemy. Such a counterfactual fantasy of asymmetrical force reaches from Cameron's *Aliens*, in which a group of cocky space marines is humiliated and decimated by an overwhelming enemy, to Cameron's *Avatar* (2009), in which a gathering of plucky natives fights a heroic and successful battle against a massive, technologically advanced military machine. Both films are grounded in traditional military values such as honor, courage, comradeship, and heroism, and, more important, both invite viewer identification with the group perceived as the underdog. This narrative scenario illustrates the mechanism by which military SF tends to disavow the historical reality of most wars launched by the United States during the American Century. Given the logic of such conflicts as Vietnam and the Gulf War, and running very much against the ideological grain of military SF, Americans should identify *not* with the rebel forces in *Star Wars* but with the imperial stormtroopers, *not* with the humans in *Independence Day* (1996) or *Falling Skies* but with the alien invaders. What better metaphor for US forces strategically deployed for the projection of American power around the globe than the alien ships hovering menacingly over Washington or London or Tokyo?

The asymmetrical nature of recent American wars provides an insight into the way actual military deployment is framed as a reasonable measure. Overwhelming force, when projected at the enemy, allows for military success; in the case of failure—or of an outcome framed as failure, though none the less devastating to an enemy, such as in the case of the Vietnam War—it serves as justification and provides a mythology of national victimization. Sent to die on behalf of an invisible corporate elite and abandoned by their incompetent officers, the space marines in *Aliens* fail honorably, heroically, and tragically. These marines return in Jonathan Liebesman's *Battle Los Angeles* (2011), visually upgraded to high-tech urban warfare to reflect US wars in the Middle East since 2001, their suffering in ideological alignment with self-declared war critics such as Michael Moore, who, in *Fahrenheit 9/11* (2004), exonerates US soldiers from individual moral accountability by foregrounding the economic inequality that "forces" them to enlist—an argument that validates its leftist credentials while drawing the criticism of conservatives, who tolerate no criticism of the militarized state at all, yet also forecloses criticism of the military *as such*, the necessity of its existence, and its moral legitimacy. If military science fiction in the 1950s served as a form of ideological recruitment for a project of empire, then the smooth interlacing of American militarism with its supposed critique in more recent years suggests one thing: Mission Accomplished.

Still, although warfare is ever more a matter of cutting-edge technologies, a sense nonetheless persists, best articulated by William Gibson, "that our future has lost that capital F we used to spell it with. The science fiction future of my childhood has had a capital F—it was assumed to be an American Future because America was the future" (Gorney). Together with the belief that the future would be inherently American, Gibson suggests that the future—or, rather, the *Future*—has lost its essence as a distinct temporal Other; we are less excited about it because, in essence, it is always already here. To the degree that this makes it more difficult to frame advanced high-tech warfare as science fiction, other genres are likely to take over SF's role. It is no coincidence that the most massive martial spectacle to appear in cinemas during the constant warfare of the Bush administration was neither a historical epic (though its roots are deep in the British experience of World War II), nor a science fiction spectacular (though its visual and technological accomplishments—especially its extensive use of CGI—place it squarely as a successor of *Star Wars*), but a piece of heroic fantasy reimagined, as if on demand, for Bush's war on terror: Peter Jackson's *The Lord of the Rings* (2001–03). To the degree that Jackson's fantasy franchise and its many imitators, not to mention the proliferation of superhero franchises spawned out of comic books, have pushed SF proper out of the cinematic mainstream, there is an opportunity for the genre to reclaim a position from which it can realize what George Slusser and Eric Rabkin see as its true function: not to become "mired in epic or chivalric models but [to] continue

... to meet the challenge of changing modes of combat" by providing "neither nostalgia nor play, but analysis" (4). If the ultimate goal of analysis is not to contribute to the continued normalization of war and the military, however, we might, together with Ursula Le Guin, have to resort to more radical visions and imagine ourselves living on an alien planet on which "nothing led to war. Quarrels, murders, feuds, forays, vendettas, assassinations, tortures and abominations, all these were in their repertory of human accomplishments; but they did not go to war. They lacked, it seemed, the capacity to *mobilize*" (48–49; emphasis in original).

Works Cited

Bacevich, Andrew. *The New American Militarism: How Americans Are Seduced by War.* New York: Oxford UP, 2005. Print.

———. *Washington Rules: America's Path to Permanent War.* New York: Henry Holt, 2010. Print.

Basinger. Jeanine. *The World War II Combat Film: Anatomy of a Genre.* Middletown, CT: Wesleyan UP, 2003. Print.

Biskind, Peter. *Easy Riders, Raging Bulls: How the Sex-Drugs-and-Rock 'n' Roll Generation Saved Hollywood.* New York: Touchstone, 1998. Print.

Clarke. I. F. *Voices Prophesying War: Future Wars, 1763–3749.* 1966. 2nd ed. New York: Oxford UP, 1992. Print.

Connors, Scott. "The Politics of Military SF." *Publishers Weekly* (Apr. 7, 2008). Web. July 26, 2013. http://www.publishersweekly.com/pw/print/20080407/3167-the-politics-of-military-sf-.html.

Franklin, H. Bruce. *War Stars: The Superweapon and the American Imagination.* 1988. Rev. ed. Amherst: U of Massachussetts P, 2008. Print.

Gannon, Charles E. *Rumors of War and Infernal Machines: Technomilitary Agenda-Setting in American and British Speculative Fiction.* Lanham, MD: Rowman & Littlefield, 2003. Print.

Gorney, Douglas. "William Gibson and the Future of the Future." *The Atlantic* (Sept. 14, 2010). Web. July 26, 2013. http://www.theatlantic.com/entertainment/archive/2010/09/william-gibson-and-the-future-of-the-future/62863/.

Grossman, Dave. *On Killing: The Psychological Cost of Learning to Kill in War and Society.* 1995. Rev. ed. New York: Little Brown, 2009. Print.

Jamilla, Nick. *Sword Fighting in the* Star Wars *Universe: Historical Origins, Style and Philosophy.* Jefferson, NC: McFarland, 2008. Print.

Le Guin, Ursula K. *The Left Hand of Darkness.* New York: Ace, 1969. Print.

Lieven, Anatol. *America Right or Wrong: An Anatomy of American Nationalism.* New York: Oxford UP, 2004. Print.

Rabkin, Eric. "How the Evil Networks of Science Fiction Became Your Best Friend." *The Network: Cisco's Technology News Site.* Sept. 19, 2011. Web. July 26, 2013. http://newsroom.cisco.com/feature-content?type=webcontent&articleId=474705.

Seed, David. *American Science Fiction and the Cold War: Literature and Film.* Edinburgh: Edinburgh UP, 1999. Print.

Shone, Tom. *Blockbuster: How the Jaws and Jedi Generation Turned Hollywood into a Boom-Town*. 2004. New York: Scribner's, 2005. Print.

Singer, Peter Warren. *Wired for War: The Robotics Revolution and Conflict in the 21st Century*. London: Penguin, 2009. Print.

Slusser, George, and Eric S. Rabkin. "Wars Old and New: The Changing Nature of Fictional Combat." *Fights of Fancy: Armed Conflict in Science Fiction and Fantasy*. Ed. George Slusser and Eric S. Rabkin. Athens: U of Georgia P, 1993. 1–11. Print.

Turse, Nick. "Bringing the War Home: The New Military-Industrial-Entertainment Complex at War and Play." *TomDispatch.com*. Oct. 16, 2003. Web. July 26, 2013. http://www.tomdispatch.com/post/1012/.

Walker, Dinah. "Trends in U.S. Military Spending." *Council on Foreign Relations*. Aug. 23, 2012. Web. July 26, 2013. http://www.cfr.org/defense-budget/trends-us-military-spending/p28855.

CHAPTER 26

ATOMIC CULTURE AND THE SPACE RACE

DAVID SEED

The echoes of the bombing of Hiroshima and Nagasaki reverberated throughout the Cold War decades because these events demonstrated both a new energy source and a weapon with unimaginable destructive force. The atomic age that followed 1945 displayed an ambivalence about whether to celebrate the former possibility or explore the negative potential of the latter. This ambivalence also characterized depictions of the space race, which veered between the extremes of disinterested scientific exploration on the one hand and the drive to militarize near space before the Soviet Union could do so on the other.

From the late 1940s to the 1980s, a subgenre of science fiction explored fears of nuclear war and an extensive body of fiction was generated (see Brians). Indeed, the subject had become so common by January 1952 that H. L. Gold, the editor of *Galaxy* magazine, complained: "Over 90% of stories submitted still nag away at atomic hydrogen and bacteriological war, the post-atomic world, reversion to barbarism, mutant children" (qtd. James 89). Over the decades that followed, numerous novels and films engaged with these dreaded possibilities, each with its own diagnosis to offer. Bernard Wolfe's *Limbo* (1952) was a black comedy canvassing attempts to neutralize aggression in the aftermath of a nuclear war—by, for example, amputating limbs. Walter M. Miller Jr.'s *A Canticle for Leibowitz* (19597) depicts a rupturing of history that triggers a rerun of events culminating in yet another war. Stanley Kubrick's 1964 film *Dr. Strangelove* famously paints the desire to deploy nuclear weapons as a self-destructive displacement of the sexual instinct. And Russell Hoban's *Riddley Walker* (1980) explores the consequences of atomic war not merely as a relapse into social barbarism but as an act of unimaginable violence committed against language itself.

By contrast with these grim scenarios, comic books during the 1960s began to promote characters positively empowered by radiation (see Szasz). The Atomic Knights, who first appeared in *Strange Adventures* in 1960, battled against the tyrannous Black Baron in the wake of the Hydrogen War of 1986. Marvel's Fantastic Four acquire superhuman powers after exposure to cosmic rays. Doctor Solar of Golden Key comics disintegrated after a nuclear accident, but by sheer force of will reassembles himself to become a crimefighter. And more famously, the physicist Dr. Bruce Banner develops a capacity to transform himself into the Incredible Hulk after the accidental detonation of a gamma bomb. Most narratives of nuclear war imply its inevitability, but the fact that the series just described appeared during some of the worst crises of the Cold War suggests that compensatory fantasies were emerging that revised radiation into a positive, enabling force that could work toward the benefit of society.

From the very beginning of the atomic age, government-sponsored attempts were made to reassure the public over the threat of attack. *Duck and Cover* (1952), the first civil-defense film, attempted to combine entertainment and direct instruction. The opening cartoon sequence, showing Bert the Turtle practising caution when attacked, was designed to reinforce drills in schools and to integrate civil-defense concepts within the daily life of the young. In a similar spirit, *Life* magazine in 1959 co-sponsored the experiment of a Miami couple to spend their honeymoon in an underground fallout shelter; though such shelters were quite rare, they were covered extensively in the popular media during the period (Boyer 353). Some early treatments of atomic energy attempted to project a blandly reassuring line, as in Walt Disney's 1957 film *Our Friend the Atom*, where the military application of the new technology is played down as far as possible. Disney himself appeared near the beginning to proclaim that "the atom is our future"; an extended lesson from the German physicist (and former Luftwaffe pilot) Heinz Haber followed on the unique potential of the atom. The book accompanying the film made the opposing possibilities of the atom starkly evident by juxtaposing the familiar image of a mushroom cloud alongside a text declaring that the atom made a "superb villain" but that it was up to humanity to give the atomic story a happy ending. Disney also engaged in an extended collaboration with Wernher von Braun, who served as technical adviser on several educational films, including *Man and the Moon* (1955), which further popularized the idea of space travel. Disney's promotion of von Braun, combined with the rocket scientist's prominent role at NASA, made him both a celebrity and, given his Nazi past, an easy target for satirical humor, such as Tom Lehrer's 1965 song portraying him as a cynical opportunist "ruled by expedience"— Von Braun, according to Arthur C. Clarke, was not amused (Neufeld 407).

In the period following the end of the Second World War, the atomic bomb was assimilated into consumer culture. Within weeks of the Hiroshima bombing, *Life* magazine promoted model Linda Christian as an "anatomic bomb," and in the same spirit the two-piece bikini swimsuit was named after the Pacific atoll where bombs were being tested in 1946, presumably due to their explosive potential for susceptible males. A similar process of assimilation can be witnessed in pop songs like Bill Haley and the Comets' "Thirteen Women (And Only One Man in Town)," from 1954, where the male singer dreams that an H-bomb has wiped out all other men, leaving him his pick of the female survivors. Andy Warhol's 1965 silkscreen *Atomic Bomb* placed the familiar mushroom cloud alongside other cultural icons of the period similarly enshrined by the artist, such as Elvis and Marilyn Monroe. Warhol's composition features five panels with negative images of the nuclear cloud increasing in number until the bottom row is almost indistinguishable darkness. These examples suggest that atomic themes became routine ingredients in postwar popular (and Pop) culture, its potentially threatening dimensions neutralized by its taming as fashion, song, or mere image.

Although satires of the atomic age had begun to appear as early as 1949 with Richard M. Field's novel *Alice's Adventures in Atomland in the Plastic Age*, it was not until the late 1950s that skepticism about civil defense began to be really evident. Jules Feiffer's 1959 cartoon sequence "Boom" ironically revealed the gaps between government statements that nuclear tests were safe and mounting anxieties about the danger of fallout. During the 1961 Berlin crisis, President John Kennedy mounted a fresh campaign for fallout shelters, but that same year an episode of Rod Serling's TV series *The Twilight Zone* graphically demonstrated the psychological consequences of the nuclear threat: in "The Shelter," a radio announcement that the United States may be under attack throws a group of dinner guests into total panic. That same year, a sketch by Marvin Kitman in Paul Krassner's satirical magazine *The Realist* ridiculed the government line of calm, practical civil-defense measures: "How I Fortified My Family Fallout Shelter" grotesquely parodies the do-it-yourself tradition promoted throughout the 1950s by presenting the real enemy as a family's neighbors, whose aggression can only be fended off by seeding the family lawn with mines and mounting machine guns at the shelter entrance. The most powerful satire of official treatments of the atomic age, however, remains the 1982 "mockumentary" film *The Atomic Cafe*, which assembles a montage of hilariously straight-faced civil-defense footage and other sequences, including grotesque attempts to incorporate atom-bomb imagery into cultural products as diverse as cocktails, pop songs, and do-it-yourself shelters. The film builds up to a grim climax, ending with massive nuclear detonations that shed a grimly ironic light on the viability and value of civil-defense measures.

The "space race" between the United States and the Soviet Union is conventionally taken to begin in 1957 with the launch of the *Sputnik 1* satellite and to have ended in the 1970s with the collaborations over the international space station. The concept of such a race dates back at least to 1945, however, implicit in the tension between the parallel developments of intercontinental ballistic missiles and space exploration, between the conflicting uses of the rocket as weapon and as vehicle. In classic SF descriptions of nuclear war such as Ray Bradbury's *The Martian Chronicles* (1950) or Miller's *A Canticle for Leibowitz*, the rocket serves both purposes: as a latter-day ark taking survivors into space in search of a refuge, an escape from a planet in the process of succumbing to a global spasm of missile-borne destruction. Furthermore, there were in effect two races simultaneously ongoing—to produce ever more destructive bombs and to control near space. The first of these accelerated with the 1949 detonation of an atomic bomb by the Soviet Union, reinvigorating what H. Bruce Franklin has called the "myth of the superweapon that would give global hegemony to a single nation" in pursuit of an elusive ultimate security (169). The resulting tensions could be perceived in the complexly overlapping agendas of military and astronautic development.

From a place of cultural marginality, science fiction came to occupy a central position, during the postwar decades, as a source of fictional and cinematic representations of space travel, even playing a role in the evolution of the relevant technology. Historians of the space race, such as Walter A. McDougall and Deborah Cadbury, have tended to ignore or downplay this crossover, yet it was evident in, for example, the career of Robert A. Heinlein, who toward the end of World War II was not only writing pathbreaking SF but also working in the aeronautical engineering section of the US Navy. As soon as the news broke about the atomic bombings of Japan, Heinlein with considerable prescience drafted a naval memorandum declaring that warfare had changed forever and that work should start immediately on a moon rocket applying V-2 technology, which would give "unique prestige" to the United States (Patterson 355). Unbeknownst to him, however, this very process was already under way through Operation Paperclip, the US program for recruiting Nazi rocket scientists and transporting them to sites such as Los Alamos, New Mexico, near the White Sands Proving Grounds where the original Trinity bomb was detonated (see Lasby).

Heinlein worked closely with director George Pal, one of the major SF filmmakers of the Cold War era, on the 1950 film *Destination Moon*, which presents one of the earliest cinematic expressions of the space race. Typical of Heinlein's fiction, the film depicts individuals whose strong patriotic commitment can achieve almost anything—in this case, extra-orbital flight. Two characters introduced at the outset of the film represent technology (the director of the project) and the military (a general who has arranged the appropriations), but their rocket fails to take off. The main opponents of the moon shot are what the general describes as "filthy, Godless Commies," a shadowy amorphous group whose agents attempt to forestall the second, successful launch. Once in space, the crew learn that the Soviet Union has brought forward a proposal for the Moon to be declared United Nations property. The military member of the crew (in Heinlein's novella adaptation of the screenplay, an admiral) insists: "This is not an attempt to insure the neutrality of the Moon; this is the same double-talk they used to stop world control of atomics. The commissars simply want to tie us up in legalisms until they have time to get to the Moon. We'll wake up one morning to find Russia with a base on the Moon and us with none—and World War Three will be over before it starts" (155). The deeply reductive logic of the Cold War is clear in these sentences: the voyage is a race against time to claim the Moon for the United States; the rocket resembles a missile but is using atomic power benignly to power its flight; and the Moon is perceived as a displaced or extended site for political power plays taking place on Earth. The filming of *Destination Moon* began in November 1949, some three months after the Soviet Union tested its first atomic bomb. A publicity brochure made the implication clear by declaring: "He who controls the Moon controls the Earth" (Heinlein n.p.). This very phrase was to be used in 1958 by a US Air Force brigadier in making his case for a lunar military base (McCurdy 84).

Destination Moon was released amidst a massive publicity campaign that proclaimed its unique authenticity and, even more important, its predictive value in projecting a flight that would actually take place within the next 10 to 15 years. The publicity hammered home the point that "other nations" may already be well at work preparing just such a rocket. According to William E. Burrows, one of the few historians to give SF a central place in Cold War debates over space, the film was part of a multipronged effort by "rocket diehards" to impel the US government to action by raising the specter of "foreign competition" (138). Thus, the claim that the crisis induced by the Soviets' launch of *Sputnik 1* in 1957 marks the beginning of the space race ignores the fact that *Destination Moon* had already popularized the notion of space travel against the backdrop of superpower rivalries, and Heinlein's name was prominent in the film's publicity not only as a leading SF author but also as a technical adviser. In 1953 he supplied the script for Richard Talmadge's *Project Moon Base*, which opens with a legend declaring the need for such a remote station: "By 1954, atom bombs and interconontinental rockets had made it a necessity.... By 1970, the Space Station had been built and free men were reaching for the Moon to consolidate the safety of the Free World." The publicity for *Destination Moon* was obviously aimed at selling the movie, but Heinlein had made the issue of fundraising for space flight central to his 1950 novella "The Man Who Sold the Moon," in which an American business tycoon mounts a campaign for a moonshot to stave off his nightmare that the Soviets will get there first.

The popular media of the early 1950s played their part in presenting space travel as an essential national enterprise. *Collier's* magazine ran features on the topic with contributions from von Braun and Willy Ley, a German rocket scientist who had close links with the SF community, including penning a long-running science column for *Galaxy* magazine. The *Collier's* articles were collected in the 1952 volume *Across the Space Frontier*, edited by Cornelius Ryan, whose introduction stressed that more was involved than simply educating the public on space. Instead, he declared, "This book is an urgent warning that the United States should immediately embark on a long-range development programme to secure for the West 'space superiority,' since a ruthless power established on a space station could actually subjugate the peoples of the world" (xiii). This possibility is woven into von Braun's own SF novel, *Project Mars* (written in 1949 but not published until 2006), where space exploration can only take place once there is peace on Earth. Here, a third world war in the 1970s has led to the defeat of the Eastern bloc, and Western hegemony is maintained by an orbiting military satellite described as the "Goddess of a new, strong peace" (11). Cold War anxieties about security focused obsessively on the skies, with the concluding lines from the 1951 film *The Thing from Another World* becoming something of a catch-phrase for the period: "Tell the world, tell everyone. Watch the skies, everywhere! Keep looking. Keep watching the skies!" The Soviet launch of *Sputnik 1* only confirmed these fears in its symbolic challenge to American presumption of technological supremacy.

In the wake of *Sputnik*, potential developments in satellite and space technology were explored in the fiction of Jeff Sutton, who turned to writing after serving as an engineer with Consolidated Aircraft in San Diego. His initial effort, *First on the Moon* (1958), outlines a situation of conflict between the superpowers: since anatomic exchange would be unacceptably destructive, there is a tacit agreement that the struggle can take any form short of outright war. In Sutton's novel, the stakes are even higher than just the Moon because reaching that planet would simply be the "first step in the world race for control of the Solar System" (13). Only the resourcefulness of the crew saves the mission from Communist sabotage, and the captain reflects with patriotic satisfaction that "an atom-powered space ship spelled complete victory over the Eastern World.... Man was on his way to the stars" (149), a whole new vista of future colonization opening up before him.

Sutton was well aware of the complex intertwining of space exploration with nuclear rivalry between the superpowers. His novel *Bombs in Orbit* (1959) describes a situation where competition for military supremacy in near space has resulted in an undeclared war in which spy vessels are pitted against each other. The novel opens with the Soviet launch of a new satellite with sophisticated radar and an accompanying facility to mount nuclear attacks from space. *Spy Eye*, however, is more than just a satellite; as a US officer explains, "It's a weapon, a deadly weapon, a giant electronic laboratory hoisted into the sky" (16). The novel thus extrapolates *Sputnik* according to the logic of the space race, the sole issue being whether and how the satellite can be disabled. Sutton's later novel *H-Bomb Over America* (1967) follows a similar scenario in which renegade Soviets opposed to detente launch an orbital missile.

Sutton was one of the first novelists to try to describe in detail the experience of flying to the Moon. *Apollo At Go*—published in 1963, two years after the Apollo program began—is unusual because the author detaches the moonshot from superpower rivalry and concentrates instead on the sensations of the astronauts. Explicitly positioning his narrative (which takes place in 1969) in relationship to recent events like the *Sputnik* launch and John Glenn's 1962 orbital flight around Earth, Sutton offers, in effect, a piece of anticipatory reportage designed to substantiate the NASA program director's assertion in the novel that "Apollo is a symbol of our scientific and industrial capacity, the determination and know-how of its people—the willingness to sacrifice" (35). There is still a strongly nationalistic impetus to the narrative, but it is dramatized as a struggle against physical dangers and technological difficulties rather than against the sinister actions of a rival power.

Sutton's evocation of space exploration uses one of the most familiar tropes of this period—namely, space as a new frontier, which aligned astronautics with grand narratives of US history such as manifest destiny. The television series *Star Trek* debuted in 1966 as a transposed Western, what creator Gene Roddenberry referred to as a "wagon train to the stars" (qtd. Telotte 15). The series dramatized the open-ended voyage of the starship *USS Enterprise*, which carried the same name as an enormous nuclear-powered aircraft carrier launched in 1960. The crew's mission, announced at the opening of each episode, was "to boldly go where no man has gone before," a phrase probably taken from the 1958 White House booklet *Introduction to Outer Space*, issued after the *Sputnik* crisis, which identifies a "compelling urge of man to explore and to discover, the thrust of curiosity that leads men to try to go where no one has gone before" (President's Science Advisory).

Apart from demonstrating the circulation of SF tropes within the culture, *Star Trek* (which numbered SF authors Harlan Ellison and Theodore Sturgeon among its script writers) also shared its optimistic evocation of space travel with the most famous independent commentator of the period, Arthur C. Clarke, whose early works—both fiction and nonfiction—had helped to educate readers on the scientific issues involved in space exploration. What gives Clarke's scientific writings, in particular, their utopian dimension is his divorce of "science" from the massive funding sources necessary to promote this kind of research. In the chapter he added to his 1951 volume *The Exploration of Space* upon its reprinting in 1958, Clarke at least recognizes the complications arising from the militarization of space: a traditional icon of hope within SF (the rocket) has become instead part of a global arms race. In his words,

> It is one of the tragic ironies of our age that the rocket, which could have been the symbol of humanity's aspirations for the stars, has become one of the weapons threatening to destroy civilization. . . . [A]lmost all research on rockets is now carried out by military establishments and is covered by various security classifications. (182–83)

The result is a predicament even more severe than that raised by atomic energy—namely, "separating the military and the peaceful uses of rockets" (183).

Clarke's steadfast opposition to the political alignments of the Cold War can be seen clearly in his 1953 novel *Childhood's End*, which revisits the traditional SF subject of invasion from space. Set in the 1980s, the novel opens with a conversation between a former Nazi rocket technologist and his American colleague in Army Technical Intelligence, with the latter revealing the worrying news that "the Russians are nearly level with us. They've got some sort of atomic drive—it may be even more efficient than ours." The German scientist Reinhold, a former worker at the V-2 plant at Peenemünde, draws the unavoidable conclusion: "The race is on—and we may not win it" (4). The story then cuts to an installation on Lake Baikal where an ex-colleague of Reinhold's is discussing Soviet technical progress with his Russian commissar. Clarke's paralleling of the two scenes reflects an internationalism rarely found in this sort of fiction, where instead the Soviet Union is usually demonized as a threatening alien force. Clarke's initial scenes are the prelude to a benign invasion by alien beings who become known as the "Overlords" and whose leader institutes a global ban on nuclear weapons. The Overlords thus embody an idealized intelligence that Clarke found lacking in the prevailing geopolitics of the Cold War.

Clarke's resistance to the militarization of space can be seen in the final version of *2001: A Space Odyssey* (1968), which he scripted. In the film, a grand narrative of evolution segues from the primeval era to the imminent future with the famous slow-motion shot of a Neolithic-era weapon gradually transforming into a spacecraft. In his 1970 log of the film, Jerome Agel includes a photograph of this craft with the caption: "Sunrise on Earth. Orbiting satellites carrying nuclear weapons make their rounds at end of Twentieth Century" (88). The 1965 screenplay was even more explicit, depicting an array of orbital missiles from the Soviet Union, United States, France, Germany, and China, with a voice-over proclaiming: "Hundreds of giant bombs had been placed in perpetual orbit above the Earth. They were capable of incinerating the entire Earth's surface from an altitude of 100 miles" (Kubrick and Clarke). As Kubrick's plans for the film evolved, he removed the military dimension of the plot, probably because of the too-obvious echoes this would have carried of his previous film, *Dr. Strangelove*, though traces of this theme can still be found in Clarke's novel version.

Although budgetary considerations drastically curtailed the space race during the 1970s, the controversy sparked by President Reagan's announcement of the Strategic Defense Initiative in 1983 could be seen as a renewal of that race with the goal of militarily controlling near space. A leading figure in this dispute was SF novelist Jerry Pournelle, who had a background in systems engineering and political science. His co-authored (with Stefan T. Possony) book *The Strategy of Technology* (1970) opens with the arresting declaration that "[t]he United States is at war" (1)—a technological struggle against the Soviet Union that commenced in 1945 and takes place everywhere, including translunar space. Since 1970 Pournelle has been a tireless commentator on politics and technology, as well as the author of a series of right-wing military-SF novels. He reportedly played a part in composing Reagan's 1983 speech advocating SDI, later popularly known as "Star Wars." In 1984 Pournelle and fellow SF writer Dean Ing published *Mutual Assured Survival*, a book that came with a ringing endorsement from Reagan on its back cover. Ing had served in the US Air Force and held a chair in communications theory at the University of Oregon before turning to SF. The volume's title seeks to reverse the pessimism of the policy of "Mutual Assured Destruction" (or MAD), which had informed American nuclear strategy since the late 1950s. Pournelle and Ing argue that the militarization of space took place as soon as intercontinental ballistic missiles were deployed and claim that, despite ineffective treaties, "the Soviets currently have the world's only operational space weapons, and are expanding broad efforts to achieve military dominance of near-Earth space" (99).

The SF writers associated with the SDI project and the related Citizens' Advisory Council on National Space Policy included, on top of Pournelle and Ing, Greg Bear, Gregory Benford, Larry Niven, and that formative figure in postwar American SF, Robert Heinlein. These and other SF authors collectively reminded readers during the 1980s that the space race was just as urgent as it was when it started. Bear's 1985 novel *Eon* features, first, a limited nuclear war (the "Little Death") and then a full-scale one ("The Death"), arising from the Soviet Union's realization in the late 1980s of its imminent defeat in the "war of technology" (102); even in the novel's present (the story is set in 2005), war remains a danger. Similarly, Ben Bova's *Privateers* (1985) evokes a near future where the United States has been compelled to leave NATO and space is now controlled by the Soviet Union. Because America has collapsed, the only hope for the future lies with a millionaire industrialist who orchestrates a plan to destroy Soviet military power in space. *Privateers* makes a case for the military, industrial, and political continuation of the space program, which had lapsed before the novel opens. A number of SF texts connected with the SDI project reanimate the trope of the frontier, which by the 1980s had become a standard feature in the vocabulary of space exploration, bringing out its military implications even more fully. In his writings on space, Pournelle repeatedly evokes a national tradition of appropriating territory, as if to suggest that ultimately the space program is merely continuing the plans of the Founding Fathers.

The consequence of the space race in general and the Apollo program specifically was that space travel entered the cultural mainstream and was no longer the exclusive concern of science fiction. This change was reflected in treatments of the subject by writers outside the genre. An early example can be seen in John Hersey's 1960 novel *The Child Buyer*. Taking the form of a legislative hearing into a conspiracy by a US company called United Lymphomilloid to purchase an unusually bright male child for a top-secret government project (a company representative tells the committee, starkly, "I buy brains" [33]), the novel critiques this commodification of scientifically gifted children in the wake of the *Sputnik* crisis. During the 1970s, Norman Mailer and Tom Wolfe wrote celebrated quasi-journalistic accounts of the space program. Mailer's *Of A Fire on the Moon* (1970) partly reports on the buildup toward the *Apollo 11* mission and partly engages in an extended reflection on the place of technology in American culture. Far from engaging in celebration, Mailer speculates on a latent streak of fascism in the whole enterprise, commenting pointedly on the assimilation of Nazi scientists like von Braun into the US space program: "Was the conquest of space . . . the unique and grand avenue for the new totalitarian?" (65). Mailer's Freudian scrutiny of the technocratic psyche was even more elaborately developed later in the decade by Thomas Pynchon, whose 1973 novel *Gravity's Rainbow* sets its main action during the 1945 transition from the Nazi V-2 program to Cold War–era US military research. The novel's labyrinthine plot moves backward to explore the German cultural matrix that spawned both rocket technology and such SF films as Fritz Lang's *Frau im Mond* (Woman in the Moon, 1929). The underground rocket assembly plant at Nordhausen is described by Pynchon in science-fictional terms—as a "Raketen-Stadt" (Rocket City) where dreamy fantasy conspires with the latest in military technology. The novel thematically links the V-2 with the bombing of Hiroshima, thus anticipating the postwar merger of both systems in the form of ICBMs (which descend at the close in an orgasmic paroxysm of destruction reminiscent of the closing sequences of *Dr. Strangelove*).

Tom Wolfe also draws on SF in his 1979 investigation of the "psychological mystery" (xiv) of why men agreed to become astronauts, *The Right Stuff*, a profile in courage framed within the evolution of the space program. In the wake of the *Sputnik* launch, Wolfe stresses the unnerving ability the Soviets demonstrated to anticipate every aim of the United States with a skill amounting to "sorcery" (55), made all the more mysterious by their refusal to disclose any information about their projects. In order to summon a figure embodying this unnerving ability, Wolfe draws on Yevgeny Zamyatin's 1921 dystopian novel *We*: the "Builder of the Integral" (55–56), accordingly, becomes the shadowy personification of the Soviet space program who dogs the activities of NASA throughout *The Right Stuff* and whose sinister background presence adds to the urgency of the Apollo launch. The same mode of reportage informs James A. Michener's 1982 novel *Space*, which traces the history of the space program, drawing on Michener's own experience on NASA's Advisory Council.

Other writers followed Mailer and Pynchon in refusing to go along with the technocratic hype surrounding the space race. In a facetious sketch, "The Moon-shot Scandal," Terry Southern (co-author, with Kubrick, of the *Dr. Strangelove* screenplay) set out to question the assumption that *"everything* which occurs in regard to these American spaceshots is immediately known by the entire public" (213; emphasis in original). Southern's "exposé" concerns a 1961 launch during which five astronauts get into a gay argument (complete with cross-dressing) so severe that the spacecraft goes off course into outer space. The primary target of Southern's brief sketch is the reverential decorum associated with the space program in much public coverage, but he was also raising an issue that other writers addressed: the fear that some astronauts may have perished in unreported missions or that survivors may have suffered psychological damage.

The latter possibility is dramatized in Barry N. Malzberg's award-winning SF novel *Beyond Apollo* (1972), which assembles the fragmentary reflections of an astronaut who has flown on a mission to Venus. Sometimes referring to himself in the third person, Harry Evans repeatedly states his intention of writing an authentic novel about his mission that will tell the whole truth for the first time. In Malzberg's future history, the Moon program has already been abandoned, replaced by Mars and then Venus as target planets. Evans displays a disturbingly erratic mindset, making it virtually impossible to decide which of his statements are reliable: the narrative comes directly from the astronaut's wavering consciousness, unlike the similar space-age tales of Jeff Sutton and Arthur C. Clarke, whose anonymous narrators adopt an un-ironic pose of serene scientific rationalism. Malzberg's novel provoked controversy when it was published because it undermined many of the pieties then circulating about the space program: the "disinterested" impulse to explore, the patriotic commitment to national values, unquestioned heroism. Very early in the novel, Evans's words suggest that he has become unhinged as a result of his voyage and may even have killed the ship's captain. His training has rendered him virtually impotent, and he simultaneously dismisses SF tropes while at the same time believing in them: his Venusians, for example, are rational creatures challenging the astronauts' actions through thought projection. Malzberg destabilizes his narrative so thoroughly that routine statements about space exploration begin to sound like diseased fantasy.

J. G. Ballard's stories about astronauts, published throughout the 1960s and 1970s and collected in 1988 as *Memories of the Space Age*, have a similar effect, although the fictional strategies they follow are quite different. As early as 1962, Ballard registered his sense that the space age would be a temporary phenomenon by writing as its archaeologist. The vast majority of narratives discussed in this chapter propel the reader's imagination forward to a future of unlimited exploration and development, but for Ballard these hopes and plans have already died. Not only have the rocket gantries begun to rust, but also the "stars" observed from Earth now include orbiting capsules carrying the corpses of dead astronauts. Occasionally, a capsule crashes, at which point "relic hunters" crounge for macabre mementoes of a lost enterprise (70). Ballard repeatedly evokes the space age as a period of cultic obsession, as if it had been a temporary religion now perceived only through the dim traces it has left on the landscape and in the skies. A former astronaut, now the inmate of a psychiatric clinic, gives a pathological interpretation of man's desire for space travel as an "evolutionary crime, a breach of the rules governing his tenancy of the universe, and of the laws of time and space" (108). Ballard does not exactly endorse this viewpoint, but he does repeatedly hint that the space age, despite its surface scientism, was deeply structured by subconscious, irrational impulses. He also contradicts the grand evolutionary narrative promoted by figures like Arthur C. Clarke, describing instead how time at Cape Kennedy has frozen or even "moved into reverse" (151).

In recent years, more technophilic hard-SF writers have taken exception to Ballard's pessimism. In 1999 Gregory Benford's *The Martian Race* attempted to recapture the halcyon days of aeronautics, but quite independently of any superpower struggle: the "race" in Benford's title refers exclusively to the heroic scientific impulse behind Martian exploration. By contrast, Bruce Sterling, looking back more critically, has paid tribute to Ballard's unique ability to stand apart from the rhetoric of the period, which generated rah-rah slogans such as "Science, the Endless Frontier" or "Storming the Cosmos." Sterling comments: "The slogans seemed to emanate from every corner of the ideological compass at the time, but in retrospect they can be recognized as notes in a single piece of period music, a brassy modernist rant." It is a measure of how distanced and disenchanted Sterling clearly feels with the grandiose promises of the space age that he should reduce the period solely to a handful of catch-phrases. In any event, during that heady era, the dreams of SF's pulp infancy were—however partially and fleetingly—fulfilled, giving the genre a cultural centrality it never had before, and has perhaps not had since.

Works Cited

Agel, Jerome. *The Making of Kubrick's 2001*. New York: Signet, 1970. Print.
Ballard, J. G. *Memories of the Space Age*. Sauk City, WI: Arkham House, 1988. Print.
Bear, Greg. *Eon*. New York: Tor, 1985. Print.
Bova, Ben. *Privateers*. New York: Tor, 1985. Print.
Boyer, Paul. *By the Bomb's Early Light: American Thought and Culture at the Dawn of the Atomic Age*. 1985. Chapel Hill: UP of North Carolina, 1994. Print.
Brians, Paul. *Nuclear Holocausts: Atomic War in Fiction, 1895–1984*. Kent, OH: Kent State UP, 1987. Print.
Burrows, William E. *This New Ocean: The Story of the First Space Age*. New York: Random House, 1998. Print.
Cadbury, Deborah. *Space Race: The Epic Battle Between America and the Soviet Union for Dominion of Space*. New York: HarperCollins, 2006. Print.
Clarke, Arthur C. *Childhood's End*. New York: Harcourt Brace and World, 1953. Print.
_____. *The Exploration of Space*. 1951. London: Penguin, 1958. Print.
_____. *2001: A Space Odyssey*. London: Hutchinson, 1968. Print.
Franklin, H. Bruce. *War Stars: The Superweapon and the American Imagination*. 1988. Rev. ed. Amherst: U of Massachusetts P, 2008. Print.

Heinlein, Robert A. *Destination Moon*. 1950. Boston: Gregg, 1979. Print.
Hersey, John. *The Child Buyer*. London: Hamish Hamilton, 1962. Print.
James, Edward. *Science Fiction in the 20th Century*. New York: Oxford UP, 1997. Print.
Kitman, Marvin. "How I Fortified My Family Fallout Shelter." *The Realist* 30 (Dec. 1961). Web. July 26, 2013. http://www.ep.tc/realist/30/index.html.
Kubrick, Stanley, and Arthur C. Clark [sic]. "The 2001 Screenplay (1965)." *The Kubrick Site*. Web. July 26, 2013. http://www.visual-memory.co.uk/amk/doc/0057.html.
Lasby, Clarence G. *Project Paperclip: German Scientists and the Cold War*. New York: Atheneum, 1971. Print.
Mailer, Norman *Of a Fire on the* Moon. 1970. New York: Signet, 1971. Print.
Malzberg, Barry N. *Beyond Apollo*. New York: Random House, 1972. Print.
McCurdy, Howard E. *Space and the American Imagination*. 1997. 2nd ed. Baltimore: Johns Hopkins UP, 2011. Print.
McDougall, Walter A. *The Heavens and the Earth: A Political History of the Space Age*. 1985. Baltimore: Johns Hopkins UP, 1997. Print.
Neufeld, Michael J. *Von Braun: Dreamer of Space, Engineer of War*. 2007. New York: Vintage, 2008. Print.
Patterson, William H. *Robert A. Heinlein*. Vol. 1: *Learning Curve 1907–1948*. New York: Tor, 2010. Print.
Possony, Stefan T., and J. E. Pournelle. *The Strategy of Technology: Winning the Decisive War*. Cambridge, MA: UP of Cambridge, 1970. Print.
Pournelle, Jerry E., and Dean Ing. *Mutual Assured Survival*. New York: Baen, 1984. Print.
President's Science Advisory Committee. *Introduction to Outer Space*. White House. March 26, 1958. *FAS: Space Policy Project*. Web. July 26, 2013. http://www.fas.org/spp/guide/usa/intro1958.html.
Pynchon, Thomas. *Gravity's Rainbow*. 1973. New York: Penguin, 1987. Print.
Ryan, Cornelius. "Introduction." *Across the Space Frontier*. Ed. Cornelius Ryan. London: Sidgwick and Jackson, 1952. xi–xiv. Print.
Southern, Terry. "The Moon-shot Scandal." *Red-Dirt Marijuana and Other Tastes*. 1967. New York: Citadel, 1990. 213–16. Print.
Sterling, Bruce. "Catscan 14: Memories of the Space Age". 1996. *Libros*. Web. July 26, 2013. http://www.libros.am/book/read/id/106004/slug/essays-catscan-columns.
Sutton, Jeff. *Apollo At Go*. New York: Ace, 1963. Print.
———. *Bombs in Orbit*. New York: Ace, 1959. Print.
———. *First on the Moon*. New York: Ace, 1958. Print.
Szasz, Ferenc M. "Atomic Comics: The Comic Book Industry Confronts the Nuclear Age." *Atomic Culture: How We Learned to Stop Worrying and Love the Bomb*. Ed. Scott C. Zeman and Micahel A. Amundson. Boulder: UP of Colorado, 2004. 11–32. Print.
Telotte, J. P. "Introduction: The Trajectory of Science Fiction Television." *The Essential Science Fiction Television Reader*. Ed. J. P. Telotte. Lexington: U of Kentucky P, 2008. 1–34. Print.
von Braun, Wernher. *Project Mars: A Technical Tale*. Trans. Henry J. White. Burlington, ON: Apogee, 2006. Print.
Wolfe, Tom. *The Right Stuff*. 1979. New York: Bantam, 1980. Print.

CHAPTER 27

UFOS, SCIENTOLOGY, AND OTHER SF RELIGIONS

GREGORY L. REECE

ALONGSIDE the development of the literary genre known as science fiction, a number of religious movements have arisen, especially since the 1950s, which share many of that genre's basic features and conventions. While it is certainly the case that "science fiction religions" have been directly influenced by the SF genre, it is probably best to understand the growth and development of both SF and the religious movements that seem to mirror its themes as products of common cultural factors. Granted, L. Ron Hubbard, the founder of Scientology, had deep roots in the SF community, and his early writings on Dianetics were promoted by influential SF editor John W. Campbell Jr. Likewise, the social phenomena associated with flying saucers were influenced by the writings of Richard Shaver and Ray Palmer in the pages of the pulp magazine *Amazing Stories*. Furthermore, George Adamski, arguably the first and perhaps most influential of the UFO contactees, was undoubtedly influenced by the 1951 science fiction film *The Day the Earth Stood Still* (Moseley and Pflock 66). It is also true, however, that SF itself, from its earliest days, drew upon religious sources for inspiration, most significantly the work of eighteenth-century Swedish theologian Emmanuel Swedenborg, who claimed contact with extraterrestrials long before such ideas became a common theme for fiction writers, and from the theosophical ideas expressed by Madame Blavatsky and others in the nineteenth century. Both science fiction and the religious movements in question came of age at a time when scientific discovery and technological advancement were at the forefront of many people's thoughts, worries, and dreams. The development of SF as a literary genre is inextricable from the scientific and technological changes that swept the world during the twentieth century, as is the development of religious movements seeking to come to terms with those very same changes. It is probably most accurate to say that the relationship between the two phenomena is a complementary, rather than a directly causal, one.

There are at least four SF-related themes that are shared, in varying degrees, across many religious movements that developed in the mid- and late twentieth century. First, these religious movements claim contact, in one form or another, with extraterrestrial entities. Second, these movements feature narratives that place alien contact in a broader context of extraterrestrial civilizations and cosmic histories. Third, these religions emphasize the evolutionary progress of the human species and its related dangers. Fourth, these religious movements place an emphasis on innovative "futuristic" technologies that promise alleviation of human problems and assistance in human evolution.

The first—and possibly defining—SF-related feature of the religious movements in question are their claims of contact with beings from other planets. Contact with these entities takes place in a variety of ways, most commonly (1) through physical encounters, (2) through the channeling of messages from outer space, and (3) through the recovery of lost memories, from both this life and past lives. Encounters of the first sort usually take place in the context of flying-saucer sightings or landings. Arguably, the first of these accounts was published in 1953 by George Adamski, along with co-author Desmond Leslie, in their book *Flying Saucers Have Landed*. Adamski described the interplanetary visitor Orthon as physically indistinguishable from an Earthman, albeit a youthful, fit, and attractive Earthman: he appeared to be around 5 feet, 6 inches tall, slender, with gray-green eyes and long, sandy-colored hair. Orthon claimed to be from the planet Venus. A year after Adamksi's account was published, two similar ones appeared: Daniel Fry's *The White Sands Incident* and Truman Bethurum's *Aboard a Flying Saucer*, and several more emerged over the next decade; indeed, Curtis Peebles, in his history of the UFO phenomenon, refers to this period as "The Contactee Era" (93–108). Bethurum's book claimed that the author had encountered an entire ship's crew of diminutive humanoids, including the female captain of the vessel, Aura Rhanes. According to Betherum's account, the vessel commanded by Captain Rhanes, a saucer some 300 feet in diameter, was known as *The Admiral's Scow* and traveled to Earth from its home planet of Clarion. Clarion, according to Captain Rhanes, is a planet in our solar system, but because of its position on the other side of our moon is always invisible from Earth.

While the extraterrestrials described by Adamski and Bethurum hailed from relatively nearby in the solar system, this is not the case for all contact reports. For example, Billy Meier a few decades later claimed contact with visitors known as the Pleiadians, or Plejaren. According to Meier, though the location of their home world lies in the direction of the constellation known as the Pleiades, the Plejaren are actually from a different space-time configuration light-years beyond the Pleiades themselves. Meier has claimed to receive telepathic messages providing a time and place for his meeting with Plejaren ships; once at the designated location, his body is reportedly lifted into the hovering craft. Meier claims to have interacted with hosts of representatives from the Plejaren civilization, most frequently with individuals named Ptaah, Samjase, and Quetzal (see Korff).

Not all of Meier's alleged contacts with extraterrestrials have been physical encounters with travelers aboard nuts-and-bolts flying saucers: he also has claimed telepathic contacts with the Plejaren. Indeed, many individuals and groups believe that their contacts with interplanetary messengers take place on the mental or spiritual plane rather than the physical one. According to the official history of the Urantia Brotherhood, for example, the original communications between founder William Sadler and extraterrestrials were delivered through the medium of a sleeping subject. The first transmission received claimed to be from a being that had traveled from a distant planet in order to observe Earth at close range. Information gathered from such sleep channeling, as well as from channeled writing, was published in 1955 as *The Urantia Book*. Likewise, George Van Tassel claimed to be able to channel messages from outer space: in July 1952 he purportedly received a message from Ashtar, identified as commandant of the Quadra sector, warning him of the dangers to Earth associated with the development of the hydrogen bomb (see Van Tassel). Van Tassel went on to organize a series of Giant Rock Spacecraft Conventions between 1953 and 1978 in Landers, California.

In addition to physical contact with space beings, usually travelers aboard flying saucers, and contact via mental telepathy or channeling, interplanetary contact has also been claimed through the recovery of lost memories. Sometimes this process reveals otherwise forgotten experiences from this life and sometimes from past lives. The first of these types of experiences is exemplified by the story of Betty and Barney Hill, who uncovered buried memories of their encounter with extraterrestrials only after participating in hypnotic therapy. Their story was made famous by the 1965 book *The Interrupted Journey: Two Lost Hours "Aboard a Flying Saucer"* by John G. Fuller and by the 1975 television film, *The UFO Incident*, that followed. The Hills's story sparked a bevy of abductee claims in the following decades, usually involving recovered memories of medical examinations by mysterious gray-skinned aliens who shared little information about their mission or their place of origin.

SF scholar Roger Luckhurst has referred to such stories as a "science-fictionalization of trauma" linked to the therapeutic practice of recovered memories, proposing that we

> situate alien abduction accounts within contemporary US memoro-politics. Without the space of possibility opened by this conjunction of a historically specific model of traumatic forgetting, and the attendant remodulation of techniques of recovery—from fantasy to hypnosis, from interpretation to affirmation—alien abduction narratives would not have materialized. (34)

This context may also account for even bolder claims about repressed memories, assertions that delving deeper into an individual's unconscious may lead to the discovery of lost memories of past lives. These sorts of claims characterize both the Unarius movement founded by Ernest and Ruth Norman and L. Ron Hubbard's Church of Scientology. Hubbard, for example, taught that auditing the current lifetime of a "preclear"—a therapeutic subject who has not yet been purified of the distorting "engrams" in his or her subconscious—can be a waste of time and effort if the "whole track technique" is not also used to delve into the past lives where these engrams may have originated (*Scientology* 5). Through the use of an E-meter (an "electropsychometer" that purportedly measures the galvanic response of the skin in order to determine unconscious states), a trained Scientology auditor may be able to uncover lost memories of previous lives, including ones lived in distant galaxies and on alien planets.

A second important SF-related feature of the religious movements in question is the inclusion of a narrative context or backstory, of varying degrees of complexity, to explain the presence of the interplanetary visitors. These narratives sometimes describe the political or cultural state of affairs in the larger galaxy, a state of affairs unknown to Earth dwellers prior to extraterrestrial contact. In other instances, these narratives describe past cosmic events that have an influence on the present-day state of affairs on Earth. These narratives take on a variety of forms and functions within the religions that accept them as true, including (1) providing origin stories that set the stage for an understanding of present conditions, (2) informing Earth dwellers of our place in cosmic societies and intergalactic organizations, and (3) making prophetic predictions concerning the future. An example from within the SF genre of precisely such a backstory, which may well have been inspirational for subsequent UFO accounts, was Richard Shaver's "I Remember Lemuria!" Published in the March 1945 issue of *Amazing Stories*, Shaver's account spun a tale of an advanced underground race that fled Earth for outer space, connecting with extraterrestrial civilizations, while leaving behind a handful of humanlike descendants as well as a horde of malign robotic drones (see Toronto). The editor of *Amazing*, Raymond Palmer, who would go on to edit the magazines *Fate* and *Flying Saucer* in the 1950s, actively cultivated what became known as the "Shaver Mysteries," thus fusing (as his biographer Fred Nadis points out) "the fantastic visions of science fiction and the separate but oddly similar components of occultist narratives" (94)—though SF fans were not always pleased with the results (Nadis 106–10).

The Church of Scientology provides one of the clearest examples of an intergalactic origin story, and one whose origins, as noted above, also derive from the SF genre via the career of the Church's founder. L. Ron Hubbard claimed that the narrative was revealed to him through the auditing process, which allowed him to retrieve buried memories from the distant past. According to the narrative, many millions of years ago, 76 planets were united as a galactic federation. This federation was ruled over by the evil Xenu who sought to alleviate overpopulation in the federation by transporting large numbers of his citizens to the planet Teegeeack, our Earth. Once on Earth, Xenu murdered the masses by dropping them from spaceships into open volcanoes and then blasting the volcanoes with hydrogen bombs. The souls, or "thetans," of the murdered were trapped, bound together into clusters, and implanted with misleading circuits and false memories. In time, these thetans became attached to the bodies of Earth's indigenous population, consequently imparting their traumatic implants to their host bodies. Multiple clusters of thetans could attach to a single human being, meaning that any one person could be covered with innumerable thetans. Opponents of Xenu waged a six-year war that finally resulted in his capture and imprisonment in a mountain prison, where he still remains.

The problems he caused are still with us, however. The only way to reverse this evil, as it turns out, is to engage in the auditing techniques of Scientology and thus remove the attached thetans and false implants from individuals. This cluster of thetans that are intertwined with human souls must be unraveled one at a time, requiring a lifelong process of auditing to become clear. In doing so, humans may be freed from delusions, physical infirmities, and psychological illnesses. The Xenu narrative provides an origin story to explain the presence of suffering and disease in human life and provides the framework for the church's mission in the world, to clear the earth of the evil influences and past terrors that continue to haunt us. Until recently, however, this narrative was known only to those who had risen in the ranks of the organization to the level known as Operating Thetan Level III—or OT III (see Reitman).

Orfeo Angelucci offered a related origin narrative in his 1955 book *The Secret of the Saucers*. Angelucci claimed to have learned from his extraterrestrial contact that Earth is the site of a cosmic battle between the forces of good and evil. At one time, a now lost planet circled the Sun, a planet that was the original home to the current inhabitants of Earth. Life on this other world was without pain, illness, sorrow, or death. In time, however, the residents of the lost world became proud and arrogant and began to war among themselves until they turned against the Great Giver of Life. In a final cataclysmic battle, they laid waste to their home world, shattering it into a million pieces. The remains of this world can be seen today in the asteroid belt that lies between the planets Mars and Jupiter. Angelluci learned that the residents of the lost world were reborn upon Earth and forced to live with pain and suffering in order to achieve redemption. Given time and a cycle of rebirth, all of Earth's residents may finally be saved. Extraterrestrial visitors, Angelluci was told, are coming to Earth to bring assistance in the struggle against evil, especially as the residents of Earth threaten to fall into the destructive practices of their home world. Angelluci claimed to have been called to help the fellowship of interplanetary visitors in their mission to redeem Earth.

Angelluci's assertion of the existence of an interplanetary society and of Earth's role in that society is also an example of a second feature of many of the central narratives of SF religions—namely, to inform Earth dwellers of our place in intergalactic society. Another instance of such a narrative is that told by George Van Tassel, in his claim of contact with Ashtar, a representative of the "Council of Seven Lights." Concerned with the development and potential use of the hydrogen bomb, Ashtar—in a plan reminiscent of the plot of *The Day the Earth Stood Still*—informed Van Tassel of the Council's willingness and readiness to take steps to stop the use of such weapons by the people of Earth (or Shan, as our planet was known). According to the transmissions received by Van Tassel, Ashtar's title was Commandant of the Vela Quadra Sector, section Schare. Among other ships in his fleet, Ashtar commanded three "sub-stations" within the "vortices" of the planet Shan, each prepared to release 500,000 "ventalas" if the need should arise. Ashtar claimed that his authority to take action came from Schnling, Lord God of the Third Dimensional Sector. Ashtar warned that though he did not have the ability to stop the people of Earth from detonating hydrogen bombs, the Council could be helpful in limiting the effects of those bombs and ensuring that total war did not break out upon the planet.

Van Tassel's relationship with Ashtar was not exclusive. Following his initial contact, the idea of "Ashtar Command," an organization dedicated to the enforcement of galactic law, became a common theme in many contactee accounts. In 1955 Elouise Moeller channeled Ashtar and revealed that ships from the Command would soon land on Earth in great numbers. In the 1970s and 1980s, Tuella (a.k.a. Thelma B. Terrill) reported, like Moeller, that a fleet of ships from the Ashtar Command was on its way to Earth to evacuate a select few humans in anticipation of a worldwide crisis. Yvonne Cole predicted that the Ashtar Command fleet would arrive on Earth in 1994 and trained her followers in the performance of tasks critical to the mission of the fleet. With the failure of the landing predictions, emphasis turned to what are called "lift-off experiences." According to Christopher Helland, in his history of the Ashtar Command phenomenon:

> In 1994 a small group of Ashtar Command members claimed that an extraordinary event had taken place: "the lift-off experience." What they communicated through the Ashtar network was that they had been taken off Earth and placed aboard the "ships of Light" that were circling the planet. . . . This involved the human consciousness (or, sometimes, the "etheric body") being raised from the physical dimension and transferred to the "Light ships." (176)

Websites provided the opportunity for participants in the lift-off experience to share their spiritual experiences aboard the Command fleet with one another. Participants described the spaceships and their crews in great detail. Since time seemed to flow at a different speed aboard the craft of the Ashtar Command, they believed that a few minutes of Earth-bound meditation was sufficient for extended missions aboard the starships.

The prediction of landings by Ashtar Command spaceships is an example of a third feature of the intergalactic narratives proffered by various religious movements: they supply predictions or prophecies concerning coming events of significant importance. As with claims made by members of the Ashtar Command movement, these prophecies usually include predictions concerning large-scale landings that will reveal the presence of the extraterrestrials to a global audience. The Unarius movement, founded in 1954 by Ernest Norman and his wife Ruth and centered in El Cajon, California, makes just such a claim. According to Unarian teaching, as articulated in Ruth Norman's *Preparation for the Landing*, an interstellar craft will one day come to Earth and land on the lost continent of Atlantis, which will rise from the depths of the Atlantic Ocean in anticipation of the event. The craft will hail from the planet Myton in the constellation of the Pleiades and will include a thousand scientists who will bring technology that will cleanse the air and restore Earth to its original purity. The visitors will also serve as moral exemplars, inspiring the citizens of Earth to overcome evil and aggression. When Earth has been purified, its citizens cleansed of their destructive ways and made ready to accept the offer to become a member of the Interplanetary Confederation, 33 spaceships with ambassadors from all Confederation planets will land together at the Unarian landing site in California and form Unarius Star Center One, an interplanetary university (see Tumminia and Kirkpatrick).

A third SF theme shared by many of these religious movements is the emphasis placed on human evolution and progress, and the present threats that stand in the way of that progress—a theme evident, as we have already seen, in the narratives of Angelluci, Van Tassel, and the Normans. The most common threat to human life and progress is, more often than not, identified with the development of atomic weapons and the consequent destruction of life on Earth. Other matters are sometimes identified as causes for worry, however. The Church of Scientology, for example, identifies traditional religion and psychiatry as two of the most pervasive threats to positive human growth and development, while contactee Howard Menger delivered a message related to the evils of Earth's diet, including the overconsumption of animal proteins, sugar, alcohol, tobacco, and, most important of all, fluoridated water.

Despite the dangers that threaten our progress, most SF religions emphasize the potential for positive growth and development. Often, the messages delivered to the contactees are messages of impending cosmic transformation. The human race, we are told, is on the verge of the next step in human evolution, in need of just a little assistance and oversight from our extraterrestrial brothers and sisters. This theme, for example, was central to the teachings of George Adamski. In his account of later contacts with visitors from beyond Earth, *Inside the Space Ships*, he told of the important things he learned from great teachers from the other planets. From one such mentor, for example, Adamski learned that life on Earth is but a stopping place for developing human souls:

> The first fact your people must realize is that the inhabitants of other worlds are not fundamentally different from Earth men. The purpose of life on other worlds is basically the same as yours. Inherent in all mankind, however deeply buried it may be, is the yearning to rise to something higher. Your school system on Earth is, in a sense, patterned after the universal progress of life. For in your schools you progress from grade to grade and from school to school, toward a higher and fuller education. In the same way, man progresses from planet to planet, and from system to system toward an ever higher understanding and evolvement in universal growth and service. (88–89)

Adamski asserted that the increasing frequency of visits by extraterrestrials was a result of their growing concern about the use of atomic weapons and the potential damage that humans might do to Earth and, indeed, the solar system. Travelers from Mars, Venus, and Jupiter came to Earth to assist in the evolution of the planet's citizens from the present stage of violent struggle to a stage of universal brotherhood and recognition of the divine presence in all life.

Similar themes can be found in the teachings of Claude Vorilhon, also known as Raël, and his followers, the Raëlians. Vorilhon claims to have been contacted by interplanetary visitors known as the Elohim who travel to Earth aboard flying saucers. These creatures revealed to Vorilhon that human beings had been created by the Elohim in the ancient past through the use of advanced genetic science. According to the Elohim, the present age is the age of apocalypse, the age when humans have reached a state of development advanced enough to accept the truth concerning their origins. Human development will move into the next stage when the Elohim return to Earth, an event that will not occur until humans achieve world peace (see Palmer).

> Human evolution was likewise a central claim for the tragic Heaven's Gate movement, founded by Marshall Herff Applewhite and Bonnie Lu Nettles. Applewhite and Nettles taught that extraterrestrials had visited the earth 2000 years ago but had found the human species too primitive for full contact and elevation to the "Next Level." Leaving behind a small number of their own to nudge the human race in the right direction, the aliens departed, planning to return again when Earth was better prepared. Applewhite and Nettles saw themselves as part of that ancient visitation, having been reincarnated throughout history to carry out their mission—a mission that was rapidly coming to a close. Seemingly abandoning the hope of preparing the entire human race for further evolution, Applewhite and Nettles fostered a small, close-knit community for which they developed a complex set of rules meant to assist their followers in achieving what they called "Human Individual Metamorphosis." Their followers were made to change their names, cut their hair, abandon their family and social connections, and abstain from sex, all in anticipation of the return to Earth of the ancient astronauts (see Bromley 37–40).

When the Halle-Bopp Comet was sighted in 1995, Applewhite pronounced that the returning spaceship was hidden in the comet's tail and would soon arrive to collect those who had completed their mission and those humans who had accepted their message. Applewhite described the arrival of Halle-Bopp as the "marker" that his group had been waiting for, heralding a mass "Exodus" or "Transit" to the Next Stage. At first he expected that he and his followers would board the arriving spacecraft in their physical bodies, but he worried that, before the ship could appear, he or members of his group might die or be incarcerated by the government. He wrote:

> It has always been our way to examine all possibilities, and be mentally prepared for whatever may come our way. For example, consider what happened at Masada around 73 A.D. A devout Jewish sect, after holding out against a siege by the Romans, to the best of their ability, and seeing that the murder, rape, and torture of their community was inevitable, determined that it was permissible for them to evacuate their bodies by a more dignified, and less agonizing method. We have thoroughly discussed this topic (of willful exit of the body under such conditions), and have mentally prepared ourselves for this possibility.... However, this act certainly does not need serious consideration at this time, and hopefully will not in the future. (qtd. Hoffman and Burke 202)

On March 29, 1997, 39 members of the group, including Applewhite (Nettles having died earlier of natural causes), were found dead in their San Diego home, dressed in matching clothes and shoes. They had apparently committed suicide as a means of leaving Earth and joining the space brothers who were coming for them.

The fourth theme prevalent in SF religions is an emphasis on alien or futuristic technology as a means to alleviate human problems and support human progress. Often this technology is related to the amazing flying saucers and spaceships that serve as transport for the extraterrestrials. In other cases, however, the technology is more directly connected to the redemption and progress of the human race. Van Tassel, for example, claimed to have received information from Ashtar, as well as from deceased scientist Nikola Tesla, concerning the construction of a device for the spiritual and physical rejuvenation of human beings and for facilitating contact with extraterrestrials: the Integratron, which stands unfinished today in Landers, California. The Integratron, when completed, would have drawn its power from an electromagnetic connection to the source of universal power and collected static electricity from the desert air, all for the purpose of reenergizing human cells, restoring their youthfulness and vigor, and prolonging the life of those who sought its therapy. Prolonged lifespans, Van Tassel taught, would make it possible for humans to rise to levels of spiritual maturity over the course of fewer incarnations (see Helland 168).

Vorilhon's Raëlian movement also proposes that human life can be improved by extraterrestrial technology. Unlike most other SF religions, Raëlians do not believe in the spiritual nature of human existence: for Raël and his followers, humans are purely material beings. Immortality is possible, however, not through the perpetuation of a soul or through reincarnation in new physical forms, but through genetic cloning, a technology they believed was first developed by the ancient aliens who were our creators. Raëlians believe that their own current technology allows the creation of human clones, something they have claimed to do successfully. The clone must then be subjected to rapid maturation, a technique Raël believes is within the grasp of his group and other human researchers in the near future. Next, the personality of an individual must be transferred to the clone, a process of memory "uploading" similar to claims made by the "transhumanist" Extropians (see Dery 300–08). For those who die prior to the perfection of these techniques by Earth scientists, all is not lost: the memories and DNA of everyone who has lived and died during the last thousand years are maintained on file by the Elohim. Vorhilon claims that when the Elohim return to Earth, cloning technology will be used to restore life to the dead.

The Church of Scientology illustrates the importance of futuristic technology perhaps better than any other religious group. The Church envisions its entire mission as a scientific and technological one, with Dianetics understood as a new science of the human mind and Scientology a new science of the human soul. In *Dianetics: The Modern Science of Mental Health* (1950), Hubbard presented Dianetics as a historically unique form of therapy, called auditing, in which painful memories, including memories from past lives, are scrutinized in order to free the individual from their influence. Auditing, as noted above, is usually performed with the use of an E-meter, a device similar to a lie detector, that can allegedly reduce stress, increase intelligence, and cure illnesses. Through persistent use of the E-meter, preclears gradually shed their engram programming, thus enabling them to reach the state of Clear and become an Operating Thetan. Hubbard also developed a vitamin compound he called Dianazene that could supposedly cure cancer, though it was impounded and destroyed by agents of the Food and Drug Administration (see Miller 227–28).

The twentieth century witnessed both massive technoscientific development and the burgeoning of the science fiction genre. With advances in our understanding of humanity's place in the universe and the development of technologies that portended radical changes to that place came a new set of concerns about who we are and where we are going, concerns that have been the subject matter of SF since its inception. But these concerns are not purely literary; they also raise significant philosophical and spiritual questions. By the mid-twentieth century, they found expression not just in the pages of pulp magazines and SF B-movies, but in the most deeply held beliefs and hopes of those seeking spiritual and religious solace and enlightenment. Questions about our place in the universe, about whether or not human beings are alone among the stars, and about what we might learn from our star cousins if we ever did meet them are at their heart religious questions even when they come clothed in science-fictional garb. It is not surprising that religious movements arose in response to these questions, offering answers where otherwise there might only be mystery.

Similar questions surround our radically transformational technologies, from rocketships, vaccines, and computers to atomic bombs, germ warfare, and genetic engineering. Do these technologies, these innovations and inventions, offer us reasons for hope or despair? Do they herald the coming conclusion of the human story, an ending marked by mushroom clouds and toxic rivers, or do they point toward a future of promise and wonder? Should we accept with bowed heads that the end is near or view the rapidly approaching future optimistically, preparing ourselves for the next step in human evolution and progress? Questions about tomorrow, about what the unseen future holds, have always elicited religious responses. They probably always will.

The multitude of new religious movements and ideas that developed alongside the rise of science fiction mirrored the literary genre's central themes. Though these movements are a diverse lot, they share many of these SF themes as a set of core beliefs. They believe that human beings have been or are now in contact with extraterrestrial entities. They believe that this contact reveals our place among truly universal humanity, our place in the grand cosmic order. They believe that with this growing awareness will come dramatic developments in human evolution and that we stand, as a species, on the brink of something new and wonderful. They believe that at least part of our future development is linked with the continued growth of our technologies, and with the revelation of new and wondrous machines and forms of knowledge that will come from contact with our space brothers and sisters. Though sometimes dark and paranoid (especially when confronted with their lack of acceptance by the larger human community), not to mention subject to the serious psychological dangers inherent in any exclusivist religious community, these religious movements are nevertheless mostly forward-looking and optimistic. Even when preaching a message of warning and danger, whether about nuclear weapons, the human diet, or the evils of psychoanalysis, they usually express a belief in the ability of humanity to overcome its limitations, to rise above its earthly trials, and to find a place and a destiny as citizens of the cosmos.

Works Cited

Adamski, George. *Inside the Space Ships.* New York: Abelard-Schuman, 1955. Print.
Angelucci, Orfeo M. *The Secret of the Saucers.* Amherst, WI: Amherst P, 1955. Print.
Bethurum, Truman. *Aboard a Flying Saucer.* Los Angeles: DeVorss, 1954. Print.
Bromley, David G. "Dramatic Denouements." *Cults, Religion, and Violence.* Ed. David G. Bromley and J. Gordon Melton. Cambridge, UK: Cambridge UP, 2002. 11–41. Print.
Dery, Mark. *Escape Velocity: Cyberculture at the End of the Century.* New York: Grove, 1996. Print.
Fuller, John G. *The Interrupted Journey: Two Lost Hours "Aboard a Flying Saucer."* New York: Dial, 1965. Print.
Helland, Christopher. "From Extraterrestrials to Ultraterrestrials: The Evolution of the Concept of Ashtar." *UFO Religions.* Ed. Christopher Partridge. London: Routledge, 2003. 162–78. Print.
Hoffman, Bill, and Cathy Burke. *Heaven's Gate: Cult Suicide in San Diego.* New York: HarperCollins, 1997. Print.
Hubbard, L. Ron. *Dianetics: The Modern Science of Mental Health.* Los Angeles: Bridge, 1950. Print.
———. *Scientology: A History of Man.* Los Angeles: Bridge, 1952. Print.
Korff, Kal K. *Spaceships of the Pleiades: The Billy Meier Story.* Amherst, NY: Prometheus, 1995. Print.
Leslie, Desmond, and George Adamski. *Flying Saucers Have Landed.* New York: British Book Center, 1953. Print.
Luckhurst, Roger. "The Science-Fictionalization of Trauma: Remarks on Narratives of Alien Abduction." *Science Fiction Studies* 25.1 (Mar. 1998): 29–52. Print.
Menger, Howard. *From Outer Space to You.* Clarksburg, WV: Saucerian, 1959. Print.
Miller, Russell. *Bare-Faced Messiah: The True Story of L. Ron Hubbard.* London: Michael Joseph, 1987. Print.
Moseley, James W., and Karl T. Pflock. *Shockingly Close to the Truth: Confessions of a Grave-Robbing Ufologist.* New York: Prometheus, 2002. Print.
Nadis, Fred. *The Man from Mars: Ray Palmer's Amazing Pulp Journey.* New York: Tarcher/Penguin, 2013. Print.
Norman, Ruth. *Preparation for the Landing.* El Cajon, CA: Unarius Educational Foundation, 1987. Print.
Palmer, Susan J. *Aliens Adored: Raël's UFO Religion.* New Brunswick, NJ: Rutgers UP, 2004. Print.
Peebles, Curtis. *Watch the Skies!: A Chronicle of the Flying Suacer Myth.* Washington, DC: Smithsonian Institution, 1994. Print.
Reitman, Janet. *Inside Scientology: The Story of America's Most Secretive Religion.* New York: Houghton Mifflin Harcourt, 2011. Print.

Toronto, Richard. *War Over Lemuria: Richard Shaver, Ray Palmer and the Strangest Chapter of 1940s Science Fiction*. Jefferson, NC: McFarland, 2013. Print.

Tumminia, Diane, and R. George Kirkpatrick. "Unarius: Emergent Aspects of an American Flying Saucer Group." *The Gods Have Landed: New Religions from Other Worlds*. Albany: SUNY P, 1995. 85–104. Print.

The Urantia Book. Chicago: Urantia Foundation, 1955. Print.

Van Tassel, George W. *I Rode a Flying Saucer: The Mystery of the Flying Saucers Revealed*. 1952. 2nd ed. Glendale, CA: New Age, n.d. Print.

CHAPTER 28

ADVERTISING AND DESIGN

JONATHAN M. WOODHAM

This chapter brings together science fiction, corporate projections of the future through advertising and product styling, and the role of first-generation industrial designers in promoting futuristic utopias. The main thrust will concentrate on the period from the 1920s to the 1960s when these interrelationships were at their most potent. The streamlined forms of industrial products—ranging from railway locomotives, automobiles, and buildings to radios, toasters, and fountain pens—found their counterparts in the dramatic illustrations of space rockets, architecture, and weaponry in contemporary SF magazines. Enticing "Worlds of Tomorrow" were promoted in national and international exhibitions where rockets, robots, and other technologically sophisticated futuristic visions were displayed.

The United States was the pulsating epicenter of activity in such spheres, especially in the practices and promotional activities of the automobile industry. Increasingly central to the American way of life (see Seiler), automobiles expressed their capacity to arouse consumer desire through a proliferation of evocative advertising images and seductive stylings—as well as through General Motors' "Motoramas," auto shows staged from 1949 to 1961. These shows drew audiences totaling more than 10 million to what became choreographed musical, dance, and media tours de force involving "futuristic," "concept," or "dream" cars that embodied the iconography of science fiction and the jet and space ages (see Temple). A number of GM shows also included seductive, futuristic Frigidaire "Kitchens of Tomorrow"; like the Motoramas, these were powerful three-dimensional futuristic advertisements that consumers likened to a science-fictional world depicting new concepts of domestic lifestyles, interior spaces, and technology. Like automobile dashboards, cooking appliances became increasingly sophisticated, with progressively complex arrays of dials and controls that symbolized a World of Tomorrow in which consumers could participate, as if piloting an SF rocketship or advanced jet fighter (see Spigel 383–84).

Of six major national and international exhibitions held in 1930s America, two in particular revealed the immense public eagerness for glimpses into the future and a growing infatuation with scientific advance: the Chicago Century of Progress

Exposition in 1933–34 and the New York World's Fair (NYWF), entitled "Building the World of Tomorrow," in 1939–40. This decade marked the rise and fall of the Technocratic Party, a dramatic growth in the readership of pulp SF magazines, increasingly sophisticated advertising techniques, and public recognition of the industrial designer. Many such designers were commissioned to set the stage for exhibitions in which large-scale corporations presented far from impartial visions of the future. In reality, these impressive promotional displays were at once living three-dimensional advertisements and test-beds of the consumer psyche, pointing to a future in which the interests of American corporate capitalism would play a central role. In some ways they anticipated the future world portrayed in Frederick Pohl and C. M. Kornbluth's 1953 SF novel *The Space Merchants*, in which large-scale multinational media and advertising corporations are all-powerful.

The late nineteenth and early twentieth centuries saw the rise of advertising agencies such as J. Walter Thompson (established in 1877) and Calkins & Holden (established in 1901), the latter highly influential in the early twentieth century. Earnest Calkins had a background writing advertising copy, which, blended with an understanding of industrial design gained through evening classes, informed his belief in the capacity of contemporary design to stimulate consumer desires through styling and planned obsolescence (see Tungate 9–22). This perspective was taken further in Roy Sheldon and Egmont Arens's influential text, *Consumer Engineering: A New Technique for Prosperity* (1932). In 1929 Arens had been appointed advertising director at Calkins & Holden where he also established the firm's industrial styling department. In fact, many of the first generation of American industrial designers had backgrounds in advertising and display: Norman Bel Geddes worked in advertising, stage design, and window display; Raymond Loewy was as an advertising designer and fashion illustrator for leading department stores on New York's Fifth Avenue; and Walter Dorwin Teague was employed in the art department at Calkins & Holden before setting up his industrial design office in 1926 (see Meikle).

Norman Bel Geddes's somewhat sensationalist 1932 book *Horizons* was a manifesto for the power of industrial design to shape the future, containing many projections of streamlined automobiles, buses, airliners, products, and buildings. Often mirroring the familiar teardrop form of futuristic vehicles in contemporary pulp SF magazines, Bel Geddes's visions of the future included his *Airliner Number 4*, boasting several decks and incorporating a promenade, gym and games deck, baths, a dining room with orchestra, a solarium, a nursery, and a doctor's surgery (see Albrecht). His futuristic buses, cars, and trains closely resembled the streamlined SF vehicles dreamed up by illustrator Frank R. Paul and others. Such visions presaged many of the dramatic displays promoting the goods and services of leading American corporations at Chicago in 1933–34 and New York in 1939–40.

Originally conceived on an international scale, the 1933 Century of Progress Exposition was downgraded to national status following the global economic consequences of the Great Depression. Planned to mark the centenary of the incorporation of the city of Chicago, its huge impact was underlined by the 39 million visitors over the

FIGURE 28.1 Norman Bel Geddes, *Automobile of the Future*, 1934. Harry Ransom Center, The University of Texas at Austin. Image courtesy of the Edith Lutyens and Norman Bel Geddes Foundation.

two seasons it was open. The May 27, 1933, issue of the *Chicago Tribune* commented that "throughout the fair, the emphasis was on the modern and futuristic," pointing out that the exhibition's dramatic lighting was activated by photoelectric cells charged with energy from the rays of the star Arcturus, which had begun their journey through space at the time of the Chicago World's Columbian Exposition of 1893 (Warren). Arcturus also featured in poster designs, logos, and stamps in 1933–34. Although not as dramatically aligned with the SF aura of technological utopias projected at the 1939 NYWF, the 1933 Exposition sought to mark the ways in which scientific achievements had impacted on the American way of life, a theme originally proposed by the US National Research Council. Nonetheless, the Exposition was dominated by large American corporations that sought to identify themselves as public benefactors through their commitment to scientific and technological discovery, epitomized by the streamlined products and services on display (see Marchand, *Creating* 249–311). Among the 20 or so powerful corporations with dominant pavilions were the Big Three motor manufacturers, Ford, GM, and Chrysler—which by 1935 controlled 90 percent of all automobile sales in the country. The GM Pavilion featured a complete working Chevrolet assembly line, the hugely successful Ford Pavilion portrayed the industrial ethos of factory manufacturing processes in a display designed by Teague, and the Chrysler Pavilion—"the world's largest showcase"—included a drop forge where new parts for cars were made in front of the visitors (Ganz 80–81).

FIGURE 28.2 Frank R. Paul, cover for *Wonder Stories*, March 1932. Image courtesy of the Frank R. Paul Estate.

At the Exposition, the public was immersed in an enthralling futuristic setting, surrounded by buildings in the art deco style, with extensive displays of colored lighting effects encapsulating a sense of drama and otherworldliness. The Firestone Factory and Exhibition display featured multicolored lighting on entrance pylons, as well as singing color fountains, a multiplane shadow sign, and interactive light-music-color displays (Findling 103). The Westinghouse and General Electric laboratories had devised many of the Exhibition's special lighting effects, including electric cascades and fireworks, color transparencies, and dramatic effects orchestrated by means of a color scintillator linked to huge banks of arc searchlights (Findling 88). These spectacular displays were reminiscent of imagery encountered in the pages of the SF pulps and the comic strips featuring Flash Gordon and Buck Rogers. In fact, Buck Rogers's screen debut—*Buck Rogers in the 25th Century: An Interplanetary Battle with the Tiger Men of Mars* (1933)—coincided with the Chicago Exposition. On the Chicago site, visitors were able to enjoy the science-fictional landscape from the top of two 628-foot towers that could be reached by high-speed elevators, from which they could alight to experience the landmark Skyride from two double-decker Rocket Cars suspended 218 feet above the lagoon (Lohr 233–34).

During the Exposition, General Electric promoted the work of its research laboratories through a series of half-hour performances in its "House of Magic," where visitors (700,000 in 1933) were introduced to the wonders of modern electrical research and imbued with "a tingling anticipation of things yet to come" (Marchand and Smith 160–63). These displays proved highly popular and continued after the end of the Exposition by means of a traveling show that toured the country satisfying consumer appetites for a "domestic life of the future served by electricity" (Ragsdale 255). Scientists entertained the public through such wonders as "popping" corn by microwaves, transforming light beams into music, and lighting incandescent bulbs without wiring. So popular was GE's House of Magic that the concept continued for more than two decades.

Following GM's Chicago display, considerable emphasis was placed on the importance of its traveling "science circus" in persuading consumers of the company's ability to roll back the frontiers of knowledge. As a result, the GM "Parade of Progress," as it became known, was initiated in 1936 and, over the next 20 years, was seen by more than 13 million inhabitants of more than 300 small towns around the United States, Canada, Mexico, and Cuba. The show arrived at these venues with a parade down the main streets in a series of distinctive, streamlined, red-and-white buses designed by Harley Earl (and from 1941 redesigned as "Futurliners" with clear driver cockpits), followed by tractor trailers and a number of brand new GM automobiles. Collectively, these provided the ingredients for stage shows, demonstrations, lectures, and an exhibition. Projected engagements with the future included the concept of a "rocket shop" launched into space for the purpose of scientific research (see "Fascinating History").

During the Chicago Exposition's 1934 season, the public experienced the latest streamlined modes of transportation, including the aerodynamic forms of Chrysler's wind-tunnel-tested Airflow automobile, often photographed alongside the Union Pacific Railroad's brand-new streamlined train, the M-10000 (later known as *The City of Salina*). The train's dramatic contours aligned it with SF illustrations of space rockets and the future train and automobile designs envisaged by Bel Geddes in *Horizons*. During 1934 the M-10000 made an exhibition tour across America, attracting nearly 1 million visitors to experience the future direction of rail transportation in the later 1930s. Another highly publicized example was Burlington's record-breaking, stainless-steel, aeronautically styled *Zephyr* train, complete with symbolic "speed-whiskers" running along its full length. Built by the Budd Company, it was center stage on the opening day of the Chicago Exposition's 1934 season, going on to inspire the 1934 film *The Silver Streak* (see Doughty). With its clear mission to whet consumer appetites and thereby stimulate the economy, the Exposition was a prelude to the much more dramatic and futuristic New York World's Fair of 1939–40, an immense, living advertisement for corporate visions of "The World of Tomorrow."

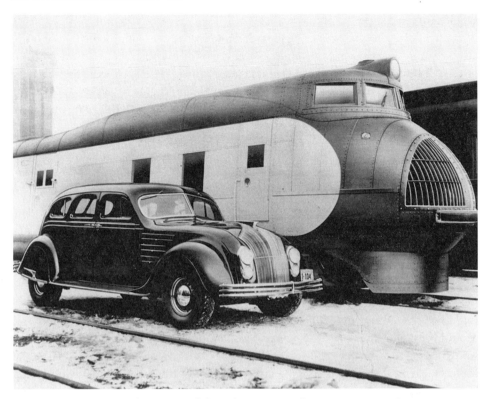

FIGURE 28.3 Chrysler Airflow automobile and Union Pacific M-10000 streamliner train, 1934. Image courtesy of Chrysler Group LLC.

This major international exhibition attracted 45 million visitors in the two seasons it was open, featuring 60 overseas nations, more than 30 US states and territories, and more than 1,000 corporations, including General Motors, Chrysler, Ford, Firestone, General Electric, Westinghouse, Consolidated Edison, American Telephone & Telegraph, Du Pont, and Eastman Kodak. The exhibition theme, "Building the World of Tomorrow with the Tools of Today," gave commercial and industrial corporations considerable scope to present themselves to the consuming public as scientific and technological public benefactors busily constructing a technoscientific utopia. Their often awe-inspiring pavilions and displays were powerful three-dimensional advertisements for the corporate presence in the World of Tomorrow (see Nye 199–224). Egmont and Arens's "consumer engineering" had truly come of age.

As at Chicago in 1933–34, the promotion of science proved controversial at the NYWF. Much to the displeasure of the science community that had anticipated great opportunities, the NYWF's vision of the future was dominated not by "the scientists' science—it was corporate science, advertisers' science, magicians' science, and entertainers' science" (Kuznick 360). It was also highly expressive of the impresariolike roles of American industrial designers such as Loewy, Teague, and Bel Geddes. Much of the architecture and street furniture at the NYWF could have been drawn from the pages of contemporary SF magazines, a sense heightened by dramatic nighttime lighting effects, including the striking stainless-steel forms of the abstract sculpture in front of the GE Building (inside which visitors could witness flashes of artificial lightning shooting 30 feet through the air and experience talking light-and-steel bars floating in magnetic space), and the light, color, and sound properties of the Westinghouse "Singing Tower of Light" (Cotter 87–90).

The NYWF drew the public into the World of Tomorrow via many ingredients, including television, whose first public broadcast showed President Franklin Roosevelt opening the Exhibition on April 30, 1939 (Kuznick 366). Furthermore, although there had been a number of experimental precedents in Europe, Russia, and the United States during the 1930s, the first 3D film viewing by a large audience took place in the Chrysler Building. Seen through Polaroid glasses and entitled *In Tune with Tomorrow*, a 15-minute, black-and-white animated film showed the assembly of a 1939 Plymouth automobile. Viewed by 1.5 million visitors, it proved so popular that, for the Fair's second season, filmmaker John Norling made a Technicolor version, *New Dimensions* (Hayes 12–13). Even more popular was the robot on display in the Westinghouse Building: created by Joseph Barnett especially for the Fair, Elektro the 7-foot-tall Moto-Man could, after a fashion, talk and walk; move his head, arms, and fingers; and smoke a cigarette. For the 1940 season, Barnett built a canine companion, Sparko the Moto-Dog, who could respond to Elektro's commands to sit and stand as well as wag his tail (Nocks 56–58).

It was the pavilions of the largest American motor manufacturers, however, that showed tomorrow's world at its most sensational, underlining the ways in which they advertised themselves as occupying the center of technological and scientific change. Loewy designed a "Rocketport of the Future" for the Chrysler Motors Building where visitors could see projected passenger travel from London to New York. According to publicity material for the exhibit,

> As many as a thousand at a time will be able to watch the presentation of the Rocketport with signal lights blinking, warning sirens sounding, machinery humming, while futuristic liners, trains, buses and automobiles discharge voyagers. When the moment of departure nears, a crane equipped with a magnet picks up the rocketship, and, as the breech of the rocketgun opens, deposits the vehicle of the future in the gun. After an interval, the rocketgun discharges and the rocketship appears to be winging its way into the stratosphere. (qtd. Novak)

Also in the Chrysler Building were Loewy's streamlined renderings of futuristic transportation, closely aligned visually with Bel Geddes's projections in *Horizons*. Loewy's conceptions included a double-decker "Transcontinental Bus of the Future" with high standards of comfort and leisure provision, an aerodynamic three-wheeled "Taxicab of the Future," and a rear-engine streamlined car (see Strohl). The sleek, low, horizontal forms of these vehicles, all using new materials such as polarized glass and

FIGURE 28.4 Rocketport of the Future at the Chrysler Motors Pavilion, New York World's Fair, 1939–40. Image courtesy of the Estate of Raymond Loewy.

equipped with blowout-proof tires, find visual parallels in the illustrated pages and covers of the SF pulps. The 1930s had also seen the rise of SF fanzines, the majority of which were characterized by fairly crude and amateurish production values; following the first national SF convention in 1938, the first World SF Convention was held in 1939 in conjunction with the NWYF. Fittingly, it welcomed one of the most celebrated illustrators of contemporary pulp science fiction, Frank R. Paul, as its guest of honor (see Moskowitz 213–24).

A socially and economically "benign" Fordist future was on show in the Ford Building, designed by Teague and Albert Kahn. Inside, visitors were able to see the impressive "Ford Cycle of Production" as well as the latest cars designed for the half-mile-long, spiral "Road of Tomorrow," where over 4 million visitors queued to experience the new, chauffer-driven model Fords, Mercurys, and Lincoln Zephyrs (Leggett 484). The corporation's documentary film, *Scenes from the World of Tomorrow*, declared that "The Road of Tomorrow is the Dream Highway of the Future," reporting how visitors could see in the Pavilion much that "will furnish inspiration for [their] lives in the future, inspiration for ideas that may be as important to the World of Tomorrow as the motor car is to the World of Today."

At the center of the 1,216-acre NYWF exhibition site were the two major symbols of the Fair: the 700-foot-tall, needlelike Trylon and the adjacent, 180-feet-in-diameter Perisphere, symbolizing the world. The futuristic dimensions of these landmarks were underscored by Frank R. Paul, who (perhaps in a fit of pique at the decision of the Fair's

Board of Design to reject him as one of the four official illustrators of the site's architecture) painted a cover for the June 1939 issue of *Science Fiction* magazine that showed these structures being attacked by an invading spaceship. Inside the Perisphere was a vast diorama of "Democracity," a utopian urban center of 2039 complete with satellite towns. Approximately 8,000 visitors per day were able to view this "perfectly integrated, futuristic metropolis pulsing with life and rhythm and music" from slowly revolving balconies, as if in a low-flying aircraft ("Building" 44). Designed by Henry Dreyfuss and supervised by Robert D. Kohn, Chair of the Fair's Theme Committee, this tour de force was only one of the dramatic representations of a futuristic utopian world on display at the NYWF.

Overshadowing Democracity and attracting considerably more media attention and public adulation was Bel Geddes's "Futurama" in the GM Pavilion. As part of a corporate promotion of the continuing centrality of the automobile in the American way of life, the major display was a projection of the "Highways and Horizons" of 1960. In 1939 alone, this highly popular metropolitan vision attracted 5 million viewers who saw a future world of streamlined transportation systems incorporating multilane highways and segregated pedestrian traffic. On a daily basis, the 36,000-square-foot exhibit attracted long queues that often stretched more than a mile, from 5,000 to 15,000 visitors at a time waiting to experience a 16-minute conveyor-belt ride in a comfortable "sound chair" (which provided an explanatory commentary) while viewing from above the model metropolis of 1960, complete with soaring skyscrapers, low-rise suburbs, factories, farms, and surrounding landscape (see Marchand, "Designers"). As Bel Geddes described the exhibit in his 1940 book *Magic Motorways*:

> We have come out with transcontinental roads built for a maximum of one hundred and a minimum of fifty miles an hour. We have come out with cars that are automatically controlled, which can be driven safely even with the driver's hands off the wheel. We have discovered that people could be driving from San Francisco to New York in twenty-four hours if roads were properly designed. (8)

As Robert W. Rydell has put it, "Futurama . . . was more than an exercise in technological utopianism; it was an exercise in planning the future" (135).

Far from the dystopian future city portrayed in Fritz Lang's 1926 film *Metropolis*, Bel Geddes's metropolis of 1960 was aligned with the futuristic portrayal of 1980 New York in the SF musical film *Just Imagine* (1930), which featured 250-story buildings and elevated multilane highways. Indeed, a number of the cityscape settings from this movie were later reused in Universal's Flash Gordon and Buck Rogers serials. Also known to Bel Geddes would have been the celebrated book *Metropolis of Tomorrow* (1929) by Hugh Ferriss, whose dramatic drawings of towering skyscrapers, elevated trafficways, and visionary urban landscapes were the architectural counterparts to Bel Geddes's ultramodern designs in *Horizons*. Such architectural vistas were also familiar to readers of pulp SF—as in Frank R. Paul's cover for the July 1934 issue of *Wonder Stories*, which featured a rocketship for travel between New York and Sydney. Cementing the

FIGURE 28.5 Visitors viewing the Futurama exhibit at the General Motors Pavilion, New York World's Fair, 1939. © Estate of Margaret Bourke-White/licensed by VAGA, New York, NY. Image courtesy of The Harry Ransom Center, University of Texas at Austin.

link between Futurama and GM's core business of enticing consumers to buy its products was the visitors' exit through a full-sized city intersection where the latest GM models could be viewed.

In 1936 Stanley Resor, CEO of the J. Walter Thompson advertising agency, had commissioned Bel Geddes to produce a series of drawings that addressed the problems of traffic congestion. These provided the basis for a series of 1937 Shell advertisements, which were supported by a detailed scale model of the "City of Tomorrow" that Bel Geddes had persuaded Thompson and Shell to finance. With its 11,000 teardrop automobiles and 19,000 pedestrians, this model anticipated the larger-scale Futurama display at the NYWF. The advertisements' text featured a strapline reading "This is the City of Tomorrow," with predictions by Norman Bel Geddes, "an authority on future trends" (Norton 249–50). A similar ethos underpinned 1930s advertisements for Firestone's Deluxe Champion Tires that showed a low-flying aerial view of a futuristic landscape with a sweeping multilane highway busy with streamlined automobiles and

FIGURE 28.6 Frank R. Paul, cover for *Wonder Stories*, July 1934. Image courtesy of the Frank R. Paul Estate.

buses, with a text reading "The Tire of Tomorrow is Here Today" and "Will the Road of Tomorrow Look Like This?" (Henthorn 151).

Nowhere was the allure of science fiction more potent in advertising than in the increasingly extravagant events and films that promoted futuristic automobiles in the decades immediately following World War II. A series of Motoramas, as they became known, were staged in several of the largest US cities between 1949 and 1961, attracting a total of 12 million visitors. Careful attention had been paid to the styling of GM automobiles since the 1920s, stimulated by the creation of the corporation's Art and Color Section in 1927, the first styling division in the American automobile industry (see Clarke). Led by Harley Earl, this section was a major influence in the promotion of what became known as "dream cars," which were aimed at capturing viewers' imaginations but were never intended for mass production. As Earl remarked: "The dream of the potential buyer must be discovered and satisfied; and the buyer must be awakened with his dreams turned into cars that he can and will buy" (qtd. Gartman 17). Often, these extravagantly styled "concept" cars were intended to test consumers' appetite for particular features, such as the sweeping tailfins, engine air-intakes, and wraparound windshields associated with SF and the jet age—which, if publicly acclaimed, would be incorporated (in rather more muted format) into future production models. Earl's dramatic 1949 Buick Le Sabre, with its built-in sensors that raised a convertible roof during rain showers, epitomized the corporate desire to increase consumer demand for new automobiles through science-fictional design (Marling 12).

Taking up the baton from the displays in the automobile manufacturers' pavilions at the NYWF, futuristic cars emerged as important corporate tools for analyzing consumer aspirations. Almost 600,000 visitors attended the Transport Unlimited Autorama held in New York and Boston in 1949. By 1953, the year in which the event was first named a Motorama, the show—complete with orchestra, singers, and dancers—was staged in a number of major American cities, attracting 1.4 million visitors. The Oldsmobile Starfire, the Cadillac Le Mans, the Buick Wildcat, and other dream cars attracted particular attention. In 1956, its peak year, the Motorama attracted a total audience of 2.3 million to its traveling shows in New York, Miami, Los Angeles, San Francisco, and Boston. The electronic "Highways of Tomorrow" feature displayed a future transportation system in which drivers could contact an operator who would take control of the vehicle, guiding it remotely to its destination. (This was not new: Bel Geddes had proposed independently controlled cars in Shell advertising in 1937, the GM Futurama in 1939, and his 1941 book *Magic Motorways*.) GM also commissioned a short promotional film entitled *Design for Dreaming* (1956), which incorporated the new 1956 models, including the year's dream cars—one of which was the rocketlike, gas-turbine–powered Firebird II. Conceived as a four-seater family car, it was equipped with reclining seats and a table at which to eat light refreshments: the driver and passengers could also take in the view from the 360-degree transparent canopy while speeding automatically down the Highway of Tomorrow for which it was planned.

Included in the film—which was eventually seen by some 8 million people—was the Frigidaire "Kitchen of Tomorrow," also displayed at the Waldorf Astoria (Holliday 79). *Design for Dreaming* was a musical in which a masked man suddenly appeared in the bedroom of a female dancer and whisked her off to the 1956 Motorama; after viewing several GM automobiles, she was taken to the Kitchen of Tomorrow, in which she baked a cake before returning to the Motorama where she danced the "Dance of Tomorrow." The film ended with the two lovers, as they inevitably became in this cinematic dream world, propelled down the "Road of Tomorrow" in their Firebird II with the immortal lines: "Firebird II to Control Tower. We are about to take off on the Highway to Tomorrow. Stand by!" This conjunction of automobiles and domestic technology also appeared in the 1961 GM-sponsored musical *A Touch of Magic*, in which a couple from the 1920s suddenly found themselves transported forward in time to the 1960s where they had trysts in the latest GM automobiles. The subsequently happily married pair

FIGURE 28.7 Harley Earl, GM Firebird II, introduced at the 1956 Motorama. Image courtesy of General Motors.

was then seen in a 1960s home of the future, complete with magic kitchen, holding a housewarming party with invisible guests.

The 1956 Motorama's vision of drivers surrendering control of their vehicles to a remote operator was echoed in the Futurama II display at the 1964 New York World's Fair, which tacitly acknowledged the negative realities of traffic congestion. Designed by GM stylists, Futurama II featured an "autoline" whereby drivers would, upon entering cities, hand over control of their vehicles to electronic traffic control centers: automobiles would be equipped with television, hi-fi, and refrigerators to provide relaxation when not being driven, thereby maintaining their position as desirable products central to American lifestyles. Visitors to the exhibit received lapel buttons reading "I Have Seen the Future!" (Samuel 108).

Many manufacturers other than GM had presented their own series of "concept" or "dream" cars at major motor shows, Ford's "space-age" cars among them. The 1954 FX Atmos (short for Future Experimental Atmosphere), shown at the 1954 Chicago Auto Show, had much in common visually with contemporary SF illustration and film. Complete with rocket-exhaust taillights, a feature of many midcentury dream cars, the FX Atmos boasted a large, bubble-top cockpit canopy under which the centrally positioned driver controlled the car with two joysticks instead of the conventional steering wheel. Antennae projecting from the front allowed the driver to access a radio-controlled traffic distancing system supported by a radar screen mounted on the dashboard (see Corn and Horrigan 102). The car was featured floating above the clouds on the July 1954 cover of *Car Life* magazine, accompanied by the question "Atomic Car Coming?"

The following year, Bill Schmidt, Lincoln-Mercury's chief stylist, designed the futuristic Lincoln Futura dream car, billed as a "spotlight on tomorrow." Although partially inspired by manta rays and mako sharks, its dramatic form clearly drew on jet aircraft design, as seen in the dramatic air intakes of the front wings, the radiator grill, and the twin-domed Plexiglas cockpit. Described in a Ford press release as the "latest development in automotive design—an experimental car from which the Lincoln division will be able to garner valuable engineering data and test public reaction to the styling innovations" (qtd. Satterfield), it made its debut at the 1955 Chicago Auto Show. A decade later, the Futura was remodeled as the Batmobile for ABC's *Batman* television series (1966–68), completing the circle of futuristic projections linking the world of consumer advertising and popular science fiction (see Satterfield). The iconography of the space age also pervaded many everyday popular objects (see Brosterman and Topham)—for example, a Seeburg jukebox of 1958 that incorporated "rocket-burn" taillights into its façade.

With the public appetite whetted by the science-fictional stylings of 1950s dream cars, the dashboards of many contemporary mass-produced cars began to feature a profusion of instruments, dials, switches, and chrome detailing, with a level of complexity apparent on both sides of the Atlantic. Writing in *Design* magazine in 1955 about what he termed "the new mythology" that characterized contemporary attitudes toward the space age, British design journalist John E. Blake commented that "[t]he dashboards of many new, particularly American, cars look, and are obviously intended to look, as though they would control nothing less than a space-ship. . . . [T]he more dials and monitors we possess, the more apparently we identify ourselves with our space heroes, the more we can bring this romantic world of science into our homes" (12). This analogy with SF-inspired instrumentation was heightened by the styling of transmission consoles that often took on quasi-sculptural form and incorporated features such as electric window switches and radio buttons, thus complementing the complexities of the dashboard and adding to the illusion of becoming a technologically sophisticated driver-pilot.

Science-fictional language pervaded both automobile advertising and the naming of specific technological features. GM transmissions systems included the Dynaflow, launched by Buick in 1948, followed by the Twin Turbine Dynaflow in 1953 and the Triple Turbine Flight Pitch Dynaflow in 1958. Later GM transmissions included the Super Turbine 300 automatic transmission (1964–69), also known as the Jetaway model for Oldsmobiles. Chrysler transmission systems were identified by similarly evocative names, such as PowerFlite (1954–61) and Torqueflite (1956). Automobile engines also had space-age names: GM's Oldsmobile Rocket Overhead V8 engine was launched in 1949, the J-2 Golden Rocket in 1957, the Sky Rocket in 1961, and the Starfire in 1964. The 1953 Chevrolet Corvette was equipped with a Blue Flame engine, evoking the color of hot jet-exhaust gases, whereas the first Chrysler OHV8 was named FirePower (1951–58) and the DeSoto versions the FireDome, Firesweep, and FireFlite (see Flory). And 1957

DeSoto advertisements invited consumers "to pilot her [the automobile] out through traffic" whether with the "New Torsion-Aire Ride," "New TorqueFlite transmission," or "New Triple-Range push button-control[s]" (Stern and Stern 92).

Just as the Motoramas of the 1950s had their roots in the extravagant futuristic projections of America's most powerful corporations at the 1939 NYWF, so the 1950s "Kitchens of Tomorrow" displays had their roots in earlier precedents, including the celebrated Libbey-Owens-Ford Glass Company's prototype Kitchen of Tomorrow, first exhibited in 1944 and overseen by H. Creston Doner, previously an architectural and design consultant at the 1939 NYWF (as he was to be for Disney's Tomorrowland, the 1964 NYWF, and Expo '67). Commencing with a showing at Macy's in New York, this exhibition—with its three full-scale models—toured major department stores across the country and was eventually seen by more than 1.6 million viewers. Visitors were invited to vote for the high-tech gadgets they most wanted to see put into production, such as foot-operated taps, glass-topped vessels that eliminated the need for pots and pans, and sliding panels that could cover the sink, cooking unit, and automatic food mixer (Pulos 42).

Underpinned by the considerable resources of GM and Frigidaire (the latter owned by GM from 1919 to 1979), the Kitchens of Tomorrow displays became a highly popular feature of the Motoramas from 1954 on. The 1956 Kitchen strongly embraced the technological utopianism of the times, complete with a "planning communication center," IBM "electro-recipe file," "thermopane" oven, "ultrasonic" dishwasher, and "rotostorage" cabinet for dry, refrigerated, and frozen goods. The iconography and appliance styling evidenced in the advertising for these kitchens were further complemented by a rhetoric that whetted consumer appetite for the future through such terms as "aquamatic," "centrifugal clutch-drive," and "jet spray"—and that was almost interchangeable with that of automobile advertising copy, in which the names of engines and transmission systems captured the imagination through allusions to the jet age and science fiction (see Woodham 76–77). Indeed, in some ways, these high-tech kitchens had already been anticipated in Ray Bradbury's SF story "There Will Come Soft Rains" (1950), in which an automated house goes about its business even in the aftermath of a nuclear holocaust.

Complementing the GM-Frigidaire Kitchens of Tomorrow, Whirlpool joined forces with RCA to launch a "Miracle Kitchen" in 1956, featuring a planning center with audiovisual remote control, a closed-circuit television monitor, a telephone, an electronic (microwave) oven, a "mechanical maid" robotic floor cleaner, and "mood lighting" that responded to the weather to create a fitting "atmosphere" (Holliday 105). The following year, this "concept kitchen" began traveling around the United States and Europe before arriving at the American National Exhibition in Moscow in 1959, at which the so-called Kitchen Debate between Soviet Premier Nikita Khrushchev and US Vice President Richard Nixon took place (Castillo 158–64). Drawing on earlier precedents of "living advertisements" such as the Westinghouse dishwashing "battle" between Mrs. Drudge and Mrs. Modern staged at the 1939 NYWF, the Miracle Kitchen involved "housewives of the future" performing domestic tasks in front of a

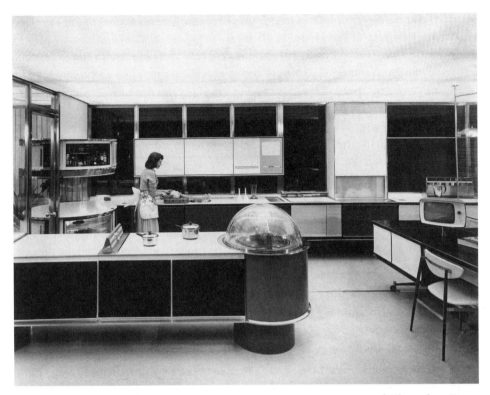

FIGURE 28.8 Frigidaire Kitchen of Tomorrow, 1956. Image courtesy of Electrolux Home Products, Inc.

live audience. A few years later, Whirlpool/RCA would design the space-age meals processor featured in Stanley Kubrick's film *2001: A Space Odyssey* (1968).

In 1967 the Philco-Ford Corporation released a short promotional film entitled *1999 AD*. Focusing on a futuristic house of 1999, it purportedly sought to show how technological change would impact the lives of American consumers (but was perhaps more concerned with linking the company with progressive ideas). A computer in the basement controlled many domestic operations throughout the house: in the kitchen, ideas for family meals were supplied on demand and viewed on a flat screen, their ingredients automatically ordered, purchased, and prepared by a microwave-freezer food processor. Dishwashing was avoided through the extrusion of plastic plates on demand, to be disposed of at the end of the meal ("*1999*"). By this time, however, the widespread commitment to ever-increasing cycles of production, consumption, and built-in obsolescence was being increasingly questioned. Imaginative projections of the future, linked to the potency of SF visions contained in the now-moribund pulp magazines, were in the 1960s overwhelmed by the realities of space exploration and the immediate prospect of a landing on the moon.

The close relationship linking advertising, design, and science fiction was particularly potent in the period from the 1920s to the 1960s, with the rise in economic power of the major corporations, the emergence of influential advertising agencies, and the burgeoning of the SF pulps. By the 1960s, the visionary future worlds promoted by GM were becoming a little shopworn when confronted with the car's social and environmental consequences, outlined in devastating detail in Ralph Nader's 1965 book *Unsafe at Any Speed: The Designed-In Dangers of the American Automobile*. On a broader front, widespread questions were being raised about manipulative advertising techniques and built-in product obsolescence, boosted by a series of regular reports issued by the Consumers' Union (established in 1936) and by popular works such as Vance Packard's *The Hidden Persuaders* (1957) and *The Wastemakers* (1960). Furthermore, the tremendous power of large-scale corporations was being challenged in the writings of economist John Kenneth Galbraith (for example, *The Affluent Society* [1958], *The New Industrial State* [1967]) and biologist and conservationist Rachel Carson, whose 1962 book *Silent Spring* was a powerful indictment of the chemical industry and a spur to the growth of the modern environmental movement. The heady utopianism of midcentury American advertising and design was one of the chief casualties of these developments.

Works Cited

Albrecht, Donald, ed. *Norman Bel Geddes Designs America*. New York: Abrams, 2012. Print.
Bel Geddes, Norman. *Horizons*. 1932. New York: Dover, 1978. Print.
———. *Magic Motorways*. New York: Random House, 1940. Print.
Blake, John E. "Space for Decoration." *Design* 77 (1955): 9–23. Print.
Brosterman, Norman. *Out of Time: Designs for the Twentieth Century Future*. New York: Abrams, 2000. Print.
"Building the World of Tomorrow": *The Official Guide Book of the New York World's Fair 1939*. New York: Exposition Publications, 1939. Print.
Castillo, Greg. *Cold War on the Home Front: The Soft Power of Midcentury Design*. Minneapolis: U of Minnesota P, 2010. Print.
Clarke, Sally. "Managing Design: The Art and Colour Section at General Motors, 1927-–1941." *Journal of Design History* 12.1 (1999): 65–79. Print.
Corn, Joseph J., and Brian Horrigan. *Yesterday's Tomorrows: Past Visions of the American Future*. Ed. Katherine Chambers. 1984. Baltimore: Johns Hopkins UP, 1996. Print.
Cotter, Bill. *The 1939–1940 New York World's Fair*. Charleston, SC: Arcadia, 2009. Print.
Doughty, Geoffrey H. *Burlington Route: The Early Zephrys*. Lynchburg, VA: TLC, 2002. Print.
"The Fascinating History of the GM Futurliner." *MotorwayAmerica*. Feb. 24, 2011. Web. Aug. 4, 2013. http://www.motorwayamerica.com/content/fascinating-history-gm-futurliner.
Ferriss, Hugh. *The Metropolis of Tomorrow*. 1929. Mineola, NY: Dover, 2005. Print.
Findling, John E. *Chicago's Great World's Fairs*. Manchester, UK: Manchester UP, 1995. Print.
Flory Jr., J. "Kelly." *American Cars, 1946 to 1959: Every Model, Year by Year*. Jefferson, NC: McFarland, 2008. Print.
Ganz, Cheryl R. *The 1933 Chicago World's Fair: A Century of Progress*. Urbana: U of Illinois P, 2012. Print.

Gartman, David. "Harley Earl and the Art and Color Section: The Birth of Styling at General Motors." *Design Issues* 10.2 (Summer 1994): 3–26. Print.

Hayes, R. M. *3-D Movies: A History and Filmography of Stereoscopic Cinema*. 1989. Jefferson, NC: McFarland Classics, 1998. Print.

Henthorn, Cynthia Lee. *From Submarines to Suburbs: Selling a Better America, 1939–1959*. Athens: Ohio UP, 2006. Print.

Holliday, Laura Scott. "Kitchen Technologies: Promises and Alibis, 1944–1966." *Camera Obscura* 16.2 (2001): 79–131.

Kuznick, Peter J. "Losing the World of Tomorrow: The Battle Over the Presentation of Science at the 1939 World's Fair." *American Quarterly* 46.3 (Sept. 1994): 341–73. Print.

Leggett, Julian. "Wonders of the New York Fair." *Popular Mechanics* 71.4 (Apr. 1939): 481–84. Print.

Lohr, Lenox R. *Fair Management: The Story of a Century of Progress Exposition*. Chicago: Cuneo, 1952. Print.

Marchand, Roland. "The Designers Go to the Fair, II: Norman Bel Geddes, The General Motors 'Futurama,' and the Visit-to-the-Factory Transformed." *Design History: An Anthology*. Ed. Dennis P. Doordan. Cambridge, MA: MIT, 1995. 103–21. Print.

———. *Creating the Corporate Soul: The Rise of Public Relations and Corporate Imagery in American Big Business*. Berkeley: U of California P, 2001. Print.

Marchand, Roland, and Michael L. Smith. "Corporate Science on Display." *Scientific Authority & Twentieth-Century America*. Ed. Ronald G. Walters. Baltimore: Johns Hopkins UP, 1997. 148–82. Print.

Marling, Karal Ann. "Autoeroticism: America's Love Affair with the Automobile in the Television Age." *Design Quarterly* 146 (1989): 5–20. Print.

Meikle, Jeffrey L. *Twentieth Century Limited: Industrial Design in America, 1925–1939*. 1979. 2nd ed. Philadelphia: Temple UP, 2001. Print.

Moskowitz, Sam. *The Immortal Storm: A History of Science Fiction Fandom*. 1954. Westport, CT: Hyperion, 1974. Print.

"1999 A.D. (1967)." *Paleo-Future*. Apr. 30, 2007. Web. Aug. 4, 2013. http://paleo-future.blogspot.com/2007/04/1999-ad-1967.html.

Nocks, Lisa. *The Robot: The Life Story of a Technology*. Westport, CT: Greenwood, 2007. Print.

Norton, Peter Daniel. *Fighting Traffic: The Dawn of the Motor Age in the American City*. Cambridge, MA: MIT, 2008. Print.

Novak, Matt. "Travel by Rocketship (1939)." *Paleo-Future*. Jan. 10, 2010. Web. Aug. 3, 2013. http://paleofuture.gizmodo.com/travel-by-rocketship-1939-512626444.

Nye, David E. *American Technological Sublime*. Cambridge, MA: MIT, 1994. Print.

Pulos, Arthur J. *The American Design Adventure, 1940–1975*. Cambridge, MA: MIT, 1988. Print.

Ragsdale, Kenneth Baxter. *The Year America Discovered Texas: Centennial '36*. College Station: Texas A&M UP, 2000. Print.

Rydell, Robert W. *World of Fairs: The Century-of-Progress Expositions*. Chicago: U of Chicago P, 1993. Print.

Samuel, Lawrence R. *End of the Innocence: The 1964–1965 New York World's Fair*. Syracuse, NY: Syracuse UP, 2007. Print.

Satterfield, Michael. "Before Batman." *TGR*. Jan. 2013. Web. Aug. 4, 2013. http://www.thegentlemanracer.com/2013/01/before-batman.html.

Seiler, Cotton. *Republic of Drivers: A Cultural History of Automobility in America*. Chicago: U of Chicago P, 2008. Print.

Spigel, Lynn. *Welcome to the Dreamhouse: Popular Media and Postwar Suburbs*. Durham, NC: Duke UP, 2001. Print.

Stern, Jane, and Michael Stern. *Auto Ads*. New York: Random House, 1978. Print.

Strohl, Daniel. "Raymond Loewy Envisions the Future of Tranportation." *Hemmins Daily* (July 21, 201). Web. Aug. 3, 2013. http://blog.hemmings.com/index.php/2011/07/21/raymond-loewy-envisions-the-future-of-transportation/.

Temple, David W. *GM's Motorama: The Glamorous Show Cars of a Cultural Phenomenon*. Ed. Dennis Adler. St. Paul, MN: Motorbooks/MBI, 2006. Print.

Topham, Sean. *Where's My Space Age?: The Rise and Fall of Futuristic Design*. New York: Prestel, 2003. Print.

Tungate, Mark. *Ad Land: A Global History of Advertising*. London: Kegan Page, 2007. Print.

Warren, Ellen. "'A Century of Progress': Science and Show Biz Come Together to Revive a City Worn Weary by Depression." *Chicago Tribune* (May 27, 1933). Web. July 31, 2013. http://www.chicagotribune.com/news/politics/chi-chicagodays-centuryofprogress story,0,4857263. story.

Woodham, Jonathan M. *Twentieth-Century Design*. New York: Oxford UP, 1997. Print.

CHAPTER 29

COUNTERCULTURES

ROB LATHAM

SCIENCE fiction has always had a close relationship with countercultural movements, especially if the allied genre of the literary utopia is included within its orbit (see Corporaal and van Leeuwen). The articulation of visions of alternative worlds in SF has often proven inspirational for those seeking to change the conditions under which they live, especially during periods of widespread social ferment. Indeed, the inspirational energies have generally flowed in both directions, with SF drawing equally on the idealistic ambitions of social reformers. As Richard Stites has shown, the Bolshevik Revolution was a "remarkable launching pad for utopian science fiction," generating some 200 titles during the 1920s, with 50 appearing in 1927 alone (172). Russian SF authors, he claims, "donned scarlet colored glasses to see what a communist society might, should, or would look like across a widely variant stretch of the ages" (168). At the same time, of course, the Revolution was producing less sanguine works, such as Yevgeny Zamyatin's *We* (1924), which depicted the Communist future as an authoritarian dystopia. In any case, the advent of Stalinism basically strangled the developing genre in its crib, but while it lasted, it gave fertile evidence of the powerful energies unleashed "in an era of drastic and willful change" (Stites 189).

Meanwhile, in the United States, the nascent pulp genre was also deeply imbricated with contemporaneous countercultural trends. As Andrew Ross has shown, the reformist zeal sparked by the Great Depression ushered in a host of left- and right-wing visions for the transformation of an ailing industrial society. "While sharing the dominant values of modernity and progress," Ross writes, "these countercultures promised to be more creative, more productive, more efficient, more growth-oriented, and more humane than the fettered capitalist management of society was proving to be" (120). In terms of specific connections with pulp SF, Ross traces compelling links between Thorstein Veblen's vision of an avant-garde of engineers, enlightened technocrats capable of organizing industrial production in a more dynamic way, and "the erector-set-inspired amateur inventor" of 1930s SF—who, though socially "anachronistic," was nonetheless "available as a protopolitical vehicle" (126), evoking the possibilities of individual autonomy in an age of "corporate technostructure" (127). Though this idealization of the inventor-hero brought with it a "romantic individualism" that could too readily descend into a conservative libertarianism (127), it still contained progressive possibilities actuated by the utopian energies of the decade.

While the rest of this chapter will be devoted to a discussion of major post–World War II countercultures that had substantial links with SF, my purpose in rehearsing the above background is to indicate that this phenomenon had deep historical roots. Moreover, it points to something critically and creatively fecund at the heart of science fiction itself. The genre's radical openness to change, so often remarked by scholars—its existence as what Brooks Landon has called a "zone of possibility" (17)—makes it uniquely serviceable during times of social turbulence: on the one hand, it is at least theoretically capable of entertaining the wildest of utopian speculations; on the other hand, this very feature is likely to prove inspirational to social utopianists of all varieties. Without necessarily becoming a tendentious vehicle for the articulation of programmatic agendas (the aesthetic danger of all utopian genres), works of SF can potently suggest both the limits of everyday "reality" and the lineaments of fresh modes of social being glimpsed dimly on the horizon. As Landon puts it, "All SF is preparation," a reorientation of perspective impelled by "the postulate that the world can best be understood through change" (xii).

While the reputation of the US 1950s has seen some scholarly rehabilitation that has shown the decade to be more diverse and bawdy than stereotypes of its prim conformism might suggest (see Foreman), it is certainly the case that influential prewar countercultures—countercultures that significantly impacted the sociopolitical landscape—had by 1960 virtually disappeared, at least as mainstream forces. This ebbing of vigor was not accidental but the result of concerted efforts at suppression (often the fate of politicized countercultures unless, like Bolshevism, they manage to seize control of the levers of power). The left-wing radicalism that had marked the 1930s was more or less systematically effaced, its sympathizers publicly shamed by the House Committee on Un-American Activities while the Communist Party was hobbled by the 1940 Smith Act and the 1950 McCarran Act, before being banned outright by the 1954 Communist Control Act (see Caute). Indeed, a rigid interpretation of these acts would virtually criminalize dissent itself, making words as such potentially treasonous (Whitfield 47). Likewise, the feminist movement—which had seen landmark accomplishments in the early decades of the century, such as women's suffrage and the advancement of reproductive rights, won via the brave advocacy of figures like Margaret Sanger and Ida B. Wells—vanished during the 1950s under what Marty Jezer calls "a sea of relentless propaganda" valorizing marriage and motherhood, an antifeminist "counter-revolution" (227–28). It would be another decade before the legacy of these progressive movements was revived, their utopian passions rekindled.

Yet the 1950s was not lacking in countercultures, though these may have lost a good measure of their overt political edge. The two I wish to discuss here are science fiction and the writings of the Beats, which had rather closer points of connection at the time than might initially appear. The most obvious link—one that has been well documented in scholarly work on both literary traditions—was William S. Burroughs's undeniable fondness for pulp SF. In a 1980 interview, Burroughs acknowledged that he had "gone through a whole wall of science fiction," even though he found much of it unconvincing—not because of its inclination to depict otherworldly spaces and altered states, which he approved, but because "it's a very difficult form" to wield effectively, its authors too often failing to activate the field's radically alienating perspectives (Skerl 119). His notorious 1959 novel *Naked Lunch*—with its weird biomorphic transformations and paranoia about mind control—was, by his own admission, a work of science fiction (Masterton and Rossabi 39), and his later "cut-up" trilogy (1961–64) borrowed liberally from the genre for its psychedelic imagery and its loose-knit "plots"—which featured extra-dimensional "Nova criminals" doing battle with the "Nova police." *Nova Express* (1964) offers extended, kaleidoscopic pastiches of SF exposition that only a writer well steeped in the genre could produce ("Flesh sheets dissolving amid vast ruins of berserk machines" [63–64], "Electric waves of resistance sweeping through mind screens of the earth" [67]), and *The Ticket That Exploded* (1962) contains, amidst its overall collage, passages lifted directly from Henry Kuttner's 1947 novel of posthuman mutants, *Fury*. (Burroughs was such a fan of this novel that, when SF author James Gunn in the mid-1980s challenged him to recite its mindbending two-word epilogue, he spontaneously did so [Gunn 54].) The SF authors to whose work Burroughs was drawn were usually minor ones—Eric Frank Russell, Barrington J. Bayley, Alan E. Nourse (whose 1974 novel *The Bladerunner* he adapted into a screenplay in 1979)—but his appreciation for the genre's ability to rescind conventional worldviews and invoke a radical otherness was undeniable.

As was his reciprocal influence on the development of science fiction. In 1963, when *The Times Literary Supplement* ran a contemptuous review-essay dismissing Burroughs's work as incoherent and repulsive, one of the responses it summoned was an angry letter from a youthful British SF fan named Michael Moorcock. One of Moorcock's main lines of defense was to argue for Burroughs as "one of the first real writers of SF to emerge to date," based on not only his key themes ("space and time, ... the place of the individual in the total universe") but also his stylistic techniques, the cut-up method being "something of a scientific as well as a literary experiment" (Letter 47–48). The following year, when Moorcock was the surprise selection to replace the hallowed John Carnell as editor of Britain's premier SF magazine, *New Worlds*, he gained a highly visible platform within the genre from which to further advance these (at the time) rather unconventional views.

The editorial in his very first issue, entitled "A New Literature for the Space Age," hailed *The Ticket That Exploded* and *Nova Express* as "the SF we've all been waiting for," a "kind of SF which is unconventional in every sense," perfectly capturing "the mood of our ad-saturated, Bomb-dominated, power-corrupted times" (2–3). The same issue contained a glowing profile of Burroughs by J. G. Ballard, whose own work was in the process of taking an experimental turn that would eventually culminate in his collage novel *The Atrocity Exhibition* (1970). The cut-up trilogy, Ballard claimed, was "the first definitive portrait of the inner landscape of our mid-century, using its own language and manipulative techniques, its own fantasies and nightmares" (121);

it was the first work of SF actually to deploy "the casual vocabulary of the space age" (126), its high-tech jargon and "medicalese" (123), against entrenched technocracy and its instrumentalized languages of control (the bulk of the contemporary genre having abdicated this social-critical responsibility). The profile ended with a direct salute to Burroughs that quoted the final lines of Allen Ginsberg's 1956 poem "Howl," with its tribute to Carl Solomon, Ginsberg's fellow inmate at New York State's Rockland County mental hospital: "I'm with you in Rockland / where we wake up electrified out of the coma by our own soul's airplanes" (qtd. Ballard 127).

New Worlds' championing of Burroughs was not exactly embraced by the genre at large; indeed, this was the first volley in what would become a protracted battle between SF's Old Guard, wedded to traditional pulp narration and generally comfortable with a technocratic worldview, and a rising "New Wave" cohort that sought radical alternatives in both style and content—and that became strongly associated, especially later in the decade, with the period's activist countercultures (see Latham). Most histories of SF have followed this basic trajectory, beginning with *New Worlds*' embrace of Burroughs's work and going on to show the genre's growing enmeshment in 1960s contexts and debates: the articulation of antitechnocratic options, the promise of the new media landscape, the embrace of experimentalism as both a literary and a social ethos (see Luckhurst 141–66). Yet no history has yet traced the thread backward, excavating the roots of SF's New Wave in 1950s US countercultural writing, despite the fact that Ballard also prominently cites Ginsberg in his Burroughs profile, thus suggesting a broader-based debt than to just one exceptional author. Indeed, the Burroughs–*New Worlds* link and its subsequent reverberations within the field have essentially become, within SF scholarship, *the* moment when the genre and postwar countercultures converged, when in fact this convergence was already well under way in the 1950s and early 1960s.

Virtually the only commentator to acknowledge this connection is Norman Spinrad, himself a celebrated New Wave author, whose essay "Science Fiction and the Beats" sees both Beat literature and SF as "the spiritual descendants of an old American bohemian tradition": "Both viewed official reality from the point of view of outsiders, both were in that sense messianic, both offered radical political and social visions, and both opposed individual liberty to social control." Both forms of writing also focused on a characteristic protagonist, the "hero as self-made psychic mutant, and the mutant as Subterranean, hipster, Dharma Bum, outlaw transformer of the world." Spinrad's essay tracks a tradition of outsider SF starting in the 1940s—including the fiction of A. E. van Vogt, Alfred Bester, Robert Sheckley, Philip K. Dick, Moorcock, William Gibson, and "of course the Cyberpunks"—that incarnates the "transcendentalist spirit" equally animating the Beats and their countercultural successors, literary and otherwise: Thomas Pynchon, Richard Fariña, Ken Kesey, Bob Dylan, Leonard Cohen, and Timothy Leary. (It is curious that he does not mention Rudy Rucker, one of the few SF writers to have frankly acknowledged his debt to the Beats [81–91].) Both vectors of work, Spinrad asserts, emerge from an even longer bohemian tradition that can be traced back through Henry Miller to Mark Twain, Henry David Thoreau, and Walt

Whitman. Even more intriguingly, in terms specifically of the Beats–SF link, Spinrad points to the fact that active "subcultures formed around both literatures": SF fandom on the one hand, and the popular "Beat Generation" on the other (contemptuously dubbed "beatniks" by the mainstream press). What these groups shared was a worldview that drew a stark contrast between countercultural and consensus perspectives—what SF fans called the difference between SF readers and "mundanes" and what the followers of the Beats saw as the split between enlightened hipsters and blinkered "squares."

Though the Beat writers did not use this terminology consistently (just as SF authors did not simply adopt the lingo of fandom), their most characteristic work usually centered on precisely such a contrast: the frenzied, quest-driven protagonists vs. the settled, conventional masses in Kerouac's *On the Road* (1957), the "angelheaded hipsters" (9) versus the soulless worshippers of "Moloch" in Ginsberg's "Howl." Burroughs's cut-up trilogy offers the most overtly science-fictional articulation of this division in the Beat canon, although Kerouac did briefly essay a work of SF himself. In his original conception, developed in the mid-1950s, this was an ambitious novel-length project limning a hypertrophied, totalitarian city of the future in which individuals were numbered ciphers tranquillized by drugs and mass media. At one point, likely knowing Burroughs's fondness for SF, he suggested their potential collaboration (Charters 222), but eventually he abandoned the effort, leaving only a brief sketch, which was published first as "The Electrocution of Block 38383939383. . ." in 1959 and then, in 1963, as "cityCityCITY" (the title by which it is more widely known). Indeed, unlike Burroughs, Kerouac turned his back on SF thereafter, declaring the genre to be one of those "[m]odern bizarre structures" that "arise from language being dead" ("Essentials" 58).

Kerouac's "cityCityCITY" has been neglected by SF scholars, which is in one way completely understandable given the derivativeness of its themes, its clear debts to Zamyatin's *We* and Aldous Huxley's *Brave New World* (1932), among many other tales about dystopian cities. The only substantial attention it has received from within the genre is a brief essay by Stuart Cormie appearing in the online speculative fiction magazine, *Strange Horizons*, in 2006. As Cormie observes, the story seems to fit neatly within the tradition of "1950s American paranoiac sci-fi . . . depict[ing] a post-apocalyptic future Earth"; were the style of its telling less addled (Kerouac confessed to Ginsberg that he wrote it largely "on weed" [qtd. Cormie]), it could readily have appeared in the SF magazine *Galaxy*, which by the mid-1950s had cornered the market on darkly ironic futurism within the genre. As Cormie observes, the story "serves to emphasize Kerouac's oft-expressed view of his own society as a rampant machine, blindly driven by a military-industrial complex, in which people exist merely to power the machine in return for the consumption of its output." In other words, it is a Beat-flavored version of such classic comic infernos as Frederik Pohl and C. M. Kornbluth's *The Space Merchants* (1953). Kerouac claimed to have penned the story while watching the 1954 Army-McCarthy hearings, intending it as "a preview of the world's future straight out of Kafka" (Amburn 204). If so, then his deflection of the satire into a science-fictional realm tallies with the work of a number of SF authors—such as Pohl and Kornbluth, Sheckley, and William Tenn—who managed to produce, in estranged form, incisive critiques of the political atmosphere of the era; as Barry N. Malzberg has pointed out, SF was, during the heyday of McCarthyism, one of "the very few mass markets where, sufficiently masked, an antiauthoritarian statement could be published" (34). Kerouac's lone work of SF further underlines the kinship between these 1950s countercultures.

The plot of "cityCityCITY," such as it is, centers on a boy named M-80 whose father, "Prime Minister" of their "Zone Block," attempts to save from the mass electrocution dictated for their sector (a routine way of thinning the excess population). "When a Zone Block was chosen for Electrocution, Elimination from life, it was because of the low Merit Average of the whole 2500-odd community" (201). As this passage suggests, the narrative voice is a wise-ass parody of technocratic jargon, satirizing a society run with crisp precision by faceless experts, who wield machines like the "Brain Halo, which divined equations, . . . balancing them together, so skillfully, so complicated, a thousand wires running into a million larger ones that grew and snaked and vined their way in the tangled Wire Room of the Brain" (201–02). Shadowy factional infighting—and periodic backstabbing—among government ministers suggest divisions underlying the surface calm, as does the abiding social presence of disaffected hipsters, "the bums of the community, . . . shiftless . . . and dreamy" (201). In the version published in 1963, M-80 winds up electrocuted along with the rest of his Zone Block (see Jones 262), but in an expanded text published in 1998 in Kerouac's collection *Good Blonde & Others*, the boy's father manages to arrange an escape route: a rocket into space, destination unknown. As the bleak vistas of the "outer chillicosm" sweep by (212), M-80 ponders his uncertain fate, while "[t]he rocket wobbled on and on, like the lonely sensation of thinking" (213). Despite Kerouac's ultimate dismissal of the genre, this inspired final line indicates how deeply he sought to reimagine its classic iconography—as well as how easily that iconography, despite its roots in technocratic discourses, could be adapted as flexible symbols in Beat improvisations.

Depending on how broadly one defines the genre, Burroughs and Kerouac were not the only Beats to dabble in SF-inspired metaphors—or, at least, imagery that had its roots in the same technocultural matrix that fed SF. Ginsberg's Blakean jeremiad against the American Moloch ("whose mind is pure machinery! . . . whose fate is a cloud of sexless hydrogen!" [21–22]), Michael McClure's vision of poetry as a "[b]io-alchemical investigation" (76), and Amiri Baraka's short story "Answers in Progress" (1967)—one of the founding texts of Afrofuturism, in which space aliens appear and demand "Art Blakey records" (136)—show the ways in which science-fictional ideas and symbolism were adopted by Beat writers in order to satirize the emptiness of "square" society and defend the value of "hip" subcultural expression. As Baraka's reference to Blakey indicates, jazz music was by this point already a clear signifier for hipness—or "coolness" (see MacAdams)—among the Beats, but a taste for jazz had also developed within certain segments of the SF authorial community during the 1950s. In fact, this was one of the strongest areas of cultural common ground between the Beats and SF; just as Beat classics such as *On the Road* hymned bebop as a transcendent experience, so a number of SF stories—Charles Beaumont's "Black Country" (1954), Fritz Leiber's "Rump-Titty-Titty-Tum-TAH-Tee" (1958), Richard Matheson's "The Jazz Machine" (1963)—drew on jazz for their subject matter and even their styles of writing. And the interest was reciprocated, most visibly and flamboyantly by composer and bandleader Sun Ra, who used the term "space music" as early as 1956 to describe the sounds of his cosmic "Arkestra" (Szwed 384). The connection between jazz and SF was so well established that, in 1960, the Jazz Book Club ran an advertisement in *Science Fantasy* magazine claiming that "the worlds of jazz and sf are parallel," both embracing "intellectual kicks and excitement; offbeatness, for people who somehow can't go all the way with the world they live in"—a world constructed by and for vacuous "[s]nobs." The ad addressed itself, in short, to a cadre of SF hipsters whose countercultural pleasures exceeded those of the mundane squares.

Direct crossover traffic between Beatdom and SF picked up in the early 1960s, thanks in large part to the mainstreaming of the Beats through journalistic profiles such as John Clellon Holmes's "The Philosophy of the Beat Generation" (1958), the appearance of popular studies such as Lawrence Lipton's *The Holy Barbarians* (1959), and the eruption of "youthsploitation" films featuring beatnik characters, such as *The Beat Generation* (1959). Most of the resultant SF stories were jocular and wacky, as if not quite able to take the phenomenon seriously (of course, Kerouac himself scorned the whole beatnik craze as "just kind of a fad" [qtd. Theado 25]). These spoofs included Dan Lindsay's "The Beatnik Werewolf" in the December 1960 issue of *The Magazine of Fantasy and Science Fiction* and Randall Garrett's "Hep-Cats of Venus" in the January 1962 issue of *Fantastic*, both of which riffed on what by then had become a popular stereotype. A considerably more substantial—though no less comical—story was Fritz Leiber's "The Beat Cluster," which appeared in the October 1961 issue of *Galaxy*.

This tale—set in the "Big Igloo," a semi-transparent bubble full of hipsters floating in orbit near a space research station—shares the lightness of tone of other "beatnik SF" stories (though, significantly, Leiber prefers the term "beat" throughout): the inhabitants of the Big Igloo wear "black leotards" (160), play guitars, and practice "freefall yoga" (160). In their gravity-free shell, they commune with the universe, periodically favoring the planet with performances of their Small Jazz Ensemble via shortwave radio. "The wild ones who yesterday would have headed for the Village or the Quarter or Big Sur, the Left Bank or North Beach, or just packed up their Zen Buddhism and hit the road, are out here now, digging cool sounds as they fall round and round Dear Old Dirty" (164)—their nickname for Mother Earth. Yet despite its deployment of typical stereotypes, the story is not mocking the Beats: rather, the objects of its scorn are the agents of the Resident Civilian Administration, especially the priggish "proctor"—the tale's prototypical square—who cannot stand the funky smell of these "sloppy long-haired floaters" (160). The plot begins with the proctor bringing a deportation notice to the denizens of the Big Igloo, ordering that these space squatters be evicted and shipped back to Earth. "Ah well," one of the Beats remarks, "we all knew this bubble would burst someday" (161).

The leader of the crew, Fats Jordan (a.k.a. "Big Daddy of the Space Beats" [159]), delivers a farewell message during their final radio performance, defending the group's unconventional lifestyle. Having come to space as manual laborers helping to build the research satellite, the original core of the group decided to remain, crafting their own orbital environment, which soon attracted from Earth the "artists and oddballs, who have a different kind of toughness" (167). Self-reflexively addressing the technocratic legacy of science fiction itself, Fats observes that those who planned "the conquest of space entirely in terms of military outposts and machine precision" failed to take into account the possibility that the wide-open expanse of this new frontier would be a draw "for the drifters and dreamers, the rebels and no-goods" (164), folks who would find the liberation of freefall "[o]ut of this world.... A good twenty thousand miles out, Captain Nemo" (164). Ultimately, Fats's speech presents the Beats as the genuine heirs of the SF tradition, who—though lacking a legal right to remain in orbit—nonetheless have "the right that's conveyed by a dream" (168). This is not only an intriguing echo of Kerouac's notion, in "cityCityCITY," that Beats would be more at home in space than on Earth, it is also a version of Spinrad's transcendentalist SF, rejecting the technocratic idea that "space belongs to soldiers and the civil service, with a slice of it for the research boys" (168), and asserting instead the claim of the outsiders—"the laziest cats in the cosmos: the ones who couldn't bear the thought of carrying their own weight around every day of their lives" (167).

Despite this imputation of indolence, however, the Beat Cluster is in fact quite industrious, becoming almost a proto-hippie commune through their cultivation of "a flourishing ecology" (171): algae to generate oxygen and yeast cultures fed on recycled wastes to provide a food supply. Indeed, it is revealed at the end that the Big Igloo is "a pilot experiment in the free migration of people into space" in order to see if it is possible to sustain a self-sufficient biosphere in orbit (172)—a revelation that effectively revokes the deportation order and makes a fool out of the dumbstruck proctor. Leiber's ingenious little parable hymning the merits of hipness—the superior insights of "the dreamers and the funsters, the singers and the studiers" (167)—operates as both a fitting capstone to a decade of collaboration between SF and the Beats and a foretaste of the sort of antitechnocratic SF that would characterize the New Wave just a few years later. Moreover, the story's pointed contrast between hip and straight worldviews not only mirrored one of the key themes of the Beat writers but also established a narrative paradigm for much 1960s countercultural SF.

A prominent example is Samuel R. Delany's Nebula Award–winning 1966 novel *Babel-17*. Delany, as a gay black man married to a lesbian poet, brought even more bohemian authenticity to the genre than had earlier SF hipsters such as Sheckley and Theodore Sturgeon; indeed, he was living in a bisexual commune in Greenwich Village not long after *Babel-17* was published (see Delany, *Heavenly*). *Babel-17* is an elaborate space opera whose intricate plot is of less concern to me here than the sharp distinction the narrative draws between two future communities: Transport, consisting of the assorted ruffians and rogues who make their livings in space, and Customs, the rather strait-laced planet-bound officials who oversee their doings. In one sense, the contrast is merely a recapitulation of the longstanding historical tension between "seadogs" and "landlubbers" (Delany at one point explicitly compares Transport's subcultural rituals to the conduct of sailors [*Babel* 30]), but it is also fairly clearly a reframing of the hip–square distinction earlier SF had adapted from the Beats.

The antagonism between these groups—suggested in their very names, with "Transport" registering a comfort in the transit between worlds, and Customs signaling a dependency on settled norms—is introduced early on in a confrontation between a rumbustious starship crew and a prim young Customs Officer named Danil D. Appleby. Appleby expresses revulsion at—though clearly is secretly fascinated by—the startling otherness of the crew's appearance and behavior: their "cosmetisurgery," which allows one of them to look like a lion, complete with fangs and claws; their tendency to consort with the "discorporate," invisible creatures who live a kind of shadowy half-life in "The Discorporate Sector" (a clear stand-in for the red-light district); and especially their unconventional sexuality, in particular the deep triune partnerships that link starship navigators. When the nature of this bond is explained to him, he inadvertently blurts out "[p]erverts!" (43). The disgust is mutual since one of the crew has already berated him with a contemptuous tirade whose rhetoric echoes typical countercultural put-downs of squares: "You don't know anything, Customs! . . . Aw, you hide in your Customs cage, cage hid in the safe gravity of Earth, Earth held firm by the sun, sun fixed headlong toward Vega, all in the predicted tide of this spiral arm. . . . And you never break free! . . . Ehhh! You have nothing to say to me!"

This mutual incomprehension and contempt exist only on the surface, however, at least when it comes to the Customs side of the equation; indeed, one of the story's subplots involves the overcoming of Appleby's uptight bias against Transport and his gradual seduction into their lifestyle. First, he has a sexual rendezvous in the Discorporate Sector, leaving him feeling "luminous amazement, fear, excitement" (44). By the end, he has had a "miniature dragon with jewelled eyes, glittering scales, and opalescent wings" cosmetisurgically implanted into his shoulder; the creature can "whistle hiss, roar, flap [its] wings, and spit sparks" at the behest of his own nervous system (192). Still, bespeaking his uneasiness with this alteration (which "just wouldn't go at the office"), Appleby is careful to ensure that the dragon can be "covered up when [he] was wearing clothes" (191). This attempt to straddle hip and straight worlds was a common theme in late 1950s and early 1960s popular culture; Dennis Lynds's 1963 paperback novel *Uptown Downtown*, for example, bore a cover blurb that reads: "By day he was a ruthless executive, by night a free-wheeling beatnik. He had the best of both worlds. . . ." Leiber alludes to this tradition in "The Beat Cluster" in the form of the "research boys" who like to sneak over from the station for "art show[s]" and "jazz Fridays" (162)—one of whom, when he hears about the imminent deportation order, complains: "You can't cut off recreation that way. I depend on the Cluster to keep my electron bugs happily abnormal" (168). Delany has merely refigured this "double life" motif for the hippie generation.

The hesitant but compelling conversion experience Customs Officer Appleby undergoes in *Babel-17* was happening all over the country by the mid- to late 1960s. It was happening, indeed, to the genre itself: SF paperbacks began sporting psychedelic cover art, with New Wave fiction in particular being marketed with the expectation that a substantial segment of its readership were, at the very least, sympathetic to the hippie phenomenon. By the late 1960s, a significant portion of the fan community had transitioned completely into the counterculture; as a fanzine columnist commented in 1968:

> There are a large number of fan "heads" coexisting (mostly) peacefully with the fan "straights." . . . Marijuana, and even acid, are growing phenomena in fandom. . . . This is probably because the type of person who would become a fan is somewhat akin to the type of person who would become a hippie. Both have similar goals and commitments, even if the more conservative fans would like to close their minds to the subject. Anyway, it's definitely the wave of the future; and fans are more conditioned than most to be in the vanguard. (Rudolph 6)

In short, becoming an SF fan already represented a kind of conversion from "mundane" ways of seeing (and being in) the world, akin to the sort of experiential transformation involved in embracing the counterculture movement.

Nor were the dynamics of this process unilateral: just as the genre was counterculturalized during the 1960s, so was the counterculture growingly science-fictionalized. What Tom Lutz has called "the hippie curriculum" (41) included, among the assorted texts on zen and shamanism, a number of popular-science works (such as John C. Lilly's books on interspecies communication) and several major SF novels—most prominent among them Robert A. Heinlein's *Stranger in a Strange Land* (1961) and Frank Herbert's *Dune* (1965), with their themes of group marriage and ecological consciousness, respectively. These books became bestsellers in the late 1960s not because SF fans were buying them but because hippies were: as Scott MacFarlane points out, Heinlein's *Stranger*—though popular within the genre (it won the 1962 Hugo Award for best novel)—did not see a second paperback edition until 1968; in the interim, "dog-eared copies of the first printing were being passed among the youthful participants of the burgeoning counterculture who used the story as a blueprint of sorts to experiment with communal relationships and religious practices" (92). H. Bruce Franklin has recounted how his students often spoke reverently of the book, in "intense personal statements that sounded like narratives of religious conversion" (127–28). In April 1962 two true believers founded the neopagan Church of All Worlds, its name borrowed from a Dionysian sect in the novel (see Cusack); later in the decade, Charles Manson, an apostle of group marriage himself, was prompted by his fondness for *Stranger* to name one of his sons Valentine Michael in honor of the book's protagonist—much to the consternation of the author (Heinlein 240–41). But Heinlein should not have been surprised, since SF's compelling ability to evoke alternative modes of being—its utopian "zone of possibility"—has always been an inspiration to those who, for whatever motives, are not content with the worlds in which they live.

WORKS CITED

Amburn, Ellis. *Subterranean Kerouac: The Hidden Life of Jack Kerouac*. 1998. New York: St. Martin's Griffin, 1999. Print.
Ballard, J. G. "Myth-Maker of the 20th Century." *New Worlds* 142 (May–June 1964): 121–27. Print.
Baraka, Amiri. "Answers in Progress." 1967. *Selected Plays and Prose of Amiri Baraka/LeRoi Jones*. New York: William Morrow, 1979. 136–39. Print.
Burroughs, William S. *Nova Express*. 1964. New York: Grove, 1992. Print.
Caute, David. *The Great Fear: The Anti-Communist Purge Under Truman and Eisenhower*. New York: Simon & Schuster, 1978. Print.
Charters, Ann. *Kerouac: A Biography*. 1973. New York: St. Martin's, 1994. Print.
Cormie, Stuart. "cityCityCITY: Jack Kerouac's Science Fiction." *Strange Horizons*. Dec. 4, 2006. Web. Sept. 15, 2013. http://www.strangehorizons.com/2006/20061204/kerouac-a.shtml.
Corporaal, Marguérite, and Evert Jan van Leeuwen, eds. *The Literary Utopias of Cultural Communities, 1790–1910*. Amsterdam: Rodopi, 2010. Print.
Cusack, Carole M. "Science Fiction as Scripture: Robert A. Heinlein's *Stranger in a Strange Land* and the Church of All Worlds." *Literature and Aesthetics* 19.2 (Dec. 2009): 72–91. Print.
Delany, Samuel R. *Babel-17*. 1966. New York: Vintage, 2001. Print.
_____. *Heavenly Breakfast: An Essay on the Winter of Love*. New York: Bantam, 1979. Print.
Foreman, Joel, ed. *The Other Fifties: Interrogating Midcentury American Icons*. Urbana: U of Illinois P, 1997. Print.
Franklin, H. Bruce. *Robert A. Heinlein: America as Science Fiction*. 1980. Oxford: Oxford UP, 1981. Print.
Ginsberg, Allen. "Howl." *Howl and Other Poems*. 1956. San Francisco: City Lights, 2002. 3–8. Print.
Gunn, James. "Introduction to Henry Kuttner's *Fury*." 1990. *Paratexts: Introductions to Science Fiction and Fantasy*. Lanham, MD: Scarecrow, 2013. 54–58. Print.
Heinlein, Robert A. *Grumbles from the Grave*. Ed. Virginia Heinlein. New York: Del Rey, 1989. Print.
Jazz Book Club. Advertisement. *Science Fantasy* 40 (Apr. 1960): 107. Print.
Jezer, Marty. *The Dark Ages: Life in the United States 1945–1960*. Boston: South End, 1982. Print.
Jones, James T. *Jack Kerouac's Duluoz Legend: The Mythic Form of an Autobiographical Fiction*. Carbondale: Southern Illinois UP, 1999. Print.
Kerouac, Jack. "cityCityCITY." 1959. *Good Blonde & Others*. 1993. Rev. ed. San Francisco: Grey Fox, 1998. 191–214. Print.
_____. "Essentials of Spontaneous Prose." 1965. *The Portable Beat Reader*. Ed. Ann Charters. New York: Penguin, 1992. 57–58. Print.
Landon, Brooks. *Science Fiction After 1900: From the Steam Man to the Stars*. 1995. New York: Routledge, 2002. Print.
Latham, Rob. "The New Wave." *A Companion to Science Fiction*. Ed. David Seed. Malden, MA: Blackwell, 2005. 202–16. Print.
Leiber, Fritz. "The Beat Cluster." *Galaxy* 20.1 (October 1961): 158–72. Print.
Luckhurst, Roger. *Science Fiction*. Malden, MA: Polity, 2005. Print.

Lutz, Tom. *Doing Nothing: A History of Loafers, Loungers, Slackers, and Bums in America.* New York: Farrar Strauss and Giroux, 2006. Print.

Lynds, Dennis. *Uptown Downtown.* New York: New American Library, 1963. Print.

MacAdams, Lewis. *Birth of the Cool: Beat, Bebop, and the American Avant-Garde.* New York: Free Press, 2001. Print.

MacFarlane, Scott. *The Hippie Narrative: A Literary Perspective on the Counterculture.* Jefferson, NC: McFarland, 2007. Print.

Malzberg, Barry N. *The Engines of the Night: Science Fiction in the Eighties.* New York: Bluejay, 1982. Print.

Masterton, Graham, and Andrew Rossabi. "William Burroughs: *Penthouse* Interview." 1972. *Conversations with William S. Burroughs.* Ed. Allen Hibbard. Jackson: U of Mississippi P, 1999. 39–50. Print.

McClure, Michael. *3 Poems: "Dolphin Skull," "Rare Angel," "Dark Brown."* New York: Penguin, 1995. Print.

Moorcock, Michael. Letter to the Editor, *Times Literary Supplement.* 1963. *William S. Burroughs at the Front: Critical Reception, 1959–1989.* Ed. Jennie Skerl and Robin Lydenberg. Carbondale: Southern Illinois UP, 1991. 47–48. Print.

———. "A New Literature for the Space Age." *New Worlds* 142 (May–June 1964): 2–3. Print.

Ross, Andrew. *Strange Weather: Culture, Science, and Technology in the Age of Limits.* New York: Verso, 1991. Print.

Rucker, Rudy. *Nested Scrolls: A Writer's Life.* Hornsea, UK: PS, 2011. Print.

Rudolph, Ken. "A Small Circle of Friends." *Shangri L'Affaires* 72 (Apr. 1, 1968): 6–7. Print.

Skerl, Jennie. "An Interview with William S. Burroughs." 1980. *Conversations with William S. Burroughs.* Ed. Allen Hibbard. Jackson: U of Mississippi P, 1999. 113–31. Print.

Spinrad, Norman. "Science Fiction and the Beats: American Literary Transcendentalism." *SFF Net.* N.d. Web. Sept. 14, 2013. http://www.sff.net/people/normanspinrad/beats.htm.

Stites, Richard. *Revolutionary Dreams: Utopian Vision and Experimental Life in the Russian Revolution.* New York: Oxford UP, 1989. Print.

Szwed, John F. *Space Is the Place: The Life and Times of Sun Ra.* 1997. New York: Da Capo, 1998. Print.

Theado, Matt. *Understanding Jack Kerouac.* Columbia: U of South Carolina P, 2000. Print.

Whitfield, Stephen J. *The Culture of the Cold War.* Baltimore: Johns Hopkins UP, 1991. Print.

CHAPTER 30

SEXUALITY

PATRICIA MELZER

SCIENCE fiction has long been heralded as a genre with the potential to radically reconceptualize society, its narratives of what Darko Suvin has famously dubbed "cognitive estrangement" enabling a denaturalization of existing social hierarchies and understandings of the human condition. Historically, however, SF has not always lived up to this potential but instead has reproduced white, male, heterosexual power fantasies of colonization and subjugation of the Other that have often relied on traditional values in their depictions of futuristic societies, including a deeply heteronormative understanding of sexuality. The general absence, in pulp SF, of serious investigations of sexuality as a force driving and defining human relations points to an inherent conservatism within the genre that was only challenged extensively during the New Wave era. Prior to the 1960s, SF was mainly asexual—or, rather, heteronormative sexuality (though taking place largely offstage) was simply projected onto the genre's visions of possible (human) futures.

The figure of the alien has been primarily constructed as "Other" (racially as well as sexually), serving to reinscribe normative power relations amidst a plethora of technological inventions and extraterrestrial presences, creating a white, middle-class "Intergalactic Suburbia," as SF writer and critic Joanna Russ noted in 1972: "Mummy and Daddy may live inside a huge amoeba and Daddy's job may be to test psychedelic drugs or cultivate yeast-vats, but the world inside their heads is the world of Westport and Rahway *and that world is never questioned*" (81; emphasis in original). White, heterosexual masculinity and bourgeois values either explicitly or implicitly defined the norm throughout virtually all the galaxies and futures of pulp-era SF. Despite their seemingly asexual content, however, the pages of the pulp magazines were riddled with images of threatening sexual "Others"—"the alien in our midst, the queer who could pass," as Wendy Pearson puts it, "wreaking havoc on the nation and destroying the family" (6).

The 1960s and 1970s brought innovation in style and content to the genre, expanding its treatment of sexuality by depicting nonnormative subjectivities and desires. Yet the potential for radically reimagining sexual relations often goes unfulfilled even today.

While the mainstream SF community generally does not tolerate openly homophobic narratives, and on its margins authors are challenging heteronormative assumptions by creating futuristic alternatives, by and large heteronormativity still prevails in most SF texts. Even though sexual practices are more freely depicted now than in the past, present-day social and political constraints still structure the vast majority of SF futures, as Candas Jane Dorsey points out in a special "Science Fiction and Sexuality" issue of *Science Fiction Studies*: "a breakthrough in paradigm," she says, is still lacking (390). Yet the sexual restrictions inherent in SF throughout its history do not mean that sexuality as an organizing principle was entirely absent or never questioned. As Wendy Gay Pearson, Veronica Hollinger, and Joan Gordon point out, Mary Shelley's *Frankenstein*, with its "extraordinary anxiety about the material outcomes of heterosexual relations" (2), serves as just one example of a simmering queer subtext in a classic SF text, one that lies at the very origins of the genre. On the other hand, SF narratives always tend to mirror the sexual morals, trends, and discourses of their time, embedding them deeply within their futuristic visions.

As a genre, SF creates hypothetical scenarios of social engineering, designing elaborate utopian and dystopian futures. Perhaps because of this, SF seems particularly susceptible to the influence of social movements and, in turn, influences them—including those politicizing sexual identities and practices. The genre's draw for social visionaries speaks to the often submerged but nonetheless potent political theory inherent in its narrative strategies and topics. As Donna Haraway observes, SF narratives do not simply *reflect* political discourses, they collectively *constitute* a form of political theory (*How Like* 120). Since its origins as a genre, SF has engaged with charged political and social issues, from colonialism to environmentalism, consistently grappling with the ethics of scientific and technological developments; as a result, it has, as Carl Freedman has pointed out, a structural affinity with critical theory and other forms of social inquiry. Gayle Rubin's claim that sexuality is both regulated through and shapes the realm of politics (sex, she says, "is always political" [4])—a claim inspired by Foucault's theory of power being produced through discourses, including literary ones—allows us to see SF as complicit with prevailing sexual ideologies, drawing upon them even as they contribute to them.

Science fiction's (re)definitions of subjects and subjectivities, and the shape their desires might and might not take, can thus be tracked alongside developments in the history of sexuality. The transformation of sexual attitudes in the West during the twentieth century—what Estelle Freedman and John D'Emilio identify as the rise of "sexual liberalism" (239–360)—has transformed the way SF handles sexual themes; reciprocally, the genre has articulated visions of sexual identity and possibility that have had a significant cultural impact. The founder of pulp SF, Hugo Gernsback, was also the editor of *Sexology: The Magazine of Sex Science*, which—from 1933 to 1967—helped to popularize the discoveries of Freud, Krafft-Ebing, Alfred Kinsey, and others. During the postwar era, the so-called sexual revolution deeply inspired SF and vice versa, with the genre becoming more explicit in its treatment of sexual themes while the counterculture began to adopt some of SF's "experimental" social attitudes. Robert

A. Heinlein's 1960s writings, beginning with *Stranger in a Strange Land* (1961), explored polyamorous possibilities in a way that proved influential in numerous arenas, from Robert Rimmer's 1966 bestseller *The Harrad Experiment* to the communal attitudes of the Manson Family (see Allyn 71–84; MacFarlane 92–103). Women writers created lesbian utopias, projecting gender-separatist societies akin to lesbian rural communes of the time, including fantasies of reproduction without men in such novels as Suzy McKee Charnas's *Motherlines* and Sally Miller Gearheart's *The Wanderground: Stories of the Hill Women* (both 1978). Feminist activists and writers used SF to explore the implications of sexual-liberationist viewpoints as well as science's impact on gender relations: works such as Marge Piercy's *Woman on the Edge of Time* and Dorothy Bryant's *The Kin of Ata Are Waiting for You* (both 1976) critiqued heterosexual relationships, including male violence against women, and offered alternative (sexual) visions.

Meanwhile, gay, lesbian, and bisexual characters began to appear in SF stories as something besides objects of scorn or sniggering humor, and—following the advent of Gay Liberation in the 1970s, a number of SF writers, such as Samuel R. Delany, came out as gay. The increased presence of nonstraight sexuality in SF texts was matched by the growing visibility of LGBT fans, who had previously, though tolerated by the fan community, rarely made their presence public. In 1986 the Gaylactic Network, a fan organization, was founded to promote LGBT concerns within the genre, while a growing strain of queer SF has proven popular with gay and lesbian readers who are not otherwise SF fans. Today, LGBT themes and characters, as well as LGBT-identified authors, are acknowledged and supported by (at least part of) the SF community through the Gaylactic Spectrum Awards, the Lambda Literary Awards, and the Golden Crown Literary Society Awards, which highlight works of SF, fantasy, and horror exploring queer themes and characters.

Scientific discourses on sexuality have played a significant role in this exchange between SF literary texts and social discourses (as science usually does for SF more generally). Theories of sexual and gender identities as located in biological and physical properties circulate in SF narratives at the same time as SF destabilizes the naturalization of knowledge about bodies and desires produced by the natural sciences as well as by sexology and psychoanalysis. The politicization of sexual identities and discursively constructed bodies in the "real" world, mounted by LGBT social movements as well as by feminist and queer theory, is reflected and developed in SF texts. For example, the increasing politicization that gender identities and sexualities have undergone the past 20 years through the transgender rights and queer movements finds representation in texts such as Melissa Scott's SF novel *Shadow Man* (1995), which thematizes the foundation of a political movement for the recognition of gender and sexual diversity in a futuristic, extraterrestrial human society. While it would be a gross generalization to insist that the genre produced *no* provocative depictions of eroticism prior to the sexual revolution, it is fair to say that the foundations for the routinely more explicit handling of sexuality in SF today were laid during the 1960s, cemented by massive social transformations in sexual views and conduct *and* by the New Wave movement, which challenged the genre's longstanding strategy of avoiding "controversial" topics.

A view of the Golden Age as a "sexless" period in SF history prevails in fans' and critics' perceptions. SF authors and scholars since the 1970s have critiqued the genre's inherent puritanism, its omission of sexuality—at least at the conscious level of its narratives—from the structure of its imaginary worlds (see, for example, Harrison; Sobchack). This reticence was attributed to a repressive sexual culture that, until the 1960s, was seldom challenged: SF magazines, still the main medium for new SF, were largely run by editors who balked at publishing material whose sexual content and language could be seen as unsuited for their readership base of adolescent boys. They censored what they considered inappropriate, such as explicit sex scenes, homosexual content, descriptions of polyamorous relationships, or the breaking of sexual taboos such as incest or pedophilia. This did not mean that SF worlds were not structured by sexuality: as noted above, heteronormativity was assumed. Nevertheless, as Rob Latham observes, even prior to the New Wave, a small handful of stories, most published during the early 1950s, framed their plots openly in relation to sexual topics long avoided by the genre, including homosexuality, incest, and sadomasochism ("Sextrapolation" 254). For example, Philip José Farmer's 1952 novella "The Lovers" dealt with the theme of interspecies miscegenation, depicting a sexual union between an Earthman and a female extraterrestrial, while Theodore Sturgeon's "The World Well Lost" (1953) sympathetically treated the plight of a pair of gay aliens exiled from their home planet due to their sexuality. Within these occasional challenges to sexual orthodoxy, one can perceive how the genre's tendency to estrange the given world offers radical and subversive means to undermine sexual norms. Curiously, this critical potential was recognized more potently by some early homosexual activists than it was by SF writers, with two stories depicting posthomophobic futures appearing in the magazine *ONE*, the official publication of the Mattachine Society, in 1954 and 1962 (see Latham, "Worlds" 189). It was only when the broader social challenge to conservative sexual morality—and the resultant generational divisions it reflected and exacerbated—struck the SF community full force during the mid-1960s that the genre took up the legacy of these rare examples.

As Latham observes, "The split between Old Guard and New Wave, coinciding as it did with an unparalleled period of erotic openness in the broader culture, inevitably came to involve fraught exchanges regarding the growing explicitness of contemporary sf's depictions of sexuality" ("Sextrapolation" 253). Increasingly strident demands for a relaxation of censorship restrictions resulted in the genre's own "sexual revolution," with young authors and editors pioneering new publishing outlets, thus changing the face of the genre. Most famously, Michael Moorcock's aggressive editing of the British magazine *New Worlds* in 1964, and Harlan Ellison's taboo-busting anthologies *Dangerous Visions* (1967) and *Again Dangerous Visions* (1972) in the United States, sparked significant conflicts within the SF community over the representation of sexuality in SF texts. As Moorcock commented in an editorial explaining his agenda, for SF to be "relevant to the world of Now" (25), it had to "use images apt for today" and feature "characters fitted for the society of today" (3). As Latham puts it: "In the view of many New Wave partisans, old-school SF was dominated by the antiquated social attitudes and claustrophobic gender ideologies of the 1950s; it could not possibly speak to an audience weaned on LSD, Vietnam, and the sexual revolution" ("Worlds" 191).

The calls for more "mature" content in SF voiced by many male authors and editors during the 1960s, however, often reflected a masculinist worldview that was firmly based in the heterosexual male credo of the sexual revolution. Ruth Rosen, in her history of postwar feminism, uses the phrase "male sexual revolution" to refer to a "libertine counterculture" that "elevated freedom over equality" in a way that merely intensified gender-based sexual exploitation (144–45). Some of the works that emerged in the wake of the New Wave offered virulent sexist scenarios, and sexual violence became the signature of many "liberated" SF texts. The focus lay more on breaking taboos than on promoting gender equality or sexual diversity, as Judith Merril observed in a critical review of the first *Dangerous Visions* anthology, many of whose stories, in her view, "substitute[d] shock for insight" (qtd. Latham, "Sextrapolation" 65). True sexual innovations among the textual orgies of the New Wave were frequently strangely absent.

There were a few writers who viewed the exploration of sexual identity and desire as a significant challenge whose results should include more than simply shocking puritanical readers. Samuel R. Delany complicated typical macho, wet-dream scenarios in stories like "Aye, and Gomorrah" (published in *Dangerous Visions*), which projects a truly unique form of futuristic sexuality, while Ursula K. Le Guin, in *The Left Hand of Darkness* (1969), imagined a planet whose denizens were biologically capable of switching sexes, forming long-lasting relationships that did not depend on the "essential" gender of their partners. Once the initial resistance against explicit sexual content on the part of editors and publishers gave way to a broader acceptance of sexuality as a feature of SF's future visions, and more feminist and queer authors emerged to counter the dominant trend of masculinist taboo-breaking and (hetero)sexual violence, the imaginative limitations of much of the New Wave's sexual experiments became clear. As Rosen's book shows, the same pattern held in the general culture, with the agenda of the "male sexual revolution" eventually being challenged by feminist and lesbian activists.

In Latham's account of New Wave "sextrapolation," there are three at times overlapping ways in which the genre's newfound sexual openness was expressed, shaping the genre's treatment of sexuality today. One was feminist SF's critique of the relentless focus on male sexuality and the resultant objectification of women that echoed the rejection, by the women's liberation movement, of the misogyny of the sexual revolution. With its critique of normative gender roles and sexual relationships, feminist SF, Latham claims, "served as a kind of conscience for the New Wave movement, seeking to ensure that the genre's newfound aesthetic freedoms would be used with some degree of moral accountability" (262), while at the same time offering explorations of lesbian desire and alternative heterosexual encounters. Examples of these early feminist challenges included Joanna Russ's *The Female Man* (1975) and the short fiction of Alice Sheldon (a.k.a. James Tiptree Jr.). Second, the New Wave pioneered new forms of pornography using SF themes and settings; while these were often merely "predictable male fantasies thinly veiled in SF trappings" (264), they could nevertheless on occasion generate "more thoughtful efforts . . . [that] use their science-fictional set-ups precisely to lay bare the pathologies of rampant machismo" (264) and heteronormativity's debilitating prescriptions. The author who has gained the most recognition for his fusion of SF and pornography is probably Delany, whose *Nevèrÿon* series (1979–87) and *Triton* (1976) explore sadomasochistic and transgender options, respectively. Finally, according to Latham, there are nonpornographic forms of sextrapolation that involve "projecting future trends based on current sexual mores or inventing novel sexual practices and relationships" (264), and that have contributed to the general movement toward less traditional ways of imagining human and nonhuman sexualities in the genre.

These forms of engagement with sexuality have shaped, and are echoed in, post-New Wave SF, from cyberpunk's virtual bodies and human–computer erotics in the 1980s to queer SF and SLASH writing in the 1990s and after. SLASH, a form of fan fiction written predominantly by women that develops sexual scenarios based on popular film and television narratives, constitutes a largely Internet-based subgenre of SF, produced by nonprofessional writers on the margins of what are still mostly male-dominated SF communities. Often, these narratives create sophisticated reflections on the implications that naturalized sex/gender systems have for our understanding of desire and pleasure. At their best, they conceptualize desire beyond homo—and heterosexuality to include bi—and pansexuality, or else they destabilize sexual identities through transgender, alien, and technological bodies of desire. They thus challenge not only a binary model of human desire, but also the discursive construction of bodies within the bounds of that desire, thus queering sexuality in SF beyond the mere inclusion of gay and lesbian characters (a by now somewhat commonplace textual strategy celebrated in anthologies like Nicola Griffith and Stephen Pagel's *Bending the Landscape* [1998]).

From the mid-1980s well into the late 1990s, the posthuman, both as a textual and a theoretical metaphor, dominated SF's anxious explorations of the human–machine interface. Donna Haraway's influential "Manifesto for Cyborgs" (1985) excavated the theoretical linkage of feminist, queer, political-economic, and technoscientific contexts surrounding the eponymous figure, celebrating the cyborg as a hybrid entity that transgresses dominant narratives, including those relating to gender and sexuality. Just one of SF's many "alien constructions" that destabilize discourses of power and identity, the cyborg keeps company with aliens, cross-species beings, and virtual bodies, all of which question the naturalized correlation of gender/sexuality relied on by heteronormativity (see Melzer, *Alien* 11–13). The fantastic settings in SF allow for a radical reimagining of what Judith Butler has called gender performativity, the idea that gender and sexual desire are not inherent but are produced discursively, through daily negotiations of political and social norms that privilege heterosexuality. Gender, Butler writes, "is an identity tenuously constituted in time, instituted in an exterior space through a *stylized repetition of acts*" (140; emphasis in original). Because of its fantastic corporeal manifestations, SF possesses a narrative logic that potentially allows the radical refiguring of sexual desires and practices and their social and political implications. Queer discourse during the mid-1980s and 1990s intersected with this narrative logic to create transgressive, distinctively queer sexualities in SF. "Queer" here signifies constellations of desire that cannot be contained within what Eve Kosofsky Sedgwick has termed the existing "taxonomy" of categories that reproduce—and rely upon—a stable correlation of gender and sexuality (23–27). Queerness undermines what Butler calls the "heterosexual matrix"—"that grid of cultural intelligibility through which bodies, genders, and desires are naturalized" (151n6). Queer theory's assertion that gender and sexual identities are discursive in origin—that desires are regulated by norms and thus that there is no one "normal" (hetero)sexual identity—challenges not only the heteronormative assumptions of many SF texts but also the binary understanding of the desire that underpins them as either heterosexual (normal) or homosexual (deviant).

During the early 1980s, the emergence of cyberpunk—in the early works of William Gibson, Bruce Sterling, Pat Cadigan, and others—injected desire into virtual spaces, especially those constructed by information technologies. In the process, they problematized essentialist understandings of sexuality by questioning whether the body is the only source for desire and identity. In fact, the main erotic thrill of novels such as Gibson's *Neuromancer* (1984) involved disposing of the "meat" (body) by "jacking-in" to a computer console, liberating oneself from the constraints of physical existence. As a character comments to the novel's protagonist, a renegade hacker, after watching him blissfully immerse himself in "cyberspace" (a term Gibson invented), "I saw you stroking that Sendai; man, it was pornographic" (47). Cyberpunk writers' eerily accurate anticipations of today's world of mobile virtual experiences conceptualized subjectivity—and consequently sexuality—as produced and channeled by online communication in a disembodied space.

This embrace of disembodiment was criticized by many feminist SF writers and critics, who dismissed much of cyberpunk's handling of the relationship between technology and the body as little more than (white) masculinist fantasies that instantiate an invidious Cartesian dualism between (male) mind and (female) body (see Squires). Historically, this ideological juxtaposition of reason vs. nature has disempowered women and nonwhite people by binding them to corporeality in ways that forestall cyberpunk fantasies of shedding the body and erotically communing in a cyberspatial realm of pure mind. This familiar dualism is reproduced in many of cyberpunk's most iconic narratives: the virtual sexual encounters that male protagonists enjoy—as well as the disembodied existence akin to a state of permanent cerebral orgasm—are contrasted to the physicality of the narratives' female characters, who are often depicted as sex workers, most famously in *Neuromancer*, where Molly Millions makes money as a "meat puppet" by prostituting her comatose body, thus "attach[ing] a subtext of femininity to the 'prison' of the flesh" (Foster 61).

Despite claims that cyberpunk's sexual politics are deformed by patriarchal ideology, even "conceal[ing] a complicity with '80s conservatism" (Nixon 231), aspects of this subgenre have been appropriated and deployed for more transgressive ends by lesbian and queer writers. Cyberpunk's eroticization of computers and affiliated technologies amounts to a form of "teledildonics" (Rheingold) that has developed side by side with real-world forms of virtual erotic play, at times drawing upon and at times stimulating them. Indeed, cybersex is an essentially science-fictional modality for the expression of amorous desire, one that has potentially queer implications. As Tom Foster points out, while "technologies of disembodiment" that make possible a decoupling of public persona from physical body are at risk of reproducing a "gendered hierarchy that equates masculinity with universal rationality and femininity with embodied particularity," they also carry the potential for revealing "that sex and gender are not related as cause and effect and that sex and gender do not necessarily exist in a one-to-one expressive relation to one another" (116). The gender performativity the subject executes in cyberspace potentially queers the body's relationship to sexual desire when it is not understood as a complete *release* from the body but as "a different way of conceptualizing a *relationship* to the human body" (Stone 40; emphasis in original). Narratives that utilize virtual technologies to complicate the links between gender and sexuality include Laura J. Mixon's *Glass Houses* (1992), Melissa Scott's *Trouble and Her Friends* (1994), and Maureen F. McHugh's stories "A Coney Island of the Mind" (1992) and "Virtual Love" (1994). By constructing and exploring complex connections between "real" and virtual identities, tales such as these, Foster observes, "interrogat[e] the naturalness of expressive assumptions" regarding desire and subjectivity (125).

Cyberpunk has not been alone in exploring the erotic implications of the human–machine interface. A different set of cyborg texts, generally produced by feminist and queer authors, place computers and the virtual worlds they sustain in the context of other technical systems, such as reproductive technologies, cloning, and biotech, as well as within social and environmental discourses. As a result, they create explicitly political narratives that do not simply center on an individual's subjectivity (though they do often feature lesbian central characters) but rather address the larger structures and ideologies that shape our world, often envisioning collective forms of resistance to them. Works such as Nicola Griffith's *Slow River* (1995), Rebecca Ore's *Gaia's Toys* (1997), and Nalo Hopkinson's *Brown Girl in the Ring* (1998) explore the impact of technology within a framework critical of heteronormative bodies and desires.

Within the general corpus of cyborg texts, the exploration of desire and pleasure manifests in a variety of ways, not always advancing SF's potential for undermining and denaturalizing heteronormativity. The cyborg body—always gendered and racialized—permits visions of technologically enhanced female and nonwhite identities whose implicit queerness threatens patriarchal normalcy. A precursor to the dangerous female cyborg body in narratives of the 1990s is Joanna Russ's Jael in *The Female Man*, an assassin of men whose politicized violence enables the parallel-world lesbian utopia of Whileaway; her technobody serves the deliberate destruction of patriarchy. Jael is echoed in Gibson's Molly, who, despite her deadly cyborg implants, lacks Jael's dangerous rage, instead being locked into a feminized corporeality that contrasts with the male protagonist's virtual experiences, while Nili in Marge Piercy's *He, She and It* (1991) represents a later feminist version of the female technoassassin. The cyborg body, however, also enables reactionary, hyperbolic male fantasies that cement polarized gender constructions in a heterosexual economy of desire. For example, alongside more radical texts such as Griffith's, Ore's, and Hopkinson's, one finds such works as Richard Calder's trilogy *Dead Girls, Dead Boys, Dead Things* (1992–96), in which a dystopian near future is overrun with hypersexualized and Orientalized female bodies that have been nanotechnologically modified to become vampiric sex-dolls. These novels rely upon and reinforce traditional heterosexual male fantasies, replete with pseudo-empowered femme fatales and orgies of sexual violence. While Calder flirts with still-taboo subjects such as fetishism and sadomasochism, his imagination fails to queer these depictions, constraining them within a predictable sexual economy of heterosexual power relations, thus echoing the more disappointing shortcomings of the New Wave some 30 years earlier.

The traditional SF encounter between humans and aliens has also generated compelling queer treatments in recent decades. In these tales, extraterrestrials are not depicted as dangerous and aberrant others, as was often the case in earlier SF, but rather as alternatives to an inflexible sex/gender system: cross-species desire and reproduction enable sexual identities that transgress and transcend binary human conceptions (*either* gay/lesbian *or* straight). Octavia E. Butler's work is a primary example of these reconfigurations: her narratives challenge readers' assumptions not only about gender and sexuality, but also about race. From novels like *Wild Seed* (1980) and the celebrated "Xenogenesis" trilogy (1987–89) all the way up to her final novel *Fledgling* (2005), Butler offers feminist queerings of desire through multifarious depictions of eroticized human–alien relationships that destabilize both sexual and racial categories of identity. Her treatments of cross-species and cross-gender shapeshifting, human–alien coupling and reproduction, and complex models of sexual symbiosis display an intricate erotics of power. Queer desire as a mechanism of community building is explored in *Fledgling*, where vampiric creatures known as Ina sustain mutually fulfilling, polyamorous relationships with their human "symbionts." Since humans rely on the Ina to survive and vice versa, pleasure becomes inseparable from power; the dynamics characteristic of BDSM communities are inherent in Butler's imagined world, with consensual power serving as an alternative to historical forms of nonconsensual exploitation, such as slavery. Human–Ina households contain humans of both sexes but Ina of only one sex, undermining the heterosexual nuclear family and foregrounding a socialized interspecies homoeroticism.

Moreover, Butler further unsettles the reader through the suggestion of even more tabooed sexual practices: the first human–Ina encounter in the narrative occurs between a seemingly 10-year-old girl (since Ina age more slowly than humans) and a man in his mid-twenties. The biological component of the cross-species relationship, grounded in a nutritional need for blood on the part of the Ina and a physical addiction to Ina "venom" on the part of the humans, thematizes desire as both physical and learned, both nonconsensual (because driven by bodily needs) and consensual (because necessary for mutual survival). *Fledgling*'s treatment of queer sexuality in *Fledgling* echoes Judith Butler's recognition that desire fundamentally underpins any subject formation, binding people together into networks and communities. In Octavia Butler's work, as I have argued elsewhere, the "body follows desire, not vice versa, disrupting the naturalized correlation between sex, gender, and sexuality; identity *is* that indeterminate state that is resolved only through the object of desire" (*Alien*

241; emphasis in original). Butler's work is representative of contemporary SF texts that use the genre's radical potential to explore forms of "queer futurity" claimed by queer writers of color in particular (see Muñoz)—futures "that seem queer from our perspective" because they "result from a resignification of the sexual customs we consider natural" (Kilgore 237).

Meanwhile, on the margins of the mainstream SF community one finds lesser-known SF texts that evoke technologically enhanced, bioengineered, and genetically altered bodies that redefine both anatomy and desire. Fan writing—especially SLASH, the erotic, usually homosexual pairing of existing SF characters (see Penley 101–46)—and hard-core queer erotica use sexuality as a science-fictional trope to shape narratives of technologized bodies and desires while also functioning as pornography. While much of this material is released online, a number of editors—such as Cecilia Tan, founder of Circlet Press—are dedicated to publishing SF and fantasy erotica in book form. Many of the short stories gathered in Tan's numerous SF erotica collections—which include *Worlds of Women: Sapphic Science Fiction Erotica* (1994), *Wired Hard: Erotica for a Gay Universe* (1994), *Fetish Fantastic: Erotica on the Edge* (1997), and *Sex in the System: Stories of Erotic Futures, Technological Stimulation, and the Sensual Life of Machines* (2006)—intersect with queer theory's criticisms of heteronormativity, featuring representations of politically transgressive desires seldom found in mainstream SF. As she states in one of her introductions, Tan views her work as a contribution to SF's ongoing project of social critique, engaging forcefully with the sexual politics of our time by releasing fiction for "all those people in the real world whose desires are marginalized, outlawed, or made taboo, . . . all those who fear being attacked or killed for being who they are, . . . anyone who has ever felt alone in their desire or who has had to hide to live it" (8). Pornographic narratives such as these celebrate specifically queer desires and practices within SF settings, creating new kinds of sexual subjects. By allowing for the articulation of new anatomies, the cyborgs and alien beings in these stories denaturalize the human body (and thus gender), but they also denaturalize sexual desires and practices, undermining the sexual taxonomy upon which heteronormativity depends. In this, they echo the lesbian transgender narratives conceptualized by Foster that have appropriated cyberspace from the heterosexual male cyberpunks in order to convert it into a politicized and transgressive social-sexual space.

The queering of desire through reimagined, technologized bodies in SF pornography intersects with discussions of prosthetics and medical interventions in disability and transgender studies. As I have observed in an earlier essay, the "cyborg is characterized by detachable extremities . . . [that] become part of the body, not its artificial extensions" ("And How Many" 164–65). By refusing a nostalgic yearning for an unalienated "natural" body and instead embracing posthuman subjectivity, these tales resist fetishistically otherizing the technologically enhanced body, whose queered desires are experienced as liberating and empowering. Some of the most sexually transgressive and political writings in the genre today can be found on the margins of the SF community, tucked on the shelves of LGBT bookstores or archived on SLASH websites. Yet they retain a presence within the genre through such fan practices as wearing

BDSM gear at conventions, sites that are themselves "marginal but mainstream spaces" that provide safe venues for fantasy role-playing (see Herman 97–98). Indeed, Staci Newmahr has argued that a taste "for alternative literature and film, especially sci-fi and fantasy," often "set[s] the stage for alternative interests, including SM"; the genre's "potential for . . . creat[ing] open-mindedness" serves as "a virtual training ground for the tolerance necessitated by SM participation" (51). As Lewis Call argues in his recent study of *BDSM in American Science Fiction and Fantasy*, S/M and SF share an inclination to violate norms and blur boundaries, an affinity that permits genre writers to offer depictions of alternative sexual practices that "can evade the twin dangers of normalization and pathologization" (16).

Following Michel Foucault's theory of the discursive operations of power (often seen as foundational for contemporary queer theory), it would be attributing too much merit to the concept of repression to claim that there was *no* sexual content in SF prior to the New Wave movement: instead of a linear progression from repressed to liberated texts, the genre has always been preoccupied with sexual orders. The fact that the most prevalent one is still heteronormativity attests to the power our norms wield over our imaginations. True challenges to a heterosexist, binary economy of desire can be found on the margins of SF: in the work of LGBT writers and writers of color, such as Delany and Butler, and in the work of queer SF pornographers and SLASH fans, whose narratives estrange the reader's sexual assumptions by using the genre's conventional icons and techniques in groundbreaking and pleasurable ways. Ultimately, SF texts and SF communities reflect our world in that they contain conservative viewpoints as well as ones that forcefully challenge the sexual status quo, offering visions of alternative futures filled with new forms of intimacy and desire.

Works Cited

Allyn, David. *Make Love, Not War: The Sexual Revolution, An Unfettered History*. New York: Routledge, 2001. Print.

Butler, Judith. *Gender Trouble: Feminism and the Subversion of Identity*. New York: Routledge, 1990. Print.

Butler, Octavia E. *Fledgling*. New York: Seven Stories, 2005. Print.

Calder, Richard. *Dead Girls, Dead Boys, Dead Things*. 1992, 1994, 1996. New York: St. Martin's Griffin, 1998. Print.

Call, Lewis. *BDSM in American Science Fiction and Fantasy*. New York: Palgrave Macmillan, 2012. Print.

Dorsey, Candas Jane. "Some Notes on the Failure of Sex and Gender Inquiry in SF." *Science Fiction Studies* 36.3 (Nov. 2009). 389–90. Print.

Foster, Thomas. *The Souls of Cyberfolk: Posthumanism as Vernacular Theory*. Minneapolis: U of Minnesota P, 2005. Print.

Freedman, Carl. *Critical Theory and Science Fiction*. Hanover, NH: Wesleyan UP, 2000. Print.

Freedman, Estelle, and John D'Emilio. *Intimate Matters: A History of Sexuality in America*. 1988. 2nd ed. Chicago: U of Chicago P, 1997. Print.

Gibson, William. *Neuromancer*. New York: Ace, 1984. Print.

Griffith, Nicola. *Slow River*. New York: Ballantine, 1995. Print.

Haraway, Donna. *How Like a Leaf: An Interview with Thyrza Nichols Goodeve*. New York: Routledge, 2000. Print.

———. "A Manifesto for Cyborgs: Science, Technology, and Socialist Feminism in the 1980s." 1985. *Coming to Terms: Feminism, Theory, Politics*. Ed. Elizabeth Weed. New York: Routledge, 173–204. Print.

Harrison, Harry. *Great Balls of Fire: An Illustrated History of Sex in Science Fiction*. London: Pierrot, 1977. Print.

Herman, RDK. "Playing with Restraints: Space, Citizenship and BDSM." *Geographies of Sexualities: Theory, Practices and Politics*. Ed. Kath Brown, Jason Lim, and Gavin Brown. Surrey, UK: Ashgate, 2009. 89–100. Print.

Kilgore, De Witt Douglas. "Queering The Coming Race?: A Utopian Historical Imperative." *Queer Universes: Sexualities in Science Fiction*. Ed. Wendy Gay Pearson, Veronica Hollinger, and Joan Gordon. Liverpool: Liverpool UP, 2008. 233–51. Print.

Latham, Rob. "Sextrapolation in New Wave Science Fiction." *Science Fiction Studies* 33.2 (July 2006): 251–74. Print.

———. "Worlds Well Lost: Homosexuality in Science Fiction." *The Golden Age of Gay Fiction*. Ed. Drewey Wayne Gunn. Albion, NY: MLR, 2009. 185–96. Print.

MacFarlane, Scott. *The Hippie Narrative: A Literary Perspective on the Counterculture*. Jefferson, NC: McFarland, 2007. Print.

Melzer, Patricia. *Alien Constructions: Science Fiction and Feminist Thought*. Austin: U of Texas P, 2006. Print.

———. "'And How Many Souls Do You Have?': Technologies of Perverse Desire and Queer Sex in Science Fiction Erotica." *Queer Universes: Sexualities in Science Fiction*. Ed. Wendy Gay Pearson, Veronica Hollinger, and Joan Gordon. Liverpool: Liverpool UP, 2008. 161–79. Print.

Moorcock, Michael. "Symbols for the Sixties." *New Worlds* 148 (1965): 2–3, 25. Print.

Muñoz, José Esteban. *Cruising Utopia: The Then and There of Queer Futurity*. New York: NYU P, 2009. Print.

Newmahr, Staci. *Playing on the Edge: Sadomasochism, Risk, and Intimacy*. Bloomington: Indiana UP, 2011. Print.

Nixon, Nicola. "Cyberpunk: Preparing the Ground for Revolution or Keeping the Boys Satisfied?" *Science Fiction Studies* 19.2 (July 1992): 219–35. Print.

Pearson, Wendy. "Alien Cryptographies: The View from Queer." *Science Fiction Studies* 26.1 (Mar. 1999): 1–22. Print.

Pearson, Wendy, Veronica Hollinger, and Joan Gordon. "Introduction." *Queer Universes: Sexualities in Science Fiction*. Ed. Wendy Gay Pearson, Veronica Hollinger, and Joan Gordon. Liverpool: Liverpool UP, 2008. 1–14. Print.

Penley, Constance. *NASA/Trek: Popular Science and Sex in America*. New York: Verso, 1997. Print.

Rheingold, Howard. "Teledildonics: Reach Out and Touch Someone." 1990. *net.seXXX: Readings on Sex, Pornography, and the Internet*. Ed. Dennis D. Waskul. New York: Peter Lang, 2004. 319–22. Print.

Rosen, Ruth. *The World Split Open: How the Modern Women's Movement Changed America*. 2000. New York: Penguin, 2001. Print.

Rubin, Gayle. "Thinking Sex: Notes for a Radical Theory of the Politics of Sexuality." 1982. *The Lesbian and Gay Studies Reader.* Ed. Henry Abelove, Michèle Aina Barale, and David M. Halperin. New York: Routledge, 1993. 3–44. Print.

Russ, Joanna. "The Image of Women in Science Fiction." 1970. *Images of Women in Fiction: Feminist Perspectives.* Ed. Susan Cornillon. Bowling Green, OH: Bowling Green U Popular P, 1972. 79–94. Print.

Sedgwick, Eve Kosofsky. *Epistemologies of the Closet.* Berkeley: U of California P, 1990. Print.

Sobchack, Vivian. "The Virginity of Astronauts: Sex and the Science Fiction Film." 1985. *Alien Zone: Cultural Theory and Contemporary Science Fiction Cinema.* Ed. Annette Kuhn. New York: Verso, 1990. 103–15. Print.

Squires, Judith. "Fabulous Feminist Futures and the Lure of Cyberspace." 1996. *The Cybercultures Reader.* Ed. David Bell and Barbara M. Kennedy. New York: Routledge, 2000. 360–73. Print.

Stone, Alluquère Rosanne. *The War of Desire and Technology at the Close of the Mechanical Age.* 1995. Cambridge, MA: MIT Press, 2001. Print.

Tan, Cecilia. "Introduction." *Sexcrime: Tales of Underground Love and Subversive Erotica.* Cambridge, MA: Circlet, 2000. 8. Print.

CHAPTER 31

BODY MODIFICATION

ROSS FARNELL

Body modification, once the domain of a marginalized subculture, has emerged into mainstream cultural visibility. The late twentieth and early twenty-first centuries have witnessed a remarkable legitimation of the more common body-modification practices—most notably, tattooing, piercing, and cosmetic surgery—while at the same time, some practices (such as cutting, scarification, branding, and elongation) have continued to be marginalized. The growing interest in body modification was heralded by the appearance, in 1989, of the pioneering RE/Search Press publication *Modern Primitives*, edited by V. Vale and Andrea Juno. This volume culminated two decades of subcultural experimentation, by punks and other marginalized groups, with "deviant" strategies of body modification; according to Victoria Pitts, these appropriations "positioned the body as a site of exploration as well as a space needing to be reclaimed from culture" (7). "Modern primitivism," a term coined by Fakir Musafar, marked an important moment in the rising popularity of body modification (see Winge 19–22); interviews with Musafar and photographs of his varied and often extreme practices—skin stretching, suspensions, "ceremonial" adornment and piercing—were pivotal to Vale and Juno's book. For Fakir, body modification was about the empowering of people who are socially isolated, permitting them to reassert control over their bodies and beliefs: "We had all rejected the Western cultural biases about ownership and use of the body. We believed that our body belonged to us" (qtd. Pitts 9).

This belief weaves a common thread through the many and varied practices of body modification, of which "modern primitivism" is but one strand. Body-modification practices range across (generally subversive) subcultures as varied as queer S/M, fetish and body-art clubs, so-called pro-sex feminism, punk and cyberpunk subcultures, alternative music scenes, performance art, New Age spiritualism, and of course tattoo culture (see Pitts 4–14). Body-modification practices are posited variously as ways of enjoying new transgressive pleasures, of reclaiming female bodies from patriarchal culture, of inventing new body technologies, of making political statements with the body, and of returning to tribalism and primitive spiritualism. As with numerous other subcultures, those that embrace body modification are now increasingly implicated in the frenetic pace and reciprocity of the feedback loop that connects margins to mainstream.

Still, some more extreme practices resist easy appropriation, and some advocates are insistent on maintaining that distance—or else, like Shannon Larratt, editor of the website *BME* (*Body Modification Ezine*), retaining subcultural control of their communal history. According to its mission statement, *BME* speaks for "an uncommon subculture and community built by and for modified people. We are the historians, practitioners and appreciators of body modification. We are the collaborative and comprehensive resource for the freedom of individuality in thought, expression and aesthetic" (Larratt). Increasingly a victim of their own popularity, body-modification subcultures are attempting to shore up the barricades and resist commodification. The statistics on tattooing, for example, are telling: according to a 2010 Pew Research Center report, 38 percent of the Millennial Generation (those born after 1981) are inked, comparing closely with 32 percent of Generation X, yet more than 50 percent of those Millennials have between two and five tattoos, and fully 18 percent have six or more. More compelling is the rise in piercings in areas other than the earlobes, with 23 percent of Millennials having them, compared to just 9 percent of Generation X and 1 percent of those over 45. The statistics are even higher for women under 30, with 35 percent having body piercings, compared to 11 percent for men ("Millennials"). The gender difference is interesting, but the generational shift is remarkable.

Just as this boundary between margins and mainstream is breached, so too is the line between cultural representations and contemporary social practices. Science fiction plays a critical role in this erasure of borders, and therefore it is unsurprising to find common themes and ideas shared between SF and the realms of body modification, most notably in the transgressive aesthetics and ideologies of cyberpunk and the cyborg, which have moved from the page to the catwalk and piercing parlor. Donna Haraway has proposed that "the boundary between science fiction and social reality is an optical illusion" ("Manifesto" 66), while Jean Baudrillard has gone further, arguing that it is no longer "necessary to write science-fiction: [our societies] have as of now ... broken the referential orbit of things" (36). Both theorists register the end of SF as a self-contained genre since contemporary culture and theory now draw regularly on some of the most basic of SF's tropes, the cyborg being perhaps the most obvious. The culture of body modification is simply one arena in which science fiction is materialized as a form of social practice.

Body modification involves not only directly altering the appearance and form of the body's outer surface but also, as Mike Featherstone notes, augmenting the body with "various forms of prostheses and technological systems" that offer "the potential for further *inner body* cyborg technological developments" (1–2; emphasis added). In conjunction with these converging modes of modification, we can identify common threads in both the subcultures and the SF narratives of body modification. For example, the tendency, within "modern primitivism" specifically and body modification in general, to "tak[e] control over and mak[e] a gesture against the body natural" (Featherstone 2) speaks to SF's persistent denaturalizations of the body, its estrangements of any "standard" conception of corporeal identity. Anne Balsamo has spoken of the convergence between SF's cyborg fantasies and such common practices as piercing and cosmetic surgery, which are in her view modes of self-definition in an era of profound social and economic change, making the body a "vehicle for staging cultural identities" (*Technologies* 78).

Faced with massive "ontological insecurity," Christian Klesse argues, "self-identity has become deliberative.... Thus, people are engaged in a permanent re-ordering of identity narratives in which a concern with the body is central" (19). Klesse points to Chris Shilling's concept of "body projects": in Shilling's words, "There is a tendency for the body to be seen as an entity which is in the process of becoming, *a project which should be worked at and accomplished as part of an individual's self-identity*" (5; emphasis in original). Such body projects are, as Elizabeth Grosz notes (143), what Foucault would call a "technique of self-production"; tribal scarifications, for example, can be seen to "mark the body as a public, collective, social category" (Grosz 140). The body, Grosz argues, has always been a cultural product and the site of innumerable inscriptions, as opposed to being some natural or innate blank canvas. Still, even though the body is socially constructed, these constructions have affective and communal force, which is why the notion of altering identity via modification of the body can be problematic. The SF narratives that explore such transgressions and self-productions of body and identity are the fictional extrapolations that intersect with, inform, and at times serve to aestheticize actual body-modification practices.

Like many of those body-modification discourses with which it intersects, science fiction is concerned with representations of posthuman otherness, depicting transformations and transfigurations of the body via prosthetics, nanotechnology, and genetic engineering. Yet neither the genre nor practices of body modification are without limitations in regard to imagining the "Other." It is debatable whether SF's modes of signification, woven as they are from preexisting codes and metaphors, can ever capture images of true alterity, as opposed to arresting refigurations of the "already-said." So too, argues Klesse, modern primitivism, for all its delirious transformations of bodies, may simply reproduce "all the inherently repressive gendered stereotypes on [sic] racialized people and their sexuality" stemming from the narratives of colonial rule embedded in the very concept of primitivism (18). The diversity of strategies in SF texts and their intersection with body modification practices, however, do have the capacity to provide valuable speculations on both the possibilities and limitations of the hybrid, modified, and transgressed body in a diversity of sociopolitical, cultural, and "alien" contexts—present and future; real and imagined. Indeed, there is perhaps no more famous example of the modified body in all of literature than that of Frankenstein's monster, a grotesque collage of recombined bodies, and Mary Shelley's creature has been followed by a long line of organically, surgically, and technologically modified bodies, from the human–animal hybrids of H. G. Wells's *Island of Dr. Moreau* (1897) to the infotech- and biotech-augmented characters of William Gibson's *Neuromancer* (1984).

In her groundbreaking anthropological work, Mary Douglas identified two opposing traits in a culture's attitude toward the body: the "autoplastic," which seeks to achieve a culture's goals through manipulations of the body, and the "alloplastic," which achieves its ends by "operating directly on the external environment" in which the body exists (116). In many schools of anthropological thought, Douglas notes, these terms were problematically presumed to correlate with "primitive" and "modern-technological" cultures, respectively; yet the latter also are subject to elaborate taboos regarding bodily integrity, body orifices, and bodily "pollution." Modern primitives would thus be an indication of the persistence of autoplastic modes in Western industrial societies. When applied to SF, the two concepts may be figured as opposing sides of a dichotomy in the ways that the genre has imagined the exploration of space: thus, modifying the body to make the (post)human form compatible with alien environments would be an autoplastic approach, whereas terraforming planets to make them more hospitable to the body as it currently exists would be alloplastic.

The original hypothesis of the cyborg proposed that "[a]ltering man's bodily functions to meet the requirements of extraterrestrial environments would be more logical than providing an earthly environment for him in space" (Clynes and Kline 26). Frederik Pohl's 1976 SF novel *Man Plus* is an excellent example of just such an autoplastic depiction of cyborgization, and it has set a telling precedent for subsequent treatments of body modification within the genre. In the novel, the "architects" of the "Exomedicine Project" radically remake astronaut Roger Torraway for a mission to Mars. A "man plus large elements of hardware" (16), Torraway has his organs and regulatory, circulatory, and nervous systems either replaced with artificial substitutes or cybernetically augmented. As a result, Torraway's body becomes a living "work of art" (106), albeit one produced through much pain and suffering—a contested site, a zone of problematic cyborg irruptions into the organic human. The dilemmas of future cyborg modifications identified by Pohl point toward the indeterminate border zones of cyberpunk and postcyberpunk SF, such as the "arcane bioaesthetics of Posthumanist philosophy" found in Sterling's "Shaper/Mechanist" stories (*Crystal* 87). The bifurcation of posthumanity in Sterling's series into the genetically refigured Shapers on the one hand and the prosthetically enhanced Mechanists on the other represents a new duality created by the incorporation of alternative forms of technology into the body. In these tales, as Craig Thompson points out, "The *design* of the body becomes a motive for power struggles" (200; emphasis in original)—for example, over commodification by the corporations and factions that control their production. Limbs and other body parts are "repossessed," children reduced to the status of "investments": the modified body has become as valuable—or as obsolete—as any other technological object.

SF that so clearly articulates a problematic future commodification of modified bodies is prescient for modern primitivism, which, though rejecting "the materialism of Western consumer culture," is nonetheless subject to the commercialization of tattooing and piercing (Klesse 21). Promoting and supplying the demand for body modification is a burgeoning business, as Klesse points out, as well as a "fashion trend [that] has to be interpreted in the context of an increasingly trendy *aestheticization and commodification of ethnic difference*" (21; emphasis in original). Bryan S. Turner concurs, asserting that tattooing is "closely related to the commercial exploitation of sexual themes in popular culture.... In short, tattoos have become a regular aspect of consumer culture, where they add cultural capital to the body's surface" (40). These mundane forms of commercial appropriation converge asymptotically with Sterling's wild extrapolations of their future possibilities, conspiring to posit the figure of a simultaneously modified and commodified (post)human body indentured to the scientific, technological, and economic power structures that produce it.

Sterling's representation of the Mechanists is best exemplified by the total-body prosthetics and wired existence of the Lobsters, "creatures . . . bored with the outmoded paradigms of blood and bone" (*Crystal* 76–77). Their cyborg body modifications—grafted shells over skin, amplified senses, cranial plugs, and drugs to overcome agoraphobic fears—not only allow existence in the vacuum of space but also create new forms of desire and pleasure. Alternatively, the Shapers, "industrial artifacts constructed of patented genes" (49), achieve their enhancements through a combination of genetic engineering and plastic surgery. Shapers and Mechs are symbols of a divided evolutionary process, two different posthuman outcomes of radical body modification, yet both display a "respective oversignification of various body parts" (Bukatman 349) evident in the foregrounding of various fetishized and decompartmentalized modification zones comprising the bodies of today's extreme modifiers.

If Victor Frankenstein is Shelley's modern Prometheus, then Sterling's Lindsay Abelard is the "posthuman Prometheus," begetting a "new Creation, where art and purpose would take the place of a billion years of evolution" (*Schismatrix* 279). Sterling's amusing appraisal of *Frankenstein* in his essay "Cyberpunk in the Nineties" contrasts Shelley's depiction of Victor's "spine-chilling transgression," his "affront against the human soul" that "is direly punished by his own creation," with a parodic synopsis of a putative "cyberpunk version" of the story: "The Monsters of cyberpunk... are already loose on the streets.... Quite likely *we* are them. The Monster would have been copyrighted through the new genetics laws, and manufactured worldwide in many thousands. Soon the monsters would all have lousy night jobs mopping up at fast food restaurants" (emphasis in original). For Sterling, the point of this cynical rendition is not only that any recourse to the burden of hubris should be redundant for a Promethean future of self-made bodies, but that the act of modification itself becomes potentially mundane as it is appropriated and commodified, losing much of the Gothic charge of sublimity that haunts Shelley's tale.

Cyberpunk SF of the 1980s and 1990s was centrally concerned with themes of body and mind invasion, "techniques radically redefining the nature of humanity, the nature of the self" (Sterling, "Preface" xiii). The movement's "impatience with borders" (xiv) provided a fertile breeding ground for the erasure of human–machine or nature–technology dichotomies, creating a veritable cyborgian laboratory of transgressive bodily possibilities. Cyberpunk's very real intersections with the subcultures of body modification stem directly from its powerful images and metaphors of prosthesis, its futuristic biotechnologies converging with contemporary (sub)cultural desire and the aesthetic, cosmetic, and technological systems that exist to fulfill it. Indeed, Victoria Pitts identifies "cyberpunk" as a marginal but significant segment of today's body-modification movement, taking modification "into cyberspace, biomedicine, and high technology ... [and] framing the body as a limitless frontier for technological innovation.... [C]yberpunk body artists have accomplished modifications previously imagined only in science fiction" (13). Describing the case of one renowned body modifier who engages in "highly deviant appropriation[s] of medical procedures to create implants and conduct self-surgery" (173), utilizing scarification, branding, and facial alterations, Pitts positions his attitude toward the body as "postmodern and cyberpunk," mixing tribal and high-tech practices to create a hybrid style (2).

According to Pitts, radical cyberpunk modifications and modern primitivism share a faith in the wonders of self-fashioning, based on a common "trope of postmodern liberalism": "We can be who we want to be, personal and social history notwithstanding" (195). Lisiunia Romanienko puts a more positive spin on this idea: agreeing that the theories and practices of body modification evince "intentional self-construction processes," she claims that these "symbols are used to expedite the process of self-actualization, and are crucial in the exchange of meaning in self-construction" (2). Private and public symbols of body modification—from the more conventional to the extreme—signify meaning via a process of "nonverbal communication" that is used by practitioners as both "a decivilizing mechanism of the transgressive" and a "mechanism of emancipatory authenticity to facilitate liberating transformation" (189–90). As we shall see, such a positioning of the body as an undifferentiated site of individuation and liberation is ultimately problematic.

Anne Balsamo argues that Pat Cadigan's *Synners* (1991) reconceptualizes the typical cyberpunk scenario in which the "meat" body is transcended in favor of ecstatic experiences in cyberspace; instead, it counters a vision of the "body-in-isolation" with one of the "body-in-connection," always plugged into the collective histories of gender and racial identity (144). Yet while Cadigan's resolutely embodied form of cyberpunk writing does offer paradigms of difference to guide the production of informed, "marked" bodies and empowered subjectivities, it is still entwined with the limiting technologics of masculinist cyberpunk tropes. Coupled with such limitation is the persistent problem of commodification for the cyberpunk subject, always functioning in a relentlessly corporatized realm of technomania, with its insistent "subjection of all individuals to preexisting systems of control and power" (Foster 74). Like body modifiers and performance artists, cyberpunk subjects are arguably commodified in the very act of resistance, their appropriation and incorporation of technology literally marking them as "fully invested in products produced by a corporate culture that maintains power only for itself" (Easterbrook 390). The problem of militarist instrumentalism is inherent, too, within the iconic figure of the cyborg.

The "cyborg" has been with us since 1960, when Manfred E. Clynes and Nathan S. Kline coined the term to describe an "exogenously extended, integrated homeostatic self-regulating man-machine system" (27). Their cyborg "invited man to take an active part in his own biological evolution" (26–27), becoming a border-effacing symbiosis of the organic and the artificial. The cyborg has become a dominant motif not only in SF but also in forms of social theory with an agenda involving the transgression of boundaries. Donna Haraway, for example, has positioned the cyborg as a "site of the potent fusions of the technical, textual, organic, mythic, and political" ("Actors" 24–25). It is this border-erasing mutability that positions the cyborg at the center of interdisciplinary discourses crossing performance, theory, science, body modification, and science fiction, which collectively explore the potential consequences of our modification through technologies.

Representations of the cyborg in SF provide a profusion of both dystopian and utopian speculative scenarios. Claudia Springer points to the dominance in popular SF films of the hyperviolent, invincible, aggressively phallic cyborg, which in her view reinforces traditional gender stereotypes and a "misogynistic resistance to change" (104). This illustrates the problem associated with appropriating a creature conceptually spawned by the technomilitarist system in order to disrupt that very system. Haraway acknowledges that the "main trouble with cyborgs . . . is that they are the illegitimate offspring of militarism and patriarchal capitalism" ("Manifesto" 68). As Mary Catherine Harper writes, despite liberating possibilities and the potential for transgression, "all cyborgs, whether in cyberpunk, feminist cyborg literature, or living in the real world" are "still undeniably the dream-children of a positivist, rationalist American technology built by middle-class men of the previous two centuries" (400, 405). These inherent contradictions and compromised origins do not necessarily disable cyborg strategies, however, so long as the practitioners—whether SF writers, social theories, or modern primitives—bear in mind the dialectic of cooptation and transgression built inexorably into them. Pitts poses the following key questions for the entire body-modification subculture when it comes to cyborg self-transformations:

> How do nonmainstream body practices reflect, and contest, contemporary norms and values about the body? What are the roles of the body in social, political, and economic relations, and how do individuals negotiate these? What is the subversive promise of radical forms of body alternation? What are the limits of radical body practices for cultural politics? To what extent are the meanings of bodies shaped by individual bodies and selves, and to what extent do collective histories, cultural values, and patterns of inequality and social stratification shape them? (14)

For Pitts (and others, such as Haraway and Grosz), the "radicalism of body modifiers is limited by social forces—sometimes the very same forces they seek to oppose, including patriarchy, Western ethnocentrism, symbolic imperialism, pathologization, and consumerism" (Pitts 189). We see these questions and concerns dynamically addressed in the public arenas where body modification emerges as art.

Occupying an interface zone between contemporary body-modification subcultures and cyborgian SF narratives of becoming-Other are performance and visual art practices foregrounding the body. Indeed, a direct historical lineage can be traced between performance art practices, body modification, and the tropes of SF. The history of body art can be traced back to the radical theater theory of Antonin Artaud, whose work contains all the essential elements of transgressive body-modification art practices: corporeality, alterity, and actualization. Drawing on Artaud, the "events" of the Viennese Actionists of the 1960s used the body as surface and site for production of their art, often in ways that were seen as violent and destructive. This prioritization of the body has continued into both contemporary performance art and body-modification practices, including fetish and body-art clubs incorporating self-torture and public scarification "performances." Body modification as performance and visual art, cyborgization, and becoming-cyberpunk have evolved in form, substance, and style, due in no small part, as Sarah Miller notes, to the availability of cheap prosthetic, medical, and even genetic technologies (7–8). The performance artist Stelarc graphically brings together discourses of the critical and the theoretical, body modification and science fiction. In sympathy with both the driving philosophies of cyborgization and many elements of body-modification subcultures, Stelarc posits the human frame as having always been "incomplete," asserting that the historical urge to extend its limited capabilities has defined our very humanity (Stelarc 47). Mirroring the Lobsters of *Schismatrix*, Stelarc's dramatic cyborgian performances and his Promethean desire to remake the external and internal body have, despite his objections to the contrary, a vast array of intersections with the narratives of SF, and Stelarc can be clearly positioned as an SF performance "practitioner" (Farnell, "In Dialogue" 136–37).

The work of another artist, Orlan, is also of importance not only for her body-modifying performances but also for the way those performances provide new contexts for the contemporary cultural penchant for—and normalization of—cosmetic surgery (not to mention the self-surgery practices of more extreme body modifiers). As with Stelarc, technology has always been integral to her events, and she posits surgical intervention as the last taboo that must be broken (Lovelace 25). Orlan is most famous for a series of performances generally known as "The Reincarnation of Saint Orlan," in which she has submitted to plastic surgery in order to reshape her features into those of classic icons of female beauty from the history of art. Orlan's aim of "re-creating the self through deliberate acts of alienation" (qtd. Rose 83) has been derided as a narcissistic "spectacle of sadomasochistic voyeurism tarted up as performance art," unable to transcend the "dominant male paradigmatic codes of fetisism and voyeurism" she ostensibly seeks to combat (Grace 106–08).

Not all assessments of her body-modification performances are negative. Jane Goodall has argued that Orlan's practices are a form of feminist "Prometheanism" that challenges the "reduction of female selfhood to embodiment," exploring the "lack of fit between identity and image with the intervention of an 'I' that refuses to take its identity from its corporeal form" (156–57). Echoing the aims of modern primitives, and by contrast with cosmetic-surgery junkies seeking some culturally inscribed and fetishized "Barbie Doll" ideal, Orlan "seeks to subvert an image culture" by taking "total control over the design and concept of her own image" and "enacting non-conformity" (160). Similarly, Kathy Davis's critical work on cosmetic surgery suggests that not all patients are victims of patriarchal and cultural interpellation—or, as she puts it, "cultural dopes" (56). Rather than victims of false consciousness, she argues, women who choose cosmetic surgery can be positioned as "female agents" who can "actively and knowledgeably transform the texts of femininity into a desire for cosmetic surgery," altering their bodies surgically "in the context of their having to 'do femininity'" (56). The high percentage of female Millennials with piercings provides graphic evidence of this female agency in practice. And yet Orlan is keen to differentiate her work from more common body-modification practices such as piercing and tattooing: according to her, "The majority of people who are into those things believe that they are liberating themselves from the dictates of a certain society, but in fact it all boils down to the same thing because they are conforming to the dictates of a smaller, mini-society" (qtd. Ayers 182).

Yet her rejection of subcultural neotribalism as its own form of conformity does not address real concerns regarding an inherent body essentialism that is common both to her own work and to the practices of the very body-modification subcultures from which she seeks to establish critical distance. The lived, material body cannot, as critics such as Grosz and Judith Butler have pointed out, be fundamentally distinguished from the social, discursive body: the former is always inscribed by the latter, rather than being a brute biological given available for self-inscription. This situation is particularly perilous for body artists such as Orlan, who seeks to make feminist statements about the social construction of femininity by mounting assaults on her own flesh. Rather than "becoming-Other" through the transgression of their bodies, body-modification practitioners, from performance artists to modern primitives, fictional cyborgs, and real cyberpunks, may be merely amplifying a process of cultural inscription that is always already at work.

The mark on the flesh, writes Clinton R. Sanders, is part of a modern-primitive sign system that uses the body as an "instrument of communication" ("Memorial" 146)—a motif of body-as-information that science fiction also frequently deploys. In reprioritizing the "marked body," William Gibson's later novels discarded both the style of cyberpunk and its impulse to escape "the meat" into the bodiless exuberance of cyberspace. Indeed, Gibson's treatment of technology and bodies starts to approach that of J. G. Ballard, for whom (as William S. Burroughs said) the "body becomes landscape" (7). The theme of modern primitivism that runs through Gibson's 1993 novel *Virtual Light* exemplifies the author's fascination with the trends of popular culture: the skin surface is both territory and map, a site of (counter)enculturation. Contemporary body fetishism, in the form of tattoos, scarification, piercings, and the like, becomes the characters' dominant mode for expressing their resistance to cultural hegemony, a type of posthuman primitivism. Gibson's conception of the body-as-site is a defiant reclamation of the body, a literal "re-embodiment" and assertion of individual identity through transgressive self-inscription (Farnell, "Posthuman" 465–66). Similarly, advocates of modern primitivism defend the practice of body modification as the "last artistic territory resisting cooptation and commodification" (Vale and Juno 5). As I have noted, this approach to body modification problematically instantiates a vision of the body as a purely material surface that one may own, positing a "hostility between culture and the body" (Mascia-Lees and Sharpe 146–47). Gibson foregrounds such an oppositional relationship, yet as potential sites of resistance are absorbed through commercial appropriation, the body itself is no longer immune but rather "written upon" by—and forced to signify for—late capitalism itself.

In *Virtual Light*, the mark of the modern primitive still operates as a codification of otherness with those who are inked, referred to as the "Colored People." As Dery notes, the novel's specific reference to tattoos utilizing the biomechanical designs of H. R. Giger is a recognition of a common "cyberpunk rite of passage" in modern-primitive style (280). The technotribal inscription of cyborglike circuitry onto the skin—as "rippers" or "peelaways"—indicates the novel's conflation of the technological and the organic, literalized in the neotribal, hivelike Bridge community. Yet the novel's seeming enthusiasm for modern-primitivist techniques is tempered in Gibson's 1996 follow-up *Idoru*, which critiques the commodification of body inscription. At the very outset of the story, we are introduced to a disco bar called "Death Cube K" that features a Disneyfied representation of Kafka's "In The Penal Colony" (1919), where the "sentence of guilt, graven in the flesh of the condemned man's back" is translated into a banal marketing device for a Tokyo nightclub (*Idoru* 3).

Greg Egan also invokes the metaphor of Kafka's punishment machine in his novel *Permutation City* (1995), exploring differences between lived, virtual, and inscribed bodies. In a literalized (self)punishment, guilt is enhanced by a ritualistic writing and rewriting on the body's surface, a self-mutilating scarification. Egan's digitized bodies crave a corporeal punishment and thus an identity through inscription that is ultimately denied them by virtue of their inconsequential existence as mere "body-as-representation" (245). That two contemporary SF narratives should literalize the Kafka metaphor is informative in a cultural context where ritualized pain is often identified as an important part of body-modification practices, affirming and thus grounding experience in the marked body (Klesse 30). Once again, science fiction's not-so-future worlds provide new contexts from which to view—and make meaning of—our cultural present.

The "artwork" known as *Tim 2006* brings together many of the marked-body themes of theory, practice, and SF in a body-modification tour de force. Belgian artist Wim Delvoye transformed Tim Steiner's back into a signed work of tattoo art, which was sold in 2006 for 150,000 euros—a commercial vending of a person as art made possible by Switzerland's prostitution laws. When he dies, Steiner's skin will be cut up and framed; he has thus literally become "a Wim Delvoye" that can be sold and resold or regularly placed on exhibition in public galleries. In keeping with the purely transactional nature of the body-as-canvas, Delvoye tattooed images that "meant nothing to Steiner" in opposition to the usual body-modification entwining of personal identity with mark-making practices (Delvoye). *Tim 2006* moves body modification out of the domain of identity and the personal into the realms of law, art, and commerce. Delvoye's work is the apotheosis of what Sanders has identified as tattooing's transition "from deviance to art," no longer tied to "its historical roots as a disvalued craft" because now "defined as a fine art form ... [,] vying for artistic legitimacy" (*Customizing* 32–33). Yet Delvoye's work also raises the specter of the world described in Ballard's 1973 novel *Crash*, where body modification is taken to extremes of fetishism, the body objectified and alienated, with the subject revelling in the pleasure of its violent aestheticization.

Body modification, Romanienko argues, is used by a diversity of individuals and communities as a "discursive, semiotic method of primitivism that formalizes the struggle for freedom, autonomy and self-determination," a process by which the body is identified as the "primary site for the struggle to maximize our potential for human emancipation" (190). But the ability of body modification to offer such hopes of self-liberation to its practitioners and proponents is increasingly called into question not only by the issues surrounding the body as a cultural site, inscribed by race, gender, and other forms of enculturation, but also by the increasing popularity and commodification of the practice. This fashionability of body modification, Pitts notes, is both a "kind of victory"—as the erstwhile negatively conceived signifiers of modification practices are adopted—and a problematic commercialization that forces "body modification communities to define and reconsider the meanings of their practices," debating "authenticity," defending the "personal and political significance" of their work, and negotiating "the boundaries of who counts as one of them" (12).

One potential site of reappraisal is the zone where the narratives of SF, the subcultures of body modification, and the spectacles of performance art collide. This is a site of compelling works that provide rich, unique extrapolations of body-modification practices and the assumptions of modern primitivism. In this arena, we witness a veritable collage of SF narratives, cultural theory, technoscientific rhetorics of prosthesis, and performance-art traditions, a nexus that indicates how fully science-fictional our culture has become.

The extrapolative near futures of SF may be one of the most effective speculative spaces and discourses through which to explore the cultural, social, physical, and ontological implications of transgressing the body, providing fresh insight into the possible consequences of our desire to "become-Other" by modifying and augmenting our bodies.

Works Cited

Ayers, Robert. "Serene and Happy and Distant: An Interview with Orlan." *Body & Society* 5.2–3 (1999): 171–84. Print.

Balsamo, Anne. *Technologies of the Gendered Body: Reading Cyborg Women*. Durham, NC: Duke UP, 1999. Print.

Baudrillard, Jean. "The Year 2000 Has Already Happened." 1985. Trans. Nai-fei Ding and Kuan-Hsing Chen. *Body Invaders: Sexuality and the Postmodern Condition*. Ed. Arthur and Marilouise Kroker. London: Macmillan, 1988. 35–44. Print.

Bukatman, Scott. "Postcards from the Posthuman Solar System." *Science Fiction Studies* 18.3 (Nov. 1991): 343–57. Print.

Burroughs, William S. "Preface." *Love and Napalm: Export U.S.A.* by J. G. Ballard. New York: Grove, 1972. 7–8. Print.

Cadigan, Pat. *Synners*. London: Grafton, 1991. Print.

Clynes, Manfred E., and Kline, Nathan S. "Cyborgs and Space." *Astronautics* 9 (Sept. 1960): 26–27, 74–76. Print.

Davis, Kathy. *Reshaping the Female Body: The Dilemma of Cosmetic Surgery*. New York: Routledge, 1995. Print.

Dery, Mark. *Escape Velocity: Cyberculture at the End of the Century.* London: Hodder & Stoughton, 1996. Print.

Delvoye, Wim. "Libération-Le Temps." *tattootim.com.* Oct. 10, 2012. Web. Aug. 11, 2013. http://tattootim.com/2012/10/10/2901/.

Douglas, Mary. *Purity and Danger: An Analysis of Concepts of Pollution and Taboo.* London: Routledge, 1966. Print.

Easterbrook, Neil. "The Arc of Our Destruction: Reversal and Erasure in Cyberpunk." *Science Fiction Studies* 19.3 (Nov. 1992): 378–94. Print.

Egan, Greg. *Permutation City.* London: Millennium, 1995. Print.

Farnell, Ross. "In Dialogue with 'Posthuman' Bodies: Interview with Stelarc." *Body & Society* 5.2–3 (1999): 129–48. Print.

———. "Posthuman Topologies: William Gibson's 'Architexture' in *Virtual Light* and *Idoru*." *Science Fiction Studies* 25.3 (Nov. 1998): 459–80. Print.

Featherstone, Mike. "Body Modification: An Introduction." *Body & Society* 5.2–3 (1999): 1–13. Print.

Foster, Thomas. *The Souls of Cyberfolk: Posthumanism as Vernacular Theory.* Minneapolis: U of Minnesota P, 2005. Print.

Gibson, William. *Virtual Light.* London, Viking, 1993. Print.

———. *Idoru.* London: Viking, 1996. Print.

Goodall, Jane. "An Order of Pure Decision: Un-Natural Selection in the Work of Stelarc and Orlan." *Body & Society* 5.2–3 (1999): 150–70. Print.

Grace, Sharon. "Introduction: The Doyenne of Divasection." *Mondo 2000* 13 (1995): 106–108. Print.

Grosz, Elizabeth. *Volatile Bodies: Toward a Corporeal Feminism.* London: Allen & Unwin, 1994. Print.

Haraway, Donna. "The Actors Are Cyborg, Nature Is Coyote, and the Geography Is Elsewhere: Postscript to 'Cyborgs at Large.'" *Technoculture.* Ed. Constance Penley and Andrew Ross. Minneapolis: U of Minnesota P, 1991. 21–26. Print.

———. "A Manifesto for Cyborgs: Science, Technology and Socialist-Feminism in the 1980's." *Socialist Review* 80 (1985): 65–107. Print.

Harper, Mary Catherine. "Incurably Alien Other: A Case for Feminist Cyborg Writers." *Science Fiction Studies* 22.3 (Nov. 1995): 399–420. Print.

Klesse, Christian. "'Modern Primitivism': Non-Mainstream Body Modification and Racialized Representation." *Body & Society* 5.2–3 (1999): 15–38. Print.

Larratt, Shannon. *BME (Body Modification Ezine).* Web. Aug. 9, 2013. http://www.bme.com.

Lovelace, Carey. "ORLAN: Offensive Acts." *Performing Arts Journal* 49 (1995): 13–25. Print.

Mascia-Lees, Frances E., and Patricia Sharpe. "The Marked and the Un(re)marked: Tattoo and Gender in Theory and Narrative." *Tattoo, Torture, Mutilation, and Adornment: The Denaturalization of the Body in Culture and Text.* Ed. Frances E. Mascia-Lees and Patricia Sharpe. New York: SUNY P, 1992. 144–69. Print.

Miller, Sarah. "A Question of Silence—Approaching the Condition of Performance." *25 Years of Performance Art in Australia: Performance Art, Performance and Events.* Ed. Nick Waterlow. Sydney: R.F. Jones, 1994. 7–12. Print.

"Millennials: A Portrait of Generation Next." Pew Research Center. Feb. 24, 2010. Web. Aug. 9, 2013. http://www.pewsocialtrends.org/files/2010/10/millennials-confident-connected-open-to-change.pdf.

Pitts, Victoria. *In The Flesh: The Cultural Politics of Body Modification.* New York: Palgrave Macmillan, 2003. Print.

Pohl, Frederik. *Man Plus.* 1976. London: Gollancz, 2004. Print.

Romanienko, Lisiunia A. *Body Piercing and Identity Construction: A Comparative Perspective.* New York: Palgrave Macmillan, 2011. Print.

Rose, Barbara. "Is It Art?: Orlan and the Transgressive Act." *Art in America* 81 (Feb. 1993): 82–87, 125. Print.

Sanders, Clinton R. "Memorial Decoration: Women, Tattooing, and the Meanings of Body Alteration." *Michigan Quarterly Review* 30.1 (1991): 146–57. Print.

Sanders, Clinton R., with D. Angus Vail. *Customizing the Body: The Art and Culture of Tattooing.* 1988. Rev. ed. Philadelphia: Temple UP, 2008. Print.

Shilling, Chris. *The Body and Social Theory.* London: SAGE, 1993. Print.

Springer, Claudia. *Electronic Eros: Bodies and Desire in the Postindustrial Age.* Austin: U of Texas P, 1996. 87–101. Print.

Stelarc. "Electronic Voodoo." Interview with Nicholas Zurbrugg. *21.C: The Magazine of the 21st Century* 2 (1995): 44–49. Print.

Sterling, Bruce. *Crystal Express.* New York: Ace, 1990. Print.

———. "Cyberpunk in the Nineties." 1990. *Technoculture.* Web. Aug. 9, 2013. http://cyber.eserver.org/sterling/interzon.txt.

———. "Preface." *Mirrorshades: The Cyberpunk Anthology.* Ed. Bruce Sterling. 1986. New York: Ace, 1988. ix–xvi. Print.

———. *Schismatrix.* London: Penguin, 1986. Print.

Thompson, Craig. "Searching for Totality: Antinomy and the 'Absolute' in Bruce Sterling's *Schismatrix.*" *Science Fiction Studies* 18.2 (July 1991): 198–209. Print.

Turner, Bryan S. "The Possibility of Primitiveness: Towards a Sociology of Body Marks in Cool Societies." *Body & Society* 5.2–3 (1999): 39–50. Print.

Vale, V., and Andrea Juno. "Introduction." *Modern Primitives: An Investigation of Contemporary Adornment and Ritual.* San Francisco: Re/Search, 1989. 4–5. Print.

Winge, Thèresa M. *Body Style.* New York: Berg, 2012. Print.

CHAPTER 32

CYBERCULTURE

THOMAS FOSTER

In popular usage, the term "cyberculture" is identified with a specific historical moment and its sensibility, usually the naïve utopianism of the dot-com boom of the 1990s. This same period saw the semantic inflation of cyberpunk and the "cyber" prefix more generally, as they began to be attached to a wide range of cultural practices and productions beyond print science fiction. This history implies a narrative of progress and accelerated obsolescence, in which the term "cyberculture" has at best a limited, residual relevance to the contemporary media environment. This chapter instead treats cyberculture as a more general interdisciplinary project of articulating cybernetics and the study of culture (or meaning production); it attends to the ongoing tension between the two components of the term, rather than assuming that this articulation can be taken for granted, already transparently installed within the texture of everyday life. By contrast with David Bell or David Silver, who see the field primarily as a form of cyberspace or Internet studies, I will define the "cyber" in cyberculture in terms of the history of cybernetics and its relevance to contemporary cultural studies. In this context, science fiction provides a primary archive of speculative responses to the emergence of cybernetics after World War II.

Cybernetics was originally defined as the science of control and communication in complex systems. Emerging out of the interdisciplinary Macy conferences held between 1943 and 1954, the term was institutionalized by Norbert Wiener's two books, *Cybernetics* (1948) and its popularization, *The Human Use of Human Beings* (1954). Wiener built on foundational work by a range of associated figures including Claude Shannon (information theory); Warren McCulloch (human neural "circuitry"); John von Neumann (games theory, self-replication, and cellular automata); and Gregory Bateson, who along with Margaret Mead (who joined the Macy group later) was one of the main representatives of a more culturally oriented humanities field—anthropology—within this interdisciplinary group (see Hayles 50–83). To define systems of information exchange and processing, early cybernetics focused on processes of self-correction (or negative feedback loops), an approach that effectively defined a level of abstraction at which both mechanical and organic systems could be described in the same terms. This redescription depended on the concept of homeostasis or self-regulation, defined as a "physiological application of the principle of feedback" and an "inner economy" of "governors," including "thermostats" (Wiener, *Cybernetics* 115). These processes were central to the design of missile guidance systems at the end of World War II, and thus the term "cybernetics," deriving from the Greek term for steersman, was metaphorically applied (11–12).

Daniel Dennett has drawn out the implications of Wiener's ideas by explaining how the simple thermostat can be seen as an example of a self-correcting system indistinguishable in principle from the human body in that both contain "governors" (or "representations of the world" that control their reactions via feedback):

> Now the reason for stressing our kinship with the thermostat should be clear. There is no magic moment in the transition from a simple thermostat to a system that *really* has an internal representation of the world around it. The thermostat has a minimally demanding representation of the world, fancier thermostats have more demanding representations of the world, fancier robots for helping around the house would have still more demanding representations of the world. Finally you reach us. (32; emphasis in original)

This rhetorical and conceptual conflation of human and machine is, Donna Haraway argues, one of the "boundary breakdowns" characteristic not only of cybernetics but of postmodern culture and late capitalism as well, and it makes possible her feminist analysis of the figure of the cyborg (a term coined by Manfred E. Clynes and Nathan S. Kline in their 1960 essay "Cyborgs and Space"). According to Haraway, cybernetics' elision of borders between humans and machines defines the kind of self required by the "control strategies" of decentralized, global forms of late capitalism, which treat "[a]ny object or persons . . . in terms of disassembly and reassembly," since "no 'natural' architectures constrain system design" (162). But the cyborg is also, for Haraway, "the self feminists' must code" in order to resist such forms of control (163). Haraway's cyborg feminism is one of the foundational models for articulating cybernetics and cultural studies—though it is perhaps less widely noted how Haraway's cyborg politics is grounded in a dialectical understanding of the "informatics of domination" (161–65), the ways in which cybernetics and postmodernism participate in the establishment of new capitalist norms of social interaction and self-definition at the same time that they define the parameters within which it is possible to create alternatives to those norms.

But the redefinition of personhood generated by cybernetics takes other forms than Haraway's cyborg. One of the basic moves of cybernetics discourse is its conceptualization of homeostatic feedback loops as flows of information. While homeostasis had "[t]raditionally . . . been understood as the ability of living organisms to maintain steady states when they are buffeted by fickle environments" (Hayles 8), within cybernetics this conservative tendency to reproduce the integrity of individual systems also means that organisms (or homeostatic machines) are always coupled with their environment through the exchange of information (2). As a result, the integrity of the boundaries that define their individuality is also jeopardized by the very processes that maintain that integrity. The system and its environment are not separate but mutually constitutive, in ways that threaten to undermine ideologies of individualism or what Hayles calls "the liberal humanist subject" (2). Dennett refers to those ideologics as belief in a "magic moment" distinguishing human from machine. It is precisely this shift from subject to system that culminates in the ideology Haraway defines, in which no clear boundaries between inside and outside, private and public, self and other, seem to "constrain system design" (162).

Gregory Bateson's "cybernetics of self" makes this point through the famous example of a blind man and his cane. Defining cybernetics' challenge to the traditional definition of control as individual free will, he begins by asserting that "self-corrective" or homeostatic systems do not possess a "governor," if that term is "taken to mean...unilateral control" (315–16). From there, he argues that "the mental characteristics of the system are immanent, not in some part, but in the system as a whole," and this system "will usually not have the same limits as the 'self'—as this term is commonly (and variously) understood" (316–17). Mind may be "immanent in the larger system—man plus environment" (317; this passage is presumably a direct source for Frederik Pohl's 1976 cyborg novel, *Man Plus*). Bateson then asks readers to "consider a blind man with a stick. Where does the blind man's self begin," he asks (318)—at the stick's tip, its handle, or somewhere halfway up?

As this example suggests, debates about the nature of homeostatic processes are a necessary framework for understanding cyborg body prostheses, because homeostasis implies a more basic prosthetic model of identity. This implication has been developed in Allucquère Rosanne Stone's work on virtual systems theory and Andy Clark's on the theory of extended mind. For cybernetics, Clark argues, we are all "natural-born cyborgs": if "it is our basic human nature to ... incorporate non-biological stuff deep into our mental profiles," as Bateson's blind man with his cane does, then we must "give up the idea of the mind and self as a kind of wafer-thin inner essence, dramatically distinct from all physical trappings" (189). Stone uses prosthetic voice technologies to reformulate Bateson's questions about where to locate the "edges" of a person (5). For Stone, virtual systems of computer-mediated communication disarticulate the seemingly natural mapping of the self onto the boundaries of the body that supposedly contains it—or, rather, participation in virtual "spaces of prosthetic communication" (36) makes visible how that mapping always had to be socially produced and maintained. As a result, virtual systems go beyond theories of social constructionism and their rejection of essentialist concepts of human nature, theories central to the analytic practices of cultural studies and, more disturbingly, as Haraway suggests, to late-capitalist practices of subject formation and workforce training. As Stone puts it: "If we consider the physical map of the body and our experience of inhabiting it as socially mediated," as social constructionists do,

> then it should not be difficult to imagine the next step in a progression toward the social—that is, to imagine the *location* of the self that inhabits the body as also

socially mediated—not in the usual ways we think of subject construction in terms of position within a social field or of capacity to experience, but of the *physical* location of the subject, *independent* of the body within which theories of the body are accustomed to ground it, within a system of symbolic exchange, that is, information technology. (92; emphasis in original)

Here, we see another model for articulating cybernetics or information technology and culture or symbolic exchange.

But homeostasis has cultural implications as well, not just as a spatial redefinition of subjectivity and location but also as a shift from spatial to temporal modes of *self*-definition. Hayles notes that the concept of homeostasis was contested within early cybernetics: on the one hand, it provided a way of arguing that systems always tend to reproduce themselves, equating any threat to such perpetuation with death rather than transformative possibility (8, 65), but on the other hand, the stability produced by homeostasis could also be conceptualized as a provisional "state that itself would become enfolded into a reflexive spiral of change" (64), central to the "second-generation" cybernetic concept of autopoiesis, which equated informational flows with change rather than resistance to it (63). The concept of homeostasis can therefore be placed in dialogue with Judith Butler's influential theory of gender performativity as a process of iteration, a *"stylized repetition of acts"* that produces a "gendered corporealization of time" (*Gender Trouble* 140–41; emphasis in original). At the same time, such acts reveal that "gender is a norm that can never be fully internalized" (141) since the repetition necessary to produce binary gender categories as normative also means that this "identity is always at risk" of being "de-instituted at every interval" (Butler, "Imitation" 315). Homeostasis implies that systemic self-continuity is produced precisely through such a series of "intervals" or "iterations," as the system is continually de- and restabilized.

Alan Turing's use of a gender "imitation game" as the basis for his famous Turing Test of machine intelligence is perhaps the classic example of this intersection between homeostatic models and gender norms as performative (433–34). In the 1973 science fiction story "The Girl Who Was Plugged In" by James Tiptree Jr. (a.k.a. Alice Sheldon), cybernetics—in the form of telepresence, or the remote operation of a robotic body—is presented as both determined by and determining of gendered and sexual embodiment specifically, not just of individual or systemic identity in general. The gap between operator and robot dramatizes Butler's "interval" between performances of gendered embodiment. C. L. Moore's 1944 story "No Woman Born" offers another example of cybernetic performativity within science fiction. In this story, a famous dancer named Deirdre receives a full-body prosthesis following a serious accident, a metallic body that problematizes other people's perceptions of her as a woman. Deirdre herself answers the question of how, "without face or body," she could be perceived as a woman at all, by invoking her "years of training" as a dancer, "engraved . . . in the habit patterns grooved into [her] brain" by repeated acts (269), which she is now able to impose upon her mechanical body, held together as it is only by "muscles of magnetic currents"

(270). The rest of the story demonstrates the effects on the male characters of Deirdre's increasing ability to exploit the potential of "de-instituting" her gendered identity through the very act of repeating or imitating her previous self. This potential results directly from her prosthetic or technological embodiment: the impression of femininity she has to work to produce is disrupted when she uses her increased strength to catch a man who tries to leap out of a window. Deirdre's new body means that she has to constantly work at homeostatic self-correction, at returning herself to a previous gendered condition whose stability increasingly begins to seem normative rather than necessary, even as "the taint of metal in her voice" (64) points toward a new stability or self-definition (see Hollinger).

But Deirdre also reads this same redefinition of embodied identity back into her "normal," organic state of being when she asserts to an admirer that "I never was beautiful"; that impression was produced through, "well, vivacity, I suppose, and muscular coordination" (270)—that is, embodied performance of a kind that she only repeats in a new way, in her new body. As in Butler's interpretation of "drag" performances, Deirdre's prosthetic embodiment "implies that all gendering is a kind of impersonation and approximation" of an impossible ideal or fantasy (Butler, "Imitation" 21). Moore's story asserts both continuities and discontinuities between Deirdre's organic negotiations and performances of cultural norms of feminine beauty and her technological performances. The story therefore offers a model for the complex and mutually determining relations between cybernetics and culture, as the interpretation of her cyborg embodiment continues to be at least partly determined by preexisting cultural assumptions about who Deirdre is or was as a woman, while at the same time that new embodiment at least threatens to transform the assumptions about women that inform the interpretation of her as a more ambiguously gendered cyborg.

Just as cybernetics privileges science fiction as a mode uniquely suited to capturing the kinship between humans and machines, so SF becomes a powerful method for articulating cybernetics with specifically cultural issues and situations. More generally, we can see this articulation in much postmodern art, which according to Fredric Jameson expresses "a new kind of flatness or depthlessness," collapsing traditional distinctions between inner, psychic life and the public or social world (9). The result is a rejection of aesthetic models of expression that presume "some conception of the subject as a monadlike container, within which things felt are then expressed by projection outward" (15). Butler sees gender performativity as precisely such a critique of expressive subjectivity, with its assumption of both the "internal fixity of the self" and "the internal locale of gender identity" (*Gender* 134). An SF story like Tiptree's "The Girl Who Was Plugged In," in which the robotic body of an actress in virtual-reality media spectacles is remotely controlled by a female "drone," is thus at once a characteristic work of postmodern art, a classic illustration of gender performativity, and a compelling demonstration of several of the key concepts of cybernetics discourse.

Stuart Hall has traced the origins of British cultural studies back to a desire to break down the distinctions between high art and popular culture (another feature of postmodernism for Jameson), linked with an anthropological focus on the symbolic practices of everyday life in general. But Hall also argues that cultural studies needs to critique this anthropological model to the extent that it defines culture "expressively," as a reflection of an overly unified or totalized "whole way of life" (27). As a result, cultural-studies methodologies emphasize a more dynamic relation between text and context, analogous to the cybernetic emphasis on the relation between system and environment (see Grossberg 55–56). While Hall turned to structuralist theories of language to critique expressive models of culture, Haraway turned to cybernetics—where, as Bateson and Stone have argued, the "edges" of cognitive systems, the distinction between inner and outer, are problematized by the homeostatic flow of information between systems and environments.

There are two versions of this theoretical rejection of interiority, espressiveness, and "depth models" (in Jameson's phraseology). The first is essentially nostalgic, emphasizing what has been lost and treating depthlessness as a kind of Marcusean one-dimensionality, evidence of "repressive desublimation" (Marcuse 56). For Jameson, that loss has to do with affect and inner feelings (what Dennett calls "internal representations"), but it also has to do with a loss of historicity or context. In terms of contemporary cyberculture, Lev Manovich has been critical of the conceptual impoverishment of Internet culture, where "the single figure of metonymy," the linking of ideas through mere proximity rather than metaphorical similarity, is "privileged at the expense of all others," resulting in a "new media culture" that functions "as *an infinite flat surface* where individual texts are placed in no particular order" (77; emphasis added). The result is precisely Jameson's "new kind of [formal] superficiality" (9), now exemplified by mash-up techniques.

In the second version of the theoretical rejection of depth models, modern forms of individual autonomy and bourgeois personhood are not simply replaced and transcended, in an ongoing narrative of cultural progress, but instead critically displaced or transformed. Jameson describes this possibility as a shift from modernist alienation, in which the private individual confronts society as an external threat, to postmodern subjective fragmentation (14). This fragmentation emerges not only from the process of the private becoming public, as in contemporary media culture, but also from the difficulty of separating the public from the private in the first place. Thus, Bateson's cybernetic extension of mind beyond the limits of body or skin is translated into Jean Baudrillard's critique of "the forced extraversion of all interiority" and the "forced introjection of all exteriority" (26)—that is, the collapse of distinctions between body/subject and society/system characteristic of postmodern image culture. Computer scientist John Walker reminds us that cyberspace is "a three-dimensional domain in which cybernetic feedback and control occur" (444), yet (as Bateson pointed out) cybernetic feedback problematizes which link in the circuit is controlling and which is controlled—in this case, the user or the system.

The best illustration of this problematic may be found in a classic trope of cyberpunk SF: the notion that users' access to cyberspace can occur via interface devices implanted in their bodies that connect their brains directly to computer networks. In William Gibson's celebrated novel *Neuromancer* (1984), the ambiguity of control analyzed by Bateson takes the form of ICE (intrusion countermeasures electronics), a mode of computer security that induces physical effects in users' bodies, including death, even as their minds are described as projected entirely into cyberspace and experienced as distinct from their bodies (28). Such effects are only possible if a feedback loop continues to couple mind and body, however attenuated or virtualized that coupling has become—as is the case with Tiptree's main character, who has a "forty-thousand-mile parenthesis in her nervous system" (92). These examples support Haraway's claims that in high-tech cybercultures, "[i]t is not clear who makes and who is made in the relation between human and machine" or "what is mind and what body in machines that resolve into coding practices" (177). Gibson's (in)famous rhetoric of escaping the "meat" body into a cyberspace of pure mind (*Neuromancer* 6) depends upon clear distinctions between inside and outside, physical and virtual, individual and society, private and public—distinctions that cyberpunk SF also calls into question by dramatizing the incorporation of individuals into cybernetic systems. But these boundary confusions do not necessarily have to result in the disappearance of differences; subjective fragmentation means that those differences reside *within* cultural identities, not *between* the individual and their culture (see Delany 355–56).

There has been, as noted above, theoretical resistance to understanding the advent of postmodernism (and its attendant cyberculture) as an ambivalent process of transformation rather than a tragic loss of subjective "depth." Moreover, Jameson's insistence on treating postmodernism as a "periodizing hypothesis" or "cultural dominant" (3–4) is also problematic because it depends on an assumption that "depth" once existed (under modernism) but has been effaced by "the cultural logic of late capitalism"—an assumption that cybernetics, which radically resists depth models, would call into question. In terms of my own argument here, we might ask if there can be cyberculture *before* cybernetics, as both Clark and Bateson suggest, or whether cyberculture is a uniquely post–World War II phenomenon, with no more extensive historical relevance. Yet what are we to make of the appearance, in L. Frank Baum's 1914 novel *Tik-Tok of Oz*, of what now reads like a classic cyberpunk rhetoric of the body as mere "meat" in relation to a clockwork automaton (79)?

What such an example would seem to dramatize are the ways in which preexisting cultural frameworks or fantasies at least partly help to determine technoscientific developments—or, at least, claims about the significance and social import of such developments. The best example for my purposes is a 15-panel episode from the newspaper comic strip *Dream of the Rarebit Fiend* (1904–25) by Winsor McCay. The episode, published in 1906, depicts an anxiety dream in which the protagonist, who misses his ferryboat, has himself ground into sausages, transmitted to the ferry by wireless telegraph, and reconstituted at the other end. At the bottom of the final panel, McCay, as he occasionally did, acknowledges that the idea for the comic came from a reader, and he offers his thanks to "Huck Gernsback." This is a reference to none other than Hugo Gernsback, who in 1926 would found *Amazing Stories*, the first pulp magazine devoted exclusively to science fiction. Thus, McCay's dream of a mechanical, steampunk

FIGURE 32.1 1906 episode from Winsor McCay's comic strip *Dream of the Rarebit Fiend*.

version of a *Star Trek*-style transporter device derives from the imagination of a future SF writer and editor.

But the episode also demonstrates the cultural origin of the fantasy or thought experiment about teleportation in which Norbert Wiener indulges, in the course of defining what he calls "pattern-identity" or the "metaphor" of "the organism . . . seen as a message," a mere pattern of replicable information (*Human Use* 95). "It is the pattern maintained by . . . homeostasis," Wiener asserts, "which is the touchstone of our personal identity . . . . We are not stuff that abides, but patterns that perpetuate themselves"—and if a "pattern is a message," then it "may be transmitted as a message" (96). Wiener goes on to suggest transmitting "the whole pattern of the human body" and "brain," to be re-embodied by a "hypothetical receiving instrument" at a remote location (96). He presents such speculations as inspired by the new discipline of information theory, but they cannot so readily be distinguished from narratives like McCay's, whose substitution of sausages for wireless signals now reads like an ironic comment on the difficult of separating physicality from information. In relation to McCay's episode, this passage reveals the dependence of Wiener's thinking about cybernetics on a fantasy structure that can be dated back to at least the nineteenth century. Within print fiction, it appeared as early as March 1877, in "The Man Without a Body," a short story originally published anonymously in the *New York Sun* and later attributed to Edward Page Mitchell, which imagines transmitting a Platonic idea of matter over telegraph lines.

The question of whether and how it is possible to read cyberculture back into earlier historical moments is especially important if we wish to make claims about the relevance of cybernetics to feminism, the study of race and colonialism, or queer theory, since those struggles and the relations of dominance or cultural norms they contest, of course, long preceded cybernetics or postmodernism as formalized concepts—a point Phillip Brian Harper makes in his critique of Jameson for failing to take into account inequities in "the historical distribution of the power to conceive of oneself as a centered, whole entity" (11). Key critical works on the topic of race and cybernetics, for example, might include Paul Gilroy's argument about how new digital imaging and visualization technologies have called into question the biologization of racial difference and the "old visual signatures of 'race'" (43). In particular, Gilroy's claims that "skin is no longer privileged as the threshold of either identity or particularity" and that "the "boundaries of 'race'" have moved "across the threshold of the skin" (47) develop the cultural implications of the postmodern/cybernetic critiques of interiority discussed above. Lisa Nakamura similarly notes the power of the Internet to de-naturalize racial difference but also points out that this de-naturalization does not mean that those differences don't continue to be produced in online contexts where there are no bodies present to instantiate them. Nakamura argues that race persists in the form of "cybertypes," reductive stereotypes that are understood not as natural but as *performative acts*, ones that establish very limited, racist parameters for what can count as "black" or "Asian" in such contexts (38–39). The kind of de-naturalization Gilroy identifies can function normatively rather than critically within the spaces of online communication and self-representation.

Nakamura's cybertyping is an example of how cyberculture challenges some of the conventional wisdom of cultural studies—that de-naturalization generates change by de-legitimating ideological forms of common sense. It therefore returns us to cyberpunk science fiction, which presumes a thoroughly de-naturalized world, as in the famous opening line of Gibson's *Neuromancer*: "The sky above the port was the color of television, tuned to a dead channel" (3). Gibson calls cyberspace a "consensual hallucination" (5) precisely to mark the fact that this metaphor names the experience of social space as explicitly de-naturalized. If, for Stone, access to cyberspace means that the "locus of sociality that would in an older dispensation be associated with [the] body goes on in a space which is quite irrelevant to it" (43), Nakamura points out that the result is not disembodiment or transcendence but a situation of generalized "passing," including cross-racial forms (31–32). By contrast, Stone herself provocatively declares that "[i]n cyberspace the transgendered body is the natural body" (180)—in other words, to use Butler's formulation, a body in which gender is not exclusively internalized as a form of expressive subjectivity, as revealing one's true nature or essence.

In his introduction to the anthology *Mirrorshades*, Bruce Sterling analyzed cyberpunk's fascination for "intimacy with machines" as a combination of body and mind "invasion" (xiii), the result of a capacity metaphorically to plug human nervous systems into computer networks. Cyberpunk SF has become almost synonymous with cyberculture in some critical circles (see Cavallaro), despite the longer history of science-fictional responses to cybernetics. This tendency is, in part, a consequence of Sterling's claims about the relation of cyberpunk to the history of the genre, specifically its attempt to synthesize the technological focus of traditional hard-SF with the cultural relevance and literacy of the New Wave, as well as its openness to influences from outside the field (x). One result of this synthesis was a privileging of the hacker, rather than the more conventional scientists or engineers of hard-SF, as a key character type. Gibson's statement "The street finds its own use for things" (186)—from his 1982 story "Burning Chrome," where he also coined the term "cyberspace"—exemplifies not only this focus on hacking but also the idea that advanced technologies are inevitably appropriated into meaning-making cultural systems or frameworks (the "street," for short). Its functionality, in other words, is not a given: technology and culture exist in a dialectical relationship of mutual determination.

As this quotation suggests, cyberpunk is a signal example of how SF requires a movement beyond the separation of culture into "high" and "low" spheres, just as Gibson's cyberspace led computer engineers like John Walker to rethink the metaphors informing computer interface design. As Walker tells it, Gibson's fiction showed him that "[w]hen you're interacting with a computer, you are not conversing with another person. You are exploring another world" (443). This insight spurred the development of the GUI (Graphical User Interface) operating system and virtual reality interfaces. Sterling has continued to explore this movement from fiction to technology and back by proposing, in his 2005 nonfiction book *Shaping Things*, the term "design fiction" to name the central role of speculative writing and thought experiments in the creation of material culture. This embedding of cyberpunk concepts within a larger sociotechnical environment is evidence of the genre's unique position in relation to cyberculture, for which it has served as both an inspiration and a critique. It is also an extension of SF's history as a genre characterized by unusually tight feedback loops between writers and fans, as exemplified by institutions of fan comment and interaction, including letter columns, fanzines, conventions, websites, and fan fiction. The fans, like the street, always find their own uses for things.

Wiener's claim that cybernetic processes of homeostasis foreground the notion of "patterns that perpetuate themselves" rather than "stuff that abides" dramatizes how cyberculture often combines a de-essentializing emphasis on the temporality of identity with a much more problematic duality between materiality and information, body and mind, physical and virtual. Wiener's teleportation scenario demonstrates how cybernetics may actually intensify Cartesian mind–body dualisms rather than producing Haraway's boundary confusions. N. Katherine Hayles has offered one of the most influential critiques of this tendency within the history of cybernetics, suggesting that it may culminate either in the "nightmare" of "a culture inhabited by posthumans who regard their bodies as fashion accessories rather than the ground of being" or else in a much more desirable "version of the posthuman" that understands how "human life is embedded" in its material environment (5). The problem is how to acknowledge that embeddedness without reifying identity as solid "stuff" rather than seeing it as an open-ended process. Stone responds to that problem by arguing that "the physical/virtual distinction" does not map directly onto "a mind/body distinction," suggesting instead that virtuality represents an opportunity to conceptualize "a relationship to the human body" in a different way than Jameson's "monad," with its sharp ego boundaries and securely interiorized individual subjectivity (40).

Within contemporary cyberculture, there have been some attempts to respond to this critique of the disembodiment of information, of the privileging of signal over noise, that Hayles makes. As exemplified by the more recent work of cyberpunk writer and computer scientist Rudy Rucker (11–14, 21), one response has been to return to Turing's early work on the "halting problem"—the idea that it is not possible to predict the outcome of a particular computational operation or software program until that program has been run or performed. This argument provides the basis for shifting away from information as such, and therefore away from the dualistic distinction between information and materiality, message and medium, that Hayles traces back to Claude Shannon's version of information theory. Instead, static concepts of information are replaced by computational processes that *transform* information, and that are therefore both dynamic and embodied: computations have to be run *on something*.

Another response to the disembodiment of information and the association, in cyberpunk SF, of cyberspace with transcendence of—or escape from—the "meat" can be found in the dialogue between science fiction and new applications of geolocative technology, ubiquitous computing or "everyware," and augmented reality interfaces, where information is layered over the real world rather than replacing it. Gibson's metaphor for these technologies is "eversion," or turning inside out. In his 2007 novel *Spook Country* (2007), a character declares flatly that cyberspace "is everting" (20)—the virtual is erupting into the physical. This process resists treating the physical/virtual distinction as a hierarchy that retains some version of Jameson's "depth model," instead insisting that the physical and the virtual coexist within the same social space. In a similar context, Sterling's speculations on the use of embedded computer chips to create an "Internet of Things" have been especially influential (see *Shaping* 92–94).

In an example of the genre's ongoing dialogue on these subjects, British SF writer Paul J. McAuley, in his 2012 novel *In the Mouth of the Whale*, has reappropriated Gibson's metaphor of eversion to describe the operation of telepresence technologies (202) and the effects of "eccentric projection" that Tiptree attributed to them (Tiptree 86). The use of this term to describe the extension of consciousness beyond the limits of the body serves, I would argue, as a reminder that the eruption of the virtual into the physical works the other way around, too—and that the meaning of these recent developments can only be evaluated in the context of the history I have outlined in this essay, of cybernetic and postmodern critiques of the privatization of subjectivity and the mapping of ego boundaries onto body boundaries. This is the issue at the heart of cyberculture, and science fiction is the quintessential discourse articulating its ongoing cultural ramifications.

Works Cited

Bateson, Gregory. *Steps to an Ecology of Mind*. New York: Ballantine, 1972. Print.
Baudrillard, Jean. "The Ecstasy of Communication." 1983. *The Ecstasy of Communication*. 1987. Trans. Bernard and Caroline Schutze. New York: Semiotext(e), 1988. 11–28. Print.
Baum, Frank L. *Tik-Tok of Oz*. Chicago: Reilly & Lee, 1914. Print.
Bell, David. *An Introduction to Cybercultures*. New York: Routledge, 2001. Print.
Butler, Judith. *Gender Trouble: Feminism and the Subversion of Identity*. New York: Routledge, 1990. Print.
———. "Imitation and Gender Insubordination." *The Lesbian and Gay Studies Reader*. Ed. Henry Abelove, Michèle Aina Barale, and David Halperin. New York: Routledge, 1993. 307–20. Print.
Cavallaro, Dani. *Cyberpunk and Cyberculture: Science Fiction and the Work of William Gibson*. New York: Continuum, 2001. Print.
Clark, Andy. *Natural-Born Cyborgs: Minds, Technologies, and the Future of Human Intelligence*. New York: Oxford UP, 2003. Print.
Delany, Samuel R. "Afterword." *Stars in My Pocket Like Grains of Sand*. 1984. Middletown, CT: Wesleyan UP, 2004. 349–56. Print.
Dennett, Daniel. *The Intentional Stance*. Cambridge, MA: MIT, 1989. Print.
Gibson, William. "Burning Chrome." 1982. *Burning Chrome and Other Stories*. 1986. New York: Ace, 1987. 168–91. Print.
———. *Neuromancer*. New York: Ace, 1984. Print.
———. *Spook Country*. New York: Putnam, 2007. Print.
Gilroy, Paul. *Against Race: Imagining Political Culture Beyond the Color Line*. Cambridge, MA: Harvard UP, 2000. Print.

Grossberg, Lawrence. *We Gotta Get Out of This Place: Popular Conservatism and Postmodern Culture*. New York: Routledge, 1992. Print.

Hall, Stuart. "Cultural Studies: Two Paradigms." 1980. *Culture, Ideology, and Social Process: A Reader*. Ed. Tony Bennett, Graham Martin, Colin Mercer, and Janet Woolacott. London: Open UP, 1981. 19–37. Print.

Haraway, Donna. "A Cyborg Manifesto: Science, Technology, and Socialist-Feminist in the Late Twentieth Century." 1985. *Simians, Cyborgs, and Women: The Reinvention of Nature*. New York: Routledge, 1991. 149–82. Print.

Harper, Phillip Brian. *Framing the Margins: The Social Logic of Postmodern Culture*. New York: Oxford UP, 1994. Print.

Hayles, N. Katherine. *How We Became Posthuman: Virtual Bodies in Cybernetics, Literature, and Informatics*. Chicago: U of Chicago P, 1999. Print.

Hollinger, Veronica. "(Re)Reading Queerly: Science, Fiction, Feminism, and the Defamiliarization of Gender." 1999. *Reload: Rethinking Women + Cyberculture*. Ed. Mary Flanagan and Austin Booth. Cambridge, MA: MIT, 2002. 301–20. Print.

Jameson, Fredric. *Postmodernism, or, The Cultural Logic of Late Capitalism*. Durham, NC: Duke UP, 1991. Print.

Manovich, Lev. *The Language of New Media*. Cambridge, MA: MIT, 2001. Print.

Marcuse, Herbert. *One-Dimensional Man: Studies in the Ideology of Advanced Industrial Society*. 1964. 2nd ed. Boston: Beacon, 1991. Print.

McAuley, Paul J. *In the Mouth of the Whale*. London: Gollancz, 2012. Print.

Moore, C. L. "No Woman Born." 1944. *Reload: Rethinking Women + Cyberculture*. Ed. Mary Flanagan and Austin Booth. Cambridge, MA: MIT, 2002. 261–300. Print.

Nakamura, Lisa. *Cybertypes: Race, Ethnicity, and Identity on the Internet*. New York: Routledge, 2002. Print.

Rucker, Rudy. *The Lifebox, The Seashell, and the Soul*. New York: Thunder's Mouth, 2005. Print.

Silver, David. "Introduction: Where Is Internet Studies?" *Critical Cyberculture Studies*. Ed. David Silver and Adrienne Massanari. New York: NYU P, 2006. 1–14. Print.

Sterling, Bruce. "Preface." *Mirrorshades: The Cyberpunk Anthology*. Ed. Bruce Sterling. New York: Ace, 1988. ix–xvi. Print.

———. *Shaping Things*. Cambridge, MA: MIT, 2005. Print.

Stone, Allucquère Roseanne. *The War of Desire and Technology at the Close of the Mechanical Age*. Cambridge, MA: MIT, 1995. Print.

Tiptree Jr., James (a.k.a. Alice Sheldon). "The Girl Who Was Plugged In." 1973. *Warm Worlds and Otherwise*. New York: Del Rey, 1975. 79–121. Print.

Turing, Alan. "Computing Machinery and Intelligence." *Mind: A Quarterly Review of Philosophy and Psychology* 59.236 (Oct. 1950): 433–60. Print.

Walker, John. "Through the Looking Glass." *The Art of Human-Computer Interface Design*. Ed. Brenda Laurel. Reading, MA: Addison-Wesley, 1990. 439–47. Print.

Wiener, Norbert. *Cybernetics, or Control and Communication in the Animal and the Machine*. 1948. 2nd ed. Cambridge, MA: MIT, 1961. Print.

———. *The Human Use of Human Beings: Cybernetics and Society*. 1950. New York: Da Capo, 1988. Print.

CHAPTER 33

RETROFUTURISM AND STEAMPUNK

ELIZABETH GUFFEY AND KATE C. LEMAY

RETROFUTURISM encompasses multiple strands and meanings in twentieth-century culture, including the identification of "the future" as a style, as well as content that highlights nostalgia, irony, and time-bending dislocation. By the late twentieth century, retrofuturism surged through popular culture, from films to comic books, buildings to television programs, engaging the relationship between the future and the past, as well as broader paradigms such as history, (post)modernity, and progress. It has become the popular futurism of many writers of speculative fiction, as well as a diverse band of scientists, philosophers, and Madison Avenue copywriters who optimistically posited technology-driven change for the future. Today, our futures feel increasingly citational: each is haunted by the "semiotic ghosts" of futures past (Gibson 35). For architecture critic Niklas Maak, "Retrofuturism is nothing more than an aesthetic feedback loop recalling a lost belief in progress, the old images of the once radically new" (117). For others, it has shifted into steampunk, a revisionist take on science fiction. However construed, retrofuturism represents a loss of faith, but it is not a meaningless exercise. Instead, it recycles overlapping material forms of collective memory, reflecting but also challenging ideals, attitudes, and values of what Daniel Rosenberg and Susan Harding have called "the escalating storms of the early 21st century" (3).

If futurism is a term that describes our anticipation of what is to come, then retrofuturism describes how we remember these visions. The term itself is laden with ambiguity, however. Where futurism is sometimes called a "science" bent on anticipating what will come, retrofuturism is the remembering of that anticipation. If the meaning of retrofuturism is nebulous, this imprecision stems, in part, from the term's unclear origins. Most recent speculation has attributed the term to the writer, editor, and musician Lloyd Dunn, who coined the word and renamed his 'zine *Retrofuturism* in 1988 (Latham 340). Nevertheless, the term should be tied to the larger phenomenon of "retro," a word that itself has roots in the beginning of the 1970s, as an articulation of a half-nostalgic, half-ironic way of looking at the past (see Guffey). But the term also cuts to the heart of our ideas of progress, thereby reflecting our current dissatisfaction with the present while creating a nostalgia for what we once considered the future.

Tales of time travel and artificial intelligence, fleets of spaceships and robotic servants are inextricably tied to futurism. But we often forget that these notions are part of a larger, collective imaginary that I. F. Clarke once called "the tale of the future" (see Clarke). Moreover, to conceive of the future, you have to imagine a past and present—two ideas that took their modern form only in the nineteenth century. Speculative optimism, however, can be traced at least back to the Renaissance. At this time, Christian ideas of paradise transmuted into the earthly ideal of a secular utopia; by the nineteenth century, a wide range of thinkers, ranging from Karl Marx and Joseph Fourier to Edward Bellamy and William Morris, looked to overhaul and improve society. But the Industrial Revolution bore two threads that come together in futurism—an insistence or faith in progress and an implicit trust that technology will bring about utopia. Ideas of progressivism, partly based on scientific discourse in the nineteenth century, including the work of Charles Lyell and Charles Darwin, and partly inspired by rapid developments in science and technology, prompted many contemporaries to believe that life would only get better and better. Continuing long into the twentieth century, and shaping scientific and technological prophesizing, this progressive model of time put its emphasis not on political change but rather on the development of applied science. For our purposes, such futurism can be broken into three eras: an early optimism that focused on the past and was rooted in the nineteenth century, an early-twentieth-century "Golden Age" that continued long into the 1960s space age, and a period of decline or loss of interest beginning in the late 1960s and 1970s.

Many early dime novels reflect the gritty applied science of factory and steam. Among them were the Edisonades or scientific romances aimed at boys and featuring Thomas Edison-like inventor heroes. In Edward Ellis's *The Huge Hunter, or the Steam Man of the Prairies* (1868) and later series such as the Frank Reade stories, young men use engineered inventions to save themselves and society. But it was the fevered imagining of the second industrial age, with its combustion engines, automation, telegraphy, and electricity, that encouraged the most expansive of optimistic speculations. The propeller-powered balloons, automatically sliding doors, and bullet-shaped spaceships of Jules Verne and H. G. Wells captured a generation's fantasies, suggesting that advanced science and technology could not only help readers transform themselves but also the world. Wells's *Anticipations of the Reactions of Mechanical and Scientific Progress Upon Human Life and Thought* (1901) presented a form of fictional "futurology," helping move what was once soothsaying and crystal-ball gazing toward what could be considered a "science." A large swathe of writers and artists alike eagerly embraced this technical alchemy, visualizing a future shaped by applied science and industrial power. This is the revolutionary discourse for a mechanized utopia that pushed the Bolshevik vision of socialist might. But it also launched new directions in popular culture, encouraging early filmmakers like George Méliès, who fantasized a *Trip to the Moon* in 1902, and the French publisher Villemard to print a series of postcards in 1910 that depicted flying firemen and speaking newspapers of the year 2000.

In many ways, the bullish form of speculative futurism, a looking to the future rather than a recalling of the past, reached an apogee in the first half of the twentieth century. During this era, science fiction became a recognized genre of literature and its cultural influence rapidly rose. Automation, widespread electrification, and air travel all helped to develop popular fascination with applied science. Pulp magazines like *Amazing Stories, Science Wonder Stories,* and *Future Science Fiction* introduced new ways of living, with flying cars and meals in pill form. These stories surveyed contemporary technologies and envisioned how they might develop. Air travel, for example, suggested the possibility of space travel; automation in the workplace encouraged fantasies of robots able to labor in the home as well as factories. Popular comic strips of the period, including Philip Francis Nowlan's *Buck Rogers* (originally published in *Amazing Stories* in 1926) and Alex Raymond's *Flash Gordon*, amplified visions of a future in space and were soon adapted into radio serials and films. Historian David Gebhard argues that the streamlined *Moderne* style of architecture was partly inspired by the sleek and aerodynamic imagery of science fiction in pulp magazines (Gebhard 13). To be sure, the high-water mark of this style, the 1939 New York World's Fair, embraced the futurist theme, "Building the World of Tomorrow." With displays including the robot Elektro and GM's Futurama, Fair planners forecast "the shape of things to come" (see Gelernter).

If futurism continued to capture the public's imagination in the immediate years after World War II, some of this interest was driven by wartime inventions and new materials that were introduced into the marketplace; indeed, many consumer products seemed to be answers to earlier futurist promises. Developments in chemistry led the Monsanto Chemical Company to open a "House of the Future," made completely out of plastic, at Disneyland's Tomorrowland. Friendly visions of nuclear-powered machines included the Ford Nucleon, an atomic car unveiled in 1958 that ran on a rechargeable power package. Fueled by the US-Soviet space race, futurism continued unabashed and debates in the 1950s began to discuss not *if* people could go into space but rather *when* this would happen. An optimistic brand of futurism shaped space-age fantasies well into the 1960s, with iterations like *The Jetsons* (1962–63) and Gene Roddenberry's *Star Trek* (1966–69).

But futurist expectations plunged just as the space age was beginning. By the mid-1970s, anticipation of nonstop progress, along with expectations that there would be infinite resources to fuel it, declined; moreover, many observers began to question scientific innovation and wondered at the ecological and social toll it was exacting. The oil crisis, the recession of the mid- to late 1970s, and environmental disasters like the pollution of Love Canal and Three Mile Island, all prompted widespread questioning of technology's benefits, without suggesting specific solutions. Even as NASA carried out its Apollo program, it was clear that pulp SF writers had taken too lightly the technical and financial means necessary to put human beings into space.

As futurism lost its hold on the popular imagination during the late 1960s and early 1970s, retrofuturism began to take its place. Where futurism looked forward with unabashed confidence, retrofuturism raised doubts. Futurism's breathless visions of what was to come, including space colonization and flying cars, were increasingly negated by retrofuturism's skeptical reactions to these dreams. The floating cities and bustling spaceports that had shaped futurist visions were not forgotten, but a subtle shift occurred as they seemed less an inevitable destination than a promise once made but gradually reneged upon. The original pledge became increasingly remembered in an ironic and nostalgic manner.

Retrofuturist themes began to express this shift in popular culture during the 1970s and 1980s, and "the future" (in ironic quotation marks) developed into a recognizable style. Translating "the future" from a vision of a time that is to come into a set of established clichés was a complex process. Stylistic apparitions of "the future" quoted visual conventions that, in other eras, tried to imagine and anticipate what was to come. At the end of the twentieth century, "the future" became associated with the forward-looking architecture and design of the earlier twentieth century. Examples include futuristic car tailfins, which were modeled on rockets, and American roadside restaurants built in gravity-defying cantilevers that resembled the space stations on pulp magazine covers.

While Niklas Maak suggests that the "future style" is "a mere quotation of its own iconographic tradition" and retrofuturism is little more than "an aesthetic feedback loop" (117), we should not reject it so quickly. Retrofuturism reveals a nostalgic longing, accompanied by a deep dissatisfaction with the present moment. One example, similar to Seattle's Space Needle and the TWA terminal at JFK Airport, is William Pereira and Charles Luckman's "Theme Building" at the Los Angeles International Airport, built in 1961. A landmark of midcentury modernist architecture, the building resembles a large, white flying saucer, with soaring arches and a revolving elevated dining room that exposes its panoramic views. After years of neglect, the restaurant was landmarked in 1992 and renovated, including being spotlighted by dramatic new lighting designed by Disney's Imagineers, reopening in 1997. Similarly, its interiors were decorated with Lava lamps and amoeba-shaped banquettes; true to the spirit of retrofuturism, its tongue-in-cheek stylings aim for a Jetsons-style fantasy.

While science fiction routinely transports readers out of the present moment, retrofuturism plays with ideas of temporality, blurring past and future. At its most unsettling, retrofuturism disrupts our understanding of the nature of time, encouraging a kind of hybrid temporality. Retrofuturism reflects a time-bending vertigo, forcing our contemporaries to confront earlier conceptions of the future. In "The Gernsback Continuum," for instance, an art historian asks the narrator to photograph decaying futurist architecture in California; when the photographer has trouble grasping the concept, she insists that he "[t]hink of it . . . as a kind of alternate America: a 1980 that never happened. An architecture of broken dreams" (Gibson 28). Gibson's text suggests that a different 1980 could exist simultaneous to the one experienced by our narrator; he becomes so enmeshed in the idea of overlapping times that he begins to see a world filled with lumbering airships and vast skyscraper-filled cities, "phantoms" of a parallel present spawned by 1930s pulp fantasies.

But Gibson's "architecture of broken dreams" isn't an empty rhetorical pose; the attitudes that suffuse his understanding of futurism were developed during a period

FIGURE 33.1 The Theme Building at the Los Angeles International Airport, built in 1961.

characterized by swift but also concentrated technological change. From the introduction of the microprocessor to the jumbo jet, the neutron bomb to the test tube baby, applied science flourished in the 1970s. Although mass production and heavy manufacturing remained a mainstay of the economy in industrialized countries, a larger and more painful shift was taking place as the technological landscape was beginning to transmute into a postindustrial economy of service, information, and finance. This economy was not based on brick-and-mortar changes of the sort heralded by the futurist writers, illustrators, and architects of a generation earlier. As Scott Bukatman writes, technology was increasingly "the face of the invisible and hence unknowable spaces of terminal culture" (62). In these unimaginable futures, retrofuturism obliquely registers a change in attitude, still acknowledging earlier prophecies but also securing a place for prediction and therefore new ideas.

By the late twentieth century, as significant dates of futurist predictions such as 1960 (the "future" imagined in GM's 1939 Futurama), 1984 (anticipated by George Orwell's 1949 novel), and 2001 (from Stanley Kubrick's 1968 film) came and passed, the world did not see the materialization of automated roadways, dinner in a pill, or commercial space travel. Gibson's "Gernsback Continuum" reflects a darker change in science fiction that included the advent of cyberpunk in the 1980s. As several observers have noted, many of the advances predicted were accurate—for example, computers in cars, phones that stream images, and babies conceived in test tubes. For the most part, however, a technological utopia masterminded by scientists and engineers has failed to appear, and retrofuturist nostalgia suggests continuing disillusionment.

Ideas of technology and the past and future have been utterly rethought in the postindustrial world. But retrofuturism's plastic paradise and its cynical vision of technology in the past, present, and future are themselves being transformed. SF writer K. W. Jeter decries "the mid-Eighties' starry-eyed, gobsmacked fascination with the siliconized future." Jeter sees this vision as dated, belonging more to "the Kennedy-era Disneyland's Carousel of Progress exhibit than [to] the life we're living now" (*Infernal Devices* 1). Jeter's indictment of dated technologies announces a newer vision of humankind and its relationship with technology. At the end of the twentieth century, many technophiles, like Jeter, turned their imaginations to an era when applied science was not encased in plastic but instead was seeable, pliable, and knowable.

In recent years, steampunk has emerged as a different way that SF and fantasy deal with the past. An offshoot of cyberpunk in the 1980s, steampunk has emerged as what one critic calls a "craft and lifestyle movement" (Forlini 72). As Mike Perschon explains, "Defining steampunk unilaterally is challenged by what aspect of steampunk culture one is trying to define: the literature, the fashion, the bricolage artworks, or the politics" (128). Brass goggles and do-it-yourself gadgetry mark steampunk aesthetics, but these characteristics are not its defining terms. Indeed, it borrows heavily from the "age of steam," the first Industrial Revolution as it took shape by the mid-nineteenth century. But one of steampunk's most significant contributions is that it forces us to reconsider the roots and historical import of the digital.

Steampunk is a malleable cultural manifestation, but one that, like retrofuturism, negotiates a present longing for a historical past; if reimagined with different applications, this past might have yielded an alternative current moment. In its selective collective memory, steampunk posits a direct agency for the individual in a postindustrial society. Moreover, its distinctive, handmade, and ornamental aesthetic sets it apart from the machine-engineered, streamlined designs associated with futurism and half-ironically, half-nostalgically recalled by retrofuturists. By making visible process and time through the mark of the hand, steampunk essentially remakes the past in the image of the present. Like retrofuturism, steampunk often recalls the older but still modern eras in which technological change seemed to anticipate a better world, one remembered as relatively innocent of industrial decline. Unlike retrofuturism, however, steampunk strives to create a desired future. While steampunk celebrates nineteenth-century technology, it usually prioritizes the period prior to the major industrial changes of the later half of that century. One of steampunk's most significant contributions is that it revises our conception of the digital, forcing us to reconsider its roots and historical import, but also insisting that we try to envision how it has impacted our expectations.

A broad and loose term that is sometimes exchanged with "clockpunk" (Dawdy 766), steampunk marks the melding of different eras of technology. The many iterations of steampunk recall and recreate the settings where steam power was widely used—usually Britain of the early to mid-nineteenth century or the fantasized "Wild West"-era United States. Steampunk combines material culture from this period of history with elements of either SF or fantasy, thereby attempting to create or encourage a utopian future. Although this essay does not analyze steampunk literature, this lifestyle movement is rooted in the literary genre of science fiction. Jeter coined the term "steampunk" in an April 1987 letter to *Locus* magazine, suggesting it as a way to refer to a growing group of writers incorporating Victorian machines into their narratives. Already the author of *Infernal Devices*, a steampunk novel issued the same year, Jeter claimed a new importance for SF rooted in "Victorian fantasies." Nevertheless, Jeter argued, this emerging subset of science fantasy needed to "come up with a fitting collective term . . . [s]omething based on the appropriate technology for the era" (qtd. "Birth"). Meant as a response to the term "cyberpunk," Jeter's steampunk deals with a subgenre of SF literature that drew heavily on elements of mid-nineteenth-century technology, culture, and design. The term, however, would be popularized by Paul DiFilippo's *Steampunk Trilogy*, published in 1995 (see Good [208]; Yaszek).

But its literary roots stretch deeper, and aficionados cite early industrial-era writers like Poe and Mary Shelley as forerunners (Hantke 10). Mike Ashley dates the genre to Ellis's publication of *The Steam Man of the Prairies*, which he claims as the first piece of steampunk SF. He argues that "steampunk was well under way by the 1880s," only to fade out when "the wonderful visions and hopes of the Victorians became overtaken by the real world" with the coming of World War I (10). It is important to note, however, that even in Ellis's time, steam was rapidly being superseded. Steampunk has a tendency to leapfrog over the second Industrial Revolution as well as much of the twentieth century. Instead, it often combines early Victorian morality, aesthetics, and technology with applied science from today.

The first fully developed steampunk writing comes from the cultural ferment of the 1980s, when authors began incorporating references to steam technology into their work, using it to question or subvert systems of power. The origins of steampunk can be traced to parodies of the Wellsian scientific romance, such as Michael Moorcock's *The Warlord of the Air* (1971). Many of these neo-Victorian texts interpret the digital revolution through comparison with the first Industrial Revolution. Pivotal works include not only Jeter's *Infernal Devices*, but also Tim Powers's *The Anubis Gates* (1983) and James P. Blaylock's *Homunculus* (1986), both of which recall scientific applications and machines from H. G. Wells's *The Time Machine* (1895) and Jules Verne's *Twenty Thousand Leagues Under the Sea* (1870). In 1990 William Gibson and Bruce Sterling published *The Difference Engine*, whose success catalyzed the popular appeal of the steampunk movement. This novel incorporates real people and locations into a fictive narrative, revealing how technological proficiency—specifically, the creation of a steam-driven computing machine—can be closely connected to the equipment of nation building and power. Like Gibson's "Gernsback Continuum," *The Difference Engine* creates a conterfactual history.

As developed in these books and elsewhere, steampunk emerges as a movement that is not antitechnology; indeed, a constant fear of Luddism suffuses steampunk fiction and culture (see Carpenter 158). Instead, at its most hopeful, steampunk combines nostalgic recall with "appropriate" applied science in order to rewrite the past and create a better future. As Rachel Bowser and Brian Croxall assert, "The tinkering and tinker-able technologies within steampunk invite us to roll up our sleeves and get to work re-shaping our contemporary world" (23). In other words, if we were to return to the past—the *usable* past—the future might not be so bad.

Steampunk has outgrown its literary roots, however, and in the late 1990s, it began to emerge as a craft and lifestyle movement. While steampunk culture can fetishize pseudo-historical artifacts, Ele Carpenter posits that, at its best, "steampunk can be seen as an aspect of radical craft, a hybrid of the digital and the analog, and an eco-aesthetic engagement with how things work" (149). Although this is only alluded to in steampunk literature, steampunk culture carries with it a strong arts-and-craft component. Nevertheless, with its focus on steam power and machinery, steampunk would seem unlikely as a latter-day reincarnation of the nineteenth-century Arts and Crafts movement since William Morris founded this movement as a direct response to the ills that accompanied nineteenth-century industrialization. But, in looking to the past for an answer to current problems, both steampunk and the Arts and Crafts movement privilege the maker and his or her individuality, as well as the materials and processes used, and each prizes a materialist form of honesty. Moreover, in a more complex manner, the cultural, aesthetic, and technological alienation voiced by Morris and other reformers is also echoed by steampunk writers—for example, the clan of "neo-Morrisites" dedicated to "mak[ing] beautiful things" in the nanotech-dominated future of Neal Stephenson's 1995 novel *The Diamond Age* (261). As Bowser and Croxall posit, steampunk's latter-day arts and crafts may be seen as a critical response to the "opacity" of contemporary technology, its imperviousness to tinkering, and its discouragement of amateur repair (17). As author Scott Westerfeld told *TIME* magazine in 2009, "The Internet is global and seemingly omniscient, while iPods and phones are all microscopic workings encased in plastic blobjects.... Compare that to a steam engine, where you can watch the pistons move and feel the heat of its boilers. I think we miss that visceral appeal of the machine" (qtd. Grossman).

Although steampunk remains more loosely defined than the movement that coalesced around William Morris, these latter-day tinkerers do subscribe to a generalized set of ethical principles. In the letter where he coined the term, Jeter calls on us to imagine applied sciences "based on the appropriate technology for the era"; nevertheless, he avers, "We live in a disposable society. Everything is plastic, everything is saturated, everything is manufactured with the least amount of design or beauty possible" (qtd. "Birth"). Building on a larger desire for "beauty" but also for technological transparency, aspects of steampunk culture foster increased sensitivity toward the environment (Forlini 81). Above all, steampunk can be understood as a "response to the realities of modern consumer technology" (Grossman): its makers reject the notion of planned obsolescence. As Stefania Forlini notes, steampunk practitioners' "belief in their ability to shape a better future through the recycling of the past" can be applied to their artistic and subcultural activities (75). Many search pawnshops, second-hand dealers, thrift stores, flea markets, and the stockrooms of antiques shops for materials. Some regularly rummage around the Internet for parts. In so doing, the tinkering process has evolved to include any found object that can be repurposed. In a similar way, steampunk do-it-yourself instructions encourage sustainable practices, recommending that readers procure their parts from "junk" stores, or "even through 'dumpster-diving,' and that they dispose of any chemicals in environmentally-friendly

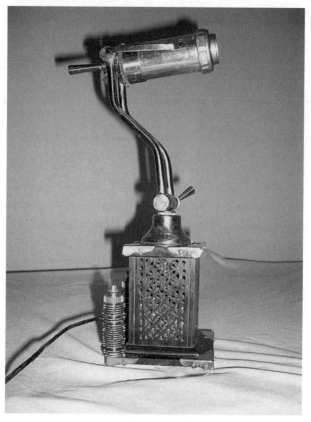

FIGURE 33.2 Steampunk webcam created by Brian Goudie, 2011. Image courtesy of the artist.

ways" (Forlini 7). Consequently, steampunk teeters between two extremes—ambivalent, pessimistic reactions to power structures and the depletion of resources and a hopeful urge to transcend time, plunder a specific historical moment, and apply its lessons to the future.

As movements in popular culture, both retrofuturism and steampunk engage the past in order to understand the future. But the two cannot be conflated. Steampunk fuses the first Industrial Revolution's hands-on machinery with a practical DIY ethos in the postdigital world, whereas retrofuturism invokes later technologies from the late nineteenth and twentieth centuries while remembering the past's vision of the future. Nevertheless, both phenomena messily integrate many temporal moments, highlighting the fact that the future is not predictable ("Introduction" 6) and that futurology is not a neutral scientific enterprise (see Kefalas). More significant, retrofuturism and steampunk both describe not just where we want to be but also our present dissatisfactions, reflecting our uneasy fascination with technology's imaginary, alternately marking a curious nostalgia combined with a sense of the speeding up of "progress," as well as registering nationalist beliefs or reflecting subversive ideologies.

If, as Svetlana Boym argues (7), the dislocating and reimagining of time lend themselves to recent constructions of nostalgia, then both retrofuturism and steampunk not only meet her criterion but also push our understanding of nostalgia in new directions. Retrofuturism emerged as a collective longing for a future that never happened, evoking "nostalgia for a time of forward-looking hope and romance" (Rosa 85), but this nostalgia is also suffused with self-conscious irony. Noting a distinct flavor of sarcasm, illustrator Bruce McCall calls retrofuturism a "faux nostalgia" (McCall). Remarking on the same quality while commenting on marketing campaigns for Pepsi, Levi Strauss, and Ralph Lauren, Arjun Appadurai calls these qualities an "ersatz nostalgia." Citing "spare, surreal, science-fictionish" television ads that are "unmistakably evocative of the sixties (or fifties)," Appadurai observes a dynamic that looks backward and forward simultaneously (77). In remembering 1950s futurism, for instance, we "create the simulacra of periods that constitute the flow of time, conceived as lost, absent, or distant"; history is rewritten in ways that suit us, not only participating in "ersatz nostalgia" but also conceiving "imagined precursory moments" that would have yielded a different present-day reality (78).

While science fiction routinely transports readers out of the present moment, retrofuturism and steampunk play with ideas of temporality, blurring past and future. At their most unsettling, each disrupts our understanding of the nature of time, encouraging a kind of hybrid temporality. They leave us with a sense of the speeding up of progress. Although ideas of secular progressivism began earlier, over much of the late nineteenth and twentieth centuries, observers felt that time was accelerating and change was occurring at an ever-quickening pace. The designations meant to mark the future, "big and small alike—seemed to be coming and going with breathtaking speed" (Rosenberg and Harding 6). When, in his 1964 publication *Understanding Media*, Marshall McLuhan spoke of a shift from mechanization to electric speed, he also expressed the sense that time itself was quickening. American writer Alvin Toffler posited that people would soon be driven mad with "future shock" triggered by the increasing pace of change (see Toffler). If, as Rosenberg and Harding suggest, society in the late twentieth century was experiencing "a crisis in modern futurity" (4), both retrofuturism and steampunk can be related to visions of the imaginary future being too quickly usurped by reality.

This disappointment with failed predictions evolves out of what political scientist Jenny Edkins refers to as "trauma time": "When there is a mismatch between expectations and event," she writes, "we have what is experienced as a betrayal—or in other words, as traumatic" (9). In retrofuturist time, irony serves to help stabilize what otherwise would be cataclysmic, in terms of expectations never met. Retrofuturism looks to collective memory as a vehicle of manipulation or prediction, and when this fails, as is often the case, time is not only destabilized but also the unrealized fantasy feels like a loss. But steampunk engages this "trauma" very differently. Instead of trying to recapitulate the future as it was once fantasized in the past, steampunk enthusiasts speak of "colonizing the past so we can dream the future" (Catastrophone 4). Adopting a flexible and proactive stance, they imagine that "[t]he future isn't one of monolithic, inescapable doom. There are several futures ahead of us, just as today there are people who live side by side but inhabit different worlds; which one you live to witness will depend largely on what you do in the meantime" (CrimethInc 80). By evoking the first Industrial Revolution's utterly knowable gadgetry, these latter-day tinkerers rediscover machines that are "not the airy intellectual fairies of algorithmic mathematics but the hulking manifestations of muscle and mind, the progeny of sweat, blood, tears and delusions. The technology of steampunk is natural; it moves, lives ages and even dies" (Catastrophone 4). Not all steampunk literature follows this course. Stephenson's *The Diamond Age*, for example, imagines a world that has adopted a neo-Victorian social structure but is run entirely on nanotechnology, and the novel traces its widespread, and often negative, social influences. But in the steampunk lexicon, trauma and betrayal result more from lack of agency than loss of vision.

This emphasis on vision can recast both retrofuturism and steampunk as critiques of social and political change in the present. As De Witt Douglas Kilgore argues, the twentieth-century space age was a frontier or "site of renewal, a place where we can resolve the domestic and global battles that have paralyzed our progress on earth" (2). Recalling this vision of the future can be construed as a political act in and of itself. For Sharon Sharp, the television series *Star Trek: Enterprise* (2001–05) and the contemporaneous attitudes of President George W. Bush assumed retrofuturist overtones for the same purpose. Sharp argues that Bush strategized to divert attention from the ill-favored international war on terrorism when "he proposed that America would return to the moon.... Meanwhile, network television was engaged in its own nostalgic appeal to the 1960s space age in the relaunch of the Star Trek franchise" (25). In these cases, both Bush and *Enterprise* were spreading "retrofuturist rhetoric," allowing them to "allegorise problems of national identity and social difference in primetime US television in response to cultural and industrial change" (25). Scholars like Henry Jenkins see a similar retrofuturist response to 9/11 in films, such as *Sky Captain and the World of Tomorrow* (2004), that "circulate a technophilia for futuristic technologies" but also use them to defeat America's enemies (10). While full of hope and wonder, retrofuturist predictions are not often realized—perhaps making it a fitting construct for the era of the Iraq War.

Conversely, although steampunk's collective memorializing of the Victorian past is transnational, it can reflect a different series of themes more tailored to the British past. Novels like *The Difference Engine* and the 2004 film *Steamboy* self-consciously look back to the days of British industrial hegemony and highlight a period when Victorian England had undisputed political and economic supremacy. Comics like *2000 AD* (1977–) and novels like Jonathan Green and Al Ewing's *Pax Britannia* (2007) describe a world ruled by Britain (in the comic, the empire is called "Neo-Britannia"). Nevertheless, steampunk enthusiasts outside the United Kingdom continue to celebrate steampunk's Victoriana, remembering this as an age where manners and dress still reigned. In the United States, for example, America's frontier in the nineteenth century has accented an alternative milieu for the steampunk imaginary; the film *Wild Wild West* (1999), for example, presents a steampunk-inspired world of bulletproof chainmail, steam tanks, and a menacing mechanical spider. But, nationalist or not, as Edkins observes, "The fantasy is only convincing if, once it has been put in place, we can forget that it is fantasy" (14).

If fantasy must be created but also hidden, then most retrofuturism and steampunk forms contain an ironic note, lending the entire genre a kind of subversive power. Retrofuturism, for example, may quote older forms of futurism, but it also subtly questions the very premises that support speculative thinking. Describing the themes found in Gibson's "Gernsback Continuum," Bruce Sterling notes not only that "[t]imes have changed since the comfortable era of Hugo Gernsback" but also that Gibson's story implicitly reimagines a time "when authority still had a comfortable margin of control" (xiii). Both Gibson and Sterling would explore aspects of this subversion in their cyberpunk writing of the 1980s. But, as Thomas Haigh observes, "The influence of retrofuturism can be seen even in the phrase 'cyber-punk' itself": the term was taken from "cybernetics," a phrase coined by Norbert Wiener in the 1940s, yet by the 1980s, "cybernetics had fallen from scientific respectability and was increasingly the domain of cranks"; fusing the term with the rebellious "punk" movement gave cybernetics a new if rather subversive life (28). Alternately, by imagining a world of Victorian-era technology, "steampunk" also distinguishes itself from cyberpunk. The very imagining of a world run on steam is a subversive rejoinder to technology as it developed after the late 1880s. Instead, steampunk enthusiasts "love machines that we can see, feel, and fear. We are amazed by artifacts but are unimpressed by 'high technology.' For the most part, we look at the modern world about us, bored to tears, and say 'no thank you. I'd rather have trees, birds and monstrous mechanical contraptions than an endless sprawl that is devoid of diversity" (Ratt 9).

When Niklas Maak, in 2005, suggested that retrofuturism is dead, there was a swift and anguished outcry. Calling Maak's position "galvanizing," architect and web commentator Tom Mallory noted that many people want it to continue because it announces the death of the futurist dream as defined in the early to mid-twentieth century (Mallory). But the situation is complex and deserves a more nuanced interpretation. Certainly, the idea of an utterly transformed future—that is, an era that will arrive and completely change the way we live—seems preposterous. The present simply evolves gradually. Cars run with computer microchips, microwave ovens almost instantly heat up our meals, and portable phones make business possible on a Caribbean beach. These technologies, however, have unceremoniously been introduced into our current reality. In older homes, WiFi networks coexist with noisy heaters, electric cars mingle in parking lots with gas guzzlers. The future continues to arrive in incremental steps.

Whether we discuss retrofuturism's sleek glamor or steampunk's gritty but also more sustainable vision, their larger implications continue to nag. When people mourn futurist expectations, they also wonder at the implicit promise of a social utopia. But even more to the point, both cultural forms clearly remind us that technology alone will never be able to engineer such a utopia.

Works Cited

Appadurai, Arjun. *Modernity at Large: Cultural Dimensions of Globalization*. Minneapolis: U of Minnesota P, 1996. Print.

Ashley, Mike, ed. *Steampunk Prime: A Vintage Steampunk Reader*. New York: Nonstop, 2010. Print.

"The Birth of Steampunk." *Letters of Note: Correspondence Deserving of a Wider Audience*. Mar. 1, 2011. Web. Aug. 17, 2013. http://www.lettersofnote.com/2011/03/birth-of-steampunk.html.

Bowser, Rachel A., and Brian Croxall. "Introduction." *Neo-Victorian Studies* 3.1 (2010): 1–45. Web. Aug. 17, 2013. http://neovictorianstudies.com/past_issues/3-1%202010/NVS%20 3-1-1%20R-Bowser%20&%20B-Croxall.pdf.

Boym, Svetlana. *The Future of Nostalgia*. New York: Basic, 2001. Print.

Bukatman, Scott. "There's Always . . . Tomorrowland: Disney and the Hypercinematic Experience." *October 57* (1991): 55–78. Print.

Carpenter, Ele. "Coal-powered Craft: A Past for the Future." *The Journal of Modern Craft* 4.2 (Aug. 2011): 147–60. Print.

Catastrophone Orchestra and Arts Collective. "What Then, Is Steampunk?: Colonizing the Past So We Can Dream the Future." *SteamPunk Magazine* 1 (Mar. 3, 2007): 4–5. Web. Aug. 17, 2013. http://www.combustionbooks.org/downloads/SPM1-printing.pdf.

Clarke, I. F. *The Pattern of Expectation: 1644–2001*. New York: Basic Books, 1979. Print.

CrimethInc. "The Future." *SteamPunk Magazine* 4 (Feb. 26, 2008): 80. Web. Aug. 17, 2013. http://www.combustionbooks.org/downloads/spm4-web.pdf.

Dawdy, Shannon Lee. "Clockpunk Anthropology and the Ruins of Modernity." *Current Anthropology* 51.6 (Dec. 2010): 761–93. Print.

Edkins, Jenny. *Trauma and the Memory of Politics*. New York: Cambridge UP, 2003. Print.

Forlini, Stefania. "Technology and Morality: The Stuff of Steampunk." *Neo-Victorian Studies* 3.1 (2010): 72–98. Web. Aug. 17, 2013. http://www.neovictorianstudies.com/past_issues/3-1%202010/NVS%203-1-3%20S-Forlini.pdf.

Gebhard, David. *The National Trust Guide to Art Deco in America*. New York: Wiley, 1996. Print.

Gelernter, David. *1939: The Lost World of the Fair*. New York: Free Press, 1995. Print.

Gibson, William. "The Gernsback Continuum." 1981. *Burning Chrome*. New York: Eos, 2003. 24–36. Print.

———, and Bruce Sterling. *The Difference Engine*. London: Gollancz, 1990. Print.

Good, Joseph. "'God Save the Queen, for Someone Must!': Sebastian O and the Steampunk Aesthetic." *Neo-Victorian Studies* 3.1 (2010): 208–15. Web. Aug. 17, 2013. http://www.neovictorianstudies.com/past_issues/3-1%202010/NVS%203-1-9%20J-Good.pdf.

Grossman, Lev. "Steampunk: Reclaiming Tech for the Masses." *TIME*. Dec. 14, 2009. Web. Aug. 17, 2013. http://www.time.com/time/magazine/article/0,9171,1945343,00.html.

Guffey, Elizabeth. *Retro: The Culture of Revival*. London: Reaktion, 2006. Print.

Haigh, Thomas. "Technology's Other Storytellers: Science Fiction as History of Technology." *Science Fiction and Computing: Essays on Interlinked Domains*. Ed. David L. Ferro and Eric G. Swedin. Jefferson, NC: McFarland, 2011. 13–37. Print.

Hantke, Steffen. "Difference Engines and Other Infernal Devices: History According to Steampunk." *Extrapolation* 40.3 (1999): 244–54. Print.

Jenkins, Henry. "The Tomorrow That Never Was"—Retrofuturism in the Comics of Dean Motter." *Comics and the City: Urban Space in Print, Picture and Sequence*. Ed. Jorn Ahrens and Arno Meteling. New York: Continuum, 2010. 63–83. Print.

Jeter, K. W. *Infernal Devices*. New York: St. Martin's, 1987. Print.

Kefalas, A. G. "The Future of Human Organizations: An Overview." *Human Systems Management* 1.1 (Winter 1980): 79–84. Print.

Kilgore, De Witt Douglas. *Astrofuturism: Science, Race, and Visions of Utopia in Space*. Philadelphia: U of Pennsylvania P, 2003. Print.

Latham, Rob. "Our Jaded Tomorrows." *Science Fiction Studies* 36.2 (July 2009): 339–49. Print.

Maak, Niklas. "Goodbye Retro-Futurism." *032c 9* (Summer 2005): 117–19. Web. Aug. 17, 2013. http://032c.com/2005/goodbye-retro-futurism/.

Mallory, Tom. "Is Nostalgia Dead? Retro-Futurism, Architecture & Film." *The Huffington Post*. July 28, 2011. Web. Aug. 17, 2013. http://www.huffingtonpost.com/tom-mallory/top-10-film-settings-in-m_b_908082.html#s314730&title=Trudelturm_Wind_Tunnel.

McCall, Bruce. "What Is Faux Nostalgia?" *TED: Ideas Worth Spreading*. Mar. 2009. Web. Aug. 17, 2013. http://www.ted.com/talks/bruce_mccall_s_faux_nostalgia.html.

McLuhan, Marshall. *Understanding Media: The Extensions of Man*. New York: McGraw Hill, 1964. Print.

Perschon, Mike. "Steam Wars." *Neo-Victorian Studies* 3.1 (2010): 127–66. Web. http://www.neovictorianstudies.com/past_issues/3-1%202010/NVS%203-1-5%20M-Perschon.pdf. August 17, 2013.

Ratt, Margaret P. "Putting the Punk Back into Steampunk." *SteamPunk Magazine 1* (Fall 2006): 2. Web. Aug. 17, 2013. http://www.combustionbooks.org/downloads/SPM1-printing.pdf.

Rosa, Joseph, ed. *Glamour: Fashion + Industrial Design + Architecture*. New Haven, CT: Yale UP, 2006. Print.

Rosenberg, Daniel, and Susan Harding. "Introduction." *Histories of the Future*. Ed. Daniel Rosenberg and Susan Harding. Durham, NC: Duke UP, 2005. 1–18. Print.

Sharp, Sharon. "Nostalgia for the Future: Retrofuturism in *Enterprise*." *Science Fiction Film and Television* 4.1 (2011): 25–40. Print.

Stephenson, Neal. *The Diamond Age: Or, a Young Lady's Illustrated Primer*. New York: Bantam Spectra, 1995. Print.

Sterling, Bruce. "Introduction." *Mirrorshades: The Cyberpunk Anthology*. 1986. Ed. Bruce Sterling. New York: Ace, 1988. ix–xvi. Print.

Toffler, Alvin. *Future Shock*. 1970. New York: Bantam, 1984. Print.

Yaszek, Lisa. "Democratizing the Past to Improve the Future: An Interview with Steampunk Godfather Paul Di Filippo." *Neo-Victorian Studies* 1.1 (2008): 189–95. Web. Aug. 17, 2013. http://www.neovictorianstudies.com/past_issues/3-1%202010/NVS%203-1-7%20L-Yaszek.pdf.

PART IV

SCIENCE FICTION AS WORLDVIEW

CHAPTER 34

THE ENLIGHTENMENT

ADAM ROBERTS

One commonsense way of distinguishing science fiction from fantasy might be to connect the former specifically to discourses of "science" as we now understand the term—to suggest that SF emerges as a distinct cultural phenomenon at the time that modern science (as both a set of specific disciplines and a broader ideological approach to the world) emerges. That is to say, during the "Enlightenment." By "Enlightenment," critics and historians of ideas mean a mostly eighteenth-century philosophical consensus that agreed (largely) on the primacy of reason and the importance of experimental and evidential science, and that challenged older religious myths and superstitions. This movement gained much of its initial impetus from the scientific advances associated with figures such as Newton and Leibniz; and by 1784—when Immanuel Kant published his essay "Answering the Question: What Is Enlightenment?"—it was a well-established enough term to have become a contested notion. Kant's answer to his own question, incidentally, was—in a nutshell—intellectual maturity: "the emancipation of the human consciousness from an immature state of ignorance and error" (Porter 1; see also Deligiorgi). Other thinkers have seen "die Aufklärung" as a less ideologically neutral process. According to Jonathan Israel, it was the function of a broad radicalization of political debates during the period, while Isaiah Berlin considered it a "fundamental type of approach to social and political problems," the approach in question being "rational and sentimental" (183). Jonathan Rée usefully summarizes:

> There might be dozens of alternative histories of the present age, but they all intersected at some point in the 18th century known as the Age of Reason, or more vividly the Enlightenment (or *le siècle des lumières*, *die Aufklärung* or *l'illuminismo*). Essentially, the Enlightenment was taken to be Europe's concerted effort to cleanse itself of the last residues of barbarism and medieval superstition and replace them with liberalism, science and secular philosophy. (21)

All of these last-named qualities, we can note, are eminently science-fictional—although most contemporary critics would argue that superstition and myth aren't so much "cleansed" as repressed and reconfigured, in both Enlightenment thought and in SF.

Complex though arguments about the nature of the Enlightenment may be, it is worth isolating one key term—"reason," newly conceived as systematic knowledge or totalization. It is this ideal that is most indicative of an Enlightenment "worldview," which in turns shapes a particular sort of science fiction. Max Horkheimer and Theodor Adorno's influential monograph *The Dialectic of Enlightment* (1947) sees the "Enlightenment program" as "the disenchantment of the world," a movement "to dispel myths, to overthrow fantasy with knowledge" (1). They add that "technology is the essence of this knowledge" (2)—which in turns means that the imaginative literature of the period can look forward with sometimes uncanny prescience to twentieth- and twenty-first century saturations of technological innovation: "The 'many things' which, according to Bacon, knowledge still held in store are themselves mere instruments: the radio as a sublimated printing press, the dive bomber as a more effective form of artillery, remote control as a more reliable compass" (2). We could replace the radio, dive bomber, and remote control with more science-fictional versions, such as the ansible, X-Wing fighter, and cyborg wetware: on a purely imaginative level, the technical fixtures articulate the same root exhilaration—and anxiety—at the heart of Enlightenment culture.

Horkheimer and Adorno's thesis is sometimes cited as being that the Enlightenment worldview can be traced in a direct line from the eighteenth century to Auschwitz (as they say, "Enlightenment is totalitarian" [4]); but the book is a little more complicated than that. Indeed, not despite but *because* of its totalizing ideological impulse, Horkheimer and Adorno see the Enlightenment as deeply conflicted and contradictory. The "dialectic" of the book's title is not mere window dressing; as they put it: "Myth is already enlightenment, and enlightenment reverts to mythology" (xviii). And although the *Dialectic of Enlightenment* is not specifically interested in SF, we can extrapolate precisely this insight into a critique of science fiction—a mode that, even today, is simultaneously the articulation of enlightened values of reason, science, and knowledge *and* is powered by an immanent quasi-mythic cultural subconscious. SF is exhilarated by and superstitiously fearful of technological advance, or alien life, or the scale of the cosmos. *Scientia*, the Latin word behind the first term in the genre's brand name, means "knowledge"; but science fiction is only a knowledge fiction in a strictly mythological sense. Horkheimer and Adorno observe that "[h]umans believe themselves free of fear when there is no longer anything unknown. This has determined the path of demythologization"; but "Enlightenment is mythical fear radicalized" (11).

In the eighteenth century, as today, this fear of the unknown manifests very often as a fear of not just unexplored topographies but also previously unencountered peoples—the alien, to use a term crucial to SF. It ought not to surprise us, indeed, that the imaginative extrapolation of Enlightenment writers tends both to celebrate and to satirize imperial expansion—to be both excited by and suspicious of the possibilities of technology and its implementation in the world. More important, there is a deeply embedded fascination with shifts of scale in much eighteenth-century SF.

By discussing first some of the varieties of Enlightenment imaginative literature, I will work up to what I consider two of the most significant SF masterpieces of the era: Jonathan Swift's *Travels into Several Remote Nations of the World. In Four Parts. By Lemuel Gulliver, First a Surgeon, and then a Captain of Several Ships* (1726), commonly known as *Gulliver's Travels*, and Voltaire's "Micromégas" (1752). It is no coincidence that both works are based upon seeing the universe anew in terms of the very large and the very small.

Nor are they alone in this. A great many Enlightenment works find the macroscopic and the microscopic to be a new imaginative resource of wondrous possibility, as well as satirical precision. This has to do, I think, with two things. First, scientific discoveries and inventions had revealed, on the one hand, that the universe is incomparably huger than had been previously thought, and on the other hand, that whole ecosystems existed that were far too small for the unaided eye to see. But there is a metaphorical as well as an empirical dimension to this new fascination with scale: knowledge itself, the cornerstone of Enlightenment praxis, had been reconceptualized as something simultaneously very large and very small—the vast overall project of total knowledge, combined with the endless minutia of accumulated data. As Kant put it in his Enlightenment essay, rationality consists in "processes of ascending to the higher genera and of descending to the lower species [by which] we obtain the idea of systematic connection in its completeness"; the resultant systematization of knowledge lies in "the connection of its parts in conformity with a single principle" (qtd. Horkheimer and Adorno 63).

Here are two contemporary examples to illustrate these two new modes of scale. The first is Dutch scientist Bernard Nieuwentyt's 1715 work *The Religious Philosopher: or the Right Use of Contemplating the Works of the Creator*. Nieuwentyt calculates that "a Cannon-Bullet will require 26 years in passing from hence to the Sun, [and] with the same Velocity wherewith it was discharged, it would require, in order to arrive at the fix'd Stars . . . almost Seven hundred thousand Years; and a Ship that can sail 50 miles in a Day and a Night, will require 30,430,400 Years" (819). The 700,000 years figure was widely cited by other eighteenth-century thinkers, emphasizing the sheer scale of the new Copernican cosmos. This sense of limitless astronomical vistas played a key role in the resurgence of interest in the Sublime—or, to give it its SF name, "sense of wonder." The second example, a key Enlightenment text, is the Encyclopédie, *ou dictionnaire raisonné des sciences, des arts et des métiers* (1751–72) edited by Denis Diderot and Jean le Rond d'Alembert, an ambitious attempt to synthesize and summarize all that was known. This "Systematic Dictionary of the Sciences, Arts and Crafts" makes no bones about the work's totalizing ambition; it eventually ran to 28 volumes, weathering difficulties created by its perceived radicalism and impiety (see Blom 283–302).

It can be argued that, conceptually and formally, science fiction possesses an "encyclopedic" logic—or, more precisely, that its synchronic encyclopedic impulses exist in dynamic tension with its diachronic narrative impulses. One of SF's main activities is "worldbuilding," a totalizing project that is often reified into appendices, maps, glossaries, and even—with more popular works such as Frank Herbert's "Dune" series

(1965–85)—a whole paratextual subculture of guides, handbooks, encyclopedias, and wikis (see McNelly). But SF embodies its worldbuilding, to varying degrees of aesthetic elegance, in terms of story, character, form, and style. Not for nothing did Isaac Asimov make the compiling of a huge *Encyclopedia Galactica* the conceit behind his most influential work, the "Foundation" series (1942–93); the accumulation of knowledge in that story is both a disinterested project of research and synthesis *and* the covert elaboration of a strategy of galactic-scale social reform—just as with the original *encyclopédistes*.

SF's fascination with other worlds, aliens, and the interplanetary fantastic voyage dates from the Enlightenment period. The *Encyclopédie* entry on "World" raised the question of whether extraterrestrial planets might be inhabited, citing Bernard Le Bovier de Fontenelle's 1686 book on the "plurality of worlds," which had inspired much debate and controversy (see Crowe). That a century after this book was published, a project as rational and radical as the *Encyclopédie* was still fretting over the theological implications of space aliens is particularly striking. The problem had to do with the uniqueness, or otherwise, of Christ's atonement for our sins: If inhabitants of Mars or Saturn were descended from Adam, then how were they saved from original sin? If they weren't, wasn't it unconscionably cruel of God to send whole planets into damnation? But if these space aliens had been saved, had they encountered their own Martian or Saturnian Christs? The notion that many, perhaps millions, possibly an infinite number of Christs had incarnated on all the various inhabited worlds in the cosmos diluted the uniqueness and significance of the Earthly Christ intolerably. This may seem to modern sensibilities like minor theological quibbling; but, in fact, it was not only a fiercely contested Enlightenment issue, it also proved—strangely enough—constitutive of science fiction itself. Twentieth- and twenty-first-century SF, still fascinated by dilemmas that have to do, at root, with incarnation, redemption, and atonement, is the way it is because it has been shaped by the vertiginous cultural moment of the Enlightenment (see Roberts 36–63). Indeed, in 1958, SF author James Blish published a novel entitled *A Case of Conscience* that centers precisely on the question of whether a sentient alien race has Christian souls and are thus open to salvation.

Certainly, the eighteenth century saw a sudden flurry of narratives that imaginatively explored this new cosmos. Bonamy Dobrée describes the new astronomy as releasing "a terrific tidal wave of imaginative description, phosphorescent with wonder" (80). In almost all these works, the authors struggle hard to find consonance between wonder and piety. For example, Richard Blackmore's *Creation: A Philosophical Poem Demonstrating the Existence and Providence of a God* (1712) is a seven-book epic poem designed to refute atheists, but its most powerful sections look outward, to the cosmos science was discovering, rather than backward to Milton and Genesis:

> Th'expanded Spheres amazing to the Sight,
> Magnificent with Stars and Globes of Light;
> The Glorious Orbs, which Heav'n's bright Host compose ... (5)

Interestingly, Blackmore takes the situation of Earth's orbit in what we now call the "Goldilocks zone" (that is, the ideal distance from the Sun to sustain a climate and atmosphere conducive to life) to be proof of divine providence—so far as I know, the first person to discuss this question. Had, he says, the earth occupied the orbits of Jupiter or Saturn "Unsufferable winter, had defac'd / Earth's blooming Charms, and made a barren Waste"; this vision of a Plutonian Earth, in the grip of "Eternal Frost, with Ice that never flows" (40) has a genuine sense-of-wonder chill about it.

Samuel Boyse's *Deity: A Poem* (1739) adopts the imperative voice ("Go!—all the sightless realms of space survey, / Returning trace the *Planetary Way!*' [23; emphasis in original]), assured that the contemplation of such a large prospect will nurture our religious awe. William Derham's *Astro-Theology, or a Demonstration of the Being and Attributes of God from a Survey of the Heavens* (1714) makes the argument that divine utility must mean the planets are inhabited: "What is the use of so many Planets as we see about the Sun, and so many as are imagined to be about the Fixt Stars... [unless] they are *Worlds*, or Places of *Habitation*" (xlvii; emphasis in original)? This judgment, as his rather touchy ill-temper makes plain ("This Conclusion is so natural, so cogent, that any thing but *stupid prejudiced Blockheads*... would have naturally and easily made it" [75; emphasis in original]), is a degree of wishful thinking. Unlike the Ptolemaic system of Dante, this new universe is frankly *too* big, ontologically hostile to the scale of human living. On the one hand, surely God has created the profusion of stellar bodies for a reason; on the other hand, science shows that most of this vast cosmos is egregiously inhospitable to human life. Henry Baker's *The Universe: A Philosophical Poem* (1729) speculates about Saturnians living on a world where "our Poles" are warmer than "its burning Zone":

> Who, there inhabit, must have other Pow'rs,
> Juices, and Veins, and Sense, and Life than Ours.
> One Moment's Cold, like their's, would pierce the Bone,
> Freeze the Heart-Blood, and turn Us all to Stone. (18)

This groping toward actually alien aliens is the very stuff of modern SF, and a completely new note—not present in earlier fantastic voyages.

David Mallet's *The Excursion* (1728) propels the narrator into a cosmos teeming with alien life:

> Ten thousand Suns blaze forth; each with his Train
> Of peopled Worlds; all beneath the Eye,
> And sovereign Rule of one eternal Lord. (49–50)

Indeed, 10,000 is such an underestimate that a little later he corrects himself: "stupendous Host! In flaming Millions thro' the Vacant hung, / Sun behind Sun, with Gulphs of Sky between" (62). Nevertheless, the impression Mallet's poem gives of outer space is chilly. Traveling to the edge of things ("last, outmost *Saturn* walks his Frontier-Round / The Boundary of Worlds; with his pale *Moons*, / Faint glimmering thro' the Gloom..."

[57; emphasis in original]), he looks back at the Sun, once an "Ocean of Flame" that now only "twinkles from afar, / A glimmering Star amid the Train of Night!" (64). Here, the beauty outweighs the terror, but as Mallet shifts into the Sublime mode, the tenor of his work becomes less comfortable still:

> While in these deep Abysses of the Sky,
> Spaces incomprehensible, new Suns,
> Crown'd with unborrowed Beams, illustrious shine...
> Myriads beyond, with blended Rays inflame
> The *Milky Way*, whose stream of azure Light,
> Pour'd from innumerable Fountains round,
> Flows trembling, from Wave on Wave, from Sun to Sun... (64; emphasis in original)

The narrator is overwhelmed by the unimaginable vastness of these cosmic processes, where worlds are born and die unceasingly:

> Dazling the view; here nameless Worlds afar,
> Yet undiscover'd: there a *dying Sun*,
> Grown dim with Age, whose Orb of Flame extinct,
> Incredible to tell!...
> Millions of Lives, that live but in his Light,
> With Horror see, from distant Spheres around,
> The Source of Day expire, and all his Worlds
> At once involv'd in everlasting Night! (66; emphasis in original)

This splendidly rebarbative portrait of wholly alien life forms facing the termination of their world takes much of its force from its cool distance from the more familiar religious conventions of the Apocalypse.

Outer space in SF, then as now, is often deployed as a metaphor for inner space. Danish writer Ludvig Holberg's 1741 hollow-earth fantasy, *Niels Klim's Journey Under the Ground*, features a penniless ex-student who narrates how he fell into a chasm through Earth's surface and into an interior cosmos, lit by a sun at the earth's center around which various worlds orbit. Klim himself falls into orbit around one of the planets of this internal system. A small cake drops out of his own pocket and goes into orbit about *him*, turning him, as he himself puts it, into a planetary body in his own right (6)—an eloquent emblem of the simultaneous conceptual expansion and shrinkage that are characteristic of Enlightenment imaginary voyages more generally. The Enlightenment saw a vogue for hollow-earth adventures, a fact that indicates a desire to internalize the cosmic enormousness revealed by the new astronomy (see Fitting).

Moreover, inner space has a social as well as a psychological valence. Many works of Enlightenment SF rendered alien worlds as distorting-mirror versions of our own world, the satirical point of the text existing in tension with its imaginative creativity—a balance very common in SF, though in the eighteenth century the balance was weighted more often toward the satirical. Le Chevalier de Béthune's *Relation du Monde de Mercure* (Relating to the World of Mercury, 1750) is unusual in specifically disavowing political or utopian satire; the author sports with his diminutive, winged Mercurian aliens (ruled by mysterious but benevolent beings who dwell in the Sun), insisting in his preface that the book is merely "une fable, dans laquelle on a essayé ... des idées amusantes par leur nouveauté" (158; that is, "a fable, in which we tried out ... fun ideas for their novelty value"). Eberhard Christian Kindermann's *The Rapid Journey by Airship to the Upper World, Recently Taken by Five People* (1744), a story of traveling to Mars by balloon, is similarly intoxicated by the imaginative possibilities of its exuberant conceit. But these sorts of text are the exception rather than the rule: much more commonly, extraterrestrial adventure is the pretext for satirical point-scoring.

To avoid contemporary political repercussions, the authors often took refuge behind pseudonyms. *A Trip to the Moon: Containing an Account of the Island of Noibla* (1764) by "Sir Humphrey Lunatic" (actually, Sir Francis Gentleman) has some knockabout fun with contemporary politicians, and in William Thomson's *The Man in the Moon; or, Travels into the Lunar Regions* (1783), published as by "The Man of the People," lunar aliens abduct English radical politician Charles Fox and subject him to various indignities. In the anonymous (published by "Aratus") *A Voyage to the Moon, Strongly Recommended to All Lovers of Real Freedom* (1793), the hero travels to the Moon by means of a balloon, where he discovers a civilization of serpentine aliens who, in a parody of Tory England, are subjected to onerous taxation in order keep a giant wheel turning endlessly.

Joshua Barnes's *Gerania* (1675)—an adventure story located upon a hitherto hidden "great lake on the utmost Borders of India" (1)—introduces the notion of a population of very small people, of which Swift and Voltaire went on to make such potent imaginative use. In Barnes's titular kingdom, the narrator encounters tiny people who not only are "able in all the sciences" but also speak English—indeed, they are "skill'd in fifty four Languages; a thing, which to the Europeans may seem incredible" (48). Barnes's British-Tory ideological biases inform his imagination: his miniature Geranians are, improbably, not only Christians but also Protestants, with a deep animus against Jesuits; they have no taxation, but instead the population spontaneously gift the exchequer with voluntary donations. But the thoroughness with which Barnes elaborates his imagined world gives it a vividness that makes it live with more than merely satirical vividness. Another example, George Psalmanazar's *Description of Formosa* (1704), a fictional account of a strange society upon a far eastern island, was believed by many to be true, a fact upon which its mysterious author capitalized (see Keevak).

These satirical-fantastic extrapolations were interpenetrated by contemporary discourses of science. Indeed, the Enlightenment is arguably the last epoch in which "scientific" and "literary" texts could be essentially the same thing. John Armstrong's long poem *The Art of Preserving Health* (1728), widely admired and reprinted, was as highly regarded by medical specialists as by literary critics. What is interesting about it for our purposes is the way it makes the human body itself the ground of an Enlightenment fascination with miniaturization. Armstrong's post-Harvey imaginative realization of blood flow turns a simple, indeed universal dynamic—the operations of the human corpus—into a narrative of the collapse of a beautifully realized alien landscape:

> The blood, the fountain whence the spirits flow,
> The generous stream that waters every part,
> And motion, vigour, and warm life conveys
> To every particle that moves or lives;
> This vital fluid, thro' unnumber'd tubes
> Pour'd by the heart, and to the heart again
> Refunded; scourg'd for ever round and round;
> Enrag'd with heat and toil, at last forgets
> Its balmy nature; virulent and thin
> It grows; and now, but that a thousand gates
> Are open to its flight, it would destroy
> The parts it cherish'd and repair'd before.
> Besides, the flexible and tender tubes
> Melt in the mildest, most nectareous tide
> That ripening nature rolls; as in the stream
> Its crumbling banks; but what the vital force
> Of plastic fluids hourly batters down,
> That very force, those plastic particles
> Rebuild: So mutable the state of man. (4)

This depiction anticipates not only Erasmus Darwin's attempts to meld epic poetry with biological instruction, it is also a forerunner of the 1966 SF film *Fantastic Voyage*, in which a group of miniaturized doctors are injected into a patient's bloodstream. As in Swift's Gulliver, the human body itself is contracted or expanded to become a whole world by means of the relative perspectives of science.

Certainly, in the best fantastic fictions of the era, the satire, no matter how obvious, does not overwhelm the imaginative possibilities of the mode. Voltaire's "Micromégas"—written in 1730 but not published until 1750—is a preeminent example. On the one hand, this is a satirical reimagining, from a cosmic scale, of the things we consider important, thus revealing their triviality. But it is more than just this; like Swift's *Gulliver's Travels*, by which it was directly inspired, it generates a memorable imaginative surplus, lifting off into the spheres of wonder that animate the best SF. Micromégas himself is a gigantic, 5-kilometer-tall alien from the star Sirius. Voyaging through the galaxy, he comes to our solar system and befriends a native of the planet Saturn (who, at only a thousand fathoms high, is a dwarf beside him). Together, they travel to Earth, where they observe an ocean-going vessel full of philosophers returning from an exploratory voyage to the Arctic Circle. Once the two extraterrestrials have gotten over their amazement that such "invisible insects" (73) could possess intelligence and soul, they engage them in conversation, interrogating their knowledge of physics—for example, the distance from Earth to the Moon, the weight of Earth's atmosphere. Humanity's knowledge of these matters impresses them; but when Micromégas discourses on the philosophy of mind ("Tell me what is the soul, and how do your ideas originate?" [75]), the philosophers reveal a multitude of conflicting theories deriving from various Earthly philosophers. Further questioning reveals man's essential ignorance. "But what dost thou understand by spirit?" asks Micromégas of the Cartesian, who replies, "I have no idea of it" (75). When one thinker insists that God has made the entire cosmos purely for the benefit of humankind, the aliens are "seized with a fit of . . . uncontrollable laughter" (76). Micromégas eventually gifts humankind a book of philosophy that he promises contains all the truth about things; when opened, its pages are revealed to be blank. Voltaire's short novel foregrounds the way using the new cosmos—of the very large and the very small—as a lens through which to view human affairs inevitably estranges us from human conventionalities. But it does more than this; it comes to life on its own terms, functioning as a compelling work of satirical SF.

Swift's *Gulliver's Travels* is perhaps the greatest melding of the satirical and the scientific that the entire era produced: a masterpiece that articulates and critiques the Enlightenment worldview that is its inspiration. Lemuel Gulliver, afflicted with a mania for travel, leaves England to sail around the world. Shipwrecked on the island of Lilliput, Gulliver discovers a kingdom of people barely 6 inches high. He takes the Lilliputian side in their war with the equally diminutive Blefuscuns, but he falls into disfavor with the monarch after pissing on his palace (to put out a dangerous fire) and leaves the island, eventually returning to England. In the second volume, Gulliver travels again, this time to the island of the Brobdingnags where everything is 12 times as large as normal, including the people. In the third volume, Gulliver sets out on a fresh voyage and encounters a number of new islands—such as Laputa, over which a magnetically powered flying island hovers. The fourth volume sees Gulliver encountering a utopian race of sapient horses, the Houyhnhnms.

Many SF critics argue that *Gulliver's Travels* is not an example of the genre. For Brian Aldiss, the work "does not count as science fiction, being satirical and/or moral in intention rather than speculative" (85). Kingsley Amis thought the difficulty in calling Swift's novel science fiction was that "there is no science (or technology) as such in the first two parts" (12). These attitudes reflect a widespread critical misunderstanding that takes the book to be "unscientific" or even antiscientific; the latter reading is advanced by critics who contrast the absurdity of life aboard the scientists' flying island with the purity of life among the Houyhnhnms, who are so removed from science that they have not even discovered metallurgy (see Patey). But the fact is that all four parts of Swift's great novel are deeply imbued with Enlightenment science to such a degree that it becomes hard to avoid reading the book as being *about* science—or, more particularly, about the relationship between science and representation.

Such a reading, I should add, is at odds with most critical analyses of the book. In Terry Eagleton's opinion, the world explored by Gulliver is actually Gulliver himself, or more specifically Gulliver's conflicted ideological situation as *homo enlightenmentensis*.

His travels reveal himself to himself as "an area traversed and devastated by intolerable contradiction" (58). The Lilliputians, for instance, function as a means of ridiculing the minute triviality of Western court politics, with wars fought over which end of the egg to break when eating it, and political office won by those able to jump the highest. But to read the novel is to be struck by how much respect, actually, Gulliver has for the way Lilliput orders its affairs. He is, for instance, full of praise for the way "they look upon fraud as a greater crime than theft" (Swift 56), the way the law not only punishes delinquency but also actively rewards virtue (anyone who obeys all the laws for "seventy-three Moons" can claim certain privileges and is paid money out of the public purse [57]), and the way the children are bred up "in the Principles of Honour, Justice, Courage, Modesty, Clemency, Religion, and Love of their Country" (59). In other words, Swift's portrait of Lilliput engages *at one and the same time* in satirical mockery and quasi-utopian celebration. The same is true of the Brobdingnagians: on the one hand, Gulliver is exhibited in their kingdom as a prisoner and freak; he is an unwilling participant in lechery and observes political infighting. On the other hand, these are a people from whom he receives uncommon wisdom and insight, such that, at the end of the book, he adjudges them "the least corrupted" of the Yahoo-humans he has encountered (268), and they live peaceful, productive, happy lives.

Amis's assertion that "there is no science" in the first two parts of the novel is flatly wrong: Swift dilates at length upon several scientific and technical fields. The Lilliputians, for instance, are most excellent mathematicians and have arrived at a great perfection in mechanics (their emperor "is a renowned Patron of Learning" [28]). Despite being very capable machinists, they have not encountered clockwork, and they react with bemusement on discovering Gulliver's pocket watch. The Brobdingnagians do possess clockwork, which technology is apparently raised to "very great Perfection" (97); but they lack military ordnance, and Gulliver tries, and fails, to interest the king in metal cannon fired by gunpowder.

The third part of *Gulliver's Travels*, "A Voyage to Laputa," is more obviously concerned with science. Gulliver is taken aboard a floating island, a huge dirigible artifact powered by magnetism (Swift knew William Gilbert's 1600 treatise *On the Magnet, Magnetic Bodies, and that Great Magnet, the Earth*, a work that conflates what we now think of as magnetism and gravity into one force and makes great claims for its possible utility in technical advances). It is populated with a culture of scientists so entirely caught up in speculative astronomy that they have lost touch with reality—or, more precisely, their sense of human reality has been overwhelmed by the enormity of the cosmic perspectives:

> Their Apprehensions arise from several Changes they dread in the Celestial Bodies. For Instance; that the Earth by the continual approaches of the Sun towards it, must in course of Time be absorbed or swallowed up. That the Face of the Sun will by Degrees be encrusted with its own Effluvia, and give no more Light to the World. That the Earth very narrowly escaped a brush from the Tail of the last Comet, which would have infallibly reduced it to Ashes ... (153)

Meanwhile, they live in squalor, and their neglected wives have sex with strangers. As a satire on a particular cast of intellect, externalizing the tendency of thinkers to "have their heads in the clouds" by imagining a whole city that is literally up in the sky is effective enough. But this is also an imaginative entry into precisely the conceptual deracination of Enlightenment science as such.

This is true in terms of both the totalizing scientific aspirations of the age, and its burgeoning totalitarian imperialism: Swift ends his novel with the rather plaintive appeal that "those Countries which I have described do not appear to have any Desire of being conquered, and enslaved, murdered or driven out by Colonies" (270). He ironically has Gulliver argue that "the Lilliputians, I think, are hardly worth the Charge of a Fleet and Army to reduce them" (268) and that the Brobdingnagians and Houyhnhnms would be too formidable as opponents, despite having already established that neither people possesses the destructive technologies of artillery or explosives (268). Of course, he knew better. Following the novel's logic and applying our sense of the ideological conditions of early-eighteenth-century Europe, we can readily imagine colonization, exploitation, expropriation, slavery, and death being visited upon Lilliputians, Brobdingagians, and Houyhnhnms alike.

Such is, of course, one of the key facets of the scientific rationalism of Swift's age. The Enlightenment worldview is, with devastating straightforwardness, a view of the whole world as open to conquest, colonization, and immiseration—in the name precisely of reason, liberty, and the perfectibility of mankind. In this regard, science fiction remains one of its principal heirs (see Csicsery-Ronay; Rieder). In both discourses, the universe has become simultaneously much bigger and much smaller, and the imaginative vertigo of that state of affairs is as relevant today as it was then.

WORKS CITED

Aldiss, Brian W., with David Wingrove. *Trillion Year Spree: The History of Science Fiction*. London: Gollancz, 1986. Print.

Amis, Kingsley. "Editor's Note." *The Golden Age of Science Fiction*. Harmondsworth, UK: Penguin, 1981. 11–15. Print.

Armstrong, John. *The Art of Preserving Health: A Poem*. 1728. London: T. Caddell, 1768. Print.

Baker, Henry. *The Universe: A Philosophical Poem. Intended to Restrain the Pride of Man*. 1729. 3rd ed. London: J. Worrall, n.d. Print.

Barnes, Joshua. *Gerania: A New Discovery of a Little Sort of People, Anciently Discoursed of, Called Pygmies*. London: W.G., 1675. Print.

Berlin, Isaiah. *Enlightening: Letters 1946–1960*. Ed. Henry Hardy and Jennifer Holmes. London: Random House UK, 2009. Print.

Béthune, Le Chevalier de. *Relation du Monde de Mercure*. 1750. *Voyages Imaginaires: Songes, Visions, et Romans Cabalistiques*. Vol. 16. Paris: A. Amsterdam, 1787. 165–478. Print.

Blackmore, Richard. *Creation: A Philosophical Poem Demonstrating the Existence and Providence of a God*. 1712. 3rd ed. London: F. Tonson, 1715. Print.

Blom, Philipp. *Enlightening the World*: Encyclopédie, *the Book That Changed the Course of History*. 2004. New York: Palgrave Mcmillan, 2005. Print.

Boyse, Samuel. *Deity: A Poem*. 1739. London. C. Corbett, 1749. Print.
Crowe, Michael J. *The Extraterrestrial Life Debate, 1750–1900*. Cambridge, UK: Cambridge UP, 1999. Print.
Csicsery-Ronay Jr., Istvan. "Science Fiction and Empire." *Science Fiction Studies* 30.2 (July 2003): 231–45. Print.
Deligiorgi, Katerina. *Kant and the Culture of Enlightenment*. New York: SUNY P, 2005. Print.
Derham, William. *Astro-Theology, or a Demonstration of the Being and Attributes of God from a Survey of the Heavens*. 1714. 6th ed. London: W. Innys, 1731. Print.
Dobrée, Bonamy. *The Broken Cistern*. London: Cohen and West, 1953. Print.
Eagleton, Terry. "Ecriture and Eighteenth-Century Fiction." *Literature, Society and the Sociology of Literature: Proceedings of the Conference Held at the University of Essex, July 1976*. Ed. Francis Barker, John Coombes, Peter Hulme, David Musselwhite, and Richard Osborne. Colchester, UK: University of Essex, 1977. 55–58. Print.
Fitting, Peter, ed. *Subterranean Worlds: A Critical Anthology*. Middletown, CT: Wesleyan UP, 2004. Print.
Holbert, Lewis [a.k.a. Ludvig]. *Niels Klim's Journey Under the Ground*. 1741. Trans. John Gierlow. Boston: Saxton, Pierce, & Co., 1845. Print.
Horkheimer, Max, and Theodor Adorno. *Dialectic of Enlightenment: Philosophical Fragments*. 1947. Trans. Edmund Jephcott. Ed. Gunzelin Schmid Noerr. Stanford, CA: Stanford UP, 2002. Print.
Israel, Jonathan. *Democratic Enlightenment: Philosophy, Revolution, and Human Rights, 1750–1790*. New York: Oxford UP, 2011. Print.
Keevak, Michael. *The Pretended Asian: George Psalmanazar's Eighteenth-Century Formosan Hoax*. Detroit, MI: Wayne State UP, 2004. Print.
Mallet, David. *The Excursion: A Poem in Two Parts*. London: J. Walthoe, 1728. Print.
McNelly, Willis. *The Dune Encyclopedia: The Complete, Authorized Guide and Companion to Frank Herbert's Masterpiece of the Imagination*. New York: Berkley, 1987. Print.
Nieuwentyt, Bernard. *The Religious Philosopher: or the Right Use of Contemplating the Works of the Creator*. 1715. Trans. John Chamberlayne. 1719. 3rd ed. London: W. Bower, 1730. Print.
Patey, Douglas Lane. "Swift's Satire on 'Science' and the Structure of *Gulliver's Travels*." *ELH* 58.4 (Winter 1991): 809–39. Print.
Porter, Roy. *The Enlightenment*. 1990. 2nd ed. New York: Palgrave, 2001. Print.
Rée, Jonathan. "The Brothers Koerbagh." *London Review of Books* 24.2 (Jan. 14, 2002): 21–24. Print.
Rieder, John. *Colonialism and the Emergence of Science Fiction*. Middletown, CT: Wesleyan UP, 2008. Print.
Roberts, Adam. *The History of Science Fiction*. New York: Palgrave Mcmillan, 2006. Print.
Swift, Jonathan. *Gulliver's Travels*. 1726. Ed. Robert DeMaria Jr. Rev. ed. London: Penguin, 2003. Print.
Voltaire. "Micromégas." 1750. *Candide and Other Stories*. Trans. Tobias Smollett; rev. by William F. Fielding. New York: Digireads, 2009. 65–76. Print.

CHAPTER 35

THE GOTHIC

WILLIAM HUGHES

Gothic is the unnatural, uncaring, and irresponsible parent of science fiction. Provocative though such a statement may be for critics who assert the generic integrity of SF, the connection between a genre initially distinguished by a taste for anachronistic medievalism and one aspiring to a futuristic technocracy cannot easily be denied. However discrete the two literary forms may have become in the twenty-first century, their origins are inextricably intertwined, and both arguably maintain to the present day an enduring concern with the same issues that preoccupied their eighteenth-century literary ancestor.

These are issues not of the concretely scientific or mechanistic fields, but of the specifically and identifiably human. The haunted and the haunter, and the robot and its inventor, share alike the quality of a human identity tested, observed, and ultimately valorized through empathy and identification. The Other of the human protagonist is always a compromised figure, its apparent distance—abhuman, inhuman, former human—from the physiologically conventional and temporally mortal being illusory, concealing but momentarily its unavoidable kinship with the familiar and the mundane. Monster and menaced, whatever their genre, are thus aspects of essentially the same imaginative and philosophical project.

The Gothic, like science fiction, is a literary laboratory, a projected experimental space that, if it does not satisfactorily claim a didactic imperative, almost invariably interrogates the limits of the human as much as those of the imaginary technological. Contentious ethical issues and projected responses to unprecedented—or else fearfully familiar—situations of horror, indecision, or ignorance are the stuff of both. If both genres disturb the comfort of the known world through the deployment of alternative histories or alternate futures, they also characteristically embody the empathetic imperatives of Aristotelian tragedy: pity—associated with greatness fallen, virtue lost, or misfortune undeserved—and fear (fear that the fictional protagonist—human, abhuman, inhuman—might bespeak a hamartia or a hubris reminiscent of the reader's own).

The genesis of Gothic science fiction can be dated to 12 significant days between June 10–22, 1816 (see Joseph 158). Between these dates, Mary Shelley, her husband Percy, and their young son made up a literary party with Lord Byron, his physician John Polidori, and Byron's sometime mistress Claire Clairmont (Mary's stepsister), at the Villa Diodati near Lake Geneva. Shelley's *Frankenstein; or, the Modern Prometheus* (1818) was one product of the occasion, as the Preface to the anonymous first edition acknowledges:

> The season was cold and rainy, and in the evenings we crowded around a blazing wood fire, and occasionally amused ourselves with some German stories of ghosts, which happened to fall into our hands. These tales excited in us a playful desire of imitation. Two other friends... and myself agreed to write each a story, founded on some supernatural occurrence. (48)

Frankenstein is thus the product of an overwhelmingly literary context, its textual reference point being the *Fantasmagoriana* of Jean-Baptiste-Benoît Eyriès, which was read and imitated by the assembled company. If the trappings of medical science in *Frankenstein* distinguish that novel from earlier Gothic fictions that drew their inspiration from superstition and religious sectarianism, its displaced but necessary "supernatural" content is embodied in the manner whereby the unprecedented becomes the uncanny, with the pointed lack of specific detail in the scene in which the Creature is brought to life functioning in much the same way as necromancy or *diablerie* do elsewhere in the genre.

As is the case with so many documents and testimonies presented within the Gothic, however, the Preface to *Frankenstein* is both fraudulent and misleading (see Sage 127). Likewise, the simplistic association of *Frankenstein* with the *Fantasmagoriana* is a product of a too rapid and easy acceptance of what is, at best, a fragmentary authority. The anonymous Preface to the first edition was written by Percy, not Mary Shelley, despite the ownership implied in its modest first-person address. The lighthearted "literary contest" between Mary, Shelley, Byron, and Polidori—as it has historically been styled in literary criticism (see Kiely 155)—is similarly undermined in its primacy in the genesis of *Frankenstein* by the Preface's explicit assertion of a more speculative (and specifically scientific) content whose presence emphatically distances the novel and its implications from any "supernatural occurrence."

Percy Shelley's Preface, indeed, frames *Frankenstein* as much as the familiar quotation from *Paradise Lost* (1667) that graces the preceding title page. Before its recollection of the reading and imitation of the *Fantasmagoriana*, however, the Preface evokes another context less readily acknowledged in criticism of *Frankenstein*, which prioritizes Shelley's knowledge of both popular fiction and prevailing philosophies of human development. Percy's Preface opens thus:

> The event on which this fiction is founded has been supposed by Dr Darwin, and some of the physiological writers of Germany, as not of impossible occurrence. I shall not be supposed as according the remotest degree of serious faith to such an imagination; yet in assuming it as the basis of a work of fancy, I have not considered

myself as merely weaving a series of supernatural terrors. The event on which the interest of the story depends is exempt from the disadvantages of a mere tale of spectres or enchantment. It was recommended by the novelty of the situations which it developes [sic]; and, however impossible as a physical fact, affords a point of view to the imagination for the delineating of human passions more comprehensive and commanding than any which the ordinary relations of existing events can yield. (47)

This is somewhat paradoxical. On the one hand, the culturally valued, "progressive" discourses of science are duly acknowledged through the contemporary work of Erasmus Darwin and his Continental associates; on the other hand, the writer distances himself from any belief in the practical possibility of returning life to dead matter. The implications of this are clear: the speculations and projections of science are as suitable a vehicle for fiction as the British folk memories from which are derived both a fear of the Roman Catholic Other and the more abstracted presence of ghosts, vampires, and demonic tempters in the Gothic novel proper.

The real interest of Shelley's statement, though, arguably lies in his aligning of contemporary scientific romance (itself a novelty) with the established tenor of supernatural fiction. Though the "disadvantages" of the latter are not enumerated here, it might well be assumed that these are almost certainly centered upon the immateriality of ghostliness or the inability for the uninitiated to satisfactorily reprise an incident of "enchantment." This being the case, any fiction that is uniquely premised upon a supernatural incident—such as the presence of a ghost or the summoning of a demon—must surely delineate "human passions" even less satisfactorily than a narrative of secular mundanity.

That Shelley's Preface goes on to suggest that *Frankenstein*, implicitly in all of its characters, strives to "preserve the truth of the elementary principles of human nature" (47) is also surely significant. The "amiableness of domestic affection" (47) that the novel supposedly illustrates is achieved, in part, under abnormal and extreme circumstances: the exile of Safie and the degradation of the De Lacey family, the functional rather than consanguine bond that links the Creature to his creator. In these occurrences, which reflect, variously, an all too human cupidity and a rhetorically emphatic juxtaposition of paternal duty and filial love, the novel implies an essentialism of sympathy and response that links a culturally and racially disparate conventional humanity with the even more hybridized body of the Creature.

The Creature's privileged function as a fabricated human is thus to comment upon the nature of his organically conventional counterparts. As a doppelgänger not merely to his Creator but with regard to the entire human species, the unnamed Creature is an everyman and an anyman—not one human but many, he yet enjoys the boundaried integrity of a singular being. He may feel for all, for he endures the sufferings that are recorded as the pain of many. Alongside the exiled Safie—whose gendered dispossession is doubly signaled by both Eastern slavery and the exclusion of women from power in Western culture—he learns of the inhumanity and barbarism of "progressive" civilization: as he intimates to his creator, "I heard of the discovery of the American hemisphere, and wept with Safie over the hapless fate of its original inhabitants" (144). The focus here is upon a monstrosity greater than that of the Creature—a monstrosity that, though it may not in reality be able to create such a chimera, is more than ready to justify inhumane behaviour, arbitrary control over life, and inequitable access to power. It is the deployment of medical discourse that successfully imbricates the technology of science with the polemic of human inequality and intolerance in *Frankenstein*.

Medical science, though, is represented with a tantalizing vagueness in the understated scene in which the dead tissue of the Creature is reanimated (84–85). If this protects the scenario from anachronism, facilitating its transmission as a Gothic interlude illuminated only by a guttering candle, it links it also to the culture of hearsay and half-understanding in which the author participated. This much was acknowledged in 1831 by Mary Shelley in her retrospective Introduction to a revised *Frankenstein*: admitting that the speculative science of the novel was inspired not so much by what Erasmus Darwin had actually done as by "what was then spoken of as having been done by him," Shelley recalled having speculated while at the Villa Diodati that "[p]erhaps a corpse would be re-animated; galvanism had given token of such things: perhaps the component parts of a creature might be manufactured, brought together, and endued with vital warmth" (357). Luigi Galvani, as Shelley doubtless knew, accidentally discovered the neural reaction that inspired his later experiments in electricity by accidentally touching dead reptilian flesh with a domestic knife, charged through contact with an adjacent electrical apparatus (Anon., "Galvanism" 2). So sufficient is the paradigm of Galvani's actions that Shelley in her Introduction not merely attributes Victor's success to "the working of some powerful engine" but considers how these may "mock the stupendous mechanism of the Creator of the world" (357). The mockery proclaimed in this latter remark may be read, however, in terms other than those of a theological outrage consequent upon the usurpation of the Deity's sole right to create life. Indeed, it is strangely germane to Percy Shelley's earlier prefatory remark regarding the "disadvantages of a mere tale of spectres," chief among which must surely be the impossibility of satisfactorily recreating a truly supernatural event.

Galvani, as popular accounts of his work insistently stress, repeated his apparent energization of dead flesh both immediately following his accidental discovery and on many subsequent occasions (Anon., "Galvanism" 2; Anon., "Deaths" 2). Victor Frankenstein, likewise, fabricates a further creature from disparate components, though he destroys it before giving it life, following an introspection of what he has already done and of what both creatures might do together (Shelley, *Frankenstein* 190–93). It is clear, though, that Frankenstein is confident the second experiment *will* succeed, for it is the realization that he was "now about to form another being, of whose dispositions I was alike ignorant" (190) that causes him first to pause and then to act decisively. The Deity, though, seems less demonstrative in the matter of creation. Adam—so often mentioned in *Frankenstein*—is formed of earthly dust, but Eve is not created in the same way, being merely an extraction from the man's already created and enlivened form. The descendants of the primal couple are the product of conventional human coitus, and are thus further distanced from the original divine act, being the product of the desire of their parents not the will of their God. The creation of Adam, therefore, is an experiment or an action never repeated, and thus not scientifically tenable. The textual mockery is exactly that: medical science has aspired to enact *twice* that which the Deity has achieved but once. God and man, seemingly, are equal. It is the consequences of creation, however, rather than the technology of unprecedented revivification, around which the novel pivots.

The extent to which *Frankenstein* functions as a paradigm for subsequent Gothic— and Gothic-inflected—science fiction cannot be overstated; indeed, Brian Aldiss has identified the novel's "diseased creation myth" (43) as the originary model for the SF genre, whose essential theme, in his view, is "[h]ubris clobbered by nemesis" (26; emphasis in original). Yet such an emphasis must be tempered by the realization that Gothic, which extensively and at times repugnantly details human degradation, supernatural predation, and abject physical dissolution, seldom fetishizes and foregrounds technology in the manner associated with generically orthodox SF. The emphasis in Gothic, as has already been suggested, is characteristically placed upon human relations and human inequalities, where science fiction would appear to address these issues via an attention— if not more detailed, then at least more protracted—to massive changes in technology and society. Yet, as Fred Botting has observed, the "Gothic parts of Shelley's fictions take their bearings from the same, modern conditions of change that allow the emergence of science fiction"—namely, "the economic, industrial and technological apparatuses of modern society" and their associated "values and procedures that shape and define individuals, making humans and making monsters at the same time" (137). Shelley's *Frankenstein*, because of its unique position at the purported close of the first phase of one genre and the initiation of another, balances both of these factors, the human and the technoscientific, though later works of Shelley's and her Gothic successors, from the nineteenth century to the present day, have been more apt to polarize them.

That polarization can be perceived in the manner in which the Gothic—and Gothic-inflected science fiction—deal with the effect of morbid or degenerate states upon the individual body and, more speculatively, upon human culture and the geoclimatic environment that sustains it. In the case of the individual body, speculations based upon human medicine, and its attempts to construct general theories out of specific interventions into empirical bodies, remain as prominent in fictions today as they did in *Frankenstein*, while treatments of the more sweeping effects on culture and the environment, with their presaging of apocalypse or even extinction, are actually far less a departure from Shelley's 1818 novel than might first appear. *Frankenstein*, if it is anything other than a generic Gothic novel, is a narrative of speculative and irresponsible medical experimentation (see Turney). As such, it anticipates a distinctive tradition in the Gothic sufficiently wide to embrace works as diverse as Wilkie Collins's *The Woman in White* (1859) and *Heart and Science* (1883), Arthur Machen's "The Great God Pan" (1894), H. G. Wells's *The Island of Dr Moreau* (1896), and Bram Stoker's *Dracula* (1897). All of these works are, in essence, novels of human transformation, fictions in which drastic—sometimes fatal—change is brought to body or mind by the imposition of innovative, unproven, or unorthodox surgical or psychological techniques.

At the center of this tradition lies a core fear of powerlessness that can be linked back to the elaborate depictions of imprisonment and persecution embodied in late-eighteenth-century Gothic. The horrors of the eighteenth-century fin de siècle, as Sade intimated (108–09), were a displacement into an imagined past of contemporary British fears associated with the French Revolution and the Terror. In the place of contemporary demagogues, Gothic authors substituted feudal noblemen and historical clerics as emblems of absolute, autocratic rule and policy by cabal. By contrast, nineteenth-century Gothic after *Frankenstein* was more inclined to channel its anxieties through representations of the near contemporary. Thus, the arbitrary chambers of the convent and the Inquisition, choice locations for wrongful and punitive incarceration in the eighteenth century, are replaced in the nineteenth by the madhouse and the prison—thoroughly modern institutions that nonetheless characteristically embody no easy process of appeal or release. Likewise, feudalism and the theocratic rule of canon law are eclipsed in nineteenth-century Gothic by the arbitrary power wielded by secular professionals in law and medicine. There is little hope for those morally right, but otherwise disabled, in such modern circumstances.

Though Collins suggests, in *The Woman in White*, that "the Law is still, in certain inevitable cases, the pre-engaged servant of the long purse" (5), medicine is its close ally in the persecution of the apparently defenseless. Laura, the novel's heroine, is confined to a lunatic asylum by the signatures of two attending doctors upon a legal document (434–35); once incarcerated there, her mental confusion is effectively maintained through up-to-date medical techniques of hypnotic suggestion and moral management (see Pearl). The incarceration of the mental patient—and, indeed, of the physiologically disordered or deviant individual—is, however, a matter of private rather than public intervention. The prison, on the other hand, is a public institution, its prime function being—until comparatively recently—to exclude and enclose, rather than reform, those who deviate from established social consensus. In postfeudal culture, the prison enforces and maintains the power of the centralized state rather than that of the localized individual.

The hospital, though, is rarely a public institution in British Gothic, and the madhouse is even more likely to be a private establishment. Medical jurisprudence imposes itself upon the body of the individual, the power of the clinical specialist extracting the patient from the otherwise absolute protection afforded to the physically and mentally sound by statute law. Within the walls of such places, the presiding doctor's word is law, and his medical decisions dictate the access those incarcerated have to communication, liberty, or relief. There is thus more to a medical institution than the administration of palliative or curative care. In the Gothic, medical institutions are places where inmates temporarily or permanently lose their identity as readily as those confined by the Inquisition, where the actions of professionals in authority may with impunity interfere with the body or the mind in the pursuit of some (hopefully present) truth, and where the self has few rights and seemingly no recourse to statute or moral law. As Ruth Bienstock Anolik puts it, "The social and psychological empathy that links people through a sense of shared humanity disappears in the face of a deviation that seems to remove the sufferer completely from the human and thus from human intercourse" (3).

Within the walls of the hospital or the asylum, the ward and the operating theater elide almost seamlessly into the laboratory and the dissecting room, and the human subject loses its distinctive humanity, becoming instead the equivalent of a dog or a monkey, experimental animals whose existence is perpetuated only to unlock, through painful science, the hidden mysteries of nature. Such laboratories of human vivisection, with their utter disregard for individuality and the simple value of life, are surprisingly common in Victorian Gothic. In Collins's *Heart and Science*, the vivisectionist Nathan Benjulia deliberately encourages the development of the morbid brain disorder that threatens the life of his patient, Carmina, just as in *Dracula* Dr. Seward systematically facilitates for experimental purposes the already advanced mental delusions of Renfield, an elderly inmate of his private asylum. In Machen's "The Great God Pan," a surgical intervention into the brain of a physiologically viable adult is justified not merely on the basis of experimental expediency but also, as the presiding surgeon intimates, because he "rescued Mary from the gutter, and from almost certain starvation, when she was a child; I think her life is mine, to use as I see fit" (8). The presiding medical professional, who represents modernity of procedure and emotionless, supposedly "progressive" thought, is a force whose influence over the lives of those he governs is as arbitrary as the whims of any feudal baron or Renaissance abbot depicted in earlier Gothic fictions.

Victimhood is enforced in such cases neither by gender nor by poverty, as is so often the case in earlier Gothic fiction. Those who are *available* to the physician—whether they are corpses looted from the grave or pauper cadavers supplied for dissection under the Anatomy Act of 1832, patients signed over to confinement by the processes of secular law, or infirm individuals passed into ostensibly protective medical custody by concerned or exasperated relatives—effectively cease to be human. They exist in no other context aside from those circumscribed by a doctor's aspirations and his theoretical extrapolation of their specific example to the greater maladies suffered by humankind. There is little to separate the attitude expressed toward an expendable—if not purchasable—humanity in these Victorian works and twenty-first-century fictions such as Kazuo Ishiguro's SF novel *Never Let Me Go* (2005), where certain individuals—cloned, derivative, but otherwise genetically identical to their originals—are experimentally nurtured, rendered subject to professional and political expediency, and ultimately deprived of life and/or limb without appeal or institutional regret. The ambiguously official twentieth-century policy at Alder Hey Children's Hospital in Liverpool, under which organs and tissue were harvested from dead bodies and subsequently retained or sold for experimental purposes without permission or acknowledgment, provides a chilling parallel to such fictional projections (see Jenkins).

This kind of experimentation may be proclaimed by some as a necessary or at least justifiable sacrifice for the greater good, yet Victorian Gothic tends to suggest that such noble aspirations are at best tangential to the egotism of the vivisectionist. Nathan Benjulia, for example, unashamedly berates his brother Lemuel, who is skeptical regarding the claims and ethics of vivisection, with a barrage of rhetoric when the question is raised as to why he has so long engaged in physically debilitating and morally questionable experiments:

> What do you say? Am I working myself into my grave, in the medical interests of humanity? *That* for humanity! I am working for my own satisfaction—for my own pride—for my own unutterable pleasure in beating other men—for the fame that will keep my name living hundreds of years hence... Knowledge for its own sake, is the one god I worship. Knowledge is its own justification and its own reward. (Collins, *Heart and Science* 190; emphasis in original)

Knowledge, as the earlier part of Benjulia's tirade intimates, is simply an outgrowth of egotism. Dr. Seward, Stoker's presiding physician, displays similar traits of egotistical ruthlessness in his own acceleration of his patient's disorder (114–15), though these are muted in comparison to the rhapsodies of Machen's Dr. Raymond, who recounts how his discovery led him to see, "mapped out in lines of light[,] a whole world, a sphere unknown; continents and islands, and great oceans in which no ship has sailed (to my belief) since a man first lifted up his eyes and beheld the sun, and the stars of heaven, and the quiet earth beneath" (5).

The godlike defiance and egotistical irresponsibility of the Victorian physician-turned-experimental-scientist was, however, nothing new. Victor Frankenstein himself on comprehending (in suitably hyperbolic terms) how he "alone should be reserved to discover so astonishing a secret" as the ability to bestow life to inanimate matter, breathlessly anticipates how a "new species would bless me as its creator and source; many happy and excellent natures would owe their being to me. No father could claim the gratitude of his child so completely as I should deserve their's [sic]" (Shelley, *Frankenstein* 82). To create, however, may equally be to destroy, and the unforeseen implications of the actions of doctors Frankenstein, Benjulia, Seward, Raymond, and Moreau have an impact that extends far beyond the death of the individual bodies of their experimental subjects.

The establishment of categories of persons that can be excluded from society is, in essence, a mode of repression that is as much prophylactic as therapeutic—to protect the human community from the contagion of their pathologies. Part of the perversity of Gothic, however, is that those who incarcerate are often as degenerate as the victims of their desires or aspirations. Whether depicted as a necessarily constrained prisoner of the law, as an inmate confined to a hospital or asylum, or else as the powerful administrator of any of these familiar institutions of incarceration, the exceptional individual, as genius or degenerate, threatens the enduring stability of consensus culture. Such a threat to the persistence of recognizable civilization lies at the core of the second preoccupation of Gothic science fiction—and, predictably, its presence is discernible in nascent form in *Frankenstein*.

When Victor Frankenstein originally aspires to imbue life into dead matter, his motivations—beyond his evident egotism—are expressed in the idealistic terms of creating a useful supplement to conventional humanity (81–84). His later assessment of how such physiologically distinctive beings may fit into an existing society of nonfabricated humanity is, however, considerably more bleak. It is not so much the prospect of simple coexistence with such a creature, however, that prompts Frankenstein's reverie.

Rather, the fear that ultimately causes him to destroy the mate he has made for his original creation centers upon the consequent independence of what would effectively be a new *and rival* species, should the two artificial beings enjoy fruitful sexual congress. Frankenstein speculates:

> Even if they were to leave Europe, and inhabit the deserts of the new world, yet one of the first results of those sympathies for which the daemon thirsted would be children, and a race of devils would be propagated upon the earth, who might make the very existence of the species of man a condition precarious and full of terror. Had I a right, for my own benefit, to inflict this curse upon everlasting generations? (190)

A similar fear of humanity threatened by a new species released by one's own ill-thought agency is voiced by Jonathan Harker when contemplating Count Dracula in his coffin (Stoker 92), a predator Harker helps to transfer to London through his professional mastery of contemporary commercial and technological instruments: real-estate transactions, bills of lading, railway timetables, and telegraphy. The eclipse of modern civilization, and indeed potentially of the human race itself, is presaged by such moments of reflection. Humanity has ceased to be the supreme predator and must take its relative place among the powerless. If not entirely in a Gothic vein, similar implications surround the blood-drinking Martians who lay waste to the communication networks and civic infrastructure of the metropolitan capital of the British Empire in Wells's 1898 invasion fantasy, *The War of the Worlds*.

If eclipse by a rival species were not sufficiently fearful a prospect for the reader of Gothic novels, the decimation of humanity by some other form of catastrophe provides an alternative outcome in the type of apocalyptic Gothic that is often aligned with SF. Mary Shelley is, again, an early pioneer in this tradition. Her third novel, *The Last Man* (1826), evokes a late twenty-first century in which a deadly plague spreads to England, having already ravaged Asia, America, and Europe. Lionel Verney—the "Last Man" of the title and the only mortal to contract and then recover from the disease—wanders across a desolate landscape of empty countryside and de-populated cities, before contemplating his lot and that of humanity in the deserted streets of Rome. En route to that city, he pauses and compares himself to the animals and insects who have not been wiped out:

> Why could I not forget myself like one of those animals, and no longer suffer the wild tumult of misery I endure? Yet, ah! what a deadly breach yawns between their state and mine! Have not they companions? Have not they each their mate—their cherished young, their home, which, though unexpressed to us, is, I doubt not, endeared and enriched, even in their eyes by the society which kind nature has created for them? It is I only that am alone ... I only cannot express to any companion my many thoughts, nor lay my throbbing head on any loved bosom, nor drink from meeting eyes an intoxicating dew, that transcends the fabulous nectar of the gods. (2:190)

Verney's attitude expresses the contemplative wanderlust of European Romanticism, but there is also much in him of the Gothic Hero, terrible in his isolation and inability to vouchsafe his agony to another human being. That isolation is the fulcrum of his despair: it is the fear of being the *last* man, without solace for or relief from his suffering and loneliness. The Last Man will die unknown, unmourned and forgotten, leaving no memorial other than a legend that may, perchance, be found accidentally—just as Verney's own testimony is encountered at the opening of the novel.

The Last Man thematically anticipates a number of subsequent works of SF that might with justification be termed apocalyptic Gothics (see Spooner 164). Such narratives depend upon the conceit of a de-populated Earth and, in most cases, the contemplation of times past and present by a loquacious individual who is destined to be the "Last Man" in recorded (or recognizable) history. Clear comparisons can be drawn, for example, with a text such as Richard Matheson's 1954 novel *I Am Legend*, with its amateur-scientist hero the last surviving human in a world ravaged by a pandemic whose symptoms resemble vampirism. Indeed, Matheson's book inherits and carries forward the two strains of Gothic SF pioneered by Mary Shelley: like Victor Frankenstein, he fears his antiquation and replacement by a competing, unsympathetic species; like Lionel Verney, he is fated to lead a solitary and disconsolate life, leaving behind only stray fragments of thought and (as the title acknowledges) an ambiguous legend.

The singular perspective of the isolated individual confronting a future bereft of humanity is also evidenced by H. G. Wells's Time Traveller in *The Time Machine* (1895), whose temporal wanderings—from the Victorian fin de siècle to the close of the earth's ecological viability—find him, momentarily at least, alone on a barren shore, contemplating "the mystery of the earth's fate" (108). Even there, though, he is subject to the menacing predation of a successor species in the form of an immense, crablike creature whose "mouth was all alive with appetite" (107). If there is *any* positive message in Wells's consideration of how civilization "must inevitably fall back upon and destroy its makers in the end" (118), it is one premised upon the endurance of human compassion: as the narrator suggests in his final sentence, "Even when mind and strength have gone, gratitude and a mutual tenderness still lived on in the heart of man" (118). There is something here of the essential humanism of *Frankenstein*, a heroic assertion of meaning in the face of an uncaring cosmos, that has found strong echoes throughout the history of SF.

Other works, though, are less optimistic in their depiction of societies succumbing to natural disasters. Depictions of plague and pestilence are rife in the apocalyptic writings of a twentieth century that has done much to eradicate disease and contagion. Terry Nation's 1976 SF novel *Survivors*, for example (based on his TV series of the same name, which ran from 1975 to 1977), charts the rapid, worldwide dissemination of a genetically engineered virus, whose vector is a single ill passenger at London's Heathrow Airport. Accompanying Nation's positive narrative of sustaining communities reformed and artisan skills rediscovered is a bleaker survivalist tone in which individuals continually struggle for control of what are, because of the massive depopulation of the United Kingdom, still surprisingly abundant resources. Scarce resources, however, are apt to produce similar reactions, as is demonstrated in J. G. Ballard's ecological disaster novel, *The Drought* (1965), whose evocation of a subsistence community living beside a sluggish sea, utterly dependent upon de-salinating the incoming tide each day for its water, reflects many of the anxieties now associated with climate change.

Disaster narratives tend to depict familiar human environments abandoned and reclaimed by a resurgent nature: the vision of a lifeless Rome in *The Last Man* has its successors in the dead London of Wells's *The War of the Worlds* and the drowned Thames Valley of another of Ballard's ecocatastrophes, *The Drowned World* (1962). Modern postapocalyptic fictions, like their Romantic and Gothic precursors, haunt and are haunted by ruins, by the spectacle of an advanced civilization subsiding into irremediable decay (see Goldstein; Yablon). If *I Am Legend* evokes a vague but credible posthuman Los Angeles, other works are inclined to dwell on what is possibly the most emblematic monument of idealistic human civilization in the modern world: the Statue of Liberty, frozen and submerged in the film *The Day After Tomorrow* (2004) after having been wrecked and half-buried in the culminating shot of the 1968 film *Planet of the Apes*. Such cultural signifiers, however grandiose and iconic, have no meaning following the eclipse of human culture: the absence of a dominant human civilization is thus equivalent to the extinction of the human(e) values the Lady Liberty ostensibly represents.

The interface of Gothic and science fiction is a phenomenon with a significant pedigree, as I have shown, and one that gives no sign of imminent demise (see Wasson and Alder). The aesthetic and moral energies of the historical Gothic seeded the nascent genre of SF, and fiction that is now created within the ambience of what have become progressively more related—though still credibly distinct—genres is inclined to dwell less on the details of technology and more extensively on the human implications of massive social or natural change. Likewise, this fiction's visions of the future are—as was often the case in eighteenth- and nineteenth-century Gothic—tempered with a deep consciousness of the past, however imaginatively that departed milieu might be rendered. As the fearful twenty-first-century West continues to oscillate between a preoccupation with looming natural disasters and the threat of global (possibly nuclear) terrorism, it is unlikely that the two genres will part ways in the foreseeable future.

Works Cited

Aldiss, Brian W., with David Wingrove. *Trillion Year Spree: The History of Science Fiction*. 1986. New York: Avon, 1988. Print.

Anolik, Ruth Bienstock. "Introduction." *Demons of the Mind and Body: Essays on Disability in Gothic Literature*. Ed. Ruth Bienstock Anolik. Jefferson, NC: McFarland, 2010. 1–19. Print.

Anonymous. "Deaths of Men of Letters on the Continent." *Oracle and Daily Advertiser* 17 (May 1799): 2. Print.

——. "Galvanism." *Hampshire Telegraph & Portsmouth Gazette* (Apr. 4, 1803): 2. Print.

Botting, Fred. *Gothic Romanced: Consumption, Gender and Technology in Contemporary Fictions*. New York: Routledge, 2008. Print.

Collins, Wilkie. *Heart and Science*. 1883. Ed. Steve Farmer. Peterborough, Ontario: Broadview, 1996. Print.

———. *The Woman in White*. 1859. Ed. John Sutherland. Oxford: Oxford UP, 1999. Print.

Goldstein, Laurence. *Ruins and Empire: The Evolution of a Theme in Augustan and Romantic Literature*. Pittsburgh: U of Pittsburgh P, 1977. Print.

Jenkins, Russell. "Next They Will Sell Organs on the Net." *The Times of London* (Jan. 27, 2001): 13. Print.

Joseph, M. K. "The Composition of *Frankenstein*." 1969. Mary Shelley, *Frankenstein: The 1818 Text*. Ed. J. Paul Hunter. New York: Norton, 1996. 157–60. Print.

Kiely, Robert. *The Romantic Novel in England*. Cambridge, MA: Harvard UP, 1972. Print.

Machen, Arthur. "The Great God Pan." 1890. *"The Great God Pan" and "The Inmost Light."* London: John Lane, 1895. 1–109. Print.

Pearl, Sharrona. "Dazed and Abused: Gender and Mesmerism in Wilkie Collins." *Victorian Literary Mesmerism*. Ed. Martin Willis and Catherine Wynne. Amsterdam: Rodopi, 2006. 163–82. Print.

Sade, Donatien Alphonse Françoise de. "Reflections on the Novel." 1800. *The 120 Days of Sodom and Other Writings*. Trans. Austryn Weinhouse and Richard Weaver. London: Arrow, 1991. 108–09. Print.

Sage, Victor. *Horror Fiction in the Protestant Tradition*. Basingstoke, UK: Macmillan, 1988. Print.

Shelley, Mary. *Frankenstein: The Original 1818 Text*. Ed. D. L. MacDonald and Kathleen Scherf. Peterborough, Ontario: Broadview, 2001. Print.

——— [as Mary W. Shelly (sic)]. *The Last Man*. 1826. 2 vols. Philadelphia: Carey, Lea, and Blanchard, 1833. Print.

Spooner, Catherine. *Fashioning Gothic Bodies*. Manchester, UK: Manchester UP, 2004. Print.

Stoker, Bram. *Dracula*. 1897. Ed. William Hughes and Diane Mason. Bath, UK: Artswork, 2007. Print.

Turney, Jon. *Frankenstein's Footsteps: Science, Genetics and Popular Culture*. New Haven, CT: Yale UP, 1998. Print.

Wasson, Sara, and Emily Alder, eds. *Gothic Science Fiction, 1980–2010*. Liverpool: Liverpool UP, 2011. Print.

Wells, H. G. *The Time Machine: An Invention*. 1895. London: Heinemann, 1968. Print.

Yablon, Nick. *Untimely Ruins: An Archaeology of American Urban Modernity, 1819–1919*. Chicago: U of Chicago P, 2009. Print.

CHAPTER 36

DARWINISM

PATRICK B. SHARP

In one sense, it is easy to understand the importance of Charles Darwin and evolutionary science to the history of science fiction. Many definitions of SF have emphasized that it is "fiction that takes place in worlds that operate according to the same physical principles as our own but that differ from our own in ways that are rationally explicable" (Booker 2). For well over a century, evolution has operated as a scientific paradigm in biology and a number of other fields. This means that evolution has served as the basic "physical principle" of organic life for practically all science fiction since the explosion of the genre in the late nineteenth century. SF scholars have long recognized the importance of evolution for the scientific extrapolations of authors such as H. G. Wells, whose Morlocks in *The Time Machine* (1895) and Martians in *The War of the Worlds* (1898) are explicit evolutionary parables about class and technological dependency, respectively. Darwin's influence on SF extends beyond such explicit extrapolations, however. His work intervened into the preexisting genre systems that shaped science fiction, bringing with it colonial assumptions about a wide range of issues such as technology, race, and gender. As a result, the interests, ideologies, and hierarchies of Victorian evolutionary science became an inseparable part of the plots, characterizations, and framing logics of the SF genre as a whole.

The rise of Darwinian evolution was a central part of the professionalization of science and the growth of scientific authority in the Victorian world. The work of Darwin and his contemporaries played an important role in transforming Victorian society and fundamentally reshaping our understanding of the universe. As such, Darwin's work was one of the many "conditions of emergence" for SF as a genre (Luckhurst 21–23). One reason—perhaps the main reason—for controversies and extreme differences of opinion over Darwin's work is that his formulation of evolution changed the very idea of what it means to be human. Though he avoided talking about humans in his *On the Origin of Species by Means of Natural Selection* (1859), the reviews and responses to his groundbreaking study immediately expounded upon what Darwin's argument meant for human origins (see Desmond and Moore 477). Many people had mused about evolutionary possibilities before *The Origin of Species*, but Darwin's powerful argument fired both the scientific and popular imaginations, leading to endless disquisitions about the meaning of humanity's supposedly bestial nature. When Darwin published *The Descent of Man, and Selection in Relation to Sex* in 1871, countless scientists, scholars, clergymen, and commentators had already weighed in on the meaning of his work for understanding who we are as a species. Still, *The Descent of Man* was to prove crucially important in shaping debates over human nature for generations to come. As historians Adrian Desmond and James Moore put it, *The Descent of Man* seemed to tell "an arm-chair adventure of the English evolving, clambering up from the apes, struggling to conquer savagery, multiplying and dispersing around the globe" (579). Darwin's book was interwoven with complex and often contradictory ideas about race, culture, gender, intelligence, progress, technology, and numerous other issues that were constantly debated within Victorian culture, and these issues also became the focus of the nascent genre of SF.

Darwin's work on evolution arose within the context of European colonial expansion, and his evolutionary narratives bear the indelible stamp of their origins. His account of human evolution proved popular, in part, because it spoke to Victorian beliefs about colonialism and the advance of English civilization. In this regard, Darwin was working within the framework European science had established centuries before. Historical studies have shown how early-modern science—and what is known as the Scientific Revolution—was deeply intertwined with European colonial expansion (MacLeod 11). Of particular importance for the understanding of SF is the narrative context in which early-modern science took shape. In the late 1400s and early 1500s, the printing press allowed accounts of the voyages of Christopher Columbus and Amerigo Vespucci to receive wide distribution in Europe. One key feature of the narratives chronicling their adventures was the detailed description of the lands and natives "discovered" from the perspective of the European male explorer. These descriptions served the colonial and mercantile purposes of such voyages: the authors were cataloging the various resources of the lands they came across to make clear (and at times exaggerate) the profits and power that could be gained from future expeditions. Francis Bacon explicitly used the voyages of discovery as an inspiration for discarding older ways of thinking about nature and pursuing new paths to knowledge (Terrall 226). Like the colonial voyages of discovery, the benefits that the new Baconian science offered included wealth, power, and prestige.

In the eighteenth century, the importance of scientific discovery and travel narratives grew within the European genre system. The colonial sciences of this period were not driven by some insular and innocent search for truth: as Sandra Harding has shown, "[They] were designed especially for increasing the profit Europe could extract from other lands and maintaining the forms of social control necessary to do so" (44). These traits were woven throughout the fictional and nonfictional travel stories that exploded in popularity during the first half of the eighteenth century (Adas 69). Narratives about voyages to exotic lands reflected and reinforced changing notions of biological difference, and assessments of technology became an important part of European accounts of other peoples and their cultures (Adas 74). In the first decades of the nineteenth century, people in Europe—as well as in Europe's current and former colonies—emphasized the unique and exceptional nature of European peoples and their civilization (Adas 134). Technology became associated with not only cultural superiority but also racial superiority in the classification systems of scientists. Male scientists and adventurers became heroic figures in narratives about the Euro-American march of civilization: they worked in their labs and traveled the world to bring both nature and "savage" races under their mastery.

When Darwin embarked on his famous voyage aboard the H.M.S. Beagle from 1831 to 1836, he took with him these assumptions and the training of a Cambridge-educated young gentleman. The Beagle surveying mission was "a showpiece for the Hydrographer's Office" (Browne 151), and the ship "was equipped as a mobile base for scientific instruments which were going to be used in counterpoint with other measurements taken on land" (179). Darwin found himself aboard a crucial colonial mission, and its scientific success is now the stuff of legend. In 1839 Darwin was elected to the Royal Society and published an account of his voyage that received positive reviews (Browne 407–19). He was familiar with the travelogues of other scientists and shaped his narrative to match the colonial genre, titling it *Journal of Researches into the Geology and Natural History of the Various Countries Visited by H.M.S. Beagle* (usually now shortened to *Voyage of the Beagle*). Darwin's travelogue maintained the Baconian perspective of the curious man who stumbles across natural facts and uses them to construct larger generalizations. At the same time, his descriptions of frontier warfare, dangerous characters, and treacherous landscapes added to the drama of the journey. Darwin came off as a heroic scientist in the mold of his predecessors, a man aboard a mobile laboratory who put his life at risk in the name of discovery and the progress of knowledge.

Darwin's adventurous narrative repeats the colonial hierarchy of race and gender that was endemic to the genre in which he was writing. In his expanded 1845 account of the inhabitants of Tierra del Fuego, he made several observations regarding what he saw as the natives' poor level of technological achievement, which he claimed evidenced a lack of the "higher powers of the mind." He went on to observe that "[t]heir skill in some respects may be compared to the instinct of animals; for it is not improved by experience: the canoe, their most ingenious work, poor as it is, has remained the same, as we know from Drake, for the last two hundred and fifty years" (216). This was not innocent observation: Darwin was drawing on contemporary colonial beliefs to size up people he saw as inferior, an inferiority reflected in their lack of scientific development and technological innovation. Darwin diagnosed their problems as stemming from the failure of Fuegian men to organize their society in a way that allowed for the accumulation of resources, finally concluding that they were "savages of the lowest grade" (220).

By the time Darwin published the second edition of *The Descent of Man* in 1874, he had developed a complex argument about the interconnection between technology, race, gender, and colonization that naturalized common Victorian beliefs. Darwin devoted two-thirds of the book to the process of sexual selection, including the importance of mating choices and the role of the sexes in the evolution and progress of humanity. His theory of natural selection in *The Origin of Species* had proven controversial even among those who accepted his argument that species evolved over time. As Kimberly Hamlin describes the problem, "If evolution by natural selection depended on slight variations increasing certain individuals' odds of survival, how, then, could one explain the endurance of traits such as the peacock's bright plumage and many species' large antlers?" (53). In *the Descent of Man*, Darwin put forward sexual selection as a force that counterbalanced natural selection: the mating preferences of species, he argued, preserved certain physical features that otherwise would prove to be harmful to their chances of survival. Among most nonhuman animals, Darwin asserted that males had become more beautiful and more virile in the contest for coy females; however, he posited that it was females who had the power of choice in most nonhuman species. In effect, peacocks evolved their cumbersome tails because peahens found them attractive, allowing those peacocks with the right plumage to leave more offspring than their less-endowed brothers.

Drawing on colonial anthropological accounts, however, Darwin also argued that for humans this situation had changed: "Man is more powerful in body and mind than woman, and in the savage state he keeps her in a far more abject state of bondage than does the male of any other animal; therefore it is not surprising that he should have gained the power of selection" (619). With men in complete control of sexual selection, Darwin asserted, "women have long been selected for beauty" and as a result "have become more beautiful, according to general opinion, than men" (619). Thus, humans seemed to be something of an exception in Darwin's picture of the animal kingdom, with brutal men in complete control of sexual selection and beautiful women having no power of choice. Darwin also eliminated women from his "man the toolmaker" narrative of progress: it was the men who had to develop more inventive brains and more adept bodies in their struggle with other men for mates. Women were mentally and physically inferior, serving the function of beautiful prizes—ready to mate with the best men and nurture their superior offspring—in Darwin's accounting of human progress (Sharp, "Darwin's Soldiers" 216–17). For Darwin, it was men who drove invention, progress, and colonization with their combination of reason, ambition, and violence.

Darwin's scientific narratives became one of the primary vehicles for the transmission of colonial assumptions about race and gender into science fiction. When creating their stories, authors, filmmakers, and cartoonists producing the early texts we now label as science fiction drew heavily from such closely related colonial genres as the scientific race treatise, the travelogue, and the "lost race" story (see Rieder 1–33; Sharp, *Savage* 36–47). Darwin and his contemporaries reconfigured these narratives in their accounts of human evolution, and SF authors of the late nineteenth and early twentieth centuries explicitly drew upon the language and ideas of evolution in telling their stories. Over time, the problematic colonial assumptions of Darwin's evolutionary narrative became encoded into the very structure of science fiction in a way that still lingers, often contradicting the explicit aims and goals of the SF texts that contain them.

The technoutopian writings of feminists in the half-century after *The Descent of Man* provide one example of the contested acceptance of Darwin's work. Feminists such as

Charlotte Perkins Gilman appealed to Darwin's concept of sexual selection to argue for women's liberation, implicitly accepting many of its problematic claims about sex, race, and civilization. For Gilman and her feminist contemporaries, such as Eliza Gamble (see Jann), control of sexual selection was essential not only for women but also for the race, since Gilman's understanding of the "force called Evolution" was that it "is always pushing, pushing, upward and onward, though a world of changing conditions... It is always there. It is 'the will to live,' and behind that is 'the will to improve'" (qtd. Davis 190). Women, Gilman argued, were the ones who cooperated by nature: it was men who were selfish and destructive, according to Darwin's own argument. Thus, some central traits associated with civilization by nineteenth-century anthropologists and sociologists—sympathy, nurturing, cooperation—were carried forward by women. As the bearers of civilization, women should logically be given more power in society and not be kept down by barbaric men. Gilman's evolutionary views led her to embrace a vision of "positive eugenics" whose goal was the systematic reform of the species (300).

One problem identified by Gilman and her contemporaries was that men in the late nineteenth century controlled marriage and made women economically helpless and dependent. The Victorian image of the "Angel in the house" became the subject of particular scorn. In her landmark 1898 treatise *Women and Economics*, Gilman argued that male control of sexual selection had exaggerated differences between the sexes in a way that was injurious to women but also to the race as a whole (51–57). The vision of evolution in Gilman's *Women and Economics* formed the basis for her famous 1915 utopia *Herland*, where three male explorers come across a lost race of women that functions perfectly well without men. These women originally seem androgynous to the explorers, but that is simply because they reproduce through a form of parthenogenesis: without the warping influence of male-dominated sexual selection, they have become physically and mentally stronger and have lost conventional feminine traits like submissiveness (Gilman, *Herland* 86). The eugenics-driven perfection of the Herlanders is possible because they are "of Aryan stock, and were once in contact with the best civilization of the old world" (48). Though Herlanders no longer have the male drive to conquer, *Herland* accepts colonial narratives of race and civilization (Hausman 498–99). Like Darwin, Gilman sees those of European descent as exceptional, especially with regard to technology and progress. While disagreeing with some of Darwin's conclusions about relations between the sexes, Gilman accepted Darwin's basic formulation of sexual selection and the evolutionary qualities he claimed contemporary men and women had inherited from their ancestors. The resultant evolutionary essentialism of her novel underscores the centrality of Darwinism as a worldview in early science fiction.

With the rise of pulp SF in the 1920s, Darwin's colonialist assumptions about technology, progress, race, gender, and the frontier continued to be encoded into the genre by SF authors and editors. As Bould and Vint argue, the "specialization, or segregation" of pulps like Hugo Gernsback's *Amazing Stories* and John W. Campbell's *Astounding Stories* "sought to separate SF out from the broader field of the fantastic and create it as a distinct genre or marketing category" (41). Evolutionary frontier stories were common in *Amazing* and *Astounding*, playing an important part in their attempts to define science fiction. Philip Francis Nowlan's "Armageddon 2419 A.D.," the story that spawned the Buck Rogers universe, which appeared in the August 1929 edition of *Amazing Stories*, was typical of such evolutionary frontier narratives: a white protagonist leads the fight against evolutionary aliens, in this case the "Hans," who descended from "human-like" aliens who "mated forcibly with the Tibetans" (191). The white heroine, Wilma, serves as a sidekick in these stories, and her main role is to get captured or threatened by the males of the alien race. Fifteen years earlier, Edgar Rice Burroughs had written similar SF adventure stories that drew explicitly and repeatedly on evolutionary ideas about colonization, the frontier, race, and gender for their plots and characterization (see Sharp, *Savage* 92–96). The popularity and influence of writers such as Burroughs can be seen in Nowlan's story, but Nowlan leaves the explicit evolutionary commentary until a coda at the end; as evolution was becoming a more familiar, encoded part of the genre, it was no longer necessary for authors to give repeated explanations of its meaning and implications.

The women authors writing in the pulp magazines tended to rely on the evolutionary perspectives of early SF as much as the men did. As Lisa Yaszek argues, women SF writers during this period had to contend with the rapidly developing "narrative conventions of the field" and "a network of socially conservative authors, editors, and fans" (28). Leslie F. Stone wrote several stories in the late 1920s and 1930s that played with concepts of gender, race, and colonization but that ultimately accepted them as universal evolutionary principles. In "Out of the Void," published in the August and September 1929 issues of *Amazing Stories*, Stone drew upon the well-established trope of the cross-dressing female soldier to put her heroine Dana Gleason in position for a voyage to Mars. Gleason is described as having been raised as a boy by her father and traveling the world before earning honors as a pilot in World War I. For the first two-thirds of the story, Gleason's bravery and strength are noted as other characters try to sort out the mystery of her trip into space. Toward the end of the story's first installment, Gleason's diary reveals that she is a woman as she asks, "Haven't I proved myself equal to any man?" (1:452). Though Stone establishes a strong female character, her tale begins to lapse into a Darwinist essentialism identical to that of Nowlan's Buck Rogers stories.

This happens through the introduction of a love interest named Richard Dorr. Before the hatch of Gleason's ship closes for the trip to Mars, Dorr forces himself into the vessel, and they set off together. Dorr, who has learned her secret, explains to the surprised Gleason why he came along: "Oh, yes, I know your records . . . I know all your courageous deeds, your researches, your science, your war experiences, your bravery. I know all that, but with it all . . . you *are* a woman. You are brave, strong, great willed, yet you *are* at a disadvantage, and you are attempting a tremendous thing" (1:454–55; emphasis and ellipses in original). Early in the second installment, Gleason shows this disadvantage, collapsing under the physical and emotion stress of the voyage. Dorr carries Gleason to the couch, kisses her, and declares, "How I love you. I loved you before I knew you were a woman, and I have adored you more each day . . . I thought that on this other world we should find love together, in the need for each other, work together, live for each other" (2:544). The initial strength of Gleason's character, and the queerness of Dorr's romantic interest in her when he thought she was a man, indicate that Stone may have been testing the possibility of subverting hegemonic notions of gender and sexuality. Once under the spell of love, however (or, in Darwinian terms, sexual selection), Gleason becomes just another plucky but swooning beauty. When the duo crash-land on Abrui, a hitherto-unknown planet beyond the orbit of Neptune, Dorr is the hero who leads an army to overthrow the repressive native government, while Gleason is repeatedly captured or threatened by alien men and has to be rescued by Dorr. Stone emphasizes racial difference with her descriptions of these aliens, one of whom has a servant who "was somewhat smaller than his master, just as finely built, and had an extremely intelligent face; but his skin was different. Whereas his masters looked silvery, he looked golden!" (1:443). Not only are sexual selection and sexual dimorphism universal in Stone's story: racial hierarchies are also universal. This Darwinian narrative of gender and race was simply an embedded part of the genre during the early pulp period, as Stone's acquiescence to it indicates.

In a later short story "The Conquest of Gola," which Stone published in *Wonder Stories* in April 1931, the author explicitly challenged the sexist assumptions of most contemporary SF by having a planet of technologically superior women easily rebuff an invading force of arrogant Earthmen bent on colonization. The story sparked a negative reaction among fans, showing the dangers of going against the genre's entrenched evolutionary gender essentialism (Yaszek 27). Some women authors writing in the pulps were more successful in questioning assumptions about gender, race, and colonization through their creative use of evolutionary ideas. C. L. Moore's "Shambleau," for example, which was published in the November 1933 issue of *Weird Tales*, drew upon horror and fantasy in a manner that scrambled the ideological assumptions built into other frontier SF stories of the period. Moore also used evolution as a means to challenge the supposed universality of sexual dimorphism.

At the outset, "Shambleau" presents itself as just another SF frontier tale, with its morally ambiguous, square-jawed antihero, Northwest Smith, ambling through "the streets of Earth's latest colony on Mars," characterized as "a raw, red little town where anything might happen" (1–2). Smith steps into a doorway and puts "a wary hand on his heat-gun's grip" when he hears a hysterical mob coming his way shouting "Shambleau!" The mob is chasing what appears to be "a berry-brown girl in a single tattered garment," who throws herself at Smith's feet, "a huddle of burning scarlet and bare, brown limbs" (2). Though Moore's narrator points out that Smith did not have "the reputation of a chivalrous man," seeing the "hopeless" girl "huddle[d] at his feet touched that chord of sympathy for the underdog that stirs in every Earthman" (2). Thus, Moore presents a classic evolutionary "damsel in distress" narrative with the frontier hero saving an exotic brown beauty from the mob.

Yet Moore troubles this generically safe reading of the story. In a prologue, she had already suggested Shambleau's otherworldly evolution as a "*creature that Earth [never] nourished*" (1; emphasis in original), and once they return to Smith's room, Moore reveals to our hero—and no doubt also to *Weird Tales*' startled readers—how truly alien Shambleau is. While Smith sleeps, he has a "strange dream" that "some nameless, unthinkable *thing* . . . was coiled about his throat . . . something like a soft snake, wet and warm" (12; emphasis and ellipses in original). What is truly unsettling, however, is the mixture of pleasure and disgust that Moore weaves into every sentence: the "soft snake"—by implication originating from the Medusa-like Shambleau—"was moving gently, very gently, with a soft, caressive pressure that sent little thrills of delight through every nerve and fiber of him, a perilous delight—beyond physical pleasure, deeper than joy of the mind" (12). The "perilous delight" Smith feels alternates with "a horror" that turns "the pleasure into a rapture of revulsion, hateful, horrible—but still most foully sweet" (12). Moore thus queers the standard, male-dominant, heterosexual narrative of evolutionary science: instead of accepting the Darwinian formulation of the feminine as did Gilman, Moore creates a distrust for simple gendered appearances throughout her story. Moore also troubles the usual racial hierarchy of such tales: the "berry brown" Shambleau is not simply another poor unfortunate from an inferior race who needs to be rescued by a white man; instead, she is a powerful, complex creature who bends the white man to her will.

Moore destroys the possibility of understanding Shambleau through any stable sense of universal biological sexual identity (and therefore of any reliable sense of gender). On their second night together, Smith is frozen as he witnesses Shambleau's true form, described as "a nest of blind, restless worms . . . it was—it was like naked entrails endowed with an unnatural aliveness, terrible beyond words" (18–19; ellipsis in original). In early SF stories, one manifestation of evolutionary essentialism involved women being overcome by weakness or hysteria when trying to do things outside their supposed domain, such as traveling through space or fighting alien men. Here, it is male hero who falls "into a blind abyss of submission" (19), a clear inversion of the gender hierarchy seemingly established at the story's outset. Not only is Darwinian sexual selection turned on its head, so is heterosexuality itself, given the overwhelming (if humiliating) pleasure Smith takes from Shambleau's wet, phallic appendages. Shambleau, we later discover, is a creature who has evolved to seduce and feast on men like a "carnivorous flower" (30). Though consistently referred to as "she," the Shambleau's real form is androgynous, troubling the common assumption that sexual dimorphism is universal and that white men are innately superior, inhabiting the apex of evolutionary development. Indeed, it becomes fairly clear that the Shambleau have evolved their demure feminine guises merely to trap their prey, thus taking advantage of species such as humans who do manifest gender and racial hierarchies. In this way, Moore uses an evolutionary idea to challenge the Darwinian account of sexual selection, race, and colonization that is accepted uncritically in so many other SF stories of the period.

More recently, SF authors such as Octavia E. Butler have used evolution to engage in pointed critiques of sexual and racial hierarchies. In her 1987 novel *Dawn*, Butler presents a postapocalyptic Earth devastated by a global thermonuclear war. The few survivors are rescued by an alien species called the Oankali, "Medusa"-like tentacled beings that bear a striking resemblance to Moore's Shambleau (12). The Oankali diagnose humans as having "a mismatched pair of genetic characteristics": humans are "intelligent" but also "hierarchical" (32, 37); and the novel dramatizes how hierarchies of gender, race, and sexuality actually impede the ability of the species to survive. In order even to continue, humans must learn how to overcome both their cultural and biological limitations—which means joining with the Oankali, a species that has three sexes and interbreeds with other alien races. While many of the characters fret that they are evolving into something that may not be human, Butler strongly suggests that our knowledge of essential human nature makes a posthuman future desirable. Like Gilman, Butler accepts much of the Darwinian narrative about human nature and colonization; however, Butler dramatizes how important it is for humans as intelligent beings to take control of our evolutionary destiny and eliminate the worst parts of ourselves. For Butler, this includes eliminating hierarchies of gender, race, and sexuality, even if that means forfeiting our humanity in the process.

It is possible to see the legacy of Darwinist narrative still at work in science fiction in the current craze surrounding Suzanne Collins's 2008 novel *The Hunger Games*. Collins challenges the essentialist formulation of the evolutionary hero as male, thus continuing the feminist critique of normative gender roles that has been common in SF since the early twentieth century. Katniss Everdeen, the protagonist, is still represented in Darwinist terms; however, she is a heroic frontierswoman with diverse survival skills—masculine hunting, feminine gathering—that can be learned from, and taught to, both sexes. Like Butler, Collins also represents the threat of self-destruction through nuclear war as a serious challenge to our survival as a species. In Collins's final novel of the series, *Mockingjay* (2010), a democracy is established to replace a totalitarian regime, and an official in the new government tells Katniss that "[w]e're fickle, stupid beings with poor memories and a great gift for self-destruction. Although who knows? Maybe this time . . . it sticks. Maybe we are witnessing the evolution of the human race" (379). This is not simply a throwaway line, it is an explicit acknowledgment of how evolutionary narrative is woven into all science fiction. Even when authors disagree with the Victorian views regarding sex, race, and colonization that are built into Darwin's narratives, they are still writing on Darwinist terrain.

Darwinian evolution incorporated and shaped countless commonly held Victorian assumptions that have been reinforced, circulated, and contested in Euro-American culture for generations. As Gillian Beer notes, "We pay Darwin the homage of our assumptions. Precisely because we live in a culture dominated by evolutionary ideas, it is difficult for us to recognise their imaginative power in our daily readings of the world" (2). Evolution is not simply a theme of some science fiction texts. The evolutionary writings of Darwin and his contemporaries were one of the primary vehicles through which Victorian ideas about technology, progress, race, gender, and the frontier found their way into SF. Understanding Darwin's impact on science fiction requires decoding the dense ideological matrix of the narratives of evolution that gave science fiction much of its form and substance. Where some authors simply accepted evolutionary views of the past in creating their visions of the future, others such as Moore and Butler used evolutionary ideas to challenge conventional thinking about gender, race, and sexuality. For all SF authors since the inception of the genre, evolution has provided the master narrative for understanding race, alien life, gender roles, technological development, and so much more that has been associated with the field. In this sense, science fiction is inherently Darwinist.

Works Cited

Adas, Michael. *Machines as the Measure of Men: Science, Technology, and Ideologies of Western Dominance*. Ithaca, NY: Cornell UP, 1989. Print.
Beer, Gillian. *Darwin's Plots: Evolutionary Narrative in Darwin, George Eliot and Nineteenth-Century Fiction*. 1983. 3rd ed. Cambridge, UK: Cambridge UP, 2009. Print.
Booker, Keith M. *Historical Dictionary of Science Fiction Cinema*. Lanham, MD: Scarecrow, 2010. Print.
Bould, Mark, and Sherryl Vint. *The Routledge Concise History of Science Fiction*. New York: Routledge, 2011. Print.
Browne, Janet. *Charles Darwin: Voyaging, Volume 1 of a Biography*. New York: Knopf, 1995. Print.
Butler, Octavia. *Dawn*. 1987. New York: Warner, 1997. Print.
Collins, Suzanne. *The Hunger Games*. New York: Scholastic, 2008. Print.
———. *Mockingjay*. New York: Scholastic, 2010. Print.
Darwin, Charles. *The Descent of Man, and Selection in Relation to Sex*. 1871. 2nd ed. 1874. Amherst, NY: Prometheus, 1998. Print.
———. *Journal of Researches into the Natural History and Geology of the Countries Visited During the Voyage of H.M.S. Beagle Round the World*. 1839. 2nd ed. London: John Murray, 1845. Print.
Davis, Cynthia J. *Charlotte Perkins Gilman: A Biography*. Stanford, CA: Stanford UP, 2010. Print.
Desmond, Adrian, and James Moore. *Darwin: The Life of a Tormented Evolutionist*. New York: Warner, 1991. Print.
Gilman, Charlotte Perkins. *Herland*. 1915. Lexington, KY: Feather Trail, 2009. Print.
———. *Women and Economics: A Study of the Economic Relation Between Men and Women as a Factor in Social Evolution*. Boston: Small, Maynard & Company, 1898. Print.
Hamlin, Kimberly A. "The Birds and the Bees: Darwin's Evolutionary Approach to Sexuality." *Darwin in Atlantic Cultures: Evolutionary Visions of Race, Gender, and Sexuality*. Ed. Jeannette Eileen Jones and Patrick B. Sharp. New York: Routledge, 2009. 53–72. Print.
Harding, Sandra. *Is Science Multicultural?: Postcolonialisms, Feminisms, and Epistemologies*. Bloomington: Indiana UP, 1998. Print.
Hausman, Bernice L. "Sex Before Gender: Charlotte Perkins Gilman and the Evolutionary Paradigm of Utopia." *Feminist Studies* 24.3 (1998): 488–510. Print.
Jann, Rosemary. "Revising the Descent of Woman: Eliza Burt Gamble." *Natural Eloquence: Women Reinscribe Science*. Ed. Barbara T. Gates and Ann B. Shteir. Madison: U of Wisconsin P, 1997. 147–63. Print.
Luckhurst, Roger. *Science Fiction*. Malden, MA: Polity, 2005. Print.
MacLeod, Roy. "Introduction." Special Issue: Nature and Empire: Science and the Colonial Enterprise. Ed. Roy MacLeod. *Osiris* 15 (2000): 1–13. Print.

Moore, C. L. "Shambleau." 1933. *The Best of C. L. Moore*. Ed. Lester Del Rey. New York: Ballantine, 1975. 1–32. Print.

Nowlan, Philip Francis. *Armageddon 2419 A.D.* 1928. LaVergne, TN: Wildside, 2011. Print.

Rieder, John. *Colonialism and the Emergence of Science Fiction*. Middletown, CT: Wesleyan UP, 2008. Print.

Sharp, Patrick B. "Darwin's Soldiers: Gender, Evolution, and Warfare in *Them!* and *Forbidden Planet*." *Science Fiction Film and Television* 1.2 (2008): 215–30. Print.

———. *Savage Perils: Racial Frontiers and Nuclear Apocalypse in American Culture*. Norman: U of Oklahoma P, 2007. Print.

Stone, Leslie F. "Out of the Void." Part 1, *Amazing Stories* 4.5 (Aug. 1929): 440–55; Part 2, *Amazing Stories* 4.6 (Sept. 1929): 544–65. Print.

Terrall, Mary. "Heroic Narratives of Quest and Discovery." *Configurations* 6.2 (1998): 223–42. Print.

Yaszek, Lisa. *Galactic Suburbia: Recovering Women's Science Fiction*. Columbus: Ohio State UP, 2008. Print.

CHAPTER 37

COLONIALISM AND POSTCOLONIALISM

JOHN RIEDER

ALTHOUGH scholars of science fiction have always acknowledged that colonialism and imperialism provide a significant context for such exemplary and classic writers as Jules Verne, H. G. Wells, and Edgar Rice Burroughs, full recognition of the depth, complexity, and scope of the relationship between SF and colonialism has only begun to emerge in the wake of recent postcolonial scholarship. After Said's persuasive demonstration in *Culture and Imperialism* (1993) that the cultural ramifications of imperialism pervade texts as apparently remote from the topic as the novels of Jane Austen (Said 80–97), it was no surprise that the first decade of the twenty-first century saw a flurry of anthologies, special issues of scholarly journals, and monographs devoted to investigating the connections between science fiction and colonialism, imperialism, and postcolonialism. It is also no surprise, given the sheer breadth of the topic, that such studies are constrained to limit their subject matter in various ways, for instance, by chronology (my *Colonialism and the Emergence of Science Fiction* [2007] ends at World War II, Ralph Pordzik's *The Quest for Postcolonial Utopia* [2001] restricts itself to the final decades of the twentieth century); by region (Carl Abbott's *Frontiers Past and Future* [2006] and Patrick B. Sharp's *Savage Perils* [2007] both restrict themselves to American SF); or by national or ethnic identity (authorial ethnicity determines candidacy for inclusion in Nalo Hopkinson and Uppinder Mehan's anthology of postcolonial science fiction, *So Long Been Dreaming* [2004]). I don't want to criticize these decisions or resist the specificity of the thematic and regional concerns to which all these efforts testify, but rather to pose a strategic counterweight to them. That is, I want to insist here that the relationship of SF to colonialism overflows all such chronological, regional, and ethnic boundaries.

At no point in the history of SF is colonialism not yet or no longer relevant, and there is no point on the earth that has not been affected by it. Nancy Batty and Robert Markley, in their introduction to a 2002 special issue of *Ariel* on "Speculative Fiction and the Politics of Postcolonialism," include "the complex issues of race, nationalism, ethnicity, gender, political authority, cultural hegemony, and economic exploitation" in their list of "postcolonial concerns" (5). An account of SF and (post)colonialism must interweave economic, epistemological, political, geographical, and technical histories with one another, all mutually co-determining one another (see Appadurai). I propose that lending the topic the full scope and force it can sustain would require conceptualizing colonialism on the same scale as capitalism itself. But while I maintain, in concert with world-systems theorists like Immanuel Wallerstein, that modern colonialism is coterminous with the emergence and consolidation of a capitalist world economy, I do not propose that it is an epiphenomenon of capitalism, determined by the inner dynamics of European science, politics, and economy. Rather, the consolidation of European capitalism has from its beginnings depended upon and incorporated the dynamics of colonialism. One of the fundamental premises of capitalist development has been European expropriation of non-European material resources and labor on a scale unprecedented in world history, as in the grand historical movements that tied together the African slave trade, New World plantations, and European industry, or in the European exploration and mapping of the globe that laid the empirical foundations for evolutionary theory and modern anthropology. If the historical impact of colonialism is framed in this capacious way, the relationship of SF and colonialism turns out to be contiguous with just about every other major historical topic in SF studies, starting with the genre's representation of the social impact of technology and of the discourses and practices of science, and equally with SF's handling of the vicissitudes of race, class, and subject formation in general.

I will return to these themes along the way, but above all I want to argue that the topic of postcoloniality, or postcolonial SF, ought to be framed by an articulation of the grand historical narratives of colonialism and capitalism that does not simply subordinate one to the other. Jessica Langer, in the most recent example of many introductory discussions of the problems and ambiguities presented by postcolonialism as a term, ably articulates the position that postcolonialism "is not an exorcism of colonial influence . . . but rather, as many postcolonial critics have suggested, a *process* by which that society negotiates its identity after it gains independence" (6; emphasis in original). Taking that emphasis on negotiating the dire legacy of colonialism as a point of departure, let me raise two points for discussion, the first having to do with structural differences between different colonial situations and the second having to do with the construction of subject positions in the attempt to narrate historical process. The importance and the difficulty of articulating colonialism and capitalism will become apparent in working through these two points.

The first has to do, not with the complexity and specificity of various regional and historical conjunctures, a complexity that is one of the hallmarks of much postcolonial scholarship to respect, but rather with a drastic and crucial structural difference between the ways two different kinds of colonial societies gain independence and hence negotiate their postcolonial identities. Most postcolonial studies, starting from the foundational work of Aimé Césaire and Frantz Fanon, have been based upon analysis of and reaction to the type of colonial situation formulated in a classic essay by

Georges Balandier: "the domination imposed by a foreign minority, racially (or ethnically) and culturally different, acting in the name of a racial (or ethnic) and cultural superiority dogmatically affirmed, and imposing itself on an indigenous population constituting a numerical majority but inferior to the dominant group from a material point of view" (54). The postcolonial process of negotiating a social identity after gaining independence in Langer's formulation implies this kind of colonial situation, and in this respect it is entirely consonant with the central work of theorists like Homi Bhabha and Gayatri Spivak, whose dominant historical focus is on India, as well as Said with his focus on Northern Africa and the Middle East.

Australian scholars Patrick Wolfe and Lorenzo Veracini point out, however, that settler colonies like Australia, Canada, the United States, and Israel do not conform to Balandier's demographic description. In fact, the indigenous populations of these settler colonies, far from being a numerical majority, have been (and are being) systematically reduced in a process that tends toward total elimination. As Veracini writes, "All settler colonial projects are foundationally premised on fantasies of ultimately 'cleansing' the settler body politic of its (indigenous and exogenous) alterities" (33). Where the primary objects of dependent colonialism of the sort Balandier describes are exploitation of native labor and expropriation of natural resources, the object of settler colonialism is primarily the takeover and permanent occupation of the land itself. The native population is therefore to be rendered invisible—if not simply by extermination (which is clearly the first and most common option), then by a myriad of strategies of assimilation, legal restriction and incarceration, ethnic redefinition, and historical revision (see Veracini 33–52). These are the strategies that comprise the process of negotiating national identity in former settler colonies. In this context, as Wolfe observes, "Invasion is a structure not an event" (2), and the colonized enjoy no properly "postcolonial" moment within this structure.

One consequence of this dichotomy is that the term "postcolonial" has a deeply bitter ring to some indigenous writers and activists. Another consequence, perhaps less profound but more relevant in the present context, is that the different processes of settler and dependent colonialism tend to generate two quite different sets of thematic concerns and motifs in SF. Those associated with the aftermath of dependent colonialism are the ones most often invoked in discussions of postcolonial SF. The keynote is sounded when Césaire attacks the bourgeois concepts of "man" and "nation" in *Discourse on Colonialism* (74–75) and when Fanon declares in *The Wretched of the Earth* that "decolonization is quite simply the replacement of a certain 'species' of men by another 'species' of men" (35). In Homi Bhabha's extended meditation on the postcolonial condition, the key terms delineating the issue of cultural identity become hybridity and mimicry. In all three cases, subject formation itself is a site of political and cultural struggle that condenses and epitomizes the tensions of what Mary Louise Pratt, in *Imperial Eyes*, calls the "contact zone" between European and non-European epistemologies and symbolic hierarchies, and what Fanon calls the "zone of nonbeing" that condemns the colonized to subhuman status within the "massive psycho-existential complex" inflicted on them by colonial society (*Black Skin* xii, xvi). Exemplary contemporary SF settings dramatizing these dynamics would be the heterogeneous metropolises of New York and Calcutta in Amitav Ghosh's *The Calcutta Chromosome* (1995) or the San Diego–Tijuana complex in Alex Rivera's film *Sleep Dealer* (2008). (Mis)communication across cultures is one of its dominant themes, as in the startling, violent, and sometimes deadly misunderstandings that emerge between colonizers and colonized around the meaning of personal identity in Gwyneth Jones's "Aleutian" trilogy (1991–98).

The dominant themes of settler colonial narratives are starkly different. According to Veracini, settler colonial narratives, in general, conspire to erase indigenous presence from the land and simultaneously to indigenize the settler. Their epic model is not the long journey home of the *Odyssey* but rather the journey to the Promised Land of the *Aeneid* or *Exodus* (Veracini 95–102). The potential Promised Land tends to be some sort of primal romance setting, a wilderness or frontier, hence the polar opposite of the postcolonial metropolis. Instead of being focused on the hybridized and conflicted self of dependent-postcolonial theory and SF, settler narratives envision the frontier as an opportunity for purification of the self, a return to innocence, or at least to first principles such as the right to exercise violence in order to establish social order in the wilderness. The proximity of SF to the western in American culture depends heavily on the common ideological ground provided by the figure of the frontier, and the lasting vigor of settler fantasy in mass cultural SF can be measured by the success of James Cameron's film *Avatar* (2009), with its full-body fantasy of indigenizing the settler. A more complex, startlingly and powerfully ambivalent rendition of settler ideology can be found in Octavia E. Butler's great "Xenogenesis" trilogy (1987–89), where alien settlers who plausibly see themselves as mankind's saviors present a doomed indigenous humankind with the stark alternative of giving up human identity or simply becoming extinct, and the planet itself is not only occupied but also literally consumed and reconstructed in the mold of the aliens' civilizing but genocidal mission.

It is not the case, of course, that the social framework or the political and economic histories of former settler colonies (or of formerly dependent ones) dictate the kinds of fictions that are produced by their writers, nor is it to be doubted that the neat contrasts I have just been making overlap and blur into one another in innumerable cases. But the crucial theoretical consequence to be drawn from recognizing the structural differences between the settler colony and the dependent one remains clear: the break represented by the historical passage from colonial to independent or "postcolonial" society has an entirely different status in the two cases. Langer accurately indicates that the postcolonial negotiation of colonialism's legacy is accentuated and intensified by the formerly dependent colony's gaining independence. According to Veracini, the de-colonization of settler colonies, in contrast, "inevitably constitutes an effective acceleration of colonising practices"; postcoloniality actively *exacerbates* colonial domination because the "zero sum game" for control of the land makes settler and indigenous sovereignties mutually incompatible (108). Thus, postcolonialism represents very different modes of continuity and discontinuity of the two types of colonial structures at the national level, and the cultural ramifications of those differences, if not predetermined, are nonetheless likely to be significant.

The same is arguably the case at the global level. An economy and government run by white settlers who have more or less confidently consolidated their grip on the land will likely find different ways of integrating themselves into the world market and geopolitics than will a former dependent colony's native elite, forced to navigate the tensions between popular anticolonialism and the persistent structures of a dependent economy. The move to a global level of analysis complicates issues of continuity in other ways as well. It is hardly news to anyone that the breaks in political power at the national level accomplished during the postwar process of de-colonization often served only to mask more enduring and powerful continuities of economic dependence at the global level as the decaying imperialist system was replaced by US world hegemony. Conversely, apparent continuities at the national level may help to obscure sharp discontinuities within the global system, as happened in the restructuring of the world economy from Fordism to the regime of "flexible accumulation" after 1970, according to David Harvey in *The Limits to Capital* (1982), or, alternatively, in the passage from imperialism to Empire, according to Michael Hardt and Antonio Negri in *Empire* (2000).

Such problems make it notoriously difficult to untangle the postcolonial from the neocolonial within the complex, ongoing interactions of colonialism and capitalism. Orienting cultural analysis in such a large and uneven terrain calls for an approach that can immerse itself in the complexity of local situations without losing its grasp on their insertion into and determination by global ones. But if the argument is correct that colonialism and capitalism have to be thought in tandem with one another, then the problem of subject position—and the attendant narration of history—arises. This presents itself first of all as the problem of the position occupied by the theorist. Postcolonial critique entails, and even coheres around, a well-founded suspicion of too much coherence—that is, of the position of power and privilege implied by assuming too panoramic a perspective. From what subject position is it possible to command the kind of comprehensive knowledge of colonialism and capitalism as interlocking global systems called for here? Does theoretical construction of such a position necessarily reproduce a fantasy of mastery and authority that is inimical to the project of postcolonial critique?

There are two closely related ways of posing this problem. The first would be to approach it as a question about models of history. How does one understand colonialism in relation to capitalism without subsuming colonialism into the developmental narratives of progress and growth endemic to capitalist societies or enfolding colonial history into the logic of capital, as even David Harvey's insistence on the "inherent spatiality of capital accumulation" (xviii) and on "reading Marx through a spatio-temporal lens" (xxi) seems to do? The second way to pose the problem would be at the level of the formation of the subject. Is it possible for the theorist to occupy the position of the subject of knowledge in relation to a totalizing conception of history without reproducing colonial hierarchies of authority and colonial dynamics of appropriation, assimilation, and erasure of the colonized Other? How can postcolonial critique articulate local and global knowledge without reproducing colonial or neocolonial patterns of power, desire, and agency?

Neither of these concerns is peculiar to the project of postcolonial critique, but the postcolonial project may well enjoy a privileged point of access to them. Robert Young argues in *White Mythologies* (1990) that suspicion of "master narratives" in postmodern and poststructuralist thought is ultimately based upon a critique of colonialist ideology:

> In the past few hundred years Europe has been, as Gayatri Chakravorty Spivak has suggested, constituted and consolidated as "sovereign subject, indeed sovereign and subject." Just as the colonized has been constructed according to the terms of the colonizer's own self-image, as the "self-consolidating other," so Europe "consolidated itself as sovereign subject by defining its colonies as 'Others,' even as it constituted them, for purposes of administration and the expansion of markets, into programmed near-images of that very sovereign self." It is this sovereign self of Europe which is today being deconstructed, showing the extent to which Europe's other has been a narcissistic self-image through which it has constituted itself while never allowing it to achieve a perfect fit. (Young, quoting Spivak, 49)

Young singles out Marxism particularly as a variety of master narrative that bears the baggage of Europe's sovereign self within its construction of history: "Marxism's universalizing narrative of the unfolding of a rational system of world history is simply a negative form of the history of European imperialism... Marxism's standing Hegel on his head may have reversed his idealism, but it did not change the mode of operation of a conceptual system which remains collusively Eurocentric" (33, 35).

But, as Jacques Derrida insists in *Specters of Marx*, there is more than one Marx (13). Thus, what Young says about the notion of "the West" in general should also be said about Marx's theory of capital in particular: an "active critique of the Eurocentric premises of Western knowledge [or Marxist theory]" does not position itself "outside 'the West' [or 'Marx'], but rather uses its own alterity and duplicity in order to effect its deconstruction" (51–52). The articulation of colonialism and capitalism that I have been calling for as the necessary framework for postcolonial cultural analysis has to resist subordinating postcolonial critique to the history of capital, but it can do so from within Marx's work itself by accepting the project of "provincializing Europe," as Dipesh Chakrabarty puts it. According to Chakrabarty, the history of capital in Marx, a history unfolding in Hegelian style from the developmental logic of capital itself, is intertwined throughout with multiple and diverse histories that emerge out of the contingencies of use rather than from the logic of profit-making (47–71). Chakrabarty charges this second version of history, or History 2, with the task of "constantly interrupting the totalizing thrusts of History 1" (66), and therefore opening up the possibility of a noncapitalist, de-colonized future that seems to be foreclosed by the dire logic of capital in History 1. The project of provincializing Europe then becomes that of writing a history that can "look toward its own death by tracing that which resists and escapes the best human effort at translation across cultural and other semiotic systems, so that the world may once again be imagined as radically heterogeneous" (45–46).

The movement away from a monolithic historical narrative that casts non-Western societies as remnants of its own past, still in the process of development toward instead a set of complexly intertwined histories enjoying various modes of visibility and audibility within the dynamics of agency and power afforded their protagonists, is one that some postcolonial SF has taken on in an admirable fashion. Its impulse proceeds from the undeniable fact that one confronts the Western subject writ large in the most prominent contours of SF itself: its fascination with science and technology, its conventional glorification of enlightened rationality, and its immersion in ideologies of progress and development. Istvan Csicsery-Ronay Jr. describes SF's distinctive generic romance as the "*technologiade*, the epic of the struggle surrounding the transformation of the cosmos into a technological regime" (*Seven Beauties* 217), and he has also written of the strong grip upon the genre as a whole exercised by the fantasy of "technoscientific empire" as a mythic destiny rooted in but surpassing the colonial and imperialist past ("Empire" 363). But against this generic set of expectations, one might well pose the postcolonial counterfantasy of Amitav Ghosh's *The Calcutta Chromosome*, which decentralizes and de-colonizes the official history of Sir Ronald Ross's discovery of the role of mosquitoes in transmitting malaria, exposing it as the cover story for a mazelike conspiracy protecting a powerful native sect's occult practices. *The Calcutta Chromosome* thus splinters colonial History into postcolonial histories along the lines suggested by Young and Chakrabarty, positioning itself within the tropes of scientific discovery but introducing into them a novel, anticolonial set of alterities and duplicities that challenges the Western narrative, subverts its illusion of mastery, and opens the way to an alternative temporality (see Smith).

One of the fundamental effects of the positioning of the subject in relation to history in colonial ideology is anachronism (see McClintock 36–44, Rieder 6–12). Colonial geography turns travel into the nonindustrialized world into a journey into the past, so that Marlowe's voyage up the Congo in Joseph Conrad's "Heart of Darkness" (1899) appears to him a return to "prehistoric earth" (138). Scientific racism, with its comparative charts demonstrating the apelike characteristics of Africans and Australians, identified the inhabitants of these "prehistoric" areas as themselves relics of prehistory, fixed by their anatomy in a pre-Western stage of development (see Gould). H. G. Wells famously reversed the anachronistic perspective of colonial ideology in *The War of the Worlds* (1898) by imagining England being invaded by a version of humanity's future, and he attacked complacent Social-Darwinist notions of progress in his rendition of the degenerate posthuman species that inhabit his future London in *The Time Machine* (1895). Indeed, playing with the anachronistic effects of colonial geography and racism is one of the hallmarks of much early SF; other prominent examples would include Jules Verne's *Journey to the Center of the Earth* (1864), Arthur Conan Doyle's *The Lost World* (1912), and Jack London's "The Red One" (1918). All of these efforts have in common that the subject of knowledge is a white male scientist or adventurer.

Some more recent postcolonial SF explores the effects of anachronism when the colonized or postcolonized Other occupies the position of the subject of knowledge, by setting these subjects adrift in time, dramatizing their struggle to achieve self-recognition in relation to the complex and tortured histories of their communities. A splendid example is Vandana Singh's short story "Delhi" (2004), whose main character wanders through past, present, and future versions of the eponymous city searching for the face of the woman who, according to an oracular computer printout, will give meaning to his life. According to Grant Hamilton, the "conceptually difficult position" occupied by the protagonist of the story "holds the seemingly divergent temporalities of the past and present immanent to its very constitution because of the simultaneity of a becoming that posits the subject as both subject and other" (70). The protagonist of "Delhi" finally comes to suspect that the meaning of his life has very little to do with his individual consciousness and that his encounter with the mysterious woman in the printout has its meaning in relation to the collective subject formed by the city of Delhi itself—a consciousness that he extrapolates from the metaphors of a beehive or a computer, with himself as merely a drone or a few bits of data in the larger gestalt. Where the classic examples of early SF tend in their critical moments to humble the illusions of a master narrative of history, the postcolonial project struggles to find a stable subject position within a radically incomprehensible field of knowledge.

One of the classic statements of the problem of the theorist's position in postcolonial theory is Gayatri Spivak's 1988 essay "Can the Subaltern Speak?" Spivak's title, as I understand it, does not call into question the subaltern's power of speech so much as the Western theorist's power of listening. Addressing herself to a published conversation between Michel Foucault and Gilles Deleuze, it is as if she were asking these two high-powered academic male theorists to please be quiet for a moment, to stop speaking for the "monolithic and anonymous" collective Subject they have invented (272) and allow the woman in the back row (or more precisely, in the imperial archive) to get a word in edgewise. Spivak's target is not intellectual arrogance, however, but rather a theoretical construction of the subaltern as a kind of allegorical representation of revolutionary desire that leads Foucault and Deleuze to an "unquestioned valorization of the oppressed as subject" (274). Spivak's charge, finally, is that the "monolithic and anonymous subjects-in-revolution" (272) that Foucault and Deleuze appropriate to their purposes "cohere with the work of imperialist subject-constitution, mingling epistemic violence with the advancement of learning and civilization" (295). Her brilliant analysis of the problem of representation posed by a class unable to speak for itself thus cautions against allowing advocacy, speaking *for* the Other, to act as cover for a kind of speaking *about* that silences and erases the subaltern subject.

Spivak's essay points toward another set of problems concerning colonial and postcolonial subject positions. These have to do with the dynamics of assimilation: challenges to culturally bound notions of the human that arise from contact between radically different societies; the negotiation of values in relation to claims of authenticity, purity, and nativism; the proliferation of countervalues based on hybridity and cosmopolitanism; the problematic ironies of mimicry and cultural ventriloquism. The ways these dynamics get played out vary according to the different structures of dependent and settler colonialism, and they return us as well to the articulation of colonial situations with the global capitalist economy. For instance, Spivak illustrates the "epistemic violence" of cultural assimilation by quoting Thomas Macaulay's "Minute on Indian Education" (1835): "We must at present do our best to form a class who may be interpreters between us and the millions whom we govern; a class of persons, Indian in blood and colour, but English in taste, in opinions, in morals, and in intellect" (qtd. Spivak 282). This project, which leads to the thematics of mimicry and the colonized position of the "not quite/not white" theorized by Bhabha (92), is sharply different from the forced assimilation—or cultural genocide—visited upon the so-called Stolen Generation of Australian Aboriginal children by taking them away from their parents and installing them in white settlers' families. Different as they are, the ultimate goal of both projects is to erase native autonomy at the level of desire, a goal that arguably falls in the long run more into the purview of mass-cultural entertainment and advertising than government-sponsored education.

The vicissitudes of the colonized subject in SF certainly span and draw upon all of these varieties of regional, ethnic, and structural struggles. A classic late-nineteenth-century instance is that of the Beast People of Wells's *The Island of Doctor Moreau* (1896), where assimilation is accomplished by torturing the body, in the first place, and then completed by imposing the grotesque imperatives of the Law upon Moreau's imperfectly humanized subjects (the Law's refrain "Are we not Men?" pointedly echoes the eighteenth-century antislavery motto "Am I Not a Man and Brother?"). A noteworthy early-twenty-first century instance is Nisi Shawl's "Deep End" (2004), where the instrumentalization of colonized bodies takes on a decidedly biopolitical slant. On a prison ship's 87-year-long interstellar trip to colonize another planet, the prisoners' consciousnesses are implanted in bodies with the DNA of rich folk back home, so that the children born on the new planet will be biological descendants of the ruling class. Midway between these two examples, one finds a horrific invasion by assimilation, the cooptation of not only bodily form but more profoundly desire itself by the Pod People of *Invasion of the Body Snatchers*. In perhaps the most chilling moments of this great 1956 film, the hero's former ally, now absorbed into the Pod collective, assures the hero that his former ally's wife has no problem with the change he has undergone: "She feels exactly the way I do." A few moments later, when the hero desperately asserts that the rest of humankind will come to destroy the invaders, the Pod People's spokesperson confidently assures him, "Tomorrow you won't want them to." Here, mimicry and cultural genocide become indistinguishable from one another in a parable often interpreted as an allegory of the Communist menace, but arguably better read as an intuition of the insidiously homogenizing effects of American mass culture itself (see Rieder 147–48).

Such inventive proliferation of forms of coercive assimilation and explorations of the matrices of knowledge, power, agency, and desire suggest that SF might well be called upon as a resource to imagine ways of theorizing the problem of the subject of knowledge within the framework of models of history and of colonial and postcolonial history in particular. Let me offer one final, canonical example, Octavia Butler's *Kindred* (1979). Like many other extraordinary voyagers in SF, Dana Franklin, in *Kindred*, is inexplicably ripped out of her present-day, realist world and thrust into a radically strange one, an antebellum Maryland slave-owning plantation. Like many other extraordinary voyages, Dana's journey drives toward the traveler's discovery of a true self, but the entire affective and conceptual thrust of the narrative moves, not toward the heroic status enjoyed by colonial adventurers such as H. Rider Haggard's Allan Quatermain and his companions in *King Solomon's Mines* (1885) and *Allan Quatermain* (1887) or Edgar Rice Burroughs's John Carter in *A Princess of Mars* (1917), but rather toward dramatizing the black female postcolonial subject's agonizing confrontation with the brute realities of her inhuman past. *Kindred* thus loads every rift of this nightmarish "contact zone" with the task of realizing—and rendering intimate—the affective and ideological tensions that beset the subject of knowledge in postcolonial critique. The unwilling time traveler Dana Franklin finds herself precipitated into the nightmare of history, forced to live as a slave alongside her own ancestors, to endure the unsanitary conditions and horrifying medical practices of the early-nineteenth-century American South, to confront the reality that she has no control over her own life, to recognize that arbitrary violence can be visited upon her by any white person without justification, and finally to kill her white slave-owning great-great-great-grandfather in order to prevent him from raping her. She pays for this last act by finding that, upon her return to the present, the very arm that freed her from her ancestral tormentor is embedded in the wall of her house, and she can only achieve some degree of autonomy from the familial and racial legacies of violence and objectification that form the infrastructure of her present by literally ripping herself free of her history's grasp, nearly killing herself in the process. Perhaps Butler is suggesting how agonizing a price the postcolonial intellectual must be willing to pay in order to attain the "detachment" of a subject of knowledge, and so put herself in the position of being able to speak for and about her history rather than being confounded with the "monolithic and anonymous" status conventionally granted her.

The problem of the capacity of different subjects to speak and be heard bears upon one more topic that is not usually held to be closely connected with that of colonialism and SF: genre theory. I have argued in my 2010 essay "On Defining Science Fiction, or Not" that SF studies ought to adopt a historical approach to genre theory, one that stresses the multiple agencies and motives involved in genre formation and in the propagation of generic categories and that pays attention to the heterogeneous, overlapping goals and values of different communities of practice. Let me add here that taking a historical rather than a formalist approach to genre theory also conforms with the de-centering impulse and de-colonizing projects of postcolonial critique. These demand an approach to genre that is as open as possible to the interweaving and interaction of different traditions, conceptions of story, venues of performance, sets of literary values, and notions of art and narrative, and that attunes itself to the neighborliness and commerce among genres rather than attempting to isolate a set of formal possibilities as its object of study. A historical genre theory's emphasis on different communities of practice should likewise pay off in its attention to the uneven effects of the global diffusion of mass-cultural products. While the homogenizing ideological and even libidinal power of globally distributed mass culture may be counted among the more subtle yet important weapons in the arsenal of US postwar hegemony, it is always attended by local, regional, and ethnic differences in reception and resistance. Thus, in counterbalance to the critical judgment I made earlier concerning *Avatar* as an example of settler-colonial ideology, consider the perspective of Mayra Vega, the head of the Women's Association of the Shuar Nation, an indigenous group opposing mining operations in the Amazon: "It's an example that makes us think a lot because the indigenous are defending their rights. We have to defend just as the indigenous so clearly defended in the movie. We had an uprising, we had a confrontation with gases; it's the same as what we just saw in the movie" ("*Avatar* in the Amazon"). While scholars and critics of SF must continue to speak against the persistence of colonialist ideology in the genre, we may also find occasions when it is better to let others have the last word.

Works Cited

Abbott, Carl. *Frontiers Past and Future: Science Fiction and the American West*. Lawrence: U of Kansas P, 2006. Print.

Appadurai, Arjun. "Disjuncture and Difference in the Global Cultural Economy." *Public Culture* 2.2 (Spring 1990): 1–24. Print.

"*Avatar* in the Amazon." *PRI's The World: Global Perspectives for an American Audience*. Jan. 29, 2010. Web. June 16, 2011. http://www.theworld.org/2010/01/avatar-in-the-amazon/.

Balandier, Georges. "The Colonial Situation: A Theoretical Approach." 1951. *Social Change: The Colonial Situation*. Ed. Immanuel Wallerstein. New York: Wiley, 1966. 34–61. Print.

Batty, Nancy, and Robert Markley. "Introduction—Writing Back: Speculative Fiction and the Politics of Postcolonialism, 2001." *Ariel* 33.1 (Jan. 2002): 5–14. Print.

Bhabha, Homi. *The Location of Culture*. New York: Routledge, 1994. Print.

Butler, Octavia E. *Kindred*. 1979. Boston: Beacon, 2003. Print.

Césaire, Aimé. *Discourse on Colonialism*. 1955. Trans. Joan Pinkham. 1972. New York: Monthly Review, 2000. Print.

Chakrabarty, Dipesh. *Provincializing Europe: Postcolonial Thought and Historical Difference*. Princeton, NJ: Princeton UP, 2000. Print.

Conrad, Joseph. "Heart of Darkness." 1899. *Heart of Darkness and Other Tales*. Ed. Cedric Watts. New York: Oxford UP, 2002. 101–87. Print.

Csicsery-Ronay Jr., Istvan. "Empire." *The Routledge Companion to Science Fiction*. Ed. Mark Bould, Andrew M. Butler, Adam Roberts, and Sherryl Vint. New York: Routledge, 2009. 362–72. Print.

———. *The Seven Beauties of Science Fiction*. Middletown, CT: Wesleyan UP, 2008. Print.

Derrida, Jacques. *Specters of Marx: The State of the Debt, the Work of Mourning, and the New International*. 1993. Trans. Peggy Kamuf. New York: Routledge, 1994. Print.

Fanon, Frantz. *Black Skin, White Masks*. 1952. Trans. Richard Philcox. New York: Grove, 2008. Print.

———. *The Wretched of the Earth*. 1961. Trans. Richard Philcox. New York: Grove, 2004. Print.

Ghosh, Amitav. *The Calcutta Chromosome: A Novel of Fevers, Delirium & Discovery*. 1995. New York: Perennial, 2001. Print.

Gould, Steven Jay. *The Mismeasure of Man*. 1981. Rev. ed. New York: Norton, 1996. Print.

Hamilton, Grant. "Organization and the Continuum: History in Vindana Singh's 'Delhi.'" *Imperialism and the Third World: Essays on Postcolonial Literature and Film*. Ed. Ericka Hoagland and Reema Sarwal. Jefferson, NC: McFarland, 2010. 65–76. Print.

Hardt, Michael, and Antonio Negri. *Empire*. Cambridge, MA: Harvard UP, 2000. Print.

Harvey, David. *The Limits to Capital*. 1982. 2nd ed. New York: Verso, 2006. Print.

Hopkinson, Nalo, and Uppinder Mehan, eds. *So Long Been Dreaming: Postcolonial Science Fiction & Fantasy*. Vancouver, BC: Arsenal Pulp, 2004. Print.

The Invasion of the Body Snatchers. Dir. Don Siegel. 1956. Olive Films, 2012. DVD.

Langer, Jessica. *Postcolonialism and Science Fiction*. New York: Palgrave Macmillan, 2012. Print.

McClintock, Anne. *Imperial Leather: Race, Gender, and Sexuality in the Colonial Contest*. New York: Routledge, 1995. Print.

Pordzik, Ralph. *The Quest for Postcolonial Utopia: A Comparative Introduction to the Utopian Novel in the New English Literatures*. New York: Peter Lang, 2001. Print.

Pratt, Mary Louise. *Imperial Eyes: Travel Writing and Transculturation*. New York: Routledge, 1992. Print.

Rieder, John. *Colonialism and the Emergence of Science Fiction*. Middletown, CT: Wesleyan UP, 2008. Print.

———. "On Defining Science Fiction, or Not: Genre Theory, SF, and History." *Science Fiction Studies* 37.2 (July 2010): 191–210. Print.

Said, Edward. *Culture and Imperialism*. 1993. New York: Vintage, 1994. Print.

Sharp, Patrick B. *Savage Perils: Racial Frontiers and Nuclear Apocalypse in American Culture*. Norman: U of Oklahoma P, 2007. Print.

Shawl, Nisi. "Deep End." *So Long Been Dreaming: Postcolonial Science Fiction & Fantasy*. Ed. Nalo Hopkinson and Uppinder Mehan. Vancouver, BC: Arsenal Pulp, 2004. 79–94. Print.

Singh, Vandana. "Delhi." *So Long Been Dreaming: Postcolonial Science Fiction & Fantasy*. Ed. Nalo Hopkinson and Uppinder Mehan. Vancouver, BC: Arsenal Pulp, 2004. 12–22. Print.

Smith, Eric. *Globalization, Utopia, and Postcolonial Science Fiction: New Maps of Hope*. New York: Palgrave Macmillan, 2012. Print.

Spivak, Gayatri. "Can the Subaltern Speak?" *Marxism and the Interpretation of Culture*. Ed. Cary Nelson and Lawrence Grossberg. Basingstoke, UK: Macmillan, 1988. 271–313. Print.

Veracini, Lorenzo. *Settler Colonialism: A Theoretical Overview*. New York: Palgrave Macmillan, 2010. Print.

Wolfe, Patrick. *Settler Colonialism and the Transformation of Anthropology*. London: Cassell, 1999. Print.

Young, Robert J. C. *White Mythologies: Writing History and the West*. 1990. 2nd ed. New York: Routledge, 2004. Print.

CHAPTER 38

PSEUDOSCIENCE

ANTHONY ENNS

Mary Shelley's *Frankenstein* (1818) is often described as the first science fiction novel, yet this is due to not only its critique of scientific hubris but also its examination of the boundaries between orthodox and unorthodox science. For example, Victor Frankenstein stops studying alchemy when he realizes that it is no longer accepted by the scientific establishment, but Professor Waldman inspires him to "return to [his] ancient studies" by suggesting that modern chemists "have acquired new and almost unlimited powers" that enable them to perform alchemical miracles (50–51). In addition to raising questions about scientific ethics, therefore, Shelley's novel also raises questions about the nature of science itself. How do scientific facts, methods, and theories evolve over time? Why are some facts, methods, and theories accepted, while others are considered nonscientific? The origin of science fiction is thus closely related to the concept of pseudoscience, which refers to concepts and practices that are rejected by the scientific establishment.

Pseudoscience represents the boundary limit of orthodox science, and it can take many different forms, including obsolete sciences that were once part of mainstream science but have since been rejected because they contradict newly accepted facts, methods, or theories; frontier sciences that challenge accepted facts, methods, or theories but have not yet been embraced by the scientific establishment; and anomalistic sciences that are conducted in isolation and have no connection to accepted facts, methods, or theories. Moreover, the boundaries between science and pseudoscience are constantly subject to revision. Pseudosciences arise when new evidence challenges accepted scientific theories, and they can potentially initiate a revolution when the number of empirical anomalies accumulates to such a degree that they can no longer be ignored (see Kuhn). The development of orthodox science thus depends on pseudosciences since these speculative theories often lead to the formation of new paradigms. According to Michel Foucault, such "subjugated knowledges" challenge the "scientific hierarchy" or "the rights of a science that is in the hands of a few" ("Society" 8–9). The history of a pseudoscience thus represents a history of power struggle, and in order to understand this struggle, it is necessary to examine all aspects of culture: "Only propositions that obey certain laws of construction belong in the domain of scientificity . . . [but] [a]rcheological territories may extend to 'literary' or 'philosophical' texts, as well as scientific ones. Knowledge is to be found not only in demonstrations, it can also be found in fiction, reflexion, narrative accounts, institutional regulations, and political decisions" (Foucault, *Archeology* 128). Fiction can thus be seen as a privileged site where extraordinary investigations are conducted without the rigid policing of scientific hierarchies.

Science fiction plays a particularly significant role in the process of knowledge formation because it challenges accepted scientific theories. As Roger Luckhurst points out, SF seizes "opportunistically on new anomalies or nascent states or breakthroughs" ("Pseudoscience" 405). In other words, science fiction examines how new scientific facts, methods, and theories potentially subvert the normative view of reality, and the genre thus occupies "the phase-space between anomaly and normalization . . . when knowledge is controversial or in flux" (404). Like Kuhn, Luckhurst also argues that these "speculative theories" have the potential to inspire new paradigms: "Such imaginative interventions can in turn influence the parameters of actual scientific research, perhaps most intensively when the boundaries of the human are thrown into flux" (404). When these phases of disturbance are over, however, "the history of science quietly erases all trace of the theories that were left behind" (405). Like Foucault, therefore, Luckhurst concludes that SF provides a valuable "cultural record of these multiple, speculative possibilities" (405). In short, science fiction can be seen as a kind of amateur laboratory that is beyond the jurisdiction of scientific hierarchies, and SF authors are thus free to extrapolate the implications of frontier sciences, to perpetuate obsolete scientific theories, and to imagine alternative methods that defy orthodox science, which makes SF a site of contestation, resistance, and dissensus.

In order to illustrate the relationship between SF and pseudoscience, I will examine the representations of three pseudosciences that have been particularly significant in the development of the genre: hollow-earth theory, the Martian canals controversy, and debates over extrasensory perception. These case studies show how the struggle over scientific facts, methods, and theories is a struggle for power, and they also reveal the important role that science fiction plays in this power struggle, as the proponents of pseudosciences often appeal to SF readers when their ideas are dismissed by the scientific establishment.

The notion that Earth is hollow was first proposed by English astronomer Edmond Halley in 1692. Halley's theory was an attempt to explain variations in magnetic pole lines, a problem that had attracted the attention of many natural philosophers, including René Descartes, Athanasius Kircher, and Robert Hooke. By analyzing compass variations, Halley determined that a magnetic pole must "turn about the Centre of the Globe, having its Centre of Gravity fixt and immoveable in the same common Centre of the Earth," but it must also be "detached from the external parts" and thus able to move independently (567). Halley concluded that Earth must have several layers divided by a liquid substance. This theory was perfectly in line with orthodox science since it was based on an accepted scientific theory, had been deduced from an accepted scientific

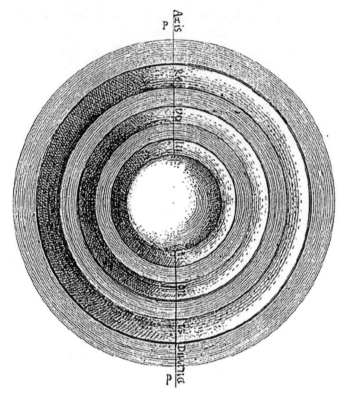

FIGURE 38.1 Edmund Halley's hollow Earth (1692).

text (Isaac Newton's 1687 treatise *Philosophiae Naturalis Principia Mathematica*), employed an accepted scientific method, and addressed an accepted scientific problem. Halley departed from orthodox science, however, when he added that the interior of Earth was habitable and illuminated: "The Concave Arches may in several places shine with such a substance as invests the Surface of the Sun" (575–76). This theory was supported by scientists such as William Whiston, who served as Newton's successor at Cambridge, but Newton himself never incorporated Halley's idea into subsequent editions of his *Principia*.

In an endnote to the 1829 edition of his book *Elements of Natural Philosophy*, Scottish physicist Sir John Leslie similarly argued that "our planet must have a very widely cavernous structure" (452) that contains a source of light: "[S]ince an absolute void is inadmissible, the vast subterranean cavity must be filled with some very diffusive medium, of astonishing elasticity or internal repulsion among its molecules. The only fluid we know possessing that character is LIGHT itself, which, when embodied, constitutes *Elemental Heat or Fire*" (452–53; emphasis in original). Leslie thus argued that the interior of Earth must be illuminated by an internal sun.

In 1818 an American army officer named John Cleves Symmes Jr. similarly claimed that "the earth is hollow, and habitable within; containing a number of solid

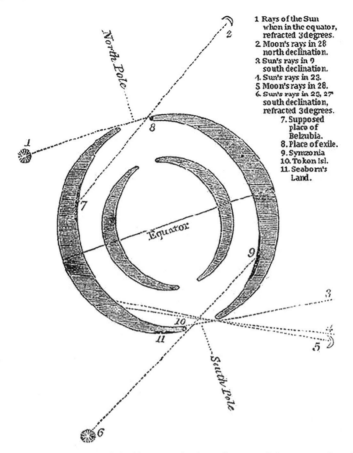

FIGURE 38.2 John Cleves Symmes's hollow Earth, from his novel *Symzonia* (1920).

concentrick spheres, one within the other" (qtd. Griffin 382). Symmes also argued that Earth is "open at the poles twelve or sixteen degrees" (qtd. Griffin 382), and these openings allowed light to be reflected into the interior. When this theory failed to arouse interest within the scientific establishment, Symmes wrote the novel *Symzonia; Voyage of Discovery* (1820), which depicts a fictional polar expedition that discovers an opening into the interior of Earth. Symmes's novel thus illustrates the important role that fiction played in the promotion and dissemination of speculative theories that had been dismissed by orthodox science.

Symmes's novel was also a tremendous source of inspiration to early SF writers. The writer who was most directly influenced was Edgar Allan Poe, whose 1831 short story "MS. Found in a Bottle" describes a ship that travels to the South Pole and is consumed in a whirlpool that drags it down into the center of Earth:

> [T]he ice opens suddenly to the right, and to the left, and we are whirling dizzily, in immense concentric circles, round and round the borders of a gigantic

amphitheatre, the summit of whose walls is lost in the darkness and the distance. But little time will be left me to ponder upon my destiny—the circles rapidly grow small—we are plunging madly within the grasp of the whirlpool—and amid a roaring, and bellowing, and shrieking of ocean and of tempest, the ship is quivering, oh God! and—going down. (126)

The conclusion of Poe's 1838 novel *The Narrative of Arthur Gordon Pym* similarly depicts a canoe heading toward the South Pole on a current of warm water, which encounters a "chasm" that "threw itself open" (206). Both of these narratives thus conclude with the discovery of Symmes's holes, although neither work follows the protagonists into the interior of Earth.

The most famous hollow-earth narrative is Jules Verne's 1864 novel *A Journey to the Centre of the Earth*, which describes a fictional expedition into the globe's interior through a dormant volcano in Iceland. When the explorers reach Earth's center, they discover an underground ocean illuminated by electric clouds that "produced an astonishing play of light" (138). L. Sprague de Camp and Willy Ley argue that this image was inspired by Leslie's theory of an internal sun (305); David Standish and Allen Debus also argue that Verne was inspired by Sir Humphry Davy's theory that seismic activity was caused by subterranean caves. According to Davy, this activity was extremely volatile when Earth was young, but it gradually subsided as the planet cooled. Davy's theory was already obsolete when Verne's novel was first published, but Verne clearly needed this theory in order to explain how his characters could survive Earth's interior (Standish 124; Debus 408). When Professor Lidenbrock proposes the expedition, for example, his nephew Axel argues that "all the theories of science demonstrate that such an undertaking is impossible"—to which his uncle replies, "Oh the nasty theories! They're going to get terribly in our way, the poor theories! . . . [N]either you nor anyone else knows for certain what happens in the Earth's interior" because "each existing theory is constantly replaced by a new one" (30). The debate continues throughout the novel until Axel is finally forced to admit that the law of central heat must be flawed: "I admit that circumstances which are still not properly explained can sometimes modify this law under the effect of certain natural phenomena" (154). Verne's novel thus not only promotes the idea that Earth is hollow, illuminated, and capable of supporting life, but it also emphasizes the importance of questioning orthodox science.

The number of hollow-earth narratives fell drastically after 1910, as it became much harder for readers to suspend their disbelief after Robert Edwin Peary and Matthew Alexander Henson reached the North Pole in 1909 and Roald Amundsen the South Pole in 1911. In Edgar Rice Burroughs's "Pellucidar" series (1914–63) and Richard Shaver's "Lemuria" series (1945–49), for example, the interior of Earth served as nothing more than a fantastic setting for escapist fiction, and there was no longer any attempt to intervene in an ongoing scientific debate.

The second pseudoscientific theory I will examine—the notion that the surface of Mars is crisscrossed by a system of canals—was originally inspired by the observations of Italian astronomer Giovanni Schiaparelli, who reported in 1877 that the surface of the planet was covered by "canali." Schiaparelli's observations were verified by French astronomers Henri Perrotin and Louis Thollon in 1886 and by American astronomers William H. Pickering and Percival Lowell in 1892 and 1894, respectively. In 1895 Lowell began publishing a series of articles in the *Atlantic*, which became the basis of several books, including *Mars* (1895), *Mars and Its Canals* (1906), and *Mars as the Abode of Life* (1908). In these books, Lowell argued that the canals were designed by an advanced race to maintain their dying world. Lowell also argued that the canals were proof of the "sagacity" of the Martians, as they had managed to set aside their differences and act as a unified collective (377–78). In response to the argument that Mars was too cold to sustain life, Lowell also claimed that animals could hibernate during the winter and that during warmer seasons the climate was comparable to the south of England. Lowell thus presented his theory as a new frontier science, which was based on anomalistic sightings that challenged existing scientific paradigms.

Robert Markley notes that most of the 232 entries on Mars published in *Nature* between 1894 and 1909 "treat the canals as either a viable, if unproved, scientific theory or as an established fact" (106), which indicates that "Lowell's theory ... offered a compelling narrative to many of his contemporaries" (62). The most sustained attack on Lowell came from English biologist Alfred Russel Wallace, whose 1907 book *Is Mars Habitable?* was written as a direct response to Lowell's 1906 book *Mars and Its Canals*. Wallace had previously argued, in his 1902 book *Man's Place in the Universe*, that Mars was not habitable, and he reiterated these claims in his response to Lowell by insisting that Mars was too cold to sustain life, that the atmospheric pressure was too low for liquid to exist on the surface, and that spectroscopic analysis had failed to find any evidence of water vapor in the atmosphere (37). Instead of recognizing Lowell's theory as a frontier science, therefore, Wallace argued that it must be false because it contradicted accepted scientific theories. Following Wallace's attack, the reviews of Lowell's books became increasingly critical. In his review of *Mars as the Abode of Life*, for example, Eliot Blackwelder asserted that Lowell knew nothing about geology and that he "unscrupulously deceives the educated public merely in order to gain a certain notoriety and a brief, but undeserved, credence for his pet theories" (661). As Norriss S. Hetherington points out, Lowell was gradually "seen very much as an interloper among professional scientists" (161). Lowell's theory was not fully discredited, however, until 1909 when the Mount Wilson Observatory in California produced a series of photographs of Mars that showed no trace of the canals. Within a year, "the astronomical communities of Europe and North America had largely abandoned their thirty-year flirtation with the idea of intelligent Martian inhabitants" (Lane 62).

The Martian canal controversy inspired a tremendous explosion of SF narratives around the turn of the twentieth century. In the late 1880s and early 1890s, for example, the Reverend W. S. Lach-Szyrma published a series of interplanetary travel stories in *Cassell's Magazine*, which were designed to illustrate popular astronomical theories. Several of these stories focused on the Martian canals, and in one installment the protagonists befriend a Martian guide who explains the origin of the canals:

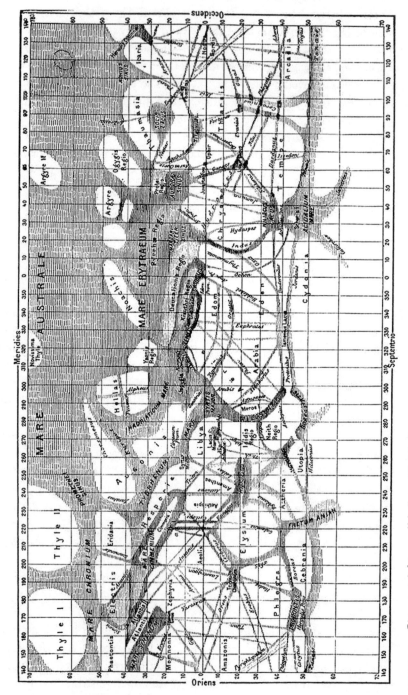

FIGURE 38.3 Giovanni Schiaparelli's "canali" (1877).

> Our population is great, and our supply of water is not enough. The rains are insufficient. If we depended on nature alone, the inner parts of many of our continents would be desert and want moisture. Now we open them up by these canals, and diffuse water everywhere on the land as is most convenient to us and likely to develop the production of the soil ... Left to themselves we should have land in one part and sea in the other, and our planet could not then support so much life as it does now. (17)

The canals thus represented a technological response to an ecological crisis, and it was only possible because the Martians "had no wars" and were "able to devote our force to the arts of peace" (17). Lach-Szyrma's narratives were thus based on Schiaparelli's findings, and they anticipated all of Lowell's major arguments, such as the notion that Mars was inhabited by intelligent life, that the planet faced an ecological crisis caused by a water shortage, that the Martians were able to resolve this crisis using their superior knowledge, and that they had the wisdom to set aside their differences and work together in peace.

H. G. Wells's 1898 novel *The War of the Worlds* did not specifically mention the Martian canals, but it described Mars as an old planet suffering from a water shortage: "Since Mars is older than our earth ... [,] it necessarily follows that it is not only more distant from life's beginning but nearer its end ... [I]ts oceans have shrunk until they cover but a third of its surface" (3). Wells's novel thus supported the theory that Martians were facing an ecological crisis and that this crisis had "brightened their intellects" and "enlarged their powers" (3).

Lowell's theory was also the basis of Garrett P. Serviss's 1898 novel *Edison's Conquest of Mars*, which was written as a sequel to *The War of the Worlds*. Serviss was already well known across the United States as "the New York *Sun*'s astronomer" (Johnson and Clareson 37), a position he held until 1892. He then became head of the astronomy department at the Brooklyn Institute and delivered lectures on astronomy around the country while continuing to work as a syndicated columnist. In 1896 Serviss published the speculative essay "If We Could Move to Mars," which was explicitly inspired by Lowell's theories. *Edison's Conquest of Mars* was essentially an expanded version of this essay, and it was clearly designed as an intervention into the canal debate.

For example, as the human scientists approach Mars in their spaceship, they see vast forests and polar ice caps: "Around the South Pole were spread immense fields of snow and ice, gleaming with great brilliance" (97). The scientists also notice the existence of artificial canals designed to channel the melting ice to other parts of the planet: "Cutting deep into the borders of these ice-fields, we could see broad channels of open water, indicating the rapid breaking of the grip of the frost" (97). As they orbit the planet, they also note that "crossing and recrossing the red continent, in every direction, were the canals of Schiaparelli" (98). The scientists immediately recognize that these topographical features represent conclusive evidence of intelligent life: "There could be no longer any question that it was a world which ... bore on every side the marks of their presence and of their incredible undertakings and achievements" (98). The canals also play an important role in the narrative, as the human scientists ultimately defeat the Martians by sabotaging their irrigation system and causing a flood that kills 90 percent of the population. Serviss's novel thus illustrates how extraordinary scientific theories migrated to science fiction after they were rejected by orthodox science.

Most of the interplanetary travel narratives published during the next decade similarly focused on the canal debate. In George Griffith's *A Honeymoon in Space* (1901), for example, a group of space explorers describe the geography of Mars as four continents "split up into semi-regular divisions by the famous canals which have so long puzzled terrestrial observers" (132). The space explorers also discover that the "canals are the remains of gulfs and straits which have been widened and deepened and lengthened by . . . Martian labour" due to the fact that "Mars is getting old" and "her seas are diminishing" (132). This discovery thus corroborates Lowell's predictions, and one of the explorers even expresses a sigh of relief that the canal controversy is finally resolved: "Well, there is one problem solved at any rate" (132).

The canals also play a prominent role in Alexander Bogdanov's 1908 novel *Red Star*, which tells the story of a human scientist named Leonid who becomes friends with a Martian named Menni and travels to Mars to learn about their socialist system. Bogdanov's representation of Mars was thoroughly consistent with Lowell's theories. As they approach the planet, for example, Leonid observes "the contours of the continents and the seas and the canal networks, which I recognized from the maps of Schiaparelli" (41). Menni's explanation of the canals is also taken directly from Lowell: "The canals are indeed immense, but they are not dozens of kilometers wide, as they would in fact have to be for your astronomers to see them. What they see are the broad bands of forest we have planted along the canals in order to maintain an even level of humidity in the air and prevent the water from evaporating too rapidly. Some of your scientists seem to have guessed as much" (56). Menni also explains that the turning point in Martian history was the drying up of the planet's water resources, which inspired the Great Canal Project. Although this project was initially financed by private enterprise, Menni explains that it gradually led to a consolidation of land resources, which precipitated a proletarian revolt against the power of the landlords. As Leonid concludes, "The famous canals served as a powerful stimulus to economic development at the same time as they firmly reinforced the political unity of all mankind" (55). Bogdanov's novel thus presents socialism as a logical extension of Lowell's theories, and in 1913 Bogdanov also published a prequel, *The Engineer Menni*, which focuses specifically on the construction of the canals and the revolution it causes.

Like Serviss, Mark Wicks was also an astronomer and public lecturer who promoted Lowell's theories by writing an SF novel, *To Mars Via the Moon* (1911). Not only is this novel dedicated to Lowell, but it also begins with the following testimonial: "Many years' careful study of the various theories . . . has convinced me that the weight of evidence is in favour of Professor Lowell's conceptions, as being not only the most reasonable but the most scientific; and that they fit the observed facts with a completeness attaching to no other theory" (xi). Wicks's personal convictions become abundantly clear when the narrator of the novel, Professor Wilfrid Poynders, delivers an extended lecture on the canal debate while en route to Mars. In this lecture, Poynders refutes the notion that the canals are optical illusions by arguing that they were deduced "from scientific fact and from the many different things which have actually been seen and confirmed by many thousands of observations" (143). In response to Wallace's argument concerning spectroscopic analysis, Poynders also asserts that "improved means will definitely show that water vapour undoubtedly exists in the Martian atmosphere" (122). Poynders thus concludes that "Professor Lowell's conceptions ... fit in with observed facts with all the accuracy of the pieces in a child's picture puzzle; whilst his logical deductions are supported and enhanced by his wide knowledge of physical science and planetology" (152).

These claims are soon proven to be correct when the space explorers land on Mars and learn the truth about the canals from a friendly Martian guide: "Our seas and other large bodies of water have long ceased to exist, and we are therefore dependent upon the water arising from the dissolving snow of our polar snow-caps for a supply of that prime necessary of life. Our canal system is, therefore, the most supremely important work which we have to maintain and develop, so that every part of the planet may be supplied with water" (186). The Martian's explanation thus supports Lowell's theories, and he even adds that the ecological crisis on Mars forced the entire population of the planet to work together, just as Lowell predicted: "Upon the adequacy and perfect working of the canals all life here is dependent; so every other matter is regarded as of lesser importance" (186). Wick's novel thus employs SF to promote and defend subjugated knowledges under attack from the scientific establishment.

Edgar Rice Burroughs's 1912 novel *A Princess of Mars* similarly describes Mars as a planet suffering from a water shortage that required the construction of the canal system, just as Lowell had claimed (63). By depicting the division of the population into warring factions and the regression of civilization into a state of primitive savagery, however, Burroughs's novel clearly rejected most of the central elements of Lowell's theory. Like his "Pellucidar" series, therefore, Burroughs's Martian novels did not represent an attempt to intervene in an ongoing scientific debate but rather simply employed the canals as a fantastic backdrop for escapist entertainment. As Robert Crossley points out, astronomical theories of Mars and literary representations of Mars began to diverge by 1912, and they became increasingly separate over the course of the twentieth century: "The old nineteenth-century ideal of using narratives about Mars to stimulate interest in astronomical research and to teach readers the state of the scientific question ceased to have much bearing on the literary imagination" (171). As a result, "the Mars of fiction became a predominantly mythic place" (171).

Unlike hollow-earth theory and the Martian canal controversy, the study of extrasensory perception has always been relegated to the margins of science. The concept of telepathy was first proposed by William F. Barrett, Professor of Experimental Physics at the Royal College of Science in Dublin, in a paper presented at the 1876 meeting of the British Association for the Advancement of Science. Barrett's paper described his observations of hypnosis experiments conducted on children in Westneath, Ireland,

and it concluded that, under hypnosis, thoughts could be communicated "without the intervention of recognized organs of sensation" (244). While Barrett was regarded as an expert in his field, William Carpenter objected to the "unscientific turn" in the proceedings and requested that Barrett's lecture be cancelled. Alfred Russel Wallace, the head of the subsection on anthropology, overruled this objection, but the Association still refused to publish Barrett's paper in its journal as it could not accept the premise that telepathic communication was possible. Barrett's paper was subsequently published in the proceedings of the Society for Psychical Research, which was formed in 1882 with the declared intention of investigating such phenomena in a serious and scientific manner. Together with Edmund Gurney and Frederic W. H. Myers, Barrett also compiled the Society's first report on "Thought-Reading" in June of that year. This report focused on the Creery sisters, who exhibited a striking capacity to guess words, numbers, and objects at which another person was looking. Their ability had first caught the attention of their father, who had asked the newly formed society to send an investigator to study their case. The sisters then participated in 382 experimental trials over the course of the following year. In each of these experiments, one of the investigators selected a playing card, number, or object while the girl being tested was out of the room. The girl was then called in and asked to name the thing they had in mind. The statistical improbability of guessing five or eight cards in a row, which the sisters occasionally achieved, seemed impossible without further explanation, and the investigators ultimately concluded that these experiments provided scientific evidence of telepathy (Barrett, Gurney, and Myers 891).

In his account of the history of telepathy, Roger Luckhurst argues that this pseudoscience emerged in the late nineteenth century due to a scientific paradigm shift from questions of matter (or mechanistic science) to questions of force (or science of energy). As a "counter-hegemonic conception of the physical universe" emerged, it generated a state of confusion in which scientific facts, methods, and theories were more loosely defined, and this opened the door for "extraordinary sciences" by allowing mechanistic models to be replaced by spiritualist theories (*Invention* 84). Luckhurst thus concludes that pseudosciences like telepathy appear at "vanishing points . . . where confident demarcations between truth and error, science and pseudoscience, could not at the time be determined" (2).

This pseudoscience became even more controversial when it attracted the attention of major research institutions. During World War I, for example, Stanford University received an endowment for the promotion of psychical research, and John E. Coover subsequently conducted the first university-funded experiments on telepathy. Coover's final report, which was published in 1917, argued that the subjects tested were not capable of thought transference, and this was regarded at the time as the only authoritative scientific treatment of the subject. In 1920 American psychologist William McDougall funded G. H. Estabrooks's research on telepathy at Harvard University. Estabrooks used a large number of subjects, each of whom was asked to guess playing cards for half an hour. During these experiments, the subject and the sender were placed in separate rooms. When a ready signal was given by a telegraph key, the sender was asked to concentrate on a card chosen by a random cut from a shuffled pack and the subject was asked to write down the name of the first card that occurred to him. In the end, the results were allegedly high enough to prove statistically that something more than random factors was affecting them. These findings were largely dismissed by professional scientists, however, and Estabrooks's papers were only published in the journals of psychical research organizations (Radin 64).

In 1927 McDougall moved to Duke University where he founded a parapsychology laboratory with research assistant Joseph Banks Rhine. Their goal was to study psychic phenomena in a way that was consistent with the experimental techniques used in scientific laboratories. In order for psychical research to be regarded as a frontier science, in other words, it was necessary to relate these anomalous facts to existing scientific methods. Rhine began by coining the term "extrasensory perception" (ESP), which represented a more scientifically precise description of the phenomenon under investigation. Rhine's colleague Karl Zener also created a special set of cards that was specifically designed for ESP experiments. Rhine then proceeded to conduct experiments for several years using a laboratory method that was similar to the one developed by Estabrooks. His first exceptional subject was Adam Linzmayer, an undergraduate student who scored very high (including a run of 21 out of 25 cards in the spring of 1931). The following year, Rhine tested another promising subject, Hubert Pearce, who even surpassed Linzmayer (Hyman 108–09). Rhine published his findings in a series of books: *Extrasensory Perception* (1934), *New Frontiers of the Mind* (1938), *The Reach of the Mind* (1947), and *New World of the Mind* (1953). In these books, Rhine repeatedly argued that the statistical evidence represented scientific proof of the existence of ESP (Rhine 290) and claimed that the goal of his experiments was to develop a means of perfecting this latent ability (295). Rhine also described the discovery of ESP as a scientific paradigm shift comparable to Einstein's theory of relativity (290). Rhine thus argued that the study of ESP represented a frontier science that was being conducted in advance of new theoretical paradigms, and it was only a matter of time before the accumulated evidence became so overwhelming that orthodox scientists would be forced to revise their theories of cognition.

As with the hollow-earth theory and the Martian canal controversy, SF played a pivotal role in the promotion and dissemination of this new pseudoscience. The postwar "psi-boom" is largely attributed to John W. Campbell, who served as editor of *Astounding Stories* (later renamed *Astounding Science-Fiction*, and eventually *Analog: Science Fiction and Fact*) from 1937 until his death in 1971. Campbell was one of Rhine's volunteer subjects during the 1930s, and he promoted ESP throughout his career by encouraging writers to examine its potential applications. In a letter written to Rhine in 1953, for example, Campbell reported that "I am trying to use fiction to induce competent thinkers to attack such problems as psi-effects" (*Letters* 225). Even toward the end of his career, in his introduction to a 1969 anthology entitled *14 Great Tales of ESP*, Campbell openly questioned the validity of orthodox science since it simply dismisses any facts that contradict the dominant scientific paradigm:

> The question of extra-sensory perception—ESP—is one of the things official science, today, dismisses with annoyance. It's nonsense ... coincidence ... sheer balderdash ... exaggerated and mistaken or misstated stories and warped memories of events. Certainly nothing real. Having gone through that sort of treatment once before with respect to such pseudo-science nonsense as atomic weapons and interplanetary rocketships, I'm a little bit less willing to be properly cowed by those Authoritative Scientific Statements. (13)

Like Luckhurst, therefore, Campbell argues that pseudosciences such as ESP are particularly relevant to SF since the genre is explicitly designed to examine speculative theories that challenge the scientific establishment.

Beginning in 1945, Campbell published a series of stories by Lewis Padgett that explored the possibility that telepathy might signal a new stage in human evolution (see Berger 129). Campbell also published several stories that examined how telepathy might be employed to prevent war. In Raymond Jones's "The Toymaker" (1946), for example, a group of pacifists create a toy that records and amplifies the thoughts of children, and as the toy is distributed to nurseries, it magnifies the children's fears of war until war itself becomes obsolete. Some of the stories published at this time also addressed the potential weaponization of telepathy. Lewis Padgett's "The Fairy Chessmen" (1946), for example, describes how a war could be won using telepathy to drive an enemy army insane. Robert A. Heinlein's "Project Nightmare," published in *Amazing Stories* in 1953, presents a scenario in which the Soviet Union has planted dozens of atomic bombs in major American cities, and these bombs can only be found by a group of psychics, who are then used to launch a retaliatory strike by detonating bombs planted in the Soviet Union. Perhaps the most famous work of postwar SF devoted to the subject is Alfred Bester's 1953 novel *The Demolished Man*, which posits that the gene for ESP is dominant and thus each succeeding generation will include more telepaths. In twenty-fourth-century America, these "Espers" have produced a dystopian surveillance state, yet the conclusion of the novel presents ESP as a potential force for good. Police Prefect Lincoln Powell provides a closing speech that praises the value of this psychic power: "*Listen, normals! You must learn what it is. You must learn how it is. You must tear the barriers down. You must tear the veils away. We see the truth you cannot see ... That there is nothing in man but love and faith, courage and kindness, generosity and sacrifice. All else is only the barrier of your blindness. One day we'll all be mind to mind and heart to heart*" (175; emphasis in original). In other words, Powell suggests that the spread of ESP will eventually lead to the formation of a utopian society based on mutual understanding and empathy. Bester's novel thus encourages readers not only to accept the existence of ESP but also to consider its positive impact on society.

All three of these pseudoscientific theories—hollow-earth theory, the Martian canal controversy, and ESP—represent "subjugated knowledges" that were buried or disqualified by orthodox science. Scientific journals refused to publish articles on these theories, and their proponents thus turned to science fiction, a genre that was primarily concerned with challenging normative views. In some cases, science fiction served as a space where obsolete scientific theories continued to be discussed after they had been dismissed by the scientific establishment. In other cases, SF extrapolated the implications of new scientific facts or theories. In other cases, the genre extrapolated the implications of anomalous facts that could not be explained according to established scientific theories and methods. All of these case studies thus illustrate the important role that SF played in the formation of knowledge, as it effectively functioned as a privileged site where the boundaries of science were constantly being negotiated, contested, and resisted.

Works Cited

Barrett, William F. "On Some Phenomena Associated with Abnormal Conditions of Mind." *Proceedings of the Society for Psychical Research, Volume 1 (Containing Parts I–IV), 1882–83*. London: Trübner, 1883. 238–44. Print.

_____, Edmund Gurney, and Frederic W. H. Myers. "Thought-Reading." *Nineteenth Century* 11 (1882): 890–901. Print.

Berger, Albert I. "Towards a Science of the Nuclear Mind: Science-Fiction Origins of Dianetics." *Science Fiction Studies* 16.2 (July 1989): 124–44. Print.

Bester, Alfred. *The Demolished Man*. New York: Signet, 1953. Print.

Blackwelder, Eliot. "Mars as the Abode of Life." *Science* 29.747 (1909): 659–61. Print.

Bogdanov, Alexander. *Red Star: The First Bolshevik Utopia*. 1908. Ed. Loren R. Graham and Richard Stites. Trans. Charles Rougle. Bloomington: Indiana UP, 1984. Print.

Burroughs, Edgar Rice. *A Princess of Mars*. 1917. New York: Ballantine, 1963. Print.

Campbell Jr., John W. "Introduction." *14 Great Tales of ESP*. Ed. Idella Purnell Stone. Greenwich, CT: Fawcett, 1969. 11–16. Print.

_____. *The John W. Campbell Letters*. Vol. 1. Ed. Perry Chapdelaine, Tony Chapdelaine, and George Hay. Franklin, TN: AC Projects, 1985. Print.

Crossley, Robert. *Imagining Mars: A Literary History*. Middletown, CT: Wesleyan UP, 2011. Print.

Debus, Allen A. "Re-Framing the Science in Jules Verne's *Journey to the Center of the Earth*." *Science Fiction Studies* 33.3 (Nov. 2006): 405–20. Print.

De Camp, L. Sprague, and Willy Ley. *Lands Beyond*. New York: Rinehart, 1952. Print.

Foucault, Michel. *The Archeology of Knowledge*. 1969. Trans. Alan Sheridan. London: Tavistock, 1974. Print.

_____. *"Society Must Be Defended": Lectures at the Collège de France, 1975–76*. Ed. Mauro Bertani and Alessandro Fontana. Trans. David Macey. New York: Picador, 2003. Print.

Griffin, Duane A. "Hollow and Habitable Within: Symmes's Theory of Earth's Internal Structure and Polar Geography." *Physical Geography* 25.5 (2004): 382–97. Print.

Griffith, George. *A Honeymoon in Space*. London: C. Arthur Pearson, 1901. Print.

Halley, Edmond. "An Account of the Cause of the Change of the Variation of the Magnetical Needle; with an Hypothesis of the Structure of the Internal Parts of the Earth; As It Was Proposed to the Royal Society in One of Their Late Meetings." *Philosophical Transactions of the Royal Society* 16 (1692): 563–78. Print.

Heinlein, Robert A. "Project Nightmare." 1953. *14 Great Tales of ESP*. Ed. Idella Purnell Stone. Greenwich, CT: Fawcett, 1969. 111–36. Print.

Hetherington, Norriss S. "Percival Lowell: Professional Scientist or Interloper?" *Journal of the History of Ideas* 42.1 (Jan.-Mar. 1981): 159–61. Print.

Hyman, Ray. *The Elusive Quarry: A Scientific Appraisal of Psychical Research*. Buffalo, NY: Prometheus, 1989. Print.

Johnson, William B., and Thomas D. Clareson. "The Interplay of Science and Fiction: The Canals of Mars." *Extrapolation* 5 (1964): 37–48. Print.

Jones, Raymond F. "The Toymaker." *Astounding Science-Fiction* 38.1 (Sept. 1946): 6–39. Print.

Kuhn, Thomas S. *The Structure of Scientific Revolutions*. Chicago: U of Chicago P, 1962.

Lach-Szyrma, W. S. "Letters from the Planets: A Ruined City in the Moon." *Worlds Apart*. Ed. George Locke. London: Cornmarket, 1972. 1–27. Print.

Lane, K. Maria D. *Geographies of Mars: Seeing and Knowing the Red Planet*. Chicago: U of Chicago P, 2011. Print.

Leslie, John. *Elements of Natural Philosophy, Volume First, Including Mechanics and Hydrostatics*. 1823. 2nd ed. Edinburgh: Oliver & Boyd, 1829. Print.

Lowell, Percival. *Mars and Its Canals*. New York: Macmillan, 1906. Print.

Luckhurst, Roger. *The Invention of Telepathy, 1870–1901*. Oxford: Oxford UP, 2002. Print.

———. "Pseudoscience." *The Routledge Companion to Science Fiction*. Ed. Mark Bould, Andrew M. Butler, Adam Roberts, and Sherryl Vint. New York: Routledge, 2009. 403–12. Print.

Markley, Robert. *Dying Planet: Mars in Science and the Imagination*. Durham, NC: Duke UP, 2005. Print.

Padgett, Lewis [a.k.a. Henry Juttner and C. L. Moore]. "The Fairy Chessmen." Part 1, *Astounding Science-Fiction* 36.5 (Jan. 1946): 7–45; Part 2, *Astounding Science-Fiction* 36.6 (Feb. 1946): 122–79. Print.

Poe, Edgar Allan. "The Narrative of Arthur Gordon Pym of Nantucket." 1837. *Collected Writings of Edgar Allan Poe. Vol. 1: The Imaginary Voyages*. Ed. Burton R. Pollin. New York: Gordian, 1994. 53–363. Print.

———. "MS. Found in a Bottle." *Tales of the Grotesque and Arabesque*. Vol. 1. Philadelphia: Lea and Blanchard, 1840. 111–26. Print.

Radin, Dean. *The Conscious Universe: The Scientific truth of Psychic Phenomena*. New York: HarperCollins, 1997. Print.

Rhine, J. B. *New Frontiers of the Mind*. London: Faber and Faber, 1938. Print.

Serviss, Garrett P. *Edison's Conquest of Mars*. 1898. Los Angeles: Carcosa House, 1947. Print.

———. "If We Could Move to Mars." *Harper's* (Feb. 25, 1896): 408–10. Print.

Shelley, Mary. *Frankenstein; or, the Modern Prometheus*. 1818. Ed. Johanna M. Smith. Boston: Bedford, 1992. Print.

Standish, David. *Hollow Earth: The Long and Curious History of Imagining Strange Lands, Fantastical Creatures, Advanced Civilizations, and Marvelous Machines Below the Earth's Surface*. Cambridge, MA: Da Capo, 2006. Print.

Verne, Jules. *A Journey to the Centre of the Earth*. 1864. Trans. William Butcher. Oxford: Oxford UP, 2008. Print.

Wallace, Alfred Russel. *Is Mars Habitable? A Critical Examination of Professor Percival Lowell's Book "Mars and Its Canals" with an Alternative Explanation*. London: Macmillan, 1907. Print.

Wells, H. G. *The War of the Worlds*. London: Heinemann, 1898. Print.

Wicks, Mark. *To Mars Via the Moon: An Astronomical Story*. Philadelphia: J.B. Lippincott, 1911. Print.

CHAPTER 39

FUTUROLOGY

ANDREW M. BUTLER

THERE is a moment in an editorial when Daniel Bell argues that "[t]he future does not exist, but a limitless number of possible futures can be created" (2). According to Charles Hartshorne, "The future of a given present consists of a limited range of real possibilities or open alternatives, which indeed *will* be replaced step by step with suitable determinate actualities as the future becomes present and past . . . [T]he future does not consist exclusively of what will happen, but also of what within limits may or may not happen, the limits being referents of the *will* and the rest of the *may*" (293; emphasis in original). Futures might be possible, with varying degrees of probability, or impossible. "Futurology," "Futurism," and "futures studies" are competing terms for the study of such futures, as well as the processes of anticipating coming scenarios. "Futurist" had been used as early as 1842 to refer to Christian eschatology; it was adopted for the 1909 manifesto by Filippo Tommaso Marinetti that kickstarted an artistic movement. This chapter will trace the idea (and some of the methods) of futures studies, examine "future shock" as a reaction to the future, and detail the uses futurology makes of science fiction. It will then briefly consider eschatology and SF as versions of the future, before concluding with a critique of futurology's deployment of SF.

"Futurology" was coined in 1943 by Ossip K. Flechtheim, a German refugee teaching at the University of Atlanta, to refer to a science of predictive probability. He advocated that futures studies should be taught in the classroom, noting that "[t]his is the first period in human history when universal basic change occurs within less than one generation" (266). This assertion is debatable—compare, say, the Industrial Revolution—but there were definitely significant geopolitical and technological shifts after World War II. Flechtheim claimed that futurology "represents a new synthesis of varied materials" that is "closely related to [the discipline of] history and could indeed be pictured as a projection of history into a new time dimension . . . [I]t will avail itself of interpretation, generalization, and speculation to a considerably higher degree" than history does (255). Futurology was seen as a discipline close to cultural anthropology, theoretical sociology, and social philosophy, and its forecasting could be short-term (for example, weather reports), medium-term (for example, flood-defense planning), and long-term (for example, contingency plans for a 1- or 2-meter rise in sea levels). Predicted events might be possible (low-probability), probable (high-probability), preferable (utopian), or wildcards (low-probability but high-risk). Flechtheim viewed it as "a science or . . . a 'prescientific' branch of knowledge" (266). As for the links with SF, the genre does deal in possible, impossible, probable, and preferable worlds, so attempts by futurologists to establish connections are understandable (if, as we shall see, more limited than they imagine).

Futures studies became an academic subject during the 1960s, dating roughly to the establishment of the World Future Society in 1966, which was designed to help organizations, communities, and individuals deal with change. The WFS still researches the impact of speculations about the future, organizes conferences, and publishes newsletters and journals, including *The Futurist*. The first issue of *Futures: The Journal of Forecasting and Planning* appeared in 1968, the same year that an offshoot of the RAND Corporation, the Institute for the Future, was established in Middletown, Connecticut. Its founder Paul Baran had been designing a communications system that could survive a nuclear war, and the organization became involved in researching ARPANet, an ancestor of the Internet, after it moved to Silicon Valley in 1969. Today, the IFF researches technology, health, and work for corporations, although initially it had planned to work for governments. Other North American organizations include the Hawai'i Research Center for Futures Studies at the University of Hawai'i at Mānoa (established in 1971), the Tellus Institute in Boston (1976), the National Intelligence Council in Washington, D.C. (1979), and the Singularity Institute for Artificial Intelligence in San Francisco (2000). In Britain, there is the Tavistock Institute of Human Relations in London (1946), the Institute for Operational Research in London (1963), and the Institute of Development Studies and the Science Policy Research Unit at the University of Sussex (1966). Scandinavia is home to the Copenhagen Institute for Futures Studies (1970), the Finland Futures Research Centre at the University of Finland in Turku (1992), and Kairos Future in Sweden (1993). Elsewhere, there is the Weizmann Institute of Science in Rehovot, Israel (1933), and the Nomura Research Institute in Tokyo, Japan (1965), among many other global think tanks, government intelligence agencies, and related university departments.

Futures studies aims "to reduce the margin of error in estimating likely developments and to introduce a measure of stability into decision-making by reducing the uncertainty that attends the contemplation of major projects in a time of rapid change" (Bell 3). It both extrapolates current trends and estimates their limits and likelihood. It also identifies points of potential intervention: "The primary supposition behind most of the work in futures is that we *do* have the ability to make some kind of change, although there is argument about its extent, and that we are not merely passengers" (Thompson 12; emphasis in original). If a community has a particular goal—say, self-sufficiency in food production—futurology should help achieve this. It can also note the problems that would arise from certain courses of behavior: "An exploratory forecast looks forward to likely technological progress from the present. A normative forecast looks back from a desirable goal in the future, and discerns the events that must be achieved in order to reach that particular goal" (Cetron and Mahinske 26).

Future population size is key information for governments as they plan for the provision of services. Patterns of cultivation and distribution of food are significant to the private enterprises that supply shops and eating places. Crop and livestock technology may improve calorific yields, but there may be unforeseen consequences such as disease, pollution, food poisoning, and technophobic panics. Thompson, for example, warns of the danger of replacing "wild strains by a single or small number of cultivated ones" (61), which could replace the diversity of existing species with a monoculture of patented seeds and breeds.

Communities also require utilities and the removal of waste, and such needs must be anticipated well in advance; overcapacity and dearth both cause problems. Housing must be planned, and town and other planners have to bear infrastructure in mind. Schools, hospitals, and prisons are also part of planned communities. Transport delivers goods, permits commuting, and facilitates leisure. Buses, trains, boats, and airplanes all need varying degrees of regulating, timetabling, and scheduling. In southeast England, for example, the airports are reaching capacity and can only expand through more night flights or the addition of runways, with consequent noise pollution and home demolitions, probably in the Heathrow area. Schools, hospitals, and prisons are also part of planned communities.

Futures studies often assumes problems have technological solutions; for example, some have suggested that face-to-face meetings might be replaced with virtual contacts, thus significantly obviating the need for plane travel: "The increasing use of telecommunication, the transmission of data and drawings by this means, and the growing use of satellite communication in our daily life could well provide all the additional speed of communication that is desired" (Boorer 224). On the other hand, advanced telecommunications and other technologies have inaugurated an information explosion, leading to an overwhelming experience of "information overload." Damien Broderick suggests that we may soon reach "the Spike," a point at which technology develops too quickly to be understood, and Vernor Vinge and Ray Kurzweil claim that technology will reach a "Singularity" with the advent of artificial intelligence, beyond which point the future cannot be predicted. For their part, Soviet futurologists feared that modern industrialized humanity, confronted with this glut of information, was degenerating into a passive receiver of signals rather than an autonomous intellectual entity (see Saifulin 302). Rafail Nudelman notes that both socialist and bourgeois futurologists seemed to be invested in "inculcat[ing] an enmity toward change into readers" (242). Yet, at the same time, hopeful prophecies abounded of technology permitting modes of decentralization that would promote fruitful social engagement, such as Robert Jungk's prediction that

> [t]hose aiming at a participative democracy of the near future might need to create a new technological infrastructure geared to the needs of the largely decentralized decision making. Information banks with numerous terminals and information

nets, linking thousands of largely autonomous local, regional, and national bodies, would help to assure the functioning of fairly small and relatively independent political and social units inside the larger framework. (36)

In the words of Dennis Gabor, "The future cannot be predicted, but futures can be invented" (161).

Of course, technology has a range of costs—research, development, and production on the one hand, pollution, obsolescence, and waste on the other—so that the benefits it offers might be questioned: "Technology *per se* will not increase wealth; it can, in fact, have precisely the opposite effect, for it is no magic formula by itself" (Thompson 54). According to many futurologists, the lifecycle of a technology has three phases: invention, when an idea is conceived by an individual or a group; innovation, when it enters into the economy; and diffusion, when it spreads through marketing and adoption. An idea can fail at any point in this process, either for lack of funding or because the market is not receptive to it. Between two competing technologies, the better version does not necessarily succeed. Paul Saffo, a technology forecaster at the Institute for the Future, observes that "[w]e tend to overestimate the short-term impacts of some threatened change, but we underestimate the long-term implications" (qtd. Wylie). The technologies of the Internet, the home computer, and the mobile phone were available for years before there was an explosion in take-up. While home portable computer terminals and small communications devices were predicted in science fiction—*Star Trek* anticipating cellphones and *2001: A Space Odyssey* (1968) anticipating the tablet computer—the futuristic technology did not quite happen as anticipated.

On top of the projections of individual futurologists, "blue-sky," and "black-sky" consultants, forecasting techniques used by think tanks include the Delphi method, developed during the Second World War, in which a group of experts individually offer their predictions on a topic, receive a distillation of the responses, and revise their suggestions accordingly. This may go through several iterations, with new technology facilitating the process greatly; the process anticipates the kind of consensus method characteristic of wikis, although it can also be designed to produce a range of differing opinions. Scenario planning was introduced in the 1950s; in it, a thick description of a possible future world is created in an attempt to locate possible problems with plausible solutions. In a sense, this is a form of collective gameplaying and has been used by the military as well as corporations such as Shell. In the 1960s, Cross Impact Analysis was developed, in which at least 10 possible events are assigned individual probabilities and then the probability of one event occurring if another has taken place is calculated—thus demonstrating the need to consider holistic systems when interpreting causal change. Computer simulations began to be used in the 1970s to speed up this process of calculation.

Futurology reached a mass audience with the publication of Alvin Toffler's 1970 bestseller *Future Shock*, which grew out of a 1965 article for the journal *Horizon*. Future shock, in Toffler's analysis, was "the shattering stress and disorientation that we induce in individuals by subjecting them to too much change in too short a time" (12). The problem was not just that the American population was facing a period of crisis in the

1960s—with the Civil Rights movement, Second Wave feminism, gay liberation, the counterculture, economic volatility, and so on—but that the experience itself was simply too much, too fast. Toffler argues that "to soften the impact of future shock, we must begin by making speculation about the future respectable" (384), and his book indeed describes a series of possible futures. Toffler asserts that ideas about the future should be taught in schools and, moreover, that the reading and watching of SF should be actively encouraged. As society faces the end of industrialization, traditional top-down economic remedies will not work, Toffler insists. Instead, he proposes a "social futurism," in which people are consulted: "We need to initiate ... a continuing plebiscite on the future" (431). A series of ad-hoc think tanks will steer policy with long-term planning, and because individuals are stakeholders, they will be wired into the machinery of social change. The individual "must master evolution ... anticipate and design the future" (438). This would, of course, require the "new technological infrastructure" forecast by Jungk.

Dennis Livingston also suggested that futures studies should look to SF for inspiration, noting that "the future is not totally unknown. In fact, inherent in science fiction is the notion that there is not one future, but many possible futures, each arising from the infinite variations that could be applied to the extension of present-day trends" (232). According to Livingston, SF provides forecasts of innovations, predictions for social and behavioral science, future sociologies, depictions of transcendental events/discoveries, and technological/sociological accounts of extraterrestrial cultures; and fictional characters' reactions to these things offer a potential range of responses for futurological study. Livingston suggests three yardsticks for evaluating individual SF works: skill in description, internal consistency, and authorial reputation. The first of these is subjective, the third may well vary across time. Livingston also admits that "the literature is relatively conservative when it comes to drawing the cultural settings within which the [future] gadgets operate" (235). In other words, the genre lacks a sufficient sense of difference in its projection of possible worlds: "[T]he pervasive assumptions [are] that human nature as we know it will remain stable, that economic incentive will remain the highest motivation, and that twentieth century cultural and moral values will continue to dominate the world" (235). It is difficult to escape contemporary assumptions, and the history of SF is a history of previous ideas of norms and innovations. But futurologists must also break with contemporary cultural and moral values.

In futurology as well as SF, "The future is no longer regarded as predestined—an existing landscape which will be revealed to us as we travel through it. It is now seen as the result of the decisions, discoveries, and efforts that we make today" (Bell 2). Futurology attempts to ensure that these decisions lead to progress rather than regression, toward utopia rather than dystopia, driven by a "belief ... that things will in some sense get better in the future" (Pollard 9). But futures studies, along with the method of thinking that it lays claim to, is not the only space for anticipating the future; and there is nothing essentially modern about it, either. As Thompson observes, "People have always had some concept of the future, and made plans for it" (15). The provision of shelter, the cultivation of plants, and the rearing of animals require a degree of forward planning—seeds need planting, plants need harvesting, and produce needs storage or preservation through the winter. Moreover, most societies have a set of transcendental beliefs that imagine an end to their world and the start of a new phase. Flechtheim suggests that Christian belief situates "human history as a brief chapter in the eternal book of God's creation, beginning with the Fall of Man and ending either with the Millennium or the Last Judgment" (265). A messianic promise of the apocalyptic transformation of the world—involving a Second Coming, a Great Tribulation, a raising of the dead, and a Last Judgment—informs Christian eschatology (see Link), and eschatological thinking also informs the decision-making of individuals in their progress toward salvation, as Allen J. Behm points out (38–39). Over two millennia, various groups have suspected that the end times were near, providing a fertile ground for religious art and literature.

Benjamin Uffenheimer argues that "eschatology encompasses not only utopias that bring history to an end, but also imminent 'reachable' utopian situations" (200), but Carl E. Braaten claims that "[t]he utopian future is projected as another time *in* history; the eschatological deals with the final fulfillment end *of* history" (43; emphasis in original). The genre of utopian literature is rather more ambivalent about the preferability of an imagined society—whether distanced spatially or temporally from the here and now—and it has been increasingly absorbed into science fiction, along with antiutopia, dystopia, and heterotopia (see Moylan). SF, like futures studies, imagines possible, probable, improbable, and preferable (as well as impossible) worlds. Yet the futurologist sees this as offering examples specifically of *prediction*. Toffler suggests that "if we view it as a kind of sociology of the future, rather than as literature, science fiction has immense value as a mind stretching force for the creation of the habit of anticipation" (384), and goes on to recommend the works of Arthur C. Clarke, William Tenn, Robert A. Heinlein, Ray Bradbury, and Robert Sheckley as exemplars of the imaginable connections among sociology, politics, and psychology. If literature is defined by the foregrounding of an aesthetic function, then the suggested utility of SF for futurology makes a virtue of its paraliterary status, even though several SF critics have rejected the supposition that most SF is written for purposes of prediction per se (see Westfahl).

But, clearly, science fiction at its core *is* concerned with the future. Indeed, according to literary historian I. F. Clarke, science fiction as a genre was not possible before what he calls "the discovery of the future"—"a new sense of perspective that discerned the shape of things-to-come in the circumstances of contemporary society" (6). The gradual mastery of nature enabled by modern science, combined with the accelerated social tempo prompted by industrial development, generated a form of literature devoted to depicting the promises and perils of change. In Edward Bellamy's *Looking Backward: 2000–1887* (1888), for example, young American Julian West falls into a mesmeric trance and awakes over a century later, where he is treated to a detailed description of the future utopian society. H. G. Wells's *The Time Machine* (1895) features travel to a distant future where society is divided into two degenerated races of humanity—a bifurcation of the species that extrapolates late-nineteenth-century class differences. In the novel, the trajectory of future evolution has eluded the control of The Time

Traveller's progress-worshipping Victorian contemporaries. This is further underlined by a later scene where he journeys even further into the future, to a dying Earth beneath a red sun, and ponders the extinction of humanity.

Mark B. Adams has labeled H. G. Wells "the inventor and head guru of futurology" (470), but he also sees in Wells's fiction a lack of faith in human agency in shaping the future: "For Wells, the most glorious fruits of the century of progress—its discovery of astronomical, physical, biological and social laws—meant that progress itself was constrained, humans were subject to inexorable natural laws beyond their control, and powerless to shape our individual or collective destiny" (473). There were limits to the power of prediction, but Wells was able to open up an evolutionary futurology. In *The Outline of History* (1919), he provided a summary of historical development from prehistoric times; in *The Shape of Things to Come* (1933), he attempted to produce a history book that could have been written in a world state of 2106. Published at a time of widespread economic depression in the West, Wells's future history predictably diverges from the future that did, in fact, occur (although he does anticipate the Second World War).

Wells influenced J. B. S. Haldane, a biologist and early geneticist whose *Daedalus; or, Science and the Future* (1924) was a best-selling pamphlet calling for the harnessing of biological processes for social ends. This "wonderfully provocative" book (Parrinder, "Siblings" 50), which includes a paper written by a Cambridge undergraduate to his tutor in the mid-twenty-first century, argues among other things for artificial forms of reproduction in order to separate sexual pleasure from procreation. Haldane's 1927 essay "The Last Judgment" describes—appropriately for its eschatological title—a number of possible ends of the world, culminating with a summary of the "most probable" outcome as narrated to a hypothetical audience of Venusian children 40 million years in the future (292). As Adams notes, "The complete destruction of life on the earth is *not* the end; and the 'spectators on another planet' who view the earth's destruction are, in fact, our descendants" (363–64; emphasis in original). Haldane imagines the slowing of Earth's rotation; the survivors travel to colonize Venus and then attempt to populate the galaxy. "The death of the Earth is a negligible event in this process," Parrinder claims (*Science Fiction* 99). Again, the long-term future may be beyond humanity's control, but technology can enable survival beyond the coming crises. Robert Crossley notes that Haldane's essay was "a cornucopia of unelaborated but provocative guesses and fancies about the future, around many of which Olaf [Stapledon] built entire episodes" (190). Stapledon's *Last and First Men: A Story of the Near and Far Future* (1930) and its sequel, *Last Men in London* (1933), project human history over the next 2 billion years through a series of rises and falls of civilizations, even of species.

These works formed the backbone of the British SF tradition in the first half of the twentieth century, but in the United States, the genre—rooted more deeply in popular (pulp) fiction—attempted to graft stronger narratives onto the vast galactic panoramas. Each of the so-called big three SF writers—Robert A. Heinlein, Isaac Asimov, and Arthur C. Clarke—constructed futurologies, a fact for which Adams credits Haldane's "vision of a long future history for humankind throughout the galaxy" (485). In 1939 Heinlein devised a plan for a "Future History," aided by John W. Campbell Jr., editor of

Astounding Science-Fiction, who published it in the March 1941 issue. Heinlein envisaged a cohesive sequence of forthcoming events, thus committing himself to writing particular titles (most of them eventually gathered in his 1967 collection *The Past Through Tomorrow*). In part, this was a marketing tool, building a readerly appetite for his future work. Many of Heinlein's novels and stories fit within his capacious Future History, which Parrinder has described as a "truncated epic based on the prospect of galactic imperialism, with its associated themes of leaving the Earth, colonizing the planets, and meeting with aliens" (*Science Fiction* 104). One novel outside of the sequence, *Beyond this Horizon* (1948), "explicitly critiqued many of Haldane's ideas while incorporating others" (Adams 485)—for example, featuring a genetically engineered protagonist.

Isaac Asimov wrote about the processes of prediction in his "Foundation" series (1942–93), which gives an account of psychohistory—a mathematical, sociological, and historical futurology developed by the character Hari Seldon. A foundation is established in order to preserve the state of knowledge of a galactic empire during a predicted period of collapse, with a second foundation created as a back-up in case the first is destroyed. Asimov had reread Edward Gibbon's *The History of the Decline and Fall of the Roman Empire* (1776–89), and he wanted to write about the fate of empires on a galactic scale. The probable worlds predicted by Seldon's psychohistory are derailed by a wildcard future, thanks to the appearance of "The Mule" in the story of the same name (1945). A powerful telepathic mutant whose appearance had not been predicted by Seldon, The Mule wreaks havoc on the projected contours of psychohistorical forecasting, thus suggesting the limitations of prediction.

Clarke had read Haldane since childhood, and "many of his subsequent writings, whether stories, novels, or popular science, are infused with Haldane's vision" (Adams 486). Clarke's *Childhood's End* (1953) echoes Stapledon in its evocation of a vast evolutionary leap undertaken by humankind. This was a characteristic theme of Clarke's, likely inherited from the tradition of British scientific romance that descends through Wells and Haldane. *2001: A Space Odyssey* (1968), developed as a script for Stanley Kubrick's film and then published as a novel, features yet another eschatological transcendence as astronaut David Bowman is transformed into a cosmic Star Child whose return to Earth heralds a new evolutionary phase. Clarke's subsequent novels in the series, *2010: Odyssey Two* (1982), *2061: Odyssey Three* (1987), and *3001: The Final Odyssey* (1997), continue humanity's historical development, as well as chronicling the fate of the transhuman Bowman. Clarke's narratives were littered with plausible technological developments that improved human life, such as the space elevator that figures in his award-winning novel *The Fountains of Paradise* (1979). His futuristic fiction was buttressed by publications in scientific journals and works of science advocacy, in which he examined many of the tropes of fantastic science, exploring the possibilities of space travel, time travel, invisibility, and so forth, often with a mix of optimism (an unshakeable belief in progress) and skepticism (an awareness of the limitations of science). The latter is expressed in one of Clarke's famous "Laws" of technoscientific development, published in his 1962 work of futurology, *Profiles of the Future*: "When a distinguished but elderly scientist states that something is possible, he is almost certainly right. When he states that something is impossible, he is very probably wrong" (25). Yet, unlike Heinlein and Asimov, who often denied their predictive aims (see Asimov 205), Clarke saw himself as a Futurist as much as an SF writer, and the Arthur C. Clarke Foundation he established endows various initiatives that bring scientists, humanists, and artists together for purposes of social betterment through technology.

In the wake of the "big three," SF has taken up the writing of future history with a vengeance. Almost every SF writer, as much for commercial as for intellectual reasons, has projected a self-consistent fictive universe, extending forward from our own, in which all manner of narratives may be set. C. J. Cherryh's "Alliance-Union" universe imagines a future space-based civilization divided into two main factions and centered on strategically located space stations and a handful of colonized planets. Meanwhile, the imagination of dystopic futures that emerge from exaggerated features of our own present day is also commonplace within the genre—and also outside it, with the work of mainstream author Margaret Atwood leading the way: her 1985 novel *The Handmaid's Tale* depicts a theocratic future where women have lost all rights, while *Oryx and Crake* (2003) deals with the imagined consequences of runaway biotechnology. At times, near-future science fiction—especially by the likes of Atwood, Bruce Sterling, and William Gibson—reads very much like futurological scenarios in narrative guise. Indeed, Sterling is a part-time Futurist, author of such works as *Tomorrow Now: Envisioning the Next Fifty Years* (2002).

Charles Elkins, in his analysis of futurology, claims that the futures of Wells, Heinlein, Asimov, and Clarke "embrace a version of Saint-Simonian utopianism with all of its techno-bureaucratic implications" (25). Elkins's allusion is to early French socialist Henri de Saint-Simon, who had argued that society should be ruled by leaders of industry and that scientists should set the moral agenda. Essentially, Elkins objects to futurology's characterization of society as a series of "problems" to be solved scientifically. By contrast, fiction does not offer the rational forms of solution demanded by science, instead providing "a strategy for dealing with a particular situation in a specific way by communicating an attitude toward that situation which either accepts, rejects, or doubts the principles upon which the order that created the situation is based" (25–26). According to Elkins, literature, including SF, is dramatic, dialogic, even dialectical: it explores multiple sides of an argument rather than didactically asserting its own views. Elkins suggests that SF, rather than being predictive, may have an inspirational and hortatory role in terms of its relationship to the future; like all art, "it must destroy old beliefs, furnish us with forms of passage from the old to the new, and finally inculcate new values in place of old beliefs" (28).

Nudelman basically agrees, arguing that "[w]hat is really significant in SF has nothing in common with the 'real future' and real prediction. SF deals with the novum and not with the future; with changes and not with prediction" (242). He suggests that futurology attempts to *limit* possible futures and thus freedom of choice. This is, in part, a turf war: Elkins and Nudelman are defending SF as a specifically *literary* genre. Theirs is an argument for aesthetics over utility: the readerly encounter with

SF involves experiences of sublimity or estrangement through its invocations of imagined (future) environments. By contrast, futurology, Futurism, and futures studies are methods of future *prediction*, with varying needs to persuade an audience into taking or avoiding particular actions; it is much more overtly tendentious than SF, advocating for (rather than merely evoking) potential futures. Despite their differences, however, it is fair to say that futurology, like SF, is a product of the modern technoscientific world, and just as SF is, in its own way, futurological (making use of extrapolation and scenario-building), so futurology can be seen as science-fictional, expressly engaging with—and accommodating readers to—the inescapable reality of technological and social change.

Works Cited

Adams, Mark B. "Last Judgment: The Visionary Biology of J. B. S. Haldane." *Journal of the History of Biology* 33.3 (2000): 457–91. Print.

Asimov, Isaac. "Prediction." 1989. *Gold: The Final Science Fiction Collection*. New York: HarperPrism, 1996. 205–10.

Behm, Allen J. "The Eschatology of the Jātakas." *Numen* 18.1 (1971): 30–44. Print.

Bell, Daniel. "Confidence from Chaos." *Futures: The Journal of Forecasting and Planning* 1.1 (1968): 2–3. Print.

Boorer, N. W. "The Future of Civil Aviation." *Futures: The Journal of Forecasting and Planning* 1.3 (1969): 206–26. Print.

Braaten, Carl E. "The Significance of the Future: An Eschatological Perspective." *Hope and the Future of Man*. Ed. Ewert H. Cousins. Philadelphia: Fortress, 1972. 40–54. Print.

Broderick, Damien. *The Spike: How Our Lives Are Being Transformed by Rapidly Advancing Technologies*. New York: Tor/Forge, 2001. Print.

Cetron, Marvin J., and Edmund B. Mahinske. "The Value of Technological Forecasting for the Research and Development Manager." *Futures: The Journal of Forecasting and Planning* 1.1 (1968): 21–33. Print.

Clarke, Arthur C. *Profiles of the Future: An Inquiry into the Limits of the Possible*. New York: Harper and Row, 1962. Print.

Clarke, I. F. *The Pattern of Expectation, 1644–2001*. New York: Basic, 1979. Print.

Crossley, Robert. *Olaf Stapledon: Speaking for the Future*. Liverpool: Liverpool UP, 1994. Print.

Elkins, Charles. "Science Fiction Versus Futurology: Dramatic Versus Rational Models." *Science Fiction Studies* 6.1 (Mar. 1979): 20–31. Print.

Flechtheim, Ossip. "Futurology—The New Science of Probability." *The Futurists*. Ed. Alvin Toffler. New York: Random House, 1972. 264–76. Print.

Gabor, Dennis. *Inventing the Future*. Harmondsworth, UK: Pelican, 1964. Print.

Haldane, J. B. S. *Daedalus; or, Science and the Future*. 1924. London: Kegan, Paul, Trench, Trübner, 1926. Print.

———. "The Last Judgment." *Possible Worlds and Other Essays*. 1927. New Brunswick, NJ: Transaction, 2009. 287–312. Print.

Hartshorne, Charles. "Necessity." *The Review of Metaphysics* 21.2 (1967): 291–96. Print.

Jungk, Robert. "Human Futures." *Futures: The Journal of Forecasting and Planning* 1.1 (1968): 34–39. Print.

Kurzweil, Ray. *The Singularity Is Near: When Humans Transcend Biology*. New York: Penguin, 2005. Print.

Link, Christian. "Points of Departure for a Christian Eschatology." *Eschatology in the Bible and in Jewish and Christian Tradition*. Ed. Henning Graf Reventlow. Sheffield, UK: Sheffield Academic, 1997. 98–110. Print.

Livingston, Dennis. "Science Fiction as a Source of Forecast Material." *Futures: The Journal of Forecasting and Planning* 1.3 (1969): 232–38. Print.

Moylan, Tom. *Scraps of the Untainted Sky: Science Fiction, Utopia, Dystopia*. Boulder, CO: Westview, 2000. Print.

Nudelman, Rafail. "On SF and Futurology." *Science Fiction Studies* 6.2 (July 1979): 241–42. Print.

Parrinder, Patrick. *Science Fiction: Its Criticism and Teaching*. London: Methuen, 1980. Print.

———. "Siblings in Space: J. B. S. Haldane and Naomi Mitchison." *Foundation* 22 (1981): 49–56. Print.

Pollard, Sidney. *The Idea of Progress: History and Society*. Harmondsworth, UK: Pelican, 1971. Print.

Saifulin, Murad, ed. *The Future of Society: A Critique of Modern Bourgeois Philosophical and Socio-Political Conceptions*. Moscow: Progress, 1973. Print.

Thompson, Alan E. *Understanding Futurology: An Introduction to Futures Study*. London: David and Charles, 1979. Print.

Toffler, Alvin. *Future Shock*. 1970. London: Pan, 1971. Print.

Uffenheimer, Benjamin. "From Prophecy to Apocalyptic Eschatology." *Eschatology in the Bible and in Jewish and Christian Tradition*. Ed. Henning Graf Reventlow. Sheffield, UK: Sheffield Academic, 1997. 200–17. Print.

Vinge, Vernor. "The Coming Technological Singularity: How to Survive in the Post-Human Era." 1993. *Vernor Vinge Home Page*. Web. Aug. 30, 2013. http://www-rohan.sdsu.edu/faculty/vinge/misc/singularity.html.

Westfahl, Gary. "Pitfalls of Prophecy: Why Science Fiction So Often Fails to Predict the Future." *Science Fiction and the Prediction of the Future: Essays on Foresight and Fallacy*. Ed. Gary Westfahl, Wong Kin Yuen, and Amy Kit-Sze Chan. Jefferson, NC: McFarland, 2011. 9–22. Print.

Wylie, Margie. "Silicon Valley Soothsayer." *CNET*. June 23, 1997. Web. Aug. 30, 2013. http://news.cnet.com/Silicon-Valley-soothsayer/2009-1082_3-233697.html.

CHAPTER 40

POSTHUMANISM

COLIN MILBURN

TIME and again, science fiction has speculated on the posthuman condition. Striving to think beyond man and humanism, to make "the post" imaginable in the here and now, the genre has entertained a diversity of posthuman scenarios. For example, some narratives consider the posthuman in a biological sense, focusing on the evolutionary future of *Homo sapiens* and the extent to which human physiology might dramatically alter over time, or even in symbiogenesis with other species (see Bruce Clarke). Biological accounts of the posthuman have appeared in H. G. Wells's *The Time Machine* (1895), Olaf Stapledon's *Last and First Men* (1930), Arthur C. Clarke's *Childhood's End* (1953), Theodore Sturgeon's *More than Human* (1953), Sheri S. Tepper's *Grass* (1989), and Greg Bear's *Darwin's Radio* (1999), among many others. Some narratives instead consider the posthuman in a technological sense, focusing on the synthetic, engineered successors of humanity or the idea of humans and machines linked ever more closely in the circuits of technoculture (see Hayles; Bukatman). Technological visions of the posthuman feature prominently in texts such as Mary Shelley's *Frankenstein* (1818), Karel Čapek's *R.U.R.* (1920), Bernard Wolfe's *Limbo* (1952), Philip K. Dick's *Do Androids Dream of Electric Sheep?* (1968), William Gibson's *Neuromancer* (1984), Bruce Sterling's *Schismatrix* (1985), and Nalo Hopkinson's *Midnight Robber* (2000), among many others. At the same time, some narratives concern the posthuman in a cultural or epistemic sense, discovering that "human nature" is a tenuous social construct open to modification and revision (see Badmington; Wolfe). The posthuman condition as an epistemological alternative to the cultural and linguistic traditions of humanism has been explored in William S. Burrough's *The Soft Machine* (1961), Ian Watson's *The Embedding* (1973), J. G. Ballard's *Crash* (1973), Joanna Russ's *The Female Man* (1975), Samuel R. Delany's *Trouble on Triton* (1976), and Gwyneth Jones's *White Queen* (1991), among many others. These different registers of the posthuman—biological, technological, and cultural—have each generated rich genealogies of scientific extrapolation and literary representation, with different lineages intermixing and cross-breeding with creative abandon.

The history of SF, as many critics have argued, offers a map of the posthuman imagination (see Csicsery-Ronay; Foster; Graham; and Vint). To the extent that representations of the posthuman suggest provocative divergences from the norms of human biology, the conventions of human society, and the limitations of human thought, science fiction often poses as a way of "going postal"—sometimes even depicting posthumanization as a function of SF itself. To be sure, there is a longstanding conceit in the discourse of science fiction that prolonged engagement with the genre might have real transformative effects. Caveat lector: reading science fiction might turn you posthuman.

Science fiction has often promoted itself as a literature of genius (scientific or otherwise), imagining its writers and fans as unusually intelligent, different from the common stock (see Huntington). For example, in his Guest of Honor speech at the 1940 World Science Fiction Convention, E. E. "Doc" Smith theorized that true fans possess "peculiar mental attributes" (10): "While we will probably never become a very large group—it seems obvious that the necessity of possessing what I may call the science-fantasy mind does now and probably always will limit our number to a very small fraction of the total population—we will continue to grow" (11). Similarly, in his Guest of Honor speech at the 1941 Worldcon, Robert A. Heinlein said: "Science fiction fans differ from most of the rest of the race by thinking in terms of racial magnitudes—not even centuries, but thousands of years" ("Guest" 14), adding "I think that science fiction fans are better prepared to face the future than the ordinary run of people around them, because they believe in change" (17). These affirmative pronouncements from famous writers in the field participate in the postal imaginary of science fiction. Indeed, the self-fashioning of the SF community as cognitively exceptional, possessing peculiar mental faculties, even goes so far as to suggest that the difference is not one of degree but of kind. The "science-fantasy mind," distinguishing fans from the "rest of the race," conceives of itself in evolutionary or eugenic terms: a hopeful monster, already admiring its preadaption to the future.

In his novel *Slan*, serialized in *Astounding Science-Fiction* during 1940 and published in book form in 1946, A. E. Van Vogt depicts a race of superhuman beings called "slans" (named after Samuel Lann, the scientist who supposedly—or so it is widely believed—created them). Slans possess psychic powers, as well as phenomenal strength, rejuvenating capabilities, and stunning intelligence. Normal humans, however, detest slans and hunt them mercilessly. The plot follows a young slan named Jommy Cross (evidently a Christ figure) who must fight for survival after his mother is executed by a human mob. He eventually discovers that slans are actually thriving in the world, passing among the normal human population and gaining access to the channels of political power. In fact, it turns out that slans are the unacknowledged legislators of the world. To some SF fans in the 1940s and 1950s, *Slan* seemed to be an allegory of fandom itself: super mutants living among "the ordinary run of people around them" (in Heinlein's terms)—scientifically talented, imaginative, downtrodden and persecuted, but waiting for their inevitable recognition. A popular slogan emerged, persisting for decades: "Fans are slans!" Some fans even founded small communes based on this idea, called "slan shacks" (Warner 33–35).

Is a slan born a slan or made a slan? This is a chicken-or-egg question, perhaps, but it haunts the narrative of Van Vogt's novel. For the human hatred of slans, as depicted in the text, is partly attributed to the belief that slans kidnap human children and turn them into slans: "You've heard what slans do to human babies?" (34). Samuel Lann, figured by rumor and prejudice as a mad scientist, is said to have invented a machine capable of transforming normal human biology into superhuman biology. Indeed, it is thought that Lann first tested the machine on his own wife and children. And yet, Jommy discovers that this story is entirely fictitious. Slans are not engineered but natural, the products of an orthogenetic force in the field of biological evolution: "You see, there is not, there never has been, a slan-making machine. All slans are natural mutations" (235). Samuel Lann therefore did not create slans; he simply helped to nurture the first slan babies he discovered in the course of his biomedical research. In the novel, then, the cultural narrative of the "slan-making machine" proves to be nothing other than a *science fiction*—that is to say, the rumor of the slan machine is a recursive representation of SF itself, indexing the genre as a speculative mode of discourse.

But the slan machine, exposed as science fiction—an imaginary and untrue account of technoscientific possibility, an artful lie about the capacities of science (as Thomas M. Disch essentially defines the genre)—becomes an *alibi* for the true conceit of the novel: the idea that posthuman beings are irrupting everywhere in the normal human population through a non-Darwinian process of orthogenetic mutation. As the slan Kier Grey explains to Jommy:

> Naturally . . . [,] your discovery that slans are naturals and not machine-made is nothing new to us. We are the mutation-after-man. The forces of that mutation were at work many years before that great day when Samuel Lann realized the pattern of perfection in some of the mutations. It is only too obvious in retrospect that nature was building for an enormous attempt . . . [I]n a single stupendous quarter of a millennium more than a billion abnormal births occurred. It was like a cataclysm . . . No preconceived plan existed. What happened seemed simply to have been a reaction to the countless intolerable pressures that were driving men mad, because neither their minds nor their bodies were capable of withstanding modern civilization. (248–49)

"Naturally" enough, a mysterious "natural" process accounts for the secret origin of slans. Yet it seems that even nature has been de-naturalized by the rapid advances of science and technology. Apparently without "preconceived plan," nature was nevertheless "building for an enormous attempt" to perfect human biology, adapting it to "modern civilization." Nature was provoked by technology; slans are nature's "reaction" to machine culture. In this regard, even the first slans were indeed "machine-made," engineered by nature to thrive in a futuristic world. Nature turns out to be nothing natural—or rather, something much more than natural.

Moreover, Jommy learns that the early slans, as if mimicking the fraudulent rumor of a "slan-making machine," took control of the genetic mechanisms of slan evolution:

> The scattered remnants of the slans finally concentrated on efforts to control the mutation force. At last they found how to shape the large molecules that made up the genes themselves ... It remained then to experiment. That took two hundred years ... They found at last how complex groups of molecules could control the form of each organ for one generation or many ... And so they changed the basic slan structure, keeping what was good and had survival value, eliminating what had proved dangerous. The genes controlling the tendrils were altered, transferring the mind-reading ability inside the brain, but insuring that the ability did not turn up for many generations—. (250)

So the speculative rumor about a "slan-making machine"—a technology of programmable evolution—proves both *scandalously fictive* and *absolutely true*. The slans have reengineered the developmental biology of their own offspring to forestall the orthogenetic force—postponing the rise of slandom until a time when the human population would no longer be such a threat, looking forward to a future that is, in the context of the novel itself, nothing but science fiction. In the reconstructed genes of their progeny, the true slans encode a message—a program—that will only be read later. The posthuman future is reverse-transcribed into the present, but indefinitely delayed—evidence of what Jacques Derrida has analyzed as the waywardness of the "post."

This resolution of the mystery posed in the narrative—are slans made or born?—thus threatens to undermine the dichotomous logic of humanism, insisting instead on cyborg ways of thinking. For slans are both natural and artificial, born mutant yet technologically transmuted to postpone their speciation. As Donna Haraway has said of all cyborgs, slans are "monstrous and illegitimate" (154). Slandom abides, yearning for a world promised but not represented in the novel, projected beyond the final pages of the text: a postal zone created within the novel as its own outside, its aftermath. The narrative of *Slan* exposes the fact that, at the root of the posthuman condition (whether biological, technological, or cultural), there lies science fiction.

Science fiction thus discovers itself as an instrument of technoevolutionary change. This is an idea ripe for satire, to be sure. In the October 1951 issue of *Other Worlds Science Stories*, Robert Bloch published a humorous fable about the alleged posthumanizing effects of the genre called "The End of Science Fiction." The story features Bloch himself as the protagonist, detailing his visit to the Tenth World Science Fiction Convention, where the author meets up with his friend Richard Ormsbee—"He'd been a fan. Then he'd turned writer" (289)—who is scheduled to deliver the Guest of Honor speech at the convention the following day. Ormsbee tells Bloch a startling tale, claiming that alien intelligences recently purloined his copy of H. P. Lovecraft's *The Outsider and Others* (1939), as well as his entire collection of pulp magazines. Ormsbee is convinced that the aliens not only identify with Lovecraft's fiction—the stories are all about "outsiders" and "others"—but also intend to use the stories as scripts for a takeover of Earth. The narrative of Lovecraft's story "The Whisperer in Darkness" (1931) seems especially resonant; in Ormsbee's opinion: "It's about the things that came from beyond ... [T]hey had a queer, superior intelligence ... They stole human intelligence, too, when they needed it. And gradually, by means of hypnotism, deception and outright violence, they planned to take control of mankind" (294). Listening to Ormsbee's story, Bloch scoffs: "Sounds like something out of Eric Frank Russell or a hundred other science-fiction yarns I've read. Trouble with you is that you've been reading too much science fiction!" (294). Ormsbee agrees that science fiction is precisely the problem:

> Exactly! . . . It's from these stories that they get their information! . . . Picture these aliens, these outsiders, arriving through a gap in the continuum of space or time. They have no direct kinship with humanity or human thought. The strongest link would naturally be through the minds of those who are at least conditioned—however unwittingly—to the possibility of their existence. To be specific, the writers of fantasy and science fiction, whose brains can conceive of such things. (294–95)

Ormsbee recognizes the brains of SF writers as distinct from those of the normal, mundane human population. Science fiction apparently requires a different kind of neurology, an abnormal cognitive apparatus, to even "conceive of such things." The alien intelligences, despite having no "kinship with humanity or human thought," can nevertheless read the minds of SF writers, and they also see their own desires reflected in the pages of the SF and fantasy magazines. Science fiction, it seems, communicates across species boundaries, beyond the limitations of merely human brains. It is posthuman literature, offering a wealth of ingenious ideas to "[o]thers who read not for pleasure but for information. Others who might plagiarize" (288). Such entities do not distinguish fiction from reality: "[P]resences from outside . . . who can plagiarize any horror, make it real" (299). For this reason, Ormsbee intends to denounce science fiction during his Guest of Honor speech. He wants to insist that fans, writers, and publishers join together to put an end to science fiction, once and for all: "We've aided the enemy unconsciously for years, and it must stop . . . We must stop writing the stories. We must seal our imaginations to those images of *outside* that seem to aid them" (295; emphasis in original).

But the next day, instead of exposing SF's correspondence with the *outside* and the *post*, Ormsbee's speech belittles the assembled fans for their blindness: "The peculiar irony of it . . . is that you—who are presumably authorities on the subject—know nothing about it . . . Still, you have unwittingly served your purpose. Ignorantly, you have opened the way to the very abysses of which you complacently scribble your childish fantasies—" (296–97). As it turns out, Ormsbee is no longer Ormsbee. Inspired by science fiction, the "presences from outside" have turned him into something radically posthuman: "It took a complete autopsy [of Ormsbee's body] to determine how the brain had been removed and the spinal cord altered. Even now they cannot account for the tangle of wires, coils and metal filaments that filled the empty skull and extended through the body" (299).

Upon discovery that Ormsbee had been turned into an alien cyborg—his mind literally *changed* because of science fiction—it is decided that SF must be banned. Everyone agrees, it seems. Yet Bloch writes this story, "The End of Science Fiction," *after* the end of science fiction, willfully violating the prohibition lest his readers forget the painful lessons learned on "that fatal day when science fiction died" (299). It is a story composed in the space of the postmortem, a scene of writing that takes place after science fiction has already died . . . and therefore has not died. Science fiction addresses itself from beyond the end—or as Bloch puts it, from *outside*—occupying its own postal destination. Hyperbolizing the extent to which SF celebrates alienation and "queer, superior intelligence," Bloch's narrative stages a powerful allegory of the cognitive functions of the genre. The shocking image of Ormsbee's upgraded cyborg neurology, his alien cognitive system ("*it wasn't made on earth!*" [299; emphasis in original]), wickedly symbolizes the capacity of science fiction to experiment with the norms of human thought, affording ways of thinking otherwise. The story is a satire, of course, with tongue planted firmly in cheek. And yet, as the Robert Bloch character suggests, sometimes wacky fictions turn out to contain serious critical propositions: "Does that sound peculiar to you? A little wacky, perhaps? I wish it were just that. But there's a grim truth behind my words" (288).

After all, the discovery of SF at the root of posthumanization is not limited to literary representations. Many nonfiction texts embraced by real-life advocates of posthuman engineering—whether they prefer the name of cyborg, transhuman, immortalist, extropian, Singularitarian, or some other avatar of superhumanity—also attend to science fiction as prefiguring real possibilities for the future and changing the way we think. For example, J. B. S. Haldane's *Daedalus; or, Science and the Future* (1924), Norbert Weiner's *The Human Use of Human Beings* (1950), K. Eric Drexler's *Engines of Creation: The Coming Era of Nanotechnology* (1986), Hans Moravac's *Mind Children: The Future of Robot and Human Intelligence* (1988), Vernor Vinge's "Technological Singularity" (1993), and other texts inclined to envision the more-than-human often engage with familiar SF novels to develop their theoretical arguments. More significant, these nonfiction texts typically represent the posthuman future—even as a real social goal or horizon for scientific research—in the mode of speculative fiction, locating the postal imaginary inside the formal conventions of literary fabulation.

Consider J. D. Bernal's 1929 book *The World, the Flesh, and the Devil*—described by Arthur C. Clarke as "the most brilliant attempt at scientific prediction ever made" (401). Bernal extrapolates upon the evolution of the universe, the inevitability of space travel, and the necessity to redesign human biology in order to survive the onrushing future. As an expert on X-ray crystallography and a pioneering figure in the history of molecular biology, Bernal composed his futurological treatise in the idiom of elite science, drawing authoritatively upon various technical fields. His vision of "mechanized man" and the scientific capacity to radically reconfigure the human body—replacing the flesh with advanced technology, extending the central nervous system across various sensors and measurement devices, biochemically engineering the substance of human evolution—has become a touchstone for later theorists of transhumanity and posthumanity. Yet even while imparting his vision in the language of science, arguing for its technical feasibility and socioevolutionary necessity,

Bernal also concedes that the concept of mechanized man is itself nothing other than fabulation: "The account I am about to give must be taken rather as a fable" (33). In other words, the posthuman future unfolds in the form of speculative fiction; where scientific extrapolation fails, the potential of mechanized man is rendered through literary narration alone.

Even so, Bernal's fable of the postal condition repeatedly runs up to the limits of literary representation. After narrating the future transformation of humanity, including the scientific mechanization of outmoded biology and the merger of human brains into a vast hive-mind, Bernal announces the end of his prophetic fable: "This is perhaps far enough; beyond that the future must direct itself" (35). But the end is not the end, for Bernal continues to rush forward into the postal zone, unable to leave the future to its own devices: "Yet why should we stop until our imaginations are exhausted. Even beyond this there are foreseeable possibilities" (45). Reaching the end of the story—the end of man and of humanism—Bernal nevertheless goes further. Indeed, he presses the faculty of cognitive estrangement beyond its own limits, speculating that the human mind may eventually go so far as to evolve itself right out of consciousness: "Consciousness itself may end or vanish in a humanity that has become completely etherealized, losing the close-knit organism, becoming masses of atoms in space communicating by radiation, and ultimately perhaps resolving itself entirely into light" (47). Upon presenting this vision of humanity disintegrated into atoms and light, Bernal again pulls back to proclaim it beyond our capacities of foresight: "This may be an end or a beginning, but from here it is out of sight" (47). But this postscript to Bernal's fable, this inscrutable exteriority ("out of sight"), is already contained inside the text. The posthuman aftermath, while yet incomprehensible "from here"—that is to say, from the perspective of mere humanity—nonetheless appears in the human present as a scientific fable that keeps venturing beyond its own end.

And in this way, it comes back around. For the end, as Bernal suggests, is also a beginning: this imaginary future comes to prescribe our own present, our ongoing technological advancement. After all, Bernal's fable demands action. Repeatedly discovering the limits of foresight only to press beyond them, Bernal's account of the posthuman future concludes yet one more time:

> We are on the point of being able to see the effects of our actions and their probable consequences in the future; we hold the future still timidly, but perceive it for the first time, as a function of our own action. Having seen it, are we to turn away from something that offends the very nature of our earliest desires, or is the recognition of our new powers sufficient to change those desires into the service of the future which they will have to bring about? (80–81)

Bernal thus asks us proactively to change ourselves in body and mind, to think and live otherwise—already, right now—in service to the future he has described. The postscript, as it turns out, is the preface.

The post arrives in advance of itself, conditioning the shape of things to come. This is a paradox, perhaps; it is nevertheless the operating principle for a number of practicing posthumans in our own world—those daring adventurers who, anticipating the high-tech future to come, have rendered themselves posthuman in advance. To be sure, they may be dead right now (or at least, not quite alive), but from their own perspective, it is only a matter of time. Frozen in cryonic suspension, they wait patiently for an era in which sufficiently advanced technoscience will bring them back to life, delivering them to a new world: a life after life. Embracing the logic of science fiction, they wager that any decision to become posthuman cannot wait for the future but must be made in the here and now (see Doyle).

The discourse of cryonics makes no secret of its intimate relationship with science fiction; in fact, cryonics traces its conceptual origins to the pulp magazines. Robert Ettinger, the founder of cryonics, first articulated the possibility of freezing dead bodies in the present and resurrecting them in the future in a 1948 short story entitled "The Penultimate Trump," which was published in *Startling Stories*. In Ettinger's fable, a wealthy tycoon funds a couple of scientists to perfect the methods of suspended animation. When he dies, the tycoon is put "to sleep in a nice refrigerator until people *really* know something about the body" (107; emphasis in original). Three hundred years later, the tycoon is resurrected, only to discover a world that no longer tolerates his attitudes of predatory capitalism; he is sentenced to a penal colony on Mars for his past crimes against humanity. Mars is no longer called Mars, however: "Now they call it Hell" (115).

The posthuman future, it would seem, remakes old myths into technological realities: Hell is recreated as a Martian penal colony, and the "last trump" of Christian apocalypticism is now preempted by biomedical science. The story's title, of course, alludes to Biblical tradition: "We shall not all sleep, but we shall all be changed, in a moment, in the twinkling of an eye, at the last trumpet. For the trumpet will sound, and the dead will be raised imperishable, and we shall be changed" (*New Oxford Annotated Bible*, 1 Cor. 15.51–52). Ettinger turns the "last trump" of Christian theology into a trope of science fiction, an ancient fable made real by the advances of medical research. In this way, "The Penultimate Trump" allegorizes the ability of prophetic narratives, rebooted in the mode of science fiction, to shape the posthuman future. Indeed, Ettinger's story itself poses as an overture or prelude—the penultimate trump—to actual biomedical immortality.

But even as it prefaces the entire cryonics movement, "The Penultimate Trump" is likewise prefaced by other speculative fictions. As Ettinger describes in his 2009 book *Youniverse: Toward a Self-Centered Philosophy of Immortalism and Cryonics*, he grew up "reading Hugo Gernsback's *Amazing Stories*," where he encountered Neil R. Jones's 1931 story "The Jameson Satellite," in which the eponymous professor is frozen in an orbiting capsule "for millions of years, during which humanity died out" (Ettinger, *Youniverse* 388). Discovered by the alien "Zoromes," creatures with "organic brains in mechanical bodies," Jameson is revived and equipped with a mechanical body of his own. As Ettinger observes: "I saw at once that the author had missed or avoided the main point of his own story. Why wait millions of years for possible aliens to rescue one eccentric? Why not have our own people do the job in the relatively near future, for everyone who chooses it? And that was the seed of cryonics, which lay dormant for many years" (388). Fertilized by science fiction, this seed would eventually grow into Ettinger's 1962 treatise, *The Prospect of Immortality*, which outlines Ettinger's mature vision of cryonics.

The Prospect of Immortality features a preface by Jean Rostand, a French biologist whose studies of cryopreservation had also inspired Ettinger. Yet while attesting to the technical plausibility of Ettinger's vision, Rostand's preface begins by recalling the fictional prehistory of cryostasis research in the work of an early SF writer named Edmond About, whose 1862 novel *The Man with the Broken Ear* had featured "a professor of biology who dries out a living man and then, after a 'suspension of life' lasting several decades, successfully resuscitates him." As Rostand comments: "What was, in 1861 [sic], only an amusing fantasy has in our time taken on a rather prophetic air; for, in the light of recent scientific developments, a similar method for preserving a human being no longer seems so impossible" (vii). Thus, the cryonic future recedes deeper into the literary past, *avant la lettre*, appearing now before its own origin—before "The Penultimate Trump," before "The Jameson Satellite." And we need not stop there: numerous stories about suspended animation, technological resurrection, and sleeping into the future were published before the official birth of cryonics, including H. P. Lovecraft's "Cool Air" (1928), E. D. Skinner's "The Corpse that Lived" (1930), and Edgar Rice Burroughs's "The Resurrection of Jimber-Jaw" (1937)—to say nothing of such foundational texts as Washington Irving's "Rip Van Winkle" (1819), Edward Bellamy's *Looking Backward: 2000–1887* (1888), and H. G. Wells's *The Sleeper Awakes* (1910). Science fiction, always getting ahead of itself, has been waiting a long time for reality to catch up.

In 1972 Ettinger wrote *Man into Superman*, an exhaustive analysis of our already existing capacity to turn posthuman. Considering the rapid acceleration of science and technology in recent history, the necessary methods to secure superhuman immortality are likely to appear at any moment, Ettinger claims. Should they fail to arrive before we die, we need merely chill out in cryonic suspension for a while: "Some have already decided to try for immortality and transhumanity, including the dozen or so chrononauts now lying frozen in their voyage through time . . . What marvelous future do they foresee, that they are determined to experience it? In that far season, what strange flowerings do they imagine, that they tug so insistently at Heinlein's 'door into summer'? (1).

Ettinger relies here on literary allusion to explain the motives of those who have already chosen to go postal. Heinlein's 1957 novel *The Door into Summer* features a cat named Petronius the Arbiter (Pete for short) who searches the house all winter long for a door that might open onto better weather. Pete's imaginary "door into summer" also comes to symbolize the technology of suspended animation that conveys Pete's frozen owner, Daniel Boone Davis, into the future (and then once more, after Daniel travels through time to intervene in his own history, back to the future). Ettinger cannily recycles Heinlein's metaphor: the coldness of winter aligned with the coldness of cryostasis, the warmth of summer aligned with the hope for a posthumous, posthuman future. Yet in the novel, this metaphor also stands for science fiction as such, for the technology of suspended animation becomes a "door into summer" to the extent that it rehearses the logic of science fiction, the prospect of radical difference from the here and now. As Daniel explains: "Oh, I had read H. G. Wells' *The Sleeper Awakes*, not only when the [suspended animation] insurance companies started giving away free copies, but before that, when it was just another classic novel . . . go beddy-bye and wake up in a different world. Maybe a better world, the way the insurance companies would have you believe . . . or maybe worse. But certainly different" (8). Heinlein's metaphor for the promise of a different world—which is to say, the promise made by science fiction throughout its history—accounts for Daniel's motivations in the novel, as well as the motivations of those who sign up for cryonic suspension in real life: "They tug so insistently at Heinlein's 'door into summer.'" Science fiction, it would seem, compels them.

Taking the inspirational force of science fiction for granted, Ettinger's book critically surveys a number of novels about superhuman evolution, including Van Vogt's *Slan*, Clarke's *Childhood's End*, Sturgeon's *Venus Plus X* (1960), and many others: "We must remake ourselves, and in planning for this we might begin by looking at previous speculations, the supermen of literature" (*Man into Superman* 22). Science fiction emerges as an important resource throughout *Man into Superman* for theorizing the challenges of building actual superhuman beings—but as much for what the genre gets wrong as for what it gets right.

In Ettinger's estimation, even as they inspire dreams of a better biology, the supermen of literature are often based on scientific impossibilities: "They provide some positive clues as to what may be, and also reveal crucial limitations in previous speculation and aspiration" (23). So it is necessary to modify the inventions of fiction, to make them work in the real world: "Instead of inventing superman, we can assemble him" (44). Ettinger imagines assembling posthuman biology from bits and pieces of already existing resources: "(1) rare human talents, (2) talents of other species, and (3) machine talents" (45). Of course, this method of "assembling superman" from existing components—inventing nothing but instead modifying and tinkering, composing the posthuman out of the resources at hand—also describes his own rhetorical method. For Ettinger takes scraps of science, morsels of philosophy, and a hefty sampling of SF stories from other authors and remixes them, assembling them into an account of a future that is already within our grasp. The posthuman comes into being as a motley patchwork of social and technical resources, held together by a backbone of science fiction.

The hybrid nature of posthumanist discourse, mashing together scientific concepts, sociological extrapolations, and SF scenarios, frequently renders the human present as a simulacrum of itself. Consider the 2010 documentary film *The Singularity Is Near: A True Story About the Future*, directed by Anthony Waller and Ray Kurzweil, based on Kurzweil's own best-selling 2005 pop-science book *The Singularity Is Near: When Humans Transcend Biology*. The documentary features a number of provocative interviews with technoscientific authorities—Eric Drexler, Marvin Minksy,

Aubrey de Grey, and others. These scientists and futurologists offer various insights on the "technological Singularity," Vernor Vinge's concept of a point in the future when the rate of technological change will rise exponentially, outstripping our capacities of foresight and thrusting us into the posthuman era. The documentary footage is constantly intercut with scenes from an SF story involving an AI named Ramona, invented by Kurzweil, as she struggles to gain legal recognition as an actual person and simultaneously stop a massive attack of "grey goo" nanobots before they devour the planet. The SF story constitutes the spine of the film, a continuous narrative punctuated by snippets of nonfiction.

Though the fictional and nonfictional components of the film are clearly demarcated, they nevertheless bleed into each other. Real-life figures—the inventor Ray Kurzweil, the lawyer Alan Dershowitz, and the self-help writer Tony Robbins—also appear as characters in the SF narrative. Dershowitz, for example, plays a pivotal role in the story: in a virtual courtroom of the future, his electronic avatar is called upon to defend the legal rights of artificial persons. Playing an avatar of himself in this scene, he draws attention to the fact that he also plays an avatar of himself in the nonfictional components of the documentary. That is to say, the film presents the mortal, human Alan Dershowitz as a mere prelude to an immortal, more-than-human Alan Dershowitz. Shifting back and forth between nonfiction and fiction—recreating our present as the preface to its "true story of the future"—all of the people in this film, real and imaginary, become fictions of themselves. Even while insisting that the Singularity will preserve and enhance the essential aspects of human nature ("We still consider it human intelligence . . . we're postbiological, not posthuman"), the film de-natures its real-life characters and makes them into puppets of the post-Singularity future. We all become characters in this storyline; as Kurzweil tells us, all humans are destined to become "much more machine than we are biological." In other words, our lived reality is made the avatar of science fiction.

Indeed, at the conclusion of the film, Ramona the AI addresses the audience directly: "It's interesting to think back now to a half of a century ago, the beginning of this twenty-first century. People actually went through each day without backing up their mind-files. Now that's frightening to contemplate! But biological humans had a golden opportunity that had never existed before. If they took care of themselves, the old-fashioned way, just for a little while longer, they had the prospect of joining me—here—on the other side." Science fiction here speaks to us from beyond the Singularity, from "the other side," compelling us to prepare for going postal—not in the future but already today.

Time and again, science fiction proves to be a mechanism by which we might think about and speculate upon the posthuman future. Whether in literary texts, pop-science books, or futurological documentaries, science fiction emerges as a mode of discourse that confronts humanism with the possibility of being otherwise. As nothing other than fiction, it performs the cognitive estrangements of the postal condition right now, opening the present to a different order of things that promises to be—or so they say—much stranger than fiction.

Works Cited

Badmington, Neil. *Alien Chic: Posthumanism and the Other Within.* London: Routledge, 2004. Print.

Bernal, J. D. *The World, the Flesh and the Devil: An Enquiry into the Future of the Three Enemies of the Rational Soul.* 1929. 2nd ed. Bloomington: Indiana UP, 1969. Print.

Bloch, Robert. "The End of Science Fiction." 1951. *The Reader's Bloch.* Vol. 1: *The Fear Planet and Other Unusual Destinations.* Ed. Stefan R. Dziemianowicz. Burton, MI: Subterranean, 2005. 287–99. Print.

Bukatman, Scott. *Terminal Identity: The Virtual Subject in Postmodern Science Fiction.* Durham, NC: Duke UP, 1993. Print.

Clarke, Arthur C. "A Choice of Futures." 1992. *Greetings, Carbon-Based Bipeds!: Collected Essays, 1934–1998.* Ed. Ian T. Macauley. New York: St. Martin's Press, 1999. 410–15. Print.

Clarke, Bruce. *Posthuman Metamorphosis: Narrative and Systems.* New York: Fordham UP, 2008. Print.

Csicsery-Ronay Jr., Istvan. *The Seven Beauties of Science Fiction.* Middletown, CT: Wesleyan UP, 2008. Print.

Derrida, Jacques. *The Post Card: From Socrates to Freud and Beyond.* 1980. Trans. Alan Bass. Chicago: U of Chicago P, 1987. Print.

Disch, Thomas M. *The Stuff Our Dream Are Made Of: How Science Fiction Conquered the World.* New York: Simon & Schuster, 1998. Print.

Doyle, Richard. *Wetwares: Experiments in Postvital Living.* Minneapolis: U of Minnesota P, 2003. Print.

Ettinger, Robert C. W. *Man into Superman: The Startling Potential of Human Evolution—and How to Be Part of It.* New York: St. Martin's, 1972. Print.

———. "The Penultimate Trump." *Startling Stories* 17.1 (March 1948): 104–15. Print.

———. *Youniverse: Toward a Self-Centered Philosophy of Immortalism and Cryonics.* Boca Raton, FL: Universal, 2009. Print.

Foster, Thomas. *The Souls of Cyberfolk: Posthumanism as Vernacular Theory.* Minneapolis: U of Minnesota P, 2005. Print.

Graham, Elaine L. *Representations of the Post/Human: Monsters, Aliens, and Others in Popular Culture.* New Brunswick, NJ: Rutgers UP, 2002. Print.

Haraway, Donna J. "A Cyborg Manifesto: Science, Technology, and Socialist-Feminism in the Late Twentieth Century." 1985. *Simians, Cyborgs, and Women: The Reinvention of Nature.* New York: Routledge, 1991. 149–81. Print.

Hayles, N. Katherine. *How We Became Posthuman: Virtual Bodies in Cybernetics, Literature, and Informatics.* Chicago: U of Chicago P, 1999. Print.

Heinlein, Robert A. *The Door into Summer.* 1957. New York: Del Rey, 1986. Print.

———. "Guest of Honor Speech: Denvention 1, The Third World Science Fiction Convention, July 4, 1941." *Worldcon Guest of Honor Speeches.* Ed. Mike Resnick and Joe Siclari. Deerfield, IL: ISFiC, 2006. 13–25. Print.

Huntington, John. *Rationalizing Genius: Ideological Strategies in the Classic American Science Fiction Short Story.* New Brunswick, NJ: Rutgers UP, 1989. Print.

New Oxford Annotated Bible, with the Apocrypha: Revised Standard Version. 1962. 2nd ed. Ed. Herbert G. May and Bruce M. Metzger. New York: Oxford UP, 1977. Print.

Rostand, Jean. "Preface." Trans. Sandra Danenberg. *The Prospect of Immortality* by Robert C. W. Ettinger. Garden City, NY: Doubleday, 1964. vii–ix. Print.

The Singularity Is Near: A True Story About the Future. Dir. Anthony Waller and Ray Kurzweil. Fighting Ant Productions/Cometstone Pictures/Exponential Films, 2010. Film.

Smith, Edward E. ("Doc"). "Guest of Honor Speech: Chicon 1, The Second World Science Fiction Convention, July 4, 1941." *Worldcon Guest of Honor Speeches*. Ed. Mike Resnick and Joe Siclari. Deerfield, IL: ISFiC, 2006. 6–12. Print.

Van Vogt, A.E. *Slan*. 1946. New York: Orb, 1998. Print.

Vinge, Vernor. "Technological Singularity." *Whole Earth Review* 81 (Winter 1993): 88–95. Print.

Vint, Sherryl. *Bodies of Tomorrow: Technology, Subjectivity, Science Fiction*. Toronto: U of Toronto P, 2007. Print.

Warner Jr., Harry. *All Our Yesterdays: An Informal History of Science Fiction Fandom in the Forties*. 1969. Chicago: Advent, 1972. Print.

Wolfe, Cary. *What Is Posthumanism?* Minneapolis: U of Minnesota P, 2009. Print.

CHAPTER 41

FEMINISM

LISA YASZEK

It is a truth universally acknowledged that there are as many definitions of science fiction as there are people within the SF community. The same can be said of "feminism," a seemingly simple word that has been used to describe a dizzying array of social activities, political stances, and analytic outlooks since Hubertine Auclert coined the term in the 1880s (Dicker 10). Yet by 1981, Joanna Russ could easily identify scores of women writing a specific kind of future-oriented fiction that celebrated female agency, community, and sexuality in reaction to "what [its] authors believe society . . . and/or women lack in the here and now" ("Recent" 144). While Russ and her cohort were the first generation to identify overtly as feminist SF authors, they were by no means the first authors to write politically charged speculative fiction about science, society, and sex. For nearly 200 years, writers have used speculative fiction consciously and collectively to dramatize the political issues most central to women living in a technocultural world and to create a sense of wonder about the interrelated possibilities of social and scientific change.

At its core, SF is naturally compatible with the project of feminism. Feminist political thinkers often employ speculative techniques that should feel very familiar to SF readers. First and foremost, feminist writers educate their audiences about sex and gender inequities by estranging them from the world as they think they know it. They do so by figuring the people who experience these inequities as alien others or strangers traveling through strange lands. After illuminating the problem at hand, feminist writers often offer solutions by forecasting alternate worlds where women can mitigate their own alienation and work to build a better future. Writers of feminist fiction use SF to intervene into social and scientific narratives not of their own making, recreating them as, in Robin Roberts's words, "the feminist fairy tales that are needed to counteract the misogynistic stories of our culture" (6). As a corollary, we can say that feminist political writers use speculative techniques to intervene in social and scientific arrangements not of their own making, recasting them in terms that stake claims for women in the future imaginary.

Indeed, the use of speculative techniques to make the case for feminist action is as old as feminism itself. Feminist history officially begins with the Seneca Falls Convention of 1848, when American women lodged their first formal, communal protest again taxation without representation (see Wellman). The beliefs of the women attending the convention are summed up in Elizabeth Cady Stanton's famous "Declaration of Sentiments and Resolutions":

> We hold these truths to be self-evident: that all men and women are created equal; that they are endowed by their Creator with certain inalienable rights; that among these are life, liberty, and the pursuit of happiness . . . Whenever any form of government becomes destructive of these ends, it is the right of those who suffer from it to refuse allegiance to it, and to insist up the institution of a new government . . . Such has been the patient sufferance of the women under this government, and such is now the necessity which constrains them to demand the equal station to which they are entitled. (252)

In good science-fictional fashion, Stanton estranges conventional assumptions about the democratic nature of the United States by strategically rewriting one of America's founding documents: the Declaration of Independence. In Stanton's version, it is not "all men" who are created equal, but "all women and men," and not all American colonists who have patiently suffered under the tyranny of Great Britain, but, more specifically, all women deprived of their natural rights under the tyrannical rule of the US government. As Stanton's alternate history suggests, the United States teeters on the brink of disaster because it fails to live up to own democratic ideals; instead, it repeats the abuses of England against its own female citizens, making them strangers in their own land and fostering calls for revolution.

The solution proposed by Stanton in her "Declaration" is one that quickly became the core of the liberal-feminist movement in America—and one that should, in its broadest dimensions, feel familiar to SF fans the world over. First, Stanton posits that "women of this country ought to be enlightened in regard to the laws under which they live"—especially when those laws contradict the natural rights of humanity as a whole (254). Next, she insists that feminists must band together with like-minded people to change the social and political system from within: "We shall employ agents, circulate tracts, petition the State and National legislatures, and endeavor to enlist the pulpit and the press on our behalf" (254). It is only by pursuing this course of action that American women—and indeed, all Americans—can hope to avoid the disaster of internal revolt, building a truly democratic future that "secur[es] to woman an equal participation with men in the various trades, professions, and commerce" (255).

While Stanton's speech employs basic techniques of SF storytelling, other feminist authors of this period more directly explored the possibility of new futures derived from new arrangements of science, society, and gender. This was especially apparent in the work of biochemist and pragmatic feminist Ellen Richards, founder of what has variously been called "euthenics," "domestic science," and "home economics." As Richards explains in the introduction to *Euthenics: The Science of Controllable Environment* (1910), the United States is confronting an imminent economic crisis because "[p]robably not more than twenty-five percent in any community are doing a full day's work such as they would be capable of doing if they were in perfect health" (4). The problem, according to Richards, is that women as housewives have been granted moral authority over their families but given little exposure to the new scientific knowledge or labor-saving devices that "in six cases out of ten ... could cut in half the housekeeping budget and double the comfort of living" (152). But if they are trained in the science of better living through nutrition, sanitation, and family management, then women will become "*an important factor and economic force in improving the national health and increasing the national wealth*" (141; emphasis in original). Again, in good science-fictional fashion, Richards estranges conventional ideas about women's work in the private sphere of the home as being essentially distinct from the public sphere of politics, economics, and technoscience. Instead, she insists that understanding women's work both in relation to and as a kind of industrial labor is critical to the long-term success of the nation.

Richards also refused the conventional notion of women's work as labor that happens only in the home, insisting that modern housewives must become "economic leaders in the body politic" (152). After citing a case where a woman trained in the principles of domestic science saved the hospital where she worked over $12,000 per year, Richards proposes that "[i]t may be said without fear of contradiction that the future well-being of society is largely in the hands of woman ... If civic authorities felt that women's leagues were informed bodies of women whose suggestions they would make no error in adopting, more legislation could be effected" (152). She went on to add that the problems of industrial society could be solved "if the aid of scientifically-trained women is brought into service to work in harmony with the engineer who has already accomplished so much" (158). While liberal feminists such as Stanton extrapolated from contemporary political ideals to make readers think differently about women's roles in a democratic society, pragmatic ones such as Richards extrapolated from emergent scientific and social developments to illustrate women's real worth in the economic arena. At their core, however, both types of feminists agreed that education and collective action were crucial to building better futures for all.

Women writing utopian fiction at this time incorporated both aspects of First Wave feminism into their storytelling. This is particularly apparent in Mary E. Bradley Lane's *Mizora: A Prophecy* (1881) and Charlotte Perkins Gilman's *Herland* (1915), both of which depict single-sex societies organized around mothering, homemaking, and community building. The women of Mizora and Herland enjoy unprecedented standards of living because they apply the principles of municipal housekeeping on the widest possible scale, abolishing the distinction between the public and private spheres and treating the entire nation as one family. Significantly, these utopian heroines are also scientists who make fantastic advances in psychology and genetics, as well as engineers who transform their Arctic and jungle homes into fertile paradises. Lane and Gilman combined the differing feminist ideals of their time to illustrate how women who traverse the private and public spheres might initiate the next stage of human evolution.

Utopian dreams also permeate the first generation of women's stories for the SF pulp magazines. Like their male counterparts, the dozens of women who helped establish SF as a distinct mode of fiction used their chosen genre to create a sense of wonder in readers regarding the possibilities of modern science and technology. Sometimes, they used their chosen genre to speculate specifically about the ways that advanced technoscience might change sex and gender relations. For example, the protagonists of Lilith Lorraine's "Into the 28th Century" (1930) enjoy labor-free banquets of jeweled food flakes and sparking beverages, while the women of Leslie F. Stone's "Women with Wings" (1930) delegate housework to autonomous robots. Meanwhile, in Sophie Wenzel Ellis's "Creatures of the Light" (1930), the dangers of childbirth are eliminated by the perfection of glass wombs, and in Stone's "Men with Wings" (1929), women are free to pursue careers outside the home because children are raised by trained professionals. Much like Lane and Gilman before them, early female SF authors made feminist ideas about women's work central to their storytelling practices. While presuffrage authors used these ideas to illustrate why women deserved the vote, however, their postsuffrage counterparts used them to remind readers that political reform must be accompanied by scientific and social reform as well.

The necessary interrelations of political, social, and scientific reform are particularly apparent in Lorraine's "Into the 28th Century." Lorraine's story relates the adventures of Anthony, an educated ex-Navy officer from the early twentieth century who longs to live in a world that combines aristocratic sensibilities with democratic freedoms. His dream is realized when he is whisked forward in time to twenty-eighth-century Corpus Christi, where war, poverty, and disease have been eliminated and people are free to pursue lives filled with art, science, and sport. It is, in many ways, a world that seems to have fully realized the liberal-feminist dream of equality between men and women: Anthony is brought to the future by a co-ed group of students using the physics of time travel to learn history, and later he enjoys a rousing (and surprisingly chaste) game of naked water-ball with his new friends. But this is also a world structured along the lines of municipal housekeeping: when they take their place as citizen-workers in the World State, the men and women of Lorraine's future do so in specifically and conventionally gendered ways. While men take the lead in "invention, mechanics, mathematics, and the more strenuous sports," women assume top government positions because they are concerned with "education, with the patronage of art, science and literature, [and] with the beautification and spiritualization of all life," making them the "ideal directors" of their world (257).

Lorraine's twenty-eighth century is more than just a reaction to the specific feminist ideals of the author's time; it is also a dramatization of the larger feminist story, demonstrating how and why educated people might work together for social and political change. As both Lorraine's protagonist and her readers soon learn, the utopian World State is the end result of a centuries-old struggle between a cohort of "Industrial Dictators" who tried to produce more efficient workers by lobotomizing the entire human race and a coalition of young "reformers, scientists, and radicals" who successfully opposed them (257). The success of "The Great Revolt" depended specifically on a "feminist movement" that began in the early twentieth century when women won economic equality, continues through the years of war when women take on all the same hardships as men while continuing to be primary caretakers for their families, and then culminates in the postwar era when a woman is installed as the first World President. Speaking on behalf of her entire sex, the World President announces that women refuse to bear any more children until men agree to a new social and moral order that respects life above all else. The men reluctantly agree because "there was nothing else to do," but within a few short generations they become genuine champions of "the new chivalry" because it leads to unprecedented advances in science, economics, and the arts (257). For Lorraine, then, the collective actions that women take to secure freedom, equality, and respect are key to the creation of a truly democratic and utopian future for all.

When American women achieved the vote with the passage of the Constitution's Nineteenth Amendment in 1920, it seemed that the goals of First Wave feminism had been achieved (see Hewitt). And it is true that while women continued the project of progressive reform, feminism as a political movement was displaced from the public consciousness by events such as the Great Depression, World War II, and the Cold War. But feminism, like other forms of progressive and radical politics, enjoyed a resurgence in the 1960s and 1970s. New political groups such as the National Organization for Women (NOW), founded in 1966, worked to create laws derived from the Civil Rights Act of 1964, which guaranteed equal access to jobs regardless of race or gender, and Title IX of the Education Amendment Acts of 1972, which banned sex discrimination in all federally funded education programs (see Rosen 70–81). Meanwhile, grassroots organizations encouraged women to assume control of their private lives by learning how to manage their own bodies and taking advantage of new household technologies to redistribute domestic labor more equitably (see Strasser 310–11).

Given that this new generation of feminists celebrated its history while setting new goals for the future, it is no surprise that authors continued to use speculative techniques in their political writing. Second Wave feminists dreamed of overtly science-fictional futures where women might overcome their alienation and secure equality with men by using science and technology to change humanity itself. As radical philosopher Shulamith Firestone argues in *The Dialectics of Sex* (1970), "Unlike economic class, sex class sprang directly from a biological reality: men and women were created different, and not equally privileged" (93). Accordingly, Firestone links the development of cultural patriarchy and the logics of domination attending it to the biological dependency women experience during pregnancy, childbirth, and childrearing. In this scenario—one that Firestone herself acknowledges is perhaps more estranging than anything previously proposed by feminists—women's alienation stems not from modern political or economic systems that limit their agency in the public sphere, but from ancient evolutionary arrangements structuring interpersonal relations in the private sphere of the home.

As Firestone reminds readers, however, "we are no longer just animals" and "'natural' is not necessarily a 'human' value" (94). Instead, new fertility technologies make it possible for women to seize "control of reproduction" and transform "the social institutions of childbearing and childrearing" (95). If artificial reproduction replaces its biological counterpart, then "children would be born to both sexes equally . . . The division of labor would be ended by the elimination of labor altogether (cybernation). The tyranny of the biological family would be broken. And with it, the psychology of power" (95). Like Ellen Richards before her, Firestone extrapolates from new techno-scientific developments to imagine brave new futures for women and men alike; but where Richards saw domestic science as a tool for eliminating male privilege, Firestone identifies new reproductive technologies as the key to eliminating sex distinction altogether. It is only by doing so, she contends, that people can build a new world characterized by truly novel human relations.

Like their activist counterparts, SF authors of the period criticized sexual and economic exploitation while celebrating women's attempts to prevent it. Stories including Lisa Tuttle's "Wives" (1979), Marge Piercy's *Woman on the Edge of Time* (1976), and Suzy McKee Charnas's *Walk to the End of the World* (1973) and *Motherlines* (1978) all imagine futures where women (or, in Tuttle's story, feminine aliens) are literally transformed into doll-like creatures for the amusement of their husband-owners. But they also imagine that women might fight these bad futures in a variety of ways. While Tuttle's alien protagonist chooses to commit suicide rather than spend the rest of her life in drag as a human wife, the women of Charnas's world unite and wage war against men to prevent individual women from ever having to make such choices. Meanwhile, in Piercy's novel, one woman from a present-day Earth much like our own gladly turns the weapons of science against men, even at the cost of her own life, to ensure that such bad futures will never occur at all.

Authors also explored the possibility of creating truly egalitarian new worlds through domestic and reproductive reform. Some, such as Ursula K. Le Guin in *The Left Hand of Darkness* (1969), used anthropology and sociology to demonstrate how androgynous cultures might distribute childbearing responsibilities and thus power relations more equitably. Others, such as Piercy in *Woman on the Edge of Time* and Joanna Russ in *The Female Man* (1975), looked to new reproductive technosciences instead. In Piercy's novel, babies gestate in mechanical wombs, while both men and women use hormone therapy to produce breast milk and experience mothering. Meanwhile, the technosciences of Russ's single-sex utopia liberate women to engage in activities ranging from farming to dueling. Like the utopian writers who preceded them, feminist SF authors challenged conventional ideas about gender by doing away with distinctions between the public and private spheres. The new worlds that emerge from such reform are not based on essentialist notions of feminine nurture and benevolence, however. Instead, they demonstrate how men and women alike might achieve full humanity by using technology to redistribute both productive and reproductive labor.

Like their literary predecessors, Second Wave feminists often included visions of both dystopia and utopia in their fiction. This is particularly apparent in Russ's *The Female Man*, which follows the adventures of four women who are variants of the same genotype but who were raised in very different worlds. Three of these four worlds are dystopias: Jeannine hails from an Earth where the Great Depression never ended and Second Wave feminism never happened; Joanna comes from a present-day Earth where women have gained a limited and somewhat schizophrenic equality by acting like stereotypical men in the workplace and stereotypical women in the bedroom; and Jael comes from a future where women and men have literally gone to war against one another. In all three worlds, men show a clear preference for women who look and act like Playboy bunnies, but in Jael's world, war breaks out because men literally try to remake the world in the image of the Playboy Club, long an object of Second Wave feminist scorn (see Steinem). Bereft of their women, the men of Jael's world force the weakest boys to undergo extensive surgery to become "femmes"—"monument[s] of irrelevancy on high heels . . . [,] pretty girl[s] with too much of the right curves and . . . bobbing, springing, pink feather boa[s]" (171). Thus, Russ demands that readers think about both the long history of economic and gendered exploitation in our own world and how that kind of exploitation might expand to transcend sex difference in the future.

Russ also demands that readers acknowledge women's anger at this history. Jael is a self-described assassin who travels through time and space to recruit other women into the war against Manland. While Jeannine and Joanna are each willing to help in their own ways, the fourth variant on the J-genotype, Janet, is not. Hailing from the all-female world of Whileaway, Janet argues that her planet must remain hidden if there is ever to be a utopian future for women. Much to everyone's surprise, Jael reveals that the plague that killed all of Whileaway's men resulted from Jael's war against Manland; as Jael affirms: "I am the plague . . . I and the war I fought built your world for you, I and those like me, we gave you a thousand years of peace and love and the Whileawayan flowers nourish themselves on the bones of the men we have slain" (211). Like Lorraine had before her, Russ imagines that women might have to take drastic collective action to fight pernicious patriarchal and capitalist futures. But earlier authors usually imagined that such action would be predicated on a kind of benevolent maternal instinct and that women would naturally ally themselves with sympathetic male scientists to rationally and peacefully prevent bad futures from unfolding. Russ, however, insists that women are not just saintly mothers but complex human beings who are just as likely to use the tools of science against men as they are to ally themselves with men of science—especially when those tools have been used against them.

While the quest for sex and gender equality continues today, the development of new information and communication technologies and the advent of global capitalism have brought new issues to the attention of activists and authors. In contrast to earlier feminists who saw science as one locus of discrimination among many, the Third Wave feminists who emerged in the 1980s propose that thinking carefully about the relations of science, society, and gender should be a central priority for all women (see Gillis, Howie, and Munford). This argument is advanced most famously in Donna Haraway's groundbreaking "Cyborg Manifesto" (1985), which appropriates the figure of the eponymous—part-organic, part-technological—entity from science and SF to illustrate how women are exploited by, enmeshed in, and even complicit with new economic and technological networks. As Haraway puts it, "The cyborg is a creature of social reality as well as a creature of fiction (174)—"the illegitimate offspring of militarism and patriarchal capitalism, not to mention state socialism" (176). Like earlier generations of feminists, Haraway begins her call to political action by estranging readers, but she departs from her predecessors by refusing conventional ideas about women as either victims of or mistresses over science and technology, insisting instead on the strange but true fact that all women—indeed, all modern people—are metaphorical cyborgs with identities created by their complex and sometime contradictory places in various technoscientific networks.

In contrast, then, to the disenfranchised housewives and alienated sex-dolls of earlier feminist writing, the cyborg represents both a frightening reality and a potentially better future. As Haraway reminds readers, the cyborg might be the accidental by-product of dystopic scientific and economic forces, but "illegitimate offspring are often exceedingly unfaithful to their origins. Their fathers are, after all, inessential" (176). Instead, the cyborg takes pleasure in its ability to interface with a wide range of other machines, animals, and people. As such, it represents the "transgressed boundaries, potent fusions, and dangerous possibilities which progressive people might explore as one part of needed political work" (178). Following her "cyborg myth" (177) to its logical conclusion, Haraway proposes a model of affinity politics in which seemingly disparate political actors come together temporarily to "subvert [the forms of] command and control" characteristic of technoscientific modernity (198); in doing so, such actors create space for meaningful change. Given that Haraway makes explicit the science-fictional and speculative nature of her cyborg myth, especially as it pertains to women in the integrated circuit of global capitalism, it is no surprise that she identifies feminist SF authors—including Anne McCaffrey, Joanna Russ, and Octavia E. Butler—as inspirational figures exploring the promises and perils of cyborg politics in their fiction.

Haraway credits recent feminist SF authors as an inspiration for her thinking about the potential future of cyborg politics, but as postcolonial feminist Chela Sandoval demonstrates, people of color have been engaging in such politics for some time:

> Colonized people of the Americas have already developed the cyborg skills required for survival under technohuman conditions as a requisite for survival under domination over the last three hundred years. Interestingly, however, theorists of globalization . . . [act] as if these politics have emerged with the advent of electronic technology alone, and not as a requirement of consciousness in opposition developed under previous forms of domination. (408)

For Sandoval, cyborg skills—what she calls "the methodologies of the oppressed"—are not just the foundation for a new kind of politics; instead, they comprise one of the most effective modes of resistance to emerge from technocultural modernity (409). For well over 300 years, people of color have evinced a steadfast commitment to "double vision," moving back and forth between dominant and subaltern points of view, using the latter to comment on and even change the former. In doing so, Sandoval contends, they build a better future for themselves, their communities, and humanity as a whole.

While feminist theorists such as Haraway and Sandoval use the notion of the cyborg metaphorically to describe certain kinds of progressive politics, their activist counterparts enact those politics quite literally. In the early 1990s, punk singer Kathleen Hanna and her sister musicians from Bikini Kill started the Riot Grrrl movement, encouraging women to appropriate guitars and related technologies of music production to create the "sense of community that we need in order to figure out how bullshit like racism, able-bodieism, ageism, speciesism, classism, thinism, sexism, anti-semitism and heterosexism figures in our own lives" (Hanna; see also Marcus). This trend continues today with the Gamer Girl movement (see Misa) and is best summed up by "The Gamer Girl Manifesto," a 2-minute video produced by YouTube user Sexy Nerd Girl Presents that took the Internet by storm in December 2011. As the anonymous women featured in this video puts it: "I am a gamer . . . and I am a woman. I don't need you to hold my hand . . . No I won't tell you what I'm wearing . . . I'm here to game, I'm here to pwn . . . Don't judge me based on my ID . . . No, I'm not one of the boys, but neither are you. We're all on the same team, we're gamers" (Sexy Nerd). As they appropriate conventionally masculine technologies such as guitars and joysticks, riot and gamer girls become the science-fictional heroines of their own lives, using technology to create temporary utopian spaces—the concert hall, the video game—where they can test new social and sexual arrangements that carry over into their daily lives.

Insights derived from Third Wave feminism are central to the imaginative practices of contemporary SF authors. For example, feminist writers often use the SF subgenre of cyberpunk to dramatize the gendered implications of life in the integrated circuit of high-tech capitalism. Novels including Pat Cadigan's *Synners* (1991) and Melissa Scott's *Trouble and her Friends* (1994) predict that the dream of a future in which people use new technologies to escape the messy problems of the material world will eventually trigger information apocalypse and social destruction. But these authors also imagine that those who recognize why bodies still matter in the world of computation might transform bad futures into better ones where women can pursue satisfying politics, work, and even romance.

Like their cyberpunk counterparts, feminist writers of color intervene into contemporary narratives of science, society, and gender in provocative ways. This is particularly true of African-American author Octavia E. Butler. Nearly every story Butler published between her literary debut in 1971 and her death in 2006 uses the classic SF theme of encounter with the alien other to complicate readers' thinking about technoscience, gender, and racial difference. Most notably, "Blood Child" (1984) and the "Xenogenesis" trilogy (1987–89) imagine that humans and aliens might use advanced technologies to breed the new, hybrid races that are both species' only hope for survival. Significantly, the offspring of these new races experience both sadness about the passing of old ways and anxiety about their uncertain futures; and yet, Butler's stories are ultimately imbued with great hope because her characters look forward to truly new futures that do not simply repeat the past but come with challenges and triumphs all their own.

The issues central to these two strands of Third Wave feminist SF come together most strikingly in Geoff Ryman's *Air: Or, Have Not Have* (2004), which fuses them with the concerns of Third World feminism (see Mohanty). Ryman's novel follows the adventures of Mae Chung, an illiterate but highly intelligent "fashion expert" from a remote, rural Asian village that serves as a beta testing site for "Air," a new information technology much like the Internet that operates within the human brain. Mae is one of the few people to successfully negotiate Air during its first test run, and the experience leaves her determined to make sure that all her people are both financially and intellectually prepared for the new technology when it goes global in one year. Capitalizing on the latest fashion trend—clothing "expressing . . . interest in Third World issues" (142)—Mae and her friend Kwan Wing use all the media technologies at their disposal to build a wildly successful business exporting traditional dress and embroidery designs to Western fashion houses. Along the way, they forge new friendships (and a few new enmities) within their village, throughout their nation, and across the globe.

Ryman is careful to explore both the perils and promises of life in the integrated circuit of global capitalism. Air is owned by the United Nations and thus technically by all the people of Earth, but it is a Western technology that requires Mae and her friends to adopt modern Western values, including the habit of "greed and gouging" (70). This new technology quickly proves to be more complex than it first appears, however, allowing Mae and Kwan to raise global awareness about the lives of women and ethnic minorities in their village—lives that have been, until that point in time, downplayed or erased from official national culture. It also enables Ryman's heroine to quite literally save her village from destruction—first by working with meteorologists across the globe to determine exactly when seasonal floods are most likely to strike her part of the world and then by narrowcasting the effects of local flooding to her fashion contacts in the West, who respond with the emergency provisions Mae's people need to survive and rebuild.

Like their real-world counterparts, the fictional women of *Air* actively appropriate new technologies and, in so doing, change conventional ideas about sex and gender. Mae is initially attracted to Air not simply because she wants to help her village become modern, but because she is afraid that her drunkard husband has taken on a bad loan that will cost them the family farm. This drives her to cast off deeply ingrained assumptions that economic dealings are "men's business" in which women "cannot interfere" and to acquire economic independence through her fashion website (45). Later, when Mae sets up a school to prepare people for Air, it is the women who take advantage of this new opportunity, using the knowledge they gain from Mae to join her business and establish competing enterprises of their own. Finally, Mae's newfound economic and intellectual autonomy leads her to sexual autonomy as well. This theme unfolds primarily in relation to the handsome widower Kuei Ken, who first becomes Mae's lover and then, later on, her domestic caretaker and partner in the creation of a "new kind of family" (382). This family includes Mae, Ken, their five children from previous marriages, the one child they are about to have together, and Siao Chung, Mae's former brother-in-law and current business partner/lover. Thus, Ryman strategically updates the classic SF tradition, ending his novel with a celebration of the visionary, technologically savvy hero—or in this case, heroine—who is rewarded for virtuous labor with both money and love.

The fact that *Air* was written by a man underscores one final, important point about feminist SF: while it is most obviously the province of women who have experienced discrimination within patriarchal scientific and social systems, men can engage feminist issues as well. This has been true since the inception of SF as a modern literary genre. In the 1920s and 1930s, *Amazing* magazine editor Hugo Gernsback vocally advocated suffrage and the modern birth control movement while fostering the careers of women writers such as Clare Winger Harris and Leslie F. Stone (see Donawerth). Around the same time, Henry Kuttner used the letters forum of *Weird Tales* as a pulpit from which to criticize the tendency toward sexually lurid SF cover art, arguing that the often misogynist nature of this art detracted from the serious issues explored by authors including his wife C. L. Moore. After World War II, SF editors—including Anthony Boucher of *The Magazine of Fantasy and Science Fiction* and Leo Margulies of *Fantastic Universe*—celebrated the new generation of women's domestic SF as a groundbreaking phenomenon that provided readers with "sensitive depictions of the future from a woman's point of view" (Boucher). While these editors and authors did not address feminist issues in their own fiction, they saw women who did so as making important contributions to the ongoing development of SF as a unique popular genre (see Yaszek).

Since the 1960s and 1970s, men have begun to incorporate feminist themes into their own fiction. For example, John Crowley's *Little, Big* (1981) and many of John Varley's "Eight Worlds" stories (1974–92) use family dramas as focusing lenses through which to explore the feminist premise that humanity is unnatural and, as such, will evolve into different—ideally, more egalitarian—forms of life. Other authors use family dramas to assess the technocultural arrangements of the information age; this is particularly apparent in Bruce Sterling's *Islands in the Net* (1988) and *Holy Fire* (1996), which explore how new information and biomedical technologies might dissolve women's traditional life patterns, thereby encouraging them to forge new relations with their family members and the larger world. Other stories examine the impact of domesticity on men as scientific and social creatures: tales in this vein include Trent Hergenrader's "From the Mouth of Babes" (2006), Albert E. Cowdrey's "Animal Magnetism" (2006), and Kim Stanley Robinson's "Science in the Capital" trilogy (2004–07). While Hergenrader and Robinson explore how straight men might try to reform science from their perspectives as lovers and fathers, Cowdry's lighthearted tale about two male werewolves and their female dog stakes out a space for gay families in the future imaginary. Taken together, such stories demonstrate how men, like women, can use SF to creatively revise dominant understandings of science, society, and gender as they structure our thinking at the beginning of the new millennium.

WORKS CITED

Boucher, Anthony. "Introduction to Alice Eleanor Jones's 'Created He Them.'" *The Best from Fantasy and Science Fiction: Fifth Series*. New York: Doubleday, 1956. 125. Print.

Dicker, Rory. *A History of U.S. Feminisms*. Berkeley, CA: Seal, 2008. Print.

Donawerth, Jane L. "Science Fiction by Women in the Early Pulps." *Utopian and Science Fiction by Women: Worlds of Difference*. Ed. Jane L. Donawerth and Carol A. Kolmerten. Syracuse, NY: Syracuse UP, 1994. 137–52. Print.

Firestone, Shulamith. *The Dialectic of Sex: The Case for Feminist Revolution*. 1970. New York: Farrar, Straus, and Giroux, 2003. Print.

Gillis, Stacy, Gillian Howie, and Rebecca Munford, eds. *Third Wave Feminism: A Critical Exploration.* 2004. 2nd ed. New York: Palgrave Mcmillan, 2007. Print.

Hanna, Kathleen. "The Riot Grrrl Manifesto." 1991. *One War Art.* Web. Sept. 4, 2013. http://onewarart.org/riot_grrrl_manifesto.htm.

Haraway, Donna. "A Manifesto for Cyborgs: Science, Technology, and Socialist Feminism in the 1980s." 1985. *Coming to Terms: Feminism, Theory, Politics.* Ed. Elizabeth Weed. 1989. New York: Routledge, 2013. 173–204. Print.

Hewitt, Nancy A. "From Seneca Falls to Suffrage: Reimagining a 'Master' Narrative in U.S. Women's History." *No Permanent Waves: Recasting Histories of U.S. Feminism.* Ed. Nancy Hewitt. New Brunswick, NJ: Rutgers UP, 2010. 15–38. Print.

Lorraine, Lilith. "Into the 28th Century." *Science Wonder Quarterly* 1.2 (Winter 1930): 250–67. Print.

Marcus, Sara. *Girls to the Front: The True Story of the Riot Grrrl Revolution.* New York: HarperCollins, 2010. Print.

Misa, Thomas J. "Gender Codes: Defining the Problem." *Gender Codes: Why Women Are Leaving Computing.* Ed. Thomas J. Misa. Hoboken, NJ: Wiley, 2010. 3–24. Print.

Mohanty, Chandra Talpade, ed. *Feminism Without Borders: Decolonizing Theory, Practicing Solidarity.* Durham, NC: Duke UP, 2003. Print.

Richards, Ellen H. *Euthenics: The Science of Controllable Environment; A Plea for Better Living Conditions as a First Step Toward Higher Human Efficiency.* Boston: Whitcomb & Barrows, 1910. Print. http://catalog.hathitrust.org/Record/006528658. September 25, 2012.

Roberts, Robin. *A New Species: Gender and Science in Science Fiction.* Urbana: U of Illinois P, 1993. Print.

Rosen, Ruth. *The World Split Open: How the Modern Women's Movement Changed America.* 2000. New York: Penguin, 2001. Print.

Russ, Joanna. *The Female Man.* 1975. Boston: Beacon P, 1986. Print.

———. "Recent Feminist Utopias." 1981. *To Write Like a Woman: Essays in Feminism and Science Fiction.* Bloomington: Indiana UP, 1995. 133–48. Print.

Ryman, Geoff. *Air: Or, Have Not Have.* New York: St. Martins, 2004. Print.

Sandoval, Chela. *Methodology of the Oppressed.* Minneapolis: U of Minnesota P, 2000. Print.

Sexy Nerd Girl Presents. "Gamer Girl Manifesto." *YouTube.* December 2011. Web. Sept. 4, 2013. http://www.youtube.com/watch?v=XrBoeMF4FYs&list=TLaA9gDOaIHNE.

Stanton, Elizabeth Cady. "Declaration of Sentiments and Resolutions." 1848. *Women, the Family, and Freedom: The Debate in Documents, Volume One: 1750–1880.* Ed. Susan Groag Bell and Karen M. Offen. Stanford, CA: Stanford UP, 1983. 252–55. Print.

Steinem, Gloria. "I Was a Playboy Bunny." 1963. *Outrageous Acts and Everyday Rebellions.* New York: Holt, Rinehart and Winston, 1983. 29–69. Print.

Strasser, Susan. *Never Done: A History of American Housework.* 1982. New York: Henry Holt, 2000. Print.

Wellman, Judith. *The Road to Seneca Falls: Elizabeth Cady Stanton and the First Woman's Rights Convention.* Champaign: U of Illinois P, 2004. Print.

Yaszek, Lisa. *Galactic Suburbia: Recovering Women's Science Fiction.* Columbus: Ohio State UP, 2008. Print.

CHAPTER 42

LIBERTARIANISM AND ANARCHISM

NEIL EASTERBROOK

IN *Science Fiction After 1900: From the Steam Man to the Stars*, Brooks Landon describes the range and diversity of science fiction within the last century. One of his central claims is that "SF works regularly interrogate political and social norms, frequently, if not usually, advancing a general libertarian philosophy that mistrusts authority in all its official guises" (109). As an "oppositional literature," most SF challenges "prevailing wisdom and received ideas," producing what he calls a "radical parallax"—where SF's alternative narratives torque the present to present the audience with a distanced, estranged perspective (109). SF has been oppositional even to itself. In *Science Fiction*, Roger Luckhurst examines how, especially since the emergence of the British New Wave in the 1960s, SF history might be charted as an explicit reworking of its own conceits and conventions: the New Space Opera or the New Weird provide examples. Luckhurst concentrates on Iain M. Banks, Ken MacLeod, and China Miéville, arguing that, in the 1990s, SF everted its own history, interrogating yet revivifying its received wisdom with an unprecedented vigor (220–44).

That two of the most sophisticated, accomplished accounts of SF's history and thematic development centrally agree on this point should surprise no one. SF has long thought of itself as a literature of ideas, and insofar as these ideas trace an alternate future or ask readers to reflect on alternate presents, it is oppositional by definition. One way that SF thinking strikes oppositional stances is its utopian invocations of *political* alternatives. Often opened up as possibilities brought about through changes in technoscience, these oppositional alternatives frequently critique the gap between what we say about ourselves and what we actually do. One articulation that describes SF's post-Enlightenment relation to both technoscience and politics comes from Ken MacLeod: "Science fiction is essentially the literature of progress, and the political philosophy of SF is essentially liberal" (231). By "liberal," MacLeod means that set of ideas that emerged in Europe during the mid- to late eighteenth century: "political liberty, personal autonomy, free thought and the free exchange of goods" (231), to which we should add the basic notion of republican representation within parliamentary democracy. The central political theorists of these views include John Locke, Adam Smith, Jean-Jacques Rousseau, John Stuart Mill, and a number of others—culminating, some would say, with John Rawls and his magisterial *A Theory of Justice* (1971).

But another series of political philosophers—William Godwin, Pierre-Joseph Proudhon, Michael Bakunin, and Peter Kropotkin—gave rise to an alternative political tradition, one that comes to fruition in contemporary versions of anarchist and libertarian thought, two very strong influences within SF. These four political thinkers—obviously selected from a vast corpus of anarchist philosophers (see Marshall; Sheehan)—share in common two central notions: a profound distrust in or absolute rejection of authority and a privileging of collective justice over individual property. Godwin challenged the legitimacy of the state and its institutions; Proudhon challenged the idea of private property and the system of state authority erected to protect it; Bakunin challenged any notion of hierarchized authority, whether political, personal, or theological; and Kropotkin challenged Darwinian models of competition, offering instead a vision of systematic human cooperation (see Ward 3–13). For almost 200 years, the word "libertarian" was roughly synonymous with the word "anarchist," and, in much of world, it still is. In the United States, however, the term has taken a very distinct trajectory. Libertarians sometimes call themselves "classical liberals," especially when invoking the ideas of Adam Smith (see Doherty). Unfortunately, the terms "anarchism" and "libertarianism" remain frustratingly overdetermined—they are used synonymously or not, pejoratively or not, consistently or not. There is anarcho-capitalism, anarchist liberalism, philosophic anarchism, anarcho-syndicalism, communist anarchism, individualist anarchism, paleoliberterianism, minarchism, revolutionary anarchism, and so on. Depending upon the historical moment, the national culture, and the political conditions, the terms are sometimes used in precisely the opposite way that they are used under different moments, cultures, or conditions.

Common usage frequently aligns anarchism with the political left and libertarianism with the political right, but generally speaking, it is a mistake—especially outside the United States—to identify anarchism with liberalism and libertarianism with conservatism. Anarchists often have more in common with libertarians than with liberals, and libertarians often have more in common with anarchists than with conservatives. The central difference between libertarians and conservatives concerns restrictions on social, not economic liberty. Charles Murray's *What It Means to Be a Libertarian*, while not a scholarly account, provides an admirably concise discussion of libertarian doctrine. Murray sees libertarian thought as being built around two key ideas—economic freedom and unconstrained civil liberties, both of which begin with the single natural right of human beings: "Each person owns himself. Self-ownership is unalienable" (6). From this single unalienable right, three philosophical principles follow: "In a free society individuals may not initiate the use of force against any other individual or group" (7); free markets provide the best opportunity to maximize and ensure individual liberty (8); and "the legitimate functions of government should be performed at the most local feasible level" (16). This view endorses absolute individual property rights, rejects any coercive authority, and favors a minimal state beyond what is necessary to defend national boundaries and maintain civic order and infrastructure. Hence, the state should have no interest in regulating business, free association, speech, education, health care, discrimination; even a person's choices about what to do with their own bodies, from sex work, to drug consumption, to abortion, are decisions left to individuals making noncoercive contracts.

Historically, these libertarian views were sometimes called anarcho-capitalism or individualist anarchism (see Barry). Growing out of the tradition of classical liberalism, its twentieth-century tenets were developed by two Austrian political economists and a Russian émigré—Ludwig von Mises, Friedrich von Hayek, and Ayn Rand. Mises and Hayek were both academics, though they often worked outside the academy; the most famous and influential of their writings was Hayek's *The Road to Serfdom* (1944), published by the University of Chicago Press, a school whose economics and law faculty—such as Milton Freidman and Richard Epstein—became famous for advocating libertarian views (see Schulak and Unterköfler). Outside of the United States, these views are most frequently called "neoliberalism." Rand, who began her experience in America as a Hollywood screenwriter, became a popular icon of libertarian thought, generally through her fiction—*Anthem* (1938), *The Fountainhead* (1943), and *Atlas Shrugged* (1957)—rather than her philosophical treatises, the most influential of which is probably *Capitalism: The Unknown Ideal* (1966). Unlike Mises, Hayek, or Friedman, Rand's enormous notoriety has sometimes seemed more a cult of personality than a set of arguments about political economy and philosophy, and so mentions of her name are as frequently the punch lines of jokes as reverent invocations of a saint (see Heller).

Anthem is an openly dystopian novella, somewhat in the manner of Yevgeny Zamyatin's *We* (1924), set in a distant future where the individual ego has been outlawed by a collectivist tyranny. A lively and imaginative version of socialist dystopia, the story culminates in the rediscovery of individuality. *The Fountainhead* was a bestseller, adapted for a 1949 Hollywood film featuring Gary Cooper, Patricia Neal, and Raymond Massey, which significantly increased the novel's fame and influence. Howard Roark, the novel's romantic architect hero, struggles against convention and collectivism: his ambitions are ruined and revived through a series of melodramatic reversals; he then gets both the girl and the commission of a lifetime. The best-known but worst of Rand's books, *Atlas Shrugged* falls into the category of what the French call a "thesis novel"— the characters and events form an allegorical sketch illustrating Rand's philosophy of "objectivism." As in *The Fountainhead*, a statist collectivism suppresses individual achievement and innovation in favor of leveling all excellence to the lowest common denominator. Business tycoons struggle against uncouth usurpers amid melodramatic intrigues considerably less interesting than in the earlier book. *Atlas Shrugged* is most notable for the long speech by its hero, John Galt, which occupies almost 10 percent of a very long novel: Galt lectures his audience on enlightened self-interest, the rational selfishness that is objectively good for all; his heroic genius promises the rising tide that floats all boats. But against his brilliance stands the maxim of distributive justice, which permits "looters" and "moochers" to steal the wealth of the creative and productive. In response, Galt leads a "strike" of the enlightened elite against the parasitic masses. His diatribe rails against empathy for anyone but oneself, making altruism of any sort the worst sin imaginable. Whatever else it is, *Atlas Shrugged* is deadly dull—a fact that has not prevented it from selling in the tens of millions.

Despite the novel's aesthetic failures, the book has had a remarkable and widespread influence, converting many readers into true believers. The most seductive aspects of Rand's fiction may well be its astonishing level of self-confident certainty and its brazen transformation of a character fault, selfish greed, into the greatest human virtue—something best reflected, perhaps, in Rand's choice of name for her philosophical disposition: objectivism. While she popularized many libertarian ideas, she has not been well received by literary critics—nor indeed by those libertarian economists and philosophers, such as Joseph Epstein or Robert Nozick, whom one might imagine to be most sympathetic to her basic commitments (see Burns 247–78). And despite involving near-future or dystopian settings, Rand's novels can hardly be seen as science fiction.

One excellent way to understand libertarian SF would be to follow the suggestions of the Prometheus Award, given by the Libertarian Futurist Society to the year's best work of fiction (see Beatty). The society also bestows a Hall of Fame Award to important libertarian novels published in earlier years, and a special award, which has gone to films, graphic novels, or anthologies. The Prometheus Award was founded by L. Neil Smith, an SF writer who also actively campaigned for public office as a libertarian. Smith won the award in 1982 for his novel *The Probability Broach* (1980). The first of seven books in a loose series called "The North American Confederacy," *The Probability Broach* opens with a near-future America "staggering toward extinction" (153): political, economic, and environmental conditions have seen a sharp decline, and the country teeters near collapse. While investigating the murder of a scientist, Win Bear, a noirish homicide cop in a Denver made dystopian by central planning and a swollen government bureaucracy that has appropriated all individual property rights, uncovers a suspicious university lab with both a remarkable new technology and an insidious undercurrent of conspiracy. The new gadget is the Probability Broach, which creates a "hole in the fabric of reality" (151). Broaching reality opens an alternate universe that differs from Bear's in its political history and economic conditions—a proverbial rabbit hole leading to another Colorado where Denver does not exist and central planning is a distant nightmare. Instead, he finds himself in the utopian North American Confederacy. Named after the United States' initial Articles of Confederation, the document that followed the Declaration of Independence and was replaced by the Constitution, this Confederacy had a historical point of divergence with our own reality in 1791, when the Whiskey Rebellion was successful. It was then declared that no government—neither federal nor state—could interfere with trade (104); libertarian ideas gained hegemony, and utopia necessarily followed.

Rather than producing a war of all against all, the Confederacy's privileging of enlightened self-interest resulted in conditions benefiting everyone. No hunger, no underclass, no capitalist cycle of boom and bust, no fear, no pollution (63–64), no political partisanship or sectarian gridlock, no religious or racial or other ideological conflict. The *sole* problem is the presence of the nefarious, cabalistic followers of early American Federalism (that is, believers in the idea of a strong, central federal government), who are named Hamiltonians, after Alexander Hamilton, the secretary of the Treasury under George Washington. Hamilton successfully argued for a national bank and for policies that made the federal government as significant in the American economy as any state or locality, company or individual.

An entertaining, pulpy romp, the novel's quick plotting and occasionally sharp wit provide some relief from its cartoonish moral clarity, which produces a cloying tone of smug certitude. Libertarian principles are simply self-evident, proved by the imagined nightmarish future: they always work; there is no serious ambiguity or difficulty. Bear's world, rife with complexities, ambiguities, and competing interpretations, evades his understanding, while the world of the Confederacy is simple and clear. A subtler problem is the book's ubiquitous tongue-in-cheek ironies, many of which elude Smith's control. Early on, we are told that "[t]o Confederates, history's Thomas Edisons mean a lot more than its Lyndon Johnsons. Inventions, ideas, philosophers are central; invasions and elections are temporary aberrations" (99). The contrast reveals a good deal of the book's prejudicial understanding of history—and how the "clarity" of the Confederacy is achieved through mere sleight-of-hand. Johnson, whose central project as president was the Great Society, which not only promoted a variety of programs that increased America's social safety net but also saw the adoption of the Civil Rights Act of 1964 and the Voting Rights Act of 1965, did indeed stand for election. While he foolishly escalated America's war in Vietnam, he was not responsible for the invasion. Johnson's policies were clearly more about philosophy and ideas, particularly concerning justice, than was true of Edison's inventions. Rather than the solitary, heroic genius, Edison was a scheming manipulator who took credit for the inventions of others—such as the 1,000 employees who staffed his laboratory—and worked tirelessly to suppress or discredit his rivals, such as Nikola Tesla.

A second example concerns Smith's joking distortions of federalism. The leader of the nefarious miscreants, for example, is named John Jay Madison (167); though a pseudonym of a foreign *agent provocateur*, the joke does not make much sense. While Madison was a framer of the US Constitution and believed in the importance of some centralized authority (with Jay and Hamilton, he wrote the Federalist Papers), he openly opposed Hamilton, and he was also central to the Bill of Rights that limited the power of the federal government. Especially troubling is the way that Smith uses the joke of the pseudonym to tar, by association, the historical Hamilton. In Smith's Confederacy, Jefferson abolished slavery. But the historical Hamilton was the true abolitionist; Jefferson merely opposed the slave trade: personally, he owned many slaves, and during his lifetime freed just nine of them—all children or relatives of Sally (Betty) Hemings, whose descendants have DNA markers of the Jefferson family's bloodline (see Gordon-Reed). What slaves he owned at his death he assigned to be sold, not freed. The failure of *The Probability Broach* is not that of distorting history, since in alternate-history or many-worlds SF much of the pleasure derives from factual divergence, whether possible or preposterous. Rather, the problem is the smugness of the narrative, which trades more in sanctimonious finger-pointing than in the estrangement that produces genuine cognition.

Neither as entertaining nor as clever as *The Probability Broach*, Dani and Eytan Kollin's "Unincorporated Man" series is nevertheless a stronger achievement. In these novels, human beings have experienced a "Grand Collapse," in which three-quarters of the species perished. An economic meltdown, a virtual-reality plague, and other sundry crises precipitated panicky national governments to commence a nuclear war, after which the surviving Alaskans reorganized the world along their own political outlines. "In an amazingly short period of time hunger, suffering, discomfort, ignorance, and fear . . . practically vanished from the human race due to the power of incorporation that capitalism unleashed" (*Unincorporated War* 81). Curiously, the libertarian ideal of treating everything according to the dictates of a capitalist free market has produced a very un-libertarian result: human beings are themselves *incorporated*, suitable to be bought and sold on the market. One does not own one's own body: at birth, one's parents own 20 percent, while the government owns 5 percent, with the remainder given to the individual as a percentage they can freely sell for goods and services, such as education, which can be a very expensive investment (*Unincorporated Man* 67). In this future, students do not take out loans; they sell shares of themselves, of their futures. The result is that until individuals buy back a majority of themselves, they are subject to the wishes of their stockholders; members of this society believe such conditions will necessarily entail civic order, since war (for example) will likely damage one's investments.

Into this future comes a Rip van Winkle figure. Justin Cord, a leading American industrialist from roughly our own time, awakes from a long period of cryogenic sleep into a radically changed society. Reborn as "unincorporated," within a few hundred pages he leads a revolt against the system of incorporation. The first novel, *The Unincorporated Man* (2009), takes place entirely on Earth, and in both substance and style is quite Randian. The second, *The Unincorporated War* (2010), opens onto the rest of the solar system, where humanity has set up colonies from the Moon and Mars to the asteroid belt and beyond. The series then traces the familiar SF motif of colonies resisting the economic dominance of their colonial masters. According to the authors, both their central novum and their didactic purpose are linked to an explicitly Randian desire to work out "a system that was truly capitalist" ("Desperation" 61); they claim, as many libertarians do, that we have yet to try "pure" or "true" capitalism. But they also hold that the capitalism they propose suffers only from the naked ambition of those who lust for power over others. In the novels, they give the romantic lead to Cord, the "unincorporated" man who represents true freedom and provides the catalyst for the revolt of the colonies against Earth and Mars. Cord "goes Galt," early and often. *The Unincorporated War* ends with Cord's rousing speech; in a blessedly crisp three pages, he claims the beginning of the revolution is not just for one unincorporated man: "You've freed me from the curse of 'one free man.' I will say it again for all to hear and rejoice. *I am no longer the one free man*, because, as of this day forward, *we are all free men*" (478; emphasis in original). The second novel is devoted to this problem: that individual freedom comes from the liberation of the larger human community and can be maintained only through the sacrifice of individual liberties. While the book never phrases things quite this way, what it implicitly manifests is the contradiction between libertarianism as an economic theory and as a political philosophy: the advantages of a market economy are twinned with the failures of a market society (see Sandel).

The Unincorporated Man won the Prometheus Award in 2010. The first Prometheus Hall of Fame winner in 1983 (in a tie with Rand's *Atlas Shrugged*) was Robert A. Heinlein's 1966 novel *The Moon Is a Harsh Mistress*, perhaps the paradigmatic example of libertarian SF. *Double Star* (1956) was Heinlein's first foray into explicitly libertarian thought, though *The Moon Is a Harsh Mistress* is both his clearest statement and perhaps his greatest achievement as a writer. In 2075–76, the Moon begins a revolt against an oppressive Earth. Originally founded as a penal colony for Earth's political and hardened criminals, Luna has developed a culture governed by natural laws (such as gravitation) and free markets (signaled by the witty slogan "TANSTAAFL"—or "There Ain't No Such Thing As a Free Lunch"). The "Loonies" face two pressing problems: an administrative authority sets prices for ice and wheat, prices that are not linked either to real costs or real value, and the Moon is depleting its natural resources, especially water: unless the wheat trade is stopped immediately, Loonies will face cannibalism within seven years (94). A revolutionary cabal emerges—the central computer (Mike), a political agitator (Wyoh), an electronics technician (Mannie), and a veteran revolutionary (Prof)—that orchestrates a coup against Warden, then commences a shooting war with Earth, dropping powerful kinetic weapons—rocks—into the planet's gravity well. This results in a final battle, an uneasy armistice, and a trade agreement to make resource shipments that match Luna's losses "tonne-for-tonne" (376–77).

The book's libertarian core is Prof's political philosophy, which advocates "rational anarchism," but which is probably best called anarcho-capitalism. He thinks the only political right is "to bargain in a free marketplace" (33) and that the only laws needed are negative ones, such as those limiting the power of the state to restrict individual freedoms (302). At the end of the novel, the principle of TANSTAAFL prevails, and Loonies pay for their revolution in two ways: first, with the deaths of Prof and Mike, and second, with the irony that the libertarian revolution has produced republican democracy, which leads to intractable bureaucracy, a failure of the Prof's project. The book ends with the suggestion that Mannie will leave the Moon and head out to the asteroids, where a new frontier and more libertarian possibilities await.

The extent to which readers will find the novel an endorsement of free markets or a systematic dramatization of the contradictions within libertarian thought relies on whether the reader trusts Mannie, Prof, and Mike—that is, on the fundamental reliability of the narrative itself. There are reasons to distrust Mannie's narrative, beginning with the fact that he admits he is neither in control nor informed. The evidence is not hard to assemble: Prof is the political schemer, the planner, the savvy veteran for whom revolution is an art (86, 123), while Mannie, Wyoh, and Mike remain naïfs. This becomes increasingly clear to Mannie—who, during the central crisis of the revolt, remarks that "Prof was the only one who seemed to know what he was doing" (296).

Indeed, it is clear that Prof alone orchestrates events: as they plan the initial cabal, Prof insists that "there are *always* betrayals" (77; emphasis in original), and since there is no demonstrable moment when either Mannie or Wyoh betrays the others' trust, an observant reader will suspect Prof. And when Mannie thinks about the fixed elections, the theft from citizens' bank accounts, the media propaganda, the fundamental dishonesty and hypocrisy—the very essence of coercion, the denial of a free market, and the exercise of tyrannical authority by some to constrain the freedom of all—he says to himself, "I told [my] conscience to go to sleep" (137).

This greatest of SF libertarian novels is thus rampant with contradiction and deception. Two problems stand out: the problem of transparency and the problem of tyranny. If the general libertarian gesture is antiauthoritarian, to promote individual liberty through a free market that cannot coerce private property, then Prof's system fails on all counts. He becomes the central—indeed, centralized—authority (356); if the book presents him as a benevolent tyrant, he is tyrannical just the same. Prof controls all streams of information, public and private, and so the system fails the test of transparency; there are even reasons to doubt Mike's prediction of the coming existential crisis (286). David Brin, one of libertarian SF's most talented and interesting writers, argues that many libertarians, especially those working in the shadow of Rand, favor property over competition. A totalized commitment to property, he thinks, would foreclose transparency, the most important quality for a fair free market; propertarians would therefore flatten opportunity and foster a system that inherently denies fairness (see "Is Libertarianism").

But understanding Brin's view also produces a clear analysis of the economic problem at the heart of libertarianism, which presupposes transparency of information and the rationality of human agents, both of which happen to be empirically false (see Stiglitz; Kahneman). Prof's tyranny produces the problem of inequality of opportunity, a failure of the level playing field necessary to individual liberty. The most compelling thing about *The Moon Is a Harsh Mistress*, like *The Unincorporated Man* but unlike *The Probability Broach*, is that the novel compels us to examine those contradictions. Unfortunately, the narrative is delivered with such confidence and charm that its ambiguities can be rationalized away, except perhaps by readers hostile to the central libertarian idea—the unalienable right to private property. The problems of libertarianism—at least insofar as the fiction of Rand, Smith, the Kollins, and Heinlein represent it—are the inequity of opportunity, the failure of transparency, and the subtle reinscription of central authority.

Some Prometheus winners—such as Ernest Cline's charming *Ready Player One* (2011), the 2012 winner, or such classics as George Orwell's *Nineteen Eighty-Four* (1949) and Zamyatin's *We*—do not express any sort of overtly libertarian view. These books are antiauthoritarian and thus appealing to libertarians, but they fall far short of endorsing libertarian arguments. Zamyatin was a communist, Orwell a socialist: both condemned totalitarianism, but neither endorsed free-market capitalism. Other Prometheus winners are actually quite hostile to libertarian views, and these turn out to be anarchist fictions. The central difference between anarchists and libertarians is the concept of private property: anarchists endorse communitarian views, while libertarians privilege personal liberty. Put another way, anarchists choose common justice before personal liberty. Although there are many widely respected examples of anarchist SF—such as Ken MacLeod's "Fall Revolution" quartet (1995–99), Kim Stanley Robinson's "Mars" trilogy (1992–96), or Samuel R. Delany's *Trouble on Triton* (1976)—Ursula K. Le Guin's *The Dispossessed: An Ambiguous Utopia* (1974) is the best-known and most widely discussed. Le Guin's narrative presents no grand, heroic triumph, but it does confront us with the real difficulties of being human, of weighing individual liberty against social justice, equality of opportunity, and simple fairness. The novel is neither comforting nor glib; moral failures or contradictions are not winked away, as in Smith or Heinlein, or rationalized as goods, as in Rand.

Openly a response to Heinlein, *The Dispossessed* concerns a parent planet (Urras) and its rebellious moon (Anarres). The largest of Urras' states, A-IO, is a capitalist plutocracy, in some respects similar to the United States, at least from an anarchist perspective. A-IO has exiled its insubordinate anarchists to their moon, where followers of Laia Odo, who seems modeled on Emma Goldman, live a communal life in harsh conditions. Organized into Syndicates, Odonian life centers around sharing—shared work, shared pain, and shared spoils. Shevek, a young, innovative physicist, despairs over the syndicates' bureaucracy, which after 170 years has ossified into hierarchal structures of power, and so he travels to A-IO, seeking greater opportunity for his unconventional science. The novel then plays out as an investigation of each political structure's advantages and disadvantages.

While just as didactic as Heinlein's book, Le Guin's treats both systems skeptically, identifying the positive and pleasurable opportunities created though capitalism and the rigidity of a communal system controlled by the moral imperative of "shared pain." Tom Moylan rightly calls *The Dispossessed* a "critical utopia," a genre where claims to certainty of any stripe are examined for their limitations and probable failures, but not faulted for their seductive appeal or possible successes. Critical utopias provide a robust distrust of any utopian blueprint. Although they may finally promote a particular view, as *The Dispossessed* does when Shevek returns to Anarres to embrace Odonian anarchism with the additional imperative to bridge the political wall between Anarres and Urras, they never try to occult or obfuscate the real, ineluctable weaknesses in that position. The pattern established in *The Dispossessed*, that of thoughtful doubt and moral hope, is characteristic, I think, of the vast majority of anarchist fiction.

Libertarian and anarchist SF are all the more interesting for the radical challenge they present to complacent conceptions of the commonweal and common woe, and hence they provide a fine representation of what SF, at its best and worst, can accomplish. Like many types of art, libertarian and anarchist fictions have had a powerful effect on real-world politics and economics. Landon argues that contemporary Western culture, and increasingly the rest of the world, has been transformed by "science fiction thinking," while Delany claims that SF provides an imaginative space for a vast, radical thought experiment of alternatives to our own culture and politics. This is certainly true for the libertarian and anarchist communities, both dedicated to a radical transformation of the status quo. The libertarian economist David Friedman found *The Moon Is a Harsh Mistress* central to his conversion to libertarian thought, perhaps as important as the work of his famous father, the Nobel laureate Milton Friedman; libertarians of every stripe embrace Heinlein, Smith, Poul Anderson, and Robert Anton Wilson as central influences (see Doherty 518–23). Similarly, Le Guin's fiction has had a profound effect on the real world: Occupy Wall Street organizers and websites frequently cite *The Dispossessed* and her other major novel, *The Left Hand of Darkness* (1969); some protesters at Occupy Oakland marched with placards depicting the cover of *The Dispossessed* (see Morton). When the anarchist ezine *Strangers in a Tangled Wilderness* assessed writers with anarchist themes, in a collection entitled *Mythmakers and Lawbreakers* (2009), most were known for their SF—such as Le Guin, Robinson, Lewis Shiner, and Michael Moorcock (see Killjoy). Tadzio Mueller, both a scholar and an anarchist activist, reports that fiction has been his inspiration, providing a way to dramatize political ideas in a concrete fashion that can stimulate debate as much as philosophical or economic theory can—perhaps more so.

Of all these writers, probably Rand remains the most influential, especially in the United States, and especially through *Atlas Shrugged*. Since the 1960s, and perhaps as a reaction against liberalism, political views in the United States have moved steadily toward the right, and much of one major political party's agenda is dominated by libertarian ideas. Hayek and Milton Friedman have been sources, but it may well be the case that no one has had more sway over the right-leaning public than Rand, whose fiction seems to be most frequently read, as the old SF joke has it, at the Golden Age of fourteen, when it can change the direction of one's life. In the United States, Rand seems as prominent now as ever she was, and it is commonplace to see "I am John Galt" signs at libertarian political rallies or in groups of fellow travelers, such as the Tea Party movement (Gary Weiss calls Rand "The First Teabagger" [138–44]).

But while both libertarianism and anarchism share a family history and several fundamental tenets, the plain truth is that one is more science-fictional than the other. Because libertarian fiction believes, with smug certainty, in the totalizing final truth of its worldview, empirical reality be damned, it is less like the SF project than its anarchist doppelgänger, which characteristically presents incomplete, ambiguous, or complex conditions that the narrative or characters still doubt, probe, and question. The difference is vividly illustrated by details in *Atlas Shrugged* and *The Dispossessed*. In the middle of John Galt's long harangue, he pronounces that "[t]here are two sides to every issue: one side is right and the other is wrong, but the middle is always evil" (1054). Compare this arrogant certitude with the modesty that concludes Le Guin's treatment of Shevek, whose "hands were empty, as they had always been" (311).

If Landon is right that the general thrust of SF has been libertarian in the sense of "mistrust[ing] authority in all its official guises" (109), then expressly libertarian SF seems especially anomalous, for as it critiques notions of authority, it at the same time reinscribes them in a way that is often quite insidious. Rand, Smith, and Heinlein are typical in this regard. But anarchist SF seems exemplary of Landon's claim, since it always questions authority, even its own.

Works Cited

Barry, Norman P. *On Classical Liberalism and Libertarianism*. New York: Palgrave Macmillan, 1986. Print.
Beatty, Greg. "Reason, Sexuality, and the Self in Libertarian Science Fiction Novels." *Strange Horizons*. Sept. 17, 2001. Web. Sept. 6, 2013. http://www.strangehorizons.com/2001/20010917/libertarian_SF.shtml.
Brin, David. "Is Libertarianism Fundamentally about Competition? Or about Property?" Jan. 17, 2012. Web. Sept. 6, 2013. http://davidbrin.blogspot.com.au/2012/01/is-libertarianism-fundamentally-about.html?commentPage=2.
Burns, Jennifer. *Goddess of the Market: Ayn Rand and the American Right*. New York: Oxford UP, 2009. Print.
Delany, Samuel R. *Starboard Wine: More Notes on the Language of Science Fiction*. Pleasantville, NY: Dragon, 1984. Print.
Doherty, Brian. *Radicals for Capitalism: A Freewheeling History of the Modern American Libertarian Movement*. New York: Public Affairs, 2007. Print.
Gordon-Reed, Annette. *The Hemingses of Monticello: An American Family*. New York: Norton, 2008. Print.
Heinlein, Robert A. *The Moon Is a Harsh Mistress*. 1966. New York: Orb, 1996. Print.
Heller, Anne C. *Ayn Rand and the World She Made*. New York: Anchor, 2009. Print.
Kahneman, Daniel. *Thinking, Fast and Slow*. New York: Macmillian, 2011. Print.
Killjoy, Margaret, ed. *Mythmakers and Lawbreakers: Anarchist Writers on Fiction*. Oakland, CA: AK, 2009. Print.
Kollin, Dani, and Eytan Kollin. "Desperation Inspiration." *Locus* 66.4 (Apr. 2011): 61–62. Print.
_____. *The Unincorporated Man*. New York: Tor, 2009. Print.
_____. *The Unincorporated War*. New York: Tor, 2010. Print.
Landon, Brooks. *Science Fiction After 1900: From the Steam Man to the Stars*. 1995. New York: Routledge, 2002. Print.
Le Guin, Ursula K. *The Dispossessed*. New York: Avon, 1974. Print.
Luckhurst, Roger. *Science Fiction*. Malden, MA: Polity, 2005. Print.
MacLeod, Ken. "Politics and Science Fiction." *The Cambridge Companion to Science Fiction*. Ed. Edward James and Farah Mendlesohn. New York: Cambridge UP, 2003. 230–40. Print.
Marshall, Peter. *Demanding the Impossible: A History of Anarchism*. 1992. Oakland, CA: PM, 2010. Print.
Morton, Paul. "Getting Away with Murder: The Millions Interviews Ursula K. Le Guin." *The Millions*. Jan. 31, 2013. Web. Sept. 6, 2013. http://www.themillions.com/2013/01/getting-away-with-murder-the-millions-interviews-ursula-k-le-guin.html.
Moylan, Tom. *Demand the Impossible: Science Fiction and the Utopian Imagination*. 1986. New York: Routledge, 1987. Print.
Mueller, Tadzio. "Empowering Anarchy: Power, Hegemony, and Anarchist Strategy." *Post-Anarchism: A Reader*. Ed. Duane Rousselle and Süreyya Evren. London: Pluto, 2011. 75–94. Print.

Murray, Charles. *What It Means to Be a Libertarian: A Personal Interpretation*. New York: Broadway, 1997. Print.

Rand, Ayn. *Atlas Shrugged*. New York: Dutton, 1957. Print.

Sandel, Michael. *What Money Can't Buy: The Moral Limits of Markets*. New York: Farrar, Straus, and Giroux, 2012. Print.

Schulak, Eugen Maria, and Herbert Unterköfler. *The Austrian School of Economics: A History of Its Ideas, Ambassadors, and Institutions*. Auburn, AL: Mises Institute, 2011. Print.

Sheehan, Seán M. *Anarchism*. London: Reaktion, 2003. Print.

Smith, L. Neil. *The Probability Broach*. 1980. New York: Orb, 2001. Print.

Stiglitz, Joseph E. *The Price of Inequality: How Today's Divided Society Endangers our Future*. New York: Norton, 2012. Print.

Ward, Colin. *Anarchism: A Very Short Introduction*. New York: Oxford UP, 2004. Print.

Weiss, Gary. *Ayn Rand Nation: The Hidden Struggle for America's Soul*. New York: St. Martin's, 2012. Print.

CHAPTER 43

AFROFUTURISM

DE WITT DOUGLAS KILGORE

In the final decade of the twentieth century, the future seemed ever more imminent. The great expansion of computer- and Internet-based technoculture had produced a renewed interest in the nature and character of tomorrow's world. Fiction writers and cultural journalists traced the advent of a virtual or digital future that they believed would usher in a more prosperous, just, and democratic order (see Gilder). Less sanguine commentators pointed to a potential digital divide, a technological separation that could reproduce old divisions between rich and poor, black and white in a new global space (see Norris). Underlying both prospects lay the tacit assumption that any future would be defined and directed by a Euro-American majority; people of color would fit into those futures merely as an afterthought.

Still, amidst the general technofuturist ferment of the era, the position and prospects of African Americans attracted the attention of a number of cultural critics. In his 1994 collection of essays *Flame Wars: The Discourse of Cyberculture*, editor Mark Dery included a chapter of his own, entitled "Black to the Future," in which he developed the term "Afrofuturism." This neologism, which referred to a mode of African-American science fiction that was contingent upon but critical of the nation's Futurist imaginary, was defined by Dery as follows: "speculative fiction that treats African-American themes and addresses African-American concerns in the context of twentieth-century technoculture—and, more generally, African-American signification that appropriates images of technology and a prosthetically enhanced future" (180). Dery positioned the concept in opposition to histories and futures in which blacks play minor roles or disappear entirely. In Euro-American Futurism, the ability to imagine things to come is the property of a dominant class distinguished from the rest of the human species by race—a situation Dery recognizes by asking, "Isn't the unreal estate of the future already owned by the technocrats, futurologists, streamliners, and set designers—white to a man—who have engineered our collective fantasies?" (180). For Dery, Afrofuturism was a way around the racial exclusion encoded in the various media of mainstream Futurism.

While the term had actually been coined the year before by a British music journalist (Eshun 299; Bould 180), it was Dery's usage that gained critical traction, especially in the United States. Identifying Afrofuturism as a material practice within American culture, Dery cast a broad net: not only was it a growingly significant minority voice within SF, but it could also be found in fine and street art, art-house and documentary film, and most especially in music (182). Indeed, subsequent Afrofuturist scholarship has been dominated by explorations of Futurist aesthetics and narratives in various forms of black music culture (see Weheliye; Zuberi). Producing material evidence for a popular Afrofuturism, Dery also cited Milestone Media's ambitious and hopeful experiment in creating comics written and drawn by African-American creators for a mainstream audience (182). Thus, Dery's Afrofuturism, while staking a claim within literary culture, displayed its significance most fully and richly in the visual and performing arts. This emphasis tracked Dery's own interests but also validated his impression that Afrofuturism is a transgeneric cultural force and, as such, may be discovered "in unlikely places, constellated from far-flung points" (182).

In a version of the original article republished in Marleen Barr's anthology *Afro-Future Females* (2008), Dery teases out the implications of Afrofuturist artistic production, arguing that it is a form of hacking, a technoperformative way of cracking a complex cultural code, as well as a survival skill that is "quintessentially black" (13). It is an Afrocentric form of Futurist expression authored by black creators who eschew SF's more metaphorical approach to the social and political realities of racial difference. In his initial search for work that could serve as models for Afrofuturism, however, Dery had included Lizzie Borden's *Born in Flames* (1983) and John Sayles's *The Brother from Another Planet* (1984), films written and directed by whites. Afrofuturism thus forces us to pay attention not only to the authorship and control of Futurist meaning-making but also to the specific communicative spaces within which raced artists intervene in the construction of racial identity.

Afrofuturism makes visible an aspect of African-American expressive culture that had been noticed before but with only a fleeting recognition of its relevance to either the black community or the general culture. A decade prior to its establishment as a distinct cultural form, for example, Thulani Davis, in a *Village Voice* article, defined the future as primarily a white affair, with no place for black communities and only a little room for black individuals. She recognized African-American writers such as Delany and Ishmael Reed as exceptions that proved the rule, seeing their experimental play with racial categories and modes of recognition as irrelevant to the street-level vibrancy she cherished in contemporary African-American culture—the customs of a community surviving and thriving on its own terms. Her general assessment of the state of the American Futurist imaginary c. 1983 was contained in her article's title, "The Future May Be Bleak, but It's Not Black." Davis hoped for but did not see artistic representations of a future we might now term Afrofuturist, one in which Euro-American culture and whiteness are presumed to be neither preeminent nor directive of history.

Davis's pessimism and Dery's relative optimism were founded on two foundational suppositions: that black expressive activity in speculative or science fiction is relatively recent and that it is rare. Dery framed his initial investigation of black Futurism with the question: "Why do so few African Americans write science fiction, a genre whose close encounters with the Other—the stranger in a strange land—would seem uniquely suited to the concerns of African-American novelists?" (179–80). He went on to locate the black community as the inhabitants of "a sci-fi nightmare in which unseen but no less impassable force fields of intolerance frustrate their movements; official histories undo what has been done; and technology is too often brought to bear on black bodies" (180). What is interesting here is the conflation of black people with the horrors they face: like Earthlings in any number of SF B-movies, they are arrayed against an invading force intent on alienating and subjugating them. Dery's implication is that, if creative engagement with this situation is limited to the protocols of social realism or historical recovery (if, in other words, the techniques of SF are eschewed), then black literature has little or nothing to say about the technoscientific episteme in which we now live.

Yet Afrofuturism does have a literary pedigree that is rather longer than Dery acknowledges. This became evident with the publication of Sheree R. Thomas's first *Dark Matter* anthology in 2000, which showed that the fantastic is an old and familiar register in African diasporic writing. Covering a broad spectrum of material, both chronologically and generically, *Dark Matter* presented a cornucopia of speculative thought and narrative emerging from black communities in the New World, charting both a substantial tradition and a vibrant contemporary practice of black writing in SF and fantasy. In her followup collection, *Dark Matter: Reading the Bones* (2004), Thomas indicated that her overall goal was to showcase stories motivated by the desire to change or influence the future (ix–x). This represents a core value of Afrofuturism: to imagine futures directed by the survival and even the resurgence of black people and their cultures, experiences, and designs. The anthologies' 29 pieces of fiction rebut Dery's impression of scarcity, replacing it with a richness that Thomas sees as generative of a deeper understanding of the diverse histories of speculative fiction.

An important part of the first anthology's project were the essays that Thomas included by Butler, Delany, Charles R. Saunders, Walter Mosley, and Paul D. Miller, which collectively offered a historical and prophetic manifesto for black involvement in SF. Noting that there has been an Africanist discourse among white writers in the genre, Saunders insists that blacks must tell their own stories or else have them told by others: "Just as our ancestors sang their songs in a strange land when they were kidnapped and sold from Africa, we must, now and in the future, continue to sing our songs under strange stars" (404). Afrofuturism is here defined as responsible storytelling, a challenge to remember a past that instructs the present and can build a future. For Walter Mosley, SF is a genre in which it is possible to throw off the chains of a realism that can imprison groups and individuals in facts as they are; he argues for SF's appeal to African Americans, heralding black creative efforts in the field that "will be the beginning of a new autonomy" (407). Miller's contribution indicates the wide range of literary and musical references that seed an Afrofuturist sensibility (409), offering not only Butler and Delany as guides but also Ursula K. Le Guin and J. G. Ballard, as well as Sylvia Plath and Countee Cullen (411). For Miller, science fiction is an integral part of the artistic education that supports his own hip-hop-inflected experiments as "DJ Spooky," the name under which he is more widely known. Finally, Butler's essay looks forward to the possibility that humanity may meet another sentience, creating a crisis in which we must finally confront the aliens that we are to one another (416). Each essayist projects an Afrofuturist sensibility that seeks to recover, change, and extend black identities beyond their mundane limits while retaining the histories and accomplishments of the African diaspora. The essays promote an opening-up of black expressive efforts to the not-yet, in order to exploit what Ernst Bloch might call the utopian surplus of contemporary technoculture (see Kellner).

Is imagining futures for peoples of African descent, especially if conventional doomsday scenarios do not limit these futures, evidence of a resurgent black nationalism? Does it constitute a simple exchange of a black future for the white futures that Daniel Bernardi has identified as a persistent trope of SF's historical imaginary? While this is certainly possible, an ethic of racial exclusivity is not central to Afrofuturist thought. Rather, the focus is on crafting an expressive mode that may also be taken up by artists from across the racial spectrum. The price of the ticket is an intimate engagement with black complexity, a self-reflexive recognition that it is inextricable from an artist's own identity and the futures he or she might foretell.

Caribbean-Canadian author Nalo Hopkinson demonstrates this aspect of Afrofuturism by using it as the nodal point in the dialogue she curates between black and white authors in her anthology *Mojo: Conjure Stories* (2003). Writers of both races share roughly equal space, showing what they can do with the dramatic political histories and rich storytelling traditions that the diverse peoples of the New World have created. Hopkinson offers the rationale behind this project in the introduction to another of her anthologies, *So Long Been Dreaming: Postcolonial Science Fiction and Fantasy* (2004), co-edited with Uppinder Mehan. "If I were to edit such an anthology on my own," she writes in her Introduction, "I would likely have chosen to include white writers, since I feel that a dialogue about the effects of colonialism is one that white folks need to have with the rest of us" (8). Thus, Afrocentric speculative fiction is cast as a mode of communication between readers and writers who occupy different points in what Delany calls the racial "system" (381); it becomes part of the "social vigilance" he sees as necessary to the creation and maintenance of "anti-racist institutions and traditions" (396–97).

This gesture betokens a generosity of spirit or, at least, a nonessentialist brand of Afrofuturism that focuses attention on "black" expression as a linguistic and cultural field for which raced bodies serve only as a conveniently visible sign. Thus, any writer or creator who is drawn to and can credibly operate within the field may be seen as Afrofuturist, no matter what identity they occupy through racial custom. This indicates that Afrofuturism can be viewed as less a marker of black authenticity and more of a cultural force, an episteme that betokens a shift in our largely unconscious assumptions about which histories matter and how they may serve as a precondition for any future we might imagine. Afrofuturism also helps SF gain a social and historical depth and sophistication it has often lacked, despite (or perhaps because of) the genre's claim to represent a "disinterested" paradigm of scientific reason.

It is worth remembering how often in SF the idea of a future controlled by an African-derived regime has been entertained and dismissed as dystopian, sometimes in the most egregiously racist of ways. In Robert A. Heinlein's *Farnham's Freehold* (1964), for example, a postholocaust America is dominated by an African tyranny that has institutionalized cannibalism and enslaved whites. An alternative to this sort of narrative is one in which Africa survives into the future but never quite escapes its colonial past, as in Mike Resnick's *Kirinyaga* (1998). This latter approach is more interesting because it at least takes African history and culture seriously enough to offer detailed individual and cultural portraits. Yet it still conforms to the sort of "American Africanism" analyzed by Toni Morrison, by which she means a form of white literature that serves "to allay internal fears and to rationalize external exploitation" (38). Resnick's vision of Africa is strongly influenced by the tradition of hunter-naturalists or safari writers such as Theodore Roosevelt and Ernest Hemingway. Resnick was the editor of St. Martin's "Library of African Adventure" in the early 1990s, and he authored a column entitled "Ask Bwana" in the fanzine *Speculations* during the late 1990s and early 2000s. Saunders has compared his work to that of Edgar Rice Burroughs, creator of Tarzan: "Each of them has taken the worst his times offered about Africa, and either ignored or discounted the positive aspects of the continent's history and culture" (403).

The cultural canvas of Afrofuturism is so large that it is possible to miss significant details as we take in the overall picture. This is especially true when considering Afrofuturist fiction. The critical tendency is to sweep the broad range of African-American literature into view as a way of substantiating the claim that we have identified a significant thread of artistic production, yet this approach may divert our attention from how Afrofuturism emerges from and is in conversation with the generic traditions of science fiction. This is especially crucial when discussing the work of black SF writers like Delany, Butler, Hopkinson, and Steven Barnes, whose reading and writing are so strongly identified with SF, its protocols and potentials.

An alternative approach would be to consider science fiction as the repository of a positive, even radical, strand of Afrofuturist speculation predating the prominence of modern Afro-diasporic writers. This thread of Afrofuturist writing can be traced as far back as the mid-nineteenth century, functioning as a political counter to the prevailing assumptions fostered by white-supremacist ideology. In books such as Herrmann Lang's *The Air Battle: A Vision of the Future* (1859), T. Shirby Hodge's *The White Man's Burden: A Satirical Forecast* (1915; pseudonymously penned by Roger S. Tracy), and Margot Bennett's *The Long Way Back* (1954), white authors imagined an Africa of advanced civilizations who could assist a fallen West or defeat its imperial ambitions. More recent fiction in this vein—such as Mack Reynolds's "North Africa" trilogy (1961–78), A. M. Lightner's *The Day of the Drones* (1969), Michael Moorcock's *The Land Leviathan* (1974), and Terry Bisson's *Fire on the Mountain* (1988)—were written in the context of the anticolonial and Civil Rights movements that became prominent in the second half of the twentieth century. Not only is this work in conversation with white debates about race, but it is also informed by a more finely tuned awareness of black history and politics. Such work may be taken as evidence that, even as it articulated a hegemonic Euro-American Futurism, SF also contained sites of critical resistance that have made a counterhegemonic Afrofuturism possible, even necessary. What the popularity of Afrofuturism as a term has done is to make it possible to see these gestures of opposition to the dominance of white futures, both inside and outside the genre.

Very few of the writers who have been typed as Afrofuturist see themselves as part of a movement or even a school. For example, even as he recognizes his popular status as the "first African-American science fiction writer," Delany also remarks that he "wear[s] that originary label as uneasily as any writer has worn the label of science fiction writer itself" (383). For scholars of the African diaspora, American studies, and SF studies, however, Afrofuturism has been exciting news. During the late 1990s, a flurry of critical activity made the term part of the nomenclature of both technoculture and pop-culture studies, where it functioned as a way of organizing and bringing into focus an aspect of black cultural production that had as yet received little attention. As a result, a broad range of work produced in a number of media was identified as newly worthy of study within this emerging field.

In the late 1990s, Alondra Nelson, then a graduate student at New York University, started an online forum called "AfroFuturism" that helped generate debates among creators and critics. Shaped, in part, by the participation of Hopkinson, Thomas, and Nnedi Okorafor, the group shared ideas about "sci-fi imagery, futurist themes, and technological innovation in the African diaspora" (Nelson 9). Their concern was to establish a constructive conversation about the relationship between black communities and technoscience that went beyond racialized notions of a digital divide. The work of the AfroFuturism listserv seeded a 2002 special issue of *Social Text*, a major academic journal. Edited by Nelson, the issue introduced Afrofuturism into the discourse of the academy, speaking in particular to critics receptive to new ways of linking literature and culture to political action. At a time when it was attractive to imagine a "postracial" cybernetic future, the articles in the issue countered by arguing that fantasies of a race-free world "smack of old racial ideologies" (Nelson 1), silencing those black voices "with other stories to tell about culture, technology and things to come" (9).

This special issue followed closely on the heels of Kodwo Eshun's book *More Brilliant Than the Sun: Adventures in Sonic Fiction* (1998), which built upon Dery's ideas about black musical culture by focusing on contemporary jazz, hip-hop, funk, and experimental music, as well as science fiction. *More Brilliant Than the Sun* engages with the work of a wide range of African-American musicians, including Miles Davis, Pharaoh Sanders, Rammellzee, Funkadelic, Sun Ra, and Alice Coltrane. While Eshun does not explicitly use the term Afrofuturism, he does operate in its spirit. As a writer, he exchanges the formal rhetoric of academic scholarship for a style that evokes a funky "computronic" stance. The biographical blurb for the book refers to him as "a concept engineer, an imagineer at the millenium's end writing on electronic music, science fiction, technoculture, gameculture, drug culture, post war movies and post war art" (n.p.). Eshun's critical positioning, coupled with his self-conscious use of a speculative-fictional style, shows the imbrication of a black writer/scholar in an Afrofuturist vocabulary even as he surveys the range of black artistic production indexed by term.

A subsequent essay, "Further Considerations on Afrofuturism" (2003), carries forward Eshun's stylized investigation of black SF through a structure that alternates a critique of science fiction as linked to what he calls the "futures industry" (290) with a fictive extrapolation in which archaeologists from a future United States of Africa pick through the cultural detritus of the twentieth century. This device allows Eshun to both create an Afrofuture that would make a credible short story for an SF magazine and to construct specific priorities for Afrofuturist discourse. Through both structure and statement, Eshun provides a strong rationale for why SF must be seen as a critical medium for black thought and expression:

> It is not that black subjectivities are waiting for science-fiction authors to articulate their lifeworlds. Rather, it is the reverse. The conventions of science fiction, marginalized within literature yet central to modern thought, can function as allegories for the systemic experience of post-slavery black subjects in the twentieth century. Science fiction, as such, is recast in the light of Afrodiasporic history. (299)

Eshun clarifies the Afrofuturist project as a recasting of the black subject in modern terms, a process of continual renewal that involves shedding the sticky past of colonialism and slavery.

Also at issue is the state of Africa as we imagine global futures. Eshun argues that the continent is always already the object of a "market futurism" that sees it as the "zone of absolute dystopia" (292). Thus, "Afrofuturism's first priority is to recognize that Africa increasingly exists as the object of futurist projection" (291). Afrofuturism must intervene to combat this discourse of Malthusian pessimism; to do so constitutes a "chronopolitical act" (292) that "expos[es] and refram[es] . . . futurisms that act to forecast and fix African dystopia" (293). Eshun does sound a cautionary note with reference to the faults of "vernacular futurologies" that generate reversals mirroring the white-supremacist ideology they react against (296–97); however, he sees Afrofuturism as mature enough to become "a space within which the critical work of manufacturing tools capable of intervention within the current political dispensation may be undertaken" (301).

By the mid-2000s, scholars in SF studies found Afrofuturism useful as a way of reimagining the field—and American literature more generally. Lisa Yaszek, for example, offers a history of Afrofuturist storytelling, relating it to genre scholarship's slender engagement with black SF over the past generation. Yaszek's aim is to develop Afrofuturism as a potent conceptual lens through which a particular strand of African-American literature may be read, allowing her to recapture a literary history that demonstrates black investment in representing the imbrication of science and technology. Afrofuturism permits her to read Ralph Ellison's *Invisible Man* (1952), for instance, as part of a tradition in black writing that includes the speculative fiction of Butler, Hopkinson, George Schuyler, and W. E. B. Du Bois. She sees Ellison's novel as "a particularly compelling example of Afrofuturism because it invites readers to think about how the rhetoric of the futures industry impacts people of color" (47). The novel thus gains a political and aesthetic relevance that would be otherwise difficult to perceive, prompting us to see African-American writing as a form of science fiction that charts the future in ways that are both subtle and complex.

Afrofuturism gained prominence in SF studies with the 2007 publication of a special issue on the subject by *Science Fiction Studies*, the major journal in the field. Edited by scholar Mark Bould and fiction author Rone Shavers, the issue draws together six essays that establish the limits and potential of Afrofuturist writing, past and present. Isiah Lavender suggests the concept of "ethnoscapes" as a new interpretive tool allowing critics to read the racial environments constructed within specific SF stories, while Darryl A. Smith presents black SF as a robust critique of the Euro-American Futurism represented by typical scenarios of the "Singularity." Mark Bould recovers the revolutionary black-power SF that, he argues, has been hidden by the "hegemonic definitional structures and practices" of academic SF studies, the popular SF genre, and the mainstream literary canon (220). Sherryl Vint argues that realist protocols are not sufficient for understanding what "neo-slave narratives" tell us about African-American history and culture, and Nabeel Zuberi, treating musical Afrofuturism, claims that Afrofuturism must broaden its range to "engage in greater dialogue with those looking at Atlantic or African-American experience from Asia and the South" (297).

Jillana Enteen's contribution to the issue, "'On the Receiving End of the Colonization': Nalo Hopkinson's 'Nansi Web," may be taken as representative of current scholarship in Afrofuturism. Enteen presents Hopkinson as an Afrofuturist visionary who "fashions unconventional scenarios premised on technological development" that provide "unorthodox versions of yet-to-come societies" (263). This represents the utopian core of what might be called Afrofuturism's political project. Through a reading of Hopkinson's novel *Midnight Robber* (2000), Enteen argues that the author's Afro-Caribbean approach to cyberpunk refashions that subgenre's conventions of a white-corporatist future that cast black history and language as exotic. She describes Hopkinson's creation of a cyberfuture that foregrounds the inventions of Caribbean culture as a kind of "hacking" (274). Hopkinson's Afrofuturism gives Enteen a way of critiquing the racial and masculinist investments of cyberpunk, yet that critique does not amount to a dismissal of the form. Her broader aim is to demonstrate how Afrofuturist fiction participates in the generic protocols of cyberpunk's futures, all the while challenging its tendency to confine the broad range of human invention within stereotyped notions of racial or cultural difference. In Enteen's usage, Afrofuturism is not simply a distinct subgenre of SF, to be discussed in isolation from debates and practices in the wider field. Instead, she reads Hopkinson's work as a part of—rather than apart from—the fiction produced by paradigmatic authors of the cyberpunk movement such as William Gibson and Bruce Sterling. At the very least, she argues, the inclusion of Afrofuturist fiction "in the cyberpunk canon supplies scenarios that expand [the subgenre's] seemingly unilateral vision of carnivorous corporate machines bent on annihilating humans and human practices" (276). In her hands, Afrofuturism provides a critique of the genre's unconscious investments, as well as a renewal of its potential as both a mode of political speculation and an expression of contemporary technoculture.

Cultural forms prove themselves not only by satisfying programmatic aims but also by demonstrating a broad appeal. Catherine S. Ramírez, a specialist in Chicana studies, illustrates this point by acknowledging her debt to Afrofuturism in her consideration of the invisibility of Mexican Americans in science fiction and the centrality of SF cinema to her childhood in Southern California. The theories, practices, and commitments indexed by the term "Afrofuturism" inspired her to conceive the complementary notion of "Chicanafuturism"—a cultural modality that "explores the ways that new and everyday technologies, including their detritus, transform Mexican American life and culture" (187). Afrofuturism thus becomes a model for how other peoples of color might view the futuristic art they create, allowing them to become conscious of their own imbrication in a technoscientific culture and to resist erasure from the narratives it sponsors. The growing alliance of historically subordinated Futurisms has recently culminated in an anthology entitled *We See a Different Frontier: A Postcolonial Speculative Fiction Anthology* (2013), edited by Fabio Fernandes and Djibril al-Ayad.

Afrofuturist writers and scholars organize their work around at least three basic assumptions: that peoples of African descent, their ways and histories, will not disappear in any credible future; that the future, indeed, will be one in which the peoples of the African diaspora operate as the directors and beneficiaries of technological progress; and that the cultural meaning of blackness will continually change as generations advance. This last point links Afrofuturism with other contemporary debates concerning the emergence of a "post-black" art. In the late 1990s, artist Glenn Ligon and museum curator Thelma Golden developed the idea that African-American art may have entered such a phase. Golden gave the concept wider currency as the framing device for a 2001 exhibition at the Studio Museum in Harlem (Touré 31–32), using the term to mark a transition between black artists whose work was defined by the racial exclusions and battles of the past century and a millennial generation whose work operates within a society where segments of black culture have been incorporated into mainstream popular culture (41). Whatever we make of this claim, the exhibition showed that some artists could create inspiring work that reconfigures narratives about race and identity in ways largely unavailable to racial politics in the last century (see Golden). As a form that seeks an imaginative engagement with Afro-diasporic history through science fiction, Afrofuturism may be seen as part of the new twenty-first-century black aesthetic that the term "post-black" attempts to describe.

An important question to confront, therefore, is the SF genre's reputation as a repository of boys' adventure stories descending from colonialist histories of racial exploitation and exclusion (see Rieder). Obviously, if this history is accepted at face value—that is, if no counterhistories to it are imagined or constructed—then any writer of color operating within the genre is open to having the "authenticity" or "seriousness" of his or her work questioned (see Tucker 50–53). After all, how can any genre contaminated by such baggage be of use in forecasting or validating the histories and potentials of peoples who, as Hopkinson has said, "are on the wrong side of the strange-looking ship that appears out of nowhere" ("Introduction" 7)? Addressing this assumption in *So Long Been Dreaming*, Hopkinson argues that, precisely *because* of this history, the tools provided by a Eurocentric culture not only belong to anyone who has been taught them but also can be used to transform meaning within the genre. Glossing her Caribbean reimagining of the Red Riding Hood story, she notes that "[i]n my hands, massa's tools don't dismantle massa's house ... [I]n fact, I don't want to destroy it so much as I want to undertake massive renovations—then build me a house of my own" (8).

Thus, the specific investments of Afrofuturist practice vindicate the spirit of the form, making it a constructive way of framing the future as complex and contradictory rather than destructive. Science fiction is claimed as a powerful tool that, in Hopkinson's words, "makes it possible to think about new ways of doing things" (9). Those new ways include not only a demolition of racial hierarchy but also an articulation of futures in languages other than English, using points of cultural reference other than those descending from a European tradition. Uppinder Mehan, Hopkinson's co-editor on *So Long Been Dreaming*, expands on this point by arguing for the necessity of postcolonial futures that allow the descendants of racial and colonial oppression to see "how life might be otherwise" (270). Afrofuturism can be viewed within this more general political and aesthetic project, imbricating the experiences of the African diaspora with those of colonized peoples in Asia, South America, and elsewhere. We thus arrive at a Futurism with the potential to evade exclusive investment with a particular population—in theory at least, a Futurism that has no country.

Whatever we make of such claims, Afrofuturism is still a minority discourse, a single current within the broad river of science fiction—and speculative literature more generally. The brute fact of the matter is that SF remains predominantly white in terms of its writers and readers. It should not be surprising, therefore, that narratives organized around black identities and histories represent a relatively small part of generic production. What Afrofuturism has helped us to appreciate, however, is that the work of this group is no longer invisible or inconsequential. Like older currents in science fiction, such as the New Wave, feminist utopia, cyberpunk, or, more recently, the New Weird and steampunk, Afrofuturism can be defined as a distinctive subgenre, marked by a particular interest and a general approach. As we have seen, it also inspires a robust scholarship that has opened up a fertile critical terrain, mapping accomplishments, limitations, and potentials. If, to paraphrase Langston Hughes, black authors and scholars of SF have faced a racial mountain, then they have scaled a good way up it.

Works Cited

Bernardi, Daniel. *Star Trek and History: Race-ing Toward a White Future*. New Brunswick, NJ: Rutgers UP, 1998. Print.

Bould, Mark. "Come Alive by Saying No: An Introduction to Black Power SF." *Science Fiction Studies* 34.2 (July 2007): 220–40. Print.

Butler, Octavia E. "The Monophobic Response." *Dark Matter: A Century of Speculative Fiction from the African Diaspora*. Ed. Sheree R. Thomas. New York: Warner, 2000. 415–16. Print.

Davis, Thulani. "The Future May Be Bleak, but It's Not Black." *The Village Voice* (Feb. 1, 1983): 17–19. Print.
Delany, Samuel R. "Racism and Science Fiction." *Dark Matter: A Century of Speculative Fiction from the African Diaspora*. Ed. Sheree R. Thomas. New York: Warner, 2000. 383–97. Print.
Dery, Mark. "Black to the Future: Afro-Futurism 1.0." *Afro-Future Females: Black Writers Chart Science Fiction's Newest New-Wave Trajectory*. Ed. Marleen Barr. Columbus: Ohio State UP, 2008. 6–13. Print.
———. "Black to the Future: Interviews with Samuel R. Delany, Greg Tate, and Tricia Rose." *Flame Wars: The Discourse of Cyberculture*. Ed. Mark Dery. Durham, NC: Duke UP, 1994. 179–222. Print.
Enteen, Jillana. "'On the Receiving End of the Colonization': Nalo Hopkinson's 'Nansi Web." *Science Fiction Studies* 34.2 (July 2007): 262–82. Print.
Eshun, Kodwo. "Further Considerations on Afrofuturism." *CR: The New Centennial Review* 3.2 (Summer 2003): 287–302. Print.
———. *More Brilliant Than the Sun: Adventures in Sonic Fiction*. London: Quartet, 1998. Print.
Gilder, George. *Life After Television: The Coming Transformation of Media and American Life*. New York: Norton, 1992. Print.
Golden, Thelma. "Introduction." *Freestyle*. New York: Studio Museum in Harlem, 2001. 14–15. Print.
Hopkinson, Nalo. "Introduction." *So Long Been Dreaming: Postcolonial Science Fiction and Fantasy*. Ed. Nalo Hopkinson and Uppinder Mehan. Vancouver, BC: Arsenal Pulp, 2004. 7–9. Print.
———, ed. *Mojo: Conjure Stories*. New York: Warner, 2003. Print.
Kellner, Douglas. "Ernst Bloch, Utopia, and Ideology Critique." *Not Yet: Reconsidering Ernst Bloch*. Ed. Jamie Owen Daniel and Tom Moylan. New York: Verso, 1997. 80–95. Print.
Lavender, Isiah, III. "Ethnoscapes: Environment and Language in Ishmael Reed's *Mumbo Jumbo*, Colson Whitehead's *The Intuitionist*, and Samuel R. Delany's *Babel-17*." *Science Fiction Studies* 34.2 (July 2007): 187–200. Print.
Mehan, Uppinder. "Final Thoughts." *So Long Been Dreaming: Postcolonial Science Fiction and Fantasy*. Ed. Nalo Hopkinson and Uppinder Mehan. Vancouver, BC: Arsenal Pulp, 2004. 269–70. Print.
Miller, Paul D. "Yet Do I Wonder." *Dark Matter: A Century of Speculative Fiction from the African Diaspora*. Ed. Sheree R. Thomas. New York: Warner, 2000. 408–14. Print.
Morrison, Toni. *Playing in the Dark: Whiteness and the Literary Imagination*. 1992. New York: Vintage, 1993. Print.
Mosley, Walter. "Black to the Future." *Dark Matter: A Century of Speculative Fiction from the African Diaspora*. Ed. Sheree R. Thomas. New York: Warner, 2000. 405–07. Print.
Nelson, Alondra. "Introduction: Future Texts." *Social Text* 20.2 (Summer 2002): 1–15. Print.
Norris, Pippa. *Digital Divide: Civic Engagement, Information Poverty, and the Internet Worldwide*. Cambridge, UK: Cambridge UP, 2001. Print.
Ramírez, Catherine R. "Afrofuturism/Chicanafuturism: Fictive Kin." *Aztlán: A Journal of Chicano Studies* 33.1 (Spring 2008): 185–94. Print.
Rieder, John. *Colonialism and the Emergence of Science Fiction*. Middletown, CT: Wesleyan UP, 2008. Print.
Saunders, Charles R. "Why Blacks Should Read (and Write) Science Fiction." *Dark Matter: A Century of Speculative Fiction from the African Diaspora*. Ed. Sheree R. Thomas. New York: Warner, 2000. 398–404. Print.

Smith, Darryl A. "Droppin' Science Fiction: Signification and Singularity in the Metapocalypse of Du Bois, Baraka, and Bell." *Science Fiction Studies* 34.2 (July 2007): 201–19. Print.

Thomas, Sheree R., ed. *Dark Matter: A Century of Speculative Fiction from the African Diaspora*. New York: Warner, 2000. Print.

———. "Introduction." *Dark Matter: Reading the Bones*. Ed. Sheree R. Thomas. New York: Warner, 2004. ix–xii. Print.

Touré. *Who's Afraid of Post-Blackness?: What It Means to Be Black Now*. New York: Free Press, 2011. Print.

Tucker, Jeffrey Allen. *A Sense of Wonder: Samuel R. Delany, Race, Identity, and Difference*. Middletown, CT: Wesleyan UP, 2004. Print.

Vint, Sherryl. "'Only by Experience': Embodiment and the Limitations of Realism in Neo-Slave Narratives." *Science Fiction Studies* 34.2 (July 2007): 241–60. Print.

Weheliye, Alexander G. "'Feenin': Posthuman Voices in Contemporary Black Popular Music." *Social Text* 20.2 (Summer 2002): 21–47. Print.

Yaszek, Lisa. "Afrofuturism, Science Fiction, and the History of the Future." *Socialism and Democracy* 20.3 (Nov. 2006): 41–60. Print.

Zuberi, Nabeel. "Is This The Future?: Black Music and Technology Discourse." *Science Fiction Studies* 34.2 (July 2007): 283–300. Print.

CHAPTER 44

UTOPIANISM

PHILLIP E. WEGNER

Utopianism is not simply one among a range of possible themes or motifs in modern science fiction—like, say, technology, time travel, telepathy, teleportation, alien encounters, alternate histories, postapocalypse, the far future, or dystopia, all of which Mark Rose usefully assembles under the more abstract categories of space, time, machine, and monster (32). Rather, it is fundamental to this vital modern genre. Such an assertion may strike some as behind the times, for there seems to be something decidedly old-fashioned about the question of SF's utopianism, redolent as it is of the unruly countercultural days of SF studies' youth, out of place in a maturing discipline that has achieved a measure of academic respectability. While SF studies often undertakes the quest for legitimacy under the aegis of a welcome cultural-studies inclusiveness that flies in the face of conservative disciplinary retrenchments such as the new-formalist "surface reading" (see Bartolovich; Levinson), the end result can often be the same: the transformation of cultural criticism (indeed, culture itself) into a kind of narrow specialization, thus becoming what Bertolt Brecht saw as an intervention that "ha[s] no particular material consequences, and foster[s] no particular change"—and which Brecht thereby identifies as the very form of "being ideological" (Jameson, *Brecht* 25).

In fact, it is precisely its utopianism that distinguishes modern science fiction both from precursor forms such as the fable, travel narrative, Gothic, and *voyage extraordinaire*, and from the contemporary practices of futurology and prognostication. Moreover, what Fredric Jameson has described as the "desire called Utopia" at work in all science fiction is a matter of narrative and not, as is often assumed, of representation, and it is here that its constitutive force resides. In order to grasp what is at stake in such a claim, however, we first need to reframe our understanding of SF's utopianism. Few would dispute the deep and intimate interactions that occur between the literary or narrative utopia and modern science fiction, or even the contributions the older genre—founded by Thomas More's *Utopia* (1516), or more precisely by those "second" writers who saw in *Utopia* a new literary technology they could imitate, repeat, and refine (see Wegner, *Imaginary* 31–33)—made to SF's development. Science fiction, like the utopia, is also part of the larger tradition of romance, which focuses on the representation of space and the building of worlds rather than on character and individual psychology, as in the more recent prose form of the novel.

Moreover, the naturalist rejoinder to the revival of utopian narratives that occurs in the late nineteenth century—inaugurated by the publication of Edward Bellamy's extraordinary international bestseller, *Looking Backward, 2000–1887* (1888)—gives rise, in works such as Jack London's *The Iron Heel* (1908), to one of the most significant subgenres of modern SF: the dystopia (see Wegner, *Life* 117–24). Finally, writing long after the establishment of the generic institution of science fiction, and in another moment of resurgence in the production of new utopias—including such classics as Ursula K. Le Guin's *The Dispossessed* (1974), Joanna Russ's *The Female Man* (1975), Marge Piercy's *Woman on the Edge of Time* (1976), and Samuel R. Delany's *Triton* (1976)—Darko Suvin maintains that we have come full circle, utopia heretofore to be understood as nothing less than "the socio-political subgenre of sf" ("Science Fiction" 38). Tom Moylan qualifies this judgment, identifying this mid-1970s outburst of what he calls the "critical utopia" as a revitalization of the utopian tradition that nonetheless maintains an "awareness of [its] limitations. . ., reject[ing] utopia as blueprint while preserving it as dream" (10). Yet Moylan ultimately agrees with Suvin in seeing SF and utopia as allied practices that estrange and critique our present-day world (35–36).

One of the most important things that the narrative utopia contributes to the development of science fiction is the latter's materialist orientation. That is, the worlds envisioned in narrative utopias—and it is this dimension that separates the genre from such kin as the pastoral—are shown to be the product of human labor: it is, after all, the all-too-human King Utopus who conquers the Abraxan peninsula, bringing its "rude and rustic people to such a perfection of culture and humanity" and ordering his new Utopian populace to excavate the trench that creates their island nation (More 113). The later, more flexible and inclusive mode of science fiction extends a similar materialist and historical agency to the natural world itself. And while in much SF the privileged figure for such an orientation is technology, in both its mechanical and its social-institutional forms, this materialism is also paradoxically evident in some of the genre's most seemingly idealist devices, such as telepathy or telekinesis: for all these need to be understood ultimately as figures of human intellectual energy made directly and immediately manifest in the world.

It is this materialism that Suvin underscores in the first part of his landmark Brechtian redefinition of science fiction as "*the literature of cognitive estrangement*" (*Metamorphoses* 4; emphasis in original); and it is also what is at stake in his more contested efforts to distinguish SF from "non-cognitive" practices of estrangement such as fantasy. Whatever the productive challenges that have emerged to Suvin's opposition of cognitive and noncognitive fictions—a binary that Suvin himself has come to reflect upon further in some of his more recent writings (see Suvin, "Considering")—it has been the second part of this definition, with its emphasis on the negative or critical labors of de-naturalization performed by SF texts, that has been its far more influential aspect. While Suvin's notion of "cognition" provides a convenient shorthand for grasping SF's specific representational strategies and his concept of "estrangement" a way of indexing its critical or modernist energies (see Wegner, "Jameson's" 8–9), there is a third aspect to Suvin's modeling of the genre that is often overshadowed by these other two. Suvin later adds that science fiction is also *"distinguished by the narrative dominance or hegemony of a fictional 'novum' (novelty, innovation) validated by cognitive logic"* (*Metamorphoses* 63; emphasis in original). Here, he borrows and, as he acknowledges, adapts or refunctions the concept of the novum from the work of the most important twentieth-century theorist of utopianism, the German philosopher, Ernst Bloch. For Bloch, utopianism, which he identifies as the utopian impulse— or, as in the title of his most important work, the "principle of hope" (*Das Prinzip Hoffnung*)—is a fundamental desire for the future in the form of the new, and it is this desire that drives all history forward.

Furthermore, this utopian impulse is manifest in *every* expression of culture and human creativity, even in its most degraded and apparently irredeemable forms. The primary task for cultural criticism, as reconceived by Bloch, is to develop a hermeneutic sensitive to the feeblest traces of this utopian hope, or anticipatory illumination, and this is what he attempts to do in the three volumes of *The Principle of Hope*, an encyclopedic work that Jameson characterizes as

> a vast and disorderly exploration of the manifestations of hope on all levels of reality: from the ontological itself, in the central and crucial analysis of human time, fanning out to touch upon existential psychology . . . ; ethics . . . ; logic . . . ; political science . . . ; the social planning inherent in the conception of Utopias of all kinds; *Technik*, not only in the sense of the scientific achievements of the world of the future, but also in terms of the way in which it alters our relationship to the objects around us; sociology, in the form of the analysis of the wish-fulfillments of advertising and popular culture; ideological and literary criticism, finally, in its all-embracing account of the archetypes of Utopia in art, myth, and religion. (*Marxism* 120–21)

Jameson's own long-standing fidelity to this hermeneutic project is made evident in a more recent book, where he notes the imperative "to change the valences on phenomena which so far exist only in our own present; and experimentally to declare positive things which are clearly negative in our own world, to affirm that dystopia is in reality Utopia if examined more closely, to isolate specific features in our empirical present so as to read them as components of a different system" (*Valences* 434). Elsewhere and more famously, Jameson develops a related reading strategy, which would also be applicable to both popular and more formally adventurous forms of science fiction, arguing that "all contemporary works of art—whether those of high culture and modernism or of mass culture and commercial culture—have as their underlying impulse—albeit in what is often distorted and repressed unconscious form—our deepest fantasies about the nature of social life, both as we live it now, and as we feel in our bones it ought rather to be lived" (*Signatures* 46).

There are two implications of Suvin's deployment of Bloch's concept of the novum that have a significant bearing on any discussion of SF's utopianism. First, a science-fictional novum represents more than the merely new, as more commonplace understandings of the notions of novelty or innovation would have it. Rather, a "novum or cognitive innovation is a totalizing phenomenon or relationship deviating from the author's and implied reader's norm of reality ... [I]ts novelty is 'totalizing' in the sense that it entails a change of the whole universe of the tale, or at least of crucially important aspects thereof" (*Metamorphoses* 64)—or, as Jameson puts it, the novum is "the utterly and unexpectedly new, the new which astonishes by its absolute and intrinsic unpredictability" (*Marxism* 126). Second, this formulation of the novum strips the notion of utopianism of any residual axiological or evaluative connotations. In other words, there is no necessary indication whether this radically and totally new world is to be taken as better (*eu-topian*) or worse (*dys-topian*) than the reader's present-day society (see Sargent 9). Indeed, for Bloch, the novum's sheer alienating *otherness* will mean those condemned to live only in this world cannot help perhaps but react to it with revulsion or even horror.

One of the primary labors of any SF text is to give figurative form to such a dramatic break from the status quo. When this utopianism is absent, the work degenerates into mere futurological speculation, projecting another modified or reformed world that is, in fact, different from our own only in the most superficial of ways. As Moylan has said of Suvin's application of Bloch's theories to the analysis of SF: "By not only tracking what was at hand in the tendencies of the historical moment as portrayed in the alternative world but also pointing, through the textual novum, toward the potential for radically new directions in the latencies of the moment, Suvin's claim for sf brought it to a level of sociopolitical value that many sensed but never fully theorized" (*Scraps* 45). By the same token, it is the very totalizing drive of these figurative efforts that quickly brings the genre up against its representational limits. In his own important contributions to our understanding of SF, Jameson maintains that any full representation of such a radical alterity is, in fact, impossible because we lack the cognitive tools, even the language, to bring into focus something that breaks so completely with the practices and structures shaping our everyday existence. As Redrick Shuart, the protagonist of Arkady and Boris Strugatsky's *Roadside Picnic* (1972), proclaims near the novel's end, in a scene that could be understood as an allegory of the representational problems confronted by all SF: "I am an animal, you see that. I don't have the words, they didn't teach me the words. I don't know how to think, the bastards didn't let me learn how to think" (145). In this sense, all SF works are, like Redrick's quest, failures.

And yet, out of such representational failure emerges a very different set of operations taking place in any SF text. On the one hand, through estrangement, science fiction "enacts and enables a structurally unique 'method' for apprehending the present as history, and this is irrespective of the 'pessimism' or 'optimism' of the imaginary future world which is the pretext for that defamiliarization" (Jameson, *Archaeologies* 288). On the other hand, Jameson argues, the genre's "deepest vocation is to bring home, in local and determinate ways and with a fullness of concrete detail, our constitutional inability to imagine Utopia itself: and this, not owing to any individual failure of imagination but as the result of the systemic, cultural and ideological closure of which we are all in one way or another prisoners" (289). In this way, Jameson begins to turn our attention away from the manifest contents of SF texts to the genre's form. In the climax of the chapter in which he advances these claims, Jameson shifts his focus to *Roadside Picnic*, maintaining that, like the other works he discusses, it "is self-referential, its narrative production determined by the structural impossibility of producing that Utopian text which it nonetheless miraculously becomes" (295). Yet still, at its climax, the reader witnesses "the unexpected emergence, as it were, beyond 'the nightmare of History' and from out of the most archaic longings of the human race, of the impossible and inexpressible Utopian impulse" (295). In this way, the "desire called Utopia," the struggle to break free of the enclosures of one world into a radically different one, becomes the motor driving the narrative forward.

Every SF narrative can thus be understood to unfold through three distinct stages: first, a critical estrangement of the author's contemporary reality; second, a pushing up against the limits of representation and the contemporary imagination; and finally, a leap into a void where language and signification themselves break down. The most concrete manifestation of any SF narrative's utopianism is to be located in those moments where the closure of the conventional realist work is displaced by an openness to the unfinished potential of historical becoming. In this way, the genre's commitment to utopianism receives figuration only through what Jameson describes as an "absolute formalism, in which the new content emerges itself from the form and is a projection of it" (*Archaeologies* 212).

A similar dynamic is evident in Mark Rose's striking reconsideration of apocalypse stories in SF. Rose argues that the narrative movement of science fiction "can be understood as an attempt to restore human meaning to time ... And, insofar as science fiction is committed to the humanization of time, it naturally tends toward fictions of apocalypse" (99). In terms that resonate with Jameson's formulation of SF's utopianism, Rose concludes his book by noting that the figurative realization of this apocalypse also signals the narrative's conclusion:

> Because it lies beyond consciousness, beyond language, the apocalyptic moment is unrealizable in narrative. And yet, because it represents the logical limit of the dialectic between the human and the non-human, science fiction inevitably moves toward apocalypse. Meaningless in itself, the idea of apocalypse is nevertheless the necessary condition for the creation of meaning in the genre. At that far point, the separation between self and other, human and non-human, collapses, as does any distinction between past and future, finite and infinite, matter and spirit, necessity and freedom. All the terms that constitute the substance of science fiction disappear. (195)

Through a series of perspicacious readings, Rose shows how this dialectic unfolds in such classic works as Olaf Stapledon's *Last and First Men* (1930), Stanislaw Lem's *Solaris*

(1961), J. G. Ballard's *The Drowned World* (1962), and Arthur C. Clarke's *2001: A Space Odyssey* (1968).

Rose similarly offers us a new way of understanding why Verne's *voyages extraordinaires*, while indispensible precursors to the genre, fall short of making the passage into science fiction proper: for what they lack is the utopianism found in the formal resolution of later works in the genre. Verne's *Journey to the Center of the Earth* (1864), for example, already embraces the materialism fundamental to SF, with the book's coda, in Rose's reading, affirming "the materialist faith that the book of nature is readable to the last word, that materialism is merely a cryptogram to be decoded" (66). And yet this is materialism as ideology, and when the narrative approaches what should, in fact, have been the story's climax in the apocalyptic breakdown of this closed system with the voyagers' arrival at the earth's core, it retreats, literally expelling its protagonists back into the "known and safe space" of southern Europe (65).

A very different narrative dynamic is evident in H. G. Wells's two great "scientific romances"—*The Time Machine* (1895) and *The War of the Worlds* (1898)—that together help stabilize the generic field from which all subsequent science fiction will emerge. The narrative of *The Time Machine* unfolds through the positing and overturning of a series of explanatory paradigms offered up by the "Time Traveller." Unlike in Verne's earlier work, however, there is no arresting of this movement until, in the narrative's penultimate paragraph, the arrival of an "apocalypse": "At that I understood. At the risk of disappointing Richardson I stayed on waiting for the Time Traveller: waiting for the second, perhaps still stranger story, and the specimens and photographs he would bring with him. But I am beginning now to fear that I must wait a lifetime. The Time Traveller vanished three years ago. And, as everybody knows now, he has never returned" (90). It is this "second, perhaps still stranger story" that pulls the narrative action forward, with its promise of a full unveiling of an estranged utopian future. This sense of the radical alterity and hence unrepresentability of such a future is then reinforced by the narrator's brief epilogue, where he states, "But to me the future is still black and blank—is a vast ignorance, lit at a few casual places by the memory of his story" (90). In the conclusion of *The War of the Worlds*, this utopian future is projected onto a larger collective canvas: "It may be that in the larger design of the universe this invasion from Mars is not without its ultimate benefit for men; it has robbed us of that serene confidence in the future which is the most fruitful source of decadence, the gifts to human science it has brought are enormous, and it has done much to promote the conception of the commonweal of mankind" (192). And yet, once again, as soon as the conditions of possibility for the emergence of this utopian otherness are established, the narrative comes to a close, this world too remaining cloaked in darkness.

In its fundamental utopianism, science fiction reveals an unexpected kinship with a set of narrative practices: the *Künstlerroman* or artist's novel, the universal history, and the comedy of remarriage. Each of these four forms serves as the utopian Other to what Jameson has identified as the four realist genres: respectively, naturalism, the *Bildungsroman*, the historical novel, and the novel of adultery ("A Note" 262). I call the former grouping, following the lead of Alain Badiou, *evental genres*. An event, in Badiou's meaning, is much like Bloch's novum: something that happens "that cannot be reduced to its ordinary inscription in 'what there is'" (*Ethics* 41). "It takes place in a situation but is not of that situation," Peter Hallward notes (xxv), and hence the event is the "void of the situation, that aspect of the situation that has absolutely no interest in preserving the status quo as such" (114). In short, the event is the very possibility of a new beginning, the inauguration of that which was unexpected, unaccounted for, and unknown. Echoing one of the major themes of *Roadside Picnic*, Badiou argues that language is inextricably intertwined with the known world; "an Event," on the other hand, "is supernumerary, and so it does not belong to the language of the situation" (*Being* 329). As a result, and in synch with the related concepts of Bloch's utopian novum and Rose's apocalypse, the event escapes every effort to represent it directly. Badiou maintains that an event cannot be communicated but rather is encountered: "It is an Ethics of the Real, if it is true that—as Lacan suggests—all access to the Real is of the order of an encounter" (*Ethics* 52).

Building further on these insights, Slavoj Žižek distinguishes between what he calls authentic and pseudo-events:

> The answer involves the way an Event relates to the Situation whose Truth it articulates: Nazism was a pseudo-Event and the October Revolution was an authentic Event, because only the latter related to the very foundations of the Situation of capitalist order, effectively undermining those foundations, in contrast to Nazism, which staged a pseudo-Event precisely in order to *save* the capitalist order. (*Ticklish* 138–39; emphasis in original)

There are some significant lessons in Žižek's distinction for an understanding of SF's utopian narrative dynamic. First, a similar dialectic is at work in all of the cognate concepts discussed in this chapter: there are pseudo-utopias, pseudo-novums, and pseudo-apocalypses, as well as pseudo-events. Second, the inaugural event or the apparent novum opening an SF narrative invariably turns out to be a pseudo-event. The other world figured in the text is thus revealed as no more than a continuation or repetition of the status quo, exposing its underlying logics in the light of SF's estranging representations. This fact is given brilliant figuration in *Roadside Picnic*, where the reader soon realizes the apparently world-changing event of the Visitation, which one character refers to as "the most important discovery not only of the past thirty years but of the entire history of mankind" (*Roadside* 5), is no more than an excuse—what the Russian Formalists called a "motivation of the device" (Erlich 194)—for the genre's critical estranging operations to begin. The world that results from the Visitation—the positing of incomprehensible alien artifacts, or perhaps no more than the detritus left over from a "roadside picnic, on some road in the cosmos" (*Roadside* 102–03)—turns out to be one where our own world's senseless bureaucratic protocols, instrumentalism, greed, and violent exploitation of the planet, its resources, and people are exposed in an extremely unflattering light. The deeper utopianism of the very best modern SF occurs in the narrative process of replacing this pseudo-event by an open figure, or placeholder, of a still-to-come authentic event (or novum, or apocalypse).

Such a movement is brilliantly on display in one of the most significant SF works of the mid-twentieth century, Alfred Bester's *The Stars My Destination* (1956). Bester's novel focuses on the accidental discovery of the new human technology of teleportation—or "jaunting"—and its profound effects on society: "Within three generations the entire solar system was on the jaunte. The transition was more spectacular than the changeover from horse and buggy to gasoline age five centuries before. On three planets and eight satellites, social, legal, and economic structures crashed while the new customs and laws demanded by universal jaunting mushroomed in their place" (13). Crucially, Bester's novel, like *Roadside Picnic*, brings home the often-hard lesson that technological developments, even the most dramatic ones (and jaunting is in no small part a figure for the 1950s communications revolutions that seemed to shrink space and tie the planet into a new "global village"), are not necessarily events. Walter Benjamin similarly argues that the promises of the architectural practices of the early nineteenth century—technologies celebrated by their enthusiasts with a furor paralleled by the champions of film in Benjamin's time, television in Bester's era, and the Internet today—remained unrealized precisely because this moment proved "incapable of responding to the new technological possibilities with a new social order" (*Arcades* 26). The twenty-fifth-century world portrayed in Bester's novel is one where the characteristic features of the 1950s—social conformism, class hierarchies, corporate power, rampant consumerism, and the postwar relegation of women to the domestic sphere—are reflected back to us in a dramatically estranging light: "After a thousand years of civilization (it says here) we're still property. Jaunting's such a danger to our virtue, our value, our mint condition, that we're locked up like gold plate in a safe. There's nothing for us to do . . . nothing respectable. No jobs. No careers. There's no getting out, Gully, unless you burst out and smash all the rules" (74; ellipsis in original).

As in *The Time Machine* and *The War of the Worlds* before it and *Roadside Picnic* later on, an actual utopian change of affairs achieves figuration only in the novel's concluding pages. During the course of events, the protagonist Gulliver (Gully) Foyle discovers that he has become the first human to develop the capacity to jaunt through space. In the midst of the marvelous formal and typographical surrealism of its conclusion, Bester writes, "He went flickering along the new near-horizontal axis, this new space-time geodesic, driven by the miracle of a human mind no longer inhibited by concepts of the impossible" (236). "The miracle of a human mind no longer inhibited by concepts of the impossible"—how better to describe the utopian shattering of the constraints of the world that occurs in what Badiou calls the event?

This personal event presages a collective one that occurs in the novel's final pages as a result of Foyle's distribution of a monstrously destructive technology, a figure for the novum or radical otherness of human freedom unexpectedly realized across the globe:

> I've handed life and death back to the people who do the living and dying. The common man's been whipped and led long enough by driven men like us . . . Compulsive men . . . Tiger men who can't help lashing the world before them. We're all tigers, the

three of us, but who the hell are we to make decisions for the world just because we're compulsive? Let the world make its own choice between life and death. Why should we be saddled with the responsibility? (254; ellipses in original)

The other world that this event opens up onto, as in Wells and the Strugatskys, remains only glimpsed at the outermost horizons of the narrative, in the figures of a far-future humanity who, in the novel's final scene, sit alongside a dreaming Foyle "prepared to await the awakening" (258).

Finally, to offer an example of this narrative dynamic at work in more contemporary SF, I turn to the climax of Ken MacLeod's *The Sky Road* (1999), the final novel in his magnificent "Fall Revolution" quartet (1995–99). The novel's protagonist, Myra Godwin, the president-dictator of the tiny International Scientific and Technical Workers' Republic (ISTWR), located within the borders of Kazakhstan, seeks military aid to protect her nation from an imminent invasion. Her failed efforts have the dire consequence of alerting the US and UN militaries to the ISTWR's cache of banned nuclear weapons hidden among the clutter of space stations, weapons platforms, communications satellites, and junk orbiting the planet. When Myra refuses to relinquish these weapons, the imperial military powers begin to level her nation's major cities and, even more sinisterly, to direct their fire at the refugee groups streaming out of them. When her own caravan comes under attack, Myra decides to detonate the orbital weapons, thereby unleashing the "ablation cascade," an event that "means the end of satellite guidance, global positioning, comsats, the nets, everything! It'll be like the world going blind!" (394). It is precisely this unexpected and undreamt event that creates the preconditions for the emergence of the postnational "utopian" world that we see figured in the alternating chapters of the novel.

In the novel's final pages, MacLeod presents this striking scene:

> Riding into the first dawn of the new world, Myra knew that the little camcopter dancing a couple of meters in front of her might well be relaying the last television news most of its watchers would ever see.
>
> Behind her, in a slow struggle that ended with the ambulances and litters of the injured and dying, the Kazakh migration spread to the horizon. The sun was rising behind them, silhouetting their scattered, tattered banners. There was only one audience, now, that was worth speaking to: the inheritors.
>
> "Nothing is written," she said. "The future is ours to shape. When you take the cities, spare the scientists and engineers. Whatever they may have done in the past you need them for the future. Let's make it a better one." (401)

The novel's (and the quartet's) final image—a statue of Myra, located in a Scottish community hundreds of years hence, "riding, at the head of her own swift cavalry ... and, floating bravely above her head and above her army, the black flag on which nothing is written" (406)—resonates with one that occurred in our world only a few years before MacLeod began publishing science fiction. As Žižek explains:

> The most sublime image that emerged in the political upheavals of the last years—and the term "sublime" is to be conceived here in the strictest Kantian sense—was undoubtedly the unique picture from the time of the violent overthrow of Ceaușescu in Romania: the rebels waving the national flag with the red star, the Communist symbol, cut out, so that instead of the symbol standing for the organizing principle of the national life, there was nothing but a hole in its center. It is difficult to imagine a more salient index of the "open" character of a historical situation "in its becoming," as Kierkegaard would have put it, of that intermediate phase when the former Master-Signifier, although it has already lost the hegemonical power, has not yet been replaced by the new one ... [W]hat really matters is that the masses who poured into the streets of Bucharest "experienced" the situation as "open," that they participated in the unique intermediate state of passage from one discourse (social link) to another, when, for a brief, passing moment, the hole in the big Other, the symbolic order, became visible. (*Tarrying* 1)

With this figuration of the "hole in the big Other," we arrive at the true utopianism of MacLeod's rich and complex narrative: dismantling any notion of rigid historical determinism and fully opening up the closure of prehistory, MacLeod's utopia cannot be identified with any of the variety of possible worlds mapped out in his work. Rather, it is the utopia of an explosive upswelling of an event, of a future as permanent revolution where we are once again endowed with the power—and the responsibility—to act as free subjects. It is in the narrative education of our desire for this kind of an event—for a novum, for apocalypse; in short, for utopia—that the continued vitality of all science fiction lies.

Works Cited

Badiou, Alain. *Being and Event*. 1988. Trans. Oliver Feltham. New York: Continuum, 2005. Print.

———. *Ethics: An Essay on the Understanding of Radical Evil*. 1998. Trans. Peter Hallward. New York: Verso, 2001. Print.

Bartolovich, Crystal. "Humanities of Scale: Marxism, Surface Reading—and Milton." *PMLA* 127.1 (Jan. 2012): 115–21. Print.

Benjamin, Walter. *The Arcades Project*. 1982. Trans. Howard Eiland and Kevin McLaughlin. Cambridge, MA: Harvard UP, 1999. Print.

Bester, Alfred. *The Stars My Destination*. 1956. New York: Vintage, 1996. Print.

Bloch, Ernst. *The Principle of Hope*. 3 vols. 1938–47. Trans. Neville Plaice, Stephen Plaice, and Paul Knight. Cambridge, MA: MIT, 1986. Print.

Erlich, Victor. *Russian Formalism*. 1955. 4th ed. The Hague: Mouton, 1980. Print.

Hallward, Peter. *Badiou: A Subject to Truth*. Minneapolis: U of Minnesota P, 2003. Print.

Jameson, Fredric. *Archaeologies of the Future: The Desire Called Utopia and Other Science Fictions*. New York: Verso, 2005. Print.

———. *Brecht and Method*. New York: Verso, 1998. Print.

———. *Marxism and Form: Twentieth-Century Dialectical Theories of Literature*. Princeton, NJ: Princeton UP, 1971. Print.

——. "A Note on Literary Realism in Conclusion." *Adventures in Realism*. Ed. Mathew Beaumont. Oxford: Blackwell, 2007. 261–71. Print.

——. *Signatures of the Visible*. 1990. New York: Routledge, 2007. Print.

——. *Valences of the Dialectic*. New York: Verso, 2009. Print.

Levinson, Marjorie. "What Is New Formalism?" *PMLA* 122.2 (Mar. 2007): 558–69. Print.

MacLeod, Ken. *The Sky Road*. 1999. New York: Tor, 2001. Print.

More, Thomas. *Utopia*. 1816. Ed. Edward Surtz and J. H. Hexter. *The Yale Edition of the Complete Works of St. Thomas More*. Vol. 4. Ed. Louis L. Martz. New Haven, CT: Yale UP, 1965. Print.

Moylan, Tom. *Demand the Impossible: Science Fiction and the Utopian Imagination*. New York: Methuen, 1986. Print.

——. *Scraps of the Untainted Sky: Science Fiction, Utopia, Dystopia*. Boulder, CO: Westview, 2001. Print.

Rose, Mark. *Alien Encounters: Anatomy of Science Fiction*. Cambridge, MA: Harvard UP, 1981. Print.

Sargent, Lyman Tower. "The Three Faces of Utopianism Revisited." *Utopian Studies* 5.1 (1994): 1–37. Print.

Strugatsky, Arkady, and Boris Strugatsky. *Roadside Picnic/Tale of the Troika*. 1972/1968. Trans. Antonia W. Bouis. New York: Macmillan, 1977. Print.

Suvin, Darko. "Considering the Sense of 'Fantasy' or 'Fantastic Fiction': An Effusion." *Extrapolation* 41.3 (2000): 209–47. Print.

——. *Metamorphoses of Science Fiction: On the Poetics and History of a Literary Genre*. New Haven, CT: Yale UP, 1979. Print.

——. "Science Fiction and Utopian Fiction: Degrees of Kinship." 1974. *Positions and Presuppositions in Science Fiction*. Kent, OH: Kent State UP, 1988. Print.

Wegner, Phillip E. *Imaginary Communities: Utopia, the Nation, and the Spatial Histories of Modernity*. Berkeley: U of California P, 2002. Print.

——. "Jameson's Modernisms; or, the Desire Called Utopia." *Diacritics* 37.4 (Winter 2007): 3–20. Print.

——. *Life Between Two Deaths, 1989–2001: U.S. Culture in the Long Nineties*. Durham, NC: Duke UP, 2009. Print.

Wells, H. G. *A Critical Edition of The War of the Worlds: H.G. Wells's Scientific Romance*. 1898. Ed. David Y. Hughes and Harry M. Geduld. Bloomington: Indiana UP, 1993. Print.

——. *The Definitive Time Machine: A Critical Edition of H.G. Wells's Scientific Romance*. 1895. Ed. Harry M. Geduld. Bloomington: Indiana UP, 1987. Print.

Žižek, Slavoj. *Tarrying with the Negative: Kant, Hegel, and the Critique of Ideology*. Durham, NC: Duke UP, 1993. Print.

——. *The Ticklish Subject: The Absent Center of Political Ontology*. New York: Verso, 1999. Print.

Index

Abbott, Carl, 486
Abé, Kobo, 49
"Abhorsen" trilogy (Nix), 134
Aboard a Flying Saucer (Bethurum), 353
About, Edmond, 532
Abramovic, Marina, 263
Absurrealismus style, 203
Accelerando (Stross), 326
Ace Books, 63, 85, 203
Acker, Kathy, 118, 119, 120
Ackerman, Forrest J., 76
Ackroyd, Peter, 117
Across the Space Frontier (Ryan, ed.), 344
Action Comics, 218
Adams, Mark B., 519
Adamski, George, 352, 353, 358
Adorno, Theodor, 268, 452
Adventure (magazine), 94
Adventures of Jonny Quest (television program), 176
Advertising and design, 12, 364–80. *See also* Chicago Century of Progress Exposition; New York World's Fair
Aesthetics, 7, 16, 35–45;
 for different forms of SF, 37;
 diversity issue, 35–37;
 notion of compulsion in, 41;
 prescriptive *vs.* descriptive, 40;
 unique account for SF, 37–38. *See also* Beauty
Affluent Society, The (Galbraith), 380
Afghanistan conflict, 330, 340
African diaspora, 17, 564, 566, 569, 570
Afro-Future Females (Barr, ed.), 562
Afrofuturism, 16–17, 206, 261, 388, 561–70;
 basic assumptions of, 569;
 defined, 561;
 literary pedigree of, 563;
 prominence gained in SF studies, 568
"AfroFuturism" (online forum), 566
Again, Dangerous Visions (Ellison, ed.), 63, 398
Agel, Jerome, 346
A.I.: Artificial Intelligence (film), 232
Air: Or, Have Not Have (Ryman), 130–31, 148, 545–47
Air Battle, The: A Vision of the Future (Lang), 565
Airflow automobile, 368, 369 (figure)
Airliner Number 4 (Bel Geddes), 365
Air Wonder Stories (magazine), 82, 198
Akira (film), 192, 217

Alas Babylon (Frank), 90
Alba (bioluminescent bunny), 241, 272
Alder, Emily, 143
Alder Hey Children's Hospital, 469
Aldiss, Brian W., 42, 50, 53, 62, 97, 98, 109, 111, 116, 187, 196, 459, 467
ALF (television program), 178
Alice's Adventures in Atomland in the Plastic Age (Field), 342
Alice's Adventures in Wonderland (Carroll), 129
Alien (fanzine), 76
Alien (film), 257, 307, 332
Alien Chic (Badmington), 146
Alien Encounters (Rose), 143, 146
Alien Nation (film), 178
Alien Nation (television program), 178, 179
Aliens: in animated works, 189, 190;
 in Enlightenment thought, 452, 454, 455;
 sexuality and, 395, 403
Aliens (film), 178, 332, 334, 336, 337
Aliens vs. Predator (video game), 230, 235
Alien Zone: Cultural Theory and Contemporary Science Fiction Cinema (Kuhn), 155
Alkon, Paul K., 49, 50
Allan Quatermain (Haggard), 495
Allen, Irwin, 177, 335
Allende, Isabel, 117
Alloplastic traits, 411
"All You Zombies" (Heinlein), 111
Alternate-reality games (ARGs), 229, 232
Alternate Worlds (Gunn), 196
Altman, Rick, 157
Alvin and the Chipmunks, 258
Amateur press association (APA), 71–72
Amazing Adventures of Kavalier and Clay, The (Chabon), 113
Amazing Detective Tales (magazine), 82
Amazing Stories (magazine), 4, 51, 60, 63, 64, 72, 76, 82, 96, 187, 325, 352, 355, 427, 436, 479–80, 547;
 artwork in, 198–200, 201, 202 (figure);
 characteristics of stories published in, 93;
 comics in, 10;
 debut of, 59, 81, 95, 213
American Century, 329, 335, 336
American Flagg! (comic), 5, 223–24
American National Exhibition, 378
American Revolution, 334, 336

Amerika (television program), 333
Amis, Kingsley, 47, 50, 117, 459, 460
Among Others (Walton), 79
Amundsen, Roald, 502
Analog (magazine), 15, 26
Anarchism, 16, 550, 556–59
"Anarchitecture" manifesto (Woods), 287
Anarcho-capitalism, 551, 555
Anatomy Act of 1832, 469
Anatomy of Wonder (Barron), 52, 53, 54, 146
Anders, Lou, 68, 88
Anderson, Paul W. S., 164, 165
Anderson, Paul Y., 170
Anderson, Poul, 90, 558
Anderson, Taylor, 89
"And He Built a Crooked House" (Heinlein), 84
Andrews, Jim, 246, 247
Andromeda (bookstore), 73
Andromeda Strain, The (film), 165, 257
Angelucci, Orfeo, 356, 358
Anger, Kenneth, 256
"Animal Magnetism" (Cowdrey), 547
Animation, 9, 184–95;
  aliens in, 189, 190;
  concept of space in, 187–88;
  as "thick text," 9, 184, 192
Anime, 74, 192, 217
Anolik, Ruth Bienstock, 468
"Another Orphan" (Kessel), 111
"Another World" (Grandville), 185
Ansible (fanzine), 79
"Answering the Question: What Is Enlightenment?" (Kant), 451
"Answers in Progress" (Baraka), 388
Antheil, George, 253
Anthem (Rand), 551
Anthony, Piers, 134
Anthropocene (performance art), 268–69
Anticipations of the Reaction of Mechanical and Scientific Progress upon Human Life and Thought (Wells), 323, 435
Anubis Gates, The (Powers), 440
Apocalyptic fiction, 471–73, 577–78, 579
Apollo At Go (Sutton), 345
Apollo space program, 345, 348, 436
A-Positive (performance art), 271, 272 (figure)
Appadurai, Arjun, 443
Applewhite, Marshall Herff, 359–60
"Ararat" (Henderson), 127–28
Aratus, 457
Archaeologies of the Future (Jameson), 278
Archigram Group, 11, 283–84, 285
Architecture, 10, 11, 277–88;
  Constructivist, 11, 279–82, 286;
  consumerism and, 283–85;
  representations of technology in, 277–79

Archive of Our Own (online community), 78
Arcologies, 285
Arctic Giant, The (cartoon), 188
"Are 'Friends' Electric?" (song), 261
Arens, Egmont, 365, 369
"Are You Experienced?" (song), 259
Argentina, 73, 216–17
Argosy (magazine), 93, 94
Ariel (magazine), 486
"Arkestra" (Sun Ra), 389
"Armageddon 2429 A. D." (Nowlan), 480
Armstrong, John, 457–58
Arnold, Ion, 95
Arnold, Jack, 335
Arnold, Matthew, 320
Ars Electronica Festival, 265, 273
Arslan (Engh), 333
Art and illustration, 9, 196–210;
  cultural impact of, 196;
  digital, 207–9;
  surrealist influence, 203–4;
  Technocracy Movement and, 200–201;
  vice movement and, 199–200
Artaud, Antonin, 267, 414–15
Arthur, Robert, Jr., 171
Arthur C. Clarke Award, 75, 140
Arthur C. Clarke Foundation, 521
Art of Preserving Health, The (Armstrong), 457–58
"Art of Technology: A New Unity" (exhibition), 265
"As Easy as A.B.C." (Kipling), 325
Ash, Brian, 52
Ashby, Hal, 333
Ashes to Ashes (television program), 182
Ashley, Mike, 49, 99, 440
Ashtar, 356–57, 360
Asimov, Isaac, 26, 29, 44, 60, 61, 78, 83, 86, 90, 106, 159, 171, 453, 519, 520, 521
Asimov's Science Fiction (magazine), 66, 87
"Ask Bwana" (Resnick), 565
"Assassination of John Fitzgerald Kennedy Considered as a Downhill Motor Race, The" (Ballard), 62
Assault on Precinct 13 (film), 257
Asteroids (video game), 226
Astounding Science Fiction (magazine), 15, 26, 61, 83–85, 90, 215, 325, 509, 520, 525
Astounding Stories (magazine), 61, 93, 97–98, 99, 100, 109, 159, 187, 479–80, 509
Astro Boy (Tezuka), 10, 217
Astro Boy (television program), 176, 191–92
Astro City (comic), 224
Astro-Theology, or a Demonstration of the Being and Attributes of God from a Survey of the Heavens (Derham), 455
Atlas of Fantasy (Post), 78
Atlas of Pern (Fostad), 78

Atlas Shrugged (Rand), 551–52, 555, 558
Atomic bomb, 325–26
Atomic Bomb (silkscreen), 341
Atomic Cafe, The (film), 342
Atomic culture, 12, 340–50. *See also* Nuclear
　weapons; Space race
Atomic Submarine, The (film), 335
Atrocity Exhibition, The (Ballard), 308, 385
"Atrocity Exhibition, The" (song), 261
Attack of the Fifty Foot Woman (film), 189
Attebery, Brian, 8, 52, 94, 214
Atwood, Margaret, 42, 105–6, 112, 145, 521
Auclert, Hubertine, 537
Austen, Jane, 65
Auster, Paul, 117
Australia, 72, 172
Authentic events, 579
"Autofac" (Dick), 318
Automania 2000 (film), 192
Automata, 319–20
Automation, 11–12, 317–26;
　coinage of term, 317;
　cultural and political effects of, 324;
　utopian-dystopian tension and, 318, 321–23
Automation (journal), 317
Automobile of the Future (design), 366 (figure)
Automobiles, advertising and design of, 364, 366
　(figure), 368, 369 (figure), 374–78
Autoplastic traits, 410–11
Autopoiesis, 424
Avatar (film), 333, 334, 336, 489, 496
"Avenging Tiger, The" (Vrooman), 94
Avon Publications, 214
Ayad, Djibril al-, 569
"Aye, and Gomorrah" (Delany), 399

Babel-17 (Delany), 13, 390–91
Babylon 5 (television program), 181
Bacevich, Andrew, 330–31
Bacigalupi, Paolo, 32, 67, 90, 148, 312–13
Bacon, Francis, 452, 476
Badiou, Alain, 578–79, 580
Bad Machine (Shiovitz), 246
Badmington, Neil, 146
Baen Books, 332
Bailey, J. O., 1, 47–48, 53
Baker, Henry, 455
Bakunin, Michael, 550
Balandier, Georges, 488
Baldwin, Craig, 310
Ballantine, Betty, 85
Ballantine, Ian, 85
Ballantine Books, 85, 203
Ballard, J. G., 29, 62, 63, 109, 110, 111, 116, 120, 144,
　203–4, 206, 261, 283, 308, 349–50, 385–86, 416,
　417, 473, 524, 563, 578

Balsamo, Anne, 410, 413
Bangs, Lester, 259
Banks, Iain M., 44, 90, 549
Bantam Books, 87
Baraka, Amiri, 388
Baran, Paul, 514
Bar Code Hotel (installation), 244–46
Barefoot in the Head (Aldiss), 42
Barnes, Joshua, 457
Barnes, Julian, 117
Barnes, Steven, 333, 565
Barnett, Joseph, 370
Barnouw, Erik, 171
Baron Münchausen (film), 191
"Baroque Cycle" (Stephenson), 44, 313–14
Barr, James, 95
Barr, Marleen, 53, 562
Barrett, Syd, 260
Barrett, William F., 507–8
Barron, Bebe, 254, 256
Barron, Louis, 254, 256
Barron, Neil, 52, 53, 54, 146
Barthelme, Donald, 118
Barthes, Roland, 161
Bartkowiak, Mathew J., 254
Basinger, Jeanine, 333
Batchelor, Joy, 192
Bateson, Gregory, 421, 423, 426, 427
Batman (character), 218, 223, 224
Batman (television program), 377
Battle of Dorking, The (Chesney), 329
Battle of Los Angeles (film), 337
Battle of the Sexes in Science Fiction, The
　(Larbalestier), 312
Battlestar Galactica (television program), 178, 181
Batty, Nancy, 486–87
Baudrillard, Jean, 91, 120, 129, 144, 145, 146, 147, 242,
　269–70, 292–93, 299–300, 409, 426
Baum, L. Frank, 427
Baxter, John, 155–56, 160
Baxter, Stephen, 67
Bayley, Barrington J., 385
BBC Radiophonic Workshop, 255
BDSM in American Science Fiction and Fantasy
　(Call), 405
Beach Boys (band), 259
Beagle, H.M.S., 15, 477
Beamer, Amelia, 140
Bear, Greg, 64, 67, 90, 148, 347, 524
Beast, The (video game), 232
Beast from 20,000 Fathoms, The (film), 190
"Beat Cluster, The" (Leiber), 389–90, 391
Beat Generation, The (film), 389
Beatles (band), 258, 259
"Beatnik Werewolf, The" (Lindsay), 389
Beats, 12–13, 384–91

Beaumont, Charles, 389
Beauty: of expression, 41–43;
    of structure, 41, 43–44;
    sublime *vs.*, 7, 38–39, 41;
    of world, 41, 44. *See also* Seven beauties of science fiction
Bedford-Jones, H., 101
Beer, Gillian, 483
Beethoven, Ludwig van, 256
Behm, Allen J., 518
Beijing International SF Conference, 74
Bel Geddes, Norman, 365, 366 (figure), 368, 369, 370, 372–73, 375
Bell, Daniel, 513
Bell, David, 421
Bellamy, Edward, 71, 105, 138, 321, 322, 435, 518, 532, 574
"Belle Dame Sans Merci, La" (Keats), 108
Bell Laboratories, 255
Bender, Amy, 123
Bending the Landscape (Griffith and Pagel), 400
Benett, Léon, 197, 198 (figure)
Benford, Gregory, 79, 347, 350
Benford, Jim, 79
Benison, Jonathan, 144, 146, 147
Benjamin, Walter, 580
Bennet, Spencer Gordon, 335
Bennett, Ed, 271
Bennett, Gertrude, 100
Bennett, Margot, 565
Berlin, Isaiah, 451
Berman, Albert, 171
Bernal, J. D., 529–30
Bernardi, Daniel, 564
Bester, Alfred, 17, 213, 386, 510, 580–81
Bethke, Bruce, 64
Béthune, Le Chevalier de, 457
Bethurum, Truman, 353
Beyond Apollo (Malzberg), 349
Beyond This Horizon (Heinlein), 84, 520
Beyond Tomorrow (radio program), 171
Bhabha, Homi, 488, 494
Bierce, Ambrose, 105
Bigend, Hubertus, 143, 146
Big Name Fans, 72, 75, 76
Bikini Kill (band), 545
Bilal, Enki, 216
Bilal, Wafaa, 264
Bill Haley and the Comets (band), 341
Billion Year Spree (Aldiss), 50, 53
Bimbos of the Death Sun (McCrumb), 79
BioCom (performance art), 265
Bionic Woman, The (television program), 178
Biopiracy, 312
Biopunk, 65

Bioshock (video game), 230, 234
Birds, The (film), 161, 165
Birkerts, Sven, 105–6, 109
Birmingham School, 4
Bishop, K. J., 67
Bishop, Michael, 111
Bisson, Terry, 333, 565
Bixby, Jerome, 86
"Black Country" (Beaumont), 389
Blackford, Russell, 54
Black Hawk Down (film), 336
Black Mask (magazine), 94
Blackmore, Richard, 454–55
Blackton, J. Stuart, 186
"Black to the Future" (Dery), 561
Blackwelder, Eliot, 503
Blade Runner (film), 49, 64, 230, 240, 257–58, 286
Blade Runner (video game), 232
Bladerunner, The (Nourse), 385
Blake, John E., 377
Blake, William, 133
Blake's Seven (radio program), 172
Blake's 7 (television program), 178
Blavatsky, Madame, 352
Blaylock, James P., 65–66, 440
Bleiler, Everett F., 1, 47, 50, 97
Blish, James, 53, 60, 148, 159, 454
Blob, The (film), 189
Bloch, Ernst, 4, 268, 564, 575, 576, 579
Bloch, Robert, 527–29
Blogging, 77–78
"Blood Child" (Butler), 545
Blood Music (Bear), 148
Bloor, David, 310
"Blowups Happen" (Heinlein), 84
BME (Body Modification Ezine) (website), 409
Bodin, Félix, 140–41
Body modification, 13, 408–18;
    commodification of, 411–12, 413, 418;
    cyborgism and, 13, 409, 410, 411, 413–14;
    generational differences in, 409;
    in performance art, 264, 414–16, 418
Bogdanov, Alexander, 506
Bolshevik Revolution, 383
Bolton, Christopher, 49, 54
Bombs in Orbit (Sutton), 345
Bonestell, Chesley, 191
Booker, M. Keith, 176, 179, 181
"Book of the Long Sun, The" (Wolfe), 136
"Book of the New Sun, The" (Wolfe), 128, 136
"Book of the Short Sun, The" (Wolfe), 136
"Boom" (cartoon), 342
Booth, Austin, 140
Borden, Lizzie, 562
Born in Flames (film), 562

Born This Way (album), 206
Boskone, 72
Bottger, Matthias, 268
Botting, Fred, 467
Boucher, Anthony, 28, 61, 62, 85, 547
Bould, Mark, 5, 9, 25, 31, 51, 52, 54, 130, 140, 141, 142, 479, 568
Bourdieu, Pierre, 142, 156
Bova, Ben, 334, 347
Bowie, David, 206, 252, 259
Bowser, Rachel, 440, 441
Boyle, Richard, 314
Boym, Svetlana, 443
Boyse, Samuel, 455
Braaten, Carl E., 518
Bradbury, Ray, 41–42, 52, 78, 109, 159–62, 171, 192, 200, 215, 255, 342, 378, 518
Bradley, Marion Zimmer, 78, 128
Braidotti, Rosi, 272, 274
Brasyl (McDonald), 207, 208 (figure)
Braun, Wernher von, 341, 344
Brave New World (Huxley), 323, 387
Brazil, 73
Brazilian Science Fiction (Ginway), 312
Breccia, Alberto, 217
Brecht, Bertolt, 573
Bretnor, Reginald, 28–29
Breton, André, 204
Briggs, Stephen, 78
Brin, David, 52, 556
Bristolcon, 73
British Science Fiction Association, 73, 78
Brittle Innings (Bishop), 111
Broderick, Damien, 33, 64, 110, 270, 515
Brooke-Rose, Christine, 48
Brooks, Terry, 88
Brosnan, John, 156, 159
Brother from Another Planet, The (film), 562
Brown, Charles, 79
Brown, Howard, 187, 200
Brown, Jeffrey, 215–16
Brown, Reynold, 201–2, 203
Brown Girl in the Ring (Hopkinson), 134, 402
Brundage, Margaret, 199
Brunner, John, 43, 62, 85, 90, 109
Bryant, Dorothy, 397
Bryman, Alan, 292, 293, 297
BSFA awards, 75
Buck Rogers (character), 9–10
Buck Rogers (radio program), 169
Buck Rogers in the 25th Century (comic strip), 82, 213, 221, 223, 436
Buck Rogers in the 25th Century (film), 367
Buck Rogers in the 25th Century (television program), 178

Buffy the Vampire Slayer (television program), 181
Bujold, Lois McMaster, 76, 79, 89
Bukatman, Scott, 4, 5, 223, 293–94, 298, 299, 438
Bunch, David R., 63
Burden, Christopher, 265
Burgum, Edwin Berry, 101
Burke, Edmund, 38
"Burning Chrome" (Gibson), 65, 207, 309, 430
Burroughs, Edgar Rice, 49, 95, 96, 128, 218, 480, 486, 495, 502, 507, 532, 565
Burroughs, William S., 62, 63, 68, 116, 117, 120, 384–86, 387, 388, 416, 524
Burrows, William E., 344
Busiek, Kurt, 224
Bush, George H. W., 339
Bush, George W., 337, 339, 340, 444
Busiek, Kurt, 224
Butler, Andrew M., 15–16, 52, 124
Butler, Judith, 400–401, 403, 416, 424, 425, 430
Butler, Octavia E., 16, 42, 90, 113, 140, 145, 148, 403–4, 405, 482–83, 489, 494–95, 544, 545, 563, 564, 565, 567
Butler, Samuel, 321–22
"By His Bootstraps" (Heinlein), 84
Byron, Lord, 464

Cadbury, Deborah, 343
Cadigan, Pat, 64, 413, 545
Cage, John, 254, 268–69
"Cage of Sand, The" (Ballard), 109
Caillois, Roger, 129
Calcutta Chromosome, The (Ghosh), 135, 489, 492
Calder, Richard, 402–3
Calkins, Dick, 221
Calkins, Earnest, 365
Calkins & Holden, 365
Call, Lewis, 405
Cambridge Companion to Science Fiction, The (James and Mendlesohn), 52, 54
Camera Obscura (journal), 3
Cameron, James, 332, 336, 489
Camouflage (Haldeman), 111
Campbell, Jack, 89
Campbell, John W., Jr., 15, 26, 27, 28, 29, 30, 50, 68, 82, 86, 87, 88, 89, 90, 91, 106, 109, 215, 479, 519–20;
    alternative science encouraged by, 509–10;
    on automation, 325;
    Dianetics promoted by, 352;
    influence on pulp SF, 93–94, 97–98, 100, 101, 102;
    influence on the marketplace, 83–85;
    influence on the SF movement, 61
Canada, 73, 172
Canadia 2056 (radio program), 172
Cannon, Danny, 49
"Can the Subaltern Speak?" (Spivak), 493
Canticle for Leibowitz, A (Miller), 90, 340, 342

Cantley, Bryan, 286
Capek, Karel, 2, 49, 53, 170, 173, 324, 524
Capellas, Michael, 296
Capitalism, 200, 209;
   anarcho-, 551, 555;
   colonialism and, 487, 490–91;
   late (*See* Late Capitalism)
Capitalism: The Unknown Ideal (Rand), 551
Cappiello, Leonetto, 190
Captain Future (magazine), 83
Captain Video (television program), 86, 172, 173
Card, Orson Scott, 90, 332, 334
Cardigan, Pat, 401
Carl, Lillian Stewart, 76
Carlos, Wendy (Walter), 256, 259
Carlyle, Thomas, 320
Carnell, John, 385
Carpenter, Ele, 441
Carpenter, John, 257, 258, 267
Carpenter, William, 322, 508
Carr, Terry, 63, 64
Carroll, Lewis, 129
"Cars" (song), 261
Carson, Rachel, 380
Case of Conscience, A (Blish), 454
Castells, Manuel, 207
Caza, Philippe, 193
Centauri Device, The (Harrison), 67
Century of Progress Exposition. *See* Chicago Century of Progress Exposition
Césaire, Aimé, 487, 488
Chabon, Michael, 112, 113
Chakrabarty, Dipesh, 491, 492
Challenge of Space (radio program), 172
Channon, Claude, 431
Chaplin, Charlie, 324
Chariots of Fire (film), 257
Charnas, Suzy McKee, 397, 542
Chaykin, Howard, 5, 223
Cheap Truth (newsletter), 64–65
Checklist of Fantastic Literature (Bleiler), 1
"Chemical Basis of Morphogenesis, The" (Turing), 239
Chengdu SF/Fantasy Conference, 74
Chernikhov, Iakov, 281
Cherryh, C. J., 521
Chesney, George Tomkyns, 329
Chiang, Ted, 52, 123
Chicago Century of Progress Exposition (1933-34), 294–95, 364–69
Chicano/a Futurism, 17, 569
Child Buyer, The (Hersey), 348
Childhood's End (Clarke), 43, 85, 106–7, 132, 203, 346, 520, 524, 533
China, 74
Chobits (comic), 217
Chomón, Segundo de, 9, 184, 186

Christian eschatology, 15, 513, 518
Chroma (Loyer), 247–50
Chrysler Motors, 366, 368, 370
Chtchetlov, Ivan, 285
Cinq études de bruits (Schaeffer), 254
Circlet Press, 404
Cisco, Michael, 66, 67
"Citadel of Fear, The" (Bennett), 100
Cité Industrielle, Une, 282
Citizens' Advisory Council on National Space Policy, 347
Città Nuova, La (exhibiton), 279, 280 (figure)
City and the City, The (Miéville), 43–44, 113
"cityCityCITY" (Kerouac), 387–88, 390
Civilization (video game), 231
Clairmont, Claire, 464
Clamp, 217
Clareson, Thomas, 47, 97
Clarion (writing workshop), 79
Clark, Andy, 423, 427
Clarke, Arthur C., 16, 43, 49, 85, 86, 90, 104, 106–7, 128, 132, 200, 203, 206, 221, 255, 270, 309, 529;
   atomic culture and, 341, 346–47, 349, 350;
   futurology and, 518, 519, 520–21;
   posthumanism and, 524, 533;
   utopianism and, 578
Clarke, I. F., 197, 435, 518
Clave, Salvador, 292, 293
Clear, Nic, 11
Clear Air Turbulence (album), 206
Clemens, George T., 174
Clement, Hal, 24, 311
Cline, Ernest, 556
Cline, John, 10, 11
Clinton, Bill, 330
Clockpunk, 439
Clockwork Orange, A (film), 157, 256
Close Encounters: Film, Feminism, and Science Fiction (Penley et al., eds), 3
"Close Encounters: The Squandered Promise of Science Fiction" (Lethem), 104
Close Encounters of the Third Kind (film), 162, 201, 257
Clute, John, 32–33, 52, 66, 139, 140, 144, 228, 288
Clynes, Manfred E., 413, 422
Cobb, Ron, 334
Coetzee, J. M., 117
Cognitive estrangement, 2, 48, 141, 144, 163, 277, 308, 395;
   the Natural Fantastic and, 131;
   performance art and, 11, 264–65, 266–67;
   utopianism and, 17, 574–75
Cohen, Leonard, 386
Cohl, Emile, 186
"Cold Equations, The" (Godwin), 24, 307, 308
Cold War, 306, 329, 332, 335, 336, 340, 341;
   music and, 255, 259;
   space race and, 343, 344, 346

Cole, Yvonne, 357
Collins, Suzanne, 483
Collins, Wilkie, 467, 468, 470
Colonialism, 15, 486–96;
    Afrofuturism and, 564, 565;
    cybernetics and, 429;
    Darwinism and, 15, 476–78;
    dependent, 15, 488, 489, 490;
    as an ideological anachronism, 492–93;
    master narratives on, 491;
    science and, 312;
    settler, 15, 488, 489, 496. *See also* Postcolonialism
Colonialism and the Emergence of Science Fiction (Rieder), 15, 312, 486
Coltrane, Alice, 566
Columbia-Princeton Electronic Music Center, 255
Columbia Workshop (radio program), 170
Comic-Con, 73, 75
Comics, 9–10, 212–24, 444;
    atomic culture depicted in, 340–41;
    censorship of, 215, 219;
    interaction with SF as a genre, 213–16;
    international scope of, 212, 216–17;
    marginalizing of, 212–13;
    superhero, 213, 218–20
Comics Code, 215, 219
Coming Home (film), 333
"Coming of the Unconscious, The" (Ballard), 203–4
Committee for the Political Advancement of Science Fiction, 60
"Common Sense" (Heinlein), 84
Communism, 324, 383, 384
Communist Control Act of 1954, 384
Companion to Science Fiction, A (Seed), 52
Computer Space (video game), 10, 226
"Computing Machinery and Intelligence" (Turing), 239, 240–41
Comsat Angels (band), 261
"Conan the Barbarian" (Howard), 78
"Coney Island of the Mind, A" (McHugh), 402
Connors, Scott, 334
"Conquest of Gola, The" (Stone), 481
Conquest of Space, The (film), 191
Conrad, Joseph, 111, 492
Constructivism, 11, 279–82, 286
Consumer Engineering: A New Technique for Prosperity (Sheldon and Arens), 365
Consuming Youth (Latham), 55
"Continuous Urban Monument" (architectural design), 284–85
Convergence culture, 232
Cook, Peter, 283
"Cool Air" (Lovecraft), 532
Cooper, Leonie, 11
Coover, John E., 508
Coover, Robert, 118
Copenhagen Institute for Futures Studies, 514

Corbusier, Le, 282
Cormie, Stuart, 387
Corn, Joseph, 173, 209–10
Cornell, Joseph, 207
Cornell, Paul, 78
"Corpse that Lived, The" (Skinner), 532
Cosmetic surgery, 415–16
Cosmic Stories (fanzine), 213
Cosplay, 74
Countercultures, 12–13, 63–64, 383–92;
    art and illustration influenced by, 203;
    Beat, 12–13, 384–91;
    disappearance of prewar, 384;
    hippie, 12–13, 392;
    sexuality and, 396–97;
    SF as an inspiration for, 383–84;
    utopianism and, 12–13, 383, 384
Count Zero (Gibson), 207
"Coventry" (Heinlein), 84
Cowdrey, Albert E., 547
Cowell, Henry, 253
Cramer, Kathryn, 32, 66, 67, 68, 88
Crary, Jonathan, 278
Crash (Ballard), 144, 206, 261, 417, 524
Crawdaddy! (magazine), 259
Creation: A Philosophical Poem Demonstrating the Existence and Providence of a God (Blackmore), 454–55
Creature from the Black Lagoon (film), 189
"Creatures of the Light" (Ellis), 540
Creekmur, Corey, 9–10
Creery sisters, 508
Critical Art Ensemble, 265
Critical iconology, 196
Critical Theory and Science Fiction (Freedman), 2
Critical utopia, 557, 574
Critique of Judgment (Kant), 39
Croatia, 72
Cross Impact Analysis, 516
Crossley, Robert, 54, 507, 519
Crowley, John, 136, 547
Croxall, Brian, 440, 441
Cryonics, 16, 531–33
Crysis 2 (video game), 227, 230
Crystal Palace, 278, 283, 288
Csicsery-Ronay, Istvan, Jr., 2, 4–5, 6, 17, 25, 30, 39–40, 41, 49, 52, 53, 54, 107–8, 120, 121, 132, 142, 143, 145, 146, 148, 212, 293, 294, 299, 492
Cubitt, Sean, 162, 163
Cullen, Countee, 563
Cultural-studies perspectives, 3–5
Culture and Imperialism (Said), 486
Culture of science, 11, 305–15;
    defined, 307;
    economic and political factors in, 307–8, 313;
    shifting paradigms in, 309–10. *See also* Science
"Culture" universe (Banks), 44

Cunningham, Michael, 112
Cure for Cancer, A (Moorcock), 308
Cushicle, 283
Cut-up trilogy (Burroughs), 385–86, 387
Cyberabad Days (McDonald), 148
Cyberculture, 13–14, 421–32. *See also* Cybernetics
Cybernetics, 13–14, 140, 241, 326, 421–32, 445;
  coinage of term, 317;
  depth models resisted by, 426, 427, 432;
  homeostasis and, 422–24, 429, 431;
  original definition of, 421;
  redefinition of personhood in, 422–23;
  of self, 423
Cybernetics (Wiener), 421
Cyberpunk, 4, 5, 7, 13–14, 67, 68, 144, 386, 426–27, 430–31, 438, 439, 440, 568;
  body modification and, 13, 412–13;
  coinage of term, 64;
  in comics, 215;
  emergence of, 64–66;
  feminism and, 545;
  sexuality and, 400, 401–2;
  slipstream and, 120–22;
  steampunk distinguished from, 445
"Cyberpunk in the Nineties" (Sterling), 412
CyberSM (performance art), 265
Cyberspace, 426–27, 430, 431–32;
  coinage of term, 401, 430;
  liquid architectures of, 11, 287. *See also* Internet
Cyborg Citizen (Gray), 146
"Cyborg Manifesto" (Haraway), 16, 148, 543–44
Cyborgs, 424–25;
  body modification and, 13, 409, 410, 411, 413–14;
  coinage of term, 413, 422;
  feminism and, 16, 242, 422, 543–45;
homeostasis and, 423;
  performance art and, 264, 266–67;
  sexuality and, 400, 402–3, 404
"Cyborgs and Space" (Clynes and Kline), 422
Cyrano de Bergerac, 52, 53, 191

Daedalus; or, Science and the Future (Haldane), 519, 529
D'Alembert, Jean le Rond, 453
Dalí, Salvador, 203
Dal Tokyo (comic strip), 215
Dan Dare, Pilot of the Future (comic), 216, 221
Dangerous Visions (Ellison, ed.), 63, 85, 109, 398, 399
Daniel, Sharon, 249
Dark Knight Rises, The (comic), 224
Dark Matter (Thomas, ed.), 563–64
Dark Matter: Reading the Bones (Thomas, ed.), 563
"Darkover" books (Bradley), 128
Dark Skies (television program), 181
Dark Star (film), 257
Dart, Harry Grant, 213

Darwin, Charles, 435, 475–79, 483
Darwin, Erasmus, 458, 465, 466
Darwinism, 15, 475–84, 550;
  colonialism and, 15, 476–78;
  concept of humanity changed by, 475–76;
  feminist disagreement with, 478–79
Darwin's Radio (Bear), 524
Davenport, Basil, 23, 27
Davies, Russell T., 182
Davis, Don, 258
Davis, Kathy, 415–16
Davis, Miles, 566
Davis, Ray, 104, 113
Davis, Thulani, 562
Davy, Sir Humphry, 502
DAW Books, 88
Dawn (Butler), 482–83
Day, Robert, 335
Day After Tomorrow, The (film), 473
Day of Creation, The (Ballard), 111
Day of the Dead (film), 165
Day of the Dolphin, The (film), 257
Day of the Drones, The (Lightner), 565
Day of the Triffids, The (radio program), 172
Day the Earth Stood Still, The (film), 171, 201, 254, 256, 336, 352, 356
DC comics, 219–20
"Dead, The" (Joyce), 110
Dead Girls, Dead Boys, Dead Things (Calder), 402–3
Dead Space (video game), 230
Debord, Guy, 203, 285
Debus, Allen, 502
De Camp, L. Sprague, 134–35, 502
De Certeau, Michel, 209
"Declaration of Sentiments and Resolutions," 538
Deep, The (Crowley), 136
"Deep End" (Shawl), 494
Deep Secret (Jones), 79
Defoe, Daniel, 53
De Grey, Aubrey, 534
Deity: A Poem (Boyse), 455
Delany, Samuel R., 2, 13, 37, 48, 79, 85, 104, 105, 107, 119, 120, 127, 128, 141, 146, 148, 242–44, 245, 246, 390–91, 557–58;
  Afrofuturism and, 562, 563, 564, 565;
  anarchism and, 557;
  posthumanism and, 524;
  sexuality, 397, 399, 400, 405;
  utopianism and, 574
Deleuze, Gilles, 267, 272, 273, 274, 493
"Delhi" (Singh), 493
De Lillo, Don, 120
Dell Books, 203
Delphi method, 516
Del Rey, Lester, 49, 62
Delvoye, Wim, 417

D'Emilio, John, 396
Demolished Man, The (Bester), 510
De Montaut, Henri, 185, 191
Denari, Neil, 286
Denmark, 72
Dennett, Daniel, 422, 423, 426
Dent, Lester, 98, 100
Dependent colonialism, 15, 488, 489, 490
Depth models, 426, 427, 432
Derham, William, 455
Derleth, August, 52
Derrida, Jacques, 120, 157, 314, 491, 527
Dershowitz, Alan, 534
Dervish House, The (McDonald), 208
Dery, Mark, 417, 561–63, 566
Descartes, René, 499
Descent of Man, and Selection in Relation to Sex, The (Darwin), 476, 477, 478
Description of Formosa (Psalmanazar), 457
Design for Dreaming (film), 375
Desmond, Adrian, 476
Destination Moon (comic), 216
Destination Moon (film), 191, 343–44
Détournement, 204
DeusEx (video game), 227
De Vaucanson, Jacques, 319, 320
Devo (band), 260
De Vries, Jetse, 68
Dexter's Laboratory (television program), 193
De Zwaan, Victoria, 8
Dialectic of Enlightenment, The (Horkheimer and Adorno), 452
Dialectics of Sex, The (Firestone), 16, 541–42
Diamond Age, The (Stephenson), 441, 444
Dianetics, 12, 352, 360. *See also* Scientology
Dianetics: The Modern Science of Mental Health (Hubbard), 360
Dick, Philip K., 63–64, 84, 85, 90, 147–48, 204–5, 206, 240, 259, 318, 326, 386, 524
Dictionary of Imaginary Places (Manguel), 78
Diderot, Denis, 453
Diebold, John, 317
Dieselpunk, 65
Dietz, William C., 89
Di Fate, Vincent, 196
Difference Engine, The (Gibson and Sterling), 66, 440, 444
Di Filippo, Paul, 65, 66, 67, 440
Digital art and illustration, 207–9
Digital arts and hypertext, 10, 239–50;
    allergorization in, 241–44, 250;
    the material-semiotic in, 240, 241, 244;
    monologic closure risk and, 243–44, 245, 247;
    participatory expression and, 247–50;
    technical closure risk and, 244, 245
Dignity of Labour, The (album), 261

Dilemma (film), 192
Dime novels, 94, 95, 99
Dimension X (radio program), 171
Disch, Thomas M., 63, 109, 116, 526
Discourse on Colonialism (Césaire), 488
Disembodiment, 401–2
Disney, Walt, 291, 292, 295, 297, 341
Disneyization of Society (Bryman), 297
Disney studios, 186
Disney theme parks, 5, 291–300;
    architecture of reassurance in, 298;
    performative labor in, 297;
    symbolism of, 292–93;
    transitional spaces in, 11, 295–98
Dispossessed, The: An Ambiguous Utopia (Le Guin), 136, 557, 558, 574
Dissensus Fantastic, the, 131, 133, 135–36
Distant Soil, A (comic), 215
"Distortion of the Product, The" (Hartwell), 87, 88
Distrust That Particular Flavor (Gibson), 149
Ditko, Lee, 219
Ditko, Steve, 219
Ditmar Awards, 72, 75
"Divine Madness" (Zelazny), 36
Dixon, Steve, 10–11
DNA Media, 245
Do Androids Dream of Electric Sheep? (Dick), 64, 206, 240, 524
Dobrée, Bonamy, 454
Doctorow, Cory, 148, 209
Doctor Who (television program), 174, 175 (figure), 176, 179, 182, 255–56
Dogme 95, 130
Dolby, Thomas, 261
Dold, William, 188
Dollhouse (television program), 181
Dome of Discovery, 283
"Dome over Manhattan" (architectural design), 284
Donaldson, Kristian, 224
Donawerth, Jane, 53
Doner, H. Creston, 378
Donner, Richard, 174
"Do Not Open for 5,000 Years" (radio adaptation), 170
Donovan's Brain (radio adaptation), 171
Doolin, Joe, 214
Doom (video game), 226, 332
Door into Summer, The (Heinlein), 532–33
"Doors of His Face, the Lamps of His Mouth, The" (Zelazny), 36
Doorway to Heaven (performance art), 265
Doran, Colleen, 215
Dorsey, Candas Jane, 396
Double Star (Heinlein), 555
Douglas, Gordon, 335
Douglas, Mary, 410–11

Dowling, Terry, 128
Downward to the Earth (Silverberg), 111
Doyle, Arthur Conan, 492
Doyle, Deborah, 78
Dozois, Gardner, 64, 67, 87
Dr. Jekyll and Mr. Hyde (radio program), 172
Dr. Strangelove (film), 332, 340, 347, 348, 349
Dracula (Stoker), 15, 467, 469, 470, 471
Dragon*Con, 75
Dragonflight (McCaffrey), 128
Drake, David, 332
Dreaming Jewels, The (Sturgeon), 108
Dream of the Rarebit Fiend (comic strip), 427–29
Dreamwidth (blog), 77
Dreamworks, 189
Drexler, K. Eric, 33, 529, 533
Dreyfuss, Henry, 372
Drought, The (Ballard), 473
Drowned World, The (Ballard), 473, 578
Druillet, Philippe, 215, 216
Du Bois, W. E. B., 567
Duck and Cover (film), 341
Duck Dodgers in the 24½th Century (cartoon), 187, 189
Duke University, 509
Duncan, Hal, 67
Dune (film), 206
Dune (Herbert), 392, 453
Dune (video game), 231
Dungeons & Dragons (game), 88
Dunn, Lloyd, 434
"Dunwich Horror, The" (radio adaptation), 171
Durrell, Lawrence, 117
Dust Devil (film), 165
Dykstra, John, 178
Dylan, Bob, 259, 386
Dymaxion, 284
Dynamation, 190
Dystopianism, 551, 565, 574, 575. *See also* Utopian-dystopian tension

Eagle (magazine), 216
Eagleton, Terry, 459
Earl, Harley, 368, 374–75, 376 (figure)
Earth 2150 (video game), 231
Earth Search (radio program), 172
Earth vs. the Flying Saucers (film), 190, 201, 336
Easterbrook, Neil, 16
Eastercon, 73, 75, 76
Eastern Standard Tribe (Doctorow), 148
EC comics, 215
Eddings, David, 88
Eddings, Leigh, 88
Edel, Leon, 106
Edison, Thomas, 309, 326, 435, 553

Edisonades, 435
Edison's Conquest of Mars (Serviss), 505–6
Edkins, Jenny, 443, 445
Edwards, Malcolm, 79
Egan, Greg, 32, 311, 417
eI (ezine), 77
"Eight Worlds" stories (Varley), 547
Einstein Intersection, The (Delany), 128
Eisenhower, Dwight, 330
Electrical Experimenter, The (magazine), 173
Electric Earthquake, The (cartoon), 188
Electric Hotel, The (stop-motion feature), 186
Electroclash, 261
Electropolis (comic), 224
Elektro (robot), 370, 436
Elements of Natural Philosophy (Leslie), 500
Elfman, Danny, 258
Elfpunk, 65
Elgin, Suzette Haden, 135
Eliot, T. S., 109, 110
Elkins, Charles, 521
Ellis, Edward, 435, 440
Ellis, John, 173
Ellis, Sophie Wenzel, 540
Ellis, Warren, 10, 215
Ellison, Harlan, 63, 64, 68, 85, 109, 132, 174, 232, 345, 398
Ellison, Ralph, 567–68
Elohim, 358–59, 360
"Elsewhen" (Heinlein), 84
Éluard, Paul, 203
Embassytown (Miéville), 44
Embedding, The (Watson), 524
Emerald City (fanzine), 77
Emergence of Latin American Science Fiction, The (Ferreira), 312
Emerson, Lake and Palmer (band), 260
Emperor: Battle for Dune (video game), 230, 231
Empire (Hardt and Negri), 490
Empire of the Senseless (Acker), 118
Emshwiller, Carol, 63, 66
Encyclopedia of Science Fiction (Clute and Nicholls), 25, 66, 146, 288
Encyclopédie (Diderot and d'Alembert, eds.), 453–54
Ender's Game (Card), 334
"End of Science Fiction, The" (Bloch), 527–29
Enframing, 323
Engel, Ludwig, 268
Engh, M. M., 333
Engineer Menni, The (Bogdanov), 506
Engines of Creation: The Coming Era of Nanotechnology (Drexler), 529
England Swings (Merril, ed.), 62
Enlightenment, 14, 24, 38, 306, 308, 311, 313, 314, 451–61;

fascination with other worlds in, 454–57;
  importance of reason in, 452;
  the macroscopic and macroscopic in, 453;
  qualities shared with SF, 451–52
Enns, Anthony, 15
Eno, Brian, 260
Enteen, Jillana, 568
Enterprise (television program), 179
Eon (Bear), 347
Epcot (Disney attraction), 292, 294, 295–96
Epstein, Joseph, 552
Epstein, Richard, 551
Erewhon (Butler), 321–22
Ernst, Max, 203
Ernst, Paul, 97
Escape (radio program), 170, 171
Escape from New York (film), 257
Eshun, Kodwo, 566–67
Estabrook, G. H., 508–9
E.T.: The Extra-Terrestrial (film), 178
Eternauta, El (comic), 216–17
Ethno-Cyberpunk Trading Post & Curio Shop on the Electronic Frontier, The (performance art), 265
Ethnoscapes, 568
Ettinger, Robert, 16, 531–33
Eureka (television program), 181
Euripides, 111
Eurocon, 73
European Science Fiction Association, 73
European Science Fiction Society, 73
Euthenics: The Science of Controllable Environment (Richards), 538–39
Evans, Arthur B., 5, 7, 52, 146
Evaporating Genres (Wolfe), 32, 140
Eventual genres, 578–79
Eve Online (video game), 231 (figure), 235–36
Everquest (video game), 249
Ewing, Al, 444
Excitement (magazine), 100
Excursion, The (Mallet), 455–56
Excursion to the Moon (film), 186
Exoskeleton (performance art), 267
Experimental fiction, 8, 118, 119
Experimental jazz, 16
Exploration of Space, The (Clarke), 346
Explorers of the Infinite (Moskowitz), 53
Explorers on the Moon (comic), 216
Explorigator, The (comic strip), 213
Extra Ear (performance art), 273
Extrapolation (journal), 1, 147, 155
Extrapolation and speculation, 6–7, 23–33;
  changed meaning of terms, 30–31;
  plausibility of, 7, 23, 27, 28, 29–30, 32;
  relationship of two terms, 23–24, 32;
  role of science in, 30–32;

  scarcity of material on, 24
Extrasensory perception, 15, 499, 507–10
Extrasensory Perception (Rhine), 509
Eyriès, Jean-Baptiste Benoît, 464
Ezquerra, Carlos, 216

Fahrenheit 9/11 (film), 337
Fahrenheit 451 (film), 159–62
Fail-Safe (film), 332
"Fairy Chessmen, The" (Padgett), 510
Fakeshop, 265–66
Falling Skies (television program), 333, 335, 337
Fallout (video game), 230
"Fall Revolution" quartet (MacLeod), 557, 581
Fancartography, 78
Fandom, 7, 60, 71–79, 96;
  comics and, 219–20;
  defined, 71;
  diversity of, 75;
  emergence of, 71–72;
  fiction writing in, 78, 404;
  interaction with writers in, 78–79;
  international scope of, 72–74;
  as a knowledge economy, 7, 75–76
Fanon, Frantz, 487, 488
Fantasmagoriana, 464
Fantastic (magazine), 389
Fantastic, the, 8, 127–37;
  definitions of, 128–29;
  Dissensus, 131, 133, 135–36;
  Natural, 131–32;
  Rationalized, 131, 132–33, 134;
  Situated, 131, 133–35;
  use of criticized, 129–30
Fantastic Four, The (comic), 218–19
Fantastic Planet (film), 193
Fantastic Romance, 131
Fantastic Universe (magazine), 547
Fantastic Voyage (film), 176, 458
Fantasy, 88, 127–28, 129, 277, 451
Fanzines, 72, 76–78
Fariña, Richard, 386
Farmer, Philip José, 63, 111, 398
Farnell, Ross, 13
Farnham's Freehold (Heinlein), 565
Farscape (television program), 181
Fascism, 325
Fate (magazine), 355
Favorite Story (radio program), 170
Fawcett Publications, 99
F.E.A.R. (video game), 230
Featherstone, Mike, 409
Federman, Raymond, 118
Feeling Very Strange: The Slipstream Anthology (Kelly and Kessel, eds.), 66, 122–23

Feiffer, Jules, 342
Feldstein, Al, 215
Female Man, The (Russ), 399, 402, 524, 542–43, 574
Feminism, 16, 242, 243, 537–47;
  coinage of term, 537;
  in comics, 215;
  counter-revolution against, 384;
  culture of science and, 311–12;
  cybernetics and, 429;
  cyborg, 16, 242, 422, 543–45;
  Darwinism contested by, 478–79;
  fandom and, 72;
  First Wave, 539–41;
  men and, 546–47;
  performance art and, 415–16;
  pro-sex, 408;
  Second Wave, 541–43;
  sexuality and, 397, 399;
  in SF criticism, 53;
  SF's natural compatibility with, 537;
  Third Wave, 543–47
Fenkl, Heinz, 66
Fenn, Jainne, 79
Fernandes, Fabio, 569
Ferreira, Rachel Haywood, 54, 312
Ferriss, Hugh, 372
Festival of Britain, 282–83
Fetish Fantastic: Erotica on the Edge (story collection), 404
Feynman, Richard, 264
Fiction House, 214
"Fictions Versus Fact" (Gernsback), 81
Fictive neology, 39, 107
Fictive novums, 39, 107
Fidelity fallacy, 158
Fiedel, Brad, 258
Field, Richard M., 342
Fifth Element, The (film), 258
Fifty Key Figures in Science Fiction, 91
Film, 9, 10, 86, 155–66;
  CGI in, 9, 334, 337;
  divergence between source and, 158–62;
  generic hybridity in, 156–58;
  marginalizing of, 155–56;
  military culture depicted in, 331–37;
  poster art for, 201–3;
  soundtracks for, 10, 254–58;
  special effects in, 3, 9, 162–66, 333–34;
  video game influence on, 226
Finder (comic), 215
Finland, 72, 73
Finland Futures Research Centre, 514
Finnegans Wake (Joyce), 42
Finney, Jack, 174
Firebird II, 375, 376 (figure)
Firefly (television program), 181, 182
Fire in the Stone, The (Ruddick), 55
Fire on the Mountain (Bisson), 565

Firestone, Shulamith, 16, 541–42
Firestone Tires, 373–74
First Kingdom, The (Katz), 215
First Man into Space (film), 335
First Men in the Moon, The (Wells), 213
First on the Moon (Sutton), 344–45
First-person perspective (FPP) (in video games), 230
First-person shooter (FPS) (video game genre), 228, 235, 332
Fitting, Peter, 54–55
Flame Wars: The Discourse of Cyberculture (Dery, ed.), 561
Flammarion, Camille, 53, 186
Flanagan, Mary, 140
Flash Gordon (comic strip), 82, 213, 221, 222 (figure), 223, 436
Flash Gordon (radio program), 170
Flash Gordon Strange Adventure Magazine, 82
Flechtheim, Ossip, 513–14, 518
Fledgling (Butler), 403
Fleischer brothers, 186, 187, 188
Flint, Eric, 78
Fly, The (film), 189
Flying Saucer (magazine), 355
"Flying Saucer Rock 'n' Roll" (song), 258
Flying Saucers Have Landed (Adamski and Leslie), 353
Foley artists, 254, 255
Fontenelle, Bernard Le Bovier de, 454
Food Force (video game), 228
Foot Hose (band), 260
Forbidden Planet (film), 201, 254, 256
Ford, Henry, 323–24
Ford, Jeffrey, 66
Fordism, 324, 490
Ford Motor Company, 317, 366, 371, 376–77
Ford Nucleon, 436
Foreger, Nikolai, 265
Forerunner Foray (Norton), 133
Forever War, The (Haldeman), 111, 332
"Forgotten Realms" novels, 88
"Fork in the Road, The" (Sedgewick), 88
Forlini, Stefania, 441–42
Formula, 286
"Formulary for a New Urbanism" (Ivain), 285
Forster, E. M., 110, 323
Foss, Chris, 197, 206, 286
Fostad, Karen Wynn, 78
Foster, Thomas, 13–14, 402, 404
Foucault, Michel, 396, 405, 410, 493, 498–99
Foundation (journal), 155
"Foundation" series (Asimov), 44, 454, 520
Foundation Trilogy, The (radio program), 172
Fountainhead, The (Rand), 551
Fountains of Paradise, The (Clarke), 520
Fourier, Joseph, 435
14 Great Tales of ESP (Stone, ed.), 509
4'33 (Cage), 254

Fowler, Alastair, 143
Fowler, Hayden, 268–69
Fowler, Karen Joy, 24, 66
Fractal Flesh (performance art), 266
France, 73, 216
France, Anatole, 268
Frank, Pat, 90
Franke, Herbert W., 52
Frankenstein (radio adaptation), 170, 172
Frankenstein; or, the Modern Prometheus (Shelley), 14, 24, 39, 50, 51, 110–11, 396, 412, 464–68, 470–71, 472, 498, 524
Frankenstein Unbound (Aldiss), 111
Franklin, H. Bruce, 4, 5, 53, 54, 105, 342, 392
Frank Reade stories (dime novels), 95, 96, 435
Frau im Mond (film), 348
Freas, Frank Kelly, 206
Freedman, Carl, 2, 3, 53, 163, 273–74, 308, 396
Freedman, Estelle, 396
Frelik, Pawel, 10
French, Paul (Asimov pseudonym), 86
Freud, Sigmund, 319, 396
Friedman, David, 558
Friedman, Milton, 551, 558
Friedrich, Mike, 215
Friel, Arthur O., 101
Frigidaire, 364, 375, 378
Fringe (television program), 181
From the Earth to the Moon (Verne), 185
"From the Mouth of Babes" (Hergenrader), 547
Frontier narratives, 479–80, 481
Frontiers Past and Future (Abbott), 486
Fry, Daniel, 353
Fuller, John G., 354
Fuller, Richard Buckminster, 284
Full Metal Apache (Tatsumi), 146
Funkadelic, 566
"Further Considerations on Afrofuturism" (Eshun), 567
Fury (Kuttner), 385
Futura (car), 377
"Futurama" (exhibit), 12, 295, 306, 372–73, 375, 436, 438
Futurama (television program), 193, 259
"Futurama II" (exhibit), 376
Future history, 39, 107
"Future History" (Heinlein), 15, 519–20
"Future May Be Bleak, but It's Not Black, The" (Davis), 562
"Future of Science Fiction, The" (Bretnor), 28
Futures: The Journal of Forecasting and Planning, 514
Future Science Fiction (magazine), 436
Future shock, 513, 516–17
Future Shock (Toffler), 516–17
Futurian Science Literary Society, 59, 60–61, 72, 78, 201
Futurian War Digest (FIDO) (fanzine), 76
Futurism. *See* Futurology

Futurist (journal), 514
Futurist Architectural Exhibition, 279
"Futurist Manifesto, The" (Marinetti), 279
Futurology, 15–16, 513–22;
    as an academic subject, 514;
    coinage of term, 513;
    purpose and applications of, 514–15;
    SF as an inspiration for, 517–18. *See also* Afrofuturism; Retrofuturism
FX Atmos, 376–77

Gabor, Dennis, 516
Gagarin, Yuri, 191, 261
Gaia's Toys (Ore), 402
Gaiman, Neil, 90
Galactic Suburbia (Yaszek), 312
Galaxian (video game), 226
Galaxy (magazine), 28, 61, 85, 318, 340, 344, 387, 389
Galaxy Awards, 74
Galbraith, John Kenneth, 380
Galileo's Dream (Robinson), 311
Galloway, Alexander R., 235
Galvani, Luigi, 466
Gamble, Eliza, 479
Gamer (film), 162
"Gamer Girl Manifesto, The" (video), 545
Gamer Girl movement, 545
Gamow, George, 132
Gandahar (film), 193
García Márquez, Gabriel, 118
Garnier, Charles, 53
Garnier, Tony, 282
Garrett, Randall, 389
Gastev, Alexei, 324
Gate to Women's Country, The (Tepper), 111
Gatiss, Mark, 78
Gaudreault, André, 163
Gaughan, Jack, 203
Gaylactic Network, 13, 397
Gaylactic Spectrum Awards, 397
Gay SF, 397, 404
Gearheart, Sally Miller, 397
Gebhard, David, 436
Geim, Andre, 307
GenCon, 75
Gender performativity, 400, 402, 424–25
General Electric (GE), 367, 368, 370
General Motors (GM), 12, 295, 306, 364, 366, 372–73, 374, 375–76, 377–78, 380, 436, 438
General pulps, 93–95, 97, 98, 99–102
Genesis (band), 260
Genesis (performance art), 272–73
Genette, Gérard, 44, 233
Genre *vs.* mode, 8–9, 139–49;
    boundary permeability, 140–42;
    shift from future to present, 143–49;
    shift from metonymy to metaphor, 143;
    sociocultural analysis, 143–44

598 INDEX

Gentleman, Sir Francis, 457
Geraghty, Lincoln, 173, 178
Gerania (Barnes), 457
German Bauhaus, 265
Germany, 72, 73
Gernsback, Hugo, 28, 50, 51, 68, 86, 89, 91, 106, 198–99, 201, 213, 309, 325, 427, 445, 479, 531;
    electronic media and, 9, 169, 173;
    fandom and, 72, 96;
    feminism supported by, 547;
    influence on pulp SF, 93, 94, 95, 96–97, 101;
    influence on the marketplace, 81–82;
    influence on the SF movement, 59–60, 61;
    popularization of term "science fiction," 81, 94, 105, 305;
    sexology popularized by, 13, 396
"Gernsback Continuum, The" (Gibson), 437, 438, 440, 445
Ghosh, Amitav, 135, 489, 492
Ghost in the Shell (film), 192
Ghost in the Shell (Shirow), 217
Giant Rock Spacecraft Conventions, 354
Gibbon, Edward, 520
Gibbons, Dave, 212, 221
Gibson, William, 4, 42–43, 64–65, 66, 68, 90, 112, 118, 132, 139, 145–46, 147, 148, 149, 207, 228, 231–32, 242, 244, 271, 287, 309, 337, 386, 401, 402, 410, 416–17, 568;
    cybernetics and, 426–27, 430, 431–32;
    futurology and, 521;
    posthumanism and, 524;
    retrofuturism and, 437, 445;
    steampunk and, 440
Giger, H. R., 417
Gilbert, William, 460
Gilbreth, Frank, 324
Gilbreth, Lillian, 324
Gilman, Charlotte Perkins, 16, 479, 482, 483, 539, 540
Gilroy, Paul, 429
Ginsberg, Allen, 386, 387, 388
Ginsburg, Mosei, 281
Ginway, Elizabeth, 312
Giraud, Jean. *See* Moebius
"Girl Who Was Plugged In, The" (Tiptree), 424, 425
Gladiator (Wylie), 214
Glass Houses (Mixon), 402
Glenn, John, 345
Glenn Gould: The New Listener (CD-ROM), 245
Gnosticism, 135, 136
Godwin, Tom, 24, 307
Godwin, William, 50, 550
Gold, H. L., 28, 61, 62, 85, 340
Golden, Thelma, 569
Golden Age of comics, 218
Golden Age of SF, 61, 109, 308–9, 398
Golden Age of SF pulps, 97

"Golden Apples of the Sun, The" (Bradbury), 41–42
Golden Crown Literary Society Awards, 397
Golden Key comics, 341
"Goldfish Bowl" (Heinlein), 84
"Goldilocks zone," 455
Gold Medal Books, 99
Goldsmith, Cele, 63
Goldsmith, Jerry, 256–57
Gómez-Peña, Guillermo, 265
Gomoll, Jeanne, 76, 79
Good, I. J., 270
Goodall, Jane, 415
Good Blonde & Others (Kerouac), 388
"Good Vibrations" (song), 259
Goonan, Kathleen Ann, 111
Gordon, Joan, 8, 52, 55, 396
Goss, Theodora, 66
Gothic fiction, 14–15, 50, 102, 143, 463–73;
    apocalyptic, 471–73;
    the automaton in, 319;
    genesis of SF form, 463–64;
    medical science depicted in, 466–70
Gothic Science Fiction (Wasson and Alder, eds.), 143
Goudie, Brian, 442
Gould, Glenn, 245
Graham, Brandon, 224
Grandville, J. J., 185
Graphene, 306–7
Grass (Tepper), 524
Grass, Günter, 118
Gravity's Rainbow (Pynchon), 104, 113, 118, 348
"Gravy Planet" (Kornbluth), 61
Gray, Chris Hables, 146
Great Exclusion Act of 1939, 60, 78
Great Exhibition (London), 278, 283
"Great God Pan, The" (Machen), 467, 469
"Great Slow Kings, The" (Zelazny), 36
Green, Jonathan, 444
Greene, David, 283
Greenland, Colin, 67
Griffith, George, 506
Griffith, Nicola, 400, 402
Grimsley, Jim, 134
Grivel, Jean-Baptiste, 53
Groensteen, Thierry, 223
Grosset & Dunlap, 86
Grossman, Dave, 334
Grosz, Elizabeth, 410, 414, 416
Grotesque, SF, 39, 107
Guattari, Felix, 267, 272, 273
Guffey, Elizabeth, 14
Gulliver's Travels (Swift), 2, 453, 458, 459–61
Gunn, James, 31–32, 47, 52, 141, 156, 196, 307, 385
Gunning, Tom, 163
Gurney, Edmund, 508

Haber, Heinz, 341
Haggard, H. Rider, 71, 495
Hagio, Moto, 217
Haigh, Thomas, 445
Halas, John, 192
Halberstam, Judith, 241
Haldane, J. B. S., 519, 520, 529
Haldeman, Joe, 90, 111–12, 332
Half-Life (video game), 227, 230
Hall, Stuart, 425–26
Halley, Edmond, 499–500
Hall of Fame Award, 552, 555
Hall of the Mountain Grill (album), 206
Halloween (film), 257
Hallward, Peter, 579
Halo (video game), 227, 230, 232, 332
Halo 2 (video game), 232
Halpern, Marty, 65
Hamilton, Alexander, 553
Hamilton, Edmond, 82, 214
Hamilton, Grant, 493
Hamilton, Peter, 67
Hamilton, Richard, 283
Hamlet (Shakespeare), 37
Hamlin, Kimberly, 478
Hampson, Frank, 216, 221
Hancock, Herbie, 206
Hand, Elizabeth, 128, 333
Handmaid's Tale, The (Atwood), 521
Handwriting (performance art), 266
Hanna, Kathleen, 545
Hannett, Martin, 261
Hantke, Steffen, 12
Haraway, Donna, 16, 91, 133, 145, 146, 147, 148, 240, 242, 396, 400, 409, 414, 422, 423, 426, 427, 431, 527, 543–44, 545
Harder, Delmar, 317
Harding, Sandra, 311–12
Harding, Susan, 434, 443
Hard SF, 7, 306, 309
Hardt, Michael, 490
Hardware (film), 165
Hardy, Phil, 159
Haredevil Hare (cartoon), 189
Hareway to the Stars (cartoon), 189
Harlequin Books, 86
Harper, Mary Catherine, 414
Harper, Phillip Brian, 429
Harrad Experiment, The, 397
Harris, Clare Winger, 547
Harrison, M. John, 66, 67
Harrison, Niall, 122
Harryhausen, Ray, 78, 184, 189
Hartshorne, Charles, 513
Hartwell, David, 67, 79, 87, 88, 91
Harvey, David, 207, 490

Hasty Hare, The (cartoon), 189
Hatfield, Charles, 223
Haussman, Raoul, 280
Hawai'i Research Center for Future Studies, 514
Hawkwind (band), 206, 260
Hawthorne, Nathaniel, 52, 105, 320
Hayden, Patrick Nielsen, 79
Hayden, Teresa Nielsen, 79
Hayden, Tom, 63
Hayek, Friedrich von, 551, 558
Hayles, N. Katherine, 4, 5, 124, 140, 146, 147, 244, 247, 326, 423, 424, 431
Hayward, Philip, 254
H-Bomb Over America (Sutton), 345
He, She and It (Piercy), 402
"Healer, The" (Bender), 123
Heart and Science (Collins), 467, 469, 470
"Heart of Darkness" (Conrad), 111, 492
"Heat Death of the Universe, The" (Zoline), 62, 143
Heaven's Gate movement, 12, 359–60
Heavy Metal (magazine), 215
Heidegger, Martin, 323
Heinlein, Robert A., 13, 15, 16, 25–26, 27, 29, 61, 90, 111, 171, 278, 309, 325, 332, 334, 392, 396–97, 510, 525, 565;
    futurology and, 518, 519–20, 521;
    influence on the marketplace, 83–84;
    libertarianism and, 555–56, 557, 558–59;
    posthumanism and, 532–33;
    space race and, 343–44, 347
Helland, Christopher, 357
"Hell Is the Absence of God" (Chiang), 123
Hemings, Sally, 553
Hemingway, Ernest, 111–12, 565
Hemingway Hoax, The (Haldeman), 111–12
Hench, John, 295
Henderson, Zenna, 86, 127–28, 137
Hendrix, Jimi, 206, 259
Henry, Pierre, 259
Henson, Matthew Alexander, 502
"Hep-Cats of Venus" (Garrett), 389
Herbert, Frank, 90, 206, 232, 392, 453
Hergé, 216
Hergenrader, Trent, 547
Herland (Gilman), 16, 479, 539
Herrmann, Bernard, 254, 256–57
Herron, Ron, 283, 284 (figure)
Hersey, John, 348
Hetherington, Norriss S., 503
Hickman, Jonathan, 224
Hidden Persuaders, The (Packard), 380
Hieroglyph project, 68
Highlander (film), 164
Highlander II: The Quickening (film), 164
"Highways of Tomorrow" (Motorama attraction), 375

Hill, Barney, 354
Hill, Betty, 354
Hippies, 12–13, 392
Hiroshima bombing, 217, 326, 340, 341, 348
Histories, 7, 47–55;
    on earliest SF prototypes, 50–51;
    new frontiers in, 54–55;
    origins of SF criticism and, 52–53;
    semiotic approach, 7, 48–49;
    shift in, 53–54;
    sociological, 49;
    theme-author based, 47–48
"History and Criticism" (Wolfe), 52
History of Science Fiction, The (Roberts), 50
"History of Science Fiction Criticism, A" (Evans), 146
Hitchcock, Alfred, 158, 160, 161–62
Hitchhiker's Guide to the Galaxy, The (radio program), 172
Hitler, Adolph, 325
Hjerstedt, Gunnar, 98, 101
Hoban, Russell, 42, 116, 118, 340
Hobbes, Thomas, 314
Hoberman, Perry, 244–45, 250
Hodge, T. Shirby, 565
Hoffman, Arthur S., 94
Hoffmann, E. T. A., 319
Hogan, Robert J., 97
Holberg, Ludvig, 53, 456
Holland, Steve, 196
Hollinger, Veronica, 4–5, 8–9, 16, 52, 55, 120, 121, 396
Hollow-earth theory, 15, 499–502
Holmes, John Clellon, 389
Holmes, Thom, 252
Holt Hinshaw Pfau Jones, 286
Holy Barbarians, The (Lipton), 389
Holy Fire (Sterling), 547
Homeostasis, 422–24, 429, 431
Homunculus (Blaylock), 440
Honegger, Arthur, 253
Honeymoon in Space, A (Griffith), 506
Hooke, Robert, 499
Hopkinson, Nalo, 17, 133, 134, 402, 486, 524, 564, 565, 566, 567, 568, 569–70
Horizon (journal), 516
Horizons (Bel Geddes), 365, 368, 370, 372
Horkheimer, Max, 452
Horrigan, Brian, 173, 209–10
Horror films, 9, 156
Host Planet Earth (radio program), 172
House Committee on Un-American Activities, 384
"House of Magic" (exhibit), 368
Howard, Robert E., 78
Howe, Irving, 63
"Howl" (Ginsberg), 386, 387
How We Became Posthuman: Virtual Bodies in Cybernetics, Literature, and Informatics (Hayles), 4, 140, 146, 244

Hubbard, Dorothy, 94
Hubbard, L. Ron, 352, 354, 355, 360–61
Huge Hunter, The, or the Steam Man of the Prairies (Ellis), 435, 440
Hughes, Langston, 570
Hughes, Rian, 206
Hughes, William, 14–15
Hugo Award, 64, 75, 76, 77, 78, 88, 113, 207, 212, 392
Hulk, The (comic), 219
Humanists, 65
Human League (band), 261
Human Use of Human Beings, The (Wiener), 421, 529
Hume, Kathryn, 129, 131
Hunger Games, The (Collins), 483
Huntington, John, 49
Huxley, Aldous, 105, 161, 323, 387
Huxley, T. H., 322
Huxtable, Ada Louise, 293
Hydra Club, 59
Hyperion (Simmons), 111
Hyperreality, 144, 145, 149

I, Robot (Asimov), 159
I, Robot (film), 159
I Am Legend (Matheson), 15, 472, 473
Ian Gillian Band, 206
ICE (intrusion countermeasures electronics), 427
"Icons of Science Fiction, The" (Jones), 220
"Idea of North, The" (Gould), 245
Idoru (Gibson), 417
"If This Goes On" (Heinlein), 84
"If We Could Move to Mars" (Serviss), 505
"I Have No Mouth, and I Must Scream" (Ellison), 132
I Have No Mouth and I Must Scream (video game), 232
I Hear a New World (album), 258
Ikin, Van, 54
ILLIAC, 255
I Love Bees (video game), 232
Imagetext, 196
Imaginary Landscape No. 1 (Cage), 254
Imaginary science, 30, 39, 107
"Imagination of Disaster, The (Sontag), 202–3
Imagining Mars (Crossley), 54
Imperial Eyes (Pratt), 488
Impossible Voyage, The (film), 185
Incal, The (comic), 223
"Incident of the Cosmos, An" (radio adaptation), 170
Incredible Change-Bots (comic), 215
Incredible Science Fiction (magazine), 215
Independence Day (film), 337
India, 73–74
Industrial Light and Magic (ILM), 190, 333–34
Industrial Revolution, 11, 308, 318, 435, 439, 440, 442, 444
Infernal Devices (Jeter), 440
Infernal War, The (Robida), 197

Infinite, The (television program), 182
Infinite Worlds (Di Fate), 196
Ing, Dean, 347
Inklings, 59, 71
Inner Sanctum (radio program), 170, 171
Innocence (film), 192
Inquiriy into Science Fiction (Davenport), 23
In Search of Wonder (Knight), 85
Inside the Space Ships (Adamski), 358
Instant City, 283
Institute for Operational Research, 514
Institute for the Future (IFF), 15, 236, 514
Institute of Development Studies, 514
Instruments and Automation (journal), 317
Interfictions: An Anthology of Interstitial Writings (Sherman and Goss, eds.), 66
International Scienc Fiction Guild, 60
Internet, 76–78, 287. *See also* Cyberspace; Digital art and illustration; Digital arts and hypertext
Interrupted Journey, The: Two Lost Hours "Aboard a Flying Saucer" (Fuller), 354
"Interstellar Overdrive" (song), 259
Interstitial Arts Foundation, 66
Interstitial movement, 66, 67
Interzone (magazine), 67, 68
In the Mouth of the Whale (McAuley), 432
"In the Penal Colony" (Kafka), 417
In the Slipstream (Sukenick and White, eds.), 118–19
"Into the 28th Century" (Lorraine), 540–41
In Tune with Tomorrow (film), 370
Invaders, The (television program), 176
Invaders from Mars (film), 336
Invasion (television program), 181
Invasion of the Body Snatchers (film), 494
Invention of Destruction, The (film), 191
Invisible Man (Ellison), 567–68
Iraq conflict, 330, 340
Ireland, 72
"I Remember Lemuria" (Shaver), 355
Iron Heel, The (London), 574
Irving, Washington, 105, 532
Ishiguro, Kazuo, 112, 469
Island of Doctor Moreau, The (Wells), 13, 410, 467, 494
Islands in the Net (Sterling), 547
Is Mars Habitable? (Wallace), 503
Israel, Jonathan, 451
Italian Futurists, 265, 279, 282
Italy, 73
It Came From Beneath the Sea (film), 190
"It's a Good Life" (Bixby), 86
It! The Terror from Beyond Space (film), 86
Ivain, Gilles, 285

J. Walter Thompson advertising agency, 365, 373
Jack of Shadows (Zelazny), 134
Jackson, Peter, 337
Jackson, Shelley, 242, 243–44, 250
James, Edward, 1–2, 38, 50, 52, 54
James, Henry, 106, 128
James, P. D., 112
Jameson, Fredric, 4, 53, 120–21, 143, 144, 146, 147, 242, 245, 247, 249, 268, 269, 278, 285, 286; cybernetics and, 425, 426, 427, 429, 431, 432; utopianism and, 563, 575, 576–77, 578
"Jameson Satellite, The" (Jones), 531–32
Janus (fanzine), 76
Japan, 74, 191–92. *See also* Manga
Japoteurs (cartoon), 188
Jaquet-Droz, Pierre, 320
Jarrold, John, 79
Jazz, 388–89
"Jazz Machine, The" (Matheson), 389
Jeanneret, Charles-Édouard, 282
Jefferson, Thomas, 553
Jefferson Airplane (band), 206
Jenkins, Henry, 224, 232, 444
Jeter, K. W., 65–66, 439–40, 441
Jetsons, The (television program), 176, 193, 436
Jezer, Marty, 384
Jigureul jikyeora! (film), 157–58
Jodorowsky, Alejandro, 206, 223
"John Carter of Mars" books (Burroughs), 128
Johnny Chase, Secret Agent of Space (radio program), 172
Johnny Got His Gun (film), 333
Johnny Mnemonic (film), 258
Johnson, Greg, 123
Johnson, Lyndon, 63, 553
Johnson-Smith, Jan, 178, 179, 182
Jones, Chuck, 187, 189
Jones, Diana Wynne, 79
Jones, Gerard, 213
Jones, Gwyneth, 220, 311, 524
Jones, Neil R., 531–32
Jones, Raymond, 510
Jorgensen, Darren, 235, 236
Journey to the Center of the Earth (film), 191
Journey to the Center of the Earth (radio adaptation), 172
Journey to the Center of the Earth (Verne), 185, 492, 502, 578
Jovovich, Milla, 165
Joyce, James, 42, 110
Joy Division (band), 261
Judge Dredd (comic), 216, 223
Judge Dredd (film), 49
"Judgment Day" (Feldstein), 215
Judgment on Janus (Norton), 134
Jünger, Ernst, 325
Jungk, Robert, 515–16
Jungle Drums (cartoon), 188
"Junkspace" (Koolhaas), 286–87
Juno, Andrea, 408
Just Imagine (film), 372

Juul, Jesper, 228

Kac, Eduardo, 241, 264, 271–73
Kafka, Franz, 417
Kairos Future, 514
Kant, Immanuel, 7, 39, 451, 453
Katz, Jack, 215
Kaveney, Roz, 184
Kaye, Lenny, 259
Keaton, Russell, 221
Keats, John, 108
Kelleghan, Fiona, 65
Keller, Evelyn Fox, 311
Keller, Helen, 241
Kellner, Douglas, 242, 244
Kelly, Frank K., 82
Kelly, James Patrick, 24, 52, 65, 66, 122–23
Kemp, Earl, 77
Kempelen, Wolfgang von, 319
Kennedy, John F., 330, 342
Kent State shootings, 260
Kepler, Johannes, 50, 52–53
Kepler 16b (Tattooine), 306
Kerouac, Jack, 387–88, 389, 390
Kerry, John, 330
Kesey, Ken, 386
Kessel, John, 52, 65, 66, 111, 122–23, 124
Ketterer, David, 49, 53
Keyhoe, Donald, 97
"Keys to December, The" (Zelazny), 36
Khachaturian, Aram, 256
Khrushchev, Nikita, 378
Kid A (album), 261
Kikauka, Laura, 270
Kilgore, De Witt Douglas, 16–17, 53, 444
Kindermann, Eberhard Christian, 457
Kindred (Butler), 494–95
King, Geoff, 163, 184
King Crimson (band), 260
King Kong (stop-motion feature), 187
King Rat (Miéville), 66–67
Kingsley, Gershon, 259
King Solomon's Mines (Haggard), 495
Kin of Ata Are Waiting for You, The (Bryant), 397
Kinsella, W. P., 117
Kinsey, Alfred, 396
Kipling, Rudyard, 325
Kirby, Jack, 218–19, 222–23
"Kirby krackle," 223
Kircher, Athanasius, 499
Kirinyaga (Resnick), 565
Kitchen Debate, 378
"Kitchens of Tomorrow" (exhibit), 12, 364, 375, 378, 379 (figure)
Kitman, Marvin, 342
Klein, Norman M., 191
Klesse, Christian, 410, 411

Kline, Nathan S., 413, 422
Klugman, Karen, 298–99
Knight, Damon, 47, 53, 60, 63, 85, 105, 160
Knotted Line, The, 249
Knowledge and Social Imagery (Bloor), 310
Koch, Howard, 170
Kohn, Robert D., 372
Kollin, Dani, 554–55, 556
Kollin, Eytan, 554–55, 556
Kon, Satoshi, 192
Koolhaas, Rem, 286–87
Korean War, 329, 335, 336
Kornbluth, C. M., 60, 61, 130, 309, 365, 387, 388
Krafft-Ebing, Richard von, 396
Kraken (Miéville), 44
Kraken Wakes, The (radio program), 172
Krassner, Paul, 342
Krautrock, 260, 261
Kress, Nancy, 65
Kropotkin, Peter, 550
Krzywinska, Tanya, 184
Kubrick, Stanley, 3, 132, 159, 206, 255, 256, 258, 270, 307, 340, 347, 349, 379, 438, 520
Kugelberg, Johan, 259
Kuhn, Annette, 155
Kuhn, Thomas, 309–10, 499
Kurosawa, Akira, 333
Kurzweil, Ray, 33, 270, 515, 533–34
Kushner, Ellen, 66
Kuttner, Henry, 214, 385, 547
Kyle, Dave, 60

Lacey, Bruce, 265
Lach-Szyrma, W. S., 503–5
Lady Gaga, 206
Lafferty, R. A., 63
Lake, Jay, 67
Laloux, René, 193
Lalumiere, Claude, 65
Lambda Literary Awards, 397
Land Leviathan, The (Moorcock), 565
Land of the Giants (television program), 176
Landon, Brooks, 3, 4, 5, 6–7, 49, 54, 96, 145, 293, 299, 384, 549, 557, 558–59
Lane, Mary E. Bradley, 539, 540
Lang, Fritz, 201, 206, 323, 348, 372
Lang, Herrmann, 565
Langer, Jessica, 487, 488, 489
Langford, David, 79
Larbalestier, Justine, 49, 53, 312
Larratt, Shannon, 409
Laser Books, 86
Lasseter, John, 195
Lasswitz, Kurd, 49
Last and First Men: A Story of the Near and Far Future (Stapledon), 519, 524, 577
"Last Judgment, The" (Haldane), 519

Last Man, The (Shelley), 471–72, 473
Last Men in London (Stapledon), 519
Last Starfighter, The (film), 226, 335
Late capitalism, 120, 121, 122, 144, 165, 298;
  architecture of, 285;
  body modification and, 416;
  cybernetics and, 422, 423, 427;
  video games and, 236
Latham, Rob, 52, 55, 122, 124, 142, 398–400
Latin America, 73, 216–17
Latour, Bruno, 157, 241, 313, 314
Lautréamont, 204
Lavender, Isiah, 568
Lazarus Organization, 203
League of Extraordinary Gentlemen, The (comic), 215
Leary, Timothy, 386
Lee, Sharon, 89
Lee, Stan, 218–19, 222
Lefanu, Sarah, 49, 53
Left Hand of Darkness, The (Le Guin), 130, 399, 542, 558
Legion of Science Fiction Improvement, 60
Le Guin, Ursula K., 2, 42, 44, 52, 85, 90, 110, 130, 133–34, 136, 267, 333, 338, 399, 542, 557, 558, 563, 574
Lehr, Paul, 203
Lehrer, Tom, 341
Leiber, Fritz, 63, 389–90, 391
Lem, Stanislaw, 2, 27, 49, 577
Lemay, Kate C., 14
"Lemuria" series (Shaver), 502
L'Engle, Madeleine, 136
Lenin Institute, 281
Leonard, Elmore, 117
Leonidov, Ivan, 281
Lesbian SF, 397, 399, 401, 402, 404
Leslie, Desmond, 353
Leslie, Sir John, 500, 502
Lessing, Doris, 116
Lethem, Jonathan, 104, 112, 113, 123, 124
Letterist International, 285
Level 7 (Roshwald), 326
Levy, Michael, 64, 65
Lewis, C. S., 59, 129, 131, 135, 136
Ley, Willy, 344, 502
Leyner, Mark, 119
LGBT SF, 13, 397, 404
Libbey-Owens-Ford Glass Company, 378
Libertarian Futurist Society, 16, 552
Libertarianism, 16, 384, 549–59;
  impact on real-world issues, 557–58;
  key ideas of, 550;
  philosophical principles of, 550–51;
  problems of, 556
Liebesman, Jonathan, 337
Life (Jones), 311
"Life and Death of Literary Forms, The" (Fowler), 143

"Life-Line" (Heinlein), 84
Life on Mars (television program), 182
Ligeti, György, 256
"Light and the Sufferer" (Lethem), 123
Lightner, A. M., 565
Ligon, Glenn, 569
"Like a Rolling Stone" (song), 259
Lilly, John C., 392
Limbo (Wolfe), 340, 524
Limits of Infinity, The: The American Science Fiction Film (Sobchack), 3, 155, 254
Limits to Capital, The (Harvey), 490
Lindsay, Dan, 389
Lindsay, David, 135, 136
Link, Kelly, 66
Linzmayer, Adam, 509
Lipton, Lawrence, 389
Liquid architecture, 11, 287
Liquid Metal: The Science Fiction Film Reader (Redmond), 155
Liquid Sky (film), 256
Lissitzky, Lazar Markovich (El Lissitzky), 280–81
Literary marketplace. *See* Marketplace
Literary movements, 7, 59–68;
  counterculture influences, 63–64;
  early factions in, 60–61;
  editors influencing, 59–60, 61–62;
  humanist influences, 65;
  optimism in, 68
Literary science fiction, 3, 8, 104–13;
  background on, 105;
  character development in, 108;
  differing demands and rewards of, 106–7;
  existence of denied, 105–6;
  literalizing of metaphor in, 107, 110;
  megatext and, 105, 110–12
Little, Big (Crowley), 547
Little Nemo in Slumberland (comic strip), 213
LiveJournal (blog), 77–78
Living Pod, 283
Livingston, Dennis, 517
Locke, John, 550
Locus (magazine), 65, 75, 76, 79, 440
Locus Award, 75
Loewy, Raymond, 365, 369, 370
Lofficier, Jean-Marc, 49, 54
Lofficier, Randy, 54
Logan's Run (film), 257
Logan's Run (television program), 177–78
"Logic of Empire" (Heinlein), 84
LogPlug, 283
London, Jack, 492, 574
Lone Gunmen, The (television program), 181
Longo, Robert, 258
Long Way Back, The (Bennett), 565
Looking Backward: 2000-1887 (Bellamy), 71, 136, 321, 518, 574

Lord of Light (Zelazny), 128
Lord of the Rings, The (film), 337
Lord of the Rings, The (Tolkien), 78
Lorraine, Lilith, 540–41
Los Angeles Interactive Media Festival, 244
Los Angeles Science Fantasy Society (LASFS), 72, 78
Lost (television program), 181
Lost in Space (television program), 176
Lost Missile, The (film), 86
Lost World, The (Doyle), 492
Lost World, The (stop-motion feature), 187
Lothar and the Hand People (band), 260
Loudon, Jane, 321
Lovecraft, H. P., 67, 71, 101, 128, 131, 135, 136, 171, 527–28, 532
"Lovers, The" (Farmer), 398
Lowell, Percival, 503, 505, 506, 507
Lowndes, Robert A. W., 60
Loyer, Erik, 247–50
Lucas, George, 172, 178, 181, 190, 257, 331, 333, 334
Luce, Henry, 329
Lucian of Samosata, 50, 52, 53
Luckhurst, Roger, 5, 11–12, 25, 31, 49, 54, 109, 122, 137, 142, 147, 217–18, 306, 310, 354, 499, 508, 510, 549
Luckman, Charles, 437
Luddism, 319, 440
Lukas, Scott A., 291, 293
Lumière, Auguste, 185
Lumière, Louis, 185
Lunatic, Sir Humphrey (pseudonym of Francis Gentleman), 457
Lundwall, Sam, 47
Lutz, Tom, 392
Lyell, Charles, 435
Lynd, Dennis, 391
Lyotard, Jean-François, 120

Maak, Niklas, 434, 437, 445
MacArthur Award, 113
Macaulay, Thomas, 494
McAuley, Paul, 67, 432
McCaffery, Larry, 4, 120, 121–22
McCaffrey, Anne, 78, 128, 132–33, 544
McCain, John, 330
McCall, Bruce, 443
McCarran Act of 1950, 384
McCarthy, Cormac, 113
McCarthyism, 388
McCay, Winsor, 186, 213, 427–29
McClintock, Barbara, 311
McClure, Michael, 388
McComas, J. Francis, 61, 62, 85
McCulley, Johnston, 96
McCulloch, Warren, 421
McDevitt, Jack, 90
McDonald, Ian, 90, 148, 207–9
McDougall, Walter A., 343

McDougall, William, 508–9
MacFarlane, Scott, 392
McGuirk, Carol, 52, 268
McHale, Brian, 120, 230
Machen, Arthur, 467, 469
"Machine Stops, The" (Forster), 323
McHugh, Maureen, 148, 402
McKean, Dave, 209
MacLeod, Ken, 16, 17, 67, 549, 557, 581–82
McLuhan, Marshall, 443
Macmillan, R. H., 318
McMorrow, Will, 96
McMullen, Sean, 54
McNeil, Carla Speed, 215
Macy conferences, 326, 421
Mad as a Mars Hare (cartoon), 189
Mad Max 2 (film), 165
Magazine of Fantasy, The, 61, 99
Magazine of Fantasy and Science Fiction, The, 28, 61, 62, 85, 87, 99, 127, 389, 547
"Magic, Inc." (Heinlein), 84
Magic Motorways (Bel Geddes), 372, 375
Magnetic Telescope, The (cartoon), 188
Mailer, Norman, 117, 348, 349
Malevich, Kazimir, 279, 280
Mallet, David, 455–56
Mallory, Tom, 445
Malmgren, Carl, 48
Malzberg, Barry N., 349, 388
"Man, Android and Machine" (Dick), 326
Man and the Moon (film), 341
Manga, 10, 74, 191, 212, 217
Manguel, Alberto, 78
Manhattan Project, 325–26
Manhattan Projects, The (comic), 224
Manhattan Research, Inc., 255
"Manifesto for Cyborgs" (Haraway), 145, 400
Man in the High Castle, The (Dick), 204–5
Man into Superman (Ettinger), 532, 533
Mann, George, 52
Mannerpunk, 65
Manovich, Lev, 190, 230, 426
Man Plus (Pohl), 411, 423
Manson, Charles, 392, 397
Man's Place in the Universe (Wallace), 503
"Man Who Sold the Moon, The" (Heinlein), 309, 344
"Man Who Was Tomorrow, The" (radio adaptation), 170
"Man Who Went Back to Save Lincoln, The" (radio adaptation), 171
"Man Without a Body, The" (Mitchell), 429
Man with the Broken Ear, The (About), 532
"Many Deaths of Science Fiction, The" (Luckhurst), 147
Margulies, Leo, 547
Mariën, Marcel, 204
Marinetti, Filippo Tommaso, 279, 513

Marketplace, 7–8, 81–91;
  early influences on, 81–82;
  formulaic plotting and, 82–83;
  juvenile literature in, 85–86;
  resistance to standardization in, 83–85;
  series fiction in, 86–90
Markley, Robert, 486–87, 503
Marks, Laura U., 163
Marling, Karal, 294, 296, 298
Mars (Lowell), 503
Mars and Its Canals (Lowell), 503
Mars as the Abode of Life (Lowell), 503
Mars Attacks! (film), 258
"Mars" trilogy (Robinson), 249, 557
Martian canals controversy, 15, 499, 502–7
Martian Chronicles, The (Bradbury), 42, 109, 342
"Martian Odyssey, The" (Weinbaum), 200
Martian Race, The (Benford), 350
Martian Through Georgia (cartoon), 189
Martinière, Stephan, 197, 207–9
Marvel comics, 215, 218–19, 220, 340–41
Marx, Karl/Marxism, 5, 321, 435, 490, 491
Marx, Leo, 320
Mass Effect (video game), 228, 232, 234(figure)
Massive, The (comic), 224
Matheson, Richard, 15, 174, 389, 472
Matrix (video game), 232
Matrix, The (film), 258, 271
Matta, Roberto, 203
Mattachine Society, 398
Matthews, Harry, 118
Matthews, James Tilly, 320
Mauzan, Achille, 190
Max Headroom: Twenty Minutes into the Future (film), 5
May, Julian, 79
Mead, Margaret, 421
Mead, Syd, 286
Mecha manga, 217
Mechanical Monsters, The (cartoon), 188
Mechanics of Wonder, The (Westfahl), 51, 59
Meek, Joe, 258–59
Megatext of SF, 27, 47, 48, 105, 110–12
Mehan, Uppinder, 486, 564, 570
Meier, Billy, 353–54
Méliès, Georges, 185, 186, 190, 213, 435
Mellotron, 259
Melville, Herman, 105, 111
Melzer, Patricia, 13
Memories of the Space Age (Ballard), 349–50
Mencken, H. L., 102
Mendlesohn, Farah, 7, 52, 54, 94
Menger, Howard, 358
Men Like Gods (Wells), 323
Menschifesto (pamphlet), 203
"Men with Wings" (Stone), 540
Menzies, William Cameron, 323, 336

Mercury Theater on the Air (radio program), 170
Merrick, Helen, 49, 53
Merril, Judith, 27–29, 48, 60, 62, 73, 78, 109, 398
Metal Hurlant (magazine), 215
Metamorphoses of Science Fiction: On the Poetics and History of a Literary Genre (Suvin), 2, 48, 53, 129
Metaphor, 107, 110, 143
Methuselah's Children (Heinlein), 84
Metropolis (film), 173, 201, 206, 324, 372
Metropolis of Tomorrow (Ferriss), 372
Meyerhold, Vsevolod, 265
Michel, John, 60
Michelism, 60, 61, 63
Michener, James A., 348
"Micromégas" (Voltaire), 14, 453, 458–59
Midnight Robber (Hopkinson), 134, 524, 568
Midwich Cuckoos, The (Wyndham), 310
Miéville, China, 43–44, 48, 66–67, 68, 90, 112, 113, 140, 277, 549
Milburn, Colin, 16, 140, 146, 147, 148
Milestone Media, 562
Military culture, 12, 329–38;
  SF aligned with specific agendas of, 335;
  SF disavowal of wars' historical reality, 336–37;
  SF on moral legitimacy of military, 337;
  visual-culture texts as key medium of, 332
Military-industrial complex, 326, 330
Milius, John, 333
Mill, John Stuart, 550
Miller, Daniel, 261
Miller, Frank, 224
Miller, Henry, 386
Miller, P. Schuyler, 62
Miller, Paul D., 563–64
Miller, Sarah, 415
Miller, Steve, 89
Miller, Walter M., Jr., 90, 340, 342
Mills, C. Wright, 331
Mills, Pat, 216
Milner, Andrew, 142
Mimesis, 129, 241
Mind Children: The Future of Robot and Human Intelligence (Moravac), 529
Minksky, Marvin, 533
"Minute on Indian Education" (Macaulay), 494
"Miracle Kitchen" (exhibit), 378–79
Miró, Joan, 203
Mirrorshades: The Cyberpunk Anthology (Sterling, ed.), 64, 430
Mises, Ludwig von, 551
"Misfit" (Heinlein), 84
Misfits (band), 260
Missile Command (video game), 226
Mission: Space (Disney attraction), 294, 295–300
Mission of Gravity (Clement), 24, 311
Mission to Horatius (Reynolds), 86
Mississippi Review (journal), 4

606 INDEX

Mister X (comic), 224
Mitchell, Edward Page, 429
Mitchell, W. J. T., 196
Mixon, Laura J., 402
Mizora: A Prophecy (Lane), 539
MMORPGs (massively multiplayer online role-playing games), 235, 249
Moby Dick (Melville), 111
Mockingjay (Collins), 483
Modern Electrics (magazine), 198, 201
Modern Primitives (Vale and Juno, eds.), 408
Modern primitivism, 13, 408, 409–10, 411, 413, 416–17
Modern Times (film), 324
Modern Utopia, A (Wells), 322, 323
Moebius, 193, 215, 216, 223
Moeller, Elouise, 357
Mojo: Conjure Stories (Hopkinson), 564
Moles, David, 123
Monáe, Janelle, 206
Mondes imaginaires et les mondes réels, Les (Flammarion), 53
Monette, Sarah, 67
Monsanto Chemical Company, 436
Monsters vs. Aliens (film), 189–90
Moog, Robert, 259, 261
Moon Is a Harsh Mistress, The (Heinlein), 555–56, 558
"Moon-shot Scandal, The" (Southern), 349
Moorcock, Michael, 28, 29, 62, 63, 68, 85, 90, 109, 116, 206, 259, 260, 308, 385, 386, 398, 440, 558, 565
Moore, Alan, 212, 215
Moore, C. L., 101, 108, 128, 140, 424–25, 481–82, 483, 547
Moore, James, 476
Moore, Michael, 337
Moravac, Hans, 529
More, Thomas, 2, 48, 50, 136, 563
More Brilliant Than the Sun: Adventures in Sonic Fiction (Eshun), 566
More than Human (Sturgeon), 108, 524
Morey, Leo, 187, 200
Morgan, Cheryl, 66, 77
Morgan, Richard, 227
Morricone, Ennio, 257
Morris, William, 59, 71, 322, 435, 441
Morrison, Toni, 117, 565
Moskowitz, Sam, 47, 48, 53, 54
Mosley, Walter, 563
Motherlines (Charnas), 397, 542
Mothra (film), 189
Motoramas, 12, 364, 374–78
Motor Stories (magazine), 96
Motter, Dean, 224
Moylan, Tom, 50, 557, 574, 576
"Mr. Roboto" (song), 260
Mr. Tompkins in Wonderland (Gamow), 132
"MS. Found in a Bottle" (Poe), 501–2
M-10000 (train), 368, 369 (figure)
Mueller, Tadzio, 558

Mulburn, Colin, 309
Mulcahy, Russel, 164
"Mule, The" (Asimov), 520
Mullen, R. D., 131
Mullen, Richard D., 5
Multiple_Dwelling (performance art), 265
Mumford, Lewis, 268
Mummy, The!: A Tale of the Twenty-Second Century (Loudon), 321
Mundane SF, 67–68, 130–31, 148
Murakami, Haruki, 112
Murray, Charles, 550
Musafar, Fakir, 408
Music, 10, 252–61, 562;
    Beats and, 388–89;
    film soundtracks, 10, 254–58;
    instrumental, 252–53;
    laboratories for electronic, 255–56;
    popular, 258–61
Musique concrète, 254, 259
"Mutation" (Campbell), 61
Mute Records, 261
Mutual Assured Survival (Pournelle and Ing), 347
Myers, Frederic W. H., 508
My Favorite Martian (television program), 176
My Philosophy of Industry (Ford), 324
Mythmakers and Lawbreakers (ezine collection), 558
Mythpunk, 65

Nachman, Gerald, 173
Nadel, Alan, 202
Nader, Ralph, 380
Nadis, Fred, 355
Nagasaki bombing, 217, 340
Nakamura, Lisa, 429–30
Naked Lunch (Burroughs), 117, 385
Nanopunk, 65
Nanovision (Milburn), 140, 146, 148
Napier, Susan, 184
Narrative of Arthur Gordon Pym, The (Poe), 502
Nash, Walter, 82
Natalini, Adolfo, 284
Nation, Terry, 472
National Convention (NatCon), 72, 75
National Intelligence Council, 514
National Organization for Women (NOW), 541
National Public Radio (NPR), 172
Natural Fantastic, the, 131–32
Natural History of the Enigma, A (performance art), 273
Natural selection, 478
Ndalianis, Angela, 291, 294, 295, 299
Nead, Lynda, 186
Nebula Award, 64, 75, 104, 113, 118, 390
Negri, Antonio, 490
Nekropolis (McHugh), 148
Nelson, Alondra, 566
Neo-Marxist theory, 17

Nettles, Bonnie Lu, 359, 360
Neumann, John von, 421
Neuromancer (Gibson), 64, 118, 132, 207, 228, 230, 242, 244, 271, 309, 401, 410, 426–27, 430, 524
Neuromancer (video game), 231
Never Let Me Go (Ishiguro), 469
Nevèrÿon series (Delany), 400
Nevins, Jess, 8
New Babylon, 285
New Dimensions (film), 370
New England Science Fiction Association (NESFA), 72
New Frontiers of the Mind (Rhine), 509
New Industrial State, The (Galbraith), 380
"New Literature for the Space Age, A" (Moorcock), 385
Newmahr, Staci, 405
Newman, James, 233
Newman, Kim, 157–58
New Maps of Hell (Amis), 50
News from Nowhere (Morris), 71, 322
News from This World (album), 206
"New Sort of Magazine, A" (Gernsback), 59, 81
New Space Opera, 67, 549
New Space Opera, The (Strahan and Dozois, eds.), 67
Newton, Sir Isaac, 313, 314, 451, 500
New Wave, 7, 29, 85, 308, 386, 392, 549;
  in art and illustration, 203, 205, 206, 207;
  in comics, 215, 216;
  emergence of, 62–63;
  literary quality of, 109–10;
  sexuality and, 397, 398–400, 405
New Weird, 66–67, 68, 549
New Weird, The (VanderMeer, ed.), 67
New World of the Mind (Rhine), 509
New Worlds (magazine), 29, 62, 63, 85, 109, 385–86, 398
New York Review of Science Fiction, The (semiprozine), 79, 104
New York World's Fair (1939–40), 281, 294–95, 306, 365, 366, 368, 369–75, 378, 436
New York World's Fair (1964), 376
Nicholls, Peter, 52, 97, 146, 159, 288
Niebur, Louis, 255
Niels Klim's Journey Under the Ground (Holberg), 456
Nieuwenhuys, Constant, 285
Nieuwentyt, Bernard, 453
"Night" (Campbell), 325
Nine Inch Nails (band), 232
"Nine Lives" (Le Guin), 110
Nineteen Eighty-Four (Orwell), 556
1999 AD (film), 379
Nio (program), 246, 248
Niven, Larry, 89, 106, 334, 347
Nix, Garth, 134
Nixon, Richard, 378
Nobel Prize, 307, 311

Noble, Maurice, 187, 189
"No Direction Home" (Spinrad), 259
Nomura Research Institute, 514
Noon, Jeff, 42, 287
Norling, John, 370
Normal, The (band), 261
Norman, Ernest, 354, 357, 358
Norman, Ruth, 354, 357, 358
North, Dan, 164
"North Africa" trilogy (Reynolds), 565
"North American Confederacy, The" series (Smith), 552
Norton, Andre, 128, 133, 134
Norton Book of Science Fiction, The (Le Guin and Attebery, eds.), 52
Nourse, Alan E., 385
Nouvelle vague, 62, 63
Novae Terrae (fanzine), 62
Nova Express (Burroughs), 385
Nova Express (fanzine), 119
Novak, Marcos, 287
Novik, Naomi, 78
Novoselov, Konstantinin, 307
Novum, 2, 4, 11, 48;
  architecture and, 277, 278;
  fictive, 39, 107;
  utopianism and, 17, 575, 576, 579
Nowlan, Philip Francis, 82, 436, 480
"No Woman Born" (Moore), 424–25
Nowpunk, 65
Nozick, Robert, 552
Nuclear weapons, 325–26, 335–36, 340–43, 345, 347
Nudelman, Rafail, 515, 521–22
Numan, Gary, 260–61
Numinous, the, 136, 137
Nuove Tendenze (exhibition), 279
Nye, David E., 196, 223

Objectivism, 234, 551, 552
Odaiba, 291
Oesterheld, H. G., 216–17
Of A Fire on the Moon (Mailer), 348
Office for Metropolitan Architecture, 286
Off the Planet: Music, Sound, and Science Fiction Cinema (Hayward, ed.), 254
OK Computer (album), 261
Okorafor, Nnedi, 566
Oldeuboi (film), 157, 158
Omega Man, The (film), 257
Omniiaveritas, Vincent (Sterling pseudonym), 64
"On Computable Numbers" (Turing), 239
"On Defining Science Fiction, Or Not" (Rieder), 142, 495
Ondes Martenot, 253, 259
Ondioline, 259
ONE (magazine), 398
101 Architectural Fantasies (Chernikhov), 281
O'Neill, Kevin, 215

Only Apparently Real (Williams), 64
On the Magnet, Magnetic Bodies, and that Great Magnet, the Earth (Gilbert), 460
On the Origin of Species by Means of Natural Selection (Darwin), 475–76, 478
"On the Receiving End of the Colonization': Nalo Hopkinson's 'Nansi Web'" (Enteen), 568
On the Road (Kerouac), 387, 388
Operation Paperclip, 343
Orbit (Knight), 63
Orbit One Zero (radio program), 172
Ordinary, The (Grimsley), 134
ORDVAC, 255
Ore, Rebecca, 402
"Origins of Science Fiction Criticism, The" (Evans), 52–53
Orlan, 10, 264–65, 266, 415–16
Orlando, Joe, 215
Ormsbee, Richard, 527–29
Orwell, George, 105, 161, 438, 556
Oryx and Crake (Atwood), 105–6, 145, 521
Oshii, Mamuro, 192
Oshiro, Noburu, 217
Other Worlds Science Stories (magazine), 527
Otomo, Katsuhiro, 192, 217
Otto, Rudolf, 136
Our Friend the Atom (film), 341
"Our Pious Hope: Science" (Cramer), 88
Outer Limits, The (television program), 174
Outland (film), 257
Outline of History, The (Wells), 519
Out of the Silent Planet (Lewis), 131
Out of the Silent Planet (radio program), 172
"Out of the Void" (Stone), 480–81
Outsider and Others, The (Lovecraft), 527
"Ozark Trilogy" (Elgin), 135

Pacific Edge (Robinson), 136
Packard, Vance, 380
Padgett, Lewis, 510
Pagel, Stephen, 400
Paik, Nam June, 265
Pal, George, 343
Palace of Labor, 281
Palace of the Soviets, 281
Palmer, Raymond, 352, 355
Pan-American Exposition, 292
"Pandora's Box" (Heinlein), 25
Panter, Gary, 215
Paperbacks, 85, 99, 203
Paprika (film), 192
Paradise Lost (Milton), 464
Parliament-Funkadelic, 206
Parrinder, Patrick, 2, 30–31, 519, 520
Past Through Tomorrow, The (Heinlein), 520
Patarra, Nick, 224

Patchwork Girl (Jackson), 242, 243–44
Patlabor (film), 191
Pattern of Expectation, The (Clarke), 197
Pattern Recognition (Gibson), 139, 140, 148
Paul, Frank R., 187, 197, 198–99, 200–201, 202 (figure), 207–8, 213, 365, 367 (figure), 371–72, 373 (figure)
Pauling, Linus, 63
Pax Britannia (Green and Ewing), 444
Paxton, Joseph, 278
Pearce, Hubert, 509
Pearson, Wendy, 55, 395, 396
Peary, Robert Edwin, 502
Peebles, Curtis, 353
"Pellucidar" series (Burroughs), 502
Penley, Constance, 3, 309
"Penultimate Trump, The" (Ettinger), 531, 532
Penultimate Truth, The (Dick), 318
People of color. *See* Race
Perdido Street Station (Miéville), 67, 140
Pereira, Willaim, 437
Performance art, 10–11, 263–74;
    actualization in, 263–64, 273–74;
    body modification in, 264, 414–16, 418;
    cyborgism in, 264, 266–67;
    historical lineage of, 265
Perisphere, 371–72
Permutation City (Egan), 417
Perrey, Jean-Jacques, 259
Perrotin, Henri, 503
Perschon, Mike, 439
Persian Gulf War, 330, 336
Person, Lawrence, 118
Peyton, Rog, 73
Philco-Ford Corporation, 379
Philip, Kavita, 312
Philip K. Dick Award, 64, 75
Philmus, Robert M., 1, 48, 53
Philosophiae Naturalis Principia Mathematica (Newton), 500
"Philosophy of the Beat Generation, The" (Holmes), 389
Pickering, Andy, 318–19
Pickering, William H., 503
Picture Theory (Mitchell), 196
Piercy, Marge, 116–17, 397, 402, 542, 574
Pierson, Michele, 164, 176
Pikal, Vaclav, 190
Pilgrims Through Space and Time: Trends and Patterns in Scientific and Utopian Fiction (Bailey), 1, 47–48, 53
Pink Floyd (band), 206, 259, 260
Pioneer Award, 142
Piper at the Gates of Dawn, The (album), 259
Pitts, Victoria, 408, 412–13, 414, 418
Pixar Studios, 9, 186, 193, 195
"Place of Science Fiction, The" (Campbell), 26

Planetary Plaza (Disney attraction), 295–98
Planet B (radio program), 172
Planet Comics, 214
Planet Man (radio program), 172
Planet of the Apes (film), 176, 257, 483
Planet of the Apes (television program), 177–78
Planet Stories (magazine), 82, 84, 213, 214
Plan Voisin, 282
Plath, Sylvia, 563
Plato, 52
Platonov, Andrei, 324
Player Piano (Vonnegut), 326
Pleiadians, 353
Plug-In City, 283
Pluto (Urasawa), 217
Pocket Books, 86–87
Poe, Edgar Allan, 50, 51, 105, 185, 305, 319, 440, 501–2
Poème électronique (Varèse), 253
Poetics, 41–43
Pohl, Frederik, 60, 63, 72, 76, 78–79, 85, 130, 141, 171, 309, 365, 387, 388, 411, 423
Pohl, Frederik, IV, 159
Poland, 73
Polidori, John, 464
Pollock, Frederick, 317, 318
Popular Astronomy (Flammarion), 186
Pordzik, Ralph, 486
Pornography, 399–400, 404
Porush, David, 4
Positive eugenics, 479
Possony, Stefan T., 347
Post, J. B., 78
Postcolonialism, 15, 486–96;
    assimilation dynamics and, 493–94;
    contact zone and, 15, 488, 495;
    neocolonialism distinguished from, 490
Posthumanism, 4, 16, 148, 241, 400, 431, 524–34;
    body modification and, 411;
    cyronics as preparation for, 531–33;
    as a function of SF, 525, 527–29;
    nonfiction texts on, 529–30
Postmodernism, 144, 422, 425–26, 427;
    cyberpunk and, 120–22;
    Disney theme parks and, 298;
    video games and, 229
Pournelle, Jerry, 332, 334, 347, 348
Powerpuff Girls, The (television program), 193
Powers, Richard, 148, 197, 203–6
Powers, Tim, 65–66, 440
Powers of Matthew Star, The (television program), 178, 179
Practices of Everyday Life, The (de Certeau), 209
Pratchett, Terry, 78, 79, 89
Pratt, Fletcher, 134–35
Pratt, Mary Louise, 488
Predator (film), 178

Prefiguring Cyberculture (Tofts et al., eds), 140
Preparation for the Landing (Norman), 357
Prey (video game), 230
Primeval: New World (television program), 182
Princess of Mars, A (Burroughs), 49, 495, 507
Principia Mathematica (Newton), 314
Principle of Hope, The (Bloch), 575
Principles of Scientific Management, The (Taylor), 323–24
Pringle, David, 67
Privateers (Bova), 347
Probability Broach, The (Smith), 552–54, 556
Profiles of the Future (Clarke), 520–21
Progressive (prog) rock, 260
"*Progress versus* Utopia, or, Can We Imagine the Future?" (Jameson), 144, 268
Project Mars (Braun), 344
Project Moon Base (film), 344
"Project Nightmare" (Heinlein), 510
Prometheus Award, 16, 552, 555, 556
Prophet (comic), 224
Pro-sex feminism, 408
Prospect of Immortality, The (Ettinger), 532
Proudhon, Pierre-Joseph, 550
Proun, 280–81
Psalmanazar, George, 457
Pseudo-events, 579
Pseudoscience, 15, 498–511;
    extrasensory perception, 15, 499, 507–10;
    hollow-earth theory, 15, 499–502;
    Martian canals controversy, 15, 499, 502–7
Psyché Rock (Henry), 259
Public Image, Ltd. (band), 260
Public Secrets (Daniel), 249
Pulitzer Prize, 113
Pulp science fiction, 2, 8, 93–102, 213–14;
    amateur writers of, 95;
    characteristics of, 93;
    Darwinist thought in, 479–80;
    demise of format for, 99, 102;
    feminist writing in, 540;
    general pulps and, 93–95, 97, 98, 99–102;
    professional writers and, 98
"Punk and His Music, A" (radio broadcast), 260
"Purple People Eater" (song), 258
Pynchon, Thomas, 48, 104, 112, 113, 118, 120, 348, 349, 386
Pyr Books, 88

Q: Are We Not Men? A: We Are Devo! (album), 260
Quake (video game), 332
Quasi-objects, 313
Quatermass Memoirs, The (radio program), 172
Queen (band), 206
Queen City Jazz (Goonan), 111
Queer theory, 397, 400–401, 403–5, 429

Queer Universes (Pearson et al., eds), 55
Quest for Postcolonial Utopia, The (Pordzik), 486

Rabkin, Eric, 52, 128–29, 337
Race: colonialism and, 492;
  cybernetics and, 429;
  the cyborg and, 544;
  Darwinism on, 481, 482;
  fandom and, 77–78;
  feminism and, 545;
  pulp SF treatment of, 100. *See also* Afrofuturism
RaceFail, 77
Radical Imagination, 249
Radio, 9, 169–73
Radio and Television (magazine), 169, 173
Radiodiffusion-francaise, 255
Radio Guild (radio program), 170
Radiohead (band), 261
Radio News (magazine), 169
Raëlian movement, 12, 358–59, 360
Rage of War (video game), 230
Railway spine, 320
Raley, Rita, 209
Ralph 124C 41+: A Romance of the Year 2660 (Gernsback), 81, 201
Ramírez, Catherine S., 569
Rammellzee, 566
Ranch Romances (magazine), 93
Rand, Ayn, 16, 234, 551–52, 555, 556, 557, 558–59
RAND Corporation, 514
Random Acts of Senseless Violence (Womack), 148
Rapid Journey by Airship to the Upper World, Recently Taken by Five People, The (Kindermann), 457
Rationalized Fantastic, the, 131, 132–33, 134
Rawls, John, 550
Ray, Gordon N., 106
Raymond, Alex, 221, 222 (figure), 436
Rayns, Tony, 158
Razorback (film), 164
RCA, 378–79
Reach of the Mind, The (Rhine), 509
Readercon, 79
"Reading Science Fiction as Science Fiction" (Gunn), 141
Ready Player One (Cline), 556
Reagan, Ronald, 334, 347
Realist, The (magazine), 342
Red Dawn (film), 333
Red Dwarf (television program), 182
Redmond, Sean, 155
"Red One, The" (London), 492
Red Sea Astrarium, 291
Red Star (Bogdanov), 506
Rée, Jonathan, 451
Reece, Gregory L., 12
Reed, Kit, 63
Reed, Robert, 67

Reincarnation of St. Orlan, The (performance art), 264, 415
Relation du Monde de Mercure (Béthune), 457
Religion, 12, 352–62;
  contact claims in, 353–55;
  contact narrative context/backstory in, 353, 355–57;
  evolutionary progress claims and, 353, 358–60;
  predictions and prophecies in, 357–58;
  technology-to-the-rescue theme in, 353, 360–61
Religious Philosopher, The: or the Right Use of Contemplating the Works of the Creator (Nieuwentyt), 453
Reload: Rethinking Women and Cyberculture (Flanagan and Austin, eds.), 140
Rendezvous with Rama (Clarke), 104
"Requiem" (Heinlein), 84
RE/Search Perss, 408
Resident Evil: Afterlife (film), 166
Resident Evil: Apocalypse (film), 165
Resident Evil: Damnation (film), 166
Resident Evil: Degeneration (film), 165, 166
Resident Evil: Extinction (film), 164–66
Resident Evil: Retribution (film), 166
Resnick, Mike, 86, 87, 565
Resor, Stanley, 373
"Resurrection of Jimber-Jaw, The" (Burroughs), 532
"Rethinking the Slipstream" (De Zwaan), 118, 122
Retrofuturism, 14, 261, 434–39;
  ambiguity of term, 434–35;
  coinage of term, 434;
  in comics, 224;
  steampunk compared with, 439, 442–45;
  themes of, 437
Retrofuturism (fanzine), 434
"Revelation Space" (Reynolds), 44
Reynolds, Alastair, 44, 67
Reynolds, John, 98
Reynolds, Mack, 86, 565
Rhen Show, 203
Rhine, Joseph Banks, 310, 509
Rhodan, Perry, 72
Ribofunk, 65
Richards, Ellen, 538–39, 542
Richards, I. A., 113
Riddley Walker (Hoban), 340
"Riders of the Purple Wage" (Farmer), 63
Rieder, John, 15, 31, 49, 53, 142, 312
Right Stuff, The (Wolfe), 348
Riley, Billy Lee, 258
Rimmer, Robert, 397
Riot Grrrl movement, 545
Riou, Edouard, 185, 191
"Rip Van Winkle" (Irving), 532
Rise and Fall of Ziggy Stardust and the Spiders from Mars, The (album), 260
Rivera, Alex, 489

River of Gods (McDonald), 208
Riverworld (Farmer), 111
Road, The (McCarthy), 113
Roadside Picnic (Strugatsky), 576–77, 580
"Roads Must Roll, The" (Heinlein), 84, 309, 325
Road to Serfdom, The (Hayek), 551
"Roaring Trumpet, The" (Pratt and De Camp), 134–35
Robbins, Tony, 534
Roberts, Adam, 14, 50, 52, 277, 288
Roberts, Garyn G., 52
Roberts, Robin, 537
Robertson, Darick, 10, 215
Robida, Albert, 185–86, 197, 198, 199 (figure), 321
Robinson, Frank M., 196
Robinson, Kim Stanley, 65, 136, 249, 310–11, 547, 557, 558
Robocop (film), 235
Robot Carnival (film), 191
Robots, 270–71, 324, 370
"Robot" series (Asimov), 44
Robson, Justina, 66
Robson, William N., 170
Robur, The Conqueror (Verne), 197, 198 (figure)
Rocannon's World (Le Guin), 134
"Rocketport of the Future" (exhibit), 370, 371 (figure)
Rockmore, Clara, 253, 259
Rocky Jones, Space Ranger (television program), 173
Rocky Starr (radio program), 172
Rod Brown of the Rocket Rangers (television program), 173
Roddenberry, Gene, 176, 177, 179, 345, 436
Rogers, Hubert, 188, 200
Rokplug, 283
Rolling Stone (magazine), 64
Roman de l'avenir (Bodin), 140–41
Romanienko, Lisiunia, 413, 417–18
Roosevelt, Franklin, 370
Roosevelt, Theodore, 565
Rope (film), 161
Rose, Mark, 143, 146, 147, 573, 577–78, 579
Rose, Nikolas, 241
"Rose for Ecclesiastes, A" (Zelazny), 36
Rosen, Ruth, 399
Rosenberg, Daniel, 434, 443
Rosenblum J. Michael, 76
Roshwald, Mordecai, 326
Rosny Aîné, J.-H., 49
Ross, Andrew, 4, 5, 200, 383
Ross, Sir Ronald, 492
Rostand, Jean, 532
Roswell (television program), 179
Roswell, New Mexico, 258
Roth, Philip, 112, 117
Rotten, Johnny, 260
Roujin Z (film), 191
Rousseau, Jean-Jacques, 550

Rousseau, Victor, 96
Routledge Companion to Science Fiction, The (Bould et al., eds), 5, 52
Routledge Concise History of Science Fiction, The (Bould and Vint), 25, 31, 51, 54, 140, 142
Roy, Simon, 224
Ruben and Lullabye (narrative app), 249
Rubin, Gayle, 396
Rucker, Rudy, 63–64, 120, 386, 431
Ruddick, Nicholas, 49, 55
Rudolph, Ken, 392
Ruins of Empire (Volney), 320
"Rump-Titty-Titty-Tum-TAH-Tee" (Leiber), 389
R.U.R. (Capek), 170, 173, 324, 524
Rush (band), 260
Rushdie, Salman, 118
Ruskin, John, 320
Russ, Joanna, 16, 37, 38, 79, 104, 105, 106, 113, 145, 148, 395, 399, 402, 524, 542–43, 544, 574
Russell, Eric Frank, 385
Russia, 72, 279–82
Russolo, Luigi, 253
Ryan, Cornelius, 344
Ryan, Marie-Laure, 230
Rydell, Robert W., 372
Ryman, Geoff, 16, 67–68, 112, 130–31, 148, 545–47

Sadler, Simon, 285
Sadler, William, 354
Saffo, Paul, 516
Saga (comic), 224
Sagan, Carl, 136
Said, Edward, 486, 488
Sainston, Steph, 66
Saint, H. F., 118
Saint-Simon, Henri de, 521
Sanders, Clinton R., 416
Sanders, Pharoah, 566
"Sandman, The" (Hoffman), 319
Sandoval, Chela, 544–45
San Francisco Science Fiction Conventions Inc. (SFSFC), 72
San Francisco Tape Music Center, 255
Sanger, Margaret, 384
Sant'Elia, Antonio, 279, 280(figure)
Sarah Jane Adventures, The (television program), 182
Sattelite Seven (radio program), 172
Saucer Wisdom (Rucker), 64
Saunders, Charles R., 563
Savage Humanists, The (Kelleghan, ed.), 65
Savage Perils (Sharp), 486
Saving Private Ryan (film), 336
Sawyer, Robert J., 90
Sayles, John, 562
Scalzi, John, 332
Scanner Darkly, A (Dick), 63–64
"Scanners Live in Vain" (Smith), 29

Scenario planning, 516
Scenes from the World of Tomorrow (film), 371
Schaeffer, Pierre, 254, 255, 259
Schaffer, Simon, 314
Schechner, Richard, 263
Schiaparelli, Giovanni, 503, 504 (figure), 505
Schild's Ladder (Egan), 311
Schismatrix (Sterling), 412, 415, 524
Schlemmer, Oscar, 265
Schmidt, Bill, 377
Schmidt, Stanley, 26–27
Scholes, Robert, 29, 48
Scholz, Carter, 115, 122
Schopenhauer, Arthur, 39
Schuiten, François, 216
Schuiten, Luke, 216
Schumacher, Patrick, 286
Schuyler, George, 567
Schwartz, Julius, 213
Science, 11, 305–15;
    conjunction of industry and, 308–9;
    in extrapolation and speculation, 30–32;
    Gernsback on accuracy of, 81, 96, 305;
    SF supplement to discourses of, 314–15;
    understanding of filtered through SF, 306–7. *See also* Pseudoscience
Science and Invention (magazine), 169, 198
Science fantasy, 127–28
Science Fantasy (magazine), 389
Science Fiction (Luckhurst), 25, 49, 549
Science Fiction (magazine), 372
"Science Fiction: Its Nature, Faults and Virtues" (Heinlein), 25–26
Science-Fiction: The Early Years (Bleiler), 50
Science Fiction Advancement Association, 60
Science Fiction After 1900: From the Steam Man to the Stars (Landon), 549
"Science-fictionality," 145, 146
Science Fiction and Fantasy Writers of America, 75
"Science Fiction and Mrs. Brown" (Le Guin), 110
"Science Fiction and Postmodernity" (Benison), 144
Science Fiction and Television (journal), 3
"Science Fiction and the Beats" (Spinrad), 386
"Science Fiction and the Scientific World-View" (Parrinder), 30–31
Science Fiction Art (Aldiss), 196
Science Fiction Association, 62
Science Fiction Before 1900 (Alkon), 50
Science Fiction Eye (magazine), 115, 121
Science Fiction Film and Television (journal), 147, 155
Science Fiction in the Cinema (Baxter), 155–56
"Science Fiction in the Real World--Revisited" (Spinrad), 88
Science Fiction in the 20th Century (James), 50
Science Fiction League, 60

Science Fiction of the Twentieth Century: An Illustrated History (Robinson), 196
Science Fiction Research Association, 142
Science Fiction Studies (journal), 1, 3, 5, 48, 119, 120, 122, 124, 146, 147, 155, 396, 568
Science Fiction Theater (television program), 171, 173, 174
Science Fiction World (magazine), 74
Science Fiction Writers of America, 118
"Science in Science Fiction, The" (Schmidt), 26–27
"Science in the Capital" trilogy (Robinson), 311, 547
Science Policy Research Unit, 514
Science Wonder Stories (magazine), 105, 201, 213, 436
Scientific Detective Monthly (magazine), 60, 82
Scientific romances, 435, 465
Scientology, 12, 352, 354–56, 358, 360–61
Sci-Fi: A Graphic History (Holland), 196
Sconce, Jeffrey, 169, 174
Scorsese, Martin, 256
Scott, Melissa, 16, 397, 402, 545
Scott, Raymond, 255
Scott, Ridley, 49, 64, 240, 286, 332, 336
Scraps of the Untainted Sky (Moylan), 50
Screamers (film), 318
Screening Space: The American Science Fiction Film (Sobchack), 155, 254, 258
Scripted spaces, 191
Scruggs, Philip, 100
Sears, Fred F., 336
Second Life, 267
"Second Variety" (Dick), 318
Secret History of Science Fiction, The (Kelly and Kessel, eds.), 52
Secret of Dominion, The (radio program), 172
Secret of the Saucers, The (Angelucci), 356
Sedgewick, Cristina, 88
Sedgwick, Eve Kosofsky, 163–64, 401
Seed, David, 12, 52
Seiun Award, 74, 75
Self-Hybridization (performance art), 264
Semiprozines, 76
"Semley's Necklace" (Le Guin), 133–34
Seneca Falls Convention, 537–38
"Sense of wonder," 7, 30, 38, 105, 108, 141, 453
Serenity (television program), 182
Serling, Rod, 173, 174, 342
Serra, Eric, 258
Serviss, Garrett P., 505–6
Settler colonialism, 15, 488, 489, 496
Seven beauties of science fiction, 39–40, 107–8
Seven Beauties of Science Fiction, The (Csicsery-Ronay), 25, 145
Sex in the System: Stories of Erotic Futures (story collection), 404
Sexology: The Magazine of Sex Science, 396
Sex Pistols (band), 260

Sextrapolation, 399
Sexuality, 13, 395–405;
    cyberpunk and, 400, 401–2;
    New Wave and, 397, 398–400, 405;
    SF's "sexual revolution" and, 398–99;
    SF's unfilled potential for reimagining, 395–96
Sexual selection, 477–78, 479, 481, 482
Sexy Nerd Girl Presents, 545
SF: The Best of the Best (Merril, ed.), 29
"SF of Theory, The" (Csicsery-Ronay), 145
SF68 (radio program), 172
"SF Tourism" (Landon), 293
Shadow, The (film), 164
Shadow Man (Scott), 397
Shakespeare, William, 37
"Shambleau" (Moore), 108, 481–82
Shannon, Claude, 421
Shape of Things to Come, The (Wells), 519
"Shaper-Mechanist" series (Sterling), 13, 411
Shapin, Steven, 308, 314
Shaping Things (Sterling), 430
Sharp, Patrick B., 15, 486
Sharp, Sharon, 444
Shaver, Richard, 352, 355, 502
Shavers, Rone, 568
Shaviro, Steven, 162, 163
Shaw, Debra Benita, 144, 148
Shaw, Greg, 259
Shaw, Joseph T., 94
Shawl, Nisi, 494
"She Blinded Me With Science" (song), 261
Sheckley, Robert, 386, 388, 390, 518
Sheehan, Perley Poore, 97
Sheldon, Alice. *See* Tiptree, James, Jr.
Sheldon, Roy, 365
Shelley, Mary, 7, 14, 24, 50, 51, 52, 110–11, 278, 320, 396, 410, 412, 440, 463–67, 471–72, 498, 524
Shelley, Percy Bysshe, 463–65, 466
Shell Oil, 373, 375
She Loves It, She Loves It Not (Tamblyn), 243
Shepard, Lucius, 65, 332
Sherman, Delia, 66
Shibano, Takumi, 74
Shilling, Chris, 410
Shine: An Anthology of Optimistic SF (de Vries, ed.), 68
Shiner, Lewis, 64, 558
Shiovitz, Dan, 246
Shippey, Tom, 38, 52, 141
Shirley, John, 64, 90, 119, 120
Shirow, Masamune, 217
Shiva, Vandana, 312
Shojo manga, 217
Shuster, Joe, 213, 218
Siegel, Don, 174
Siegel, Jerry, 213, 218

Sight and Sound (journal), 157
Silberberg, Mrs. L., 199–200
Silent Running (film), 257
"Silent Smith and the Hounds of Death" (Hjerstedt), 101
Silent Spring (Carson), 380
Silver, David, 421
Silver Age of comics, 218
Silver Apples (band), 260
Silverberg, Robert, 79, 109, 111, 285, 309
Silver Streak, The (film), 368
Simak, Clifford, 83, 171
SimCity (video game), 231
Simmons, Dan, 90, 111
Simulacra, 129, 144, 269–70, 293, 533
"Simulacra and Science Fiction" (Baudrillard), 144
Singer, Peter Warren, 334
Singh, Vandana, 493
Singularity, 24, 33, 270–71, 515, 533–34, 568
Singularity (video game), 234
Singularity Institute for Artificial Intelligence, 514
Singularity Is Near, The: A True Story About the Future (film), 533–34
Singularity Is Near, The: When Humans Transcend Biology (Kurzweil), 270, 533
Siodmak, Curt, 171
Siringer, Norman, 85, 89
Situated Fantastic, the, 131, 133–35
Situated knowledges, 133
Situationist International, 203, 204, 285
Six Millin Dollar Man, The (television program), 178
Sixth Column (Heinlein), 84
Skinner, E. D., 532
Sky Captain and the World of Tomorrow (film), 444
Skylark of Space, The (Smith), 82
Skylon Tower, 283
Sky Road, The (MacLeod), 581–82
Slan (Van Vogt), 310, 525–27, 533
SLASH writing, 400, 404, 405
Slater, Ken, 76
Sleep Dealer (Rivera), 489
Sleeper Awakes, The (Wells), 532
Slide, The (radio program), 172
Slipstream, 8, 29, 48, 68, 112, 115–24, 143;
    in comics, 215–16;
    cyberpunk and, 120–22;
    emergence of, 66;
    reasons for attractiveness of, 122;
    Sterling's definition of, 115;
    Sterling's list of writers, 116–17
"Slipstream" (De Zwaan), 118
"Slipstream" (Sterling), 115–16
"Slipstream 2" (Sterling), 119
Slow River (Griffith), 402
Slusser, George, 337
Smith, Adam, 550

Smith, Clark Ashton, 67, 128
Smith, Cordwainer, 29
Smith, Darryl A., 568
Smith, E. E. ("Doc"), 82, 106, 525
Smith, L. Neil, 16, 552–54, 556, 557, 558–59
Smith, Tony, 77
Smith Act of 1940, 384
Smofcon, 75
Snow, C. P., 97
Sobchack, Vivian, 3, 54, 155, 156–57, 252, 254, 256, 258
"Social Science Fiction" (Asimov), 26
Social Text (journal), 566
Sociology of Science, The (Merton), 308
Sofia, Zoë, 142
Soft Machine, The (Burroughs), 524
Solano Lopez, Francisco, 216–17
Solaris (Lem), 49, 577
Soleri, Paoli, 285
Solomon, Carl, 386
So Long Been Dreaming (Hopkinson and Mehan, eds.), 486, 564, 569–70
"Solution Unsatisfactory" (Heinlein), 84
"Some Kinds of Life" (Dick), 318
Someone Comes to Town, Someone Leaves Town (Cory), 209
Somnium (Kepler), 52–53
Sonic Arts Union, 255
Sontag, Susan, 202–3
Sorkin, Michael, 297
S.O.S.--Tidal Wave (film), 173
Sounds of the Future: Essays on Music in Science Fiction Film (Bartkowiak, ed.), 254
South Africa, 172
Southern, Terry, 349
Soviet Union, 73, 324. See also Space race
Soylent Green (film), 257
Space (Mitchener), 348
Space Force (radio program), 172
Space Invaders (video game), 226
Space Merchants, The (Pohl and Kornbluth), 61, 130, 365, 387
"Space Oddity" (song), 252, 259
Space opera, 85, 89, 213, 260;
  coinage of term, 82;
  in comics, 219;
  new, 67, 549;
  on radio, 169, 172;
  on television, 173, 181
Space Opera Renaissance, The (Hartwell and Cramer, eds.), 67
Space Patrol (radio program), 172
Space Patrol (television program), 172, 173
Space race, 12, 340, 342–50;
  mainstream work on, 348;
  nuclear rivalry intertwined with, 345;
  SF use of frontier trope for, 345, 347–48

Spacewar! (video game), 10, 226
Spain, 73
Spark, Muriel, 117
Sparko (robot), 370
Specters of Marx (Derrida), 491
Speculation. See Extrapolation and speculation
Speculations (fanzine), 565
Speculative fiction, 11, 27–28, 29, 91, 252, 278, 305
Speculative music, 252, 254
Spider-Man (comic), 219
Spielberg, Steven, 232, 257, 332, 336
Spike, the, 515
Spike, The (Broderick), 270
Spiller, Neil, 287
Spinrad, Norman, 63, 64, 83, 88, 259, 309, 386–87, 390
Spivak, Gayatri, 488, 493–94
Splatterpunk, 65
Split Infinity (Anthony), 134
Spook Country (Gibson), 431–32
Springer, Claudia, 414
Sputnik 1, 258, 294, 342, 344, 345, 348
St. Clair, Justin, 124
Stableford, Brian, 47, 49, 53, 95, 321
S.T.A.L.K.E.R. (video game), 231
Stam, Robert, 157
Standish, David, 502
Stand on Zanzibar (Brunner), 90
Stanford University, 508
Stanley, Richard, 165
Stanton, Elizabeth Cady, 538
Stapledon, Olaf, 105, 519, 520, 524, 577
Staples, Fiona, 224
Star Craft (video game), 231
StarCraft 2: Wings of Liberty (video game), 231
Stargate SG-1 (television program), 181
Starman (film), 257
Starman (television program), 178
*Star*Reach* (Friedrich, ed.), 215
Star Ship Sofa (podcast), 77
Starship Troopers (Heinlein), 332, 334
Stars My Destination, The (Bester), 580–81
Startling Stories (magazine), 531
Star Trek (novelizations), 86–87
Star Trek (television program), 174–76, 177 (figure), 181, 182, 331, 345–46, 436, 516
Star Trek: Deep Space Nine (television program), 179
Star Trek: Enterprise (television program), 444
Star Trek: The Next Generation (television program), 179, 180 (figure)
Star Trek: Voyager (television program), 179
Star Trek Experience, The (hotel attraction), 291–92
Star Wars (film), 12, 102, 162, 178, 226, 257, 307, 331–37
Star Wars (radio adaptation), 172
Star Wars (video game), 232
Star Wars: Episode II--Attack of the Clones (film), 162
Star Wars: The Clone Wars (television program), 181

Stasheff, Christopher, 134
Steamboy (film), 444
Steampunk, 14, 190, 434, 435, 439–45;
    challenge of defining, 439;
    coinage of term, 439–40;
    in comics, 215, 444;
    emergence of, 65–66;
    literary roots of, 440;
    retrofuturism compared with, 439, 442–45
Steampunk Trilogy, The (Di Filippo), 66, 440
Stefano, Joseph, 174
Steiner, Tim, 417
Stelarc, 10, 264, 265, 266–67, 273, 415
Stensie, Stahl, 265
Stephenson, Neal, 44, 68, 90, 112, 287, 313–14, 441, 444
Stereolab (band), 261
Sterling, Bruce, 6, 8, 13, 64–65, 66, 115–24, 350, 401, 411, 412, 430, 432, 440, 445, 521, 524, 547, 568
Stites, Richard, 383
Stockhausen, Karlheinz, 255, 259, 260
Stockton, Frank, 23
Stockwell, Peter, 7
Stoddard, Jason, 68
Stoker, Bram, 15, 467, 470
Stolen Generation of Aboriginal children, 494
Stomach Sculpture (performance art), 266
Stone, Allucquère Roseanne, 309, 423–24, 426, 430, 431
Stone, Leslie F., 82, 480–81, 540, 547
Storming the Reality Studio: A Casebook of Cyberpunk and Postmodern Fiction (McCaffery, ed.), 4, 120, 122
"Story of the Days to Come, A" (Wells), 323
Strahan, Jonathan, 66, 67
Strange Adventures (comic), 340
Strange Horizons (magazine), 387
Stranger in a Strange Land (Heinlein), 13, 392, 397
Strangers in a Tangled Wilderness (ezine), 558
Strange Weather: Culture, Science and Technology in the Age of Limits (Ross), 4
Strange Worlds (comic), 214
Strategic Defense Initiative (SDI; "Star Wars"), 12, 334, 347
Strategy of Technology, The (Pournelle and Possony), 347
Stratemeyer Syndicate, 85–86
"Strato-Shooters" (Bedford-Jones), 101
Strauss, Johan II, 256
Strauss, Richard, 256
Stross, Charles, 42, 79, 90, 326
Structure of Scientific Revolutions, The (Kuhn), 309–10
Strugatsky, Arkady, 17, 49, 232, 576–77, 581
Strugatsky, Boris, 17, 49, 232, 576–77, 581
Stuart, Don A. (Campbell pseudonym), 83
Studio Museum, 569

Sturgeon, Theodore, 61, 83, 104, 108, 109, 148, 213, 345, 390, 398, 524, 533
"Sturgeon's Law," 90
Styx (band), 260
Sublime: beauty *vs.*, 7, 38–39, 41;
    SF, 39, 107, 132;
    technological, 196–97, 223
Subterranean Worlds (Fitting), 55
Suitaloon, 283
Sukenick, Ronald, 118–19
Sun Ra, 206, 389, 566
Superman (character), 187, 188–89, 213, 214, 218, 223
Superstruct (video game), 236
Superstudio, 284–85
Superworld Comics, 213
Suprematism, 279, 280
Surrealism, 203–4
Survival Research Laboratories, 265
Survivors (Nation), 472
Suspense (radio program), 170–71
Sutton, Jeff, 344–45, 349
Suvin, Darko, 2–3, 4, 5, 9, 11, 17, 48–49, 53, 129–30, 131, 141, 163, 264, 266–67, 277, 278, 308, 395, 574–75, 576
Swainston, Steph, 67
Swancon, 72
Swanwick, Michael, 65
Sweden, 72
Swedenborg, Emmanuel, 352
Swift, Jonathan, 2, 53, 453, 457, 458, 459–61
Switched-On Bach (album), 259
SyFy Channel, 181–82
Symmes, John Cleves, Jr., 500–502
Symzonia; Voyage of Discovery (Symmes), 501
Syndicate (video game), 227
Synners (Cadigan), 413, 545
System of the World, The (Newton), 314

Tafuri, Manfredo, 278
Taken (television program), 181
Tales from the Other Side (radio program), 172
Tales of Tomorrow (radio program), 171
Talmadge, Richard, 344
Tamblyn, Christine, 243, 250
Tan, Celia, 404
Tanguy, Yves, 203, 204
Tarantino, Quentin, 256
Tarantula (film), 336
Tatlin, Vladimir, 279–80
"Tatlin at Home" (collage), 280
Tatlin's Tower, 279–80
Tatsumi, Takayuki, 54, 146
Tattoos, 408, 409, 411–12, 417
Tausk, Victor, 320
Tavistock Institute of Human Relations, 514
Taylor, Frederick Winslow, 323–24

Taylorism, 323–25
Teague, Walter Dorwin, 365, 366, 369
Technocracy, 200–201, 318, 325
Technocracy Review, The (magazine), 325
Technocratic Party, 365
Technoculture, 3–5
Technologiade, 17, 39, 107
"Technological Singularity" (Vinge), 529
Technological Stimulation and the Sensual Life of Machines (story collection), 404
Technology fiction, 277
Techno-optimism, 68
Tehlharmonium, 253
Teige, Karel, 190
Teledildonics, 401
Television, 9, 86, 169, 171, 172–82, 370;
 ambitious nature of SF programming, 176–77;
 identity struggle for SF programming, 177–78;
 importance of as SF media, 181–82
Tellus Institute, 514
Telotte, J. P., 9, 54, 145, 188, 298–99
"Telstar" (song), 258
Tenn, William, 388, 518
Tepper, Sheri S., 111, 524
Terminal City (comic), 224
Terminal Identity: The Virtual Subject in Postmodern Science Fiction (Bukatman), 4
Terminator (films), 12, 235, 258, 326, 332
Terminator Salvation (video game), 232
Terminator 2: Judgment Day (film), 165, 270
Terrill, Thelma B., 357
Tesla, Nikola, 360, 553
Teslapunk, 65
Tetsujin 28-go (Yokoyama), 217
Tetsuwan Atomu (Tezuka), 191
Tezuka, Osamu, 10, 191, 217
Thacker, Eugene, 265–66, 274
"Thank You!" (Gernsback), 81
That Hideous Strength (Lewis), 135
Them! (film), 335
Theme Building, 437, 438 (figure)
Theme parks, 11, 291–300. *See also* Disney theme parks
Them Fuckin' Robots (performance art), 270
Theory of Justice, A (Rawls), 550
"There Is No Such Thing as Science Fiction" (Bould and Vint), 31, 141
Theremin (musical instrument), 10, 171, 253, 259
Theremin, Leon, 253–54, 256
"There Will Come Soft Rains" (Bradbury), 109, 192, 378
Thetans, 355–56
"They" (Heinlein), 84
They Were 11 (Hagio), 217
"Thick text," 9, 184, 192
Thing, The (film), 83, 257, 267

Thing from Another World, The (film), 171, 344
Things to Come (film), 323
"Think Like a Dinosaur" (Kelley), 24
3rd I (performance art), 264
Third-person perspective (TPP) (in video games), 230
"3rd Stone From the Sun" (song), 259
"Thirteen Women (And Only One Man in Town)" (song), 341
32 Short Films About Glenn Gould (film), 245
This Island Earth (film), 202, 203
"This Is Tomorrow" (exhibition), 283
Thollon, Louis, 503
Thomas, Sheree R., 17, 563, 566
Thompson, Alan E., 515, 517–18
Thompson, Craig, 411
Thompson, E. P., 321
Thomson, Rupert, 118
Thoreau, Henry David, 386
3001: The Final Odyssey (Clarke), 520
Thrill Book (magazine), 95–96
"Thunder and Roses" (Sturgeon), 108
Ticket That Exploded, The (Burroughs), 385
Tiffany, J. A., 95
Tik-Tok of Oz (Baum), 427
Tim (artwork), 417
Time Capsule (performance art), 264, 271–72
Time Machine, The (radio adaptation), 170, 171
Time Machine, The (television adaptation), 173
Time Machine, The (Wells), 11–12, 322, 440, 472, 475, 492, 518–19, 524, 578, 580
Times Literary Supplement, The, 385
Time Tunnel (television program), 176, 335
Tintin comic series, 216
Tiptree, James, Jr., 24, 140, 399, 424, 425, 427, 432
Tiptree Award, 75
Tobias, James, 10
Todd, Julian, 67
Todd, Loretta, 248
Todorov, Tzvetan, 128, 129, 131, 137
Toffler, Alvin, 15, 516–17, 518
Tofts, Darren, 140
Tokyo Forum, 286
Tolkien, J. R. R., 59, 78, 88
To Mars Via the Moon (Wicks), 506–7
Tom Corbett, Space Cadet (radio program), 172
Tom Corbett, Space Cadet (television program), 172, 173
Tomkins, Dave, 255
Tomkins, Walker, 101
Tomorrowland (Disney attraction), 5, 292, 294–95, 299, 378, 436
Tomorrow Now: Envisioning the Next Fifty Years (Sterling), 521
Tonto's Expanding Headband (band), 260
Topor, Roland, 193

Toraldo di Francia, Cristiano, 284
TOR Books, 79, 88
Torchwood (television program), 182
Tornados (band), 258
Tors, Ivan, 173
Total Recall (film), 257, 334
Touch of Magic, A (film), 375
Tourneur, Jacques, 174
"Towards an Aesthetic of Science Fiction" (Russ), 106
Toyen, 190
"Toymaker, The" (Jones), 510
Transgender movement, 397
Transmetropolitan (Ellis and Robertson), 10, 215
Transport Unlimited Autorama, 375
Transrealism, 63–64
Transrealist Fiction: Writing in the Slipstream of Science (Broderick), 64
"Transrealist Manifesto" (Rucker), 64
Traviss, Karen, 89
Tremaine, F. Orlin, 83
Triem, Frank, 97
Trillion Year Spree (Aldiss), 50
Triple Revolution Statement, 63
Trip to the Moon, A (film), 185, 213, 435
Trip to the Moon, A: Containing an Account of the Island of Noibla (Lunatic/Gentleman), 457
Trojan Women, The (Euripides), 111
TRON (film), 5, 226
Trouble and Her Friends (Scott), 402, 545
Trouble on Triton (Delany), 400, 524, 557
"True Life Science Fiction" (Jones), 311
Truffaut, François, 159–62
Trumbo, Dalton, 333
Trylon, 371–72
Tubb, E. C., 78
Tubeway Army (band), 260
Tucker, Wilson, 82
Tuella, 357
Tulyakhodzhayev, Nazim, 192
Turing, Alan, 239–41, 244, 246, 250, 424, 431
Turing Test, 240, 424
Turk (automaton), 319–20
Turner, Bryan S., 411–12
Turner, Harry, 76
"Turn of the Screw, The" (James), 128
Turse, Nick, 334
Turtledove, Harry, 332
Tuttle, Lisa, 542
Twain, Mark, 105, 111, 386
Twentieth Century, The (Robida), 197, 199(figure)
Twentieth Century, The: The Electric Life (film), 185–86
"Twenty-First-Century Stories" (Wolfe and Beamer), 140
20 Million Miles to Earth (film), 190
20,000 Leagues Under the Sea (radio adaptation), 170, 172
Twenty Thousand Leagues Under the Sea (Verne), 440
"Twilight" (Campbell), 83, 325
Twilight Zone, The (television program), 171, 173, 174, 175(figure), 182, 342
"Two Cultures" (Snow), 97
2000 AD (comic), 216, 223, 444
2001: A Space Odyssey (film), 3, 43, 132, 157, 176, 206, 255, 256, 270, 307, 346–47, 379, 516, 520, 578
2000 Plus (radio program), 171
2061: Odyssey Three (Clarke), 520
2010: Odyssey (Clarke), 520
Tyng, Christopher, 259

Uffenheimer, Benjamin, 518
UFO contactees, 12, 352
UFO Incident, The (television film), 354
Understanding Media (McLuhan), 443
Unexpected Destruction of the Elaborately Engineered Artifacts, The (performance art), 265
Unincorporated Man, The (Kollin), 554–55, 556
Unitary Urbanism, 285
United Kingdom: architecture of, 282–83;
    comics of, 216;
    fandom in, 72–73;
    radio programming in, 172;
    television programming in, 173, 182
United States of America, The (band), 260
Unites, 282
Universe (Carr), 63
"Universe" (Heinlein), 84
Universe, The: A Philosophical Poem (Baker), 455
University of Chicago Press, 551
University of Illinois at Urbana-Champaign, 255
Unknown (magazine), 83
Unknown Worlds (magazine), 83
"Unpleasant Profession of Jonathan Hoag, The" (Heinlein), 84
Unsafe at Any Speed (Nader), 380
Upgrade (narrative app), 249
Uptown Downtown (Lynd), 391
Uranius movement, 357–60
Urantia Book, The (Sadler), 354
Urantia Brotherhood, 354
Urasawa, Naoki, 217
Ure, Andrew, 321
"Useful Phrases" (Wolfe), 110
"User's Guide to the Postmoderns, A" (Swanwick), 65
Usual Suspects, The (film), 157
Utopia (More), 2, 48, 136, 573
Utopian-dystopian tension: in Afrofuturism, 17;
    animation and, 186, 188, 189;
    automation and, 318, 321–23;
    the cyborg and, 414;
    digital arts and hypertext and, 239–40, 242, 249, 250;
    feminism and, 542–43

Utopianism, 17, 573–82;
  architecture and, 278, 282;
  countercultures and, 12–13, 383, 384;
  critical, 557, 574;
  digital arts and hypertext and, 245, 246–47;
  Disney theme parks and, 292, 293, 299;
  the fantastic and, 131, 136;
  feminism and, 16, 539–40;
  as fundamental to SF genre, 573;
  futurology and, 518;
  libertarianism and, 549;
  materialist orientation of, 574, 578;
  narrative practices allied to, 578;
  in performance art, 268–69;
  space race and, 346

V (television program), 178
Vale, V., 408
Valente, Catherynne, 65
Vance, Jack, 128
Van der Graaf Generator (band), 260
VanderMeer, Ann, 67
VanderMeer, Jeff, 66, 67
Van Gelder, Gordon, 87
Vangelis, 232, 257–58
Van Tassel, George, 354, 356–57, 358, 360
Van Vogt, A. E., 61, 83, 310, 386, 525–27, 533
Varèse, Edgard, 253–54, 256
Varley, John, 547
Vaughan, Brian K., 224
Veblen, Thorstein, 325, 383
Vega, Mayra, 496
Venus Plus X (Sturgeon), 108, 533
Veracini, Lorenzo, 488, 489
Verhoeven, Paul, 332
Verne, Jules, 24, 50, 51, 54, 71, 185, 190–91, 197, 198, 213, 215, 216, 278, 305, 435, 440, 486, 492, 502, 578
Vertigo (film), 161
Vesnin Brothers, 281
Vice movement, 199–200
Video games, 10, 226–37;
  as distributed narratives, 229, 231–32;
  future worlds portrayed by, 229, 233–34;
  intersection with SF as a genre, 226–27;
  military culture depicted in, 332;
  as performative simulations, 229, 234–36;
  as space narratives, 229–31
Vidler, Anthony, 282
Viennese Actionists, 415
Vietnam War, 329, 336, 337
Village Voice (newspaper), 104, 562
Ville Contemporaine, 282
Villemard, 435
Ville Radieuse, 282
Vincent, Harl, 82
Vinge, Vernor, 33, 64, 67, 89, 270, 515, 529, 534
Vingtième Siècle, Le (Robida), 321

Vint, Sherryl, 11, 25, 31, 51, 52, 54, 140, 141, 142, 479, 568
Viriconium (Harrison), 67
Viriolio, Paul, 179
Virtual Light (Gibson), 416–17
"Virtual Love" (McHugh), 402
Visual Music, 246
Vocoder, 255
Voices of Time, The (Ballard), 204
Vollmann, William T., 120
Volney, C. F., 320
Voltaire, 14, 453, 457, 458–59
Vonnegut, Kurt, 42, 116, 326
Vorilhon, Claude (Raël), 358–59, 360
Voyage of the Beagle (Darwin), 477
Voyages Extraordinaire (Verne), 197
Voyages imaginaires, songes, visions, et romans cabalistiques (Garnier, ed.), 53
Voyage to Arcturus, A (Lindsay), 135
Voyage to Jupiter (film), 186
Voyage to Mars (Oshiro), 217
Voyage to the Bottom of the Sea (television program), 176, 177, 335
Voyage to the Moon, Strongly Recommended to All Lovers of Real Freedom (anonymous), 457
Vrooman, H. Wellington, 94

Wagner, John, 216
"Waldo" (Heinlein), 84, 309
Walker, John, 426, 430
Walking Cities, 283, 284(figure)
Walking Head (performance art), 267
Walk to the End of the World (Charnas), 542
Wallace, Alfred Russel, 503, 508
Wallace, David Foster, 118
Wall-E (film), 186, 193–94
Waller, Anthony, 533
Wallerstein, Immanuel, 487
Walter, Damien, 68
Walton, Jo, 79
Wanderground, The: Stories of the Hill Women (Gearheart), 397
Wandering Star (comic), 215
Warehouse (television program), 181
Warhammer (video game), 332
Warhol, Andy, 203, 265, 341–42
War in the Air, The (Wells), 329
Wark, McKenzie, 230
Warlock in Spite of Himself, The (Stasheff), 134
Warlord of the Air, The (Moorcock), 440
"Warm Leatherette" (song), 261
Warner Brothers, 187
War of the Worlds (film), 201, 332
War of the Worlds (television program), 178
War of the Worlds, The (radio adaptation), 170, 172
War of the Worlds, The (Wells), 200, 471, 473, 475, 492, 505, 578, 580

War Stars: The Superweapon and the American Imagination (Franklin), 4
Washington Post Book World, 64
Wasson, Sara, 143
Wastemakers, The (Packard), 380
Watchmen (comic), 212, 223–24
Watson, Ian, 524
We (Zamyatin), 90, 288, 324, 348, 383, 387, 551, 556
"We Also Walk Dogs" (Heinlein), 84
Webb, Mike, 283
Webcam (steampunk), 442 (figure)
Weber, David, 89, 332
Wegner, Phillip, 17
Weinbaum, Stanley, 200
Weiner, Norbert, 317
Weird Fantasy (magazine), 215
Weird Science (magazine), 215
Weird Science-Fantasy (magazine), 215
Weird Tales (magazine), 96, 108, 128, 199, 481, 547
Weisinger, Mort, 213
Weiss, Gary, 558
Weizmann Institute of Science, 514
Welles, Orson, 170
Wellman, Manly Wade, 214
Wells, H. G., 1, 2, 7, 11–12, 13, 24, 50, 51, 52, 53, 71, 90, 106, 135, 173, 185, 200, 213, 215, 278, 305, 329, 332, 410, 467, 471, 472, 473, 475, 486, 492, 494, 505;
  on automation, 318, 322–23, 324;
  futurology and, 518–19, 521;
  posthumanism and, 524, 532;
  steampunk and, 435, 440;
  utopianism and, 578, 581
Wells, Ida B., 384
Wells, Paul, 9
We See a Different Frontier (Fernandes and al-Ayad, eds.), 569
Wesleyan Anthology of Science Fiction (Evans et al., eds), 52
Wesso, H. W., 200
West Coast Gateway, 286
Westdeutscher Rundfunk, 255
Westerfeld, Scott, 441
Western Story Magazine, 94
Westfahl, Gary, 7–8, 51, 59, 95, 122
Westinghouse, 367, 370
Weston, Pete, 76
Westworld (film), 257
"What Do You Mean: Science? Fiction?" (Merril), 28
"What I Didn't See" (Fowlers), 24
What It Means to Be a Libertarian (Murray), 550
Whedon, Joss, 181
When It Changed: 'Real Science' Science Fiction (Ryman, ed), 68
"Which Way to Inner Space" (Ballard), 109
Whirlpool, 378–79
"Whisperer in Darkness, The" (Lovecraft), 527
Whiston, William, 500

White, Curtis, 118–19
White, James, 86
White, Norman, 270
White Man's Burden, The: A Satirical Forecast (Hodge), 565
White Mythologies (Young), 491
White Noise (band), 260
White Queen (Jones), 524
White Sands Incident, The (Fry), 353
Whitman, Walt, 386–87
"Who Goes There?" (Campbell), 83
Wicks, Mark, 506–7
Wiener, Norbert, 326, 421, 422, 429, 431, 445, 529
Wilde, Oscar, 59
Wild Seed (Butler), 403
Wild Wild West (film), 444–45
Willard, Nancy, 117
Williams, Charles, 59
Williams, John, 257
Williams, Paul, 64, 259
Williams, Raymond, 4
Williamson, Al, 215
Williamson, Jack, 52, 61, 82
Willis, Connie, 65, 89
Wilson, Robert Anton, 558
Wilson, Robert M., 97
Wilson, William, 305
Windling, Terri, 66
Windup Girl, The (Bacigalupi), 32, 148, 312–13
Wind Whales of Ishmael, The (Farmer), 111
Wingrove, David, 159
Winter, Jerome, 9
"Winterlong" trilogy (Hand), 128
Wired Hard: Erotica for a Gay Universe (story collection), 404
WisCon, 72, 76
Wise, Robert, 336
"Witch World" books (Norton), 128
Witpunk, 65
"Wives" (Tuttle), 542
Wizard of Earthsea, A (Le Guin), 130
Wodehouse, P. G., 65
Wolf, Mark J. P., 228
Wolfe, Bernard, 340, 524
Wolfe, Gary K., 7, 32, 48, 52, 105, 124, 129, 140, 146, 305
Wolfe, Gene, 90, 110, 128, 136
Wolfe, Patrick, 488
Wolfe, Tom, 348
Wollen, Peter, 324
Wollheim, Betsy, 88
Wollheim, Donald A., 60, 62, 85, 86, 88, 203
Wolmark, Jenny, 53
Womack, Jack, 112, 116, 148
Woman in White, The (Collins), 467, 468
Woman on the Edge of Time (Piercy), 116–17, 397, 542, 574

Women: Darwinist themes explored by, 480–83; pulp SF depiction of, 100. *See also* Feminism
Women and Economics (Gilman), 479
"Women Men Don't See, The" (Tiptree), 24
"Women with Wings" (Stone), 540
Wonder Quarterly (magazine), 198
Wonder Stories (magazine), 60, 200, 367(figure), 372, 373(figure), 481
Wood, Brian, 224
Wood, Teri Sue, 215
Wood, Wally, 214, 215, 222
Woodham, Jonathan M., 12, 14
Woods, Lebbeus, 287
Woof, Virginia, 110
Wooley, Sheb, 258
Woolford, Kirk, 265
Word for World Is Forest, The (Le Guin), 333
Workers Leaving the Lumière Factory (newsreel), 185
"Works as Assemblage" (Hayles), 232
World, the Flesh, and the Devil, The (Bernal), 529–30
World building, 219–20, 230, 233, 453–54
World Chinese Science Fiction Association, 74
World Fantasy Award, 75
World Future Society (WFS), 15, 514
World Inside, The (Silverberg), 285
World of Warcraft (video game), 249, 332
World Policy Journal, 68
World Science Fiction Convention (Worldcon), 60, 63, 72, 73, 74–75, 201, 371
World Science Fiction Society (WSFS), 72, 74–75
World's Fair. *See* New York World's Fair
Worlds of Women: Sapphic Science Fiction Erotica (story collection), 404
World War II, 325, 329, 330
"World Well Lost, The" (Sturgeon), 398
Wretched of the Earth, The (Fanon), 488
Wrinkle in Time, A (L'Engle), 136
Wrong Man, The (film), 161
Wylie, Philip, 214

Wyndham, John, 310

"Xenogenesis" trilogy (Butler), 403, 489, 545
X-Files (television program), 179, 180–81, 182
Xingyun Awards, 74
X-Men (comic), 219
X Minus One (radio program), 171
X-2 shuttle (Disney ride), 296, 297–98

Yager, Rick, 221
Yaszek, Lisa, 16, 24, 53, 312, 480, 567–68
Year of the Flood, The (Atwood), 145
Year's Best S-F (Merril, ed.), 28, 29
Years of Rice and Salt, The (Robinson), 136, 310–11
Year Zero (video game), 232
Yeats, W. B., 41
Yes (band), 260
Yesterday's Tomorrows (Corn and Horrigan), 209–10
Yiddish Policemen's Union, The (Chabon), 113
Yokoyama, Mitsuteru, 217
Yonder Comes the Other End of Time (Elgin), 135
Young, Robert, 491, 492
Youniverse: Toward a Self-Centered Philosophy of Immortalism and Cryonics (Ettinger), 531
Yugoslavia, 73

Zaha Hadid Architects, 286
Zahn, Timothy, 332
Zamyatin, Yevgeny, 90, 161, 288, 324, 348, 383, 387, 551, 556
Zardoz (film), 257
Zelazny, Roger, 36–37, 63, 128, 134
Zeman, Karel, 190–91
Zener, Karl, 509
Zenith (fanzine), 76
Zephyr (train), 368
Ziv, Maurice, 173
Žižek, Slavoj, 273, 579, 581–82
Zoline, Pamela, 62, 63, 143
Zone of possibility, 384
Zuberi, Nabeel, 568